INFANTS, CHILDREN, AND ADOLESCENTS

Infants, Children, and Adolescents

SECOND EDITION

LAURA E. BERK

ILLINOIS STATE UNIVERSITY

ALLYN AND BACON

BOSTON LONDON TORONTO SYDNEY TOKYO SINGAPORE

Vice President and Publisher: Susan Badger
Executive Editor: Laura Pearson
Editorial Assistant: Jennifer Normandin
Senior Developmental Editor: Sue Gleason
Developmental Editor: Anne Reid
Executive Marketing Manager: Joyce Nilsen
Editorial-Production Service: Thomas E. Dorsaneo
Text Designer: Seventeenth Street Studios
Text Composition: Seventeenth Street Studios
Prepress Buyer: Linda Cox
Cover Coordinator: Linda Knowles

ABOUT THE ART

The sixteen works of art that serve as chapter openings come from the International Museum of Children's Art in Oslo, Norway. Founded in 1986, the museum houses 100,000 drawings, paintings, sculptures, and crafts by children from over 130 countries. The works provide a feast of imagination, feeling, and color as they express the fantasy, freedom, and creativity of childhood. Each piece has been carefully chosen to reflect the theme of the chapter with which it appears.

Library of Congress Cataloging-In-Publication Data

Berk, Laura E.
Infants, children, and adolescents / Laura E. Berk. — 2nd ed.
p. cm.
Includes bibliographical references (p.) and index.
ISBN 0-205-16449-8
1. Child development. 2. Infants—Development. 3. Adolescence. I. Title.
RJ131.B387 1996
305.23'1—dc20 94-43710
CIP

Printed in the United States of America

10 9 8 7 6 5 4 3 2 99 98 97 96

TO MINNIE PERRIN BERSON,
INSPIRING MENTOR, COLLEAGUE, AND FRIEND

BRIEF CONTENTS

I
THEORY AND RESEARCH IN CHILD DEVELOPMENT

- 1. HISTORY, THEORY, AND RESEARCH STRATEGIES 2

II
FOUNDATIONS OF DEVELOPMENT

- 2. BIOLOGICAL AND ENVIRONMENTAL FOUNDATIONS 50
- 3. PRENATAL DEVELOPMENT 96
- 4. BIRTH AND THE NEWBORN BABY 132

III
INFANCY AND TODDLERHOOD: THE FIRST TWO YEARS

- 5. PHYSICAL DEVELOPMENT IN INFANCY AND TODDLERHOOD 168
- 6. COGNITIVE DEVELOPMENT IN INFANCY AND TODDLERHOOD 208
- 7. EMOTIONAL AND SOCIAL DEVELOPMENT IN INFANCY AND TODDLERHOOD 246

IV
EARLY CHILDHOOD: TWO TO SIX YEARS

- 8. PHYSICAL DEVELOPMENT IN EARLY CHILDHOOD 284
- 9. COGNITIVE DEVELOPMENT IN EARLY CHILDHOOD 312
- 10. EMOTIONAL AND SOCIAL DEVELOPMENT IN EARLY CHILDHOOD 352

V
MIDDLE CHILDHOOD: SIX TO ELEVEN YEARS

- 11. PHYSICAL DEVELOPMENT IN MIDDLE CHILDHOOD 394
- 12. COGNITIVE DEVELOPMENT IN MIDDLE CHILDHOOD 420
- 13. EMOTIONAL AND SOCIAL DEVELOPMENT IN MIDDLE CHILDHOOD 464

VI
ADOLESCENCE: THE TRANSITION TO ADULTHOOD

- 14. PHYSICAL DEVELOPMENT IN ADOLESCENCE 508
- 15. COGNITIVE DEVELOPMENT IN ADOLESCENCE 546
- 16. EMOTIONAL AND SOCIAL DEVELOPMENT IN ADOLESCENCE 582

Glossary G-1
References R-1
Name Index I-1
Subject Index I-9

CULTURAL INFLUENCES

- SCHOOL MATTERS IN MEXICAN-AMERICAN HOMES: AN ETHNOGRAPHIC STUDY 38
- THE AFRICAN-AMERICAN EXTENDED FAMILY 83
- CHILDBIRTH PRACTICES AROUND THE WORLD 139
- CULTURAL VARIATION IN INFANT SLEEPING ARRANGEMENTS 183
- YOUNG CHILDREN'S ATTACHMENT TO SOFT OBJECTS 265
- CHILD HEALTH CARE IN THE UNITED STATES AND EUROPEAN NATIONS 298
- CHILDREN'S UNDERSTANDING OF HEALTH AND ILLNESS 408
- EDUCATION IN JAPAN, TAIWAN, AND THE UNITED STATES 459
- CHILDREN'S MORAL CONCEPTS IN INDIA AND THE UNITED STATES 479
- ADOLESCENT INITIATION CEREMONIES 521
- WORK–STUDY APPRENTICESHIPS IN GERMANY 577
- IDENTITY DEVELOPMENT AMONG ETHNIC MINORITY ADOLESCENTS 588

SOCIAL ISSUES

- SOCIAL CHANGE AND CHILD-REARING ADVICE TO PARENTS 14
- THE PROS AND CONS OF REPRODUCTIVE TECHNOLOGIES 70
- THE CHILDREN'S DEFENSE FUND 85
- A GLOBAL PERSPECTIVE ON FAMILY PLANNING 100
- PRENATAL TRANSMISSION OF AIDS 119
- A CROSS-NATIONAL PERSPECTIVE ON INFANT MORTALITY 151
- THE CAROLINA ABECEDARIAN PROJECT: A MODEL OF INFANT–TODDLER INTERVENTION 233
- INFANT DAY CARE AND ATTACHMENT 273
- LEAD POISONING IN CHILDHOOD 294
- PROJECT HEAD START: A SOCIAL POLICY SUCCESS STORY 342
- REGULATING CHILDREN'S TELEVISION 374
- ARE ADULT-ORGANIZED SPORTS GOOD FOR CHILDREN? 415
- BILINGUAL EDUCATION IN THE UNITED STATES 449
- CHILDREN OF WAR 498
- THE NATION'S REPORT CARD: HOW ACADEMICALLY COMPETENT ARE AMERICAN ADOLESCENTS? 568
- YOUTH GANGS 617

FROM RESEARCH TO PRACTICE

- INTERVENING WITH PRENATALLY MALNOURISHED INFANTS 121
- POSTPARTUM DEPRESSION AND THE MOTHER–INFANT RELATIONSHIP 164
- THE MYSTERIOUS TRAGEDY OF SUDDEN INFANT DEATH SYNDROME 194
- PARENT–TODDLER INTERACTION AND EARLY MAKE-BELIEVE PLAY 226
- DIFFICULT CHILDREN: WHEN PARENTS ESTABLISH A "GOOD FIT" 262
- DAY CARE AND INFECTIOUS DISEASE 300
- YOUNG CHILDREN'S UNDERSTANDING OF DEATH 323
- HELPING YOUNG CHILDREN MANAGE FEARS 360
- CHILDREN WITH ATTENTION-DEFICIT HYPERACTIVITY DISORDER 430
- CHILDREN'S EYEWITNESS TESTIMONY 500
- A NEW APOACH TO SEX EDUCATION 536
- MORAL EDUCATION: THE JUST COMMUNITY 598

MILESTONES OF DEVELOPMENT

- IN INFANCY AND TODDLERHOOD 282
- IN EARLY CHILDHOOD 392
- IN MIDDLE CHILDHOOD 506
- IN ADOLESCENCE 622

DETAILED CONTENTS

Preface xvii

I THEORY AND RESEARCH IN CHILD DEVELOPMENT

1. HISTORY, THEORY, AND RESEARCH STRATEGIES 2

Child Development as an Interdisciplinary, Scientific, and Applied Field 4

Basic Themes and Issues 5
- *Organismic Versus Mechanistic Child* 6
- *Continuity Versus Discontinuity in Development* 6
- *Nature Versus Nurture* 7
- *A Balanced Point of View* 8

Historical Foundations 9
- *Medieval Times* 9
- *The Reformation* 10
- *Philosophies of the Enlightenment* 10
- *Darwin's Theory of Evolution* 11
- *Early Scientific Beginnings* 12

Mid-Twentieth-Century Theories 15
- *The Psychoanalytic Perspective* 15
- *Behaviorism and Social Learning Theory* 19
- *Piaget's Cognitive-Developmental Theory* 21

Recent Perspectives 24
- *Information Processing* 24
- *Ethology* 26
- *Ecological Systems Theory* 27
- *Cross-Cultural Research and Vygotsky's Sociocultural Theory* 29

Comparing Child Development Theories 31

Studying the Child 33
- *Common Methods Used to Study Children* 33
- *General Research Designs* 37
- *Designs for Studying Development* 41
- *Ethics in Research on Children* 44

The Chronological Approach of this Book 46

Summary 47

Important Terms and Concepts 49

■ SOCIAL ISSUES: SOCIAL CHANGE AND CHILD-REARING ADVICE TO PARENTS 14

■ CULTURAL INFLUENCES: SCHOOL MATTERS IN MEXICAN-AMERICAN HOMES: AN ETHNOGRAPHIC STUDY 38

II FOUNDATIONS OF DEVELOPMENT

2. BIOLOGICAL AND ENVIRONMENTAL FOUNDATIONS 50

Genetic Foundations 52
- *The Genetic Code* 52
- *The Sex Cells* 53
- *Conception* 55
- *Boy or Girl?* 56
- *Multiple Births* 57
- *Patterns of Genetic Inheritance* 58

Chromosomal Abnormalities 65
- *Down Syndrome* 65
- *Abnormalities of the Sex Chromosomes* 65

Reproductive Choices 67
- *Genetic Counseling* 67
- *Prenatal Diagnosis and Fetal Medicine* 68
- *The Alternative of Abortion* 68
- *The Alternative of Adoption* 72

Environmental Contexts for Development 73
- *The Family* 74
- *Social Class and Family Functioning* 76
- *The Impact of Poverty* 77
- *Beyond the Family: Neighborhoods, Schools, Towns, and Cities* 78
- *The Cultural Context* 81

Understanding the Relationship Between Heredity and Environment 86
The Question of "How Much?" 87
The Question of "How?" 89

Summary 93

Important Terms and Concepts 94

For Further Information and Special Help 95

■ SOCIAL ISSUES: THE PROS AND CONS OF REPRODUCTIVE TECHNOLOGIES 70

■ CULTURAL INFLUENCES: THE AFRICAN-AMERICAN EXTENDED FAMILY 83

■ SOCIAL ISSUES: THE CHILDREN'S DEFENSE FUND 85

3. PRENATAL DEVELOPMENT 96

Motivations for Parenthood 98
Why Have Children? 98
How Large a Family? 99
Is There a Best Time During Adulthood to Have a Child? 102

Prenatal Development 103
The Period of the Zygote 103
The Period of the Embryo 105
The Period of the Fetus 106

Prenatal Environmental Influences 110
Teratogens 110
Other Maternal Factors 118
The Importance of Prenatal Health Care 124

Preparing for Parenthood 126
Seeking Information 126
The Baby Becomes a Reality 126
Models of Effective Parenthood 127
Practical Concerns 127
The Marital Relationship 128

Summary 129

Important Terms and Concepts 130

For Further Information and Special Help 131

■ SOCIAL ISSUES: A GLOBAL PERSPECTIVE ON FAMILY PLANNING 100

■ SOCIAL ISSUES: PRENATAL TRANSMISSION OF AIDS 119

■ FROM RESEARCH TO PRACTICE: INTERVENING WITH PRENATALLY MALNOURISHED INFANTS 121

4. BIRTH AND THE NEWBORN BABY 132

The Stages of Childbirth 134
Stage 1: Dilation and Effacement of the Cervix 135
Stage 2: Delivery of the Baby 136
Stage 3: Birth of the Placenta 136
The Baby's Adaptation to Labor and Delivery 136
The Newborn Baby's Appearance 137
Assessing the Newborn's Physical Condition: The Apgar Scale 137

Approaches to Childbirth 138
Natural, or Prepared, Childbirth 140
Home Delivery 140

Medical Interventions 142
Fetal Monitoring 142
Labor and Delivery Medication 143
Instrument Delivery 143
Induced Labor 144
Cesarean Delivery 144

Birth Complications 146
Oxygen Deprivation 146
Preterm and Low-Birth-Weight Infants 147
Postterm Infants 150
Understanding Birth Complications 150

Precious Moments after Birth 152

The Newborn Baby's Capacities 153
Newborn Reflexes 153
Sensory Capacities 156
Newborn States 159
Neonatal Behavioral Assessment 162

The Transition to Parenthood 163

Summary 165

Important Terms and Concepts 166

For Further Information and Special Help 167

■ CULTURAL INFLUENCES: CHILDBIRTH PRACTICES AROUND THE WORLD 139

■ SOCIAL ISSUES: A CROSS-NATIONAL PERSPECTIVE ON INFANT MORTALITY 151

■ FROM RESEARCH TO PRACTICE: POSTPARTUM DEPRESSION AND THE MOTHER-INFANT RELATIONSHIP 164

III

INFANCY AND TODDLERHOOD: THE FIRST TWO YEARS

5. PHYSICAL DEVELOPMENT IN INFANCY AND TODDLERHOOD 168

Body Growth in the First Two Years 170
Changes in Body Size 170
Changes in Body Proportions 170
Changes in Muscle–Fat Makeup 172

Early Skeletal Growth 173
Appearance of Teeth 173

Brain Development 174
Development of Neurons 174
Development of the Cerebral Cortex 175

Factors Affecting Early Physical Growth 177
Heredity 178
Nutrition 178
Malnutrition 180
Affection and Stimulation 181

Changing States of Arousal 182

Motor Development During the First Two Years 183
The Sequence of Motor Development 184
Motor Skills as Complex Systems of Action 184
Maturation, Experience, and the Development of Motor Skills 186
Fine Motor Development: The Special Case of Voluntary Reaching 188
Bowel and Bladder Control 189

Basic Learning Mechanisms 190
Classical Conditioning 190
Operant Conditioning 192
Habituation and Dishabituation 193
Imitation 195

Perceptual Development in Infancy 197
Hearing 197
Vision 198
Intermodal Perception 203

Understanding Perceptual Development 204

Summary 205

Important Terms and Concepts 207

For Further Information and Special Help 207

CULTURAL INFLUENCES: CULTURAL VARIATION IN INFANT SLEEPING ARRANGEMENTS 183

FROM RESEARCH TO PRACTICE: THE MYSTERIOUS TRAGEDY OF SUDDEN INFANT DEATH SYNDROME 194

6. COGNITIVE DEVELOPMENT IN INFANCY AND TODDLERHOOD 208

Piaget's Cognitive-Developmental Theory 210
Key Piagetian Concepts 210
The Sensorimotor Stage 213
Recent Research on Sensorimotor Development 217
Evaluation of the Sensorimotor Stage 219

Information Processing During the First Two Years 220
A Model of Human Information Processing 221
Attention and Memory 222
Categorization 223
Evalution of Information-Processing Findings 224

The Social Context of Early Cognitive Development 225

Individual Differences in Early Mental Development 227
Infant Intelligence Tests 228
Early Environment and Mental Development 229
Early Intervention for At-Risk Infants and Toddlers 232

Language Development During the First Two Years 234
Three Theories of Language Development 235
Getting Ready to Talk 236
First Words 238
The Two-Word Utterance Phase 239
Comprehension Versus Production 240
Individual Differences in Language Development 240
Supporting Early Language Development 241

Summary 243

Important Terms and Concepts 245

For Further Information and Special Help 245

FROM RESEARCH TO PRACTICE: PARENT–TODDLER INTERACTION AND EARLY MAKE-BELIEVE PLAY 226

SOCIAL ISSUES: THE CAROLINA ABECEDARIAN PROJECT: A MODEL OF INFANT–TODDLER INTERVENTION 233

7. EMOTIONAL AND SOCIAL DEVELOPMENT IN INFANCY AND TODDLERHOOD 246

Theories of Infant and Toddler Personality 248
Erik Erikson: Trust and Autonomy 248
Margaret Mahler: Separation–Individuation 249
Similarities Between Erikson's and Mahler's Theories 251

Emotional Development During the First Two Years 251
Development of Some Basic Emotions 252
Understanding and Responding to the Emotions of Others 254
Emergence of Self-Conscious Emotions 254
The Beginnings of Emotional Self-Regulation 255

Temperament and Development 257
Measuring Temperament 257
Stability of Temperament 259
Genetic Influences 259
Environmental Influences 260
Temperament and Child Rearing: The Goodness-of-Fit Model 261

Development of Attachment 263
Early Theories of Attachment 263
Bowlby's Ethological Theory 265
Measuring the Security of Attachment 267
Cultural Variations 268
Factors That Affect Attachment Security 269
Multiple Attachments 272
Attachment and Later Development 275

Self-Development During the First Two Years 276
Self-Recognition 277
Categorizing the Self 278
Emergence of Self-Control 279

Summary 280

Important Terms and Concepts 281

■ FROM RESEARCH TO PRACTICE: DIFFICULT CHILDREN: WHEN PARENTS ESTABLISH "GOOD FIT" 262
■ CULTURAL INFLUENCES: YOUNG CHILDREN'S ATTACHMENT TO SOFT OBJECTS 265
■ SOCIAL ISSUES: INFANT DAY CARE AND ATTACHMENT 273

MILESTONES OF DEVELOPMENT IN INFANCY AND TODDLERHOOD 282

IV
EARLY CHILDHOOD: TWO TO SIX YEARS

8. PHYSICAL DEVELOPMENT IN EARLY CHILDHOOD 284

Body Growth in Early Childhood 286
Changes in Body Size and Proportions 286
Skeletal Growth 287
Asynchronies in Physical Growth 288

Brain Development in Early Childhood 289
Lateralization and Handedness 290
Other Advances in Brain Development 291

Factors Affecting Physical Growth and Health in Early Childhood 292
Hereditary and Hormonal Influences 292
Emotional Well-Being 293
Nutrition 293
Infectious Disease 296
Childhood Injuries 297

Motor Development in Early Childhood 302
Gross Motor Development 302
Fine Motor Development 304
Factors That Affect Early Childhood Motor Skills 306

Perceptual Development in Early Childhood 308

Summary 309

Important Terms and Concepts 311

For Further Information and Special Help 311

■ SOCIAL ISSUES: LEAD POISONING IN CHILDHOOD 294
■ CULTURAL INFLUENCES: CHILD HEALTH CARE IN THE UNITED STATES AND EUROPEAN NATIONS 298
■ FROM RESEARCH TO PRACTICE: DAY CARE AND INFECTIOUS DISEASE 300

9. COGNITIVE DEVELOPMENT IN EARLY CHILDHOOD 312

Piaget's Theory: The Preoperational Stage 314
Advances in Mental Representation 314
Make-Believe Play 315
Limitations of Preoperational Thought 316
Recent Research on Preoperational Thought 321
Evaluation of the Preoperational Stage 325
Piaget and Education 325

Vygotsky's Sociocultural Theory 326
Children's Private Speech 327
Social Origins of Early Childhood Cognition 328
Vygotsky and Education 329

Information Processing In Early Childhood 330
Attention 330
Memory 330
The Young Child's Theory of Mind 333
Early Literacy and Mathematical Development 334
A Note on Academics in Early Childhood 336

Individual Differences in Mental Development During Early Childhood 337
Early Childhood Intelligence Tests 337
Home Environment and Mental Development 338
Preschool and Day Care 339
Educational Television 343

Language Development in Early Childhood 344
Vocabulary Development 344
Grammatical Development 346
Becoming an Effective Conversationalist 346
Supporting Language Learning in Early Childhood 348

Summary 349

Important Terms and Concepts 351

For Further Information and Special Help 351

■ FROM RESEARCH TO PRACTICE: YOUNG CHILDREN'S UNDERSTANDING OF DEATH 323
■ SOCIAL ISSUES: PROJECT HEAD START: A SOCIAL POLICY SUCCESS STORY 342

10. EMOTIONAL AND SOCIAL DEVELOPMENT IN EARLY CHILDHOOD 352

Erikson's Theory: Initiative Versus Guilt 354

Self-Development in Early Childhood 355
Foundations of Self-Concept 355
Understanding Intentions 356
Emergence of Self-Esteem 357

Emotional Development in Early Childhood 357
Understanding Emotion 357
Improvements in Emotional Self-Regulation 358
Changes in Self-Conscious Emotions 359
Development of Empathy 361

Peer Relations in Early Childhood 362
Advances in Peer Sociability 362
First Friendships 365

Foundations of Morality in Early Childhood 366
The Psychoanalytic Perspective 367
Behaviorism and Social Learning Theory 368
The Cognitive-Developmental Perspective 370
The Other Side of Morality: Development of Aggression 371

Gender Typing in Early Childhood 375
Preschoolers' Gender-Stereotyped Beliefs and Behavior 376
Genetic Influences on Gender Typing 376
Environmental Influences on Gender Typing 377
Gender-Role Identity 379
Reducing Gender Stereotyping in Young Children 380

Child Rearing and Emotional and Social Development in Early Childhood 382
Styles of Child Rearing 382
What Makes Authoritative Child Rearing So Effective? 383
Cultural and Situational Influences on Child-Rearing Styles 384
Child Maltreatment 385

Summary 389

Important Terms and Concepts 391

For Further Information and Special Help 391

■ FROM RESEARCH TO PRACTICE: HELPING YOUNG CHILDREN MANAGE FEARS 360

■ SOCIAL ISSUES: REGULATING CHILDREN'S TELEVISION 374

MILESTONES OF DEVELOPMENT IN EARLY CHILDHOOD 392

V

MIDDLE CHILDHOOD: SIX TO ELEVEN YEARS

11. PHYSICAL DEVELOPMENT IN MIDDLE CHILDHOOD 394

Body Growth in Middle Childhood 396
Changes in Body Size and Proportions 396
Secular Trends in Physical Growth 397
Skeletal Growth 398
Brain Development 398

Common Health Problems in Middle Childhood 399
Vision and Hearing 400
Malnutrition 400
Obesity 401
Type A Behavior 403
Bedwetting 404
Illnesses 405
Unintentional Injuries 405

Health Education in Middle Childhood 406

Motor Development and Play in Middle Childhood 409
Gross Motor Development 409
Fine Motor Development 410
Individual and Group Differences in Motor Development 413
Organized Games with Rules 413
Shadows of Our Evolutionary Past 414
Physical Education 416

Summary 417

Important Terms and Concepts 418

For Further Information and Special Help 419

■ CULTURAL INFLUENCES: CHILDREN'S UNDERSTANDING OF HEALTH AND ILLNESS 408

■ SOCIAL ISSUES: ARE ADULT-ORGANIZED SPORTS GOOD FOR CHILDREN? 415

12. COGNITIVE DEVELOPMENT IN MIDDLE CHILDHOOD 420

Piaget's Theory: The Concrete Operational Stage 422
Conservation 422
Classification 422
Seriation 424
Spatial Reasoning 424
Limitations of Concrete Operational Thought 425
Recent Research on Concrete Operational Thought 425
Evaluation of the Concrete Operational Stage 427

Information Processing in Middle Childhood 428
Attention 428
Memory Strategies 429
The Knowledge Base and Memory Performance 431
Culture and Memory Strategies 432
The School-Age Child's Theory of Mind 433
Self-Regulation 434
Applications of Information Processing to Academic Learning 434

Individual Differences in Mental Development During Middle Childhood 436
Defining and Measuring Intelligence 437
Explaining Individual Differences in IQ 442
Overcoming Cultural Bias in Intelligence Tests 444

Language Development in Middle Childhood 446
Vocabulary 446
Grammar 447
Pragmatics 447
Learning Two Languages at a Time 447

Children's Learning in School 448
The Educational Philosophy 448
Teacher–Pupil Interaction 451
Computers in the Classroom 452
Teaching Children with Special Needs 453

How Well Educated Are America's Children? 458

Summary 461

Important Terms and Concepts 463

For Further Information and Special Help 463

■ FROM RESEARCH TO PRACTICE: CHILDREN WITH ATTENTION-DEFICIT HYPERACTIVITY DISORDER 430

■ SOCIAL ISSUES: BILINGUAL EDUCATION IN THE UNITED STATES 449

■ CULTURAL INFLUENCES: EDUCATION IN JAPAN, TAIWAN, AND THE UNITED STATES 459

13. EMOTIONAL AND SOCIAL DEVELOPMENT IN MIDDLE CHILDHOOD 464

Erikson's Theory: Industry Versus Inferiority 466

Self-Development in Middle Childhood 467
Changes in Self-Concept 467
Development of Self-Esteem 468
Influences on Self-Esteem 469

Emotional Development in Middle Childhood 473

Understanding Others 474
Selman's Stages of Perspective Taking 474
Perspective Taking and Social Behavior 475

Moral Development in Middle Childhood 476
Learning About Justice Through Sharing 477
Changes in Moral and Social-Conventional Understanding 478

Peer Relations in Middle Childhood 480
Changes in Peer Sociability 480
Peer Groups 480
Friendships 481
Peer Acceptance 482

Gender Typing in Middle Childhood 484
Gender-Stereotyped Beliefs 484
Gender-Role Identity and Behavior 485
Cultural Influences on Gender Typing 485

Family Influences in Middle Childhood 486
Parent–Child Relationships 486
Siblings 488
Divorce 488
Remarriage 492
Maternal Employment 494

Some Common Problems of Development 496
Fears and Anxieties 496
Child Sexual Abuse 497

Stress and Coping: The Resilient Child 502

Summary 503

Important Terms and Concepts 505

For Further Information and Special Help 505

■ CULTURAL INFLUENCES: CHILDREN'S MORAL CONCEPTS IN INDIA AND THE UNITED STATES 479

■ SOCIAL INFLUENCES: CHILDREN OF WAR 498

■ FROM RESEARCH TO PRACTICE: CHILDREN'S EYEWITNESS TESTIMONY 500

MILESTONES OF DEVELOPMENT IN MIDDLE CHILDHOOD 506

VI

ADOLESCENCE: THE TRANSITION TO ADULTHOOD

14. PHYSICAL DEVELOPMENT IN ADOLESCENCE 508

Conceptions of Adolescence 510
Biologically Oriented Views 510
The Environmental Perspective 511
A Balanced Point of View 511

Puberty: The Physical Transition to Adulthood 512
Hormonal Changes 512
Changes in Body Size and Proportions 514
Muscle–Fat Makeup and Other Internal Changes 514
Sexual Maturation 515
Individual and Group Differences in Pubertal Growth 517
The Secular Trend 517

The Psychological Impact of Pubertal Events 518
Reactions to Pubertal Changes 519
Pubertal Change, Emotion, and Social Behavior 520
Early Versus Late Maturation 522

Health Issues During Adolescence 526
Nutritional Needs 526
Serious Eating Disturbances 527
Sexual Activity 529
Teenage Pregnancy and Childbearing 533
Sexually Transmitted Disease 537
Substance Use and Abuse 538
Unintentional Injuries 540

Motor Development in Adolescence 541

Summary 543

Important Terms and Concepts 544

For Further Information and Special Help 545

CULTURAL INFLUENCES: ADOLESCENT INITIATION CEREMONIES 521

FROM RESEARCH TO PRACTICE: A NEW APPROACH TO SEX EDUCATION 536

15. COGNITIVE DEVELOPMENT IN ADOLESCENCE 546

Piaget's Theory: The Formal Operational Stage 548
- *Hypothetico-Deductive Reasoning* 548
- *Propositional Thought* 550
- *Recent Research on Formal Operational Thought* 551

An Information-Processing View of Adolescent Cognitive Development 552
- *Siegler's Rule-Assessment Approach* 553
- *Gradual Mastery of Formal Operational Abilities* 554

Consequences of Abstract Thinking 555
- *Argumentativeness* 555
- *Self-Consciousness and Self-Focusing* 556
- *Idealism and Criticism* 558
- *Planning and Decision Making* 558

Sex Differences in Mental Abilities 559

Language Development in Adolescence 560
- *Vocabulary and Grammar* 561
- *Pragmatics* 561
- *Second-Language Learning* 562

Learning in School 563
- *School Transitions* 563
- *Academic Achievement* 565
- *Dropping Out* 569

Vocational Development 572
- *Selecting a Career* 573
- *Making the Transition from School to Work* 576

Summary 579

Important Terms and Concepts 580

For Further Information and Special Help 581

SOCIAL ISSUES: THE NATION'S REPORT CARD:HOW ACADEMICALLY COMPETENT ARE AMERICAN ADOLESCENTS? 568

CULTURAL INFLUENCES: WORK-STUDY APPRENTICESHIPS IN GERMANY 577

16. EMOTIONAL AND SOCIAL DEVELOPMENT IN ADOLESCENCE 582

Erikson's Theory: Identity Versus Identity Diffusion 584

Self-Development in Adolescence 585
- *Changes in Self-Concept* 585
- *Changes in Self-Esteem* 586
- *Paths to Identity* 587
- *Identity Status and Personality Characteristics* 588
- *Factors That Affect Identity* 589

Moral Development in Adolescence 591
- *Piaget's Theory of Moral Development* 591
- *Kohlberg's Extension of Piaget's Theory* 592
- *Environmental Influences on Moral Reasoning* 596
- *Are There Sex Differences in Moral Reasoning?* 599
- *Moral Reasoning and Behavior* 600

Gender Typing in Adolescence 601

The Family in Adolescence 601
- *Parent–Child Relationships* 602
- *Siblings* 603

Peer Relations in Adolescence 604
- *Adolescent Friendships* 604
- *Cliques and Crowds* 606
- *Dating* 608
- *Peer Pressure and Conformity* 608

Problems of Development 610
- *Depression* 610
- *Suicide* 612
- *Delinquency* 614

At the Threshold 618

Summary 619

Important Terms and Concepts 621

For Further Information and Special Help 621

CULTURAL INFLUENCES: IDENTITY DEVELOPMENT AMONG ETHNIC MINORITY ADOLESCENTS 588

FROM RESEARCH TO PRACTICE: MORAL EDUCATION: THE JUST COMMUNITY 598

SOCIAL ISSUES: YOUTH GANGS 617

MILESTONES OF DEVELOPMENT IN ADOLESCENCE 622

Glossary G-1

References R-1

Name Index I-1

Subject Index I-9

PREFACE

My twenty-six years of teaching child development have brought me in contact with thousands of students having diverse college majors, future goals, interests, and needs. Some are affiliated with my own department, psychology, but many come from other child-related fields—education, sociology, anthropology, family studies, and biology, to name just a few. Each semester, my students' aspirations have proved to be as varied as their fields of study. Many look toward careers in applied work with children—teaching, caregiving, nursing, counseling, social work, school psychology, and program administration. Some plan to teach child development, and a few want to do research. Most hope someday to have children, whereas others are already parents who come with a desire to better understand and rear their own youngsters. And almost all my students arrive with a deep curiosity about how they themselves developed from tiny infants into the complex human beings they are today.

My goal in preparing this second edition of *Infants, Children, and Adolescents* is to provide a textbook that meets the instructional goals of the course as well as the varied needs of students. I aimed for a text that is intellectually stimulating, that provides depth as well as breadth of coverage, and that portrays the complexities of child development in a way that captures student interest while helping them learn.

To achieve these objectives, I have grounded this book in a carefully selected body of classic and current research brought to life with stories and vignettes about children and families, many of whom I have known personally. In addition, the text discussion emphasizes how the research process helps solve real-world problems and pays special attention to policy issues that are critical to the overall condition of children in today's world. I have also used a clear, engaging writing style and provided a unique pedagogical program that assists students in mastering information, integrating the various aspects of development, critically examining controversial issues, and applying what they have learned.

TEXT PHILOSOPHY

The basic approach of this book has been shaped by my own professional and personal history as a teacher, researcher, and parent. It consists of five philosophical ingredients that I regard as essential for students to emerge from a course with a thorough understanding of child development. Each theme is woven into every chapter:

■ 1. **AN UNDERSTANDING OF MAJOR THEORIES AND THE STRENGTHS AND SHORTCOMINGS OF EACH.** The first chapter begins by emphasizing that only knowledge of multiple theories can do justice to the richness of child development. As I take up each age sector and aspect of development, I present a variety of theoretical perspectives, indicate how each approach highlights previously overlooked aspects of development, and discuss research that has been used to evaluate them. Discussion of contrasting theories also serves as the context for an evenhanded analysis of many controversial issues throughout the text.

■ 2. **KNOWLEDGE OF BOTH THE SEQUENCE OF CHILD DEVELOPMENT AND THE PROCESSES THAT UNDERLIE IT.** Students are provided a description of the organized sequence of development along with a discussion of processes of change. An understanding of process—how complex combinations of biological and environmental events produce development—has been the focus of most recent research. Accordingly, the text reflects this emphasis. But new information about the timetable of change has also emerged. In many ways, children have proved to be far more competent beings than they were believed to be in the past. Current evidence on the timing and sequence of development, along with its implications for process, is presented throughout the book.

■ 3. **AN APPRECIATION OF THE IMPACT OF CONTEXT AND CULTURE ON CHILD DEVELOPMENT.** A wealth of new research indicates more powerfully than ever before that children live in rich physical and social contexts that affect all aspects of development. In each chapter, the student travels to distant parts of the world as I review a growing body of cross-cultural evidence. The text narrative also discusses many findings on socioeconomically and ethnically diverse children within the United States. Besides highlighting the role of immediate settings, such as family, neighborhood, and school, I make a concerted effort to underscore the impact of larger social structures—societal values, laws, and government programs—on children's well-being.

■ 4. **A SENSE OF THE INTERDEPENDENCY OF ALL ASPECTS OF DEVELOPMENT—PHYSICAL, COGNITIVE, EMOTIONAL, AND SOCIAL.** In every chapter, an integrated approach to understanding children is emphasized. I show how physical, cognitive, emotional, and social development are interwoven. Within the text narrative, students are referred to other sections of the book to deepen their grasp of relationships among various aspects of change.

■ 5. **AN APPRECIATION OF THE INTERRELATEDNESS OF THEORY, RESEARCH, AND APPLICATIONS.** Throughout this book, I emphasize that theories of child development and the research stimulated by them provide the foundation for sound, effective practices with children. The link between theory, research, and applications is reinforced by an organizational format in which theory and research are presented first, followed by implications for practice. In addition, a current focus in the field—harnessing child development knowledge to shape social policies that support children's needs—is reflected in every chapter. The text addresses the current condition of children in the United States and around the world and shows how theory and research have sparked successful interventions. Many important applied topics are considered—prenatal AIDS infection, family planning, infant mortality, maternal employment and day care, mainstreaming children with learning difficulties, bilingual education, child sexual abuse, children of war, teenage pregnancy and childbearing, and youth gangs, to name just a few.

TEXT ORGANIZATION

I have chosen a chronological organization for this text. The book begins with an introductory chapter that describes the history of the field, modern theories, and research strategies. It is followed by three chapters that cover the foundations of development. Chapter 2 combines an overview of biological and environmental contexts into a single, integrated discussion of these multifaceted determinants of development. Chapter 3 is devoted to prenatal development, Chapter 4 to birth and the newborn baby. With this foundation, students are ready to take a close look at four major age periods of change: infancy and toddlerhood, early childhood, middle childhood, and adolescence. Each chronological division contains a trio of topical chapters: physical development, cognitive development, and emotional and social development.

The chronological approach has the advantage of enabling students to get to know children of a given age period very well. It also eases the task of integrating the various aspects of development, since each is discussed in close proximity. At the same time, a chronologically organized book requires that theories covering several age periods be presented piecemeal. This creates a challenge for students, who must link the various parts together. To assist with this task, I remind students of important earlier achievements before discussing new developments. Also, chapters devoted to the same topic (for example, Cognitive Development in Early Childhood, Cognitive Development in Middle Childhood) are similarly organized, making it easier for students to draw connections across age periods and construct a continuous vision of developmental change.

PEDAGOGICAL FEATURES

The pedagogical features of the text have been revised and expanded. A highly accessible writing style—one that is lucid and engaging without being simplistic—continues to be one of the text's strong points. I frequently converse with students and encourage them to relate what they read to their own lives. In doing so, I hope to make the study of child development involving and pleasurable.

■ **STORIES AND VIGNETTES ABOUT CHILDREN.** To help students construct a clear image of development and to enliven the text narrative, each chronological age division is unified by case examples woven throughout the set of chapters. For example, within the infancy and toddlerhood section, students accompany me as I sit in on periodic gatherings of three mothers and their babies, observe dramatic changes and striking individual differences in the children's capabilities, and address their mothers' questions and concerns. Besides a set of main characters, many additional vignettes offer vivid examples of development and diversity among children. Instructor and student response to this feature has been so positive that I have made a special effort to enhance it in this edition.

■ **CHAPTER INTRODUCTIONS AND END-OF-CHAPTER SUMMARIES.** To provide students with a helpful preview of what they are about to read, I include an outline and overview of chapter content in each chapter introduction. Especially comprehensive end-of-chapter summaries, organized according to the major divisions of each chapter and highlighting important terms, remind students of key points in the text discussion. In this edition, review questions have been added to the summaries to encourage students to study actively.

■ **BRIEF REVIEWS.** Interim summaries of text content appear at the end of most major sections in each chapter. They enhance retention by encouraging students to reflect on information they have just read before moving on to a new section.

■ **BOXES.** Three types of boxes accentuate the philosophical themes of this book. *Cultural Influences* boxes highlight the impact of context and culture on all aspects of development. *Social Issues* boxes discuss the condition of children in the United States and around the world and emphasize the need for sensitive social policies to ensure their well-being. *From Research to Practice* boxes integrate theory, research, and applications.

■ **TRY THIS. . .** In each Social Issues box, I encourage students to become actively involved with the material by suggesting activities that extend their understanding of child development. Additional activities can also be found within the text narrative. In many places, students are invited to make observations, talk to children and parents, find out about the status of children in their community and nation, and reflect on their own experiences. Each activity can serve as a course assignment and stimulus for class discussion.

■ **ASK YOURSELF. . .** Active engagement with the subject matter is also supported by critical thinking questions, which can be found in the margins at the end of major sections. The focus of these questions is divided between theory and applications. Many describe problematic situations faced by parents, teachers, and children and ask students to resolve them in light of what they have learned. In this way, the questions inspire high-level thinking and new insights.

■ **CONCEPT TABLES.** I have created a special series of tables that group together related concepts, summarize the important point conveyed by each, and provide vivid examples. These tables help ensure that challenging sets of concepts will be interrelated and fully understood.

■ **MILESTONES TABLES.** A milestones table appears at the end of each chronological age division of the text. These tables summarize major physical, cognitive, language, and emotional and social developments of each age span.

■ **ADDITIONAL TABLES, ILLUSTRATIONS, AND PHOTOGRAPHS.** Additional tables are liberally included to help students grasp essential points in the text discussion, extend information on a topic, and consider applications. The many full-color illustrations throughout the book depict important theories, methods, and research findings. In this edition, the photo program has been extended. Each photo has been carefully selected to portray the text discussion and to represent the diversity of children in the United States and around the world.

■ **MARGINAL GLOSSARY, END-OF-CHAPTER TERM LIST, AND END-OF-BOOK GLOSSARY.** Mastery of terms that make up the central vocabulary of the field is promoted through a marginal glossary, an end-of-chapter term list, and an end-of-book glossary. Important terms and concepts also appear in boldface type in the text narrative.

■ **FOR FURTHER INFORMATION AND SPECIAL HELP.** Students in my own classes frequently ask where they can go to find out more about high-interest topics or to seek help in areas related to their own lives. To meet this need, I have included an annotated section at the end of each chapter that provides the names, addresses, and phone numbers of organizations that disseminate information about child development and offer special services.

ACKNOWLEDGMENTS

The dedicated contributions of a great many individuals helped make this book a reality. In the months before I began writing the first edition, Allyn and Bacon sponsored focus groups in which instructors of child development discussed features of a text that would best meet their teaching goals. The insightful comments of the following participants were critical in shaping the organization and content of this book:

Carol Chamberlin
Santa Monica City College

Linda Cravens
Moorpark College

Louise Dean
Los Angeles Valley College

Rosalind Frye
Richard J. Daley College

Robert Freudenthal
Moraine Valley Community College

Diana Hiatt
Pepperdine University

Sandy Hoffman
Oakton Community College

Barbara Kuczen-Schaller
Chicago State University

Jeri Lopton
Oxnard Community College

Maurice Page
South Suburban College

Patricia Schmolze
Los Angeles City College

Francine Smolucha
Moraine Valley Community College

Joyce West
Moraine Valley Community College

As I completed each chapter, an impressive cast of reviewers provided many helpful suggestions, constructive criticisms, and encouragement and enthusiasm for the organization and content of the book. I am grateful to each one of them.

REVIEWERS OF THE FIRST EDITION

Jerry Bruce
Sam Houston State College

Kathleen Bey
Palm Beach Community College

Donald Bowers
Community College of Philadelphia

Joseph J. Campos
University of California, Berkeley

Nancy Taylor Coghill
University of Southwest Louisiana

Roswell Cox
Berea College

Janice Hartgrove-Freile
North Harris Community College

Vernon Haynes
Youngstown State University

Malia Huchendorf
Normandale Community College

Clementine Hansley Hurt
Radford University

John S. Klein
Castleton State College

Carole Kremer
Hudson Valley Community College

Gary W. Ladd
University of Illinois, Urbana-Champaign

Linda Lavine
State University of New York at Cortland

Frank Manis
University of Southern California

Cloe Merrill
Weber State University

Mary Ann McLaughlin
Clarion University of Pennsylvania

Tizrah Schutzengel
Bergen Community College

Gregory Smith
Dickinson College

Marcia Summers
Ball State University

Judith Ward
Central Connecticut State University

Shawn Ward
Le Moyne College

Alida Westman
Eastern Michigan University

Sue Williams
Southwest Texas State University

REVIEWERS OF THE SECOND EDITION

Jennifer Cook
Kent State University

Sheridan DeWolf
Grossmont College

Constance DiMaria-Kross
Union County College

Kathleen Fite
Southwest Texas State University

Vivian Harper
San Joaquin Delta College

Paula Hillmann
University of Wisconsin, Waukesha

Eugene Krebs
California State University, Fresno

Gail Lee
Jersey City State College

Peter Oliver
University of Hartford

Virginia Parsons
Carroll College

Johnna Shapiro
Illinois Wesleyan University

Thomas Spencer
San Francisco State University

Carolyn Spies
Bloomfield College

Deborah Winters
New Mexico State University

I am also indebted to colleagues at Illinois State University and Illinois Wesleyan University—Gary Creasey, Carolyn Jarvis, Patricia Jarvis, Steven Landau, and Mark Swerdlik—for providing consultation in areas of their expertise. Eugie Foster and Lisa Otte, my graduate assistants, helped with literature reviews and securing permissions for use of copyrighted material.

I have been fortunate to work with an outstanding publishing staff at Allyn and Bacon. Laura Pearson, Executive Editor, has done a wonderful job of ushering this book through its development and publication in both editions. Her generous moral support, keen insight into the needs of instructors and students, and warm sense of humor have energized my work. Her creative approach to text publishing has sparked the innovative pedagogical program in this book. I thank Laura, especially, for arranging meetings in Boston that resulted in vital changes in the production procedures for my texts. These made it possible for me to undertake the challenging work of this revision while continuing with my teaching, research, and administrative responsibilities at Illinois State University.

Anne Reid, developmental editor, worked closely with me during the first edition to ensure that every line and paragraph of this book would be clear, every thought and concept precisely expressed and well developed. I have been especially pleased at her willingness to take on several additional tasks for the new edition. Annie managed the preparation of text supplements and planned the CNN videotape that accompanies the book. The text and its package are immeasurably better because of her involvement.

Tom Dorsaneo coordinated the complex production tasks that resulted in an exceptionally beautiful second edition. His competence, courtesy, and interest in the subject matter have made working with him a special pleasure. Elsa Peterson conducted the photo research, obtaining outstanding photographs of culturally diverse children and families. She also worked closely with the International Museum of Children's Art in Oslo, Norway, to select drawings and paintings that not only reflect each chapter's content, but accentuate the beauty, wonderment, and potential of childhood. Jennifer Normandin, Editorial Assistant, handled many details through all phases of this project. Her prompt and patient responses to my many concerns and queries have been very much appreciated.

My husband, Ken, deserves a special expression of gratitude for his unfailing patience with the many evening and weekend hours I have devoted to research and writing. David and Peter, our sons, have recently completed the journey described in this book and stand on the threshold of adulthood. Over the years, I have learned much from them about parenting and child development, and they have graciously permitted me to share some of these insights in the text's vignettes.

Finally, this book is dedicated to Minnie Perrin Berson, whose extensive knowledge and sympathetic vision of childhood were a constant source of inspiration as I wrote *Infants, Children, and Adolescents.* Years ago, we built collaborative bridges between psychology and early childhood education at Illinois State University. Today, from greater distance, she continues to serve as an extraordinary model of dedication, wisdom, and caring for children. Her influence graces each page of this text.

—Laura E. Berk

ABOUT THE AUTHOR

LAURA E. BERK is Distinguished Professor of Psychology at Illinois State University, where she has taught child development to undergraduate and graduate students for twenty-six years. She received her bachelor's degree in psychology from the University of California, Berkeley, and her masters and doctoral degrees in early childhood development and education from the University of Chicago. She has been visiting scholar at Cornell University, UCLA, and Stanford University. Berk has published widely on the effects of school environments on children's development and, more recently, on the development of children's private speech. Her research has been funded by the U.S. Office of Education and the National Institute of Child Health and Human Development. It has appeared in many prominent journals, including *Child Development, Developmental Psychology, Merrill-Palmer Quarterly, Journal of Abnormal Child Psychology,* and *Development and Psychopathology.* Her empirical studies have also attracted the attention of the general public, leading to contributions to *Psychology Today* and *Scientific American.* Berk has served as research editor of *Young Children* and and is currently consulting editor of *Early Childhood Research Quarterly*. She is author of *Scaffolding Children's Learning: Vygotsky and Early Childhood Education,* recently released by National Association for the Education of Young Children, and the topically organized text *Child Development,* published by Allyn and Bacon. Berk is recipient of the DeLissa Fellowship in Early Childhood and Family Studies and will be visiting scholar at the DeLissa Institute, University of South Australia, in 1996.

INFANTS, CHILDREN, AND ADOLESCENTS

"My family"
Bilgundi T. M. Tarkewada
5 years, India

This painting of a mother and her young children strolling through a richly colored, abstract world reminds us that development is multifaceted and, in many ways, mystifying. As you read Chapter 1, it will open the door to new ways of thinking about and studying child development.

Reprinted by permission from The International Museum of Children's Art, Oslo, Norway.

1

History, Theory, and Research Strategies

CHILD DEVELOPMENT AS AN INTERDISCIPLINARY, SCIENTIFIC, AND APPLIED FIELD

BASIC THEMES AND ISSUES

Organismic Versus Mechanistic Child • Continuity Versus Discontinuity in Development • Nature Versus Nurture • A Balanced Point of View

HISTORICAL FOUNDATIONS

Medieval Times • The Reformation • Philosophies of the Enlightenment •Darwin's Theory of Evolution • Early Scientific Beginnings

MID-TWENTIETH-CENTURY THEORIES

The Psychoanalytic Perspective • Behaviorism and Social Learning Theory • Piaget's Cognitive-Developmental Theory

RECENT PERSPECTIVES

Information Processing • Ethology • Ecological Systems Theory • Cross-Cultural Research and Vygotsky's Sociocultural Theory

COMPARING CHILD DEVELOPMENT THEORIES

STUDYING THE CHILD

Common Methods Used to Study Children • General Research Designs • Designs for Studying Development • Ethics in Research on Children

THE CHRONOLOGICAL APPROACH OF THIS BOOK

Not long ago, I left my midwestern home to live for a year near the small city in northern California where I spent my childhood years. One morning, I visited the neighborhood where I grew up—a place to which I had not returned since I was 12 years old. I stood at the entrance to my old schoolyard. Buildings and grounds that looked large to me as a child now seemed strangely small from my grown-up vantage point. I peered through the window of my first-grade classroom. The desks were no longer arranged in rows, but grouped in intimate clusters around the room. A computer rested against the far wall, near the spot where I once sat. I walked my old route home from school, the distance shrunken by my larger stride. I stopped in front of my best friend Kathryn's house, where we once drew sidewalk pictures, crossed the street to play kickball, produced plays for neighborhood audiences in the garage, and traded marbles and stamps in the backyard. In place of the small shop where I had purchased penny candy stood a neighborhood day care center, filled with the voices and vigorous activity of toddlers and preschoolers.

As I walked, I reflected on early experiences that contributed to who I am and what I am like today—weekends helping my father in his downtown clothing shop, the year during which my mother studied to become a high school teacher, moments of companionship and rivalry with my sister and brother, Sunday trips to museums and the seashore, and overnight visits to my grandmother's house where I became someone extra special.

As I passed the homes of my childhood friends, I thought of what I knew about their present lives. My close friend Kathryn, star pupil and president of our sixth-grade class—today a successful corporate lawyer and mother of two children. Shy, withdrawn Phil, cruelly teased because of his cleft lip—now owner of a thriving chain of hardware stores and member of the city council. Julio, immigrant from Mexico who joined our class in third grade—today director of an elementary school bilingual education program and single parent of an adopted Mexican boy. And finally, my next-door neighbor Rick, who picked fights at recess, struggled with reading, repeated fourth grade, dropped out of high school, and (so I heard) moved from one job to another over the following ten years.

As you begin this course in child development, perhaps you, too, have wondered about some of the same questions that crossed my mind during that nostalgic neighborhood walk:

- What determines the features human beings have in common and those that make each of us unique—in physical characteristics, capabilities, interests, and behaviors?
- Is the infant and young child's perception of the world much the same as the adult's, or is it different in basic respects?
- Why do some of us, like Kathryn and Rick, retain the same styles of responding that characterized us as children, whereas others, like Phil, change in essential ways?
- How did Julio, transplanted to a foreign culture at 8 years of age, master its language and customs and succeed in its society, yet remain strongly identified with his ethnic community?
- In what ways are children's home, school, and neighborhood experiences the same today as they were in generations past, and in what ways are they different? How does generational change—employed mothers, day care, divorce, smaller families, and new technologies—affect children's characteristics and skills?

These are central questions addressed by **child development**, a field of study devoted to understanding all aspects of human growth and change from conception through adolescence. Child development is part of a larger discipline known as **developmental psychology**, or (as it is referred to in its interdisciplinary sense) **human development**, which includes all changes we experience throughout the life span. Great diversity characterizes the interests and concerns of the thousands of investigators who study child development. But all have a single goal in common: the desire to describe and identify those factors that influence the dramatic changes in young people during the first two decades of life.

Child development
A field of study devoted to understanding all aspects of human growth from conception through adolescence.

Developmental psychology
A branch of psychology devoted to understanding all changes that human beings experience throughout the life span.

Human development
An interdisciplinary field of study devoted to understanding all changes that human beings experience throughout the life span.

CHILD DEVELOPMENT AS AN INTERDISCIPLINARY, SCIENTIFIC, AND APPLIED FIELD

Look again at the questions about children just listed, and you will see that they are not just of scientific interest. Each is of *applied,* or practical importance, as well. In fact, scientific curiosity is just one factor that led child development to become the exciting field of study it is today. Research about development has also been stimulated by social pressures to better the lives of children. For example, the beginning of public education in the early part of this century led to a demand for knowledge about what and how to teach children of different ages. The interest of pediatricians in improving children's health required an understanding of physical growth and nutrition.

The social service profession's desire to treat children's anxieties and behavior problems required information about personality and social development. And parents have continually asked for advice about child-rearing practices and experiences that would promote the growth of their child.

Our vast storehouse of information about child development is *interdisciplinary.* It has grown through the combined efforts of people from many fields of study. Because of the need for solutions to everyday problems concerning children, academic scientists from psychology, sociology, anthropology, and biology joined forces in research with professionals from a variety of applied fields, including education, home economics, medicine, and social service, to name just a few. Today, the field of child development is a melting pot of contributions. Its body of knowledge is not just scientifically important, but relevant and useful.

BASIC THEMES AND ISSUES

Before scientific study of the child, questions about children were answered by turning to common sense, opinion, and belief. Research on children did not begin until the early part of the twentieth century. Gradually it led to the construction of theories of child development, to which professionals and parents could turn for understanding and guidance. Although there are a great many definitions, for our purposes we can think of a **theory** as an orderly, integrated set of statements that describes, explains, and predicts behavior. For example, a good theory of infant–mother attachment would *describe* the behaviors that lead up to babies' strong desire to seek the affection and comfort of their mothers around 6 to 8 months of age. It would also *explain* why infants have such a strong desire. And it might also try to *predict* what might happen if babies do not develop this close emotional bond.

Theories are vital tools in child development (and any other scientific endeavor) for two reasons. First, they provide organizing frameworks for our observations of children. In other words, they *guide and give meaning* to what we see. Second, theories that are verified by research often serve as a sound basis for practical action. Once a theory helps us *understand* development, we are in a much better position to know *what to do* in our efforts to improve the welfare and treatment of children.

As we will see later, theories are influenced by the cultural values and belief systems of their times. But theories differ in one important way from mere opinion and belief: a theory's continued existence depends on *scientific verification* (Scarr, 1985). This means that the theory must be tested by using a fair set of research procedures agreed on by the scientific community.

In the field of child development, there are many theories with very different ideas about what children are like and how they develop. The study of child development provides no ultimate truth, since investigators do not always agree on the meaning of what they see. In addition, children are complex beings; they grow physically, mentally, emotionally, and socially. As yet, no single theory has been able to explain all these aspects. Finally, the existence of many theories helps advance knowledge, since researchers are continually trying to support, contradict, and integrate these different points of view.

This chapter introduces you to the major child development theories and the research strategies that have been used to test them. Then, we will return to each theory in greater detail in later parts of this book. Although there are many theories, we can easily organize them, since almost all take a stand on three basic issues about childhood and child development. To help you remember these controversial issues, they are briefly summarized in Table 1.1. Let's take a close look at each in the following sections.

Theory
An orderly, integrated set of statements that describes, explains, and predicts behavior.

TABLE 1.1

Basic Issues in Child Development

ISSUE	QUESTION RAISED ABOUT DEVELOPMENT
Organismic versus mechanistic child	Are children active beings with psychological structures that underlie and control development, or are they passive recipients of environmental inputs?
Continuous versus discontinuous	Is child development a matter of cumulative adding on of skills and behaviors, or does it involve qualitative, stagewise changes?
Nature versus nurture	Are genetic or environmental factors the most important determinants of child development and behavior?

ORGANISMIC VERSUS MECHANISTIC CHILD

Recently, the mother of a 16-month-old boy named Angelo reported to me with amazement that her young son pushed a toy car across the livingroom floor while making a motorlike sound, "Brmmmm, brmmmm," for the first time. "We've never shown him how to do that!" exclaimed Angelo's mother. "Did he make up that sound himself," she inquired, "or did he copy it from some other child at day care?"

Angelo's mother has asked a puzzling question about the nature of children. It contrasts two basic perspectives: the organismic, or *active* position, with the mechanistic, or *passive* point of view.

Organismic theories assume that change is stimulated from *within the organism*—more specifically, that psychological structures exist inside the child that underlie and control development. Children are viewed as active, purposeful beings who make sense of their world and determine their own learning. For an organismic theorist, the surrounding environment supports development, as Angelo's mother did when she provided him with stimulating toys. But since children invent their own ways of understanding and responding to events around them, the environment does not bring about the child's growth.

In contrast, **mechanistic theories** focus on relationships between environmental inputs and behavioral outputs. The approach is called *mechanistic* because children's development is compared to the workings of a machine. Change is stimulated by the environment, which shapes the behavior of the child, who is a passive reactor. For example, when Angelo's playmate says, "Brmmmm," Angelo responds similarly. According to this view, new capacities result from external forces acting on the child. Development is treated as a straightforward, predictable consequence of events in the surrounding world (Miller, 1993).

CONTINUITY VERSUS DISCONTINUITY IN DEVELOPMENT

How can we best describe the differences in capacities and behavior that exist between small infants, young children, adolescents, and adults? As Figure 1.1 illustrates, major theories recognize two possibilities.

On the one hand, babies and preschoolers may respond to the world in much the same way as adults. The difference between the immature and mature being may simply be one of *amount* or *complexity* of behavior. For example, little Angelo's thinking might be just as logical and well organized as our own. Perhaps (as his mother reports) Angelo can sort objects into simple categories, recognize whether

Organismic theories
Theories that assume the existence of psychological structures inside the child that underlie and control development.

Mechanistic theories
Theories that regard the child as a passive reactor to environmental inputs.

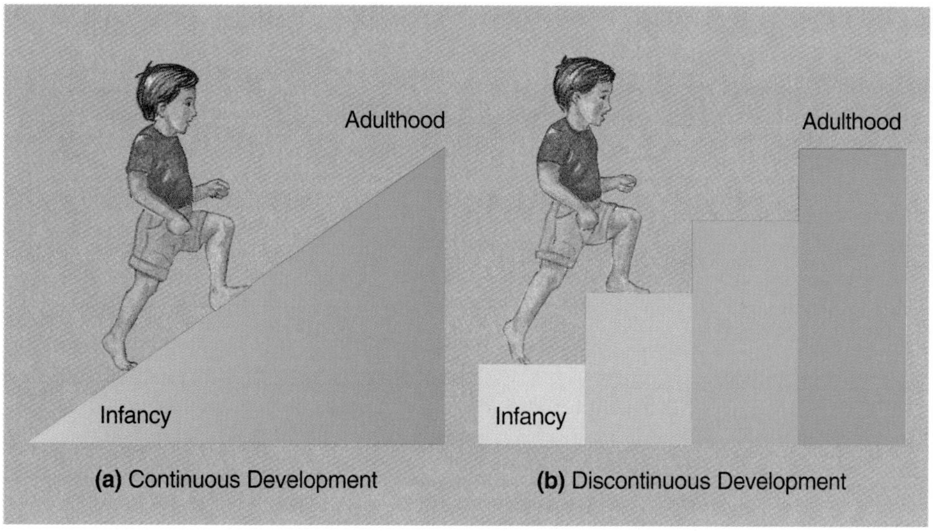

FIGURE 1.1

Is development continuous or discontinuous?
(a) Some theorists believe that development is a smooth, continuous process. Children gradually add more of the same types of skills. (b) Other theorists think that development takes place in abrupt, discontinuous stages. Children change rapidly as they step up to a new level of development and then change very little for a while. With each new step, the child interprets and responds to the world in a qualitatively different way.

there are more of one kind than another, and remember where he left his favorite toy at day care the week before. Angelo's only limitation may be that he cannot perform these skills with as many pieces of information as we can. If this is true, then changes in Angelo's thinking must be **continuous**—a process that consists of gradually adding on more of the same types of skills that were there to begin with.

On the other hand, Angelo may have *unique ways of thinking, feeling, and behaving* that must be understood on their own terms—ones quite different from our own. If so, then development is a **discontinuous** process in which new ways of understanding and responding to the world emerge at particular time periods. From this perspective, Angelo is not yet able to organize objects or remember experiences in the same way as adults. Instead, he will move through a series of developmental steps, each of which has unique features, until he reaches a final transformation that marks the beginning of adulthood.

Theories that accept the discontinuous perspective include a vital developmental concept: the concept of **stage.** Stages are *qualitative changes* in thinking, feeling, and behaving that characterize particular time periods of development. In stage theories, development is much like climbing a staircase, with each step corresponding to a more mature, reorganized way of functioning than the one that came before. The stage concept also assumes that children undergo periods of rapid transformation as they step up from one stage to the next, followed by plateaus during which they stand solidly within a stage. In other words, change is fairly sudden rather than gradual and always ongoing. Finally, stages are always assumed to be universal across children and cultures. That is, stage theories propose that children everywhere follow the same sequence of development.

Does development actually take place in a neat, orderly stepwise sequence that is identical for all human beings? For now, let's note that this is a very ambitious assumption that has not gone unchallenged. We will review some very influential stage theories later in this chapter.

NATURE VERSUS NURTURE

In addition to describing the course of child development, each theory takes a stand on a major question about its underlying causes: Are genetic or environmental factors most important? This is the age-old **nature–nurture controversy.** By *nature,* we mean inborn biological givens—the hereditary information we receive from our parents at the moment of conception that signals the body to grow and affects all

Continuous development
A view that regards development as a cumulative process of adding on more of the same types of skills that were there to begin with.

Discontinuous development
A view in which new and different ways of interpreting and responding to the world emerge at particular time periods.

Stage
A qualitative change in thinking, feeling, and behaving that characterizes a particular time period of development.

Nature–nurture controversy
Disagreement among theorists about whether genetic or environmental factors are the most important determinants of development and behavior.

our characteristics and skills. By *nurture,* we mean the complex forces of the physical and social world that children encounter in their homes, neighborhoods, schools, and communities.

Although all theories grant at least some role to both nature and nurture, they vary in the emphasis placed on each. For example, consider the following questions: Is the older child's ability to think in more complex ways largely the result of an inborn timetable of growth? Or is it primarily influenced by the way parents and teachers stimulate and encourage the child? Do children acquire language because they are genetically predisposed to do so, or because parents intensively tutor them from an early age? And what accounts for the vast individual differences among children—in height, weight, physical coordination, intelligence, personality, and social skills? Is nature or nurture largely responsible?

In later sections of this chapter and throughout this book, we will see that theories offer strikingly different answers to these questions. And the answers they provide are of great applied significance. If you believe that development is largely due to nature, then providing children with experiences aimed at stimulating change would seem to be of little value. If, on the other hand, you are convinced that the environment has a profound impact on development, then you would want to offer a rich variety of learning experiences designed to help children realize their potential.

A BALANCED POINT OF VIEW

So far, we have discussed the three basic issues of child development in terms of extremes—solutions on one side or the other. As we trace the unfolding of the field of child development in the rest of this chapter, you will see that the thinking of many theorists has softened. Modern ones, especially, recognize the merits of both sides. Some theories take an intermediate stand between an organismic versus mechanistic perspective. They regard both the child and the surrounding environment as active and as collaborating to produce development. Similarly, some contemporary researchers believe that both continuous and discontinuous changes characterize development and alternate with one another. Finally, recent investigators have moved away from asking which is more important—heredity or environment. Instead, they want to know precisely *how nature and nurture work together* to influence the child's traits and capacities.

BRIEF REVIEW

Child development is a field of study devoted to understanding human growth and change from conception through adolescence. Investigators from many disciplines have contributed to its vast knowledge base, which has been stimulated both by scientific curiosity and efforts to better the lives of children. Theories lend structure and meaning to observations of children and provide a sound basis for practical action. Almost all theories take a stand on three basic issues about what children are like and how they develop: (1) Is the child an organismic or mechanistic being? (2) Is development a continuous or discontinuous process? (3) Is nature or nurture more important in development?

ASK YOURSELF . . .

- Why is there no single theory that can explain all aspects of child development?
- A school counselor advises a parent, "Don't worry about your teenager's argumentative behavior. It shows that she's beginning to see the world in a different way than she did as a young child. A rise in conflict with parents is a stage that all adolescents pass through." What stand is the counselor taking on the three basic issues about childhood and child development?

HISTORICAL FOUNDATIONS

Modern theories of child development are the result of centuries of change in Western cultural values, philosophical thinking about children, and scientific progress. To understand the field as it exists today, we must return to its early beginnings—to influences that long preceded scientific child study. We will see that many early ideas about children linger on as important forces in current theory and research.

MEDIEVAL TIMES

In medieval times (the sixth through the fifteenth centuries), little importance was placed on childhood as a separate phase of the life cycle. The idea accepted by many theories today, that the child's nature is unique and different from that of youths and adults, was much less common then. Instead, once children emerged from infancy, they were regarded as miniature, already formed adults, a view called **preformationism.** This attitude is reflected in the art, everyday entertainment, and language of the times. If you look carefully at medieval paintings, you will see that children are depicted in dress and expression as immature adults. Before the sixteenth century, toys and games were not designed to occupy and amuse children but were for all people. And consider age, so important an aspect of modern personal identity that today's children can recite how old they are almost as soon as they can talk. Age was unimportant in medieval custom and usage. People did not refer to it in everyday conversation, and it was not even recorded in family and civil records until the fifteenth and sixteenth centuries (Ariès, 1962).

Nevertheless, faint glimmerings of the idea that children are unique emerged during medieval times. The Church defended the innocence of children and encouraged parents to provide spiritual training. Medical works had sections acknowledging the fragility of infants and children and providing special instructions for their care.

In this medieval painting, the young child is depicted as a miniature adult. His dress, expression, and activities resemble those of his elders. Through the fifteenth century, little emphasis was placed on childhood as a unique phase of the life cycle. *(Giraudon/ Art Resources)*

Preformationism
Medieval view of the child as a miniature adult.

And some laws recognized that children needed protection from adults who might mistreat or take advantage of them. But even though in a practical sense there was some awareness of the smallness and vulnerability of children, as yet there were no theories about the uniqueness of childhood or separate developmental periods (Borstelmann, 1983; Sommerville, 1982).

THE REFORMATION

In the sixteenth century, a revised image of childhood sprang from the religious movement that gave birth to Protestantism—in particular, from the Puritan belief in original sin. According to Puritan doctrine, the child was a fragile creature of God who needed to be safeguarded but who also needed to be reformed. Born evil and stubborn, children had to be civilized toward a destiny of virtue and salvation (Ariès, 1962; Shahar, 1990).

Harsh, restrictive child-rearing practices were recommended as the most efficient means for taming the depraved child. Infants were tightly swaddled, and children were dressed in stiff, uncomfortable clothing that held them in adultlike postures. In schools, disobedient pupils were routinely beaten by their schoolmasters (Stone, 1977). Although these attitudes represented the prevailing child-rearing philosophy of the time, it is important to note that they probably were not typical of everyday practices in Puritan families. Recent historical evidence suggests that love and affection for their children made many Puritan parents reluctant to exercise extremely repressive measures (Moran & Vinovskis, 1986).

As the Puritans emigrated from England to the United States, they brought with them the belief that child rearing was one of their most important obligations. Although they continued to regard the child's soul as tainted by original sin, they tried to promote reason in their sons and daughters so they would be able to separate right from wrong and resist temptation. The Puritans were the first to develop special reading materials for children that instructed them in religious and moral ideals. As they trained their children in self-reliance and self-control, Puritan parents gradually adopted a moderate balance between discipline and indulgence, severity and permissiveness (Pollock, 1987).

PHILOSOPHIES OF THE ENLIGHTENMENT

The seventeenth-century Enlightenment brought new philosophies of reason and emphasized ideals of human dignity and respect. Conceptions of childhood appeared that were more humane than those of centuries past.

■ JOHN LOCKE. The writings of John Locke (1632–1704), a leading British philosopher, served as the forerunner of an important twentieth-century perspective that we will discuss shortly: *behaviorism.* Locke viewed the child as a **tabula rasa.** Translated from Latin, this means "a blank slate" or "white piece of paper." According to this idea, children were not basically evil. They were, to begin with, nothing at all, and their characters could be shaped by all kinds of experiences during the course of growing up. Locke (1690/1892) described parents as rational tutors who could mold the child in any way they wished, through careful instruction, effective example, and rewards for good behavior. In addition, Locke was ahead of his time in recommending to parents child-rearing practices that were eventually supported by twentieth-century research. For example, he suggested that parents not reward children with money or sweets, but rather with praise and approval. Locke also opposed physical punishment: "The child repeatedly beaten in school cannot look upon books and teachers without experiencing fear and anger." Locke's philosophy led to a change from harshness toward children to kindness and compassion.

Tabula rasa
Locke's view of the child as a blank slate whose character is shaped by experience.

Look carefully at Locke's ideas, and you will see that he took a firm stand on each of the basic issues we discussed earlier in this chapter. As blank slates, children are viewed in passive, *mechanistic* terms. The course of growth is written upon them by the environment. Locke also regarded development as *continuous*. Adultlike behaviors are gradually built up through the warm, consistent teachings of parents. Finally, Locke was a champion of *nurture*—of the power of the environment to determine whether children become good or bad, bright or dull, kind or selfish.

■ JEAN JACQUES ROUSSEAU. In the eighteenth century, a new theory of childhood was introduced by the French philosopher of the Enlightenment, Jean Jacques Rousseau (1712–1778). Children, Rousseau (1762/1955) thought, were not blank slates and empty containers to be filled by adult instruction. Instead, they were **noble savages,** naturally endowed with a sense of right and wrong and with an innate plan for orderly, healthy growth. Unlike Locke, Rousseau thought children's built-in moral sense and unique ways of thinking and feeling would only be harmed by adult training. His was a permissive philosophy in which the adult should be receptive to the child's needs at each of four stages of development: infancy, childhood, late childhood, and adolescence.

Rousseau's philosophy includes two vitally important concepts that are found in modern theories. The first is the concept of *stage*, which we discussed earlier in this chapter. The second is the concept of **maturation,** which refers to a genetically determined, naturally unfolding course of growth. If you accept the notion that children mature through a sequence of stages, then they cannot be preformed, miniature adults. Instead, they are unique and different from adults, and their development is determined by their own inner nature. Compared to Locke, Rousseau took a very different stand on basic developmental issues. He saw children as *organismic* (active shapers of their own destiny), development as a *discontinuous* stagewise process, and *nature* as having mapped out the path and timetable of growth.

DARWIN'S THEORY OF EVOLUTION

A century after Rousseau, another ancestor of modern child study—this time, of its scientific foundations—emerged. In the mid-nineteenth century, Charles Darwin (1809–1882), a British naturalist, joined an expedition to distant parts of the world, where he made careful observations of fossils and animal and plant life. Darwin (1859/1936) noticed the infinite variation among species. He also saw that within a species, no two individuals are exactly alike. From these observations, he constructed his famous theory of evolution.

The theory emphasized two related principles: *natural selection* and *survival of the fittest.* Darwin explained that certain species were selected by nature to survive in particular parts of the world because they had characteristics that fit with, or were adapted to, their surroundings. Other species died off because they were not as well suited to their environments. Individuals within a species who best met the survival requirements of the environment lived long enough to reproduce and pass their more favorable characteristics to future generations. Darwin's emphasis on the adaptive value of physical characteristics and behavior eventually found its way into important twentieth-century theories.

During his explorations, Darwin discovered that the early prenatal growth of many species was strikingly similar. This suggested that all species, including human beings, were descended from a few common ancestors. Other scientists concluded from Darwin's observation that the development of the human child, from conception to maturity, followed the same general plan as the evolution of the human species. Although this belief eventually proved to be inaccurate, efforts to chart parallels between child growth and human evolution prompted researchers to make careful observations of all aspects of children's behavior. Out of these first attempts to document an idea about development, the science of child study was born.

Noble savage
Rousseau's view of the child as naturally endowed with an innate plan for orderly, healthy growth.

Maturation
A genetically determined, naturally unfolding course of growth.

EARLY SCIENTIFIC BEGINNINGS

Scientific child study evolved quickly during the early part of the twentieth century. As we will see in the following sections, rudimentary observations of single children were soon followed by improved methods and theories. Each advance contributed to the firm foundation on which the field rests today.

THE BABY BIOGRAPHIES. Imagine yourself as a forerunner in the field of child development, confronted with studying children for the first time. How might you go about this challenging task? Scientists of the late nineteenth and early twentieth century did what most of us would probably do in their place. They selected a child of their own or of a close relative. Then, beginning in early infancy, they jotted down day-by-day descriptions and impressions of the youngster's behavior. Dozens of these baby biographies were published by the early twentieth century. In the following excerpt from one of them, the author reflects on the birth of her young niece, whose growth she followed during the first year of life:

> Its first act is a cry, not of wrath, . . . nor a shout of joy, . . . but a snuffling, and then a long, thin, tearless á—á, with the timbre of a Scotch bagpipe, purely automatic, but of discomfort. With this monotonous and dismal cry, with its red, shriveled, parboiled skin. . . , squinting, cross-eyed, pot-bellied, and bow-legged, it is not strange that, if the mother . . . has not come to love her child before birth, there is a brief interval occasionally dangerous to the child before the maternal instinct is fully aroused.
>
> It cannot be denied that this unflattering description is fair enough, and our baby was no handsomer than the rest of her kind. . . . Yet she did not lack admirers. I have never noticed that women (even those who are not mothers) mind a few little aesthetic defects, . . . with so many counterbalancing charms in the little warm, soft, living thing. (Shinn, 1900, pp. 20–21)

Can you tell from this passage why the baby biographies have sometimes been upheld as examples of how *not* to study children? These first investigators tended to be emotionally invested in the infants they observed, and they seldom began with a clear idea of what they wanted to find out about the child. Not surprisingly, many of the records made were eventually discarded as biased. However, we must keep in mind that the baby biographers were like explorers first setting foot on alien soil. When a field is new, we cannot expect its theories and methods to be well formulated.

The baby biographies were clearly a step in the right direction. In fact, two theorists of the nineteenth century, Darwin (1877) and German biologist William Preyer (1882/1888), contributed to these early records of children's behavior. Preyer, especially, set high standards for making observations. He recorded what he saw immediately, as completely as possible, and at regular intervals. And he checked the accuracy of his own notes against those of a second observer (Cairns, 1983). These are the same high standards that modern researchers use when observing children. As the result of the biographers' pioneering efforts, in succeeding decades the child became a common focus of scientific research.

THE NORMATIVE PERIOD OF CHILD STUDY. G. Stanley Hall (1846–1924), one of the most influential American psychologists of the early twentieth century, is generally regarded as the founder of the child study movement (Dixon & Lerner, 1992). Inspired by Darwin's work, Hall and his well-known student Arnold Gesell (1880–1961) developed theories based on evolutionary ideas. These early leaders regarded child development as a genetically determined series of events that unfolds automatically, much like a blooming flower (Gesell, 1933; Hall, 1904).

Hall and Gesell are remembered less for their one-sided theories than for their intensive efforts to describe all aspects of child development. Aware of the limita-

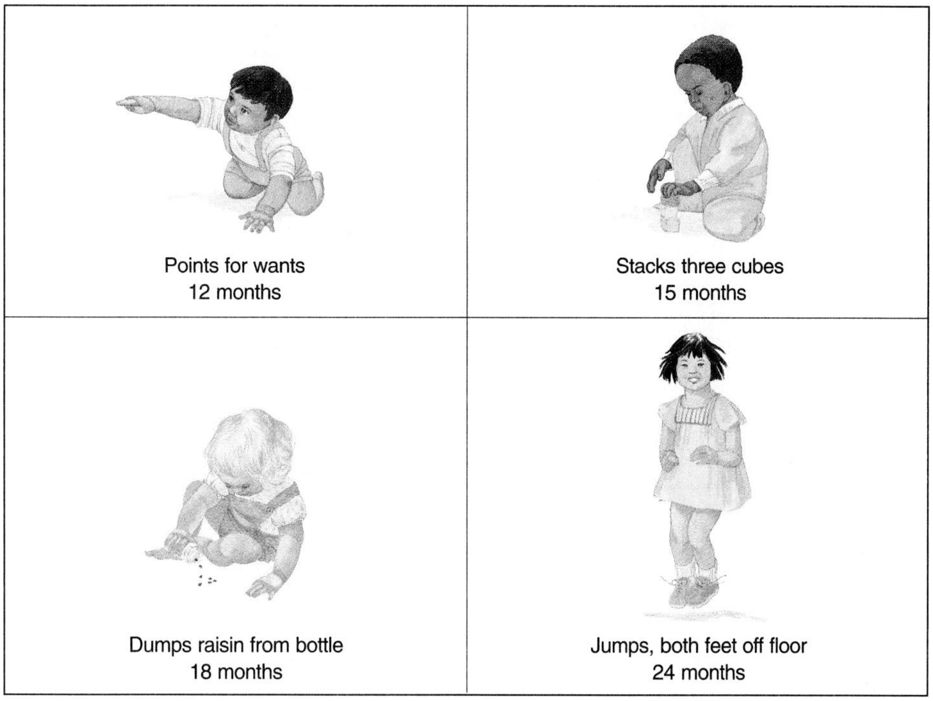

FIGURE 1.2

Sample milestones from the most recent revision of Gesell's schedules of infant development, which include norms on hundreds of motor, mental, language, and social skills.
Gesell's efforts to describe the course of development continue to be useful today. *(Adapted from Knobloch, Stevens, and Malone, 1980.)*

tions of the baby biographies, Hall set out to collect a sound body of objective facts about children. This goal launched the **normative approach** to child study. In a normative investigation, measurements of behavior are taken on large numbers of children. Then age-related averages are computed to represent the typical child's development. Using this method, Hall constructed elaborate questionnaires asking children of different ages almost everything they could tell about themselves—interests, fears, imaginary playmates, dreams, friendships, everyday knowledge, and more (White, 1992).

In the same tradition, Gesell devoted a major part of his career to collecting detailed normative information on the behavior of infants and children. His schedules of infant development were particularly complete, and revised versions continue to be used today (see Figure 1.2). Gesell was also among the first to make knowledge about child development meaningful to parents. He provided them with descriptions of motor achievements, social behaviors, and personality characteristics (Gesell & Ilg, 1943/1949, 1946/1949). Gesell hoped to relieve parents' anxieties by informing them of what to expect at each age. If, as he believed, the timetable of development is the product of millions of years of evolution, then children are naturally knowledgeable about their needs. His child-rearing advice, in the tradition of Rousseau, was a permissive approach that recommended sensitivity and responsiveness to children's cues (Thelen & Adolph, 1992).

Gesell's books were widely read. Along with Benjamin Spock's famous *Baby and Child Care,* they became a central part of a rapidly expanding literature for parents published over the course of this century (see the Social Issues box on page 14).

THE MENTAL TESTING MOVEMENT. While Hall and Gesell were developing their theories and methods in the United States, French psychologist Alfred Binet (1857–1911) also took a normative approach to child development, but for a different reason. In the early 1900s, Binet and his colleague Theodore Simon were asked to find a way to identify retarded children in the Paris school system who needed to be placed in special classes. The first successful intelligence test, which they constructed for this purpose, grew out of practical educational concerns.

Normative approach
An approach in which age-related averages are computed to represent the typical child's development.

Previous attempts to create a useful intelligence test had met with little success. But Binet's effort was unique in that he began with a well-developed theory. In contrast to earlier views, which reduced intelligence to simple elements of reaction time and sensitivity to physical stimuli, Binet captured the complexity of children's thinking (Siegler, 1992). He defined intelligence as good judgment, planning, and critical reflection. Then he selected test questions that directly measured these abilities, creating a series of age-graded items that permitted him to compare the intellectual progress of different children.

In 1916, at Stanford University, Binet's test was translated into English and adapted for use with American children. It became known as the *Stanford-Binet Intelligence Scale*. Besides providing a score that could successfully predict school

SOCIAL ISSUES

SOCIAL CHANGE AND CHILD-REARING ADVICE TO PARENTS

Almost all parents—new ones especially—feel a need for sound advice on how to rear their children. To meet this need, the field of child development has long been communicating what it knows to the general public through a wide variety of popular books and magazines. A recent survey looked at the types of advice that experts gave to parents of infants from 1955 to 1984 (Young, 1990). Two widely read sources were carefully examined: *Parents* magazine (to which scholars regularly contribute articles) and *Infant Care* (a pamphlet written by pediatricians and other child development specialists and published at regular intervals by the United States Children's Bureau).

Parents often turn to books and magazines for expert advice on how to rear their children. The information they find reflects cultural beliefs and social realities of the times. *(Innervisions)*

From the 1950s to the 1980s, advice to parents changed in ways that reflected new social realities, cultural beliefs about children, and scientific discoveries. Prior to the 1970s, the publications emphasized the central role of the mother in healthy infant development. Although mothers were encouraged to include fathers in the care of the baby, they were cautioned not to expect fathers to participate equally. The succeeding decade brought considerably fewer references to the primacy of the mother until, in the mid-1980s, an about-face was evident. Experts suggested that fathers might share in the full range of caregiving responsibilities, since new evidence revealed that the father's role is unique and important to all aspects of development.

Around this time, information about maternal employment and day care also appeared in the publications. In contrast to the earlier view of the maternal role as a full-time commitment, experts reassured the modern mother that her baby did not require her continuous presence and offered advice about how to select good day care. Recommendations on this score, however, displayed some ambivalence. Mothers were also told that staying with the infant "can be a great human experience," and they were discouraged from entrusting the care of their babies to others. As we will see in Chapter 7, controversy exists in both American culture and in the scientific community about the advisability of placing infants in day care, and it is reflected in contemporary advice to parents.

During the three decades studied, some child-rearing themes did not change. Parents were continuously told that they play a large role in guiding their baby's development, that infants are active learners who benefit from a rich variety of physical and social stimulation, and that early experiences have a lasting impact. As you read the rest of this chapter, try to identify major theories of the mid- and late-twentieth century that may have prompted these statements.

TRY THIS . . .

- Visit your library and examine several issues of *Infant Care* published by the federal government earlier in this century and today. How have parenting practices related to feeding, sleeping, and toilet training changed?
- Check your local bookstore for current parenting titles that extend beyond the period of infancy. Can you find additional examples of how advice to parents is both driven by new discoveries and influenced by the larger social context in which child rearing takes place?

achievement, the Binet test sparked tremendous interest in individual differences in development. The mental testing movement was in motion. Comparisons of the intelligence test scores of children who vary in sex, ethnicity, birth order, family background, and other characteristics became a major focus of research. Intelligence tests also rose quickly to the forefront of the controversy over nature versus nurture that has continued throughout this century.

BRIEF REVIEW

The modern field of child development has roots dating far back into the past. In medieval times, children were regarded as miniature adults. By the sixteenth century, childhood became a distinct phase of the life cycle. The Puritan belief in original sin fostered a harsh, authoritarian approach to child rearing. During the seventeenth-century Enlightenment, Locke's "blank slate" and Rousseau's "inherently good" child promoted more humane views of children. Darwin's evolutionary ideas inspired maturational theories and the first attempts to study the child directly, in the form of baby biographies and Hall and Gesell's normative investigations. Out of the normative tradition arose Binet's first successful intelligence test and a concern with individual differences among children.

ASK YOURSELF . . .

- If you could interview people of medieval times to find out whether they thought child development was a continuous or discontinuous process, how do you think they would respond?
- Suppose we could arrange a debate between John Locke and Jean Jacques Rousseau on the nature–nurture controversy. Summarize the argument that each of these historical figures is likely to present.

MID-TWENTIETH-CENTURY THEORIES

In the mid-twentieth century, the field of child development expanded into a legitimate discipline. Specialized societies were founded, and research journals were launched. As child development attracted increasing interest, a variety of mid-twentieth-century theories emerged, each of which continues to have followers today. In these theories, the European concern with the inner thoughts and feelings of the child contrasts sharply with the focus of American academic psychology on scientific precision and concrete, observable behavior.

THE PSYCHOANALYTIC PERSPECTIVE

By the 1930s and 1940s, many parents whose children suffered from serious emotional stress and behavior problems sought help from psychiatrists and social workers. The earlier normative movement had answered the question, What are children like? But child guidance professionals had to address the question, How and why did children become the way they are? to treat their difficulties. They turned for help to the **psychoanalytic perspective** on personality development because of its emphasis on understanding the unique developmental history of each child.

According to the psychoanalytic approach, children move through a series of stages in which they confront conflicts between biological drives and social expectations. The way these conflicts are resolved determines the person's ability to learn, to get along with others, and to cope with anxiety. Although many individuals contributed to the psychoanalytic perspective, two have been especially influential: Sigmund Freud, founder of the psychoanalytic movement, and Erik Erikson.

■ FREUD'S THEORY. Freud (1856–1939), a Viennese physician, saw patients in his practice with a variety of nervous symptoms, such as hallucinations, fears, and paralyses, that appeared to have no physical basis. Seeking a cure for these troubled adults, Freud found that their symptoms could be relieved by having patients talk freely about painful events of their childhood. Using this "talking cure," he carefully examined the unconscious motivations of his patients. Startling

Psychoanalytic perspective An approach to personality development introduced by Freud that assumes children move through a series of stages in which they confront conflicts between biological drives and social expectations. The way these conflicts are resolved determines psychological adjustment.

TABLE 1.2

Freud's Psychosexual Stages

PSYCHOSEXUAL STAGE	PERIOD OF DEVELOPMENT	DESCRIPTION
Oral	Birth–1 year	The new ego directs the baby's sucking activities toward breast or bottle. If oral needs are not met appropriately, the individual may develop such habits as thumb sucking, fingernail biting, and pencil chewing in childhood and overeating and smoking in later life.
Anal	1–3 years	Young toddlers and preschoolers enjoy holding and releasing urine and feces. Toilet training becomes a major issue between parent and child. If parents insist that children be trained before they are ready or make too few demands, conflicts about anal control may appear in the form of extreme orderliness and cleanliness or messiness and disorder.
Phallic	3–6 years	Id impulses transfer to the genitals, and the child finds pleasure in genital stimulation. Freud's *Oedipus conflict* for boys and *Electra conflict* for girls take place. Young children feel a sexual desire for the opposite-sex parent. To avoid punishment, they give up this desire and, instead, adopt the same-sex parent's characteristics and values. As a result, the superego is formed. The relations between id, ego, and superego established at this time determine the individual's basic personality orientation.
Latency	6–11 years	Sexual instincts die down, and the superego develops further. The child acquires new social values from adults outside the family and from play with same-sex peers.
Genital	Adolescence	Puberty causes the sexual impulses of the phallic stage to reappear. If development has been successful during earlier stages, it leads to marriage, mature sexuality, and the birth and rearing of children.

the straightlaced Victorian society in which he lived, Freud concluded that infants and young children were sexual beings and that the way they were permitted to express their impulses lay at the heart of their adult behavior. Freud constructed his **psychosexual theory** of development on the basis of adult remembrances. It emphasizes that how parents manage their child's sexual and aggressive drives in the first few years of life is crucial for healthy personality development.

Three Portions of the Personality. In Freud's theory, three parts of the personality—id, ego, and superego—become integrated during a sequence of five stages of development. The **id,** the largest portion of the mind, is inherited and present at birth. It is the source of basic biological needs and desires. The id seeks to satisfy its impulses head on, without delay. As a result, young babies cry vigorously when they are hungry, wet, or need to be held and cuddled.

The **ego**—the conscious, rational part of personality—emerges in early infancy to ensure that the id's desires are satisfied in accordance with reality. Recalling times when parents helped the baby gratify the id, the ego redirects the impulses so they are discharged on appropriate objects at acceptable times and places. Aided by the ego, the hungry baby of a few months of age stops crying when he sees his mother unfasten her clothing for breast-feeding or warm a bottle. And the more competent preschooler goes into the kitchen and gets a snack on her own.

Between 3 and 6 years of age, the **superego,** or seat of conscience, appears. It contains the values of society and is often in conflict with the id's desires. The superego develops from interactions with parents, who eventually insist that children control their biological impulses. Once the superego is formed, the ego is faced with the increasingly complex task of reconciling the demands of the id, the external world, and conscience (Freud, 1923/1974). For example, when the ego is tempted to gratify an id impulse by hitting a playmate to get an attractive toy, the superego may warn that such behavior is wrong. The ego must decide which of the two forces (id or superego) will win this inner struggle or work out a reasonable

Psychosexual theory
Freud's theory, which emphasizes that how parents manage children's sexual and aggressive drives during the first few years is crucial for healthy personality development.

Id
In Freud's theory, the part of personality that is the source of basic biological needs and desires.

Ego
In Freud's theory, the rational part of personality that reconciles the demands of the id, the external world, and the conscience.

Superego
In Freud's theory, the part of personality that is the seat of conscience and is often in conflict with the id's desires.

compromise, such as asking for a turn with the toy. According to Freud, the relations established between id, ego, and superego during the preschool years determine the individual's basic personality.

Sigmund Freud founded the psychoanalytic movement. His psychosexual theory was the first approach to stress the importance of early experience for later development. *(Lyrl Ahern)*

Psychosexual Development. Freud (1938/1973) believed that over the course of childhood, sexual impulses shift their focus from the oral to the anal to the genital regions of the body. In each stage of development, parents walk a fine line between permitting too much or too little gratification of their child's basic needs. Either extreme can cause the child's psychic energies to be *fixated,* or arrested, at a particular stage. Too much satisfaction makes the child unwilling to move on to a more mature level of behavior; too little leads the child to continue seeking gratification of the frustrated drive. If parents strike an appropriate balance, then children grow into well-adjusted adults with the capacity for mature sexual behavior, investment in family life, and rearing of the next generation. Table 1.2 summarizes each of Freud's stages.

Freud's psychosexual theory highlighted the importance of family relationships for children's development. It was the first theory to stress the importance of early experience for later development. But Freud's perspective was eventually criticized for several reasons. First, the theory overemphasized the influence of sexual feelings in development. Second, because it was based on the problems of sexually repressed, well-to-do adults, some aspects of Freud's theory did not apply in cultures differing from nineteenth-century Victorian society. Finally, Freud's ideas were called into question because he did not study children directly.

Erik Erikson expanded Freud's theory, emphasizing the psychosocial outcomes of development. At each psychosexual stage, a major psychological conflict is resolved. If the outcome is positive, individuals acquire attitudes and skills that permit them to contribute constructively to society. *(Lyrl Ahern)*

■ ERIKSON'S THEORY. Several of Freud's followers took what was useful from his theory and stretched and rearranged it in ways that improved upon his vision. The most important of these neo-Freudians for the field of child development was Erik Erikson (1902–1994).

Although Erikson (1950) accepted Freud's basic psychosexual framework, he expanded the picture of development at each stage. In his **psychosocial theory,** Erikson emphasized that social experiences at each Freudian stage do not just lead to an embattled ego that mediates between id impulses and superego demands. The ego is also a positive force in development. At each stage, it acquires attitudes and skills that make the individual an active, contributing member of society. A basic psychological conflict, which is resolved along a continuum from positive to negative, determines healthy or maladaptive outcomes at each stage. As you can see in Table 1.3, Erikson's first five stages parallel Freud's stages. However, Erikson did not regard important developmental tasks as limited to early childhood. He believed that they occur throughout life. Note that Erikson added three adult stages to Freud's model and was one of the first to recognize the life-span nature of development.

Finally, unlike Freud, Erikson pointed out that normal development must be understood in relation to each culture's unique life situation. For example, among the Yurok Indians (a tribe of fishermen and acorn gatherers in the Pacific Northwest of the United States), babies are deprived of breast-feeding for the first 10 days after birth and instead are fed a thin soup from a small shell. At 6 months of age, infants are abruptly weaned, an event enforced, if necessary, by having the mother leave for a few days. These experiences, from our cultural vantage point, seem like cruel attempts to frustrate the child's oral needs. But Erikson explained that the Yurok live in a world in which salmon fill the river just once a year, a circumstance that requires the development of considerable self-restraint for survival. In this way, he showed that child-rearing experiences are affected by a culture's general life condi-

Psychosocial theory
Erikson's theory, which emphasizes that the demands of society at each Freudian stage not only promote the development of a unique personality, but also ensure that individuals acquire attitudes and skills that help them become active, contributing members of their society.

TABLE 1.3

Erikson's Psychosocial Stages

PSYCHOSOCIAL STAGE	PERIOD OF DEVELOPMENT	DESCRIPTION	CORRESPONDING PSYCHOSEXUAL STAGE
Basic trust versus mistrust	Birth–1 year	From warm, responsive care, infants gain a sense of trust, or confidence, that the world is good. Mistrust occurs when infants have to wait too long for comfort and are handled harshly.	Oral
Autonomy versus shame and doubt	1–3 years	Using new mental and motor skills, children want to choose and decide for themselves. Autonomy is fostered when parents permit reasonable free choice and do not force or shame the child.	Anal
Initiative versus guilt	3–6 years	Through make-believe play, children experiment with the kind of person they can become. Initiative—a sense of ambition and responsibility—develops when parents support their child's new sense of purpose and direction. The danger is that parents will demand too much self-control, which leads to overcontrol, or too much guilt.	Phallic
Industry versus inferiority	6–11 years	At school, children develop the capacity to work and cooperate with others. Inferiority develops when negative experiences at home, at school, or with peers lead to feelings of incompetence.	Latency
Identity versus identity diffusion	Adolescence	The adolescent tries to answer the question, Who am I, and what is my place in society? Self-chosen values and vocational goals lead to a lasting personal identity. The negative outcome is confusion about future adult roles.	Genital
Intimacy versus isolation	Young adulthood	Young people work on establishing intimate ties to others. Because of earlier disappointments, some individuals cannot form close relationships and remain isolated from others.	
Generativity versus stagnation	Middle adulthood	Generativity means giving to the next generation through child rearing, caring for other people, or productive work. The person who fails in these ways feels an absence of meaningful accomplishment.	
Ego integrity versus despair	Old age	In this final stage, individuals reflect on the kind of person they have been. Integrity results from feeling that life was worth living as it happened. Old people who are dissatisfied with their lives fear death.	

tion. They can only be understood by making reference to the competencies valued and needed by the child's society as a whole.

CONTRIBUTIONS AND LIMITATIONS OF PSYCHOANALYTIC THEORY. A special strength of the psychoanalytic perspective is its emphasis on the individual's unique life history as worthy of study and understanding (Emde, 1992). Consistent with this view, psychoanalytic theorists accept the *clinical method* as the most effective way to find out about development. It combines data from a variety of sources—interviews with the child, family members, and others who know the child well; responses to psychological tests, and observations in the clinic setting and sometimes in everyday environments as well. The information is synthesized into a detailed picture of the personality functioning of a single child. (We will discuss the strengths and limitations of the clinical method, along with others, at the end of this chapter.) Psychoanalytic theory has also inspired a wealth of research on many aspects of emotional and social development, including infant–caregiver attachment, aggression, sibling relationships, child-rearing practices, morality, gender roles, and adolescent identity.

Despite its extensive contributions, the psychoanalytic perspective is no longer in the mainstream of child development research. There are various speculations as to why this is the case. Psychoanalytic theorists may have become isolated from the rest of the field because they were so strongly committed to the clinical approach that they failed to consider other methods. In addition, many psychoanalytic ideas, such as Freud's Oedipus conflict and the psychosexual stages, were so vague and full of interpretation that they were difficult or impossible to test empirically (Miller, 1993).

BEHAVIORISM AND SOCIAL LEARNING THEORY

At the same time that psychoanalytic theory gained in prominence, child study was also influenced by a very different perspective: **behaviorism,** a tradition consistent with Locke's image of the tabula rasa. American behaviorism began with the work of psychologist John Watson (1878–1958) in the early part of the twentieth century. Watson wanted to create an objective science of psychology. Unlike psychoanalytic theorists, he believed in studying directly observable events—stimuli and responses—rather than the unseen workings of the mind (Horowitz, 1992).

B. F. Skinner, a leading behaviorist, rejected Hull's idea that primary drive reduction is the basis of all learning. He emphasized an alternative learning principle, operant conditioning, that has been widely applied in the field of child development. *(Lyrl Ahern)*

■ TRADITIONAL BEHAVIORISM. Watson was inspired by some studies of animal learning carried out by famous Russian physiologist Ivan Pavlov. Pavlov knew that dogs release saliva as an innate reflex when they are given food. But he noticed that his dogs were salivating before they tasted any food—when they saw the trainer who usually fed them. The dogs, Pavlov reasoned, must have learned to associate a neutral stimulus (the trainer) with another stimulus (food) that produces a reflexive response (salivation). As a result of this association, the neutral stimulus could bring about the response by itself. Anxious to test this idea, Pavlov successfully taught dogs to salivate at the sound of a bell by pairing it with the presentation of food. He had discovered *classical conditioning.*

Watson wanted to find out if classical conditioning could be applied to children's behavior. In a historic experiment, he taught Albert, a 9-month-old infant, to fear a neutral stimulus—a soft white rat—by presenting it several times with a sharp, loud sound, which naturally scared the baby. Little Albert, who at first had reached out eagerly to touch the furry rat, soon cried and turned his head away when he caught sight of it (Watson & Raynor, 1920). In fact, Albert's fear was so intense that researchers eventually questioned the ethics of studies like this one (an issue we will take up later in this chapter). On the basis of findings like these, Watson concluded that environment was the supreme force in child development. Adults could mold children's behavior in any way they wished, he thought, by carefully controlling stimulus–response associations.

After Watson, American behaviorism developed along several lines. The first was Clark Hull's *drive reduction theory.* According to this view, children continually act to satisfy physiological needs and reduce states of tension. As *primary* drives of hunger, thirst, and sex are met, a wide variety of stimuli associated with them become *secondary,* or *learned, drives.* For example, a Hullian theorist believes that infants prefer the closeness and attention of adults who have given them food and relieved their discomfort. To ensure adults' affection, children will acquire all sorts of responses that adults desire of them—politeness, honesty, patience, persistence, obedience, and more.

Another form of behaviorism was B. F. Skinner's (1904–1990) *operant conditioning theory.* Skinner rejected Hull's idea that primary drive reduction is the only way to get children to learn. According to Skinner, a child's behavior can be increased by following it with a wide variety of *reinforcers* besides food and drink, such as praise,

Behaviorism
An approach that views directly observable events—stimuli and responses—as the appropriate focus of study and the development of behavior as taking place through classical and operant conditioning.

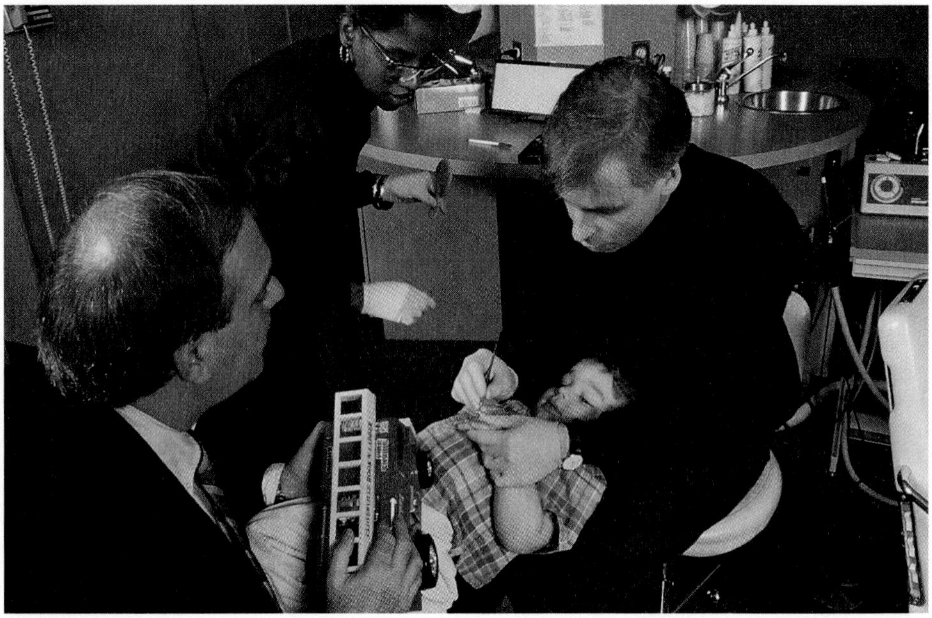

Applied behavior analysis can be used to reduce a child's anxious reactions during dental treatment. This dentist engages in a counting game to relax his young patient before conducting an examination. While the dentist works on the boy's teeth, the boy's father will distract him with a toy fire engine. After the session is over, the father will reinforce the boy's cooperative behavior by permitting him to play with the toy. *(Jacques Chenet/Woodfin Camp & Associates)*

a friendly smile, or a new toy. It can also be decreased through *punishment,* such as withdrawal of privileges, parental disapproval, or being sent to be alone in one's room. As a result of Skinner's work, operant conditioning became a broadly applied learning principle in child psychology. We will consider these conditioning principles more fully when we explore the infant's learning capacities in Chapter 5.

SOCIAL LEARNING THEORY. Psychologists quickly became interested in whether behaviorism might offer a more direct and effective explanation of the development of children's social behavior than the less precise concepts of psychoanalytic theory. This concern sparked the emergence of **social learning theory.** Social learning theorists accepted the principles of conditioning and reinforcement that came before them. They also built on these principles, offering expanded views of how children and adults acquire new responses. By the 1950s, social learning theory became a major force in child development research.

Several kinds of social learning theory emerged. The most influential was devised by Albert Bandura and his colleagues. Bandura (1977) demonstrated that *modeling,* otherwise known as *imitation* or *observational learning,* is the basis for a wide variety of children's behaviors. He recognized that children acquire many favorable and unfavorable responses simply by watching and listening to others around them. The baby who claps her hands after her mother does so, the child who angrily hits a playmate in the same way that he has been punished at home, and the teenager who wears the same clothes and hairstyle as her friends at school are all displaying observational learning.

Bandura's work continues to influence much research on children's social development. However, like changes in the field of child development as a whole, today his theory stresses the importance of *cognition,* or thinking. Bandura has shown that children's ability to listen, remember, and abstract general rules from complex sets of observed behavior affects their imitation and learning. In fact, the most recent revision of Bandura's (1986, 1989) theory places such strong emphasis on how children think about themselves and other people that he calls it a *social-cognitive* rather than a social learning approach. According to this view, children gradually become more selective in what they imitate. From watching others engage in self-praise and self-blame and through feedback about the worth of their own actions, children develop *personal standards* for behavior and a *sense of self-efficacy*—beliefs about their own abilities and characteristics—that guide responses in particular situations (Grusec, 1992). For example, imagine a parent who often remarks, "I'm glad I kept

Social learning theory
An approach that emphasizes the role of modeling, or observational learning, in the development of behavior.

working on that task, even though it was hard," who explains the value of persistence to her child, and who encourages it by saying, "I know you can do that homework very well!" As a result, the child starts to view himself as hard working and high achieving and, from the many people available in the environment, selects models with these characteristics to copy.

Through careful observations of and clinical interviews with children, Jean Piaget developed his comprehensive theory of cognitive development. His work has inspired more research on children than any other single theory. *(Yves de Braine/Black Star)*

CONTRIBUTIONS AND LIMITATIONS OF BEHAVIORISM AND SOCIAL LEARNING THEORY. Like psychoanalytic theory, behaviorism and social learning theory have had a major impact on applied work with children. Yet the techniques used are decidedly different. **Applied behavior analysis** refers to procedures that combine conditioning and modeling to eliminate children's undesirable behaviors and increase their socially acceptable responses. It has been used largely with children who have serious developmental problems, such as persistent aggression and language delays (Patterson, 1982; Whitehurst et al., 1989). But it is also effective in dealing with more common difficulties of childhood. For example, in one study, preschoolers' anxious reactions during dental treatment were reduced by reinforcing them with small toys for answering questions about a story read to them while the dentist worked. Because the children could not listen to the story and kick and cry at the same time, their disruptive behaviors subsided (Stark et al., 1989).

Although the techniques of behaviorism are helpful in treating many problems, we must keep in mind that making something happen through modeling and reinforcement does not mean that these principles provide a complete account of development (Horowitz, 1987). We will see in later sections that many theorists believe that behaviorism offers too narrow a view of important environmental influences. These extend beyond immediate reinforcements and modeled behaviors to the richness of children's physical and social worlds. Finally, in emphasizing cognition, Bandura is unique among theorists whose work grew out of the behaviorist tradition in granting children an active role in their own learning. As we will see when we discuss Piaget's theory in the next section, behaviorism and social learning theory have been criticized for underestimating children's contributions to their own development.

PIAGET'S COGNITIVE-DEVELOPMENTAL THEORY

If there is one individual who has influenced the modern field of child development more than any other, it is the Swiss cognitive theorist Jean Piaget (1896–1980). Although American investigators had been aware of Piaget's work since 1930, they did not grant it much attention until the 1960s. A major reason is that Piaget's ideas and methods of studying children were very much at odds with behaviorism, which dominated American psychology during the middle of the twentieth century (Beilin, 1992).

Recall that behaviorists did not study the child's mental life. In their view, thinking could be reduced to connections between stimuli and responses, and development was a continuous process, consisting of a gradual increase in the number and strength of these connections with age. In contrast, Piaget did not believe that knowledge was imposed on a passive, reinforced child. According to his **cognitive-developmental theory,** children actively construct knowledge as they manipulate and explore their world, and their cognitive development takes place in stages.

PIAGET'S STAGES. Piaget's view of development was greatly influenced by his early training in biology. Central to his theory is the biological concept of *adaptation* (Piaget, 1971). Just as the structures of the body are adapted to fit with the environment, so the structures of the mind develop over the course of childhood to better fit with, or represent, the external world. In infancy and early childhood, children's understanding is markedly different from that of adults. For example, Piaget believed that young babies do not realize that an object hidden from view—

Applied behavior analysis
A set of practical procedures that combine reinforcement, modeling, and the manipulation of situational cues to change behavior.

Cognitive-developmental theory
An approach introduced by Piaget that views the child as actively building psychological structures and cognitive development as taking place in stages.

According to Piaget's theory, at first schemes are motor action patterns. As this 1-year-old takes apart, bangs, and drops these nesting cups, she discovers that her movements have predictable effects on objects and that objects influence one another in regular ways. *(Erika Stone)*

a favorite toy or even the mother—continues to exist. He also concluded that preschoolers' thinking is full of faulty logic and fantasy. For example, children younger than age 7 commonly say that the amount of milk or lemonade changes when it is poured into a differently shaped container. And some of them insist that the images in their dreams are real objects that miraculously appear beside their beds at night! According to Piaget, children eventually revise these incorrect ideas in their ongoing efforts to achieve an *equilibrium,* or balance, between internal structures and information they encounter in their everyday worlds (Beilin, 1992; Kuhn, 1992).

In Piaget's theory, children move through four broad stages of development, each of which is characterized by qualitatively distinct ways of thinking. Table 1.4 provides a brief description of Piaget's stages. In the *sensorimotor stage,* cognitive development begins with the baby's use of the senses and movements to explore the world. These action patterns evolve into the symbolic but illogical thinking of the preschooler in the *preoperational stage.* Then cognition is transformed into the more organized reasoning of the school-age child in the *concrete operational stage.* Finally, in the *formal operational stage,* thought becomes the complex, abstract reasoning system of the adolescent and adult.

■ **PIAGET'S METHODS OF STUDY.** Piaget devised special methods for investigating how children think. In the early part of his career, he carefully observed his three infant children and also presented them with little problems, such as an attractive object that could be grasped, mouthed, kicked, or searched for when hidden from view. From their reactions, Piaget derived his ideas about cognitive changes that take place during the first two years of life.

In studying childhood and adolescent thought, Piaget took advantage of children's ability to describe their thinking. He adapted the clinical method of psychoanalysis, conducting open-ended *clinical interviews* in which a child's initial response to a task served as the basis for the next question he would ask. We will look at an example of a Piagetian clinical interview, as well as the strengths and weaknesses of this technique, when we discuss research methods later in this chapter.

■ **CONTRIBUTIONS AND LIMITATIONS OF PIAGET'S THEORY.** Piaget's cognitive-developmental perspective has stimulated more research on children than any other single theory. It also convinced many child development specialists that children are active learners whose minds are inhabited by rich structures of knowledge. Besides investigating children's understanding of the physical world, Piaget began some explorations into how children reason about the social world. As we will see in later chapters, Piaget's stages of cognitive development have sparked a wealth of research on children's conceptions of themselves, other people, and human relationships.

Practically speaking, Piaget's theory encouraged the development of educational philosophies and programs that emphasize children's discovery learning and direct contact with the environment. A Piagetian classroom contains richly equipped activity areas designed to stimulate children to revise their immature cognitive structures.

In Piaget's preoperational stage, preschool children represent their earlier sensorimotor discoveries with symbols. Language and make-believe play develop rapidly. These 4-year-olds create an imaginative play scene with dress-up clothes and the assistance of a very cooperative family pet. *(Tom McCarthy/Stock South)*

TABLE 1.4

Piaget's Stages of Cognitive Development

STAGE	PERIOD OF DEVELOPMENT	DESCRIPTION
Sensorimotor	Birth–2 years	Infants "think" by acting on the world with their eyes, ears, and hands. As a result, they invent ways of solving sensorimotor problems, such as pulling a lever to hear the sound of a music box, finding hidden toys, and putting objects in and taking them out of containers.
Preoperational	2–7 years	Preschool children use symbols to represent their earlier sensorimotor discoveries. Development of language and make-believe play takes place. However, thinking lacks the logical qualities of the two remaining stages.
Concrete operational	7–11 years	Children's reasoning becomes logical. School-age children understand that a certain amount of lemonade or play dough remains the same even after its appearance changes. They also organize objects into hierarchies of classes and subclasses. However, thinking falls short of adult intelligence. It is not yet abstract.
Formal operational	11 years on	The capacity for abstraction permits adolescents to reason with symbols that do not refer to objects in the real world, as in advanced mathematics. They can also think of all possible outcomes in a scientific problem, not just the most obvious ones.

Despite Piaget's overwhelming contribution to child development and education, in recent years his theory has been challenged. New evidence indicates that Piaget underestimated the competencies of infants and preschoolers. We will see in later chapters that when young children are given tasks scaled down in difficulty, their understanding appears closer to that of the older child and adult than Piaget believed. This discovery has led many investigators to conclude that the maturity of children's thinking may depend on their familiarity with the investigator's task and the kind of knowledge sampled. Finally, many studies show that children's performance on Piagetian problems can be improved with training. This finding raises questions about his assumption that discovery learning rather than adult teaching is the best way to foster development.

Today, the field of child development is divided over its loyalty to Piaget's ideas. Those who continue to find merit in Piaget's approach accept a modified view of his cognitive stages—one in which changes in children's thinking are not sudden and abrupt, but take place much more gradually than Piaget believed (Case, 1985, 1992; Fischer & Pipp, 1984). Others have given up the idea of cognitive stages in favor of a continuous approach to development—information processing—that we will take up in the next section (Gelman & Baillargeon, 1983).

In Piaget's concrete operational stage, school-age children think in an organized and logical fashion about concrete objects. This 8-year-old boy understands that the hamster on one side of the balance scale is just as heavy as the metal weights on the other, even though the two types of objects look and feel quite different from each other. *(Tim Davis/Photo Researchers)*

In Piaget's formal operational stage, adolescents can think logically and abstractly. These high school students solve a complex scientific problem by thinking of all possible outcomes, not just the most obvious. Then they systematically test each possibility to see if it occurs in the real world. *(Will Faller)*

ASK YOURSELF . . .

- A 4-year-old becomes frightened of the dark and refuses to go to sleep at night. How would a psychoanalyst and a behaviorist differ in their views of how this problem developed?
- What biological concept is emphasized in Piaget's cognitive-developmental approach? From which nineteenth-century theory did Piaget borrow this idea?

BRIEF REVIEW

Three perspectives dominated child development research in the middle of the twentieth century. Child guidance professionals turned to Freud's psychoanalytic approach, and Erikson's expansion of it, for help in understanding personality development and children's emotional difficulties. Behaviorism and social learning theory use conditioning and modeling to explain the appearance of new responses and to treat behavior problems. Piaget's stage theory of cognitive development revolutionized the field with its view of children as active beings who take responsibility for their own learning.

RECENT PERSPECTIVES

New ways of understanding the child are constantly emerging—questioning, building on, and enhancing the discoveries of earlier theories. Today, a burst of fresh approaches and research emphases, including information processing, ethology, ecological systems theory, and Vygotsky's sociocultural theory, is broadening our understanding of children's development.

INFORMATION PROCESSING

During the 1970s, child development researchers became disenchanted with behaviorism as a complete account of children's learning and disappointed in their efforts to fully verify Piaget's ideas. They turned to new trends in the field of cognitive psychology for ways to understand the development of children's thinking. Today, a leading perspective is **information processing.** It is a general approach that emerged with the design of complex computers that use mathematically specified steps to solve problems. These systems suggested to psychologists that the human mind might also be viewed as a symbol-manipulating system through which information flows (Klahr, 1992). From presentation to the senses at *input* and behavioral responses at *output,* information is actively coded, transformed, and organized.

Information processing is often thought of as a field of scripts, frames, and flowcharts. Diagrams are used to map the precise series of steps people use to solve problems and complete tasks, much like the plans devised by programmers to get computers to perform a series of "mental operations." Let's look at an example to clarify the usefulness of this approach. The left-hand side of Figure 1.3 shows the steps that Andrea, an academically successful 8-year-old, used to complete a two-digit subtraction problem. The right-hand side displays the faulty procedure of Jody, who arrived at the wrong answer. The flowchart approach ensures that models of child and adult thinking will be very clear. For example, by comparing the two procedures shown in Figure 1.3, we know exactly what is necessary for effective problem solving and where Jody went wrong in searching for a solution. As a result, we can pinpoint Jody's difficulties and design an intervention to improve her reasoning.

A wide variety of information-processing models exist. Some (like the one in Figure 1.3) are fairly narrow in that they track children's mastery of one or a few tasks. Others describe the human information-processing system as a whole (Atkinson & Shiffrin, 1968; Craik & Lockhart, 1972). These general models are used as guides for asking questions about broad age changes in children's thinking. For example, does a child's ability to search the environment for information needed to solve a problem become more organized and planful with age? How much new information can preschoolers hold in memory compared to older children and

Information processing
An approach that views the human mind as a symbol-manipulating system through which information flows and regards cognitive development as a continuous process.

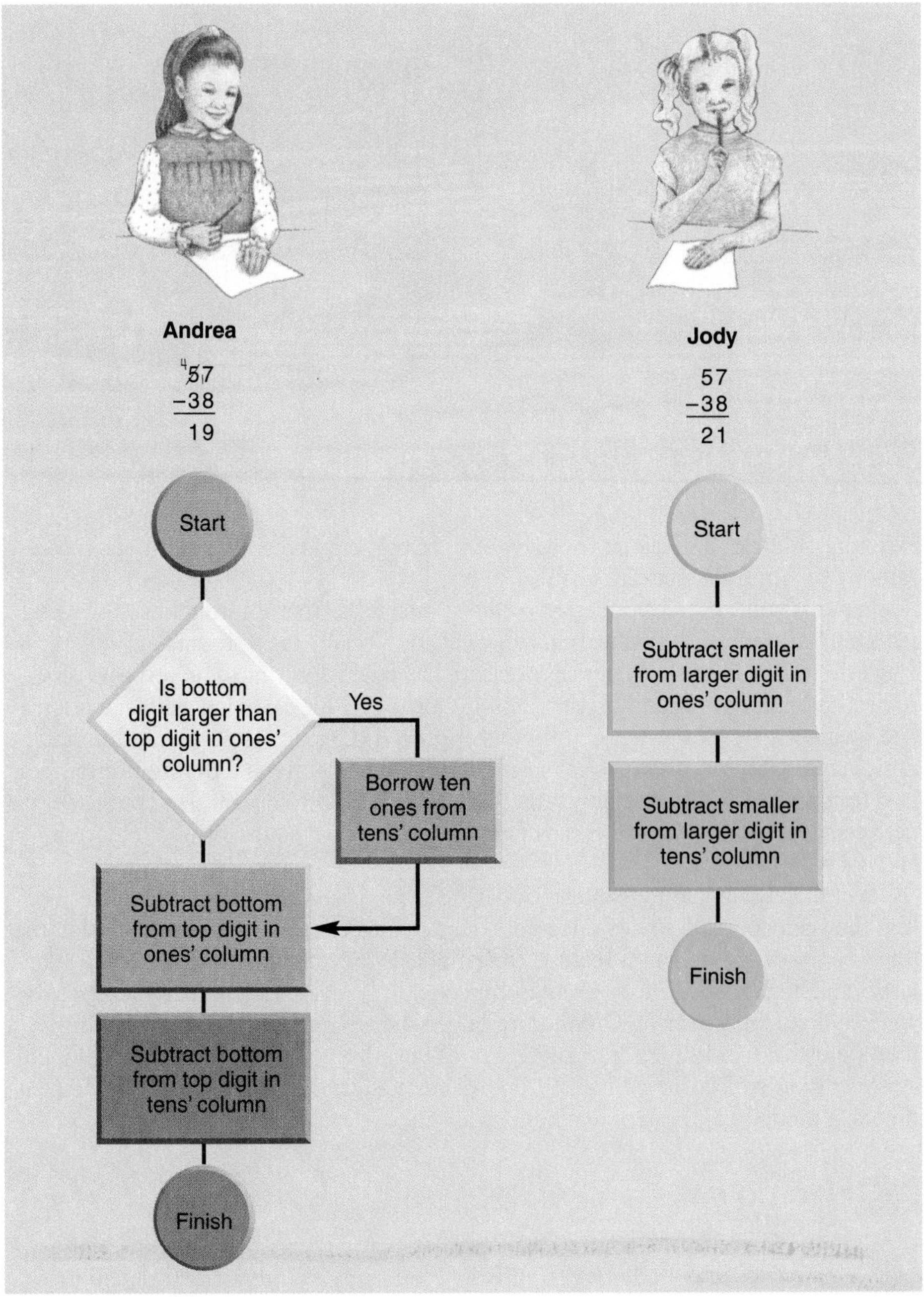

FIGURE 1.3

Information-processing flowcharts showing the steps that two 8-year-olds used to solve a math problem. In this two-digit subtraction problem with a borrowing operation, you can see that Andrea's procedure is correct, whereas Jody's results in a wrong answer.

adults? To what extent does a child's current knowledge influence her ability to learn more? The information-processing approach is also being used to clarify the processing of social information—for example, how children come to view themselves and others in gender-linked terms (Martin & Halverson, 1987). If we can identify how rigid gender stereotypes arise in childhood, then we are in a good position to design interventions that promote more flexible conceptions of male and female role possibilities at an early age.

Like Piaget's theory, the information-processing approach regards children as active, sense-making beings who modify their own thinking in response to environmental demands (Klahr, 1992). But unlike Piaget, there are no stages of development. Rather, the thought processes studied—perception, attention, memory, planning strategies, categorization of information, and comprehension of written and spoken prose—are assumed to be similar at all ages but present to a lesser

Konrad Lorenz was one of the founders of ethology and a keen observer of animal behavior. He developed the concept of imprinting. Here, young geese who were separated from their mother and placed in the company of Lorenz during an early, critical period show that they have imprinted on him. They follow him about as he swims through the water, a response that promotes survival. *(Nina Leen/*LIFE *Magazine* © *Time Warner)*

extent in children. Therefore, the view of development is one of continuous increase rather than abrupt, stagewise change.

Perhaps you can tell from what we have said so far that information-processing research has important implications for education (Hall, 1989; Resnick, 1989; Siegler, 1983b). But information processing has fallen short in some respects. Aspects of children's cognition that are not linear and logical, such as imagination and creativity, are all but ignored by this approach (Greeno, 1989). In addition, critics complain that information processing isolates children's thinking from important features of real-life learning situations. So far, it has told us little about the links between cognition and other areas of development, such as motivation, emotion, and social experience.

Fortunately, a major advantage of having many child development theories is that they can compensate for one another's weaknesses. A unique feature of the final three perspectives we will discuss is the emphasis they place on *contexts for development.* The impact of context, or environment, can be examined at many levels. We will see that family, school, community, larger society, and culture all affect children's growth. In addition, human capacities have been shaped by a long evolutionary history in which our brains and bodies adapted to their surroundings. The next theory, ethology, emphasizes this biological side of development.

ETHOLOGY

Ethology is concerned with the adaptive, or survival, value of behavior and its evolutionary history (Hinde, 1989). It began to be applied to research on children in the 1960s but has become even more influential today. The origins of ethology can be traced to the work of Darwin. Its modern foundations were laid by two European zoologists, Konrad Lorenz and Niko Tinbergen.

Watching the behaviors of diverse animal species in their natural habitats, Lorenz and Tinbergen observed behavior patterns that promote survival. The best known of these is *imprinting,* the early following behavior of certain baby birds that ensures that the young will stay close to the mother and be fed and protected from danger. Imprinting takes place during an early, restricted time period of development. If the mother goose is not present during this time, but an object resembling her in important features is, young goslings may imprint on it instead (Lorenz, 1952).

Observations of imprinting led to a major concept that has been widely applied in child development: the *critical period.* It refers to a time span during which the child is biologically prepared to acquire certain capacities but needs the support of an appropriately stimulating environment. Many researchers have conducted studies to find out whether complex cognitive and social behaviors must be learned during

Ethology
An approach concerned with the adaptive, or survival, value of behavior and its evolutionary history.

certain time periods. For example, if children are deprived of adequate food or physical and social stimulation during the early years of life, will their intelligence be impaired? If language is not mastered during the preschool years, is the child's capacity to acquire it reduced?

As we address these and other similar questions in later chapters, we will discover that the term *sensitive period* offers a better account of human development than does the strict notion of a critical period (Bornstein, 1989). A **sensitive period** is a time that is optimal for certain capacities to emerge and in which the individual is especially responsive to environmental influences. However, its boundaries are less well defined than those of a critical period. It is possible for development to occur later, but it is harder to induce it at that time.

Inspired by observations of imprinting, British psychoanalyst John Bowlby (1969) applied ethological theory to the understanding of the human infant–caregiver relationship. He argued that attachment behaviors of babies, such as smiling, babbling, grasping, and crying, were built-in social signals that encourage the parent to approach, care for, and interact with the baby. By keeping the mother near, these behaviors help ensure that the baby will be fed, protected from danger, and provided with stimulation and affection necessary for healthy growth. The development of attachment in human infants is a lengthy process involving changes in psychological structures that lead the baby to form a deep affectional tie with the caregiver (Bretherton, 1992). As we will see in Chapter 7, it is far more complex than imprinting in baby birds. But for now, note how the ethological view of attachment, which emphasizes the role of innate infant signals, differs sharply from the behaviorist drive reduction explanation we mentioned earlier—that the baby's desire for closeness to the mother is a learned response based on feeding.

Observations by ethologists have shown that many aspects of children's social behavior, including emotional expressions, aggression, cooperation, and social play, resemble those of our primate ancestors. Although ethology emphasizes the genetic and biological roots of development, learning is also considered important because it lends flexibility and greater adaptiveness to behavior. Since ethologists believe that children's behavior can best be understood in terms of its adaptive value, they seek a full understanding of the environment, including physical, social, and cultural aspects. The interests of ethologists are broad. They want to understand the entire organism–environment system (Hinde, 1989; Miller, 1993). The next contextual perspective we will discuss, ecological systems theory, serves as an excellent complement to ethology, since it shows how various aspects of the environment, from immediate human relationships to larger societal forces, work together to affect children's development.

ECOLOGICAL SYSTEMS THEORY

Urie Bronfenbrenner (1979, 1989), an American psychologist, is responsible for an approach to child development that has risen to the forefront of the field over the past decade. **Ecological systems theory** views the child as developing within a complex *system* of relationships affected by multiple levels of the surrounding environment. To illustrate the main features of this perspective, let's visit the families of two 4-year-old boys:

> Jonathan lives in a stable middle-class family with happily married parents, Susan and Jim, both of whom are employed. An active, demanding preschooler, Jonathan often strains his parents' endurance with his boundless energy and difficulty sitting still. Susan returned to work when Jonathan was 6 months old. During the day, Jonathan is cared for in the home of a kind, patient woman who has two young children of her own. When Susan and Jim pick up Jonathan after work, they stop in to find out how his day has gone. On Saturday mornings, Jim takes Jonathan to gymnastics class, an activity that helps meet his high need

Sensitive period
A time span that is optimal for certain capacities to emerge and in which the individual is especially responsive to environmental influences.

Ecological systems theory
Bronfenbrenner's approach, which views the child as developing within a complex system of relationships affected by multiple levels of the environment, from immediate settings of family and school to broad cultural values and programs.

Urie Bronfenbrenner is the originator of ecological systems theory. He views the child as developing within a complex system of relationships affected by multiple levels of the surrounding environment, from immediate settings to broad cultural values, laws, and customs. *(Courtesy of Urie Bronfenbrenner, Cornell University)*

for physical activity. When Jonathan's spirited behavior becomes too much for Susan, Jim quickly distracts him. And both parents set aside special times during the week to spend with their son. Susan and Jim are relieved that Jonathan's pace is beginning to slow down before he enters kindergarten next year.

Eric, an equally active child, experiences a very different kind of home life. His mother Greta was recently divorced. When Eric's dad left, Greta had trouble making ends meet. She moved to a small apartment in a low-rental neighborhood and took a job as a cashier. Greta had to find inexpensive child care for Eric quickly. She put him in a day-care center that she knew had too many children and too little supervision. But little else was available nearby, and she didn't have time to shop around. Greta misses her previous next-door neighbor, with whom she used to talk about her family problems and Eric's angry reaction to the divorce. Most days, Greta feels overwhelmed by financial worries, loneliness, the demands of her job, household chores, and Eric's increasingly defiant behavior. Evenings often end with Eric refusing to go to bed and Greta, exhausted and in tears, shouting and threatening to spank him.

Ecological systems theory highlights the many reasons that Jonathan is happy and well adjusted, whereas Eric is at risk for future problems. As Figure 1.4 shows, the environment is made up of four nested structures that include but extend beyond the settings in which children spend their everyday lives.

THE MICROSYSTEM. The innermost level of the environment is the *microsystem,* which refers to activities and interaction patterns in the child's immediate surroundings. Bronfenbrenner emphasizes that to understand child development at this level, we must keep in mind that all relationships are *bidirectional and reciprocal.* That is, adults affect children's behavior, but children's characteristics—their personality styles and ways of thinking—also influence the behavior of adults. Both Jonathan and Eric are especially lively youngsters who would challenge the resources of just about any parent! But why are Jonathan's parents sensitive but firm, whereas Eric's mother is inconsistent, impatient, and punitive? To answer this question, we must look at environmental support systems that surround and influence parent–child relationships.

Within the microsystem, interaction is affected by the presence of *third parties.* If other people in the setting are supportive, then the quality of the parent–child relationship is enhanced. Notice how Susan and Jim help one another in their parent-

FIGURE 1.4

The four layers of the environment in ecological systems theory.
The *microsystem* refers to relations between the child and the immediate environment, the *mesosystem* to connections among the child's immediate settings, the *exosystem* to social settings that affect but do not contain the child, and the *macrosystem* to values, laws, and customs of the child's culture. *(Adapted from Kopp & Krakow, 1982.)*

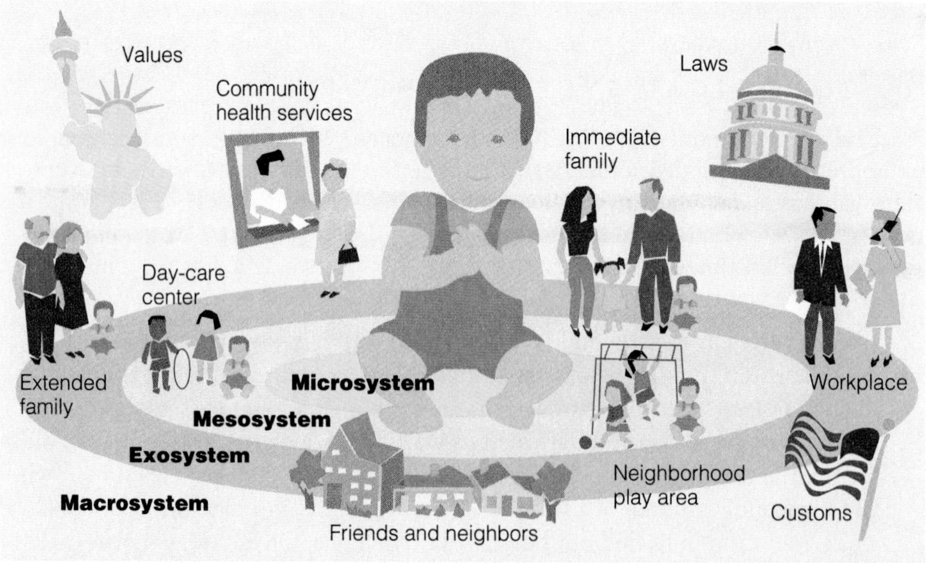

ing roles. In contrast, Greta has no one with whom to share family responsibilities and discuss Eric's needs.

■ **THE MESOSYSTEM.** For children to develop at their best, child-rearing supports must also exist in the larger environment. The second level in Bronfenbrenner's theory is the *mesosystem.* It refers to connections among microsystems, such as home, school, neighborhood, and day care center, that foster children's development. Jonathan benefits from ample mesosystem support. For example, Susan and Jim talk often with his caregiver, and Jim visits Jonathan's gymnastics class and touches base with his teacher. This is not true for Eric, whose mother has little time to check on his day care experiences and whose caregiver has too many children to spend time with parents.

■ **THE EXOSYSTEM.** The *exosystem* refers to social settings that do not contain children, but that affect their experiences in immediate settings. These can be formal organizations, such as the parents' workplace or health and welfare services in the community. For example, flexible work schedules, paid maternity and paternity leave, and sick leave for parents whose children are ill are ways that work settings can help parents in their child-rearing roles and, indirectly, enhance development. Exosystem supports can also be informal, such as parents' *social networks*—friends and extended family members who provide advice, companionship, and even financial assistance. Notice how Greta lost a meaningful exosystem tie with a neighbor when she had to move. Because she has few personal and community-based relationships on which to rely, she feels isolated and unhappy. This is one reason that she has become harsh and punitive with her son (Emery, 1989).

■ **THE MACROSYSTEM.** The outermost level of Bronfenbrenner's model is the *macrosystem.* It is not a specific context. Instead, it refers to the values, laws, and customs of a particular culture. The priority that the macrosystem gives to children's needs affects the support they receive at lower levels of the environment. For example, in countries that require high-quality standards for day care and workplace benefits for employed parents, children are more likely to have favorable experiences in their immediate settings. As we will see in greater detail in later chapters, although most European nations have such programs in place, they are not yet widely available in the United States to help Greta do a better job of raising Eric (Children's Defense Fund, 1994).

■ **INTERVENING IN THE ENVIRONMENT.** Perhaps you have already noticed that ecological systems theory is of tremendous applied significance, since it suggests that interventions at any level of the environment can enhance development. For example, at the level of the exosystem, providing Greta with access to a parenting group, where she can discuss her own and Eric's problems and experience gratifying social relationships, would help to relieve her distress and improve her relationship with Eric. Bronfenbrenner (1989) emphasizes that change at the level of the macrosystem is particularly important. Because the macrosystem affects all other environmental levels, revising established values and government programs in ways more favorable to child development has the most far-reaching impact on children's well-being.

CROSS-CULTURAL RESEARCH AND VYGOTSKY'S SOCIOCULTURAL THEORY

Ecological systems theory, as well as Erikson's psychoanalytic theory, underscores the connection between culture and development. In line with this emphasis, child development research has recently seen a dramatic increase in cross-cultural studies. Investigations that make comparisons across cultures, and between ethnic and social-class groups within cultures, provide insight into

According to Lev Semenovich Vygotsky, many cognitive processes and skills are socially transferred from more knowledgeable members of society to children. Vygotsky's sociocultural theory helps us understand the wide variation in cognitive competencies from culture to culture. Vygotsky is pictured here with his daughter. *(Courtesy of James V. Wertsch, Clark University)*

This South American child candy seller is learning to solve arithmetic problems involving large currency values through everyday street vending activities. Her mathematical skills illustrate how culture and social experience influence cognitive development. *(David Bartruff/Stock Boston)*

whether developmental theories apply to all children or are limited to particular environmental conditions. In doing so, cross-cultural research helps us untangle the contributions of biological and environmental factors to the timing and order of appearance of children's behaviors.

In the past, cross-cultural studies focused on broad cultural differences in development—for example, whether children in one culture are more advanced in motor development or do better on intellectual tasks than children in another. However, this approach can lead us to conclude incorrectly that one culture is superior in enhancing development, whereas another is deficient. In addition, it does not help us understand the precise experiences that contribute to cultural differences in children's behavior.

Today, more research is examining the relationship of *culturally specific practices* to child development. The contributions of the Russian psychologist Lev Semenovich Vygotsky (1896–1934) have played a major role in this trend. Vygotsky's (1934/1987) perspective is called **sociocultural theory.** It focuses on how *culture*—the values, beliefs, customs, and skills of a social group—is transmitted to the next generation. According to Vygotsky, *social interaction*—in particular, cooperative dialogues between children and more knowledgeable members of society—is necessary for children to acquire the ways of thinking and behaving that make up a community's culture (Wertsch & Tulviste, 1992). Vygotsky believed that as adults and more expert peers help children master culturally meaningful activities, the communication between them becomes part of children's thinking. Once children internalize the essential features of these dialogues, they can use the language within them to guide their actions and accomplish skills on their own. The young child instructing herself while working a puzzle or tying her shoes has started to produce the same kind of guiding comments that an adult previously used to help her master important tasks (Berk, 1992a).

Perhaps you can tell from this brief description that Vygotsky's theory has been especially influential in the study of children's cognition. But Vygotsky's approach to cognitive development is quite different from Piaget's. Recall that Piaget did not regard direct teaching by adults as important for cognitive development. Instead, he emphasized children's active, independent efforts to make sense of their world. Vygotsky agreed with Piaget that children are active, constructive beings. But unlike Piaget, he viewed cognitive development as a *socially mediated process*—as dependent on the support that adults and more mature peers provide as children try new tasks. Finally, Vygotsky did not regard all children as moving through the same sequence of stages. Instead, as soon as children acquire language, their enhanced ability to communicate with others leads to continuous, step-by-step changes in thought and behavior that can vary greatly from culture to culture.

A major finding of cross-cultural research is that cultures select different tasks for children's learning. In line with Vygotsky's theory, social interaction surrounding these tasks leads to knowledge and skills essential for success in a particular culture. For example, among the Zinacanteco Indians of southern Mexico, young girls become expert weavers of complex garments through the informal guidance of adults (Childs & Greenfield, 1982). In Brazil, child candy sellers with little or no schooling develop sophisticated mathematical abilities as the result of buying candy from wholesalers, pricing it in collaboration with adults and experienced peers, and bargaining with customers on city streets (Saxe, 1988).

Sociocultural theory
Vygotsky's theory, in which children acquire the ways of thinking and behaving that make up a community's culture through cooperative dialogues with more knowledgeable members of society.

Findings like these reveal that children develop unique strengths in every culture that are not present in others. The field of child development has again borrowed from another discipline—anthropology—to achieve this understanding. A cross-cultural perspective reminds us that the majority of child development specialists reside in the United States, and their research includes only a small minority of humankind. We cannot assume that the developmental sequences observed in our own children are "natural" or that the experiences fostering them are "ideal" without looking around the world.

BRIEF REVIEW

New child development theories are constantly emerging, questioning and building on earlier discoveries. Using computerlike models of mental activity, information processing has brought exactness and precision to the study of children's thinking. Ethology highlights the adaptive, or survival, value of children's behavior and its evolutionary history. Ecological systems theory stresses that adult–child interaction is a two-way street affected by a range of environmental influences, from immediate settings of home and school to broad cultural values and programs. Vygotsky's sociocultural theory takes a closer look at social relationships that foster development. Through cooperative dialogues with mature members of society, children acquire unique, culturally adaptive competencies. .

ASK YOURSELF . . .

- What shortcoming of the information-processing approach is a strength of ethology, ecological systems theory, and Vygotsky's sociocultural theory?
- Return to the story about Greta and her son Eric on page 28. Describe an intervention at each level of Bronfenbrenner's model that would reduce Eric's distress and support his development.
- What features of Vygotsky's sociocultural theory make it very different from Piaget's theory?

COMPARING CHILD DEVELOPMENT THEORIES

In the previous sections, we reviewed seven theoretical perspectives that are major forces in modern child development research. They differ in many respects. First, they focus on different aspects of development. Some, such as the psychoanalytic perspective and ethology, emphasize children's social and emotional development. Others, such as Piaget's cognitive-developmental theory, information processing, and Vygotsky's sociocultural theory, stress important changes in children's thinking. The remaining approaches—behaviorism, social learning theory, and ecological systems theory—discuss factors assumed to affect all aspects of children's functioning.

Second, every theory contains a point of view about what the process of development is like. As we conclude our review of theoretical perspectives, take a moment to identify the stand that each theory takes on the three controversial issues presented at the beginning of this chapter. Then check your own analysis of theories against the information given in Table 1.5. If you had difficulty classifying any of them, return to the relevant section of this chapter and reread the description of that theory.

Finally, we have seen that theories have strengths and weaknesses. This may remind you of an important point we made earlier in this chapter—that no theory provides a complete account of development. Perhaps you found that you were attracted to some theories, but you had doubts about others. As you read more about child development research in later chapters of this book, you may find it useful to keep a notebook in which you test your own theoretical likes and dislikes against the evidence. Do not be surprised if you revise your ideas many times, just as theorists have done throughout this century. By the end of the course, you will have built your own personal perspective on child development. It might turn out to be a blend of several theories, because each viewpoint we have discussed has contributed in important ways to what we know about children. And like the field of child development as a whole, you will be left with some unanswered questions. I hope they will motivate you to continue your quest to understand children in the years to come.

TABLE 1.5

Stance of Major Developmental Theories on Three Basic Issues in Child Development

THEORY	ORGANISMIC VERSUS MECHANISTIC CHILD	CONTINUOUS VERSUS DISCONTINUOUS DEVELOPMENT	NATURE VERSUS NURTURE
Psychoanalytic perspective	*Organismic:* Relations among structures of the mind (id, ego, and superego) determine personality.	*Discontinuous:* Stages of psychosexual and psychosocial development are emphasized.	*Both:* Innate impulses are channeled and controlled through child-rearing experiences.
Behaviorism and social learning theory	*Mechanistic:* Development is the result of connections established between stimulus inputs and behavioral responses.	*Continuous:* Quantitative increase in learned behaviors occurs with age.	*Emphasis on nurture:* Learning principles of conditioning and modeling determine development.
Piaget's cognitive-developmental theory	*Organismic:* Psychological structures determine the child's understanding of the world. The child actively constructs knowledge.	*Discontinuous:* Stages of cognitive development are emphasized.	*Both:* Children's innate drive to discover reality is emphasized. However, it must be supported by a rich, stimulating environment.
Information processing	*Both:* Active processing structures combine with a mechanistic, computerlike model of stimulus input and behavioral output to produce development.	*Continuous:* A quantitative increase in perception, attention, memory, and problem-solving skills takes place with age.	*Both:* Maturation and learning opportunities affect information-processing skills.
Ethology	*Organismic:* The infant is biologically prepared with social signals that actively promote survival. Over time, psychological structures develop that underlie infant–caregiver attachment and other adaptive behavior patterns.	*Both:* Adaptive behavior patterns increase in quantity over time. But sensitive periods—restricted time periods in which qualitatively distinct capacities and responses emerge fairly suddenly—are also emphasized.	*Both:* Biologically based, evolved behavior patterns are stressed, but an appropriately stimulating environment is necessary to elicit them. Also, learning can improve the adaptiveness of behavior.
Ecological systems theory	*Organismic:* Children's personality characteristics and ways of thinking actively contribute to their development.	*Not specified*	*Both:* Children's characteristics and the reactions of others affect each other in a bidirectional fashion. Layers of the environment influence child-rearing experiences.
Vygotsky's sociocultural theory	*Organismic:* Children internalize essential features of social dialogues, forming psychological structures that they use to guide their own behavior.	*Continuous:* Interaction of the child with mature members of society leads to step-by-step changes in thought and behavior.	*Both:* Maturation and opportunities to interact with knowledgeable members of society affect the development of psychological structures and culturally adaptive skills.

STUDYING THE CHILD

In the preceding sections, we saw how theories guide the collection of information about the child, its interpretation, and its application to practices with children. In fact, research usually begins with a prediction about behavior drawn directly from a theory, or what we call a *hypothesis.* But theories and hypotheses are only the beginning of the many activities that result in sound research on child development. Conducting research according to scientifically accepted procedures involves many important steps and choices. Investigators must decide which participants, and how many, to include. Then they must figure out what the participants will be asked to do and when, where, and how many times each will need to be seen. Finally, they must examine relationships and draw conclusions from their data.

In the following sections, we take a look at research strategies commonly used to study children. We begin with *research methods,* the specific activities of participants, such as taking tests, answering questionnaires, responding to interviews, or being observed. Then we turn to *research designs*—overall plans for research studies that permit the best possible test of the investigator's hypothesis. Finally, we discuss special ethical issues involved in doing research on children.

At this point, you may be wondering, Why learn about research strategies? Why not leave these matters to research specialists and concentrate on what is already known about the child and how this knowledge can be applied? There are two reasons. First, each of us must be wise and critical consumers of knowledge, not naive sponges who soak up facts about children. A basic appreciation of the strengths and weaknesses of research strategies becomes important in separating dependable information from misleading results. Second, individuals who work directly with children are sometimes in a position to carry out research studies, either on their own or with an experienced investigator. At other times, they may have to provide information on how well their goals for children are being realized to justify continued financial support for their programs and activities. Under these circumstances, an understanding of research becomes essential practical knowledge.

COMMON METHODS USED TO STUDY CHILDREN

How does a researcher choose a basic approach to gathering information about children? Common methods in the field of child development include systematic observation, self-reports (such as questionnaires and interviews), and clinical or case studies of a single child. As you read about these methods, you may find it helpful to refer to Table 1.6, which summarizes the strengths and limitations of each.

■ **SYSTEMATIC OBSERVATION.** To find out how children actually behave, a researcher may choose systematic observation. Observations of the behavior of children, and of the adults who are important in their lives, can be made in different ways. One approach is to go into the field, or natural environment, and observe the behavior of interest, a method called **naturalistic observation.**

A study of children's social development provides a good example of this technique (Barrett & Yarrow, 1977). Observing 5- to 8-year-olds at a summer camp, the researchers recorded the number of times each child provided another person with physical or emotional support in the form of comforting, sharing, helping, or expressing sympathy. The great strength of naturalistic observation in studies like this one is that investigators can see directly the everyday behaviors they hope to explain (Miller, 1987).

Naturalistic observation also has a major limitation: not all children have the same opportunity to display a particular behavior in everyday life. In this study, some children happened to be exposed to more cues for positive social responses

Naturalistic observation A method in which the researcher goes into the natural environment to observe the behavior of interest.

TABLE 1.6

Strengths and Limitations of Common Research Methods

METHOD	DESCRIPTION	STRENGTHS	LIMITATIONS
Systematic Observation			
Naturalistic observation	Observation of behavior in natural contexts	Observations reflect participants' everyday lives	Conditions under which participants are observed cannot be controlled
Structured observation	Observation of behavior in a laboratory	Conditions of observation are the same for all children	Observations may not be typical of the way participants behave in everyday life
Self-Reports			
Clinical interview	Flexible interviewing procedure in which the investigator obtains a complete account of the participant's thoughts	Comes as close as possible to the way participants think in everyday life; great breadth and depth of information can be obtained in a short time	Participants may not report information accurately; flexible procedure makes comparing individuals' responses difficult
Structured interview, questionnaires, and tests	Self-report instruments in which each participant is asked the same questions in the same way	Standardized method of asking questions permits comparisons of participants' responses and efficient data collection and scoring	Does not yield the same depth of information as a clinical interview; responses still subject to inaccurate reporting
Clinical Method (Case Study)	A full picture of a single individual's psychological functioning, obtained by combining interviews, observations, and test scores	Provides rich, descriptive insights into processes of development	May be biased by researcher's theoretical preferences; findings cannot be applied to individuals other than the paticipant
Ethnography	Understanding a culture or distinct social group through participant observation; by making extensive field notes, the researcher tries to capture the culture's unique values and social processes	Provides a more complete and accurate description than can be derived from a single observational visit, interview, or questionnaire	May be biased by researcher's values and theoretical preferences; findings cannot be applied to individuals and settings other than the ones studied

(such as a tearful playmate), and for this reason they showed more helpful and comforting behavior. Researchers commonly deal with this difficulty by making **structured observations** in a laboratory. In this approach, the investigator sets up a situation that evokes the behavior of interest so every participant has an equal opportunity to display the response. In one study, structured observations of children's helping behavior were made by having an adult "accidentally" spill a box of gold stars and recording how each child reacted (Stanhope, Bell, & Parker-Cohen, 1987). This approach gives investigators more control over the research situation. But the great disadvantage of structured observations is that children do not always behave in the laboratory as they do in everyday life.

Structured observation A method in which the investigator sets up a situation that evokes the behavior of interest and observes it in a laboratory.

The procedures used to collect systematic observations may vary considerably, depending on the nature of the research problem. Some investigators need to describe the entire stream of behavior—everything said and done over a certain time period. In one of my own studies, I wanted to find out how sensitive, responsive, and verbally stimulating caregivers were when they interacted with children in day care centers (Berk, 1985). In this case, everything each caregiver said and did—even the amount of time she spent away from the children taking coffee breaks and talking on the phone—was important. In other studies, only one or a few kinds of behavior are needed, and it is not necessary to preserve the entire behavior stream. In these instances, researchers use more efficient observation procedures in which they record only certain events or mark off behaviors on checklists.

Systematic observation provides invaluable information on how children and adults actually behave, but it tells us little about the reasoning that lies behind their responses. For this kind of information, researchers must turn to another type of method: self-reports.

SELF-REPORTS: INTERVIEWS AND QUESTIONNAIRES. Self-reports are instruments that ask research participants to answer questions about their perceptions, thoughts, abilities, feelings, attitudes, beliefs, and past experiences. They range from relatively unstructured clinical interviews, the method used by Piaget to study children's thinking, to highly structured interviews, questionnaires, and tests.

Let's look at an example of a **clinical interview** in which Piaget questioned a 5-year-old child about his understanding of dreams:

> Where does the dream come from?—*I think you sleep so well that you dream.*—Does it come from us or from outside?—*From outside.*—What do we dream with?—*I don't know.*—With the hands? . . . With nothing?—*Yes, with nothing.*—When you are in bed and you dream, where is the dream?—*In my bed, under the blanket. I don't really know. If it was in my stomach, the bones would be in the way and I shouldn't see it.*—Is the dream there when you sleep?—*Yes, it is in the bed beside me . . .* —You see the dream when you are in the room, but if I were in the room, too, should I see it?—*No, grownups don't ever dream.*—Can two people ever have the same dream?—*No, never.*—When the dream is in the room, is it near you?—*Yes, there!* (pointing to 30 cm. in front of his eyes). (Piaget, 1926/1930, pp. 97–98)

Notice how Piaget used a flexible, conversational style to encourage the child to expand his ideas. Prompts are given to obtain a fuller picture of the child's reasoning.

The clinical interview has two major strengths. First, it permits people to display their thoughts in terms that are as close as possible to the way they think in everyday life. Second, the clinical interview can provide a large amount of information in a fairly brief period of time. For example, in an hour-long session, we can obtain a wide range of child-rearing information from a parent—much more than we could capture by observing parent–child interaction for the same amount of time.

A major limitation of the clinical interview has to do with the accuracy with which people report their thoughts, feelings, and experiences. Some participants, desiring to please the interviewer, may make up answers that do not represent their actual thinking. When asked about past events, they may have trouble recalling exactly what happened. And because the clinical interview depends on verbal ability and expressiveness, it may underestimate the capacities of individuals who have difficulty putting their thoughts into words.

The clinical interview has also been criticized because of its flexibility. When questions are phrased differently for each participant, responses may be due to the manner of interviewing rather than to real differences in the way people think about a certain topic. **Structured interviews,** in which each participant is asked the same set of questions in the same way, can eliminate this problem. In addition, these techniques are much more efficient. Answers are briefer, and researchers can obtain written responses from an entire class of children or group of parents at the same time. Also, when structured interviews use multiple-choice, yes–no, and true–false

Clinical interview
A method in which the researcher uses a flexible, conversational style to probe for the participant's point of view.

Structured interview
A method in which each participant is asked the same questions in the same way.

Using the clinical interview, this researcher asks a mother to describe her child's development. The method permits large amounts of information to be gathered in a relatively short period of time. However, a major drawback of this method is that subjects do not always report information accurately. *(Tony Freeman/ Photo Edit)*

formats, as is done on many tests and questionnaires, responses can be tabulated by machine. However, we must keep in mind that these approaches do not yield the same depth of information as a clinical interview. And they can still be affected by the problem of inaccurate reporting.

■ THE CLINICAL METHOD. Earlier in this chapter, we discussed the **clinical method** (sometimes called the *case study approach)* as an outgrowth of psychoanalytic theory, which stressed the importance of understanding the individual. Recall that the clinical method brings together a wide range of information on a single child, including interviews, test scores, and observations. The aim is to obtain as complete a picture as possible of that child's psychological functioning and the experiences that led up to it.

Although clinical studies are usually carried out on children who have serious emotional problems, they sometimes focus on well-adjusted youngsters. In one recent investigation, the researchers wanted to find out what contributes to the accomplishments of children with extraordinary intellectual talents. Among the six prodigies studied intensively was Adam, a boy who read, wrote, and composed musical pieces before he was out of diapers. Adam's parents provided a home rich in stimulation and raised him with affection, firmness, and humor. They searched for schools in which he could both develop his abilities and form rewarding social relationships. By age 4, Adam was intensively involved in mastering human symbol systems—BASIC for the computer, French, German, Russian, Sanskrit, Greek, ancient hieroglyphs, music, and mathematics. Would Adam have realized his abilities without the chance combination of his special gift with nurturing, committed parents? Probably not, the investigators concluded (Feldman, 1991). Adam's case illustrates the unique strengths of the clinic method. It yields case narratives that are rich in descriptive detail and that offer valuable insights into development.

The clinical method, like all others, has drawbacks. It is subject to the same problems as the clinical interview. Also, more than other methods, the theoretical preferences of the researcher can bias the interpretations of clinical data. Finally, investigators cannot assume that their conclusions apply to anyone other than the particular child being studied. The insights drawn from clinical investigations need to be tested further with other research methods.

Clinical method
A method in which the researcher attempts to understand the unique individual child by combining interview data, observations, and sometimes test scores.

Ethnography
A method in which the researcher attempts to understand the unique values and social processes of a culture or a distinct social group by living with its members and taking field notes for an extended period of time.

■ ETHNOGRAPHY. Because of a growing interest in the impact of culture, child development researchers have begun to rely increasingly on a method used often by anthropologists—**ethnography.** Like the clinical method, ethnographic research is a descriptive, qualitative technique. But instead of aiming to understand a single individual, it is directed toward understanding a culture or distinct social group (Winthrop, 1991).

The ethnographic method achieves its goals through *participant observation.* Typically, the researcher lives with the cultural community for a period of months or years, participating in its daily life. Extensive field notes, which consist of a mix of observations, self-reports from members of the culture, and interpretations by the investigator, are gathered. Later, these notes are put together into a description of the community that tries to capture its unique values and social processes.

Ethnographies of children from diverse cultures currently exist, and many more are being compiled. In some, investigators focus on all aspects of children's experience, as one researcher did in describing what it is like to grow up in a small American town (Peshkin, 1978). In other instances, the study is limited to one or a few settings, such as home or school life (Chang, 1992; Miller & Sperry, 1987). Because the ethnographic method is committed to trying to understand others' perspectives, it often overturns widely held stereotypes, as the Cultural Influences box on page 38 reveals.

Ethnographers try to minimize their influence on the culture being studied by becoming part of it. Nevertheless, at times their presence does alter the situation. In addition, as with clinical research, investigators' cultural values and theoretical commitments sometimes lead them to observe selectively or misinterpret what they see. Finally, the findings of ethnographic studies cannot be assumed to apply to people and settings other than those in which the research was originally conducted (Hammersley, 1992).

BRIEF REVIEW

Systematic observation, self-reports, clinical or case studies, and ethnographies are commonly used methods in the field of child development. Naturalistic observation provides information on children's everyday behaviors. When it is necessary to control the conditions of observation, researchers often make structured observations in a laboratory. The flexible, conversational style of the clinical interview provides a wealth of information on the reasoning behind behavior. However, participants may not report their thoughts accurately, and comparing their responses is difficult. The structured interview is a more efficient method that questions each person in the same way, but it does not yield the same depth of information as a clinical interview. Clinical studies of individual children provide rich insights into the processes of development. However, information obtained is often unsystematic and subjective. In ethnographic research, an investigator tries to understand a distinct social group through participant observation. Like clinical studies, ethnographies can be affected by researchers' theoretical biases, and the findings may not generalize beyond the people studied.

ASK YOURSELF . . .

- Why is it important for students of child development and individuals who work directly with children to understand research strategies?
- A researcher wants to study the thoughts and feelings of children who have experienced their parents' divorce. Which method is best suited for investigating this question?
- What limitations do the clinical method and ethnography have in common?

GENERAL RESEARCH DESIGNS

In deciding on a research design, investigators choose a way of setting up a study that permits them to test their hypotheses with the greatest certainty possible. Two main types of designs are used in all research on human behavior: correlational and experimental.

CORRELATIONAL DESIGN. In a **correlational design,** researchers gather information on already existing groups of individuals without altering their experiences in any way. Suppose we want to answer such questions as: Does attending a day care center promote children's friendliness with peers? Do mothers' styles of interacting with children have any bearing on children's intelligence? How do child abuse and neglect affect children's feelings about themselves and relationships with peers? In these and many other instances, it is either very difficult or ethically impossible to arrange and control the conditions of interest.

Correlational design
A research design in which the researcher gathers information without altering participants' experiences and examines relationships between variables. Does not permit inferences about cause and effect.

CULTURAL INFLUENCES

SCHOOL MATTERS IN MEXICAN-AMERICAN HOMES: AN ETHNOGRAPHIC STUDY

For many years, the poor school achievement of low-income minority children was attributed to "cultural deficits"—home environments that place little value on education. A recent ethnographic study of Mexican-American families challenges this assumption. Concha Delgado-Gaitan (1992) spent many months getting to know the residents of a Mexican-American community located in a small California city. There she collected extensive field notes on six families, each with a second-grade child. While in their homes, she carefully examined children's experiences related to education.

Although the Mexican-American parents had little schooling themselves, they regarded education as a great privilege and supported their children's learning in many ways. Their homes were cramped, one-bedroom apartments, occasionally shared with relatives. Still, parents did their best to create a stable environment that encouraged children to think positively about school. They offered material rewards for good grades (such as a new book or dinner at a favorite restaurant), set regular bedtime hours, and where possible provided a special place for doing schoolwork. And they frequently spoke to their children about their own educational limitations and the importance of taking advantage of the opportunity to study.

During the week, most parent–child conversations revolved around homework. All parents did their best to help with assignments and foster behaviors valued in school. But how well they succeeded depended on social networks through which they could obtain information about educational matters. Some parents relied on relatives who had more experience in dealing with the school system. Others sought out individuals at church or work as advisers.

When social support was available, perplexing school problems were quickly resolved. For example, one parent, Mrs. Matias, received repeated reports from her son Jorge's teacher about his unruly behavior. Finally, a note arrived threatening suspension if Jorge did not improve. Mrs. Matias consulted one of her coworkers, who suggested that she ask for permission to leave during the lunch hour to talk with Jorge's teacher. After a conference revealed that Jorge needed to stay away from certain boys who were provoking him, his fighting subsided.

Despite sincere efforts, lack of familiarity with school tasks often hampered Mexican-American parents' ability to help their children. Mrs. Serna insisted that her poorly achieving daughter Norma do her homework at regularly scheduled times, and she checked to make sure that Norma completed her assignments. But when she tried to assist Norma, Mrs. Serna frequently misinterpreted the instructions. And she did not understand the school environment well enough to contact teachers for information about how to support her child. As a result, Norma's progress remained below average.

Although the Mexican-American families had limited income and material resources, this did not detract from their desire to create a home environment conducive to learning. The major barrier parents faced was how to assist children with actual tasks. Delgado-Gaitan recommends that schools establish open lines of communication with minority parents to make sure they have access to the resources they need to strengthen their children's learning.

This Mexican-American mother tries to support her children's academic development by helping with homework and providing a quiet place for study. Ethnographic research reveals that how well she will succeed depends on access to information and resources from the school. *(Comstock)*

The correlational design offers a way of looking at relationships between children's experiences or characteristics and their behavior or development. But correlational studies have one major limitation: we cannot infer cause and effect. For example, if we find in a correlational study that maternal interaction does relate to children's intelligence, we would not know whether mothers' behavior actually causes intellectual differences among children. In fact, the opposite is certainly possible. The behaviors of highly intelligent children may be so attractive that they cause mothers to interact more favorably. Or a third variable that we did not even think about studying, such as amount of noise and distraction in the home, may be causing both maternal interaction and children's intelligence to change together in the same direction.

In correlational studies, and in other types of research designs, investigators often examine relationships by using a **correlation coefficient.** It is a number that describes how two measures, or variables, are associated with one another. We will encounter the correlation coefficient in discussing research findings throughout this book. So let's look at what it is and how it is interpreted. A correlation coefficient can range in value from +1.00 to –1.00. The *magnitude, or size, of the number* shows the *strength of the relationship.* A zero correlation indicates no relationship, but the closer the value is to +1.00 or –1.00, the stronger the relationship that exists. The *sign of the number* (+ or –) refers to the *direction of the relationship.* A positive sign (+) means that as one variable *increases,* the other also *increases.* A negative sign (–) indicates that as one variable *increases,* the other *decreases.*

Let's take a couple of examples to illustrate how a correlation coefficient works. In one study, a researcher found that a measure of maternal attention at 11 months of age was positively correlated with infant intelligence during the second year of life, at +.60. This is a moderately high correlation, which indicates that the more attentive the mothers were to their babies in infancy, the better their children did on an intelligence test several months later (Clarke-Stewart, 1973). In another study, a researcher reported that the extent to which mothers ignored their 10-month-olds' bids for attention was negatively correlated with children's willingness to comply with parental demands one year later—at –.46 for boys and –.36 for girls (Martin, 1981). These moderate correlations reveal that the more mothers ignored their babies, the less cooperative their children were during the second year of life.

Both of these investigations found a relationship between maternal behavior in the first year and children's behavior in the second year. Although the researchers suspected that maternal behavior affected the children's responses, in neither study could they really be sure about cause and effect. However, if we find a relationship in a correlational study, this suggests that it would be worthwhile to track down its cause with a more powerful experimental research strategy, if possible.

■ EXPERIMENTAL DESIGN. Unlike correlational studies, an **experimental design** permits us to make inferences about cause and effect. In an experiment, the events and behaviors of interest are divided into two types: independent and dependent variables. The **independent variable** is the one anticipated by the investigator to cause changes in another variable. The **dependent variable** is the one the investigator expects to be influenced by the independent variable. Inferences about cause-and-effect relationships are possible because the researcher directly *controls* or *manipulates* changes in the independent variable. This is done by exposing participants to two or more treatment conditions and comparing their performance on measures of the dependent variable.

In one *laboratory experiment,* researchers wanted to know if quality of interaction between adults (independent variable) affects young children's emotional reactions while playing with a familiar peer (dependent variable). Pairs of 2-year-olds were brought into a laboratory set up to look much like a family home. One group was exposed to a *warm treatment,* in which two adults in the kitchen spoke in a friendly way while the children played in the living room. A second group received an *angry*

Correlation coefficient
A number, ranging from +1.00 to –1.00, that describes the strength and direction of the relationship between two variables.

Experimental design
A research design in which the investigator randomly assigns participants to treatment conditions. Permits inferences about cause and effect.

Independent variable
The variable manipulated by the researcher in an experiment.

Dependent variable
The variable the researcher expects to be influenced by the independent variable in an experiment.

treatment, in which positive communication between the adults was interrupted by an argument in which they shouted, complained, and slammed the door. Children in the angry condition displayed much more distress (such as freezing in place, anxious facial expressions, and crying). They also showed more aggression toward their playmates than did children in the warm treatment (Cummings, Iannotti, & Zahn-Waxler, 1985). The experiment revealed that exposure to even short episodes of intense adult anger can trigger negative emotion and antisocial behavior in very young children.

In experimental studies, investigators must take special precautions to control for unknown characteristics of participants that could reduce the accuracy of their findings. For example, in the study just described, if a greater number of children who had already learned to behave in hostile and aggressive ways happened to end up in the angry treatment, we could not tell whether the independent variable or children's background characteristics produced the results. *Random assignment* of participants to treatment conditions offers protection against this problem. By using an evenhanded procedure, such as drawing numbers out of a hat or flipping a coin, the experimenter increases the chances that children's characteristics will be equally distributed across treatment groups.

Sometimes researchers combine random assignment with another technique called *matching.* In this procedure, participants are measured ahead of time on the factor in question—in our example, aggression. Then an equal number of high- and low-aggressive children are randomly assigned to each treatment condition. In this way, the experimental groups are deliberately matched, or made equivalent, on characteristics that are likely to distort the results.

MODIFIED EXPERIMENTAL DESIGNS: FIELD AND NATURAL EXPERIMENTS. Most experiments are conducted in laboratories where researchers can achieve the maximum possible control over treatment conditions. But, as we have already indicated, findings obtained in laboratories may not always apply to everyday situations. The ideal solution to this problem is to do experiments in the field as a complement to laboratory investigations. In *field experiments,* investigators capitalize on rare opportunities to randomly assign people to different treatments in natural settings. In the experiment we just considered, we can conclude that the emotional climate established by adults affects children's behavior in the laboratory. But does it also do so in daily life?

How does attending day care affect children's development? To answer this question, it is unlikely that researchers can randomly assign children and manipulate conditions in the real world. But they may be able to conduct a natural experiment by selecting groups of day care and non-day care children whose characteristics are as much alike as possible. *(Will Faller)*

Another study helps answer this question. This time, the research was carried out in a day care center. A caregiver deliberately interacted differently with two groups of preschoolers. In one condition (nurturant treatment), she modeled many instances of warmth, helpfulness, and concern for others. In the second condition (the control, since it involved no treatment), she behaved as usual, with no special concern for others. Two weeks later, the researchers created several situations that called for helpfulness. For example, a visiting mother asked each child to watch her baby for a few moments, but the baby's toys had fallen out of the playpen. The investigators recorded whether or not each child returned the toys to the baby. As Figure 1.5 shows, children exposed to the nurturant treatment behaved in a much more helpful way than those in the control condition (Yarrow, Scott, & Waxler, 1973).

In testing many hypotheses, researchers cannot randomly assign participants and manipulate conditions in the real world, as these investigators were able to do. Sometimes researchers can compromise by conducting *natural experiments.* Treatments that already exist, such as different school environments, day care centers, and preschool programs, are compared. These studies differ from correlational research only in that groups of participants are carefully chosen to ensure that their characteristics are as much alike as possible. In this way, investigators rule out as best as they can alternative explanations for their treatment effects. But despite these efforts, natural experiments are unable to achieve the precision and rigor of true experimental research.

To help you compare the correlational and experimental designs we have discussed, Table 1.7 summarizes their strengths and limitations. It also includes an overview of designs for studying development, to which we now turn.

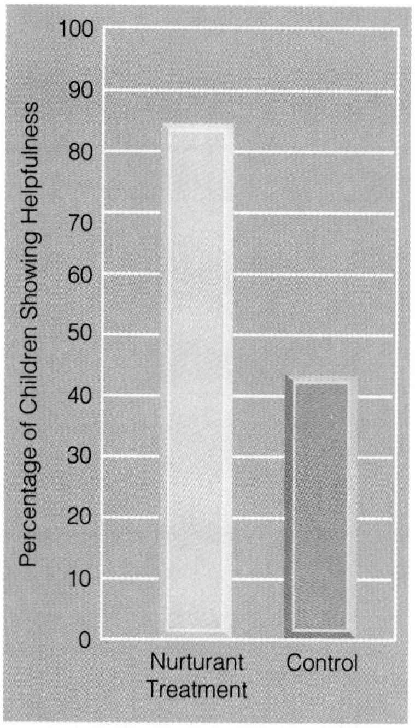

FIGURE 1.5

Does the emotional climate established by adults affect children's behavior in everyday life?
In a field experiment conducted in a day care center, children exposed to a nurturant treatment in which a caregiver modeled helpfulness and concern for others were far more likely than children in the control condition to show helpfulness themselves. *(Adapted from Yarrow, Scott, & Waxler, 1973.)*

DESIGNS FOR STUDYING DEVELOPMENT

Scientists interested in child development require information about the way research participants change over time. To answer questions about development, they must extend correlational and experimental approaches to include measurements at different ages. Longitudinal and cross-sectional designs are special *developmental* research strategies. In each, age comparisons form the basis of the research plan.

THE LONGITUDINAL DESIGN. In a **longitudinal design,** a group of participants is studied repeatedly at different ages, and changes are noted as they mature. The time spanned may be relatively short (a few months to several years) or very long (a decade or even a lifetime). The longitudinal approach has two major strengths. First, since it tracks the performance of each person over time, researchers can identify common patterns of development as well as individual differences in the paths children follow to maturity. Second, longitudinal studies permit investigators to examine relationships between early and later events and behaviors. Let's take an example to illustrate these ideas.

Recently, a group of researchers wondered whether children who display extreme personality styles—either angry and explosive or shy and withdrawn—retain the same dispositions when they become adults. In addition, they wanted to know what kinds of experiences promote stability or change in personality and what consequences explosiveness and shyness have for long-term adjustment. To answer these questions, the researchers delved into the archives of the Guidance Study, a well-known longitudinal investigation initiated in 1928 at the University of California, Berkeley, and continued over several decades (Caspi, Elder, & Bem, 1987, 1988).

Results revealed that the two personality styles were only moderately stable. Between ages 8 and 30, a good number of individuals remained the same, whereas others changed substantially. When stability did occur, it appeared to be due to a "snowballing effect," in which children evoked responses from adults and peers that acted to maintain their dispositions. In other words, explosive youngsters were likely to be treated with anger and hostility (to which they reacted with even greater unruliness), whereas shy children were apt to be ignored.

Persistence of extreme personality styles affected many areas of adult adjustment, but these outcomes were different for males and females. For men, the results of early explosiveness were most apparent in their work lives, in the form of conflicts with supervisors, frequent job changes, and unemployment. Since few women in this sample of an earlier generation worked after marriage, their family lives were most affected. Explosive girls grew up to be hotheaded wives and parents who were

Longitudinal design
A research design in which one group of participants studied repeatedly at different ages.

TABLE 1.7

Strengths and Limitations of Research Designs

DESIGN	DESCRIPTION	STRENGTHS	LIMITATIONS
General			
Correlational	The investigator obtains information on already existing groups, without altering participants' experiences	Permits study of relationships between variables	Does not permit inferences about cause-and-effect relationships
Experimental	The investigator manipulates an independent variable and looks at its effect on a dependent variable; can be conducted in the laboratory or natural environment	Permits inferences about cause-and-effect relationships	When conducted in the laboratory, findings may not apply to the real world; when conducted in the field, control over treatment is usually weaker than in the laboratory
Developmental			
Longitudinal	The investigator studies the same group of participants repeatedly at different ages	Permits study of common patterns and individual differences in development and relationships between early and later events and behaviors	Age-related changes may be distorted because of dropout and test-wiseness of participants and cohort effects
Cross-sectional	The investigator studies groups of participants differing in age at the same point in time	More efficient than the longitudinal design	Does not permit study of individual developmental trends. Age differences may be distorted because of cohort effects
Longitudinal-sequential	The investigator studies two or more groups of participants born in different years repeatedly at different ages	Permits both longitudinal and cross-sectional comparisons; reveals existence of cohort effects	May have the same problems as longitudinal and cross-sectional strategies, but the design itself helps identify difficulties

especially prone to divorce. Sex differences in the long-term consequences of shyness were even greater. Men who had been withdrawn in childhood were delayed in marrying, becoming fathers, and developing stable careers. Because a withdrawn, unassertive style was socially acceptable for females, women who had shy personalities showed no special adjustment problems.

PROBLEMS IN CONDUCTING LONGITUDINAL RESEARCH. Despite their many strengths, longitudinal investigations pose a number of problems. For example, participants may move away or drop out of the research for other reasons. This changes the original sample so it no longer represents the population to whom researchers would like to generalize their findings. Also, from repeated study, people may become "test-wise." As a result, the behavior they present to investigators may become unnatural.

But the most widely discussed threat to the accuracy of longitudinal findings is cultural-historical change, or what are commonly called **cohort effects.** Longitudinal studies examine the development of *cohorts*—children born in the

Cohort effects
The effects of cultural-historical change on the accuracy of findings: Children born in one period of time are influenced by particular cultural and historical conditions.

same time period who are influenced by a particular set of cultural and historical conditions. Results based on one cohort may not apply to children growing up at other points in time. For example, in the study of personality styles described in the preceding section, we might ask whether the sex differences obtained are still true, in view of recent changes in gender roles in our society.

■ THE CROSS-SECTIONAL DESIGN. The length of time it takes for many behaviors to change, even in limited longitudinal studies, has led researchers to turn toward a more convenient strategy for studying development. In the **cross-sectional design**, groups of people differing in age are studied at the same point in time.

A recent investigation provides a good illustration. Children in grades 3, 6, 9, and 12 filled out a questionnaire asking about their sibling relationships. Findings revealed that sibling interaction was characterized by greater equality and less power assertion with age. Also, feelings of sibling companionship declined during adolescence. The researchers thought that these age changes were due to several factors. As later-born children become more competent and independent, they no longer need and are probably less willing to accept direction from older siblings. In addition, as adolescents move from psychological dependence on the family to greater involvement with peers, they may have less time and emotional need to invest in siblings (Buhrmester & Furman, 1990). These are intriguing ideas about the impact of development on sibling relationships that deserve to be followed up in future research.

■ PROBLEMS IN CONDUCTING CROSS-SECTIONAL RESEARCH. The cross-sectional design is a very efficient strategy for describing age-related trends. But when researchers choose it, they are shortchanged in the kind of information they can obtain about development. Evidence about change at the level at which it actually occurs—the individual—is not available. For example, in the study of sibling relationships that we just discussed, comparisons are limited to age-group averages. We cannot tell if important individual differences exist in the development of sibling relationships, some becoming more supportive and intimate and others becoming increasingly distant with age.

Cross-sectional studies that cover a wide age span have another problem. Like longitudinal research, they can be threatened by cohort effects. For example, comparisons of 5-year-old cohorts and 15-year-old cohorts—groups of children born and reared in different years—may not really represent age-related changes. Instead, they may reflect unique experiences associated with the different time periods in which the age groups were growing up.

■ IMPROVING DEVELOPMENTAL DESIGNS. To overcome some of the limitations of longitudinal and cross-sectional research, investigators sometimes combine the two approaches. One way of doing so is the **longitudinal-sequential** design. It is called a *sequential* design because it is composed of two or more different age groups of participants, each of which is followed longitudinally for a number of years.

The design has three advantages. First, it permits researchers to find out whether cohort effects are operating by comparing children of the same age who were born in different years. Using the example shown in Figure 1.6, we can compare the behaviors of the two samples at ages 6 and 9. If they do not differ, then we can rule out cohort effects. Second, it is possible to do both longitudinal and cross-sectional comparisons. If outcomes are similar in both, then we can be especially confident about our findings. Third, the design is efficient. In the example shown in Figure 1.6, the researcher can find out about change over a 9-year period by following each cohort for just 6 years. Although the longitudinal-sequential design is used only occasionally, it provides researchers with a convenient way to profit from the strengths of both longitudinal and cross-sectional approaches.

Cross-sectional design
A research design in which groups of participants of different ages are studied at the same point in time.

Longitudinal-sequential design
A research design with both longitudinal and cross-sectional components in which groups of participants born in different years are followed over time.

FIGURE 1.6

Example of a longitudinal-sequential design. Two samples of children, one born in 1982 and the other in 1985, are observed longitudinally from 3 to 12 years of age. The design permits the researcher to check for cohort effects by comparing children of the same age who were born in different years. Also, both longitudinal and cross-sectional comparisons can be made.

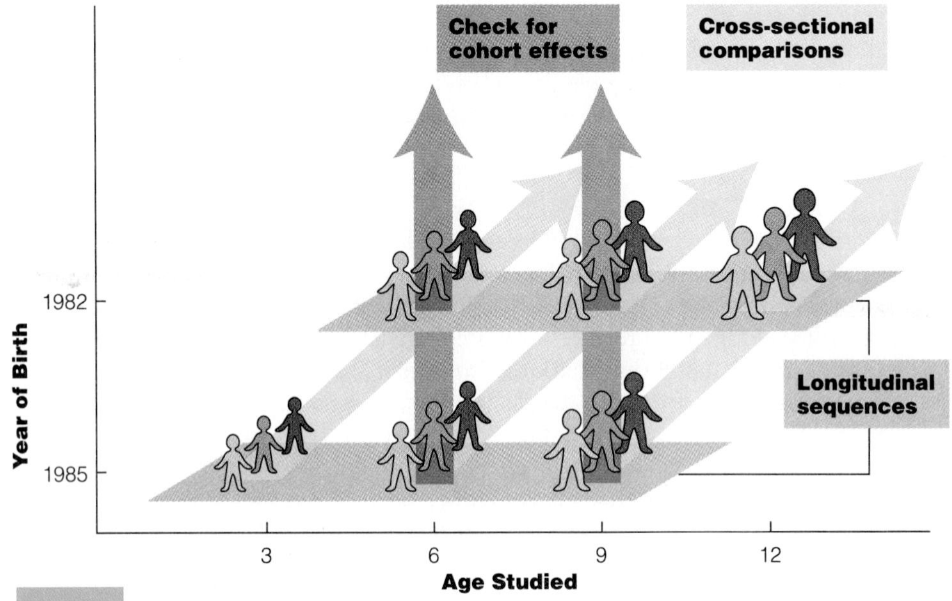

ASK YOURSELF . . .

- A researcher compares children who went to summer leadership camps with children who attended athletic camps. She finds that those who attended leadership camps are friendlier. Should the investigator tell parents that sending children to leadership camps will cause them to be more sociable? Why or why not?
- A researcher wants to find out if children who go to day care centers during the first few years of life do as well in school as those who did not attend day care. Which developmental design, longitudinal or cross-sectional, is appropriate for answering this question? Explain why.

BRIEF REVIEW

A variety of research designs are commonly used to study children. In correlational research, information is gathered on existing groups of individuals. Investigators can examine relationships between variables, but they cannot infer cause and effect. Because experimental design involves random assignment of participants to treatment groups, researchers can find out if an independent variable causes change in a dependent variable. Field and natural experiments permit generalization to everyday life, but they sacrifice rigorous experimental control. Longitudinal and cross-sectional designs are uniquely suited for studying development. In longitudinal research, participants are studied repeatedly at different ages, an approach that provides information on common patterns as well as individual differences in development and the relationship between early and later events and behaviors. The cross-sectional approach is more efficient because groups of participants differing in age are studied at the same point in time. However, comparisons are limited to age-group averages. The longitudinal-sequential approach permits researchers to reap the benefits of both longitudinal and cross-sectional strategies.

ETHICS IN RESEARCH ON CHILDREN

Research into human behavior creates ethical issues because, unfortunately, the quest for scientific knowledge can sometimes exploit people. When children take part in research, the ethical concerns are especially complex. Children are more vulnerable than adults to physical and psychological harm. In addition, immaturity makes it difficult or impossible for children to evaluate for themselves what participation in research will mean. For these reasons, special ethical guidelines for research on children have been developed by the federal government, by funding agencies, and by research-oriented associations such as the American Psychological Association (1992) and the Society for Research in Child Development (1993).

Table 1.8 presents a summary of children's basic research rights drawn from these guidelines. Once you have examined them, read the following research situations, each of which poses a serious ethical dilemma. What precautions do you think should be taken in each instance? Is either so threatening to children's well-being that it should not be carried out?

- To study the development of children's willingness to separate from their caregivers, an investigator decides to ask mothers of 1- and 2-year-olds to leave their youngsters alone for a brief time period in an unfamiliar playroom. The researcher knows that under these circumstances, some children become very upset.
- In a study of moral development, an investigator wants to assess children's ability to resist temptation by videotaping their behavior without their knowledge. Seven-year-olds are promised an attractive prize for solving some very difficult puzzles. They are also told not to look at a classmate's correct solutions, which are deliberately placed at the back of the room. If the researcher has to tell children ahead of time that cheating is being studied or that their behavior is being closely monitored, she will destroy the purpose of her study.

Did you find it difficult to decide on the best course of action in these examples? Virtually every committee that has worked on developing ethical principles for research has concluded that the conflicts raised by studies like these cannot be resolved with simple right-or-wrong answers. The ultimate responsibility for the ethical integrity of research lies with the investigator. However, researchers are advised or, in the case of federally funded research, required to seek advice from others. Special committees exist in colleges, universities, and other institutions for this purpose. These committees weigh the costs of the research to the participant in terms of time, stress, and inconvenience against its value for advancing knowledge and improving children's conditions of life. If there are any negative implications for the safety and welfare of participants that the worth of the research does not justify, then preference is always given to the interests of the research participant.

TABLE 1.8

Children's Research Rights

RESEARCH RIGHT	DESCRIPTION
Protection from harm	Children have the right to be protected from physical or psychological harm in research. If in doubt about the harmful effects of research, investigators should seek the opinion of others. When harm seems possible, investigators should find other means for obtaining the desired information or abandon the research.
Informed consent	All research participants, including children, have the right to have explained to them, in language appropriate to their level of understanding, all aspects of the research that may affect their willingness to participate. When children are participants, informed consent of parents as well as others who act on the child's behalf (such as school officials) should be obtained, preferably in writing. Children, and the adults responsible for them, have the right to discontinue participation in the research at any time.
Privacy	Children have the right to concealment of their identity on all information collected in the course of research. They also have this right with respect to written reports and any informal discussions about the research.
Knowledge of results	Children have the right to be informed of the results of research in language that is appropriate to their level of understanding.
Beneficial treatments	If experimental treatments believed to be beneficial are under investigation, children in control groups have the right to alternative beneficial treatments if they are available.

Sources: American Psychological Association, 1992; Society for Research in Child Development, 1993.

The ethical principle of *informed consent* requires special interpretation when research participants are children. The competence of youngsters of different ages to make choices about their own participation must be taken into account. Parental consent is meant to protect the safety of children whose ability to make these decisions is not yet fully mature. Besides parental consent, researchers should obtain the agreement of other individuals who act on children's behalf, such as institutional officials when research is conducted in schools, day care centers, or hospitals. This is especially important when research includes special groups of children, such as abused youngsters, whose parents may not always represent their best interests (Fisher, 1993; Thompson, 1990b).

For children 7 years and older, their own informed consent should be obtained in addition to parental consent. Around age 7, changes in children's thinking permit them to better understand simple scientific principles and the needs of others. Researchers should respect and enhance these new capacities by providing school-age children with a full explanation of research activities in language that children can understand (Fisher, 1993). Extra care needs to be taken when informing children that the information they provide will be kept confidential and that they can end their participation at any time. Children may not understand, and sometimes do not believe, these promises from researchers (Abramovitch et al., 1991).

Finally, young children rely on a basic faith in adults to feel secure in unfamiliar situations. For this reason, it is possible for some types of research to be particularly disturbing to them. All ethical guidelines advise that special precautions be taken in the use of deception and concealment, as occurs when researchers observe children from behind one-way mirrors, give them false feedback about their performance, or do not tell them the truth regarding what the research is all about. When these kinds of procedures are used with adults, *debriefing,* in which the experimenter provides a full account and justification of the activities, occurs after the research session is over. Debriefing should also take place with children, but it does not always work as well. Despite explanations, children may come away from the research situation with their belief in the honesty of adults undermined. Ethical standards permit deception in research with children if investigators satisfy institutional committees that such practices are necessary. Nevertheless, since deception may have serious emotional consequences for some youngsters, many child development specialists believe that its use is always unethical and that researchers should come up with other research procedures when children are involved (Cooke, 1982; Ferguson, 1978).

ASK YOURSELF . . .

- An investigator decides to conduct a study of teacher–pupil interaction in a fourth-grade classroom. From whom should she seek informed consent for research participation?
- A researcher interested in recruiting preschoolers from low-income families for a study of cognitive development decides to offer $50 to each mother who permits her child to participate. How might this practice violate research rights?
- An investigator wants to assess the effectiveness of an intervention designed to promote independence and assertiveness in 10-year-olds. After the study is underway, several parents complain that in their ethnic group it is not appropriate for children to behave in these ways. How should the researcher respond? What could he have done to avoid this problem?

THE CHRONOLOGICAL APPROACH OF THIS BOOK

With the completion of this overview of theory and research, we are ready to chart the course of child development itself. In the following chapters, the story of childhood unfolds in chronological sequence. We begin with a chapter on biological and environmental foundations—the basics of human heredity and how it combines with environmental influences to shape children's characteristics and skills. Then we turn to particular time spans of development.

There are many ways to divide the first two decades of life into separate age periods. I have chosen the following divisions because they serve as major transition points in most theories of child development. Each brings with it a diverse array of new capacities and, consequently, new social expectations of children in cultures around the world:

- Prenatal development and birth
- Infancy and toddlerhood—the first 2 years
- Early childhood—2 to 6 years
- Middle childhood—6 to 11 years
- Adolescence—11 to 20 years

Within each age period, a separate chapter is devoted to each of the following aspects of development:

- Physical development—growth in body size and proportions, brain development, perceptual and motor capacities, and physical health
- Cognitive development—development of a wide variety of intellectual abilities, including attention, memory, academic and everyday knowledge, problem solving, imagination, creativity, and the uniquely human capacity to represent the world through language
- Emotional and social development—development of emotional communication, self-understanding, knowledge about other people, interpersonal skills, and moral reasoning and behavior

You are already aware from reading this chapter that the aspects of development listed here are not really distinct; they overlap and interact a great deal. A major advantage of discussing them as a unit within each age period is that we can easily see how they are interwoven. As our discussion proceeds, we will continuously point out relationships among all aspects of development.

Finally, it is my hope that the content, organization, and instructional features of this book will help meet the needs and interests of you, its readers. Perhaps you aspire to a career in applied work with children, want to teach child development or advance its knowledge base, plan someday to raise children, are already a parent, or are simply curious about how you yourself developed from a tiny infant into the complex adult you are today. Whichever goals happen to be yours, as you embark on the study of children I wish you a stimulating and rewarding journey.

SUMMARY

CHILD DEVELOPMENT AS AN INTERDISCIPLINARY, SCIENTIFIC, AND APPLIED FIELD

What is child development, and what factors stimulated expansion of the field?

- **Child development** is the study of human growth and change from conception through adolescence. It is part of a larger field known as **developmental psychology,** or **human development,** which includes all changes that take place throughout the life span. Research on child development has been stimulated by both scientific curiosity and social pressures to better the lives of children.

BASIC THEMES AND ISSUES

Identify three basic issues on which child development theories take a stand.

- Child development **theories** can be organized according to the stand they take on three controversial issues: (1) Is the child an **organismic** or **mechanistic** being? (2) Is development a **continuous** process, or does it follow a series of **discontinuous stages?** (3) Is development primarily determined by **nature** or **nurture?**

HISTORICAL FOUNDATIONS

Describe major historical influences on modern theories of child development.

- Modern theories of child development have roots extending far back into the past. In medieval times, children were thought of as miniature adults, a view called **preformationism.** By the sixteenth and seventeenth centuries, childhood became a distinct phase of the life cycle. However, the Puritan conception of original sin led to a harsh philosophy of child rearing.
- The Enlightenment brought new ideas favoring more humane child

treatment. Locke's notion of the **tabula rasa** furnished the basis for twentieth-century behaviorism, and Rousseau's idea of the **noble savage** foreshadowed the concepts of stage and **maturation.** A century later, Darwin's theory of evolution stimulated scientific child study.

- Efforts to observe the child directly began in the late nineteenth and early twentieth centuries with the baby biographies. Soon after, Hall and Gesell introduced the **normative approach,** which produced a large body of descriptive facts about children. Binet and Simon constructed the first successful intelligence test, which initiated the mental testing movement.

MID-TWENTIETH-CENTURY THEORIES

What theories influenced child development research in the mid-twentieth century?

- In the 1930s and 1940s, child guidance professionals turned to the **psychoanalytic perspective** for help in understanding children with emotional problems. In Freud's **psychosexual theory,** children move through five stages, during which three portions of the personality—**id, ego,** and **superego**—become integrated. Erikson's **psychosocial theory** builds on Freud's theory by emphasizing the development of culturally relevant attitudes and skills and the lifespan nature of development.
- Academic psychology also influenced child study. From **behaviorism** and **social learning theory** came the principles of conditioning and modeling and practical procedures of **applied behavior analysis** with children.
- In contrast to behaviorism, Piaget's **cognitive-developmental theory** emphasizes an active child with a mind inhabited by rich structures of knowledge. According to Piaget, children move through five stages, beginning with the baby's sensorimotor action patterns and ending with the elaborate, abstract reasoning system of the adolescent. Piaget's work has stimulated a wealth of research on children's thinking and encouraged educational programs that emphasize discovery learning.

RECENT PERSPECTIVES

Describe four recent theoretical perspectives on child development.

- The field of child development continues to seek new directions. **Information processing** views the mind as a complex, symbol-manipulating system, operating much like a computer. This approach helps investigators achieve a detailed understanding of what children of different ages do when faced with tasks and problems.
- Three modern theories place special emphasis on contexts for development. **Ethology** stresses the adaptive, or survival, value of behavior and its origins in evolutionary history. In **ecological systems theory,** nested layers of the environment, which range from the child's immediate settings to broad cultural values and programs, are seen as major influences on children's well-being. Vygotsky's **sociocultural theory** has enhanced our understanding of cultural influences, especially in the area of cognitive development. Through cooperative dialogues with mature members of society, children acquire culturally relevant knowledge and skills.

STUDYING THE CHILD

Describe research methods commonly used to study children.

- Common research methods in child development include systematic observation, self-reports, the clinical or case study approach, and ethnography. **Naturalistic observations** are gathered in children's everyday environments, whereas **structured observations** take place in laboratories, where investigators deliberately set up cues to elicit the behaviors of interest.
- Self-report methods, such as the **clinical interview,** can be flexible and open-ended. Alternatively, **structured interviews** and questionnaires, which permit efficient administration and scoring, can be given. Investigators use the **clinical method** when they desire an in-depth understanding of a single child.
- A growing interest in the impact of culture has prompted child development researchers to rely increasingly on **ethnography.** It uses participant observation to capture the unique values and social processes of a culture or distinct social group.

Distinguish between correlational and experimental research designs, noting the strengths and limitations of each.

- Two main types of designs are used in all research on human behavior. The **correlational design** examines relationships between variables as they happen to occur, without any intervention. The **correlation coefficient** is often used to measure the association between variables. Correlational studies do not permit statements about cause and effect. However, their use is justified when it is difficult or impossible to control the variables of interest.
- An **experimental design** permits inferences about cause and effect. Researchers randomly assign participants to treatment conditions and manipulate an **independent variable.** Then they determine what impact this has on a **dependent variable.** To achieve high degrees of control, most experiments are conducted in laboratories, but their

findings may not apply to everyday life. Field and natural experiments are strategies used to compare treatments in natural environments.

Describe designs for studying development, noting the strengths and limitations of each.

- Longitudinal and cross-sectional designs are uniquely suited for studying development. The **longitudinal design** permits study of common patterns as well as individual differences in development and the relationship between early and later events and behaviors. The **cross-sectional design** offers an efficient approach to investigating development. However, it is limited to comparisons of age group averages.
- Findings of longitudinal and cross-sectional research can be distorted by **cohort effects.** To overcome some of the limitations of these designs, investigators sometimes combine the two approaches, as in the **longitudinal-sequential design.**

What special ethical concerns arise in doing research on children?

- Research on children raises special ethical concerns. Ethical guidelines help ensure that children's research rights are protected. Besides parental consent, researchers should seek the informed consent of children 7 years and older for research participation. The use of deception in research with children is especially risky, since it may undermine their basic faith in the trustworthiness of adults.

IMPORTANT TERMS AND CONCEPTS

child development (p. 4)
developmental psychology (p. 4)
human development (p. 4)
theory (p. 5)
organismic theories (p. 6)
mechanistic theories (p. 6)
continuous development (p. 7)
discontinuous development (p. 7)
stage (p. 7)
nature–nurture controversy (p. 7)
preformationism (p. 9)
tabula rasa (p. 10)
noble savage (p. 11)
maturation (p. 11)
normative approach (p. 13)
psychoanalytic perspective (p. 15)
psychosexual theory (p. 16)
id (p. 16)
ego (p. 16)
superego (p. 16)
psychosocial theory (p. 17)
behaviorism (p. 19)
social learning theory (p. 20)
applied behavior analysis (p. 21)
cognitive-developmental theory (p. 22)
information processing (p. 24)
ethology (p. 26)
sensitive period (p. 27)
ecological systems theory (p. 27)
sociocultural theory (p. 30)
naturalistic observation (p. 33)
structured observation (p. 34)
clinical interview (p. 35)
structured interview (p. 35)
clinical method (p. 36)
ethnography (p. 36)
correlational design (p. 37)
correlation coefficient (p. 39)
experimental design (p. 39)
independent variable (p. 39)
dependent variable (p. 39)
longitudinal design (p. 41)
cohort effects (p. 42)
cross-sectional design (p. 43)
longitudinal-sequential design (p. 43)

"Mother"
Nadia Huzina
12 years, Russia

This tranquil image of mother and child suggests an unusually warm, close relationship. Is family resemblance in personality, interests, and capabilities partly responsible? Chapter 2 will introduce you to the complex blend of genetic and environmental forces that lead parents and children to be both alike and different.

Reprinted by permission from The International Museum of Children's Art, Oslo, Norway.

2

Biological and Environmental Foundations

■
GENETIC FOUNDATIONS

The Genetic Code • The Sex Cells • Conception • Boy or Girl? • Multiple Births • Patterns of Genetic Inheritance

■
CHROMOSOMAL ABNORMALITIES

Down Syndrome • Abnormalities of the Sex Chromosomes

■
REPRODUCTIVE CHOICES

Genetic Counseling • Prenatal Diagnosis and Fetal Medicine • The Alternative of Abortion • The Alternative of Adoption

■
ENVIRONMENTAL CONTEXTS FOR DEVELOPMENT

The Family • Social Class and Family Functioning • The Impact of Poverty • Beyond the Family: Neighborhoods, Schools, Towns, and Cities • The Cultural Context

■
UNDERSTANDING THE RELATIONSHIP BETWEEN HEREDITY AND ENVIRONMENT

The Question of "How Much?" • The Question of "How?"

"It's a girl," announces the doctor, who holds up the squalling little creature, while her new parents gaze with amazement at their miraculous creation.

"A girl! We've named her Sarah!" exclaims the proud father to eager relatives waiting by the telephone for word about their new family member.

As we join these parents in thinking about how this wondrous being came into existence and imagining her future, we are struck by many questions. How could this well-formed baby, equipped with everything necessary for life outside the womb, have developed from the union of two tiny cells? What ensures that Sarah will, in due time, roll over, reach for objects, walk, talk, make friends, imagine, and create—just like every other normal child born before her? Why is she a girl and not a boy, dark-haired rather than blond, calm and cuddly instead of wiry and energetic? What difference will it make that Sarah is given a name and place in one family, community, nation, and culture rather than another?

To answer these questions, this chapter takes a close look at the foundations of development: heredity and environment. Because nature has prepared us for survival, all human beings have many features in common. Yet a brief period of time spent in the company of any child and his or her family reveals that each human being is unique. Take a moment to jot down the most obvious similarities in physical characteristics and behavior for several children and parents whom you know well. Did you find that one child shows combined features of both parents, another resembles just one parent, whereas still a third is not like either parent? These directly observable characteristics are called **phenotypes.** They depend in part on the individual's **genotype**—the complex blend of genetic information transmitted from one generation to the next that determines our species and influences all our unique characteristics. Throughout life, phenotypes are also affected by the person's history of experiences in the environment.

We begin our discussion of development at the moment of conception, an event that establishes the hereditary makeup of the new individual. In the first section of this chapter, we review basic genetic principles that help explain similarities and differences among us in appearance and behavior. Next, we turn to a variety of aspects of the environment that play a powerful role in children's lives.

As our discussion proceeds, you will quickly see that both nature and nurture are involved in all aspects of development. In fact, some findings and conclusions in this chapter may surprise you. For example, many people believe that when children inherit unfavorable characteristics, not much can be done to help them. Others are convinced that when environments are harmful, the damage done to children can easily be corrected. We will see that neither of these assumptions is true. In the final section of this chapter, we take up the question of how nature and nurture *work together* to shape the course of development.

GENETIC FOUNDATIONS

Basic principles of genetics were unknown until the mid-nineteenth century, when the Austrian monk and botanist Gregor Mendel began a series of experiments with pea plants in his monastery garden. Recording the number of times white- and pink-flowered plants had offspring with white or pink flowers, Mendel found that he could predict the characteristics of each new generation. Mendel inferred the presence of genes, factors controlling the physical traits he studied. Although peas and humans may seem completely unrelated, today we know that heredity operates in similar ways among all forms of life. Since Mendel's ground-breaking observations, our understanding of how genetic messages are coded and inherited has vastly expanded.

THE GENETIC CODE

Each of us is made up of trillions of independent units called *cells*. Inside every cell is a control center, or nucleus. When cells are chemically stained and viewed through a powerful microscope, rodlike structures called **chromosomes** are visible in the nucleus. Chromosomes store and transmit genetic information. Their number varies from species to species—48 for chimpanzees, 64 for horses, 40 for mice, and 46 for human beings. Chromosomes come in matching pairs (an exception is the XY pair in males, which we will discuss shortly). Each member of a pair corresponds to the other in size, shape, and genetic functions. One is inherited from the mother and one from the father. Therefore, in humans, we speak of 23 *pairs* of chromosomes residing in each human cell (see Figure 2.1).

Chromosomes are made up of a chemical substance called **deoxyribonucleic acid,** or **DNA.** In the early 1950s, James Watson and Francis Crick's (1953) discovery of the structure of the DNA molecule unlocked the genetic code. As Figure 2.2 on page 54 shows, DNA is a long, double-stranded molecule that looks like a twisted ladder. Notice that each rung of the ladder consists of a specific pair of chemical substances called *bases*, joined together between the two sides. Although the bases always pair up in the same way across the ladder rungs—A with T and C with G—they can occur in any order along its sides. It is this sequence of bases that provides genetic instructions. A **gene** is a segment of DNA along the length of the

Phenotype
The individual's physical and behavioral characteristics, which are determined by both genetic and environmental factors.

Genotype
The genetic makeup of the individual.

Chromosomes
Rodlike structures in the cell nucleus that store and transmit genetic information.

Deoxyribonucleic acid (DNA)
Long, double-stranded molecules that make up chromosomes.

Gene
A segment of a DNA molecule that contains hereditary instructions.

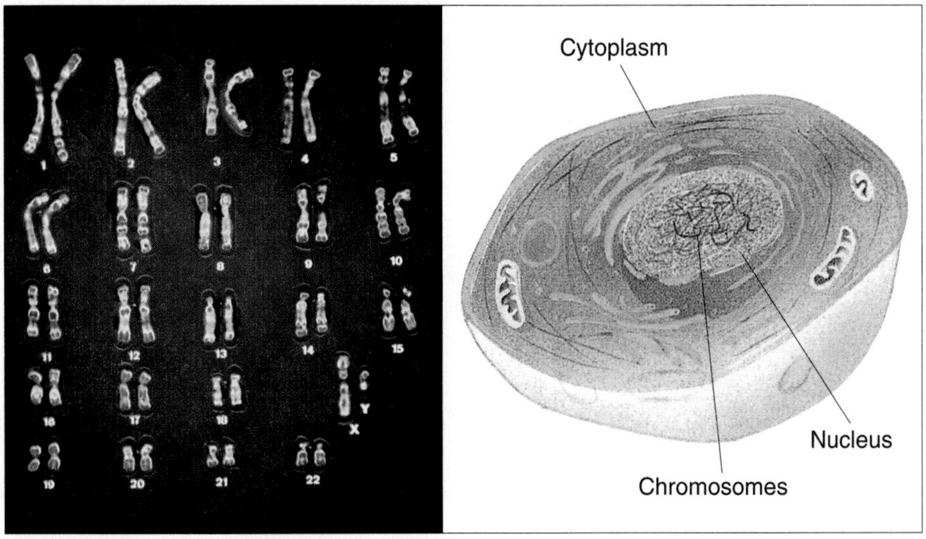

FIGURE 2.1

A karyotype, or photograph, of human chromosomes. The 46 chromosomes shown here were isolated from a body cell, stained, greatly magnified, and arranged in pairs according to decreasing size of the upper arm of each chromosome. Note the twenty-third pair, XY. The cell donor is a male. In females, the twenty-third pair would be XX. *(CNRI/ Science Photo Library/ Photo Researchers)*

chromosome. Genes can be of different lengths—perhaps 100 to several thousand ladder rungs long—and each differs from the next because of its special sequence of base pairs. Altogether, about 100,000 genes lie along the human chromosomes.

Genes accomplish their task by sending instructions for making a rich assortment of proteins to the cytoplasm, the area surrounding the nucleus of the cell. Proteins, which trigger chemical reactions throughout the body, are the biological foundation from which our characteristics and capacities are built.

A unique feature of DNA is that it can duplicate itself. This special ability makes it possible for the one-celled fertilized ovum to develop into a complex human being composed of a great many cells. The process of cell duplication is called **mitosis.** In mitosis, the DNA ladder splits down the middle, opening somewhat like a zipper (refer again to Figure 2.2). Then each base is free to pair up with a new mate from the area surrounding the nucleus of the cell. Notice how this process creates two identical DNA ladders, each containing one new side and one old side from the previous ladder. At the level of chromosomes, during mitosis each chromosome copies itself. As a result, each new body cell contains the same number of chromosomes and the identical genetic information.

THE SEX CELLS

If babies developed from the joining of two regular body cells (one from the mother and one from the father), they would have too many chromosomes to grow normally. Instead, new individuals are created when two special cells called **gametes,** or sex cells—the sperm and ovum—combine. Gametes are unique in that they contain only 23 chromosomes, half as many as a regular body cell. They are formed through a special process of cell division called **meiosis,** which halves the number of chromosomes normally present in body cells.

Meiosis takes place according to the steps in Figure 2.3. First, chromosomes pair up within the original cell, and each one copies itself. Then a special event called **crossing over** takes place. In crossing over, chromosomes next to each other break at one or more points along their length and exchange segments, so that genes from one are replaced by genes from another. This shuffling of genes in crossing over creates new hereditary combinations. Next, the paired chromosomes separate into different cells, but chance determines which member of each pair will gather with others and eventually end up in the same gamete. Finally, in the last phase of meiosis, each chromosome leaves its duplicate and becomes part of a sex cell containing 23 chromosomes instead of the usual 46.

Mitosis
The process of cell duplication, in which each new cell receives an exact copy of the original chromosomes.

Gametes
Human sperm and ova, which contain half as many chromosomes as a regular body cell.

Meiosis
The process of cell division through which gametes are formed and in which the number of chromosomes in each cell is halved.

Crossing over
Exchange of genes between chromosomes next to each other during meiosis.

FIGURE 2.2

DNA's ladderlike structure. The figure on the left shows that the pairings of bases across the rungs of the ladder are very specific: adenine (A) always appears with thymine (T), and cytosine (C) always appears with guanine (G). Here, the DNA ladder duplicates by splitting down the middle of its ladder rungs. Each free base picks up a new complementary partner from the area surrounding the cell nucleus.

The photo on the right shows a computer-generated model of DNA. By simulating and color-coding DNA's structure, scientists can rotate the image and study it from different vantage points. *(Jean-Claude Revy/ Phototake)*

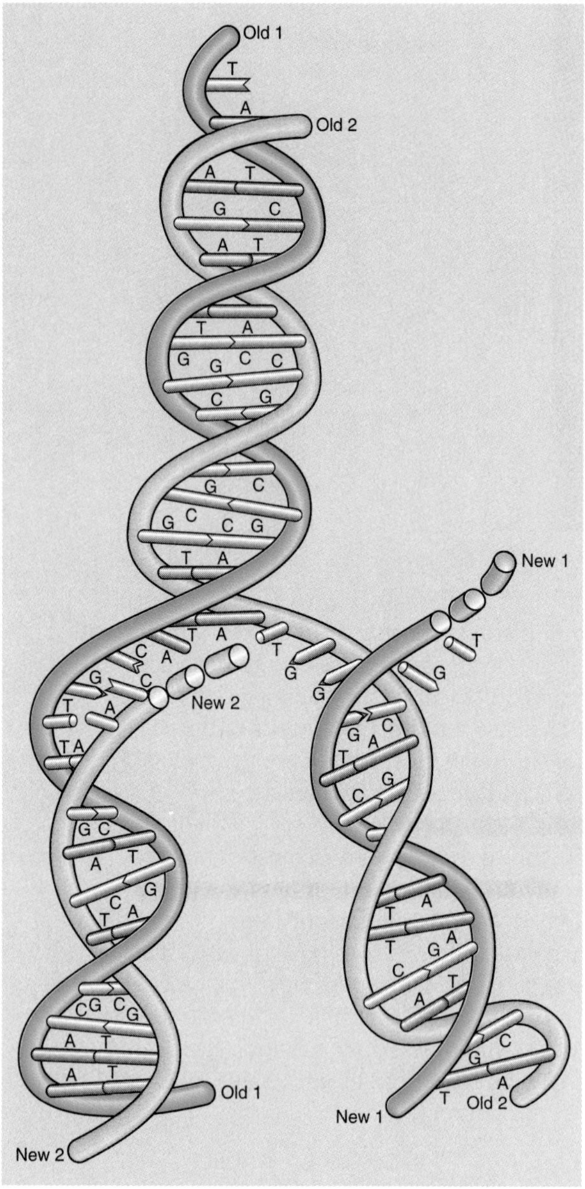

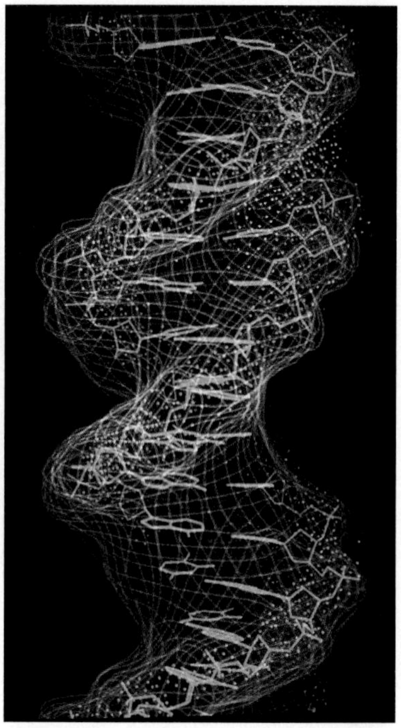

In the male, four sperm are produced each time meiosis occurs. Also, the cells from which sperm arise are produced continuously throughout life. For this reason, a healthy man can father a child at any age after sexual maturity. In the female, gamete production is much more limited. Each cell division produces just one ovum. In addition, the female is born with all her ova already present in her ovaries, and she can only bear children for three to four decades. Most women stop ovulating between the ages of 45 and 53. Still, there are plenty of female sex cells. About 1 to 2 million are present at birth, 40,000 remain at adolescence, and approximately 350 to 450 will mature during a woman's childbearing years (Moore & Persaud, 1993).

Look again at the steps of meiosis displayed in Figure 2.3, and notice how they ensure that a constant quantity of genetic material (46 chromosomes in each cell) is transmitted from one generation to the next. Can you also see how meiosis leads to genetic differences among offspring? Crossing over and random sorting of each member of a chromosome pair into separate sex cells mean that no two gametes will ever be the same. Meiosis explains why siblings differ from each other, even though they also have features in common, since their genotypes come from a common pool of parental genes.

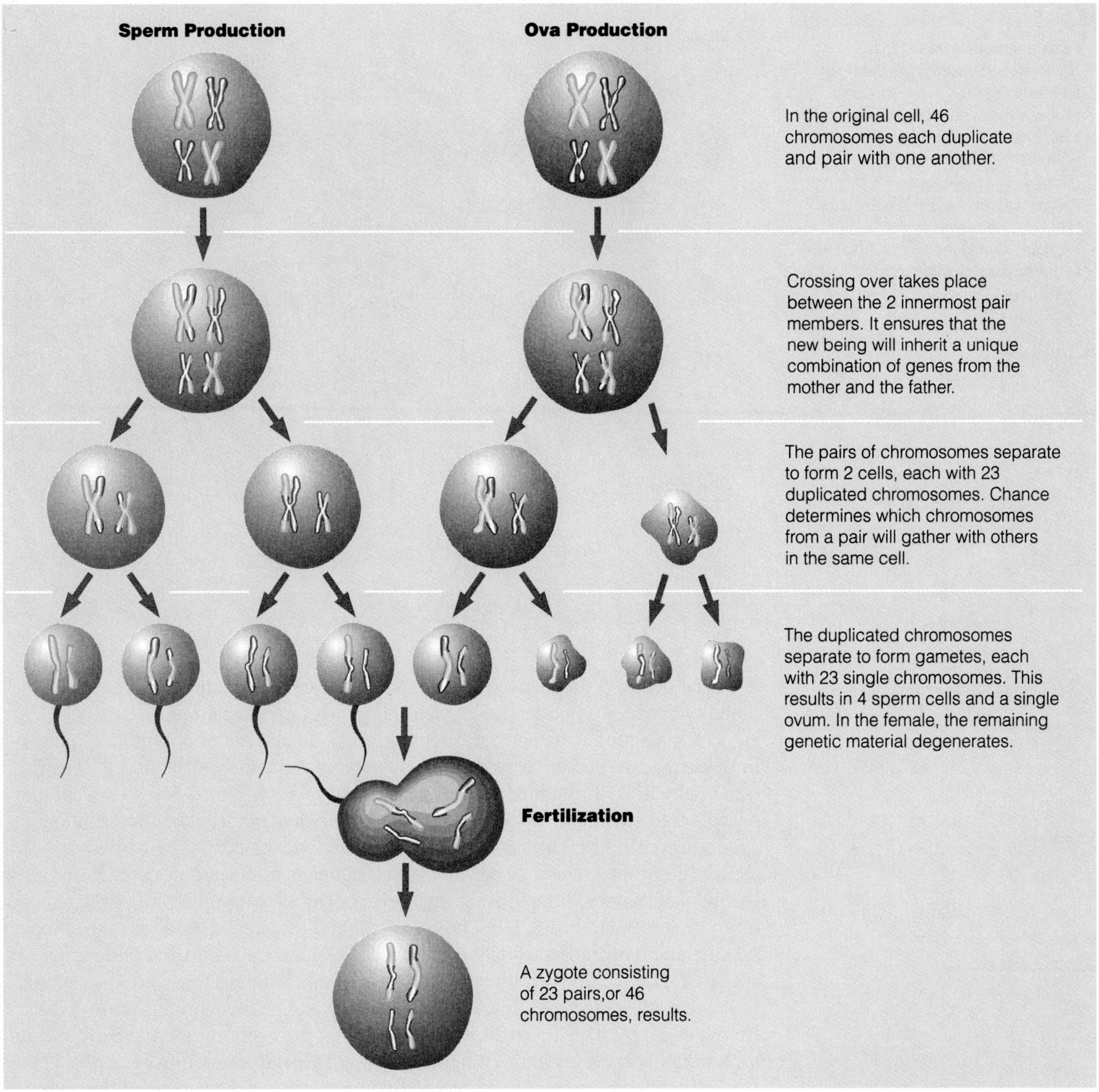
Sperm Production
Ova Production
In the original cell, 46 chromosomes each duplicate and pair with one another.
Crossing over takes place between the 2 innermost pair members. It ensures that the new being will inherit a unique combination of genes from the mother and the father.
The pairs of chromosomes separate to form 2 cells, each with 23 duplicated chromosomes. Chance determines which chromosomes from a pair will gather with others in the same cell.
The duplicated chromosomes separate to form gametes, each with 23 single chromosomes. This results in 4 sperm cells and a single ovum. In the female, the remaining genetic material degenerates.
Fertilization
A zygote consisting of 23 pairs,or 46 chromosomes, results.

FIGURE 2.3

The cell division process of meiosis leading to gamete formation. (Here, original cells are depicted with 2 rather than the full complement of 23 chromosome pairs.) Meiosis creates gametes with only half the usual number of chromosomes. When sperm and ovum unite at fertilization, the first cell of the new individual (the zygote) has the correct, full number of chromosomes.

CONCEPTION

Once formed, male and female gametes are ready to fuse with each other. The human sperm and ovum are uniquely suited for the task of reproduction. The ovum is a tiny sphere, measuring 1/175 of an inch in diameter, that is barely visible to the naked eye as a dot the size of the period at the end of this sentence. But in its microscopic world it is a giant—the largest cell in the human body. The ovum's size makes it a perfect target for the much smaller sperm, which measure only 1/500 of an inch.

About once every 28 days, in the middle of a woman's menstrual cycle, an ovum bursts from one of her *ovaries,* two walnut-sized organs located deep inside her abdomen (see Figure 2.4). Surrounded by thousands of nurse cells that will feed and protect it along its path, the ovum is drawn into one of two *fallopian tubes*—long, thin structures that lead to the hollow, soft-lined uterus. While the ovum is traveling, the spot on the ovary from which it was released, now called the *corpus luteum,* begins to secrete hormones that prepare the lining of the uterus to receive a

FIGURE 2.4

Female reproductive organs. An ovum is released from the ovary and fertilized high in the fallopian tube. As the zygote begins to duplicate, it travels toward the uterus and burrows into the uterine lining. *(From K. L. Moore and T. V. N. Persaud, 1993, Before We Are Born (4th ed.), Philadelphia: W. B. Saunders Company, p. 33. Adapted by permission of the publisher and the author.)*

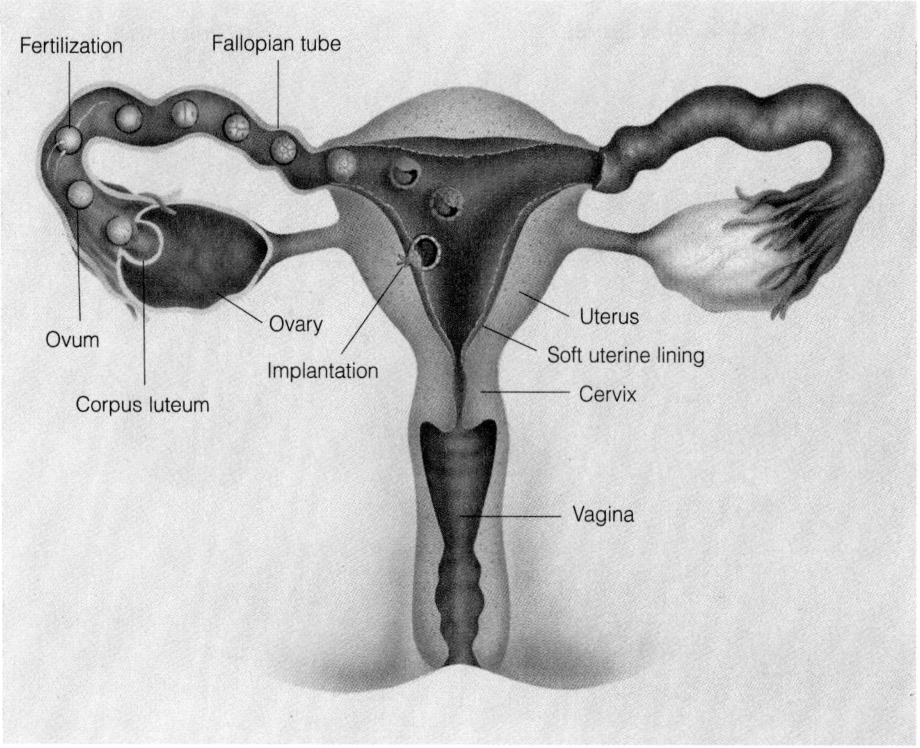

fertilized ovum. If pregnancy does not occur, the corpus luteum shrinks, and the lining of the uterus is discarded 2 weeks later with menstruation.

The male produces sperm in vast numbers—an average of 300 million a day—in the *testes,* two glands located in the *scrotum,* sacs that lie just behind the penis (see Figure 2.5). In the final process of maturation, each sperm develops a tail that permits it to swim long distances. During sexual intercourse, about 360 million sperm move through the *vas deferens,* a thin tube in which they are bathed in a protective fluid called *semen.* At sexual climax, semen is ejaculated from the penis into the woman's vagina. Immediately, the sperm begin to swim upstream in the female reproductive tract, through the *cervix* (opening of the uterus), and into the fallopian tube, where fertilization usually takes place. The journey is difficult, and many sperm die. Only 300 to 500 reach the ovum, if one happens to be present. Sperm have an average life of 48 hours and can lie in wait for the ovum for up to 2 days. An ovum survives for up to 24 hours. Therefore, the maximum fertile period during each monthly cycle is about 72 hours (Nilsson & Hamberger, 1990).

Only a single sperm will be successful in penetrating the surface of the enormous ovum, although others that arrive release chemicals that help break down its protective barrier. Once the winner of the race comes in contact with the ovum's inner cellular material, any remaining competitors are immediately turned away. In this way, the first cell of the new individual is formed. Called a **zygote,** it is ready to begin multiplying into a new human being.

Zygote
The newly fertilized cell formed by the union of sperm and ovum at conception.

Autosomes
The 22 matching chromosome pairs in each human cell.

Sex chromosomes
The twenty-third pair of chromosomes, which determines the sex of the child. In females, called XX; in males, called XY.

BOY OR GIRL?

Using special microscopic techniques, the 23 pairs of chromosomes in each human cell can be distinguished from one another. Twenty-two of them are matching pairs, called **autosomes.** They are numbered by geneticists from longest (1) to shortest (22) (refer back to Figure 2.1). The twenty-third pair consists of **sex chromosomes.** In females, this pair is called *XX;* in males, it is called *XY.* The X is a relatively long chromosome, whereas the Y is short and carries very little genetic material. When gametes are formed in males, the X and Y chromosomes separate

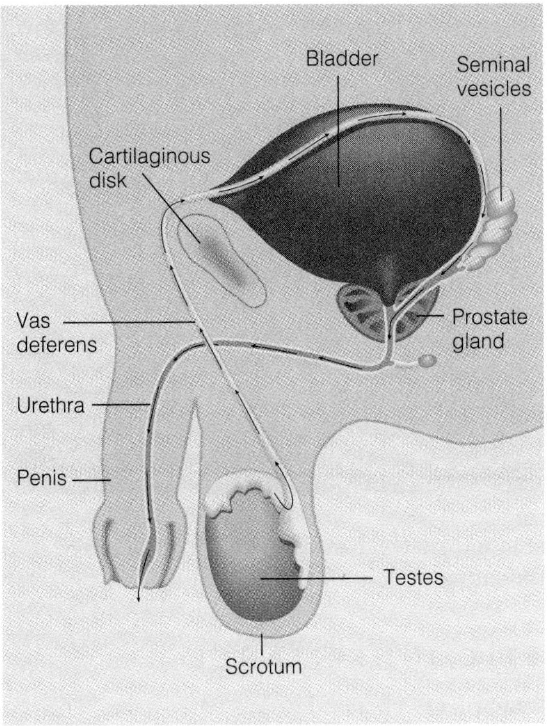

FIGURE 2.5

Male reproductive organs.
Sperm produced in the testes move through the vas deferens, where they are mixed with semen from the prostate gland and seminal vesicles. Then they are released through the urethra in the penis.

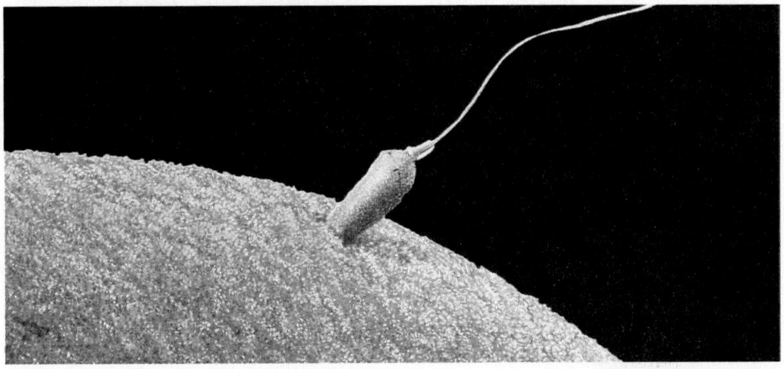

In this photograph of fertilization taken with the aid of a powerful microscope, a tiny sperm completes its journey and starts to penetrate the surface of an enormous-looking ovum, the largest cell in the human body. *(Francis Leroy, Biocosmos/ Science Photo Library/Photo Researchers)*

into different sperm cells. In females, all gametes carry an X chromosome. The sex of the new organism is determined by whether an X-bearing or a Y-bearing sperm fertilizes the ovum. In fact, scientists have isolated a single gene on the Y chromosome that triggers male sexual development by switching on the production of male sex hormones. When that gene is absent, the fetus that develops is female (Page et al., 1987).

MULTIPLE BIRTHS

Ruth and Peter, a couple I know well, tried for several years to have a child, without success. Ruth's doctor finally prescribed a fertility drug, and twins—Jeannie and Jason—were born. Jeannie and Jason are **fraternal,** or **dizygotic, twins,** the most common type of multiple birth. The drug that Ruth took caused two ova to be released from her ovaries, and both were fertilized. Therefore, Jeannie and Jason are genetically no more alike than ordinary siblings. Fertility drugs are only one cause of fraternal twinning (and occasionally more offspring). As Table 2.1 shows, other genetic and environmental factors are also involved.

There is another way that twins can be created. Sometimes a zygote that has started to duplicate separates into two clusters of cells that develop into two individuals. These are called **identical,** or **monozygotic, twins** because they have the same genetic makeup. The frequency of identical twins is unrelated to the factors listed in Table 2.1. It is about the same around the world—4 out of every 1,000 births. Scientists do not know what causes this type of twinning in humans. In animals, it can be produced by temperature changes, variation in oxygen levels, and late fertilization of the ovum.

During their early years, children of single births are often healthier and develop more rapidly than do twins (Moilanen, 1989). Ruth and Peter's experience indicates why this is the case. Jeannie and Jason were born early (as most twins are)—3 weeks before Ruth's due date. Like other premature infants (as we will see in Chapter 4), they required special care after birth. When the twins came home from the hospital, Ruth and Peter had to divide time between them, and neither baby got quite as much attention as the average single infant. As a result, Jeannie

Fraternal, or dizygotic, twins
Twins resulting from the release and fertilization of two ova. They are genetically no more alike than ordinary siblings.

Identical, or monozygotic, twins
Pairs of twins that result when a zygote, during the early stages of cell duplication, divides in two. They have the same genetic makeup.

These identical, or monozygotic, twins were created when a duplicating zygote separated into two clusters of cells, and two individuals with the same genetic makeup developed. Identical twins look alike, and as we will see later in this chapter, tend to resemble each other in a variety of psychological characteristics. *(Porter/The Image Works)*

and Jason walked and talked several months later than other children their age, although both caught up in development by middle childhood.

PATTERNS OF GENETIC INHERITANCE

Jeannie has her parents' dark, straight hair, whereas Jason is curly-haired and blond. Patterns of genetic inheritance—the way genes from each parent interact—explain why this is the case. Earlier we indicated that except for the XY pair in males, all chromosomes come in matching pairs. Two forms of each gene occur at the same place on the autosomes, one inherited from the mother and one from the father. Each different form of a gene is called an **allele.** If the alleles from both parents are alike, the child is **homozygous** and will display the inherited trait. If the alleles are different, then the child is **heterozygous**, and relationships between alleles determine the trait that will appear.

DOMINANT–RECESSIVE RELATIONSHIPS. In many heterozygous pairings, only one allele affects the child's characteristics. It is called *dominant;* the second allele, which has no effect, is called *recessive.* Hair color is an example of **dominant–recessive inheritance.** The allele for dark hair is dominant (we can represent it with a capital *D*), whereas the one for blond hair is recessive (symbolized by a lowercase *b*). Children who inherit either a homozygous pair of dominant alleles (*DD*) or a heterozygous pair (*Db*) will be dark-haired, even though their

Allele
Each of two forms of a gene located at the same place on the autosomes.

Homozygous
Having two identical alleles at the same place on a pair of chromosomes.

Heterozygous
Having two different alleles at the same place on a pair of chromosomes.

Dominant–recessive inheritance
A pattern of inheritance in which, under heterozygous conditions, the influence of only one allele is apparent.

TABLE 2.1

Maternal Factors Linked to Fraternal Twinning

FACTOR	DESCRIPTION
Ethnicity	About 8 per 1,000 births among whites, 12 to 16 per 1,000 among blacks, and 4 per 1,000 among Asians
Age	Rises with maternal age, peaking at 35 years, and then rapidly falls
Nutrition	Occurs less often among women with poor diets; occurs more often among women who are tall and overweight or of normal weight as opposed to slight body build
Number of births	Chances increase with each additional birth
Exposure to fertility drugs	Treatment of infertility with the hormones increases the likelihood of multiple fraternal births, from twins to quintuplets

Source: Cohen, 1984.

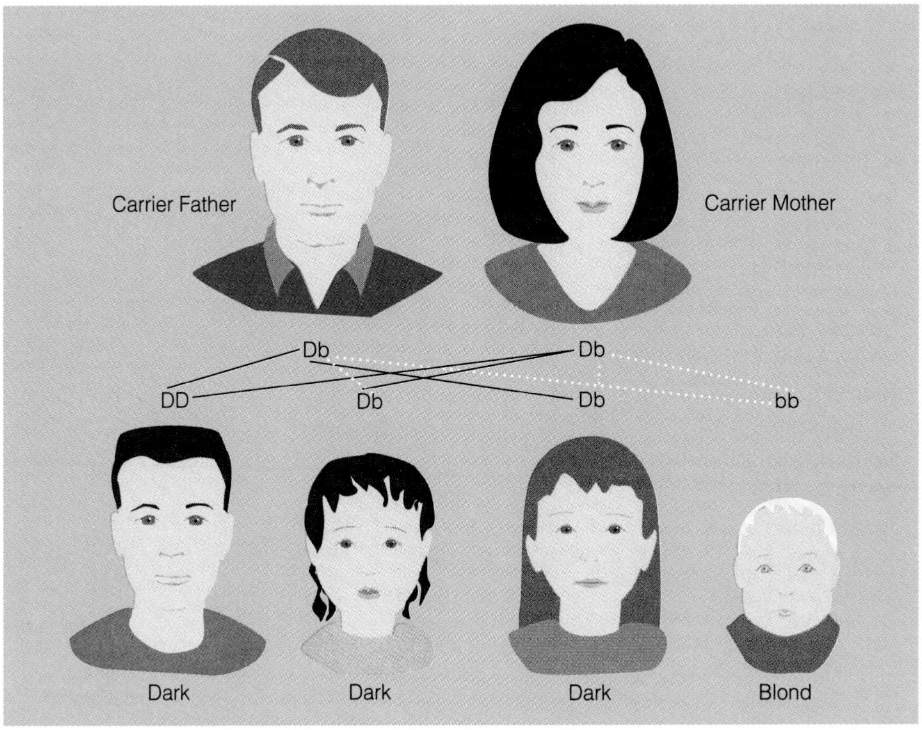

FIGURE 2.6

Dominant–recessive model of inheritance as illustrated by hair color.
By looking at the possible combinations of the parents' genes, we can predict that 25 percent of their children are likely to inherit two dominant genes for dark hair; 50 percent are likely to receive one dominant and one recessive gene, resulting in dark hair; and 25 percent are likely to receive two recessive genes for blond hair.

genetic makeup is different. Blond hair (like Jason's) can result only from having two recessive alleles (*bb*). Still, heterozygous individuals with just one recessive allele (*Db*) can pass on that trait to their children. Therefore, they are called **carriers** of the trait.

In dominant–recessive inheritance, if we know the genetic makeup of the parents, we can predict the percentage of children in a family who are likely to display a trait or be carriers of it. Figure 2.6 shows the pattern of inheritance for hair color. Note that for Jason to be blond, both Peter and Ruth must be carriers of a recessive allele (*b*). The figure also indicates that if Peter and Ruth decide to have more children, most are likely to be dark-haired like Jeannie. Peter and Ruth's children, whether dark- or blond-haired, may vary in precise shade of hair color. *Modifier genes* often act on alleles controlling particular traits, slightly altering their effects.

Some human characteristics and disorders that follow the rules of dominant–recessive inheritance are given in Table 2.2 on page 60 and Table 2.3 on pages 62–63. As you can see, many disabilities and diseases are the product of recessive alleles. One of the most frequently occurring recessive disorders is *phenylketonuria*, or *PKU*. PKU is an especially good example, since it shows that inheriting unfavorable genes does not always mean that the child's condition cannot be treated.

PKU affects the way the body breaks down proteins contained in many foods, such as cow's milk, bread, eggs, and fish. Infants born with two recessive alleles lack an enzyme that converts one of the basic amino acids that make up proteins (phenylalanine) into a by-product essential for body functioning (tyrosine). Without this enzyme, phenylalanine quickly builds to toxic levels that damage the central nervous system. Around 3 to 5 months of age, infants with untreated PKU start to lose interest in their surroundings. By 1 year, they are permanently retarded. All U.S. states require that each newborn be given a blood test for PKU. If the disease is found, treatment involves placing the baby on a diet low in phenylalanine. Children who receive this treatment attain an average level of intelligence and have a normal life span. Nevertheless, they display subtle difficulties with planning and problem solving, since the presence of even small amounts of phenylalanine interferes with normal brain functioning (Welsh et al., 1990).

Carrier
A heterozygous individual who can pass a recessive gene to his or her children.

TABLE 2.2

Examples of Dominant and Recessive Characteristics

DOMINANT	RECESSIVE
Dark hair	Blond hair
Normal hair	Pattern baldness
Curly hair	Straight hair
Nonred hair	Red hair
Facial dimples	No dimples
Normal hearing	Some forms of deafness
Normal vision	Nearsightedness
Farsightedness	Normal vision
Normal vision	Congenital eye cataracts
Normal color vision	Red–green color blindness
Normally pigmented skin	Albinism
Double-jointedness	Normal joints
Type A blood	Type O blood
Type B blood	Type O blood
Rh-positive blood	Rh-negative blood

Note: Many normal characteristics previously thought to be due to dominant–recessive inheritance, such as eye color, are now regarded as due to multiple genes. For the characteristics listed here, there still seems to be fairly common agreement that the simple dominant–recessive relationship holds.
Source: McKusick, 1992.

As Table 2.3 suggests, only rarely are serious diseases due to dominant alleles. Think about why this is the case. Children who inherited the dominant allele would always develop the disorder. They would seldom live long enough to reproduce, and the harmful dominant allele would be eliminated from the family's heredity in a single generation. Some dominant disorders, however, do persist. One of them is *Huntington disease,* a condition in which the central nervous system degenerates. Why has this disorder endured in some families? The reason is that its symptoms usually do not appear until age 35 or later, after the person has passed the dominant gene to his or her children.

CODOMINANCE. In some heterozygous circumstances, the dominant–recessive relationship does not hold completely. Instead, we see **codominance,** a pattern of inheritance in which both alleles influence the person's characteristics.

The *sickle cell trait,* a heterozygous condition present in many black Africans, provides an example. *Sickle cell anemia* (see Table 2.3) occurs in full form when a child inherits two recessive alleles. They cause the usually round red blood cells to assume a sickle shape, a response that is especially great under low oxygen conditions. The sickled cells clog the blood vessels and block the flow of blood. Individuals who have the disorder suffer severe attacks involving intense pain, swelling, and tissue damage. They generally die in the first 20 years of life; few live past age 40. Heterozygous individuals are protected from the disease under most circumstances. However, when they experience oxygen deprivation—for example, at high altitudes or after intense physical exercise—the single recessive allele asserts itself, and a temporary, mild form of the illness occurs (Sullivan, 1987).

The sickle cell allele is common among black Africans for a special reason. Carriers of it are more resistant to malaria than individuals with two alleles for normal red blood cells. In Africa, where malaria is common, these carriers survived and reproduced more frequently than others, leading the gene to be maintained in the black population.

Codominance
A pattern of inheritance in which both alleles, in a heterozygous combination, are expressed.

MUTATION AND UNFAVORABLE GENES. At this point, you may be wondering, How are harmful genes created in the first place? The answer is **mutation,** a sudden but permanent change in a segment of DNA. A mutation may affect only one or two genes, or it may involve many genes, as is the case for the chromosomal disorders we will discuss shortly. Some mutations occur spontaneously, simply by chance. Others are caused by a wide variety of hazardous environmental agents that enter our food supply or are present in the air we breathe.

For many years, ionizing radiation has been known to cause mutations. Women who receive repeated doses of radiation before conception are more likely to miscarry and give birth to children with hereditary defects (Zhang, Cai, & Lee, 1992). Genetic abnormalities are also higher when fathers are exposed to radiation in their occupations. In one instance, men who worked at a reprocessing plant for nuclear fuel in England were fathers of an usually high number of children who developed cancer. Exposure to radiation at the plant is believed to have damaged chromosomes in the male sex cells, causing cancer in their children years later (Gardner et al., 1990). Does this mean that routine chest and dental X-rays are dangerous to future generations? Research indicates that infrequent and mild exposure to radiation does not cause genetic damage. Instead, high doses over a long period of time appear to be required.

X-LINKED INHERITANCE. Males and females have an equal chance of inheriting recessive disorders carried on the autosomes, such as PKU and sickle cell anemia. But when a harmful allele is carried on the X chromosome, **X-linked inheritance** applies. Males are more likely to be affected because their sex chromosomes do not match. In females, any recessive allele on one X chromosome has a good chance of being suppressed by a dominant allele on the other X. But the Y chromosome is only about one-third as long and therefore lacks many corresponding alleles to override those on the X.

Red–green color blindness (a condition in which individuals cannot tell the difference between shades of red and green) is one example of an X-linked recessive trait. It affects males twice as often as females (Cohen, 1984). In one 3-year-old boy I know, the problem was discovered when he had difficulty learning the names of colors at nursery school. The boy's maternal grandfather was also color blind. Although his mother was unaffected, she was a carrier who passed an X chromosome with the recessive allele to her son. Return to Table 2.3 and review the diseases that are X-linked. A well-known example is *hemophilia,* a disorder in which the blood fails to clot normally. Figure 2.7 on page 64 shows its greater likelihood of inheritance by male children whose mothers carry the abnormal allele.

Besides X-linked disorders, many sex differences reveal the male to be at a disadvantage. Rates of miscarriage and infant and childhood deaths are greater for males. Learning disabilities, behavior disorders, and mental retardation are also more common among boys (Richardson, Koller, & Katz, 1986). It is possible that these sex differences can be traced to the genetic code. The female, with two X chromosomes, benefits from a greater variety of genes. Nature, however, seems to have adjusted for the male's disadvantage. About 106 boys are born for every 100 girls, and judging from miscarriage and abortion statistics, a still greater number of boys appear to be conceived (Shettles & Rorvik, 1984).

GENETIC IMPRINTING. Over 1,000 human characteristics follow the rules of dominant–recessive and codominant inheritance (McKusick, 1992). In these cases, regardless of which parent contributes a gene to the new individual, the gene responds in the same way. Geneticists, however, have identified some exceptions governed by a newly discovered mode of inheritance. In **genetic imprinting,** alleles are *imprinted,* or chemically *marked,* in such a way that one pair member (either the mother's or the father's) is activated, regardless of its makeup. The

Mutation
A sudden but permanent change in a segment of DNA.

X-linked inheritance
A pattern of inheritance in which a recessive gene is carried on the X chromosome. Males are more likely to be affected.

Genetic imprinting
A pattern of inheritance in which alleles are imprinted, or chemically marked, in such a way that one pair member is activated, regardless of its makeup.

TABLE 2.3

Examples of Dominant and Recessive Diseases

DISEASE	DESCRIPTION	MODE OF INHERITANCE	INCIDENCE	TREATMENT	PRENATAL DIAGNOSIS	CARRIER IDENTIFICATION[a]
Autosomal Diseases						
Cooley's anemia	Pale appearance, retarded physical growth, and lethargic behavior begin in infancy.	Recessive	1 in 500 births toparents of Mediterranean descent	Frequent blood transfusions; death from complications usually occurs by adolescence.	Yes	Yes
Cystic fibrosis	Lungs, liver, and pancreas secrete large amounts of thick mucus, leading to breathing and digestive difficulties.	Recessive births	1 in 2,000 to 2,500 Caucasian births; 1 in 16,000 African-American infections;	Bronchial drainage; prompt treatment of respiratory dietary management. Advances in medical care allow survival with good life quality into adulthood.	Yes	Yes
Phenylketonuria (PKU)	Inability to neutralize the amino acid phenylalanine, contained in many proteins, causes severe central nervous system damage in the first year of life.	Recessive	1 in 8,000 births	Placing the child on a special diet results in average intelligence and normal life span. Subtle difficulties with planning and problem solving are often present.	Yes	Yes
Sickle cell anemia	Abnormal sickling of red blood cells causes oxygen deprivation, pain, swelling, and tissue damage. Anemia and susceptibility to infections, especially pneumonia, occur.	Recessive	1 in 500 African-American births	Blood transfusions, painkillers, prompt treatment of infections. No known cure; 50 percent die by age 20.	Yes	Yes
Tay-Sachs disease	Inability to metabolize fatty substances in neural tissue leads to central nervous system degeneration, with onset at about 6 months. Results in poor muscle tone, blindness, deafness, and convulsions.	Recessive	1 in 3,600 births to Jews of European descent	None. Death by 3 to 4 years of age.	Yes	Yes
Huntington disease	Central nervous system degeneration leads to muscular coordination difficulties, mental deterioration, and personality changes. Symptoms usually do not appear until age 35 or later.	Dominant	1 in 18,000 to 25,000 American births	None. Death occurs 10 to 20 years after symptom onset.	Yes	Not applicable

TABLE 2.3, Continued

Examples of Dominant and Recessive Diseases

DISEASE	DESCRIPTION	MODE OF INHERITANCE	INCIDENCE	TREATMENT	PRENATAL DIAGNOSIS	CARRIER IDENTIFICATION[a]
Autosomal Diseases						
Marfan syndrome	Tall, slender build; thin, elongated arms and legs. Heart defects and eye abnormalities, especially of the lens. Excessive lengthening of the body results in a variety of skeletal defects.	Dominant	1 in 20,000 births	Correction of heart and eye defects sometimes possible. Death from heart failure in young adulthood common.	Yes	Not applicable
X-Linked Diseases						
Duchenne muscular dystrophy	Degenerative muscle disease. Abnormal gait, loss of ability to walk between 7 and 13 years of age.	Recessive	1 in 3,000 to 5,000 male births	None. Death from respiratory infection or weakening of the heart muscle usually occurs in adolescence.	Yes	Yes
Hemophilia	Blood fails to clot normally. Can lead to severe internal bleeding and tissue damage.	Recessive	1 in 4,000 to 7,000 male births	Blood transfusions. Safety precautions to prevent injury.	Yes	Yes
Diabetes insipidus	A form of diabetes present at birth caused by insuffcent production of the hormone vasopressin. Results in excessive thirst and urination. Dehydration can cause central nervous system damage.	Recessive	1 in 2,500 male births	Hormone replacement.	No	No

[a]Carrier status detectable in prospective parents through blood test or genetic analyses.
Sources: Behrman & Vaughan, 1987; Cohen, 1984; Fackelmann, 1992; Gilfillan et al., 1992; Martin, 1987; McKusick, 1992; Simpson & Harding, 1993.

imprint is often temporary: it may be erased in the next generation, and it may not occur in all individuals (Sapienza, 1990).

Imprinting helps us understand the confusion in genetic inheritance for some disorders. For example, children are more likely to develop diabetes if their father, rather than their mother, suffers from it. And people with asthma or hay fever tend to have mothers, as opposed to fathers, with the illness. Scientists do not yet know what causes this parent-specific form of inheritance. At times, it reveals itself in heart-breaking ways. Imprinting is involved in several childhood cancers and in *Praeder-Willi syndrome,* a disorder with symptoms of mental retardation and severe obesity. It may also explain why Huntington disease, when inherited from the father, tends to emerge at an earlier age and progress more rapidly (Day, 1993; Reik, 1992).

In these examples, genetic imprinting affects traits carried on the autosomes. It can also operate on the sex chromosomes, as *fragile X syndrome* reveals. In this disorder, an abnormal break appears in a special spot on the X chromosome, damaging

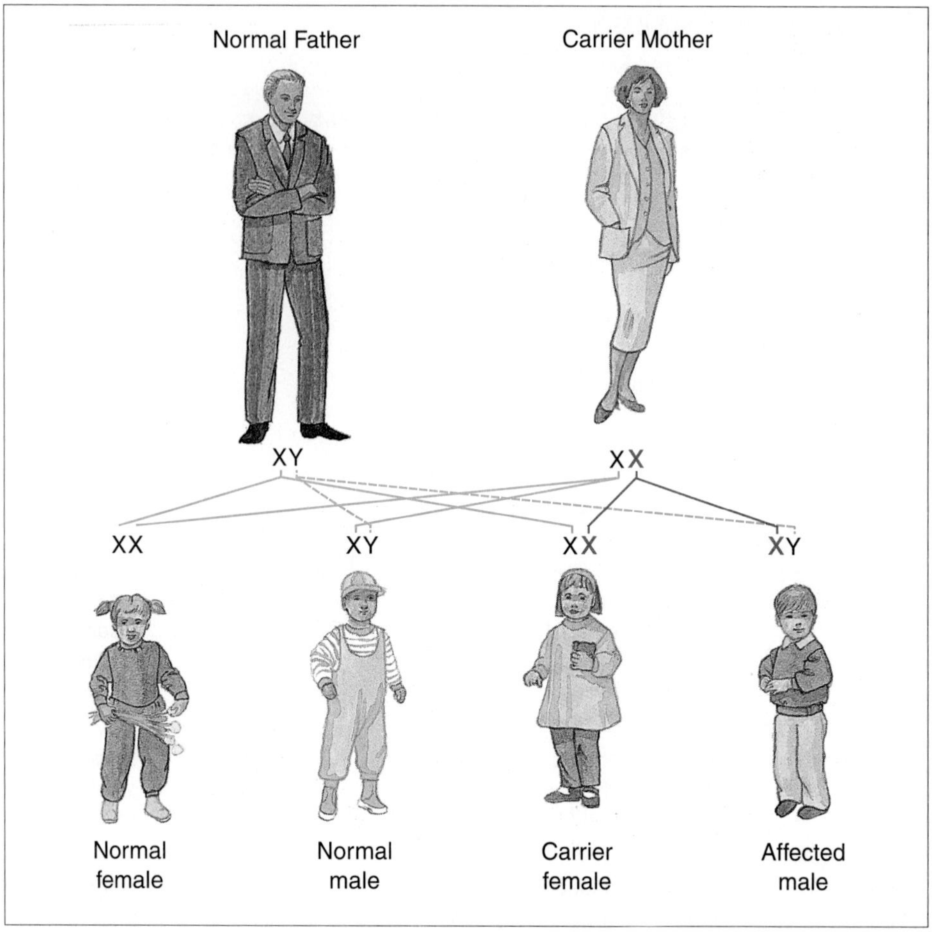

FIGURE 2.7

X-linked inheritance.
In the example shown here, the allele on the father's X chromosome is normal. The mother has one normal and one abnormal recessive allele on her X chromosomes. By looking at the possible combinations of the parents' alleles, we can predict that 50 percent of male children will have the disorder and 50 percent of female children will be carriers of it.

a particular gene. Fragile X syndrome is a common inherited cause of moderate mental retardation. It has also been linked to infantile autism, a serious emotional disorder of early childhood involving bizarre, self-stimulating behavior and delayed or absent language and communication (Hagerman, 1991). Recent evidence indicates that the defective gene at the fragile site is expressed only when it is passed from mother to child (Bodurtha, Tams, & Jackson-Cook, 1992; Day, 1993).

POLYGENIC INHERITANCE. So far, we have discussed patterns of inheritance in which people either display a particular trait or do not. These cut-and-dried individual differences are much easier to trace to their genetic origins than characteristics that vary continuously among people. Many traits of interest to child development specialists, such as height, weight, intelligence, and personality, are of this type. People are not just tall or short, bright or dull, outgoing or shy. Instead, they show gradations between these extremes. Continuous traits like these are due to **polygenic inheritance,** in which many genes determine the characteristic in question. Polygenic inheritance is complex, and much about it is still unknown. So far, scientists have had to study the influence of polygenic inheritance on important human characteristics indirectly. In the final section of this chapter, we will discuss ways that have been used to infer the influence of heredity on human attributes when knowledge of precise patterns of inheritance is unavailable.

Polygenic inheritance
A pattern of inheritance in which many genes determine a characteristic.

CHROMOSOMAL ABNORMALITIES

Besides inheriting harmful recessive alleles, abnormalities of the chromosomes are a major cause of serious developmental problems. Most chromosomal defects are the result of mistakes during meiosis when the ovum and sperm are formed. A chromosome pair does not separate properly or part of a chromosome breaks off. Since these errors involve far more DNA than problems due to single genes, they usually produce disorders with many physical and mental symptoms.

DOWN SYNDROME

The most common chromosomal disorder, occurring in 1 out of every 800 live births, is *Down syndrome*. In most cases, it results from a failure of the twenty-first pair of chromosomes to separate during meiosis, so the new individual inherits three of these chromosomes rather than the normal two. For this reason, Down syndrome is sometimes called *trisomy 21*. In other less frequent forms, an extra broken piece of a twenty-first chromosome is present. Or an error occurs during the early stages of mitosis, causing some but not all body cells to have the defective chromosomal makeup (called a *mosaic* pattern). In these instances, the child's characteristics can vary from practically normal to the typical characteristics of Down syndrome, depending on how much extra genetic material is present (Rosenberg & Pettigrew, 1983).

Children with Down syndrome have distinct physical features—a short, stocky build, a flattened face, a protruding tongue, almond-shaped eyes, and an unusual crease running across the palm of the hand. In addition, infants with Down syndrome are often born with eye cataracts and heart and intestinal defects. Because of medical advances, fewer Down syndrome children die early than was the case in the past, but early death is still common. About 14 percent die by age 1, and 21 percent by age 10. The rest live until middle adulthood (Baird & Sadovnick, 1987).

The behavioral consequences of Down syndrome include mental retardation, speech problems, limited vocabulary, and slow motor development. These problems become more evident with age, since Down syndrome children show a gradual slowing in development from infancy onward when compared to normal children (Kopp, 1983). Parents who give birth to a Down syndrome infant need special help in adjusting to the news that their baby is not normal and in raising their child.

As Table 2.4 shows, the incidence of Down syndrome rises dramatically with maternal age. Why is this so? Geneticists believe that the ova, present in the woman's body since her own prenatal period, weaken over time because of the aging process or increased exposure to harmful environmental agents. As a result, chromosomes do not separate properly during meiosis (Antonarakis, 1992). The mother's gamete, however, is not always the cause of a Down syndrome child. In about 20 percent of cases, the extra genetic material originates with the father. However, Down syndrome and other chromosomal abnormalities are not related to advanced paternal age. In these instances, the mutation occurs for other unknown reasons (Phillips & Elias, 1993).

TABLE 2.4

Risk of Giving Birth to a Down Syndrome Child by Maternal Age

MATERNAL AGE	RISK
20	1 in 1900 births
25	1 in 1200
30	1 in 900
33	1 in 600
36	1 in 300
39	1 in 140
42	1 in 70
45	1 in 30
48	1 in 15

Source: Adapted from Hook, 1982.

The flattened face and almond-shaped eyes of the younger child in this photo are typical physical features of Down syndrome. Although his intellectual development is impaired, this boy is doing well because he is growing up in a family in which his special needs are met and he is loved and accepted. *(Frank Siteman/Stock Boston)*

ABNORMALITIES OF THE SEX CHROMOSOMES

Disorders of the autosomes other than Down syndrome usually disrupt development so severely that miscarriage occurs. When such babies are born, they rarely survive beyond early childhood. In contrast, abnormalities of the sex chromosomes usually lead to fewer problems. In fact, sex chromosome disorders are often not recognized until adolescence when, in some of the deviations, puberty is delayed. The most common problems involve the presence of an extra chromosome (either X or Y) or the absence of one X chromosome in females (see Table 2.5).

TABLE 2.5

Sex Chromosomal Disorders

DISORDER	DESCRIPTION	INCIDENCE	TREATMENT
XYY syndrome	Inheritance of an extra Y chromosome. Typical characteristics are above-average height, large teeth, and sometimes severe acne. Intelligence, development of male sexual characteristics, and fertility are normal.	1 in 1,000 male births	No special treatment necessary.
Triple X syndrome (XXX)	Inheritance of an extra X chromosome. Impaired verbal intelligence. Affected girls are no different in appearance or sexual development from normal agemates, except for a greater tendency toward tallness.	1 in 500 to 1,250 female births	Special education to treat verbal ability problems.
Klinefelter syndrome (XXY)	Inheritance of an extra X chromosome. Impaired verbal intelligence. Affected boys are unusually tall, have a body fat distribution resembling females, and show incomplete development of sex characteristics at puberty. They are usually sterile.	1 in 500 to 1,000 male births	Hormone therapy at puberty to stimulate development of sex characteristics. Special education to treat verbal ability problems.
Turner syndrome (XO)	All or part of the second X chromosome is missing. Impaired spatial intelligence. Ovaries usually do not develop prenatally. Incomplete development of sex characteristics at puberty. Other features include short stature and webbed neck.	1 in 2,500 to 8,000 female births	Hormone therapy in childhood to stimulate physical growth and at puberty to promote development of sex characteristics. Special education to treat spatial ability problems.

Sources: Bancroft, Axworthy, & Ratcliff, 1982; Borghraef et al., 1987; Cohen, 1984; Hall et al., 1982; Ho, Glahn, & Ho, 1988; Netley, 1986; Pennington et al., 1982; Schaivi et al., 1984.

A variety of myths about individuals with sex chromosome disorders exist. For example, many people believe that males with *XYY syndrome* are more aggressive and antisocial than XY males. Yet by examining Table 2.5, you will see that this is not the case. Also, it is widely believed that children with sex chromosome disorders are retarded. Yet most are not. The intelligence of XYY syndrome boys is similar to that of normal children (Stewart, 1982; Netley, 1986). And the intellectual problems of children with *triple X, Klinefelter, and Turner syndromes* are very specific. Verbal difficulties (for example, with reading and vocabulary) are common among girls with triple X and boys with Klinefelter syndrome, each of whom inherits an extra X chromosome. In contrast, Turner syndrome girls, who are missing an X, have trouble with spatial relationships. Their handwriting is poor, and they have difficulty telling right from left and finding their way around the neighborhood during the early school years. When they get to high school, they avoid courses like geometry and those that demand drawing skills (Hall et al., 1982; Netley, 1986; Pennington et al., 1982). These findings tell us that adding to or subtracting from the usual number of X chromosomes results in particular intellectual deficits. At present, geneticists do not know why this is the case.

BRIEF REVIEW

Each individual is made up of trillions of cells. Inside each cell nucleus are chromosomes, which contain a chemical molecule called DNA. Genes are segments of DNA that determine our species and unique characteristics. Gametes, or sex cells, are formed through a special process of cell division called meiosis that halves the usual number of chromosomes in human cells. Then, when sperm and ovum unite at conception, each new being has the correct number of chromosomes. A different combination of sex chromosomes establishes whether a child will be boy or girl. Two types of twins—fraternal and identical—are possible. Fraternal twins are genetically no more alike than other siblings, whereas identical twins have the same genetic makeup. Four patterns of inheritance—dominant–recessive, codominant, X-linked, and genetic imprinting—underlie many traits as well as disorders. Continuous characteristics, such as height and intelligence, result from the enormous complexities of polygenic inheritance, which involves many genes. Chromosomal abnormalities occur when meiosis is disrupted during gamete formation.

ASK YOURSELF . . .

- Two brothers, Todd and Blake, look strikingly different. Todd is tall and thin; Blake is short and stocky. What events taking place during meiosis contributed to these differences?
- Gilbert and Jan are planning to have children. Gilbert's genetic makeup is homozygous for dark hair; Jan's is heterozygous for blond hair. What color is Gilbert's hair? How about Jan's? What proportion of their children are likely to be dark haired?
- Ashley and Harold both carry the defective gene for fragile X syndrome. Explain why Ashley's child inherited the disorder but Harold's did not.

REPRODUCTIVE CHOICES

Two years after they were married, Ted and Marianne gave birth to their first child. Kendra appeared to be a healthy and lively infant, but by 4 months her growth slowed. Diagnosed as having Tay-Sachs disease (see Table 2.3), Kendra died at 2 years of age. Ted and Marianne were devastated by Kendra's death. Although they did not want to bring another infant into the world who would endure such suffering, they badly wanted to have a child. When Ted and Marianne took walks in the neighborhood, they would see children in strollers, and tears would come to their eyes. They began to avoid family get-togethers where little nieces and nephews were constant reminders of the void in their lives.

In the past, many couples with genetic disorders in their families chose not to bear a child at all rather than risk having an abnormal baby. Today, genetic counseling and prenatal diagnosis help people make informed decisions about conceiving, carrying a pregnancy to term, or adopting a child. In addition, the legalization of abortion has meant that women, whether or not they have an increased likelihood of bearing a child with defects, can decide after conception whether they wish to give birth.

GENETIC COUNSELING

Genetic counseling helps couples assess their chances of giving birth to a baby with a hereditary disorder. Individuals likely to seek it are those who have had difficulties bearing children, such as repeated miscarriages, or who know that genetic problems exist in their families. In addition, women who delay childbearing past age 35 are candidates for genetic counseling. After this time, the overall rate of chromosomal abnormalities rises sharply, from 1 in every 100 to as many as 1 in every 3 pregnancies at age 48 (Hook, 1988).

If a family history of mental retardation, physical defects, or inherited diseases exists, the genetic counselor interviews the couple and prepares a *pedigree,* a picture of the family tree in which affected relatives are identified. The pedigree is used to estimate the likelihood that parents will have an abnormal child, using the same genetic principles we discussed earlier in this chapter. In the case of many disor-

Genetic counseling
Counseling that helps couples assess the likelihood of giving birth to a baby with a hereditary disorder.

TABLE 2.6

Prenatal Diagnostic Methods

METHOD	DESCRIPTION
Amniocentesis	The most widely used technique. A hollow needle is inserted through the abdominal wall to obtain a sample of fluid in the uterus. Cells are examined for genetic defects. Can be performed by 11 to 14 weeks after conception; 1 to 2 more weeks are required for test results. Small risk of miscarriage.
Chorionic villus sampling	A procedure that can be used if results are desired or needed very early in pregnancy. A thin tube is inserted into the uterus through the vagina or a hollow needle is inserted through the abdominal wall. A small plug of tissue is removed from the end of one or more chorionic villi, the hairlike projections on the membrane surrounding the developing baby. Cells are examined for genetic defects. Can be performed at 6 to 8 weeks after conception, and results are available within 24 hours. Entails a slightly greater risk of miscarriage than does amniocentesis. Also associated with a small risk of limb deformities, which increases the earlier the procedure is performed.
Ultrasound	High-frequency sound waves are beamed at the uterus; their reflection is translated into a picture on a videoscreen that reveals the size, shape, and placement of the fetus. By itself, permits assessment of fetal age, detection of multiple pregnancies, and identification of gross physical defects. Also used to guide amniocentesis, chorionic villus sampling, and fetoscopy (see below).
Fetoscopy	A small tube with a light source at one end is inserted into the uterus to inspect the fetus for defects of the limbs and face. Also allows a sample of fetal blood to be obtained, permitting diagnosis of such disorders as hemophilia and sickle cell anemia as well as neural defects. Usually performed between 15 to 18 weeks after conception, although can be done as early as 5 weeks. Entails some risk of miscarriage.
Maternal blood analysis	By the second month of pregnancy, some of the baby's cells enter the maternal blood stream. An elevated level of alpha-fetoprotein may indicate kidney disease, abnormal closure of the esophagus, or neural defects, such as anencephaly (absence of most of the brain) and spina bifida (bulging of the spinal cord from the spinal column).

Sources: Benacerraf et al., 1988; Burton, 1992; Canick & Saller, 1993; Holmes, 1993; Quintero, Puder, & Cotton, 1993.

ders, blood tests or genetic analyses can reveal whether the parent is a carrier of the harmful gene. Turn back to pages 62–63, and you will see that carrier detection is possible for most of the diseases listed in Table 2.3.

When all the relevant information is in, the genetic counselor helps people consider appropriate options. These include "taking a chance" and conceiving, choosing from among a variety of reproductive technologies (see the Social Issues box on pages 70–71), or adopting a child.

PRENATAL DIAGNOSIS AND FETAL MEDICINE

If couples who might bear an abnormal child decide to conceive, several **prenatal diagnostic methods**—medical procedures that permit detection of problems before birth—are available (see Table 2.6). Women of advanced maternal age are prime candidates for *amniocentesis* or *chorionic villus sampling* (see Figure 2.8). Except for *ultrasound* and *maternal blood analysis,* prenatal diagnosis should not be used routinely, since other methods have some chance of injuring the developing organism.

Improvements in prenatal diagnosis have led to new advances in fetal medicine. Today, some medical problems are being treated before birth. For example, by inserting a needle into the uterus, drugs can be delivered to the fetus. Surgery has been performed to repair such problems as urinary tract obstructions and neural defects. Nevertheless, these practices remain controversial. Although some babies are saved, the techniques frequently result in complications or miscarriage. Yet when parents are told that their unborn child has a serious defect, they may be willing to try almost any option, even if there is only a slim chance of success. Currently, the medical profession is struggling with how to help parents make informed decisions about fetal surgery. One suggestion is that the advice of an independent counselor be provided—a doctor or nurse who understands the risks but is not involved in doing research on or performing the procedure (Harrison, 1993).

Prenatal diagnostic methods
Medical procedures that permit detection of developmental problems before birth.

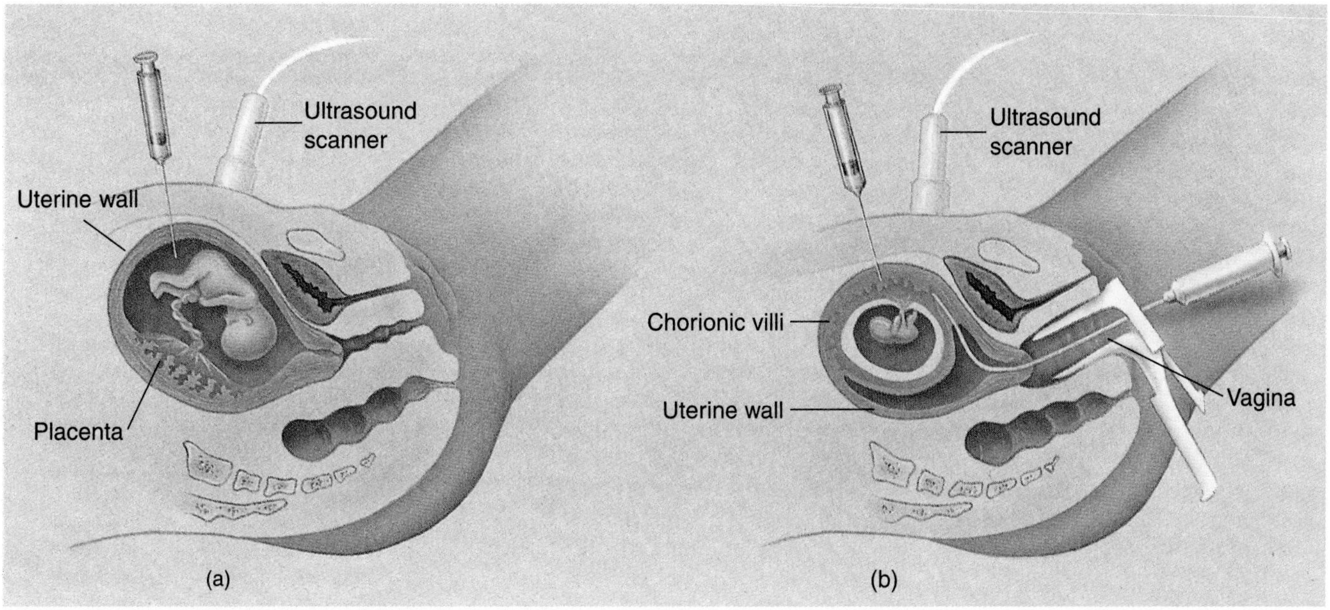

FIGURE 2.8

Amniocentesis and chorionic villus sampling.
Today, more than 250 defects and diseases can be detected before birth using these procedures. (a) In amniocentesis, a hollow needle is inserted through the abdominal wall into the uterus. Fluid is withdrawn and fetal cells are cultured, a process that takes about 1 to 2 weeks. (b) Chorionic villus sampling can be performed much earlier in pregnancy, at 6 to 8 weeks after conception, and results are available within 24 hours. Two approaches to obtaining a sample of chorionic villi are shown: inserting a thin tube through the vagina into the uterus or a needle through the abdominal wall. In both amniocentesis and chorionic villus sampling, an ultrasound scanner is used for guidance. *(From K. L. Moore & T. V. N. Persaud, 1993,* Before We Are Born, *4th ed., Philadelphia: Saunders, p. 89. Adapted by permission of the publisher and author.)*

Advances in *genetic engineering* also offer new hope for correcting hereditary defects. Genetic repair of the prenatal organism, once inconceivable, is a goal of today's genetic engineers. Researchers are mapping human chromosomes, finding the precise location of genes for specific traits and cloning (copying) these genes using chemical techniques in the laboratory. Of the approximately 3,000 known inherited diseases, genes have been found for about 100, including cystic fibrosis, Huntington disease, and Duchenne muscular dystrophy (NIH/CEPH Collaborative Mapping Group, 1992). Scientists are using this information to identify abnormal conditions with greater accuracy before birth. Eventually, *gene splicing* (replacing a harmful gene with a good one in the early zygote or in cells in the affected part of the body) may permit many defects to be corrected.

THE ALTERNATIVE OF ABORTION

If prenatal diagnosis shows that the fetus has an abnormal condition that cannot be corrected, parents are faced with the difficult choice of whether or not to have an abortion. The decision to terminate a desired pregnancy is painful for all who have to make it. Parents must deal with the emotional shock of the news and decide within a very short period of time. If they choose to have an abortion, they face the grief that comes with having lost a wanted child, worries about future pregnancies, and possible guilt about the abortion itself.

Fortunately, 95 percent of developing babies examined through prenatal diagnosis are normal. It is not surprising, then, that women who accidentally become pregnant account for far more abortions than women who know their infants will be born with serious defects. Adolescents who conceive before they are mature enough to raise a child have the highest rate of abortion. In the United States, about 40 percent of over one million teenage pregnancies are aborted each year (Henshaw, 1993).

SOCIAL ISSUES

THE PROS AND CONS OF REPRODUCTIVE TECHNOLOGIES

Some couples decide not to risk pregnancy because of a history of genetic disease. And many others—in fact, one-sixth of all couples who try to conceive—discover that they are sterile. Today, increasing numbers of people are turning to alternative methods of conception—technologies that, although fulfilling the wish of parenthood, have become the subject of heated debate.

DONOR INSEMINATION AND IN VITRO FERTILIZATION. For several decades, *donor insemination*—injection of sperm from an anonymous man into a woman—has been used to overcome male reproductive difficulties. In recent years, it has also permitted women without a heterosexual partner to bear children. In the United States alone, 30,000 children are conceived through donor insemination each year (Swanson, 1993).

In vitro fertilization is another reproductive technology that has become increasingly common. Since the first "test tube" baby was born in England in 1978, more than 7,000 infants have been created this way (Ryan, 1989). In in vitro fertilization, hormones are given to a woman, stimulating ripening of several ova. These are removed surgically and placed in a dish of nutrients, to which sperm are added. Once an ovum is fertilized and begins to duplicate into several cells, it is injected into the mother's uterus, where, hopefully, it will implant and develop.

In vitro fertilization is usually used to treat women whose fallopian tubes are permanently damaged, and it is successful for 20 percent of those who try it. These results have been encouraging enough that the technique has been expanded. By mixing and matching gametes, pregnancies can be brought about when either or both partners have a reproductive problem. In cases where couples might transmit harmful genes, single cells can be plucked from the duplicating zygote and screened for hereditary defects. Fertilized ova can even be frozen and stored in embryo banks for use at some future time, thereby guaranteeing healthy zygotes to older women (Edwards, 1991).

Clearly donor insemination and in vitro fertilization have many benefits. Nevertheless, serious questions have arisen about their use. Many states have no legal guidelines for these procedures. As a result, donors are not always screened for genetic or sexually transmitted diseases. In addition, only a minority of doctors keep records of donor characteristics. Yet the resulting children may someday want information about their genetic background or need it for medical reasons (Nachtigall, 1993).

SURROGATE MOTHERHOOD. A more controversial form of medically assisted conception is *surrogate motherhood.* Typically in this procedure, sperm from a man whose wife is infertile are used to inseminate a woman, who is paid a fee for her childbearing services. In return, the surrogate agrees to turn the baby over to the man (who is the natural father). The child is then adopted by his wife.

Although most of these arrangements proceed smoothly, those that end up in court highlight serious risks for all concerned. In one case, both parties rejected the disabled infant that resulted from the pregnancy. In several others, the surrogate mother changed her mind and wanted to keep the baby. These children came into the world in midst of family conflict that threatened to last for years to come. Most surrogates already have children of their own,

Mary Beth Whitehead was the surrogate mother in the highly publicized case of Baby M. She changed her mind about giving the baby to the natural father (who donated sperm for artificial insemination) and permitting adoption by his wife. Baby M entered the world in midst of intense family conflict. Whitehead's sad expression highlights the serious emotional risks of surrogacy. *(Bergen Record)*

who may be deeply affected by the pregnancy. Knowledge that their mother would give away a baby for profit may cause these youngsters to worry about the security of their own family circumstances (McGinty & Zafran, 1988; Ryan, 1989).

NEW REPRODUCTIVE FRONTIERS. Reproductive technologies are evolving faster than societies can weigh the ethics of these procedures. Doctors have used donor ova from younger women in combination with in vitro fertilization to help postmenopausal women become pregnant (see Figure 2.9). Most recipients are in their forties, but in 1993, a 62-year-old woman gave birth in Italy (Beck, 1994). Even though candidates for postmenopausal intervention are selected on the basis of good health, serious questions arise about bringing children into the world whose parents may not live to see them reach adulthood.

Currently, experts are debating other reproductive options. At donor banks, customers can select ova or sperm on the basis of physical characteristics and even the IQ of potential donors. Some worry that this practice is a dangerous step toward selective breeding of the human species. Researchers recently delivered baby mice using the transplanted ovaries of aborted fetuses (Hashimoto, Noguchi, & Nakatsuji, 1992). If the same procedure were eventually applied to human beings, it would create babies whose genetic mothers had never been born.

Finally, scientists have successfully cloned (made multiple copies of) fertilized ova in sheep and cattle, and they are working on effective ways of doing so in humans. (Kolberg, 1993). By providing extra ova for injection, cloning might improve the success rate of in vitro fertilization. But it also opens the possibility of mass-producing genetically identical people.

Although new reproductive technologies permit many barren couples to rear healthy newborn babies, laws are needed to regulate them. In the case of surrogate motherhood, the ethical problems are so complex that 18 U.S. states have sharply restricted the practice, and many European governments have banned it (Belkin, 1992; Charo, 1994). Recently, England, France, and Italy took steps to prohibit in vitro fertilization for women past menopause (Beck, 1994). At present, nothing is known about the psychological consequences of being a product of these procedures. Research on how such children grow up, including what they know and how they feel about their origins, is important for weighing the pros and cons of these techniques.

TRY THIS . . .

- Locate newspaper and magazine articles on two highly publicized surrogate motherhood cases: Baby M of New Jersey (1987) and the Calvert case of California (1990). Do you think the problems that arose in each case justify limiting or banning the practice of surrogacy?

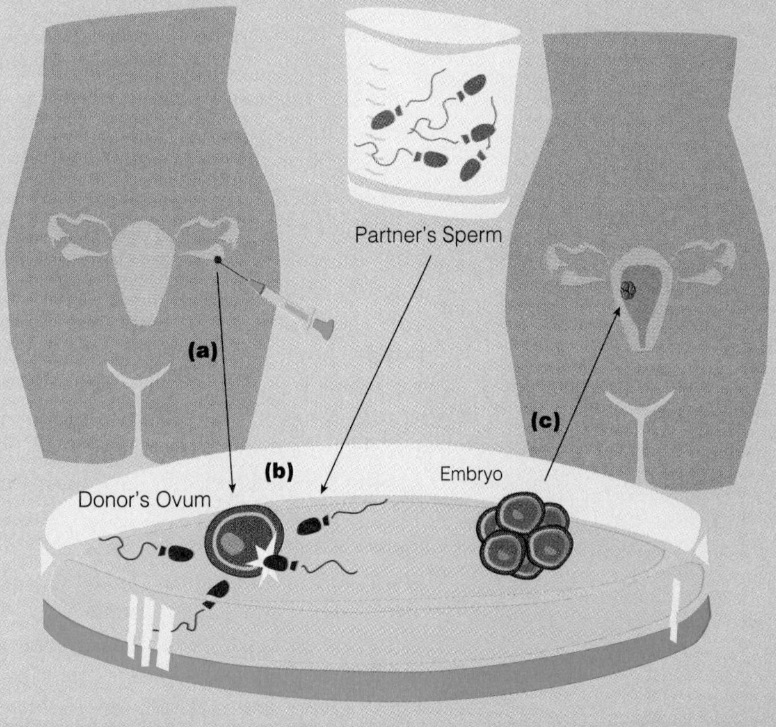

FIGURE 2.9

In vitro fertilization procedure that can help postmenopausal women become pregnant. (a) A young female donor is given hormones to stimulate ovulation. Then a needle is inserted into her ovary, and several ova are extracted. (b) The donor's ova are fertilized in a dish of nutrients using sperm from the recipient's partner or from another male donor. (c) The prospective mother is given hormones to prepare her uterus to receive the fertilized ova, which are inserted.

A wealth of research suggests that being wanted by parents who have established a clear sense of direction for their own lives is important for healthy development. As we will see in Chapter 14, adolescent girls who become pregnant usually have too many pressing concerns of their own to be effective parents. As a result, their children often have serious developmental problems. A study carried out in Czechoslovakia revealed that unwanted children in general—not just those born to adolescents—develop less favorably. Children of Czech mothers whose requests for an abortion had been denied were compared to controls whose mothers had not asked for an abortion. Unwanted children were less physically healthy and emotionally stable and achieved less well in school. By young adulthood, they were less satisfied with their lives, and they blamed their unhappiness on a poor relationship with their parents (David et al., 1988).

Nevertheless, science cannot inform pregnant women or society as a whole about whether abortion is a morally justifiable act. The issue of when personhood begins—at conception or sometime later during pregnancy—divides people into fiercely opposing camps. Other concerns also arise in evaluating the ethics of abortion. Is the quality of life experienced by unwanted and defective children so unfavorable that they should not be brought into the world at all? Is the burden that their care places on family members and the general public enough reason to end a pregnancy? To what extent should abortion be a woman's choice, and to what extent should it be controlled by the state? These are complex questions that do not have easy answers.

THE ALTERNATIVE OF ADOPTION

Many parents who cannot have children or who are likely to pass along a genetic disorder decide to adopt. Adoption agencies try to find parents of the same ethnic and religious background as the child. Where possible, they also try to choose parents who are the same age as most natural parents. When matches of these kinds cannot be made, agencies place children with adoptive parents having other characteristics rather than delaying their entry into a family.

Selection of adoptive parents is important, since sometimes adoptive relationships do not work out, and the child must be removed from the home. The risk of adoption failure is greatest for children with disabilities and youngsters adopted at older ages, but it is not high. Over 85 percent of these children do well in their adoptive homes. Of those who do not, 90 percent are successfully placed with a new family (Churchill, 1984; Glidden & Pursley, 1989). The outcomes are good because of careful pairing of children with parents along with advice and guidance provided to adopting families by well-trained social service professionals.

Still, adopted children have more emotional and learning difficulties than occur in the general child population (Verhulst, Althaus, & Versluis-Den Bieman, 1990). There are many reasons for this trend. The natural mother may have been unable to care for the child because of emotional problems believed to be partly genetic, such as alcoholism and schizophrenia.[1] She may have passed this tendency to her offspring. Or perhaps the mother experienced stress, poor diet, or inadequate medical care during pregnancy—factors that (as we will see in Chapter 3) can affect the child. Finally, children adopted at older ages often have a history of conflict-ridden family relationships and lack of parental affection. But rearing children under any reproductive alternative entails risks, and it is still the case that most adopted children have happy childhoods and grow up to be well-adjusted, productive citizens.

As we conclude our discussion of reproductive choices, perhaps you are won-

[1]Schizophrenia is a disorder involving serious difficulty in distinguishing fantasy from reality, frequent delusions and hallucinations, and irrational and inappropriate behaviors.

dering how things turned out for Ted and Marianne. They were my next-door neighbors for many years, and I am glad to report that their story had a happy ending. Through genetic counseling, Marianne discovered a history of Tay-Sachs disease on her mother's side of the family. Ted had a distant cousin who died of the disorder. The genetic counselor explained that the chances of giving birth to another affected baby were 1 in 4. Ted and Marianne took the risk. Their son Douglas is now 12 years old. Although Douglas is a carrier of the recessive allele, he is a normal, healthy boy. In a few years, Ted and Marianne will tell Douglas about his genetic history and explain the importance of genetic counseling and testing before he has children of his own.

BRIEF REVIEW

Genetic counseling helps couples who have a family history of reproductive problems or hereditary defects make informed decisions about bearing a child. For those who decide to conceive, prenatal diagnostic methods permit early detection of fetal problems. Reproductive technologies, such as donor insemination, in vitro fertilization, and surrogate motherhood, are also available, but they raise serious ethical concerns. The majority of abortions are to women who accidentally become pregnant, many of them teenagers, rather than to women carrying a baby with a serious disorder. Although developmental problems are more common among adopted children than children in general, careful selection of adoptive parents and family support services make adoption successful in the large majority of cases.

ASK YOURSELF . . .

- A woman over 35 has just learned that she is pregnant. Although she would like to find out as soon as possible whether her baby has a chromosomal disorder, she wants to minimize the risk of injury to the developing baby. Which prenatal diagnostic method is she likely to choose?
- Describe the ethical pros and cons of fetal surgery, surrogate motherhood, and postmenopausal-assisted childbearing.

ENVIRONMENTAL CONTEXTS FOR DEVELOPMENT

Just as complex as the heredity that sets the stage for development is the child's environment—a many-layered set of influences that combine with one another to help or hinder the course of growth. Take a moment to think back to your own childhood, and jot down a brief description of the first ten memories that come to mind. When I ask my students to do this, about half the events they list involve their families. This emphasis on the family is not surprising, since it is the child's first and longest-lasting context for development. But other settings turn out to be important as well. Friends, scouting troops, clubs at church or synagogue, and successes and disappointments at school generally make the top ten.

Finally, there is one very important context my students rarely mention. Its influence is so widespread that we seldom stop to think about it in our everyday lives. This is the broad social climate of society—its values and programs that support and protect children's development. All families need help in rearing their children—safe neighborhoods, well-equipped parks and playgrounds, good schools, affordable health services, and more. And some families, because of poverty or special tragedies, need considerably more help than others.

In the following sections, we take up the role of each of these contexts in children's lives. Since they affect every age period and aspect of development, we will return to them in later chapters. For now, our discussion emphasizes that besides heredity, environments can enhance growth or create risks for children. And when a vulnerable child—a youngster with physical or psychological problems—is exposed to unfavorable child-rearing contexts, then development is seriously threatened.

THE FAMILY

In power and breadth of influence, no context for development equals the family. The family introduces children to the physical world through the opportunities it provides for play and exploration of objects. It also creates bonds between people that are unique. The attachments children form with parents and siblings usually last a lifetime, and they serve as models for relationships in the wider world of neighborhood and school. Within the family, children also experience their first social conflicts. Discipline by parents and arguments with siblings provide children with important lessons in compliance and cooperation and opportunities to learn how to influence the behavior of others. Finally, within the family, children learn the language, skills, and social and moral values of their culture.

In the section on *ecological systems theory* in Chapter 1, we saw that modern investigators view the family as a complex set of interacting relationships. The **social systems perspective** on family functioning, which has much in common with Bronfenbrenner's (1979, 1989) ecological model, grew out of researchers' efforts to describe and explain the patterns of interaction that take place in families. It regards the family as a complex system in which the behaviors of each family member affect those of others. Let's take a closer look at its basic features.

THE FAMILY AS A SOCIAL SYSTEM. When child development specialists first studied the family in the middle part of this century, they investigated it in a very limited way. Most research focused on the mother–child relationship and emphasized one-way effects of the mother's child-rearing practices on children's behavior. Today, family systems theorists recognize that children are not mechanically shaped by the inputs of others. Instead, *bidirectional* influences exist in which the behaviors of each family member affect those around them. The very term *family system* implies that the responses of all family members are related (Kantor & Lehr, 1975; Minuchin, 1988). These system influences operate in both *direct* and *indirect* ways.

Direct Influences. Keep a sharp lookout the next time you pass through the checkout counter at your local supermarket. Recently, I witnessed the following two episodes, in which parents and children directly affected each other:

- Little Danny stood next to tempting rows of candy as his mom lifted groceries from the cart onto the counter. "Pleeeeease, can I have it, Mom?" begged Danny, holding up a large package of bubble gum. "Do you have a dollar? Just one?"

  "No, not today," his mother answered softly. "Remember, we picked out your special cereal. That's what I need the dollar for." Danny's mother handed him the cereal while gently taking the bubble gum from his hand and returning it to the shelf. "Here, let's pay the man," she said, as she lifted Danny into the empty grocery cart where he could see the cash register.

- Three-year-old Meg sat in the cart while her mom transferred groceries to the counter. Meg turned around, grabbed a bunch of bananas, and started to pull them apart.

  "Stop it, Meg!" shouted her mom, who snatched the bananas from Meg's hand. Meg reached for a chocolate bar from a nearby shelf while her mother wrote the check. "Meg, how many times have I told you, DON'T TOUCH!" Loosening the candy from Meg's tight little grip, Meg's mother slapped her hand. Meg's face turned red with anger as she began to wail. "Keep this up, and you'll get it when we get home," threatened Meg's mom as they left the store.

These observations fit with a wealth of research on the family system. Many studies show that when parents (like Danny's mom) are firm but patient, children

Social systems perspective
A view of the family as a complex system in which the behaviors of each family member affect those of others.

The family is a complex social system in which each person's behavior influences the behavior of others, in both direct and indirect ways. The positive mealtime atmosphere in this family is probably a product of many forces, including parents who respond to children with warmth and patience, aunts and uncles who support parents in their child-rearing roles, and children who have developed cooperative dispositions. *(Michal Heron/Woodfin Camp & Associates)*

tend to comply with their requests. And when children cooperate, their parents are likely to be warm and gentle in the future (Baumrind, 1983; Lewis, 1981). In contrast, parents (like Meg's mom) who discipline with harshness and impatience have children who refuse and rebel. And because children's misbehavior is stressful for parents, they may increase their use of punishment, leading to more unruliness by the child (Patterson, DeBaryshe, & Ramsey, 1989). In these examples, the behavior of one family member helps sustain a form of interaction in another that either promotes or undermines children's well-being.

Indirect Influences. The impact of family relationships on child development becomes even more complicated when we consider that interaction between any two members is affected by others present in the setting. Recall from Chapter 1 that Bronfenbrenner called these indirect influences the effect of *third parties.* Researchers have become intensely interested in how a range of relationships—mother with father, parent with sibling, grandparent with parent—modifies the child's direct experiences in the family.

Third parties can serve as effective supports for child development. For example, when parents' marital relationship is warm and considerate, mothers and fathers praise and stimulate their children more and nag and scold them less. In contrast, when a marriage is tense and hostile, parents are likely to criticize and punish (Cox et al., 1989; Howes & Markman, 1989; Simons et al., 1992). Findings like these help us understand the stressful impact of divorce on children, a topic we will take up in Chapter 13. Yet even when children's adjustment is strained by arguments between their parents, other family members may help restore effective interaction. Grandparents are a case in point. They can promote children's development in many ways—both directly, by responding warmly to the child, and indirectly, by providing parents with child-rearing advice, models of child-rearing skill, and even financial assistance (Cherlin & Furstenberg, 1986). Of course, like any indirect influence, grandparents can sometimes have harmful effects. When quarrelsome relations exist between parents and grandparents, children may suffer.

A Dynamic, Ever-Changing System. The social systems approach views the interplay of forces within the family as dynamic and ever-changing. Important events, such as a move to a new neighborhood or the birth of a baby, create challenges that modify existing relationships. For example, a mother once told me that when her second child was born, her 2-year-old daughter Trina reacted (as many children do) with some "creative" attention-getting behaviors. Trina would throw her cup, demand to be taken to the toilet, or squeeze into her mother's lap during the baby's feeding time. "I was exhausted from trying to take care of both children," the mother explained. "One day I stopped and listened to myself speak to Trina. I realized how impatient I'd become." The way new events affect parent–child interaction depends on the support provided by other family members as well as the age of the child. Suppose that Trina had been a school-age youngster, with many satisfying activities beyond the family, when the new baby was born. Clearly she would have responded very differently!

In addition to new events, a child's development itself is another dynamic aspect of family life. As children grow and change, parents must adjust their style of interaction to fit with their child's expanding abilities. When you next have a chance, notice the way that a parent relates to a tiny baby as opposed to a walking, talking toddler. During the first few months of life, much time is spent in caregiving—feeding, changing, bathing, and cuddling the infant. Within a year, things change dramatically. The 1-year-old points, shows, names objects, and makes his way through the household cupboards. In response, parents spend less time in physical care and more in talking and playing games. These new ways of interacting encourage the child's expanding cognitive, language, and motor skills (Green, Gustafson, & West, 1980).

Despite the family's flexible and changing nature, child development specialists have discovered some general rules about good parenting practices. As we will see in later chapters, parental *responsiveness* is repeatedly associated with better development. In infancy, responsive parents sensitively adapt their own behaviors to those of the baby. They hold the infant tenderly, wait until she is ready for the next spoonful of food, and gaze into her eyes, smile, and talk softly when she indicates she is ready for social stimulation. Babies who receive such care are likely to develop into especially competent toddlers and preschoolers, both cognitively and socially (Frankel & Bates, 1990; Suess, Grossmann, & Sroufe, 1992).

During childhood and adolescence, responsive parents communicate in a warm, affectionate manner and listen patiently to their youngster's point of view. And when they combine this sensitivity with another crucial feature of effective parenting—*reasonable demands for mature behavior*—their children tend to be socially active and responsible and to achieve well in school (Baumrind, 1971, 1991). In fact, research examining parenting in over 180 societies indicates that a style that is warm but moderately demanding is the most common pattern around the world. Many cultures seem to have discovered for themselves the link between this style of child rearing and healthy psychological development (Rohner & Rohner, 1981). Nevertheless, consistent differences in parenting practices do exist. In the United States and other Western nations, one important source of these differences is social class.

SOCIAL CLASS AND FAMILY FUNCTIONING

When asked about qualities they would like to encourage in their children, parents who work in skilled and semiskilled manual occupations (for example, machinists, truck drivers, and custodians) tend to place a higher value on external characteristics, such as obedience, neatness, and cleanliness. In contrast, parents in white-collar and professional occupations tend to emphasize inner psychological traits, such as curiosity, happiness, and self-control. These differences in values are reflected in parents' behaviors. Middle-class parents talk to and stimulate their infants more and grant them greater freedom to explore. When their children are older, they use more explanations and verbal praise. In contrast, lower-class parents are more likely to be restrictive. Because they think that infants can easily be spoiled, they limit the amount of rocking and cuddling they do (Luster et al., 1989). Later on, commands, such as "You do that because I told you to," as well as criticism and physical punishment occur more often in low-income households (Laosa, 1981).

Social-class differences in child rearing can be understood in terms of the different life conditions in low-income and middle-income families. Low-income parents often feel a sense of powerlessness and lack of influence in their relationships beyond the home. For example, at work they must obey the rules of others in positions of power and authority. When they get home, their parent–child interaction seems to duplicate these experiences, only with them in the authority roles. In contrast, middle-class parents have a greater sense of control over their own lives. At work, they are used to making independent decisions and convincing others of their point of view. At home, they teach these same skills to their children (Kohn, 1979).

Education also contributes to social-class differences in child rearing. Middle-class parents' interest in developing their child's inner characteristics is supported by years of schooling, during which they learned to think about abstract, subjective ideas. In a study carried out in Mexico, where female school enrollment has recently increased, the more years of education a mother had, the more she stimulated her young child through face-to-face conversation (Richman, Miller, & LeVine, 1992).

Furthermore, the greater economic security of middle-class parents frees them from the burden of having to worry about making ends meet on a daily basis. They can devote more energy and attention to their own inner characteristics and those of their children. And they can also provide many more experiences—from toys to special outings to after-school lessons—that encourage these characteristics (Hoffman, 1984).

As early as the second year of life, middle-class children tend to be advanced in cognitive and language development over their lower-class agemates. And throughout childhood and adolescence, middle-class children do better in school (Brody, 1992; Walker et al., 1994). Child development specialists believe that social-class differences in parenting practices have much to do with these outcomes.

THE IMPACT OF POVERTY

When families become so low-income that they slip into poverty, effective parenting and children's development is seriously threatened. Shirley Brice Heath (1990), an anthropologist who has spent many years studying children and families of poverty, describes the case of Zinnia Mae, who grew up in Trackton, a close-knit black community located in a small southeastern American city. As unemployment struck Trackton in the 1980s and citizens moved away, 16-year-old Zinnia Mae caught a ride to Atlanta. Two years later, Heath visited her there. By then, Zinnia Mae was the mother of three children—a 16-month-old daughter named Donna and 2-month-old twin boys. She had moved into a high-rise public housing project, one of eight concrete buildings surrounding a dirt plot scattered with broken swings, see-saws, and benches. Describing her life to Heath, Zinnia Mae said,

> "My days, you know, I just do what I can, can't get away much . . . . I can't haul [Donna] up and down those six flights of steps to get her out with them other kids, and the place here is too cramped as it is; . . . so me and Donna, we pretty much stay in here with the babies by ourselves 'cept when I get the neighbor girl to come in so I can go get some food for us to eat . . . ." (p. 504)

Each of Zinnia Mae's days was much the same. She watched TV and talked with girlfriends on the phone. The children had only one set meal (breakfast) and otherwise ate whenever they were hungry or bored. Their play space was limited to the living room sofa and a mattress on the floor. Toys consisted of scraps of a blanket, spoons and food cartons, a small rubber ball, a few plastic cars, and a roller skate abandoned in the building. Zinnia Mae's most frequent words were "I'm so tired." She worried about how to get papers to the welfare office, where to find a baby-

Homelessness in the United States has risen over the past 15 years. Families like this one travel from place to place in search of employment and a safe and secure place to live. At night, they sleep in the family car. Because of constant stresses, homeless children are usually behind in development, have frequent health problems, and show poor psychological adjustment. *(Rick Browne/ Stock Boston)*

sitter so she could go to the laundry or grocery, and what she would do if she located the twins' father, who had stopped sending money. She rarely had enough energy to spend time with her children.

Over the past 25 years, economic changes in the United States have caused the poverty rate among families with children to climb substantially, from 15 to 22 percent. Today, 14.6 million children are affected. Families hit hardest include parents under age 25 with preschool children, the growing number of mother-only families (teenage mothers like Zinnia Mae are especially vulnerable), and ethnic minorities. Poverty is as high as 54 percent among children in single-parent households, 40 percent among Hispanic children, and 47 percent among black children. And poverty is far more likely to persist for most of childhood among African-Americans and Hispanics than Caucasian-Americans (Chase-Lansdale & Brooks-Gunn, 1994; Children's Defense Fund, 1994).

The constant stresses that accompany poverty gradually weaken the family system. Poor families have many daily hassles—bills to pay, the car breaking down, loss of welfare and unemployment payments, something stolen from the house, to name just a few. When daily crises arise, parents become distressed, irritable, and distracted, hostile interactions between family members increase, and children's development suffers (Conger et al., 1992; Garrett, Ng'andu, & Ferron, 1994). These outcomes are especially severe in families that must live in poor housing and dangerous neighborhoods—conditions that make everyday existence even more difficult (Duncan, Brooks-Gunn, & Klebanov, 1994; McLoyd, 1990).

Besides poverty, another problem—one that was quite uncommon 15 years ago—has reduced the life chances of poor children in the United States. By the early 1990s, approximately 3 million people had no place to live. Over 40 percent of America's homeless population is made up of families, and 1 in every 4 homeless individuals is believed to be a child. The rise in child homelessness is due to a number of factors, the most important of which is a dramatic decline in the availability of government-supported low-cost housing for the poor (Children's Defense Fund, 1994).

Most homeless families consist of women on their own with young children—usually under the age of 5 (Milburn & D'Ercole, 1991). These children suffer from developmental delays and serious emotional stress (Rafferty & Shinn, 1991). Homeless youngsters also have many health problems due to inadequate diets, living outdoors or in crowded, unsanitary public shelters, and lack of immunization against childhood diseases (Wright, 1991).

An estimated 25 to 50 percent of homeless children who are old enough do not attend school. Some have difficulty enrolling because they lack a permanent address or prior school records. Others do not have transportation, a change of clothes, or school supplies. And still others stay away because they are embarrassed about having no home or find it difficult to adjust to new teachers and classmates every few months. Because of poor school attendance and health and emotional problems, homeless children who do go to school achieve less well than other poor children, and they are more likely to repeat a grade (Rafferty & Shinn, 1991).

BEYOND THE FAMILY: NEIGHBORHOODS, SCHOOLS, TOWNS, AND CITIES

Family systems theory emphasizes that ties between family and community are important for children's well-being. From our discussion of child poverty, perhaps you can see why this is the case. In poverty-stricken urban areas, community life is usually disrupted. Families move often, parks and playgrounds are in disarray, and community centers providing organized leisure time activities do not exist (Wilson, 1991). Research indicates that child abuse and neglect are greatest in neighborhoods

These parents of pupils enrolled in a bilingual classroom attend an open house, where the teacher informs them about their children's school experiences. Supportive ties between family and school enhance children's development. *(J. Koontz)*

in which residents are dissatisfied with their community, describing it as a socially isolated place to live. In contrast, when family ties to the community are strong—as indicated by regular church attendance and frequent contact with friends and relatives—family stress and child adjustment problems are reduced (Garbarino & Kostelny, 1992; Werner & Smith, 1982).

■ NEIGHBORHOODS. Let's take a closer look at the functions that communities serve in the lives of children by beginning with the neighborhood. What were your childhood experiences like in the yards, streets, and parks surrounding your home? How did you spend your time, whom did you get to know, and how important were these moments to you? To most children, the neighborhood is not just an outdoor play space—"it is a social universe" (Medrich et al., 1982, p. 33).

Neighborhoods differ in the extent to which they encourage play and exploration among children. In one study, researchers compared the impact of several neighborhoods in the same large city on children's social lives. One of them was Monterey, a well-to-do, hilly area with homes set back on large lots and streets without sidewalks. The arrangement of this neighborhood restricted children's freedom to move about and gather together. In contrast, the flat, densely populated city neighborhood of Yuba provided children with rich social experiences. Children played often in large groups, used the sidewalks and streets for spontaneous games, built secret hideaways in empty lots, and traveled together to make purchases in nearby shops (Berg & Medrich, 1980).

The resources offered by neighborhoods play an important part in children's development. One study found that the more varied children's neighborhood experiences—membership in organizations (such as scouting and 4-H), contact with adults of their grandparents' generation, visits to mother's workplace, and places to go off by themselves or with friends (a treehouse, a fort, or a neighbor's garage)—the better they scored on a battery of tests designed to measure their social and emotional adjustment (Bryant, 1985).

■ SCHOOLS. Unlike the informal worlds of family and neighborhood, school is a formal institution designed to transmit knowledge and skills that children need to become productive members of their society. Children spend many long hours in school—6 hours a day, 5 days a week, 36 a year—totaling, altogether, about 15,000 hours by graduation from high school. In fact, if we consider that during the first 5 years of life many more children are entering day care centers and preschools that are "school-like," then the impact of schooling begins earlier and is even more powerful than these figures suggest.

Schools themselves are complex social systems bringing together a wide variety of factors that affect many aspects of development (Goodlad, 1984; Minuchin & Shapiro, 1983). Schools differ in the quality of their physical environments—how many children are enrolled, how much space is available for work and play, and how classrooms are furnished and arranged. They also vary in their educational philosophies—whether teachers regard children as passive learners to be molded by adult instruction; as active, curious beings who determine their own learning; or somewhere in between. Finally, social life among children varies from school to school—for example, in the degree to which pupils are cooperative or competitive and in the extent to which children of different ethnic groups spend time together. We will discuss the importance of each of these aspects of schooling in later chapters.

At all ages, regular contact between families and teachers supports children's development. In one study, parents who were involved in school activities and who attended parent–teacher conferences had children who showed superior academic achievement (Stevenson & Baker, 1987). Phone calls and visits to school are common among middle-class parents, whose backgrounds and values are like those of teachers. In contrast, low-income and ethnic minority parents often feel uncomfortable about coming to school (Delgado-Gaitan, 1992; Heath, 1989). Contact between parents and teachers is also more frequent in small towns, where most citizens know each other and schools serve as centers of community life (Peshkin, 1978). Extra steps must be taken with low-income and minority families and in large urban areas to build supportive ties between family and school.

TOWNS AND CITIES. Besides family–school contact, other aspects of life are different for children growing up in small towns than in large cities. A well-known study examined the kinds of community settings children entered and the roles they played in a midwestern town with a population of 700 (Barker, 1955). Many settings existed, and children were granted important responsibilities in them. For example, they helped stock shelves at Kane's Grocery Store, played in the town band, and operated the snow plow when help was short. As children joined in these activities, they did so alongside adults, who taught them the skills they needed to become responsible members of the community.

Of course, children in small towns cannot visit aquariums, take rides in subways and buses, eat pizza in Italian restaurants, go to professional baseball games, or attend orchestra concerts on a regular basis. The variety of settings is somewhat reduced compared to large cities. In small towns, however, children's active involvement in the community is likely to be greater. In addition, public places in small towns are safe and secure environments for children. All the streets and people are familiar, and responsible adults are present in almost all settings—a situation hard to match in today's urban environments.

Think back to the case of Zinnia Mae and her three young children, described on pages 77–78. It reveals that community life is especially undermined in high-rise urban housing projects. In these dwellings, social contact is particularly important, since many residents have been uprooted from neighborhoods where they felt a strong sense of cultural identity and belonging. Typically, high rises are heavily populated with young single mothers, who are separated from family and friends by the cost and inconvenience of cross-town transportation. They report intense feelings of loneliness in the small, cramped apartments. At Heath's (1990) request, Zinnia Mae agreed to tape-record her interactions with her children over a two-year period. In

500 hours of tape, (other than simple directions or questions about what the children were doing) Zinnia Mae started a conversation with Donna and the boys only 18 times. Cut off from community ties, Zinnia Mae found it difficult to join in activities with her children. As a result, Donna and her brothers experienced a barren, understimulating early environment—one very different from the home and community in which Zinnia Mae herself had grown up.

THE CULTURAL CONTEXT

In Chapter 1, we pointed out that child development can only be fully understood when it is viewed in the larger cultural context in which it takes place. In the following sections, we expand on this important theme. First, we discuss ways in which cultural values and life conditions affect the environments in which children grow up. Second, we show how children are deeply influenced by the political and economic conditions of their nation. We will see that healthy development depends on laws and government programs that shield children from harm and foster their well-being.

CULTURE AND CHILD-REARING ENVIRONMENTS. Cultures shape family interaction, school experiences, and community settings beyond the home—in short, all aspects of the child's daily life. Many of us remain blind to aspects of our own cultural heritage until we see them in relation to the practices of others (Rogoff & Morelli, 1989).

Each year, I ask my students to think about the following question: "Who should be responsible for rearing young children?" Here are some typical answers: "If parents decide to have a baby, then they should be ready to care for it." "Most people are not happy about others intruding into family life." These statements reflect a widely held opinion in the United States—that the care and rearing of children during the early years is the duty of parents, and only parents (Goffin, 1988). This view has a long history—one in which independence, self-reliance, and the privacy of family life emerged as central American values. It is one reason, among others, that the American public has been slow to accept the idea of publicly supported day care, even though the majority of mothers of young children in the United States are employed (Hayghe, 1990). This strong emphasis on individualism also helps us understand why, among middle-class families (who best represent American cultural values), only a small percentage of grandparents and other relatives participate actively and regularly in the rearing of children (Thompson et al., 1989).

Do cultures everywhere share the belief that the responsibility for early child rearing should rest in the hands of parents? Apparently not. Among the Efe hunters and gatherers of Zaire, Africa, a collective caregiving system exists in which infants are passed from one adult to another—relatives and nonrelatives alike—as often as three to eight times an hour (Winn, Tronick, & Morelli, 1989). The Efe may have developed this style of infant care because their babies are unusually fussy and difficult to console. The responsibility for soothing the infant is shared among members of the group, reducing the burden on the baby's mother (Brazelton, 1989). In small agricultural societies in which mothers must spend many hours in the gardens and fields, *sibling caregiving,* in which older sisters (and sometimes brothers) take charge of younger children throughout the day, is widespread (Weisner & Gallimore, 1977).

Although American middle-class families value independence and privacy, cooperative family structures can be found in the United States. In large industrialized nations like ours, not all citizens share the same set of values. **Subcultures** exist—groups of people with beliefs and customs that differ from those of the larger culture. The values and practices of some ethnic minority groups protect children against the harmful effects of poverty. A case in point is the African-American family.

Subculture
A group of people with beliefs and customs that differ from those of the larger culture.

As the Cultural Influences box on the following page indicates, the black cultural tradition of **extended-family households,** in which parent and child live with one or more adult relatives, is a vital feature of black family life that has enabled its members to survive generations of economic deprivation and racism. Active and involved extended families also characterize other American minorities, such as Asian-American, Native-American, and Hispanic subcultures (Harrison et al., 1990).

Children growing up in different cultures also encounter unique experiences in their neighborhoods and schools. Among the !Kung hunters and gatherers of Botswana, Africa, the "neighborhood" is the barren desert region surrounding the group campground. Little exists to draw children into exploration of their surroundings. Instead, they spend most of their time near home, conversing and playing with adults and peers and developing especially close bonds with others (Draper & Cashdan, 1988). Also, since !Kung children are not strong enough to keep up on lengthy hunting and gathering missions, they are "schooled" in adult work roles informally, by listening as their elders describe previous hunts and swap exciting stories and tales (Super, 1980).

Even in industrialized nations, schooling varies considerably from one culture to the next. In recent years, many investigators have looked carefully at education in Asian countries. They hope to find out why, in cross-national comparisons of mathematics and science achievement, Japanese and Chinese children are top performers, whereas American pupils do poorly. Indeed, as we will see in Chapter 12, many variables, including more intensive instruction, a longer school year, and more frequent communication between Asian parents and teachers, contribute to this achievement gap (Stevenson, Chen, & Lee, 1993).

■ PUBLIC POLICIES AND CHILD DEVELOPMENT. When widespread social problems arise, such as poverty, homelessness, hunger, and disease, nations attempt to solve them by developing **public policies**—laws and government programs designed to improve the condition of children and families. For example, when poverty increases and families become homeless, a country might decide to build more low-cost housing, raise the minimum wage, and increase welfare benefits. When reports indicate that many children are not achieving well in school, federal and state governments might grant more tax money to school districts and make sure that help reaches children who need it most.

We have already seen in previous sections that although many American children fare well, a large number grow up in environments that threaten their development. Because of global economic conditions, the overall status of children worldwide has also declined, especially in developing countries (Grant, 1993). Yet the United States is among the wealthiest nations and has the broadest knowledge base for intervening effectively in children's lives. Still, as Table 2.7 reveals, it does not rank among the top countries on any key measure of children's health and well-being.

Like many people who care about children, you may deeply disturbed by these findings. Why has the United States not yet created conditions that protect the development of its youngest citizens? A complex set of political and economic forces is involved. Earlier we mentioned the American ideals of self-reliance and privacy. These beliefs have led government to hesitate to become involved in family matters. In addition, there is more disagreement among American than European citizens on issues of child and family policy. Americans differ sharply about government support for such programs as day care, medical benefits, and special educational services for minority youth (Wilensky, 1983). Finally, good social programs are expensive, and they must compete for a fair share of a country's economic resources. Children can easily remain unrecognized in this process, since they cannot vote or speak out to protect their own interests, as adult citizens do. Instead, they must rely on the goodwill of others to become an important government priority (Garwood et al., 1989).

Extended-family household
A household in which parent and child live with one or more adult relatives.

Public policies
Laws and government programs designed to improve current conditions.

CULTURAL INFLUENCES

THE AFRICAN-AMERICAN EXTENDED FAMILY

The African-American extended family can be traced to the African heritage of most black Americans. In many African societies, newly married couples do not start their own households. Instead, they marry into a large extended family that assists its members with all aspects of daily life. This tradition of a broad network of kinship ties traveled to the United States during the period of slavery. Since then, it has served as a protective shield against the destructive impact of poverty and prejudice on black family life (Harrison et al., 1990; McLoyd, 1990). Today, more black than white adults have relatives other than their own children living in the same household. African-American parents also see more kin during the week and perceive them as more important figures in their lives, respecting the advice of relatives and caring deeply about what they think is important (Wilson, 1986).

By providing emotional support and sharing income and essential resources, the African-American extended family helps reduce the stress of poverty and single parenthood. In addition, extended-family members often help with the rearing of children (Pearson et al., 1990). The presence of grandmothers in the households of black teenagers and their infants can protect babies from the negative influence of an overwhelmed and inexperienced mother. In one study, black grandmothers displayed more sensitive interaction with the babies of their teenage daughters than did the teenage mothers themselves. The grandmothers also provided basic information about infant development to these young mothers (Stevens, 1984). Furthermore, adolescent mothers who live in extended families are more likely to complete high school and get a job and less likely to be on welfare than mothers living on their own—factors that return to benefit children's well-being (Furstenberg & Crawford, 1978).

For single mothers who were very young at the time of their child's birth, extended family living continues to be associated with more positive adult–child interaction during the preschool years. Otherwise, establishing an independent household with the help of nearby relatives is related to improved child rearing. Perhaps this arrangement permits the more mature mother who has developed effective parenting skills to implement them (Chase-Lansdale, Brooks-Gunn, & Zamsky, 1994). In families with adolescents, kinship support continues to increase the likelihood of effective parenting, which, in turn, is related to self-reliance, emotional well-being, and reduced delinquency (Taylor, Casten, & Flickinger, 1993).

Finally, the African-American extended family plays an important role in transmitting black cultural values to children. Compared to nuclear families, extended family arrangements place more emphasis on cooperation and moral and religious values (Tolson & Wilson, 1990). These factors strengthen family bonds, protect children's development, and increase the chances that the extended family lifestyle will carry over to the next generation.

Strong bonds with extended-family members have helped to protect the development of many African-American children growing up under conditions of poverty and single parenthood. *(Karen Kasmauski/Woodfin Camp & Associates)*

TABLE 2.7

How Does the United States Compare to Other Nations on Indicators of Child Health and Well-Being?

INDICATOR	U.S. RANK	SOME COUNTRIES THE UNITED STATES TRAILS
Childhood poverty	8th (among 8 industrialized nations studied)	Australia, Canada, Germany, Great Britain, Norway, Sweden, Switzerland
Infant deaths in the first year of life	22nd (worldwide)	Hong Kong, Ireland, Singapore, Spain
Low birth weight newborns	28th (worldwide)	Bulgaria, Egypt, Greece, Iran, Jordan, Kuwait, Paraguay, Romania, Saudi Arabia
Percent of young children immunized against measles	21st (worldwide)	Chile, Czechoslovakia, Jordan, Poland
Number of school-age children per teacher	12th (worldwide)	Cuba, Lebanon, Libya
Mathematics achievement of college-bound high school students	12th (among 15 nations studied)	Belgium, Canada (Ontario), Finland, Israel, Scotland
Expenditures on education as the percentage of gross national product[a]	14th (among 16 industrialized nations studied)	Canada, France, Great Britain, the Netherlands, Sweden
Teenage pregnancy rate	6th (among 6 industrialized nations studied)	Canada, England, France, the Netherlands, Sweden

[a]Gross national product is the value of all goods and services produced by a nation during a specified time period. It serves as an overall measure of a nation's wealth.

Sources: Children's Defense Fund, 1994; Grant, 1993; McKnight et al., 1987; Sivard, 1993; Smeeding, Torrey, & Rein, 1988; Wegman, 1994.

Despite the worrisome state of America's children, progress is being made in improving their condition. Throughout this book we will discuss many successful programs that could be expanded. Another positive sign is that child development specialists are more involved than ever before in conducting research relevant to policies and communicating their findings to the country as a whole (Zigler & Finn-Stevenson, 1992). When citizens learn about the problems of children, they may write to lawmakers, support organizations working for children's needs, or become directly involved in helping children themselves.

Finally, growing awareness of the gap between what we know and what we do to improve children's lives has led child development specialists to join with concerned citizens as advocates for children's causes (Jacobs & Davies, 1991). Over the past few decades, several influential interest groups with children's well-being as their central purpose have emerged in the United States. One of the most vigorous is the Children's Defense Fund. To learn about its activities, refer to the Social Issues box on the following page. As efforts like these continue, there is every reason to expect increased responsiveness to children's needs in the years to come.

SOCIAL ISSUES

THE CHILDREN'S DEFENSE FUND

Moments in America:

- Every 30 seconds a baby is born into poverty.
- Every night 100,000 children go to sleep without homes.
- Every 14 minutes an infant dies in the first year of life.
- Every 59 seconds an infant is born to a teenage mother.
- Every 5 seconds a youth drops out of public school.
- Every month at least 225,000 children are abused or neglected.
- Every day 1,222,000 school-age children go home to an empty house where there is a gun. (Children's Defense Fund, 1994)

Many people are not aware of the problems experienced by large numbers of children in the United States. To sensitize the public, the Children's Defense Fund presents dramatic images like these in media ads and nationwide mailings. Besides promoting public awareness, the Children's Defense Fund provides government officials with a steady stream of facts about the status of children and encourages them to support legislation responsive to children's needs.

The Children's Defense Fund is the most avid interest group for children in the United States. It was founded in 1973 by Marion Wright Edelman, who remains its president today. Edelman grew up in a small, segregated South Carolina town, where she became deeply involved in community work at an early age. Her parents taught her that through struggle and commitment, the world's problems could be changed. As a young adult, Edelman carried this sense of mission to Yale University Law School. After graduating in the mid-1960s, she devoted herself to civil rights issues and became the first black woman admitted to the Mississippi bar. A few years later, Edelman moved to Washington, DC, where she established the Children's Defense Fund. Since then, its voice has grown steadily more powerful. Today, it has a staff of 120 people and an annual budget of 9 million dollars.

To accomplish its goals, the Children's Defense Fund engages in research, public education, legal action, drafting of legislation, congressional testimony, and community organizing. Each year, it publishes *The State of America's Children,* which provides a comprehensive analysis of the current condition of children, government-sponsored programs serving them, and proposals for improving child and family programs. Periodically, it issues special reports on burning issues affecting children's welfare. In one recent publication on the high cost of child poverty, the Children's Defense Fund estimated annual losses to the nation from just one year in which 22 percent of American children live in dire economic straits at tens of billions of dollars in special education, medical treatment, and reduced future worker productivity (Sherman, 1994).

The Children's Defense Fund supports an extensive network of state and local organizations that have children's needs as their central purpose. Two of its most significant projects are an adolescent pregnancy prevention program and a prenatal care campaign designed to reduce the high rates of death, illness, and developmental problems among poverty-stricken infants. Dissemination of information on how communities can develop more effective child and family services and preparation of a monthly newsletter on what people across the nation are doing to solve children's problems are among its many activities.

The Children's Defense Fund is supported by private foundations, corporate grants, and individual donations. To inquire about its publications and efforts on children's behalf, contact The Children's Defense Fund, 122 C Street, N.W., Washington, DC 20001. Telephone (800) 424-9602.

In 1973, Marion Wright Edelman founded the Children's Defense Fund, a private, non-profit organization that provides a strong, effective voice for American children, who cannot vote, lobby, or speak for themselves. Edelman continues to serve as president of the Children's Defense Fund today. *(Westenberger/Liaiso, USA)*

TRY THIS . . .

- Obtain the most recent issue of *The State of America's Children* from the Children's Defense Fund or your library. Consult the section entitled "Children in the States." How do children in your state fare on such indicators as poverty, infant mortality, immunization against disease, child abuse and neglect, and teenage childbearing?

ASK YOURSELF . . .

- On one of your trips to the local shopping center, you see a father getting very angry at his young son. Using the family systems perspective, list as many factors as you can that might account for the father's behavior.
- Links between family and community are essential for children's well-being. Provide examples and research findings from our discussion that support this idea.
- Check your local newspaper and one or two national news magazines to see how often articles appear on the condition of children and families. Why is it important for researchers to communicate with the general public about children's needs?

BRIEF REVIEW

Just as complex as heredity are the environments in which children grow up. First and foremost is the family—a complex system of mutually influencing relationships that changes over time. Child rearing in families is modified by social class, and it is seriously threatened by poverty and homelessness. A variety of additional contexts—neighborhoods that offer worthwhile activities and frequent contact with peers and adults, high-quality schools that establish ties with families, and communities in which children participate actively—support development. These aspects of the environment vary considerably among cultures and subcultures. In the complex world in which we live, favorable public policies are essential for children's well-being.

UNDERSTANDING THE RELATIONSHIP BETWEEN HEREDITY AND ENVIRONMENT

So far in this chapter, we have discussed a wide variety of hereditary and environmental influences, each of which has the power to alter the course of development. Yet many examples exist in which children born into the same family (and who therefore share genes and environments) are quite different in characteristics. We also know that some children are affected more than others by their environments. Cases exist in which a child provided with all the advantages in life does poorly, whereas a second child exposed to the worst of rearing conditions does well. How do scientists explain the impact of heredity and environment when they seem to work in so many different ways?

All child development specialists agree that both heredity and environment are involved in every aspect of development. There is no real controversy on this point because an environment is always needed for genetic information to be expressed (Scarr, 1988). But for polygenic traits (due to many genes) such as intelligence and personality, scientists are a long way from knowing the precise hereditary influences involved. They must study the impact of genes on these characteristics indirectly,

Identical twins Jim Lewis and Jim Springer were separated 4 weeks after birth, grew up in different homes, and led separate adult lives until, at age 39, they were reunited. The two Jims discovered that they were alike in many ways. Both drove the same model car, chain smoked, chewed their fingernails, and vacationed at the beach. On personality tests, they scored almost exactly the same. Not all separated twins match up as well as this pair. Nevertheless, the study of identical twins reared apart reveals that heredity contributes to many psychological characteristics. *(D. Gordon/Time Magazine)*

CONCEPT REVIEW TABLE

Methods Used to Estimate the Importance of Heredity in Complex Characteristics

CONCEPT	IMPORTANT POINT	EXAMPLE
Heritability estimate	To study the role of heredity in continuous traits, such as intelligence and personality, researchers compute heritability estimates from kinship studies. A proportion that ranges from 0 to 1.00, a heritability estimate measures the extent to which individual differences in a trait are due to genetic factors.	By comparing the correlation of intelligence test scores for identical twins with that for fraternal twins, researchers have arrived at a heritability estimate of about .50. It indicates that heredity plays a moderate role.
Concordance rate	Researchers use concordance rates to study the role of heredity in emotional and behavior disorders, which can be judged as either present or absent. A concordance rate is a percentage indicating the extent to which both members of a twin pair show a trait when it is present in one pair member. By comparing concordance rates for identical and fraternal twins, researchers can estimate the importance of heredity.	Since the concordance rate for severe depression is much higher in identical than in fraternal twins, heredity probably plays an important role.

and the nature–nurture controversy remains unresolved because researchers do not agree on how heredity and environment influence these complex characteristics.

Some believe that it is useful and possible to answer the question of *how much* each factor contributes to differences among children. These researchers use special methods to find out which factor plays the major role. A second group of investigators regards the question of which factor is more important as neither useful nor answerable. They believe that heredity and environment do not make separate contributions to behavior. Instead, they are always related, and the real question we need to explore is *how* they work together. Let's consider each of these two positions in turn.

THE QUESTION OF "HOW MUCH?"

Two methods—heritability estimates and concordance rates—are used to infer the importance of heredity in complex human characteristics. Each is summarized in the Concept Review Table above.

■ HERITABILITY. **Heritability estimates** measure the extent to which individual differences in continuous traits, such as intelligence and personality, are due to genetic factors. They are obtained from **kinship studies,** which compare the characteristics of family members. The most common type of kinship study com-

Heritability estimate
A statistic that measures the extent to which individual differences in complex traits, such as intelligence or personality, are due to genetic factors.

Kinship studies
Studies comparing the characteristics of family members to determine the importance of heredity in complex human characteristics.

pares identical twins, who share all their genes, with fraternal twins, who share only some. If people who are genetically more alike are also more similar in intelligence and personality test scores, then the researcher assumes that heredity plays an important role.

Kinship studies of intelligence provide some of the most controversial findings in the field of child development. Some experts claim a strong role for heredity, whereas others believe that genetic factors are barely involved. Currently, most researchers support a moderate role for heredity. When many twin studies are examined, correlations between the scores of identicals are consistently higher than those of fraternals. In one summary of over 30 such investigations, the correlation for intelligence was .86 for identical twins and .60 for fraternal twins (Bouchard & McGue, 1981). Researchers use a complex statistical procedure to compare these correlations, arriving at a heritability estimate ranging from 0 to 1.00. The value for intelligence is about .50, which indicates that half of the variation in intelligence among children can be explained by differences in their genetic makeup (Loehlin, 1989). The fact that the intelligence of adopted children is more strongly related to the scores of their biological parents than their adoptive parents offers further support for the role of heredity (Horn, 1983; Scarr & Weinberg, 1983).

Heritability research also reveals that genetic factors are important in personality. In fact, for personality traits that have been studied a great deal, such as sociability, emotional expressiveness, and activity level, heritability estimates are at about the same moderate level as that reported for intelligence (Braungart et al., 1992; Plomin, 1989).

CONCORDANCE. A second measure that has been used to infer the contribution of heredity to complex characteristics is the **concordance rate.** It refers to the percentage of instances in which both twins show a trait when it is present in one pair member. Researchers typically use concordance to study the contribution of heredity to emotional and behavior disorders, which can be judged as either present or absent. A concordance rate ranges from 0 to 100 percent. A score of 0 indicates that if one twin has the trait, the other twin never has it. A score of 100 means that if one twin has the trait, the other one always has it. When a concordance rate is much higher for identical twins than for fraternal twins, then heredity is believed to play a major role. Twin studies of schizophrenia and severe depression show this pattern of findings. In the case of schizophrenia, the concordance rate for identical twins is 30 percent, that for fraternal twins only 6 percent. The figures are 69 percent and 13 percent for depression (Gershon et al., 1977; Kendler & Robinette, 1983). Once again, adoption studies are consistent with these results. Biological relatives of schizophrenic and depressed adoptees are more likely to share the same disorder than are adoptive relatives (Loehlin, Willerman, & Horn, 1988).

Taken together, concordance and adoption research suggest that the strong tendency for schizophrenia and depression to run in families is partly due to genetic factors (Gershon et al., 1977; Reich et al., 1987). However, we also know that environment is involved, since the concordance rate for identical twins would need to be 100 percent if heredity were the only influence operating. In later chapters, we will see that environmental stresses, such as poverty, family conflict, and a disorganized home life, are often associated with emotional and behavior disorders.

LIMITATIONS OF HERITABILITY AND CONCORDANCE. Although heritability estimates and concordance rates provide evidence that genetic factors contribute to complex human characteristics, questions have been raised about their accuracy. Both measures are heavily influenced by the range of environments to which twin pairs are exposed. For example, identical twins reared together under highly similar conditions have more strongly correlated intelligence test scores than those reared apart in very different environments. When the former are used to compute heritability estimates, the higher cor-

Concordance rate
The percentage of instances in which both members of a twin pair show a trait when it is present in one pair member. Used to study the role of heredity in emotional and behavior disorders, which can be judged as either present or absent.

relation causes the importance of heredity to be overestimated. To overcome this difficulty, researchers try to find twins who have been reared apart in adoptive families. But few separated twin pairs are available for study, and when they are, social service agencies often place them in advantaged homes that are similar in many ways (Bronfenbrenner & Crouter, 1983; Scarr & Kidd, 1983). Because the environments of most twin pairs do not represent the broad range of environments found in the general population, it is often difficult to generalize heritability and concordance findings to the population as a whole.

Heritability estimates are controversial measures because they can easily be misapplied. For example, high heritabilities have been used to suggest that ethnic differences in intelligence, such as the poorer performance of black children compared to whites, have a genetic basis (Jensen, 1969, 1985b). Yet this line of reasoning is widely regarded as inaccurate. Heritabilities computed on mostly white twin samples do not tell us what is responsible for test score differences between ethnic groups. We have already indicated that large economic and cultural differences are involved. As we will see in Chapter 12, research shows that when black children are adopted into economically advantaged homes at an early age, their scores are well above average and substantially higher than those of children growing up in impoverished families.

Perhaps the most serious criticism of heritability estimates and concordance rates has to do with their usefulness. Although they are interesting statistics that tell us heredity is undoubtedly involved in complex traits such intelligence and personality, they give us no precise information about how these traits develop or how children might respond when exposed to environments designed to help them develop as far as possible. Investigators who conduct heritability research argue that their studies are a first step. As more evidence accumulates to show that heredity underlies important human characteristics, then scientists can begin to ask better questions—about the specific genes involved, the way they affect development, and how their impact is modified by environmental factors.

THE QUESTION OF "HOW?"

According to a second perspective, heredity and environment cannot be divided into separate influences. Instead, behavior is the result of a dynamic interplay between these two forces. How do heredity and environment work together to affect development? Several important concepts shed light on this complex question. As you read about them, you may find it useful to refer to the Concept Review Table on page 90, which provides a summary.

REACTION RANGE. The first of these ideas is **range of reaction** (Gottesman, 1963). It emphasizes that each person responds to the environment in a unique way because of his or her genetic makeup. Let's explore this idea by taking a look at Figure 2.10 on page 91. Reaction range can apply to any characteristic; here it is illustrated for intelligence. Notice that when environments vary from extremely unstimulating to highly enriched, Ben's intelligence increases dramatically, Linda's only slightly, and Ron's hardly at all.

Reaction range highlights two important points about the relationship between heredity and environment. First, it shows that because each of us has a unique genetic makeup, we respond quite differently to the same environment. Again, look carefully at Figure 2.10, and notice how a poor environment results in a lower intelligence test score for Ron than Ben. Also, an advantaged environment raises Ben's score far above what is possible for Ron. Second, sometimes different genetic–environmental combinations can make two children look the same! For example, if Ben is reared in an unstimulating environment, his score will be about 100—average for children in general. Linda can also obtain this score, but to do so she must grow up in a very advantaged home. In other words, the concept of range of reaction tells us

Range of reaction
Each person's unique, genetically determined response to a range of environmental conditions.

CONCEPT REVIEW TABLE

Concepts Describing How Heredity and Environment Work Together

CONCEPT	IMPORTANT POINT	EXAMPLE
Range of reaction	Each child responds uniquely to the environment because of his or her genetic makeup.	Ben's intelligence increases much more than Linda's or Ron's in an advantaged home environment (see Figure 2.9).
Canalization	Heredity restricts the development of some characteristics more than others. Harmful environments can also limit future development.	Motor development is more strongly canalized than intelligence. Intelligence can become canalized when children are reared in very deprived environments.
Genetic–environmental correlation	Heredity affects the environments to which children are exposed. This relationship becomes stronger with age.	Parents with genes for athletic talent encourage physical exercise in their children, who may have inherited their parents' favorable genes. With age, athletically inclined children seek out physical activities.

that children differ in their range of possible responses to the environment. And unique blends of heredity and environment lead to both similarities and differences in behavior.

■ CANALIZATION. The concept of **canalization** provides another way of understanding how heredity and environment combine. Canalization is the tendency of heredity to restrict the development of some characteristics to just one or a few outcomes. A behavior that is strongly canalized follows a genetically set growth plan, and only strong environmental forces can change it (Waddington, 1957). For example, infant perceptual and motor development seems to be strongly canalized, since all normal human babies eventually roll over, reach for objects, sit up, crawl, and walk. It takes extreme conditions to modify these behaviors or cause them not to appear. In contrast, intelligence and personality are less strongly canalized, since they respond easily to changes in the environment.

Recently, scientists expanded the notion of canalization to include environmental influences. We now know that environments can also limit development (Gottlieb, 1991). For example, when children are exposed to harmful environments early in life, there may be little that later experiences can do to change characteristics (such as intelligence) that were quite flexible to begin with. In Chapter 3, we will see that this is the case for babies exposed prenatally to high levels of alcohol, radiation, or oxygen deprivation. And later in this book, we will find that it is also true for children who spend many years living in extremely deprived homes and institutions (Turkheimer & Gottesman, 1991).

Using the concept of canalization, we learn that genes restrict the development of some characteristics more than others. And over time, even very flexible behaviors can become fixed and canalized, depending on the environments to which children were exposed.

Canalization
The tendency of heredity to restrict the development of some characteristics to just one or a few outcomes.

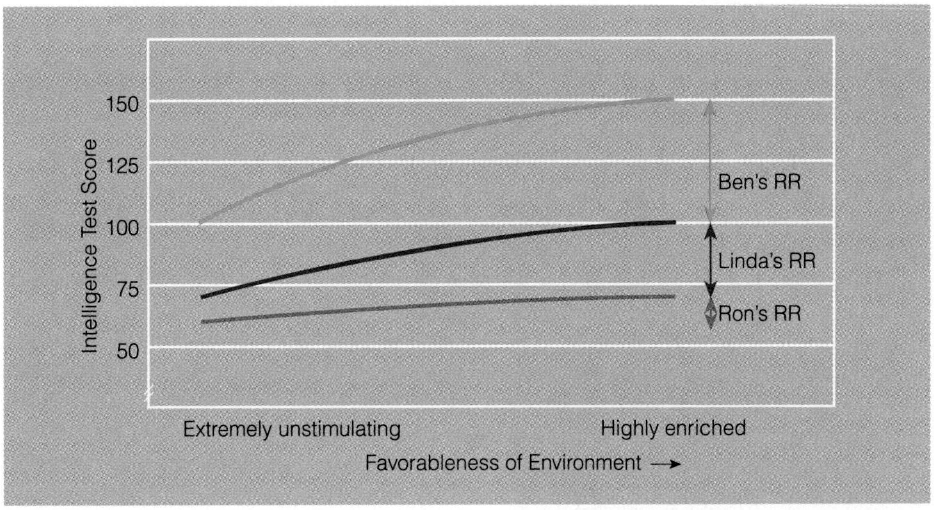

FIGURE 2.10

Intellectual ranges of reaction (RR) for three children in environments that vary from unstimulating to highly enriched.
(From I. I. Gottesman, 1963, "Genetic Aspects of Intelligent Behavior," in N. R. Ellis, ed., Handbook of Mental Deficiency, *New York: McGraw-Hill, p. 255. Adapted by permission.)*

■ GENETIC–ENVIRONMENTAL CORRELATION. There is still another way in which nature and nurture work together. Sandra Scarr and Kathleen McCartney (1983) point out that a major problem in trying to separate heredity and environment is that they are often correlated. According to the concept of **genetic–environmental correlation,** our genes influence the environments to which we are exposed. In support of this idea, a recent study showed that the greater the genetic similarity between pairs of adolescents, the more alike they were on many aspects of child rearing, including parental discipline, affection, conflict, and monitoring of the young person's activities (Plomin et al., 1994).

These findings indicate that children's heredity plays a role in molding their experiences. The way this happens changes with development.

Passive and Evocative Correlation. At younger ages, two types of genetic–environmental correlation are common. The first is called *passive* correlation because the child has no control over it. Early on, parents provide environments that are influenced by their own heredity. For example, parents who are good athletes are likely to emphasize outdoor activities and enroll their children in swimming and gymnastics lessons. Besides getting exposed to an "athletic environment," the children may have inherited their parents' athletic ability. As a result, they are likely to become good athletes for both genetic and environmental reasons.

The second type of genetic–environmental correlation is *evocative.* Children evoke responses from others that are influenced by the child's heredity, and these responses strengthen the child's original style of responding. For example, an active, friendly baby is likely to receive more social stimulation from those around her than a passive, quiet infant. And a cooperative, attentive preschooler will probably receive more patient and sensitive interactions from parents than an inattentive, distractible child.

Active Correlation. At older ages, *active* genetic–environmental correlation becomes common. As children extend their experiences beyond the immediate family to school, neighborhood, and community and are given the freedom to make more of their own choices, they play an increasingly active role in seeking out environments that fit with their genetic tendencies. The well-coordinated, muscular child spends more time at after-school sports, the musically talented youngster joins the school orchestra and practices his violin, and the intellectually curious child is a well-known visitor at her local library.

This tendency to actively choose environments that complement our heredity is called **niche-picking** (Scarr & McCartney, 1983). Infants and young children cannot do much niche-picking, since adults select environments for them. In contrast,

Genetic–environmental correlation
The idea that heredity influences the environments to which individuals are exposed.

Niche-picking
A type of genetic–environmental correlation in which individuals actively choose environments that complement their heredity.

Sandra Scarr is a leading investigator of genetic and environmental contributions to complex human characteristics. With Kathleen McCartney, she developed broadly influential ideas about genetic-environmental correlation. Her adoption research addressing the heritability of intelligence is widely known. *(University of Virginia)*

older children and adolescents are much more in charge of their own environments. The niche-picking idea explains why pairs of identical twins reared apart during childhood and later reunited often find, to their great surprise, that they have similar hobbies, food preferences, friendship choices, and vocations (Bouchard et al., 1990; Plomin, 1994). It also helps us understand some curious longitudinal findings indicating that identical twins become somewhat more similar and fraternal twins and adopted siblings less similar from infancy to adolescence (Scarr & Weinberg, 1983; Wilson, 1983). The influence of heredity and environment is not constant but changes over time. With age, genetic factors may become more important in determining the environments we experience and choose for ourselves.

A major reason that child development specialists are interested in the nature–nurture issue is that they want to find ways to improve environments in order to help children develop as far as possible. The concepts of range of reaction, canalization, and niche-picking remind us that development is best understood as a series of complex exchanges between nature and nurture. When a characteristic is strongly determined by heredity, it can still be modified. However, children cannot be changed in any way we might desire. The success of any attempt to improve development depends on the characteristics we want to change, the genetic makeup of the child, and the type and timing of our intervention.

ASK YOURSELF . . .

- A researcher wants to know whether bedwetting in middle childhood is influenced by genetic factors. Which method of inferring the importance of heredity in complex human characteristics could help answer this question?
- Bianca's parents are both accomplished musicians. Bianca began taking piano lessons when she was 4 and was accompanying her school choir by age 10. When she reached adolescence, she asked her parents if she could attend a special music high school. Explain how genetic and environmental factors work together to promote Bianca's talent.

SUMMARY

GENETIC FOUNDATIONS

What are genes, and how are they transmitted from one generation to the next?

- Development begins at conception, when sperm and ovum unite to form the one-celled **zygote.** Within the cell nucleus are 23 pairs of **chromosomes.** Along their length are **genes,** segments of **DNA** that make us distinctly human and play an important role in determining our development and characteristics.
- The **gametes,** or sex cells, are produced by the process of cell division known as **meiosis.** Since each zygote receives a unique set of genes from each parent, meiosis ensures that children will be genetically different from one another. Once the zygote forms, it starts to develop into a complex human being through cell duplication, or **mitosis.**
- If the fertilizing sperm carries an X chromosome, the child will be a girl; if it contains a Y chromosome, a boy will be born. **Fraternal,** or **dizygotic, twins** result when two ova are released from the mother's ovaries and each is fertilized. In contrast, **identical,** or **monozygotic, twins** develop when a zygote divides in two during the early stages of cell duplication.

Describe various patterns of genetic inheritance.

- **Dominant–recessive** and **codominant** relationships are patterns of inheritance that apply to many traits controlled by single genes. When recessive disorders are **X-linked** (carried on the X chromosome), males are more likely to be affected. Unfavorable genes arise from **mutations,** which can occur spontaneously or be induced by hazardous environmental agents. **Genetic imprinting** is a newly discovered pattern of inheritance in which one parent's allele is activated, regardless of its makeup.
- Human traits that vary continuously, such as intelligence and personality, are **polygenic,** or influenced by many genes. Since the genetic principles involved are unknown, scientists must study the influence of heredity on these characteristics indirectly.

CHROMOSOMAL ABNORMALITIES

Describe major chromosomal abnormalities, and explain how they occur.

- Most chromosomal abnormalities are due to errors in meiosis. The most common chromosomal disorder is Down syndrome, which results in physical defects and mental retardation. Disorders of the **sex chromosomes** are milder than defects of the **autosomes.** Contrary to popular belief, males with XYY syndrome are not prone to aggression. Studies of children with triple X, Klinefelter, and Turner syndromes reveal that adding to or subtracting from the usual number of X chromosomes leads to specific intellectual problems.

REPRODUCTIVE CHOICES

What procedures are available to assist prospective parents in having healthy, wanted children?

- **Genetic counseling** helps couples at risk for giving birth to children with genetic abnormalities decide whether or not to conceive. **Prenatal diagnostic methods** make early detection of genetic problems possible. Although reproductive technologies, such as donor insemination, in vitro fertilization, and surrogate motherhood, permit many individuals to become parents who otherwise would not, they raise serious legal and ethical concerns.
- When a prenatal condition cannot be corrected, some women opt for an abortion. However, the large majority of abortions are to women who accidentally become pregnant, many of them teenagers. Research indicates that unwanted children develop less favorably than other children. However, scientific studies cannot provide answers to the complex ethical questions surrounding abortion.
- Many parents who cannot conceive or who have a high likelihood of transmitting a genetic disorder decide to adopt. Although adopted children have more developmental problems than children in general, most fare quite well.

ENVIRONMENTAL CONTEXTS FOR DEVELOPMENT

Describe the social systems perspective on family functioning, along with aspects of the environment that support family well-being and children's development.

- Just as complex as heredity are the environments in which children grow up. The family is the child's first and foremost context for development. The **social systems perspective** emphasizes that the behaviors of each family member affect those of others. The family system is also dynamic and ever-changing, constantly adjusting to new events and developmental changes in its members.
- Two aspects of parenting promote effective development at all ages: (1) responsiveness and (2) reasonable demands for mature behavior. Although warm, moderately demanding child rearing is the

most common pattern around the world, it is modified by social class. Effective parenting, along with all aspects of children's development, is seriously undermined by poverty and homelessness.

- Children profit from supportive ties between the family and the surrounding environment. Neighborhoods that provide constructive leisure time activities, high-quality schools that communicate often with parents, and communities that promote children's active participation alongside adults enhance child development.
- The values and life conditions of cultures and **subcultures** mold the environments in which children grow up. In contrast to the American middle-class family, in many cultures grandparents, siblings, and other relatives share child-rearing responsibilities. **Extended family households,** in which parent and child live with one or more adult relatives, are common among ethnic minorities. They protect children's development under conditions of high life stress.
- In the complex world in which we live today, children's well-being depends on favorable **public policies.** Effective social programs are influenced by many factors, including cultural values, a nation's economic resources, and organizations and individuals that work for children's causes.

UNDERSTANDING THE RELATIONSHIP BETWEEN HEREDITY AND ENVIRONMENT

Explain the various ways in which heredity and environment may combine to influence complex traits.

- Scientists do not agree on how heredity and environment influence complex characteristics, such as intelligence and personality. Some believe that it is useful and possible to determine "how much" each factor contributes to individual differences. These investigators compute **heritability estimates** and **concordance rates** from **kinship studies.**
- Other scientists believe that the important question is "how" heredity and environment work together. The concepts of **range of reaction, canalization,** and **genetic–environmental correlation** remind us that development is best understood as a series of complex exchanges between nature and nurture.

IMPORTANT TERMS AND CONCEPTS

phenotype (p. 52)
genotype (p. 52)
chromosomes (p. 52)
deoxyribonucleic acid (DNA) (p. 52)
gene (p. 52)
mitosis (p. 53)
gametes (p. 53)
meiosis (p. 53)
crossing over (p. 53)
zygote (p. 56)
autosomes (p. 56)
sex chromosomes (p. 56)
fraternal, or dizygotic, twins (p. 57)
identical, or monozygotic, twins (p. 57)
allele (p. 58)
homozygous (p. 58)
heterozygous (p. 58)
dominant–recessive inheritance (p. 58)
carrier (p. 59)
codominance (p. 60)
mutation (p. 61)
X-linked inheritance (p. 61)
genetic imprinting (p. 61)
polygenic inheritance (p. 64)
genetic counseling (p. 67)
prenatal diagnostic methods (p. 68)
social systems perspective (p. 74)
subculture (p. 81)
extended family household (p. 82)
public policies (p. 82)
heritability estimate (p. 87)
kinship study (p. 87)
concordance rate (p. 88)
range of reaction (p. 89)
canalization (p. 90)
genetic–environmental correlation (p. 91)
niche-picking (p. 91)

FYI...

FOR FURTHER INFORMATION AND SPECIAL HELP, CONSULT THE FOLLOWING ORGANIZATIONS:

CAUSES OF MUTATION

Environmental Mutagen Society
1730 N. Lynn Street
Suite 502
Arlington, VA 22209
(703) 525-1191

Provides information on environmental agents that cause mutation.

GENETIC DISORDERS

March of Dimes Birth Defects Foundation
1275 Mamaroneck Avenue
White Plains, NY 10605
(914) 428-7100

Works to prevent genetic disorders and other birth defects through public education and community service programs.

PKU Parents
8 Myrtle Lane
San Anselmo, CA 94960
(415) 457-4632

Provides support and education for parents of children with PKU.

National Association for Sickle Cell Disease
4221 Wilshire Blvd. Suite 360
Los Angeles, CA 90010
(213) 736-5455

Provides information and assists local groups that serve individuals with sickle cell anemia.

National Down Syndrome Congress
1800 Dempster Street
Park Ridge, IL 60068-1146
(312) 823-7550

Assists parents in finding solutions to the needs of children with Down syndrome. Local groups exist across the United States.

INFERTILITY

Resolve, Inc.
1310 Broadway
Somerville, MA 02144-1731
(608) 791-4747

Offers counseling referral and support to persons with fertility problems.

ADOPTION

National Adoption Information
11426 Rockville Pike, Suite 410
Rockville, MD 20852
(301) 231-6512

Provides information on all aspects of adoption, including children from other countries, children with special needs, and state and federal adoption laws.

PUBLIC POLICY

The Children's Defense Fund
122 C Street N. W.
Washington, DC 20001
(202) 628-8787
(800) 424-9602

An active child advocacy organization. Provides information on the condition of children and government-sponsored programs serving them.

National Center for Children in Poverty
Columbia University School of Public Health
154 Haven Avenue
New York, NY 10032
(212) 927-8793

Aims to strengthen programs and policies for young children and their families who live in poverty in the United States. Seeks to achieve this goal through disseminating information about early education and maternal and child health and proposing promising new initiatives to policymakers.

"My mother"
Milena Jovic
10 years, Yugoslavia

This painting captures the anticipation and wonder experienced by many expectant parents as they await the arrival of a new being. How is the one-celled organism gradually transformed into a baby with the human capacity to play, dream, and create? What factors support or undermine this earliest phase of development? Chapter 3 provides answers to these questions.

Reprinted by permission from The International Museum of Children's Art, Oslo, Norway.

3

Prenatal Development

After months of wondering if the time in their own lives was right, Yolanda and Jay decided to have a baby. I met them one fall in my child development class, when Yolanda was just 2 months pregnant. Both were full of questions: "How does the baby grow before birth? When are different organs formed? Has its heart begun to beat? Can it hear, feel, or sense our presence in other ways?" Already, Yolanda and Jay had scanned the shelves of the public library and local bookstores, picking up a dozen or more sources on pregnancy, childbirth, and caring for the newborn.

Most of all, Yolanda and Jay wanted to do everything possible to make sure that their baby would be born healthy. At one time, they believed that the developing organism was completely shielded by the uterus from any dangers in the environment. All babies born with problems, they thought, had unfavorable genes. After browsing through several pregnancy books, Yolanda and Jay realized that they were wrong. Yolanda started to wonder about her diet and whether she should keep up her daily aerobics routine. And she asked me whether an aspirin for a headache, a sleeping pill before bedtime, a glass of wine at dinnertime, or a few cups of coffee during study hours might be harmful.

In this chapter, we answer Yolanda and Jay's questions, along with a great many more that scientists have asked about the events before birth. We begin our discussion during the time period before pregnancy with these puzzling questions: Why is it that, generation after generation, most couples who fall in love and marry want to

MOTIVATIONS FOR PARENTHOOD

Why Have Children? • How Large a Family? • Is There a Best Time During Adulthood to Have a Child?

PRENATAL DEVELOPMENT

The Period of the Zygote • The Period of the Embryo • The Period of the Fetus

PRENATAL ENVIRONMENTAL INFLUENCES

Teratogens • Other Maternal Factors • The Importance of Prenatal Health Care

PREPARING FOR PARENTHOOD

Seeking Information • The Baby Becomes a Reality • Models of Effective Parenthood • Practical Concerns • The Marital Relationship

become parents? And how do they decide whether to have just one child or more than one?

Then we trace prenatal development—the 9-month period before birth. Our discussion pays special attention to environmental supports that are necessary for healthy growth as well as damaging influences that threaten the child's health and survival. Finally, the prenatal period marks an important transitional phase in the lives of expectant parents—one that creates challenges as well as opportunities for personal growth. We look at ways in which couples prepare psychologically for the arrival of the baby and how a new sense of self as mother or father begins to emerge.

MOTIVATIONS FOR PARENTHOOD

As part of her semester project for my class, Yolanda interviewed her grandmother, asking why she wanted to have children and how she settled on a particular family size. Yolanda's grandmother, whose children were born in the early 1940s, replied,

> We didn't think much about whether or not to have children in those days. We just had them—everybody did. It would have seemed odd not to! I was 22 years old when I had the first of my four children, and I had four because—well, I wouldn't have had just one since we all thought children needed brothers and sisters, and only children could end up spoiled and selfish. Life is more interesting with children, you know. And now that we're older, we've got family we can depend on and grandchildren to enjoy.

WHY HAVE CHILDREN?

In some ways, the reasons given by Yolanda's grandmother for wanting children are like those of modern parents. In other ways, they are very different. In the past, the issue of whether to have children was, for many adults, "a biological given or unavoidable cultural demand" (Michaels, 1988, p. 23). Today, in Western industrialized nations, it is a matter of true individual choice. Effective birth control techniques permit adults who do not want to become parents to avoid having children in most instances. And changing social values allow people to remain childless with much less fear of social criticism and rejection than was the case a generation or two ago.

When modern American couples are asked about their desire to have children, they mention a variety of advantages and disadvantages, which are listed in Table 3.1. Take a moment to consider which ones are most important to you. Although some ethnic and regional differences exist, reasons for having children that are most important to all groups include the desire for a warm, affectionate relationship and the stimulation and fun that children provide. Also frequently mentioned are growth and learning experiences that children bring into the lives of adults, the desire to have someone carry on after one's own death, and feelings of accomplishment and creativity that come from helping children grow (Hoffman, Thornton, & Manis, 1978).

Most young adults are also aware that having children means years of extra burdens and responsibilities. When asked about the disadvantages of parenthood, they mention "loss of freedom" most often, followed by "financial strain." Indeed, the cost of child rearing is a major factor in modern family planning. According to

[1]This figure is based on a 1988 estimate, corrected for later inflation (Glick, 1990; U.S. Department of Labor, 1994). The figure includes basic expenses related to food, housing, clothing, medical care, and education.

TABLE 3.1

Advantages and Disadvantages of Parenthood Mentioned by Modern American Couples

ADVANTAGES	DISADVANTAGES
Giving and receiving warmth and affection	Loss of freedom, being tied down
Experiencing the stimulation and fun that children add to life	Financial strain
Being accepted as a responsible and mature member of the community	Worries over children's health, safety and well-being
Experiencing new growth and learning opportunities that add meaning to life	Interference with mother's employment opportunities
Having someone carry on after one's own death	Risks of bringing up children in a world plagued by crime, war, and pollution
Gaining a sense of accomplishment and creativity from helping children grow	Reduced time to spend with husband or wife
Learning to become less selfish and to sacrifice	Loss of privacy
Having offspring who help with parents' work or add their own income to the family's resources	Fear that children will turn out badly, through no fault of one's own

Source: Michaels, 1988.

a conservative estimate, parents will spend about $200,000[1] to raise a child from birth through four years of college. Finally, many adults worry greatly about bringing children into a troubled world—one filled with crime, war, and pollution (Michaels, 1988).

Careful weighing of the pros and cons of having children was rare in Yolanda's grandmother's time, yet it is increasingly common today. Child development specialists view this change as positive. It means that many more couples are making informed and personally meaningful choices about becoming parents—a trend that should increase the chances that they are ready to have children and that their own lives will be enriched by their decision.

HOW LARGE A FAMILY?

In contrast to her grandmother, Yolanda plans to have no more than two children. And she and Jay are talking about whether to limit their family to a single child. In 1960, the average number of children in an American family was 3.1. Today, it is 2.1, a downward trend that is expected to continue into the twenty-first century (U.S. Bureau of the Census, 1994). In addition to more effective birth control, a major reason that family size has declined in industrialized nations is that many women are experiencing the economic and personal rewards of a career. A family size of one or two children is certainly more compatible with a woman's decision to divide her energies between work and family.

Research also indicates that modern children benefit from growing up in small families. Parents who have fewer children are more patient and use less punishment. They also have more time to devote to each child's activities, schoolwork, and other special needs. Furthermore, in smaller families, siblings are more likely to be widely spaced (born more than 2 years apart), which adds to the attention and resources parents can invest in each child. Together, these findings may account for the fact that children growing up in small families are healthier, have somewhat

SOCIAL ISSUES

A GLOBAL PERSPECTIVE ON FAMILY PLANNING

Approximately one-fifth of the world's population—one billion people in all—live in extreme poverty, the majority in slums and shantytowns of developing countries. If current trends in population growth continue, the number of poor will quadruple within the next 60 to 70 years. Poverty and rapid population growth are intertwined: Poverty leads to high birthrates, and rising birthrates heighten poverty and deprivation. Why is this so?

There are many reasons. First, in poor regions of the world where child death rates are high, parents have more children to compensate for the fact that some will certainly die. Second, lack of status, education, and opportunities for women, characteristic of most nonindustrialized societies, restrict life choices to early marriage and prolonged childbearing. Third, in regions where few basic services and labor-saving technologies exist, families often depend on children to help in the fields and at home. Fourth, poverty is associated with absence of family planning services, which causes birthrates to remain high even when people begin to realize the advantages of smaller families. And finally, lack of hope in the future is a major obstacle to life planning in general and family planning in particular (Grant, 1994).

As a country's population grows, poverty worsens. The labor force expands more quickly than available work, and a new generation of unemployed or underemployed parents emerge. Basic resources, including food, water, land, and fuel, are in shorter supply, and health and educational services are increasingly strained. As a result, overcrowding in urban areas along with malnutrition, disease, illiteracy, and hopelessness spreads. A circuit forms through which poverty and high birthrates perpetuate one another.

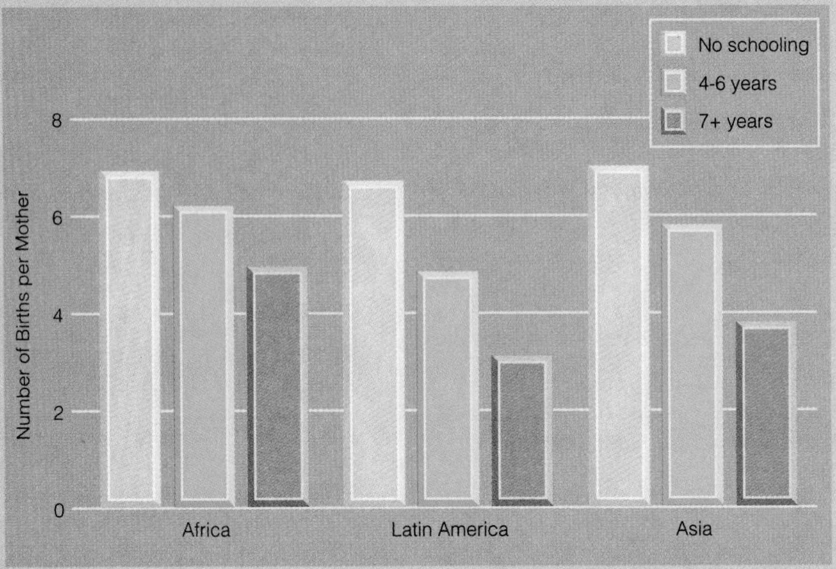

FIGURE 3.1

Number of births per mother by years of education in Africa, Latin America, and Asia.
Educated women have considerably fewer children. *(From Black, 1993.)*

Two interrelated strategies are especially effective for intervening in this cycle:

- Making family planning information and services available to all who want them, in ways that are compatible with each country's cultural and religious traditions. Over the last 30 years, the proportion of married women in the developing world using birth control has increased from 10 to 50 percent, demonstrating that substantial change in practices can be brought about in a relatively short period of time (Grant, 1994). Still, in almost all developing countries, the unmet demand for family planning remains high.
- Emphasizing education and literacy, particularly for girls. As Figure 3.1 shows, education is a strong determinant of smaller family size. Because women with more years of education have better life opportunities, they are more likely to take advantage of family planning services. As a result, they have fewer, more widely spaced, and healthier children (World Bank, 1992).

Family planning combined with education leads to substantial declines in birthrates and resulting improvements in quality of life for both mothers and children. These benefits carry over to future generations.

TRY THIS . . .

- Contact the United Nation's Children's Fund (UNICEF), 3 U.N. Plaza, New York, NY 10017, for a copy of its annual report, *The State of the World's Children.* Notice how much of the report is devoted to issues of poverty, population control, and family planning in developing countries. Find examples of nations in which the strategies just described resulted in important gains in quality of life for women and children.

higher intelligence test scores, do better in school, and attain higher levels of education (Blake, 1989; Grant, 1994; Powell & Steelman, 1993).

However, recall from Chapter 1 that a correlation between family size and children's characteristics does not tell us for sure about causation! Large families are usually less well off economically than smaller ones. Factors associated with low income—crowded housing, poor nutrition, and parental stress—may be responsible for the negative relationship between family size and children's development (Rutter & Madge, 1976). Indeed, there is evidence to support this idea. When children grow up in large, well-to-do families, the unfavorable outcomes typically associated with large family size are reduced, but they are not eliminated (Powell & Steelman, 1993). As the Social Issues box on the opposite page indicates, family planning is a major consideration in improving the quality of children's lives, especially in poverty-stricken regions of the world.

A doctor explains birth control options to two women visiting a clinic in Nepal. Family planning combined with education helps limit rising birthrates in developing countries. Smaller families mean an enhanced quality of life for both mothers and children. *(Takeshi Takahara/Photo Researchers, Inc.)*

Is Yolanda's grandmother right that parents who have just one child are likely to end up with a spoiled, selfish youngster? A great deal of research indicates this commonly held belief is not correct. Only children are just as socially well adjusted as children with siblings, and they achieve better in school. This is true not just in Western nations, but also in China, where a one-child family policy is strictly enforced to control overpopulation (Falbo & Poston, 1993). One reason for these positive outcomes may be that only children have somewhat more affectionate relationships with their parents than do children with siblings. And they also experience more pressure at home for mastery and accomplishment. As long as these demands are not unreasonable, they seem to have positive effects on children's development (Claudy, 1984; Falbo & Polit, 1986).

Still, the one-child family has both pros and cons, as does every family lifestyle. In a survey in which only children and their parents were asked what they liked and disliked about living in a single-child family, each mentioned a set of advantages and disadvantages, which are summarized in Table 3.2. The list is a useful one for parents to consider when deciding how many children would best fit their own personal and family life plans.

TABLE 3.2

Advantages and Disadvantages of a One-Child Family

ADVANTAGES		DISADVANTAGES	
Mentioned by Parents	Mentioned by Children	Mentioned by Parents	Mentioned by Children
Having time to pursue one's own interests and career	Avoiding sibling rivalry	Walking a "tightrope" between healthy attention and overindulgence	Not getting to experience the closeness of a sibling relationship
Less financial pressure	Having more privacy	Having only one chance to "make good" as a parent	Feeling too much pressure from parents to succeed
Not having to worry about "playing favorites" among children	Enjoying greater affluence	Being left childless in case of the child's death	Having no one to help care for parents when they get old
	Having a closer parent–child relationship		

Source: Hawke & Knox, 1978.

IS THERE A BEST TIME DURING ADULTHOOD TO HAVE A CHILD?

Yolanda's grandmother had her first child in her early twenties, shortly after she was married. Yolanda is pregnant for the first time at age 28. Many people believe that giving birth during the twenties is ideal, not only because the risk of having a baby with a chromosomal disorder is reduced (see Chapter 2), but also because younger parents have more energy to keep up with active children.

However, as Figure 3.2 reveals, first births to women in their thirties have increased greatly over the past two decades. Many more couples are putting off childbearing until their careers are well established and they know they can support a child (Ventura, 1989). Older parents may be somewhat less energetic than they were at earlier ages, but they are financially better off and more mature emotionally. For these reasons, they may be better able to invest in parenting (Ragozin et al., 1982). In support of this idea, when individuals who grew up with older parents are asked to reflect back on their childhoods, they often mention emotional stability as a distinct advantage (Yarrow, 1991).

Nevertheless, adult children of older parents do mention drawbacks. Some felt jealous of childhood friends because their parents seemed more active, playful, and fun loving. In addition, as they reached young adulthood, a great many began to worry about losing their parents. They had to come to terms with the fact that they would probably live much of their lives without their mothers and fathers (Yarrow, 1991).

Finally, fertility does decline with age. Older women who want to have children may find it more difficult to conceive, and a greater number of miscarriages occur with advancing age (Cohen-Overbeek et al., 1990; Phillips & Elias, 1993). Although there is no best time during adulthood to begin rearing children, individuals who decide to put off childbirth until well into their thirties or early forties do risk the possibility that they may not have children at all.

FIGURE 3.2

First births to American women of different ages in 1970 and 1992. The birthrate decreased over this time period for women 20–24 years of age, whereas it increased for women 25 years and older. For women in their thirties, the birthrate more than doubled. *(Adapted from Ventura, 1989; U.S. Department of Health and Human Services, 1994.)*

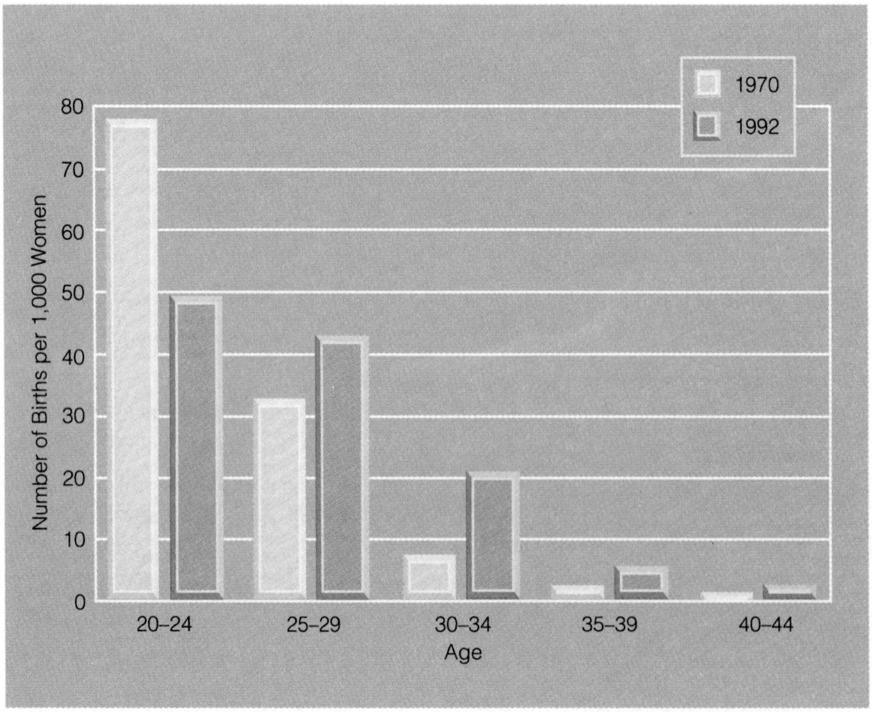

BRIEF REVIEW

Today, more couples in industrialized nations weigh the pros and cons of parenthood before deciding to have children than was the case in the past. The current trend toward smaller families fits with the greater career commitment of modern women, and it also has benefits for children. Contrary to popular belief, parents who limit their families to a single child are just as likely to raise a socially well-adjusted youngster as families with several children. Like all family lifestyles, the decision to postpone childbearing to a later age has both advantages and disadvantages.

ASK YOURSELF . . .

- In what ways are couples' reasons for having children the same today as they were in Yolanda's grandmother's time? In what ways has the decision to have children changed?
- Rhonda and Mark are career-oriented, 35-year-old parents of an only child. They are thinking about having a second baby. What factors should they keep in mind as they decide whether to add to their family at this time in their lives?

PRENATAL DEVELOPMENT

During Yolanda's pregnancy, the one-celled zygote will grow into a complex human infant fully ready to be born. The vast changes that take place during these 38 weeks are usually divided into three phases: (1) the period of the zygote; (2) the period of the embryo; and (3) the period of the fetus. As we take a look at what happens in each, you may find it useful to refer to Table 3.3 on page 104 and the photos on pages 108–109, which summarize the milestones of prenatal development.

THE PERIOD OF THE ZYGOTE

The period of the zygote lasts about 2 weeks, from fertilization until the tiny mass of cells drifts down and out of the fallopian tube and attaches itself to the wall of the uterus. The zygote's first cell duplication is long and drawn out; it is not complete until about 30 hours after conception. Gradually, new cells are added at a faster rate. By the fourth day, 60 to 70 cells exist that form a hollow, fluid-filled ball called a **blastocyst** (see Figure 3.3). The cells on the inside, called the **embryonic disk,** will become the new organism; the outer ring will provide protective covering.

■ IMPLANTATION. Sometime between the seventh and ninth day, **implantation** occurs: the blastocyst burrows deep into the uterine lining. Surrounded by the woman's nourishing blood, now it starts to grow in earnest. At first, the protective outer layer multiplies fastest. A membrane, called the **amnion,** is formed that encloses the developing organism in **amniotic fluid.** It helps keep the temperature of the prenatal world constant and provides a cushion against any jolts caused by the woman's movement. A *yolk sac* also appears. It produces blood cells until the developing liver, spleen, and bone marrow are mature enough to take over this function (Moore & Persaud, 1993).

The events of these first 2 weeks are delicate and uncertain. As many as 30 percent of zygotes do not make it through this phase. In some, the sperm and ovum do not join properly. In others, for some unknown reason, cell duplication never begins. By preventing implantation in these cases, nature eliminates most prenatal abnormalities in the very earliest stages of development (Sadler, 1990).

■ THE PLACENTA AND UMBILICAL CORD. By the end of the second week, another protective membrane, called the **chorion,** surrounds the amnion. From the chorion, tiny fingerlike *villi,* or blood vessels, begin to emerge.[2]

[2]Recall from Chapter 2 that chorionic villus sampling is the prenatal diagnostic method that can be performed earliest, by 6 to 8 weeks after conception. In this procedure, tissue from the ends of the villi are removed and examined for genetic abnormalities.

Blastocyst
The zygote 4 days after fertilization, when the tiny mass of cells forms a hollow, fluid-filled ball.

Embryonic disk
A small cluster of cells on the inside of the blastocyst, from which the embryo will develop.

Implantation
Attachment of the blastocyst to the uterine lining 7 to 9 days after fertilization.

Amnion
The inner membrane that forms a protective covering around the prenatal organism.

Amniotic fluid
The fluid that fills the amnion, helping to keep temperature constant and to provide a cushion against jolts caused by the mother's movement.

Chorion
The outer membrane that forms a protective covering around the prenatal organism. It sends out tiny, fingerlike villi, from which the placenta begins to emerge.

TABLE 3.3

Major Milestones of Prenatal Development

TRIMESTER	PERIOD	WEEKS	LENGTH AND WEIGHT	MAJOR EVENTS
First	Zygote	1		The one-celled zygote multiplies and forms a blastocyst.
		2		The blastocyst burrows into the uterine lining. Structures that feed and protect the developing organism begin to form—amnion, chorion, yolk sac, placenta, and umbilical cord.
	Embryo	3–4	1/4 inch	A primitive brain and spinal cord appear. Heart, muscles, backbone, ribs, and digestive tract begin to develop.
	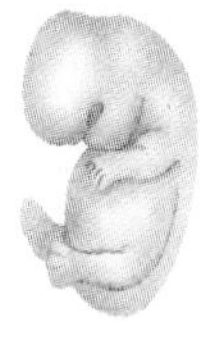	5–8	1 inch	Many external body structures (e.g., face, arms, legs, toes, fingers) and internal organs form. The sense of touch begins to develop, and the embryo can move.
	Fetus 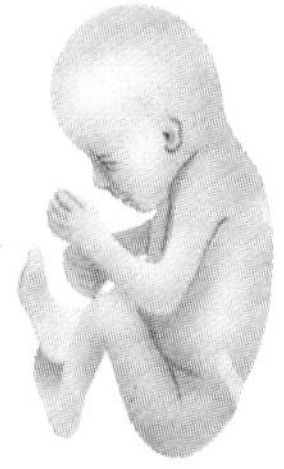	9–12	3 inches; less than 1 ounce	Rapid increase in size begins. Nervous system, organs, and muscles become organized and connected, and new behavioral capacities (kicking, thumb sucking, mouth opening, and rehearsal of breathing) appear. External genitals are well formed, and the fetus's sex is evident.
Second		13–24	12 inches; 1.8 pounds	The fetus continues to enlarge rapidly. In the middle of this period, fetal movements can be felt by the mother. Vernix and lanugo keep the fetus's skin from chapping in the amniotic fluid. All of the neurons that will ever be produced in the brain are present by 24 weeks. Eyes are sensitive to light, and the fetus reacts to sound.
Third		25–38	20 inches; 7.5 pounds	The fetus has a chance of survival if born around this time. Size continues to increase. Lungs gradually mature. Rapid brain development causes sensory and behavioral capacities to expand. In the middle of this period, a layer of fat is added under the skin. Antibodies are transmitted from mother to fetus to protect against disease. Most fetuses rotate into an upside-down position in preparation for birth.

Sources: Moore & Persaud, 1993; Nilsson & Hamberger, 1990.

As these villi burrow into the uterine wall, a special organ called the **placenta** starts to develop. By bringing the mother's and embryo's blood close together, the placenta will permit food and oxygen to reach the developing organism and waste products to be carried away. A special membrane forms that allows these substances to be exchanged but prevents the mother's and embryo's blood from mixing directly (see Figure 3.4).

The placenta is connected to the developing organism by the **umbilical cord.** In the period of the zygote, it first appears as a primitive body stalk, but during the course of pregnancy, it grows to a length of 1 to 3 feet. The umbilical cord contains one large vein that delivers blood loaded with nutrients and two arteries that remove waste products. The force of blood flowing through the cord keeps it firm, much like a garden hose, so it seldom tangles while the embryo, like a spacewalking astronaut, floats freely in its fluid-filled chamber (Moore & Persaud, 1993).

Placenta
The organ that separates the mother's bloodstream from the embryo or fetal bloodstream but permits exchange of nutrients and waste products.

Umbilical cord
The long cord connecting the prenatal organism to the placenta that delivers nutrients and removes waste products.

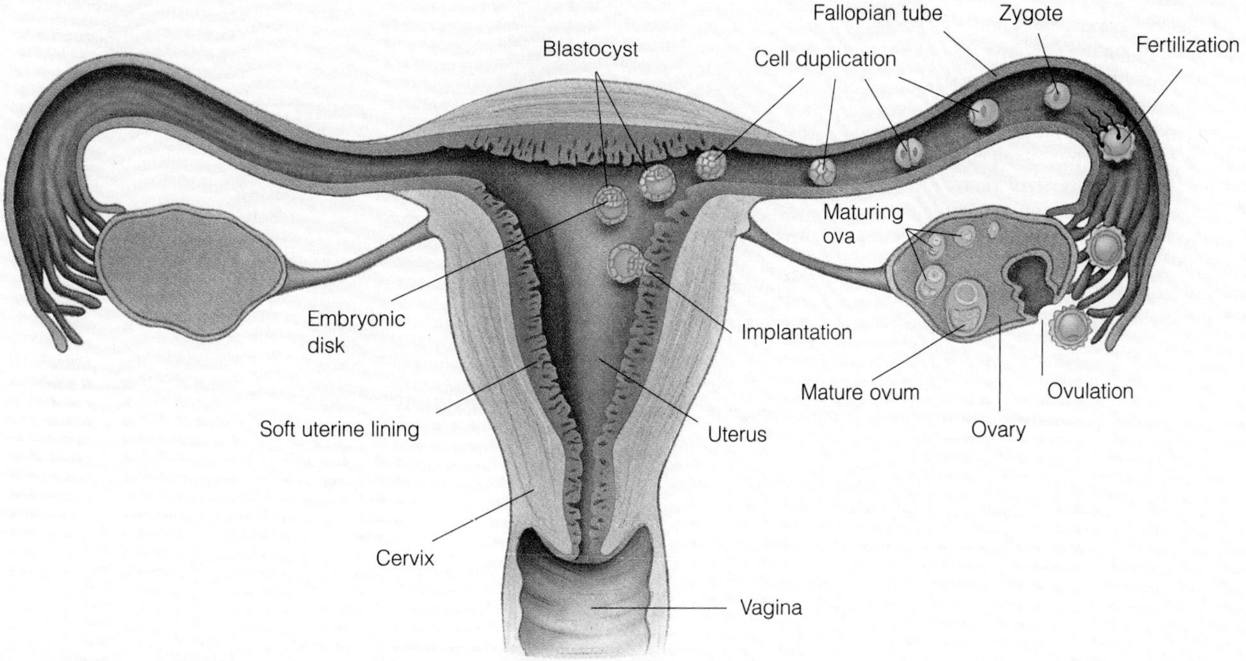

FIGURE 3.3

Development of the blastocyst.
As the zygote moves down the fallopian tube, it begins to duplicate, at first slowly and then more rapidly. By the fourth day, it forms a hollow, fluid-filled ball called a blastocyst. The inner cells will become the new organism; the outer cells will provide protective covering. At the end of the first week, the blastocyst begins to implant in the uterine lining. *(From K. L. Moore and T. V. N. Persaud, 1993,* Before We Are Born, *4th ed., Philadelphia: Saunders, p. 33. Reprinted by permission of the publisher and the author.)*

By the end of the period of the zygote, the developing organism has found food and shelter in the uterus. Already, it is a very complex being. These dramatic beginnings take place before all but the most sensitive mother knows she is pregnant.

THE PERIOD OF THE EMBRYO

The period of the **embryo** lasts from implantation through the eighth week of pregnancy. During these brief 6 weeks, the most rapid prenatal changes take place as the groundwork for all body structures and internal organs is laid down. Because all parts of the body are forming, the embryo is especially vulnerable to interference in healthy development. But the fact that embryonic growth takes place over a fairly short time span helps limit opportunities for serious harm to occur.

Embryo
The prenatal organism from 2 to 8 weeks after conception, during which time the foundations of all body structures and internal organs are laid down.

■ LAST HALF OF THE FIRST MONTH. In the first week of this period, the embryonic disk folds over to form three layers of cells: (1) the *ectoderm,* which will become the nervous system and skin; (2) the *mesoderm,* from which will develop the muscles, skeleton, circulatory system, and other internal organs; and (3) the *endoderm,* which will become the digestive system, lungs, urinary tract, and glands. These three layers give rise to all parts of the body.

FIGURE 3.4

Cross-section of the uterus showing the placenta.
The mother's blood circulates in spaces surrounding the chorionic villi. A membrane between the two blood supplies permits food and oxygen to be delivered and waste products to be carried away. The two blood supplies do not mix directly. *(From L. L. Moore and T. V. N. Persaud, 1993,* Before We Are Born, *4th ed., Philadelphia: Saunders, p. 98. Reprinted by permission of the publisher and the author.)*

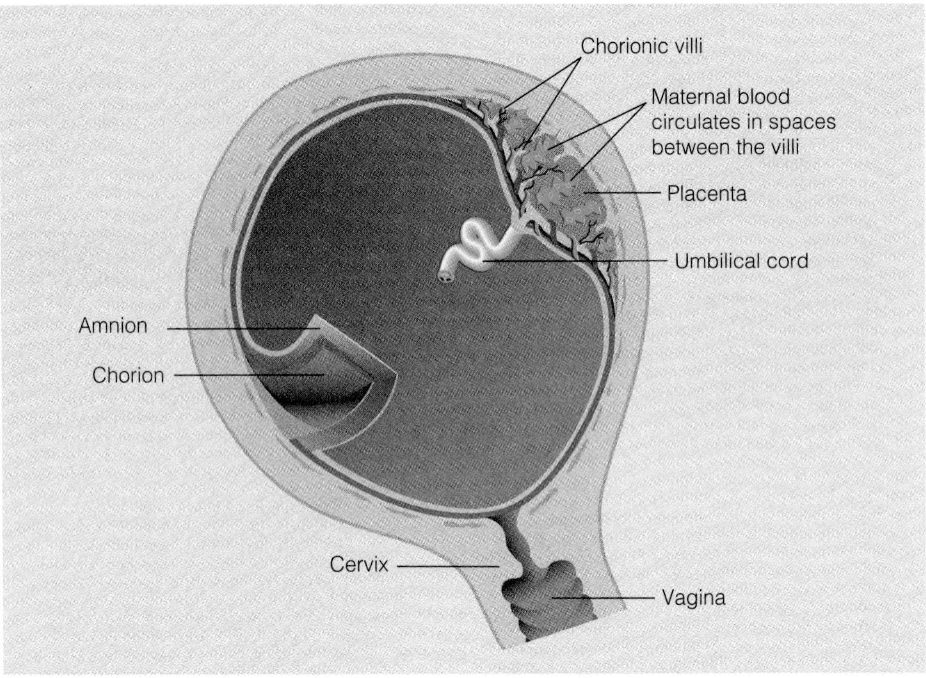

At first, the nervous system develops fastest. The ectoderm folds over to form a **neural tube,** or primitive spinal cord. At 3 1/2 weeks, the top swells to form a brain. Production of *neurons* (brain cells that store and transmit information) begins deep inside the neural tube. Once formed, neurons travel along tiny threads to their permanent locations, where they will form the major parts of the brain (Nowakowski, 1987).

While the nervous system is developing, the heart begins to pump blood around the embryo's circulatory system, and muscles, backbone, ribs, and digestive tract start to appear. At the end of the first month, the curled embryo consists of millions of organized groups of cells with specific functions, although it is only one-fourth of an inch long.

■ THE SECOND MONTH. In the second month, growth continues rapidly. The eyes, ears, nose, jaw, and neck form. Tiny buds become arms, legs, fingers, and toes. Internal organs are more distinct: the intestines grow, the heart develops separate chambers, and the liver and spleen take over production of blood cells so that the yolk sac is no longer needed. Changing body proportions cause the embryo's posture to become more upright. Now an inch long and one-seventh of an ounce in weight, the embryo can already sense its world. It responds to touch, particularly in the mouth area and on the soles of the feet. And it can move, although its tiny flutters are still too light to be felt by the mother (Nilsson & Hamberger, 1990).

Neural tube
The primitive spinal cord that develops from the ectoderm, the top of which swells to form the brain.

Fetus
The prenatal organism from the beginning of the third month to the end of pregnancy, during which time completion of body structures and dramatic growth in size takes place.

THE PERIOD OF THE FETUS

Lasting until the end of pregnancy, the period of the **fetus** is the "growth and finishing" phase. During this longest prenatal period, the developing organism begins to increase rapidly in size. As Figure 3.5 shows, the rate of body growth is extraordinary, especially from the ninth to the twentieth week (Moore & Persaud, 1993).

■ THE THIRD MONTH. In the third month, the organs, muscles, and nervous system start to become organized and connected. The brain signals, and in response, the fetus kicks, bends its arms, forms a fist, curls its toes, opens its mouth, and even sucks its thumb. The tiny lungs begin to expand and contract in

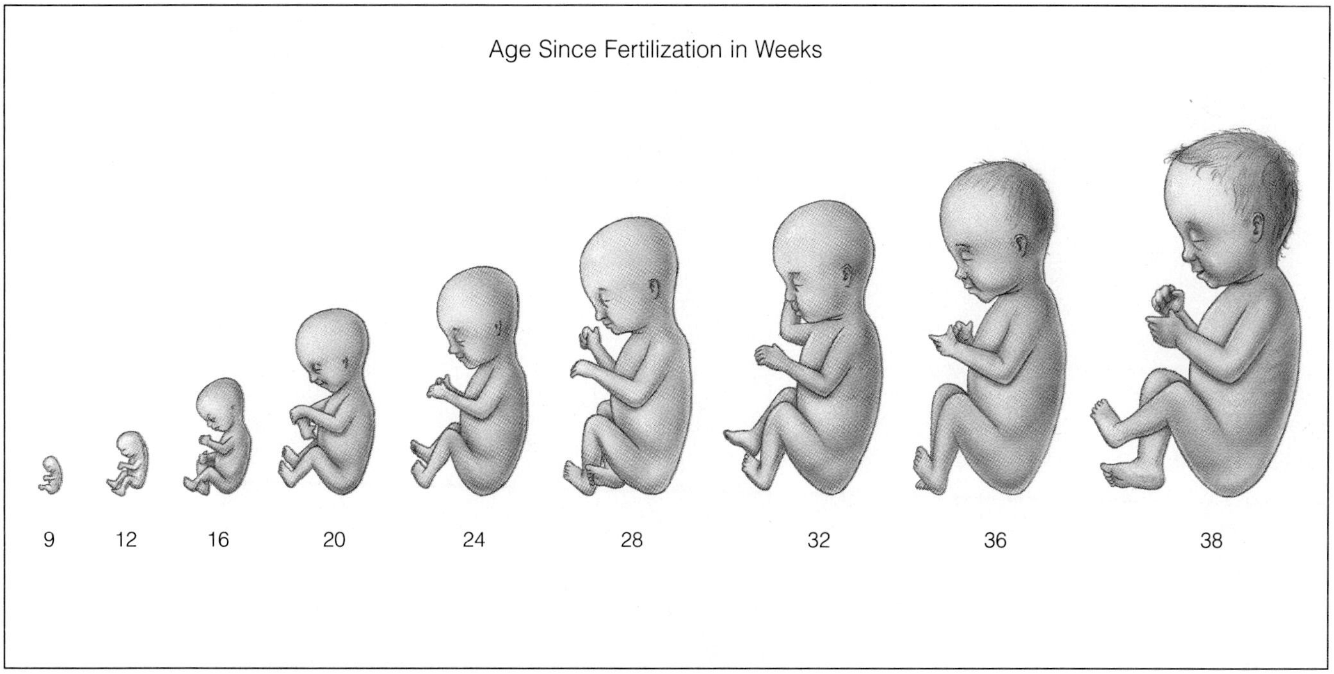

FIGURE 3.5

Rate of body growth during the fetal period.
Increase in size is especially dramatic from the ninth to the twentieth week. The drawings are about one-fifth actual size. *(From K. L. Moore & T. V. N. Persaud, 1993,* Before We Are Born, *4th ed., Philadelphia: Saunders, p. 79. Reprinted by permission of the publisher and the author.)*

an early rehearsal of breathing movements. By the twelfth week, the external genitals are well formed, and the sex of the fetus is evident. Using ultrasound, Yolanda's doctor could see that she would have a boy (although Yolanda and Jay asked not to be told the fetus's sex). Other finishing touches appear, such as fingernails, toenails, tooth buds, and eyelids that open and close. The heartbeat is now stronger and can be heard through a stethoscope.

Prenatal development is sometimes divided into **trimesters,** or three equal periods of time. At the end of the third month, the first trimester is complete. Two more must pass before the fetus is fully prepared to survive outside the womb.

■ THE SECOND TRIMESTER. By the middle of the second trimester, between 17 and 20 weeks, the new being has grown large enough that its movements can be felt by the mother. If we could look inside the uterus at this time, we would find the fetus to be completely covered with a white cheeselike substance called **vernix.** It protects the skin from chapping during the long months spent bathing in the amniotic fluid. A white, downy hair covering called **lanugo** also appears over the entire body, helping the vernix stick to the skin.

At the end of the second trimester, many organs are quite well developed. And a major milestone is reached in brain development, in that all the neurons are now in place. No more will be produced in the individual's lifetime. However, *glial cells,* which support and feed the neurons, continue to increase at a rapid rate throughout the remaining months of pregnancy, as well as after birth (Nowakowski, 1987).

Brain growth means new behavioral capacities. The 20-week-old fetus can be stimulated as well as irritated by sounds. And, if a doctor has reason to look inside the uterus with fetoscopy (see Chapter 2, page 68), fetuses try to shield their eyes from the light with their hands, indicating that the sense of sight has begun to emerge (Nilsson & Hamberger, 1990). Still, a fetus born at this time cannot survive. Its lungs are quite immature, and the brain has not yet developed to the point at which it can control breathing movements and body temperature.

Trimesters
Three equal time periods in prenatal development, each of which lasts 3 months.

Vernix
A white, cheeselike substance covering the fetus and preventing the skin from chapping due to constant exposure to the amniotic fluid.

Lanugo
A white, downy hair that covers the entire body of the fetus, helping the vernix stick to the skin.

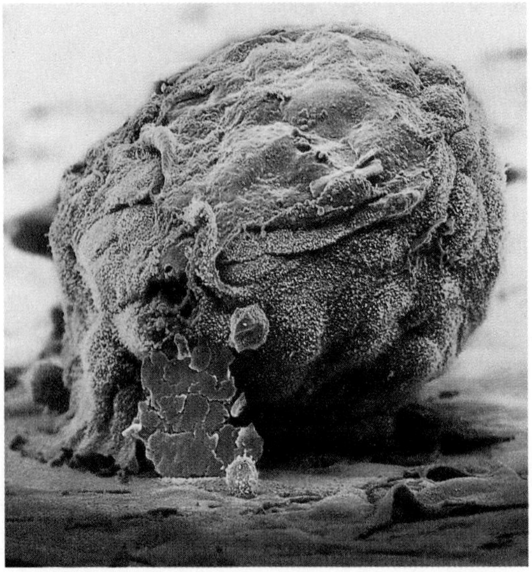

Period of the zygote: seventh to ninth day.
During the period of the zygote, the fertilized ovum begins to duplicate at an increasingly rapid rate, forming a hollow ball of cells, or blastocyst, by the fourth day after fertilization. Here the blastocyst, magnified thousands of times, burrows into the uterine lining between the seventh and ninth day. *(© Lennart Nilsson,* A Child Is Born/*Bonniers)*

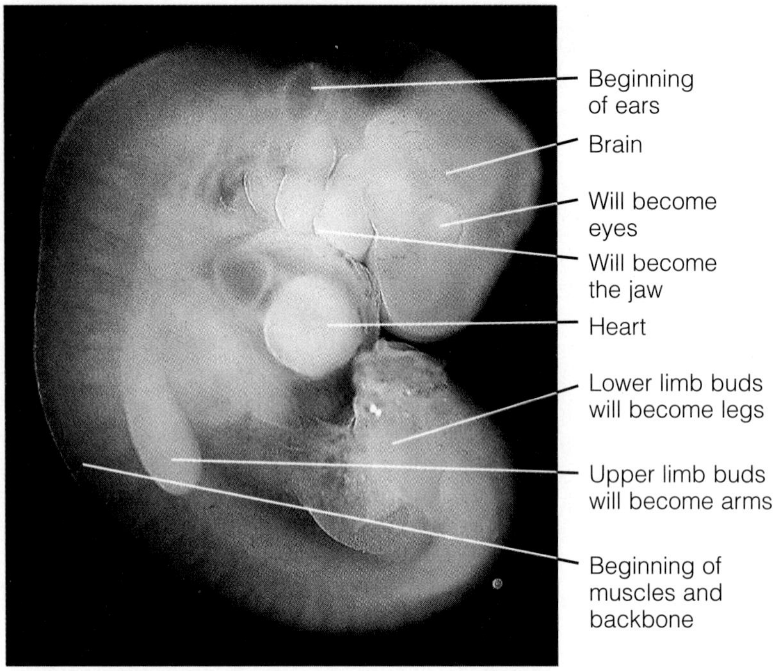

Period of the embryo: fourth week.
In actual size, this 4-week-old embryo is only 1/4-inch long, but many body structures have begun to form. The primitive tail will disappear by the end of the embryonic period. *(© Lennart Nilsson,* A Child Is Born/*Bonniers)*

THE THIRD TRIMESTER. During the final trimester, a fetus born early has a chance for survival outside the womb. The point at which the baby can first survive is called the **age of viability.** It occurs sometime between 22 and 26 weeks (Moore & Persaud, 1993). If born between the seventh and eighth month, breathing would still be a problem, and oxygen assistance would be necessary. Although the respiratory center of the brain is now mature, tiny air sacs in the lungs are not yet ready to inflate and exchange carbon dioxide for oxygen.

The brain continues to make great strides during the last 3 months. The *cerebral cortex,* the most highly evolved part of our brain and the seat of human intelligence, enlarges. At the same time, the fetus responds more clearly to sounds in the external world. Yolanda told me that one day she turned on an electric mixer. The fetus reacted with a forceful startle. By 28 weeks, fetuses blink their eyes in reaction to nearby sounds (Birnholz & Benacerraf, 1983). And in the last weeks of pregnancy, they learn to prefer the tone and rhythm of their mother's voice. In one clever study, mothers were asked to read aloud Dr. Seuss's lively poem *The Cat in the Hat* to their unborn babies for the last 6 weeks of pregnancy. After birth, their infants were given a chance to suck on nipples that turned on recordings of the mother reading this poem or different rhyming stories. The infants sucked hardest to hear *The Cat in the Hat,* the sound they had come to know while still in the womb (DeCasper & Spence, 1986).

During the final 3 months, the fetus gains more than 5 pounds and grows 7 inches. As it fills the uterus, it gradually becomes less active. In the eighth month, a layer of fat is added under its skin to assist with temperature regulation. The fetus also receives antibodies from the mother's blood that protect against illnesses, since the newborn's own immune system will not work well until several months after birth.

In the last weeks, most fetuses assume an upside-down position, partly because of the shape of the uterus and because the head is heavier than the feet. Growth of the fetus starts to slow, and birth is about to take place.

Age of viability
The age at which the fetus can first survive if born early. Occurs sometime between 22 and 26 weeks.

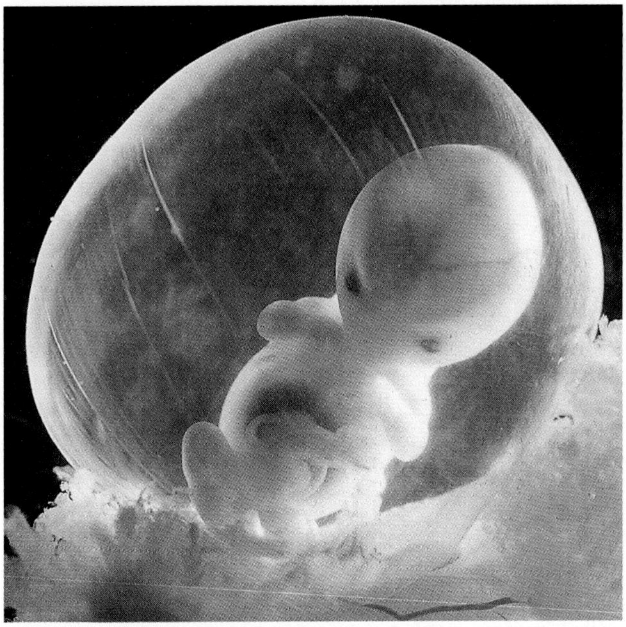

Period of the embryo: seventh week.
At 7 weeks, the embryo's posture is more upright. Body structures—eyes, nose, arms, legs, and internal organs—are more distinct. An embryo of this age responds to touch. It can also move, although at less than an inch long and an ounce in weight, it is still too tiny to be felt by the mother. *(© Lennart Nilsson,* A Child Is Born*/Bonniers)*

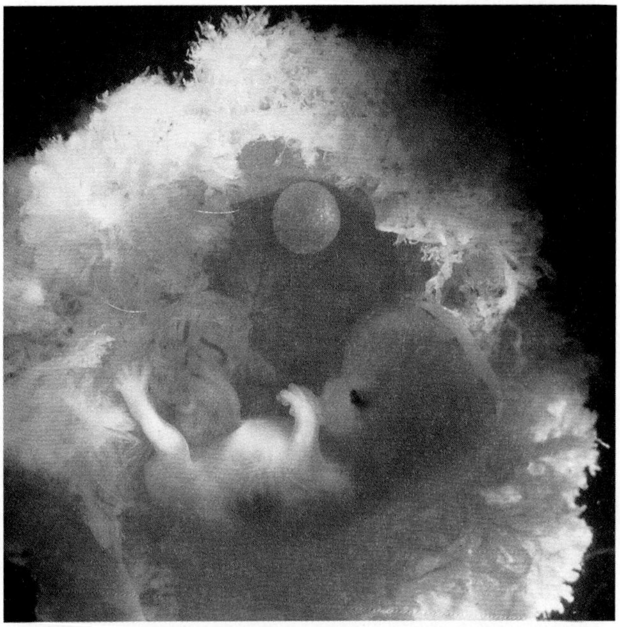

Period of the fetus: eleventh week.
During the period of the fetus, the organism increases rapidly in size, and body structures are completed. At 11 weeks, the brain and muscles are better connected. The fetus can kick, bend its arms, open and close its hands and mouth, and suck its thumb. Notice the yolk sac, which shrinks as pregnancy advances. The internal organs have taken over its function of producing blood cells. *(© Lennart Nilsson,* A Child Is Born*/Bonniers)*

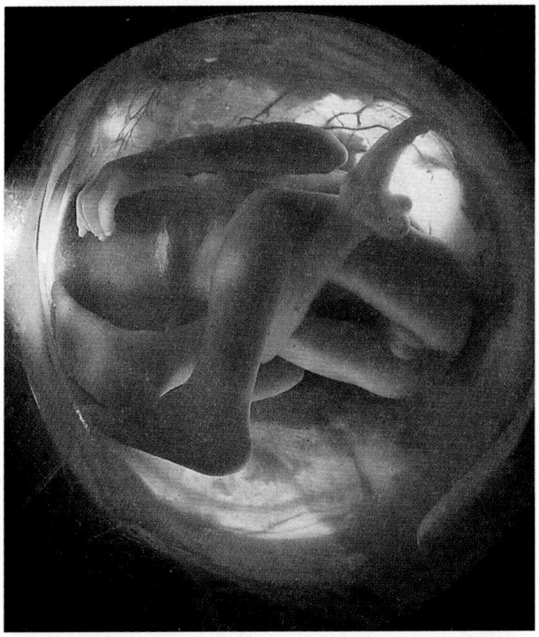

Period of the fetus: twenty-second week.
At 22 weeks, this fetus is almost a foot long and slightly over a pound in weight. Its movements can be easily felt by the mother and by other family members who place a hand on her abdomen. If born at this time, a baby has a slim chance of surviving. *(© Lennart Nilsson,* A Child Is Born*/Bonniers)*

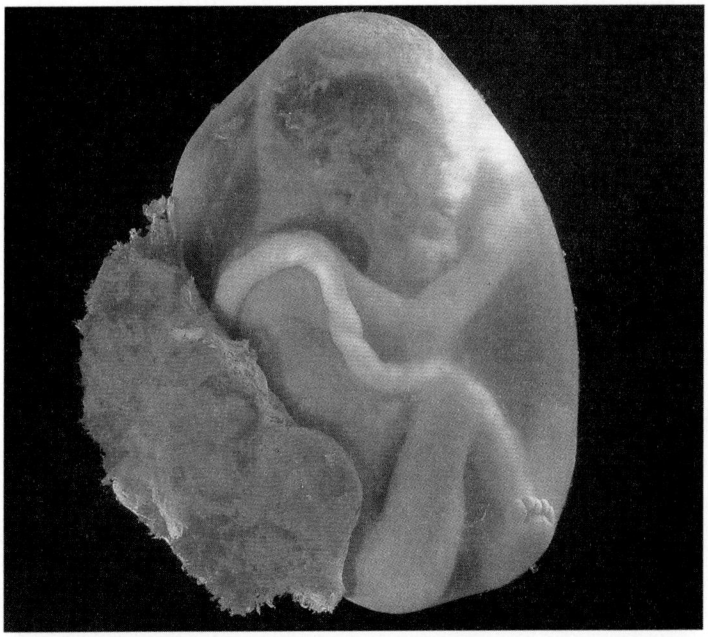

Period of the fetus: thirty-sixth week.
This 36-week-old fetus fills the uterus. To support its need for nourishment, the umbilical cord and placenta have grown very large. Notice the vernix (cheeselike substance) on the skin, which protects it from chapping. The fetus has accumulated a layer of fat to assist with temperature regulation after birth. In another 2 weeks, it would be full term. *(© Lennart Nilsson,* A Child Is Born*/Bonniers)*

ASK YOURSELF . . .

- Amy, who is 2 months pregnant, wonders how the embryo is being fed and what parts of the body have formed. Amy imagines that very little development has yet taken place. How would you answer Amy's questions? Will she be surprised at your response?

BRIEF REVIEW

The vast changes that take place during pregnancy are usually divided into three periods. In the period of the zygote, the tiny one-celled fertilized ovum begins to duplicate and implants itself in the uterine lining. Structures that will feed and protect the developing organism begin to form. During the period of the embryo, the foundations for all body tissues and organs are rapidly laid down. The longest prenatal phase, the period of the fetus, is devoted to growth in size and completion of body systems. Turn back to Table 3.3 on page 104 to review the specific changes during the 9 months before birth.

PRENATAL ENVIRONMENTAL INFLUENCES

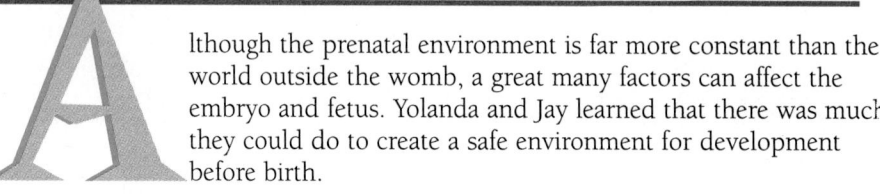

Although the prenatal environment is far more constant than the world outside the womb, a great many factors can affect the embryo and fetus. Yolanda and Jay learned that there was much they could do to create a safe environment for development before birth.

TERATOGENS

The term **teratogen** refers to any environmental agent that causes damage during the prenatal period. It comes from the Greek word *teras,* meaning "malformation" or "monstrosity." This label was selected because scientists first learned about harmful prenatal influences from cases in which babies had been profoundly damaged.

Yet the harm done by teratogens is not always simple and straightforward. It depends on several factors. First, we will see as we discuss particular teratogens that larger doses over longer time periods usually have more negative effects. Second, the genetic makeup of the mother and the developing organism plays an important role. Some individuals are better able to withstand harmful environments. Third, the presence of several negative factors at once, such as poor nutrition, lack of medical care, and additional teratogens, can worsen the impact of a single harmful agent. Fourth, the effects of teratogens vary with the age of the organism at time of exposure. We can best understand this idea if we think of prenatal development in terms of the *sensitive period* concept introduced in Chapter 1. Recall that a sensitive period is a limited time span in which a part of the body or a behavior is biologically prepared to develop rapidly. During that time, it is especially vulnerable to its surroundings. If the environment is harmful, then damage occurs that would not have otherwise happened, and recovery is difficult and sometimes impossible.

Figure 3.6 summarizes sensitive periods during prenatal development. Look carefully at it, and you will see that some parts of the body, such as the brain and eye, have long sensitive periods that extend throughout the prenatal phase. Other sensitive periods, such as those for the limbs and palate, are much shorter. Figure 3.6 also indicates that we can make some general statements about the timing of harmful influences. During the period of the zygote, before implantation, teratogens rarely have any impact. If they do, the tiny mass of cells is usually so completely damaged that it dies. The embryonic period is the time when serious defects are most likely to occur, since the foundations for all body parts are being laid down. During the fetal period, damage caused by teratogens is usually minor. However, some organs, such as the brain, eye, and genitals, can still be strongly affected.

Teratogen
Any environmental agent that causes damage during the prenatal period.

The effects of teratogens are not limited to immediate physical damage. Although deformities of the body are easy to notice, important psychological consequences are harder to identify. Some may not show up until later in development. Others may occur as an indirect effect of physical damage. For example, a defect resulting from drugs the mother took during pregnancy can change reactions of others to the child as well as the child's ability to move about the environment. Over time, parent–child interaction, peer relations, and opportunities to explore may suffer. These experiences, in turn, can have far-reaching consequences for cognitive, emotional, and social development (Kopp & Kaler, 1989; Vorhees & Mollnow, 1987). Notice how an important idea about development that we discussed in earlier chapters is at work here—that of *bidirectional* influences between child and environment. Now let's take a look at what scientists have discovered about a variety of teratogens.

■ PRESCRIPTION AND NONPRESCRIPTION DRUGS. Just about any drug taken by the mother can enter the embryonic or fetal bloodstream. In the early 1960s, the world learned a tragic lesson about drugs and prena-

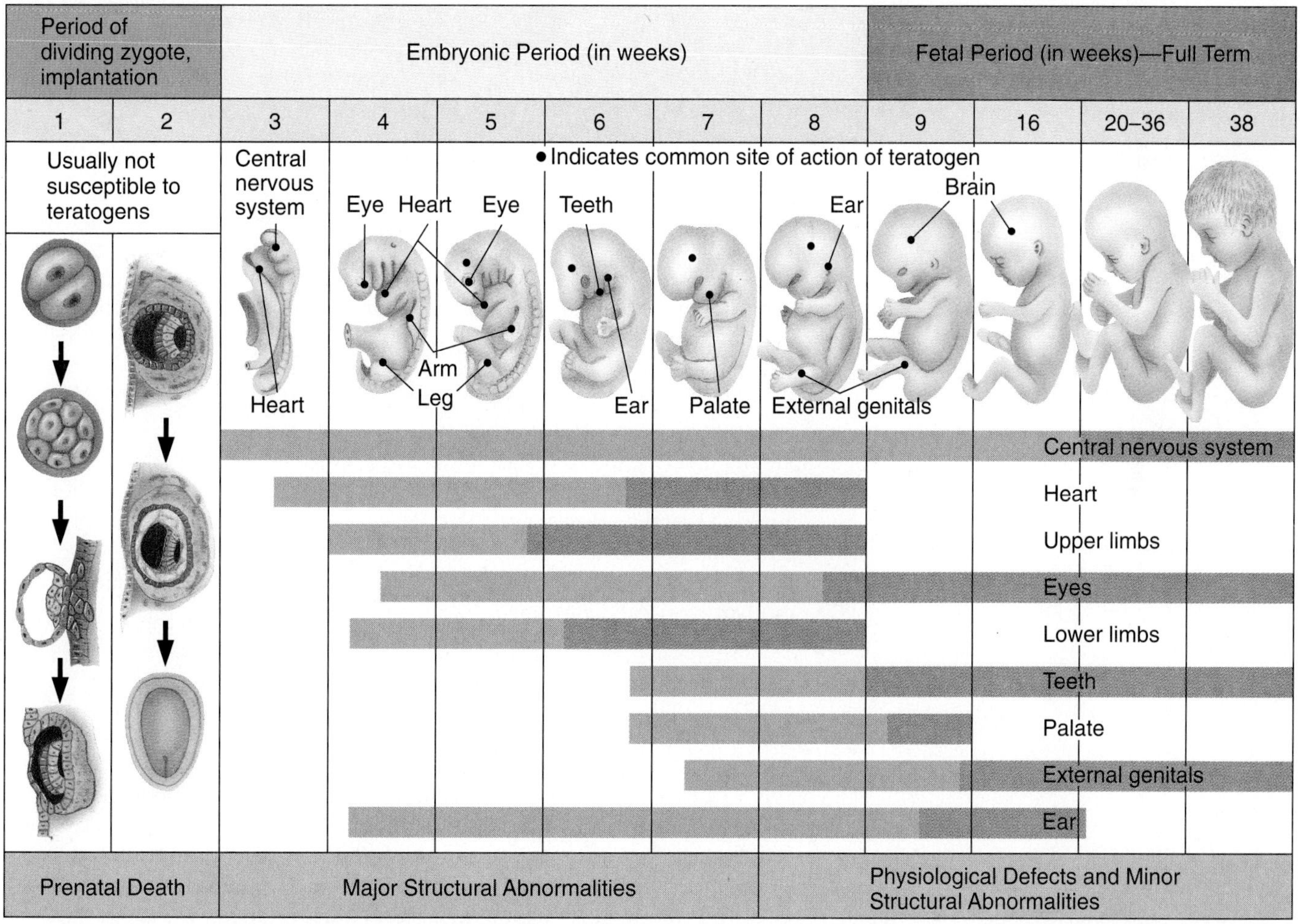

FIGURE 3.6

Sensitive periods in prenatal development.
Each organ or structure has a sensitive period during which its development may be disturbed. Gray horizontal lines indicate highly sensitive periods. Pink horizontal lines indicate periods that are somewhat less sensitive to teratogens, although damage can occur. *(From K. L. Moore & T. V. N. Persaud, 1993,* Before We Are Born, *4th ed., Philadelphia: Saunders, p. 130. Reprinted by permission of the publisher and the author.)*

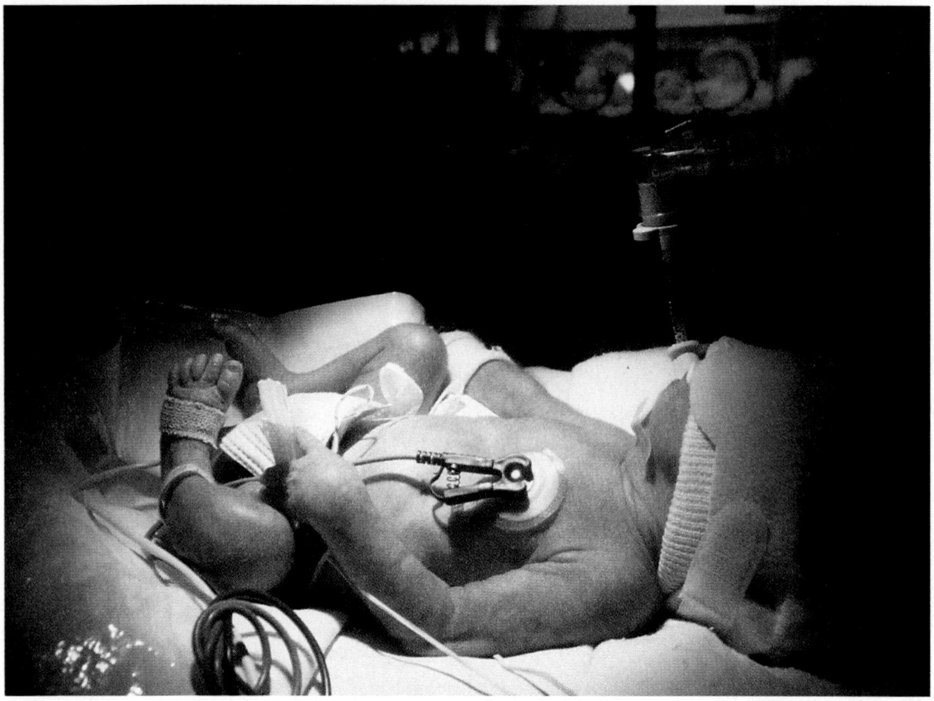

This baby, whose mother took crack during pregnancy, was born many weeks premature. He breathes with the aid of a respirator. His central nervous system may be seriously damaged. Researchers do not yet know if these outcomes are actually caused by crack or by the many other high-risk behaviors of drug users. *(John Giordano/Saba)*

tal development. At that time, a sedative called **thalidomide** was widely available in Europe, Canada, and South America. Although the embryos of test animals were not harmed by it, in humans it had drastic effects. When taken by mothers between the fourth and sixth week after conception, thalidomide produced gross deformities of the embryo's developing arms and legs. About 7,000 infants around the world were affected (Moore & Persaud, 1993). As children exposed to thalidomide grew older, a large number of them scored below average in intelligence. Perhaps the drug damaged the central nervous system directly. Or the child-rearing conditions of these severely deformed youngsters may have impaired their intellectual development (Vorhees & Mollnow, 1987).

Despite the bitter lesson of thalidomide, many pregnant women continue to take over-the-counter drugs without consulting their doctors. Aspirin is one of the most common. Several studies suggest that repeated use of aspirin is linked to low birth weight, infant death around the time of birth, poorer motor development, and lower intelligence test scores in early childhood (Barr et al., 1990; Streissguth et al., 1987). Another frequently consumed drug is caffeine, contained in coffee. Heavy caffeine intake (over 3 cups per day) is associated with prematurity, miscarriage, and newborn withdrawal symptoms, such as irritability and vomiting (Aaronson & MacNee, 1989; Dlugosz & Bracken, 1992).

Because children's lives are involved, we must take findings like these quite seriously. At the same time, it is important to note that we cannot yet be sure that these drugs actually cause the problems just mentioned. Imagine how difficult it is to study the effects of many substances on the unborn! Often mothers take more than one kind of drug. If the prenatal organism is injured, it is hard to tell which drug might be responsible or if other factors correlated with drug taking are really at fault. Until we have more information, the safest course of action is the one that Yolanda took: cut down on or avoid these drugs entirely.

Thalidomide
A sedative widely available in Europe, Canada, and South America in the early 1960s. When taken by mothers between the fourth to sixth week after conception, it produced gross deformities of the embryo's arms and legs.

■ ILLEGAL DRUGS. The use of highly addictive mood-altering drugs, such as cocaine and heroin, is become more widespread, especially in poverty-stricken inner-city areas where they provide a temporary escape from a daily life of hopelessness. The number of "cocaine babies" born in the United States has reached crisis levels in recent years. About 400,000 infants are affected annually (Waller, 1993). Here is a brief account of what two of these hospitalized newborns looked like:

> Guillermo . . . has spent his whole short life crying. He is jittery and goes into spasms when he is touched. His eyes don't focus. He can't stick out his tongue, or suck. Born a week ago to a cocaine addict, Guillermo is described by his doctors as an addict himself. Nearby, . . . Paul lies motionless in an incubator, feeding tubes riddling his tiny body. He needs a respirator to breathe and a daily spinal tap to relieve fluid buildup on his brain. Only one month old, he has already suffered two strokes. (Barol, 1986, p. 56)

Babies born to users of cocaine, heroin, or methadone (a less addictive drug used to wean people away from heroin) are at risk for a wide variety of problems, including prematurity, low birth weight, physical defects, breathing difficulties, and death around the time of birth. In addition, these infants arrive drug-addicted. Guillermo and Paul were feverish and irritable at birth. They had trouble sleeping, and their cries were abnormally shrill and piercing—a common symptom among stressed newborns that we will discuss in Chapter 4 (Allen et al., 1991; Little et al., 1989). When mothers with many problems of their own must take care of these babies, who are difficult to calm down, cuddle, and feed, behavior problems are likely to persist.

Throughout the first year of life, heroin- and methadone-exposed infants are less attentive to the environment, and their motor development is slow. After infancy, some children get better, whereas others remain jittery and inattentive. Researchers believe that the kind of parenting these youngsters receive may explain why there are lasting problems for some but not for others (Vorhees & Mollnow, 1987).

Unlike findings on heroin and methadone, growing evidence on cocaine suggests that large numbers of prenatally exposed babies have lasting difficulties. Cocaine is linked to a specific set of physical defects. These include genital, urinary tract, kidney, and heart deformities as well as brain seizures (Chasnoff et al., 1989). Throughout the first year, cocaine-exposed infants are less responsive to new stimulation, and they learn more slowly than their nonexposed agemates (Alessandri et al., 1993). Babies born to mothers who smoke crack (a cheap form of cocaine that delivers high doses quickly through the lungs) seem to be worst off in terms of low birth weight and damage to the central nervous system (Kaye et al., 1989). Fathers may also contribute to these effects. Research suggests that cocaine can attach itself to sperm, "hitchhike" its way into the zygote, and cause birth defects (Yazigi, Odem, & Polakoski, 1991). Still, it is difficult to isolate the precise damage caused by cocaine, since users often take several drugs and engage in other high-risk behaviors (Gonzalez & Campbell, 1994).

Marijuana is another illegal drug that is used more widely than cocaine and heroin. Studies examining its relationship to low birth weight and prematurity reveal mixed findings (Fried & O'Connell, 1987; Zuckerman, Frank, & Hingson, 1989). Nevertheless, prenatal marijuana exposure is related to newborn startles, an abnormally high-pitched cry, and reduced attention to the environment (Fried & Makin, 1987; Lester & Dreher, 1989). These outcomes certainly put newborn babies at risk for future problems, even though long-term effects have not been established.

■ **CIGARETTE SMOKING.** Although smoking has recently declined in the United States, an estimated 29 percent of men and 26 percent of women continue to use cigarettes (U.S. Bureau of the Census, 1994). The most well-known effect of smoking during pregnancy is low birth weight. But the likelihood of other serious consequences, such as prematurity, miscarriage, and infant death, is also increased. The more cigarettes a mother smokes, the greater the chances that her baby will be affected. If a pregnant woman decides to stop smoking at any time,

Smoking during pregnancy is associated with low birth weight, prematurity, miscarriage, and infant death. During childhood, youngsters who were prenatally exposed to nicotine may be at risk for attentional and learning problems. This mother can still protect her child by giving up smoking immediately. *(Innervisions)*

even during the last trimester, she can help her baby. She immediately reduces the chances that the infant will be born underweight and suffer from future problems (Ahlsten, Cnattingius, & Lindmark, 1993; Li, Windsor, & Perkins, 1993).

Even when a baby of a smoking mother appears to be born in good physical condition, slight behavioral abnormalities may threaten the child's development. Newborns of smoking mothers are less attentive to sounds and display more muscle tension (Fried & Makin, 1987). An unresponsive, restless baby may not evoke the kind of interaction from adults that promotes healthy psychological development. Some long-term studies report that prenatally exposed children have shorter attention spans and poorer mental test scores in early childhood, even after many other factors have been controlled (Fried & Watkinson, 1990; Fergusson, Horwood, & Lynskey, 1993). But other researchers have not been able to confirm these findings, so lasting effects remain uncertain (Barr et al., 1990; Streissguth et al., 1989).

Exactly how can smoking harm the fetus? Nicotine, the addictive substance in tobacco, causes the placenta to grow abnormally. As a result, transfer of nutrients is reduced, and the fetus gains weight poorly. Also, smoking raises the concentration of carbon monoxide in the bloodstreams of both mother and fetus. Carbon monoxide displaces oxygen from red blood cells. It damages the central nervous system and reduces birth weight in the fetuses of laboratory animals. Similar effects may occur in humans (Aaronson & MacNee, 1989; Nash & Persaud, 1988).

Finally, Jay made a special effort to give up cigarettes when Yolanda became pregnant. Newborn infants of fathers who smoke are also likely to be underweight! Jay realized that a smoke-filled environment at home could harm the fetus by turning Yolanda into a "passive smoker" who inhaled nicotine and carbon monoxide from the air around her (Makin, Fried, & Watkinson, 1991; Schwartz-Bickenbach et al., 1987).

■ ALCOHOL. Recently, Michael Dorris (1989), a Dartmouth University anthropology professor, wrote *The Broken Cord.* In this moving story, Dorris describes what it was like to raise his adopted son Adam, whose biological mother drank heavily throughout pregnancy and died of alcohol poisoning shortly after his birth. A Sioux Indian boy, Adam was 3 years old when he came into Dorris's life. He was short and underweight and had a vocabulary of only 20 words. But Dorris was sure that with extra care and attention, Adam would overcome these problems.

Unfortunately, Adam's difficulties did not go away. Although he ate well, Adam grew slowly and remained painfully thin. He was prone to infection and had repeated brain seizures. His vocabulary did not expand like that of normal preschoolers. When he was 7, special testing revealed that Adam's intelligence was below average and that he had difficulty concentrating. At age 12, he could not add, subtract, or identify the town in which he lived.

Around that time, Dorris learned the cause of Adam's problems. A counselor who worked with Native-American adolescents looked at a photograph of Adam and noticed his small head, flat nose, and droopy eyelids. "FAS, too, huh?" he remarked (p. 138). Now an adult, Adam has difficulty keeping a routine job and suffers from poor judgment. He might buy something and not wait for change, open a window on a cold night and fail to close it, or wander off in the middle of a task. His case, along with many others like it, reveals that the damage done by alcohol to the embryo and fetus cannot be undone.

Fetal alcohol syndrome (FAS)
A set of defects that results when women consume large amounts of alcohol during most or all of pregnancy. Includes mental retardation, slow physical growth, and facial abnormalities.

Fetal alcohol syndrome (FAS) is the scientific name for Adam's condition. Mental retardation, poor attention, and overactivity are typical of children with the disorder (Steinhausen, Willms, & Spohr, 1993). Distinct physical symptoms also accompany it. These include slow physical growth and a particular pattern of facial abnormalities: widely spaced eyes, short eyelid openings, a small upturned nose, and a thin upper lip. The small heads of these children indicate that the brain has been prevented from reaching full development. Other defects—of the eyes, ears, nose, throat, heart, genitals, urinary tract, or immune system—might also be present. In all babies born with FAS, the mother drank heavily through most or all of her pregnancy (Aaronson & MacNee, 1989; Hoyseth & Jones, 1989).

Sometimes children do not display all the abnormalities just described—only some of them. In these cases, the child is said to suffer from **fetal alcohol effects (FAE).** Usually, the mothers of these children drank alcohol in smaller quantities. The particular defects of FAE children vary with the timing and length of alcohol exposure during pregnancy (Hoyseth & Jones, 1989).

How does alcohol produce its devastating consequences? Researchers believe it does so in two ways. First, alcohol interferes with cell duplication and migration in the primitive neural tube. Autopsies of FAS babies show a reduced number of brain cells and major structural abnormalities (Nowakowski, 1987). Second, large quantities of oxygen are required to metabolize alcohol in the human body. When pregnant women drink heavily, they draw oxygen away from the embryo or fetus that is vital for cell growth in the brain and other parts of the body (Vorhees & Mollnow, 1987).

Like heroin and cocaine, alcohol abuse is higher in poverty-stricken sectors of the population, especially among Native Americans. On the reservation where Adam was born, many children show symptoms of prenatal alcohol exposure. Unfortunately, when girls with FAS or FAE later become pregnant, the poor judgment caused by the syndrome often prevents them from understanding why they should avoid alcohol themselves. Thus, the tragic cycle is likely to repeat itself in the next generation.

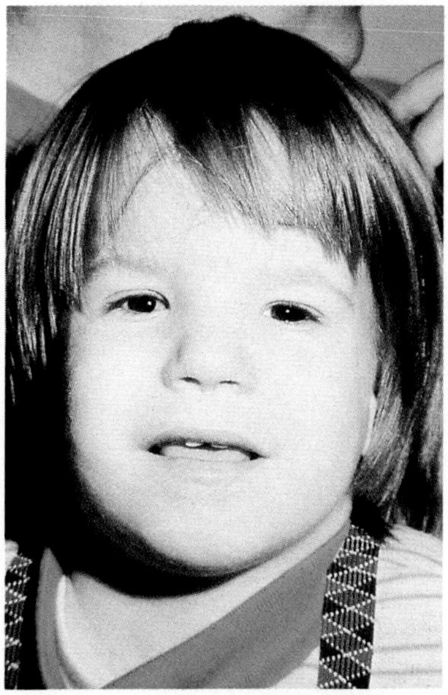

The mother of this severely retarded boy drank heavily during pregnancy. His widely spaced eyes, thin upper lip, and short eyelid openings are typical of fetal alcohol syndrome. *(Fetal Alcohol Syndrome Research Fund, University of Washington)*

At this point, you may be wondering: How much alcohol is safe during pregnancy? Is it all right to have a drink or two, either on a daily basis or occasionally? A recent study found that as little as 2 ounces of alcohol a day, taken very early in pregnancy, was associated with FAS-like facial features (Astley et al., 1992). But recall that other factors—both genetic and environmental—can make some fetuses more vulnerable to teratogenic effects. Therefore, a precise dividing line between safe and dangerous drinking levels cannot be established. Research shows that the more alcohol consumed during pregnancy, the poorer a child's motor coordination, speed of information processing, and intelligence and achievement test scores during the preschool and school years (Barr et al., 1990; Jacobson et al., 1993; Streissguth et al., 1989). These dose-related effects indicate that it is best for pregnant women to avoid alcohol entirely.

■ HORMONES. In Chapter 2, we saw that the Y chromosome causes male sex hormones (called *androgens*) to be secreted prenatally, leading to formation of male reproductive organs. In the absence of male hormones, female structures develop. Hormones are released as part of a delicately balanced system. If their quantity or timing is off, then defects of the genitals as well as other organs can occur.

Between 1945 and 1970, a synthetic hormone called **diethylstilbestrol** (DES) was widely used to prevent miscarriages in women who had a history of pregnancy problems. As the daughters of these mothers reached adolescence and young adulthood, they showed an unusually high rate of cancer of the vagina and malformations of the uterus. When they tried to have children, their pregnancies more often resulted in prematurity, low birth weight, and miscarriage than those of non-DES-exposed women. Young men whose mothers took DES prenatally were also affected. They showed an increased risk of genital abnormalities and cancer of the testes (Linn et al., 1988; Stillman, 1982). Because of these findings, pregnant women are no longer treated with DES. But many individuals whose mothers took it are now of childbearing age, and they need to be carefully monitored by their doctors.

Sometimes mothers take other hormones that could damage the embryo or fetus. For example, occasionally a woman continues to use birth control pills during the early weeks after conception, before she knows she is pregnant. Research has linked oral contraceptives to heart and limb deformities, although additional studies are needed to confirm this relationship (Grimes & Mishell, 1988; Kricker et al., 1986).

Fetal alcohol effects (FAE) The condition of children who display some but not all the defects of fetal alcohol syndrome. Usually their mothers drank alcohol in smaller quantities during pregnancy.

Diethylstilbestrol (DES) A synthetic hormone widely used between 1945 and 1970 to prevent miscarriage. It increases the chances of genital tract abnormalities and cancer of the vagina and testes in adolescence and young adulthood.

RADIATION. In Chapter 2, we saw that ionizing radiation can cause mutation, damaging the DNA in ova and sperm. When mothers are exposed to radiation during pregnancy, additional harm can come to the embryo or fetus. Defects due to radiation were tragically apparent in the children born to pregnant Japanese women who survived the bombing of Hiroshima and Nagasaki during World War II. Miscarriage, slow physical growth, an underdeveloped brain, and malformations of the skeleton and eyes were common (Michel, 1989). Even when an exposed child appears normal at birth, the possibility of later problems cannot be ruled out. For example, research suggests that even low-level radiation, as the result of industrial leakage or medical X-rays, can increase the risk of childhood cancer (Smith, 1992). Women need to tell their doctors if they are pregnant or trying to become pregnant before X-ray examinations. In addition, they should avoid work environments in which they might be exposed to X-rays.

ENVIRONMENTAL POLLUTION. Yolanda and Jay like to refinish antique furniture in their garage, and Jay is an enthusiastic grower of fruit trees in the backyard. When Yolanda became pregnant, they postponed work on several pieces of furniture, and Jay did not spray the fruit trees in the fall and spring of that year. Continuing to do so, they learned, might expose Yolanda and the embryo or fetus to chemical levels thousands of times greater than judged safe by the federal government (Samuels & Samuels, 1986).

An astounding number of potentially dangerous chemicals are released into the environment in industrialized nations. In the United States, 100,000 are in common use, and 1,000 new ones are introduced each year. Although many chemicals cause serious birth defects in laboratory animals, the impact on the human embryo and fetus is known for only a small number of them.

Mercury and Lead. Among heavy metals, mercury and lead are established teratogens. In the 1950s, an industrial plant released waste containing high levels of mercury into a bay providing food and water for the town of Minimata, Japan. Many children born at the time were mentally retarded and showed other serious symptoms, including abnormal speech, difficulty in chewing and swallowing, and uncoordinated movements. Autopsies of those who died revealed widespread brain damage (Vorhees & Mollnow, 1987).

Pregnant women can absorb lead from car exhaust, lead-based paint flaking off the walls in old houses and apartment buildings, and other materials used in industrial occupations. High levels of lead exposure are consistently linked to prematurity, low birth weight, brain damage, and a wide variety of physical defects (Dye-White, 1986). Even a very low level of prenatal lead exposure seems to be dangerous. Affected babies show slightly poorer mental development during the first 2 years of life (Bellinger et al., 1987; Ernhart et al., 1985).

Polychlorinated Biphenyls (PCBs). For many years, polychlorinated biphenyls (PCBs) were used to insulate electrical equipment. In 1977, they were banned by the federal government after research showed that, like mercury, they found their way into waterways and entered the food supply. In one study, newborn babies of women who frequently ate PCB-contaminated fish caught in Lake Michigan were compared to newborns whose mothers ate little or no fish. The PCB-exposed babies had a variety of problems, including slightly lower than average birth weight, smaller heads (suggesting brain damage), and less interest in their surroundings (Jacobson et al., 1984). When studied again at 7 months of age, infants whose mothers ate fish during pregnancy did more poorly on memory tests (Jacobson et al., 1985). A follow-up at 4 years of age showed persisting memory difficulties and lower verbal intelligence test scores (Jacobson, Jacobson, & Humphrey, 1990; Jacobson et al., 1992).

TABLE 3.4

Effects of Some Infectious Diseases during Pregnancy

DISEASE	MISCARRIAGE	PHYSICAL MALFORMATIONS	MENTAL RETARDATION	LOW BIRTH WEIGHT AND PREMATURITY
Viral				
Acquired immune deficiency syndrome (AIDS)	0	?	+	?
Chicken pox	0	+	+	+
Cytomegalovirus	+	+	+	+
Herpes simplex 2 (genital herpes)	+	+	+	+
Mumps	+	?	0	0
Rubella	+	+	+	+
Bacterial				
Syphilis	+	+	+	?
Tuberculosis	+	?	+	+
Parasitic				
Malaria	+	0	0	+
Toxoplasmosis	+	+	+	+

Note: + established finding, 0 = no present evidence, ? = possible effect that is not clearly established.

Adapted from F. L. Cohen, 1984, *Clinical Genetics in Nursing Practice*, Philadelphia: Lippincott, p. 33. Reprinted by permission.

Additional *Sources:* Chatkupt et al., 1989; Cohen, 1993a; Peckham & Logan, 1993; Samson, 1988; Sever, 1983; Vorhees, 1986; Qazi et al., 1988.

■ MATERNAL DISEASE. On her first prenatal visit, Yolanda's doctor asked if she and Jay had already had measles, mumps, chicken pox, as well as other illnesses. In addition, Yolanda was checked for the presence of several infections, and for good reason. As you can see in Table 3.4, certain diseases during pregnancy are major causes of miscarriage and birth defects.

Five percent of women catch a virus of some sort while pregnant, such as the common cold or a strain of the flu. Most of these illnesses appear to have no impact on the embryo or fetus. However, a few viruses can cause extensive damage. The best known of these is **rubella** (three-day or German measles). In the mid-1960s, a worldwide epidemic of rubella led to the birth of over 20,000 American babies with serious defects. Consistent with the sensitive period concept, the greatest damage occurs when rubella strikes during the embryonic period. Over 50 percent of infants whose mothers became ill during that time show heart defects; eye cataracts; deafness; genital, urinary, and intestinal abnormalities; and mental retardation. Infection during the fetal period is less harmful, but low birth weight, hearing loss, and bone defects may still occur (Eberhart-Phillips et al., 1993; Samson, 1988). Since 1966, infants and young children have been routinely vaccinated against rubella, so the number of prenatal cases today is much less than it was a generation ago. Still, 10 to 20 percent of American women of childbearing age lack the rubella antibody, so new outbreaks of the disease are still possible (Lee et al., 1992).

Table 3.4 summarizes the harmful effects of other common viruses. The developing organism is especially sensitive to the family of herpes viruses, for which there is no vaccine or treatment. Among these, cytomegalovirus (the most frequent prenatal infection, transmitted through respiratory or sexual contact) and herpes simplex 2 (which is sexually transmitted) are especially dangerous. In both, the

Rubella
Three-day German measles. Causes a wide variety of prenatal abnormalities, especially when it strikes during the embryonic period.

virus invades the mother's genital tract. Babies can be infected either during pregnancy or at birth. **Acquired immune deficiency syndrome (AIDS)** is a relatively new, deadly viral disease that is infecting increasing numbers of newborn babies. To find out about its prenatal transmission, refer to the Social Issues box on the following page.

Table 3.4 also includes several bacterial and parasitic diseases. Among the most common is **toxoplasmosis,** caused by a parasite found in many animals. Pregnant women may become infected from eating raw or undercooked meat or from contact with the feces of infected cats. About 40 percent of women who have the disease transmit it to the developing organism. When they do, the effects can be devastating. During the first trimester, the disease often leads to severe eye and brain damage. Later infection is linked to mild visual and cognitive impairments (Bobak, Jensen, & Zalar, 1989; Peckham & Logan, 1993). Expectant mothers can avoid toxoplasmosis by making sure that the meat they eat is well cooked. Also, pet cats should be checked for the disease and care of their litter boxes turned over to other family members. Outdoor garden areas that cats may have used should be avoided as well.

OTHER MATERNAL FACTORS

Besides avoiding teratogens, expectant parents can support the development of the embryo or fetus in other ways. Regular exercise, good nutrition, and emotional well-being of the mother are crucially important. Blood type differences between mother and fetus can create difficulties. Finally, many expectant parents wonder how a mother's age and previous births affect the course of a particular pregnancy. We examine each of these factors in the following sections.

EXERCISE. Yolanda continued her daily half-hour of aerobics into the third trimester, although her doctor cautioned her to avoid bouncing, jolting, and jogging movements that might subject the fetus to too many shocks and startles. In healthy, physically fit women, regular exercise, such as swimming, hiking, and aerobics, is related to increased birth weight (Hatch et al., 1993). Hospital-sponsored childbirth education programs frequently offer special exercise classes and suggest particular routines that help prepare for labor and delivery. Exercises that strengthen the back, abdominal, pelvic, and thigh muscles are emphasized, since the growing fetus places some strain on these parts of the body (Nilsson & Hamberger, 1990; Samuels & Samuels, 1986).

During the last trimester, when the abdomen grows very large, mothers find it difficult to move freely and often need to cut back on exercise. In most cases, a mother who has remained fit during the earlier months is likely to experience fewer of the physical discomforts that arise at this time, such as back pain, upward pressure on the chest, and difficulty in breathing.

Finally, pregnant women with health problems, such as circulatory difficulties or a history of miscarriages, should consult their doctors before beginning or continuing a physical fitness routine. For these mothers, exercise (especially the wrong kind) can endanger the pregnancy.

NUTRITION. Children grow more rapidly during the prenatal period than at any other phase of development. During this time, they depend totally on the mother for nutrients to support their growth. Many people believe that the embryo or fetus, much like a parasite, simply takes what it needs from the mother's body. They think that if the mother is poorly nourished, only she (and not the baby) will suffer. Since the 1940s and 1950s, a great many studies have proved this parasite theory to be incorrect. Children born to mothers with inadequate diets are more likely to be born premature and underweight, to die within the first year of life, and to have physical defects (Burke et al., 1943; Jeans, Smith, & Stearns, 1955; Kaplan, 1972; Philipps & Johnson, 1977).

Acquired immune deficiency syndrome (AIDS)
A relatively new viral infection that destroys the immune system and is spread through transfer of body fluids from one person to another. It can be transmitted prenatally.

Toxoplasmosis
A parasitic disease caused by eating raw or undercooked meat or contact with the feces of infected cats. During the first trimester, it leads to eye and brain damage.

SOCIAL ISSUES

PRENATAL TRANSMISSION OF AIDS

The first-born child of Jean and Claire, Ginette was diagnosed with AIDS when she was 6 months old. She died from respiratory infections and a failure to grow normally at 11 months of age. Immigrants from the Caribbean to Florida, Jean and Claire could not understand the social worker's explanation of why Ginette died. After all, neither parent felt sick. At the time, Claire was pregnant with a second baby. Several weeks after Ginette's death, Jeanine was born. In the meantime, friends learned that AIDS caused Ginette's death. When word spread, Jean lost his job, the family was evicted from their apartment, and friends and relatives started to avoid Jean and Claire. Over the next year, Claire gave birth to a son, Junior, and also became pregnant for a fourth time. During this pregnancy, both Claire and Jeanine began to show symptoms of AIDS infection. Claire's condition worsened. Her fourth child was born prematurely, and Claire and the baby died soon after. Jean was grief-stricken over Claire's death. Many months later, an uncle brought Jeanine and Junior to the hospital; they were eventually placed in foster care. Junior was tested for the AIDS virus. Unlike his sisters, he managed to escape it. Jean, who left the family and may have died of AIDS, was never heard from again. (Paraphrased from Siebert et al., 1989, pp. 36–38)

AIDS is a relatively new viral disease that destroys the immune system. Affected individuals like Jean, Claire, and their children eventually die of a wide variety of illnesses that their bodies can no longer fight. Adults at greatest risk include male homosexuals and bisexuals, users of illegal drugs who share needles, and their heterosexual partners. Transfer of body fluids from one person to another is necessary for AIDS to spread.

The percentage of AIDS victims who are female has risen dramatically over the past decade, from 3 to 12 percent. When women carrying the AIDS virus become pregnant, about 20 to 30 percent of the time they pass the deadly disease to the embryo or fetus. The likelihood of transmission is greatest when a woman already has AIDS symptoms, but (as Claire's case reveals) it can occur beforehand as well. Exactly why only some offspring are affected is not well understood. It may depend on timing of maternal infection, the condition of the placenta, heredity, and other factors. Besides prenatal infection, infants can contract the AIDS virus during the birth process, when exposure to maternal fluids increases. According to the U.S. Centers for Disease Control, nearly 4,000 childhood cases of AIDS have been diagnosed in the United States since 1981. Worldwide, about 1 million children are infected. The large majority (85 percent) are infants who received the virus before or during birth, often from a drug-abusing mother (Cohen, 1993a, 1993b; Grant, 1994).

AIDS symptoms generally take a long time to emerge in older children and adults—up to 5 years after infection with the virus. In contrast, the disease proceeds rapidly in infants. Most infected babies are born with abnormalities of the immune system (Mayers et al., 1991). By 6 months of age, weight loss, fever, diarrhea, and repeated respiratory illnesses are common. The virus also causes serious brain damage. Infants with AIDS show a loss in brain weight over time, accompanied by seizures, delayed mental and motor development, and abnormal muscle tone and movements. Like Ginette, most infants survive for only 5 to 8 months after the appearance of these symptoms (Chamberlain, Nichols, & Chase, 1991; Chatkupt et al., 1989).

Prenatal AIDS babies are generally born to urban, poverty-stricken parents. Lack of money to pay for medical treatment, rejection by relatives and friends who do not understand the disease, and anxiety about the child's future cause tremendous stress in these families. Medical services for young children with AIDS and counseling for their parents are badly needed (Kurth, 1993).

Currently, scientists are exploring ways to interrupt prenatal AIDS transmission using the drug AZT and other antiviral agents (Ferrazin, De Maria, & Gotta, 1993). Until a preventive method or cure is found, education of adolescents and adults about the disease and outreach programs that get women at high risk for infection into drug treatment programs are the only ways to stop continued spread of the virus to children (Kneisl, 1993).

TRY THIS . . .

- When is testing of prospective mothers warranted to find out if they carry the AIDS virus? Consult your library to find the stance of major professional organizations, such as the American Nurses Association and the American Academy of Pediatrics, on this issue. Why should such testing always be done confidentially and with counseling services available?

Mild, regular exercise keeps a mother fit during pregnancy and helps her prepare for the hard physical work of labor and delivery. It is also related to increased birth weight. *(Mike Malyszko/Stock Boston)*

During World War II, a severe famine occurred in the Netherlands, giving scientists a rare opportunity to study the impact of nutrition on prenatal development. Findings revealed that the sensitive period concept operates with nutrition, just as it does with the teratogens discussed earlier in this chapter. Women affected by the famine during the first trimester were more likely to have miscarriages or to give birth to babies with physical defects. When women were past the first trimester, fetuses were more likely to survive, but many were born underweight and had small heads (suggesting an underdeveloped brain) (Stein et al., 1975).

We now know that prenatal malnutrition can damage the central nervous system and other parts of the body. Autopsies of malnourished babies who died at or shortly after birth reveal fewer brain cells, a brain weight that is as much as 36 percent below average, and abnormal brain organization. The poorer the mother's diet, the greater the loss in brain weight, especially if malnutrition occurred during the last trimester. During that time, the brain is growing rapidly in size, and a maternal diet high in all the basic nutrients is necessary for it to reach its full potential (Morgane et al., 1993; Parekh et al., 1970; Winick, Rosso, & Waterlow, 1970). Prenatal malnutrition distorts the structure of other organs, including the pancreas, liver, and blood vessels, thereby increasing the risk of heart disease and diabetes in adulthood (Barker et al., 1993).

Prenatally malnourished babies enter the world with serious problems. They frequently catch respiratory illnesses, since poor nutrition suppresses development of the immune system (Chandra, 1991). In addition, these infants are irritable and unresponsive to stimulation around them. Like drug-addicted newborns, they have a high-pitched cry that is particularly distressing to their caregivers. Since malnutrition is highest in poverty-stricken areas of the world, the effects of poor nutrition quickly combine with a stressful home life. With age, low intelligence test scores and serious learning problems become more apparent (Lozoff, 1989). As the From Research to Practice box on the following page indicates, scientists know how to intervene when poverty is the cause of inadequate diet during pregnancy, although the resources for doing so are not always available.

At this point, it is important to note that the fetuses of some middle-class expectant mothers are also poorly nourished. Pregnancy is not the time for a woman to worry about her figure! A weight gain of 25 to 30 pounds is normal and helps ensure the health of both mother and baby. Yet in the United States, where thinness is the feminine ideal, women often feel uneasy about gaining this much weight, and they may try to limit their food intake. When they do so, they risk their infant's development in all of the ways just described.

FROM RESEARCH TO PRACTICE

INTERVENING WITH PRENATALLY MALNOURISHED INFANTS

Margarita, 2 months pregnant with her second child, walked into a public health clinic in a rural area of Guatemala with her 6-month-old daughter Rosita in her arms. Rosita was pale and listless. Her body looked wasted, and she was several inches shorter than the average baby of her age. Because she was so poorly nourished, Rosita was less resistant to disease. She had difficulty breathing due to a respiratory infection that her body could not fight. Carlotta, the nurse on duty, noticed that Margarita was also frail, anemic, and withdrawn. In addition to poor diet, Margarita's closely spaced pregnancies had depleted her body of iron and other essential nutrients. Unless Margarita's own malnourished condition could be quickly reversed, her unborn child was in serious danger as well.

Many studies show that providing poor mothers with food supplements improves their health and the condition of their newborn babies. Carlotta sent Margarita to a food distribution center near the small village where she lived. Twice a day, she received a protein-rich cereal along with a high-calorie drink that contained vitamins and minerals.

As a result of the food program, Margarita gained more weight during her second pregnancy than she did with her first, and her chances of miscarriage and premature birth were reduced (Institute of Medicine, 1990; Kramer, 1993). When little Juan arrived, he was a pound and a half heavier than Rosita had been at birth. His active, curious behavior caused Margarita to respond to him more, and this encouraged his development even further. Food supplementation during the prenatal period and the first 2 years for babies at risk for malnutrition is associated with improvements in school achievement and information-processing efficiency that persist into adolescence (Pollitt et al., 1993).

When poor nutrition is allowed to continue throughout pregnancy, infants often require more than dietary enrichment. Rosita's restless behavior led Margarita to be less sensitive and stimulating in caring for her. In response, Rosita became even more passive and withdrawn, and her intellectual and motor progress fell far behind that of other babies her age.

Successful intervention programs must break this bidirectional cycle of apathetic mother–baby interaction. Some do so by teaching parents how to interact effectively with their infants. Margarita was fortunate to become part of a program in which a health aide visited her home regularly over a three-year period, teaching her how to play with and stimulate her children. As a result, the large difference in intellectual skills between Rosita and adequately fed children in the village was reduced (Grantham-McGregor et al., 1994; Grantham-McGregor, Schofield, & Powell, 1987).

Other interventions focus on infants. In one study, newborns were provided with a highly stimulating and responsive day care environment in addition to an enriched diet. By 15 months of age, their intellectual development was equal to that of well-nourished babies of the same social-class background. And it was much more advanced than that of infants who had received only dietary supplements (Zeskind & Ramey, 1978, 1981).

Although prenatal malnutrition is highest in poverty-stricken regions of the world, it is not limited to developing countries. Each year, 80,000 to 120,000 American infants are born seriously undernourished. The federal government does provide food packages to impoverished pregnant women through its *Special Supplemental Food Program for Women, Infants, and Children.* Although funding was recently increased, the program serves only 50 percent of those who are eligible (Children's Defense Fund, 1994).

This government clinic in Kenya prevents early malnutrition by promoting a proper diet for pregnant women and young children, including breast-feeding in infancy (see Chapter 5, p. 178–179). *(Betty Press/Woodfin Camp & Associates)*

Finally, overweight and obesity are health hazards during pregnancy, just as they are at other times of life. A mother who tips the scales in the wrong direction at the beginning of pregnancy or who gains too much weight is at risk for high blood pressure and other complications. In addition, she is likely to find pregnancy and childbirth especially exhausting.

■ EMOTIONAL STRESS. When women experience severe emotional stress during pregnancy, their babies are at risk for a wide variety of difficulties. Intense anxiety is associated with a higher rate of miscarriage, prematurity, low birth weight, and newborn respiratory illness. It is also related to certain physical defects, such as cleft palate and pyloric stenosis (tightening of the infant's stomach outlet, which must be treated surgically) (Norbeck & Tilden, 1983; Omer & Everly, 1988).

How can maternal stress affect the developing organism? To understand this process, think back to how your own body felt the last time you were under considerable stress. When we experience fear and anxiety, stimulant hormones are released into our bloodstream. These cause us to be "poised for action." Large amounts of blood are sent to parts of the body involved in the defensive response—the brain, the heart, and muscles in the arms, legs, and trunk. Blood flow to other organs, including the uterus, is reduced. As a result, the fetus is deprived of a full supply of oxygen and nutrients. Stress hormones also cross the placenta, leading the fetus's heart rate and activity level to rise dramatically. In fact, long-term exposure to these hormones might be responsible for the irritability and digestive disturbances observed in babies of highly stressed mothers after birth (Omer & Everly, 1988). Finally, women who experience long-term anxiety are more likely to smoke, drink, eat poorly, and engage in other behaviors that harm the embryo and fetus. These factors probably contribute to the negative outcomes just described (Istvan, 1986).

But women under severe emotional stress do not always give birth to babies with problems. The risks are greatly reduced when mothers have husbands, other family members, and friends to whom they can turn for emotional support (Norbeck & Tilden, 1983). In one study of expectant women experiencing high life stress, those who reported having people on whom they could count for help had a pregnancy complication rate of only 33 percent, compared to 91 percent for those who had few or no social supports (Nuckolls, Cassel, & Kaplan, 1972). These results suggest that finding ways to provide isolated women with supportive social ties during pregnancy can help prevent prenatal complications.

■ RH BLOOD INCOMPATIBILITY. When inherited blood types of mother and fetus differ, in some instances the incompatibility can cause serious problems. The most common cause of these difficulties involves a blood protein called the **Rh factor.** When the mother is Rh negative (lacks the protein) and the father is Rh positive (has the protein), the baby may inherit the father's Rh-positive blood type. (Recall from Table 2.2 in Chapter 2 that Rh-positive blood is dominant and Rh-negative blood is recessive, so the chances are good that a baby will be Rh positive.) During the third trimester and at the time of birth, some maternal and fetal blood cells usually cross the placenta, in small enough amounts to be quite safe. But if even a little of the baby's Rh-positive blood passes into a mother's Rh-negative bloodstream, she begins to form antibodies to the foreign Rh protein. If these enter the baby's system, they destroy red blood cells, reducing the supply of oxygen. Mental retardation, damage to the heart muscle, and infant death can occur.

Since it takes time for the mother to produce Rh antibodies, first-born children are rarely affected. The danger increases with each additional pregnancy. Fortunately, the harmful effects of Rh incompatibility can be prevented in most cases. After the birth of each Rh-positive baby, Rh negative mothers are routinely given a vaccine called RhoGam, which prevents the buildup of antibodies in the mother's system. However, sometimes errors are made in maternal blood typing, and the mother's production of antibodies is not controlled. In these cases, if the baby is in

Rh factor
A protein that, when present in the fetus's blood but not in the mother's, can cause the mother to build up antibodies. If these return to the fetus's system, they destroy red blood cells, reducing the oxygen supply to organs and tissues.

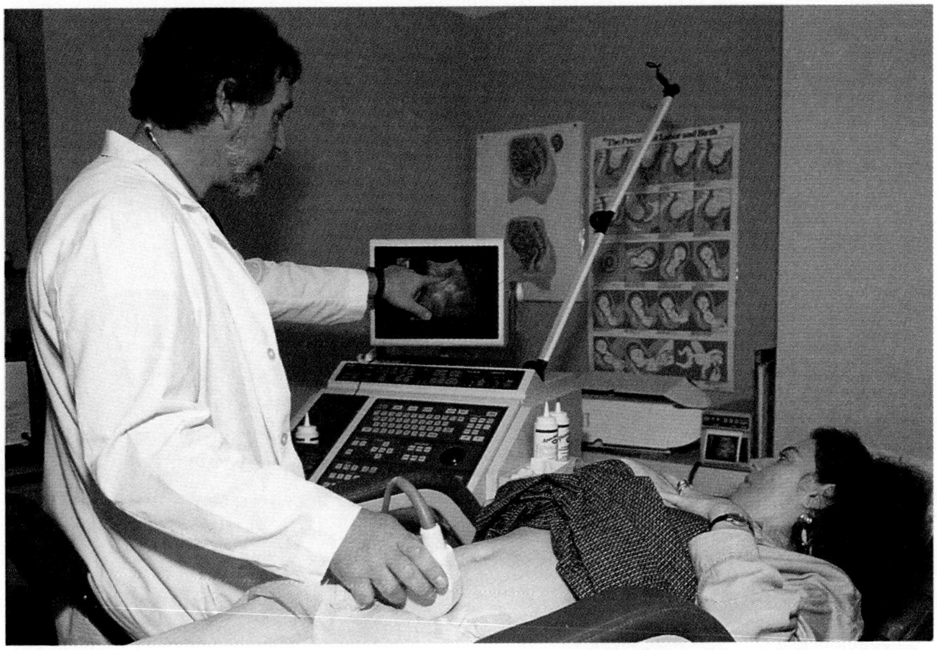

During a routine prenatal visit, this doctor uses ultrasound to show an expectant mother an image of her fetus and to evaluate its development. All pregnant women should receive early and regular prenatal care—to protect their own health and the health of their babies. *(Collins/Monkmeyer Press)*

danger blood transfusions can be performed immediately after birth or, if necessary, even before the baby is born (Simkin, Whalley, & Keppler, 1984).

■ MATERNAL AGE. Earlier we indicated that women who delay having children until their thirties or forties face a greater risk of infertility, miscarriage, and babies born with chromosomal defects. Are other pregnancy problems more common for older mothers?

For many years, scientists thought that aging of the mother's reproductive organs increased the likelihood of a wide variety of pregnancy complications. Recently, this idea has been questioned. When women without serious health difficulties are considered, even those in their forties do not experience more prenatal problems than those in their twenties (Ales, Druzin, & Santini, 1990; Spellacy, Miller, & Winegar, 1986). As long as an older woman is in good health, she can carry a baby successfully.

In the case of teenage mothers, does physical immaturity cause prenatal problems? Again, research indicates that it does not. A teenager's body is large enough and strong enough to support pregnancy. In fact, as we will see in Chapter 14, young adolescent girls grow taller and heavier and their hips broaden (in preparation for childbearing) *before* their menstrual periods begin. Nature tries to ensure that once a girl can conceive, she is physically ready to carry and give birth to a baby. Infants of teenagers are born with a higher rate of problems for quite different reasons. Many adolescents do not have access to medical care or are afraid to seek it. In addition, most pregnant teenagers come from low-income backgrounds where stress, poor nutrition, and health problems are common (Ketterlinus, Henderson, & Lamb, 1990; Roosa, 1984).

■ PREVIOUS BIRTHS. When a mother has already had several children, does her uterus start to wear out, so that more problems are experienced by later-born babies? This is another commonly held belief that has not been confirmed by research. One large study of over 50,000 pregnancies showed no relationship between number of previous births and prenatal problems (Heinonen, Slone, & Shapiro, 1977).

A few birth defects are more likely to occur in later pregnancies, but a worn-out uterus is not the cause of them. Instead, health problems have built up in these mothers over time, usually from long-term exposure to a harmful environment.

Maternal alcohol abuse is a good example. Only rarely do first-born children of alcoholic mothers show all the signs of fetal alcohol syndrome. The disorder is more likely to occur in later births. As each child is born, the complications of alcoholism (poor nutrition, anemia, and liver, kidney, and pancreatic disease) make things worse and worse for the embryo and fetus. Over time, some of these mothers become so dependent on alcohol that they eat little food and actually lose weight during later pregnancies. As a result, their later-born children feed on little else besides alcohol as well (Abel, 1988; Dorris, 1989).

THE IMPORTANCE OF PRENATAL HEALTH CARE

Yolanda had her first prenatal appointment 3 weeks after her first missed menstrual period. After that, she visited the doctor's office once a month until she was 7 months pregnant, then twice during the eighth month. As birth grew near, Yolanda's appointments increased to once a week. The doctor kept track of Yolanda's general health, weight gain, and the capacity of her uterus and cervix to support the fetus. The fetus's growth was also carefully monitored. During these visits, Yolanda had plenty of opportunity to ask questions, pick up literature in the waiting room, get to know the person who would deliver her baby, and plan the kind of birth experience she and Jay desired.

Yolanda's pregnancy, like most others, was uneventful. But unexpected difficulties can arise, especially if mothers have health problems to begin with. For example, women with diabetes need careful monitoring during pregnancy. The presence of extra sugar in the diabetic mother's bloodstream causes the fetus to grow larger than average, although it is physically less mature than the fetus of a nondiabetic mother. As a result, problems at birth are common for both mother and infant. Another pregnancy risk is **toxemia** (sometimes called *eclampsia*). In the 5 to 10 percent of women who develop this illness in the last half of their pregnancies, blood pressure increases sharply and the face, hands, and feet swell. If untreated, serious harm can result, including convulsions in the mother and death of the fetus. Usually, toxemia can be brought under control through hospitalization, bed rest, and drugs to bring blood pressure down. If not, the baby needs to be delivered at once (Samuels & Samuels, 1986).

Unfortunately, 6 percent of pregnant women in the United States wait until the end of pregnancy to seek prenatal care or never get any at all. Most of these mothers are adolescents, unmarried, and members of America's poverty-stricken ethnic minority groups. Their infants are far more likely to be born underweight and to die before birth or during the first year of life than the babies of mothers who receive early medical attention (Children's Defense Fund, 1994).

Financial problems are a major barrier to early prenatal care. Most American women who delay going to the doctor do not receive health insurance as a fringe benefit of their jobs. Others have no insurance because they are unemployed. Although the very poorest of these mothers are eligible for government-sponsored health services, many women who have low incomes and need benefits do not qualify. In Europe, where affordable health care is universally available, the percentage of late-care pregnancies is greatly reduced. Some countries offer special financial incentives. For example, in France, every expectant mother who maintains a regular schedule of prenatal visits throughout pregnancy receives a monetary allowance (Buekens et al., 1993).

Besides financial hardship, there are other reasons that some mothers do not seek prenatal care. In several recent studies, women who first went to the doctor late in pregnancy were asked why they waited so long. A wide variety of personal problems were mentioned, including psychological stress, the demands of taking care of other young children, lack of transportation, ambivalence about the pregnancy, and family crises. The researchers also discovered that many of their participants were engaging in high-risk behaviors, such as smoking and drug abuse

Toxemia
An illness of the last half of pregnancy in which the mother's blood pressure increases sharply and her face, hands, and feet swell. If untreated, it can cause convulsions in the mother and death of the fetus.

TABLE 3.5

Do's and Don'ts for a Healthy Pregnancy

DO	DON'T
Do make sure that you have been vaccinated against infectious diseases dangerous to the embryo and fetus, such as rubella, before you get pregnant. Most vaccinations are not safe during pregnancy.	Don't take any drugs without consulting your doctor.
Do see a doctor as soon as you suspect that you are pregnant—within a few weeks after a missed menstrual period.	Don't smoke cigarettes. If you have already smoked during part of your pregnancy, you can protect your baby by cutting down or (better yet) quitting at any time. If other members of your family are smokers, ask them to smoke outside or in areas of the household that you can easily avoid.
Do continue to get regular medical checkups throughout pregnancy.	Don't drink alcohol from the time you decide to get pregnant. If you find it difficult to give up alcohol, ask for help from your doctor, local family service agency, or nearest chapter of Alcoholics Anonymous.
Do obtain literature from your doctor, local library, and bookstore about prenatal development and care. Ask questions about anything you do not understand.	Don't engage in activities that might expose your baby to environmental hazards, such as radiation or chemical pollutants. If you work in an occupation that involves these agents, ask for a safer assignment or a leave of absence.
Do eat a well-balanced diet. On the average, a woman should increase her intake by 300 calories a day over her usual needs—less at the beginning and more at the end of pregnancy. Gain 25 to 30 pounds gradually.	Don't engage in activities that might expose your baby to harmful infectious diseases, such as childhood illnesses and toxoplasmosis.
Do keep physically fit through mild daily exercise. If possible, join a special exercise class for expectant mothers.	Don't choose pregnancy as a time to go on a diet.
Do avoid emotional stress. If you are a single parent, find a relative or friend whom you can count on for emotional support.	Don't overeat and gain too much weight during pregnancy. A very large weight gain is associated with complications.
Do get plenty of rest. An overtired mother is at risk for pregnancy complications.	
Do enroll in a prenatal and childbirth education class along with the baby's father. When parents know what to expect, the 9 months before birth can be one of the most joyful times of life.	

(Melnikow & Alemagno, 1993; Young et al., 1989). These women, who had no medical attention for most of their pregnancies, were among those who needed it most!

Clearly, public education about the importance of early prenatal care and medical services that reach all pregnant women, especially those who are young, single, and poor, are badly needed. Table 3.5 provides a summary of "do's and don'ts" for a healthy pregnancy, based on our discussion of the prenatal environment.

BRIEF REVIEW

Teratogens—cigarettes, alcohol, certain drugs, radiation, environmental pollutants, and diseases—can seriously harm the embryo and fetus. The effects of teratogens are complex. They depend on amount and length of exposure, the genetic makeup of mother and baby, and the presence of other harmful environmental agents. Teratogens operate according to the sensitive period concept. In general, greatest damage occurs during the embryonic phase, when all parts of the body are forming. Poor maternal nutrition, severe emotional stress, and Rh blood incompatibility can also endanger the developing organism. As long as they are in good health, teenagers, women in their thirties and forties, and women who have given birth to several children have a high likelihood of problem-free pregnancies. Regular medical checkups are important for all expectant mothers, and they are crucial for women with a history of health difficulties.

ASK YOURSELF . . .

- Why is it difficult to determine the effects of some environmental agents, such as over-the-counter drugs and pollution, on the embryo and fetus?
- Nora, who is expecting for the first time at age 40, wonders whether she is likely to have a difficult pregnancy because of her age. How would you respond to Nora's concern?
- Trixie has just learned she is pregnant. Since she has always been healthy and feels good right now, she cannot understand why the doctor wants her to come in for checkups so often. Why is early and regular prenatal care important for Trixie?

PREPARING FOR PARENTHOOD

We have discussed a great many ways that normal development can be thrown off course during the prenatal period. When we consider them together, it may seem surprising that any infants arrive intact, but the vast majority do. Over 90 percent of pregnancies in the United States result in normal newborn babies. For most expectant parents, the prenatal period is not a time of medical hazard. Instead, it is a period of major life change accompanied by excitement, anticipation, and looking inward. The 9 months before birth not only permit the fetus to grow, but also give men and women time to develop a new sense of themselves as mothers and fathers. This period of psychological preparation is vital. When asked, one-third of young Americans say they do not feel ready to deal with the demands and responsibilities of parenthood (Duncan & Markman, 1988). How effectively individuals construct a new parental identity during pregnancy has important consequences for the parent–infant relationship. A great many factors contribute to the personal adjustments that take place.

SEEKING INFORMATION

We know most about how mothers adapt to the psychological challenges of pregnancy, although some evidence suggests that fathers use many of the same techniques (Colman & Colman, 1991). One common strategy is to seek information, as Yolanda and Jay did when they read books on pregnancy and childbirth and enrolled in my class. In fact, expectant mothers regard books as an extremely valuable source of information, rating them as second in importance only to their doctors. And the more a pregnant woman seeks information—by reading or in other ways, such as asking friends, consulting her own mother, or attending a prenatal class—the more confident she tends to feel about her own ability to be a good mother (Deutsch et al., 1988).

Why does information seeking promote adjustment during pregnancy? First, when people gather information about an unfamiliar event, it often becomes less threatening. Second, pregnant women who learn a great deal about what they are about to experience start to imagine themselves engaging in the activities of motherhood. For example, when they read about breast-feeding, they see themselves nursing their own baby. Expectant mothers who imagine themselves as competent caregivers make better adjustments after birth and report greater satisfaction in caring for their babies (Deutsch et al., 1988; Leifer, 1980).

THE BABY BECOMES A REALITY

At the beginning of pregnancy, the baby seems far off in the future. Except for a missed period and some morning sickness (nausea that most women experience during the first trimester), the woman's body has not changed much. But gradually, her abdomen enlarges, and the baby starts to become more of a reality. A major turning point occurs when expectant parents are presented with concrete proof that a fetus is, indeed, developing inside the uterus. For Yolanda and Jay, this happened 13 weeks into the pregnancy. Jay went with Yolanda to the doctor, who showed them an image of the fetus using ultrasound. As Jay described this experience, "We saw it, these little hands and feet waving and kicking. It had the cord and everything. It's really a baby in there!" Sensing the fetus's movements for the first time can be just as thrilling. Of course, the mother feels these "kicks" first, but soon after the father (and any siblings) can participate by touching her abdomen.

Mothers begin to get to know the child as an individual through these first signs of life. From the vigor of its movements and its daily cycles of activity and rest, the fetus takes on the beginnings of a personality. Both parents start to dream of a relationship with the baby, to talk about names, and to make plans to welcome the newcomer into their lives.

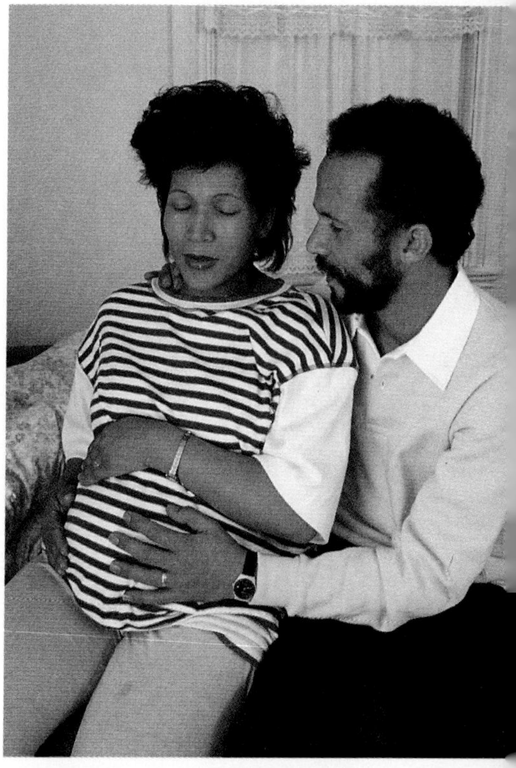

As this man and woman share the thrill of sensing the fetus's movements, parenthood starts to become more of a reality. Mother and father begin to get to know their child. *(Carol Palmer/Picture Cube)*

MODELS OF EFFECTIVE PARENTHOOD

As pregnancy proceeds, expectant parents think about important models of parenthood in their own lives—for the woman, her mother, and for the man, his father. Research indicates that when women have had good relationships with their own mothers, they are more likely to develop positive images of themselves as mothers during pregnancy (Deutsch et al., 1988). These images, in turn, predict favorable relationships with infants during the first two years of life (Fonagy, Steele, & Steele, 1991; van IJzendoorn et al., 1991).

If their own parental relationships are mixed or negative, expectant mothers and fathers may have trouble building a healthy picture of themselves as parents. Some adults handle this problem constructively, by seeking out other examples of effective parenthood. One father named Roger shared these thoughts with his wife and several expectant couples who met regularly with a counselor to talk about their concerns during pregnancy:

> I rethink past experiences with my father and my family and am aware of how I was raised. I just think I don't want to do that again, I want to change that; I don't want to be like my father in that way. I wish there had been more connection and closeness and a lot more respect for who I was. For me, my father-in-law combines spontaneity, sincerity, and warmth. He is a mix of empathy and warmth plus stepping back and being objective that I want to be as a father. (Colman & Colman, 1991, p. 148)

A warm, secure relationship with their own parents is helpful to adults in developing an optimistic view of themselves as parents, but it is not a necessity. Like Roger, many people come to terms with negative experiences in their own childhoods, recognize that other options are available to them as parents, and build healthier and happier relationships with their children (Main, Kaplan, & Cassidy, 1985). Roger achieved this understanding after he participated in a special intervention program designed to help expectant mothers and fathers prepare for parenthood. Couples who take part in such programs feel better about themselves and their marital relationships, regard the demands of caring for the new baby as less stressful, and adapt more easily when family problems arise (Duncan & Markman, 1988).

PRACTICAL CONCERNS

When women first learn they are pregnant, they often wonder how long they will be able to continue their usual activities. Culture has a major impact on answers to this question. In the United States, women in good health often work and travel until the very end of their pregnancies, without any apparent harm to the fetus. And as long as the pregnancy has gone well, American doctors advise that sexual intercourse can be continued through most or all of the 9 months before birth (Mills, Harlap, & Harley, 1981; Samuels & Samuels, 1986).

In contrast, when a Japanese woman learns that she is pregnant, she changes her daily life considerably, out of a belief that this is necessary to protect the health of her baby. Nancy Engel (1989), an American nurse, described her experience of becoming pregnant for the first time while living in Japan:

> When I announced my pregnancy it was assumed that I would quit my teaching position and drop out of language school. My teacher told me that language study was stressful, and the increased (hormone levels) it caused were harmful to the baby. Similarly, I was advised that the noise of train travel, typing, or using a sewing machine should be avoided. My colleagues at college . . . were particularly concerned when I revealed plans to go to Thailand on vacation during the fourth month. They told me that airplane travel would cause miscarriage, and they cited numerous examples. . . . My doctor assumed that I would not engage in sexual activity, to ensure a healthy newborn. (p. 83)

As the seventh or eighth month of pregnancy approaches, the Japanese woman returns to her mother's home, where she rests until birth and recuperates for several months afterward.

Although Engel could not accept these practices for herself, she realized that they were based on cultural values that hold the maternal role in high esteem and place the safety of the infant first. This investment in the child's well-being makes Japan an excellent place to have a baby. It has the lowest rate of pregnancy and birth complications in the world (Grant, 1992).

THE MARITAL RELATIONSHIP

The most important preparation for parenthood takes place in the context of the marital relationship. Expectant couples who are unhappy in their marriages during pregnancy continue to be dissatisfied after the baby is born (Belsky, Spanier, & Rovine, 1983; Cowan et al., 1985). Deciding to have a baby in hopes of improving a troubled marriage is a serious mistake. There is good evidence that pregnancy adds to rather than subtracts from family conflict if a marriage is in danger of falling apart (Snowden et al., 1988).

When a couple's relationship is faring well and both partners want and planned for the baby, the excitement of a first pregnancy may bring husband and wife closer together. At the same time, pregnancy does change a marriage. Expectant parents do not just add parenting to their existing responsibilities. They must adjust their established roles to make room for children. Women start to plan how they will juggle the demands of work and child rearing. Men reconsider the adequacy of their jobs and the size of the family bank account. In addition, each partner is likely to develop new expectations of the other. Women look for greater demonstrations of affection, interest in the pregnancy, and help with household chores from their husbands. They see these behaviors as important signs of the husband's continued acceptance of his wife, the pregnancy, and the baby to come (Richardson, 1983). Similarly, men are particularly sensitive to expressions of warmth from their pregnant wives. These reassure the husband that he will continue to occupy a central place in the new mother's emotional life after the baby is born (Fedele et al., 1988).

When a marriage rests on a solid foundation of love and respect, parents are well equipped to master the challenges of pregnancy. They are also prepared to handle the much more demanding changes that will take place in the family as soon as the baby is born.

ASK YOURSELF . . .

- Muriel, who is expecting her first child, recalls her own mother as cold and distant. Muriel is worried about whether she will be effective at caring for her new baby. What factors during pregnancy are likely to affect the quality of Muriel's maternal behavior?

SUMMARY

MOTIVATIONS FOR PARENTHOOD

List the advantages and disadvantages of parenthood, and explain the impact of family size and parental age on child rearing and child development.

- Today, adults in Western industrialized nations are more likely to weigh the advantages and disadvantages of becoming parents before having children than they were a generation or two ago. Parents are also having smaller families, a trend that has positive consequences for children's development.
- When couples limit their families to just one child, their youngsters are just as socially well adjusted as children with siblings, and they also achieve better in school. Many adults are waiting until later in their own lives to have children, when their careers are well established and they are emotionally more mature.

PRENATAL DEVELOPMENT

List the three phases of prenatal development, and describe the major milestones of each.

- Prenatal development is usually divided into three phases. The period of the zygote lasts about 2 weeks, from fertilization until the **blastocyst** becomes deeply **implanted** into the uterine lining. During this time, structures that will support prenatal growth begin to form. The **embryonic disk** is surrounded by the **amnion,** which is filled with **amniotic fluid.** From the **chorion,** villi emerge that burrow into the uterine wall, and the **placenta** starts to develop. The developing organism is connected to the placenta by the **umbilical cord.**
- The period of the **embryo** lasts from 2 to 8 weeks, during which the foundations for all body structures are laid down. In the first week of this period, the **neural tube** forms, and the nervous system starts to develop. Other organs follow and also grow rapidly. At the end of this phase, the embryo responds to touch and can move.
- The period of the **fetus,** lasting until the end of pregnancy, involves a dramatic increase in body size and completion of physical structures. It is the longest prenatal phase and includes the second and third **trimesters.** By the middle of the second trimester, the mother can feel movement. The fetus becomes covered with **vernix,** which protects the skin from chapping. White, downy hair called **lanugo** helps the vernix stick to the skin. At the end of the second trimester, the production of neurons in the brain is complete.
- The **age of viability** occurs at the beginning of the final trimester, sometime between 22 and 26 weeks. The brain continues to develop rapidly, and new sensory and behavioral capacities emerge. Gradually the lungs mature, the fetus fills the uterus, and birth is near.

PRENATAL ENVIRONMENTAL INFLUENCES

What factors influence the impact of teratogens on the developing organism?

- **Teratogens** are environmental agents that cause damage during the prenatal period. Their effects conform to the sensitive period concept. The developing organism is especially vulnerable during the embryonic period, since all essential body structures are rapidly emerging. The impact of teratogens differs from one case to the next, due to amount and length of exposure, the genetic makeup of mother and fetus, and the presence or absence of other harmful agents. The effects of teratogens are not limited to immediate physical damage. Serious psychological consequences may appear later in development. Some are indirectly caused by physical defects through bidirectional exchanges between child and environment.

List agents known or suspected of being teratogens, and discuss evidence supporting the harmful impact of each.

- Drugs, cigarette smoking, alcohol, hormones, radiation, environmental pollution, and infectious diseases are teratogens that can endanger the developing organism. **Thalidomide,** a sedative widely available in the early 1960s, showed without a doubt that drugs could cross the placenta and cause serious damage. Babies whose mothers took heroin, methadone, or cocaine during pregnancy have withdrawal symptoms after birth and are jittery and inattentive. Cocaine is especially risky, since it is associated with physical defects and central nervous system damage.
- Infants of parents who smoke cigarettes are often born underweight and may display inattentiveness and learning problems in childhood. When mothers consume alcohol in large quantities, **fetal alcohol syndrome (FAS),** a disorder involving mental retardation, poor attention, overactivity, slow physical growth, and facial abnormalities, often results. Smaller amounts of alcohol may lead to some of these problems—a condition known as **fetal alcohol effects (FAE).**

- A hormone called **diethylstilbestrol (DES)** has a delayed impact on the child, increasing the chances of genital tract abnormalities and cancer of the vagina and testes in adolescence and young adulthood. Radiation, mercury, and lead can result in a wide variety of problems, including physical malformations and severe brain damage. PCBs have been linked to decreased responsiveness to the environment and memory difficulties during infancy and poorer memory and verbal intelligence in early childhood.
- Many diseases can harm the embryo and fetus. **Rubella** causes a wide variety of abnormalities, which vary with its time of occurrence during pregnancy. **Acquired immune deficiency syndrome (AIDS)** can be transmitted prenatally and is linked to brain damage, delayed development, and early death. **Toxoplasmosis** in the first trimester may lead to eye and brain damage.

Describe the impact of additional maternal factors on prenatal development.

- Other maternal factors can either support or complicate prenatal development. In healthy, physically fit women, regular exercise contributes to an expectant woman's general health and readiness for childbirth and is related to increased birth weight. When the mother's diet is inadequate, low birth weight and brain damage are major concerns.
- Severe emotional stress is linked to many pregnancy complications, although its impact can be reduced by providing the mother with emotional support. If the **Rh factor** of the mother's blood is negative and the fetus's is positive, special precautions must be taken to ensure that antibodies to the Rh protein do not pass from mother to fetus.
- Maternal age and number of previous births were once thought to be major causes of prenatal problems. Aside from the risk of chromosomal abnormalities in older women, this is not the case. Instead, poor health and environmental risks associated with poverty are the strongest predictors of pregnancy complications.

Why is early and regular health care vital during the prenatal period?

- Early and regular prenatal health care is important for all pregnant women. Unexpected difficulties, such as **toxemia,** can arise, especially when mothers have health problems to begin with. Prenatal care is especially crucial for women unlikely to seek it—in particular, those who are young, single, and poor.

PREPARING FOR PARENTHOOD

What factors contribute to preparation for parenthood during the prenatal period?

- Pregnancy is an important period of psychological transition. Mothers and fathers prepare for their new role by seeking information from books and other sources and becoming acquainted with the movements and daily cycles of the fetus. They also rely on effective models of parenthood as they build images of themselves as mothers and fathers.
- The most important preparation for parenthood takes place in the context of the marital relationship. During the nine months preceding birth, parents adjust their various roles and expectations of one another as they prepare to welcome the baby into the family.

IMPORTANT TERMS AND CONCEPTS

blastocyst (p. 103)
embryonic disk (p. 103)
implantation (p. 103)
amnion (p. 103)
amniotic fluid (p. 103)
chorion (p. 103)
placenta (p. 104)
umbilical cord (p. 104)
embryo (p. 105)
neural tube (p. 106)
fetus (p. 106)
trimester (p. 107)
vernix (p. 107)
lanugo (p. 107)
age of viability (p. 108)
teratogen (p. 110)
thalidomide (p. 112)
fetal alcohol syndrome (FAS) (p. 114)
fetal alcohol effects (FAE) (p. 115)
diethylstilbestrol (DES) (p. 115)
rubella (p. 117)
acquired immune deficiency syndrome (AIDS) (p. 118)
toxoplasmosis (p. 118)
Rh factor (p. 122)
toxemia (p. 124)

FYI...

FOR FURTHER INFORMATION AND SPECIAL HELP, CONSULT THE FOLLOWING ORGANIZATIONS:

PRENATAL HEALTH

National Center for Education in Maternal and Child Health
2000 15th Street N., Suite 701
Arlington, VA 22201-2617
(703) 524-7802

Government-sponsored agency that provides information on all aspects of maternal and child health.

ALCOHOL ABUSE

National Clearinghouse for Alcohol and Drug Information
P.O. Box 2345
Rockville, MD 20852
(301) 468-2600

Government-sponsored agency that provides information on all aspects of alcohol and drug abuse.

Alcoholics Anonymous
475 Riverside Drive
New York, NY 10163
(212) 870-3400

An international organization aimed at helping people recover from alcoholism. Local chapters exist in many countries.

National Council on Alcoholism and Drug Dependence
12 West 21st Street
New York, NY 10010
(212) 206-6770

Works for prevention and control of alcoholism by providing information on the problem.

BIRTH DEFECTS

National Easter Seal Society for Crippled Children and Adults
70 E. Lake Street
Chicago, IL 60601
(312) 726-6200

Provides information on birth defects. Works with other agencies to help the disabled.

National Information Center for Children and Youth with Disabilities
P. O. Box 1492
Washington, DC 20013
(703) 893-6061

Provides information to parents and educators on services for children with handicaps.

March of Dimes Birth Defects Foundation
1275 Mamaroneck Avenue
White Plains, NY 10605
(914) 428-7100

Works to prevent birth defects through public education and community service programs.

Parents Helping Parents
535 Race Street, Suite 220
San Jose, CA 95126
(408) 288-5010

Offers a wide variety of services and educational programs to help parents raise children with special needs, including those with birth defects.

DES

DES Action U.S.A.
1615 Broadway, Suite 510
Oakland, CA 94617
(510) 465-4011

Attempts to reach DES-exposed individuals. Offers support, counseling, and medical referral.

AIDS

National AIDS Information Clearinghouse
P.O. Box 6003
Rockville, MD 20849-6003
(860) 458-5231

Government-sponsored agency that provides information about AIDS and AIDS-related services.

"Mexican mother"
Cyntia Arrieta Rodriguez
11 years, Mexico

This idyllic scene suggests a birth that went smoothly and an infant who has successfully made the transition to life outside the womb with the support of a loving parent. Chapter 4 explores the birth process and the marvelous competencies of newborn babies.

4

Birth and the Newborn Baby

THE STAGES OF CHILDBIRTH

Stage 1: Dilation and Effacement of the Cervix • Stage 2: Delivery of the Baby • Stage 3: Birth of the Placenta • The Baby's Adaptation to Labor and Delivery • The Newborn Baby's Appearance • Assessing the Newborn's Physical Condition: The Apgar Scale

APPROACHES TO CHILDBIRTH

Natural, or Prepared, Childbirth • Home Delivery

MEDICAL INTERVENTIONS

Fetal Monitoring • Labor and Delivery Medication • Instrument Delivery • Induced Labor • Cesarean Delivery

BIRTH COMPLICATIONS

Oxygen Deprivation • Preterm and Low-Birth-Weight Infants • Postterm Infants • Understanding Birth Complications

PRECIOUS MOMENTS AFTER BIRTH

THE NEWBORN BABY'S CAPACITIES

Newborn Reflexes • Sensory Capacities • Newborn States • Neonatal Behavioral Assessment

THE TRANSITION TO PARENTHOOD

Although Yolanda and Jay completed my course 3 months before their baby was born, both agreed to return the following spring to share their reactions to birth and new parenthood with my next class of students. When the long-awaited day arrived, little Joshua, who was 2 weeks old at the time, came along as well. The story that Yolanda and Jay told revealed that the birth of a baby is one of the most dramatic and emotional events in human experience. Jay was present throughout Yolanda's labor and delivery. Yolanda explained,

> By morning, we knew I was in labor. It was Thursday, so we went in for my usual weekly appointment. The doctor said, yes, the baby was on the way, but it would be a while. He told us to go home and relax or take a leisurely walk and come to the hospital in 3 or 4 hours. We checked in at 3 in the afternoon; Joshua arrived at 2 o'clock the next morning. When, finally, I was ready to deliver, it went quickly; a half hour or so and some good hard pushes, and there he was! His body had stuff all over it, his face was red and puffy, and his head was misshapen, but I thought, "Oh! he's beautiful. I can't believe he's really here!"

Jay was also elated by Joshua's birth. "I wanted to support Yolanda and to experience as much as I could. It was awesome, indescribable," he said, holding little Joshua over his shoulder and patting and kissing him gently. "For me, it meant everything to be there."

In this chapter, we explore the experience of childbirth, from both the parents' and the baby's point of view. A generation or two ago, the birth process was treated more like an illness than a natural and normal part of life. When her first child was born, Yolanda's mother remembers being left alone in a small room during most of the long hours of labor. She knew little about what was happening, was frightened by the powerful contractions of her uterus, and felt lonely and helpless. Fortunately, childbirth is rarely like this today. Women in industrialized nations have many more choices about where and how they give birth than at any time in the past, and modern hospitals often go to great lengths to make the arrival of a new baby a rewarding, family-centered event.

Joshua reaped the benefits of Yolanda and Jay's careful attention to his needs during pregnancy. He was strong, alert, and healthy at birth. Nevertheless, as we saw in Chapter 3, some mothers are at serious risk for birth complications, and even when they are not, the birth process does not always go smoothly. We will pay special attention to the problems of infants who are born underweight or arrive too early, before the prenatal period is complete. Our discussion will also examine the pros and cons of medical interventions, such as pain-relieving drugs and surgical deliveries, designed to ease a difficult birth and protect the health of mother and baby.

Finally, Yolanda and Jay spoke candidly about how, since Joshua's arrival, life at home had changed. "It's exciting and wonderful," reflected Yolanda, "but the adjustments are enormous. I wasn't quite prepared for the intensity of Joshua's 24-hour-a-day demands." In the last part of this chapter, we take a close look at the remarkable ability of newborn babies to adapt to the external world and to communicate their needs. We also consider how parents adjust to the realities of everyday life with a new baby.

THE STAGES OF CHILDBIRTH

It is not surprising that childbirth is often referred to as *labor.* It is the hardest physical work that a woman may ever do. A complex series of hormonal changes initiates the process. Yolanda's whole system, which for 9 months supported and protected Joshua's growth, now turned toward a new goal: getting him safely out of the uterus.

The events that lead to childbirth begin slowly in the ninth month of pregnancy and gradually pick up speed. Several signs indicate that labor is near. First, Yolanda felt the upper part of her uterus contract once in a while. These contractions are often called *false labor* or *prelabor,* since they remain brief and unpredictable for several weeks. Second, about 2 weeks before birth, an event called *lightening* occurred; Joshua's head dropped down low into the uterus. The reason was that Yolanda's cervix had begun to soften, thin, and open in preparation for delivery. As a result, it no longer supported Joshua's weight so easily. Lightening relieved some of the breathing and abdominal discomfort that Yolanda felt by the end of pregnancy, although it brought other symptoms, such as low backache and difficulty in walking. Finally, a sure sign that labor is only hours or days away is the *bloody show.* As the cervix widens more, the plug of mucus that sealed it during pregnancy is released, producing a reddish discharge (Samuels & Samuels, 1986). Soon after this happens, contractions of the uterus become more frequent, and mother and baby have entered the first of three stages of labor (see Figure 4.1).

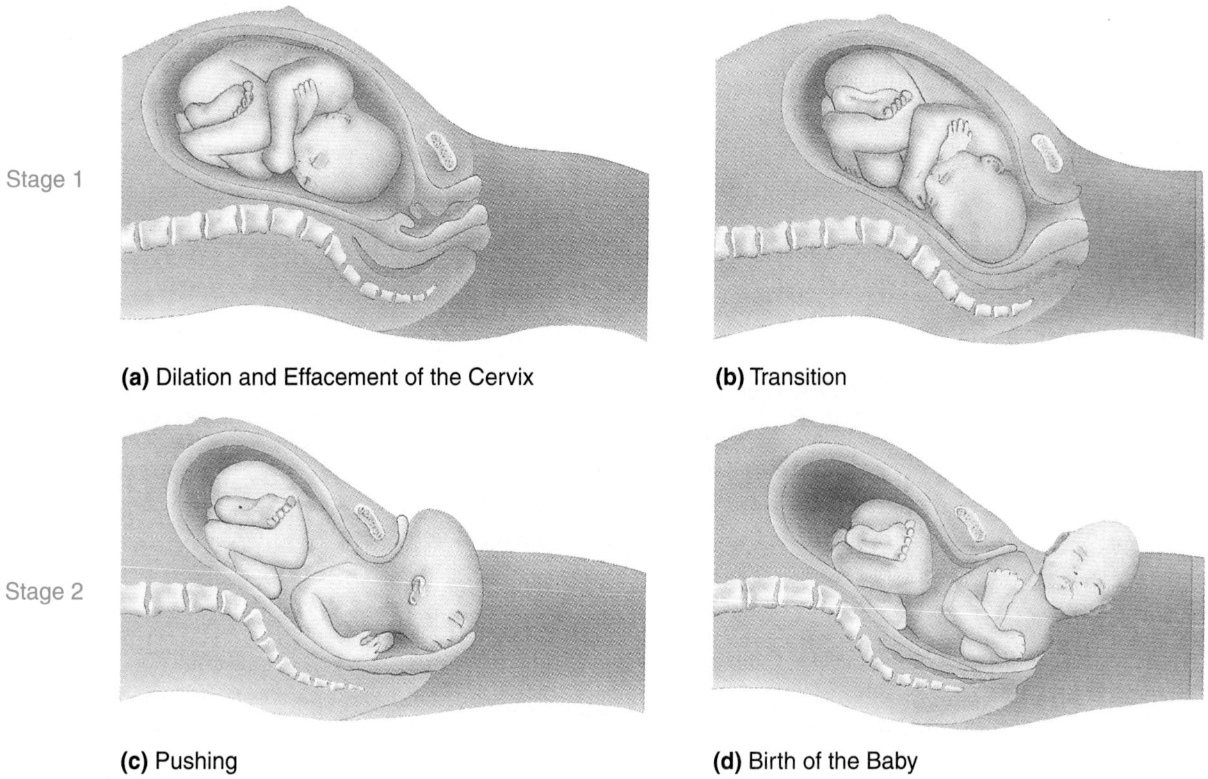

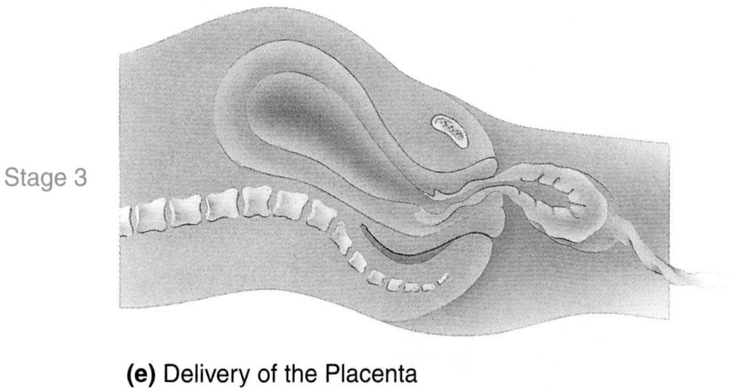

FIGURE 4.1

The three stages of labor.
Stage 1: (a) Contractions of the uterus cause dilation and effacement of the cervix. (b) Transition is reached when the frequency and strength of the contractions are at their peak and the cervix opens completely. Stage 2: (c) The mother pushes with each contraction, forcing the baby down the birth canal, and the head appears. (d) Near the end of Stage 2, the shoulders emerge and are followed quickly by the rest of the baby's body. Stage 3: (e) With a few final pushes, the placenta is delivered.

STAGE 1: DILATION AND EFFACEMENT OF THE CERVIX

This is the longest stage of labor, lasting, on the average, 12 to 14 hours with a first baby and 4 to 6 hours with later births. **Dilation and effacement of the cervix** take place—that is, the cervix widens and thins to nothing. As a result, a clear channel from the uterus into the birth canal, or vagina, is formed. Uterine contractions that open the cervix are forceful and regular, starting out 10 to 20 minutes apart and lasting about 15 to 20 seconds. Gradually, they get closer together, occurring every 2 to 3 minutes. In addition, they become more powerful, continuing for as long as 60 seconds.

Dilation and effacement of the cervix
Widening and thinning of the cervix during the first stage of labor.

During this stage, there was nothing Yolanda could do to speed up the process. She was urged to relax; Jay held her hand, provided sips of juice and water, and helped her get comfortable. Throughout the first few hours, Yolanda walked, stood, or sat upright. As the contractions became more intense, she leaned against pillows or lay on her side.

The climax of the first stage of labor is a brief period called **transition,** in which the frequency and strength of contractions are at their peak and the cervix opens completely. Although transition is the most uncomfortable part of childbirth, it is especially important that the mother relax during this time. If she tenses or bears down with her muscles before the cervix is completely dilated and effaced, she is likely to bruise the cervix and slow the progress of labor.

STAGE 2: DELIVERY OF THE BABY

Once the cervix is fully open, the infant is ready to be born. This second stage is much shorter than the first. It lasts about 50 minutes for a first baby and 20 minutes in later births. Strong contractions of the uterus continue, but they do not do the entire job. The most important factor is a natural urge that the mother feels to squeeze and push with her abdominal muscles. As she does so with each contraction, she forces the baby down and out.

Yolanda dozed lightly between contractions. As each new wave came, "I pushed with all my might," she said. In the meantime, the doctor performed an **episiotomy,** or small incision that increases the size of the vaginal opening, permitting the baby to pass without tearing the mother's tissues. When the doctor announced that the baby's head was *crowning*—the vaginal opening had stretched around the entire head—Yolanda felt a sense of renewed energy; she knew that soon the baby would arrive. Quickly, with several more pushes, Joshua's forehead, nose, and chin emerged, then his upper body and trunk. The doctor held him up, wet with amniotic fluid and still attached to the umbilical cord. Air rushed into his lungs, and Joshua cried. When the umbilical cord stopped pulsing, it was clamped and cut. Joshua was placed on Yolanda's chest, where she and Jay could see, touch, and gently talk to him. Then he was wrapped snugly to help with temperature regulation.

STAGE 3: BIRTH OF THE PLACENTA

Labor comes to an end with a few final contractions and pushes. These cause the placenta to separate from the wall of the uterus and be delivered, a stage that usually lasts about 5 to 10 minutes. Yolanda and Jay were surprised at the large size of the thick 1 1/2-pound red–gray organ that had taken care of Joshua's basic needs for the previous 9 months.

THE BABY'S ADAPTATION TO LABOR AND DELIVERY

In the preceding sections, we described the events of childbirth from the outside looking in. Let's consider, for a moment, what the experience must be like for the baby. Joshua, after being squeezed and pushed for many hours, was forced to leave Yolanda's warm, protective uterus for a cold, brightly lit external world. The strong contractions exposed his head to a great deal of pressure, and they squeezed the placenta and the umbilical cord repeatedly. Each time, Joshua's supply of oxygen was temporarily reduced.

At first glance, these events may strike you as a dangerous ordeal. Fortunately, healthy babies are well equipped to withstand the trauma of childbirth. The force of

Transition
Climax of the first stage of labor, in which the frequency and strength of contractions are at their peak and the cervix opens completely.

Episiotomy
A small incision made during childbirth to increase the size of the vaginal opening.

the contractions causes the infant to produce high levels of stress hormones. Recall from Chapter 3 that during pregnancy, the effects of maternal stress can endanger the baby. In contrast, during childbirth the infant's production of stress hormones is adaptive. It helps the baby withstand oxygen deprivation by sending a rich supply of blood to the brain and heart. In addition, it prepares the baby to breathe effectively by causing the lungs to absorb excess liquid and expanding the bronchial tubes (passages leading to the lungs). Finally, stress hormones arouse the infant into alertness at birth. Joshua was born wide awake, ready to interact with the surrounding world (Emory & Toomey, 1988; Lagercrantz & Slotkin, 1986).

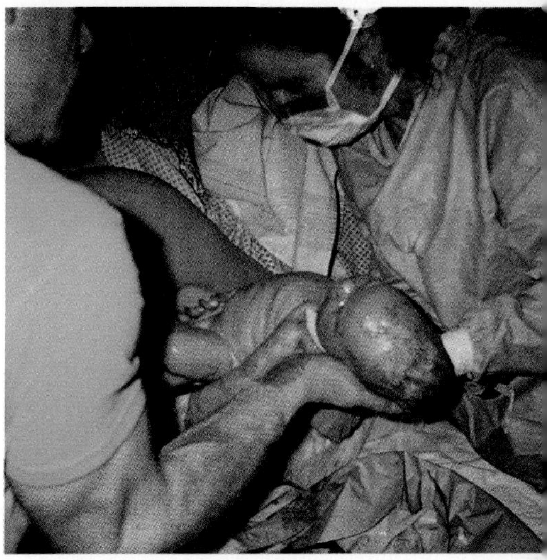

This newborn baby is held by his mother's birthing coach (on the left) and midwife (on the right) just after delivery. The umbilical cord has not yet been cut. Notice how the infant's head is molded from being squeezed through the birth canal for many hours. It is also very large in relation to his body. As the infant takes his first few breaths, his body turns from blue to pink. He is wide awake and ready to get to know his new surroundings. *(Courtesy of Dakoda Brandon Dorsaneo)*

THE NEWBORN BABY'S APPEARANCE

What do babies look like after birth? My students asked Yolanda and Jay this question. "Come to think of it," Jay smiled, "Yolanda and I are probably the only people in the world who thought Joshua was beautiful!" The average newborn is 20 inches long and 7 1/2 pounds in weight; boys tend to be slightly longer and heavier than girls. Body proportions contribute to the baby's strange appearance. The head is very large in comparison to the trunk and legs, which are short and bowed. In fact, if your head were as large as that of a newborn infant, you would be balancing something about the size of a watermelon between your shoulders! As we will see in later chapters, the combination of a big head (with its well-developed brain) and a small body means that human infants learn quickly in the first few weeks and months of life. But unlike most mammals, they cannot get around on their own until much later, during the second half of the first year.

Even though newborn babies may not match the idealized image many parents created in their minds during pregnancy, some features do make them attractive. Their round faces, chubby cheeks, large foreheads, and big eyes are just those characteristics that make adults feel like picking them up and cuddling them (Berman, 1980; Lorenz, 1943). The skin is also soft and smooth, although temporary rashes may appear on the face, which result from hormonal changes or plugged skin ducts. These clear up without treatment.

ASSESSING THE NEWBORN'S PHYSICAL CONDITION: THE APGAR SCALE

Infants who have difficulty making the transition to life outside the uterus must be given special help at once. To quickly assess the infant's physical condition, doctors and nurses use the **Apgar Scale.** As Table 4.1 shows, a rating from 0 to 2 on each of five characteristics is made at 1 and 5 minutes after birth. An Apgar score of 7 or better indicates that the infant is in good physical condition. If the score is between 4 and 6, the baby requires assistance in establishing breathing and other vital signs. If the score is 3 or below, the infant is in serious danger, and emergency medical attention is needed. Two Apgar ratings are given, since some babies have trouble adjusting at first but are doing quite well after a few minutes (Apgar, 1953).

After looking at Table 4.1, you may be wondering how infants like Joshua, who are black or are members of other dark-skinned ethnic groups, can be rated on color, the last of the five Apgar signs. Color is the least dependable of the Apgar ratings. The skin tone of nonwhite babies cannot be judged easily for pinkness and blueness. However, all newborns can be rated for a rosy glow that results from the flow of oxygen through body tissues once the baby starts to breathe, since skin tone is usually lighter at birth than the baby's inherited pigmentation.

Apgar Scale
A rating used to assess the newborn baby's physical condition immediately after birth.

TABLE 4.1

The Apgar Scale

	SCORE		
SIGN[a]	0	1	2
Heart rate	No heartbeat	Under 100 beats per minute	100 to 140 beats per minute
Respiratory effort	No breathing for 60 seconds	Irregular, shallow breathing	Strong breathing and crying
Reflex irritability (sneezing, coughing, and grimacing)	No response	Weak reflexive response	Strong reflexive response
Muscle tone	Completely limp	Weak movements of arms and legs	Strong movements of arms and legs
Color	Blue body, arms, and legs	Body pink with blue arms and legs	Body, arms, and legs completely pink

[a]To remember these signs, you may find it helpful to use a technique in which the original labels are reordered and renamed as follows: color = Appearance, heart rate = Pulse, reflex irritability = Grimace, muscle tone = Activity, and respiratory effort = Respiration. Together, the first letters of the new labels spell Apgar.

Source: Apgar, 1953.

ASK YOURSELF . . .

- What factors help newborn babies withstand the trauma of labor and delivery?
- Explain why first-time parents are often surprised at the appearance of the newborn baby.

BRIEF REVIEW

The hard work of labor takes place in three stages. In the first and longest stage, the cervix dilates and effaces to permit the baby to pass out of the uterus. In the second stage, the mother assists by pushing with each contraction, and the baby is born. In the third stage, the placenta is delivered. Stress hormones help the infant withstand the trauma of childbirth, and breathing generally starts easily and automatically. The Apgar Scale provides a quick rating of the baby's physical condition immediately after birth.

APPROACHES TO CHILDBIRTH

Childbirth practices, like other aspects of family life, are molded by the society of which mother and baby are a part. The extent to which birth is affected by culture is brought into bold relief when we look at the very different approaches to childbirth around the world (see the Cultural Influences box on the following page). Even in large Western nations, childbirth has changed dramatically over the centuries.

Before the 1800s, birth usually took place at home and was a family-centered event. Relatives, friends, and children were often present. As a result, when young people had children of their own, they knew just what to expect and were supported by family members. The nineteenth-century industrial revolution brought greater crowding to cities along with new health problems. Childbirth moved from home to hospital, where the health of mothers and babies could be protected. Once the responsibility for childbirth was placed in the hands of doctors, women's knowledge about it was reduced, and relatives and friends were no longer welcome to participate (Lindell, 1988).

By the 1950s and 1960s, women started to question the medical procedures that came to be used routinely during labor and delivery. Many felt that frequent use of strong drugs and delivery instruments had robbed them of a precious experience and were often not necessary or safe for the baby. Gradually, a new natural

CULTURAL INFLUENCES

CHILDBIRTH PRACTICES AROUND THE WORLD

In cultures everywhere, birth is regarded as a special event, often magical and mysterious and cause for celebration. When we look at how tribal and village societies handle childbirth, we become aware of the wide range of ways in which babies can be ushered into the world.

Cultures vary greatly in whether they consider birth to be an illness or a natural body function. Among the Cuna Indians of Panama, childbirth is regarded as so abnormal that the pregnant mother visits the medicine man daily for drugs to help her. Throughout labor, she is constantly medicated. Cuna children are kept ignorant about the facts of life as long as possible. They are told that babies miraculously appear in the forest between deers' horns or are put on the beach by dolphins.

In contrast, the Jarara of South America and the Pukapukans of the Pacific Islands treat birth as a normal part of life. The Jarara mother gives birth in a passageway or shelter in full view of the entire community, including small children. The Pukapukan girl is so familiar with the events of labor and delivery that she can frequently be seen playing at it. Using a coconut to represent the baby, she stuffs it inside her dress, imitates the mother's pushing, and lets the nut fall at the proper moment.

In most cultures, women are assisted during childbirth, usually by two or more helpers. The type of support given varies, but in many cases, the mother is physically held from behind. Among the Mayans of the Yucatán, she is propped up by the body and arms of a woman called the "head helper," who sits in back. The helper supports the mother's weight and pushes and breathes with her during each contraction.

The majority of cultures have the mother give birth in a vertical position—sometimes on the knees, at other times, sitting, squatting, or standing. The Siriono of South America are an exception. The mother lies in a hammock slung low to the ground. A crowd of women keeps her company, standing by or sitting in nearby hammocks. Unlike the Mayan helpers, these women do not actively take part. The mother delivers the baby herself, and the infant, once born, is allowed to slide off the hammock onto the soft earth below. The mild jolt of falling a few inches is enough to stimulate the baby's first breath.

Sensory and physical stimulation is often provided during labor. The Laotians of Indochina and the Navaho of North America play special music for the mother. The Punjab of India rub melted butter across the mother's abdomen. Among the Comanche, warmed rocks are placed on the mother's back. The Tübatulabel Indians of California dig a trench, in which they build a fire. The trench is covered with slabs of stone, layers of earth, and mats. There, the mother lies down and gives birth.

When expectant mothers in our own culture know something about the great variety of birth practices around the world, they become more aware of their own alternatives. As a result, they may be more likely to explore childbirth options and choose ones that best fit with their own life circumstances and personal needs.

Sources: Jordan, 1993; Mead & Newton, 1967.

Among the !Kung of Botswana, Africa, a mother gives birth in a sitting position, and she is surrounded by women who encourage and help her. (Shostak/Anthro-Photo)

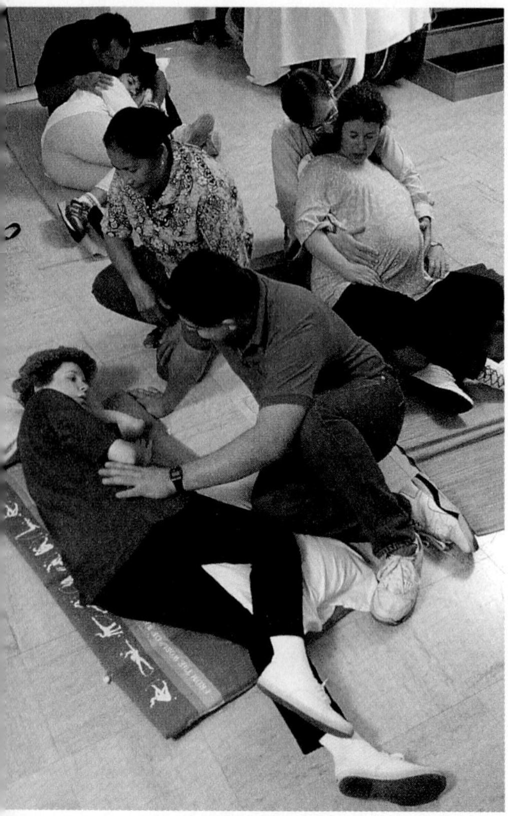

In this natural, or prepared, childbirth class, husbands learn how to be "labor coaches." Research suggests that the presence of a supportive companion during labor and delivery is an important part of the success of natural childbirth techniques. *(Lawrence Migdale)*

childbirth movement arose in Europe and spread to the United States. Its purpose was to make hospital birth as comfortable and rewarding for mothers as possible. Today, most hospitals carry this theme further by offering birth centers that are family centered in approach and home-like in appearance. *Freestanding birth centers,* which operate independently of hospitals and offer less in the way of backup medical care, also exist. And a small but growing number of American women are rejecting institutional birth entirely by choosing to have their babies at home.

Each of these places of childbirth—hospital delivery room, birth center, and home—has advantages and disadvantages that an expectant mother should consider before deciding where to have her baby. Hospitals are best equipped to handle patients with complications, since emergency medical equipment is readily available. However, hospitals usually have rigid rules that grant mothers little control over birth and post-birth experiences. Birth centers are less likely than traditional hospitals to use unnecessary medical procedures, have less rigid rules, and encourage early contact between parents and baby. Their informal, homelike birth settings are less expensive than hospital delivery rooms, but they are more expensive than home deliveries. Mothers who decide to give birth at home are in a familiar environment best suited to early parent–infant contact. But training of birth attendants can vary widely, and routine medical procedures, if needed, are usually not available. And in case of emergency, mother and baby must be transported to a hospital, delaying necessary intervention.

In the following sections, we take a closer look at two childbirth approaches that have grown in popularity in recent years: natural childbirth and home delivery.

NATURAL, OR PREPARED, CHILDBIRTH

Yolanda chose **natural, or prepared, childbirth** as the way she wanted to have her baby. Although there are many natural childbirth techniques, all try to rid mothers of the idea that birth is a painful ordeal that requires extensive medical intervention. Most programs draw on methods developed by Grantly Dick-Read (1959) in England and Ferdinand Lamaze (1958) in France. These physicians emphasized that cultural attitudes had taught women to fear the birth experience. An anxious, frightened woman in labor tenses muscles throughout her body, including those of the uterus. This turns the mild pain that sometimes accompanies strong contractions into a great deal of pain.

Yolanda and Jay enrolled in a typical natural childbirth program offered by a hospital birth center. The program consisted of three parts:

1. *Classes.* Yolanda and Jay attended a series of classes in which they learned about the anatomy and physiology of labor and delivery. Natural childbirth classes are based on the idea that knowledge about the birth process reduces a mother's fear.

2. *Relaxation and breathing techniques.* After each lecture, Yolanda was taught relaxation and breathing exercises aimed at counteracting any pain she might feel during uterine contractions. She also practiced creating pleasant visual images in her mind instead of thinking about pain.

3. *Labor coach.* While Yolanda mastered breathing and visualization techniques, Jay was taught to be a "labor coach." He learned how to help Yolanda during childbirth—by reminding her to relax and breathe, massaging her back, supporting her body during labor and delivery, and offering words of encouragement and affection.

When natural childbirth is combined with delivery in a birth center or at home, mothers often give birth in an upright position rather than lying flat on their backs with their feet in stirrups (which is the traditional hospital delivery room practice).

Natural, or prepared, childbirth
An approach designed to reduce pain and medical intervention and to make childbirth a rewarding experience for parents.

Doctors have become increasingly aware that gravity can speed up the second stage of labor. When mothers are upright, labor is shortened because pushing is easier and more effective. Also, the baby benefits because blood flow to the placenta is increased (Barnett, 1982; Davidson et al., 1993). In Europe, women are typically encouraged to give birth on their sides rather than on their backs, the position most often used in United States. The side-lying position reduces the need for an episiotomy, since pressure of the baby's head against the vaginal opening is less intense (Bobak, Jensen, & Zalar, 1989).

Studies comparing mothers who experience natural childbirth with those who do not reveal many benefits. Mothers' attitudes toward labor and delivery are more positive, and they feel less pain (Lindell, 1988). As a result, they require less medication—usually very little or none at all (Hetherington, 1990). Research suggests that social support may be an important part of the success of natural childbirth techniques. In Guatemalan and American hospitals in which patients were routinely prevented from having friends and relatives with them during childbirth, some mothers were randomly assigned a companion who stayed with them throughout labor, talking to them, holding their hands, and rubbing their backs to promote relaxation. These mothers had fewer birth complications, and their labors were several hours shorter than those of women who did not have supportive companionship. Observations of Guatemalan mothers in the first hour after delivery showed that those receiving social support were more likely to respond to their babies by talking, smiling, and gently stroking (Kennell et al., 1991; Sosa et al., 1980).

HOME DELIVERY

Home birth has always been popular in certain industrialized nations, such as England, the Netherlands, and Sweden. The number of American women choosing to have their babies at home has increased in recent years, although it is still small, amounting to about 1 percent. These mothers want to recapture the time when

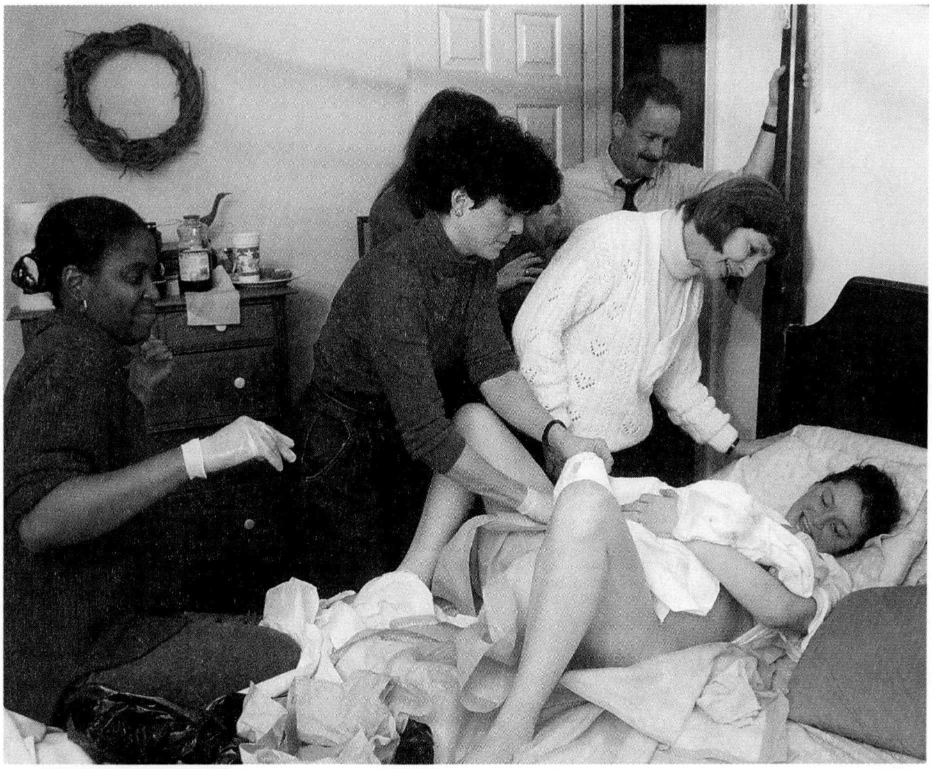

Women who choose home birth want to share the joy of childbirth with family members, avoid unnecessary medical procedures, and exercise greater control over their own care and that of their babies. When assisted by a well-trained doctor or midwife, healthy women can give birth at home safely. *(Franck Logue/ Stock South)*

birth was an important part of family life. In addition, most want to avoid unnecessary medical procedures and exercise greater control over their own care and that of their babies than most hospitals permit (Bastian, 1993; Declercq, 1992). Although some home births are attended by doctors, many more are handled by certified *nurse-midwives* who have degrees in nursing and additional training in childbirth management.

The joys and perils of home delivery are well illustrated by the story that Don, who painted my house as I worked on this book, told me as we took several coffee breaks together. Don is the father of four children, two of whom were born at home. "Our first child was delivered in the hospital," he said. "Even though I was present, Kathy and I found the whole atmosphere to be rigid and insensitive. We wanted a warmer, more personal environment in which to have our children." Don and Kathy's second child Cindy was born at their farmhouse, three miles out of town. A nurse-midwife was present. She coached Don, and he delivered Cindy himself. When, 3 years later, Kathy was in labor with Marnie, a heavy snowstorm prevented the midwife from getting to the house on time. Don delivered the baby alone, but the birth was difficult. Marnie failed to breathe for several minutes; with great effort, Don managed to revive her. The frightening memory of those moments when Marnie's body was limp and blue convinced Don and Kathy to return to the hospital to have their last child. By then, the hospital's birth practices had changed greatly. Don and Kathy got to know their doctor well, and he learned that Don had delivered Cindy and Marnie. This time, Kathy's labor proceeded easily and quickly. When the baby's head crowned, the doctor stepped aside and permitted Don to bring his youngest child into the world himself.

Don and Kathy's experience raises the question of whether it is just as safe to give birth at home as in a hospital. For healthy women who are assisted by a well-trained doctor or midwife, it seems so, since complications rarely occur. However, when attendants are not carefully trained and prepared to handle emergencies, the rate of infant death is high (Schramm, Barnes, & Bakewell, 1987). When mothers are at risk for any kind of complication, the appropriate place for labor and delivery is the hospital, where life-saving treatment is available should it be needed.

MEDICAL INTERVENTIONS

Medical interventions during childbirth are not practiced only in industrialized nations. They can also be found in much smaller and simpler cultures. For example, some preliterate tribal and village societies have discovered drugs that stimulate labor and have developed surgical techniques to deliver babies. Yet more so than anywhere else in the world, childbirth in the United States is a medically monitored and controlled event (Jordan, 1990; Notzon, 1990). What medical techniques are doctors likely to use during labor and delivery? When are they justified, and what dangers do they pose to mothers and babies? These are questions we take up in the following sections.

FETAL MONITORING

Fetal monitors are electronic instruments that track the baby's heart rate during labor. An abnormal heartbeat pattern may indicate that the baby is in distress due to lack of oxygen and needs to be delivered immediately. Fetal monitors are required in almost all American hospitals. Two types are in common use. The most popular kind is strapped across the mother's abdomen throughout labor (see Figure 4.2). A second more accurate method involves threading a recording device through the cervix and placing it directly under the baby's scalp.

Fetal monitors
Electronic instruments that track the baby's heart rate during labor.

Fetal monitoring is a safe medical procedure that has been shown to save the lives of many babies when mothers have a history of pregnancy and birth complications. Nevertheless, the devices have stimulated a great deal of controversy. In mothers who have had healthy pregnancies, fetal monitoring does not reduce the rate of infant brain damage or death (Rosen & Dickinson, 1992). Some critics also point out that use of fetal monitors is linked to an increase in the number of emergency cesarean (surgical) deliveries, a practice that we will discuss shortly. They worry that fetal monitors identify many babies as in danger who, in fact, are not (Prentice & Lind, 1987).

There is another reason that fetal monitors are controversial. Some women complain that the devices are uncomfortable, prevent them from moving easily, and interfere with the normal course of labor. Still, it is likely that fetal monitors will continue to be used routinely, even though they might not be necessary in most cases. Today, doctors can be sued for malpractice if an infant dies or is born with problems and they cannot show that they did everything possible to protect the baby (McRae, 1993). And despite lack of evidence, some doctors firmly believe that fetal monitoring contributes to healthy outcomes in all types of mothers.

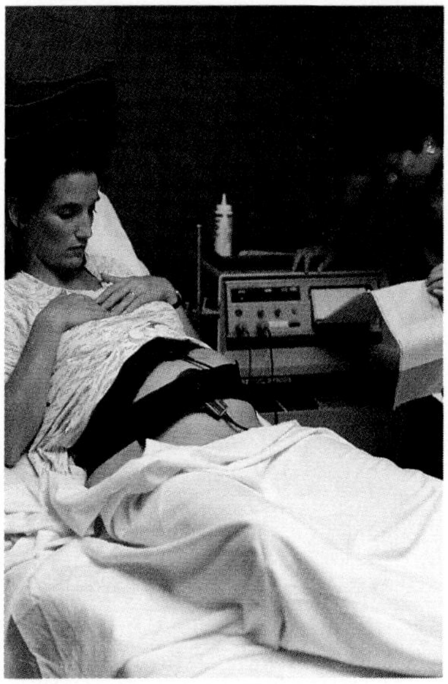

FIGURE 4.2

External fetal monitor, which is attached to the mother's abdomen and records fetal heart rate using ultrasound.
This type of fetal monitoring is used routinely in American hospitals. When mothers have a history of pregnancy and birth complications, fetal monitoring saves many lives. But it may also lead to an increase in unnecessary cesarean (surgical) deliveries. And some women complain that the monitors are uncomfortable and restrict their freedom of movement. *(George White)*

LABOR AND DELIVERY MEDICATION

Some form of medication is used in 80 to 95 percent of births in the United States. **Analgesics** are drugs used to relieve pain. When given during labor, the dose is usually mild and intended to help a mother relax. **Anesthetics** are a stronger type of painkiller that blocks sensation. General anesthesia, which puts the mother to sleep, is rarely used during childbirth today. More common are regional painkillers injected into the spinal column to numb the lower half of the body.

In complicated deliveries, pain-relieving drugs are essential because they permit life-saving medical interventions to be carried out. But when used routinely, they can cause problems. Anesthesia interferes with the mother's ability to feel contractions during the second stage of labor. As a result, she may not push effectively, increasing the likelihood of an instrument delivery (see next section).

Labor and delivery medication rapidly crosses the placenta. When given in fairly large doses, it produces a depressed state in the newborn baby that may last for days. The infant is sleepy and withdrawn, sucks poorly during feedings, and is likely to be irritable when awake (Brackbill, McManus, & Woodward, 1985; Brazelton, Nugent, & Lester, 1987). One study found that mothers who received anesthesia viewed their babies as more difficult and less rewarding to care for in the weeks after birth (Murray et al., 1981).

Does the use of medication during childbirth have a lasting impact on the physical and mental development of the child? Some researchers claim so (Brackbill, McManus, & Woodward, 1985), but their findings have been challenged, and contrary results exist (Broman, 1983). Anesthesia may be related to other risk factors that could account for the long-term consequences in some studies, and more research is needed to sort out these effects. In the meantime, the negative impact of these drugs on the early infant–mother relationship is well established, and this alone is good reason to limit their use.

Analgesic
A mild pain-relieving drug.

Anesthetic
A strong pain-killing drug that blocks sensation.

Forceps
Metal clamps placed around the baby's head, used to pull the infant from the birth canal.

Vacuum extractor
A plastic cup attached to a suction tube, used to deliver the baby.

INSTRUMENT DELIVERY

Forceps, metal clamps placed around the baby's head to pull the infant from the birth canal, have been used since the sixteenth century to speed up delivery (see Figure 4.3). A more recent instrument, the **vacuum extractor,** consists of a plastic cup (placed on the baby's head) attached to a suction tube. Instrument delivery is appropriate if the mother's pushing during the second stage of labor does not cause the baby to move through the birth canal in a reasonable period of time.

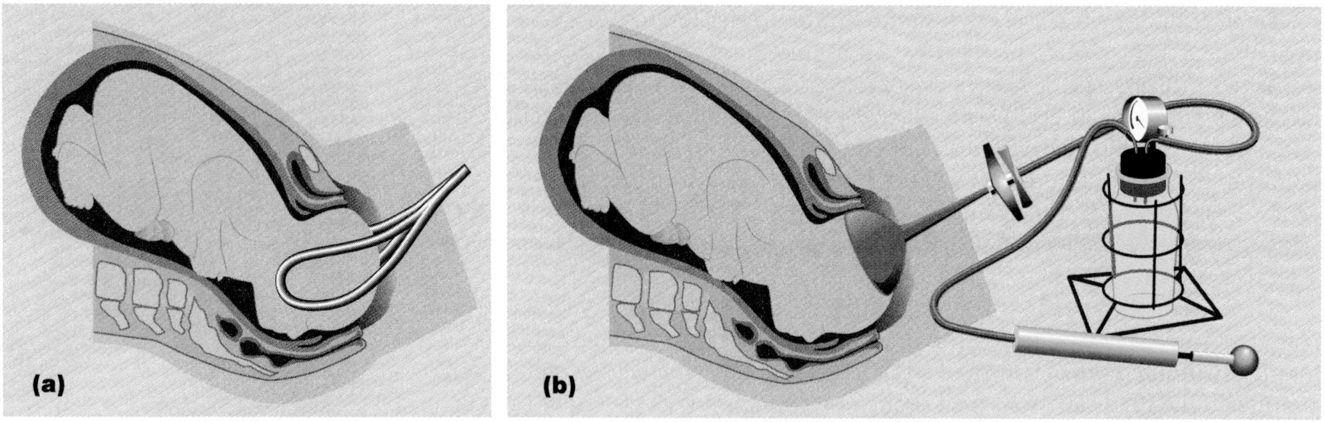

FIGURE 4.3

Instrument delivery.
(a) The pressure that must be applied to pull the infant from the birth canal with forceps involves risk of injury to the baby's head. (b) An alternative method, the vacuum extractor, is not used as often in North America. Although vacuum extraction is less likely than forceps to injure the mother, it is just as risky for the infant. Scalp injuries are common.

In the United States, forceps or vacuum extractors are used in 20 to 30 percent of births. In contrast, they are used less than 5 percent of the time in Europe. These figures suggest that instruments may be applied too freely in American hospitals (Korte & Scaer, 1990). When a doctor uses forceps to pull the baby through most or all of the birth canal, deliveries are associated with higher rates of brain damage. As a result, forceps are seldom used this way today. Low-forceps delivery (carried out when the baby is most of the way through the vagina) is not associated with poorer intellectual functioning in childhood and adolescence (Seidman et al., 1991; Wesley, van den Berg, & Reece, 1993). Still, some risk of injury to the baby's head remains. Vacuum extractors are less likely to tear the mother's tissues than are forceps, but the chances of harming the infant are just as great (Hanigan et al., 1990; Johanson et al., 1993). For these reasons, neither method should be used when the mother can still be encouraged to deliver normally and there is no special reason to hurry the birth.

INDUCED LABOR

An **induced labor** is one that is started artificially. This is usually done by breaking the amnion or bag of waters (an event that usually takes place naturally in the first stage of labor) and giving the mother synthetic oxytocin, a hormone involved in stimulating contractions.

Are there good reasons to induce labor? Yes, when continuing the pregnancy threatens the well-being of mother or baby. Too often, though, labors are induced for reasons of convenience rather than health. Perhaps the doctor is planning to go on vacation or would prefer not to be called into the hospital in the middle of the night. Parents might also desire to arrange the birth of the baby to fit with their other plans.

In a healthy mother, the onset of labor should not be scheduled like her doctor's appointment. An induced labor often proceeds differently from a naturally occurring one. The contractions are longer, harder, and closer together. The possibility of inadequate oxygen supply to the baby is increased because there is less time between contractions for a full supply of oxygen to cross the placenta. In addition, mothers often find it more difficult to stay in control of an induced labor, even when they have been coached in natural childbirth techniques. As a result, labor and delivery medication is likely to be used in larger amounts, and there is a greater chance of instrument delivery (Brindley & Sokol, 1988).

Induced labor
A labor started artificially by breaking the amnion and giving the mother a hormone that stimulates contractions.

Cesarean delivery
A surgical delivery in which the doctor makes an incision in the mother's abdomen and lifts the baby out of the uterus.

CESAREAN DELIVERY

A **cesarean delivery** is a surgical birth; the doctor makes an incision in the mother's abdomen and lifts the baby out of the uterus. Thirty years ago, cesarean delivery was rare in the United States, performed only when the life of mother or

TABLE 4.2

Common Reasons for Cesarean Delivery in the United States

REASON	PERCENTAGE OF CESAREANS
Previous cesarean	35
Abnormal labor	28
Baby in breech position	10
Infant distress due to oxygen deprivation	10
Other emergencies	17
Serious maternal illness—diabetes, heart disease, or infection (such as herpes simplex 2) that can be transmitted to the fetus during vaginal delivery. Medical emergencies, such as premature separation of the placenta from the uterus or Rh incompatibility.	

Source: Korte & Scaer, 1990.

baby was in immediate danger. In 1970, 3 percent of babies were born in this way. Since that time, the cesarean rate has climbed steadily. In 1992, the practice accounted for 23.5 percent of American births, the highest rate in the world (U.S. Bureau of the Census, 1994).

Birth complications that lead to cesarean deliveries are summarized in Table 4.2. Cesareans have always been warranted by the serious medical emergencies noted in the last entry of the table. In contrast, there is growing evidence that surgical delivery is not always needed to deal with the other four problems listed. Together, these account for over 80 percent of cesarean births.

Earlier we mentioned that fetal monitoring increases the likelihood of cesarean delivery and that some infants identified as in distress may be "false positives." Cesareans are also routinely performed when babies are in **breech position,** or turned in such a way that the buttocks or feet would be delivered first, a circumstance that affects about 1 in every 25 births. Delivering a breech baby through the vagina can be risky. The breech position increases the possibility that the umbilical cord may be squeezed as the large head moves through the birth canal, depriving the infant of oxygen. Head injuries are also more likely. Cesareans are justified in many of these cases (Cheng & Hannah, 1993). However, the exact positioning of the infant (which can be felt by the doctor) makes a difference. Certain breech babies fare just as well with a normal delivery as they do with a cesarean (Collea, Chein, & Quilligan, 1980). Sometimes the doctor can gently turn a breech baby into a head-down position during the early part of labor.

The two most common reasons for cesareans are a failure of labor to progress normally and a previous history of cesarean birth (Silver & Wolfe, 1989). Many physicians take the position that "once a cesarean, always a cesarean" because the uterine scar might rupture if the mother is permitted to deliver vaginally in a later birth. However, the surgical technique used today—a small horizontal cut in the lower part of the uterus—makes this possibility unlikely. Even when it does occur, it is not life threatening to mother or baby (Jakobi et al., 1993).

Because many unnecessary cesareans are performed in the United States, pregnant women should ask questions about the procedure before choosing a doctor. When a mother does end up having a cesarean, she and her baby need extra support. The operation itself is quite safe, but it requires more time for recovery. Cesarean newborns are more likely to be sleepy and unresponsive and to have breathing difficulties. Anesthesia may have crossed the placenta, and the rush of stress hormones stimulated by labor contractions is not present to promote arousal and respiration. Any one of these factors can negatively affect the early mother–infant relationship (Cox & Schwartz, 1990).

Breech position
A position of the baby in the uterus that would cause the buttocks or feet to be delivered first.

ASK YOURSELF . . .

- Use of any single medical intervention during childbirth increases the likelihood that others will also be used. Provide as many examples as you can to illustrate this idea.
- Sharon, a heavy smoker, has just arrived at the hospital in labor. Which one of the medical interventions discussed in the preceding sections is her doctor justified in using? (For help in answering this question, return to our discussion of the prenatal effects of smoking in Chapter 3, pages 113–114).

BRIEF REVIEW

In modern industrialized nations, a woman can choose to have her baby in a traditional hospital setting, a birth center, or at home. Natural, or prepared, childbirth programs are widely available. Home births are safe for healthy women, provided attendants are well trained.

Medical interventions during childbirth are more likely to be used in the United States than anywhere else in the world. Although often justified, these procedures can cause problems. In some instances, fetal monitoring may mistakenly identify babies as distressed. Pain-relieving drugs can cross the placenta, producing a withdrawn state in the infant. Because induced labors are more difficult, they are associated with greater use of medication. Instrument deliveries involve some risk of head injury. Cesarean births require extra recovery time for the mother, and babies tend to be less alert and more likely to have breathing difficulties.

BIRTH COMPLICATIONS

In the preceding sections and throughout Chapter 3, we indicated that some babies—in particular those whose mothers are in poor health, who do not receive good medical care, or who have a history of pregnancy problems—are especially likely to experience birth complications. Inadequate oxygen, a pregnancy that ends too early, and a baby who is born underweight are serious complications that we have mentioned many times. Another risk factor is a pregnancy in which the baby remains in the uterus too long. Let's look at the impact of each of these complications on later development.

OXYGEN DEPRIVATION

Some years ago, I got to know 2-year-old Melinda and her mother Judy, both of whom participated in a special program for infants with disabilities at our laboratory school. Melinda has **cerebral palsy,** which is a general term for a variety of problems that result from brain damage before, during, or just after birth. Difficulties in muscle coordination are always involved, such as a clumsy walk, uncontrolled movements, and unclear speech. The disorder can range from very mild tremors to severe crippling accompanied by mental retardation. One out of every 500 children born in the United States has cerebral palsy. Twenty-two percent of these youngsters experienced **anoxia,** or inadequate oxygen supply, during labor and delivery (Torfs et al., 1990).

Melinda walks with a halting, lumbering gait, and she has difficulty keeping her balance. "Some mothers don't know how the palsy happened," confided Judy, "but I do. I got pregnant accidentally, and my boyfriend didn't want to have anything to do with it. I was frightened and alone most of the time. I arrived at the hospital at the last minute. Melinda was breech, and the cord was wrapped around her neck."

Squeezing of the umbilical cord, which happened in Melinda's case, is one cause of anoxia. Another cause is *placenta previa,* or premature separation of the placenta, a life-threatening event that requires immediately delivery. Although the reasons for placenta previa are not well understood, teratogens (such as cigarette smoking) that cause abnormal development of the placenta are strongly related to it (Kramer et al., 1991). In still other instances, the birth seems to go along all right, but the baby fails to start breathing within a few minutes. Newborns can survive periods without oxygen longer than adults, but there is risk of brain damage if breathing is delayed for more than 3 minutes (Stechler & Halton, 1982). Can you think of other possi-

Cerebral palsy
A general term for a variety of problems, all of which involve muscle coordination, that result from brain damage before, during, or just after birth.

Anoxia
Inadequate oxygen supply.

ble causes of oxygen deprivation that you learned about as you studied prenatal development and birth?

How do children who experience anoxia during labor and delivery fare as they get older? Melinda's physical handicap was permanent, but otherwise she did well. The same is true for most oxygen-deprived newborns. These infants remain behind their agemates in intellectual and motor progress throughout early childhood. But by the school years, most catch up in development (Corah et al., 1965; Graham et al., 1962).

When problems do persist, the oxygen deprivation was probably extreme. Perhaps it was caused by prenatal damage to the baby's respiratory system, or it may have happened because the infant's lungs were not yet mature enough to breathe. For example, infants born more than 6 weeks early commonly have a disorder called **respiratory distress syndrome** (otherwise known as *hyaline membrane disease*). Their tiny lungs are so poorly developed that the air sacs collapse, causing serious breathing difficulties and sometimes death. Today, mechanical ventilators keep many such infants alive. In spite of these measures, some babies suffer permanent damage from lack of oxygen, and in other cases their delicate lungs are harmed by the treatment itself (Vohr & Garcia-Coll, 1988). Respiratory distress syndrome is only one of many risks for babies born too soon, as we will see in the following section.

PRETERM AND LOW-BIRTH-WEIGHT INFANTS

> Janet, just under 6 months pregnant, and her husband Rick boarded a flight at the Hartford, Connecticut, airport, on their way to a vacation in Hawaii. The plane was scheduled to make two stops before the long journey across the Pacific Ocean. In Chicago, Janet emerged from the restroom and told Rick she was bleeding. When the plane stopped again, this time in San Francisco, Janet realized she was in trouble. Rushed to a hospital, she gave birth to Keith, who weighed less than 1 1/2 pounds.
>
> During Keith's first month, he experienced one crisis after another, all of which are common in very premature infants. Three days after birth, an ultrasound scan suggested that fragile blood vessels feeding Keith's brain had hemorrhaged, a complication that can cause brain damage. Within three weeks, Keith had surgery to close a valve in his heart that seals automatically in full-term babies. Keith's immature immune system made infections difficult to contain. Repeated illnesses and the drugs used to treat them caused permanent hearing loss. He also had respiratory distress syndrome and was attached to a ventilator. Soon, there was evidence of lung damage, and Keith's vision was threatened because of constant exposure to oxygen. It took over 3 months of hospitalization for Keith's rough course of complications and treatment to ease.
> (Paraphrased from Turiel, 1991a, pp. D13–D14)

Babies born 3 weeks or more before the end of a full 38-week pregnancy or who weigh less than 5 1/2 pounds (2,500 grams) have for many years been referred to as "premature." A wealth of research indicates that premature babies are at risk for many problems. Birth weight is the best available predictor of infant survival and healthy development. Many newborns who weigh less than 3 1/3 pounds (1,500 grams) experience difficulties that are not overcome, an effect that becomes stronger as birth weight decreases. Frequent illness, visual impairments, inattention, overactivity, low intelligence test scores, and school learning problems are some of the difficulties that extend into the childhood years (Hack et al., 1994; Liaw & Brooks-Gunn, 1993; McCormick, Gortmaker, & Sobol, 1990).

About 1 in 14 infants is born underweight in the United States. The problem can strike unexpectedly, as it did for Janet and Rick. It is highest among low-income

Respiratory distress syndrome
A disorder of preterm infants in which the lungs are so immature that the air sacs collapse, causing serious breathing difficulties.

pregnant women, especially ethnic minorities (Children's Defense Fund, 1994). These mothers, as we indicated in Chapter 3, are more likely to be undernourished and to be exposed to other harmful environmental influences—factors strongly linked to low birth weight. In addition, they often do not receive the prenatal care necessary to protect their vulnerable babies.

You may recall from Chapter 2 that prematurity is also common when mothers are carrying twins. Twins are usually born about 3 weeks early, and because of restricted space inside the uterus, they gain less weight than singleton babies after the twentieth week of pregnancy.

PRETERM VERSUS SMALL FOR DATE. Although low-birth-weight infants face many obstacles to healthy development, individual differences exist in how well they do. Over half go on to lead normal lives—even some who weighed only a couple of pounds at birth (Vohr & Garcia-Coll, 1988). To better understand why some of these babies do better than others, researchers have divided them into two groups. The first is called **preterm.** These infants are born several weeks or more before their due date. Although small in size, their weight may still be appropriate for the amount of time they spent in the uterus. The second group is called **small for date.** These babies are below their expected weight when length of the pregnancy is taken into account. Some small-for-date infants are actually full term. Others are preterm infants who are especially underweight.

Of the two types of babies, small-for-date infants usually have more serious problems. During the first year, they are more likely to die, catch infections, and show evidence of brain damage. By middle childhood, they have lower intelligence test scores, are less attentive, and achieve more poorly in school (Copper et al., 1993; Teberg, Walther, & Pena, 1988). Small-for-date infants probably experienced inadequate nutrition before birth. Perhaps their mothers did not eat properly, the placenta did not function normally, or the babies themselves had defects that prevented them from growing as they should.

CHARACTERISTICS OF PRETERM INFANTS: CONSEQUENCES FOR CAREGIVING. Imagine a scrawny, thin-skinned infant whose body is only a little larger than the size of your hand. You try to play with the baby by stroking and talking softly, but he is sleepy and unresponsive. When you feed him, he sucks poorly. He is usually irritable during the short, unpredictable periods in which he is awake.

Unfortunately, the appearance and behavior of preterm babies can lead parents to be less sensitive and responsive in caring for them. Compared to full-term infants, preterm babies—especially those who are very ill at birth—are less often held close, touched, and talked to gently. At times, mothers of these infants are overly intrusive, engaging in interfering pokes and verbal commands in an effort to obtain a higher level of response from a baby who is a passive, unrewarding social partner (Patteson & Barnard, 1990). Some parents may step up these intrusive acts when faced with continuing ungratifying infant behavior. This may explain why preterm babies as a group are at risk for child abuse. When these infants are born to isolated, poverty-stricken mothers who have difficulty managing their own lives, the chances for unfavorable outcomes are increased. In contrast, parents with stable life circumstances and social supports can usually overcome the stresses of caring for a preterm infant. In these cases, even sick preterm babies have a good chance of catching up in development by middle childhood (Liaw & Brooks-Gunn, 1993).

These findings suggest that how well preterm babies develop has a great deal to do with the kind of relationship established between parent and child, to which both partners contribute. If a good relationship between parent and baby can help prevent the negative effects of early birth, then intervention programs directed at supporting this relationship should help these infants recover.

Preterm
Infants born several weeks or more before their due date. Although small in size, their weight may still be appropriate for the time they spent in the uterus.

Small for date
Infants whose birth weight is below normal when length of pregnancy is taken into account.

INTERVENING WITH PRETERM INFANTS. A preterm baby is cared for in a special bed called an *isolette*. It is a plexiglass-enclosed box in which temperature is carefully controlled, since these infants cannot yet regulate their own body temperature effectively. Air is filtered before it enters the isolette to help protect the baby from infection. When a preterm infant is fed through a stomach tube, breathes with the aid of a respirator, and receives medication through an intravenous needle, the isolette can be very isolating indeed! Physical needs that otherwise would lead to close contact and other forms of stimulation from an adult are met mechanically. At one time doctors believed that stimulating such a fragile baby could be harmful. Now we know that certain kinds of stimulation in proper doses can help preterm infants develop.

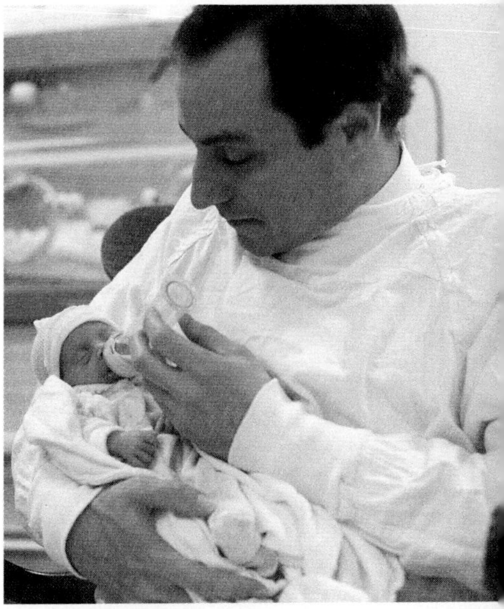

This father feeds his preterm baby in a hospital intensive care nursery. A good parent–infant relationship, the stimulation of touch, and a soft, gentle voice are likely to help this infant recover and catch up in development. *(Joseph Nettis/Photo Researchers)*

Special Infant Stimulation. In some intensive care nurseries, preterm babies can be seen rocking in suspended hammocks or lying on waterbeds—interventions designed to replace the gentle motion they would have received while being carried in the mother's uterus. Other forms of stimulation have also been used—for example, an attractive mobile or a tape recording of a heartbeat, soft music, or the mother's voice. Many studies show that these experiences promote faster weight gain, more predictable sleep patterns, and greater alertness during the weeks after birth (Cornell & Gottfried, 1976; Schaefer, Hatcher, & Bargelow, 1980).

Touch is an especially important form of stimulation for preterm newborns. In studies of baby animals, touching the skin releases certain brain chemicals that support physical growth. These effects are believed to occur in humans as well (Schanberg & Field, 1987). In one study, preterm infants who were gently massaged several times each day in the hospital gained weight faster and, at the end of the first year, were advanced in mental and motor development over preterm babies not given this stimulation (Field et al., 1986). In developing countries where hospitalization is not always possible, skin-to-skin "kangaroo baby care," in which the preterm infant is tucked between the mother's breasts and peers over the top of her clothing, is being encouraged. The technique is used often in Europe as a supplement to hospital intensive care. It fosters oxygenation of the baby's body, temperature regulation, improved feeding, and infant survival (Anderson, 1991; Hamelin & Ramachandran, 1993).

Some very small or sick babies are too weak to handle much stimulation. The noise, bright lights, and constant medical monitoring of the intensive care nursery are already quite overwhelming for them. Doctors and nurses need to carefully adjust the amount and kind of stimulation to fit the baby's individual needs (Korner, 1987).

Training Parents in Infant Caregiving Skills. When effective stimulation helps preterm babies develop, parents are likely to feel good about their infant's growth and interact with the baby more effectively. Interventions that support the parenting side of this relationship generally teach parents about the infant's characteristics and promote caregiving skills. Those that work best include enough sessions so parents can establish a warm relationship with the intervener (Patteson & Barnard, 1990).

In one program, a specially trained nurse met with mothers daily during the week before hospital discharge and in four sessions in the home over the next 3 months. The nurse helped each mother appreciate her baby's unique ways of signaling discomfort and readiness for interaction and taught her to respond sensitively to the baby's cues. Infants of mothers who received the intervention, in comparison to infants of mothers who did not, gained steadily in mental test performance over infancy and early childhood until their scores equaled those of full-term youngsters. These findings indicate that even a relatively brief effort to help mothers adjust to the care of a low-birth-weight baby can have long-term benefits for development (Achenbach et al., 1990). When preterm infants live in stressed, low-income households, intensive intervention that combines parent training with enrollment of the child in cognitively stimulating day care for several years is effective in reducing intellectual and behavior problems (Brooks-Gunn et al., 1993).

As we conclude our discussion of preterm and low-birth-weight infants, I would like to tell you more about Keith, the very sick baby whom you met at the beginning of this section. Because of advanced medical technology and new ways of helping parents, many preterm infants survive and eventually catch up in development, but Keith was not one of the lucky ones. Even with the best of care, from 30 to 70 percent of babies born as early as Keith either die or end up with serious disabilities. Eventually, Keith was transferred to a hospital near Janet and Rick's home. For a while, he could be held for several hours a day outside the isolette, but soon he suffered new setbacks. He stopped gaining weight and caught more infections. The respirator that had helped him live left his lungs so badly damaged that there was not much chance of survival. Six months after he was born, Keith died (Turiel, 1991b).

Keith's premature birth was unavoidable, but the high rate of underweight babies in the United States—one of the worst in the industrialized world—could be greatly reduced by improving the health and social conditions described in the Social Issues box on the following page. Fortunately, today we can save many preterm babies, but an even better course of action would be to prevent this serious threat to infant survival and development before it happens.

POSTTERM INFANTS

The normal length of pregnancy is 38 weeks. Infants born after 42 weeks are **postterm.** About 10 percent fall into this category. Most of these late-arriving newborns are quite normal. However, a small number start to lose weight at the end of pregnancy because the placenta no longer functions properly. As the baby becomes more overdue, the amount of amniotic fluid drops sharply. This increases the chances that the infant's movements in the uterus will squeeze the umbilical cord. Also, since postterm infants grow larger during the extra weeks spent in the uterus, they may have difficulty moving through the birth canal. Because of all these factors, the possibility of oxygen deprivation and head injuries in a postterm birth is great (Rosen & Dickinson, 1992).

Since the likelihood of birth complications and infant death rises steeply as a pregnancy continues past 42 weeks, doctors usually induce labor in these mothers (Resnick, 1988). Once born, most postterm babies do well. Their mental development may be slightly behind during infancy and early childhood, but it generally evens out by school entry (Shime, 1988).

UNDERSTANDING BIRTH COMPLICATIONS

In the preceding sections, we discussed a variety of birth complications that threaten children's well-being. Now let's try to put the evidence together. Are there any general principles that might help us understand how infants who survive a traumatic birth are likely to develop? A landmark study carried out in Hawaii provides answers to this question.

In 1955, Emmy Werner began to follow nearly 700 infants on the island of Kauai who experienced either mild, moderate, or severe complications at birth. Each was matched, on the basis of social class and ethnicity, with a healthy newborn. The study had two goals: (1) to discover the long-term effects of birth complications, and (2) to find out how family environments affect the child's chances for recovery. The findings indicated that the likelihood of long-term difficulties increased if birth trauma was severe. But among mild to moderately stressed children, the most powerful clue to how well they did in later years was the quality of their home environments. Children growing up in stable families did

Infant mortality
The number of deaths in the first year of life per 1,000 live births.

Neonatal mortality
The number of deaths in the first month of life per 1,000 live births.

Postterm
Infants who spend a longer than average time period in the uterus—more than 42 weeks.

SOCIAL ISSUES

A CROSS-NATIONAL PERSPECTIVE ON INFANT MORTALITY

Infant mortality is an index used around the world to assess the overall health of a nation's children. It refers to the number of deaths in the first year of life per 1,000 live births. How do you think the United States compares to other industrialized nations in infant mortality? The information in Figure 4.4 may surprise you. Although the United States has the most up-to-date health care technology in the world, it has made less progress than many other countries in reducing infant deaths. Over the past three decades, it slipped down in the international rankings, from seventh in the 1950s to twenty-second in the early 1990s. Members of America's poor ethnic minorities, black babies especially, are at greatest risk. Black infants are two-and-one-half times as likely as white infants to die in the first year of life (Children's Defense Fund, 1994; Wegman, 1994).

Neonatal mortality, the rate of death within the first month of life, accounts for 67 percent of the high infant death rate in the United States. Two factors are largely responsible for neonatal mortality. The first is serious physical defects, most of which cannot be prevented. The percentage of babies born with physical defects is about the same in all ethnic and income groups. The second leading cause of neonatal mortality is low birth weight, which is largely preventable. Black babies are more than four times more likely to die because they are born early and underweight than are white infants. On an international scale, the number of underweight babies born in the United States is alarmingly high. It is greater than that of 28 other countries (Children's Defense Fund, 1994; Wegman, 1994).

Why are American babies more likely to be born underweight and to die than infants in so many other nations? Experts agree that widespread poverty and weak health care programs for mothers and young children are responsible. Except for the United States, each country listed in Figure 4.4 provides all its citizens with government-sponsored health care benefits. And each takes extra steps to make sure that pregnant mothers and babies have access to good nutrition, high-quality medical care, and social and economic supports that promote effective parenting.

For example, all western European nations guarantee women a certain number of prenatal visits at very low or no cost. A health professional routinely visits the home after a baby is born to provide counseling about infant care and to arrange continuing medical services. Home assistance is especially extensive in the Netherlands. For a token fee, each mother is granted the services of a specially trained maternity helper, who assists with infant care, shopping, housekeeping, meal preparation, and the care of other children during the 10 days after delivery (Kamerman, 1993).

Paid employment leave for expectant and new parents is also widely available in western Europe. It ranges from about 2 to 10 months, depending on the country. A few nations, such as Denmark, Finland, Norway, and Sweden, permit the father to take childbirth leave if he is the principal caregiver. The period of leave can usually be extended on an unpaid basis, and additional paid leave is granted in the event of maternal or child illness (Kamerman, 1993).

In countries with low infant mortality rates, expectant mothers need not wonder how or where they will get health and child care assistance, or who will pay for it. The clear link between high-quality maternal and infant health services and reduced infant mortality provides strong justification for implementing similar programs in the United States.

TRY THIS . . .

- Why has the United States been slow to develop a national system of health care, whereas European nations have had these programs in place for many years? For help in answering this question, return to our discussion of public policies and child development in Chapter 2, pages 82–85.
- List all the factors discussed in Chapter 3 and in this chapter that increase the chances that a baby will be born underweight. How many of these factors could be prevented by better health care for mothers and babies?

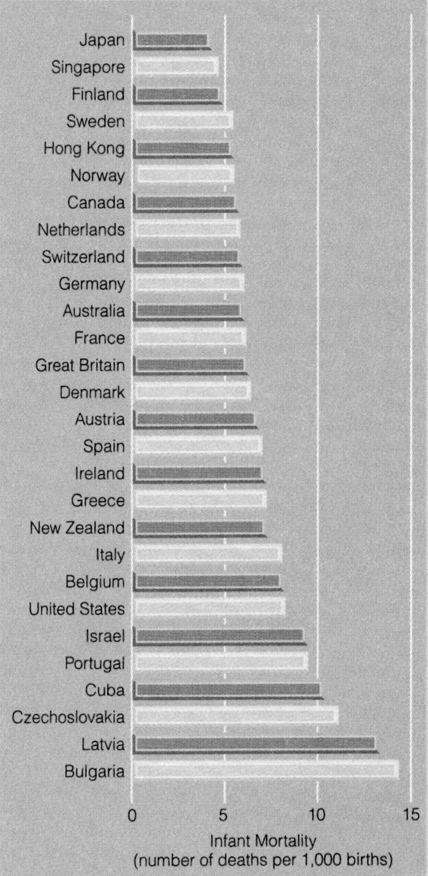

FIGURE 4.4

Infant mortality in 28 nations. Despite its advanced health care technology, the United States ranks poorly. It is twenty-second in the world, with a death rate of 8.9 infants per 1,000 births. *(Adapted from United Nations, 1994; Wegman, 1994.)*

almost as well on measures of intelligence and psychological adjustment as those with no birth difficulties. Those exposed to poverty, family disorganization, and mentally ill parents often developed serious learning difficulties, behavior problems, and emotional disturbance (Werner & Smith, 1982).

The Kauai study tells us that as long as birth injuries are not overwhelming, a supportive home environment can restore children's growth. However, the most intriguing cases in this study were the handful of exceptions to this rule. A few youngsters with both fairly serious birth complications and very troubled families grew into competent adults who fared as well as controls in career attainment and psychological adjustment. Werner found that these resilient children relied on factors outside the family and within themselves to overcome stress. Some had especially attractive personalities that caused them to receive positive responses from relatives, neighbors, and peers. In other cases, a grandparent, aunt, uncle, or baby-sitter established a warm relationship with the child and provided the needed emotional support (Werner, 1989; Werner & Smith, 1992).

The Kauai study reveals that as long as the overall balance of life events tips toward the favorable side, children with serious birth problems can develop successfully. When negative factors outweigh positive ones, even the sturdiest of newborn babies may become a lifelong casualty.

ASK YOURSELF . . .

- Explain how the long-term outcomes reported for oxygen-deprived and preterm babies fit with findings of the Kauai study.
- Sensitive care can help preterm infants recover, but unfortunately they are less likely to receive this kind of care than full-term newborns. Explain why.

BRIEF REVIEW

Birth complications can threaten children's development. Oxygen deprivation, when extreme, causes lasting brain damage. Preterm and small-for-date babies are at risk for many problems. Providing these infants with special stimulation and teaching parents how to care for and interact with them helps restore favorable growth. The longer a postterm infant remains in the uterus, the greater the likelihood of birth difficulties. When newborns with serious complications grow up in positive social environments, they have a good chance of catching up in development.

PRECIOUS MOMENTS AFTER BIRTH

Yolanda and Jay's account of Joshua's birth revealed that the time spent holding and touching him right after delivery was a memorable period filled with intense emotion. A mother given her infant at this time will usually stroke the baby gently, look into the infant's eyes, and talk softly (Klaus & Kennell, 1982). Observations of and interviews with fathers indicate that they respond similarly. Most are overjoyed at the birth of the baby, characterize the experience as "awesome," "indescribable," or "unforgettable," and display intense interest and involvement in their newborn child (Greenberg & Morris, 1974; Nichols, 1993). Regardless of their social class or whether they participated in childbirth classes, fathers touch, look at, talk to, and kiss their newborn infants just as much as mothers. When they hold the baby, sometimes they exceed mothers in stimulation and affection (Parke & Tinsley, 1981).

Many nonhuman animals engage in specific caregiving behaviors immediately after birth that are critical for survival of the young. For example, a mother cat licks her newborn kittens and then encircles them with her body (Schneirla et al., 1963). Rats, sheep, and goats engage in similar licking behaviors. But if the mother is separated from the young during the time period following delivery, her responsiveness declines until finally she rejects the infant (Poindron & Le Neindre, 1980; Rosenblatt & Lehrman, 1963).

Do human parents also require close physical contact with their babies in the hours after birth for **bonding,** or feelings of affection and concern for the infant, to develop? A few investigators used to think so, but current evidence indicates that the parent–infant relationship does not depend on a precise period of togetherness in human beings (Eyer, 1992; Lamb, 1994). Some parents report sudden, deep feelings of affection on first holding their babies. For others, these emotions emerge gradually, over the first few weeks of life (MacFarlane, Smith, & Garrow, 1978). In adoptive parents, a warm, affectionate relationship can develop quite successfully even if the child enters the family months or years after birth (Dontas et al., 1985; Hodges & Tizard, 1989). Taken together, these findings indicate that human bonding is a complex process that depends on many factors, not just what happens during a short time interval.

Still, contact with the infant after birth might be one of several factors that helps build a good relationship between parent and baby. When nurses take the infant away after delivery, they convey a message to parents that professionals are capable of caring for the baby but mothers and fathers are not. Recent research shows that mothers learn to discriminate their own newborn baby from other infants on the basis of touch, smell, and sight (a photograph) after as little as one hour of contact (Kaitz et al., 1987, 1988; Kaitz et al., 1992). This early recognition probably facilitates responsiveness to the infant, although it is not critical for the development of a warm relationship.

Today, hospitals realize that early contact between parents and babies can be helpful. An arrangement called **rooming in,** in which the baby stays in the mother's hospital room all or most of the time, is widely available. If parents choose not to take advantage of this option or cannot do so for medical reasons, there is no evidence that their competence as caregivers will be compromised or that the baby will suffer emotionally (Lamb, 1994).

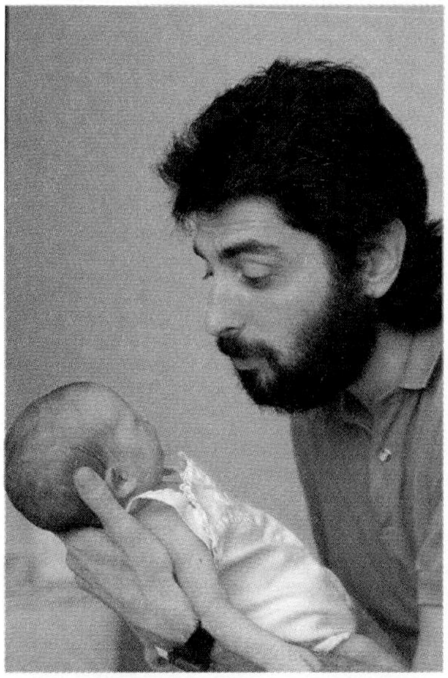

This father displays intense interest in and involvement with his newborn child. Parents typically express their elation at the baby's arrival by stroking the infant gently, looking into the baby's eyes, and talking softly. *(Erika Stone)*

THE NEWBORN BABY'S CAPACITIES

As recently as fifty years ago, scientists considered the newborn baby to be a passive, disorganized being whose world was, in the words of turn-of-the-century psychologist William James, a "blooming, buzzing confusion." The newly arrived infant, it was commonly believed, could see, hear, feel, and do very little. Today, we know that this image of an incompetent newborn is wrong. Newborn babies have a remarkable set of capacities that are crucial for survival and that are profoundly important in evoking the attention and care they receive from parents. In relating to the physical world and building their first social relationships, babies are active from the very start.

NEWBORN REFLEXES

A **reflex** is an inborn, automatic response to a particular form of stimulation. Reflexes are the newborn baby's most obvious organized patterns of behavior. Human infants come into the world with dozens of them. As Jay put Joshua down on a table in my classroom, we saw several. When Jay bumped the side of the table, Joshua reacted by flinging his arms wide and bringing them back toward his body. As Yolanda stroked Joshua's cheek, he turned his head in her direction. When she put her finger in the palm of Joshua's hand, he grabbed on tightly. Jay held Joshua upright with his feet touching the table, and he made little stepping movements. Table 4.3 provides a description of the major newborn reflexes. See if you can name the ones that Joshua displayed. Then let's look at the meaning and purpose of these curious behaviors.

Bonding
Parents' feelings of affection and concern for the newborn baby.

Rooming in
An arrangement in which the newborn baby stays in the mother's hospital room all or most of the time.

Reflex
An inborn, automatic response to a particular form of stimulation.

TABLE 4.3

Some Newborn Reflexes

REFLEX	STIMULATION	RESPONSE	AGE OF DISAPPEARANCE	FUNCTION
Eye blink	Shine bright light at eyes or clap hand near head	Infant quickly closes eyelids	Permanent	Protects infant from strong stimulation
Rooting	Stroke cheek near corner of mouth	Head turns toward source of stimulation	3 weeks (becomes voluntary head turning at this time)	Helps infant find the nipple
Sucking	Place finger in infant's mouth	Infant sucks finger rhythmically	Permanent	Permits feeding
Swimming	Place infant face down in pool of water	Baby paddles and kicks in swimming motion	4–6 months	Helps infant survive if dropped into body of water
Moro	Hold infant horizontally on back and let head drop slightly, or produce a sudden loud sound against surface supporting infant	Infant makes an "embracing" motion by arching back, extending legs, throwing arms outward, and then bringing them in toward the body	6 months	In human evolutionary past, may have helped infant cling to mother
Palmar grasp	Place finger in infant's hand and press against palm	Spontaneous grasp of adult's finger	3–4 months	Prepares infant for voluntary grasping
Tonic neck	Turn baby's head to one side while lying awake on back	Infant lies in a "fencing position." One arm is extended in front of eyes on side to which head is turned, other arm is flexed	4 months	May prepare infant for voluntary reaching
Stepping	Hold infant under arms and permit bare feet to touch a flat surface	Infant lifts one foot after another in stepping response	2 months	Prepares infant for voluntary walking
Babinski	Stroke sole of foot from toe toward heel	Toes fan out and curl as foot twists in	8–12 months	Unknown

Sources: Knobloch & Pasamanick, 1974; Prechtl & Beintema, 1965.

■ SURVIVAL VALUE OF REFLEXES. Some reflexes have survival value. The rooting reflex helps a breast-fed baby find the mother's nipple. Once found, imagine what it would be like if we had to teach young infants the complex lip and tongue movements involved in sucking. If sucking were not automatic, our species would be unlikely to survive for a single generation! The swimming reflex helps a baby who is accidentally dropped into a body of water stay afloat, increasing the chances of retrieval by the caregiver.

Other reflexes probably helped babies survive during our evolutionary past but no longer serve any special purpose. For example, the Moro or "embracing" reflex is believed to have helped infants cling to their mothers during a time period when babies were carried about all day. If the baby happened to lose support, the reflex caused the infant to embrace and, along with the grasp reflex, regain its hold on the mother's body (Kessen, 1967; Prechtl, 1958).

REFLEXES AND THE DEVELOPMENT OF MOTOR SKILLS. A few reflexes form the basis for complex motor skills that will develop later. For example, the tonic neck reflex may prepare the baby for voluntary reaching. When infants lie on their backs in this "fencing position," they naturally gaze at the hand in front of their eyes. The reflex may encourage them to combine vision with arm movements and, eventually, reach for objects (Knobloch & Pasamanick, 1974).

The stepping reflex looks like a primitive walking response. In infants who gain weight quickly in the weeks after birth, the stepping reflex drops out because thigh and calf muscles are not strong enough to lift the baby's increasingly chubby legs. However, the capacity for stepping movements is still there. If the lower part of the infant's body is dipped in water, the reflex reappears, since the buoyancy of the water lightens the load on the baby's muscles (Thelen, Fisher, & Ridley-Johnson, 1984). When the stepping reflex is exercised regularly, babies display more spontaneous stepping movements and are likely to walk several weeks earlier than if it is not practiced (Zelazo, 1983; Zelazo et al., 1993). However, there is no special need for parents to get their infants to use the stepping reflex, since all normal babies walk in due time.

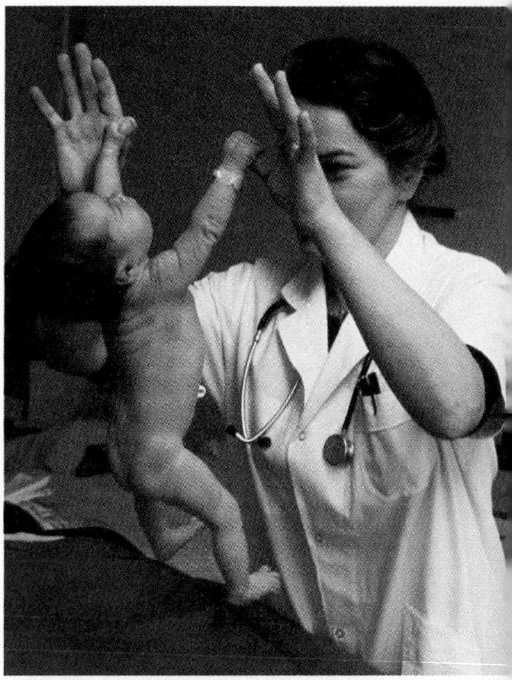

The Palmer grasp reflex is so strong during the first week after birth that many infants can use it to support their entire weight. *(J. da Cunha/Petit Format/Photo Researchers)*

REFLEXES AND EARLY SOCIAL RELATIONSHIPS. A baby who searches for and successfully finds the nipple, sucks easily during feedings, and grasps when the hand is touched encourages parents to respond lovingly and strengthens their sense of competence as caregivers. Reflexes can also help parents comfort the baby, since they permit infants to control distress and amount of stimulation to some degree themselves. For example, on short trips with Joshua to the grocery store, Yolanda brought along a pacifier. If he became fussy, sucking helped quiet him until she could feed, change, or hold and rock him.

The next time you have a chance to watch a young baby nursing, look carefully. You will see that the baby's sucking behavior is highly organized. Bursts of sucks separated by pauses occur, a style of feeding that is unique to the human species. Some researchers believe that this burst–pause rhythm is an evolved behavior pattern that helps parents and infants establish satisfying interaction as soon as possible. Notice what most mothers do during the baby's pause: they jiggle the infant. If you ask them why, they say that jiggling "wakes the baby up" and encourages more sucking. In response, newborn babies learn during the first few weeks of life to expect and wait for their mother's jiggle. As a result, mothers and infants build an early sequence of interaction during feeding that resembles the turn taking of human conversation. Using the primitive sucking reflex, the young baby participates in this dialogue as an active, cooperative partner (Kaye & Wells, 1980).

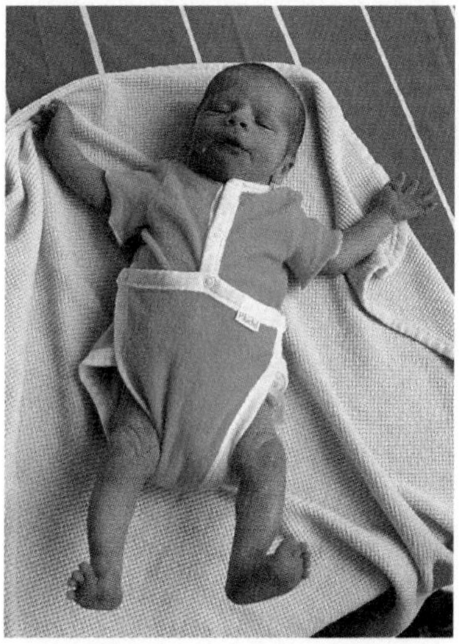

In the Moro reflex, loss of support or a sudden loud sound causes this baby to arch his back, extend his arms outward, and then bring them in toward his body. *(Elizabeth Crews)*

THE IMPORTANCE OF ASSESSING NEWBORN REFLEXES. Look at Table 4.3 again, and you will see that most newborn reflexes disappear during the first six months of life. Researchers believe this is due to a gradual increase in voluntary control over behavior as the cortex of the brain matures.

Pediatricians test reflexes carefully, especially if a newborn has experienced birth trauma, since reflexes provide one way of assessing the health of the baby's nervous system. In brain-damaged infants, reflexes may be weak or absent, or in some cases exaggerated and overly rigid. Brain damage may also be indicated when reflexes persist past the point in development when they should normally disappear. However, individual differences in reflexive responses exist that are not cause for concern. Newborn reflexes must be combined with other observations of the baby to accurately distinguish normal from abnormal central nervous system functioning (Touwen, 1984).

This baby shows Babinski reflex. When an adult strokes the sole of the foot, the toes fan out. Then they curl as the foot twists in. *(Innervisions)*

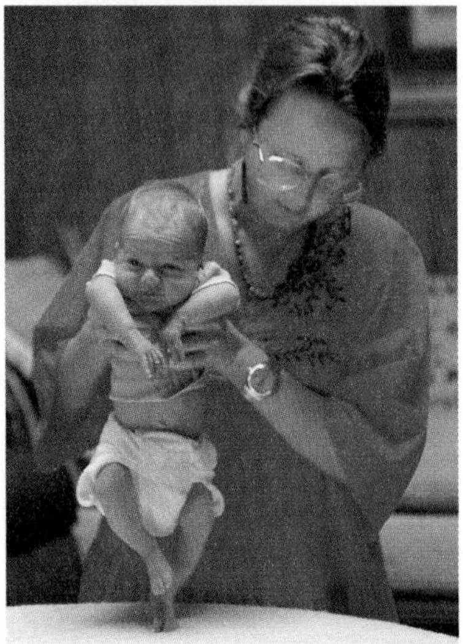

When held upright under the arms, newborn babies show reflexive stepping movements. *(Innervisions)*

SENSORY CAPACITIES

What can babies perceive with the senses at birth? On his visit to my class, Joshua looked wide-eyed at my bright pink blouse and turned to the sound of his mother's voice. During feedings, he lets Yolanda know by the way he sucks that he prefers the taste of breast milk to a bottle of plain water. Clearly, Joshua has some well-developed sensory capacities. In the following sections, we explore the newborn baby's responsiveness to touch, taste, smell, sound, and visual stimulation. See Table 4.4 for a summary of these remarkable abilities.

TOUCH. In our discussion of preterm infants, we indicated that touch helps stimulate early physical growth, and as we will see in Chapter 7, it is important for emotional development as well. Therefore, it is not surprising that sensitivity to touch is well developed at birth. Return once more to the reflexes listed in Table 4.3. They reveal that the newborn baby responds to touch, especially around the mouth and on the palms of the hands and soles of the feet. During the prenatal period, these areas, along with the genitals, are the first to become sensitive to touch, followed by other regions of the body (Humphrey, 1978).

TABLE 4.4

The Newborn Baby's Sensory Capacities

SENSE	FUNCTIONING IN THE NEWBORN
Touch	Responsive to touch, temperature change, and pain
Taste	Prefers sweetness; can distinguish sweet, salty, sour, and bitter tastes
Smell	Reacts to the smell of certain foods in the same way as adults; can identify the location of an odor and turn away from unpleasant odors; prefers the smell of a lactating woman (if breast fed, can distinguish own mother's breast odor).
Hearing	Prefers complex sounds to pure tones; can distinguish some sound patterns; recognizes differences among almost all human speech sounds; turns in the general direction of a sound; prefers high-pitched, expressive voices with rising intonation and sound of own mother's voice
Vision	Least well developed sense at birth; focusing ability and visual acuity limited; scans visual field and attempts to track moving objects; color vision not yet well developed

Reactions to temperature change are also present at birth. When Yolanda and Jay undress Joshua, he often expresses his discomfort by crying and becoming more active. Newborn babies are more sensitive to stimuli that are colder than body temperature than to those that are warmer (Humphrey, 1978).

At birth, infants are quite sensitive to pain. When male newborns are circumcised, anesthetics are usually not used because of the risk of giving pain-relieving drugs to a very young infant. Babies often respond with an intense, high-pitched, stressful cry (Porter, Porges, & Marshall, 1988). In addition, heart rate and blood pressure rise, irritability increases, and sleep is disturbed for hours afterward (Anand, Phil, & Hickey, 1987). Recent research aimed at developing safe pain-relieving techniques for newborns promises to ease the severe stress of these procedures. One helpful approach is to offer a nipple that delivers a sugar solution, which quickly reduces crying and discomfort in young babies (Blass & Ciaramitare, 1994). Doctors are becoming more aware than ever before that small infants, just like older children and adults, cannot be treated as if they were insensitive to pain.

■ TASTE. All babies come into the world with the ability to communicate their taste preferences to caregivers. When given a sweet liquid instead of water, Joshua uses longer sucks with fewer pauses, indicating that he prefers sweetness and tries to savor the taste of his favorite food (Crook & Lipsitt, 1976). If water is made salty, Joshua shortens his sucking bursts, as if to avoid an unpleasant taste (Crook, 1978). Facial expressions also reveal that infants can distinguish among several tastes. Much like adults, newborn babies relax their facial muscles in response to sweetness, purse their lips when the taste is sour, and show a distinct archlike mouth opening when it is bitter (Steiner, 1979). These reactions are important for survival, since (as we will see in Chapter 5) the food that is ideally suited to support the infant's early growth is the sweet-tasting milk of the mother's breast.

■ SMELL. Like taste, the newborn baby's responsiveness to the smell of certain foods is surprisingly similar to that of adults, suggesting that some odor preferences are innate. For example, the smell of bananas or chocolate causes a relaxed, pleasant facial expression, whereas the odor of rotten eggs makes the infant frown (Steiner, 1979). Newborns can also identify the location of an odor and, if it is unpleasant, defend themselves. When a whiff of ammonia is presented to one side of the baby's nostrils, infants less than 6 days old quickly turn their heads in the other direction (Reiser, Yonas, & Wikner, 1976).

In many mammals, the sense of smell plays an important role in eating and protecting the young from predators by helping mothers and babies recognize each other. Although smell is less well developed in humans than in other mammals, traces of its survival value are still present. In one study, newborns were exposed to the odor of their own mother's breast pad and that of a strange mother. By 6 days of age, they turned more often in the direction of their own mother's odor (MacFarlane, 1975). The ability to recognize the mother's smell occurs only in breast-fed newborns (Cernoch & Porter, 1985). However, bottle-fed babies prefer the smell of any lactating (milk-producing) woman to the smell of a nonlactating woman. And when given a choice between the smell of the lactating breast and their familiar formula, once again they choose the former (Makin & Porter, 1989; Porter et al., 1992). Newborn infants' attraction to the odor of the lactating breast probably helps them locate an appropriate food source and, in the process, learn to identify their own mother.

■ HEARING. Newborn infants can hear a wide variety of sounds, but they are more responsive to some than others. For example, they prefer complex sounds, such as noises and voices, to pure tones (Bench et al., 1976). In the first few days, infants can already tell the difference between a few sound patterns, such as a series of tones arranged in ascending and descending order and utterances with two as opposed to three syllables (Bijeljac-Babic, Bertoncini, & Mehler, 1993; Morrongiello, 1986).

These capacities, as well as others, indicate that the newborn baby is marvelously prepared for the awesome task of acquiring language. Tiny infants are especially sensitive to the sounds of human speech. They can make fine-grained distinctions among a wide variety of speech sounds—"ba" and "ga," "ma" and "na," and the short vowel sounds "a" and "i," to name just a few. For example, when given a nipple that turns on the "ba" sound, babies suck vigorously for a period of time, and then sucking slows down. When the sound switches to "ga," sucking picks up again, indicating that infants can detect this subtle sound difference. Using this method, researchers have found that there are only a few speech sounds that newborns cannot discriminate (Aslin, Pisoni, & Jusczyk, 1983). Infants seems to come into the world biologically prepared to respond to the sounds of any human language.

Responsiveness to sound provides support for the newborn baby's visual exploration of the environment. Infants as young as 3 days turn their eyes and head in the general direction of a sound. The ability to identify the precise location of a sound will improve greatly over the first 6 months and show further gains into the second year (Ashmead et al., 1991; Hillier, Hewitt, & Morrongiello, 1992).

Listen carefully to yourself the next time you talk to a young baby. You will probably speak in a high-pitched, expressive voice and use a rising tone at the ends of phrases and sentences. Adults probably communicate this way with infants because they notice that babies are more attentive when they do so. Indeed, newborns prefer speech with these characteristics (Sullivan & Horowitz, 1983). They will also suck more on a nipple to hear a recording of their own mother's voice than that of an unfamiliar woman, and to hear their mother's native language as opposed to a foreign language (Mehler et al., 1988; Spence & DeCasper, 1987). These preferences probably developed from hearing the muffled sounds of the mother's voice before birth. Infants' special responsiveness to speech encourages parents to talk to the baby. As they do so, both readiness for language and the emotional bond between parent and child are strengthened.

■ VISION. Humans depend on vision more than any other sense for active exploration of the environment. Yet vision is the least mature of the newborn baby's senses. Visual centers in the brain as well as the eye itself continue to develop after birth. For example, cells in the *retina,* the membrane lining the inside of the eye that captures light and transforms it into messages that are sent to the brain, are not as mature or as densely packed as they will be in several months. Also, the muscles of the *lens,* that part of the eye that permits us to adjust our focus to varying distances of objects, are weak at birth (Appleton, Clifton, & Goldberg, 1975).

Because of these factors, newborn babies cannot focus their eyes as well as an adult can, and visual acuity, or fineness of discrimination, is limited. When you have your vision tested, the doctor provides an estimate of your **visual acuity,** which indicates how finely you perceive stimuli in comparison to a normal adult. Applying this same index to newborn babies, researchers have found that they perceive objects at a distance of 20 feet about as clearly as adults do at 660 feet (Courage & Adams, 1990). In addition, unlike adults (who see nearby objects most clearly), newborn babies see equally unclearly across a wide range of distances (Banks, 1980). As a result, images such as the parent's face, even from close up, look much like the blur shown in Figure 4.5.

Although newborn infants cannot yet see well, they actively explore their environment with the limited visual abilities that they have. They scan the visual field for interesting sights and try to track moving objects. However, their eye movements are slow and inaccurate (Aslin, 1987; Kreminitzer et al., 1979). Joshua's captivation with my pink blouse reveals that he is attracted to bright objects. Nevertheless, once newborns focus on an object, they do not examine it as thoroughly as an older infant. Instead, they tend to look only at a single feature—for example, the corner of a triangle instead of the entire shape. Although newborn babies prefer to look at colored rather than gray stimuli, they are not yet good at

Visual acuity
Fineness of visual discrimination.

(a) Newborn View (b) Adult View

FIGURE 4.5

The newborn baby's limited focusing ability and poor visual acuity lead the mother's face, even when viewed from close up, to look much like the fuzzy image in part (a) rather than the clear image in part (b).

discriminating colors. It will take a month or two for color vision to improve (Adams, 1987; Clavadetscher et al., 1988).

NEWBORN STATES

Throughout the day and night, newborn infants move in and out of five different **states of arousal,** or degrees of sleep and wakefulness, which are described in Table 4.5. During the first month, these states alternate frequently. Quiet alertness is the most fleeting. It usually moves toward fussing and crying relatively quickly. Much to the relief of their fatigued parents, newborns spend the greatest amount of time asleep—on the average, about 16 to 18 hours a day.

Although sleep is the dominant state in all newborns, striking individual differences in daily rhythms exist that affect parents' attitudes toward and interactions with the baby. A few infants sleep for long periods at an early age, increasing the rest their parents get and the energy they have for sensitive, responsive care. Babies who cry a great deal require that parents try harder to soothe them. If these efforts are not successful, parents' positive feelings for the infant and sense of competence may suffer. Babies who spend more time in the alert state are likely to receive more social stimulation. And since this state provides opportunities to explore the environment, infants who favor it may have a slight advantage in cognitive development (Moss et al., 1988).

Of the five states listed in Table 4.5, the two extremes—sleep and crying—have been of greatest interest to researchers. Each tells us something about normal and abnormal early development.

■ SLEEP. One day, Yolanda and Jay watched Joshua while he slept and wondered why his eyelids and body twitched and his rate of breathing varied, speeding up at some points and slowing down at others. "Is this how babies are supposed to sleep?" they asked, somewhat worried. "Indeed, it is," I responded.

Sleep is made up of at least two states. Irregular, or **rapid-eye-movement (REM) sleep,** is the one that Yolanda and Jay happened to observe. The expression, "sleeping like a baby" was probably not meant to describe this state! During REM sleep, the brain and parts of the body are highly active. Electrical brain wave activity is remarkably similar to that of the waking state. The eyes dart beneath the lids; heart rate, blood pressure, and breathing are uneven; and slight body movements occur. In contrast, during regular, or **non-rapid-eye movement (NREM) sleep,** the body is quiet, and heart rate, breathing, and brain wave activity are slow and regular (Dittrichova et al., 1982).

States of arousal
Different degrees of sleep and wakefulness.

Rapid-eye-movement (REM) sleep
An "irregular" sleep state in which brain wave activity is similar to that of the waking state; eyes dart beneath the lids, heart rate, blood pressure, and breathing are uneven, and slight body movements occur.

Non-rapid-eye movement (NREM) sleep
A "regular" sleep state in which the body is quiet and heart rate, breathing, and brain wave activity are slow and regular.

TABLE 4.5

Infant States of Arousal

STATE	DESCRIPTION	DAILY DURATION IN NEWBORN
Regular sleep	The infant is at full rest and shows little or no body activity. The eyelids are closed, no eye movements occur, the face is relaxed, and breathing is slow and regular.	8–9 hours
Irregular sleep	Gentle limb movements, occasional stirring, and facial grimacing occur. Although the eylids are closed, occasional rapid eye movements can be seen beneath them. Breathing is irregular.	8–9 hours
Drowsiness	The infant is either falling asleep or waking up. Body is less active than in irregular sleep but more active than in regular sleep. The eyes open and close; when open, they have a glazed look. Breathing is even but somewhat faster than in regular sleep.	Varies
Quiet alertness	The infant's body is relatively inactive, with eyes open and attentive. Breathing is even.	2–3 hours
Waking activity and crying	The infant shows frequent bursts of uncoordinated body activity. Breathing is very irregular. Face may be relaxed or tense and wrinkled. Crying may occur.	1–4 hours

Source: Wolff, 1966.

Like children and adults, newborns alternate back and forth between REM and NREM sleep. However, they spend far more time in the REM state than they ever will again throughout their lives. REM sleep accounts for 50 percent of the newborn baby's sleep time. It declines steadily to 20 percent between 3 and 5 years of age, which is about the same percentage it consumes in adulthood (Roffwarg, Muzio, & Dement, 1966).

Why do young infants spend so much time in REM sleep? In older children and adults, the REM state is associated with dreaming. Babies probably do not dream, at least not in the same way we do. Young infants are believed to have a special need for the stimulation of REM sleep because they spend little time in an alert state, when they can get input from the environment. REM sleep seems to be a way in which the brain stimulates itself. Sleep researchers believe that this stimulation is vital for growth of the central nervous system. In support of this idea, the percentage of REM sleep is especially great in preterm babies, who are even less able to take advantage of external stimulation than are full-term newborns (Parmelee et al., 1967).

Because the normal sleep behavior of the newborn baby is organized and patterned, observations of sleep states can help identify central nervous system abnormalities. In infants who are brain damaged or who have experienced serious birth trauma, disturbed REM–NREM sleep cycles are often present (Theorell, Prechtl, & Vos, 1974).

CRYING. Crying is the first way that babies communicate, letting parents know that they need food, comfort, and stimulation. During the weeks after birth, all babies seem to have some fussy periods when they are difficult to console. But most of the time, the nature of the cry helps guide parents toward its cause. The baby's cry is actually a complex stimulus that varies in intensity, from a whimper to a message of all-out distress (Gustafson & Harris, 1990). The more intense the cry, the more likely parents are to rush to the infant, anxious and worried.

Events that cause newborn infants to cry usually have to do with physical needs. Hunger is the most common cause, but young infants may also cry in response to temperature change when undressed, a sudden loud sound, or a painful stimulus. Interestingly, newborn crying can also be caused by the sound of another crying baby. Some researchers believe this response reflects an inborn capacity to react to the suffering of others (Hoffman, 1988; Martin & Clark, 1982).

The next time you hear a baby cry, take a moment to observe your own mental and physical reaction. A crying baby stimulates strong feelings of arousal and discomfort in just about anyone—men and women and parents and nonparents alike (Boukydis & Burgess, 1982; Murray, 1985). The powerful effect of the infant's cry is probably innately programmed in all human beings to make sure that babies receive the care and protection they need to survive.

Although parents are not always correct in interpreting the meaning of the baby's cry, experience quickly improves their accuracy (Green, Jones, & Gustafson, 1987). Even when parents are fairly certain about the cause of the cry, the baby may not always calm down. Fortunately, as Table 4.6 indicates, there are many ways to soothe a crying newborn when feeding and diaper changing do not work. The technique parents usually try first is lifting the baby to the shoulder; it is also the one that works the best. Being held upright against the parent's gently moving body not only encourages infants to stop crying, but also causes them to become quietly alert and attentive to the environment (Reisman, 1987). Other common soothing methods are offering the baby a pacifier, talking gently or singing, and swaddling (wrapping the baby's body snugly in a blanket). During some fussy periods, Yolanda and Jay took Joshua on short car rides around the neighborhood. Nestled in his car seat and soothed by the motion and hum of the car motor, Joshua fell peacefully asleep.

Like reflexes and sleep patterns, the infant's cry offers a clue to central nervous system distress. The cries of brain-damaged babies and those who have experienced prenatal and birth complications are often shrill and piercing (Huntington, Hans, & Zeskind, 1990; Lester, 1987). Most parents try to respond to a sick baby's call for help with extra care and attention. In some cases, however, the cry is so unpleasant and the infant so difficult to soothe that parents become frustrated, resentful, and angry. Research reveals that preterm and sick babies are more likely to be abused by

To soothe her crying infant, this mother holds the baby upright against her gently moving body. Besides encouraging infants to stop crying, this technique causes them to become quietly alert and attentive to the environment. *(Frank Sitman/Stock Boston)*

TABLE 4.6

Ways of Soothing a Crying Newborn

METHOD	EXPLANATION
Lift the baby to the shoulder and rock or walk.	This provides a combination of physical contact, upright posture, and motion. It is the most effective soothing technique.
Swaddle the baby.	Restricting movement and increasing warmth often soothes a young infant.
Offer a pacifier.	Sucking helps babies control their own level of arousal.
Talk softly or play rhythmic sounds.	Continuous, monotonous, rhythmic sounds, such as a clock ticking, a fan whirring, or peaceful music, are more effective than intermittent sounds.
Take the baby for a short car ride or walk in a baby carriage; swing the baby in a cradle.	Gentle, rhythmic motion of any kind helps lull the baby to sleep.
Massage the baby's body.	Stroke the baby's torso and limbs with continuous, gentle motions. This technique is used in some non-Western cultures to relax the baby's muscles.
Combine several of the methods just listed.	Stimulating several of the baby's senses at once is often more effective than stimulating only one.
If these methods do not work, let the baby cry for a short period of time.	Occasionally, a baby responds well to just being put down and will, after a few minutes, fall asleep.

Sources: Campos, 1989; Heinl, 1983; Lester, 1985; Reisman, 1987.

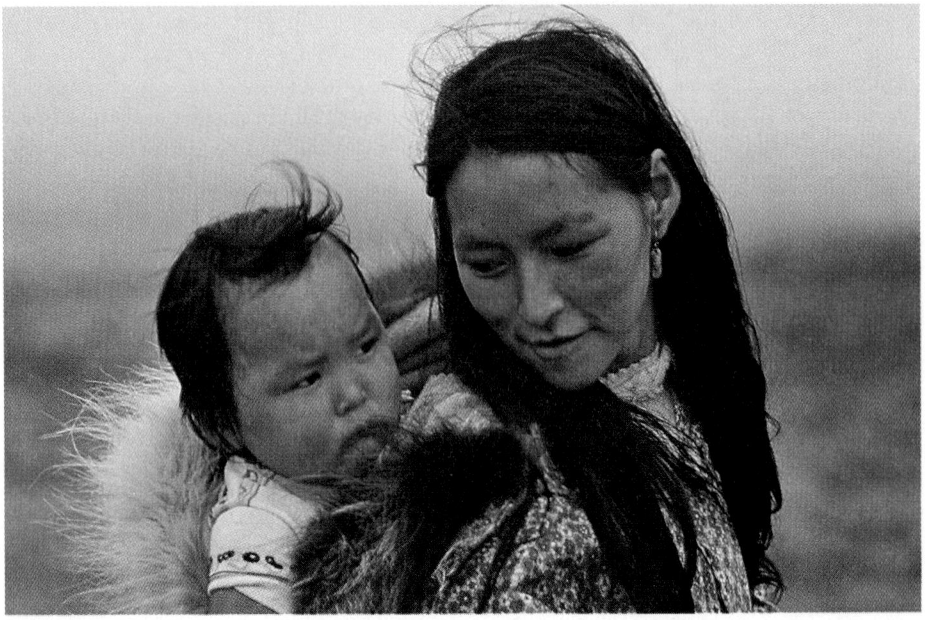

Similar to women in the Zambian culture, this Inuit mother of Northern Canada carries her baby about all day, providing close physical contact and a rich variety of stimulation. *(Eastcott/Momatiak; Woodfin Camp & Associates)*

their parents than healthy infants. Often these parents mention a high-pitched, grating cry as one factor that caused them to lose control and harm the baby (Boukydis, 1985; Frodi, 1985).

NEONATAL BEHAVIORAL ASSESSMENT

The many capacities described in the preceding sections have been put together into tests that permit doctors, nurses, and researchers to assess the behavior of the infant during the newborn period. The most widely used of these tests is T. Berry Brazelton's (1984) **Neonatal Behavioral Assessment Scale (NBAS).** With it, the examiner can look at the baby's reflexes, state changes, responsiveness to physical and social stimuli, and other reactions.

The NBAS has been given to many infants around the world. As a result, researchers have learned a great deal about individual and cultural differences in newborn behavior and how a baby's reactions can be maintained or changed by child-rearing practices. For example, NBAS scores of Asian and Native American babies reveal that they are less irritable than Caucasian infants. Mothers in these cultures often encourage their babies' calm dispositions through swaddling, close physical contact, and nursing at the first signs of discomfort (Chisholm, 1989; Freedman & Freedman, 1969; Murrett-Wagstaff & Moore, 1989). In contrast, the poor NBAS scores of undernourished infants born in Zambia, Africa, are quickly changed by the way their mothers care for them. The Zambian mother carries her baby about on her hip all day, providing a rich variety of sensory stimulation. As a result, by 1 week of age a once unresponsive newborn has been transformed into an alert, contented baby (Brazelton, Koslowski, & Tronick, 1976).

Can you tell from these examples why a single NBAS score is not a good predictor of later development? Since newborn behavior and parenting styles combine to shape development, *changes in NBAS scores* over the first week or two of life (rather than a single score) provide the best estimate of the baby's ability to recover from the stress of birth. NBAS "recovery curves" predict intelligence with moderate success well into the preschool years (Brazelton, Nugent, & Lester, 1987).

The NBAS has also been used to help parents get to know their infants. In some hospitals, the examination is given in the presence of parents to teach them about their newborn baby's capacities. Parents of both preterm and full-term newborns who participate in these programs have been found to interact more confidently and effectively with their babies (Brazelton, Nugent, & Lester, 1987; Tedder, 1991).

Neonatal Behavioral Assessment Scale (NBAS)
A test developed to assess the behavior of the infant during the newborn period.

Although lasting effects on development have not been demonstrated, NBAS-based interventions are clearly useful in helping the parent–infant relationship get off to a good start.

BRIEF REVIEW

The newborn baby is equipped with a wide variety of capacities for relating to the surrounding world. Reflexes are the infant's most obvious organized behavior patterns. Some, like sucking, have survival value, whereas others, like stepping, form the basis for motor skills that will develop later. The senses of touch, taste, smell, and hearing are well developed in the newborn baby. Vision is least mature, but newborns actively explore the environment with the visual abilities that they have. Infants move in and out of five states of arousal throughout the day and night. Sleep is the dominant state; young infants spend far more time in REM sleep than they will at later ages. A crying baby stimulates strong feelings of discomfort in nearby adults. Fortunately, there are many ways to soothe a crying newborn. Neonatal behavioral assessment permits doctors, nurses, and researchers to assess the remarkable capacities of the newborn baby.

ASK YOURSELF . . .

- How do the capacities of newborn babies contribute to their first social relationships? In answering this question, provide as many examples as you can.
- Jackie, who had a difficult birth, observes her 2-day-old daughter Kelly being given the NBAS. Kelly scores poorly on many items. Jackie wonders if this means that Kelly will not develop normally. How would you respond to Jackie's concern?

THE TRANSITION TO PARENTHOOD

The early weeks after a new baby enters the family are full of profound changes. The mother needs to recover from childbirth and adjust to massive hormone changes that have taken place in her body. If she is breast-feeding, energies must be devoted to working out this intimate relationship. The father also needs to become a part of this new threesome while supporting the mother in her recovery. At times, he may feel somewhat jealous of the baby, who constantly demands and gets his wife's attention (Berman & Pedersen, 1987; Jordan, 1990). And as we will see in Chapter 7, in families with other children, siblings—especially those who are young and first born—understandably feel displaced. They often react with jealously and anger.

While all this is going on, the tiny infant is very assertive about his urgent physical needs, demanding to be fed, changed, and comforted at odd times of the day and night. A family schedule that was once routine and predictable is now irregular and uncertain. Yolanda spoke candidly about the changes that she and Jay experienced:

> Our emotions were running high the first few days after Joshua's birth. When we brought Joshua home, we had to come down to earth and deal with the realities of our new responsibility. Both of us were struck by how small and helpless Joshua was, and we worried about whether we would be able to take proper care of him. It took us 20 minutes to change the first diaper. I rarely feel well rested, because I'm up two to four times every night, and I spend a good part of my waking hours trying to anticipate Joshua's rhythms and needs. If Jay weren't so willing to help by holding and walking Joshua, I think I'd find it much harder.

The demands of new parenthood—disrupted sleep schedules, less time for husband and wife to devote to one another, and new financial responsibilities—often lead to a mild decline in a couple's marital happiness. In addition, entry of the baby into the family usually causes the roles of husband and wife to become more traditional (Cowan & Cowan, 1988; Palkovitz & Copes, 1988). This is even true for couples like Yolanda and Jay, who are strongly committed to gender role equality and were used to sharing household tasks. Yolanda took a leave of absence from work, whereas Jay's career life continued just as it had before. As a result, Yolanda spent much more time at home with the baby, whereas Jay focused more on his

FROM RESEARCH TO PRACTICE

POSTPARTUM DEPRESSION AND THE MOTHER–INFANT RELATIONSHIP

For as many as 50 to 80 percent of first-time mothers, the excitement of the baby's arrival gives way to an emotional letdown during the first week after delivery, a reaction known as the *postpartum* (or after-birth) *blues.* The blues are temporary. They die down as new mothers adjust to hormonal changes following childbirth, gain confidence in caring for the baby, and are reassured by their husbands, family members, and friends.

However, as many as 10 percent of women do not bounce back from childbirth so easily. They experience **postpartum depression,** mild to severe feelings of sadness and withdrawal that continue for weeks or months (Gotlib et al., 1989; Ziporyn, 1992). Stella was one of these women. Her genetic makeup may have predisposed her to develop postpartum depression, but social and cultural factors were also involved. Stella's pregnancy went well until the last month, when her husband Kyle's lack of interest in the baby caused her to worry that having a child might be a mistake. Five days after Lucy was born, Stella's mood plunged. She was anxious and weepy, overwhelmed by Lucy's needs, and angry that she no longer had control over her own schedule. When Stella approached Kyle about her own fatigue and his unwillingness to help with the baby, he snapped that she overreacted to every move he made. Stella's friends, who did not have children, stopped by once to see Lucy and did not call again.

Stella's depressed mood quickly affected her relationship with the baby. As Lucy started to spend more time awake and alert, Stella rarely smiled and talked to her. Lucy responded to Stella's sad, vacant gaze by turning away, crying, and often looking sad or angry herself (Cohn et al., 1990; Pickens & Field, 1993). Each time this happened, Stella felt guilty and inadequate as a mother, and her depression deepened. Soon Lucy showed signs of serious cognitive and emotional problems, known to affect children of depressed mothers as early as 2 months of age (Cytryn et al., 1986; Whiffen & Gotlib, 1989).

Six weeks after childbirth, Stella made a routine visit to her doctor. He sensed that she was edgy and asked what was wrong. Stella described her tearfulness, fatigue, and inability to comfort Lucy. The doctor also took note of Stella's marital problems and lack of social support—factors commonly associated with postpartum depression (Albright, 1993).

Stella was referred to a special treatment program for depressed mothers and their babies. A counselor worked with the family, helping Stella and Kyle with their own problems and encouraging them to be more sensitive and patient with Lucy. In most cases of postpartum depression, treatment is successful. After several months, mother, father, and baby were doing well (Steiner, 1990).

Postpartum depression strikes women of different social classes and ages equally often. About half the time, signs of the depressive mood are already present during pregnancy (Gotlib et al., 1989). Early treatment is vital, to prevent the disorder from undermining the mother–infant relationship and harming the baby's development.

ASK YOURSELF . . .

- Suggest several ways in which a new mother and father can help each other make an effective adjustment to parenthood.

Postpartum depression Feelings of sadness and withdrawal that appear shortly after childbirth and that continue for weeks or months.

provider role. This movement toward traditional roles is hardest on new mothers who have been used to active involvement in a career (LaRossa & LaRossa, 1981). It may be one reason, among others, that women typically experience a more difficult period of adaptation to new parenthood than do men (see the From Research to Practice box above).

How long does this time of adjustment to parenthood last? One pair of counselors, who have worked with many new parents, once joked that it lasts about 15 years! Actually, when husband and wife set aside time to listen to one another and try to support each other's needs, the stress caused by new parenthood stays at manageable levels. Family relationships and routine care of the baby are worked out after a few months. Nevertheless, the counselors pointed out, "As long as children are dependent on their parents, those parents find themselves preoccupied with thoughts of their children. This does not keep them from enjoying other aspects of their lives, but it does mean that they never return to being quite the same people they were before they became parents" (Colman & Colman, 1991, p. 198).

SUMMARY

THE STAGES OF CHILDBIRTH

Describe the three stages of childbirth, the baby's adaptation to labor and delivery, and the newborn baby's appearance.

- Childbirth takes place in three stages. In the first stage, **dilation and effacement of the cervix** occur as uterine contractions increase in strength and frequency. This stage culminates in **transition,** a brief period in which contractions are strongest and closest together and the cervix opens completely. In the second stage, the mother feels an urge to bear down with her abdominal muscles, and the baby is born. In the final stage, the placenta is delivered.
- During labor, infants produce high levels of stress hormones, which help them withstand oxygen deprivation and arouse them into alertness at birth. When the baby is born, the chest springs outward, causing breathing to start automatically. Newborn infants have large heads, small bodies, and facial features that make adults feel like picking them up and cuddling them. The **Apgar Scale** is used to assess the newborn baby's physical condition at birth.

APPROACHES TO CHILDBIRTH

Describe natural childbirth and home delivery, noting any benefits and concerns associated with each.

- **Natural, or prepared, childbirth** involves classes in which prospective parents learn about labor and delivery, instruction of the mother in relaxation and breathing techniques, and a companion who serves as a coach during childbirth. The method helps reduce stress and pain during labor and delivery. As a result, most mothers require little or no medication, and they feel more positively about the birth experience. As long as mothers are healthy and assisted by a well-trained doctor or midwife, it is just as safe to give birth at home as in a hospital.

MEDICAL INTERVENTIONS

List common medical interventions during childbirth, circumstances that justify their use, and any dangers associated with each.

- Medical interventions during childbirth are more common in the United States than anywhere else in the world. When women have a history of pregnancy and birth complications, **fetal monitors** help save the lives of many babies. However, when used routinely, they may identify infants as in danger who, in fact, are not.
- **Analgesics** and **anesthetics** are necessary in complicated deliveries. When given in large doses, these drugs produce a depressed state in the newborn that affects the early mother–infant relationship. They also increase the likelihood of an instrument delivery. **Forceps** or **vacuum extractors** are appropriate if the mother's pushing does not cause the infant to move through the birth canal in a reasonable period of time, but they can cause head injuries.
- Since **induced labors** are more difficult than naturally occurring ones, they should not be scheduled for reasons of convenience. **Cesarean deliveries** are justified in cases of medical emergency and when babies are in **breech position.** Many unnecessary cesareans are performed in the United States.

BIRTH COMPLICATIONS

What risks are associated with oxygen deprivation, preterm and low birth weight, and postterm birth, and what factors can help infants who survive a traumatic birth develop?

- Although most births proceed normally, serious complications can occur. A major cause of **cerebral palsy** is lack of oxygen. As long as oxygen deprivation is not extreme, most oxygen deprived newborns catch up in development by the school years. **Respiratory distress syndrome,** which can cause permanent damage due to lack of oxygen, is common in infants who are more than 6 weeks premature.
- Premature births are high among low-income pregnant women and mothers of twins. Compared to **preterm** babies whose weight is appropriate for time spent in the uterus, **small-for-date** infants are more likely to develop poorly. The fragile appearance and unresponsive, irritable behavior of preterm infants affect the kind of care they receive. Some interventions provide special stimulation in the intensive care nursery. Others teach parents how to care for and interact with their babies. A major cause of **neonatal** and **infant mortality** is low birth weight.
- **Postterm** infants are at risk for serious birth complications. Therefore, doctors usually induce labor in mothers whose pregnancies have continued for more than 42 weeks.
- When babies experience birth trauma, a supportive home environment can help restore their growth. Even infants with severe birth complications can recover with the help of favorable life events.

PRECIOUS MOMENTS AFTER BIRTH

Is close parent–infant contact shortly after birth necessary for bonding to occur?

- Human parents do not require close physical contact with the baby immediately after birth for **bonding** and effective parenting behavior to occur. Nevertheless, most parents find early contact with the infant especially meaningful, and it may help them build a good relationship with the baby.

THE NEWBORN BABY'S CAPACITIES

Describe the newborn baby's reflexes and sensory capacities.

- Infants begin life with remarkable skills for relating to their physical and social worlds. **Reflexes** are the newborn baby's most obvious organized patterns of behavior. Some have survival value, whereas others provide the foundation for voluntary motor skills that will develop later.
- The senses of touch, taste, smell, and sound are well developed at birth. Newborns are especially responsive to high-pitched expressive voices, and they prefer the sound of their mother's voice. They can distinguish almost all speech sounds in human languages.
- Vision is the least mature of the newborn's senses. At birth, focusing ability and **visual acuity** are limited. In exploring the visual field, newborn babies are attracted to bright objects, but they limit their looking to single features. The newborn infant has difficulty discriminating colors.

Describe newborn states of arousal, including sleep characteristics and ways to soothe a crying baby.

- Although newborns alternate frequently among five different states of arousal, they spend most of their time asleep. Sleep consists of at least two states: **rapid-eye-movement (REM)** and **non-rapid-eye movement (NREM) sleep.** REM sleep is greater during the newborn period than at any later age. It provides young infants with stimulation essential for central nervous development.
- A crying baby stimulates strong feelings of discomfort in nearby adults. The intensity of the cry and the experiences that led up to it help parents tell what is wrong. Once feeding and diaper changing have been tried, lifting the baby to the shoulder is the most effective soothing technique. Many other soothing methods are helpful.

Why is neonatal behavioral assessment useful?

- The most widely used instrument for assessing the behavior of the newborn infant is Brazelton's **Neonatal Behavioral Assessment Scale (NBAS).** The NBAS has helped researchers understand individual and cultural differences in newborn behavior. Sometimes it is used to teach parents about their baby's capacities.

THE TRANSITION TO PARENTHOOD

Describe typical changes in the family after the birth of a new baby.

- The new baby's arrival is exciting but stressful. The demands of new parenthood often lead to a slight drop in marital happiness, and family roles become more traditional. When husband and wife are sensitive to each other's needs, adjustment problems are usually temporary, and the transition to parenthood goes well.

IMPORTANT TERMS AND CONCEPTS

dilation and effacement of the cervix (p. 135)
transition (p. 136)
episiotomy (p. 136)
Apgar Scale (p. 137)
natural, or prepared, childbirth (p. 140)
fetal monitors (p. 142)
analgesic (p. 143)
anesthetic (p. 143)
forceps (p. 143)
vacuum extractor (p. 143)
induced labor (p. 144)
cesarean delivery (p. 144)
breech position (p. 145)
cerebral palsy (p. 146)
anoxia (p. 146)
respiratory distress syndrome (p. 147)
preterm (p. 148)
small for date (p. 148)
infant mortality (p. 150)
neonatal mortality (p. 150)
postterm (p. 150)
bonding (p. 153)
rooming in (p. 153)
reflex (p. 153)
visual acuity (p. 158)
states of arousal (p. 159)
rapid-eye-movement (REM) sleep (p. 159)
non-rapid-eye-movement (REM) sleep (p. 159)
Neonatal Behavioral Assessment Scale (NBAS) (p. 162)
postpartum depression (p. 164)

FYI...

FOR FURTHER INFORMATION AND SPECIAL HELP, CONSULT THE FOLLOWING ORGANIZATIONS:

GENERAL CHILDBIRTH INFORMATION

National Association of Parents and Professionals for Safe Alternatives in Childbirth
Route 1, Box 646
Marble Hill, MO 63764-9725
(314) 238-2010

Provides information on all aspects of childbirth. Places special emphasis on choosing safe childbirth alternatives.

American Foundation for Maternal and Child Health
439 East 51st Street, 4th Floor
New York, NY 10022
(212) 759-5510

Provides information on maternal and child health during the birth period.

INDEPENDENT BIRTH CENTERS

National Association of Childbearing Centers
3123 Gottschall Road
Perkiomenville, PA 18074
(215) 2341-8068

Offers referrals to birth centers that operate independently of hospitals.

NATURAL CHILDBIRTH

American Society for Psycho-prophylaxis in Obstetrics (ASPO)
1101 Connecticut Avenue, N.W., Suite 700
Washington, DC 20036
(202) 857-1128

Trains and certifies instructors in Lamaze method of natural childbirth. Provides information to expectant parents.

American Academy of Husband-Coached Childbirth
P.O. Box 5224
Sherman Oaks, CA 91413
(818) 788-6662
(800) 423-2397

Certifies instructors in the Bradley method of natural childbirth, which emphasizes coaching by the husband.

HOME BIRTH

Association for Childbirth at Home, International
P.O. Box 430
Glendale, CA 91205
(213) 667-0839

Provides information on and support for home birth.

Informed Homebirth/Informed Birth and Parenting
P.O. Box 3675
Ann Arbor, MI 48106
(313) 662-6857

Trains and certifies home birth attendants. Offers information to couples interested in home birth.

MIDWIVES

American College of Nurse-Midwives
1522 K Street, N.W.
Suite 1000
Washington, DC 20005
(202) 289-0171

Certifies nurse-midwives and provides referrals to expectant parents.

CESAREAN DELIVERY

Cesareans/Support, Education, and Concern, Inc. (C/Sec, Inc.)
22 Forest Road
Framingham, MA 01701
(508) 877-8266

Provides information on and support for cesarean mothers, including vaginal birth after cesarean.

CEREBRAL PALSY

United Cerebral Palsy Associations
1522 K Street, N.W.
Suite 1112
Washington, DC 20005
(202) 842-1266

Provides assistance to people with cerebral palsy and their families. Local and state chapters offer medical, therapeutic, and social services

"Happy family"
Xiang Xiaowen
5 years, China

The wide-eyed expressions and animated behavior of the children in this scene suggest a strong drive to explore, understand, and gain control over their world. Immediately after birth, infants display these tendencies. During the first year, they grow quickly, move on their own, and make sense of complicated sights and sounds. Chapter 5 traces these awesome achievements.

object permanence
habituation
attachment
mother-ease
receptive/expressive language
physical/gross/fine motor skills
cognitive

5

Physical Development in Infancy and Toddlerhood

BODY GROWTH IN THE FIRST TWO YEARS

Changes in Body Size • Changes in Body Proportions • Changes in Muscle–Fat Makeup • Early Skeletal Growth • Appearance of Teeth

BRAIN DEVELOPMENT

Development of Neurons • Development of the Cerebral Cortex

FACTORS AFFECTING EARLY PHYSICAL GROWTH

Heredity • Nutrition • Malnutrition • Affection and Stimulation

CHANGING STATES OF AROUSAL

MOTOR DEVELOPMENT DURING THE FIRST TWO YEARS

The Sequence of Motor Development • Motor Skills as Complex Systems of Action • Maturation, Experience, and the Development of Motor Skills • Fine Motor Development: The Special Case of Voluntary Reaching • Bowel and Bladder Control

BASIC LEARNING MECHANISMS

Classical Conditioning • Operant Conditioning • Habituation and Dishabituation • Imitation

PERCEPTUAL DEVELOPMENT IN INFANCY

Hearing • Vision • Intermodal Perception

UNDERSTANDING PERCEPTUAL DEVELOPMENT

Within a two-day period, Lisa, Beth, and Felicia each gave birth to their first child at the same hospital. During their stay, the three mothers got to know one another. Over the next 2 years, they met once a month to talk over questions and concerns about the development of their babies—Byron, Rachel, and April. The mothers permitted me to sit in on several of these meetings, and I watched and listened as the infants changed from immobile lap babies into cruising 1-year-olds, and finally, into walking, talking toddlers.

As the infants grew, the mothers' conversations changed accordingly. In the beginning, they worried most about physical care—how well breast-feeding was going, how soon to introduce solid foods, and when the baby's sleep–waking schedule would become more predictable. Between 2 and 3 months, each mother noticed that her baby's daily rhythms had become more organized and patterned, and all three youngsters were much more alert. "Two months seems like a real turning point," commented Felicia. "Life is easier now that I can anticipate April's feedings and naptimes. She seems like more of a little person, and she's much more interested in the world around her."

As the infants' motor skills changed, the home setting in which the mothers gathered changed as well. By the second half of the first year, mothers and babies no longer sat quietly in pairs on the sofa. Instead, the floor was covered with toys, and all three infants crawled about while their mothers kept a watchful eye for coffee table corners, lamp cords, and electric sockets. Soon crawling became walking. This marked the beginning of *toddlerhood*—a period that spans the second year of life—and the children's approach to the world changed again. At first, the

New motor skills have a dramatic impact on the baby's approach to the world. As infants sit up and begin to crawl, their whole view of the environment and capacity to explore it changes. *(Margaret Miller/Photo Researchers)*

youngsters did, indeed, "toddle" with an awkward gait, rocking from side to side and tipping over frequently. But their faces reflected the thrill of being upright, and they explored enthusiastically. As their 2-year-old birthdays approached, the mothers reflected on the astounding changes that had taken place since the newborn period. "Byron is nearly twice as tall and four times as heavy," said Lisa. "He's starting to look more like a little boy than a baby."

This chapter traces physical growth during the first 2 years—one of the most remarkable and busiest times of development. We will see how rapid changes in the infant's body and brain support new motor skills, learning mechanisms, and perceptual capacities. Byron, Rachel, and April will join us along the way, to illustrate individual differences and environmental influences on physical development.

BODY GROWTH IN THE FIRST TWO YEARS

The next time you have a chance, briefly observe several infants and toddlers while walking in your neighborhood or at a nearby shopping center. You will see that their capabilities are vastly different. One reason for the change in what children can do over the first 2 years is that their bodies change enormously—so much so that relatives who visit just after a baby is born and return again a year or two later often remark that the child does not seem like the same individual!

CHANGES IN BODY SIZE

To parents, the most obvious signs of physical growth are changes in the size of the child's body as a whole. During the first 2 years, these changes are rapid—faster than they will be at any time after birth. As shown in Figure 5.1, by the end of the first year the infant's length is 50 percent greater than it was at birth, and by 2 years of age it is 75 percent greater. Weight shows similar dramatic gains. By 5 months of age, birth weight has doubled, at 1 year it has tripled, and at 2 years it has quadrupled.

Researchers who have carefully tracked height changes in infancy and toddlerhood report that rather than steady gains, little growth spurts occur. In one study, children followed over the first 21 months of life went for periods of 7 to 63 days with no growth and then added as much as a half-inch in a 24-hour period. Almost always, parents described their babies as irritable, restless, and very hungry on the day before the spurt (Lampl, 1993; Lampl, Veldhuis, & Johnson, 1992).

In body size, as in all aspects of development, differences among children exist. In infancy, girls are slightly shorter and lighter than boys. This small but typical sex difference continues throughout early and middle childhood, and it will be greatly magnified at adolescence. Ethnic differences in body size are apparent as well. Look again at Figure 5.1, and you will see that Rachel, a Japanese-American child, is below the growth norms (height and weight averages) for youngsters her age. In contrast, April is above average, as African-American children tend to be (Tanner, 1990).

CHANGES IN BODY PROPORTIONS

As the child's overall size increases, different parts of the body grow at different rates. Recall from Chapter 3 that during the prenatal period, the head develops first from the primitive embryonic disk, followed by the lower part of the body. After birth, the head and chest continue to have a growth advantage, but the baby's trunk and legs gradually pick up speed. This organized pattern of physical growth is called the **cephalocaudal trend**, which, translated from Latin, means "head to tail."

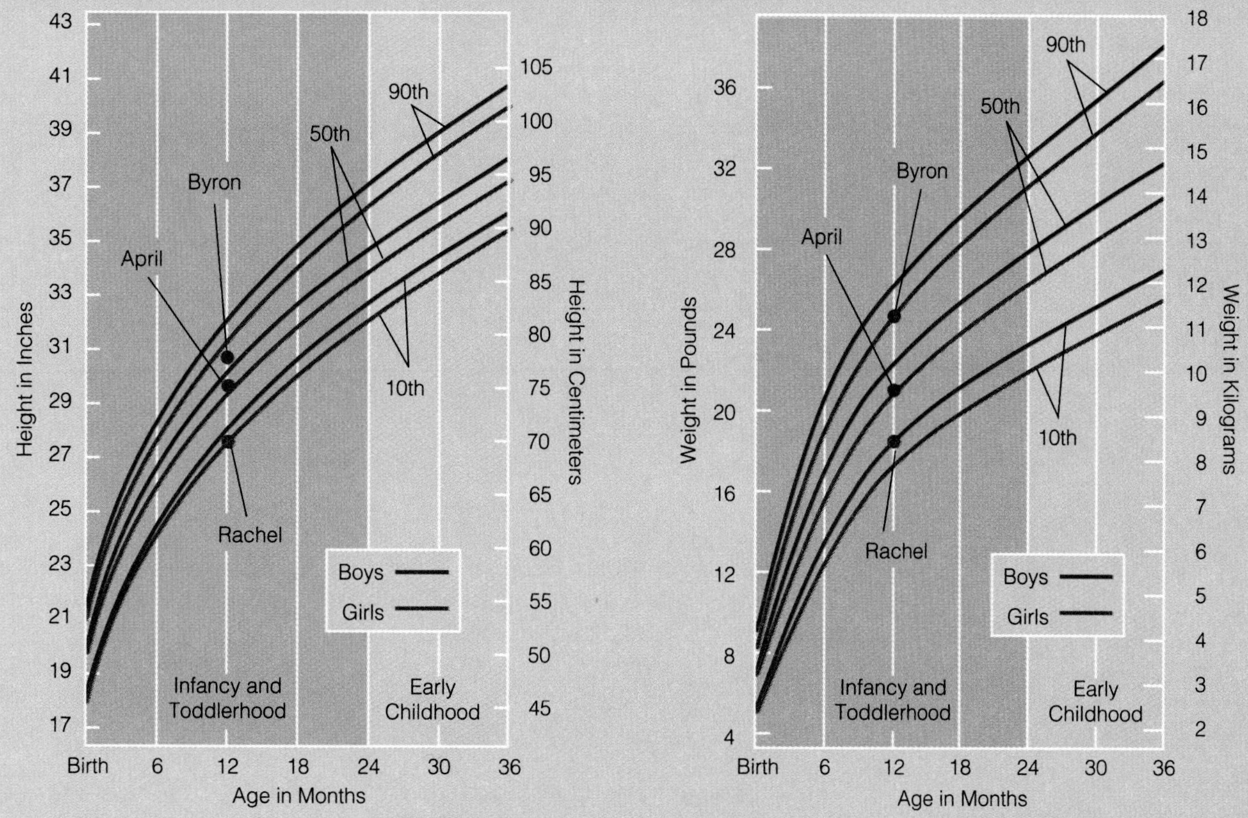

FIGURE 5.1

Gains in height and weight during infancy and toddlerhood among American children.
The steep rise in these growth curves shows that children grow rapidly from birth to 2 years. At the same time, wide individual differences in body size exist. Infants and toddlers who fall at the fiftieth percentile are average in height and weight. Those who fall at the ninetieth percentile are taller and heavier than 90 percent of their agemates. Those who fall at the tenth percentile are taller and heavier than only 10 percent of their peers. Notice that girls are slightly shorter and lighter than boys. As children move into early childhood, rate of growth slows.

You can see it depicted in Figure 5.2. At birth, the head takes up 1/4 of the body, the legs only 1/3. Notice how the lower portion of the body catches up by age 2. At that time, the head accounts for only 1/5 and the legs for nearly 1/2 of total body length.

There is a second growth pattern that describes changes in body proportions. It is called the **proximodistal trend,** meaning that growth proceeds from the center of the body outward. Again, this is what happened during the prenatal period. The head, chest, and trunk grew first, followed by the arms and legs, and finally by the hands and feet. During infancy and childhood, growth of the arms and legs continues to proceed somewhat ahead of the hands and feet.

The Concept Review Table on page 172 summarizes these important growth trends. Look carefully at the examples in the table. They show that not just body growth, but motor development (which we will discuss in a later section) follows these same developmental patterns.

Proximodistal trend
An organized pattern of physical growth and motor control that proceeds from the center of the body outward.

FIGURE 5.2

Changes in body proportions from the early prenatal period to adulthood.
This figure illustrates the cephalocaudal trend of physical growth. The head gradually becomes smaller, and the legs longer, in proportion to the rest of the body.

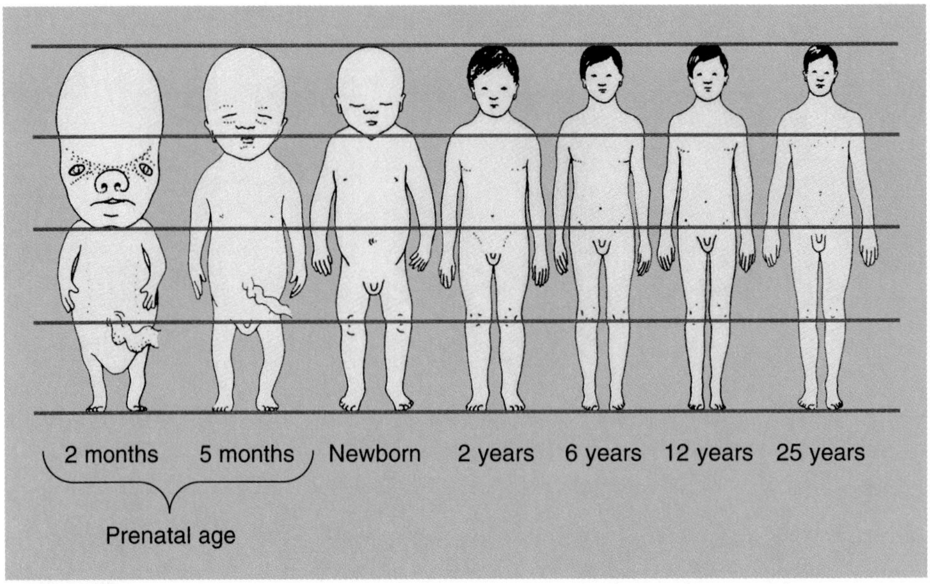

CHANGES IN MUSCLE–FAT MAKEUP

One of the most obvious changes in Byron, Rachel, and April's appearance was their transformation into round, plump babies by the middle of the first year. Body fat (most of which lies just beneath the skin) begins to increase in the last few weeks of prenatal life and continues to do so after birth, reaching a peak at about 9 months of age. Then, during the second year, toddlers start to become more slender, a trend that continues into middle childhood. This very early rise in "baby fat" helps the small infant keep a constant body temperature (Tanner, 1990).

Muscle tissue grows according to a different plan than fat. It increases very slowly during infancy and childhood and will not reach a peak until adolescence. Babies are not very muscular creatures, and their strength and physical coordination are limited.

As with body size, slight differences between boys and girls in muscle–fat makeup exist. From the beginning, girls have a higher ratio of fat to muscle than boys, a difference that will increase in middle childhood and become very large during adolescence (Malina & Bouchard, 1991).

CONCEPT REVIEW TABLE

Trends in Body Growth and Motor Control

CONCEPT	IMPORTANT POINT	EXAMPLE
Cephalocaudal trend	Parts of the body grow at different rates. Physical growth and motor control of the upper regions proceeds ahead of growth and control of the lower regions.	At birth the baby's head is large in comparison to the trunk and legs. During the first year, infants lift their heads and chests before they sit, crawl, and walk.
Proximodistal trend	Physical growth and motor control proceed from the center of the body outward.	The head, chest, and trunk grow earliest, followed by the arms and legs, and then the hands and feet. During infancy, head and chest control are achieved before control of the arms and, finally, the hands.

EARLY SKELETAL GROWTH

Children of the same age differ in *rate* of physical growth. In other words, some make faster progress toward a mature body size than others. We cannot tell how quickly a child's physical growth is moving along just by looking at current body size, since children grow to different heights and weights in adulthood. For example, Byron is slightly larger and heavier than Rachel and April, but he is not physically more mature. In a moment, you will see why.

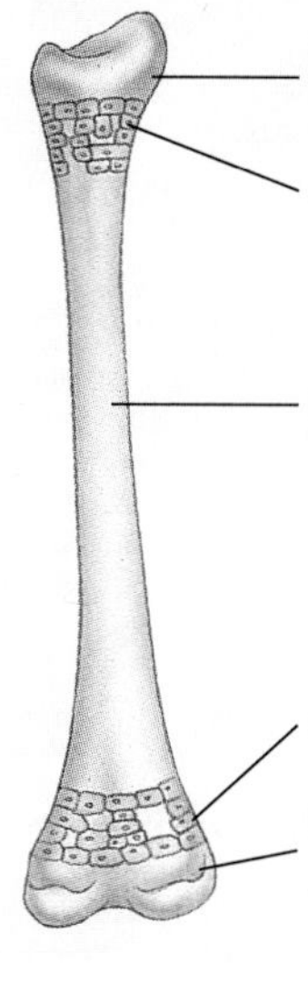

FIGURE 5.3

Diagram of a long bone showing upper and lower epiphyses. Cartilage cells are produced at the growth plates and gradually harden into bone. *(From J. M. Tanner,* Foetus into Man (2nd ed.), *Cambridge, MA: Harvard University Press,* p. 32. *Copyright © 1990 by J. M. Tanner. All rights reserved. Reprinted by permission of the publisher and author.)*

■ GENERAL SKELETAL GROWTH. The best way of estimating a child's physical maturity is to use **skeletal age,** a measure of development of the bones of the body. The embryonic skeleton is first formed out of soft, pliable tissue called *cartilage*. Then, beginning in the sixth week of pregnancy, cartilage cells gradually harden into bone, a very gradual process that continues throughout childhood and adolescence. Once bones have taken on their basic shape, special growth centers called **epiphyses** appear just before birth (see Figure 5.3). In the long bones of the body, the epiphyses emerge at the two extreme ends of each bone. There, new cartilage cells are produced and gradually harden. As growth continues, the epiphyses get thinner and disappear. When this occurs, no more growth of the bone is possible. Skeletal age can be estimated by X-raying the bones and seeing how many epiphyses there are and the extent to which they are fused. These X-rays are compared to norms established for bone maturity based on large numbers of children (Malina & Bouchard, 1991).

When the skeletal ages of infants and children are examined, they reveal that African-American children tend to be slightly ahead of white children at all ages. In addition, girls are considerably ahead of boys. At birth, the difference between the sexes amounts to about 4 to 6 weeks, a gap that widens over infancy and childhood and is responsible for the fact that girls reach their full body size several years before boys. Girls are advanced in development of other organs of the body as well. Their greater physical maturity may contribute to the fact that they are more resistant to harmful environmental influences throughout development. As we pointed out in Chapter 2, girls experience fewer developmental problems, and infant and childhood mortality for girls is also lower (Tanner, 1990).

■ GROWTH OF THE SKULL. Doctors are concerned with another aspect of skeletal development when they routinely measure the head sizes of children between birth and 2 years of age. Skull growth is especially rapid during the first 2 years because of large increases in brain size. At birth, the bones of the skull are separated by six gaps, or "soft spots," called **fontanels** (see Figure 5.4). The gaps permit the bones to overlap as the large head of the baby passes through the mother's narrow birth canal. You can easily feel the largest gap, the anterior fontanel, at the top of a baby's skull. It is slightly more than an inch across. It gradually shrinks and is filled in during the second year. The other fontanels are smaller and close more quickly. As the skull bones come in contact with one another, they form *sutures,* or seams. These permit the skull to expand easily as the brain grows during the first few years of life.

APPEARANCE OF TEETH

On the average, a Caucasian baby's first tooth appears at about 6 months, an African-American baby's around 4 months, although there are wide individual differences. April already had a tooth when she was born; a few infants do not get their first tooth until 1 year of age. After the first tooth erupts, new ones appear every month or two. By age 2, the child has 20 teeth. Dental development provides a rough clue to overall rate of skeletal development. A child who gets teeth early is likely to be advanced in physical maturity (Mott, James, & Sperhac, 1990).

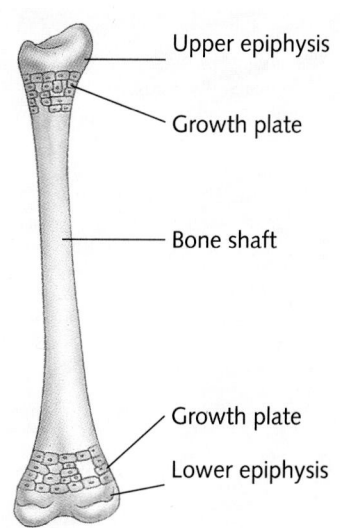

Skeletal age
An estimate of physical maturity based on development of the bones of the body.

Epiphyses
Growth centers in the bones where new cartilage cells are produced and gradually harden.

Fontanels
Six soft spots that separate the bones of the skull at birth.

FIGURE 5.4

The skull at birth, showing the fontanels and sutures.
(From P. M. Hill & P. Humphrey, 1982, Human Growth and Development Throughout Life: A Nursing Perspective, *Delmar Publishers, Inc., p. 42. Copyright 1982. Reprinted by permission.)*

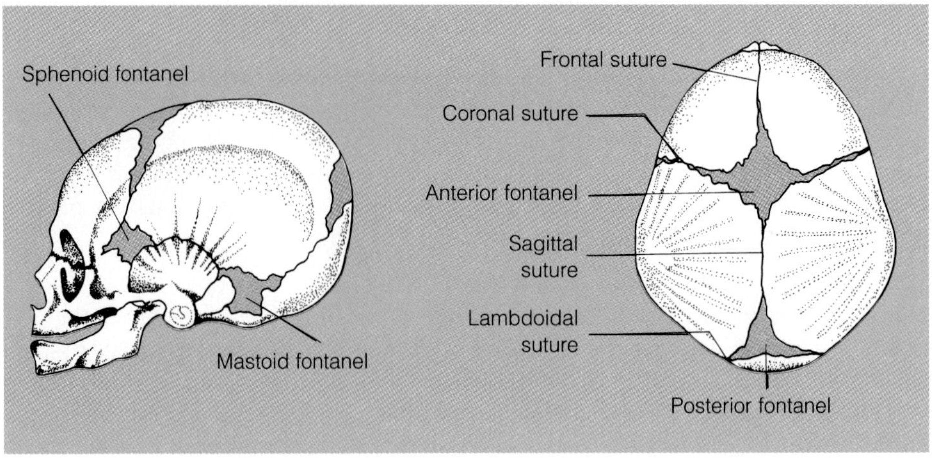

Teething is often accompanied by the baby's first illnesses, but it does not cause them. Around the time that the teeth appear, antibodies that the baby received from the mother during the prenatal period begin to decline. As a result, infants are somewhat less resistant to infection.

BRAIN DEVELOPMENT

At birth, the brain is nearer to its adult size than any other physical structure, and it continues to develop at an astounding pace throughout infancy and toddlerhood. To best understand brain growth, we need to look at it from two vantage points. The first is at the microscopic level of individual brain cells. The second is at the larger level of the cerebral cortex, the most complex brain structure and the one responsible for the highly developed intelligence of our species.

DEVELOPMENT OF NEURONS

The human brain has 100 to 200 billion **neurons,** or nerve cells that store and transmit information, many of which have thousands of direct connections with other neurons. Neurons differ from other body cells in that they are not tightly packed together. There are tiny gaps, or **synapses,** between them where fibers from different neurons come close together but do not touch. Neurons release chemicals that cross the synapse, thereby sending messages to one another.

The basic story of brain growth concerns how neurons develop and form this elaborate communication system. In Chapter 3, we indicated that neurons are produced in the primitive neural tube of the embryo, from which they travel to form the major parts of the brain. Recall that by the end of the second trimester of pregnancy, this process is complete; no more neurons will ever again be produced. After birth, the neurons form complex networks of synaptic connections. As Figure 5.5 shows, during infancy and toddlerhood, growth of neural fibers and synapses increases at an astounding pace (Huttenlocher, 1994; Moore & Persaud, 1993).

Once neurons form connections, a new factor becomes important in their survival: *stimulation.* Neurons that are stimulated by input from the surrounding environment continue to establish new synapses. Those that are seldom stimulated soon die off. This suggests that appropriate stimulation of the child's brain is critically important during periods in which the formation of synapses is at its peak (Greenough, Black, & Wallace, 1987). Indeed, a great deal of animal research supports this idea. For example, there seems to be a sensitive period during which rich

Neurons
Nerve cells that store and transmit information.

Synapses
The gaps between neurons, across which chemical messages are sent.

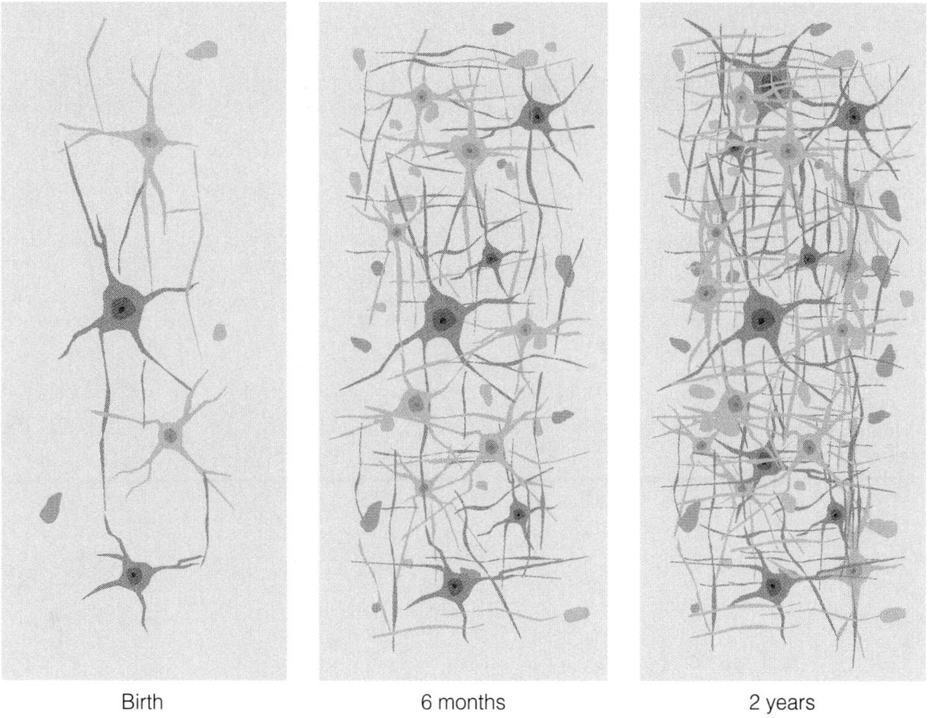

FIGURE 5.5

Development of neurons. Growth of neural fibers takes place rapidly from birth to 2 years. During this time, new synapses are formed at an astounding pace, supporting the emergence of many new capacities. Stimulation is vitally important for maintaining and increasing this complex communication network. *(From J. L. Conel,* The Postnatal Development of the Human Cerebral Cortex. *Cambridge, MA: Harvard University Press. Copyright © 1959 by the President and Fellows of Harvard College. All rights reserved.)*

and varied visual experiences must occur for the visual centers of the brain to develop normally. If a month-old kitten is deprived of light for as brief a time as 3 or 4 days, these areas of the brain start to degenerate. If the kitten is kept in the dark for as long as 2 months, the damage is permanent (Hubel & Weisel, 1970).

At this point, you may be wondering: If no more neurons are produced after the prenatal period, what causes the dramatic increase in skull size that we mentioned earlier in this chapter? Growth of neural fibers results in some increase in brain weight, but not as much as a second type of cell in the brain. About half the brain's volume is made up of **glial cells,** which do not carry messages. Instead, their most important function is **myelinization**, a process in which neural fibers are coated with an insulating fatty sheath (called *myelin*) that improves the efficiency of message transfer. Glial cells multiply dramatically from the fourth month of pregnancy through the second year of life, after which their rate of production slows down (Spreen et al., 1984). Myelinization is responsible for the rapid gain in overall size of the brain (see Figure 5.6). By the time toddlerhood is complete, the brain is already about 70 percent of its adult weight.

DEVELOPMENT OF THE CEREBRAL CORTEX

The **cerebral cortex** is the largest structure of the human brain, accounting for 85 percent of its weight and containing the greatest number of neurons and synapses. The cortex surrounds the rest of the brain, much like a half-shelled walnut. Of all brain structures, the cerebral cortex is the last to stop growing. For this reason, it is believed to be much more sensitive to environmental influences than any other part of the brain (Suomi, 1982).

As Figure 5.7 on page 177 shows, different regions of the cerebral cortex have specific functions, such as receiving information from the senses, instructing the body to move, and thinking. Scientists study the development of these regions by analyzing the chemical makeup and myelinization of the brains of young children who have died. Their findings reveal that the order in which areas of the cortex develop corresponds to the order in which various capacities emerge in the infant and growing child. For example, among areas that control body movement, neurons

Glial cells
Cells that serve the function of myelinization.

Myelinization
A process in which neural fibers are coated with an insulating fatty sheath (called *myelin*) that improves the efficiency of message transfer.

Cerebral cortex
The largest structure of the human brain that accounts for the highly developed intelligence of the human species. Surrounds the rest of the brain, much like a half-shelled walnut.

FIGURE 5.6

Increase in weight of the human brain from the prenatal period to adulthood.
The rise in brain weight is especially rapid between the fetal period and the child's second birthday (see red line), when glial cells are multiplying at a dramatic pace. As brain weight increases, the cortex becomes more convoluted, or folded. *(From R. J. Lemire, J. D. Loeser, R. W. Leech, & E. C. Alvord, 1975,* Normal and Abnormal Development of the Human Nervous System, *p. 236. New York: Harper & Row. Adapted by permission.)*

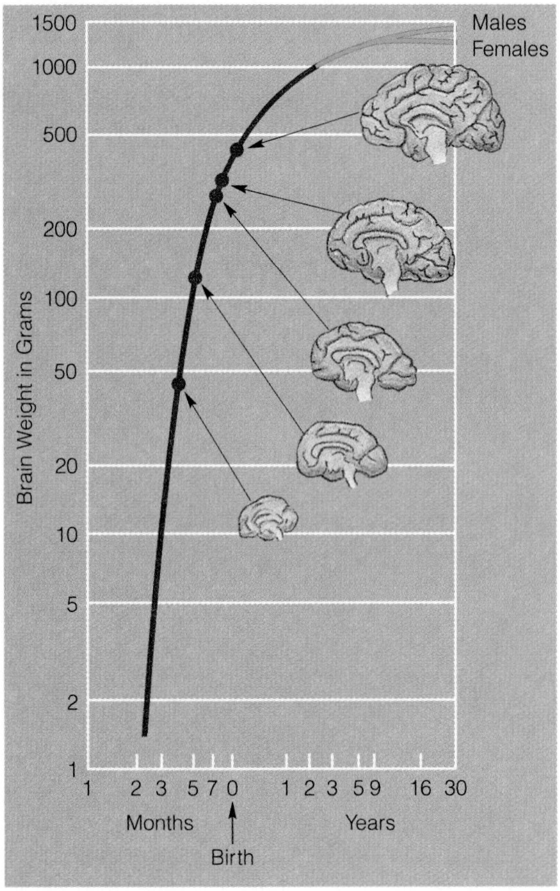

that control the head, arms, and chest mature ahead of those that control the trunk and legs. Do you recognize a familiar developmental trend? The last portion of the cortex to develop and myelinate is the frontal lobe, which is responsible for thought and consciousness. From age 2 months onward, this area functions more effectively, and it continues its growth for years, well into the second and third decades of life (Spreen et al., 1984).

■ LATERALIZATION OF THE CORTEX. Figure 5.7 shows only one *hemisphere,* or side, of the cortex. If you could turn the brain around, you would see that it has two hemispheres—left and right. Although the hemispheres look alike, they do not have precisely the same functions. Some tasks are done mostly by one hemisphere and some by the other. For example, each hemisphere receives sensory information from and controls only one side of the body—the one opposite to it.[1] For most of us, the left hemisphere is responsible for verbal abilities (such as spoken and written language) and positive emotion (for example, joy), whereas the right hemisphere handles spatial abilities (judging distances, reading maps, and recognizing geometric shapes) and negative emotion (such as distress). This pattern may be reversed in left-handed people, but more often, the cortex of left-handers is less clearly specialized than that of right-handers.

Specialization of the two hemispheres is called **lateralization.** Few topics in child development have stimulated more interest than the question of when brain lateralization occurs. Scientists are interested in this issue because they want to know more about **brain plasticity.** A highly *plastic* cortex is still adaptable because many areas are not yet committed to specific functions. If a part of the brain is damaged, other parts can take over tasks that would have been handled by the

Lateralization
Specialization of functions of the two hemispheres of the cortex.

Brain plasticity
The ability of other parts of the brain to take over functions of damaged regions.

[1]The eyes are an exception. Messages from the right half of each retina go to the left hemisphere; messages from the left half of each retina go to the right hemisphere. Thus, visual information from both eyes is received by both hemispheres.

damaged region. But once the hemispheres lateralize, damage to a particular region means that the abilities controlled by it will be lost forever.

Researchers used to think that lateralization of the cortex did not begin until after 2 years of age (Lenneberg, 1967). Today we know that this is not the case. Electrical brain-wave recordings taken as infants react to different kinds of stimulation suggest that the hemispheres have already started to specialize at birth. For example, most newborns favor the right side of the body in their reflexive reactions (Grattan et al., 1992). And like adults, they show greater electrical brain-wave activity in the left hemisphere while listening to speech sounds. In contrast, the right hemisphere reacts more strongly to nonspeech sounds as well as stimuli (such as a sour-tasting fluid) that cause infants to display negative emotion (Fox & Davidson, 1986; Hahn, 1987).

Although brain lateralization begins early in life, it is not yet complete. Dramatic evidence for early plasticity comes from research in which infants had part or all of one hemisphere removed to control violent brain seizures. The remaining hemisphere, whether right or left, took over language and spatial functions as the child matured. But because lateralization had already begun, full recovery from injury did not take place. As these brain-injured infants reached middle childhood and adolescence, they showed many normal abilities, but they had difficulty with very complex verbal and spatial tasks (Goodman & Whitaker, 1985).

Before 1 year of age, the brain is more plastic than at any later time of life, perhaps because a great many of its synapses have not yet been established (Huttenlocher, 1994). Still, the cortex seems to be programmed from the start for the hemispheric specialization that is typical of our species. A lateralized brain is certainly adaptive. It permits a much greater variety of talents to be represented in the two hemispheres than if both sides of the cortex served exactly the same functions.

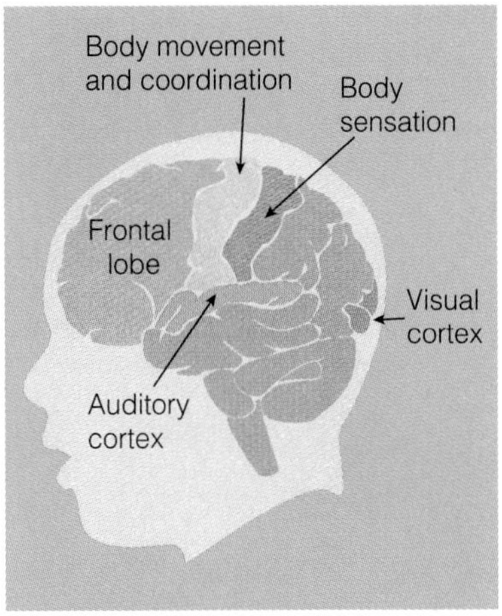

FIGURE 5.7

The left side of the human brain, showing the cerebral cortex. The cortex is divided into different lobes, each of which contains a variety of regions with specific functions. Some major ones are labeled here.

BRIEF REVIEW

The infant's body increases rapidly in overall size during the first 2 years of life. Different parts of the body grow at different rates, following cephalocaudal and proximodistal trends. During the first year, body fat increases much faster than muscle. The skull expands rapidly as the brain grows. Around 6 months of age, the first teeth emerge. The human brain grows faster early in development than any other organ of the body. During the first 2 years, synapses, or connections between neurons, are rapidly laid down. Myelinization is responsible for efficient communication among neurons and a dramatic increase in brain weight. The cerebral cortex is the last part of the brain to stop growing. It is also the structure most affected by stimulation. The cortex has already begun to lateralize at birth, but it retains considerable plasticity during the first year of life.

ASK YOURSELF . . .

- When Joey was born, the doctor found that his anterior fontanel had started to close prematurely. Joey had surgery to open the fontanel when he was 3 months old. From what you know about the function of the fontanels, why was early surgery necessary?
- Felicia commented that at 2 months of age April's daily schedule seemed more predictable, and she was much more alert. What aspects of brain development might be responsible for this change?

FACTORS AFFECTING EARLY PHYSICAL GROWTH

Physical growth, like other aspects of development, results from the continuous and complex interplay between heredity and environment. April, who has tall parents, is likely to be tall herself. Lisa, who constantly has to watch her weight, wonders whether Byron will have the same problem. Although all three children are growing up in homes where there is plenty to eat and they receive much love and stimulation, many infants are not so fortunate. Each of these factors affects early physical growth, as we will see in the following sections.

HEREDITY

Since identical twins are much more alike in height and weight than are fraternal twins, we know that heredity is important in physical growth. However, this resemblance depends on when infant twins are measured. At birth, the differences in weights and lengths of identical twins are actually greater than those of fraternals. The reason is that identical twins share the same placenta, and one baby usually manages to get more nourishment. As long as negative environmental factors are not severe, the smaller baby recovers and swings back to her genetically determined path of growth within a few months (Wilson, 1976). This tendency is called **catch-up growth,** and it persists throughout childhood and adolescence.

When environmental conditions are adequate, height and rate of physical growth (as measured by skeletal age) are largely determined by heredity. Body weight is also affected by genetic makeup, since the weights of adopted children correlate more strongly with those of their biological than adoptive parents. However, as far as weight is concerned, environment—in particular, nutrition—plays an especially important role (Stunkard et al., 1986).

NUTRITION

Good nutrition is important at any time of development, but it is especially critical in infancy because the baby's brain and body are growing so rapidly. Pound for pound, a young baby's energy needs are twice as great as those of an adult. This is because 25 percent of the infant's total caloric intake is devoted to growth, and extra calories are needed to keep rapidly developing organs of the body functioning properly (Pipes, 1989).

Babies not only need enough food, they need the right kind of food. In early infancy, breast milk is especially suited to their needs, and bottled formulas try to imitate it. Later, infants require well-balanced solid foods. If a baby's diet is deficient in either quantity or quality, growth can be permanently stunted.

BREAST- VERSUS BOTTLE-FEEDING. For thousands of years, all human babies were fed the ultimate human health food: breast milk. Only within the last hundred years has bottle-feeding been available. As formulas became easier to prepare, breast-feeding declined from the 1940s into the 1970s when over 75 percent of American infants were bottle-fed. Partly as a result of the natural childbirth movement (see Chapter 4), efforts were made in the 1970s and 1980s to encourage mothers to breast-feed. Soon breast-feeding became more common, especially among well-educated, middle-class women. Today, over 60 percent of American mothers breast-feed their babies (National Center for Health Statistics, 1994).

Table 5.1 summarizes the major nutritional and health advantages of breast-feeding. Because of these benefits, breast-fed babies in poverty-stricken regions of the world are much less likely to be malnourished and 6 to 14 times more likely to survive the first year of life. Too often, bottle-fed infants in developing countries are given low-grade nutrients, such as rice water or highly dilute cow's and goat's milk. When formula is available, it is generally contaminated due to poor sanitation. Also, because a mother is less likely to get pregnant while she is nursing, breast-feeding helps increase spacing among siblings, a major factor in reducing infant and childhood deaths in economically depressed populations (Grant, 1994). (Note, however, that breast-feeding is not a reliable method of birth control.)

In industrialized nations, most women who choose breast-feeding find it to be an emotionally satisfying experience, but breast-feeding is not for everyone. Some mothers simply do not like it, or they are embarrassed by it. A few others, for physiological reasons, are unable to produce enough milk. Occasionally, medical reasons prevent a mother from nursing. If she is taking certain drugs, they can be transmit-

Catch-up growth
Physical growth that returns to its genetically determined path after being delayed by environmental factors.

ted to the baby through the milk. If she has a serious viral or bacterial disease, such as AIDS or tuberculosis, she runs the risk of infecting her baby (Seltzer & Benjamin, 1990; Van de Perre et al., 1993).

Breast milk is so easily digestible that a breast-fed infant becomes hungry quite often—every 1 1/2 to 2 hours in comparison to the 3- to 4-hour schedule of the bottle-fed baby. This makes breast-feeding inconvenient for many women who are employed. However, a mother who cannot be with her baby all the time can still breast-feed or combine it with bottle-feeding. For example, Lisa returned to her job part-time when Byron was 2 months old. Before she left for work, she pumped her milk into a bottle for later feeding by his caregiver (Hills-Banczyk et al., 1993). The same technique can be used for infants who are hospitalized. Preterm infants, especially, benefit from the antibodies and easy digestibility of breast milk. The breast milk produced for a preterm baby is different from that produced for a full-term infant. It is higher in protein and certain minerals and believed to be specially adapted to the preterm infant's growth needs (Gross, Geller, & Tomarelli, 1981).

Some women who cannot or do not want to breast-feed worry that they might be depriving the baby of an experience that is critical for emotional development. As we will see in Chapter 7, emotional well-being is affected by the warmth and sensitivity that accompanies infant feeding, not by the type of milk offered. Regardless of the feeding method a mother chooses, she can respond promptly to her hungry baby and hold and stroke the infant gently. Research reveals that breast- and bottle-fed youngsters do not differ in psychological development (Fergusson, Horwood, & Shanon, 1987).

Breast-feeding is especially important in developing countries, where infants are at risk for malnutrition and early death due to widespread poverty. This Huastec baby of southern Mexico is likely to grow normally during the first year because his mother decided to breast-feed. *(Jean Gerard Sidaner/Photo Researchers)*

ARE CHUBBY BABIES AT RISK FOR LATER OVERWEIGHT AND OBESITY? Overweight and *obesity* are common problems in industrialized nations where food is plentiful. In the United States alone, about 45 percent of adults are affected. The health risks are serious. They include high blood pressure, heart disease, diabetes, and a shorter life span (Stamler, 1993). Fatness also has social and emotional consequences. As we will see in Chapter 11 when we take up obesity in detail, fat children tend to be very unhappy youngsters who are often disliked by their peers.

Byron was an enthusiastic eater from early infancy. He nursed vigorously and gained weight quickly. By 5 months, he indicated his need for solid foods by whimpering after a feeding and reaching for food from his parents' plates. Lisa had heard about research in which rats were overfed early in development. Their bodies

TABLE 5.1

Nutritional and Health Advantages of Breast-Feeding

ADVANTAGE	DESCRIPTION
Correct balance of fat and protein	Compared to the milk of other mammals, human milk is higher in fat and lower in protein. This balance, as well as the unique proteins and fats contained in human milk, is ideal for a rapidly myelinating nervous system.
Nutritional completeness	A mother who breast-feeds need not add other foods to her infant's diet until the baby is 6 months old. At that time, her baby is better able to swallow solids, and the digestive tract is mature enough to handle them. The milks of all mammals are low in iron, but the iron contained in breast milk is much more easily absorbed by the baby's system. Consequently, bottle-fed infants need iron-fortified formula.
Protection against disease	Through breast-feeding, antibodies are transferred from mother to child. As a result, breast-fed babies have far fewer respiratory and intestinal illnesses and allergic reactions than do bottle-fed infants.
Digestibility	Since breast-fed babies have a different kind of bacteria growing in their intestines than do bottle-fed infants, they rarely become constipated or have diarrhea.

Sources: American Academy of Pediatrics, 1984; Ford & Labbok, 1993.

responded by producing too many fat cells, which acted to maintain the overweight condition (Knittle & Hirsch, 1968; Winick & Noble, 1966). Like many other American women who live in a culture preoccupied with thinness, Lisa wondered: Was she overfeeding Byron and, thereby, increasing his chances of being permanently overweight?

As yet, there is no evidence that a well-nourished human infant—even a very chubby one—can accumulate too many fat cells. Only a slight correlation exists between fatness in infancy and obesity at older ages (Roche, 1981; Shapiro et al., 1984). Most chubby infants thin out during toddlerhood and the preschool years, as weight gain slows and they become more active.

Infants and toddlers can eat nutritious foods freely, without risk of becoming too fat. In fact, parents who try to put their babies on diets may cause malnutrition (a topic we discuss next). When infants are first given solid foods, iron-fortified cereal mixed with whole milk satisfies their needs. Between 6 and 12 months, mashed and minced cooked fruits, vegetables, starches, and meats should gradually be added. Around 1 year, most infants have enough teeth to make the transition to chopped table foods, which should include all the basic food groups (Mott, James, & Sperhac, 1990).

Although a baby's food intake should not be limited, concerned parents can prevent their infants from becoming overweight children and adults in other ways. One approach is to encourage good eating habits. Candy, soft drinks, french fries, and other high-calorie foods loaded with sugar, salt, and saturated fats are not appropriate treats for toddlers. When given such foods regularly, young children start to prefer them (Birch, 1990; Harris & Booth, 1987). Regular physical exercise also guards against excessive weight gain. Once toddlers learn to walk, climb, and run, parents should encourage their natural delight at being able to control their bodies by providing opportunities for physically active play.

MALNUTRITION

Osita is an Ethiopian 2-year-old whose mother has never had to worry about his gaining too much weight. When she weaned him at 1 year, there was little for him to eat besides starchy rice flour cakes. Soon his belly enlarged, his feet swelled, his hair began to fall out, and a rash appeared on his skin. His bright-eyed, curious behavior vanished, and he became irritable and listless.

In developing countries and war-torn areas where food resources are limited, malnutrition is widespread. Recent evidence indicates that 40 to 60 percent of the world's children do not get enough to eat (Bread for the World Institute, 1994). Among the 4 to 7 percent who are severely affected, malnutrition leads to two dietary diseases: marasmus and kwashiorkor.

Marasmus is a wasted condition of the body that usually appears in the first year of life. It is caused by a diet that is low in all essential nutrients. The disease often occurs when a baby's mother is severely malnourished. As a result, she cannot produce enough breast milk, and bottle-feeding is also inadequate. Her starving baby becomes painfully thin and is in danger of dying.

Osita has **kwashiorkor.** Unlike marasmus, it is not the result of general starvation. Instead, it is due to an unbalanced diet, one that is very low in protein. Kwashiorkor usually strikes after weaning, between 1 and 3 years of age. It is common in areas of the world where children get just enough calories from starchy foods, but protein resources are scarce. The child's body responds by breaking down its own protein reserves. This causes the swelling and other symptoms that Osita experienced.

Children who manage to survive these extreme forms of malnutrition grow to be smaller in all body dimensions (Galler, Ramsey, & Solimano, 1985a). In addition, the brain is seriously affected. One long-term study of marasmic children revealed

Marasmus
A disease usually appearing in the first year of life that is caused by a diet low in all essential nutrients. Leads to a wasted condition of the body.

Kwashiorkor
A disease usually appearing between 1 and 3 years of age that is caused by a diet low in protein. Symptoms include an enlarged belly, swollen feet, hair loss, skin rash, and irritable, listless behavior.

that an improved diet led to some catch-up growth in height, but the children failed to catch up in head size (Stoch et al., 1982). The malnutrition probably interfered with myelinization, causing a permanent loss in brain weight. By the time these youngsters reach middle childhood, they score low on intelligence and achievement tests, show poor fine motor coordination, and have difficulty paying attention in school (Galler et al., 1984, 1990; Galler, Ramsey, & Solimano, 1985b).

Recall from our discussion of prenatal malnutrition in Chapter 3 that poverty and stressful living conditions make the impact of poor diet even worse. For this reason, interventions for severely malnourished children must improve the family situation as well as the child's nutrition. But even better are efforts at prevention—providing food supplements and medical care to at-risk mothers and children before the effects of early malnutrition are allowed to run their course.

In Chapter 3, we noted that prenatal malnutrition is not confined to developing countries. The same is true for malnutrition after birth. A recent survey revealed that over 12 percent of American children go to bed hungry at night (Food Research and Action Center, 1991). Although few of these children have marasmus or kwashiorkor, their physical growth and ability to learn in school are still affected. Malnutrition is clearly a national and international crisis—one of the most serious problems confronting the human species today.

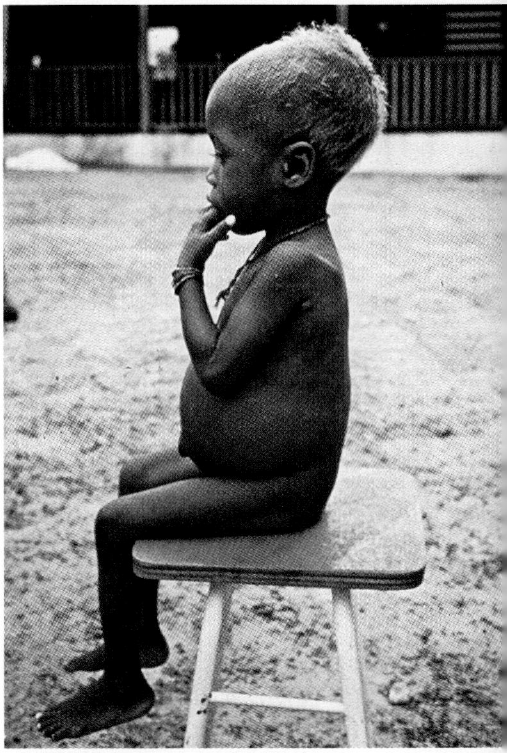

The swollen abdomen and listless behavior of this child are classic symptoms of kwashiorkor, a nutritional illness that results from a diet very low in protein. *(CNRI/Phototake)*

AFFECTION AND STIMULATION

We are not used to thinking of affection and stimulation as necessary for healthy physical growth, but they are just as vital to infants as food. **Nonorganic failure to thrive** is a growth disorder resulting from lack of parental love that is usually present by 18 months of age. Infants who have it show all the signs of marasmus, described in the previous section. Their bodies look wasted, and they are withdrawn and apathetic. However, no organic (or biological) cause for the baby's failure to grow can be found. Enough food is offered, and the infant does not have a serious illness.

Lana, an observant nurse, noticed signs of failure to thrive in Melanie, whose mother brought her to a public health clinic at 8 months of age. Melanie was three pounds lighter than she had been 2 months earlier. Her mother claimed to feed her often and could not understand why she did not grow. Lana took a close look at Melanie's behavior. Unlike most infants her age, she did not mind separating from her mother. Lana tried offering Melanie a toy, but she showed little interest. Instead, she kept her eyes on adults in the room, anxiously watching their every move. When Lana tried to interact with Melanie by looking into her eyes and smiling, Melanie turned her head away (Leonard, Rhymes, & Solnit, 1986; Oates, 1984).

The family circumstances surrounding failure to thrive help explain these typical reactions. During feeding and diaper changing, Melanie's mother sometimes acted cold and distant, at other times impatient and hostile. Melanie tried to protect herself by keeping track of her mother's whereabouts and, when her mother approached, avoiding her gaze (Haynes et al., 1983). Often an unhappy marriage or other family pressures contribute to these serious caregiving problems (Gorman, Leifer, & Grossman, 1993). In Melanie's case, her father was an alcoholic who was out of work, and her parents argued constantly. Her mother had little energy to meet the psychological needs of Melanie and her other three children. Sometimes the baby displays abnormal feeding behaviors, such as poor sucking or vomiting—circumstances that stress the parent–child relationship further (Ramsay, Gisel, & Boutry, 1993).

When treated early, by helping parents or placing the baby in a caring foster home, failure-to-thrive infants show quick catch-up growth. But if the disorder is not corrected in infancy, some children remain small and show lasting cognitive and emotional difficulties (Altemeier et al., 1984; Drotar & Sturm, 1988).

Nonorganic failure to thrive
A growth disorder usually present by 18 months of age that is caused by lack of affection and stimulation.

ASK YOURSELF . . .

- Explain why breast-feeding offers babies protection against disease and early death in poverty-stricken regions of the world.
- Ten-month-old Shaun is below average in height and painfully thin. He has one of two serious growth disorders. Name them, and indicate what clues you would look for to tell which one Shaun has.

BRIEF REVIEW

Heredity, nutrition, and affection and stimulation all contribute to early physical growth. Studies of twins show that height and weight are affected by genetic makeup. Breast milk provides babies with the ideal nutrition between birth and 6 months of age. Breast-feeding protects many poverty-stricken infants against malnutrition, disease, and early death. However, bottle- and breast-fed babies do not differ in psychological development. A mother who feeds her baby nutritious foods need not worry about a chubby infant becoming an overweight child. Malnutrition is a serious global problem. When marasmus and kwashiorkor are allowed to persist, physical size, brain growth, and ability to learn are permanently affected. Inorganic failure to thrive reminds us of the close connection between sensitive, loving care and how children grow.

CHANGING STATES OF AROUSAL

Between birth and 2 years, the organization of sleep and wakefulness changes substantially, and fussiness and crying also decline. Recall from Chapter 4 that the newborn baby takes round-the-clock naps that add up to about 16 hours of sleep. The decline in total sleep time from birth to 2 years is not great; the average 2-year-old still needs 12 to 13 hours. Instead, the greatest change in sleep and wakefulness is that short periods of each are gradually put together, and they start to coincide with a night and day schedule (Berg & Berg, 1987). While the newborn baby might take five or six naps during the day, the older infant remains awake for longer daytime periods and needs fewer naps—by the second year, only one or two. Still, there are great individual differences in sleep needs that remain fairly stable over infancy and early childhood (Jacklin et al., 1980).

The changes in infants' patterns of arousal are largely due to brain maturation, but they are affected by the social environment as well. Lisa and Felicia were delighted when, around 4 months of age, their babies slept through the night. In the United States and other Western nations, night waking is regarded as inconvenient. Parents try to get their babies to sleep through by offering an evening feeding before putting them down in a separate, quiet room. In this way, they push young infants to the limits of their neurological capacities. Yet as the Cultural Influences box on the following page shows, the practice of isolating infants to promote sleep is rare elsewhere in the world. Influenced by Japanese child-rearing customs, Beth held Rachel close for much of the day. At night, she lay in her mother's bed, sleeping and waking to nurse at will. For infants experiencing this type of care, the average sleep period remains constant at 3 hours, from 1 to 8 months of age. Only at the end of the first year do these babies move in the direction of an adultlike sleep–waking schedule (Super & Harkness, 1982).

More mature arousal patterns are a welcome relief to many parents, but they also bring new challenges. We will see in the following sections that the baby's growing alertness supports the development of many new motor skills and perceptual capacities. Parents must constantly adjust their caregiving to fit with the infant's rapidly changing approach to the world.

MOTOR DEVELOPMENT DURING THE FIRST TWO YEARS

Lisa, Beth, and Felicia each kept baby books, filling them with proud notations about when the three children held up their heads, reached for objects, sat by themselves, and walked alone. Parents' enthusiasm for these achievements makes perfect sense. They are, indeed, milestones of development. With each new motor skill, babies master their bodies and the environment in a new way. For example, sitting alone grants infants an entirely different perspective on the world compared to when they spent much of the day lying on their backs and stomachs. Voluntary reaching permits babies to find out about objects by acting on them. And when infants can move on their own, their opportunities for exploration are multiplied.

Babies' motor achievements have a powerful effect on their social relationships. April was the first of the three babies to master crawling. Suddenly Felicia had to "child-proof" the household and restrict April's movements in ways that were

CULTURAL INFLUENCES

CULTURAL VARIATION IN INFANT SLEEPING ARRANGEMENTS

While awaiting the birth of a new baby, American middle-class parents typically furnish a special room as the infant's sleeping quarters. At first, young babies may be placed in a bassinet or cradle in the parents' bedroom for reasons of convenience, but most are moved by 3 to 6 months of age. Many adults in the United States regard this nighttime separation of baby from parent as perfectly natural. Throughout this century, child-rearing advice from experts has strongly encouraged it. For example, Benjamin Spock, in each edition of *Baby and Child Care* from 1945 to the present, states with authority, "I think it is a sensible rule not to take a child into the parents' bed for any reason" (Spock & Rothenberg, 1992, p. 213).

Yet parent–infant "cosleeping" is common around the globe, in industrialized and nonindustrialized countries alike. Japanese children usually lie next to their mothers throughout infancy and early childhood and continue to sleep with a parent or other family member until adolescence (Takahashi, 1990). Among the Maya of rural Guatemala, mother–infant cosleeping is interrupted only by the birth of a new baby, at which time the older child is moved beside the father or to another bed in the same room (Morelli et al., 1992). Cosleeping is also frequent in some American subcultures. African-American children are more likely than Caucasian-American children to fall asleep with parents and to remain with them for part or all of the night (Lozoff, Wolf, & Davis, 1984). Appalachian children of eastern Kentucky typically sleep with their parents for the first 2 years of life (Abbott, 1992).

Available household space plays a minor role in infant sleeping arrangements. Dominant child-rearing beliefs are much more important. In one study, researchers interviewed middle-class American mothers and Guatemalan Mayan mothers about their sleeping practices. American mothers frequently mentioned the importance of early independence training, preventing bad habits, and protecting their own privacy. In contrast, Mayan mothers explained that cosleeping helps build a close parent–child bond, which is necessary for children to learn the ways of people around them. When told that American infants sleep by themselves, Mayan mothers reacted with shock and disbelief, stating that it would be painful for them to leave their babies alone at night (Morelli et al., 1992).

Infant sleeping practices affect other aspects of family life. Sleep problems are not an issue for Mayan parents. Babies doze off in the midst of ongoing social activities and are carried to bed by their mothers. In the United States, getting young children ready for bed often requires an elaborate ritual that takes a good part of the evening. Perhaps bedtime struggles, so common in American middle-class homes but rare elsewhere in the world, are related to the stress young children feel when they are required to fall asleep without assistance.

Infant sleeping arrangements, like other parenting practices, are meant to foster culturally valued characteristics in the young. American middle-class parents view babies as dependent beings who must be urged toward independence, and so they usually require them to sleep alone. In contrast, Japanese, Mayan, and Appalachian parents regard young infants as separate beings who need to establish an interdependent relationship with the community to survive.

unnecessary when, placed on a blanket, she would stay there! A gate was placed at the top of the staircase, breakable objects were removed from the coffee table, and April was picked up when she crawled into places that might endanger her safety. At the same time, playful activities expanded. At the end of the first year, April and her parents played a gleeful game of hide-and-seek around the living room sofa. Soon after, April could turn the pages of a cardboard picture book and point while Felicia named the objects. April's expressions of delight—laughing, smiling, and babbling—as she worked on new motor competencies triggered pleasurable reactions in others, which encouraged her efforts further (Mayes & Zigler, 1992). Motor skills, social competencies, cognition, and language were developing together and supporting one another.

THE SEQUENCE OF MOTOR DEVELOPMENT

Gross motor development refers to control over actions that help infants get around in the environment, such as crawling, standing, and walking. In contrast, *fine motor development* has to do with smaller movements, such as reaching and grasping. Figure 5.8 shows the average age at which a variety of gross and fine motor skills are achieved during infancy and toddlerhood. Most children follow this sequence fairly closely.

Notice that Figure 5.8 also presents the age ranges during which the majority of babies accomplish each skill. These indicate that although the sequence of motor development is fairly uniform across children, there are large individual differences in the rate at which motor development proceeds. Also, a baby who is a late reacher is not necessarily going to be a late crawler or walker. We would only be concerned about a child's development if a large number of motor skills were seriously delayed.

Look at Figure 5.8 once more, and you will see that there is organization and direction to the infant's motor achievements. The *cephalocaudal trend* discussed earlier in this chapter is clearly evident. Motor control of the head comes before control of the arms and trunk, and control of the arms and trunk is mastered before control of the legs. The *proximodistal trend* can also be seen in that head, trunk, and arm control is advanced over coordination of the hands and fingers. Because physical and motor development follow the same general sequence, the cephalocaudal and proximodistal trends are believed to be genetically determined, maturational patterns.

MOTOR SKILLS AS COMPLEX SYSTEMS OF ACTION

We must be careful not to think of infant motor skills as a series of isolated, unrelated accomplishments. Earlier in this century, researchers made this mistake, but today we know that motor development is a matter of acquiring increasingly complex **systems of action.** When motor skills work as a *system,* separate abilities blend together, each cooperating with others to produce more advanced ways of exploring and controlling the environment. During infancy, new systems of action emerge constantly. For example, control of the head and upper chest are combined into sitting with support. Kicking, rocking on all fours, and reaching are gradually put together into crawling. Then crawling, standing, and stepping are united into walking alone (Hofsten, 1989; Pick, 1989; Thelen, 1989).

The way simple motor acts are coordinated into more effective motor systems is most obvious in the area of fine motor skills. As we will see when we discuss the development of voluntary reaching, the various components—grasping, looking, and arm movements—at first emerge independently. Then they are combined into successful reaching for objects (Manchester, 1988). Once reaching is accomplished, it can be coordinated with other actions to produce even more complex skills, such as stacking blocks, putting objects in containers, and eating with a spoon (Connolly & Dagleish, 1989).

Systems of action
In motor development, combinations of previously acquired skills that lead to more advanced ways of exploring and controlling the environment.

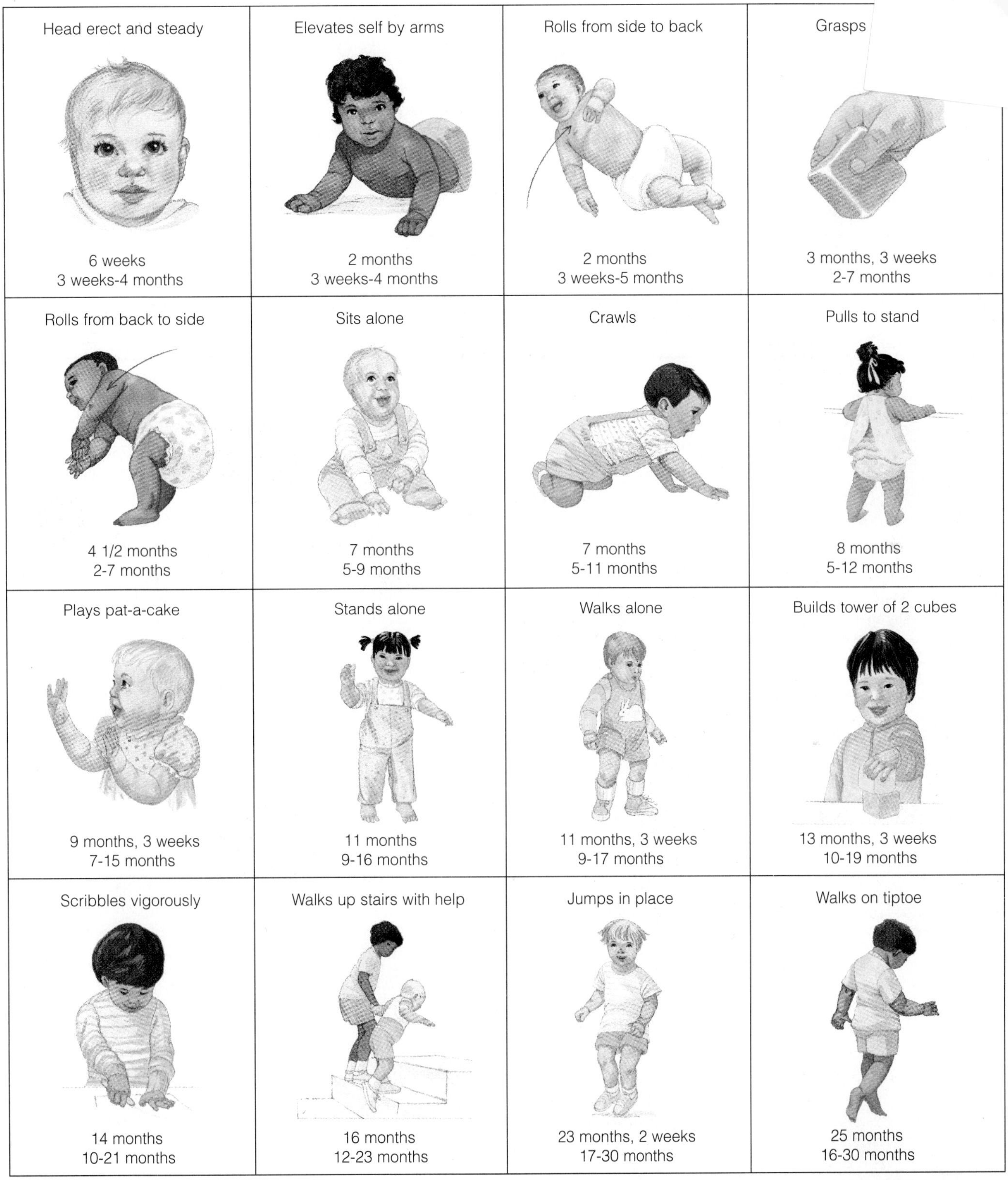
Head erect and steady
6 weeks
3 weeks-4 months
Elevates self by arms
2 months
3 weeks-4 months
Rolls from side to back
2 months
3 weeks-5 months
Grasps
3 months, 3 weeks
2-7 months
Rolls from back to side
4 1/2 months
2-7 months
Sits alone
7 months
5-9 months
Crawls
7 months
5-11 months
Pulls to stand
8 months
5-12 months
Plays pat-a-cake
9 months, 3 weeks
7-15 months
Stands alone
11 months
9-16 months
Walks alone
11 months, 3 weeks
9-17 months
Builds tower of 2 cubes
13 months, 3 weeks
10-19 months
Scribbles vigorously
14 months
10-21 months
Walks up stairs with help
16 months
12-23 months
Jumps in place
23 months, 2 weeks
17-30 months
Walks on tiptoe
25 months
16-30 months

FIGURE 5.8

Gross and fine motor skills achieved during the first two years.
The average age at which each skill is attained is presented, followed by the age range during which 90 percent of infants master the skill. *(From Bayley, 1969.)*

Like the Hopi Indians studied by Wayne and Marsena Dennis, this Shoshone baby spends the day tightly bound to a cradle board. The Dennises found that this did not hinder the development of walking. They concluded that the emergence of motor skills is largely due to biological maturation. Later studies revealed that both maturation and experience influence the course of motor development. *(Victor Englebert/Photo Researchers)*

MATURATION, EXPERIENCE, AND THE DEVELOPMENT OF MOTOR SKILLS

What explains the appearance of new motor skills? Over the past half century, cross-cultural research has suggested some thought-provoking answers. The earliest of these studies, carried out in the 1930s and 1940s, led investigators to the one-sided conclusion that motor development was almost entirely due to biological maturation. For example, Wayne and Marsena Dennis (1940) studied age of walking among the Hopi Indians. Some Hopi mothers bound their infants to cradle boards, whereas others had given up this practice. Even though cradle-board babies could not move their arms, trunk, and legs throughout the day, they walked at the same age as unbound infants—a finding that seemed to suggest experience was unimportant. But note how comparisons like this pay little attention to subtle experiences that could have affected the motor skill in question. For example, the upright position of the cradle board and the opportunity to move freely when taken off at night might have made up for lack of activity during the day.

Much later in his career, when Dennis (1960) observed infants raised in very deprived Iranian institutions, he realized that early movement opportunities and a stimulating environment do contribute to motor development. The Iranian babies spent their days lying on their backs in cribs, without toys to play with. Most did not move about on their own until after 2 years of age. When they finally did move, the constant experience of lying on their backs led them to scoot in a sitting position rather than crawl on their hands and knees the way infants raised in families do. This preference for scooting probably slowed the infants' motor development even further. Babies who scoot come up against furniture with their feet, not their hands. Consequently, they are far less likely to pull themselves to a standing position in preparation for walking.

Culture also affects the rate of motor development. Take a quick survey of several parents you know, asking these questions: Can young babies profit from training? Should sitting, crawling, and walking be deliberately encouraged? Answers vary widely from culture to culture. Japanese mothers believe such efforts are unnecessary and unimportant (Caudill, 1973). And among the Zinacanteco Indians of Southern Mexico, rapid motor progress is actively discouraged. Babies who walk before they know enough to keep away from cooking fires and weaving looms are viewed as dangerous to themselves and disruptive to others (Greenfield, 1992).

But in other parts of the world, direct stimulation of motor skills is common. Among the Baganda of Uganda and the West Indians of Jamaica, babies hold their heads up, sit alone, and walk considerably earlier than North American infants. Infant caregiving customs are believed to be responsible, since babies are advanced only in those motor skills that are trained. Children do not become true members of the Baganda community until they can sit alone. Between 1 and 3 months, Baganda babies are seated on the adult's lap with one arm held around the waist. At 3 to 4 months, they are placed on a mat or in a basin, and cloths are wrapped around them for support (Kilbride & Kilbride, 1975). Throughout the first year, West Indian babies experience a highly stimulating, formal handling routine (see Figure 5.9). Asked why they use the routine, West Indian mothers refer to the traditions of their culture and the need to help babies grow up strong, healthy, and physically attractive (Hopkins & Westra, 1988).

Putting all the evidence together, we must conclude that early motor skills, like other aspects of development, are due to complex transactions between nature and nurture. Although heredity ensures that all babies will follow a similar sequence of motor development, experience can alter this sequence to some degree. And it can greatly change the rate at which early motor milestones are reached.

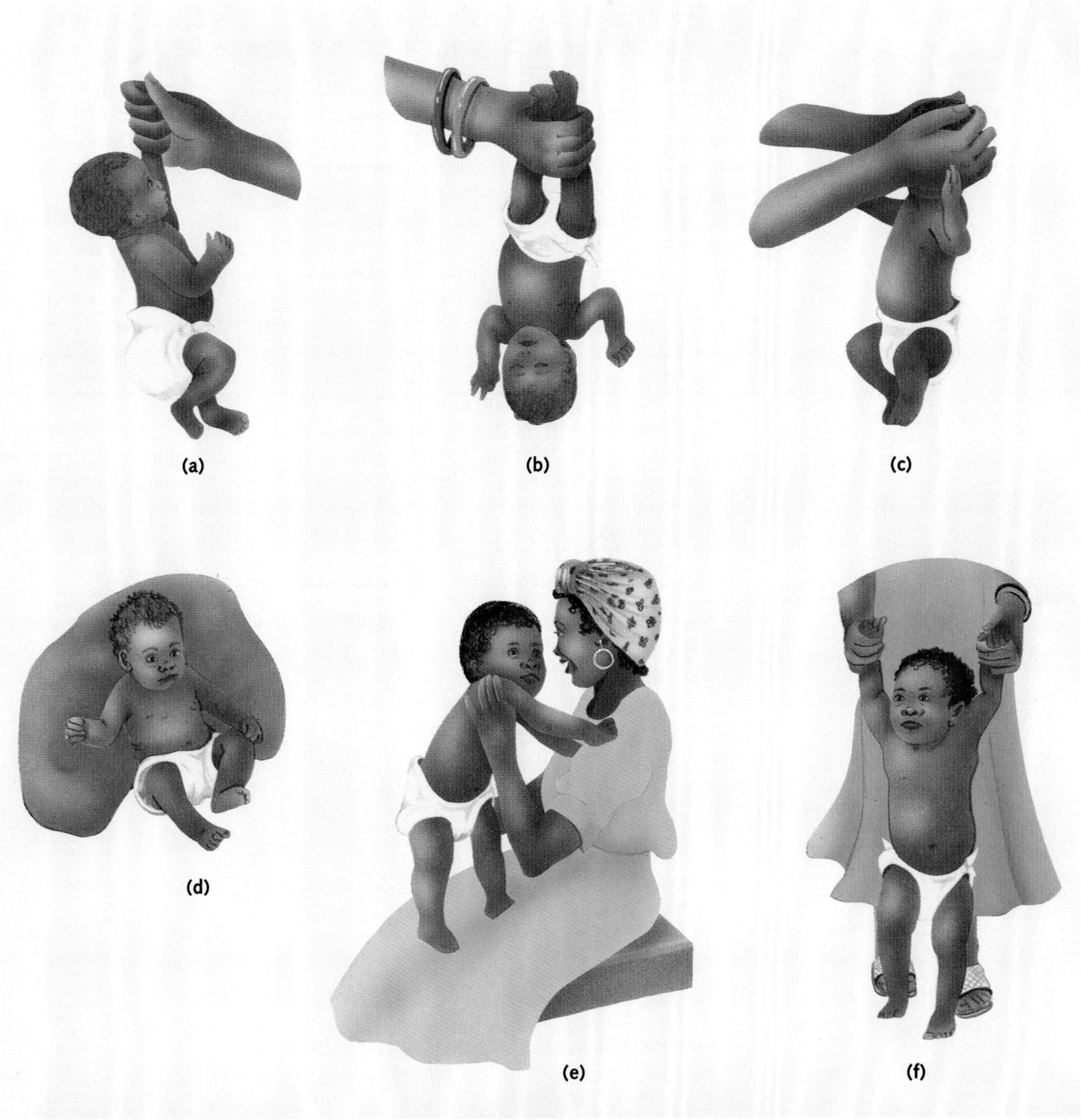

FIGURE 5.9

West Indians of Jamaica use a formal handling routine with their babies.
Exercises practiced in the first few months include stretching each arm while suspending the baby (a); holding the infant upside-down by the ankles (b); grasping the baby's head on both sides, lifting upward, and stretching the neck (c); and propping the infant with cushions that are gradually removed as the baby begins to sit independently (d). Later in the first year, the baby is "walked" up the mother's body (e) and encouraged to take steps on the floor while supported (f). *(Adapted from B. Hopkins & T. Westra, 1988, "Maternal handling and motor development: An intracultural study,"* Genetic, Social and General Psychology Monographs, *14, pp. 385, 388, 389. Reprinted by permission of the Helen Dwight Reid Educational Foundation. Published by Heldref Publications, 1319 Eighteenth St., N.W., Washington, DC 20036-1802.)*

FINE MOTOR DEVELOPMENT: THE SPECIAL CASE OF VOLUNTARY REACHING

Of all motor skills, voluntary reaching is believed to play the greatest role in infant cognitive development, since it opens up a whole new way of exploring the environment (Piaget, 1936/1952). By grasping things, turning them over, and seeing what happens when they are released, infants learn a great deal about the sights, sounds, and feel of objects.

The development of reaching and grasping, shown in Figure 5.10, provides an excellent example of how motor skills start out as gross, diffuse activity and move toward mastery of fine movements. When newborns are held in an upright posture, they direct their arms toward an object dangled in front of them. These movements are called **prereaching,** since they resemble poorly coordinated swipes or swings. Because newborn babies cannot control their arms and hands, they are rarely successful in contacting the object. Like the reflexes we discussed in Chapter 4, prereaching eventually drops out, around 7 weeks of age.

At about 3 months, voluntary reaching appears and gradually improves in accuracy (Bushnell, 1985; Hofsten, 1984). Infants of this age reach just as effectively for a sounding object in the dark as for an object in the light. This indicates that early reaching does not require visual guidance of the arms and hands. Instead, it is controlled by *proprioception,* our sense of movement and location arising from stimuli

FIGURE 5.10

Some milestones of voluntary reaching.
The average age at which each skill is attained is given. *(Ages from Bayley, 1969; Rochat, 1989.)*

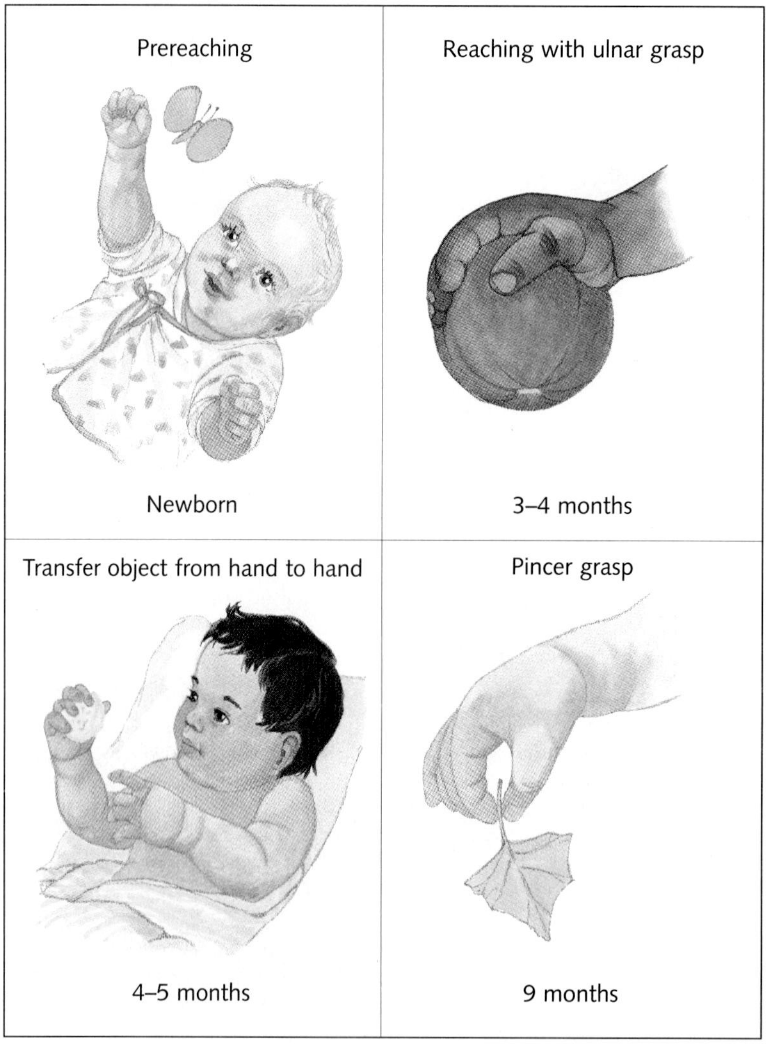

Prereaching
The poorly coordinated, primitive reaching movements of newborn babies.

within the body (Clifton et al., 1993). As a result, vision is freed from the basic act of reaching so it can focus on more complex adjustments. By 5 months, babies sensitively reduce their reaching behavior when an object is moved just beyond their reach (Yonas & Hartman, 1993). And at 9 months, they can redirect their reach to obtain a moving object that changes direction (Ashmead et al. 1993).

Individual differences in how babies develop the reaching motion exist. For example, Brian's spontaneous movements were large and forceful, and he had to make them less vigorous to reach for a toy. In contrast, Rachel's quiet, gentle actions became faster and more energetic as she perfected her reach (Thelen et al., 1993). Clearly, the act of reaching is not programmed into the brain from the start. Instead, each infant builds it in a slightly different way by exploring the match between current movements and those demanded by the task.

Once infants can reach, they start to modify the nature of their grasp. When the grasp reflex of the newborn period weakens, it is replaced by the **ulnar grasp**, a clumsy motion in which the fingers close against the palm. Around 4 to 5 months, both hands become coordinated in exploring objects. Babies of this age can hold an object in one hand while the other scans it with the tips of the fingers, and they frequently transfer objects from hand to hand (Rochat, 1989). By the end of the first year, infants use the thumb and index finger opposably in a well-coordinated **pincer grasp** (Halverson, 1931). Once the pincer grasp appears, the ability to manipulate objects greatly expands. The 1-year-old can pick up raisins and blades of grass, turn knobs, and open and close small boxes.

Between 8 and 11 months, reaching and grasping are so well practiced that they are executed smoothly and effortlessly. As a result, attention is released from coordinating the motor skill itself to events that occur before and after obtaining the object. As we will see in Chapter 6, around this time infants can first solve simple problems involving reaching, such as searching for and finding a hidden toy.

Like other motor milestones, voluntary reaching is affected by early experience. In a well-known study, Burton White and Richard Held (1966) found that institutionalized babies provided with a moderate amount of visual stimulation—at first, simple designs and later, a mobile hung over their cribs—reached for objects 6 weeks earlier than infants given nothing to look at. A third group of babies provided with massive stimulation—patterned crib bumpers and mobiles at an early age—also reached sooner than unstimulated babies. But this heavy dose of enrichment took its toll. These infants looked away and cried a great deal, and they were not as advanced in reaching as the moderately stimulated group. White and Held's findings remind us that more stimulation is not necessarily better. Trying to push infants beyond their current readiness to handle stimulation can undermine the development of important motor skills.

Toddlers are not ready for toilet training until around age 2, when they can control bladder and rectal muscles consistently. The parents of this 2-year-old boy bought a small toilet on which he can sit comfortably, and they make toileting a pleasant experience. He is likely to be fully trained within a few months. *(Margaret Miller/Photo Researchers)*

BOWEL AND BLADDER CONTROL

More than any other aspect of early muscular development, parents wonder about bowel and bladder control. Lisa admitted that she once tried sitting Byron on a child-size potty at 15 months. "That lasted for about two seconds," she said. "Byron is so absorbed in walking and exploring right now that he doesn't have the patience to sit there, waiting for something to happen."

Two or three generations ago, many mothers tried to toilet train small infants. However, they did not really succeed in teaching anything. They only caught the baby's urine or bowel movement at a convenient moment. Toilet training is best delayed until the end of the second or beginning of the third year. Not until then can toddlers consistently identify the signals from a full rectum or bladder and wait until they are in the right place to permit these muscles to open. Research indicates that mothers who postpone training until age 2 succeed in having infants who are

Ulnar grasp
The clumsy grasp of the young infant, in which the fingers close against the palm.

Pincer grasp
The well-coordinated grasp emerging at the end of the first year, involving thumb and forefinger opposition.

fully trained within 4 months. Starting earlier does not produce a more reliably trained preschooler. The whole process just takes longer (Brazelton, 1962). Trying to toilet train too early simply amounts to "a lot of effort for not much reward" (Leach, 1989, p. 246). In addition, as we will see in Chapter 7, pressuring too much in this area, as well as in others, can negatively affect the toddler's emotional well-being.

ASK YOURSELF . . .

- Rosanne read in a magazine that infant motor development could be speeded up through exercise and visual stimulation. She hung mobiles and pictures all over her newborn baby's crib, and she massages and manipulates his body daily. Is Rosanne doing the right thing? Why or why not?

BRIEF REVIEW

The overall sequence of motor development follows the cephalocaudal and proximodistal trends. Each new skill is a matter of developing increasingly complex systems of action. Large individual differences in rate of motor development exist. Besides maturation, motor development is affected by movement opportunities, infant-rearing practices, and a generally stimulating environment. Visually guided reaching begins with the uncoordinated prereaching movements of the newborn baby and gradually evolves into a refined pincer grasp around 1 year of age. Toddlers are not ready for toilet training until the end of the second or beginning of the third year.

BASIC LEARNING MECHANISMS

The term *learning* refers to changes in behavior as the result of experience. At birth, the human brain is set up to profit from experience immediately. Infants are capable of two basic learning mechanisms, which we introduced in Chapter 1: classical and operant conditioning. Now we will discuss them in greater detail. Besides conditioning, infants learn through a natural preference they have for novel stimulation. Finally, one early learning mechanism is bound to surprise you: newborn babies have a remarkable ability to imitate the facial expressions and gestures of adults. The Concept Review Table on page 192 summarizes these four ways of learning.

CLASSICAL CONDITIONING

In Chapter 4, we discussed a variety of newborn reflexes. These make **classical conditioning** possible in the young infant. In this form of learning, a new stimulus is paired with a stimulus that leads to a reflexive response. Once the baby's nervous system makes the connection between the two stimuli, then the new stimulus by itself produces the behavior.

Recall from Chapter 1 that Russian physiologist Ivan Pavlov first demonstrated classical conditioning in some famous research he conducted with dogs (see page 19). Classical conditioning is of great value to human infants, as well as other animals, because it helps them recognize which events usually occur together in the everyday world. As a result, they can anticipate what is about to happen next, and the environment becomes more orderly and predicable (Rovee-Collier, 1987). Let's take a closer look at the steps of classical conditioning.

As Beth settled down in the rocking chair to nurse Rachel, she often gently stroked Rachel's forehead. Soon Beth noticed that each time Rachel's forehead was stroked, she made active sucking movements. Rachel had been classically conditioned. Here is how it happened (see Figure 5.11):

Classical conditioning A form of learning that involves associating a neutral stimulus with a stimulus that leads to a reflexive response.

Unconditioned stimulus (UCS) In classical conditioning, a stimulus that leads to a reflexive response.

Unconditioned response (UCR) In classical conditioning, a reflexive response that is produced by an unconditioned stimulus (UCS).

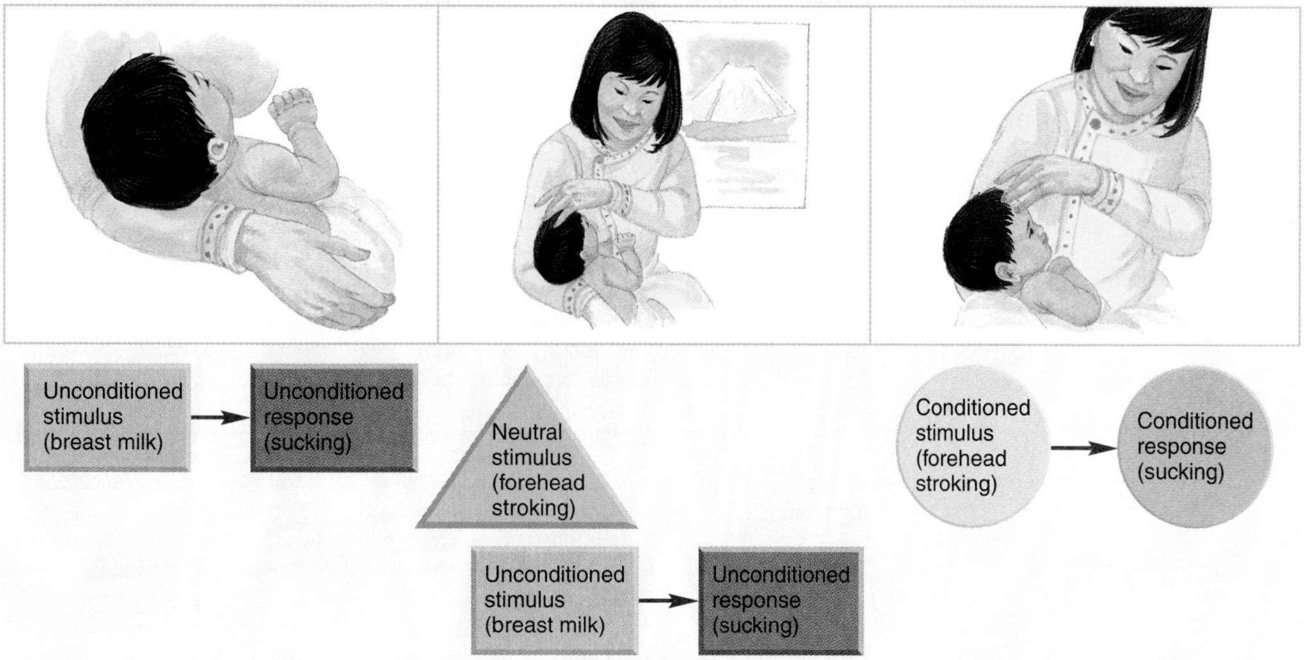

FIGURE 5.11

The steps of classical conditioning. The example here shows how Rachel was classically conditioned to make sucking movements when her forehead was stroked.

1. Before learning takes place, an **unconditioned stimulus (UCS)** must consistently produce a reflexive, or **unconditioned, response (UCR).** In Rachel's case, the stimulus of sweet breast milk (UCS) resulted in sucking (UCR).
2. To produce learning, a *neutral stimulus* that does not lead to the reflex is presented at about the same time as the UCS. Ideally, the neutral stimulus should occur just before the UCS. Beth stroked Rachel's forehead as each nursing period began. Therefore, the stroking (neutral stimulus) was paired with the taste of milk (UCS).
3. If learning has occurred, the neutral stimulus by itself produces the reflexive response. The neutral stimulus is then called a **conditioned stimulus (CS),** and the response it elicits is called a **conditioned response (CR).** We know that Rachel has been classically conditioned because stroking her forehead outside the feeding situation (CS) results in sucking (CR).

If the CS is presented alone enough times, without being paired with the UCS, the CR will no longer occur. In other words, if Beth strokes Rachel's forehead again and again without feeding her, Rachel will gradually stop sucking in response to stroking. This is referred to as **extinction.** In a classical conditioning experiment, the occurrence of responses to the CS during the extinction phase shows that learning has taken place.

Although young babies can be classically conditioned, they will not respond to just any pairing of stimuli. To be easily learned, the association between a UCS and a CS must have survival value. Rachel learned quickly in the feeding situation, since learning which stimuli regularly accompany feeding improves the infant's ability to get food and survive (Blass, Ganchrow, & Steiner, 1984).

Some responses are very difficult to condition in young babies. Fear is one of them. Until the last half of the first year, infants do not have the motor skills to escape unpleasant events. Because they depend on their parents for this kind of protection, they do not have a biological need to form these associations. But between 8 and 12 months, the conditioning of fear is easily accomplished, as the famous example of little Albert, conditioned by John Watson to withdraw and cry at the

Conditioned stimulus (CS)
In classical conditioning, a neutral stimulus that through pairing with an unconditioned stimulus (UCS) leads to a new response (CR).

Conditioned response (CR)
In classical conditioning, an originally reflexive response that is produced by a conditioned stimulus (CS).

Extinction
In classical conditioning, decline of the conditioned response (CR) as a result of presenting the conditioned stimulus (CS) enough times without the unconditioned stimulus (UCS).

CONCEPT REVIEW TABLE

Basic Learning Mechanisms

CONCEPT	IMPORTANT POINT	EXAMPLE
Classical Conditioning	When a neutral stimulus is paired with a stimulus that leads to a reflexive response, eventually the neutral stimulus produces that response. Permits infants to build associations between stimuli that regularly occur together.	A mother often places her baby in an infant seat to feed him solid foods. Each time the baby is placed in the infant seat when it is not time to eat, he mouths and moves his head forward in preparation for feeding.
Operant Conditioning	A behavior is followed by a stimulus that either increases (reinforces) or decreases (punishes) its occurrence. Enables infants to control stimuli to which they are exposed.	A mother smiles and talks gently each time her baby smiles. Soon the baby's smiling increases in frequency. A second mother frowns and speaks sharply when her baby smiles. The baby eventually stops smiling.
Habituation and Dishabituation	When a repetitive stimulus is presented, responsiveness to it declines over time (habituation). Introduction of a new stimulus causes responsiveness to return to a high level (dishabituation). This preference for novelty increases the efficiency of learning.	A baby looks with interest at a bright red ring. Soon looking decreases. Later, when shown the red ring alongside a new green one, the baby spends much more time looking at the green ring.
Imitation	The newborn's ability to copy the facial expressions and gestures of adults appears to be a voluntary capacity that promotes positive interaction between caregiver and infant.	When a parent opens her mouth, purses her lips, or moves her head, a newborn infant observing her is likely to display a similar expression or gesture.

sight of a furry white rat, clearly indicates. Return to Chapter 1, page 19, to review this well-known experiment. Then test your knowledge of classical conditioning by identifying the UCS, UCR, CS, and CR in Watson's study. In Chapter 7, we will discuss the development of fear, as well as other emotional reactions, in detail.

Operant conditioning
A form of learning in which a spontaneous behavior is followed by a stimulus that changes the probability that the behavior will occur again.

OPERANT CONDITIONING

In classical conditioning, babies build expectations about stimulus events in the environment, but they do not influence the stimuli that occur. **Operant conditioning** is quite different. In this form of learning, infants act (or operate) on the environment, and stimuli that follow their behavior change the probability that the behavior will occur again. Recall from Chapter 4 that newborn babies take longer sucks when a nipple delivers sweet liquid as opposed to plain water. If they are given a sour-tasting fluid, they purse their lips and stop sucking entirely. When you read about this research, you were actually studying operant conditioning. A stimulus that increases the occurrence of a response is called a **reinforcer.** Removing a desirable stimulus or presenting an unpleasant one to decrease the occurrence of a response is called **punishment.** In the example just described, sweet liquid *reinforces* the sucking response, whereas a sour-tasting fluid *punishes* it.

Operant conditioning of newborn babies has been demonstrated in many studies. Because the young infant can only control a few behaviors, successful operant conditioning is limited to sucking and head-turning responses. However, many stimuli besides food can serve as reinforcers. For example, researchers have created special laboratory conditions in which the baby's rate of sucking on a nipple produces a variety of interesting sights and sounds. Newborns will suck faster to see visual designs or to hear music and human voices (Rovee-Collier, 1987). Even preterm babies will seek and make contact with reinforcing stimulation. In one study, they increased their contact with a soft teddy bear placed in the isolette that "breathed" quietly at a rate reflecting the infant's respiration, whereas they decreased their contact with a nonbreathing bear (Thoman & Ingersoll, 1993). As these findings suggest, operant conditioning has become a powerful tool for finding out what stimuli babies can perceive and which ones they prefer.

As infants get older, operant conditioning expands to include a wider range of responses and stimuli. For example, special mobiles have been hung over the cribs of 2- to 6-month-olds. When the baby's foot is attached to the mobile with a long cord, the infant can, by kicking, make the mobile turn. Under these conditions, it takes only a few minutes for the infant to start kicking vigorously (Rovee-Collier, 1984). Operant conditioning soon modifies parents' and babies' reactions to each other. As the infant gazes into the adult's eyes, the adult looks and smiles back, and then the infant looks and smiles again. The behavior of each partner reinforces the other, and as a result, both parent and baby continue their pleasurable interaction. In Chapter 7, we will see that this kind of contingent responsiveness plays an important role in the development of infant–caregiver attachment.

Recall from Chapter 1 that classical and operant conditioning originated with behaviorism, an approach that views the child as a relatively passive responder to environmental stimuli. If you look carefully at the findings just described, you will see that young babies are not passive. Instead, they use any means they can to explore and control their surroundings. In fact, when infants' environments are so disorganized that their behavior does not lead to predictable outcomes, serious developmental problems, ranging from intellectual retardation to apathy and depression, can result (Cicchetti & Aber, 1986; Seligman, 1975). In addition, as the From Research to Practice box on page 194 reveals, problems in brain functioning may prevent some babies from actively learning certain life-saving responses; and the absence of such responses may lead to sudden infant death syndrome, a major cause of infant mortality.

HABITUATION AND DISHABITUATION

Take a moment to walk through the rooms of the library, your home, or wherever you happen to be reading this book. What did you notice? Probably those things that are new and different caught your attention first, such as a recently purchased picture on the wall or a piece of furniture that has been moved. At birth, the human brain is set up to be attracted to novelty. **Habituation** refers to a gradual reduction in the strength of a response due to repetitive stimulation. Looking, heart rate, and respiration may all decline, indicating a loss of interest. Once this has

Reinforcer
In operant conditioning, a stimulus that increases the occurrence of a response.

Punishment
In operant conditioning, removing a desirable stimulus or presenting an unpleasant one to decrease the occurrence of a response.

Habituation
A gradual reduction in the strength of a response as the result of repetitive stimulation.

FROM RESEARCH TO PRACTICE

THE MYSTERIOUS TRAGEDY OF SUDDEN INFANT DEATH SYNDROME

Before they went to bed, Millie and Stuart looked in on 3-month-old Sasha. She was sleeping soundly, her breathing no longer as labored as it had been 2 days before, when she caught her first cold. There had been reasons to worry about Sasha at birth. She was born 3 weeks early, and it took over a minute before she started breathing. "Sasha's muscle tone seems a little weak," Millie remembered the doctor saying. "She just needs to get busy and gain a little weight, and then she'll be well on her way." As Millie and Stuart stood over Sasha's crib, they reflected on how much she had grown and changed since those early days.

Millie awoke with a start the next morning and looked at the clock. It was 7:30, and Sasha had missed her night waking and early morning feeding. Wondering if she was all right, Millie tiptoed into the room. Sasha lay still, curled up under her blanket. She had died silently during her sleep.

Sasha was a victim of **sudden infant death syndrome (SIDS).** In industrialized nations, SIDS is the leading cause of infant mortality. It accounts for over one-third of these deaths in the United States (Keens & Ward, 1993; Wilson & Neidich, 1991). Millie and Stuart's grief was especially hard to bear because no one could give them a definite answer about why Sasha died. They felt guilty and under attack by relatives, and their other daughter, 5-year-old Jill, reacted with sorrow that lasted for months. Eventually, Millie and Stuart sought help from a support group for parents who have lost a baby. And Millie started to read about the disorder, in hopes of finding out about ways to prevent it. Here is some of what she learned:

Although the precise cause of SIDS is not known, infants who die of it show physical abnormalities from the very beginning. Early medical records of SIDS babies reveal higher rates of prematurity and low birth weight, poor Apgar scores, and limp muscle tone (Buck et al., 1989; Lipsitt, Sturner, & Burke, 1979; Shannon et al., 1987). Abnormal heart rate and respiration as well as disturbances in sleep–waking activity are also involved (Froggatt et al., 1988). At the time of death, over half of SIDS babies have a mild respiratory infection. This seems to increase the chances of respiratory failure in an already vulnerable baby (Cotton, 1990).

One hypothesis about the cause of SIDS is that problems in brain functioning prevent these infants from learning how to respond when their survival is threatened—for example, when respiration is suddenly interrupted (Lipsitt, 1990). Between 2 and 4 months of age, when SIDS is most likely to occur, reflexes decline and are replaced by voluntary, learned responses. Respiratory and muscular weaknesses may stop SIDS babies from acquiring behaviors that replace defensive reflexes. As a result, when breathing difficulties occur during sleep, they do not wake up, shift the position of their bodies, or cry out for help. Instead, they simply give in to oxygen deprivation and death.

In an effort to reduce the occurrence of SIDS, researchers are studying environmental factors associated with it. Maternal smoking, both during and after pregnancy, is highly correlated with the disorder. A baby of a smoking mother is two to three times more likely to die of SIDS than is an infant of a nonsmoker (Schoendorf & Kiely, 1992). Other consistent findings are that SIDS babies are more likely to sleep on their stomachs than on their backs, and often they are wrapped very warmly in clothing and blankets (Fleming et al., 1990). Why are these factors associated with SIDS? Scientists think that smoke and excessive body warmth (which can be encouraged by putting babies down on their stomachs) place a strain on the respiratory control system in the brain. In an at-risk baby, the respiratory center may stop functioning. In other cases, healthy babies sleeping face down in soft bedding may simply die from continually breathing their own exhaled breath (Kemp & Thach, 1993).

Can simple procedures such as quitting smoking, changing an infant's sleeping position, and removing a few bedclothes prevent SIDS? Research suggests so. For example, recent efforts to discourage parents from putting babies down on their stomachs were followed by a reduction in SIDS in England and New Zealand (Taylor, 1991; Wigfield et al., 1992). When SIDS does occur, surviving family members require a great deal of emotional support (DeFrain, Ernst, & Jakub, 1991). As Millie commented 6 months after Sasha's death, "It's the worst crisis we've ever been through. What's helped us most are the comforting words of parents in our support group who've experienced the same tragedy."

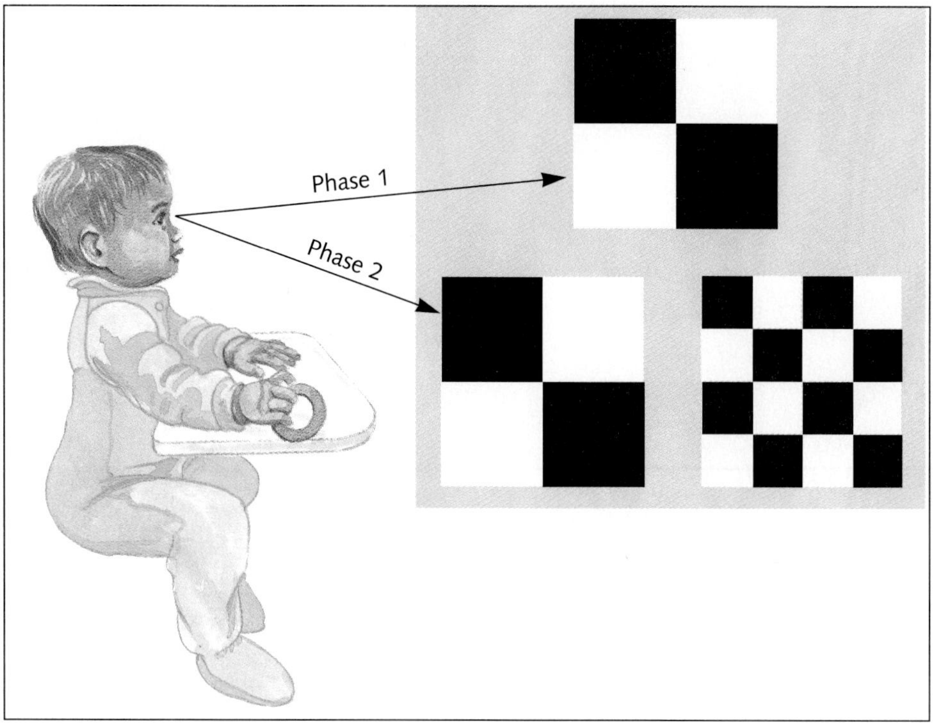

FIGURE 5.12

Example of how the habituation–dishabituation sequence can be used to study infant perception and cognition.
In Phase 1, an infant is permitted to look at (habituate to) a 2 × 2 checkerboard, but this time it appears alongside a new, 4 × 4 checkerboard. If the infant dishabituates to (spends more time looking at) the 4 × 4 checkerboard, then we know the baby remembers the first stimulus and can tell that the second one is different from it.

occurred, a new stimulus—some kind of change in the environment—causes responsiveness to return to a high level. This recovery is called **dishabituation.**

Habituation and dishabituation enable us to focus our attention on those aspects of the environment we know least about. As a result, learning is more efficient (Lipsitt, 1986). By studying the stimuli that infants of different ages habituate and dishabituate to, researchers can tell much about the infant's understanding of the world. For example, a baby who first habituates to a visual pattern (e.g., a 2 × 2 checkerboard) and then dishabituates to a new one (a 4 × 4 checkerboard) clearly remembers the first stimulus and perceives the second one as new and different from it. This method of studying infant perception and cognition, which is illustrated in Figure 5.12, can be used with newborn babies—even those who are five weeks preterm (Rose, 1980; Werner & Siqueland, 1978). We will return to habituation research later in this chapter when we discuss perceptual development, and in Chapter 6, when we consider infant attention and memory.

IMITATION

For many years, scientists believed that **imitation**—learning by copying the behavior of another person—was beyond the capacity of very young infants. They were not expected to imitate until several months after birth (Bayley, 1969; Piaget, 1945/1951). Then a growing number of studies began to report that newborn babies come into the world with a primitive ability to imitate the behavior of their caregivers.

Figure 5.13 shows examples of responses obtained in two of the first studies of newborn imitation (Field et al., 1982; Meltzoff & Moore, 1977). As you can see, the babies appeared to imitate a wide variety of adult facial expressions. These results are so extraordinary that it is not surprising they have been challenged. Other researchers who tried to get young babies to imitate were much less successful (see, for example, Abravanel & Sigafoos, 1984; Kaitz et al., 1988). Yet in all these follow-ups, exposure of newborns to labor and delivery medication could have interfered

Sudden infant death syndrome (SIDS)
Death of a seemingly healthy baby, who stops breathing, usually during the night, without apparent cause.

Dishabituation
Increase in responsiveness after stimulation changes.

Imitation
Learning by copying the behavior of another person. Also called *modeling* or *observational learning.*

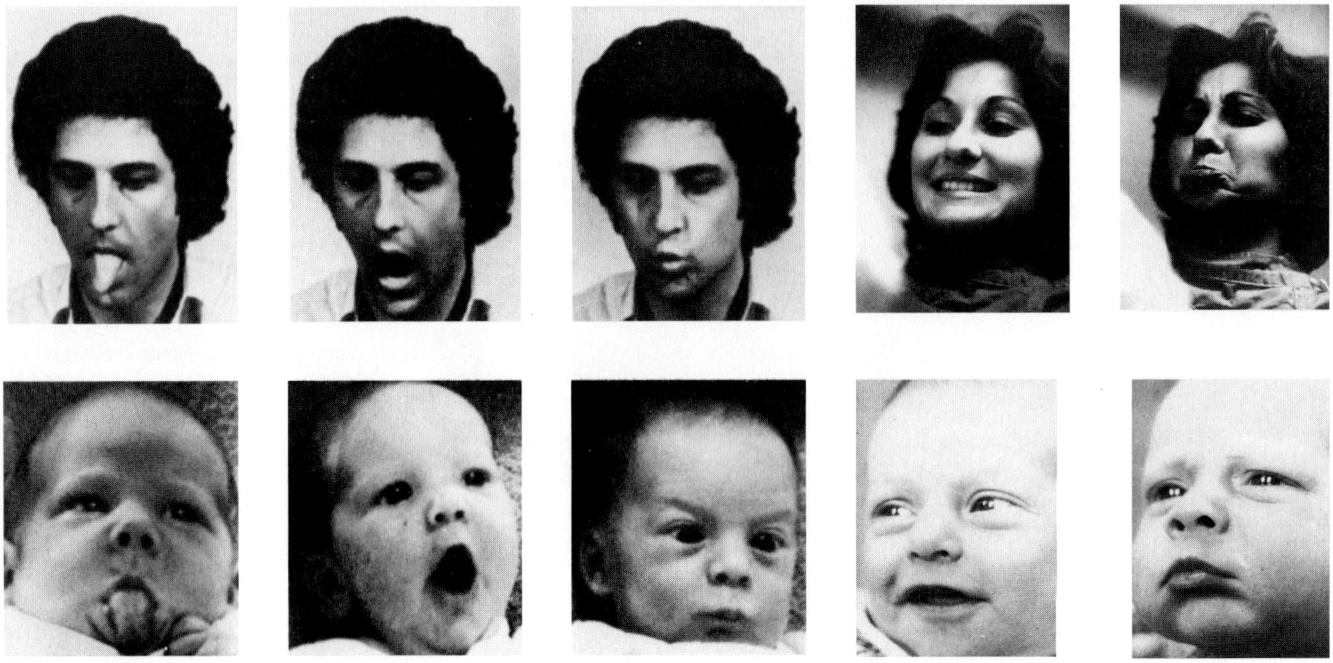

(a) (b) (c) (d) (e)

FIGURE 5.13

Photographs from two of the first studies of newborn imitation.
Those on the left show 2- to 3-week-old infants imitating tongue protrusion (a), mouth opening (b), and lip protrusion (c) of an adult experimenter. Those on the right show 2-day-old infants imitating happy (d) and sad (e) adult facial expressions. *(From A. N. Meltzoff & M. K. Moore, 1977, "Imitation of Facial and Manual Gestures by Human Neonates,"* Science, *198, p. 75; and T. M. Field et al., 1992, "Discrimination and Imitation of Facial Expressions by Neonates,"* Science, *218, p. 180. Copyright 1977 and 1982, respectively, by the AAAS. Reprinted by permission.)*

with this amazing capacity. Studies of alert newborns reveal that besides facial expressions, they imitate head movements as well (Meltzoff & Moore, 1989; Reissland, 1988).

Today, few researchers question the neonate's capacity to imitate. Explanations of the response are more controversial. Some researchers regard the capacity as little more than an automatic response to particular stimuli, much like a reflex. But newborns model a wide variety of facial expressions, and they do so even after short delays—when the adult is no longer demonstrating the behavior. This suggests that they imitate in much the same way we do—by actively trying to match body movements they "see" with ones they "feel" themselves make. Later in this chapter, we will encounter evidence that young babies are surprisingly good at coordinating information across sensory systems. Taken together, these findings support a view of newborn imitation as a flexible, voluntary capacity (Meltzoff & Moore, 1992).

As we will see in Chapter 6, a baby's capacity to imitate changes greatly over the first 2 years. But however limited it is at birth, imitation provides the young baby with a powerful means of learning. Through imitation, adults can get young infants to express desirable behaviors, and once they do, adults can encourage these further. In addition, adults take great pleasure in a baby who imitates their facial gestures and actions. Perhaps newborn imitation is one of those capacities that helps get the baby's relationship with parents off to a good start.

BRIEF REVIEW

Infants are marvelously equipped to learn immediately after birth. Through classical conditioning, infants acquire stimulus associations that have survival value. Operant conditioning permits them to control events in the surrounding world. Habituation and dishabituation reveal that infants, much like adults, are naturally attracted to novel stimulation. Finally, newborns' amazing ability to imitate the facial expressions and gestures of adults may promote early social interaction with caregivers.

ASK YOURSELF . . .

- Byron has a music box hung on the side of his crib. Each time he pulls a lever, the music box plays a nursery tune. Which learning mechanism is the manufacturer of this toy taking advantage of?
- Earlier in this chapter, we indicated that infants with nonorganic failure to thrive are unlikely to smile at a friendly adult. Also, they keep track of nearby adults in an anxious and fearful way. Explain these reactions using the learning mechanisms discussed in the preceding sections.
- Return to the section on intervening with preterm infants on page 149 of Chapter 4. Why might a preterm baby seek contact with a soft, "breathing" teddy bear, as reported in our discussion of operant conditioning on page 193?

PERCEPTUAL DEVELOPMENT IN INFANCY

In Chapter 4, you learned that touch, taste, smell, and hearing were remarkably well developed at birth. Now let's turn to a related question: How does perception change over the first year of life?

Our discussion will focus on infant hearing and vision because almost all research addresses these two aspects of perceptual development. Unfortunately, we know little about how touch, taste, and smell develop after birth. Also, in Chapter 4 we used the word *sensation* to talk about these capacities. Now we are using the word *perception.* The reason is that sensation suggests a fairly passive process—what the baby's receptors detect when they are exposed to stimulation. In contrast, perception is much more active. When we perceive, we organize and interpret what we see. As we look at the perceptual achievements of infancy, you will probably find it hard to tell where perception leaves off and thinking begins. Thus, the research we are about to discuss provides an excellent bridge to the topic of Chapter 6—infant cognitive development.

HEARING

On Byron's first birthday, Lisa bought several tapes of nursery songs, and she turned one on each afternoon at naptime. Soon Byron let her know his favorite tune. If she put on the tape with "Twinkle, Twinkle," he stood up in his crib and whimpered until she replaced it with "Jack and Jill." Byron's behavior illustrates the greatest change that takes place in hearing over the first year of life: babies start to organize sounds into complex patterns. If two melodies differing only slightly are played, 1-year-olds can tell that they are not the same (Morrongiello, 1986).

As we will see in the next chapter, throughout the first year babies are preparing to acquire language. Recall from our discussion in Chapter 4 that newborns recognize the difference between almost all sounds in human languages. As infants continue to listen actively to the talk of people around them, they learn to focus on meaningful sound variations. By 6 months of age, long before they are ready to talk, babies start to focus on the speech sounds of their own language. In other words, they stop responding to sound distinctions that are not useful in their language community (Kuhl et al., 1992).

In the second half of the first year, infants focus on larger speech units that are crucial for figuring out the meaning of what they hear. In one study, researchers recorded two versions of a mother telling a story. In the first, she spoke naturally, with pauses occurring between clauses, like this: "Cinderella lived in a great big house [pause], but it was sort of dark [pause] because she had this mean stepmother." In the second version, the mother inserted pauses in unnatural places—in the middle of clauses: "Cinderella lived in a great big house, but it was [pause] sort of dark because she had [pause] this mean stepmother." Did you find it difficult to pay attention to the second of these examples? So do 7-month-olds. They clearly prefer speech with natural breaks (Hirsh-Pasek et al., 1987). By 9 months, infants extend this rhythmic sensitivity to individual words. American babies of this age listen much longer to words in which the first rather than the second syllable is stressed—a pattern typical in the English language (Jusczyk, Cutler, & Redanz, 1993).

VISION

Suppose you lived in a world in which you were allowed to choose between hearing and vision, but you could not have both. Which would you select? Most people decide on vision, for good reason. More than any other sense, humans depend on vision for active exploration of the environment. Although at first the baby's visual world is fragmented, it undergoes extraordinary changes during the first 7 to 8 months of life.

Visual development is supported by rapid maturation of the eye and visual centers in the brain. Recall from Chapter 4 that the newborn baby's focusing ability and color perception are poor. By 2 months of age, infants can discriminate colors across the entire spectrum, and at 3 months they can focus on objects just as well as adults can (Banks, 1980; Clavadetscher et al., 1988). Visual acuity (fineness of discrimination) improves steadily throughout the first year. In Chapter 4, we noted that newborns see about as clearly at 20 feet as adults do at 660 feet. By 6 months, their acuity has improved greatly, to about 20/100. At 11 months, it reaches a near-adult level (Courage & Adams, 1990). The ability to hold fixation on a moving object and track it with the eyes improves steadily over the first 6 months of life (Hainline, 1985).

As babies see more clearly and explore their visual field more adeptly, they work on figuring out the characteristics of objects and how they are arranged in space. We can best understand how they do so by examining the development of two aspects of vision: depth and pattern perception.

DEPTH PERCEPTION. *Depth perception* is the ability to judge the distance of objects from one another and from ourselves. It is important for understanding the layout of the environment and for guiding motor activity. To reach for objects, babies must have some idea about depth. Later, when infants learn to crawl, depth perception helps prevent them from bumping into furniture and falling down staircases. However, as we will see shortly, parents are unwise to trust the baby's judgment in these situations entirely!

The earliest studies of depth perception used a well-known apparatus called the *visual cliff* (see Figure 5.14). Devised by Eleanor Gibson and Richard Walk (1960), it consists of a table covered by glass, at the center of which is a platform. On one side of the platform (the shallow side) is a checkerboard pattern just under the surface of the glass. On the other (the deep side), the checkerboard is several feet beneath the glass. The researchers placed crawling infants on the platform and asked their mothers to entice them across both the deep and shallow sides by calling to them and holding out a toy. Although the babies readily crossed the shallow side, all but a few reacted with fear to the deep side. The researchers concluded that around the time that infants crawl, most distinguish deep and shallow surfaces and avoid drop-offs that look dangerous (Walk & Gibson, 1961).

Gibson and Walk's research shows that crawling and avoidance of drop-offs are linked, but it does not tell us how they are related. Also, from studies of crawling infants, we cannot tell when depth perception first appears. To better understand the development of depth perception, recent research has looked at babies' ability to detect particular depth cues, using methods that do not require that they crawl.

FIGURE 5.14

The visual cliff.
By refusing to cross the deep side and showing a preference for the shallow surface, this infant demonstrates the ability to perceive depth. *(William Vandivert/*Scientific American*)*

The Emergence of Depth Perception. How do we know when an object is near rather than far away? Try these exercises to find out. Look toward the far wall while moving your head from side to side. Notice that objects close to your eye move past your field of vision more quickly than those far away. Next, pick up a small object (such as your cup) and move it toward and away from your face. Did its image grow larger as it approached and smaller as it receded?

Motion provides us with a great deal of information about depth, and it is the first type of depth cue to which infants are sensitive. Around 3 weeks of age, babies blink their eyes defensively to an object moved toward their face that looks as if it were going to hit (Nanez, 1987). As they are carried about and as people and things turn and move before their eyes, infants learn more about depth. For example, by 3 months, motion has helped them figure out that objects are not flat shapes. Instead, they are three-dimensional (Arterberry & Yonas, 1988).

Motion is not the only important depth cue. Our eyes are separated, and each receives a slightly different view of the visual field. In children and adults, the brain blends these two images but also registers the difference between them, providing us with *binocular* (meaning two eyes) depth cues. Researchers have used ingenious methods to find out if infants are sensitive to binocular cues. One way is to project two overlapping images before the baby, who wears special goggles to ensure that each eye receives one of them. If babies use binocular cues, they see and visually track an organized form rather than random dots. Results reveal that binocular sensitivity emerges between 2 and 3 months and gradually improves over the first half year (Banks & Salapatek, 1983). Infants quickly make use of binocular depth perception in their reaching, adjusting arm and hand movements to match the distance of objects from the eye.

We also use a final set of depth cues—the same ones that artists use to make a painting look three-dimensional. These are called *pictorial* depth cues. Examples are lines that create the illusion of perspective, changes in texture (nearby textures are more detailed than ones far away), and overlapping objects (an object partially hidden by another object is perceived to be more distant). Investigators have explored infants' sensitivity to pictorial cues by covering one eye (so the baby cannot rely on binocular vision), presenting stimuli with certain cues, and seeing which ones babies reach for. These experiments show that 7-month-old babies are sensitive to a variety of pictorial cues, but 5-month-olds are not (Yonas et al., 1986). Thus, pictorial depth perception is last to develop, emerging around the middle of the first year.

TABLE 5.2

Development of Depth Perception

AGE	PERCEPTUAL CAPACITY
3 weeks–3 months	Sensitivity to motion cues appears and improves.
3–6 months	Sensitivity to binocular cues appears and improves.
6–7 months	Sensitivity to pictorial cues appears.
6–11 months	Wariness of heights develops and is encouraged by the ability to move about independently.

Table 5.2 summarizes the infant's developing sensitivity to depth. Why does perception of depth cues emerge in the order just described? Researchers speculate that motor development is involved. For example, control of the head during the early weeks of life may help babies notice motion cues. Improved focusing ability at 3 months may permit detection of binocular cues. And around 5 to 6 months, the ability to turn, poke, and feel the surface of objects may promote perception of pictorial cues as infants use their hands to pick up information about the size, texture, and shape of objects (Bushnell & Boudreau, 1993). Indeed, as we will see next, research shows that one aspect of motor progress—the baby's ability to move about independently—plays a vital role in the refinement of depth perception.

Independent Movement and Depth Perception. Just before she reached the 6-month mark, April started crawling. "She's like a fearless daredevil," exclaimed Felicia to the other mothers. "If I put her down in the middle of our bed, she crawls right over the edge. Several times I stopped her just before she went overboard. The same thing's also happened by the stairs."

Will April become more wary of the side of the bed and the staircase as she becomes a more experienced crawler? Research suggests that she will. In one study, infants with more crawling experience (regardless of when they started to crawl) were far more likely to refuse to cross the deep side of the visual cliff (Bertenthal, Campos, & Barrett, 1984). Avoidance of heights, the investigators concluded, is "made possible by independent locomotion" (Bertenthal & Campos, 1987, p. 563).

Crawling promotes three-dimensional understanding, such as wariness of dropoffs and memory for object locations. As babies crawl about, they experience the visual world in new ways, taking note of how to get from place to place, where objects are located, and what they look like from different points of view. *(Peter Southwick/Stock Boston)*

Independent movement does not just influence wariness of drop-offs. It is related to other aspects of three-dimensional understanding as well. For example, crawling infants are better at remembering object locations and finding hidden objects than are their noncrawling agemates. And the more crawling experience they have, the better their performance on these tasks (Bai & Bertenthal, 1992; Campos & Bertenthal, 1989). Why does crawling make such a difference? Compare your own experience of the environment when you are driven from one place to another as opposed to when you walk or drive yourself. When you move on your own, you are much more aware of landmarks and routes of travel, and you take more careful note of what things look like from different points of view. The same is true for infants. In fact, researchers believe that crawling is so important in structuring babies' experience of the world that it may promote a new level of brain organization by strengthening certain synaptic connections in the cortex (Bertenthal & Campos, 1987).

An estimated 80 to 90 percent of American parents place babies who are not yet crawling in "walkers" (Marcella & McDonald, 1990). These mechanical devices consist of a seat with a frame on castors in which babies can move around independently by pushing with their feet. Do walkers help stimulate development in the ways just described? Research suggests that they do (Bertenthal, Campos, & Barrett, 1984; Kermoian & Campos, 1988). However, there is no evidence that walkers have lasting effects on development, and they can be dangerous. Infants frequently tip over in them and careen down staircases, perhaps because the frame and seat provide a false sense of security. In the United States, walkers account for almost

28,000 infant injuries annually (Trinkoff & Parks, 1993). For safety's sake, it is best not to put babies in these devices. The reorganization of experience linked to independent movement eventually takes place for all normal infants. The risks involved in trying to accelerate it far outweigh the benefits.

PATTERN PERCEPTION. Are young babies sensitive to the pattern, or form, of things they see, and do they prefer some patterns to others? Early research revealed that even newborns prefer to look at patterned as opposed to plain stimuli—for example, a drawing of the human face or one with scrambled facial features to a black-and-white oval (Fantz, 1961, 1963). Since then, many studies have shown that as infants get older, they prefer more complex patterns. For example, when shown black-and-white checkerboards, 3-week-old infants look longest at ones with a few large squares, whereas 8- and 14-week-olds prefer those with many squares (Brennan, Ames, & Moore, 1966). Infant preferences for many other patterned stimuli have been tested—curved versus straight lines, connected versus disconnected elements, and whether a pattern is organized around a central focus (as in a bull's eye), to name just a few.

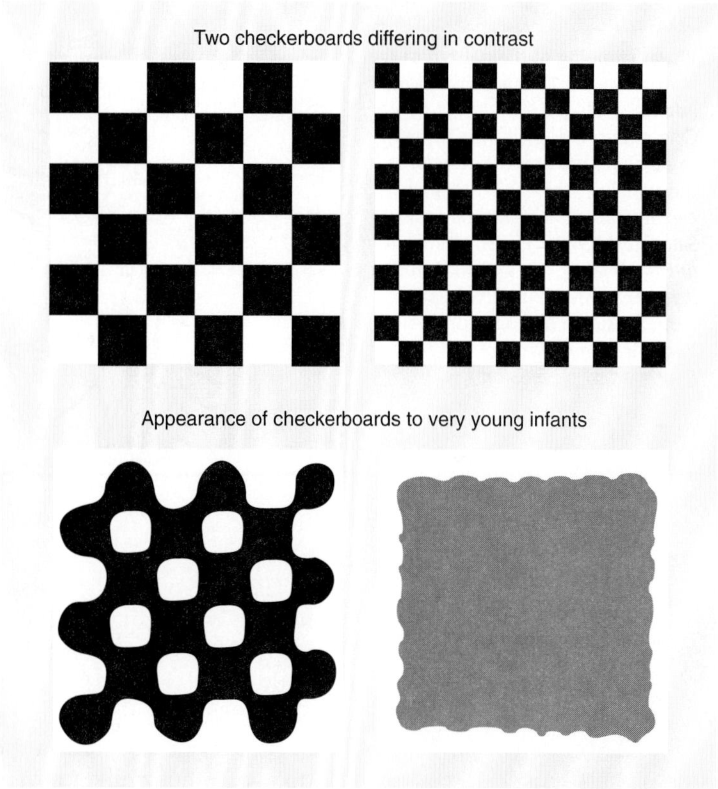

FIGURE 5.15

The way two checkerboards differing in complexity look to infants in the first few weeks of life. Because of their poor vision, very young infants cannot resolve the fine detail in the more complex checkerboard. It appears blurred, like a gray field. The large, bold checkerboard appears to have more contrast, so babies prefer to look at it. *(Adapted from M. S. Banks & P. Salapatek, 1983, "Infant Visual Perception," in M. M. Haith & J. J. Campos (Eds.),* Handbook of Child Psychology: Vol. 2. Infancy and Developmental Psychobiology *(4th ed.), New York: Wile, p. 504. Copyright © 1983 by John Wiley & Sons. Reprinted by permission.)*

Contrast Sensitivity. For many years, investigators did not understand why babies of different ages find certain patterns more attractive than others. Then a general principle was discovered that accounts for early pattern preferences. It is called **contrast sensitivity** (Banks & Ginsburg, 1985; Banks & Salapatek, 1981). *Contrast* refers to the overall quantity of light–dark transitions in a pattern. If babies are *sensitive to* (can detect) a difference in contrast between two patterns, they will prefer the one with more contrast. To understand this idea, look at the two checkerboards in the top row of Figure 5.15. To the mature viewer, the one with many small squares has more contrast. Now look at the bottom row, which shows how these checkerboards appear to infants in the first few weeks of life. Because of their poor vision, young babies cannot resolve the small features in more complex patterns. To them, the large, bold checkerboard has more contrast, so they prefer to look at it. By 2 months of age, detection of fine-grained detail has improved considerably. As a result, infants become sensitive to the greater contrast in complex patterns and start to spend much more time looking at them (Dodwell, Humphrey & Muir, 1987).

Combining Pattern Elements. In the early weeks of life, infants respond to the separate parts of a pattern. For example, when shown drawings of human faces, 1-month-olds limit their visual exploration to the border of the stimulus, and they stare at single high-contrast features, such as the hairline or chin (see Figure 5.16). At about 2 months, when scanning ability and contrast sensitivity have improved, infants start to thoroughly explore a pattern's internal features by moving their eyes quickly around the figure and pausing briefly to look at each salient part (Bronson, 1991; Salapatek, 1975).

Once babies can detect all aspects of a pattern, they combine pattern elements, integrating them into a unified whole. In fact, infants of 6 or 7 months are so good at detecting pattern organization that they even perceive subjective boundaries that are not really present. For example, look at Figure 5.17. Seven-month-old babies perceive a square in the center of this pattern, just as you do (Bertenthal, Campos,

Contrast sensitivity
A general principle accounting for early pattern preferences, which states that if babies can detect a difference in contrast between two patterns, they will prefer the one with more contrast.

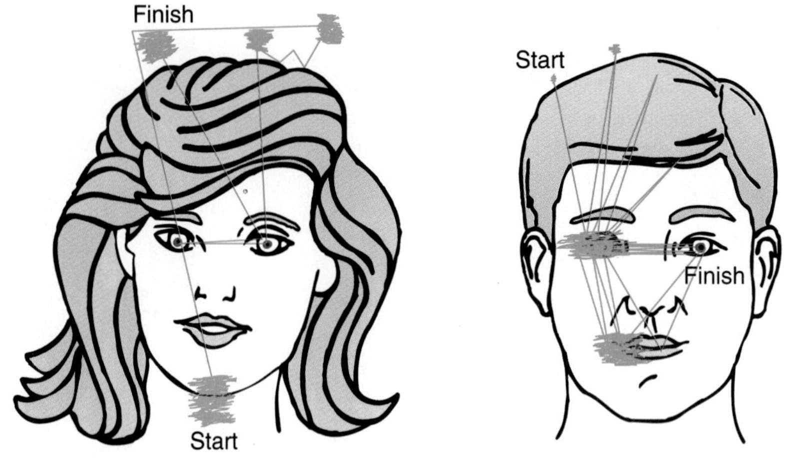

FIGURE 5.16

Visual scanning of the pattern of the human face by 1- and 2-month-old infants.
One-month-olds limit their scanning to single features on the boarder of the stimulus, whereas 2-month-olds explore internal features. *(From P. Salapatek, 1975, "Pattern Perception in Early Infancy," in L. B. Cohen & P. Salapatek (Eds.),* Infant Perception: From Sensation to Cognition, *New York: Academic Press, p. 201. Reprinted by permission.)*

FIGURE 5.17

Subjective boundaries in a visual pattern.
Do you perceive a square in the middle of this figure? By 7 months of age, infants do, too. *(Adapted from Bertenthal, Campos, & Haith, 1980.)*

& Haith, 1980). Older infants carry this responsiveness to subjective form even further. Nine-month-olds can detect the organized meaningful pattern in a series of moving lights that resemble a human being walking, in that they look much longer at this display than they do at upside-down or disorganized versions (Bertenthal et al., 1985). Although 3- to 5-month-olds can tell the difference between these patterns, they do not show a special preference for one with both an upright orientation and a humanlike movement pattern (Bertenthal et al., 1987).

Perception of the Human Face. Do newborn babies have an innate capacity to recognize and respond to the human face? Although some early work suggested that they do (Fantz, 1961), recent research indicates that they do not. Infants under 2 months do not look longer at a facial pattern than a pattern of equal complexity, such as one with scrambled facial features, largely because (as we noted earlier) 1-month-olds do not explore the internal features of a stimulus.[2] At 2 to 3 months, when infants look at an entire pattern, they do prefer a face to other stimulus arrangements (Dannemiller & Stephens, 1988; Maurer, 1985). But the perception of faces is not a built-in perceptual capacity. Instead, it follows the same sequence of development as sensitivity to other patterned stimuli.

The baby's tendency to search for structure in a patterned stimulus is quickly applied to face perception. By 3 months of age, infants make fine distinctions among the features of different faces. For example, they can tell the difference between the photos of two strangers, even when the faces are moderately similar (Barrera & Maurer, 1981a). Around this time, babies also recognize their mother's face in a photo, since they look longer at it than at the face of a stranger (Barrera & Maurer, 1981b). Between 7 and 10 months, infants start to perceive emotional expressions as organized wholes. They treat positive faces (happy and surprised) as different from negative ones (sad and fearful), even when these expressions are demonstrated in slightly varying ways by different people (Ludemann, 1991). In Chapter 7 we will see that as face perception improves, infants recognize and respond to the expressive behavior of others. Like many other early capacities, perception of the human face plays an important role in infants' earliest social relationships.

The development of pattern perception in general, and face perception in particular, is summarized in Table 5.3. Note the close parallels between them. The table shows that several important developments in pattern perception take place around 2

[2]Perhaps you are wondering how newborns can display the remarkable imitative capacities described earlier in this chapter if they do not scan the internal features of a face. Recall that the facial expressions in newborn imitation research were not static poses but live demonstrations. Their dynamic quality probably caused infants to notice them.

TABLE 5.3

Development of Pattern and Face Perception

	0–1 MONTH	2–3 MONTHS	4–10 MONTHS
Pattern perception	Preference for patterns with large elements Visual exploration limited to the border of a stimulus and single features	Preference for patterns with fine details Visual exploration of entire stimulus, including internal features Combining pattern elements into an organized whole	Detection of increasingly complex pattern arrangements
Face perception	Absence of preference for the human facial pattern	Preference for a facial pattern over patterns with scrambled facial features Recognition of the mother's face in a photo	More fine-grained discrimination of faces, including the ability to perceive facial expressions as organized wholes

months of age. Recall that 2 months is also a time when the cortex develops rapidly and when babies become more alert and interested in the world around them. Brain growth supports the baby's improved ability to make sense of patterned stimuli.

INTERMODAL PERCEPTION

So far, we have discussed the infant's perceptual abilities one by one. However, when we take in information from the environment, we often use **intermodal perception.** That is, we combine stimulation from more than one *modality,* or sensory system, at a time. For example, we know that the shape of an object is the same whether we see it or touch it, that lip movements are closely coordinated with the sound of a voice, and that dropping a rigid object on a hard surface will cause a sharp, banging sound.

Are young infants, like adults, capable of intermodal perception, or do they have to learn how to put different types of sensory input together? Although researchers have debated this issue for years, recent evidence reveals that from the start, babies perceive the world in an intermodal fashion (Meltzoff, 1990; Spelke, 1987). Recall that newborns turn in the general direction of a sound, and they reach for objects in a primitive way. These behaviors suggest that infants expect sight, sound, and touch to go together.

By a few weeks after birth, infants show some impressive intermodal associations. In one study, 1-month-old babies were given a pacifier to suck with either a smooth surface or a surface with nubs on it. After exploring it in their mouths, the infants were shown two pacifiers—one smooth and one nubbed. They preferred to look at the shape they had sucked, indicating that they could match touch and visual stimulation without spending months seeing and feeling objects (Meltzoff & Borton, 1979).

Other research reveals that by 4 months, vision and hearing are well coordinated. Infants of this age were shown two films side by side, one with two blocks banging and the other with two sponges being squashed together. At the same time, the sound track for only one of the films (either a sharp, banging noise or a soft, squashing sound) could be heard. Infants looked at the film that went with the sound track, indicating that they detected a common rhythm in what they saw and heard (Bahrick, 1983). In similar research, 4-month-olds related the shape of an adult's lips to the corresponding vowel sound in speech (Kuhl & Meltzoff, 1984). And 7-month-olds matched a happy- or angry-sounding voice with the appropriate face of a speaking person (Soken & Pick, 1992).

Intermodal perception
Perception that combines information from more than one sensory system.

Of course, a great many intermodal matches, such as the way a train sounds or a teddy bear feels, must be based on experience. But what is so remarkable about intermodal perception is how quickly infants acquire these associations. Most of the time, they need just one exposure to a new situation (Spelke, 1987). In addition, when researchers try to teach intermodal relationships by pairing sights and sounds that do not naturally go together, babies will not learn them (Bahrick, 1988, 1992). Intermodal perception is yet another capacity that helps infants build an orderly, predictable perceptual world.

ASK YOURSELF . . .

- Five-month-old Tyrone sat in his infant seat, passing a teething biscuit from hand to hand, moving it up close to his face and far away, and finally dropping it overboard on the floor below. What aspect of visual development is Tyrone probably learning about? Explain your answer.
- Diane put up bright wall paper with detailed pictures of animals in Jana's room before she was born. During the first 2 months of life, Jana hardly noticed the wallpaper. Then, around 2 months, she showed keen interest. What new visual abilities probably account for this change?

BRIEF REVIEW

During the first year, infants gradually organize sounds into more complex patterns, and they become sensitive to the sound patterns of their own language. Changes in visual abilities are striking. Depth perception improves as infants detect motion, binocular, and pictorial depth cues. Experience in independent movement plays an important role in avoidance of heights as well as other aspects of three-dimensional understanding. The principle of contrast sensitivity accounts for young babies' pattern preferences. As vision improves, infants perceive the parts of a pattern as an organized whole. Face perception follows the same sequence of development as pattern perception in general. Young infants have a remarkable ability to combine information across different sensory modalities.

UNDERSTANDING PERCEPTUAL DEVELOPMENT

Now that we have reviewed the development of infant perceptual capacities, these questions arise: How can we put this diverse array of amazing achievements together? Does any general principle account for perceptual development? Eleanor and James Gibson's **differentiation theory** provides widely accepted answers. According to the Gibsons, infants actively search for **invariant features** of the environment—those that remain stable—in a constantly changing perceptual world. For example, in pattern perception, at first babies are confronted with a confusing mass of stimulation. But very quickly, they search for features that stand out along the border of a stimulus. Then they explore its internal features, and as they do so, they notice *stable relationships* among those features. As a result, they detect overall patterns, such as crosses, squares, and faces. The development of intermodal perception also reflects this principle. Again, what babies seem to do is seek out invariant relationships, such as a similar tempo in an object's motion and sound, that unite information across different modalities.

The Gibsons use the word *differentiation* (which means analyze or break down) to describe their theory because over time, the baby makes finer and finer distinctions among stimuli. For example, the human face is initially perceived in terms of single, high-contrast features, such as the hairline or chin. Then eyes, nose, and mouth are detected and combined into a pattern. Soon subtle distinctions between one face and another are made, and babies can tell mother, father, and stranger apart. Similarly, depth perception moves from sensitivity to overall motion and binocular cues to detection of a diverse array of fine-grained pictorial features. So one way of understanding perceptual development is to think of it as a built-in tendency to search for order and stability in the surrounding world, a capacity that becomes increasingly fine-tuned with age (Gibson, 1970; Gibson, 1979).

Differentiation theory
The view that perceptual development involves the detection of increasingly fine-grained, invariant features in the environment.

Invariant features
In differentiation theory of perceptual development, features that remain stable in a constantly changing perceptual world.

According to the Gibsons, acting on the environment plays a major role in perceptual differentiation. Think back to the links between motor milestones and perceptual development discussed in this chapter. Infants constantly look for ways in which the environment affords opportunities for action. As they do so, they expand their perceptual knowledge, and they also learn about the varied ways in which they can physically control their world (Adolf, Eppler, & Gibson, 1993).

As we conclude this chapter, it is only fair to note that some researchers believe that babies do not just make sense of experience by searching for invariant features. Instead, they impose *meaning* on what they perceive, constructing categories of objects and events in the surrounding environment. We have already seen the glimmerings of this cognitive point of view in some of the evidence reviewed in this chapter. For example, older babies *interpret* a familiar face as a source of pleasure and affection and a pattern of blinking lights as a moving human being. We will save our discussion of infant cognition for the next chapter, acknowledging for now that the cognitive perspective also has merit in understanding the achievements of infancy. In fact, many researchers combine these two positions, regarding infant development as proceeding from a perceptual to a cognitive emphasis over the first year of life (Mandler, 1992a; Salapatek & Cohen, 1987).

SUMMARY

BODY GROWTH IN THE FIRST TWO YEARS

Describe major changes in body size, proportions, and muscle–fat makeup and skeletal growth over the first 2 years.

- Changes in height and weight are rapid during the first 2 years. Physical growth of parts of the body follows **cephalocaudal** and **proximodistal trends.** Body fat is laid down quickly during the first 9 months, whereas muscle development is slow and gradual.
- **Skeletal age,** a measure based on the number of **epiphyses** and the extent to which they are fused, is the best way to estimate the child's overall physical maturity. At birth, infants have six **fontanels,** which permit skull bones to expand as the brain grows. The first tooth emerges around 6 months of age.

BRAIN DEVELOPMENT

Describe brain development during infancy and toddlerhood, at the level of individual brain cells and the level of the cerebral cortex.

- Early in development the brain grows faster than any other organ of the body. During infancy, **neurons** form **synapses,** or complex communication networks, at a rapid rate. Stimulation determines which neurons will survive and which will die off. **Glial cells,** which are responsible for **myelinization,** multiply dramatically through the second year and result in large gains in brain size.
- The development of different regions of the **cerebral cortex** corresponds to the order in which various capacities emerge in the infant and child. **Lateralization** refers to specialization of the hemispheres of the cortex. In early infancy, before many regions have taken on specialized roles, there is high **brain plasticity.** However, some brain specialization already exists at birth.

FACTORS AFFECTING EARLY PHYSICAL GROWTH

Cite evidence indicating that heredity, nutrition, and affection and stimulation contribute to early physical growth.

- Physical growth results from a continuous and complex interplay between heredity and environment. Twin and adoption studies reveal that heredity contributes to body size and rate of maturation.
- Breast milk is ideally suited to the growth needs of young babies and offers protection against disease. Breast-feeding prevents malnutrition and infant death in poverty-stricken areas of the world. Breast-fed and bottle-fed babies do not differ in psychological development.
- Although overweight and obesity are widespread problems in industrialized nations, chubby babies are not at risk for accumulating too many fat cells. Trying to put a baby on a diet can endanger development.
- **Marasmus** and **kwashiorkor** are dietary diseases caused by malnutrition that affect many children in

developing countries. If allowed to continue, body growth and brain development can be permanently stunted. **Nonorganic failure to thrive** illustrates the importance of stimulation and affection for normal physical growth.

CHANGING STATES OF AROUSAL

How does the organization of sleep and wakefulness change over the first 2 years?

- During infancy, short periods of sleep and wakefulness are put together, and they start to coincide with a night and day schedule. Changing arousal patterns are affected by brain development, but the social environment also plays a role. Infants in Western nations sleep through the night much earlier than those in many Asian and African cultures.

MOTOR DEVELOPMENT DURING THE FIRST TWO YEARS

Describe the general course of motor development during the first 2 years along with factors that influence it.

- Like physical development, motor development follows the cephalocaudal and proximodistal trends. New motor skills are a matter of combining existing skills into increasingly complex systems of action.
- Experience has a profound effect on motor development, as shown by research on infants raised in deprived institutions. Stimulation of infant motor abilities accounts for cross-cultural differences in motor development.
- During the first year, infants gradually perfect their reaching and grasping. The poorly coordinated **prereaching** of the newborn period eventually drops out. Once voluntary reaching appears, the clumsy **ulnar grasp** is gradually transformed into a refined **pincer grasp.**
- Young children are not physically and psychologically ready for toilet training until the end of the second or beginning of the third year of life.

BASIC LEARNING MECHANISMS

Describe four basic infant learning mechanisms, the conditions under which they occur, and the unique value of each.

- Infants can be **classically conditioned** when the pairing of an **unconditioned stimulus (UCS)** and **conditioned stimulus (CS)** has survival value. Young babies are easily conditioned in the feeding situation. Classical conditioning of fear is difficult before 8 to 12 months.
- **Operant conditioning** of infants has been demonstrated in many studies. In addition to food, interesting sights and sounds serve as effective **reinforcers,** increasing the occurrence of a preceding behavior.
- **Habituation** and **dishabituation** reveal that at birth, babies are attracted to novelty. Newborn infants also have a primitive ability to **imitate** the facial expressions and gestures of adults, a capacity that may promote the early parent–infant relationship.

PERCEPTUAL DEVELOPMENT IN INFANCY

What changes in perception of speech sounds, depth and pattern perception, and intermodal perception take place during infancy?

- Over the first year, infants organize sounds into more complex patterns. They also become more sensitive to the speech sounds and clause units of their own language.
- Rapid development of the eye and visual centers in the brain supports the development of focusing, color discrimination, and visual acuity during the first half year. The abili ty to track a moving object also improves.
- Research on depth perception reveals that responsiveness to motion develops first, followed by sensitivity to binocular and then pictorial cues. Experience in moving about independently affects babies' three-dimensional understanding, including avoidance of edges and drop-offs, such as the deep side of the visual cliff.
- **Contrast sensitivity** accounts for babies' early pattern preferences. At first, infants look at the border of a stimulus and at single features. Around 2 months of age, they explore the internal features of a pattern and start to detect pattern organization. Over time, they discriminate increasingly complex patterns. Perception of the human face follows the same sequence of development as sensitivity to other patterned stimuli.
- Research suggests that from the start, infants are capable of **intermodal perception.** During the first year, they quickly combine information across sensory modalities, often after just one exposure to a new situation.

UNDERSTANDING PERCEPTUAL DEVELOPMENT

Explain differentiation theory of perceptual development.

- The Gibsons' **differentiation theory** is a widely accepted account of perceptual development. Over time, infants detect increasingly fine-grained **invariant features** in a constantly changing perceptual world. Others take a more cognitive viewpoint in suggesting that at an early age, infants impose meaning on what they perceive. Many researchers combine these two ideas.

IMPORTANT TERMS AND CONCEPTS

cephalocaudal trend (p. 170)
proximodistal trend (p. 171)
skeletal age (p. 173)
epiphyses (p. 173)
fontanels (p. 173)
neurons (p. 174)
synapses (p. 174)
glial cells (p. 175)
myelinization (p. 175)
cerebral cortex (p. 175)
lateralization (p. 176)
brain plasticity (p. 176)
catch-up growth (p. 178)
marasmus (p. 180)
kwashiorkor (p. 180)
nonorganic failure to thrive (p. 181)
systems of action (p. 184)
prereaching (p. 188)
ulnar grasp (p. 189)
pincer grasp (p. 189)
classical conditioning (p. 190)
unconditioned stimulus (UCS) (p. 190)
unconditioned response (UCR) (p. 190)
conditioned stimulus (CS) (p. 191)
conditioned response (CR) (p. 191)
extinction (p. 191)
operant conditioning (p. 192)
reinforcer (p. 193)
punishment (p. 193)
habituation (p. 193)
sudden infant death syndrome (SIDS) (p. 195)
dishabituation (p. 195)
imitation (p. 195)
contrast sensitivity (p. 201)
intermodal perception (p. 203)
differentiation theory (p. 204)
invariant features (p. 204)

FYI...

FOR FURTHER INFORMATION AND SPECIAL HELP, CONSULT THE FOLLOWING ORGANIZATIONS:

PHYSICAL GROWTH AND HEALTH

Healthy Mothers, Healthy Babies
409 Twelfth Street, S.W., Suite 309
Washington, DC 20024-2188
(202) 863-2458

A coalition of national and state organizations concerned with maternal and child health. Serves as a network through which information on nutrition, injury prevention, and infant mortality is shared.

United Nations Children's Fund (UNICEF)
3 United Nations Plaza
New York, NY 10017
(212) 326-7000

International organization dedicated to addressing the problems of children around the world. Develops and implements health and nutrition programs, campaigns to have children vaccinated against disease, and coordinates delivery of food and other aid to disaster-stricken areas.

Word Health Organization (WHO)
Avenue Appia
CH–1211 Geneva 27
Switzerland
(22) 791-2111

International health agency of the United Nations that seeks to obtain the highest level of health care for all people. Promotes prevention and treatment of disease and strives to eliminate poverty. Places special emphasis on the health needs of developing countries.

BREAST-FEEDING

La Leche League International
P.O. Box 1209
Franklin Park, IL 60131
(708) 455-7730

Provides information and support to breast-feeding mothers. Local chapters exist in many cities.

MALNUTRITION

Food Research and Action Center
1875 Connecticut Avenue, N.W., Suite 540
Washington, DC 20009
(202) 986-2200

Provides assistance to community organizations trying to make federal food programs more responsive to the needs of millions of hungry Americans. Seeks to enhance public awareness of the problems of hunger and poverty in the United States.

SUDDEN INFANT DEATH SYNDROME (SIDS)

National Sudden Infant Death Syndrome Clearinghouse
8201 Greensboro Drive, Suite 600
McLean, VA 22102
(703) 821-8955

Provides information to health professionals and the public on SIDS.

National Sudden Infant Death Syndrome Foundation (NSIDSF)
10500 Little Patuxent Pkwy, No. 420
Columbia, MD 21044
(410) 964-8000

Provides assistance to parents who have lost a child to SIDS. Works with families and health professionals in caring for infants at risk due to heart and respiratory problems.

"Family life"
Chiu Wing-yi
15 years, Hong Kong

A young baby, perched on his father's shoulders, surveys the complexities of his physical and social world. Already, he is an integral part of family life. In Chapter 6, you will see that a stimulating environment combined with the guidance of a sensitive parent helps ensure that cognition will develop at its best.

6

Cognitive Development in Infancy and Toddlerhood

PIAGET'S COGNITIVE-DEVELOPMENTAL THEORY

Key Piagetian Concepts • The Sensorimotor Stage • Recent Research on Sensorimotor Development • Evaluation of the Sensorimotor Stage

INFORMATION PROCESSING DURING THE FIRST TWO YEARS

A Model of Human Information Processing • Attention and Memory • Categorization • Evaluation of Information-Processing Findings

THE SOCIAL CONTEXT OF EARLY COGNITIVE DEVELOPMENT

INDIVIDUAL DIFFERENCES IN EARLY MENTAL DEVELOPMENT

Infant Intelligence Tests • Early Environment and Mental Development • Early Intervention for At-Risk Infants and Toddlers

LANGUAGE DEVELOPMENT DURING THE FIRST TWO YEARS

Three Theories of Language Development • Getting Ready to Talk • First Words • The Two-Word Utterance Phase • Comprehension Versus Production • Individual Differences in Language Development • Supporting Early Language Development

When Byron, Rachel, and April were brought together by their mothers at age 18 months, the room was alive with activity. I sat back in a corner and watched as the events of the next hour unfolded. The three spirited explorers were bent on discovery. Rachel dropped shapes through holes in a plastic box that Beth held and adjusted so the harder ones would fall smoothly into the container. Once a few shapes were inside, Rachel grabbed and shook the box, squealing with delight as the lid fell open and the shapes scattered around her. The clatter of the falling shapes attracted Byron, who picked one up, carried it to the railing at the top of the basement steps, and dropped it overboard. Byron watched with interest as the shape tumbled down the stairs, then followed it with a teddy bear, a large rubber ball, his shoe, and a spoon. In the meantime, April pulled open a drawer, unloaded a set of wooden bowls, stacked them in a pile, knocked it over, then banged two bowls together like cymbals. With each action, the youngsters seemed to be asking, "What's out here in this world? Which behavior leads to which consequence? What events can I control?"

As the toddlers experimented with things around them, I could see the beginnings of language—a whole new way of influencing the world. April was the most vocal of the three youngsters. "All gone baw!" she exclaimed as Byron tossed the bright red ball down the basement steps. Although Byron was not yet talking, he was preparing to become a speaker in many ways. A stream of babbled syllables could be heard as he moved around the room, and he skillfully used gestures to communicate his desires. A close look at Rachel revealed that the capacity to represent experience through words and gestures had opened up a whole new realm of play possibilities. Rachel could pretend. "Night-night," she said as she put her head down on her hands and closed her eyes, ever so pleased that in the world of make-believe she could decide for herself when and where to go to bed.

Over the first 2 years, the small, reflexive newborn baby becomes a self-assertive, purposeful being who solves simple problems and has started to master the most amazing of human abilities—language. "How does all this happen so quickly?" asked Felicia, turning to me. In this chapter, we consider three perspectives on early cognitive development—Piaget's *cognitive-developmental theory, information processing*, and Vygotsky's *sociocultural theory.* We will see that each casts a different light on Felicia's question.

Lisa raised another concern. "Byron isn't talking yet, and he rarely stacks things and puts shapes in containers like Rachel and April. If he isn't developing as quickly as other children now, will that still be true when he goes to school?" Mental tests permit direct comparisons of the cognitive progress of children of the same age. We will carefully consider the usefulness of these tests during this earliest phase of development.

Our discussion concludes with the beginnings of language. We will see how toddlers' first words and word combinations build on early cognitive achievements. But very soon, new words and expressions greatly increase the speed and flexibility of human thinking. Throughout development, cognition and language are related, and they mutually support one another.

PIAGET'S COGNITIVE-DEVELOPMENTAL THEORY

The Swiss theorist Jean Piaget is the great twentieth-century giant of cognitive development. His work led researchers all over the world to view children as busy, motivated explorers whose thinking develops as they act directly on the environment. Perhaps you remember from Chapter 1 that Piaget's theory was greatly influenced by his background in biology. He believed that the child's mind forms and modifies psychological structures to achieve a better adaptive fit with external reality.

KEY PIAGETIAN CONCEPTS

According to Piaget, between infancy and adolescence, children move through four stages of development. The most elaborate is the **sensorimotor stage,** which spans the first 2 years of life. As the name of this stage implies, Piaget believed that infants and toddlers "think" with their eyes, ears, hands, and other sensorimotor equipment. They cannot yet carry out many activities inside their heads. But by the end of toddlerhood, children are very different. At 18 months, Byron, Rachel, and April could solve practical, everyday problems and represent their experiences in speech, gesture, and play. To understand Piaget's view of how these vast changes take place, we need to look at some important Piagetian concepts, which are summarized in the Concept Review Table on page 212. These convey Piaget's ideas about *what changes with development,* and *how cognitive change takes place.*

Sensorimotor stage
Piaget's first stage, during which infants and toddlers "think" with their eyes, ears, hands, and other sensorimotor equipment. Spans the first 2 years of life.

Scheme
In Piaget's theory, a specific structure, or organized way of making sense of experience, that changes with age.

■ WHAT CHANGES WITH DEVELOPMENT. Piaget believed that *psychological structures*—the child's organized ways of making sense of experience—change with age. He referred to specific structures as **schemes.** At first, schemes are motor action patterns. For example, at age 6 months, Byron dropped objects in a fairly rigid way, simply by letting go of a rattle or teething ring in his hand. Each time, he looked with interest as the object fell on the floor in front of him. By age 18 months, Byron's "dropping scheme" had become much more deliberate and creative. He tossed all sorts of objects down the basement stairs, throwing some up in the air, bouncing others off walls, releasing some gently and others with all the force his little body could muster. Soon Byron's schemes will move from an *action-based level* to a *mental level.* When this happens, Byron will not just act on objects around him. He will show evidence of thinking before he acts (Ginsburg & Opper, 1988). This change, as we will see later, marks the transition from sensorimotor to preoperational thought.

Behaviors that create work for caregivers can be important learning experiences for infants and toddlers. This 18-month-old experiments with his "dropping scheme." As he pushes a piece of pineapple over the edge of his tray, he looks with interest, and his sensorimotor understanding of the world expands. *(Courtesy of Laura Berk)*

■ HOW COGNITIVE CHANGE TAKES PLACE. In Piaget's theory, two processes are responsible for changes in schemes: adaptation and organization.

Adaptation. The next time you have a chance to observe infants and toddlers, notice how they tirelessly repeat actions that lead to interesting effects. For example, Byron dropped objects over and over, gradually noticing that varying the way he held his hand and the type of object released produced fascinating new results. Byron was changing his "dropping scheme" through **adaptation,** a process that involves building schemes through direct interaction with the environment.

Adaptation is made up of two complementary activities: *assimilation* and *accommodation.* During **assimilation,** we interpret the external world in terms of our current schemes. For example, when Byron dropped objects, he was assimilating them all into his sensorimotor "dropping scheme." Beth described another instance of assimilation that occurred when Rachel visited the zoo on her second birthday. On seeing her first camel, Rachel sifted through her collection of schemes until she found one that resembled the strange-looking creature. "Horse!" she called out, after looking puzzled for a moment. In **accommodation,** we create new schemes or adjust old ones after noticing that our current ways of thinking do not capture the environment completely. When Byron dropped objects in different ways, he was modifying his dropping scheme to take account of the varied properties of objects. And when Rachel started to refer to camels as "lumpy horses," she realized that certain characteristics of camels are not like horses and revised her "horse scheme" accordingly.

So far, we have referred to assimilation and accommodation as separate activities, but Piaget regarded them as always working together. That is, in every interchange with the environment, we interpret information using our existing structures, and we also refine them to achieve a better fit with experience. But the balance between assimilation and accommodation varies from one time period to another. When children are not changing very much, they assimilate more than they accommodate. Piaget called this a state of cognitive *equilibrium,* implying a steady, comfortable condition. During times of rapid cognitive change, however, children are in a state of *disequilibrium,* or cognitive discomfort. They realize that new information does not match their current schemes, so they shift away from assimilation toward accommodation. Once they have modified their schemes, they move back toward assimilation, exercising their newly changed structures until they are ready to be modified again.

Piaget used the term **equilibration** to sum up this back-and-forth movement between equilibrium and disequilibrium throughout development. Each time it occurs, more effective schemes are produced. They take in a wider range of aspects of the environment, and there is less and less to throw them out of balance (Piaget, 1985). Because the times of greatest accommodation are the earliest ones, the sensorimotor stage is Piaget's most complex period of development.

Organization. Besides adaptation, schemes change through a second process called **organization.** It takes place internally, apart from direct contact with the environment. Once children form new structures, they start to rearrange them, linking them with other schemes so they are part of a strongly interconnected cog-

Adaptation
In Piaget's theory, the process of building schemes through direct interaction with the environment. Made up of two complementary processes: *assimilation* and *accommodation.*

Assimilation
That part of adaptation in which the external world is interpreted in terms of current schemes.

Accommodation
That part of adaptation in which new schemes are created and old ones adjusted to produce a better fit with the environment.

Equilibration
In Piaget's theory, back-and-forth movement between cognitive equilibrium and disequilibrium throughout development, which leads to more effective schemes.

Organization
In Piaget's theory, the internal rearrangement and linking together of schemes so that they form a strongly interconnected cognitive system.

CONCEPT REVIEW TABLE

Basic Piagetian Concepts

CONCEPT	IMPORTANT POINT	EXAMPLE
Schemes	Specific mental structures, or organized ways of making sense of experience, that change with age. The first schemes are motor action patterns that infants and toddlers use to find out about their world.	At 1 month, Randy's "grasping scheme" is fairly rigid; he grasps anything placed in his hand in much the same way. By 4 months, he adjusts his hand opening to the size of the object offered.
Adaptation	The process of changing schemes through direct interaction with the environment. Combines assimilation and accommodation.	At 20 months, Irene sees a kangaroo for the first time in her picture book. She tries to adapt her schemes to make sense of the object.
Assimilation	Interpreting the world in terms of current schemes. Children strive to assimilate, or use schemes to understand the environment. Successful use of schemes produces a state of equilibrium, a pleasurable cognitive condition.	At first, Irene applies a current scheme to the kangaroo, calling it a "bunny."
Accommodation	Creating new schemes or changing old ones to take account of new aspects of the environment. When children do more accommodating than assimilating, they are in a state of disequilibrium, or cognitive discomfort.	Later Irene notices that kangaroos are not just like bunnies. She modifies her scheme for interpreting the object, calling it a "funny bunny."
Equilibration	The back-and-forth movement between equilibrium and disequilibrium that occurs throughout development. Gradually produces more effective schemes.	As Randy modifies his "grasping scheme" and Irene her "bunny scheme," their new cognitive structures achieve a better fit with the environment and are less likely to be challenged in the future.
Organization	The process of linking schemes together into a strongly interconnected system so they can be applied jointly to the environment.	Over time, Irene links her schemes for "bunnies," "kitties," and "kangaroos" together. She can easily pick out similarities and differences among them.

nitive system. For example, eventually Byron will relate "dropping" to "throwing" and to his developing understanding of "nearness" and "farness." And Rachel will construct a separate "camel scheme" that will be connected by similarities and differences to her understanding of horses and other animals. According to Piaget, schemes reach a true state of equilibrium when they become part of a broad network of structures that can be jointly applied to the surrounding world (Flavell, 1963; Piaget, 1936/1952).

TABLE 6.1

Summary of Cognitive Development During the Sensorimotor Stage

SENSORIMOTOR SUBSTAGE	TYPICAL ADAPTIVE BEHAVIORS	OBJECT PERMANENCE
1. Reflexive schemes (birth to 1 month)	Newborn reflexes (see Chapter 4, page 154)	None
2. Primary circular reactions (1–4 months)	Simple motor habits centered around the infant's own body; limited anticipation of events	None
3. Secondary circular reactions (4–8 months)	Actions aimed at repeating interesting effects in the surrounding world; imitation of familiar behaviors	None
4. Coordination of secondary circular reactions (8–12 months)	Intentional, or goal-directed, action sequences; improved anticipation of events; imitation of behaviors slightly different from those the infant usually performs	Ability to find a hidden object in the first location in which it is hidden
5. Tertiary circular reactions (12–18 months)	Exploration of the properties of objects by acting on them in novel ways; imitation of unfamiliar behaviors	Ability to search in several locations for a hidden object
6. Mental combinations (18 months–2 years)	Internal representation of objects and events; deferred imitation and make-believe play	Ability to find an object that has been moved while out of sight

THE SENSORIMOTOR STAGE

The difference between the newborn baby and the 2-year-old child is so vast that the sensorimotor stage is divided into six substages. Piaget's observations of his own three children served as the basis for this sequence of development. Although this is a very small sample, Piaget watched carefully and also presented his son and two daughters with little tasks (such as hidden objects) that helped reveal their understanding of the world. In the following sections, we will first describe infant development as Piaget saw it. Then we will consider evidence indicating that in some ways, the structures of young infants are more advanced than Piaget imagined them to be.

THE CIRCULAR REACTION. At the beginning of the sensorimotor stage, infants know so little about the world that they cannot purposefully explore it. This presents a problem for young babies, since they need some way of adapting their first schemes. The **circular reaction** provides them with a special means of doing so. It involves stumbling onto a new experience caused by the baby's own motor activity. The reaction is "circular" because the infant tries to repeat the event again and again. As a result, a sensorimotor response that first occurred by chance becomes strengthened into a new scheme. For example, at age 2 months, Rachel accidentally made a smacking sound after finishing a feeding. The sound was new and intriguing, so Rachel tried to repeat it until, after a few days, she became quite expert at smacking her lips.

During the first 2 years, the circular reaction changes in several ways. At first, it is centered around the infant's own body. Later, it turns outward, toward manipulation of objects. Finally, it becomes experimental and creative, aimed at producing novel effects in the environment. Piaget considered these revisions in the circular reaction so important that he named the sensorimotor substages after them. You may find it helpful to refer to the summary of sensorimotor development in Table 6.1 as you read about each substage.

SUBSTAGE 1: REFLEXIVE SCHEMES (BIRTH TO 1 MONTH). Piaget regarded newborn reflexes as the building blocks of sensorimotor intelligence. As we will see in Substage 2, sucking, grasping, and looking quickly change as they are applied to the environment. But at first, babies suck, grasp, and look in much the same way, no matter what experiences they encounter (see Figure

Circular reaction
In Piaget's theory, a means of building schemes in which infants try to repeat a chance event caused by their own motor activity.

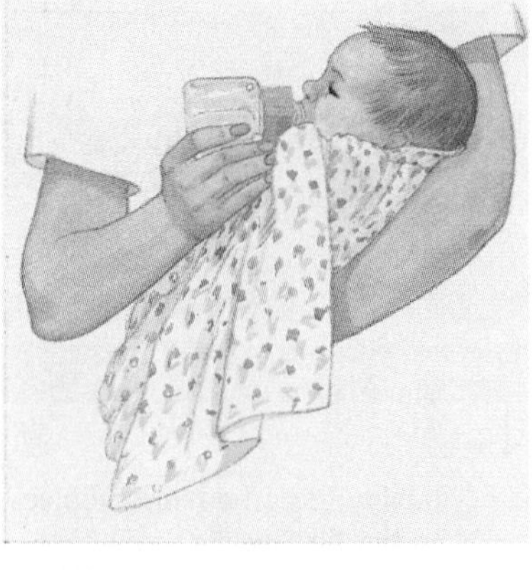

FIGURE 6.1

The newborn baby's schemes consist of reflexes, which will gradually be modified as they are applied to the surrounding environment.

6.1). Beth reported an amusing example of Rachel's indiscriminate sucking at 2 weeks of age. She lay on the bed next to her father while he took a nap. Suddenly, he awoke with a start. Rachel had latched on and begun to suck on his back!

■ SUBSTAGE 2: PRIMARY CIRCULAR REACTIONS—THE FIRST LEARNED ADAPTATIONS (1 TO 4 MONTHS). Infants start to gain voluntary control over their actions by repeating chance behaviors that lead to satisfying results. Consequently, they develop some simple motor habits, such as sucking their fists or thumbs and opening and closing their hands (see Figure 6.2). Babies of this substage also begin to vary their behavior in response to environmental demands. For example, they open their mouths differently for a nipple than a spoon. Young infants also show a limited ability to anticipate events. For example, at age 3 months, when Byron awoke from his nap, he cried out with hunger. But as soon as Lisa entered the room and moved toward his crib, Byron's crying stopped. He knew that feeding time was near.

Piaget called the first circular reactions *primary,* and he regarded them as quite limited. Notice how, in the examples just given, infants' adaptations are oriented toward their own bodies and motivated by basic needs. According to Piaget, babies of this age are not yet very concerned with the effects of their actions on the external world.

■ SUBSTAGE 3: SECONDARY CIRCULAR REACTIONS—MAKING INTERESTING SIGHTS LAST (4 TO 8 MONTHS). Think back to our discussion of motor development in Chapter 5. Between 4 and 8 months, infants sit up and become skilled at reaching for, grasping, and manipulating objects. These motor achievements play a major role in turning babies' attention outward toward the environment. Using the *secondary* circular reaction, they try to repeat interesting effects in the surrounding world that are caused by their own actions. In the following illustration, notice how Piaget's 4-month-old son Laurent gradually builds the sensorimotor scheme of "hitting" over a 10-day period (see Figure 6.3):

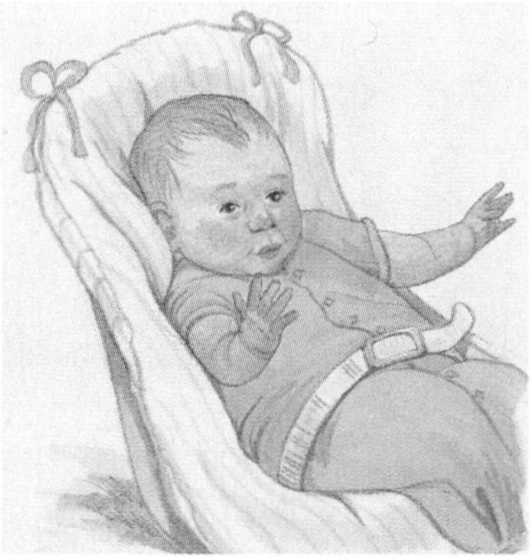

FIGURE 6.2

At 2 months, Byron sees his hand open and close and tries to repeat this action, in a primary circular reaction.

> At 4 months 7 days [Laurent] looks at a letter opener tangled in the strings of a doll hung in front of him. He tries to grasp (a scheme he already knows) the doll or the letter opener but each time, his attempts only result in his knocking the objects (so they swing out of his reach). . . . At 4 months 15 days, with another doll hung in front of him, Laurent tries to grasp it, then shakes himself to make it swing, knocks it accidentally, and then tries simply to hit it. . . . At 4 months 18 days, Laurent hits my hands without trying to grasp them, but he started by simply waving his arms around, and only afterwards went on to hit my hands. The next day, finally, Laurent immediately hits a doll hung in front of him. The [hitting] scheme is now completely differentiated [from grasping]. (Piaget, 1936/1952, pp. 167–168)

Improved control over their own behavior permits infants of this substage to imitate the behavior of others. However, babies under 8 months only imitate actions that they themselves have practiced many times. They cannot adapt flexibly and quickly, imitating behaviors that are new and unfamiliar (Kaye & Marcus, 1981).

■ SUBSTAGE 4: COORDINATION OF SECONDARY CIRCULAR REACTIONS (8 TO 12 MONTHS). Now infants start to organize schemes. They combine secondary circular reactions into new, more complex action sequences. As a result, two landmark cognitive changes take place.

Intentional, or goal-directed, behavior
A sequence of actions in which schemes are deliberately combined to solve a problem.

First, babies can engage in **intentional,** or **goal-directed, behavior.** Before this substage, actions that led to new schemes had a random, hit-or-miss quality to them—for example, *accidentally* bringing the thumb to mouth or *happening* to hit the doll hung over the crib. But by 8 months, infants have had enough practice with a variety of schemes that they coordinate them deliberately to solve sensorimo-

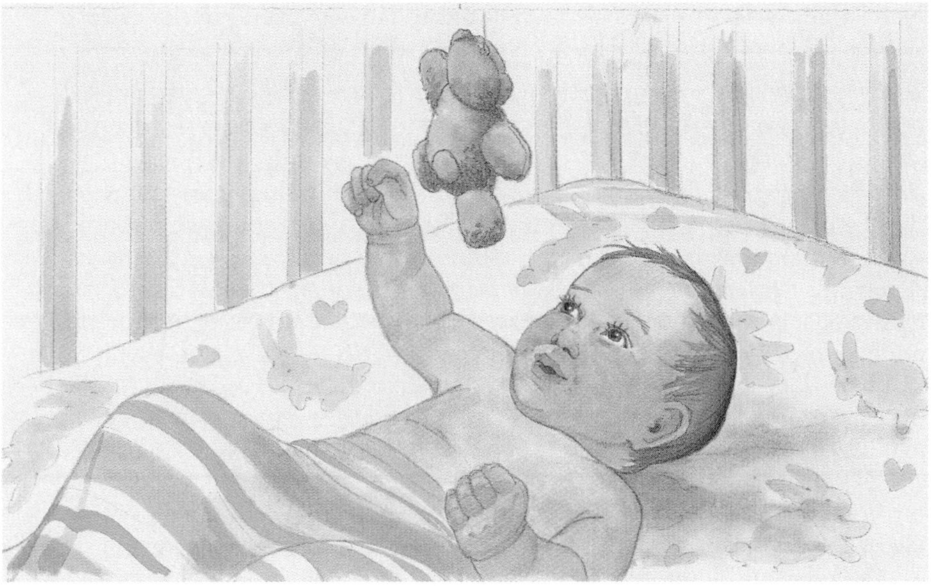

FIGURE 6.3

At 4 months, Piaget's son Laurent accidentally hits a doll hung in front of him. He tries to recapture the interesting effect of the swinging doll. In doing so, he builds a new "hitting scheme" through the secondary circular reaction.

tor problems. The clearest example is provided by Piaget's *object-hiding tasks,* in which he shows the baby an attractive toy and then hides it behind his hand or under a cover. Infants of this substage can find the object. In doing so, they coordinate two schemes—"pushing" aside the obstacle and "grasping" the toy.

The fact that infants can retrieve hidden objects reveals that they have begun to attain a second cognitive milestone: **object permanence,** the understanding that objects continue to exist when they are out of sight (see Figure 6.4). But awareness of object permanence is not yet complete. If an object is moved from one hiding place (A) to another (B), babies will search for it only in the first hiding place (A). Because 8- to 12-month-olds make this **AB search error,** Piaget concluded that they do not have a clear image of the object as persisting when hidden from view.

Finally, Substage 4 brings two additional advances. First, infants can anticipate events much more effectively than before, and using their new capacity for intentional behavior, they sometimes try to change those experiences. For example, at 10 months, Byron crawled after Lisa when she put on her coat, whimpering and hanging on to keep her from leaving. Second, now babies imitate behaviors that are slightly different from those they usually perform. After watching someone else, they try to stir with a spoon, push a toy car, or drop raisins in a cup. Once again, they do so by drawing on their capacity for intentional behavior—purposefully modifying schemes to fit an observed action (Piaget, 1945/1951).

FIGURE 6.4

Around 8 months, infants combine schemes deliberately in the solution of sensorimotor problems. They show the beginnings of object permanence, since they can find an object in the first place in which it is hidden.

■ SUBSTAGE 5: TERTIARY CIRCULAR REACTIONS—DISCOVERING NEW MEANS THROUGH ACTIVE EXPERIMENTATION (12 TO 18 MONTHS). At this substage, the circular reaction—now called *tertiary*—becomes experimental and creative. Toddlers do not just repeat behaviors that lead to familiar results. They *repeat with variation,* provoking new outcomes. Recall how Byron dropped objects over the basement steps, trying this, then that, and then another action (see Figure 6.5). Because they approach the world in this deliberately exploratory way, 12- to 18-month-olds are far better sensorimotor problem solvers than they were before. For example, Rachel could figure out how to fit a shape through a hole in a container by turning and twisting it until it fell through, and she discovered how to use a stick to get toys that were out of reach.

According to Piaget, this new capacity to experiment leads to a more advanced understanding of object permanence. Toddlers look in not just one, but several locations to find a hidden toy. Thus, they no longer make the AB search error. Their

Object permanence
The understanding that objects continue to exist when they are out of sight.

AB search error
The error made by 8- to 12-month-olds after an object is moved from hiding place A to hiding place B. Infants in Piaget's Substage 4 search for it only in the first hiding place (A).

FIGURE 6.5

At 18 months, Byron dropped a variety of objects down the basement stairs, throwing some up in the air, bouncing others off the wall, releasing some gently and others forcefully, in a deliberately experimental approach. Byron displayed a tertiary circular reaction.

more flexible action patterns also permit them to imitate many more behaviors, such as stacking blocks, scribbling on paper, and making funny faces.

SUBSTAGE 6: MENTAL REPRESENTATION—INVENTING NEW MEANS THROUGH MENTAL COMBINATIONS (18 MONTHS TO 2 YEARS). Substage 5 is the last truly *sensorimotor* stage, since Substage 6 brings with it the ability to create **mental representations** of reality—internal images of absent objects and past events. As a result, the older toddler can solve problems through symbolic means instead of trial-and-error behavior. One sign of this new capacity is that children arrive at solutions to sensorimotor problems suddenly, suggesting that they experiment with actions inside their heads. For example, at 19 months, April received a new push toy. As she played with it for the first time, she rolled it over the carpet and ran into the sofa. Faced with this problem, she paused for a moment, as if to "think," and then immediately turned the toy in a new direction. Had she been in Substage 5, she would have pushed, pulled, and bumped it in a random fashion until it was free to move again.

With the capacity to represent, toddlers arrive at a more advanced understanding of object permanence—that objects can move or be moved when out of sight. Try the following object-hiding task with an 18- to 24-month-old as well as a younger child: Put a small toy inside a box and the box under a cover. While the box is out of sight, dump the toy out, and then show the toddler the empty box. The Substage 6 child will easily find the hidden toy. Younger toddlers are baffled by this situation.

Representation also brings with it the capacity for **deferred imitation**—the ability to remember and copy the behavior of models who are not immediately present. A famous and amusing example is Piaget's daughter Jacqueline's imitation of another child's temper tantrum:

> Jacqueline had a visit from a little boy . . . who, in the course of the afternoon, got into a terrible temper. He screamed as he tried to get out of a playpen and pushed it backwards, stamping his feet. Jacqueline stood watching him in amazement . . . . The next day, she herself screamed in her playpen and tried to move it, stamping her foot lightly several times in succession. (Piaget, 1936/1952, p. 63)

Finally, the sixth substage leads to a major change in the nature of play. Throughout the first year and a half, infants and toddlers engage in **functional play**—pleasurable motor activity with or without objects through which they practice sensorimotor schemes. At the end of the second year, children's growing capac-

FIGURE 6.6

When Rachel engaged in make-believe by pretending to go to sleep, she created a mental representation of reality. With the capacity for mental representation, the sensorimotor stage draws to a close.

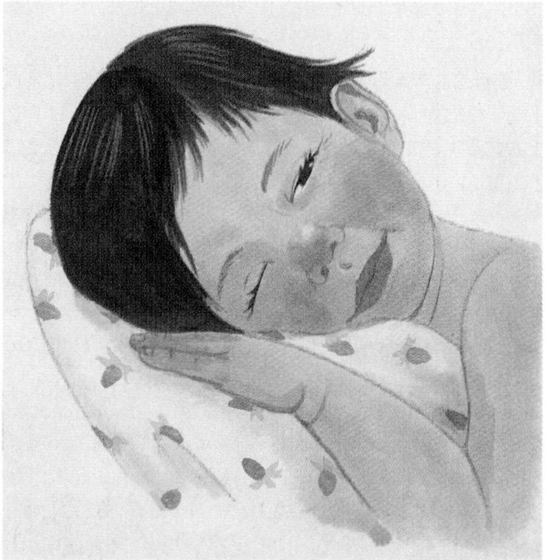

Mental representation
An internal image of an absent object or a past event.

Deferred imitation
The ability to remember and copy the behavior of models who are not immediately present.

Functional play
A type of play involving pleasurable motor activity with or without objects. Enables infants and toddlers to practice sensorimotor schemes.

ity to represent experience permits them to engage in **make-believe play,** or pretend, in which they act out everyday and imaginary activities. The make-believe of the toddler is very simple, as Rachel's pretending to go to sleep at the beginning of this chapter indicates (see Figure 6.6). However, make-believe expands greatly in early childhood, and it is so important for psychological development that we will devote a great deal of attention to it in Chapters 9 and 10. In addition, we will return to the question of how make-believe play first emerges when we take up Vygotsky's sociocultural theory later in this chapter.

RECENT RESEARCH ON SENSORIMOTOR DEVELOPMENT

Over the past 20 years, many researchers have tried to confirm Piaget's observations of sensorimotor development. New studies show that infants display certain cognitive capacities earlier than Piaget believed. Already, you have read about some of these findings. Think back to the operant conditioning research reviewed in Chapter 5. Recall that newborns will suck vigorously on a nipple that controls a variety of interesting sights and sounds, a behavior that closely resembles Piaget's secondary circular reaction. It appears that babies try to explore and control the external world much earlier than 4 to 8 months of age. In fact, they start to do so as soon as they are born.

Piaget may have underestimated infant capacities because he did not have the sophisticated experimental techniques for studying early cognition that we have today (Flavell, Miller, & Miller, 1993). As we consider recent research on sensorimotor development as well as information processing (covered in a later section), we will see that operant conditioning and the habituation–dishabituation response have been used ingeniously to find out what the young baby knows.

■ **OBJECT PERMANENCE.** Before 8 months, do babies really believe that an object spirited out of sight no longer exists? It appears not. In a remarkable series of studies in which babies did not have to engage in active search, Renée Baillargeon (1987; Baillargeon & DeVos, 1991) found evidence for object permanence as early as 3 1/2 months of age! In one investigation, infants were habituated to both a short and a tall smiley-faced carrot, each of which passed behind a screen on alternate trials (see Figure 6.7a). Then, using a screen with a large window in its upper half, the experimenter presented two test events, again on alternate trials. The first was a *possible event,* in which the short carrot (which was shorter than the window's lower edge) passed behind the screen and reappeared on the other side (Figure 6.7b). The second was an *impossible event,* in which the tall carrot passed behind the screen, did not appear in the window (although it was taller than the window's lower edge), and then miraculously emerged intact on the other side (Figure 6.7c). Young infants dishabituated to, or looked with much greater interest and surprise at, the impossible event than the possible one. This finding suggests that young babies must have some notion of object permanence—that an object continues to exist when it is hidden from view.

If 3 1/2-month-olds grasp the idea of object permanence, then what explains Piaget's finding that much older infants (who are quite capable of voluntary reaching) do not try to search for hidden objects? One explanation is that, just as Piaget's theory suggests, they cannot yet put together the separate schemes—pushing aside the obstacle and grasping the object—necessary to retrieve a hidden toy. In other words, what they *know* about object permanence is not yet *evident* in their searching behavior (Baillargeon et al., 1990).

Once 8- to 12-month-olds actively search for a hidden object, they make the AB search error. For some years, researchers thought that babies had trouble remembering an object's new location after it was hidden in more than one place. But recent findings reveal that poor memory cannot fully account for infants' unsuccessful per-

Make-believe play
A type of play in which children pretend, acting out everyday and imaginary activities.

FIGURE 6.7

Study in which infants were tested for object permanence using the habituation–dishabituation response. (a) First, infants were habituated to two events: a short carrot and a tall carrot moving behind a yellow screen, on alternate trials. Then two test events were presented, in which the color of the screen was changed to blue to help the infant notice that now it had a window. (b) In the possible event, the short carrot (which was shorter than the window's lower edge) moved behind the blue screen and reappeared on the other side. (c) In the impossible event, the tall carrot (which was taller than the window's lower edge) moved behind the screen, did not appear in the window, but then emerged intact on the other side. Infants as young as 3 1/2 months dishabituated to the impossible event, suggesting that they understood object permanence. *(Adapted from R. Baillargeon & J. DeVos, 1991, "Object Permanence in Young Infants: Further Evidence,"* Child Development, *62, p. 1230. © The Society for Research in Child Development. Reprinted by permission.)*

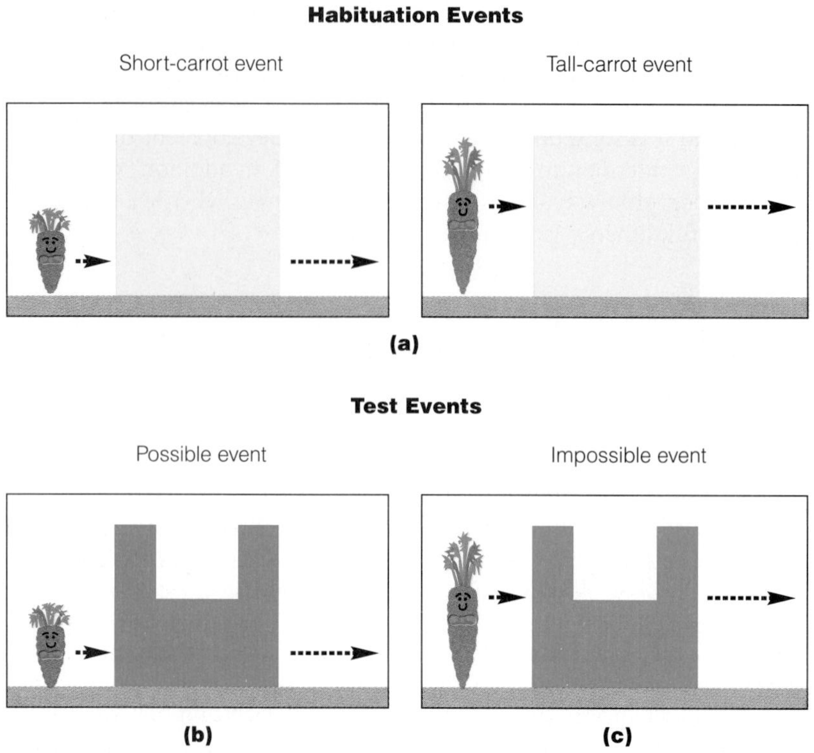

formance on these tasks (Diamond, Cruttenden, & Neiderman, 1994). Why don't they search in the right place when given an opportunity? Once again, before 12 months, infants seem to have difficulty translating what they know about an object moving from one place to another into a successful search strategy. This ability to integrate knowledge with action may depend on rapid maturation of the cortex at the end of the first year (Bell & Fox, 1992; Diamond, 1991).

■ DEFERRED IMITATION. Piaget studied imitation by noting when his own three children demonstrated it in their everyday behavior. Under these conditions, a great deal has to be known about the infant's daily life to be sure that deferred imitation has occurred. Also, some babies might be capable of deferred imitation but have very few opportunities to display it.

Recently, Andrew Meltzoff and Keith Moore (1994) brought 6-week-old babies into the laboratory and deliberately tried to induce deferred imitation of facial expressions. Infants who watched an adult demonstrate mouth opening or tongue protrusion imitated the facial gesture when exposed to the passive face of the same adult 24 hours later. These findings show that deferred imitation, a form of representation, is present by the second month of life. Perhaps young babies use it as a way to identify and communicate with persons they have seen before.

As motor capacities improve, infants start to copy adults' actions on objects. In one study, Meltzoff (1988b) showed 9-month-olds three novel toys—an L-shaped piece of wood that could be bent, a box with a button that could be pushed, and a plastic egg filled with metal nuts that could be shaken. When tested after a 24-hour delay, infants who saw these actions modeled were far more likely to reproduce them than were babies exposed to the objects but not shown how they work. By 14 months, toddlers use deferred imitation skillfully to enrich their range of sensorimotor schemes. They can retain as many as 6 modeled behaviors over a 1-week period, copy the actions of peers as well as adults, and imitate across a change in contexts—for example, enact a behavior learned at day care in the home (Hanna & Meltzoff, 1993; Meltzoff, 1988a).

At the end of the second year, toddlers imitate not only an adult's behavior, but the actions he or she *tries* to produce, even if these are not fully realized (Meltzoff, 1995). And during make-believe play, 2-year-olds duplicate entire social roles, such as mommy, daddy, or baby.

In sum, deferred imitation is present in early infancy. It does not conclude sensorimotor development, as Piaget believed. Nevertheless, deferred imitation becomes far more flexible and complex by the end of toddlerhood. It moves beyond specific behaviors to mimicking of people's intentions and perspectives. This advance permits young children to better understand and predict others' behaviors.

EVALUATION OF THE SENSORIMOTOR STAGE

In view of the evidence just discussed, how should we evaluate the accuracy of Piaget's sensorimotor stage? Clearly, important cognitive capacities emerge in preliminary form long before Piaget expected them to do so. At the same time, when these capacities first appear, they may not be secure enough to make a large difference in the baby's understanding of the world or to serve as the foundation for new knowledge. Piaget's substages do mark the full-blown achievement of many infant cognitive milestones, if not their first appearance. Follow-up research consistently shows that infants anticipate events, actively search for hidden objects, flexibly vary the circular reaction, and engage in deferred imitation of intricate action sequences within the general time frame that Piaget said they do (Corman & Escalona, 1969; Užgiris & Hunt, 1975).

The disagreements between Piaget's observations and those of recent research raise more questions about *how* early development takes place than what infants and toddlers achieve during the first 2 years. Consistent with Piaget's ideas, new research shows that motor activity does facilitate the early construction of knowledge. For example, in Chapter 5, we showed that crawling babies are better at finding hidden objects, and they have a keener appreciation of depth on the visual cliff. And we also saw that manipulating objects with the hands is a major means through which babies find out about their world (see page 189). But infants may not need to construct all aspects of experience through motor action. The beginnings of some schemes may be prewired into the human brain from the start. For example, recall the research on newborn imitation discussed in Chapter 5. It supports the idea that infants are "set up" to copy others' facial expressions and gestures of at birth. And within the first few months, babies have a basic appreciation of the properties of objects—that they are solid, cannot pass through other objects, and continue to exist when out of sight (Spelke, 1991). Important schemes may also be constructed through purely perceptual learning—by looking and listening—rather than through acting directly on the world (Baillargeon, 1993; Mandler, 1992a, 1992b).

Finally, infants do not develop in the neat stepwise fashion implied by Piaget's theory, in which a variety of skills change together and abruptly as each new substage is attained. Instead, many sensorimotor capacities appear to develop separately and gradually, depending on the infant's rate of biological maturation and the specific experiences encountered. For example, a baby at one level of progress on imitation is likely to be at quite another on object permanence (Harris, 1983). These ideas—that adultlike capacities are present during infancy in primitive form, that cognitive development is gradual and continuous, and that it must be described separately for each skill—serve as the basis for a major competing approach to Piaget's theory: information processing, which we take up next.

But before we turn to this alternative point of view, let's conclude our discussion of the sensorimotor stage by recognizing Piaget's enormous contributions. Although not all his conclusions were correct, Piaget's work inspired a wealth of new research on infant cognition, including studies that eventually challenged his ideas. In addition, Piaget's observations of infants have been of great practical value. Teachers and

Deferred imitation plays a major role in enriching the young child's range of sensorimotor schemes. This toddler may have watched an older brother or sister hit a ball with a plastic bat. After storing the behavior in memory, she practices it at a later time, when her sibling is conveniently not around to prevent her from playing with the toys. *(Elizabeth Crews/The Image Works)*

TABLE 6.2

Playthings That Support the Development of Sensorimotor and Early Representational Schemes

FROM 2 MONTHS	FROM 6 MONTHS	FROM 1 YEAR
Crib mobile	Squeezing toys	Large dolls
Rattles	Nesting cups	Toy dishes
	Foam rubber ball	Toy telephone
	Stuffed animals (without glass or button eyes that can be swallowed)	Hammer and peg toy
	Filling and emptying toys	Pull and push toys
	Large and small blocks	Cars and trucks
	Pots, pans, and spoons from the kitchen	Simple puzzles
	Bath toys	Sand box, shovel, and pail
	Picture books	Shallow wading pool and water toys

caregivers continue to look to the sensorimotor stage for guidelines on how to create developmentally appropriate environments for infants and toddlers. Now that you are familiar with Piaget's sequence of infant development, take some time to apply it. For example, what kinds of playthings would support the building of sensorimotor and early representational schemes? Prepare your own list of infant and toddler toys, and justify it by making reference to Piaget's substages. Then compare your suggestions to the ones given in Table 6.2.

ASK YOURSELF . . .

- Tony pushed his toy bunny through the slats of his crib onto a nearby table. Using his "pulling scheme," he tried to retrieve it, but it would not fit back through the slats. Next Tony tried jerking, turning, and throwing the bunny. Is Tony in a state of equilibrium or disequilibrium? How do you know?
- Mimi banged her rattle again and again on the tray of her high chair. Then she dropped the rattle, which fell out of sight on her lap, but Mimi did not try to retrieve it. Which sensorimotor substage is Mimi in? Why do you think so?

BRIEF REVIEW

According to Piaget, children actively build psychological structures, or schemes, as they manipulate and explore their world. Two processes, adaptation (which combines assimilation and accommodation) and organization, account for the development of schemes. The vast changes that take place during the sensorimotor stage are divided into six substages. The circular reaction, a special means that infants use to adapt schemes, changes from being oriented toward the infant's own body, to being directed outward toward objects, to producing novel effects in the surrounding world. During the last three substages, infants make strides in intentional behavior and understanding object permanence. By the final substage, they start to represent reality and show the beginnings of make-believe play. Recent research reveals that secondary circular reactions, object permanence, and deferred imitation are present much earlier than Piaget believed. These findings raise questions about Piaget's claim that babies must construct all aspects of their cognitive world through motor activity and that sensorimotor development takes place in stages.

INFORMATION PROCESSING DURING THE FIRST TWO YEARS

Information-processing theorists agree with Piaget that children are active, inquiring beings, but otherwise their view of human thinking is decidedly different. Unlike Piaget, information processing does not provide a single, unified theory of cognitive development. Instead, it is an approach that focuses on many different aspects of thinking, from attention, memory, and categorization skills to complex problem solving.

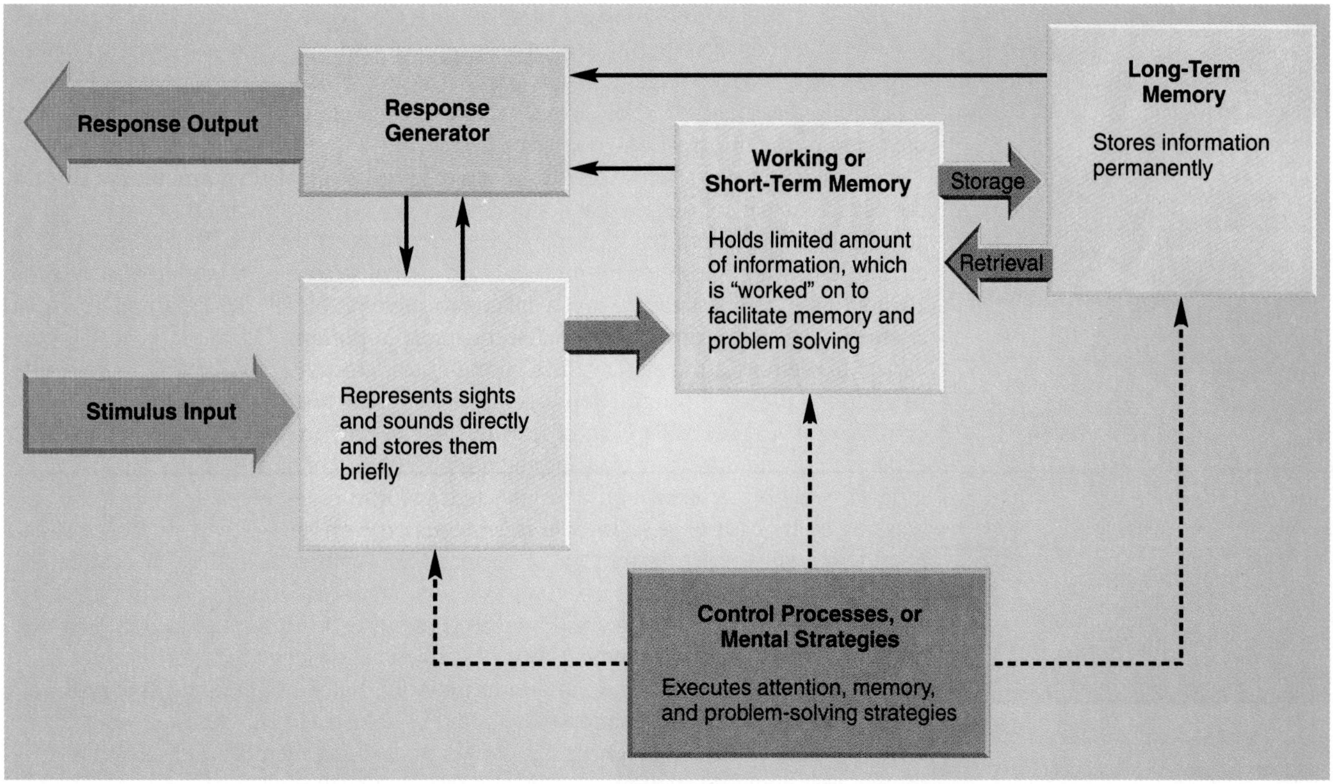

FIGURE 6.8

Atkinson and Shiffrin's model of the human information-processing system.
Stimulus input flows through three parts of the mental system: the sensory register; working, or short-term, memory; and long-term memory, In each, control processes, or mental strategies, can be used to manipulate information, increasing the efficiency of thinking and the chances that information will be retained. *(Adapted from R. M. Shiffrin & R. C. Atkinson, 1969, "Storage and retrieval processes in long-term memory,"* Psychological Review, *76, p. 180. Copyright © 1969 by the American Psychological Association. Adapted by permission of the publisher and author.)*

In Chapter 1, we saw that the information-processing approach relies on scripts, frames, and flowcharts to describe the human cognitive system. Often the steps of thinking are likened to the operations a computer performs when it stores, interprets, and responds to incoming information. The computer model of human thinking is very attractive because it is explicit and precise. Information-processing researchers find it useful because they are not satisfied with global concepts, such as assimilation and accommodation, to describe how children think. Instead, they want to know exactly what individuals of different ages do when faced with a task or problem (Klahr, 1989; Kuhn, 1992; Siegler, 1991).

A MODEL OF HUMAN INFORMATION PROCESSING

Although many flowcharts of human information processing exist, Richard Atkinson and Richard Shiffrin's (1968) computerlike model has inspired more research than any other. As Figure 6.8 shows, Atkinson and Shiffrin divide the mind into three basic parts: the *sensory register; working,* or *short-term, memory;* and *long-term memory.* As information flows through each, it can be operated on and transformed using **control processes,** or **mental strategies.** When we use strategies to manipulate input in various ways, we increase the efficiency of thinking as well as the chances that information will be retained for later use. To understand this idea more clearly, let's take a brief look at each aspect of Atkinson and Shiffrin's model.

First, information enters the **sensory register.** Here, sights and sounds are represented directly, but they cannot be held for long. For example, take a moment to

Control processes, or mental strategies
In information processing, procedures that operate on and transform information, increasing the efficiency of thinking as well as the chances that information will be retained.

Sensory register
In information processing, that part of the mental system in which sights and sounds are held briefly before they decay or are transferred to working, or short-term, memory.

Using an operant conditioning method in which babies make a mobile move by kicking a foot tied to it with a long cord, Carolyn Rovee-Collier has made many discoveries about infant learning, memory, and categorization. *(Courtesy of Carolyn Rovee-Collier, Rutgers University)*

look around, and then close your eyes. An image of what you saw probably persists for a few seconds, but then it decays or disappears, unless you use mental strategies to preserve it. For example, you can *attend* to some information more carefully than others, thereby increasing the chances that the selected input will transfer to the next step of the information-processing system.

The second waystation of the mind is **working,** or **short-term, memory.** This is the conscious part of our mental system, where we actively "work" on a limited amount of information. For example, if you are studying this book effectively, you are constantly applying control processes, or mental strategies, manipulating input to ensure that it will be retained and available to solve problems. Perhaps you are attending to certain information that seems most important. Or you may be using a variety of memory strategies, such as taking notes, repeating information to yourself, or grouping pieces of information together—a strategy much like Piaget's notion of organization. Organization is an especially effective way to remember the many new concepts flowing into your working memory at the moment. If you permit stimulus input to remain piecemeal and disconnected, you can hold very little in your working memory at once, since you must focus on each item separately. But organize it, and you will not just improve your memory. You will increase the chances that information will be transferred to the third, and largest, storage area of your system.

Unlike the sensory register and working memory, the amount of information that can be held in **long-term memory,** our permanent knowledge base, is limitless. In fact, so much input is stored in long-term memory that we sometimes have problems in *retrieval,* or getting information back from the system. To aid retrieval, we apply strategies in long-term memory just as we do in working memory. For example, think about how information in your long-term memory is arranged. According to Atkinson and Shiffrin (1968, p. 181), it is *categorized* according to a master plan based on contents, much like a "library shelving system which is based upon the contents of books." When information is filed in this way, it can be retrieved quite easily by following the same network of associations used to store it in the first place.

Information-processing researchers believe that the basic structure of the human mental system is similar throughout life. However, the *capacity* of the system—the amount of information that can be retained and processed at once—expands, making possible more complex forms of thinking with age (Case, 1992; Halford, 1993). Gains in information-processing capacity are partly due to brain maturation. But they are largely the result of improvements in strategies, such as attending to information and categorizing it effectively. Do infants use these processing strategies? How does memory—so essential to all cognitive activity—improve over the first 2 years? These are questions that information-processing researchers ask, and you will find answers to them in the following sections.

ATTENTION AND MEMORY

If you think back to our discussion of perceptual development in Chapter 5, you will discover that you already know something about how attention develops in early infancy. Recall that between 1 and 2 months of age, infants shift from attending to a single high-contrast feature of their visual world to exploring objects and patterns more thoroughly.

Besides attending to more aspects of the environment, infants gradually become more efficient at managing their attention, taking information into their mental systems more quickly with age. The habituation–dishabituation response has been used to study this aspect of cognitive change. Recall from Chapter 5 that habituation refers to a decline in attention as babies become familiar with a stimulus. In dishabituation, attention recovers when babies are exposed to a second stimulus—one new and different from the first. Research reveals that preterm infants require a long time to habituate and dishabituate to novel stimuli—for example, 5 minutes or more for visual patterns (Werner & Siqueland, 1978). But by 5 months, babies process new

Working, or short-term, memory
In information processing, the conscious part of the mental system, where we actively "work" on a limited amount of information to ensure that it will be retained.

Long-term memory
In information processing, the part of the mental system that contains our permanent knowledge base.

information rapidly, requiring as little as 5 to 10 seconds to take in a complex visual stimulus and recognize that it is different from a second one (Fagan, 1971, 1977).

Habituation does not just tell us about changes in the efficiency of infant attention. It also provides a window into infant memory capacities. For example, infants can be exposed to a stimulus until they habituate. Then they can be shown the same stimulus at a later time. If habituation takes place more rapidly on the second occasion, this indicates that babies must recognize that they have seen the stimulus before. Using this method, studies show that by 3 months, infants remember a visual stimulus for 24 hours (Martin, 1975). By the end of the first year, their retention increases to several days, and in the case of very familiar stimuli (such as a photo of the human face), even weeks (Fagan, 1973).

At this point, let's note that habituation–dishabituation research tells us how long babies retain a new stimulus in the context of the laboratory, but it underestimates their ability to remember real-world events that they can actively control. Using operant conditioning, Carolyn Rovee-Collier (1991) studied infant memory in a familiar setting—at home while babies lay in their cribs. First, 2- and 3-month-olds were taught how to make a mobile move by kicking a foot tied to it with a long cord. Then the mobile was removed, and after a week's delay, the infants were reattached to it. Right away they kicked vigorously, showing that indeed they remembered. And as long as they were reminded of the mobile's dancing motion (the experimenter briefly rotated it for the baby), infants started kicking again as long as two weeks after they were first trained (Linde, Morrongiello, & Rovee-Collier, 1985; Rovee-Collier, Patterson, & Hayne, 1985). Much like older children and adults, babies seem to remember best when experiences take place in familiar contexts and when they participate actively (Lipsitt, 1990).

So far, we have discussed only one type of memory—**recognition.** It is the simplest form of retrieval because all babies have to do is indicate (by looking or kicking) whether a new stimulus is identical or similar to one previously experienced. **Recall** is a second, more challenging form of memory, since it involves remembering something that is not present. To recall, you must generate an image of the absent stimulus. Can infants engage in recall? By the middle of the first year, they can. Felicia reported that one day when her husband telephoned, 7-month-old April listened to him speak through the receiver and immediately crawled to the front door. April seemed to be *recalling* times when she had heard the sound of her father's muffled voice through the door as he was about to arrive home from work (Ashmead & Perlmutter, 1980). By the end of toddlerhood, recall for people, places, and objects is excellent. For example, at age 2, Byron recalled a friend whom he had not seen for several months when he passed the friend's house (Nelson & Ross, 1980).

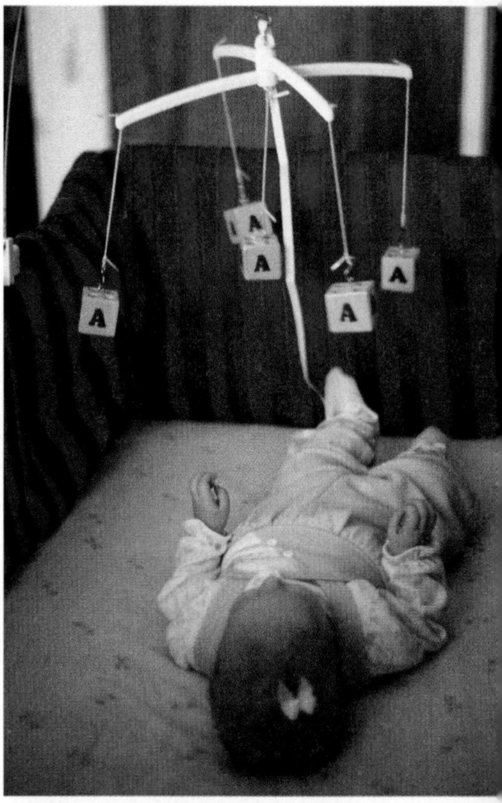

This 3-month-old infant discovered that by kicking, she could shake a mobile made of small blocks with the letter A on them. After a delay, the baby continued to kick vigorously only if the mobile she saw was labeled with the same form (the letter A). She did not kick when given a mobile with a different form (the number 2). The infant's behavior shows that she groups similar stimuli into categories and can distinguish the category A from the category 2. *(Courtesy of Carolyn Rovee-Collier/Rutgers University)*

CATEGORIZATION

As infants gradually remember more information, they seem to store it in a remarkably orderly fashion. Even young babies categorize stimulus events. In fact, they do so at such an early age that categorization is among the strongest pieces of evidence that babies' brains are set up from the start to structure experience in adultlike ways (Bornstein & Sigman, 1986; Mervis, 1985).

To find out about infant categorization, Rovee-Collier conducted some creative variations of her operant conditioning research, described in the previous section. This time, 3-month-olds were taught to kick to make a mobile move that was made of a uniform set of stimuli—for example, small blocks, all with the letter *A* on them. After a delay, kicking returned to a high level only if the babies were shown a mobile whose elements were labeled with the same form (the letter *A*). If the form was changed (from *A*'s to 2's), infants no longer kicked vigorously. While learning to make the mobile move, the babies had grouped together its features, associating the kicking response with the category "*A*" and, at later testing, distinguishing it from the category "2" (Hayne, Rovee-Collier, & Perris, 1987).

Recognition
A type of memory that involves noticing whether a stimulus is identical or similar to one previously experienced.

Recall
A type of memory that involves remembering a stimulus that is not present.

Habituation–dishabituation research has also been used to study infant categorization. For example, infants can be shown a series of pictures belonging to one category (such as hot dog, piece of bread, slice of salami). Then the investigator observes whether they look longer at, or dishabituate to, a picture that is not a member of the category (chair) than one that is (apple). The findings of such studies reveal that 9- to 12-month-olds structure objects into an impressive array of categories—food items, furniture, birds, animals, vehicles, and more (Mandler & McDonough, 1993; Oakes, Madole, & Cohen, 1991; Ross, 1980; Younger, 1985, 1993). Besides organizing the physical world, infants of this age also categorize their emotional and social worlds. For example, they can sort people and the sounds of their voices into male and female (Francis & McCroy, 1983; Poulin-DuBois et al., 1994). And they can distinguish positive from negative facial expressions, even when the expressions are demonstrated in slightly varying ways by different people (Ludemann, 1991).

During the second year, children become active categorizers during their play. Try giving a toddler a set of objects that differ in shape and color (such as small blocks). See if the child spontaneously categorizes them. Research shows that around 12 months, toddlers merely touch objects that belong together, without grouping them. A little later, they form single categories. For example, when given four balls and four boxes, a 16-month-old will put all the balls together but not the boxes. And finally, around 18 months of age, toddlers can sort objects correctly into two classes.

Interestingly, this advanced object-sorting behavior appears at about the same time that toddlers show a "naming explosion," or a sharp rise in vocabulary in which they label many more objects (Gopnik & Meltzoff, 1987, 1992). Language development seems to facilitate as well as build on improved categorization. In support of this idea, research indicates that adult labeling of objects helps direct toddlers' attention to object categories (Waxman & Hall, 1993). And Korean children, who learn a language in which object names are often omitted from sentences, develop object-grouping skills later than do their English-speaking counterparts (Gopnik & Choi, 1990).

EVALUATION OF INFORMATION-PROCESSING FINDINGS

The information-processing research discussed in the preceding sections underscores the *continuity* of human thinking from infancy into adult life. In attending to the environment, remembering everyday events, and categorizing objects, Byron, Rachel, and April think in ways that are remarkably similar to our own, even though they are far from being the proficient mental processors we are. Findings on infant memory and categorization join with other research in challenging Piaget's view of early cognitive development as taking place in discrete stages. If 3-month-olds can hold events in memory for as long as 2 weeks and categorize stimuli around them, then they must have some ability to mentally represent their experiences. Representation seems to be another cognitive skill that does not have to wait until babies have had many months of sensorimotor experience (even though there is no dispute that it flourishes during the second year of life).

Information processing has contributed greatly to our view of young infants as sophisticated cognitive beings. Still, it has drawbacks. Perhaps the greatest one stems from its central strength: By analyzing cognition into its components (such as perception, attention, and memory), information processing has had difficulty putting them back together into a broad, comprehensive theory. For this reason, many child development specialists still resist abandoning Piaget's ideas in favor of it. During the past decade, several attempts have been made to improve on Piaget's theory by combining it with the information-processing approach (Case, 1985,

1992; Fischer & Pipp, 1984). We will discuss these efforts in Chapter 12. Although none is yet widely accepted, by drawing on the strengths of both of these perspectives, the field of child development may be moving closer to a new, more powerful view of how the mind of the infant and child develops.

THE SOCIAL CONTEXT OF EARLY COGNITIVE DEVELOPMENT

If a new, broader theory eventually emerges out of Piagetian and information-processing views, it is likely to be deficient in one important respect: Both approaches pay little attention to the idea that children live in rich social contexts that affect the way their cognitive world is structured. Vygotsky's sociocultural theory has brought the field of child development to this realization (Bruner, 1990; Rogoff, 1990).

Take a moment to review the short episode at the beginning of this chapter in which Rachel dropped shapes into a container. Notice that Rachel is not an independent explorer who discovers how to use the toy on her own. Instead, she learns about it with her mother's help. With Beth's support, Rachel will gradually become better at matching shapes to openings and dropping them into the container. Then she will be able to perform the activity (and others like it) on her own.

Vygotsky (1930–1935/1978) believed that complex mental functions, such as voluntary attention, memory, and problem solving, have their origins in social interaction. Through joint activities with more mature members of their society, children come to master activities and think in ways that have meaning in their culture. A special concept, the **zone of proximal** (or potential) **development**, explains how this happens. It refers to a range of tasks that the child cannot yet handle alone but can accomplish with the help of more skilled partners. To understand this idea, think of a sensitive teacher or parent (such as Beth) who introduces a child to a new activity. The adult picks a task that the child can master but one challenging enough that the child cannot do it by herself. Thus, the activity is especially suited for spurring development forward. Then the adult guides and supports, breaking the task down into manageable units and calling the child's attention to specific features. By joining in the interaction, the child picks up mental strategies, and her competence increases. When this happens, the adult steps back, permitting the child to take over more responsibility for the task.

This mother assists her baby in making a jack-in-the-box work. By presenting a task within the child's zone of proximal development and fine-tuning her support to the infant's momentary needs, the mother promotes her son's cognitive development. *(Innervisions)*

As we will see in Chapters 9 and 12, Vygotsky's ideas have mostly been applied at older ages, when children become skilled at language and their ability to engage in social communication expands. But recently, Vygotsky's theory has been extended downward to infancy. In earlier parts of this book, we showed how babies are equipped with ways of ensuring that caregivers will interact with them. Then adults adjust the environment and their communication in ways that promote learning.

A study by Barbara Rogoff and her collaborators (1984) illustrates this process. The researchers watched how several adults played with Rogoff's son and daughter over the first 2 years, while a jack-in-the-box toy was nearby. In the early months, adults tried to focus the baby's attention by showing the toy and, as the bunny popped out, saying something like "My, what happened?" By the end of the first year (when the baby's cognitive and motor skills had improved), interaction centered on how to use the jack-in-the-box. When the infant reached for the toy, adults guided the baby's hand in turning the crank and putting the bunny back in the box. As the youngsters became toddlers, adults helped from a distance. They used verbal instructions and gestures, such as rotating a hand in a turning motion near the crank, while the child tried to make the toy work. Research suggests that this fine-tuned support is related to cognitive competence. Infants whose mothers gently direct their attention and (as they get older) encourage them to manipulate the envi-

Zone of proximal development
In Vygotsky's theory, a range of tasks that the child cannot yet handle alone but can do with the help of more skilled partners.

FROM RESEARCH TO PRACTICE

PARENT–TODDLER INTERACTION AND EARLY MAKE-BELIEVE PLAY

One of my husband Ken's shared activities with our two sons when they were young was to bake pineapple upside-down cake, a favorite treat. At age 4 1/2, David was already well versed in the process—how to arrange the pineapple slices, mix the batter, pour it into the pan, and transfer it to the oven. I remember well one Sunday afternoon when a cake was in the making. Little Peter, then 21 months old, stood on a chair at the kitchen sink, busy pouring water from one cup to another.

"He's in the way, Dad!" complained David, trying to pull Peter away from the sink. Peter let out a sharp yell and refused to budge, turning back to his pouring.

"Maybe if we let him help, then he'll give us some room at the sink," Ken suggested. As David stirred the batter, Ken poured some into a small bowl for Peter, moved his chair to the side of the sink, and handed him a spoon.

"Here's how you do it, Petey," instructed David, with an air of superiority. Peter watched as David stirred, then tried to copy his motion. When it was time to pour the batter, Ken helped Peter hold and tip the small bowl so its contents flowed into the pan.

"Time to bake it," said Ken.

"Bake it, bake it," repeated Peter, as he watched Ken slip the pan into the oven.

Several hours later, when the cake was cool and the dishes washed, we observed one of Peter's earliest instances of make-believe play. He got his pail from the sandbox and, after filling it with a handful of sand, carried it into the kitchen and put it down on the floor in front of the oven. "Bake it, bake it," Peter called to Ken. Together, father and son lifted the pretend cake inside the oven.

Historically, the emergence of make-believe play was studied in isolation from the social environment in which it usually occurs. Until recently, most researchers observed young children while playing alone. Probably for this reason, Piaget and his followers concluded that toddlers discover make-believe independently, as soon as they are capable of representational schemes. Vygotsky's theory has challenged this view. He believed that society provides children with opportunities to represent culturally meaningful activities in play. Make-believe, like other mental functions, is initially learned under the guidance of expert partners (Garvey, 1990; Smolucha, 1992). In the example just described, Peter's capacity to represent daily events was extended when Ken drew him into the baking task and helped him act it out in play.

New research supports the idea that early make-believe is the combined result of children's readiness to engage in it and social experiences that promote it. An observational study of middle-class American toddlers at play in their homes revealed that 75 to 80 percent of make-believe during the second year involved mother–child interaction. At 12 months, make-believe was fairly one-sided; almost all play episodes were initiated by caregivers. By the end of the second year, caregivers and children displayed mutual interest in getting make-believe started; half of pretend episodes were initiated by each. At all ages, caregivers elaborated on the child's contribution, resulting in joint activity in which both partners participated actively in an imaginative dialogue. Over time, the adult gradually released responsibility to the child for creating and guiding the fantasy theme (Haight & Miller, 1993).

What are the consequences of adult involvement in young children's pretending? In several studies, researchers compared toddlers' solitary play with their play while interacting with their mothers. In each case, caregiver support led early make-believe to move toward a more advanced level (Fiese, 1990; O'Reilly & Bornstein, 1993; Slade, 1987; Zukow, 1986). For example, when adults took part, play themes were more varied, and maternal commentary was especially effective in extending the duration of make-believe. In addition, toddlers were more likely to combine representational schemes into more complex sequences, as Peter did when he put sand in the bucket ("making the batter"), carried it into the kitchen, and (with Ken's help) put it in the oven ("baking the cake").

In many cultures, adults do not spend much time playing with young children. Instead, older siblings fill in by letting toddlers join in their play and by modeling appropriate actions (Zukow, 1989). Notice how, in the episode described here, David showed Peter how to stir the batter, and Peter was quickly drawn into the baking activity.

As we will see in Chapter 9, make-believe is a major means through which children extend their cognitive skills and learn about important activities in their culture. Vygotsky's theory, and the findings that support it, tell us that providing a stimulating physical environment is only part of what is necessary to promote early cognitive growth. In addition, toddlers must be invited and encouraged by their elders to become active participants in the social world around them.

ronment are advanced in play, language, and problem-solving skills during the second year (Belsky, Goode, & Most, 1980; Tamis-LeMonda & Bornstein, 1989).

In previous sections of this chapter, we saw how infants create new schemes by acting on the physical world (Piaget) and how certain prewired skills become better developed as infants and toddlers represent their experiences in more efficient and meaningful ways (information processing). Vygotsky adds a third dimension to our understanding by emphasizing that important aspects of cognitive development are socially mediated. In the From Research to Practice box on the opposite page, you will find additional evidence for this idea. And we will see even more in the next section, as we look at individual differences in mental development during the first 2 years.

BRIEF REVIEW

Using flowcharts of the human mental system, information-processing researchers analyze thinking into separate elements and study how each changes with age. Atkinson and Shiffrin's computerlike model divides the mind into three parts: the sensory register; working, or short-term, memory; and long-term memory. As information flows through the system, control processes, or mental strategies, operate on it, increasing the likelihood that information will be retained. Mental strategies gradually improve with age. Infants attend to more aspects of the environment, manage their attention more efficiently, and remember information over longer periods of time. Findings on categorization support the view that infants' brains are set up to structure experience in adultlike ways. Although information processing has helped us appreciate the remarkable cognitive abilities of infants, it has not yet provided a way of linking these diverse skills together. According to Vygotsky's sociocultural theory, early cognitive development is socially mediated as adults help infants and toddlers master tasks within the zone of proximal development.

ASK YOURSELF . . .

- When Rachel was 3 months old, she stared at a little toy dog that Beth dangled in front of her and then looked away. The next day, Beth held up the toy dog again and Rachel looked at it, but more briefly. What can we conclude about Rachel's processing of the toy?
- At age 18 months, Byron's father stood behind him, helping him throw a large rubber ball into a box. When Byron showed that he could throw the ball, his father stepped back and let him try on his own. Using Vygotsky's ideas, explain how Byron's father is supporting his cognitive development.

INDIVIDUAL DIFFERENCES IN EARLY MENTAL DEVELOPMENT

As he neared age 2, Byron had only a handful of words in his vocabulary, continued to play in a less mature way than Rachel and April, and seemed restless and overactive. Lisa, increasingly concerned about Byron's progress, decided to take him to a psychological clinic, where he was given one of many tests available for assessing the mental development of infants and toddlers.

The testing approach is different from the cognitive theories we have discussed so far, which try to explain the *process* of development—how children's thinking changes over time. In contrast, designers of mental tests are much more concerned with cognitive *products*. Their aim is to measure behaviors that reflect mental development and arrive at scores that predict future performance, such as later intelligence, school achievement, and adult vocational success. Recall from Chapter 1 that this concern with prediction arose nearly a century ago, when French psychologist Alfred Binet was asked to identify children unlikely to succeed in regular school classes. Binet's first successful intelligence test, which predicted school achievement, inspired the design of many new tests, including ones that measure intelligence at very early ages. If ways could be found to identify infants and toddlers at risk for developing poorly, then special help could be provided early in life, when there is greatest hope of preventing later problems.

French psychologist Alfred Binet (1857–1911) developed the first successful intelligence test. His work inspired the design of many new tests, including ones that measure infant mental development.
(The Bettmann Archive)

INFANT INTELLIGENCE TESTS

As you can probably imagine, accurately measuring the intelligence of infants is an especially challenging task. Unlike children, babies cannot answer questions or follow directions. All we can do is present them with stimuli, coax them to respond, and observe their behavior. As a result, most infant tests consist of perceptual and motor responses along with some tasks that tap early language and problem solving. One commonly used infant test is the *Bayley Scales of Infant Development*, designed to assess children between 1 month and 3 1/2 years. It is made up of two scales: (1) the Mental Scale, which includes such items as turning to a sound, looking for a fallen object, building a tower of cubes, and naming pictures; and (2) the Motor Scale, which assesses gross and fine motor skills, such as grasping, sitting, drinking from a cup, and jumping (Bayley, 1993).

When taking such tests, babies are not necessarily willing and cooperative. They often get hungry, distracted, or tired during the testing period. As we will see shortly, both the makeup of infant tests and the immaturity of these young test takers affect the ability of infant tests to predict later performance. But before we examine the issue of prediction, we need to look at how intelligence test scores are computed.

COMPUTING INTELLIGENCE TEST SCORES. Scores on intelligence tests, whether designed for infants, children, or adults, are arrived at in much the same way. When a test is constructed, it is given to a large, representative sample of individuals. Performances of people at each age level form a *normal* or *bell-shaped curve* in which most scores fall near the center (the mean or average) and progressively fewer fall out toward the extremes. On the basis of this distribution, the test designer computes *norms,* or standards against which future test takers can be compared. For example, the number of items that Byron passes at age 2 will be compared to that of 2-year-olds in general. If Byron does better than 50 percent of his agemates, his score will be 100, an average test score. If he exceeds most youngsters his age, his score will be much higher. If he does better than only a small percentage of 2-year-olds, his score will be much lower.

Scores computed in this way are called **intelligence quotients,** or **IQs,** a term you have undoubtedly heard before. Table 6.3 describes the meaning of a range of IQ scores. Notice how the IQ offers a way of finding out whether a child is ahead, behind, or on time (average) in mental development in relation to other children of the same age. The great majority of individuals (96 percent) have IQs that fall between 70 and 130; only a very few achieve higher or lower scores.

PREDICTING LATER PERFORMANCE FROM INFANT TESTS. Many people assume that IQ is a measure of inborn ability that does not change with

TABLE 6.3

Meaning of Different IQ Scores

SCORE	PERCENTILE RANK (CHILD DOES BETTER THAN . . . PERCENT OF SAME-AGE CHILDREN)
70	2
85	16
100 (average IQ)	50
115	84
130	98

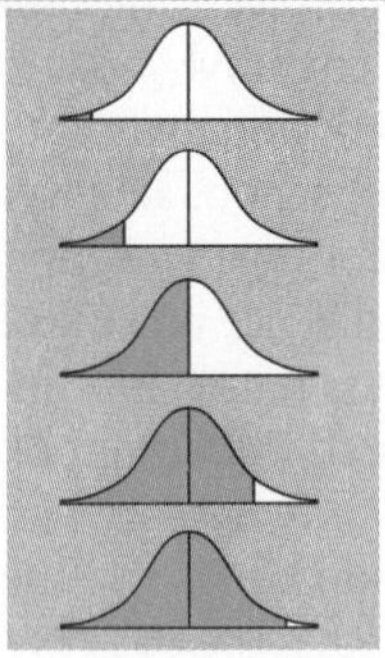

Intelligence quotient, or IQ
A score that permits an individual's performance on an intelligence test to be compared to the performances of other individuals of the same age.

age. Research on the stability of IQ shows that this is incorrect. Despite the careful construction of many infant tests, they predict later intelligence poorly (Lewis & McGurk, 1972). In one longitudinal study, the same group of children was tested repeatedly from infancy through adolescence (McCall, Appelbaum, & Hogarty, 1973). The scores of most youngsters changed considerably. In fact, the average IQ shift between 21/2 and 17 years of age was as great as 28.5 points! In addition, high scorers during the early years were not necessarily high scorers later.

We have already seen that infants and toddlers are especially likely to become distracted, fatigued, or bored during testing. As a result, scores often do not reflect their true abilities. But there is a second reason that early intellectual measures are not good predictors of later IQ. The perceptual and motor tasks that appear on infant tests are quite different from the test questions given to older children, which emphasize verbal, conceptual, and problem-solving skills. Because of concerns that infant test scores do not tap the same dimensions of intelligence measured at older ages, they are conservatively labeled **developmental quotients,** or **DQs,** rather than IQs. Not until age 6 do IQ scores become stable, serving as reasonably good predictors of later performance (Honzik, Macfarlane, & Allen, 1948; Sontag, Baker, & Nelson, 1958).

It is important to note that infant tests do show somewhat better long-term prediction for extremely low-scoring babies (Honzik, 1983). Today, infant tests are largely used for *screening*—helping to identify for further observation and intervention babies whose very low scores mean that they have a high likelihood of experiencing developmental problems in the future (Kopp, 1994).

Because infant tests do not predict later IQ for most children, researchers have turned to information processing for new ways to assess early mental functioning. Their findings show that habituation and dishabituation to visual stimuli are the best available infant predictors of childhood intelligence. Correlations between the speed of these responses and 3- to 8-year-old IQ consistently range from the .30s to the .60s (McCall & Carriger, 1993). Perhaps the habituation–dishabituation response is a more effective predictor of later IQ than traditional infant tests because it taps basic cognitive processes—attention, memory, and response to novelty—that underlie intelligent behavior at all ages.

Recently, a new test made up entirely of habituation–dishabituation items, the *Fagan Test of Infant Intelligence,* was constructed. To take it, the infant sits on the mother's lap and views a series of pictures. After exposure to each one, looking time toward a novel picture that is paired with the familiar one is recorded. Besides predicting preschool IQ, the Fagan test is highly effective in identifying babies who (without intervention) will soon show serious delays in intellectual development (Fagan & Montie, 1988; Fagan, Shepherd, & Knevel, 1991).

For many years, infant tests based on Piaget's theory have been available (Escalona & Corman, 1969; Užgiris & Hunt, 1975). Like habituation–dishabituation, object permanence is a better predictor of preschool IQ than traditional infant tests, perhaps because it, too, reflects a basic intellectual process—problem solving (Wachs, 1975). The consistency of these findings has prompted designers of the most recent edition of the Bayley test to include several items that tap higher-order cognitive skills, such as preference for novel stimuli, categorization, and ability to find hidden objects (Bayley, 1993).

EARLY ENVIRONMENT AND MENTAL DEVELOPMENT

In Chapter 2, we indicated that intelligence is a complex blend of hereditary and environmental influences. Because infant scores are so unstable, researchers have not been able to study genetic contributions to intelligence at such an early age. In contrast, many studies have examined the relationship of environmental factors to infant and toddler mental test scores.

Developmental quotient, or DQ
A score on an infant intelligence test, based primarily on perceptual and motor responses. Computed in the same manner as an IQ.

TABLE 6.4

Home Observation for the Measurement of the Environment (HOME): Infancy and Toddler Subscales

SUBSCALE	SAMPLE ITEM
Emotional and verbal responsiveness of the parent	Parent caresses or kisses child at least once during observer's visit.
Acceptance of the child	Parent does not interfere with child's actions or restrict child's movements more than three times during observer's visit.
Organization of the physical environment	Child's play environment appears safe and free of hazards.
Provision of appropriate play materials	Parent provides toys or interesting activities for child during observer's visit.
Maternal involvement with the child	Parent tends to keep the child within visual range and to look at the child often during observer's visit.
Variety in daily stimulation	Child eats at least one meal per day with mother and father, according to parental report.

Source: Elardo & Bradley, 1981.

THE HOME ENVIRONMENT. From what you have learned so far in this chapter, what aspects of young children's home experiences would you expect to influence early mental development? To answer this question, Robert Bradley, Bettye Caldwell, and their collaborators developed the **Home Observation for Measurement of the Environment (HOME)**, a checklist for gathering information about the quality of children's home lives through observation and parental interview. Factors measured by HOME during the first 3 years are listed in Table 6.4. Each is positively related to toddlers' mental test performance. In addition, high HOME scores are associated with IQ gains between 1 and 3 years of age, whereas low HOME scores predict declines as large as 15 to 20 points (Bradley et al., 1989).

When researchers look at different social-class and ethnic groups, the findings on early home environment are much the same. Stimulation provided by the physical setting and parental encouragement, involvement, and affection repeatedly predict infant and early childhood IQ, no matter what the child's background (Bradley & Caldwell, 1982; Bradley et al., 1989).

Can the research summarized so far help us understand Lisa's concern about Byron's development? Indeed, it can. Andrew, the psychologist who tested Byron, found that he scored slightly below average but well within normal range. Besides giving the test, Andrew interviewed Lisa about her child-rearing practices and watched her play with Byron. He noticed that Lisa, anxious about how well Byron was doing, tended to pressure him a great deal. She constantly bombarded him with questions and instructions that were not related to his ongoing actions. Andrew explained that when parents are intrusive in these ways, infants and toddlers are likely to be distractible, show less mature forms of play, and do poorly on mental tests (Bradley et al., 1989; Fiese, 1990). He coached Lisa in how to establish a sensitive give-and-take in the way that she played with Byron. At the same time, he assured her that Byron's current performance need not forecast his future development, since warm, responsive parenting that builds on toddlers' current capacities is a much better indicator of how they will do later than an early mental test score.

Home Observation for Measurement of the Environment (HOME) A checklist for gathering information about the quality of children's home lives through observation and parental interview.

INFANT AND TODDLER DAY CARE. Home environments are not the only influential settings in which young children spend their days. During the past two decades, women in industrialized nations have entered the labor force in large numbers. Today, over 60 percent of mothers with a child under age 2 are employed (U.S. Bureau of the Census, 1994). Day care for infants and toddlers has

TABLE 6.5

Signs of Developmentally Appropriate Infant and Toddler Day Care

PROGRAM CHARACTERISTIC	SIGNS OF QUALITY
Physical setting	Indoor environment is clean, in good repair, well lighted, and well ventilated. Fenced outdoor play space is available. Setting does not appear overcrowded when children are present.
Toys and equipment	Play materials are appropriate for infants and toddlers (see Table 6.2) and stored on low shelves within easy reach. Cribs, high chairs, infant seats, and child-sized tables and chairs are available. Outdoor equipment includes small riding toys, swings, slide, and sandbox.
Caregiver–child ratio	In day care centers, caregiver–child ratio is no greater than 1 to 3 for infants and 1 to 6 for toddlers. Group size (number of children in one room) is no greater than 6 infants with 2 caregivers and 12 toddlers with 2 caregivers. In day care homes, care giver is responsible for no more than 6 children; within this group, no more than 2 are infants and toddlers. Staffing is consistent, so infants and toddlers can form relationships with particular caregivers.
Daily activities	Daily schedule includes times for active play, quiet play, naps, snacks, and meals. It is flexible rather than rigid, to meet the needs of individual children. Atmosphere is warm and supportive, and children are never left unsupervised.
Interactions among adults and children	Caregivers respond promptly to infants' and toddlers' distress; hold, talk to, sing, and read to them; and interact with them in a contingent manner that respects the individual child's interests and tolerance for stimulation.
Caregiver qualifications	Caregiver has at least some training in child development, first aid, and safety.
Relationships with parents	Parents are welcome anytime. Caregivers talk daily with parents about children's behavior and development.
Licensing and accreditation	Day care setting, whether a center or home, is licensed by the state. If a center, accreditation by the National Academy of Early Childhood Programs is evidence of an especially high-quality program.

Sources: Berezin, 1990; Bredekamp, 1987; National Association for the Education of Young Children, 1991.

become common, and its quality has a major impact on mental development. In one series of studies, researchers examined the development of young children in Bermuda, where 85 percent enter day care before age 2. Verbal stimulation by caregivers and an overall rating of day care center quality predicted enhanced cognitive, language, and social skills during the preschool years (McCartney et al., 1985; Phillips, McCartney, & Scarr, 1987). Similarly, in Sweden, entering high-quality day care before age 1 is associated with cognitive, emotional, and social competence in middle childhood and adolescence (Andersson, 1989, 1992).

Arrange to visit some day care settings, and take notes on what you see. In contrast to most European countries, where day care is nationally regulated and liberally funded to ensure its quality, reports on American day care are cause for deep concern. Standards are set by the states, and they vary greatly across the nation. In some places, caregivers need no special training in child development, and one adult is permitted to care for as many as 8 to 12 babies at once. Large numbers of infants and toddlers attend unlicensed day care homes, where no one checks to see that minimum health and safety standards are met (Zigler & Gilman, 1993). Children who enter poor-quality day care during their first year and remain there during the preschool years are rated by teachers as distractible, low in task involvement, and inconsiderate of others when they reach kindergarten (Howes, 1990).

Unfortunately, children most likely to have inadequate day care come from low-income and poverty-stricken families, where parents cannot afford to pay for the kind of services their youngsters need (Phillips et al., 1994). As a result, these children receive a double dose of vulnerability, both at home and in the day care environment. Table 6.5 lists signs of high-quality programs that can be used in choosing a day care setting for an infant or toddler, based on standards for **developmentally appropriate practice** devised by the National Association for the Education of Young Children (Bredekamp, 1987). These standards specify program characteristics that meet the developmental and individual needs of young children of varying ages, based on current research and the consensus of experts.

Of course, for parents to select day care that is developmentally appropriate, there must be enough of it available. Recognizing that American day care is in a state of crisis, in 1992 Congress allocated additional funds to upgrade its quality and assist parents—especially those with low incomes—in paying for it (Barnett, 1993). A recent survey indicated that although far from meeting the total need, the increase in resources is having a positive impact on the quality and accessibility of day care services for low-income families (Children's Defense Fund, 1994). This is a hopeful sign, since good day care protects the well-being of all children, and it can serve as effective early intervention for youngsters whose development is at risk, much like the programs we are about to consider in the next section.

EARLY INTERVENTION FOR AT-RISK INFANTS AND TODDLERS

Many studies indicate that children of poverty are likely to show gradual declines in intelligence test scores and to achieve poorly when they reach school age (Brody, 1992). These problems are largely due to home environments that, from the earliest ages, undermine children's ability to learn and increase the chances that they will remain poor throughout their own lives. A variety of intervention programs have been developed to break this tragic cycle of poverty. Although most begin during the preschool years (we will discuss these in Chapter 9), a few start during infancy and continue to provide supports for development through early childhood.

Interventions for infants and toddlers go about the task of helping them in different ways. Some are center based. Children come to classrooms for educational experiences, well-balanced meals, and health services designed to compensate for their underprivileged home lives. In addition, parents may receive training in child-rearing skills. The Carolina Abecedarian Project is a well-known center-based intervention; you can find out about it by reading the Social Issues box on page 233. Other interventions are home based. A skilled adult visits the home and works with parents, teaching them how to stimulate a very young child's development. In most intervention programs, participating youngsters score higher on mental tests than untreated controls by age 2—gains that persist as long as the program lasts and occasionally longer. The more intense the intervention (for example, full-day, year-round, high-quality day care plus support services for parents), the greater the intellectual gains of participating children (Bryant & Ramey, 1987).

Without some form of early intervention, large numbers of children born into economically disadvantaged families will not reach their full potential. Recognition of this reality recently led the United States Congress to provide limited funding for intervention services directed at infants and toddlers who already have serious developmental problems or who are at risk for them because of poverty (Barnett, 1993). At present, available programs are not nearly enough to meet the need. Nevertheless, the ones that exist are a promising beginning in a new effort aimed at preventing the serious learning difficulties of millions of poor children by starting to help them at a very early age.

Developmentally appropriate practice
A set of standards devised by the National Association for the Education of Young Children that specify program characteristics that meet the developmental and individual needs of young children of varying ages, based on current research and the consensus of experts.

SOCIAL ISSUES

THE CAROLINA ABECEDARIAN PROJECT: A MODEL OF INFANT–TODDLER INTERVENTION

In the 1970s, an experiment was begun to find out if educational enrichment at a very early age could prevent the declines in mental development known to affect children born into extreme poverty. The Carolina Abecedarian Project identified over a hundred infants at serious risk for school failure, based on parental education and income, a history of poor school achievement among older siblings, and other family problems. Shortly after birth, the babies were randomly assigned to either a treatment or control group.

Between 3 weeks and 3 months of age, infants in the treatment group were enrolled in a full-time, year-round day care program, where they remained until they entered school. During the first 3 years, the children received stimulation aimed at promoting motor, cognitive, language, and social skills. After age 3, the goals of the program expanded to include prereading and math concepts. At all ages, special emphasis was placed on adult–child communication. Teachers were trained to engage in informative, helpful, and nondirective interaction with the children, who were talked to and read to daily. Both treatment and control children received nutrition and health services. The primary difference between them was the day care experience, designed to support the treatment group's mental development.

Intelligence test scores were gathered on the children regularly, and (as Figure 6.9 indicates) by 12 months the performance of the two groups began to diverge. Treatment children scored substantially higher than controls throughout the preschool years (Ramey & Campbell, 1984). Although the high-risk backgrounds of both groups led their IQs to drop during the school years, follow-up testing at ages 8 and 12 revealed that treatment children maintained their advantage in IQ over controls. In addition, at age 12 treatment youngsters were achieving considerably better in school, especially in reading, writing, and general knowledge. And they were less likely to have been placed in special education or to have repeated a grade (Campbell & Ramey, 1991, 1994; Martin, Ramey, & Ramey, 1990). When the Carolina Abecedarian children entered elementary school, the researchers conducted a second experiment to compare the impact of early and later intervention. From kindergarten through second grade, half of the treatment and half of the control group were provided with a special resource teacher. She introduced supplementary educational activities into the home addressing the child's specific learning needs. Findings revealed that school-age intervention had some positive effects, but these were not nearly as great as the impact of very early intervention (Campbell & Ramey, 1994). As we will see in Chapter 9, intervention programs that start later and last for shorter periods of time do not have an enduring impact on intelligence test scores (although they do show long-term academic and social benefits). The findings of the Carolina Abecedarian Project, and others like it, indicate that intensive intervention beginning in infancy is the most effective way to combat the devastating effects of poverty on children's mental development.

TRY THIS . . .

- Evaluate a day care program serving infants and toddlers on the basis of standards for developmentally appropriate practice given in Table 6.5 on page 232. Ask staff members to indicate the proportion of children enrolled who are low income. In view of its quality, do you think the program could serve as a protective factor in the mental development of poverty-stricken children? How easy is it for parents with limited resources to find good day care in your community?

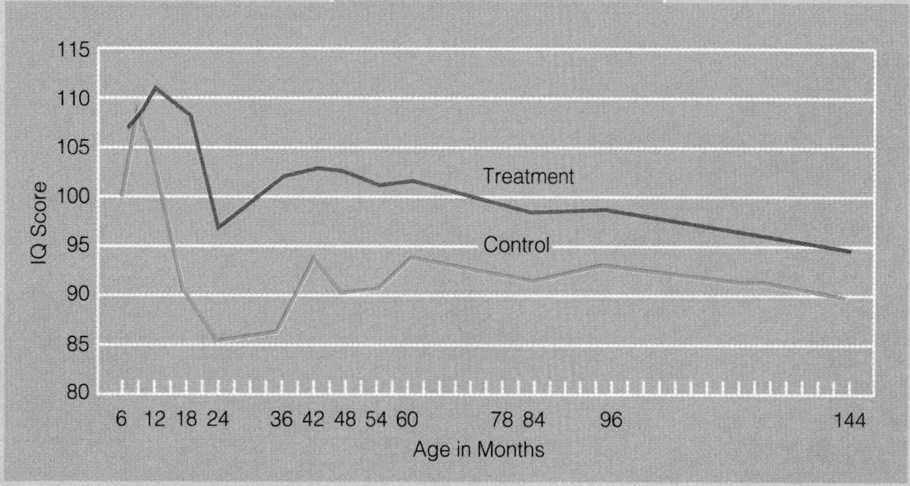

FIGURE 6.9

IQ scores of treatment and control children from 6 months to 12 years of age in the Carolina Abecedarian Project.

From F. A. Campbell & C. T. Ramey, 1991, The Carolina Abecedarian Project. *In M. Burchinal (Chair), Early experience and children's competencies: New findings from four longitudinal studies, Symposium presented at the biennial meeting of the Society for Research in Child Development, Seattle, WA. Reprinted by permission of the author.*

ASK YOURSELF . . .

- Fifteen-month-old Joey's developmental quotient (DQ) is 115. His mother wants to know exactly what this means and what she should do at home to support his mental development. How would you respond to her questions?
- Using what you learned about brain growth in Chapter 5, explain why intensive intervention for poverty-stricken children beginning in the first 2 years has a greater impact on IQ scores than intervention at a later age.

BRIEF REVIEW

The mental testing approach arrives at IQ scores that compare a child's performance to that of same-age children. Infant intelligence tests consist largely of perceptual and motor responses, and they predict later intelligence poorly. Measures of recognition memory and object permanence show better prediction into the preschool years. Factors in the home environment—stimulation provided by the physical setting and parental encouragement, involvement, and affection—are consistently related to early test scores. High-quality day care supports mental development, whereas poor-quality care undermines it. Intensive early intervention for poverty-stricken infants and toddlers has been successful in producing improvements in IQ.

LANGUAGE DEVELOPMENT DURING THE FIRST TWO YEARS

As perception and cognition improve during infancy, they pave the way for an extraordinary human achievement—language. On the average, children say their first word at 12 months of age, with a range of about 8 to 18 months (Whitehurst, 1982). Once words appear, language develops rapidly. Sometime between 1 1/2 and 2 years, toddlers combine two words. Soon their utterances increase in length and complexity. By age 6, they have a vocabulary of about 10,000 words, are speaking in elaborate sentences, and are well on the way to becoming skilled conversationalists.

To appreciate what an awesome task this is, think about the many abilities involved in your own flexible use of language. When you speak, you must select words that match the underlying concepts you want to convey. Then you must combine them into phrases and sentences using a complex set of grammatical rules. Next, you must pronounce these utterances correctly, or you will not be understood. Finally, you must follow the rules of everyday conversation. For example, if you do not take turns, make comments that are relevant to what your partner just said, and use an appropriate tone of voice, then no matter how clear and correct your language, others may refuse to listen to you.

Infants and toddlers are still newcomers to their physical and social worlds, but they make remarkable progress in getting these skills underway. How do they manage to do so? There are several theories of how early language development takes place. Let's examine and evaluate each, based on what we know about the beginnings of language in the first 2 years.

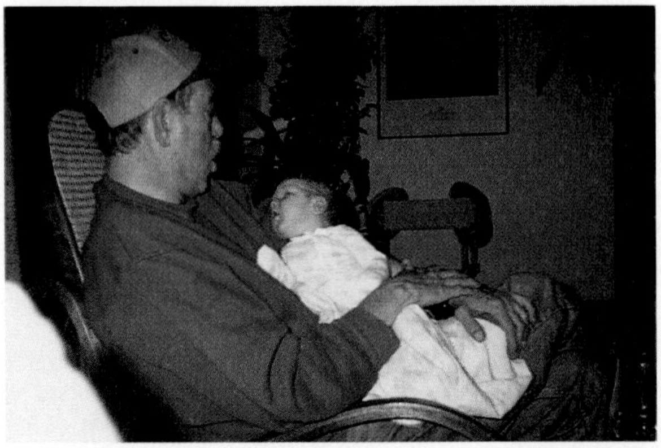

Infants are communicative beings from the start, as this interchange between a 3-month-old and his grandfather indicates. How will this child accomplish the awesome task of becoming a fluent speaker of his native tongue during the first few years of life? Theorists disagree sharply on answers to this question. *(Courtesy of Dakoda Brandon Dorsaneo)*

THREE THEORIES OF LANGUAGE DEVELOPMENT

In the 1950s, researchers had little notion that infants and toddlers were as competent as we know they are today. They did not take seriously the idea that very young children might be able to figure out important properties of the language they hear, just as they organize the world of objects into meaningful units. As a result, the first two theories of how children acquire language were extreme views. One, *behaviorism,* regarded language development as entirely due to environmental influences—in particular, intensive training by parents. The second, *nativism* (meaning inborn), assumed that children were prewired to master the intricate rules of their language.

THE BEHAVIORIST PERSPECTIVE. The leader of this view was the well-known behaviorist B. F. Skinner (1957). He proposed that language, just like any other behavior, is acquired through *operant conditioning* (see Chapter 5, pages 192–193). As the baby makes sounds, parents reinforce those that are most like words with smiles, hugs, and speech in return. For example, at 12 months, my older son David could often be heard babbling something like this: "book-a-book-a-dook-a-dook-a-book-a-nook-a-book-aaa." One day, I held up his picture book while he babbled away and said, "Book!" Very soon David was saying "book-aaa" in the presence of books. Some behaviorists rely on *imitation* to explain how children rapidly acquire complex utterances, such as whole phrases and sentences (Whitehurst & Vasta, 1975). And imitation can combine with reinforcement to promote language learning, as when the parent coaxes, "Say I want a cookie" and delivers praise and a treat after the toddler responds with "wanna cookie!"

As these examples indicate, reinforcement and imitation contribute to early language development. At the same time, there is wide agreement that they are not the whole story. As Felicia remarked one day, "It's amazing how creative April is with language. She combines words in ways she's never heard before, such as 'needle it' when she wants me to sew up her teddy bear and 'allgone outside' when she has to come in from the backyard." Felicia's observations reveal that young children do not just copy the speech of others. A great many things they say are not directly taught. So conditioning and imitation are best viewed as supporting early language learning rather than fully explaining it.

Linguist Noam Chomsky proposed a nativist theory of language development. According to Chomsky, children are born with an innate language acquisition device (LAD) that permits them to combine words into grammatically consistent utterances at an early age. *(Donna Coveney)*

THE NATIVIST PERSPECTIVE. Linguist Noam Chomsky (1957) was the first to recognize that even small children assume much responsibility for their own language learning. But his alternative to Skinner's view was just the opposite: a nativist theory that regards the young child's amazing language skill as etched into the structure of the human brain.

Chomsky's main interest was in one aspect of language—grammar. He believed that grammatical rules are much too complex to be directly taught to or independently discovered by a young child. Instead, he argued, all children are born with a **language acquisition device (LAD),** a biologically based innate system for picking up language. It permits them, as soon as they have learned enough words, to combine them into grammatically consistent expressions and to understand the meaning of sentences they hear. According to Chomsky, the LAD contains a set of rules common to all languages. Therefore, no matter which language children hear, they speak it in a rule-oriented fashion from the very beginning.

Are children biologically primed to acquire language? There is evidence that they are. Recall from Chapter 4 that newborn babies are remarkably sensitive to speech sounds and prefer to listen to the human voice. In addition, children the world over reach the major milestones of language development in a similar sequence. This regularity of development certainly fits with Chomsky's idea of a biologically determined language program.

Language acquisition device (LAD)
In Chomsky's theory, a biologically based innate system for picking up language that permits children, as soon as they have learned enough words, to combine them into grammatically consistent expressions and to understand the meaning of sentences they hear.

At the same time, there are challenges to Chomsky's theory, suggesting that it, too, provides only a partial account of language development. First, researchers have had great difficulty identifying the single system of grammar that Chomsky believes underlies all languages (Moerk, 1989). Second, careful study of children's first word combinations reveals that they do not follow basic grammatical rules (Maratsos & Chalkley, 1980; Radford, 1988). Finally, language acquisition is no longer regarded as accomplished quite as quickly as nativist theory suggests. Although extraordinary strides are made during the early years, children's progress in mastering many sentence constructions is not immediate, but steady and gradual. As we will see in Chapter 12, complete mastery of some grammatical forms is not achieved until well into middle childhood, and subtle aspects of grammar continue to be refined into the adult years (Menyuk, 1977). This suggests that more learning and discovery are involved in language development than Chomsky assumed.

THE INTERACTIONIST PERSPECTIVE. In recent years, new ideas about language development have emerged, emphasizing that innate abilities and environmental influences *interact* to produce children's extraordinary language achievements. Although several interactionist theories exist, all stress the social context of language learning. An active child, well endowed for acquiring language, observes and participates in social exchanges. From these experiences, children gradually discover the functions and regularities of language. According to the interactionist position, native capacity, a strong desire to interact with others, and a rich linguistic and social environment combine to assist children in building a communicative system (Bohannon & Warren-Leubecker, 1989).

As we chart the course of early language growth, we will come across a great deal of evidence that supports this new position. Table 6.6 provides an overview of early language milestones that we will take up in the next few sections.

GETTING READY TO TALK

Before babies say their first word, they are preparing for language in many ways. They listen attentively to human speech, and they make speechlike sounds. As adults, we can hardly help but respond.

COOING AND BABBLING. Around 2 months, babies begin to make vowel-like noises, called **cooing** because of their pleasant "oo" quality. Gradually, consonants are added, and around 6 months **babbling** appears, in which infants repeat consonant–vowel combinations in long strings, such as "babababababa" or "nanananana."

The timing of early babbling seems to be due to maturation, since babies everywhere (even those who are deaf) start babbling at about the same age and produce a similar range of early sounds (Stoel-Gammon & Otomo, 1986). But for babbling to develop further, infants must be able to hear human speech. Around 7 months, babbling starts to include the sounds of mature spoken languages. However, if a baby's hearing is impaired, these speechlike sounds are greatly delayed, and in the case of deaf infants they are totally absent (Oller & Eilers, 1988). When deaf infants are exposed to sign language from birth, they babble with their hands in much the same way hearing infants do through speech (Petitto & Marentette, 1991).

When a baby coos or babbles and gazes at you, what are you likely to do? One day while I was standing in line at the post office, a mother and her 7-month-old daughter entered. As we waited, the baby babbled, and three adults—myself and two people standing beside me—started to talk to the infant. We cooed and babbled ourselves, imitating the baby, and also said such things as "My, you're a big girl, aren't you? Out to help Mommy mail letters today?" Then the baby smiled and babbled all the more. As adults interact with infants and they listen to spoken lan-

Cooing
Pleasant vowel-like noises made by infants beginning around 2 months of age.

Babbling
Repetition of consonant–vowel combinations in long strings, beginning around 6 months of age.

TABLE 6.6

Milestones of Language Development During the First Two Years

APPROXIMATE AGE	MILESTONE
2 months	Infants coo, making pleasurable vowel sounds.
4 months on	Infants and parents establish joint attention, and parents often verbally label what the baby is looking at.
6–14 months	Infants babble, adding consonants to the sounds of the cooing period and repeating syllables. By 7 months, babbling of hearing infants starts to include many sounds of mature spoken languages. Deaf babies exposed to sign language babble with their hands.
6–14 months	Infants become capable of playing simple games, such as pat-a-cake and peekaboo. These provide practice in conversational turn-taking and also highlight the meaning and function of spoken words.
8–12 months	Infants begin using preverbal gestures, such as showing and pointing, to influence the behavior of others. Word comprehension first appears.
12 months	Infants say their first recognizable word.
18–24 months	Vocabulary expands from about 50 to 200 words.
20–26 months	Toddlers combine two words.

guage, babbling increases. By the end of the first year, it reflects the consonant–vowel and intonation patterns of the infant's language community (Boysson-Bardies & Vihman, 1991; Levitt & Wang, 1991). Through babbling, babies seem to experiment with a great many sounds that later can be blended into their first words.

BECOMING A COMMUNICATOR. Adults do not just interact with infants when they coo and babble; they also do so in many other situations. By age 4 months, infants start to gaze in the same direction adults are looking, and adults follow the baby's line of vision as well. When this happens, parents often comment on what the infant sees. In this way, the environment is labeled for the baby. Researchers believe that this kind of joint attention may be quite important for early language development. Infants and toddlers who experience it often are likely to talk earlier and show faster vocabulary development (Dunham & Dunham, 1992; Dunham, Dunham, & Curwin, 1993).

Around 6 months, interaction between parent and baby begins to include give-and-take. Turn-taking games, such as pat-a-cake and peekaboo, appear. At first, the parent starts the game and the baby is an amused observer. But by 12 months, babies actively participate, exchanging roles with the parent. As they do so, they practice the turn-taking pattern of human conversation, and they also hear words paired with the actions they perform. Simple infant games like these are ideal contexts for infants to grasp the meaning and function of spoken words (Ratner & Bruner, 1978).

At the end of the first year, as infants become capable of intentional behavior, they use preverbal gestures to influence the behavior of others (Bates, 1979; Fenson et al., 1994). For example, they hold up a toy to show it or point to the cupboard to ask for a cookie. When adults respond to babies' gestures and also label them ("Oh, you want a cookie!"), infants learn that using language quickly leads to desired results. Soon toddlers utter words along with these reaching and pointing gestures, the gestures recede, and spoken language is underway (Goldin-Meadow & Morford, 1985).

This infant uses the protodeclarative, a preverbal gesture in which he points to communicate something about these flowers. Soon words will be uttered along with these gestures, which will diminish as the child makes the transition to verbal communication. *(Stan Ries/Picture Cube)*

FIRST WORDS

Ask several parents of toddlers to tell you which words appeared first in their children's vocabularies. Note how the words build on the sensorimotor foundations that Piaget described. Children's first words usually refer to objects that move (such as "car," "ball," "cat"), familiar actions ("bye-bye," "up," "more"), or outcomes of familiar actions ("dirty," "wet," "hot"). In their first 50 words, toddlers rarely name things that just *sit there,* like table or vase (Nelson, 1973). Sensorimotor contributions to early language are also supported by evidence that hearing children exposed to both signed and spoken words are slightly advanced in learning signed symbols (Goodwyn & Acredolo, 1993).

Some early words are linked to specific cognitive achievements. For example, use of disappearance words, like "all gone," occurs at about the same time toddlers master advanced object permanence problems. And success and failure expressions, such as "there!" and "uh-oh!" appear when toddlers can solve sensorimotor problems suddenly, in Piaget's Substage 6. As one pair of researchers concluded, "Children seem to be motivated to acquire words that are relevant to the particular cognitive problems they are working on at the moment" (Gopnik & Meltzoff, 1986, p. 1057).

When young children first learn a new word, they often do not use it in just the way we do. Sometimes they apply the word too narrowly, an error called **underextension.** For example, at 16 months, April used the word "doll" only to refer to the worn and tattered doll that she carried around with her much of the day. A more common error is **overextension**—applying a word to a wider collection of objects and events than is appropriate. For example, when Rachel learned the word "car," she used it in the presence of a great many objects, including buses, trains, trucks, and fire engines. Toddlers' overextensions reflect a remarkable sensitivity to categorical relations. They do not overextend randomly. Instead, they apply a new word to

Underextension
An early vocabulary error in which a word is applied too narrowly, to a smaller number of objects and events than is appropriate.

Overextension
An early vocabulary error in which a word is applied too broadly, to a wider collection of objects and events than is appropriate.

a group of similar experiences, such as "car" to represent wheeled objects, "dog" to refer to four-legged animals, and "open" to mean opening a door, peeling fruit, and undoing shoelaces (Behrend, 1988; Clark, 1983). As their vocabularies enlarge, children start to make finer distinctions, and overextensions gradually disappear.

THE TWO-WORD UTTERANCE PHASE

At first, toddlers add to their vocabularies slowly, at a rate of 1 to 3 words a month. Over time, the number of words learned accelerates. Between 18 and 24 months, a spurt in vocabulary usually takes place. Many children add 10 to 20 new words a week (Fenson et al., 1994; Reznick & Goldfield, 1992). As vocabulary size moves toward 200 words, toddlers start to combine two words, such as "Mommy shoe," "go car," and "more cookie." These utterances are called **telegraphic speech.** Like a telegram, they focus on high-content words and leave out smaller and less important ones, such as "can," "the," and "to." Also, word endings like "-s" and "-ed" are not yet present (Brown, 1973). Even though the two-word utterance is very limited, children the world over use it to express an impressive variety of meanings (see Table 6.7).

At one time, researchers thought that there was a consistent grammar built into these expressions, but now they know that there is not. Two-word speech contains some simple formulas for use of particular words, such as "want *X*" and "more *X*" (which toddlers apply creatively by inserting many different words in the *X* position). But this does not mean that they know the rules of language, since they make many grammatical errors. For example, at 20 months, Rachel said "more hot" and "more read," but these combinations are not acceptable in English grammar (Braine, 1976; Maratsos & Chalkley, 1980).

These findings tell us that in learning to talk, toddlers are absorbed in figuring out the meanings of words and using their limited vocabularies in whatever way possible to get their thoughts across to others. This is an ambitious enough task for such a young child. But it does not take long for children to figure out basic grammatical rules. As we will see in Chapter 9, the beginnings of grammar are in place by age 2 1/2.

TABLE 6.7

Common Meanings Expressed in Toddlers' Two-Word Utterances

MEANING	EXAMPLE
Agent + action	"Tommy hit"
Action + object	"Give cookie"
Agent + object	"Mommy truck" (meaning Mommy push the truck)
Action + location	"Put table" (meaning put X on the table)
Entity + location	"Daddy outside"
Entity + attribute	"Big ball"
Possessor + possession	"My truck"
Demonstrative + entity	"That doggie"
Notice + noticed object	"Hi mommy," "Hi truck"
Recurrence	"More milk"
Nonexistent object	"No shirt," "No more milk"

Source: Brown, 1973.

Telegraphic speech
Toddlers' two-word utterances that, like a telegram, leave out smaller and less important words.

COMPREHENSION VERSUS PRODUCTION

So far, we have focused on language **production**—the words and word combinations that children use. What about **comprehension**—the language that children understand? At all ages, comprehension develops ahead of production. For example, the 8-month-old whose mother says, "Where's the doggie?" is likely to look around the room for the family's pet dog. And toddlers follow many simple directions, such as "Bring me your book" or "Don't touch the lamp," even though they cannot yet express all these words in their own speech.

Why is language comprehension ahead of production? Think back to the distinction made earlier in this chapter between two types of memory—recognition and recall. Comprehension requires only that children recognize the meaning of a word, whereas production demands that they recall, or actively retrieve from their memories, the word as well as the concept for which it stands (Kuczaj, 1986). Language production is clearly a more difficult task. Failure to say a word does not mean that toddlers do not understand it. When we evaluate a child's language development, we need to keep both of these processes in mind. If we rely only on what children say, we will underestimate their knowledge of language.

INDIVIDUAL DIFFERENCES IN LANGUAGE DEVELOPMENT

So far, we have discussed steps in language development that characterize children everywhere. But on the basis of what we have said about Byron, Rachel, and April, it should come as no surprise that there are great individual differences in how quickly language learning proceeds. Each child's progress results from a complex blend of biological and environmental influences. For example, earlier we saw that Byron's spoken language was delayed, in part because Lisa pressured him a great deal. But Byron is also a boy, and many studies show that girls are slightly ahead of boys in early vocabulary growth (Fenson et al., 1994; Jacklin & Maccoby, 1983). Besides the child's sex, personality makes a difference. Toddlers who are very reserved and cautious often wait until they understand a great deal before trying to speak. When they finally do speak, their vocabularies grow rapidly (Nelson, 1973).

Listen closely to what toddlers say, and you are likely to observe some striking differences in the words and phrases they produce. Young children have unique *styles* of early language learning. April (like most toddlers) used a **referential style**; her vocabulary consisted of many words that referred to objects. In contrast, Rachel used an **expressive style.** She produced many more pronouns and social formulas, such as "stop it," "thank you," and "I want it," which she uttered as compressed phrases, much like single words (as in "Iwannit"). Toddlers who use these styles have different early ideas about the functions of language. April thought words were for naming objects, whereas Rachel believed they were for talking about the feelings and needs of herself and other people. April's vocabulary grew faster, since all languages contain many more object labels than social phrases (Bates, Bretherton, & Snyder, 1988; Nelson, 1973).

What accounts for a toddler's choice of a particular language style? Once again, both biological and environmental factors seem to be involved. April had an especially active interest in exploring objects and parents who eagerly responded with names of things to her first attempts to talk. Rachel's personality was more social, and she listened carefully as her parents used verbal routines ("How are you?" "It's no trouble") designed to support social relationships (Furrow & Nelson, 1984; Goldfield, 1987; Nelson, 1981). Indeed, research shows that when speaking to infants and toddlers, American mothers label objects more frequently than do Japanese mothers. In contrast, Japanese mothers more often engage young children

Production
In language development, the words and word combinations that children use.

Comprehension
In language development, the words and word combinations that children understand.

Referential style
A style of early language learning in which toddlers use language mainly to label objects.

Expressive style
A style of early language learning in which toddlers use language mainly to talk about the feelings and needs of themselves and other people. Initial vocabulary emphasizes pronouns and social formulas.

in social routines, perhaps because their culture stresses the importance of membership in the social group (Fernald & Morikawa, 1993). April and Rachel's vocabularies gradually became more similar as they revised their first notions of what language is all about.

At what point should parents be concerned if their child does not talk or says very little? If a toddler's language is greatly delayed when compared to the norms given in Table 6.6 (page 237), then parents should consult the child's doctor or arrange for an evaluation by a speech and language therapist. Some toddlers who do not follow simple directions could have a hearing problem. A child over age 2 who has great difficulty putting thoughts into words may have a serious language disorder that requires immediate and intensive treatment (Warren & Kaiser, 1988).

SUPPORTING EARLY LANGUAGE DEVELOPMENT

There is little doubt that children are specially prepared for acquiring language, since no other species can develop as flexible and creative a capacity for communication as we can (Berko Gleason, 1989). At the same time, a great deal of evidence fits with the interactionist approach—that a rich social environment builds on young children's natural readiness to speak their native tongue. During infancy and toddlerhood, parents establish the contexts in which language development takes place. We have already seen several examples of how they capitalize on infants' native abilities—labeling objects babies look at, responding to coos and babbles, and playing social games.

Watch several parents talk to infants and toddlers, and you will find further evidence for the interactionist perspective. Adults in many countries speak to young children in **motherese**, a form of language made up of short sentences with exaggerated expression and very clear pronunciation (Fernald et al., 1989; Newport, Gleitman, & Gleitman, 1977). Motherese also contains many simplified words, such as "night-night," "bye-bye," "daddy," and "tummy," that are easy for toddlers to pronounce. In addition, speakers of motherese often repeat phrases, ask questions, and give directions, perhaps as a way of checking to see if their message has been properly received. Here is an example of Felicia speaking motherese to 18-month-old April as together they get ready to leave for home:

Felicia: "Time to go, April."

April: "Go car."

Felicia: "Yes, time to go in the car. Where's your jacket?"

April: (looks around, walks to the closet) "Dacket!" (pointing to her jacket)

Felicia: "There's that jacket! Let's put it on. (She helps April into the jacket.) On it goes! Let's zip up. (Zips up the jacket.) Now, say bye-bye to Byron and Rachel."

April: "Bye-bye, By-on."

Felicia: "What about Rachel? Bye to Rachel?"

April: "Bye-bye, Ta-tel (Rachel)."

Felicia: "Where's your doll? Don't forget your doll."

April: (looks around)

Felicia: "Look by the sofa. See? Go get the doll. By the sofa." (April gets the doll.)

Parents do not seem to be deliberately trying to teach children to talk when they use motherese, since many of the same speech qualities appear when adults commu-

Motherese
A form of language used by adults to speak to infants and toddlers that consists of short sentences with exaggerated expression and very clear pronunciation.

nicate with foreigners. Motherese probably arises from adults' unconscious desire to keep young children's attention and ease their task of understanding, and it works effectively in these ways. From birth on, children prefer to listen to motherese over other kinds of adult talk, and by 5 months they are more emotionally responsive to it (Cooper & Aslin, 1990; Fernald, 1993). Also, parents constantly fine-tune motherese to fit with children's needs. Notice how Felicia used an utterance length that was just ahead of April's, creating a sensitive match between the stimulation she provided and what April was capable of understanding and producing.

Motherese contains many features shown by research to support early language development. For example, parents who frequently repeat part of their own or the child's previous utterance and use simple questions have 2-year-olds who make faster language progress (Barnes et al., 1983; Hoff-Ginsburg, 1986). But this does not mean that we should deliberately load our speech to toddlers with repetitions, questions, and other characteristics of motherese! These qualities occur naturally as adults draw young children into dialogues in which their attempts to talk are accepted as meaningful and worthwhile. Conversational give-and-take between parent and toddler is one of the best predictors of early language development and academic competence during the school years. It provides many examples of speech just ahead of the child's current level and a sympathetic environment in which children pick up many new cognitive skills (Huttenlocher et al., 1991; Walker et al., 1994). In fact, a major reason that twins and later-born children often acquire early language more slowly than singletons is that they have fewer opportunities to converse with parents, who must divide their time between several youngsters (Jones & Adamson, 1987; Tomasello, Mannle, & Kruger, 1986).

As early as the second year, reading to children facilitates language progress. Adult–toddler story reading is related to language ability and a variety of reading readiness measures during the preschool years (Crain-Thoreson & Dale, 1992). When caregivers engage children in dialogues about books and respond contingently to their verbalizations, reading exposes them to great breadth of language knowledge, from vocabulary, grammar, and communicative conventions to information about print and story structures. Picture book reading can be an especially helpful intervention for low-income toddlers at risk for later language and literacy problems. Two- and three-year-olds who participate in daily reading experiences in day care or at home, compared to those who do not, are greatly advanced in language comprehension and production (Valdez-Menchaca & Whitehurst, 1992; Whitehurst et al., 1994).

Do social experiences that promote language development remind you of ones discussed earlier in this chapter that strengthen cognitive development in general? Notice how parent–child conversation and the motherese that is a part of it create a *zone of proximal development* in which children's language expands. In contrast, impatience and rejection of children's efforts to talk lead them to stop trying and result in immature language skills (Nelson, 1973). In the next chapter, we will see that the very same sensitivity to children's needs and capacities that supports cognition and language is at the heart of their emotional and social development as well.

ASK YOURSELF . . .

- Erin's first words included "see," "give," and "thank you," and her vocabulary grew slowly during the second year. What style of early language learning did she display, and what factors might explain it?
- On the basis of research presented in this chapter, list as many ways as you can think of that parents and other caregivers can foster language development in infants and toddlers.

SUMMARY

PIAGET'S COGNITIVE-DEVELOPMENTAL THEORY

According to Piaget, how do schemes change over the course of development?

- Influenced by his background in biology, Piaget viewed cognitive development as an adaptive process. By acting directly on the environment, children move through four stages in which internal structures achieve a better fit with external reality.
- In Piaget's theory, psychological structures, or **schemes,** change in two ways. The first is through **adaptation,** which is made up of two complementary activities—**assimilation** and **accommodation.** The second is through **organization,** the internal rearrangement of schemes so that they form a strongly interconnected cognitive system.

Describe the major cognitive achievements of the sensorimotor stage.

- Piaget's **sensorimotor stage** is divided into six substages. Through the **circular reaction,** the newborn baby's reflexes are gradually transformed into the more flexible action patterns of the older infant and finally into the representational schemes of the 2-year-old child. During Substage 4, infants develop **intentional,** or **goal-directed, behavior** and begin to understand **object permanence.** By Substage 6, they can represent reality and are capable of **deferred imitation** and **make-believe play.**

What does recent research have to say about the accuracy of Piaget's sensorimotor stage.

- Although Piaget's overall sequence of sensorimotor development has been confirmed, he underestimated the capacities of young infants. Secondary circular reactions, object permanence, and deferred imitation are present earlier than Piaget believed. It is possible that infants do not have to construct all aspects of their cognitive world through motor activity. The beginnings of some schemes may be there from the start, and others may be built through purely perceptual learning.

INFORMATION PROCESSING DURING THE FIRST TWO YEARS

Describe the information-processing view of cognitive development and Atkinson and Shiffrin's model of the information-processing system.

- Unlike Piaget's stage theory, information processing views development as a continuous process; the cognitive approach of children and adults is assumed to be much the same. Information-processing researchers study many different aspects of thinking. They want to know exactly what individuals of different ages do when faced with a task or problem.
- According to Atkinson and Shiffrin, the human mental system is divided into three parts: the **sensory register; working,** or **short-term, memory;** and **long-term memory.** As information flows through each, **control processes** or **mental strategies** operate on it to increase the efficiency of thinking as well as the chances that information will be retained.

What changes in attention, memory, and categorization take place over the first 2 years?

- With age, infants attend to more aspects of the environment, take information into their mental systems more quickly, and remember experiences longer. Young infants are capable of **recognition** memory; by 7 months, they can **recall** events that are not present.
- Infants remember information in a remarkably orderly fashion. During the first year, they group stimuli into increasingly complex categories. In the second year, they become active categorizers, spontaneously sorting objects during their play.

Describe the contributions and limitations of the information-processing approach to our understanding of early cognitive development.

- Information processing has contributed greatly to our view of young infants as sophisticated cognitive beings. It challenges Piaget's view of early cognitive development as taking place in discrete stages. However, it has not yet provided a broad, comprehensive theory of children's thinking.

THE SOCIAL CONTEXT OF EARLY COGNITIVE DEVELOPMENT

How does Vygotsky's concept of the zone of proximal development expand our understanding of early cognitive development?

- According to Vygotsky's sociocultural theory, complex mental functions have their origins in social interaction. By engaging in joint activities with more skilled partners, infants master tasks within the **zone of proximal development**—ones just ahead of their current capacities. Through the support and guidance of others, cognitive competence increases.

INDIVIDUAL DIFFERENCES IN EARLY MENTAL DEVELOPMENT

Describe the mental testing approach, the meaning of intelligence test scores, and the extent to which infant tests predict later performance.

- The mental testing approach measures intellectual development in an effort to predict future performance. **Intelligence quotients,** or **IQs,** are scores on mental tests that compare a child's performance to that of same-age children. Infant tests consist largely of perceptual and motor responses; they predict later intelligence poorly. As a result, scores on infant tests are called **developmental quotients,** or **DQs,** rather than IQs. The habituation–dishabituation response and object permanence, which tap basic cognitive processes, show better predictability.

Discuss environmental influences on early mental development, including home, day care, and early intervention for at-risk infants and toddlers.

- Stimulation provided by the home environment and parental encouragement, involvement, and affection repeatedly predict early mental test scores, no matter what the child's social class and cultural background. The quality of infant and toddler day care also has a major impact on mental development. Standards for **developmentally appropriate practice** specify program characteristics that meet the developmental needs of young children. Intensive early intervention is required to prevent the gradual declines in intelligence so often experienced by poverty-stricken children.

LANGUAGE DEVELOPMENT DURING THE FIRST TWO YEARS

Describe three theories of language development, and indicate the emphasis each places on innate abilities and environmental influences.

- Three theories provide different accounts of how young children develop language. According to the behaviorist perspective, parents train children in language skills by relying on operant conditioning and imitation. In contrast, Chomsky's nativist view regards children as naturally endowed with a **language acquisition device (LAD).** New interactionist theories offer a compromise between these extreme views, stressing that innate abilities and social contexts combine to promote language development.

Describe major milestones of language development in the first 2 years, individual differences, and ways in which adults support infants' and toddlers' emerging capacities.

- During the first year, a great deal of preparation for language takes place. Infants begin **cooing** at 2 months and **babbling** around 6 months. When adults respond to infants' coos and babbles, play turn-taking games with them, and acknowledge their preverbal gestures, they encourage language progress.

- Around 12 months, toddlers say their first word. When picking up new words, young children make errors involving **underextension** and **overextension.** Between 18 months and 2 years, two-word utterances called **telegraphic speech** appear. At all ages, language **comprehension** develops ahead of **production.**

- Individual differences in early language development exist. Girls show faster progress than boys, and reserved, cautious toddlers may wait for a period of time before trying to speak. Most toddlers use a **referential style** of language learning, in which early words consist largely of names for objects. A few use an **expressive style,** in which social formulas are common and vocabulary grows more slowly.

- Adults the world over speak to young children in **motherese,** a simplified form of language that is well suited to their learning needs. Motherese occurs naturally when parents engage toddlers in conversations that accept and encourage their early efforts to talk.

IMPORTANT TERMS AND CONCEPTS

sensorimotor stage (p. 210)
scheme (p. 210)
adaptation (p. 211)
assimilation (p. 211)
accommodation (p. 211)
equilibration (p. 211)
organization (p. 211)
circular reaction (p. 213)
intentional, or goal-directed, behavior (p. 214)
object permanence (p. 215)
AB search error (p. 215)
mental representation (p. 216)
deferred imitation (p. 216)
functional play (p. 216)
make-believe play (p. 217)
control processes, or mental strategies (p. 221)
sensory register (p. 221)
working, or short-term, memory (p. 222)
long-term memory (p. 222)
recognition (p. 223)
recall (p. 223)
zone of proximal development (p. 225)
intelligence quotient, (IQ) (p. 228)
developmental quotient, or DQ (p. 229)
Home Observation for Measurement of the Environment, (HOME) (p. 230)
developmentally appropriate practice (p. 232)
language acquisition device, LAD (p. 235)
cooing (p. 236)
babbling (p. 236)
underextension (p. 238)
overextension (p. 238)
telegraphic speech (p. 239)
production (p. 240)
comprehension (p. 240)
referential style (p. 240)
expressive style (p. 240)
motherese (p. 241)

FYI...

FOR FURTHER INFORMATION AND SPECIAL HELP, CONSULT THE FOLLOWING ORGANIZATIONS:

INFANT AND TODDLER DEVELOPMENT AND EDUCATION

Association for Childhood Education International (ACEI)
11501 Georgia Avenue, Suite 312
Wheaton, MD 20902
(301) 942-2443

Organization interested in promoting sound educational practice from infancy through early adolescence. Student membership is available and includes a subscription to Childhood Education, *a bimonthly journal covering research, practice, and public policy issues.*

National Association for the Education of Young Children (NAEYC)
1509 16th Street, N.W.
Washington, DC 20036-1426
(202) 232-8777 (800) 424-2460

Organization open to all people interested in acting on behalf of young children's needs, with primary focus on educational services. Student membership is available and includes a subscription to Young Children, *a bimonthly journal covering theory, research, and practice in infant and early childhood development and education.*

EARLY INTERVENTION

National Center for Clinical Infant Programs
2000 14th Street, N., Suite 380
Arlington, VA 22201-2500
(703) 528-4300

Seeks to promote optimum development of infants and toddlers through encouraging high-quality intervention services. Publishes public policy reports and a bulletin that reviews research and lists training opportunities.

High/Scope Educational Research Foundation
600 N. River Street
Ypsilanti, MI 48198-2898
(313) 485-2000

Devoted to improving development and education from infancy through the high school years. Has designed a parent–infant education program. Conducts longitudinal research to determine the effects of early intervention on development.

DAY CARE

Child Care Resource and Referral, Inc.
2116 Campus Drive, S.E.
Rochester, MN 55904
(507) 287-2220

Represents more than 260 local agencies that work for high-quality day care and provide information on available services.

National Association for Family Day Care
725 15th Street, N.W., Suite 928
Washington, DC 20005
(202) 347-3356

Organization open to caregivers, parents, and other individuals involved or interested in family day care. Serves as a national voice that promotes high-quality day care.

"Brothers"
Barbara Belle
10 years, Hungary

This child's vision of an intimate sibling relationship, bodies and lives intertwined, captures the rapid development of emotional and social capacities during the first few years. The importance of early family relationships is a major theme of Chapter 7.

Reprinted by permission from The International Museum of Children's Art, Oslo, Norway.

7

Emotional and Social Development in Infancy and Toddlerhood

THEORIES OF INFANT AND TODDLER PERSONALITY

Erik Erikson: Trust and Autonomy • Margaret Mahler: Separation–Individuation • Similarities Between Erikson's and Mahler's Theories

EMOTIONAL DEVELOPMENT DURING THE FIRST TWO YEARS

Development of Some Basic Emotions • Understanding and Responding to the Emotions of Others • Emergence of Self-Conscious Emotions • The Beginnings of Emotional Self-Regulation

TEMPERAMENT AND DEVELOPMENT

Measuring Temperament • Stability of Temperament • Genetic Influences • Environmental Influences • Temperament and Child Rearing: The Goodness-of-Fit Model

DEVELOPMENT OF ATTACHMENT

Early Theories of Attachment • Bowlby's Ethological Theory • Measuring the Security of Attachment • Cultural Variations • Factors that Affect Attachment Security • Multiple Attachments • Attachment and Later Development

SELF-DEVELOPMENT DURING THE FIRST TWO YEARS

Self-Recognition • Categorizing the Self • Emergence of Self-Control

Lisa, Beth, and Felicia's monthly conversations often focused on the emotional and social sides of their infants' development. As the babies reached 8 months of age, Beth noticed some important changes: "For some reason, Rachel's become more fearful in the last few weeks. Recently, I took her to the airport to meet my parents, who were arriving from Japan. When they stepped off the plane and tried to hug her, she didn't return their enthusiasm, as she would have a month or two ago. Instead, she turned her head away and buried it against my shoulder. Several days later, I left Rachel with my parents for several hours—the first time I'd been away from her since she was born. She wailed as soon as she saw me head for the door. And when I returned, Rachel seemed angry. She insisted on being held but also pushed me away and continued to cry. It took 5 or 10 minutes before I was able to calm her down."

Lisa and Felicia also reported an increasing wariness of strangers and a strong desire to remain close to familiar adults in Byron and April. At the same time, each baby seemed more willful. An object removed from the hand at 5 months produced little response, but at 8 months Byron actively resisted when Lisa took away a table knife he had managed to reach. And he could not be consoled by a variety of toys that she offered in its place. Taken together, these reactions reflect two related aspects of personality that begin to develop during the first 2 years: *close ties to others* and *a sense of self*—an awareness of one's own separateness and uniqueness.

Our discussion begins with major theories that provide an overall picture of personality development during infancy and toddlerhood. Then we take a look at factors that contribute to these changes. First, we chart the general course of emotional development. As we do so, we will discover why fear and anger became more apparent in Byron, Rachel, and April's range of emotions by the end of the first year.

Second, our attention turns to individual differences in temperament and personality. We will examine biological and environmental contributions to these differences and their consequences for future development.

Next, we take up attachment to the caregiver, the child's first affectional tie that develops over the course of infancy. We will see how the feelings of security that grow out of this important bond provide a vital source of support for the child's exploration, sense of independence, and expanding social relationships.

Finally, we focus on early self-development. By the end of toddlerhood, April recognized herself in mirrors and photographs, labeled herself as a girl, and showed the beginnings of self-control. "Don't touch!" she instructed herself one day as she resisted the desire to pull a lamp cord out of its socket. Cognitive advances combine with social experiences to produce these changes during the second year.

THEORIES OF INFANT AND TODDLER PERSONALITY

In Chapter 1, we pointed out that psychoanalytic theory is no longer in the mainstream of child development research. But one of its lasting contributions has been its ability to capture the essence of personality development during each phase of life. Recall from Chapter 1 that Sigmund Freud, founder of the psychoanalytic movement, believed that psychological health and maladjustment could be traced to the early years—in particular, to the quality of the child's relationships with parents.

Return to page 17 of Chapter 1 and reread the brief description of Freud's *psychosexual stages.* He focused on how parents help their children, during the first 3 years of life, discharge instinctual drives originating from the oral and then from the anal zone of the body. Freud's limited concern with the channeling of instincts and his neglect of important experiences after the early years came to be heavily criticized. But the basic outlines of his theory were accepted and elaborated by several noted psychoanalysts who came after him. The leader of these neo-Freudians is Erik Erikson, whose ***psychosocial theory*** we introduced in Chapter 1.

In the following sections, we take a closer look at the emotional and social tasks of infancy and toddlerhood, as Erikson and a second well-known psychoanalyst—Margaret Mahler—saw them. Although each emphasized somewhat different features of early experience as central to development, we will see that the two theories have much in common.

ERIK ERIKSON: TRUST AND AUTONOMY

Erikson (1950) characterized each Freudian stage as an inner conflict, which is resolved toward the positive or negative side, depending on the child's experiences with caregivers. When parenting supports the child's needs, the first year leads to feelings of trust in others and the next 2 years to a sense of personal autonomy. These early attitudes provide the foundation for healthy emotional and social development throughout life.

■ BASIC TRUST VERSUS MISTRUST. Freud called the first year the **oral stage,** during which infants obtain pleasure through the mouth—at first by sucking, and later, after teeth erupt, by biting and chewing. Gratification of the baby's need for food and pleasurable oral stimulation rests in the hands of the mother, whose task is to provide the right amount of oral satisfaction. If she feeds the baby when hungry, provides suitable objects for the infant to suck and bite, and weans neither too early nor too late, then energies transfer smoothly to the anal region, and the infant is prepared for the next stage of development.

Oral stage
Freud's first psychosexual stage, during which infants obtain pleasure through the mouth.

Erikson accepted Freud's emphasis on the importance of feeding, but he expanded and enriched Freud's view. A healthy outcome during infancy, Erikson believed, does not depend on the *amount* of food or oral stimulation offered, but rather on the *quality* of the mother's behavior. A mother who supports her baby's development relieves discomfort promptly and sensitively. For example, she holds the infant gently during feedings, patiently waits until the baby has had enough milk, and weans when the infant shows less interest in the breast and sucking.

Erikson recognized that no mother can be constantly and perfectly in tune with her baby's needs. Many factors affect her responsiveness—her own feelings of personal happiness, her momentary life condition (for example, whether she has one or several small children to care for), and child-rearing practices encouraged by her culture. But when the ***balance of care*** is sympathetic and loving, then the psychological conflict of the first year—**basic trust versus mistrust**—is resolved on the positive side. The trusting infant expects the world to be good and gratifying, so he feels confident about venturing out and exploring it. The mistrustful baby cannot count on the kindness and compassion of others, so he protects himself by withdrawing from people and things around him.

According to Erikson, basic trust grows out of the quality of the mother's relationship with the baby. A mother who relieves her infant's discomfort promptly and holds the baby tenderly, especially during feedings, promotes basic trust. *(Jeffrey W. Myers/Stock Boston)*

■ AUTONOMY VERSUS SHAME AND DOUBT. During Freud's **anal stage,** instinctual energies shift to the anal region of the body. Toddlers take pleasure in retaining and releasing urine and feces at will. At the same time, society requires that elimination occur at appropriate times and places. As a result, Freud viewed toilet training, in which children must bring their anal impulses in line with social requirements, as having a crucial impact on personality development. If parents insist that children be trained before they are physically ready, or wait too long before expecting self-control, an unresolved battle of wills is initiated between parent and child. Then anal conflicts persist, and instinctual energies are not free to move on to the next stage.

Erikson agreed that the parent's manner of toilet training is critical for psychological health. But he viewed bladder and bowel control as only one of a broad range of important experiences encountered by newly walking, talking toddlers. Their familiar refrains—"No!" and "Do it myself!"—reveal that they want to decide for themselves with all their powers, not just in toileting, but in other situations as well. The great conflict of this stage, **autonomy versus shame and doubt,** is resolved favorably when parents provide young children with suitable guidance and reasonable choices. A self-confident, secure 2-year-old has been encouraged not just to use the toilet, but also to eat with a spoon and to help pick up his toys. His parents do not criticize or attack him when he fails in these new skills. And they meet his assertions of independence with tolerance and understanding. For example, they grant him an extra 5 minutes to finish his play before leaving for the grocery store and wait patiently while he tries to zip his jacket. According to Erikson, the parent who is over- or undercontrolling in toileting is likely to be so in other aspects of the toddler's life. The outcome is a child who feels forced and shamed and who doubts his ability to control his impulses and act competently on his own.

MARGARET MAHLER: SEPARATION-INDIVIDUATION

Erikson's theory describes how sensitive channeling of the baby's drives leads to positive attitudes toward others (trust) and to good feelings about the self

Basic trust versus mistrust
In Erikson's theory, the psychological conflict of infancy, which is resolved positively if caregiving, especially during feeding, is sympathetic and loving.

Anal stage
Freud's second psychosexual stage, in which toddlers take pleasure in retaining and releasing urine and feces at will.

Autonomy versus shame and doubt
In Erikson's theory, the psychological conflict of toddlerhood, which is resolved positively if parents provide young children with suitable guidance and appropriate choices.

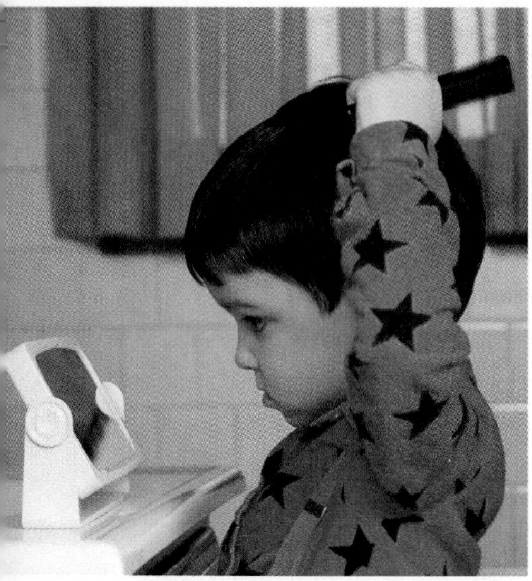

This 2-year-old is intent on combing his hair. Toddlers who are allowed to decide and do things for themselves in appropiate situations develop a sense of autonomy—the feeling that they can control their bodies and act competently on their own. *(Brent Jones/Stock Boston)*

(autonomy). Mahler carries this theme further, focusing on how the infant's early relationship with the mother provides the foundation for a sense of self that emerges in the second year (Mahler, Pine, & Bergman, 1975). According to Mahler, awareness of the self as separate and unique is the outcome of events that take place in two phases of development: symbiosis and separation–individuation.

SYMBIOSIS. During the first 2 months, babies are only minimally aware of the surrounding world, spending most of the day asleep, waking when hunger and other tensions cause them to cry, and sinking back into sleep when basic needs are satisfied and discomforts are relieved. But from the second month on, the phase of **symbiosis** (meaning the blending of two people into an intimate, harmonious relationship) begins. At this time, infants become increasingly alert and interested in sights and sounds around them (see Chapter 5). But unlike the older child and adult, they do not realize that these events exist outside themselves. Instead, the self and surrounding world (including the person they depend on most for survival—the mother) are completely fused. According to Mahler, this oneness with the mother is a necessary first step on the way to developing a sense of self. It is promoted by her responsiveness to infant emotional signals. As the baby cries, coos, and smiles, the mother reacts promptly and with positive emotional tone. The more she does so, the more confidently and easily the infant will separate from her during the next phase. In contrast, infants handled harshly and impatiently are likely to have great difficulty distancing themselves from their mothers.

SEPARATION–INDIVIDUATION. In Mahler's second phase, **separation–individuation,** the baby's capacity to move away from the mother triggers self-awareness (individuation). The process of separating from the mother begins around 4 to 5 months, when the infant, held in his mother's arms, leans away from her body to scan the environment. But the decisive events of this phase are crawling and then walking—that is, the baby's growing capacity to leave the mother at his own initiative.

Newly crawling 8- to 10-month-olds venture away from the mother to explore their world, but they remain very dependent on her for emotional support. Infants of this age wander only a short distance away. They look back frequently for reassurance and return to the mother's side to re-experience the safety and security of close body contact. Yet as crawling babies come and go, they experience the mother from a new, distant vantage point and become dimly aware of their own separateness.

Walking brings a dramatic advance in individuation. The upright posture is accompanied by greater freedom of movement and a new delight in exploration. As toddlers venture further from the mother and test their own capacities, they become even more conscious that the mother and the self are distinct beings. Around 18 months, this realization is full-blown, and at first it is frightening. Older toddlers may engage in all kinds of behaviors aimed at resisting and undoing this separateness—following and clinging to the mother, filling her lap with objects retrieved from the surrounding environment, and darting away in hopes of being chased, caught, and reminded of her continuing commitment. According to Mahler, the temper tantrums that often occur around this time—referred to as the "terrible twos" by many parents—are signs of the new self's desire to assert itself, mixed with feelings of helpless dependence at not being able to manage all the challenges of the environment.

The mother's patience and reassurance eventually help toddlers surmount this temporary crisis. Between 2 and 3 years of age, children whose mothering experiences have been gratifying and supportive emerge from this second phase with a sturdy sense of themselves as separate people. They are affectionate, caring, and cooperative; play energetically; and can cope with mild frustration. And gains in representation and language (see Chapter 6) enable children to create a positive inner image of the mother that they can rely on in her absence, so that separations from her are easier.

Symbiosis
In Mahler's theory, the baby's intimate sense of oneness with the mother, encouraged by warm, physical closeness and gentle handling.

Separation–individuation
In Mahler's theory, the process of separating from the mother and becoming aware of the self, which is triggered by crawling and walking.

SIMILARITIES BETWEEN ERIKSON'S AND MAHLER'S THEORIES

As you read about Erikson's and Mahler's theories, undoubtedly you noticed several common themes. Each regards warm, sensitive parenting as vital for personality development. In addition, each theorist views toddlerhood as a time of budding selfhood. For Erikson, it is a stage when children achieve autonomous control over basic impulses; for Mahler, it is a period during which they learn to separate confidently from the parent. Both theorists also agree that when children emerge from the first few years without sufficient trust in caregivers and a healthy sense of individuality, the seeds are sown for adjustment problems. Adults who have difficulty establishing intimate ties to others, who are overly dependent on a loved one, or who continually doubt their own ability to meet new challenges may not have fully mastered the tasks of trust, autonomy, and individuation during infancy and toddlerhood.

Erikson and Mahler arrived at their conclusions by using the clinical method (see Chapter 1) to study normal mother–infant pairs as well as children and adults with serious emotional problems. As we examine research based on other methods in the remainder of this chapter, we will return many times to the perceptive observations of these two theorists.

BRIEF REVIEW

Erikson's and Mahler's psychoanalytic theories provide an overview of the emotional and social tasks of infancy and toddlerhood. According to Erikson, basic trust and autonomy grow out of warm, supportive parenting and reasonable expectations for impulse control during the second year. Mahler's theory suggests that sensitive exchange of emotional signals between mother and baby leads to a symbiotic bond, which provides the foundation for a confident sense of self as infants crawl and then walk on their own. Both theorists agree that the development of trust and individuality during infancy and toddlerhood have lasting consequences for personality development.

ASK YOURSELF . . .

- Derek's mother fed him in a warm and loving manner during the first year. But when he became a toddler, she kept him in a playpen for many hours because he got into too much mischief while exploring freely. Use Erikson's theory to evaluate Derek's early experiences.
- Around 18 months, Betina became clingy and dependent. She followed her mother around the house and asked to be held often. How would Mahler account for Betina's behavior? How should Betina's parents respond?

EMOTIONAL DEVELOPMENT DURING THE FIRST TWO YEARS

In the previous chapter, I suggested that you find some time to observe several infants and parents, noting babies' increasingly effective schemes for controlling the environment and ways that adults support cognitive and language development. Now focus on another aspect of infant and caregiver behavior: the expression and exchange of emotions. While you observe, note the various emotions the infant displays, the cues you rely on to interpret the baby's feelings, and how the caregiver responds.

Over the past 20 years, researchers have conducted many such observations to find out how effectively babies communicate their feelings and interpret those of others. They have discovered that emotions play a powerful role in organizing the events that Erikson and Mahler regarded as so important during the early years—relationships with caregivers, exploration of the environment, and discovery of the self (Barrett & Campos, 1987; Campos et al., 1983).

DEVELOPMENT OF SOME BASIC EMOTIONS

Since infants cannot describe their feelings, researchers face a challenging task in determining exactly which emotions they are experiencing. Sounds (a cheerful squeal or an intense, loud cry) and body movements (a joyful strut or furious kicking and stomping) provide some information, but facial expressions seem to offer the most reliable cues. Cross-cultural evidence indicates that when looking at photographs of different facial gestures, people around the world associate them with emotions in the same way (Ekman & Friesen, 1972). These findings inspired researchers to carefully analyze infants' facial expressions to determine the range of emotions they display at different ages. A commonly used method for doing so is illustrated in Figure 7.1.

Do infants come into the world with the ability to express a wide variety of emotions? Some investigators regard the emotional life of the newborn baby as quite limited. For example, according to one view, discrete emotions gradually emerge over the first year out of two global arousal states: the newborn baby's tendency to approach pleasant and withdraw from unpleasant stimulation (Fox, 1991; Sroufe, 1979). Other theorists believe that all the **basic emotions**—those that can be directly inferred from facial expressions, such as happiness, interest, surprise, fear, anger, sadness, and disgust—are present in the first few weeks of life (Campos et al., 1983; Izard, 1991).

Research on young babies' facial patterns suggests that their expressive capacity may lie somewhere in between these two extremes. When adults are asked to label the emotion reflected in a variety of infant facial gestures or facial expressions are rated using the system described in Figure 7.1, positive emotions can be identified with ease, but specific negative emotions are difficult to detect (Matias & Cohn, 1993; Oster, Hegley, & Nagel, 1992). These findings suggest that facial expressions, and perhaps the experience of emotion, are less differentiated in infants than in older individuals. Still, most researchers agree that signs of almost all the basic emotions are present in early infancy and that each becomes more recognizable with age (Malatesta-Magai, Izard, & Camras, 1991; Sroufe, 1979). Three emotions—happiness, anger, and fear—have received the most research attention. Let's see how they change over the first year.

HAPPINESS. Happiness—first in terms of blissful smiles and later through exuberant laughter—contributes to many aspects of development. Infants smile and laugh when they conquer new skills, expressing their delight in cognitive and physical mastery. The smile also encourages caregivers to be affectionate as well as stimulating, so the baby will smile even more. Happiness binds parent and baby into a warm, supportive relationship and, at the same time, fosters the infant's developing competence.

During the early weeks, newborn babies smile when full, during sleep, and in response to gentle touches and sounds, such as stroking of the skin, rocking, and the mother's soft, high-pitched voice (Emde & Koenig, 1969). By the end of the first month, infants start to smile at interesting sights, but these must be dynamic, eye-catching events, such as a bright object jumping suddenly across the baby's field of vision. Between 6 and 10 weeks, the human face evokes a broad grin called the **social smile**, which is soon accompanied by pleasurable cooing (Sroufe & Waters, 1976). By 3 months, infants smile most often when interacting with people, indicating that they identify human beings as having unique social qualities (Ellsworth, Muir, & Hains, 1993). Perhaps you can already tell that early changes in smiling parallel the development of infant perceptual capacities—in particular, babies' increasing sensitivity to visual patterns, including the human face—that we discussed in Chapter 5.

Laughter, which appears around 3 to 4 months, reflects faster processing of information than smiling. But like smiling, the first laughs occur in response to very

Basic emotions
Emotions that can be directly inferred from facial expressions, such as happiness, interest, surprise, fear, anger, sadness, and disgust.

Social smile
The smile evoked by the stimulus of the human face. First appears between 6 and 10 weeks.

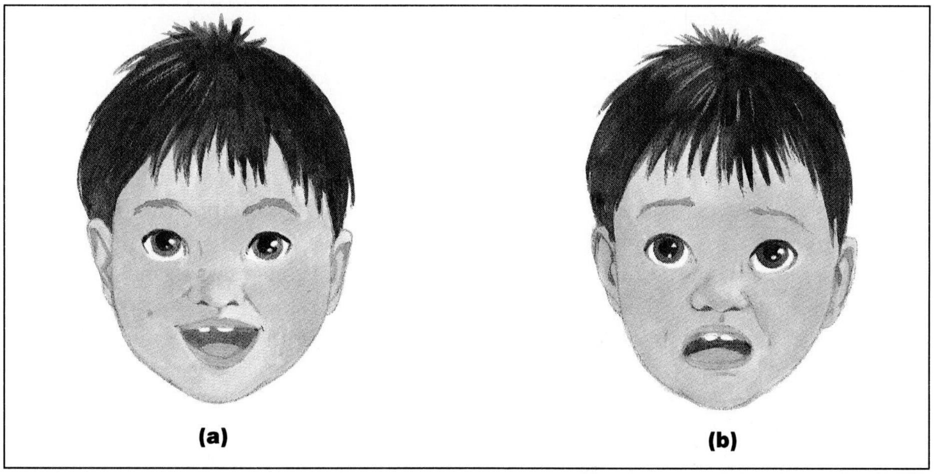

FIGURE 7.1

Which emotions are these babies displaying?
The MAX (Maximally Discriminative Facial Movement) System is a widely used method for classifying infants' emotional expressions. Facial muscle movements are carefully rated to determine their correspondence with basic feeling states. For example, cheeks raised and corners of the mouth pulled back and up signal happiness (a). Eyebrows raised, eyes widened, and mouth opened with corners pulled straight back denote fear (b). *(From Izard, 1979.)*

active stimuli, such as the mother saying playfully, "I'm gonna get you!" and kissing the baby's tummy. Over time, as infants understand more about their world, they laugh at events that contain more subtle elements of surprise. At 10 months, Byron chuckled as Lisa played a silent game of peekaboo. At 1 year, he laughed heartily as she crawled on all fours and then walked like a penguin (Sroufe & Wunsch, 1972).

Around the middle of the first year, infants smile and laugh more often when interacting with familiar people, a preference that supports and strengthens the parent–child bond. During the second year, the smile becomes a deliberate social signal. Toddlers break their play with an interesting toy to turn around and communicate their delight to an attentive adult (Jones & Raag, 1989).

■ ANGER AND FEAR. Newborn babies respond with generalized distress to a variety of unpleasant experiences, including hunger, painful medical procedures, changes in body temperature, and too much or too little stimulation (see Chapter 4). During the first 2 months, fleeting expressions that seem like anger appear as babies cry. These gradually increase in frequency and intensity from 4 to 6 months into the second year. At the same time, babies show anger in wider range of situations—for example, when an interesting object or event is removed, their arms are restrained, the caregiver leaves for a brief time, or they are put down for a nap (Camras et al., 1992; Stenberg & Campos, 1990).

Like anger, fear rises during the second half of the first year. Older infants hesitate before playing with new toy that they would have grasped immediately at an earlier age. And, as we saw in Chapter 5, research with the visual cliff reveals that they start to show fear of heights by avoiding edges and drop-offs around this time. But the most frequent expression of fear is to unfamiliar adults, a response called **stranger anxiety.** Many infants and toddlers are quite wary of strangers, although the reaction does not always occur. It depends on several factors: the infant's temperament (some babies are generally more fearful), past experiences with strangers, and the situation in which baby and stranger meet (Thompson & Limber, 1991).

To understand these influences, let's return for a moment to Rachel's fearful withdrawal from her grandparents, described at the beginning of this chapter. From birth, Rachel's mother cared for her continuously. She had little opportunity to get to know strange adults. Also, she met her grandparents for the first time in an unfamiliar environment (a crowded airport), and they rushed over and tried to hold her. Under these conditions, babies are most likely to display fearful reactions (Emde, Gaensbauer, & Harmon, 1976). Later, at home, Rachel watched with interest and approached as her grandmother sat quietly on the sofa, smiling and holding out a teddy bear. A familiar setting, the opportunity to become acquainted from a distance, and warmth and friendliness on the part of the stranger reduced Rachel's fear (Horner, 1980).

Stranger anxiety
The infant's expression of fear in response to unfamiliar adults. Appears in many babies after 6 months of age.

At this point, you may be wondering: Just what is the significance of this rise in anger and fear after 6 months of age? Researchers believe that these emotions have special survival value as infants' motor capacities improve. Older babies can use the energy mobilized by anger to defend themselves or overcome obstacles to blocked goals. Fear becomes especially adaptive as infants begin to crawl and walk. It keeps babies' enthusiasm for exploration in check, making it more likely that they will remain close to the caregiver's side and be careful about approaching unfamiliar people and objects. Anger and fear are also strong social signals that motivate caregivers to approach and comfort a suffering infant and, in the case of separation, may discourage them from leaving again soon.

Finally, cognitive development plays an important role in infants' angry and fearful reactions, just as it does in their expressions of happiness. Between 8 and 12 months, when (as Piaget pointed out) babies grasp the notion of intentional behavior, they have a better understanding of the cause of their frustrations. Therefore, they know whom or what to get angry at. In the case of fear, improved memories permit older infants to distinguish familiar events from strange ones better than they could before.

UNDERSTANDING AND RESPONDING TO THE EMOTIONS OF OTHERS

Infants' emotional expressions are closely tied to their ability to understand and respond to the feelings of others. In Chapter 5, we noted that between 2 and 3 months, babies begin to inspect the internal features of faces. Around this time, they respond in kind to an adult's facial expressions. When the mother smiles and gently talks, babies react with interest and joy. When she displays a depressed, frozen gaze, they show sadness and look away. And when she expresses anger, infants are likely to respond with angry sounds, facial gestures, and body movements (Haviland & Lelwica, 1987; Toda & Fogel, 1993). Between 7 and 10 months, infants perceive facial expressions as organized patterns, and they can match the emotional tone of a voice with the appropriate face of a speaking person (Soken & Pick, 1992).

These observations reveal that the capacity to recognize and interpret emotional signals in meaningful ways improves over the first year. Soon babies realize that an emotional expression not only has meaning, but is a meaningful reaction to a specific object or event (Bornstein & Lamb, 1992). Once these understandings are in place, infants engage in **social referencing,** in which they actively seek information about a trusted person's feelings in an uncertain situation. Beginning at 8 to 10 months, when infants start to evaluate events with regard to their safety and security, social referencing occurs often. Many studies show that a caregiver's emotional expression (happy, angry, or fearful) influences whether a 1-year-old will show wariness of strangers, play with an unfamiliar toy, or cross the deep side of the visual cliff (Rosen, Adamson, & Bakeman, 1992; Sorce et al., 1985; Walden & Ogan, 1988).

Social referencing provides infants with a powerful means of learning about the world through indirect experience. By recognizing and responding to caregivers' emotional cues, babies can avoid harmful situations (such as a shock from an electric outlet or a fall down a steep staircase) without first experiencing their unpleasant consequences. And through social referencing, parents teach their newly crawling and walking youngsters, whose capacity to explore the environment is rapidly expanding, how to react to a great many novel events.

Social referencing
Relying on a trusted person's emotional reaction to decide how to respond in an uncertain situation.

Self-conscious emotions
Emotions that involve injury to or enhancement of the sense of self. Examples are shame, embarrassment, guilt, envy, and pride.

EMERGENCE OF SELF-CONSCIOUS EMOTIONS

Besides basic emotions, humans are capable of a second, higher-order set of feelings, including shame, embarrassment, guilt, envy, and pride. These are called **self-conscious emotions** because each involves injury to or enhancement of our sense of self. For example, when we are ashamed or

Among the !Kung of Botswana, Africa, very young children are encouraged to help and share. Perhaps this toddler already feels a sense of pride as she tries to assist her grandmother with food preparation. *(Konner/Anthro-Photo)*

embarrassed, we feel negatively about ourselves. In contrast, pride reflects delight in the self's achievements (Campos et al., 1983).

Self-conscious emotions appear at the end of the second year, as the sense of self emerges. Between 18 and 24 months, children can be seen feeling ashamed and embarrassed as they lower their eyes, hang their heads, and hide their faces with their hands. Pride also emerges around this time, and envy and guilt are present by age 3 (Lewis et al., 1989; Sroufe, 1979). Besides self-awareness, self-conscious emotions require an additional ingredient: adult instruction in ***when*** to feel proud, ashamed, or guilty. Parents begin to provide this tutoring early, when they say to the toddler and preschooler, "My, look at how far you can throw that ball!" or "Shame on you for grabbing that toy from Billy!"

As these comments indicate, self-conscious emotions help children acquire socially valued behaviors and goals. The situations in which adults encourage children to experience these feelings vary considerably from culture to culture. In most of the United States, children are taught to feel pride over personal achievement—throwing a ball the farthest, winning a game, and (later on) getting good grades. Among the Zuni Indians, shame and embarrassment occur in response to purely personal success, whereas pride is evoked by generosity, helpfulness, and sharing (Benedict, 1934a). In Japan, violating cultural standards of concern for others' feelings and needs—those of a parent, a teacher, or an employer—is cause for intense shame (Lewis, 1992a).

THE BEGINNINGS OF EMOTIONAL SELF-REGULATION

Besides expanding their range of emotional reactions, infants and toddlers begin to find ways to manage their emotional experiences. **Emotional self-regulation** refers to the strategies we use to adjust our emotional state to a comfortable level of intensity so we can accomplish our goals (Dodge, 1989; Thompson, 1990a, 1994). If you drank a cup of coffee to wake yourself up this morning, reminded yourself that an anxiety-provoking event would be over soon, or decided not to see a horror movie because it might frighten you, you were engaging in emotional self-regulation.

In the early months of life, infants have only a limited capacity to regulate their emotional states. Although they can turn away from unpleasant stimulation and mouth and suck when their feelings get too intense, they are easily overwhelmed by internal and external stimuli. As a result, they depend on the soothing interventions of caregivers—lifting the distressed infant to the shoulder, rocking, and talking softly—for help in adjusting their emotional reactions.

Rapid development of the cortex (see Chapter 5) gradually increases the baby's tolerance for stimulation. Between 2 and 4 months, caregivers start to build on this capacity by initiating face-to-face play and attention to objects. In these rich interactional sequences in which emotional signals are exchanged, parents arouse pleasure in the baby while adjusting the pace of their own behavior so the infant does not

Emotional self-regulation
Strategies for adjusting our emotional state to a comfortable level of intensity.

become overwhelmed and distressed. As a result, the baby's tolerance for stimulation increases further (Kopp, 1989, Thompson, 1990a). By the end of the first year, infants' ability to move about permits them to regulate feelings more effectively by approaching or retreating from various stimuli.

As caregivers help infants regulate their emotional states, they also provide lessons in socially approved ways of expressing feelings. The unrestrained expression of negative emotion is not acceptable in most cultures because it interferes with successful social interaction. Beginning in the first few months, American middle-class mothers match their baby's positive feelings far more often than the negative ones. In this way, they encourage happiness and discourage anger and sadness. Interestingly, boys get much more of this training than do girls. Mothers respond less often to a baby boy's cries of distress than to a girl's. The well-known sex difference—females as emotionally expressive and males as emotionally controlled—is promoted at a very tender age (Malatesta & Haviland, 1982; Malatesta et al., 1986).

By the second year, growth in representation and language leads to new ways of regulating emotions. A vocabulary of words for talking about feelings, such as "happy," "love," "surprised," "scary," "yucky," and "mad," develops rapidly after 18 months (Bretherton et al., 1986; Dunn, Bretherton, & Munn, 1987). By describing their emotions, toddlers can guide caregivers in ways that will help them feel better. For example, when 2-year-old Rachel listened in on a story about monsters that Lisa was reading to Byron, she could tell her mother that she felt afraid:

Rachel: Mommy! (whining)

Beth: What's wrong, Rachel?

Rachel: Scary.

Beth: What? The book?

Rachel: Yes. Scary book. Put away.

Beth: We can't put it away yet. Byron's looking at it.

Rachel: (Walks toward her mother, about to cry). Hug Rachel.

Toddlers' use of words to label feelings shows that they already have a remarkable understanding of themselves and others as emotional beings. As we will see in later chapters, development of the ability to think about feelings leads emotional self-regulation to improve greatly during early and middle childhood.

ASK YOURSELF . . .

- Dana is planning to meet her 10-month-old niece Laureen for the first time. How should Dana expect Laureen to react? How would you advise Dana to go about establishing a positive relationship with Laureen?
- One of Byron's favorite games was dancing with his mother while she sang "Old MacDonald," clapping his hands and stepping from side to side. At 14 months, Byron danced joyfully as Beth and Felicia watched. At 20 months, he began to show signs of embarrassment—smiling, looking away, and covering his eyes with his hands. What explains this change in Byron's emotional reaction?

BRIEF REVIEW

Changes in infants' ability to express emotion and respond to the emotions of others reflect their developing cognitive capacities and serve social as well as survival functions. The social smile appears between 6 and 10 weeks, laughter around 3 to 4 months. In the middle of the first year, anger and fear start to increase. Young infants match the feeling tone of their caregivers' facial expressions. At 8 to 10 months, they begin to engage in social referencing, actively seeking information about the caregiver's feelings in an uncertain situation. Self-conscious emotions, such as shame, embarrassment, and pride, emerge at the end of the second year as toddlers develop self-awareness. Emotional self-regulation is supported by brain maturation, improvements in cognition and language, and sensitive child-rearing practices.

TEMPERAMENT AND DEVELOPMENT

Throughout the first year, Byron, Rachel, and April each showed joy, anger, sadness, fear, interest, and higher or lower activity levels in certain situations. But as I got to know them well, their unique patterns of emotional responding became apparent. Byron was constantly in motion. As early as the first few weeks of life, he wriggled about in his crib and squirmed vigorously on the diaper table. When he crawled and walked, his parents found themselves chasing after him as he dropped one toy, moved on to the next, and climbed on chairs and tables. Lisa envied Beth's calm, relaxed experience with Rachel. At 7 months, she managed to sit through a lengthy family celebration at a restaurant, remaining contented in her high chair for almost 2 hours. And April's sociability was unmistakable to everyone who met her. She smiled and laughed at adults and was especially at ease in the company of other children, whom she readily approached during the second year.

When we describe one person as cheerful and "upbeat," another as active and energetic, and still others as calm, cautious, or prone to angry outbursts, we are referring to **temperament**—stable individual differences in quality and intensity of emotional reaction (Goldsmith, 1987). Researchers have become increasingly interested in temperamental differences among infants and children, since the child's style of emotional responding is believed to form the cornerstone of the adult personality.

The New York Longitudinal Study, initiated in 1956 by Alexander Thomas and Stella Chess, is the most comprehensive and longest-lasting study of temperament to date. A total of 141 children were followed from the first few months of life over a period that now extends well into adulthood. Results showed that temperament is a major factor in increasing the chances that a child will experience psychological problems or, alternatively, be protected from the effects of a highly stressful home life. However, Thomas and Chess (1977) also found that temperament is not fixed and unchangeable. Parenting practices can modify children's emotional styles considerably.

These findings inspired a growing body of research on temperament, including its stability, its biological roots, and its interaction with child-rearing experiences. But before we review what is known about these issues, let's look at how temperament is measured.

MEASURING TEMPERAMENT

Temperament is usually assessed in one of three ways: through interviews and questionnaires given to parents; through behavior ratings by doctors, nurses, or caregivers who know the child well; or through direct observation by researchers (Bates, 1987). Recently, physiological measures have been used to supplement these techniques. For example, highly inhibited, shy children show greater electrical activity in the right than in the left hemisphere of the cortex, whereas their more sociable counterparts show the reverse pattern (Fox, Bell, & Jones, 1992).[1] And as we will see later, the heart rates of many inhibited children speed up in response to unfamiliar or stressful events, and they also produce more cortisol (a hormone that regulates blood pressure) than do their uninhibited agemates (Gunnar & Nelson, 1994; Kagan & Snidman, 1991). Researchers hope that these measures will shed light on the genetic basis and role of various brain structures in the development of temperament.

Most often, parental reports are used to assess temperament because parents have a depth of knowledge about the child that cannot be matched by any other

[1]Recall from Chapter 5 that the right cortical hemisphere is specialized to mediate the display of negative emotion, the left hemisphere positive emotion (see page 176).

Temperament
Stable individual differences in quality and intensity of emotional reaction.

TABLE 7.1

Nine Dimensions of Temperament

DIMENSION	DESCRIPTION AND EXAMPLE
Activity level	Proportion of active periods to inactive ones. Some babies are always in motion. Others move about very little.
Rhythmicity	Regularity of body functions. Some infants fall asleep, wake up, get hungry, and have bowel movements on a regular schedule, whereas others are much less predictable.
Distractibility	Degree to which stimulation from the environment alters behavior. Some hungry babies stop crying temporarily if offered a pacifier or a toy to play with. Others continue to cry until fed.
Approach–withdrawal	Response to a new object or person. Some babies accept new foods and smile and babble at strangers, whereas others pull back and cry on first exposure.
Adaptability	Ease with which the child adapts to changes in the environment. Although some infants withdraw when faced with new experiences, they quickly adapt, accepting the new food or person on the next occasion. Others continue to fuss and cry over an extended period of time.
Attention span and persistence	Amount of time devoted to an activity. Some babies watch a mobile or play with a toy for a long time, whereas others lose interest after a few minutes.
Intensity of reaction	Intensity or energy level of response. Some infants laugh and cry loudly, whereas others react only mildly.
Threshold of responsiveness	Intensity of stimulation required to evoke a response. Some babies startle at the slightest change in sound or lighting. Others take little notice of these changes in stimulation.
Quality of mood	Amount of friendly, joyful behavior as opposed to unpleasant, unfriendly behavior. Some babies smile and laugh frequently when playing and interacting with people. Others fuss and cry often.

Source: Thomas, Chess, & Birch, 1970.

source. Information from parents has been criticized for being biased and subjective, but it is useful for understanding the way parents view and respond to their child (Sirignano & Lachman, 1985). And when parents describe a baby as extreme in some aspect of temperament, independent observations usually confirm their judgments. For example, babies regarded as irritable and difficult by their mothers do show high levels of fussing and crying (Worobey & Blajda, 1989).

In the New York Longitudinal Study, detailed descriptions of each child's behavior were collected regularly from parents. When carefully analyzed, these yielded nine dimensions of temperament, which are summarized in Table 7.1. The researchers noticed that certain characteristics clustered together, producing three types of children that described the majority of their sample:

- The **easy child** (40 percent of the sample). This child quickly establishes regular routines in infancy, is generally cheerful, and adapts easily to new experiences.
- The **difficult child** (10 percent of the sample). This child is irregular in daily routines, is slow to accept new experiences, and tends to react negatively and intensely.
- The **slow-to-warm-up child** (15 percent of the sample). This child is inactive, shows mild, low-key reactions to environmental stimuli, is negative in mood, and adjusts slowly to new experiences.

Notice that 35 percent of the children did not fit any of these patterns. Instead, they showed unique blends of temperamental characteristics. Although other systems for classifying temperament do exist (Buss & Plomin, 1984; Rothbart, 1981), these nine dimensions and three styles provide a fairly complete picture of the traits most often studied.

Easy child
A child whose temperament is such that he or she quickly establishes regular routines in infancy, is generally cheerful, and adapts easily to new experiences.

Difficult child
A child whose temperament is such that he or she is irregular in daily routines, is slow to accept new experiences, and tends to react negatively and intensely.

Slow-to-warm-up child
A child whose temperament is such that he or she is inactive, shows mild, low-key reactions to environmental stimuli, is negative in mood, and adjusts slowly when faced with new experiences.

STABILITY OF TEMPERAMENT

It would be difficult to claim that something like temperament really exists if children's emotional styles were not stable over time. Indeed, the findings of many studies provide support for the long-term stability of temperament. An infant who scores low or high on activity level, rhythmicity, attention span, irritability, sociability, or shyness is likely to respond similarly when assessed again in childhood and, occasionally, even into the adult years (Caspi, Elder, & Bem, 1987, 1988; Goldsmith & Gottesman, 1981; Kochanska & Radke-Yarrow, 1992; Pedlow et al., 1993; Riese, 1987; Ruff et al., 1990). The temperamental styles identified in the New York Longitudinal Study are also fairly stable. Compared to easy children, difficult preschoolers are more likely to show problems in concentrating and getting along with peers after they enter school. And slow-to-warm-up youngsters are often overwhelmed by demands that they adapt quickly to new experiences in school, a circumstance that may intensify their withdrawal in middle childhood (Chess & Thomas, 1984; Thomas, Chess, & Korn, 1982).

When the evidence as a whole is examined carefully, however, temperamental stability from one age period to the next is usually modest. Although quite a few children remain the same, a good number have changed when assessed again as soon as a year or two later. In fact, some characteristics, such as shyness and sociability, are stable over the long term only in children at the extremes—those who are very inhibited or very outgoing to begin with (Kerr et al., 1994; Robinson et al., 1992).

A story that a mother recently told me about her two daughters illustrates the finding that early temperament persists for some but not all youngsters. The older girl, Allie, was active and sociable as a baby and remained so. On moving to a new neighborhood at age 6, she boldly went from house to house knocking on doors, asking if there were any children to play with. Throughout her school years, Allie was a joiner. By the time she graduated from high school, she had been cheerleader, prom queen, president of the senior class, captain of the tennis team, and an active participant in several clubs. In contrast, Allie's younger sister Keri was shy and withdrawn. As her mother put it, during infancy "she just sat there." At age 3, Keri reacted to the move to a new neighborhood by hiding behind her mother when children approached. Throughout middle childhood, she needed time to "warm up"—to new foods, new people, and new challenges in school. But by eighth grade, Keri began to look different. "We were astonished when she tried out for the basketball team and made it, especially since basketball requires so much physical assertiveness," her mother commented. The following year, Keri joined the tennis team and, like her sister, became president of her high school class. Her schoolmates valued her patient, considerate style of relating to others.

The fact that early in life, children show marked individual differences in temperament, some of which are related to physiological reactions, indicates that biological factors play an important role. At the same time, the changes shown by children such as Keri suggest that temperament can be modified by experience (although shy children rarely become highly sociable). Let's take a close look at genetic and environmental contributions to temperament in the following sections.

Alexander Thomas and Stella Chess initiated the New York Longitudinal Study, a comprehensive investigation of temperament in which 141 children were followed from infancy into adulthood. Thomas and Chess's groundbreaking methods and findings inspired a burst of research on the role of temperament in development. *(Courtesy of Alexander Thomas and Stella Chase)*

GENETIC INFLUENCES

The very word *temperament* implies a genetic foundation for individual differences in emotional style. In recent years, many studies have compared identical with fraternal twins to find out if heredity is involved. The findings reveal that identicals are more similar than fraternals across a wide range of temperamental traits (activity level, sociability, intensity of emotional reaction, attention span, and persistence) and personality measures (introversion, extroversion, anxiety, and impulsivity)

(Emde et al., 1992; Plomin, Chipuer, & Loehlin, 1990; Robinson et al., 1992; Saudino & Eaton, 1991). In Chapter 2, we indicated that heritability estimates derived from twin studies suggest a moderate role for genetic factors in temperament and personality: About half of the individual differences among us can be traced to differences in our genetic makeup.

New research on shyness provides further support for the importance of heredity. Early in life, children who are cautious and reserved differ in physiological reactions from those who are outgoing and emotionally expressive. At 4 months, inhibited, withdrawn babies show high rates of motor activity, fretting and crying when faced with new sights and sounds (Kagan & Snidman, 1991). By the end of the first year, highly stimulating, unfamiliar experiences (such as a battery-powered robot or a bingo cage filled with noisy, colorful balls) cause their hearts to race, their pupils to dilate, and their muscles to tense up. Under the same conditions, sociable infants remain relaxed and composed (Kagan, 1992). Shy people are also more likely to have certain physical traits—blue eyes, thin faces, and hay fever—known to be influenced by heredity. Researchers believe that the genes controlling these characteristics may also contribute to a fearful, reactive temperamental style (Kagan, Reznick, & Snidman, 1988).

Finally, consistent ethnic and sex differences in early temperament exist, again implying a role for heredity. Compared to Caucasian infants, Chinese and Japanese babies tend to be less active, irritable, and vocal, more easily soothed when upset, and better at quieting themselves (Kagan et al., 1994; Lewis, Ramsay, & Kawakami, 1993). Rachel's capacity to remain contentedly seated in her high chair through a long family dinner certainly fits with this evidence. And Byron's high rate of activity is consistent with sex differences in emotional styles. From an early age, boys tend to be more active and daring and girls more anxious and timid—a difference reflected in boys' higher accident rates throughout childhood and adolescence (Jacklin & Maccoby, 1983; Richardson, Koller, & Katz, 1986).

ENVIRONMENTAL INFLUENCES

Although hereditary influences on temperament are clear, no study has shown that infants maintain their early emotional styles in the absence of environmental supports. Instead, heredity and environment combine to strengthen the stability of temperament, since (as we saw in Chapter 2), the child's approach to the world affects the experiences to which she is exposed. To see how this works, let's take a second look at sex and ethnic differences in temperament.

As I watched Beth care for Rachel as a 3-month-old baby, her calm, soothing manner and use of gentle rocking and touching contrasted with Lisa and Felicia's stimulation of their infants through lively facial expressions and talking. These differences in caregiving appear repeatedly in studies comparing American with Asian infant–mother pairs (Fogel, Toda, & Kawai, 1988; Otaki et al., 1986). The findings suggest that some differences in early temperament are encouraged by cultural beliefs and practices. When Japanese mothers are asked about their approach to child rearing, they respond that babies come into the world as independent beings who must learn to rely on their mothers through close physical contact. American mothers are likely to believe just the opposite—that they must wean the baby away from dependence into autonomy (Doi, 1973; Kojima, 1986). As a result, Japanese mothers do more comforting and American mothers more stimulating—behaviors that enhance early temperamental differences between their infants.

A similar process seems to be at work as far as sex differences in temperament are concerned. Within the first 24 hours after birth (before they could have had much experience with the baby), parents already perceive male and female newborns differently. Sons are rated as larger, better coordinated, more alert, and stronger.

Daughters are viewed as softer, more awkward, weaker, and more delicate (Rubin, Provenzano, & Luria, 1974; Stern & Karraker, 1989). These gender-stereotyped beliefs carry over into the way parents treat their infants and toddlers. For example, parents more often encourage infant sons to be physically active and daughters to seek help and physical closeness. These practices promote and sustain temperamental differences between boys and girls (Fagot, 1978; Smith & Lloyd, 1978).

In families with several children, an additional influence on temperament is at work. Parents often look for and emphasize each child's unique characteristics (Plomin, 1989). You can see this in the comments parents make after the birth of a second baby: "He's so much calmer," "She's a lot more active," or "He's more sociable." Research shows that when one child in a family is viewed as easy, another is likely to be perceived as difficult, even though the second child might not be very difficult when compared to children in general (Schachter & Stone, 1985). Each child, in turn, evokes responses from caregivers that are consistent with parental views and with the child's actual temperamental style. These findings demonstrate that temperament and personality can only be understood in terms of complex interdependencies between genetic and environmental factors.

TEMPERAMENT AND CHILD REARING: THE GOODNESS-OF-FIT MODEL

We have already indicated that the temperaments of many children do change over time. For example, only half of shy, "slow-to-warm-up" babies like Keri will remain so at age 6. Even fewer will qualify as timid and withdrawn by the time they reach young adulthood, although these children rarely become highly sociable. This suggests that environments do not always act in the same direction as a child's temperament. In fact, if a child's disposition interferes with learning or getting along with others, it is important for adults to gently but consistently counteract the child's maladaptive behavior.

The concept of **goodness of fit** describes how temperament and environmental pressures can work together to produce favorable outcomes (Thomas & Chess, 1977). Goodness of fit involves creating child-rearing environments that recognize each child's temperament while helping the youngster achieve more adaptive functioning. In short, children with different temperaments have unique child-rearing needs. In the case of sociable Allie, a neighborhood rich in playmates was sufficient for her to reach out and develop rewarding friendships. But Keri's inhibited behavior required quite different handling. In infancy, her parents needed to sit quietly by, slowly drawing her into interaction with other people. And during the preschool years, surrounding her with several children at once was overwhelming. She needed one playmate at a time, help from adults in getting an activity started, and several meetings arranged by her mother until she felt comfortable with the new child. Had Keri been forced into social situations or criticized for her shyness, she might not have developed into the self-confident, popular youngster that she became by early adolescence.

Research shows how a "good fit" between child rearing and a related aspect of temperament—activity level—promotes exploration, which is crucial for cognitive mastery. Inactive toddlers whose mothers engage in rich verbal stimulation (frequently instructing, questioning, and pointing out objects) benefit from this encouragement; they explore the environment more freely. But for active toddlers, this style of parenting seems to interfere with their ability to provide themselves with stimulation, and exploration is reduced (Gandour, 1989). Recall from Chapter 6 that Lisa often behaved in a highly stimulating, intrusive way with Byron. A "poor fit" between her behavior and Byron's active temperament may have contributed to his tendency to move from one activity to the next with little involvement.

Goodness of fit
An effective match between child-rearing practices and a child's temperament, leading to favorable adjustment.

As the From Research to Practice box below indicates, parenting that is in tune with the child's temperament is particularly important for difficult youngsters, who are at special risk for adjustment problems. In infancy, difficult children are far less likely than easy children to receive sensitive care (Crockenberg, 1986). By the second year, their parents often resort to angry, punitive discipline. In response, the child reacts with defiance and disobedience. Then parents are likely to behave inconsistently, rewarding the child's noncompliant behavior by giving into it, although they initially resisted (Lee & Bates, 1985). The difficult child's temperament combined with harsh child rearing forms a poor fit that maintains and increases the child's irritable, conflict-ridden style. In contrast, when parents are warm and responsive and establish a happy, stable home life despite their child's negative behavior, infant difficultness declines (Belsky, Fish, & Isabella, 1991; Crockenberg, 1986).

The concept of goodness of fit reminds us that babies come into the world with unique dispositions that adults need to accept. Children cannot be molded in ways

FROM RESEARCH TO PRACTICE

DIFFICULT CHILDREN: WHEN PARENTS ESTABLISH A "GOOD FIT"

In the New York Longitudinal Study, 70 percent of children who were temperamentally difficult in the early years developed serious behavior problems by middle childhood. But in no case was this outcome the result of temperament alone. Instead, it occurred because the negative behaviors of difficult children often provoked parental reactions that fit poorly with their basic dispositions. The case of Carl, one of the most difficult youngsters in the New York Longitudinal sample, illustrates how long-term outcomes for these children are a function of rearing experiences (Thomas & Chess, 1977).

As a baby, Carl rejected almost all new situations, such as his first bath and spoonfuls of solid food. He shrieked, cried, and struggled to get away. Yet his mother and father recognized that his behavior did not mean they were "bad parents." To the contrary, Carl's father viewed his emotional intensity as a sign of strength and vigor. And both parents believed that if they were patient, reduced the number of new situations that Carl had to deal with at one time, and provided him with opportunities for repeated exposure, he would, in the end, adapt positively.

By the time Carl reached school age, he was doing remarkably well. The energies that he put into rebellious tantrums were now channeled constructively. He was a good student and became enthusiastically involved in several activities. One of these was playing the piano—lessons that he had asked for but (as with other new experiences) at first disliked intensely. Carl's mother had granted the piano instruction on one condition: that he stick to the lessons for 6 months. Held to this bargain, Carl came to love his introduction to music. His parents' patience and consistency had helped him reorganize his behavior, accept and benefit from new learning opportunities, and avoid adjustment difficulties.

Harmony between rearing environments and child temperament is best accomplished early, before unfavorable temperament–environment relationships have had a chance to produce adjustment problems that are hard to undo. Parents of difficult infants and toddlers, especially, can benefit from interventions that encourage them to be warm and accepting while making firm, reasonable, and consistent demands for mastering new experiences and situations.

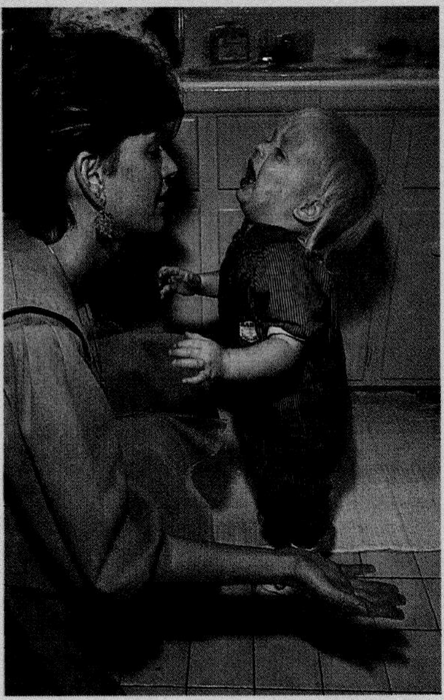

This mother is perplexed because her 1-year-old baby is not responding to her efforts to help him calm down. Difficult children react negatively and intensely to many new experiences. When parents are patient and provide opportunities for gradual, repeated exposure to new situations, difficultness often subsides. *(Nubar Alexanian/Stock Boston)*

that do not blend with their basic styles. This means that parents can neither take full credit for their children's virtues nor be blamed for all their faults—attitudes that were common a generation ago. But parents can turn an environment that exaggerates a child's problems into one that builds on the youngster's strengths, helping each child master the challenges of development.

In the following sections, we will see that goodness of fit is also at the heart of infant–caregiver attachment. This first intimate social relationship grows out of interaction between parent and baby, to which the emotional styles of both partners contribute.

BRIEF REVIEW

Children's unique temperamental styles are apparent in early infancy. However, the long-term stability of temperament is only modest; some children retain their original dispositions, while others change over time. Heredity influences early temperament, but child-rearing experiences determine whether a child's emotional style is sustained or modified over time. A good fit between parenting practices and child temperament helps children whose dispositions predispose them to adjustment problems achieve more adaptive functioning.

ASK YOURSELF . . .

- Rachel, like many other Asian infants, is calm and easily soothed when upset. What factors contribute to her temperamental style?
- At age 18 months, highly active Byron climbed out of his high chair long before his meal was finished. Exasperated with Byron's behavior, his father made him sit at the table until he had eaten all his food. Soon Byron's behavior escalated into a full-blown tantrum. Using the concept of goodness of fit, suggest another way of handling Byron.

DEVELOPMENT OF ATTACHMENT

Attachment is the strong, affectional tie we feel for special people in our lives that leads us to feel pleasure and joy when we interact with them and to be comforted by their nearness during times of stress. By the end of the first year, infants have become attached to familiar people who have responded to their need for physical care and stimulation. Watch babies of this age, and notice how parents are singled out for special attention. A whole range of responses are reserved just for them. For example, when the mother enters the room, the baby breaks into a broad, friendly smile. When she picks him up, he pats her face, explores her hair, and snuggles against her body. When he feels anxious or afraid, he crawls into her lap and clings closely.

EARLY THEORIES OF ATTACHMENT

Freud first suggested that the infant's emotional tie to the mother provides the foundation for all later relationships. We will see shortly that research on children deprived of an early caregiving relationship supports Freud's belief in the importance of the attachment bond. But attachment has also been the subject of intense theoretical debate for decades. Behaviorist and psychoanalytic theories were early views that competed with one another to explain how attachment developed. The problems with these theories eventually led to a new perspective, ethological theory, which is most popular today. As we take up each of these viewpoints, you may find it helpful to refer to the summary provided in Table 7.2.

■ BEHAVIORISM. Behaviorists believe that infants' attachment behaviors—seeking closeness to the mother, following her about, and crying and calling in her absence—are learned responses. The best-known behaviorist account is a **drive reduction explanation** that grants feeding a central role in the infant–caregiver relationship. As the baby's hunger (*primary drive*) is satisfied repeatedly by the

Attachment
The strong, affectional tie that humans feel toward special people in their lives.

Drive reduction explanation of attachment
A behaviorist view that regards the mother's satisfaction of the baby's hunger (primary drive) as the basis for the infant's preference for her (secondary drive).

TABLE 7.2

Three Theories of Attachment

THEORY	DESCRIPTION
Drive reduction (behaviorism)	As the mother satisfies the baby's hunger (primary drive), her presence is paired with tension relief and becomes a secondary or learned drive. This theory has been discredited by evidence that babies become attached to people who do not feed them.
Psychoanalytic	From warm, sensitive care, babies develop a sense of trust and a positive, inner image of the mother that enables them to separate from her and explore their world. This explanation has been criticized for placing too much emphasis on feeding and too little on the baby's contribution to the attachment bond.
Ethological	Attachment has evolved over the history of our species to promote survival, and both infant characteristics and quality of caregiving contribute to it. Babies move through four phases of development in which they develop a strong affectional tie to a familiar caregiver.

mother, her presence becomes a ***secondary*** or ***learned drive*** because it is paired with tension relief. As a result, the baby learns to prefer all kinds of stimuli that accompany feeding, including the mother's soft caresses, warm smiles, and tender words of comfort (Sears, Maccoby, & Levin, 1957).

Although feeding is an important context in which mothers and babies build a close relationship, today we know that the attachment bond does not depend on satisfying an infant's hunger. In the 1950s, a famous study of rhesus monkeys challenged the drive reduction explanation. Baby monkeys separated from their mothers at birth and reared with terrycloth and wire mesh "surrogate mothers" spent their days clinging to the terrycloth substitute, even though the wire mesh "mother" held the bottle and infants had to climb on it to be fed. The baby monkeys preferred the terrycloth (which resembled the soft body of a monkey mother), even though it had never been paired with feeding (Harlow & Zimmerman, 1959).

Observations of human infants also revealed that they become attached to family members who seldom if ever feed them, including fathers, siblings, and grandparents (Schaffer & Emerson, 1964). And perhaps you have noticed that toddlers, at least in Western cultures, develop strong emotional ties to cuddly objects, such as blankets and teddy bears (see the Cultural Influences box on the following page). Yet such objects have never played a role in infant feeding!

A second problem with the drive reduction account is that it cannot explain why the attachment relationship, once formed, tends to persist over long periods in which attachment figures are absent. Think about your own feelings of attachment for people whom you have not seen (and been reinforced by) in many months. Behaviorism would predict that your desire for closeness should ***extinguish,*** or disappear. Yet clearly it does not. Drive reduction has great difficulty explaining the remarkable endurance of human attachments over time and distance.

Baby monkeys reared with "surrogate mothers" from birth preferred to cling to a soft terry cloth "mother" instead of a wire mesh "mother" that held a bottle. These findings reveal that the drive reduction explanation of attachment, which assumes that the mother–infant relationship is based on feeding. *(Martin Rogers/Stock Boston)*

THE PSYCHOANALYTIC PERSPECTIVE. Psychoanalytic theorists, such as Erikson and Mahler, emphasize that the central ingredient in attachment is ***the quality of the mother's interaction*** with her baby. Once the infant develops a sense of trust that the mother will satisfy his needs, he can separate from her for short periods to explore the environment. Eventually the child forms a permanent, positive inner image of the mother that can be relied on for emotional support during brief absences.

Compared to behaviorism, the psychoanalytic approach provides a much richer view of the attachment bond, viewing it as critical for exploration of the environment, cognitive mastery, and emotional security. Psychoanalytic theories also recognize that deep affectional bonds, once formed, can endure over separations from loved individuals.

CULTURAL INFLUENCES

YOUNG CHILDREN'S ATTACHMENT TO SOFT OBJECTS

When Bruce was born, he received a soft, cuddly Pooh Bear—bright yellow with a red vest and a warm, smiling face. During his first few months, Bruce's mother made the bear nod and dance before his eyes. Soon Bruce laughed merrily at the bear's antics. The bear remained a favorite source of amusement for mother and baby throughout the first year.

When Bruce walked at 12 months, his interest in nursing at his mother's breast declined while his enthusiasm for exploration increased. At the same time, Pooh Bear became a special toy, accompanying Bruce everywhere he went during the day and to bed at night. During moments of fatigue and frustration, Bruce pressed the bear against his face and stroked it with his fingers, as if to substitute for the warm closeness he felt when cradled in his mother's arms.

The importance to small children of special objects, such as blankets, teddy bears, and other cuddly toys, has long been recognized by parents. Such attachments are highly frequent in Western cultures, where babies sleep in a separate room at night and experience frequent daytime separations from their caregivers. In contrast, objects of attachment are entirely absent in village and tribal societies in which caregivers are continuously available to infants (Hong & Townes, 1976; Morelli et al., 1992). This suggests that soft objects help children manage the stress of parental separation and serve as substitutes for special people when they are not available. In support of this idea, research shows that toddlers use attachment objects as a secure base of exploration in a strange playroom, in much the same way that they depend on their mothers for support when exposed to unfamiliar environments (Passman, 1976).

Soft, cuddly toys are normal and effective sources of security during a developmental period in which children increase their physical and psychological separateness from parents. Such objects help children recapture the comfort of physical closeness to the mother and provide emotional support when children are tired, upset, or exposed to unfamiliar, fear-arousing situations. Object-attached children are just as securely attached to parents and as well adjusted as other children (Mahalski, Silva, & Spears, 1985; Passman, 1987). No harm results from allowing a child who so chooses to become dependent on a cuddly comforter.

This toddler is attached to a soft, cuddly teddy bear and finds it comforting when she is fatigued, upset, or afraid. Objects of attachment are common in Western cultures, where infants and toddlers sleep in a separate room at night and experience frequent daytime separations from their caregivers. Object-attached children are just as well adjusted as other children. *(Elizabeth Crews)*

Despite its strengths, the psychoanalytic perspective has been criticized on two grounds. First, because it builds on Freud' oral stage, it (like the drive reduction explanation) overemphasizes the importance of feeding in the development of attachment. Second, if you return to Erikson's and Mahler's theories at the beginning of this chapter, you will see that a great deal is said about the mother's contribution to the attachment relationship. But much less attention is given to the importance of infants' characteristics and behavior. As we will see in the following section, ethological theory is unique in recognizing that babies contribute actively to ties established with their caregivers.

Ethological theory of attachment
A theory formulated by Bowlby, which views the infant's emotional tie to the caregiver as an evolved response that promotes survival.

BOWLBY'S ETHOLOGICAL THEORY

Today, **ethological theory of attachment** is the most widely accepted view of the infant's emotional tie to the caregiver. Recall from Chapter 1 that according to

This 1-year-old uses her mother as a secure base from which to explore. As long as the familiar caregiver is nearby, newly mobile infants typically approach their surroundings with enthusiasm. *(John Coletti/The Picture Cube)*

ethology, many human behaviors have evolved over the history of our species because they promote survival. John Bowlby (1969), who first applied this idea to the infant–caregiver bond, was originally a psychoanalyst. As you will see shortly, his theory retains a number of psychoanalytic features. At the same time, Bowlby was inspired by Konrad Lorenz's studies of imprinting in baby geese (see Chapter 1). He believed that the human infant, like the young of other animal species, is endowed with a set of built-in behaviors that help keep the parent nearby, increasing the chances that the infant will be protected from danger. Contact with the parent also ensures that the baby will be fed, but Bowlby was careful to point out that feeding is not the basis for attachment. Instead, the attachment bond has strong biological roots. It can best be understood within an evolutionary framework in which survival of the species is of utmost importance.

According to Bowlby, the infant's relationship to the parent begins as a set of innate signals that call the adult to the baby's side. Over time, a true affectional bond develops, which is supported by new emotional and cognitive capacities as well as a history of warm, responsive care. The development of attachment takes place in four phases:

1. *The preattachment phase* (birth to 6 weeks). A variety of built-in signals—grasping, smiling, crying, and gazing into the adult's eyes—help bring newborn babies into close contact with other humans. Once an adult responds, infants encourage her to remain nearby, since they are comforted when picked up, stroked, and talked to softly. Babies of this age can recognize their own mother's smell and voice (see Chapter 4). However, they are not yet attached to her, since they do not mind being left with an unfamiliar adult.

2. *The "attachment in the making" phase* (6 weeks to 6–8 months). During this phase, infants start to respond differently to a familiar caregiver than to a stranger. For example, at 4 months, Byron smiled, laughed, and babbled more freely when interacting with his mother and quieted more quickly when she picked him up. As infants engage in face-to-face interaction with the parent and experience relief from distress, they learn that their own actions affect the behavior of those around them. They begin to develop a sense of trust—the expectation that the caregiver will respond when signaled. But babies still do not protest when separated from the parent, despite the fact that they can recognize and distinguish her from unfamiliar people.

3. *The phase of "clear-cut" attachment* (6–8 months to 18 months–2 years). Now, attachment to the familiar caregiver is evident. Babies of this phase display **separation anxiety**, in that they become upset when the adult whom they have come to rely on leaves. Separation anxiety appears universally around the world after 6 months of age, increasing until about 15 months (see Figure 7.2). Its appearance suggests that infants have a clear understanding that the caregiver continues to exist when not in view. Consistent with this idea, babies who have not yet mastered Piagetian object permanence usually do not become anxious when separated from their mothers (Lester et al., 1974).

   Besides protesting the parent's departure, older infants and toddlers act more deliberately to maintain her presence. They approach, follow, and climb on her in preference to others. And they use her as a **secure base** from which to explore, venturing into the environment and then returning for emotional support, as we indicated earlier in this chapter.

4. *Formation of a reciprocal relationship* (18 months–2 years and on). By the end of the second year, rapid growth in representation and language permits toddlers to understand some of the factors that influence the parent's coming and going and to predict her return. As a result, separation protest declines. Now children start to negotiate with the caregiver, using requests and persuasion to alter her

Separation anxiety
An infant's distressed reaction to the departure of the familiar caregiver.

Secure base
The use of the familiar caregiver as a base from which the infant confidently explores the environment and returns for emotional support.

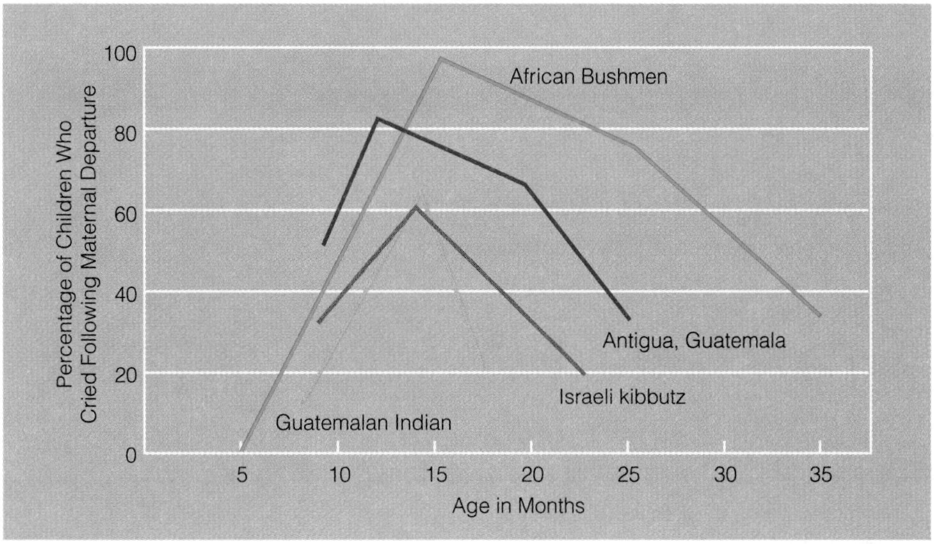

FIGURE 7.2

Development of separation anxiety.
In cultures around the world, separation anxiety emerges in the second half of the first year, increasing until about 15 months and then declining. *(From J. Kagan, R. B. Kearsley, & P. R. Zelazo, 1978,* Infancy: Its Place in Human Development, *Cambridge, MA: Harvard University Press, p. 107. Copyright © 1978 by the President and Fellows of Harvard College. All rights reserved. Reprinted by permission.)*

goals rather than crawling after and clinging to her. For example, at age 2 April asked Felicia to read a story before leaving her with a baby-sitter. The extra time with her mother, along with a better understanding of where Felicia was going ("to a movie with Daddy") and when she would be back ("right after you go to sleep"), helped April withstand her mother's absence.

According to Bowlby (1980), out of their experiences during these four phases, children construct an inner representation of the parent–child bond that becomes a vital part of their personality. It serves as an **internal working model,** or set of expectations about the availability of attachment figures and their likelihood of providing support during times of stress. This image becomes the model, or guide, for all future close relationships—through childhood and adolescence and into adult life (Bretherton, 1992).

MEASURING THE SECURITY OF ATTACHMENT

Although virtually all family-reared babies become attached to a familiar caregiver by the second year, the quality of this relationship differs greatly from child to child. Some infants appear especially relaxed and secure in the presence of the caregiver; they know they can count on her for protection and support. Others seem more anxious and uncertain. Researchers have developed special methods for assessing attachment security so they can study the factors that influence it and its impact on later development.

The **Strange Situation** is the most widely used technique for measuring the quality of attachment between 1 and 2 years of age. In designing it, Mary Ainsworth and her colleagues (1978) reasoned that if the development of attachment has gone along well, infants and toddlers should use the parent as a secure base from which to explore an unfamiliar playroom. In addition, when the parent leaves for a brief period of time, the child should show separation anxiety, and a strange adult should be less comforting than the parent. As summarized in Table 7.3, the Strange Situation takes the baby through eight short episodes in which brief separations from and reunions with the parent take place.

Observing the responses of infants to these episodes, researchers have identified a secure attachment pattern and three patterns of insecurity (Ainsworth et al., 1978; Main & Solomon, 1990). As you read about these four attachment classifications, see if you can identify the one that Rachel displayed, described at the beginning of this chapter.

Internal working model
A set of expectations derived from early caregiving experiences concerning the availability of attachment figures and their likelihood of providing support during times of stress. Becomes a model, or guide, for all future close relationships.

Strange Situation
A procedure involving short separations from and reunions with the parent that assesses the quality of the attachment bond.

TABLE 7.3

Episodes in the Strange Situation

EPISODE	EVENTS	ATTACHMENT BEHAVIORS OBSERVED
1	Experimenter introduces parent and baby to playroom and then leaves.	
2	Parent is seated while baby plays with toys.	Parent as a secure base
3	Stranger enters, is seated, and talks to parent.	Reaction to unfamiliar adult
4	Parent leaves room. Stranger responds to baby and offers comfort if upset.	Separation anxiety
5	Parent returns, greets baby, and if necessary offers comfort. Stranger leaves room.	Reaction to reunion
6	Parent leaves room.	Separation anxiety
7	Stranger enters room and offers comfort.	Ability to be soothed by stranger
8	Parent returns, greets baby, if necessary offers comfort, and tries to reinterest baby in toys.	Reaction to reunion

Note: Episode 1 lasts about 30 seconds; the remaining episodes each last about 3 minutes. Separation episodes are cut short if the baby becomes very upset. Reunion episodes are extended if the baby needs more time to calm down and return to play.
Source: Ainsworth et al., 1978.

- **Secure attachment.** These infants use the parent as a secure base from which to explore. When separated, they may or may not cry, but if they do, it is due to the parent's absence, since they show a strong preference for her over the stranger. When the parent returns, they actively seek contact, and their crying is reduced immediately.
- **Avoidant attachment.** These babies seem unresponsive to the parent when she is present. When she leaves, they are usually not distressed, and they react to the stranger in much the same way as the parent. During reunion, they avoid or are slow to greet the parent, and when picked up, they often fail to cling.
- **Resistant attachment.** Before separation, these infants seek closeness to the parent and often fail to explore. When she returns, they display angry, resistive behavior, sometimes hitting and pushing. In addition, many continue to cry after being picked up and cannot be comforted easily.
- **Disorganized/disoriented attachment.** This pattern seems to reflect the greatest insecurity. At reunion, these infants show a variety of confused, contradictory behaviors. For example, they might look away while being held by the parent or approach her with a flat, depressed gaze. Most of these babies communicate their disorientation with a dazed facial expression. A few cry out unexpectedly after having calmed down or display odd, frozen postures.

Secure attachment
The quality of attachment characterizing infants who are distressed by parental separation and easily comforted by the parent when she returns.

Avoidant attachment
The quality of insecure attachment characterizing infants who are usually not distressed by parental separation and who avoid the parent when she returns.

Resistant attachment
The quality of insecure attachment characterizing infants who remain close to the parent before departure and display angry, resistive behavior when she returns.

Disorganized/disoriented attachment
The quality of insecure attachment characterizing infants who respond in a confused, contradictory fashion when reunited with the parent.

Infants' reactions in the Strange Situation closely resemble their use of the parent as a secure base and their response to separation in the home environment (Blanchard & Main, 1979; Vaughn & Waters, 1990). For this reason, the procedure is a powerful tool for assessing attachment security.

CULTURAL VARIATIONS

Despite the usefulness of the Strange Situation, cross-cultural evidence indicates that infants' responses must be interpreted cautiously in other cultures. For example, as Figure 7.3 indicates, German infants show considerably more avoidant attachment than American babies. But German parents encourage their infants to be nonclingy and independent, so the baby's behavior may be an intended outcome of cultural beliefs and practices (Grossmann et al., 1985). Did you classify Rachel's attachment behavior as resistant? An unusually high number of Japanese infants display a resistant response, but the reaction may not represent true insecurity. Japanese mothers rarely leave their babies in the care of strange people, so the Strange Situation probably creates far greater stress for them than it does for infants who frequently experience maternal separations (Miyake, Chen, & Campos, 1985; Takahashi, 1990). Despite these cultural variations, the secure pattern is still the most common attachment classification in all societies studied to date (van IJzendoorn & Kroonenberg, 1988).

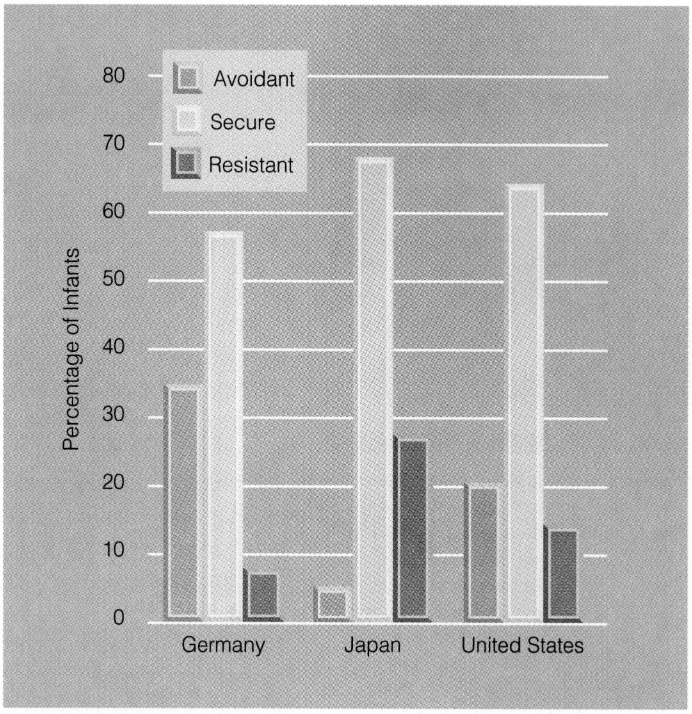

FIGURE 7.3

A cross-cultural comparison of infants' reactions in the Strange Situation. A high percentage of German babies seem avoidantly attached, whereas a substantial number of Japanese infants appear resistantly attached. Note that these responses may not reflect true insecurity. Instead, they are probably due to cultural differences in rearing practices. *(Adapted from van IJzendoorn & Kroonenberg, 1988.)*

FACTORS THAT AFFECT ATTACHMENT SECURITY

What factors might influence attachment security? First, simply having an opportunity to establish a close relationship with one or a few caregivers should be crucially important. Second, warm, sensitive parenting should lead to greater attachment security. Third, since babies actively contribute to the attachment relationship, an infant's characteristics should make a difference in how well it proceeds. And finally, because children and parents are embedded in larger contexts, family circumstances should influence attachment quality. In the following sections, we examine each of these factors.

■ MATERNAL DEPRIVATION. The powerful effect of the baby's affectional tie to the mother is most evident when it is absent. In a series of landmark studies, René Spitz (1945, 1946) observed institutionalized babies who had been given up by their mothers between the third month and the end of the first year. The infants were placed on a large ward where they shared a nurse with at least seven other babies. In contrast to the happy, outgoing behavior they had shown before separation, they wept and withdrew from their surroundings, lost weight, and had difficulty sleeping. If a caregiver whom the baby could get to know did not replace the mother, the depression deepened rapidly.

According to Spitz, institutionalized infants experienced emotional difficulties not because they were separated from their mothers, but because they were prevented from forming a bond with one or a few adults. A more recent study of maternally deprived children supports this conclusion. Researchers followed the development of infants reared in an institution that offered a good caregiver–child ratio and a rich selection of books and toys. However, staff turnover was so rapid that the average child had a total of 50 different caregivers by the age of 4 1/2! Many of these children became "late adoptees" who were placed in homes after age 4. Since most developed deep ties with their adoptive parents, this study indicates

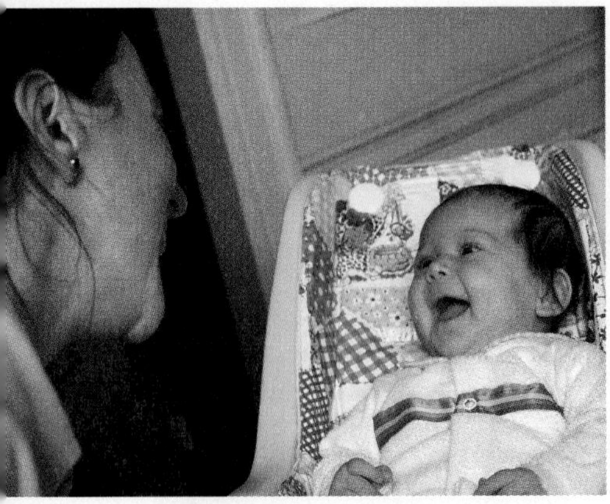

This mother and baby engage in a sensitively tuned form of communication called interactional synchrony in which they match emotional states, especially the positive ones. Interactional syncrhony may support the development of secure attachment, but it does not characterize mother–infant interaction in all cultures. *(Julie O'Neil/The Picture Cube)*

that a first attachment bond can develop as late as 4 to 6 years of age. But throughout childhood and adolescence, these youngsters were more likely to display emotional and social problems, including an excessive desire for adult attention, "over-friendliness" to unfamiliar adults and peers, and difficulties in establishing friendships (Hodges & Tizard, 1989; Tizard & Hodges, 1978; Tizard & Rees, 1975). Although follow-ups into adulthood are necessary to be sure, these results leave open the possibility that fully normal development depends on establishing close bonds with caregivers during the first few years of life.

■ QUALITY OF CAREGIVING. Even when infants experience the closeness of one or a few caregivers, parental behavior that is insensitive to their signals and needs should lead to insecure attachment. To test this idea, researchers have related various aspects of maternal caregiving to the quality of the attachment bond. The findings of many studies reveal that securely attached infants have mothers who respond promptly to infant signals, express positive emotion, and handle their babies tenderly and carefully. In contrast, insecurely attached infants have mothers who dislike physical contact, handle them awkwardly, behave in a "routine" manner when meeting the infant's needs, and are sometimes negative, resentful, and rejecting (Ainsworth et al., 1978; Belsky, Rovine, & Taylor, 1984; Isabella, 1993; Kiser et al., 1986).

Exactly what is it that mothers of securely attached babies do to support their infants' feelings of trust? In one study, mother–infant interaction was videotaped and carefully coded for each partner's behavior. Findings indicated that a special form of communication called **interactional synchrony** separated the experiences of secure from insecure babies (Isabella & Belsky, 1991). It is best described as a sensitively tuned "emotional dance" in which the caregiver responds to infant signals in a well-timed, appropriate fashion. In addition, both partners match emotional states, especially the positive ones. Watching Felicia interact with April in this way, I saw her react to April's excited shaking of a rattle with an enthusiastic "That-a-girl!" When April babbled and looked at her mother, Felicia smiled and spoke expressively in return. When she fussed and cried, Felicia soothed with gentle touches and soft words. At signs of drowsiness, Felicia reduced the amount of stimulation she offered and rocked April to sleep. Through these coordinated exchanges, Felicia seemed to be saying to April, "I understand just how you feel" (Stern, 1985).

But more evidence is needed to document the link between interactional synchrony and secure attachment. Other research reveals that only 30 percent of the time are exchanges between mothers and their babies perfectly "in sync" with one another. The remaining 70 percent of the time, interactive errors occur (Tronick, 1989). Perhaps warm, sensitive caregivers become especially skilled at repairing these errors and returning to a synchronous state. Nevertheless, finely tuned, coordinated interaction does not characterize mother–infant interaction everywhere. Among the Gusii of Kenya, mothers rarely cuddle, hug, and interact playfully with their babies, although they are very responsive to their infants' needs (LeVine & LeVine, 1988). This suggests that secure attachment depends on attentive caregiving, but its association with moment-by-moment contingent interaction is probably limited to certain cultures (MacDonald, 1992).

Compared to securely attached infants, insecure babies have mothers who are far less sensitive. Avoidant infants tend to receive overstimulating and intrusive care. Their mothers might, for example, talk energetically to a baby who is looking away or falling asleep. Resistant infants often experience interaction at the other extreme. Their mothers are minimally involved in caregiving and unresponsive to infant signals (Isabella & Belsky, 1991; Malatesta et al., 1989). It is as if avoidant babies try to escape from overwhelming, poorly paced interaction that they cannot control, whereas resistant infants react with anger and frustration to a lack of maternal involvement.

Interactional synchrony
A sensitively tuned "emotional dance," in which the caregiver responds to infant signals in a well-timed, appropriate fashion and both partners match emotional states, especially the positive ones.

When caregiving is extremely inadequate, it is a powerful predictor of disruptions in attachment. Child abuse and neglect (a topic we will consider in Chapter 10) are associated with all three forms of attachment insecurity. Among maltreated infants, the most worrisome classification—disorganized/disoriented attachment—is especially high (Carlson et al., 1989). Infants of depressed mothers also show the uncertain behaviors of this pattern, mixing closeness, resistance, and avoidance while looking very sad and depressed themselves (Lyons-Ruth et al., 1990; Radke-Yarrow et al., 1985).

■ **INFANT CHARACTERISTICS.** Since attachment is the result of a ***relationship*** that builds between two partners, infant characteristics should affect how easily it is established. Indeed, there is good evidence that this is the case. In Chapters 3 and 4, we saw that prematurity, birth complications, and newborn illness make caregiving more taxing for parents. In poverty-stricken, stressed families, these infant conditions are linked to attachment insecurity (Wille, 1991). But when parents have the time and patience to care for a baby with special needs and the infant is not very sick, at-risk newborns fare quite well in the development of attachment security (Easterbrooks, 1989).

Infants also vary considerably in temperament, but the precise role that temperament plays in attachment security has been a matter of considerable debate. Some researchers think that temperament is largely responsible for the way that babies respond in the Strange Situation. They believe, for example, that infants who are irritable and fearful may simply react to brief separations from their mothers with intense anxiety, regardless of the parent's sensitivity to the baby (Kagan, 1989). Although a few studies report relationships between distress in early infancy and insecure attachment, overall the relationship is weak and inconsistent (Izard et al., 1991; Mangelsdorf et al., 1990; Vaughn et al., 1989, 1992).

Other evidence confirms that caregiving can override the impact of infant characteristics on attachment security. In a recent study, researchers combined data from more than a thousand mother–infant pairs. As Figure 7.4 shows, they found that maternal problems—such as mental illness, teenage parenthood, and child abuse—were associated with a sharp rise in attachment insecurity. In contrast, infant problems—ranging from prematurity and developmental delays to serious physical disabilities—had little impact on attachment quality (van IJzendoorn et al., 1992).

A major reason that temperament and other infant characteristics do not show strong relationships with attachment security may be that their influence depends on goodness of fit. From this perspective, *many* child attributes can lead to secure attachment as long as the caregiver sensitively adjusts her behavior to fit the needs of the baby (Sroufe, 1985). But when mothers' capacity to do so is strained—for example, by lack of help and encouragement from husbands, relatives, and friends—

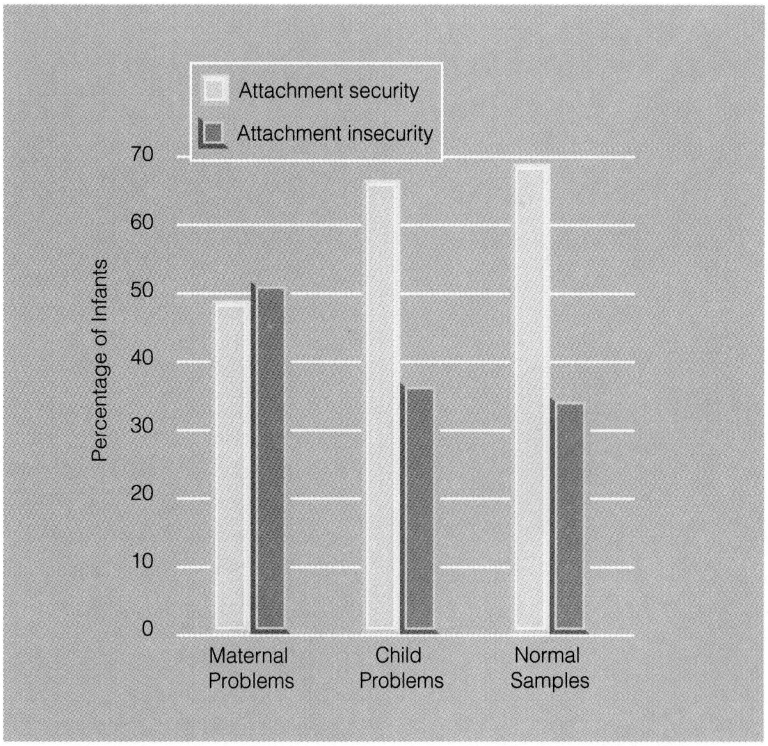

FIGURE 7.4

Comparison of the effects of maternal and child problem behaviors on the attachment bond.
Maternal problems were associated with a sharp rise in attachment insecurity. In contrast, child problems had little impact on the rate of attachment security and insecurity, which resembled that of normal samples. *(Adapted from van IJzendoorn et al., 1992.)*

then difficult babies are at greater risk for attachment insecurity (Crockenberg, 1981). These findings reveal that conditions of family life have much to do with the kind of relationship that develops between mother and baby. Indeed, in the next section we will see that this is the case.

FAMILY CIRCUMSTANCES. Around April's first birthday, Felicia and her husband Lonnie experienced a period of great emotional strain. Lonnie was laid off his job, and constant arguments with Felicia over how they would pay the monthly bills caused him to leave the family for a time. Although Felicia tried not to let these worries affect her caregiving, April sensed the tension in the air. Several times, Felicia left April at Beth's house while she looked for employment herself. April, who had previously taken such separations quite well, cried desperately on her mother's departure and clung for a long time after she returned. April's behavior reflects a repeated finding in the attachment literature: When families experience major life changes, such as a shift in employment or marital status, the quality of attachment often changes—sometimes in a positive and at other times in a negative direction (Thompson, Lamb, & Estes, 1982; Vaughn et al., 1989). This is an expected outcome, since family transitions affect parent–child interaction, which, in turn, influences the attachment bond. As Felicia and Lonnie resolved their difficulties, April's clinginess declined and she felt more secure.

Parents bring to the family context a long history of attachment experiences, out of which they construct internal working models that they apply to the bonds established with their babies. Lisa remembered her mother as tense and preoccupied and expressed regret that she and her mother had not had a closer relationship. Felicia recalled her mother as deeply affectionate and caring but much too strict and controlling. Her mother's strictness, she explained, was probably influenced by the dangerous inner-city neighborhood in which the family lived. Do these images of parenthood affect the quality of Byron and April's attachments to their mothers?

To answer this question, researchers have assessed adults' internal working models by having them describe childhood memories of attachment experiences (George, Kaplan, & Main, 1985). Parents who show objectivity and balance in discussing their childhoods, regardless of whether they were positive or negative, tend to have securely attached infants. In contrast, parents who dismiss the importance of early relationships or describe them in angry, confused ways tend to have insecurely attached babies (Cox et al., 1992; Crowell & Feldman, 1991; Main & Goldwyn, 1994). These findings reveal that adults with unhappy upbringings are not destined to become insensitive parents. Instead, the way parents ***view*** their childhoods—their ability to look back on their own parents in an understanding, forgiving way—is much more influential in how they rear their children than the actual history of care they received.

Felicia eventually took a job; Lisa had returned to work many months before. When mothers divide their time between work and parenting and place their infants in day care, is the quality of attachment affected? This question is important, since over 60 percent of American mothers with children under age 2 are employed. However, researchers disagree sharply on how to answer it. The Social Issues box on the following page reviews the controversy over whether infant day care threatens attachment security.

MULTIPLE ATTACHMENTS

We have already indicated that babies develop attachments to a variety of familiar people—not just mothers, but fathers, siblings, grandparents, and professional caregivers as well. Although Bowlby (1969) made room for multiple attachments in his theory, he believed that infants are predisposed to direct their attachment behaviors

SOCIAL ISSUES

INFANT DAY CARE AND ATTACHMENT

Recent studies indicate that American infants placed in full-time day care (more than 20 hours per week) before 12 months of age are more likely than home-reared babies to display insecure attachment in the Strange Situation. Does this mean that infants who experience daily separations from their employed mothers and early placement in day care are at risk for developmental problems? Some researchers think so (Belsky & Braungart, 1991; Sroufe, 1988), whereas others disagree (Clarke-Stewart, 1989; Scarr, Phillips, & McCartney, 1990). Yet a close look at the evidence reveals that we should be extremely cautious about concluding that day care is harmful to babies.

First, the rate of attachment insecurity among day care infants is only slightly higher than that of infants who do not attend day care (36 versus 29 percent), and it is similar to the overall figure reported for children in industrialized countries around the world (Lamb, Sternberg, & Prodromidis, 1992). In fact, most infants of employed mothers are securely attached! This suggests that the early emotional development of day care youngsters is probably within normal range.

Second, we have seen that family conditions affect attachment security. Many employed women find the pressures of handling two full-time jobs (work and motherhood) stressful. Some respond less sensitively to their babies because they are fatigued and harried, thereby risking the infant's security (Owen & Cox, 1988). Other employed mothers probably value and encourage their infant's independence. In these cases, avoidance in the Strange Situation may represent healthy autonomy rather than insecurity.

Third, poor-quality day care may contribute to the slightly higher rate of insecure attachment in infants of employed mothers. In one study, babies classified as insecurely attached to both mother and caregiver tended to be placed in day care environments with many children and few adults, where their bids for attention were frequently ignored (Howes et al., 1988).

Finally, when young children first enter day care, they must adjust to new routines and daily separations from the mother. Under these conditions, signs of distress are expected. But after a few months, infants and toddlers enrolled in high-quality programs become more comfortable. They smile, play actively, and begin to interact with agemates. These findings reveal that assessing attachment security during the period of adaptation to day care may not provide an accurate picture of its impact on early emotional adjustment (Fein, Gariboldi, & Boni, 1993). Indeed, having the opportunity to form a secure attachment bond with a stable professional caregiver can be helpful to children whose relationship with one or both parents is insecure (Goossens & van IJzendoorn, 1990). Warm bonds with caregivers in infant day care predict socially skilled behavior with peers during the preschool years (Howes, Hamilton, & Matheson, 1994).

In summary, research suggests that a small number of infants may be at risk for attachment insecurity due to inadequate day care and joint pressures of full-time employment and parenthood experienced by their mothers. However, using this evidence to justify a reduction in infant day care services is inappropriate. When family incomes are limited and mothers who want to work are forced to stay at home, children's emotional security is not promoted (Hock & DeMeis, 1987). Instead, it makes sense to increase the availability of high-quality day care and to educate parents about the vital role of sensitive, responsive caregiving in early emotional development.

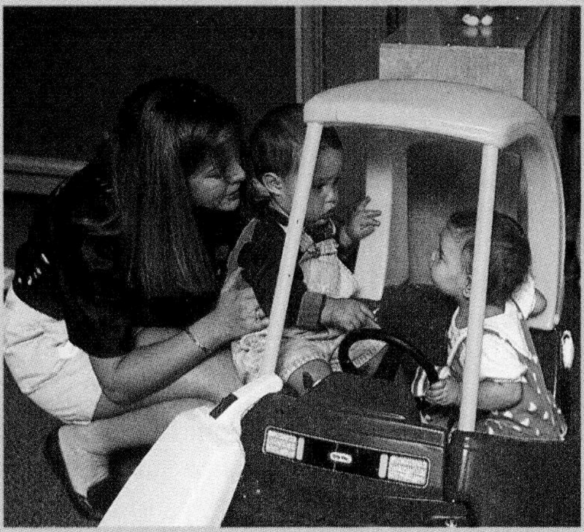

When caregivers are warm, responsive, and stable and infants' needs for physical care and stimulation are met, day care is unlikely to interfere with attachment security. *(Will Faller)*

TRY THIS . . .

- Return to Chapter 6 and review the signs of developmentally appropriate day care for infants and toddlers on page 231. Which ones are especially important for ensuring early emotional adjustment?

When playing with their babies, especially sons, fathers tend to engage in highly physical, bouncing and lifting games. *(Steve Starr/Stock Boston)*

to a single attachment figure, especially when they are distressed. Observations of infants support this idea. When an anxious, unhappy 1-year-old is permitted to choose between the mother and father as a source of comfort and security, the infant usually chooses the mother (Lamb, 1976). This preference declines over the second year of life until, around 18 months, it is no longer present. An expanding world of attachments enriches the emotional and social lives of many babies.

FATHERS. Like mothers', fathers' sensitive caregiving predicts secure attachment—an effect that becomes stronger the more time they spend with their babies (Cox et al., 1992). But as infancy progresses, mothers and fathers from a variety of cultures—Australia, India, Israel, Italy, Japan, and the United States—relate to babies in different ways. Mothers devote more time to physical care, such as changing, bathing, and feeding. In contrast, fathers spend more time in playful interaction (Lamb, 1987; Roopnarine et al., 1990). Also, when mothers and fathers play with babies, their interactions tend to be different. Mothers more often provide toys, talk to infants, and initiate conventional games like pat-a-cake and peekaboo. In contrast, fathers tend to engage in more exciting, highly physical bouncing and lifting games, especially with their infant sons (Yogman, 1981). In view of these differences, it is not surprising that babies tend to look to their mothers when distressed and to their fathers for playful stimulation.

However, this picture of "mother as caregiver" and "father as playmate" has changed in some families as a result of the revised work status of women. Employed mothers tend to engage in more playful stimulation of their babies than do unemployed mothers, and their husbands are somewhat more involved in caregiving (Cox et al., 1992). When fathers are the primary caregivers, they retain their arousing play style in addition to looking after the baby's physical well-being (Lamb & Oppenheim, 1989). Such highly involved fathers are less gender stereotyped in their beliefs; have sympathetic, friendly personalities; and regard parenthood as an especially enriching experience (Lamb, 1987; Levy-Shiff & Israelashvili, 1988).

A warm, gratifying marital relationship supports both parents' involvement with babies, but cross-cultural evidence suggests that it is particularly important as far as fathers are concerned. Among the Aka hunters and gatherers of Central Africa, fathers devote more time to infant care than in any other known society. The relationship between Aka husband and wife is unusually cooperative and intimate. Throughout the day, they share hunting, food preparation, and social activities. The more they are together, the greater the Aka father's interaction with his baby (Hewlett, 1992).

SIBLINGS. Despite a smaller family size than in generations past (see Chapter 3), 80 percent of American children still grow up with at least one sibling. In a survey that asked married couples why they desired more than one child, the most frequent reason was sibling companionship (Bulatao & Arnold, 1977). Yet the arrival of a baby brother or sister is a difficult experience for most preschoolers, who quickly realize that now they must share their parents' attention and affection. They often become demanding and clingy for a time and engage in instances of "deliberate naughtiness," especially when the mother is caring for the baby (Dunn & Kendrick, 1982).

However, resentment about being displaced is only one feature of a rich emotional relationship that starts to build between siblings after a baby's birth. The older child can also be seen kissing, patting, and calling out when the baby cries, "Mom, he needs you"—signs of growing caring and affection. By the time the baby is about 8 months old, siblings typically spend much time together, with the preschooler helping, sharing toys with, imitating, and expressing friendliness in addition to showing signs of rivalry and resentment (Dunn & Kendrick, 1982). Infants of this age are comforted by the presence of their preschool-age brother or sister during short absences of the mother (Stewart, 1983). And during the second year, they often imitate and join in play with the older child (Dunn, 1989).

TABLE 7.4

Suggestions for Encouraging Affectional Ties Between Infants and Their Preschool Siblings

SUGGESTION	DESCRIPTION
Spend extra time with the older child	To minimize feelings of being deprived of affection and attention, set aside time to spend with the older child. Fathers can be especially helpful in this regard, planning special outings with the preschooler and taking over care of the baby so the mother can be with the older child.
Handle sibling misbehavior with patience	Respond patiently to the older sibling's misbehavior and demands for attention, recognizing that these reactions are temporary. Give the preschooler opportunities to feel proud of being more grownup than the baby. For example, encourage the older child to assist with feeding, bathing, dressing, and offering toys, and show appreciation for these efforts.
Discuss the baby's wants and needs	Discuss the baby's feelings and intentions with the preschooler, such as "He's so little that he just can't wait to be fed" or "He's trying to reach his rattle and can't." By helping the older sibling understand the baby's point of view, parents can promote friendly, considerate behavior.

Sources: Dunn & Kendrick, 1982; Howe & Ross, 1990.

Nevertheless, individual differences in the quality of sibling relationships appear shortly after a baby's birth and persist through early childhood (Dunn, 1992). Temperament plays an important role. For example, conflict increases when one sibling is emotionally intense or highly active (Brody, Stoneman, & Burke, 1987; Stocker, Dunn, & Plomin, 1989). Parental behavior also makes a difference. Secure infant–mother attachment and warmth toward both children are related to positive sibling interaction, whereas coldness is associated with sibling friction (Volling & Belsky, 1992). Still, when a mother is very positive and playful with a new baby, her preschool-age child is likely to feel slighted and act in a less friendly way toward the infant. This does not mean that parents should limit the attention they give to infants, but it does indicate the importance of setting aside special times to devote to the older child. In addition, mothers who often discuss the baby's feelings and intentions have preschoolers who are more likely to comment on the infant as a person with special wants and needs. And such children behave in an especially considerate and friendly manner when interacting with the baby (Dunn & Kendrick, 1982; Howe & Ross, 1990).

A list of suggestions for promoting positive relationships between babies and their preschool siblings is given in Table 7.4. Research on brothers and sisters as attachment figures reminds us of the complex, multidimensional nature of the infant's social world. Siblings offer a rich social context in which children learn and practice a wide range of skills, including affectionate caring, conflict resolution, and control of hostile and envious feelings. Warm, enduring bonds among brothers and sisters occur especially often in large families. Having more children means that parents have less time to devote to each one, and this seems to intensify children's attachment to one another (Bossard & Boll, 1956).

ATTACHMENT AND LATER DEVELOPMENT

According to psychoanalytic and ethological theories, the inner feelings of affection and security that result from a healthy attachment relationship support all aspects of psychological development. Consistent with this view, research indicates that quality of attachment to the mother in infancy is related to cognitive and social development. Preschoolers who were securely attached as babies show greater enthusiasm and persistence on problem-solving tasks. And such children also have favorable relationships with peers, both in early and middle childhood (Elicker, Englund, & Sroufe, 1992; Frankel & Bates, 1990; Matas, Arend, & Sroufe, 1978).

These findings have been taken by some researchers to mean that secure attachment in infancy ***causes*** increased cognitive and social competence during later years. Yet more evidence is needed before we can be certain of this conclusion. Earlier in this chapter, we saw that infants deprived of a familiar caregiver show long-term adjustment difficulties. But similar outcomes do not always occur for babies who do become attached but for whom the relationship is less than ideal. In some studies, insecurely attached infants became preschoolers with serious adjustment difficulties; in others they did not (Bates & Bayles, 1988; Fagot & Kavanaugh, 1990; Lyons-Ruth, Alpern, & Repacholi, 1993).

Michael Lamb and his colleagues (1985) suggest that *continuity of caregiving* determines whether attachment insecurity is linked to later problems. When parents react insensitively for a very long time, children have a good chance of becoming maladjusted. But infants and young children are resilient beings. A child who has compensating, affectional ties outside the family or whose parent's caregiving improves is likely to fare well. This suggests that efforts to create warm, responsive environments are not just important in infancy; they are also worthwhile at later ages. Indeed, we will discover that this is the case in subsequent chapters.

ASK YOURSELF . . .

- Return to Chapter 6 and list the child-rearing practices that promote early cognitive development. How do they compare with those that foster secure attachment?
- Recall from Chapter 6 that Lisa tended to overwhelm Byron with questions and instructions that were not related to his ongoing actions. How would you expect Byron to respond in the Strange Situation? Explain your answer.
- Maggy works full time and leaves her 14-month-old son Vincent at a day care center. When she arrives to pick him up at the end of the day, Vincent keeps on playing and ignores her. Maggy wonders whether Vincent is securely attached. Is Maggy's concern warranted?

BRIEF REVIEW

Drive reduction (behaviorist) and psychoanalytic theories have been criticized for overemphasizing feeding and paying little attention to the baby's active role in establishing an attachment bond. According to ethological theory, infant–caregiver attachment has evolved because it promotes survival. In early infancy, babies' innate signals help keep the parent nearby. By 6 to 8 months, separation anxiety and use of the mother as a secure base indicate that a true attachment has formed. Representation and language help toddlers tolerate brief separations from the parent. Research on infants deprived of a consistent caregiver suggests that fully normal development depends on establishing a close affectional bond in the first few years of life. Caregiving that is responsive to babies' needs supports the development of secure attachment; insensitive caregiving is linked to attachment insecurity. Family conditions, such as a change in marital or employment status, can affect the quality of attachment. Besides mothers, fathers and siblings are influential attachment figures. Early attachment security predicts cognitive and social competence at later ages, but continuity of caregiving may be largely responsible for this relationship.

SELF-DEVELOPMENT DURING THE FIRST TWO YEARS

Infancy is a rich, formative period for the development of physical and social understanding. In Chapter 6, you learned that infants develop an appreciation of the permanence of objects—that they continue to exist when no longer in view. And in this chapter, we saw that over the first year, infants recognize and respond appropriately to others' emotions and distinguish familiar people from strangers. The fact that both objects and people achieve an independent, stable existence in infancy implies that knowledge of the self as a separate, permanent entity emerges around this time. Once self-awareness develops, it supports a diverse array of social and emotional achievements, as we will see in the following sections.

SELF-RECOGNITION

Felicia hung a large, plastic mirror on the side of April's crib. As early as the first few months, April smiled and returned friendly behaviors to her image. At what age did she realize that the charming baby gazing and grinning back was really herself?

To answer this question, researchers have conducted clever laboratory observations in which they expose infants and toddlers to images of themselves in mirrors, on videotapes, and in photos. In one study, 9- to 24-month-olds were placed in front of a mirror. Then, under the pretext of wiping the baby's face, each mother was asked to rub red dye on her infant's nose. Younger infants touched the mirror as if the red mark had nothing to do with any aspect of themselves. But by 15 months, toddlers began to rub their strange-looking little red noses—a response that indicates the beginnings of self-recognition (Bullock & Lutkenhaus, 1990; Lewis & Brooks-Gunn, 1979).

Between 15 and 18 months, toddlers become even more responsive to images of themselves. At this age, they react differently to a videotape of a strange child than to one of themselves—smiling and attending more closely to the unfamiliar youngster but imitating movements of the self. By the end of toddlerhood, self-recognition is well established. Two-year-olds look and smile more at a photo of themselves than one of another child. And almost all of them use their name or a personal pronoun ("I" or "me") to label their own image or refer to themselves (Lewis & Brooks-Gunn, 1979).

How do toddlers develop an awareness of the self's existence? As yet, there is little evidence to answer this question. Many theorists believe that the beginnings of self lie in infants' *sense of agency*—recognition that their own actions cause objects and people to react in predictable ways. Parents who encourage babies to explore the environment and who respond to their signals consistently and sensitively help them construct a sense of agency. Then, as infants act on the environment, they notice different effects that may help them sort out self from other people and objects. For example, batting a mobile and seeing it swing in a pattern different from the infant's own actions informs the baby about the relation between self and physical world. Smiling and vocalizing at a caregiver who smiles and vocalizes back helps specify the relation between self and social world. And watching the movement of one's own hand provides still another kind of feedback—one under much more direct control than other people or objects. The contrast among these experiences may help them build an image of self as separate from external reality (Case, 1991; Lewis, 1991).

This toddler notices the correspondence between his own movements and the movements of the image in the mirror, a cue that helps him figure out that the grinning child is really himself. *(Laura Dwight/Omni-Photo Communications)*

Empathy first appears in toddlerhood. It depends on the cognitive capacity to distinguish self from other. *(Michael Kornafel/FPG)*

Self-awareness quickly becomes a central part of children's emotional and social lives. Earlier you learned that self-conscious emotions depend on toddlers' emerging sense of self. Self-recognition also leads to the first signs of **empathy**—the ability to understand and respond sympathetically to the feelings of others. For example, toddlers start to give to others what they themselves find comforting—a hug, a reassuring comment, or a favorite doll or blanket (Hoffman, 1984; Zahn-Waxler et al., 1992). And along with an increase in empathic behavior comes a much clearer awareness of how to upset and frustrate other people (Dunn, 1989). One 18-month-old heard her mother comment to another adult, "Anny (sibling) is really frightened of spiders. In fact, there's a particular toy spider that we've got that she just hates" (p. 107). The innocent-looking toddler ran to get the spider out of the toy box, returned, and pushed it in front of Anny's face!

CATEGORIZING THE SELF

Self-awareness permits toddlers to compare themselves to other people, in much the same way that they group together physical objects (see Chapter 6). Between 18 and 30 months, children categorize themselves and others on the basis of age ("baby," "boy," or "man"), sex ("boy" or "girl" and "lady" or "man"), physical characteristics ("big," "strong"), and even goodness and badness ("I good girl." "Tommy mean!") (Stipek, Gralinski, & Kopp, 1990). Toddlers' understanding of these social categories is quite limited. But as soon as this knowledge appears, children use it to organize their own behavior. For example, toddlers' ability to label their own gender is associated with a sharp rise in gender-stereotyped responses (Fagot & Leinbach, 1989). As early as 18 months, children select and play in a more involved way with toys that are stereotyped for their own gender—dolls and tea sets for girls, trucks and cars for boys. Then parents encourage these preferences further by responding more positively when toddlers display them (Fagot, Leinbach, & O'Boyle, 1992). As we will see in Chapter 10, gender-typed behavior increases dramatically over early childhood.

Empathy
The ability to understand and respond sympathetically to the feelings of others.

EMERGENCE OF SELF-CONTROL

Self-awareness also provides the foundation for **self-control,** the capacity to resist a momentary impulse to engage in socially disapproved behavior. Self-control is essential for morality, another dimension of the self that will flourish during childhood and adolescence. To behave in a self-controlled fashion, children must have some ability to think of themselves as separate, autonomous beings who can direct their own actions. And they must also have the representational and memory capacities to recall a caregiver's directive (such as "April, don't touch that light socket!") and apply it to their own behavior (Kopp, 1987).

As these abilities mature, the first glimmerings of self-control appear in the form of **compliance.** Between 12 and 18 months, children start to show clear awareness of caregivers' wishes and expectations and can voluntarily obey simple requests and commands (Kaler & Kopp, 1990). And, as every parent knows, they can also decide to do just the opposite! One way toddlers assert their emerging sense of autonomy is by resisting adult directives. But think back to Erikson's theory, which suggests that parenting practices have much to do with a healthy sense of self. Consistent with this idea, among toddlers who experience warm, sensitive caregiving and reasonable expectations for mature behavior, opposition is far less common than compliance and cooperation (Crockenberg & Litman, 1990). Compliance quickly leads to toddlers' first morally relevant verbalizations—for example, correcting the self by saying "no, can't" before touching a light socket or jumping on the sofa (Kochanska, 1993).

Around 18 months, the capacity for self-control appears, and it improves steadily into early childhood. In one study, toddlers were given three tasks that required them to resist temptation. In the first, they were asked not to touch an interesting toy telephone that was within arm's reach. In the second, raisins were hidden under cups, and they were instructed to wait until the experimenter said it was all right to pick up a cup and eat a raisin. In the third, they were told not to open a gift until the experimenter had finished her work. On all three problems, the ability to wait increased steadily between 18 and 30 months of age. Toddlers who were especially self-controlled were also advanced in language development. In fact, some could be seen using verbal techniques, such as singing and talking to themselves, to keep from touching the desired objects (Vaughn, Kopp, & Krakow, 1984).

As self-control improves, mothers increase the rules they require toddlers to follow, from safety and respect for property and people to family routines, manners, and simple chores (Gralinksi & Kopp, 1993). Still, toddlers' control over their own actions is very fragile. It depends on constant oversight and reminders by parents. Young children also have more difficulty controlling their behavior in some situations than others. For example, waiting before engaging in a desired action is easier than stopping an enjoyable activity (Pressley, 1979). To get a toddler to calmly give up playing with an attractive toy to accompany the parent on an errand, several prompts ("Remember, we're going to go in just a minute") and gentle insistence are usually necessary.

As the second year of life drew to a close, Lisa, Beth, and Felicia were delighted at their youngsters' new-found capacity for compliance and self-control. It signaled that the three toddlers were ready to learn the rules of social life. As we will see in Chapter 10, advances in cognition and language, along with parental warmth and reasonable maturity demands, lead children to make tremendous strides in this area during the early childhood years.

ASK YOURSELF . . .

- Nine-month-old Harry turned his cup upside down and spilled juice all over the tray of his high chair. His mother said sharply, "Harry, put your cup back the right way!" Can Harry comply with his mother's request? Why or why not?

Self-control
The capacity to resist a momentary impulse to engage in socially disapproved behavior.

Compliance
Voluntary obedience to adult requests and commands.

SUMMARY

THEORIES OF INFANT AND TODDLER PERSONALITY

Explain Erikson's and Mahler's theories of infant and toddler personality.

- The psychoanalytic theories of Erikson and Mahler capture salient features of personality development during infancy and toddlerhood. According to Erikson, warm, responsive caregiving leads infants to resolve the psychological conflict of Freud's **oral stage—basic trust versus mistrust**—on the positive side. During the **anal stage,** the conflict of **autonomy versus shame and doubt** is resolved favorably when parents provide appropriate guidance and reasonable choices.

- According to Mahler, sensitive, loving care fosters symbiosis, which provides the foundation for separation–individuation during toddlerhood. The capacity to move away from the mother, by crawling and then walking, leads to self-awareness. Gains in representation and language help create a positive, inner image of the mother that can be relied on for emotional support in her absence.

EMOTIONAL DEVELOPMENT DURING THE FIRST TWO YEARS

Describe changes in happiness, anger, and fear over the first year, noting the adaptive function of each.

- Signs of almost all the **basic emotions** are present in infancy, each of which becomes more recognizable with age. The **social smile** appears between 6 and 10 weeks, laughter around 3 to 4 months. Happiness strengthens the parent–child bond and reflects as well as supports physical and cognitive mastery. Anger and fear, especially in the form of **stranger anxiety,** increase in the second half of the first year. These reactions have survival value as infants' motor capacities improve.

Summarize changes in understanding others' emotions, expression of self-conscious emotions, and emotional self-regulation during the first 2 years.

- The ability to understand the feelings of others expands over the first year as babies perceive facial expressions as organized patterns. Around 8 to 10 months, **social referencing** appears; infants actively seek emotional information from caregivers in uncertain situations.

- During toddlerhood, self-awareness and adult instruction provide the foundation for **self-conscious emotions,** such as shame, embarrassment, and pride. Caregivers help infants with **emotional self-regulation** by relieving distress, engaging in stimulating play, and discouraging negative emotion. During the second year, growth in representation and language leads to more effective ways of regulating emotion.

TEMPERAMENT AND DEVELOPMENT

What is temperament, and how is it measured?

- Infants differ greatly in **temperament,** or style of emotional responding. Temperament is most often assessed through parental reports, although behavior ratings by others familiar with the child and direct observations are also used. Researchers are beginning to identify physiological reactions that are markers of temperament. On the basis of parental descriptions of children's behavior, three temperamental patterns—the **easy child,** the **difficult child,** and the **slow-to-warm-up child**—were identified in the New York Longitudinal Study.

Discuss the role of heredity and environment in the stability of temperament, including the goodness-of-fit model.

- Many temperamental characteristics show moderate stability over time. Difficult children, especially, are likely to experience adjustment difficulties by school age. Temperament has biological roots, but child rearing has much to do with whether a child's emotional style remains the same or changes over time.

- **Goodness of fit** describes how temperament and environmental pressures work together to affect later development. Parenting practices that create a good fit with the child's basic emotional style help difficult, withdrawn, and highly active children achieve more adaptive functioning.

DEVELOPMENT OF ATTACHMENT

What are the unique features of ethological theory of attachment in comparison to drive reduction and psychoanalytic views?

- The development of **attachment,** infants' strong affectional tie to familiar caregivers, has been the subject of intense theoretical debate. Although **drive reduction** (behaviorist) and **psychoanalytic** explanations exist, the most widely accepted perspective is **ethological theory.** It views babies as biologically prepared to contribute actively to ties established with their caregivers, which promote survival.

- In early infancy, a set of built-in behaviors encourages the parent to remain close to the baby. Around 6 to 8 months, **separation anxiety** and use of the parent as a **secure base** indicate that a true attachment bond has formed. As representation and language develop, toddlers try to alter the mother's coming and going through requests and persuasion rather than following and clinging. Out of early caregiving experiences, children construct an **internal working model** that serves as a guide for all future close relationships.

Describe the Strange Situation, the four attachment patterns assessed by it, and factors that affect attachment security.

- The **Strange Situation** is the most widely used technique for measuring the quality of attachment between 1 and 2 years of age. Four attachment patterns have been identified: **secure, avoidant, resistant,** and **disorganized/disoriented.** Cultural conditions must be considered in interpreting reactions in the Strange Situation.

- A variety of factors affect the development of attachment. Infants deprived of affectional ties with one or a few adults show lasting emotional and social problems. Sensitive, responsive caregiving promotes secure attachment. Even difficult-to-care-for infants are likely to become securely attached if parents adapt their caregiving to suit the baby's needs. Family conditions, such as a change in employment or marital status, affect parent–infant interaction and, in turn, attachment security.

Discuss infants' attachments to fathers and siblings.

- Besides attachments to mothers, infants develop strong ties to fathers, usually through stimulating, playful interaction. Early in the first year, infants begin to build rich emotional relationships with siblings that mix affection and caring with rivalry and resentment. Individual differences in the quality of sibling relationships are influenced by temperament and parenting practices.

Describe and interpret the relationship between secure attachment in infancy and cognitive and social competence in childhood.

- Infants who are securely attached to their mothers show more effective cognitive and social development in childhood. However, continuity of parental care may be the crucial factor that determines whether an infant who is insecurely attached shows later adjustment problems.

SELF-DEVELOPMENT DURING THE FIRST TWO YEARS

When does self-recognition develop, and to what emotional and social capacities does it contribute?

- Reactions of infants to images of themselves in mirrors, on videotapes, and in photos show that self-recognition is well established by the end of the second year. Self-awareness permits toddlers to form primitive social categories based on age, sex, and goodness and badness. It also provides the foundation for self-conscious emotions, **empathy, compliance,** and **self-control.**

IMPORTANT TERMS AND CONCEPTS

oral stage (p. 248)
basic trust versus mistrust (p. 249)
anal stage (p. 249)
autonomy versus shame and doubt (p. 249)
symbiosis (p. 250)
separation–individuation (p. 250)
basic emotions (p. 252)
social smile (p. 252)
stranger anxiety (p. 253)
social referencing (p. 254)
self-conscious emotions (p. 254)
emotional self-regulation (p. 255)
temperament (p. 257)
easy child (p. 258)
difficult child (p. 258)
slow-to-warm-up child (p. 258)
goodness of fit (p. 261)
attachment (p. 263)
drive reduction explanation of attachment(p. 263)
ethological theory of attachment (p. 265)
separation anxiety (p. 266)
secure base (p. 266)
internal working model (p. 267)
Strange Situation (p. 267)
secure attachment (p. 268)
avoidant attachment (p. 268)
resistant attachment (p. 268)
disorganized/disoriented attachment (p. 268)
interactional synchrony (p. 270)
empathy (p. 278)
self-control (p. 279)
compliance (p. 279)

MILESTONES OF DEVELOPMENT IN INFANCY AND TODDLERHOOD

AGE	PHYSICAL	COGNITIVE	LANGUAGE	EMOTIONAL/SOCIAL
Birth–6 months	■ Rapid height and weight gain. ■ Reflexes decline. ■ Sleep organized into a day–night schedule. ■ Holds head up, rolls over, and reaches for objects. ■ Can be classically and operantly conditioned. ■ Habituates to unchanging stimuli. ■ Hearing well developed; by the end of this period, displays greater sensitivity to speech sounds of own language. ■ Depth and pattern perception emerge and improve.	■ Engages in immediate imitation and deferred imitation of adults' facial expressions. ■ Repeats chance behaviors leading to pleasurable and interesting results. ■ Displays object permanence in habituation–dishabituation task. ■ Recognition memory for people, places, and objects improves. ■ Can categorize simple stimuli.	■ Engages in cooing, and by the end of this period, babbling. ■ Establishes joint attention with caregiver, who labels objects and events.	■ Expresses signs of almost all basic emotions (happiness, interest, surprise, fear, anger, sadness, disgust). ■ Social smile and laughter emerge. ■ Matches adults' emotional expressions during face-to face interaction.
7–12 months	■ Sits alone, crawls, and walks. ■ Shows refined pincer grasp. ■ Perceives larger speech units critical to understanding meaning. ■ Depth and pattern perception improve further.	■ Combines sensorimotor schemes. ■ Engages in intentional, or goal-directed, behavior. ■ Finds objects hidden in one place. ■ Engages in deferred imitation of adults' actions on objects. ■ Recall memory for people, places, and objects improves. ■ Groups stimuli into wider range of categories.	■ Babbling expands to include sounds of spoken languages. ■ Uses preverbal gestures (showing, pointing) to communicate.	■ Anger and fear increase in frequency and intensity. ■ Stranger anxiety and separation anxiety appear. ■ Uses caregiver as a secure base for exploration. ■ Engages in social referencing. ■ Shows "clearcut" attachment to familiar caregivers.

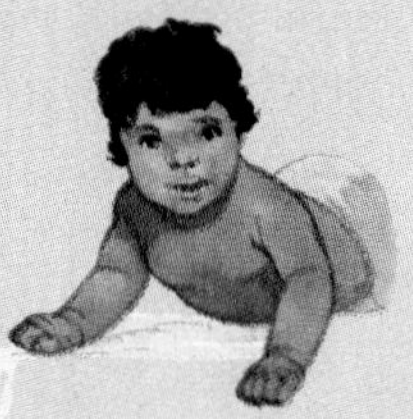

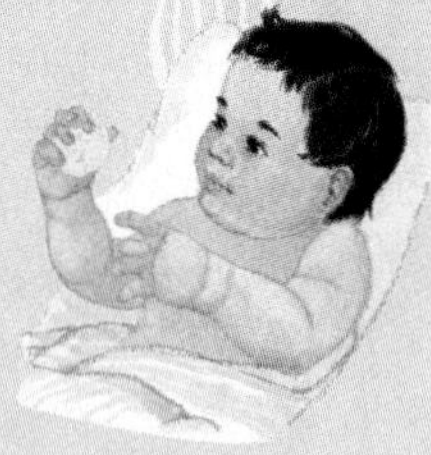

AGE	PHYSICAL	COGNITIVE	LANGUAGE	EMOTIONAL/SOCIAL
13–18 months	■ Height and weight gain rapid, but not as great as in first year. ■ Walking better coordinated. ■ Scribbles with pencil. ■ Builds tower of 2–3 cubes.	■ Experiments with objects in a trial-and-error fashion. ■ Finds objects hidden in more than one place. ■ Actively categorizes objects. ■ Imitates actions across a change in contexts—for example, a behavior learned at day care in the home.	■ Actively joins in turn-taking games, such as pat-a-cake and peekaboo. ■ Says first words. ■ Makes errors of underextension and overextension.	■ Actively joins in play with siblings. ■ Recognizes image of self in mirrors and on videotape. ■ Shows signs of empathy. ■ Capable of compliance.

AGE	PHYSICAL	COGNITIVE	LANGUAGE	EMOTIONAL/SOCIAL
19–24 months	■ Jumps, runs, and climbs. ■ Manipulates objects with good coordination. ■ Builds tower of 4–5 cubes.	■ Solves sensorimotor problems suddenly. ■ Finds objects moved while out of sight. ■ Engages in deferred imitation of complex action sequences, such as those an adult tries to produce, even if they are not fully realized. ■ Engages in make-believe play. ■ Actively categorizes objects more efficiently.	■ Vocabulary increases to 200 words; consistent grammar not yet present.	■ Self-conscious emotions (shame and embarrassment) emerge. ■ Acquires a vocabulary of emotional terms. ■ Starts to use language to assist with emotional self-regulation. ■ Begins to tolerate caregiver absences more easily. ■ Uses own name or personal pronoun to label image of self. ■ Categorizes the self and others on the basis of age and sex. ■ Shows gender-stereotyped toy choices. ■ Self-control appears.

"Weight lifting"
Shohai Takeda
7 years, Japan

A transformed body and explosion of new motor skills contribute to an expanding sense of competence in early childhood, forcefully captured in this image of strength and power. Chapter 8 highlights the close link between early childhood physical growth and other aspects of development.

8

Physical Development in Early Childhood

For more than a decade, my fourth-floor office window overlooked the preschool and kindergarten play yard of our university laboratory school. Sitting at my desk, I spent many fascinating moments watching young children at play. On mild fall and spring mornings, the doors of the preschool and kindergarten swung open, and sand table, woodworking bench, easels, and large blocks spilled out into a small, fenced courtyard. Around the side of the building was a grassy area with jungle gyms, swings, a small playhouse, and a flower garden planted by the children. Beyond it, I could see a circular path lined with tricycles and wagons. Each day the setting was alive with activity.

As I looked on from my distant vantage point, the physical changes of early childhood were clearly evident. Children's bodies were longer and leaner than they had been a year or two earlier. The awkward gait of toddlerhood had disappeared in favor of more refined movements that included climbing, jumping, galloping, and skipping. Throughout the morning, children scaled the jungle gym, searched for imaginary pirates behind trees and bushes, chased one another across the play yard, and peddled tricycles vigorously over the pavement.

Just as impressive as these gross motor achievements were gains in fine motor skills. At the sand table, children built hills, valleys, caves, and roads and prepared trays of pretend cookies and cupcakes. Nearby, blocks of wood were hammered into small sculptures. And as children grew older, the paintings that hung out to dry took on greater form and detail as family members, houses, trees, birds, sky, monsters, and letterlike forms appeared in the colorful creations.

The years from 2 to 6 are often called "the play years," and aptly so, since play blossoms during this time and supports every aspect of development. We begin our consideration of early childhood by tracing the physical achievements of this

BODY GROWTH IN EARLY CHILDHOOD

Changes in Body Size and Proportions • Skeletal Growth • Asynchronies in Physical Growth

BRAIN DEVELOPMENT IN EARLY CHILDHOOD

Lateralization and Handedness • Other Advances in Brain Development

FACTORS AFFECTING GROWTH AND HEALTH IN EARLY CHILDHOOD

Hereditary and Hormonal Influences • Emotional Well-Being • Nutrition • Infectious Disease • Childhood Injuries

MOTOR DEVELOPMENT IN EARLY CHILDHOOD

Gross Motor Development • Fine Motor Development • Factors That Affect Early Childhood Motor Skills

PERCEPTUAL DEVELOPMENT IN EARLY CHILDHOOD

period—growth in body size, improvements in motor coordination, and refinements in perception. Our discussion pays special attention to biological and environmental factors that support these changes, as well as to their intimate connection with other aspects of development. The preschool children whom I came to know well, first by watching from my office window and later by observing at close range in their classrooms, will provide us with many examples of developmental trends and individual differences. In this chapter, we will meet Lynette, a child so small that at age 4 she was no taller and heavier than the average 2 1/2-year-old. We will also get to know Hallie, whose impoverished home life left him vulnerable to serious health problems due to poor diet and infectious disease. Several of Lynette and Hallie's classmates will also join us along the way.

BODY GROWTH IN EARLY CHILDHOOD

CHANGES IN BODY SIZE AND PROPORTIONS

Look at Figure 8.1, and you will see that the rapid increase in body size that took place in infancy tapers off into a slower pattern of growth during early childhood. On the average, 2 to 3 inches in height and about 5 pounds in weight are added each year. Boys continue to be slightly larger than girls (Mott, James, & Sperhac, 1990). At the same time, the "baby fat" that began to decline in toddlerhood drops off further. The child gradually becomes thinner, although girls retain somewhat more body fat, and boys are slightly more muscular. As the torso lengthens and widens, internal organs tuck neatly inside, and the spine straightens. By age 5, the top-heavy, bowlegged, potbellied toddler has become a more streamlined, flat-tummied, longer-legged child with body proportions similar to that of adults (Tanner, 1990). Consequently, posture and balance improve—changes that support the gains in motor coordination that we will take up later in this chapter.

Individual differences in body size that existed in infancy are even more apparent during early childhood. Looking down at the play yard one day, I watched 5-year-old Darryl speed around the bike path. At 48 inches in height and 55 pounds in weight, he towered over his kindergarten classmates and was, as his mother put it, "off the growth charts" at the doctor's office (the average American 5-year-old boy is 43 inches tall and weighs 42 pounds). Priti, a girl from India, and Lynette, a Caucasian child, were at the other extreme. Priti was small because of her cultural heritage, Lynette and Hallie for reasons that we will discuss shortly.

Toddlers and 5-year-olds have very different body shapes. During early childhood, body fat declines, the torso enlarges to better accommodate the internal organs, and the spine straightens. Compared to her younger brother, this girl looks more streamlined. Her body proportions resemble those of an adult. *(Bob Daemmrich/Stock Boston)*

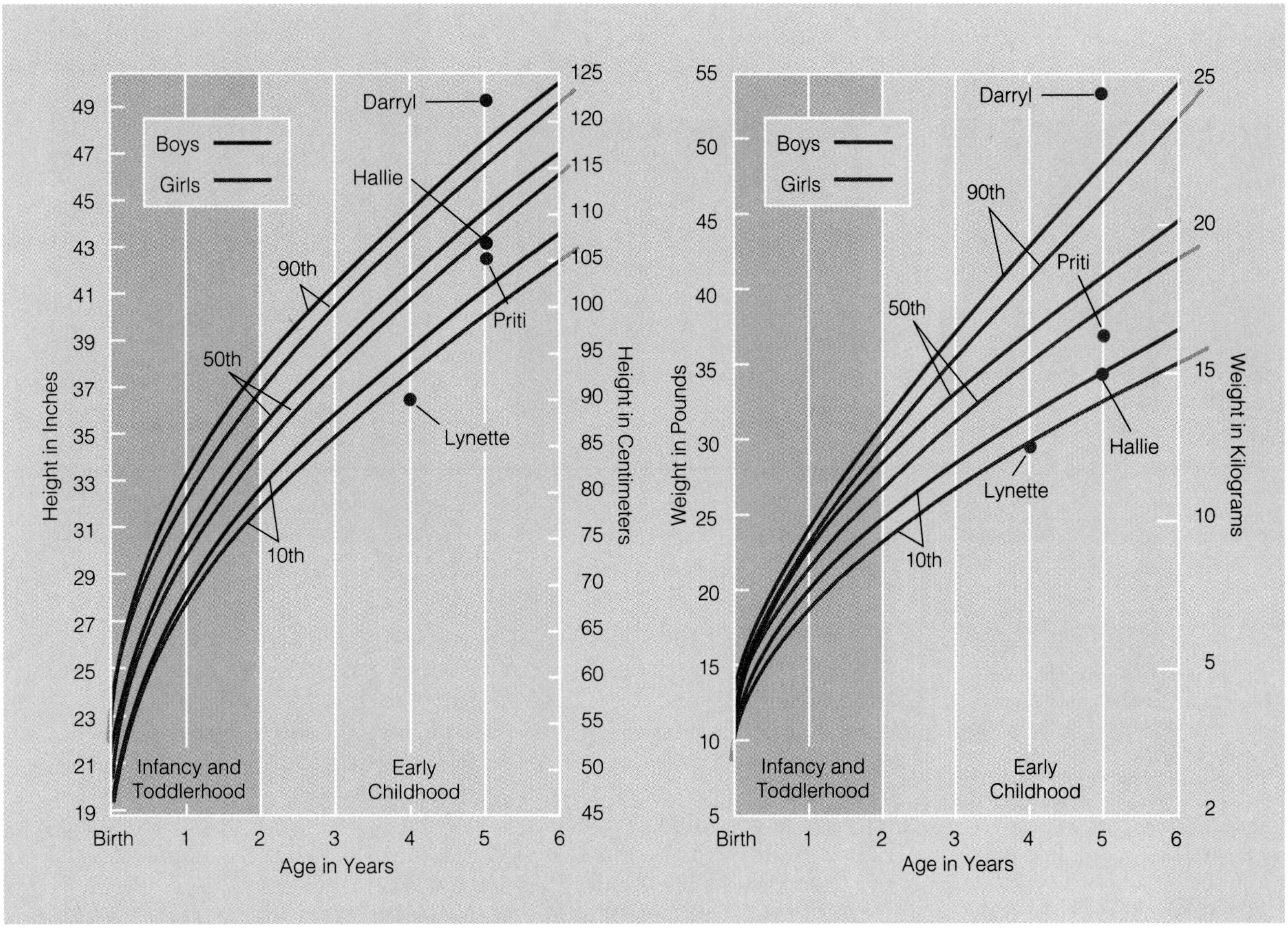

FIGURE 8.1

Gains in height and weight during early childhood among American youngsters.
Compared to the first 2 years of life, growth is slower. Girls continue to be slightly shorter and lighter than boys. Wide individual differences in body size exist, as the percentiles on these charts reveal. Darryl, Priti, Lynette, and Hallie's heights and weights differ greatly.

The existence of cultural differences in body size reminds us that growth norms for one population (those in Figure 8.1 apply to American children) are not good standards for many youngsters around the world. Consider the Efe of Zaire, an African people who normally grow to an adult height of less than 5 feet. A recent study of the early physical growth of Efe children revealed that between 1 and 6 years, their growth tapers off to a greater extent than that of American preschoolers. By age 5, the average Efe child is shorter than over 97 percent of 5-year-olds in the United States. For genetic reasons, the hormones controlling body size have less effect on Efe youngsters than they do on other children (Bailey, 1990). In view of these findings, we would be mistaken to take the Efe youngster's small stature as a sign of serious growth or health problems, although this concern is warranted for an extremely slow-growing Caucasian child, such as Lynette.

SKELETAL GROWTH

The skeletal changes that we discussed in Chapter 5 continue throughout early childhood. Between ages 2 and 6, approximately 45 new *epiphyses,* or growth centers in which cartilage hardens into bone, emerge in various parts of the skeleton. Others will appear in middle childhood. Figure 8.2, which shows X-rays of a

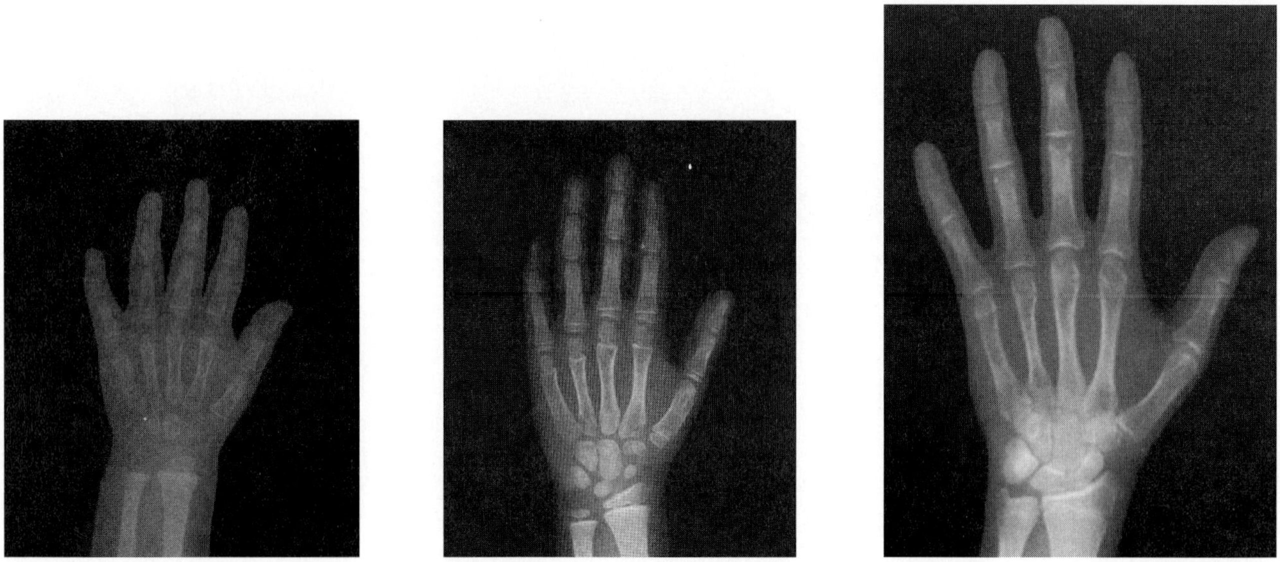

$2\frac{1}{2}$ years $6\frac{1}{2}$ years $14\frac{1}{2}$ years

FIGURE 8.2

X-rays of a girl's hand, showing skeletal maturity at three ages. Notice how the wrist bones and the epiphyses on the long bones of the fingers and forearms gradually close. *(From J. M. Tanner, R. H. Whitehouse, N. Cameron, W. A. Marshall, M. J. R. Healey, & H. Goldstein, 1983,* Assessment of Skeletal Maturity and Prediction of Adult Height *[TW2 Method], 2nd ed., Academic Press [London, Ltd.], p. 86. Reprinted by permission.)*

girl's hand at three ages, illustrates changes in the epiphyses over time. Notice how, at age 2 1/2, wide gaps exist between the wrist bones and at the ends of the finger and arm bones. By age 5 1/2, these have filled in considerably. At age 14 1/2 (when this girl reached her adult size), the wrist and long bones are completely fused. Such X-rays permit doctors to estimate children's *skeletal age,* the best available measure of progress toward physical maturity (see Chapter 5, page 173). During early and middle childhood, information about skeletal age is helpful in diagnosing growth disorders. It also provides a rough estimate of children's chronological age in areas of the world where birth dates are not customarily recorded.

Parents and children are especially aware of another aspect of skeletal growth: maturation of the teeth. By the end of the preschool years, children start to lose their primary or "baby" teeth. The age at which they do so varies from child to child and is heavily influenced by genetic factors. Girls, who are ahead of boys in physical development, lose their primary teeth sooner. Cultural heritage also makes a difference. For example, American children get their first secondary tooth at 6 1/2 years, children in Ghana at just over 5 years, and children in Hong Kong around the sixth birthday. Environmental influences, especially prolonged malnutrition, can delay the age at which children cut their permanent teeth (Mott, James, & Sperhac, 1990).

Even though preschoolers will eventually lose their primary teeth, care of them is important, since diseased baby teeth can affect the health of permanent teeth. Consistent brushing, avoiding sugary foods, and regular dental visits prevent tooth cavities. Since the early 1970s, childhood cavities in the United States have dropped by more than half. Today, 50 percent of children reach young adulthood with no tooth decay at all. Unfortunately, these improvements do not apply to all sectors of the American or world's population. Tooth decay remains high among low-income youngsters in the United States and among children in developing countries because of poor diet, lack of fluoridation, and inadequate health care (Louie et al., 1990; Margolis, Hunt, & Vann, 1994).

ASYNCHRONIES IN PHYSICAL GROWTH

General growth curve
A curve that represents overall changes in body size—rapid growth during infancy, slower gains in early and middle childhood, and rapid growth once more during adolescence.

From what you have learned so far in this chapter and in Chapter 5, can you come up with a single overall description of early physical growth? If you found yourself answering no to this question, you are correct. Figure 8.3 shows that physical growth is an *asynchronous* process. Different body systems have their own unique, carefully timed patterns of maturation. The term **general growth curve** refers to change in overall body size (as measured by height and weight). It takes its name from the fact that outer dimensions of the body as well as a variety of internal organs follow the same pattern—rapid growth during infancy, slower gains in early and middle childhood, and rapid growth again during adolescence. Yet there are important exceptions to this trend. The development of the genitals shows a slight rise from birth to age 4, followed by a period of little change throughout middle childhood, after which growth is especially rapid during adolescence. In contrast, the lymph tissue (small clusters of glands found throughout the body) grows at an astounding pace in infancy and childhood, reaching a peak just before adolescence, at which point it declines. The lymph system plays a central role in the body's ability to fight infection and also assists in the absorption of nutrients from foods (Malina & Bouchard, 1991). Rapid early growth of lymph tissue helps ensure children's health and survival.

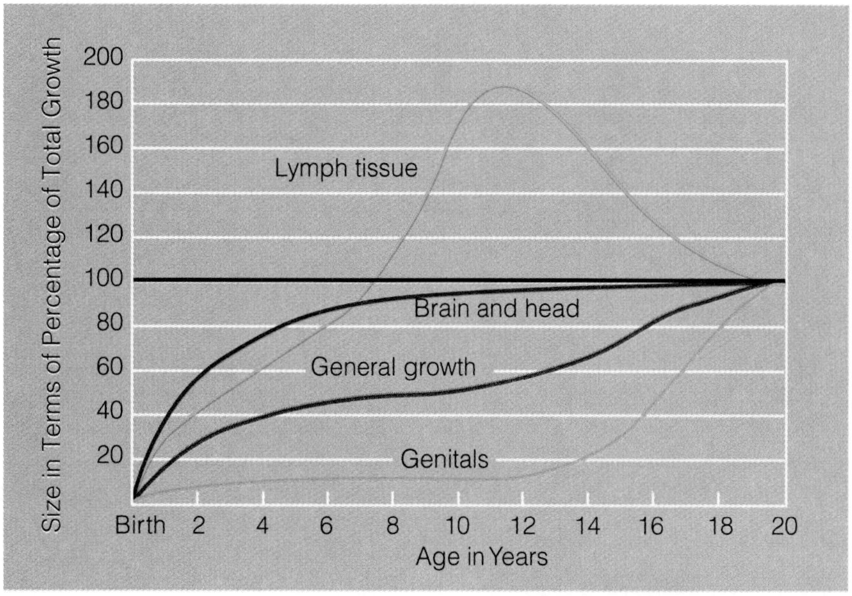

FIGURE 8.3

Growth of three different organ systems and tissues contrasted with the body's general growth. Growth is plotted in terms of percentage of change from birth to 20 years. Notice how the lymph tissue rises to twice its adult level by the end of childhood. Then it declines. *(Reprinted by permission of the publisher from J. M. Tanner, 1990,* Foetus into Man, *2nd ed., Cambridge, MA: Harvard University Press, p. 16. Copyright © 1990 by J. M. Tanner. All rights reserved.)*

Figure 8.3 shows another growth trend with which you are familiar: During the first few years, the brain grows faster than any other part of the body. Recall from Chapter 5 that the brain develops especially rapidly during infancy and toddlerhood. It continues to enlarge in size throughout early childhood, increasing from 70 percent of its adult weight at age 2 to 90 percent by age 6 (Tanner, 1990). Let's look at some highlights of brain development during early childhood.

BRAIN DEVELOPMENT IN EARLY CHILDHOOD

Between the years of 2 and 6, children gain in a wide variety of skills—physical coordination, perception, attention, memory, language, logical thinking, and imagination. Virtually all theorists agree that brain maturation contributes importantly to these changes.

During early childhood, the brain continues to *myelinate,* as it did during infancy and toddlerhood (return to Chapter 5, page 175, if you need to review this concept).

In Chapter 5, we saw that the cortex is made up of two *hemispheres* with distinct functions. A recent study measured the electrical activity of various cortical regions at different ages. The results revealed that the two hemispheres develop at different rates. For most children, the left hemisphere shows a dramatic growth spurt between 3 and 6 years and then levels off. In contrast, the right hemisphere matures slowly throughout early and middle childhood, showing a slight growth spurt between ages 8 and 10 (Thatcher, Walker, & Giudice, 1987).

These findings fit nicely with what we know about several aspects of cognitive development. Language skills (typically housed in the left hemisphere) increase at an astonishing pace in early childhood. In contrast, spatial skills (such as finding one's way from place to place, drawing pictures, and recognizing geometric shapes) develop very gradually over childhood and adolescence. Differences in rate of maturation of the two hemispheres also suggest that they are continuing to *lateralize* (specialize in cognitive functions). In the following sections, we examine brain lateralization during early childhood by focusing on the development of handedness. Then we take up some additional aspects of brain maturation during the preschool years.

Although left-handedness is associated with developmental problems, the large majority of left-handed children are completely normal. *(Gael Zucker/ Stock Boston)*

LATERALIZATION AND HANDEDNESS

One morning on a visit to the preschool, I followed the activities of 3-year-old Moira as she drew pictures, worked puzzles, joined in snack time, and played outside. Unlike most of her classmates, Moira does most things—drawing, eating, and zipping her jacket—with her left hand. But she also performs a few activities with her right hand, such as throwing a ball. By 5 to 6 months, more infants reach for objects with their right hand than with their left hand. By age 2, hand preference is stable, and it increases during early and middle childhood. As we will see, this indicates that specialization of brain regions strengthens during this time.

A strong hand preference reflects the greater capacity of one side of the brain—often referred to as the individual's **dominant cerebral hemisphere**—to carry out skilled motor action. Other abilities located on the dominant side may be superior as well. In support of this idea, for right-handed people—who make up 90 percent of the population—language is housed with hand control in the left hemisphere. For the remaining 10 percent who are left-handed, language is often shared between the hemispheres, rather than located in only one. This indicates that the brains of left-handers tend to be less strongly lateralized than those of right-handers (Hiscock & Kinsbourne, 1987). Consistent with this idea, many left-handed individuals (like Moira) are also *ambidextrous.* That is, although they prefer their left hand, they sometimes use their right hand skillfully as well (McManus et al., 1988).

Is handedness and, along with it, specialization of brain functions hereditary? Although researchers disagree on this issue, certain findings argue against a genetic explanation. Twins—whether identical or fraternal—are more likely than ordinary siblings to display opposite-handedness, yet we would expect identical twins to be more alike if heredity played a powerful role. Furthermore, the hand preference of each twin is related to positioning in the uterus (twins usually lie in opposite orientations). According to one theory, lateralization can be traced to prenatal events. New evidence indicates that the way most fetuses lie in the uterus—turned toward the left—may promote greater postural control by the right side of the body (Previc, 1991).

What about children whose hand use suggests an unusual organization of brain functions? Do these youngsters develop normally? Perhaps you have also heard that left-handedness is more frequent among severely retarded and mentally ill people than it is in the general population. Although research supports this conclusion, you also know that when two variables are correlated, this does not mean that one causes the other. Atypical lateralization is probably not responsible for the problems of these individuals. Instead, they may have suffered early damage to the left hemisphere, which caused their disabilities and, at the same time, led to a shift in handedness. In support of this idea, left-handedness shows a slight association with prenatal and birth difficulties that can result in brain damage, including prolonged labor, prematurity, Rh incompatibility, and breech delivery (Coren & Halpern, 1991; Williams, Buss, & Eskenazi, 1992).

Cross-sectional research reveals that with age, the proportion of left-handers in the population declines. On the basis of this evidence, some researchers have concluded left-handers do not live as long as right-handers (Coren & Halpern, 1991; Halpern & Coren, 1993). Others believe this age decline is largely due to a *cohort effect.* (To review this concept, return to Chapter 1, page 42). In previous generations, left-handed children were pressured to switch to their right. Today, there is greater cultural acceptance of left-handedness (Harris, 1993). If further research confirms that left-handers have a shorter life span, their greater risk of physical injury in a world built for right-handers may be largely responsible. Research confirms that left-handed children are more injury prone, and the risk of dying from an accident-related cause is greater in left-handed than right-handed adults (Graham et al., 1993; Halpern & Coren, 1991).

Finally, in considering the evidence on handedness and development, keep in mind that only a small number of left-handers show developmental problems of any

Dominant cerebral hemisphere
The hemisphere of the brain responsible for skilled motor action. The left hemisphere is dominant in right-handed individuals. In left-handed individuals, the right hemisphere may be dominant, or motor and language skills may be shared between the hemispheres.

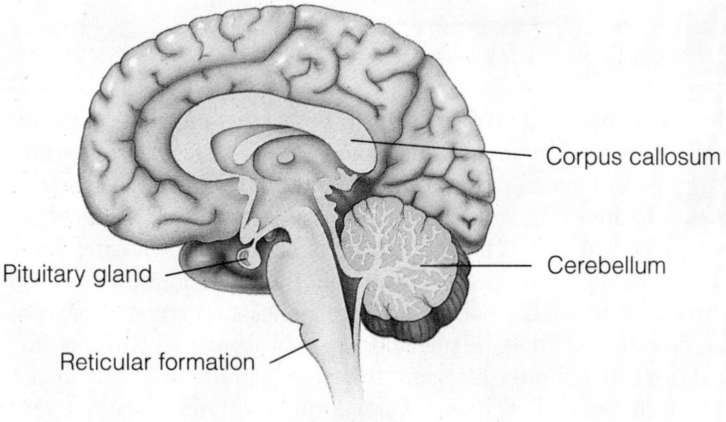

FIGURE 8.4

Cross section of the human brain, showing the location of the cerebellum, the reticular formation, and the corpus callosum.
These structures undergo considerable development during early childhood. Also shown is the pituitary gland, which secretes hormones that control body growth (see page 292).

kind. The great majority, like Moira, are normal in every respect. In fact, the unusual cortical lateralization of left-handed children may have certain advantages. Although we do not yet know why, left- and mixed-handed youngsters are more likely than their right-handed agemates to develop outstanding verbal and mathematical talents by adolescence (Benbow, 1986).

OTHER ADVANCES IN BRAIN DEVELOPMENT

Besides the cortex, several other areas of the brain make strides during early childhood. Figure 8.4 shows where each of these structures is located. As we look at these changes, you will see that they have one feature in common. They all involve establishing links among different parts of the brain, increasing the coordinated functioning of the central nervous system.

At the rear and base of the brain is the **cerebellum,** a structure that aids in balance and control of body movement. Fibers linking the cerebellum to the cerebral cortex begin to myelinate after birth, but they do not complete this process until about age 4 (Tanner, 1990). This change undoubtedly contributes to dramatic gains in motor control, so that by the end of the preschool years children can play a simple game of hopscotch, use their bodies to pump a playground swing, and throw a ball with a well-organized set of movements.

The **reticular formation,** a structure in the brain stem that maintains alertness and consciousness, myelinates throughout early childhood, continuing its growth into adolescence. Neurons in the reticular formation send out fibers to other areas of the brain. Many go to the frontal lobe of the cortex (McGuinness & Pribram, 1980). Maturation of the reticular formation contributes to improvements in sustained, controlled attention that we will discuss in Chapters 9 and 12.

A final brain structure that undergoes major changes during early childhood is the **corpus callosum.** It is a large bundle of fibers that connects the two hemispheres so that they can communicate, thereby increasing the efficiency of thinking. Myelinization of the corpus callosum does not begin until the end of the first year of life. By age 4 to 5, its development is fairly advanced (Spreen et al., 1984; Witelson & Kigar, 1988). By watching how young children solve certain problems, you can see evidence that the corpus callosum is developing. In one study, preschoolers played a matching game in which, with eyes closed, they felt a small textured pillow with one hand. While doing so, they had to tell whether a pillow rubbed across the other hand was made of the same fabric. Since each half of the brain receives information from only one side of the body, to match textures successfully, the hemispheres must communicate across the corpus callosum. Three-year-olds had great difficulty with this task, but by age 5 performance improved considerably (Galin et al., 1979).

Cerebellum
A brain structure that aids in balance and control of body movements.

Reticular formation
A brain structure that maintains alertness and consciousness.

Corpus callosum
The large bundle of fibers that connects the two hemispheres of the brain.

ASK YOURSELF . . .

- After graduating from dental school, Norm entered the Peace Corps and was assigned to rural India. He found that many Indian children had extensive tooth decay. In contrast, the young patients of his dental school friends in the United States had very little. What factors probably account for this difference?
- Crystal has a left-handed cousin who is mentally retarded. Recently she noticed that her 2-year-old daughter Shana is also left-handed. Crystal has heard that left-handedness is a sign of developmental problems, so she is worried about Shana. How would you respond to Crystal's concern?

BRIEF REVIEW

Compared to infancy, gains in body size take place more slowly during early childhood, and the child's body becomes more streamlined. The skeleton adds new epiphyses, and by the end of the preschool years children start to lose their primary teeth. Physical growth is an asynchronous process; different parts of the body have their own carefully timed patterns of maturation. During early childhood, the brain continues to grow more rapidly than the rest of the body. Hand preference strengthens, a sign of increasing brain lateralization. Although left-handedness is associated with developmental abnormalities and a shorter life span, the large majority of left-handed children show no developmental problems of any kind. The cerebellum, the reticular formation, and the corpus callosum undergo considerable development during early childhood, contributing to connections between different parts of the brain.

FACTORS AFFECTING GROWTH AND HEALTH IN EARLY CHILDHOOD

In earlier chapters, we considered a wide variety of influences on physical growth during the prenatal period and infancy. In the following sections, as we discuss growth and health in early childhood, you will encounter a variety of familiar themes. Although heredity remains powerfully important, environmental factors continue to play crucial roles. Emotional well-being, good nutrition, and relative freedom from disease remain essential for healthy physical growth. Also, as the Social Issues box on page 294 illustrates, environmental pollutants pose a serious threat to the physical health of hundreds of thousands of American children. Finally, we will see that like infant mortality, childhood mortality is largely preventable. Unintentional injuries are the leading cause of death during the preschool years.

HEREDITARY AND HORMONAL INFLUENCES

The impact of heredity on physical growth is evident throughout childhood. Children's physical size and rate of growth (as measured by skeletal age) are related to their parents'. Two tall parents are likely to have a tall child, two short parents a short child, and one tall and one short parent a child who falls somewhere in between. Also, children who show faster progress toward physical maturity tend to have parents who, as children, were advanced in physical growth themselves (Malina & Bouchard, 1991; Tanner, 1990).

Genes influence growth by controlling the body's production of hormones. The most important hormones for human growth are released by the **pituitary gland,** located near the base of the brain (return to Figure 8.4). Two pituitary hormones are especially influential. The first is **growth hormone (GH),** the only pituitary secretion produced continuously throughout life. It affects the development of all body tissues, except the central nervous system and the genitals. Although GH does not seem to affect prenatal growth, it is necessary for physical development from birth on. Children who lack it reach a mature height of only 4 feet, 4 inches, although they are normal in physical proportions and healthy in all other respects. When treated with injections of GH, such children show catch-up growth and then grow at a normal rate. Reaching their genetically expected height depends on starting treatment early, before the epiphyses of the skeleton are very mature (Tanner, 1990).

Pituitary gland
A gland located near the base of the brain that releases hormones affecting physical growth.

Growth hormone (GH)
A pituitary hormone that affects the development of almost all body tissues, except the central nervous system and the genitals.

A second pituitary hormone affecting children's growth is **thyroid-stimulating hormone (TSH).** It stimulates the thyroid gland (located in the neck) to release *thyroxine,* which is necessary for normal development of the nerve cells of the brain and for GH to have its full impact on body size. Infants born with a deficiency of thyroxine must receive it at once, or they will be mentally retarded. At later ages, children with too little thyroxine grow at a below-average rate. However, the central nervous system is no longer affected, since the most rapid period of brain development is complete. With prompt treatment, such children catch up in body growth and eventually reach normal size (Tanner, 1990).

EMOTIONAL WELL-BEING

In Chapter 5, we showed that emotional well-being can have a profound effect on growth and health in infancy. During the childhood years, mind and body continue to be closely linked. Preschoolers with very stressful home lives (due to divorce, financial difficulties, or a change in their parents' employment status) suffer more respiratory and intestinal illnesses as well as unintentional injuries (Beautrais, Fergusson, & Shannon, 1982).

When emotional deprivation is extreme, it can interfere with the production of growth hormone and lead to **deprivation dwarfism,** a growth disorder observed in children between 2 and 15 years of age. Lynette, the very small 4-year-old mentioned at the beginning of this chapter, was diagnosed as having this condition. Lynette had been taken from her parents' home and placed in foster care after child welfare authorities discovered that she spent most of her daytime hours by herself, unsupervised. Also, she may have been physically abused. To help her recover, she was enrolled in our laboratory preschool. Lynette showed the typical characteristics of deprivation dwarfism—very short stature, weight in proportion to her height, immature skeletal age, and decreased GH secretion. When such children are removed from their emotionally inadequate environments, their GH levels quickly return to normal, and they grow rapidly. But if treatment is delayed until late in development, the dwarfism can be permanent (Oates, Peacock, & Forrest, 1985).

NUTRITION

At the beginning of early childhood, there is often a dramatic change in the quantity and variety of foods that children will eat. Suddenly, the preschooler's appetite becomes unpredictable. Children may eat well at one meal and barely touch their food at the next. As a result, parents worry about the adequacy of the child's diet. Also, many children who as toddlers tried anything and everything become picky eaters (Pelchat & Pliner, 1986). One father wistfully recalled his son's eager sampling of the cuisine at a Chinese restaurant during toddlerhood. "He ate rice, chicken chow mein, egg rolls, and more. Now, at age 3, the only thing he'll try is the ice cream!"

This decline in the young child's appetite is normal. It occurs because growth has slowed. And preschoolers' wariness of new foods may be adaptive. Young children are still learning which items are safe to eat and which are not. By sticking to familiar foods, they are less likely swallow dangerous substances when adults are not around to protect them (Rozin, 1990). Adults need not worry about variations in the amount preschoolers eat from meal to meal. Over the course of a day, their food intake is fairly constant. In most cases, they compensate for a meal in which they ate little with a later one in which they eat more (Birch et al., 1991).

Because caloric intake is reduced, preschoolers need a high-quality diet. They require the same foods that make up a healthy adult diet—only smaller amounts. Milk and milk products, meat or meat alternatives (such as eggs, dried peas or beans, and peanut butter), vegetables and fruits, and breads and cereals should be

Thyroid-stimulating hormone (TSH)
A pituitary hormone that stimulates the thyroid gland to release thyroxine, which is necessary for normal brain development and body growth.

Deprivation dwarfism
A growth disorder observed between 2 and 15 years of age. Characterized by very short stature, weight that is usually appropriate for height, immature skeletal age, and decreased GH secretion. Caused by emotional deprivation.

SOCIAL ISSUES

LEAD POISONING IN CHILDHOOD

Five-year-old Desonia lives in an old, dilapidated tenement in a slum area of a large American city. Layers of paint applied over the years can be seen flaking off the inside walls and the back porch. The oldest paint chips are lead based. As an infant and young preschooler, Desonia picked them up and put them in her mouth. The slightly sweet taste of the leaded flakes encouraged her to nibble more. Soon Desonia became listless, apathetic, and irritable. Her appetite dropped off, her stomach hurt, and she vomited frequently. When Desonia complained of constant headaches, began to walk with an awkward gait, and experienced repeated convulsions (involuntary muscle contractions), her parents realized that she had more than a passing illness. At a nearby public health clinic, Desonia's blood was analyzed and her bones X-rayed. The tests showed that she had severe lead poisoning, a condition that results in permanent brain damage and (if allowed to persist) early death (Friedman & Weinberger, 1990; Veerula & Noah, 1990).

Despite years of public education, many parents remain unaware of the consequences of exposure to lead paint. In the United States, as many as three million children are believed to have dangerously high levels of lead in their bodies (Tesman & Hills, 1994). Inner-city youngsters growing up in deteriorated housing are at greatest risk, but the problem is not limited to low-income families. Children of advantaged parents who purchase older homes (built before 1978) can also be affected.

Severe lead poisoning like that experienced by Desonia has declined over the past 25 years in the United States, following passage of laws restricting use of lead-based paint. But lead already present in home environments is difficult to remove. As a result, many children continue to receive low doses that can lead to cognitive and behavioral impairments. In one study, young children with varying degrees of low-level lead exposure were followed over an 11-year period. The more lead in their bodies during the early years of life, the lower their IQ scores and the more likely they were to have a wide variety of academic difficulties during the school years, including problems with reading, vocabulary, fine motor coordination, and sustained attention. During adolescence, they earned poorer grades than their agemates, and they were seven times more likely to drop out of high school (Needleman et al., 1979, 1990).

Childhood lead poisoning has been called "the silent epidemic of American cities" (Fee, 1990, p. 570). Communities should require that lead-based paint be removed from older housing before children become residents. Until children's environments can be made safe, health professionals need to educate parents of all social classes about the hazards of lead exposure. High-risk children should be tested regularly and, if the lead concentration in their blood is too high, treated immediately. Recent evidence suggests that the effects of moderate lead exposure are partially reversible. In one study, the greater the reduction in children's blood lead level, the more their IQ scores rose over the following 6 months (Ruff et al., 1993).

TRY THIS . . .

- Return to Chapter 3, page 116, and review the impact of lead exposure during the prenatal period on children's development. How is it similar to the findings described here?
- Telephone a pediatrician's office or health clinic. Ask what kind of lead testing is routinely done (by law or otherwise) as part of children's physical exams in your community.

included (Kendrick, Kaufmann, & Messenger, 1991). Although fats, oils, and salt are also needed, these should be kept to a minimum because of their link to high blood pressure and heart disease in adulthood (U.S. Department of Health and Human Services, 1988). Foods high in sugar should also be avoided. In addition to causing tooth decay, sugary cereals, cookies, cakes, soft drinks, and candy are high-energy items, with little nutritional value, that lessen young children's appetite for healthy foods.

The wide variety of foods eaten in cultures around the world indicates that the social environment has a powerful impact on young children's food preferences. For example, Mexican preschoolers enthusiastically eat chili peppers, whereas American children quickly reject them. What accounts for this difference? Children tend to imitate the food choices of people they admire—peers as well as adults. In Mexico,

Unpredictable appetites and picky eating are common during early childhood. At dinnertime, this 3-year-old girl seems more interested in playing than eating. Fortunately, her parents are sensitive to her nutritional needs. They offer a well-balanced meal and put only a small portion on her plate. *(Joel Gordon)*

children often see family members delighting in the taste of peppery foods (Birch, Zimmerman, & Hind, 1980; Rozin & Schiller, 1980).

Repeated exposure to a new food (without any direct pressure to eat it) also increases children's acceptance. In one study, preschoolers were given one of three versions of a food they had never eaten before (sweet, salty, or plain tofu). After 8 to 15 exposures, they readily ate the food. But they preferred the version they had already tasted. For example, children in the "sweet" condition liked sweet tofu best, and those in the "plain" condition liked plain tofu best (Sullivan & Birch, 1990). These findings reveal that children's tastes are trained by foods they encounter repeatedly in the environment. Adding sugar or salt in hopes of increasing a young child's willingness to eat healthy foods is not necessary. It simply teaches the child to like a sugary or salty taste.

The emotional climate at mealtimes has a powerful impact on children's eating habits. For many parents, feeding preschoolers is a major source of anxiety, and meals become unpleasant and stressful. At times, food becomes a bribe. Parents coax their children by saying, "Finish your vegetables, and you can have an extra cookie." Unfortunately, trying to reinforce eating of healthy foods with treats causes children to like the healthy food less and the treat more (Birch, Johnson, & Fisher, 1995; Birch et al., 1987). There are many ways that parents, teachers, and caregivers can promote healthy, varied eating in young children. Table 8.1 offers some suggestions.

Finally, as we indicated in earlier chapters, many children in the United States and in developing countries are deprived of diets that support healthy growth. Hallie is a 5-year-old boy who was bused to our laboratory preschool from a poor neighborhood on the west side of town. His mother's welfare check was barely enough to cover cost of housing, let alone food. Hallie's diet was deficient in protein as well as vitamins and minerals essential for healthy body growth and functioning—iron (to prevent anemia), calcium (to support development of bones and teeth), vitamin C (to facilitate iron absorption and wound healing), and vitamin A (to help maintain eyes, skin, and a variety of internal organs). These are the most common dietary deficiencies of the preschool years. Not surprisingly, Hallie was thin and pale, and he often seemed tired. By age 7 low-income children in the United States are, on the average, about 1 inch shorter than their middle-class counterparts (Yip, Scanlon, & Trowbridge, 1993). In contrast, there are no social-class differences in body size in Sweden, where generous government food programs provide all children with access to nutritious diets (Children's Defense Fund, 1991a; Lindgren, 1976).

TABLE 8.1

Ways to Encourage Good Nutrition in Early Childhood

SUGGESTION	DESCRIPTION
Offer a varied, healthy diet	Provide a well-balanced variety of nutritious foods that are colorful and attractively served. Avoid serving sweets and "junk" foods as a regular part of meals and snacks.
Offer predictable meals as well as several snacks each day	Preschoolers' stomachs are small, and they may not be able to eat enough in three meals to satisfy energy requirements. They benefit from extra opportunities to eat.
Offer small portions, and permit the child to ask for seconds	When too much food is put on the plate, preschoolers may be overwhelmed and not even try to eat.
Offer new foods early in the meal and over several meals; respond with patience if the child rejects the food	Introduce new foods before the child's appetite is satisfied. Let children see you eating and enjoying the new food. If the child rejects it, accept the refusal and serve it again at another meal. As foods become more familiar, they are more readily accepted.
Keep mealtimes pleasant, and include the child in mealtime conversations.	A pleasant, relaxed eating environment helps children develop positive attitudes about food. Avoid confrontations over disliked foods and table manners.
Avoid using food as a reward	Saying "No dessert until you clean your plate" tells children that they must eat regardless of how hungry they are and that dessert is the best part of the meal.

Source: Birch, Johnson, & Fisher, 1995; Kendrick, Kaufmann, & Messenger, 1991.

INFECTIOUS DISEASE

Two weeks into the school year, I looked outside my window and noticed that Hallie was absent from the play yard. Several weeks passed; still I did not see him. Finally, I asked Leslie, his preschool teacher, what had happened. "Hallie's been hospitalized with the measles," she explained. "He's had a difficult time recovering—lost weight when there wasn't much to lose in the first place. He's better now, but still very weak. The doctor's trying to build him up before letting him return to school again." In well-nourished children, ordinary childhood illnesses have no effect on physical growth. But when children are poorly fed, disease interacts with malnutrition in a vicious spiral, and the consequences for physical growth can be severe.

To inform parents about the importance of immunizations, the U.S. Department of Health and Human Services distributes this poster free of charge. In the poster's next printing, chicken pox will be added to the list of preventable childhood diseases. A chicken pox vaccine was approved by the federal government in 1995.

Hallie's reaction to the measles is commonplace among children in developing nations, where a large proportion of the population lives in poverty. In these countries, many children do not receive a program of immunizations. Illnesses such as measles and chicken pox, which typically do not appear until after age 3 in industrialized nations, occur much earlier. This is because poor diet depresses the body's immune system, making children far more susceptible to disease (Tanner, 1990).

Disease, in turn, is a major cause of malnutrition and, through it, affects physical growth. Illness reduces appetite, and it limits the body's ability to absorb foods that children do eat. These outcomes are especially severe for children with intestinal infections. Diarrhea is widespread in developing countries and increases during early childhood due to contaminated foods (Grant, 1994). Research in poverty-stricken Guatemalan villages showed that 7-year-olds who had been relatively free of diarrhea since birth were nearly 1 1/2 inches taller and 3 1/2 pounds heavier than their frequently ill peers. This difference is especially large, since the Guatemalan children were quite small to begin with—5 inches shorter and 11 pounds lighter, on the average, than well-nourished children in the United States (Martorell, 1980).

In industrialized nations, childhood diseases have declined dramatically during the past half century, largely due to widespread immunization of infants and young children. Hallie got the measles because, unlike his classmates from more advantaged homes, he did not receive a full program of immunizations during his first 2 years of life. Although the majority of preschoolers in the United States are immunized, some do not receive this protection until 5 or 6 years of age, when it is required for school entry. As a result, cases of preventable disease have increased in

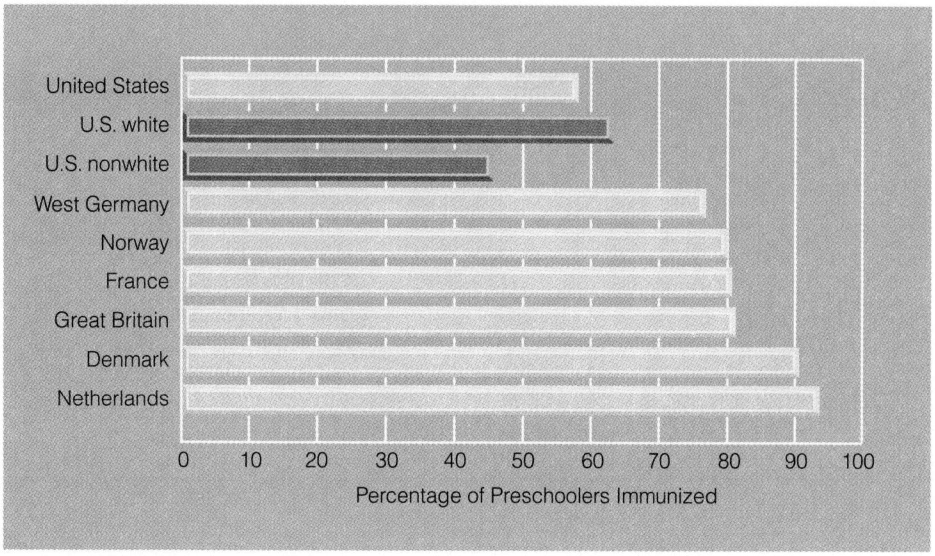

FIGURE 8.5

Immunization rates for preschool children in the United States and European nations, based on the most recent cross-national data. Children were immunized for diphetheria, tetanus, pertussis (whooping cough), measles, and polio. *(Adapted from Williams, 1990.)*

recent years. For example, in 1990 there were over 25,000 cases of measles, 16 times the number in 1983 (Children's Defense Fund, 1991b).

Figure 8.5 compares the immunization rates for preschoolers in the United States and a variety of European nations. The large number of low-income, ethnic minority youngsters who are not immunized is of special concern, since their overall poorer health makes them more vulnerable to complications when disease strikes. But note that immunization of white preschoolers also falls below the figures for other countries.

How is it that European nations (several of which also have large foreign-born and minority populations) have managed to achieve high rates of immunization, whereas the United States' record is so poor? In earlier chapters, we noted that many children in the United States do not have access to the medical care they need. The Cultural Influences box on page 298 examines child health care in the United States and European nations. Beginning in 1994, all medically uninsured American children were guaranteed free vaccinations through public health clinics.

Inability to pay for vaccines, however, is only one cause of low immunization rates. Misconceptions about safe medical practices also contribute. American parents often report that they delay bringing their child in for a vaccination because they fear that a mild illness might reduce its effectiveness or that their child might have an adverse reaction (Abbotts & Osborn, 1993; Shalala, 1993). In one case, a mother whose child reacted poorly to her first diphtheria–tetnanus–pertussis (DTP) shot decided not to let her have any more of the vaccine. Two years later, the child caught pertussis (whooping cough) and infected her 1-month-old sister, who battled for her life (Friedman & Weiss, 1993). Public education programs directed at increasing parental knowledge about the importance of timely immunizations are badly needed.

A final point regarding communicable disease in early childhood deserves mention. In recent years, doctors, nurses, and parents have noticed that day care attendance increases the potential for spread of infection. To explore this issue, turn to the From Research to Practice box on page 300.

CHILDHOOD INJURIES

Three-year-old Tory caught my eye as I visited the preschool classroom one day. More than any other child, he had trouble sitting still and paying attention at story time. Outside, I saw him dart from one place to another, spending little time at a single activity. On a field trip to our campus museum, Tory ran across the street

CULTURAL INFLUENCES

CHILD HEALTH CARE IN THE UNITED STATES AND EUROPEAN NATIONS

In the United States, economically disadvantaged children are far less likely than well-off youngsters to receive basic health care. Because of the high cost of medical treatment, low-income children see a doctor only half as often as middle-class children with similar illnesses (Newacheck & Starfield, 1988). Estimates indicate that 60 per cent of American children under 5 who come from poverty-stricken families are in less than excellent health (Children's Defense Fund, 1992).

American health insurance is an optional, employment-related fringe benefit. Many American businesses that rely on low-wage and part-time help do not insure their employees. If they do, they often do not cover other family members, including children. Although a variety of public health programs are available in the United States, they reach only the most needy individuals. This leaves nearly 8.3 million children from poor, low-income, and moderate-income families uninsured and, therefore, without affordable medical care (Children's Defense Fund, 1994).

The inadequacies of American child health care stand in sharp contrast to services provided in other industrialized nations, where medical insurance is government sponsored and available to all citizens regardless of income. Let's look at two examples.

In the Netherlands, each child receives free medical examinations from birth through adolescence. During the early years, health care also includes parental counseling in nutrition, disease prevention, and child development. The Netherlands achieves its extraordinarily high childhood immunization rate (refer to Figure 8.5) by giving parents of every newborn baby a written schedule that shows exactly when and where the child should be immunized. If the child is not brought in at the specified time, a public health nurse calls the family. In instances of repeated missed appointments, the nurse goes to the home to ensure that the child receives the recommended immunizations (Verbrugge, 1990a, 1990b).

In Norway, federal law requires that well baby and child clinics be established in all communities and that examinations by physicians take place three times during the first year and at ages 2 and 4. Specialized nurses see children on additional occasions, monitoring their growth and development, providing immunizations, and counseling parents on physical and mental health. Although citizens pay a small fee for routine medical visits, hospital services are free of charge. Parents with a seriously ill hospitalized child are given leave from work with full salary, a benefit financed by the government (Lie, 1990).

In Chapter 2, we noted that Americans have historically been strongly committed to the idea that parents should assume total responsibility for the care and rearing of children. This belief, in addition to powerful economic interests in the medical community, has prevented government-sponsored health services from being offered to all children. In European nations, child health care is regarded as a fundamental human right, no different from the right to education (Williams, 1990). Currently, many organizations, government officials, and concerned citizens committed to child health are working to find ways to guarantee every American child necessary medical care.

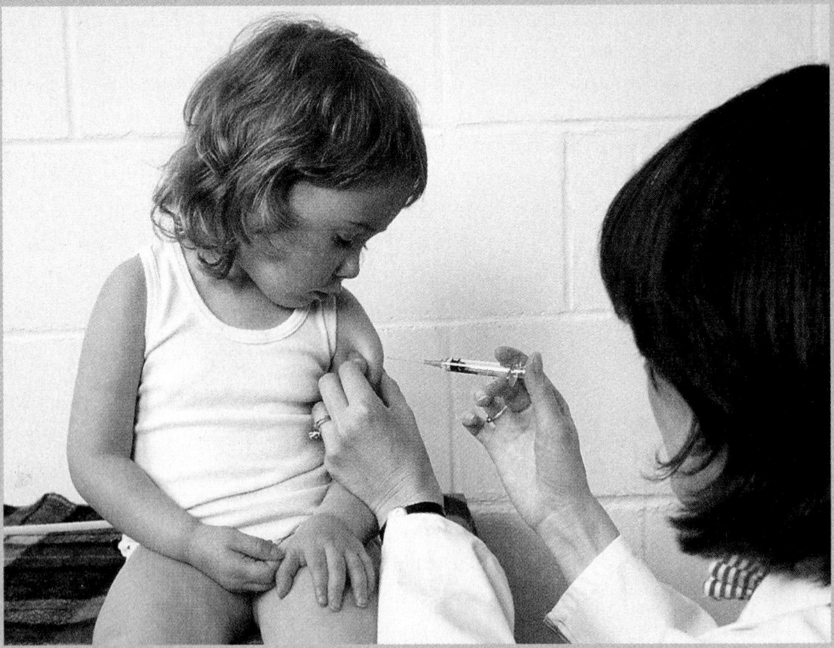

Regular medical checkups and immunizations help ensure that this preschooler will remain free of serious illnesses. In most industrialized nations, health care is regarded as a fundamental human right and is guaranteed to all children. The United States lags behind other countries in government-sponsored child health services. *(Jim Scully/Photo Researchers)*

without holding his partner's hand, even though his teacher had just reminded the children of appropriate safety precautions. Later in the year, I read about Tory on the front page of our local newspaper:

> A 3-year-old boy escaped serious injury yesterday when he shifted his mother's car into gear while she was scraping its windows, causing the vehicle to roll over the side of an overpass. Tory Flint was treated for bumps and bruises at BroMenn Hospital and released.
>
> Police said his mother, 24-year-old Deborah Flint, parked her car in the driveway and put Tory in the front passenger seat. She told police she was outside the car scraping the windows free of ice when her son put the car into gear.
>
> When the car moved forward, it went through a metal guardrail, took a nose dive over the side of a 10-foot concrete underpass, and hung there until rescue workers arrived. Police charged Mrs. Flint with a violation of state child restraint laws, which require use of child restraint seats for children under age 5.

Today, the greatest threat to children's health comes from a large collection of unintentional injuries—auto collisions, pedestrian accidents, drownings, poisonings, firearm wounds, burns, falls, swallowing of foreign objects, and others. Taken together, these events account for 40 to 50 percent of deaths in early and middle childhood and as many as 75 percent during adolescence. Approximately 22,000 youngsters die from these incidents each year. And for each death, thousands of other injured children survive but suffer pain, brain damage, and permanent physical handicaps (Brooks & Roberts, 1990). As Figure 8.6 shows, auto accidents, fires, and drownings are the most common injuries during the early childhood years. Motor vehicle collisions are by far the most frequent source of injury at all ages. They are the leading cause of death among children over 1 year of age (Fawcett, Seekins, & Jason, 1987).

■ **FACTORS RELATED TO CHILDHOOD INJURIES.** We are used to thinking of childhood injuries as "accidental," a word that encourages us to believe that chance is responsible for them and that they cannot be prevented (Christophersen, 1989). But a close look at childhood injuries reveals that a variety of individual, environmental, and societal factors are related to them. This suggests that meaningful causes underlie childhood injuries, and we can, indeed, do something about them.

As Tory's case suggests, individual differences exist in the safety level of children's everyday behaviors. Because of their higher activity level and greater willingness to take risks during play, boys are more likely to be injury victims than girls. (Look again at Figure 8.6.) Temperamental characteristics—irritability, inattentiveness, and negative mood—are also related to childhood injuries. As we saw in Chapter 7, children with these traits present parents with special child-rearing challenges. Where safety is concerned, these youngsters are likely to protest when placed in auto seat restraints, refuse to take a companion's hand when crossing the street, and disobey after repeated adult instruction and discipline (Matheny, 1987, 1991).

At the same time, families whose preschoolers get injured tend to have characteristics that increase the likelihood of exposure to danger. Poverty and low parental education are strongly associated with injury deaths. Parents who must cope with many daily stresses often have little time and energy to monitor the safety of their youngsters. And the homes and neighborhoods of such families pose further risks. Noise, crowding, and confusion characterize these households, and they tend to be

FIGURE 8.6

Rate of injury mortality in the United States for children between 1 and 4 years of age by type of injury and sex.
Note that for all kinds of injuries, mortality is higher for boys than girls. *(Adapted from Williams & Kotch, 1990.)*

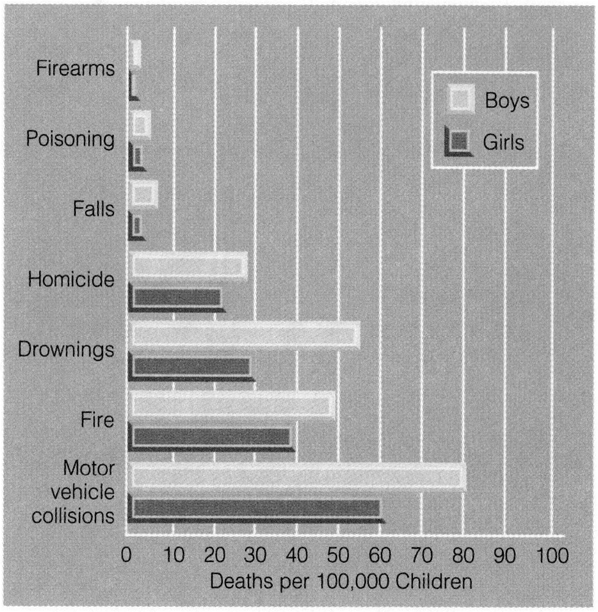

FROM RESEARCH TO PRACTICE

DAY CARE AND INFECTIOUS DISEASE

During his first 12 months in day care, 3-year-old Zach caught five colds, had the flu on two occasions, experienced one bout of diarrhea, and developed an ear infection. His mother Madge, an assembly-line worker at a manufacturing plant, had to leave her job on the spur-of-the-moment five times to pick Zach up because of illness. Madge stayed home to care for Zach for a total of 15 days during the year. After using up her own sick leave of 7 days, she was forced to take nonpaid leave for the remainder. Madge thought to herself, "Missing extra days of work has already strained our limited family budget. Is day care increasing Zach's exposure to disease?"

In the past, infectious illnesses commonly occurred between 5 and 9 years of age, when children gathered in large groups for the first time in school. Today, millions of children enroll in day care, creating earlier opportunities for children to come in close contact and increasing the exposure of infants and preschoolers to infection. Research in Europe and the United States indicates that childhood illness rises with day care attendance. Diseases that spread most rapidly are respiratory infections (the most frequent illness suffered by young children) and diarrhea (Thacker et al., 1992). Childhood viral illnesses, such as measles, mumps, diphtheria, and whooping cough, are not more common among day care than home-reared children. The reason is that licensed day care settings require immunization. But as many as 10 to 20 percent of children attending day care are not immunized, so rapid transmission of these illnesses is still possible (Hinman, 1987).

Spread of communicable disease in day care can be controlled in the following ways:

- Proper hygiene is essential. Illness rates decline when adults and children routinely wash their hands—before handling food, after toileting, and after handling clothing or objects contaminated with body secretions.
- Regular cleaning of the day care environment reduces the spread of illness. Because infants and young children often put toys in their mouths, these objects should be rinsed frequently with a disinfectant solution.
- Design of the day care setting can help control infection. Areas for food preparation and toileting should be physically separated. Spacious, well-ventilated rooms and small group sizes limit the spread of illness.
- Children admitted to day care should have a full program of infant and early childhood immunization.
- Isolation of children with communicable diseases that spread rapidly, such as viral illnesses and diarrhea, is important. As long as good hygiene is followed, children with mild respiratory infections (such as the common cold) can continue to attend day care with little impact on the health of other youngsters.

On the average, a day care infant becomes sick 9 to 10 times a year, a day care preschool child 6 to 7 times (Jordan, 1987; Wald, Guerra, & Byers, 1991). Unfortunately, most employed parents, like Madge, have no adequate solution to the problem of providing child care when their youngster is ill. Currently, only one-third to one-half of American employees receive paid sick leave of any kind. Time off or opportunities to work at home when children are ill would greatly assist employed parents in raising healthy, secure youngsters. A few day care centers have special "get well" rooms for mildly ill children and care at separate sites for more seriously ill youngsters (Giebink, 1993). Many parents need these backup systems, and they should be more widely available.

located in run-down, inner-city neighborhoods where children have few places to play other than the streets (Matheny, 1987; Rivara & Barber, 1985).

Broad societal conditions also affect childhood injury. In Chapter 5, we pointed out that the United States has slipped down in the international rankings in infant mortality. Unfortunately, this pattern repeats itself for deaths due to childhood injuries. Among Western industrialized nations, the United States ranks among the highest in childhood injury mortality. Furthermore, although injury deaths have declined steadily in nearly all developed countries during the past 30 years, they seem to be on the rise in the United States (Williams & Kotch, 1990).

What factors account for this worrisome picture? Widespread poverty, a shortage of high-quality day care (to supervise children in their parents' absence), and an alarmingly high rate of births to teenagers (who are neither psychologically nor financially ready to raise a child) are believed to play important roles. But children from advantaged families are also at somewhat greater risk for injury in the United

States than they are in European nations (Williams & Kotch, 1990). This indicates that besides reducing poverty and teenage pregnancy and upgrading the status of day care, additional steps must be taken to ensure the safety of American children.

PREVENTING CHILDHOOD INJURIES. Childhood injuries have many causes, so a variety of approaches are needed to control them. Laws prevent a great many injuries by requiring that young children ride in car safety seats, that medicine bottles have child-resistant caps, that clothing be flame-proof, and that backyard swimming pools (the site of 90 percent of early childhood drownings) be fenced. Communities can also help by modifying their physical environments. Inexpensive and widely available public transportation can reduce the time that children spend in cars. Playgrounds, a common site of injury, can be covered with protective surfaces, such as rubber matting, sand, and wood chips (Wilson & Baker, 1987). Free, easily installed window guards can be given to families living in high-rise apartment buildings to prevent falls. And public education—in the form of widespread media campaigns and information distributed in doctors' offices, schools, and day care centers—helps inform parents and children about safety issues (Pless & Arsenault, 1987).

Nevertheless, many dangers cannot be eliminated from the environment. And even though they know better, many parents and children continue to behave in ways that compromise safety. For example, 50 percent of parents (like Tory's mother) fail to place their infants and preschoolers in car safety seats (Wilson & Baker, 1987). Adults often leave caps off medicine bottles, neglect to replace batteries in home smoke detectors, and leave handguns within reach of children. In addition to the preventive measures just described, ways must be found to change human behavior.

A variety of programs based on the principles of behaviorism (modeling and reinforcement) have successfully improved the safety practices of adults and children alike. In one, counselors helped parents identify a variety of dangers in the home—fire hazards, objects that young children might swallow, poisonous substances, firearms, and others. Then they demonstrated specific ways to eliminate the dangers (Tertinger, Greene, & Lutzker, 1984). In several other interventions, parents and children were rewarded with prizes if the children arrived at day care or school each morning properly restrained in car seats (Roberts, Alexander, & Knapp, 1990; Roberts, Fanurik, & Wilson, 1988). Efforts like these have been remarkably successful in reducing the dangers to which children are exposed. They also add to the examples we have seen in earlier chapters of the practical usefulness of behaviorist theory.

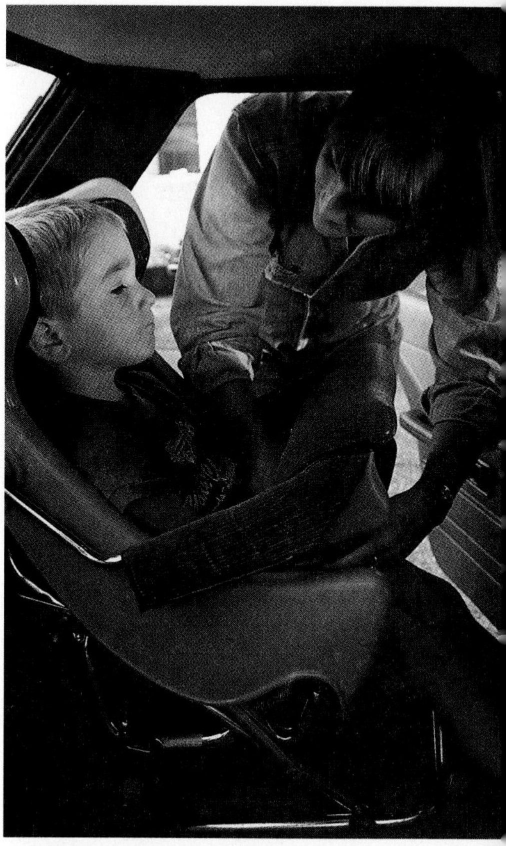

This mother reduces her son's chances of injury by insisting that he ride in a car safety seat. In doing so, she also teaches him good safety practices. *(George White)*

BRIEF REVIEW

Heredity influences physical growth by regulating the production of hormones. Two pituitary hormones, growth hormone (GH) and thyroid-stimulating hormone (TSH), play important roles in children's growth. Many environmental factors affect growth and health in early childhood. Extreme emotional deprivation can interfere with the production of GH, resulting in deprivation dwarfism. Although preschoolers' appetites decline and they resist new foods, good nutrition remains important in early childhood. The emotional climate of mealtimes influences the quality and range of foods that young children will eat. Disease can interact with malnutrition to seriously undermine children's growth, an effect that is especially common in developing countries. Unintentional injuries are the leading cause of childhood mortality. Injury rates are related to child and family characteristics as well as to broad societal conditions. Consequently, a variety of approaches are needed to prevent them.

ASK YOURSELF . . .

- One day, Leslie prepared a new snack to serve at preschool: celery stuffed with ricotta cheese and pineapple. The first time she served it, few of the children touched it. What techniques can Leslie use to encourage her pupils to accept the snack? What methods should she avoid?
- Chapter 1 introduced you to ecological systems theory, which shows how children's well-being is affected by several levels of the environment. Review ecological systems theory. Then list ways to reduce childhood injuries by intervening in the microsystem, mesosystem, and macrosystem.

MOTOR DEVELOPMENT IN EARLY CHILDHOOD

Visit a playground at a neighborhood park, preschool, or day care center, and select several children between 2 and 6 years for observation. Jot down descriptions of their activities and movements, paying special attention to differences between the younger and older children. You will see that an explosion of new motor skills occurs in early childhood, each of which builds on the simpler movement patterns of toddlerhood.

The same principle that governs motor development during the first 2 years of life continues to operate during the preschool years. Children integrate previously acquired skills into more complex *systems of action.* (Return to Chapter 5, page 184, if you need to review this concept.) Then they revise each new skill as their bodies become larger and stronger, their central nervous systems become better developed, and their environments present them with new challenges. This means that although the motor skills of early childhood tend to appear in a regular sequence, they are not simply due to a genetically determined, maturational pattern (Clark, Phillips, & Petersen, 1989). Instead, a variety of factors—both genetic and environmental—combine to produce these accomplishments. Let's look closely at young children's gross and fine motor skills to illustrate this idea.

GROSS MOTOR DEVELOPMENT

Toddlers walk with toes turned out, teetering from side to side and frequently toppling over. As children's bodies become more streamlined and less top-heavy, their center of gravity shifts downward, toward the trunk. As a result, balance improves greatly, a change that paves the way for new motor skills involving large muscles of the body (Ulrich & Ulrich, 1985). By age 2, preschoolers' gaits become smooth and rhythmic—secure enough so that soon they leave the ground, at first by running and later by jumping, hopping, galloping, and skipping. As children become steadier on their feet, their arms and torsos are freed to experiment with new skills—throwing and catching balls, steering tricycles, and swinging on horizontal bars and rings. Then upper and lower body skills combine into more refined actions. Five- and 6-year-olds dash across the play yard to catch a ball, simultaneously steer and peddle a tricycle, and flexibly move their whole body when hopping and jumping. Table 8.2 provides an overview of refinements in gross motor skills during the preschool years.

WALKING AND RUNNING. Ask a toddler to run for you. What you will see is a hurried walk, not a true run. Before age 2, children's feet are in constant contact with the floor, and their arms do not swing in opposition to their legs, helping to balance the body. During the third year, the left arm swings forward when the right foot steps, and children no longer need to keep their legs widely spaced to stay upright. As a result, feet come closer together and point straight ahead in a well-coordinated walk. Soon the child is airborne into a full-fledged run, lifting both feet off the ground during each stride. Gradually, preschoolers find that by contacting the ground with only the ball of the foot and vigorously thrusting the knees upward, they can run faster. Five-year-olds run about twice as quickly as they did at age 2—over 11 feet per second (Cratty, 1986).

Additional variations on the theme of walking appear as children experiment with movements and imitate the motor skills of playmates. Around age 4, gallops and one-step skips (in which a step on one foot alternates with a step-shuffle on the other) appear. Older preschoolers can climb up and down ladders, scale jungle gyms, and walk balance beams easily. And around 6 years, they can skip in a well-coordinated fashion (Malina & Bouchard, 1991).

TABLE 8.2

Changes in Gross Motor Skills During Early Childhood

AGE	WALKING AND RUNNING	JUMPING	HOPPING	THROWING AND CATCHING	PEDDLING AND STEERING
2–3 years	Walks more rhythmically; widely spaced feet narrow; opposite arm–leg swing appears. Hurried walk changes to true run.	Jumps down from step. Jumps several inches off floor with both feet, no arm action.	Hops 1 to 3 times on same foot with stiff upper body and nonhopping leg held still.	Throws ball with forearm extension only; feet remain stationary. Awaits thrown ball with rigid arms outstretched.	Pushes riding toy with feet; little steering.
3–4 years	Walks up stairs, alternating feet. Walks downstairs, leading with one foot. Walks straight line.	Jumps off floor, coordinated arm action. Broad-jumps about 1 foot.	Hops 4 to 6 times on same foot, flexing upper body and swinging nonhopping leg.	Throws ball with slight body rotation but little or no transfer of weight with feet. Flexes elbows in preparation for catching; traps ball against chest.	Peddles and steers tricycle.
4–5 years	Walks downstairs, alternating feet. Walks circular line. Walks awkwardly on balance beam. Runs more smoothly. Gallops and skips with one foot.	Jumps upward and forward more effectively; travels greater distance.	Hops 7 to 9 times on same foot; improved speed of hopping.	Throws ball with increased body rotation and some transfer of weight forward. Catches ball with hands; if unsuccessful, may still trap ball against chest.	Rides tricycle rapidly, steers smoothly.
5–6 years	Walks securely on balance beam. Increases speed of run. Gallops more smoothly. Engages in true skipping.	Jumps off floor about 1 foot. Broad jumps 3 feet.	Hops 50 feet on same foot in 10 seconds. Hops with rhythmic alteration (2 hops on one foot and 2 on the other).	Has mature throwing and catching pattern. Moves arm more and steps forward during throw. Awaits thrown ball with relaxed posture, adjusting body to path and size of ball.	Rides bicycle with training wheels.

Sources: Cratty, 1986; Getchell & Roberton, 1989; Newborg, Stock, & Wnek, 1984; Roberton, 1984.

JUMPING AND HOPPING. As toddlers watch others jump, they try it themselves, but they are usually unsuccessful. One 18-month-old I observed bent her knees in preparation for liftoff but could not figure out what to do next! Not only is the appropriate body movement absent, but leg muscles probably lack the strength and power needed to overcome the child's weight. The first jumps, around age 2, are awkward. The young preschooler pushes off with one foot, while the other absorbs the shock of landing. During the middle of the third year, the first two-footed takeoffs and landings can be seen. The child can jump upward as well as forward, but movements of the arms are not yet used to propel the body (Roberton, 1984). For example, when asked to broad jump, the 3-year-old's arms move back into a winging position and remain there. In contrast, 6-year-olds move their arms forward during the jump, increasing the distance traveled.

Hopping shows a similar pattern of development. Initially, the child focuses on only the footwork. Between ages 2 and 3, children can hop a few times in succession, but they land flat-footed and hold the nonhopping leg still, usually in front of the body. Over the next year, the entire motion becomes more flexible as the child experiments with ways to allow a softer, more comfortable landing (Roberton & Halverson, 1988). Five- and 6-year-olds hop skillfully. They can repeat the motion many times, moving swiftly across the floor (Getchell & Roberton, 1989).

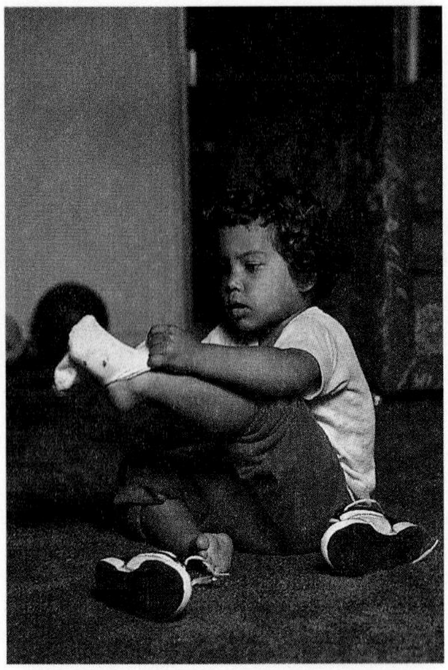

To a preschooler, putting on clothing is challenging but rewarding. Young children enjoy a new sense of independence when they can dress themselves. *(Mary Kate Denny/PhotoEdit)*

BALL SKILLS. Play a game of catch with a 2- or 3-year-old, and watch the child's body carefully. Young preschoolers stand still facing the target, throwing with their arm thrust forward. Once again, at first appearance of the skill, other parts of the body are not involved. Catching is equally awkward. Two-year-olds extend their arms and hands rigidly, using them as a single unit to trap the ball. By age 3, children flex their elbows enough to trap the ball against the chest. But if the ball arrives too quickly, younger preschoolers cannot adapt, and it may simply bounce off the child's body (Roberton, 1984).

Gradually, children call on the shoulders, torso, trunk, and legs to support throwing and catching. By age 4, the body rotates as the child throws, and at 5 years preschoolers begin to shift their weight forward, stepping as they release the ball. As a result, the ball travels faster and farther. When the ball is returned, older preschoolers predict its place of landing by moving forward, backward, or sideways. Then they catch it with their hands and fingers, "giving" with arms and body to absorb the force of the ball (see Figure 8.7).

FINE MOTOR DEVELOPMENT

Like gross motor development, fine motor skills take a giant leap forward during early childhood (see Table 8.3). Because control of the hands and fingers improves, young children at play put puzzles together, build structures out of small blocks, cut and paste, and string beads. To parents, the fine motor progress of the preschool years is most apparent in two areas: (1) children's increasing ability to care for their own bodies, and (2) the drawings and paintings that fill the walls at home, day care, and nursery school.

SELF-HELP SKILLS. During early childhood, children gradually become self-sufficient at dressing and feeding. Two-year-olds put on and take off simple items of clothing. By age 3, they do so well enough to take care of toileting needs by themselves. Between ages 4 and 5, children can dress and undress without supervision. At mealtimes, young preschoolers use a spoon well, and they can serve themselves. By age 4, they are adept with a fork, and around 5 to 6 years they can use a knife to cut soft foods. Roomy clothing with large buttons and zippers and child-sized eating utensils help children master these skills.

Preschoolers get great satisfaction from managing their own bodies. They are proud of their independence, and their new skills also make life easier for adults. But parents need to be patient about these abilities. When tired and in a hurry, young children often revert to eating with their fingers. And the 3-year-old who

TABLE 8.3

Changes in Fine Motor Skills During Early Childhood

AGE	DRESSING	FEEDING	OTHER
2–3 years	Puts on and removes simple items of clothing. Zips and unzips large zippers.	Uses spoon effectively.	Opens door by turning knob. Strings large beads.
3–4 years	Fastens and unfastens large buttons.	Serves self food without assistance.	Uses scissors to cut paper. Copies vertical line and circle.
4–5 years	Dresses and undresses without assistance.	Uses fork effectively.	Cuts with scissors following line. Copies triangle, cross, and some letters.
5–6 years		Uses knife to cut soft food.	Ties single overhand knot; around age 6, ties shoes. Draws person with six parts. Copies some numerals and simple words.

Sources: Furuno et al., 1987; Newborg, Stock, & Wnek, 1984.

FIGURE 8.7

Changes in catching during early childhood.
At age 2, children extend their arms rigidly, and the ball tends to bounce off the body. At age 3, they flex their elbows in preparation for catching, trapping the ball against the chest. By ages 5 and 6, children involve the entire body, catching with the hands and fingers.

dresses himself in the morning sometimes ends up with his shirt on inside out, his pants on backward, and his left snow boot on his right foot! Perhaps the most complex self-help skill of early childhood is shoe tying, which children master around age 6. Success requires a longer attention span, memory for an intricate series of hand movements, and the dexterity to perform them. Shoe tying illustrates the close connection between cognitive and motor development. We will see additional examples of this relationship as we look at the development of young children's drawing and writing.

DRAWING AND WRITING. When given crayon and paper, even young toddlers scribble in imitation of others, but their scrawls seem like little more than random tangles of lines. As the young child's ability to mentally represent the world expands, marks on the page take on definite meaning. At first, children's artful representation takes the form of gestures rather than pictures. For example, one 18-month-old took her crayon and hopped it around the page, explaining as she made a series of dots, "Rabbit goes hop-hop." By age 3, children's scribbles start to become pictures. Often this happens after they make a gesture with the crayon, notice that they have drawn a recognizable shape, and then decide to label it. In one case, a 2-year-old made some random marks on a page and then, realizing the resemblance between his scribbles and noodles, named the creation "chicken pie and noodles" (Winner, 1986).

A major milestone in children's drawing occurs when they begin to use lines to represent the boundaries of objects. This permits them to draw their first picture of a person by age 3 or 4. Look at the tadpole image on the left in Figure 8.8. It is a universal one in which the limits of the preschooler's fine motor skills reduce the figure down to the simplest form that still looks like a human being (Gardner, 1980; Winner, 1986).

Unlike many adults, young children do not demand that a drawing be realistic. But as cognitive and fine motor skills improve, they learn to desire greater realism. As a result, they create more complex drawings, like the one shown on the right in Figure 8.8 made by a 6-year-old child. Still, children of this age are not very particular about mirroring reality. Their drawings contain perceptual distortions, since only gradually do they figure out how to represent depth. The missing third dimension helps make the preschool child's artwork look fanciful and inventive. Accomplished artists, who also try to represent reality freely, often must work hard to do deliberately what they did without effort as 5- and 6-year-olds (Winner, 1986).

FIGURE 8.8

Examples of young children's drawings.
The universal tadpolelike shape that children use to draw their first picture of a person is shown on the left. The tadpole soon becomes an anchor for greater detail as arms, fingers, toes, and facial features sprout from the basic shape. By the end of the preschool years, children produce more complex, differentiated pictures like the one on the right, drawn by a 6-year-old child. *(Tadpole drawings from H. Gardner, 1980,* Artful Scribbles: The Significance of Children's Drawings, *New York: Basic Books, p. 64. Reprinted by permission of Basic Books, a division of HarperCollins Publishers, Inc. Six-year-old's picture from E. Winner, August 1986,* "Where *Pelicans Kiss Seals,"* Psychology Today, *20[8], p. 35. Reprinted by permission of the author.)*

As young children experiment with lines and shapes, notice print in storybooks, and observe the writing of others, they try to print letters and, later on, words. Often the first word printed is the child's name. Initially, it may be represented by a single letter. "How do you make a *D*?" my older son David asked at 3 years of age. When I printed a large uppercase *D* for him, he tried to copy. "*D* for *David*," he said as he wrote, quite satisfied with his backward, imperfect creation. A year later, David added several additional letters, and around age 5, he wrote his name clearly enough so that others could read it. In addition to gains in fine motor control, advances in perception contribute to the ability to form letters and words. Like many children, David continued to reverse some letters in his printing until well into second grade. When we take up early childhood perceptual development in the last section of this chapter, you will discover why these letter reversals are so common.

FACTORS THAT AFFECT EARLY CHILDHOOD MOTOR SKILLS

We have been discussing motor milestones in terms of the average age at which children reach them, but, of course, there are wide individual differences. Many factors affect the motor progress of young children.

■ **BODY BUILD, ETHNICITY, AND SEX.** Body build influences gross motor abilities. Compared to a short, stocky youngster, a tall, muscular child tends to move more quickly and acquire certain skills earlier. Researchers believe that body build contributes to the superior performance of African-American over Caucasian children in running and jumping. African-American youngsters tend to have longer limbs, so they have better leverage (Lee, 1980; Wakat, 1978).

Sex differences in motor skills are also evident in early childhood. Boys are slightly ahead of girls in skills that emphasize force and power. By age 5, they can jump slightly farther, run slightly faster, and throw a ball much farther (about 5 feet beyond the distance covered by girls). At the same time, girls have an edge in fine motor skills and in certain gross motor skills that require a combination of good balance and foot movement, such as hopping and skipping. Boys' greater muscle mass and (in the case of throwing) their slightly longer forearms may contribute to their skill advantages. And in Chapter 5, we indicated that girls are ahead of boys in overall physical maturity. This difference may be partly responsible for girls' better balance and precision of movement.

From an early age, boys and girls are usually encouraged into different physical activities. For example, fathers often play catch in the backyard with their sons, but they seldom do so with their daughters. Baseballs and footballs are purchased for boys, jump ropes, hula hoops, and games of jacks for girls. As children get older, differences in motor skills between boys and girls get larger, yet sex differences in physical capacity remain small until adolescence. These trends suggest that social pressures for boys to be active and physically skilled and for girls to play quietly at fine motor activities may exaggerate small, genetically based differences that are there in the first place (Thomas & French, 1985).

When play spaces are properly equipped for preschoolers and adults encourage children to use them, motor development is enhanced. *(Erika Stone)*

ENHANCING EARLY CHILDHOOD MOTOR DEVELOPMENT. Today, many parents provide preschoolers with early training in motor skills in the form of gymnastics, tumbling, and other lessons. These experiences offer excellent opportunities for physical exercise and social interaction. But aside from throwing (where direct instruction seems to make some difference), there is no evidence that preschoolers exposed to formal lessons are ahead in motor development. Instead, children seem to master the motor skills of early childhood naturally, as part of their everyday play (Espenschade & Eckert, 1980; Roberton, 1984).

Does this mean that adults can do little to promote motor development? The physical environment in which informal play takes place can make a difference in children's mastery of complex motor skills. When children have play spaces and equipment appropriate for running, climbing, jumping, and throwing, along with encouragement to use them, they respond eagerly to these challenges. But if balls are too large and heavy to be properly grasped and thrown, or jungle gyms, ladders, and horizontal bars are suitable for only the largest and strongest youngsters, then children's motor skills are likely to be poorly learned. Preschools, day care centers, and city playgrounds need to accommodate a wide range of physical abilities by offering a variety of pieces of equipment that differ in size or that can be adjusted to fit the needs of individual children (Herkowitz, 1984).

Finally, the social climate created by adults can enhance or dampen preschoolers' motor skills. When parents criticize their child's performance, push specific motor skills, or promote a competitive attitude, they risk undermining young children's self-confidence and, in turn, their motor progress. The appropriate goal of adult involvement in preschoolers' motor development should be fun rather than learning the "correct" technique (Kutner, 1993).

ASK YOURSELF . . .

- Mabel and Chad want to do everything they can to support their 3-year-old daughter's athletic development. What advice would you give them?

BRIEF REVIEW

Motor development proceeds at a rapid pace during early childhood. Improvements in balance support mastery of a variety of gross motor skills, including running, jumping, hopping, galloping, skipping, throwing, and catching. At first, new skills are awkward and involve only isolated regions of the body. Gradually, they become more flexible and include whole-body action. Advances in fine motor development can be seen in children's ability to dress themselves and eat efficiently with utensils. Preschoolers also start to draw and print, making use of fine motor skills to represent the world through pictures and written symbols. Many factors are related to early childhood motor development, including body build, ethnicity, sex, and the richness and appropriateness of the child's physical and social environment.

PERCEPTUAL DEVELOPMENT IN EARLY CHILDHOOD

Think back to our discussion of infant perceptual development in Chapter 5. The most striking changes occurred in vision, the sense on which humans depend most for obtaining information from environment. For infants, the initial perceptual task is one of figuring out how the space around them is organized. Once objects are located in space, they begin to sort them out. For example, they start to discriminate faces as well as other visual patterns. Recall that Eleanor and James Gibson's *differentiation theory* helped us understand this process. Over time, infants search for invariant features (those that remain stable in a changing perceptual world), making finer and finer distinctions among stimuli (to review this theory, return to page 204).

During early childhood, the trends in perceptual development that began in infancy continue. Brain maturation contributes to better integration between the visual and motor systems. As a result, older preschoolers can visually track a thrown ball while moving to a nearby point to catch it. And besides recognizing several geometric shapes and letters of the alphabet, 4- to 6-year-olds can copy them with reasonable accuracy.

Researchers have been especially interested in how detection of the fine-grained structure of visual patterns improves during early childhood, since it helps us understand how children go about the awesome task of discriminating written symbols as they learn to read. Eleanor Gibson has applied differentiation theory to this process. Her research shows that preschoolers begin by recognizing letters as a set of items. By age 3 or 4, they can tell writing from nonwriting (scribbling and pictures), even though they cannot yet identify very many letters of the alphabet. Then they go about discriminating particular letters. Those that are alike in shape are most difficult to tell apart. For example, because the invariant features of *C* and *G*, *E* and *F*, and *M* and *W* are very subtle, many preschoolers confuse these letter pairs (Gibson, 1970).

Letters that are mirror images of one another, such as *b* and *d* and *p* and *q*, are especially hard for young children to tell apart. This finding may remind you of a point made earlier in our discussion of preschoolers' writing. Until age 7 or 8, children print many letters backward. One reason is that until they learn to read, children do not find it especially useful to notice the difference between mirror image forms. In everyday life, left-right reversals occur only when objects are twin aspects of the same thing. For example, two cups, one with a handle on the left and one with a handle on the right, are identical to young preschoolers. In contrast, children easily discriminate a cup turned upside down, one placed right side up, and one turned over on its side, since they have many daily experiences in which objects must be placed right side up to be used effectively (Bornstein, 1992). Research reveals that the ability to tune into mirror images, as well as to scan a printed line carefully from left to right, depends in part on experience with reading materials (Casey, 1986). Thus, the very activity of learning to read helps children notice the distinctive features of each letter of the alphabet.

According to Eleanor Gibson, the early phase of learning to read involves detection of the invariant features of written symbols. At first, preschoolers distinguish letters from nonletters. Gradually they start to discriminate particular letters. *(George Goodwin/Monkmeyer Press)*

Of course, becoming a skilled reader is a very long process, entailing much more than discriminating visual forms. Children must combine what they perceive on the printed page with a variety of information-processing activities, including sustained attention, memory, comprehension, and inference making. But perceptual skills do seem to be essential, since children with advanced visual abilities read at higher levels (Fisher, Bornstein, & Gross, 1985; Kavale, 1982). We will consider other aspects of early literacy development when we take up cognitive development in the next chapter.

SUMMARY

BODY GROWTH IN EARLY CHILDHOOD

Describe changes in body size, proportions, and skeletal maturity during early childhood.

- Compared to infancy, gains in body size taper off into a slower pattern of growth in early childhood. Body fat also declines, and children become longer and leaner. New epiphyses appear in the skeleton, where cartilage gradually hardens into bone. Individual differences in body size and rate of physical growth become even more apparent during the preschool years.
- By the end of early childhood, children start to lose their primary teeth. Improved dental care and water fluoridation have led to dramatic declines in childhood tooth decay. Low-income children, however, continue to suffer from poor dental health.

What makes physical growth an asynchronous process?

- Physical growth is an asynchronous process. Different parts of the body grow at different rates. The **general growth curve** describes change in overall body size—rapid during infancy, slower during early and middle childhood, rapid again during adolescence. Exceptions to this trend include the genitals, the lymph tissue, and the brain.

BRAIN DEVELOPMENT IN EARLY CHILDHOOD

Describe brain development during early childhood, including lateralization (as reflected in handedness) and myelinization of specific structures.

- During early childhood, the left cerebral hemisphere grows more rapidly than the right, supporting young children's rapidly expanding language skills.
- Hand preference is stable by age 2 and increases during early and middle childhood, indicating that lateralization strengthens during this time. Handedness indicates an individual's **dominant cerebral hemisphere.** For right-handed people, language and hand control are housed in the left hemisphere. Left-handers tend to be less strongly lateralized than right-handers. Although left-handedness is associated with developmental problems and injury proneness, the great majority of left-handed children show no abnormalities of any kind.
- During early childhood, connections are established among differ-

ent brain structures. Fibers linking the **cerebellum** to the cerebral cortex myelinate, enhancing balance and motor control. The **reticular formation,** responsible for alertness and consciousness, and the **corpus callosum,** which connects the two cerebral hemispheres, also myelinate rapidly.

FACTORS AFFECTING GROWTH AND HEALTH IN EARLY CHILDHOOD

Explain how heredity influences physical growth.

- Heredity influences physical growth by controlling the release of hormones from the **pituitary gland.** The most important pituitary hormones for childhood growth are **growth hormone (GH)** and **thyroid-stimulating hormone (TSH).**

What are the effects of emotional well-being, nutrition, and infectious disease on physical growth in early childhood?

- Emotional well-being continues to influence body growth in middle childhood. An emotionally inadequate home life can lead to **deprivation dwarfism.**
- Preschoolers' slower growth rate causes their appetite to decline, and often they become picky eaters. Young children's social environments have a powerful impact on food preferences. Modeling by others, repeated exposure to new foods, and a positive emotional climate at mealtimes can promote healthy, varied eating in young children.
- Malnutrition can combine with infectious disease to undermine healthy growth. In developing countries, many children do not receive early immunizations that would protect them from childhood illnesses. Immunization rates have been lower in the United States than in other industrialized nations because many economically disadvantaged children do not have access to health insurance and good medical care. In addition, parental misconceptions about safe immunization practices are not always corrected through public education.

What factors increase the risk of unintentional injuries, and how can childhood injuries be prevented?

- Unintentional injuries are the leading cause of childhood mortality. Injury victims are more likely to be boys, to be temperamentally irritable, inattentive, and negative in mood, and to be growing up in poor, inner-city families. A variety of approaches are needed to prevent childhood injuries. These include laws that promote child safety, modification of home and play environments, public education, and interventions designed to change parent and child behaviors.

MOTOR DEVELOPMENT IN EARLY CHILDHOOD

Cite major milestones of gross and fine motor development in early childhood.

- During early childhood, children continue to integrate previously acquired motor skills into more complex systems of action. Body growth causes the child's center of gravity to shift toward the trunk, and balance improves, paving the way for an explosion of gross motor milestones. Preschoolers' gaits become smooth and rhythmic, and they run, jump, hop, gallop, and eventually skip. These abilities, as well as throwing and catching, become better coordinated as movements of the entire body support each new skill.
- Gains in control of the hands and fingers lead to dramatic changes in fine motor skills. Preschoolers gradually become self-sufficient at dressing themselves and using a fork and knife at mealtimes. By age 3, children's scribbles become pictures. Their drawings increase in complexity with age. Young children also try to print letters of the alphabet, an ability that gradually improves.

What factors influence early childhood motor skills?

- A variety of factors affect early childhood motor development, including body build, ethnicity, and sex. Differences in motor skills between boys and girls are partly genetic, but environmental pressures seem to exaggerate them.
- Children master the motor skills of early childhood through informal play experiences. Richly equipped play environments that accommodate a wide range of physical abilities are important during the preschool years.

PERCEPTUAL DEVELOPMENT IN EARLY CHILDHOOD

Summarize perceptual development in early childhood, paying special attention to the discrimination of written symbols.

- During early childhood, brain maturation contributes to improvements in integrating the visual and motor systems. The Gibsons' differentiation theory helps explain how children discriminate written symbols as they learn to read. Because preschoolers have little need to distinguish mirror image forms in everyday life, left–right letter reversals are common in early childhood. Exposure to reading materials increases the variety of perceptual cues to which children are sensitive.

IMPORTANT TERMS AND CONCEPTS

general growth curve (p. 288)
dominant cerebral hemisphere (p. 290)
cerebellum (p. 291)
reticular formation (p. 291)
corpus callosum (p. 291)
pituitary gland (p. 292
growth hormone (p. 292)
thyroid-stimulating hormone (TSH) (p. 293)
deprivation dwarfism (p. 293)

FYI...

FOR FURTHER INFORMATION AND SPECIAL HELP, CONSULT THE FOLLOWING ORGANIZATIONS:

INFECTIOUS DISEASE IN CHILDHOOD

U.S. Centers for Disease Control
5600 Fishers Lane
Rockville, MD 20857
(301) 443-2610

Surveys national disease trends and environmental health problems. Has organized an agency network to address problems of infectious disease in day care, including distributing information to day care staff on techniques that prevent the spread of infection.

American Academy of Pediatrics
P.O. Box 927
Elk Grove Village, IL 60009-0927
(708) 228-5005

Provides public education on a variety of childhood health issues. Among the many pamphlets and publications available are written guidelines for effective control of infectious disease.

Child Care Information Exchange
Box 2890
Redmond, WA 98052
(206) 883-9394

A bimonthly publication written especially for day care directors that addresses the practical issues of running a center. Articles discussing health and safety are often included.

U.S. Department of Health and Human Services
U.S. Government Printing Office
Superintendent of Documents
723 N. Capitol Street, N.W.
Washington, DC 20401
(202) 783-3283

Publishes What to Do to Stop Disease in Child Day Care Centers: A Kit for Child Day Care Directors, Caregivers, and Parents, *Document No. 017-023-00172-8. The kit includes handbooks, posters, and other items with specific advice on health-related issues.*

CHILDHOOD INJURY CONTROL

U.S. Consumer Product Safety Commission
5401 Westbard Avenue
Bethesda, MD 20207
(800) 638-2772

Establishes and enforces product safety standards. Operates a hot line providing information on safety issues and recall of dangerous consumer products.

"Myself"
Bilgundi G. Mallinat
7 years, India

This image of an observant young painter portrays the most striking cognitive achievement of early childhood. As Chapter 9 reveals, mental representation takes a giant leap forward.

Reprinted by permission from The International Museum of Children's Art, Oslo, Norway.

9

Cognitive Development in Early Childhood

PIAGET'S THEORY: THE PREOPERATIONAL STAGE

Advances in Mental Representation • Make-Believe Play • Limitations of Preoperational Thought • Recent Research on Preoperational Thought • Evaluation of the Preoperational Stage • Piaget and Education

VYGOTSKY'S SOCIOCULTURAL THEORY

Children's Private Speech • Social Origins of Early Childhood Cognition • Vygotsky and Education

INFORMATION PROCESSING IN EARLY CHILDHOOD

Attention • Memory • The Young Child's Theory of Mind • Early Literacy and Mathematical Development • A Note on Academics in Early Childhood

INDIVIDUAL DIFFERENCES IN MENTAL DEVELOPMENT DURING EARLY CHILDHOOD

Early Childhood Intelligence Tests • Home Environment and Mental Development • Preschool and Day Care • Educational Television

LANGUAGE DEVELOPMENT IN EARLY CHILDHOOD

Vocabulary Development • Grammatical Development • Becoming an Effective Conversationalist • Supporting Language Learning in Early Childhood

One rainy morning, as I observed in our laboratory preschool, Leslie, the children's teacher, joined me at the back of the room to watch for a moment herself. "Preschoolers' minds are such a curious blend of logic, fantasy, and faulty reasoning," Leslie reflected. "Every day, I'm startled by the maturity and originality of many things they say and do. Yet at other times, their thinking seems limited and inflexible."

Leslie's comments sum up the puzzling contradictions of early childhood cognition. Over the previous week, I had seen many examples as I followed the activities of 3-year-old Jason. That day, I found him at the puzzle table, moments after a loud clash of thunder occurred outside. Jason looked up, startled, then turned to Leslie and pronounced, "The man turned on the thunder!" Leslie patiently explained that people can't turn thunder on or off. But Jason persisted. "Then a lady did it," he stated with certainty.

In other respects, Jason's cognitive skills seemed surprisingly advanced. At snack time, he accurately counted, "One, two, three, four!" and then got four cartons of milk, giving one to each child at his table. Jason's keen memory and ability to categorize were also evident. As he sat in the reading corner, I heard him recite by heart *The Very Hungry Caterpillar* (Carle, 1969), a story he had heard many times before. Jason's favorite picture books were about animals, and he could name and group together dozens of them.

Still, Jason's cognitive skills seemed fragile and insecure. When more than four children joined his snack group, Jason's counting broke down. And some of his notions about quantity seemed as fantastic as his understanding of thunder. Across the snack table, Priti dumped out her raisins, and they scattered in front of her. "How come you got lots, and I only got this little bit?" asked Jason, failing to realize that he had just as many; they were simply all bunched up in a tiny red box.

In this chapter, we explore the many facets of early childhood cognition, drawing from three theories with which you are already familiar. We begin with Piaget's preoperational stage, which, for the most part, emphasizes preschool children's deficits rather than their strengths. Recent research on preoperational thought along with two additional perspectives—Vygotsky's sociocultural theory and information processing—extends our understanding of preschoolers' cognitive competencies. Then we turn to a variety of factors that contribute to individual differences in early childhood mental development—the home environment, the quality of preschool and day care, and the many hours young children spend watching television. Our chapter concludes with language development, the most awesome achievement of early childhood.

As our discussion proceeds, we will consider the controversial question of how language and thought are related. Do young children first master ideas and then translate them into words? Or does the capacity for language open new cognitive doors, permitting children to think in more mature ways? Major theorists differ sharply on this issue. We begin with Piaget's viewpoint in the next section.

PIAGET'S THEORY: THE PREOPERATIONAL STAGE

As children move from the sensorimotor to the **preoperational stage**, the most obvious change is an extraordinary increase in representational, or symbolic, activity. Recall that infants and toddlers have some ability to mentally represent the world. Between the ages of 2 and 7, this capacity blossoms.

ADVANCES IN MENTAL REPRESENTATION

As I looked around the preschool classroom, signs of developing representation were everywhere—in the children's drawings and paintings, in their re-creations of family life in the housekeeping area, and in their delight at story time. Especially impressive were strides in language skill. During free play, a hum of chattering voices rose from the classroom.

Piaget acknowledged that language is our most flexible means of mental representation. By detaching thought from action, it permits cognition to be far more efficient than it was during the sensorimotor stage. When we think in words, we overcome the limits of our momentary perceptions. We can deal with the past, present, and future all at once, creating larger, interconnected images of reality. And we can combine parts of the world in unique ways, as when we think about a hungry caterpillar eating bananas or monsters flying through the forest at night (Miller, 1993).

Yet despite the power of language, Piaget did not believe that it plays a major role in cognitive development. According to Piaget, language does not give rise to representational thought. Instead, sensorimotor activity provides the foundation that makes language possible, just as it leads to deferred imitation and make-believe play. Can you think of evidence that supports Piaget's view? Recall from Chapter 6 that the first words toddlers use have a strong sensorimotor basis. In addition, toddlers acquire an impressive range of cognitive categories long before they use words to label them (see pages 223–224). These findings are consistent with Piaget's belief that early language builds on advances in nonverbal cognitive skills, rather than the other way around. Still, Piaget's account of the link between language and thought is regarded by others as incomplete, as we will see later in this chapter.

Preoperational stage
Piaget's second stage, in which rapid growth in representation takes place. However, thought is not yet logical. Spans the years from 2 to 7.

MAKE-BELIEVE PLAY

Make-believe play provides another excellent example of the development of representation during the preoperational stage. Like language, it increases dramatically during early childhood (Singer & Singer, 1990). Piaget believed that through pretending, young children practice and strengthen newly acquired representational schemes. Drawing on Piaget's ideas, several investigators have traced changes in make-believe play during the preschool years.

THE DEVELOPMENT OF MAKE-BELIEVE. One day, Jason's 18-month-old brother Dwayne came to visit the classroom. Dwayne wandered around, picked up the receiver of a toy telephone, said, "Hi, Mommy," and then dropped it. In the housekeeping area, he found a cup, pretended to drink, and toddled off again.

In the meantime, Jason joined a group of children in the block area for a space shuttle launch. "That can be our control tower," he suggested to Vance, pointing to a corner by a bookshelf.

"Wait, I gotta get it all ready," said Lynette, who was still arranging the astronauts (two dolls and a teddy bear) inside a circle of large blocks, which represented the rocket.

"Countdown!" Jason announced, speaking into a small wooden block, his pretend walkie-talkie.

"Five, six, two, four, one, blastoff!" responded Vance, commander of the control tower.

Lynette made one of the dolls push a pretend button and reported, "Brrrm, brrrm, they're going up!"

A comparison of Dwayne's pretend with that of Jason and his classmates illustrates three important changes in make-believe. Each reflects the preschool child's growing symbolic mastery. First, over time, play becomes increasingly detached from the real-life conditions associated with it. In early pretending, toddlers use only realistic objects—for example, a toy telephone to talk into or a cup to drink from. Around age 2, use of less realistic toys, such as a block for a telephone receiver, becomes more frequent. Sometime during the third year, children can imagine objects and events without support from the real world, as when Jason invented the control tower in a corner of the room. We can see that children's representations are becoming more flexible, since a play symbol no longer has to resemble the object for which it stands (Bretherton et al., 1984; Corrigan, 1987).

During the preschool years, make-believe play blossoms. This child uses objects as active agents in a complex play scene. *(M. Siluk/The Image Works)*

Second, the way in which the "child as self" participates in play changes with age. When make-believe first appears, it is directed toward the self—for example, Dwayne pretends to feed only himself. A short time later, children direct pretend actions toward other objects, as when the child feeds a doll. And early in the third year, they use objects as active agents, and the child becomes a detached participant who makes a doll feed itself or (in Lynette's case) push a button to launch a rocket. This sequence reveals that make-believe gradually becomes less self-centered, as children realize that agents and recipients of pretend actions can be independent of themselves (Corrigan, 1987; McCune, 1993).

Finally, over time, make-believe includes increasingly complex scheme combinations. For example, Dwayne can pretend to drink from a cup, but he does not yet combine pouring and drinking. Later on, children combine schemes, especially in **sociodramatic play**, the make-believe with peers that appears around age 2 1/2 and increases rapidly until 4 to 5 years (Corrigan, 1987; Haight & Miller, 1993). Already, Jason and his classmates can create and coordinate several roles in an elaborate plot. By the end of early childhood, children have a sophisticated understanding of role relationships and story lines.

■ ADVANTAGES OF MAKE-BELIEVE. Today, Piaget's view of make-believe as mere practice of representational schemes is regarded as too limited. Research indicates that play not only reflects, but also contributes to children's cognitive and social skills (Singer & Singer, 1990). Sociodramatic play has been studied most thoroughly. In comparison to social nonpretend activities (such as drawing or putting puzzles together), during social pretend preschoolers' interactions last longer, show more involvement, draw larger numbers of children into the activity, and are more cooperative (Connolly, Doyle, & Reznick, 1988). When we consider these findings, it is not surprising that preschoolers who spend more time at sociodramatic play are advanced in general intellectual development and seen as more socially competent by their teachers (Burns & Brainerd, 1979; Connolly & Doyle, 1984). And many studies reveal that make-believe strengthens a wide variety of mental abilities, including memory, language, logical reasoning, imagination, and creativity (Dias & Harris, 1990; Ervin-Tripp, 1991; Newman, 1990; Pepler & Ross, 1981). We will return to the topic of early childhood play in Chapter 10.

LIMITATIONS OF PREOPERATIONAL THOUGHT

Aside from the development of representation, Piaget described preschool children in terms of what they *cannot,* rather than *can,* understand. The very name of the stage—*pre*operational—indicates that Piaget compared preschoolers to older, more capable concrete operational children. As a result, he discovered little of a positive nature about the young child's thinking. Later, when we discuss new research on preoperational thought, we will see that Piaget underestimated the cognitive competencies of early childhood, just as he did with infancy.

To appreciate the characteristics of the preoperational stage, you will need to master some concepts Piaget used to describe children's thought. These are summarized in the Concept Review Table on the following page. As you look over these characteristics, you will see that for Piaget, **operations**—mental representations of actions that obey logical rules—are where cognitive development is going. In the preoperational stage, children are not capable of operations. Instead, their thinking is rigid, limited to one aspect of a situation at a time, and strongly influenced by the way things appear at the moment. When judged by adult standards, preoperational reasoning often seems distorted and incorrect.

Sociodramatic play
The make-believe play with peers that first appears around age 2 1/2 and increases rapidly until 4 to 5 years.

Operations
Mental representations of actions that obey logical rules.

CONCEPT REVIEW TABLE

Limitations of Preoperational Thought

CONCEPT	IMPORTANT POINT	EXAMPLE
Egocentrism	Preoperational children assume that others perceive, think, and feel just the way they do. According to Piaget, this belief underlies all other limitations of the preoperational stage.	Three-year-old Josie turned on the TV in the living room while her father ate breakfast in the kitchen. "What's that boy doing?" called Josie while pointing to the screen, failing to realize that her father couldn't see the TV from where he was sitting.
Animistic thinking	Preoperational children regard inanimate objects as having lifelike qualities, just like the self.	Josie and her parents watched the sunset after spending a day at the seashore. As the sun started to sink below the horizon and the sky darkened, Josie remarked, "That sunshine's getting very sleepy."
Perception-bound thought	Preoperational children make judgments based on the immediate, perceptual appearance of objects.	Josie's mother handed her a large glass half full of lemonade and her brother a small glass filled to the top. "Fill mine up like Billie's so I'll have just as much," said Josie.
Centration	Preoperational children tend to center on one aspect of a situation to the neglect of other important features.	At preschool, it was Hallie's fourth birthday. Although Amy was only 3, Josie announced, "Amy's older 'cause she's taller," centering on height as a measure of age.
States versus transformations	Preoperational children focus on momentary states, failing to consider dynamic transformations between them. As a result, they have difficulty relating beginning and ending states in a situation.	Josie saw her little cousin Susie, whom she'd played with several times before, dressed up in a bathing suit and cap. "What's that baby's name?" Josie asked. Later, when Susie had her shirt and shorts on, Josie said, "Oh, it's Susie again."
Irreversibility	Preoperational children cannot think through a series of steps in a problem and then go backward, mentally returning to the starting point.	Josie's mother tried to explain, "When Susie puts on a bathing suit, she's still the same person." But Josie insisted that the bathing suit baby was not Susie. She failed to imagine Susie changing from her shorts and shirt into her suit and then back again.
Transductive reasoning	Preoperational children reason from particular event to particular event, rather than in an appropriately causal fashion.	"Why does it get dark at night?" the teacher asked the children at preschool one day. "Because we go to bed," responded Josie.
Lack of hierarchical classification	Preoperational children have difficulty grouping objects into hierarchies of classes and subclasses.	Josie's teacher gave her some paper shapes to sort—red and blue squares and circles. Josie put all the red ones in one pile and the blue ones in another, but she had difficulty separating the groups further, by shape.

FIGURE 9.1

Piaget's three-mountains problem.
Each mountain is distinguished by its color and by its summit. One has a red cross, another a small house, and the third a snow-capped peak. Children at the preoperational stage are egocentric. They canot select a picture that shows the mountains from the doll's perspective. Instead, they simply choose the photo that shows their own vantage point.

Egocentrism
The inability to distinguish the symbolic viewpoints of others from one's own.

Animistic thinking
The belief that inanimate objects have lifelike qualities, such as thoughts, wishes, feelings, and intentions.

■ EGOCENTRISM. According to Piaget, the most serious deficiency of preoperational thinking, the one that underlies all others, is **egocentrism.** The word *ego* means self, so the term *egocentrism* suggests that preschoolers are self-centered. By this, Piaget did not mean selfish or inconsiderate. Instead, he believed that when children first begin to mentally represent the world, they are egocentric with respect to their symbolic viewpoints. They are unaware of any perspectives other than their own, and they believe that everyone else perceives, thinks, and feels the same way they do (Piaget, 1950).

Piaget's most convincing demonstration of egocentrism involves a task called the *three-mountains problem* (see Figure 9.1). A child is permitted to walk around a display of three mountains of different heights arranged on a table. Then the child stands on one side, and a doll is placed at various locations around the display. The child must choose a photograph that shows what the display looks like from the doll's perspective. Before age 6 or 7, most children simply select the photo that shows the mountains from their own point of view (Piaget & Inhelder, 1948/1956).

Egocentrism, Piaget pointed out, shows up in other aspects of children's reasoning. Recall Jason's firm insistence that someone must have turned on the thunder, in much the same way that he uses a switch to turn on a light or radio. Similarly, Piaget regarded egocentrism as responsible for preoperational children's **animistic thinking**—the belief that inanimate objects have lifelike qualities, such as thoughts, wishes, feelings, and intentions, just like themselves. The 3-year-old who charmingly explains that the sun is angry at the clouds and has chased them away is demonstrating this kind of reasoning. According to Piaget, because young children egocentrically assign human purposes to physical events, magical thinking is especially common during the preschool years.

Piaget argued that egocentrism is responsible for the rigidity and illogical nature of young children's thinking. Thought proceeds so strongly from a single point of view that children do not *accommodate,* or revise their reasoning in response to their physical and social worlds. Egocentric thought is not reflective thought, which critically examines itself. A child who assumes that everyone else's viewpoint is the same as his own cannot think reflectively and is not even motivated to do so! But to fully appreciate these shortcomings of the preoperational stage, let's consider some additional tasks that Piaget presented to children.

INABILITY TO CONSERVE. Piaget's most important tasks are the conservation problems. **Conservation** refers to the idea that certain physical characteristics of objects remain the same, even when their outward appearance changes. At snack time, Jason revealed that he had difficulty with conservation of number. Priti and Jason each had identical boxes of raisins, but after Priti spread hers out on the table, Jason was convinced that she had more.

Another type of conservation task involves liquid. In this problem, the child is presented with two identical tall glasses of water and asked if they contain equal amounts. Once the child agrees, the water in one glass is poured into a short, wide container, changing the appearance of the water but not its amount. Then the child is asked whether the amount of water is still the same or whether it has changed. Preoperational children think that the quantity of water is no longer the same. They explain their reasoning in ways like this: "There is less now because the water is way down here" (that is, its level is so low in the short, wide container) or "There is more water now because it is all spread out." In Figure 9.2, you will find other conservation tasks that you can try with children.

Preoperational children's inability to conserve highlights several related aspects of their thinking. First, their understanding is **perception-bound.** They are easily distracted by the concrete, perceptual appearance of objects (it *looks* like there is less water in the short, wide container, so there *must be* less water). Second, their thinking is *centered,* or characterized by **centration**. In other words, they focus on one aspect of a situation and neglect other important features. In the case of conservation of liquid, the child centers on the height of the water in the two containers, failing to realize that all changes in height are compensated by changes in width. Third, children of this stage focus on *momentary states* rather than *dynamic transformations* between them. For example, in the conservation of liquid problem, they treat the initial and final states of the water as completely unrelated events. This tendency to emphasize **states versus transformations** is dramatically illustrated by another problem Piaget presented to children. A bar is allowed to fall freely from an upright position to a horizontal one. Then the child is asked either to draw or select a picture that shows what happened. Preoperational children focus only on the beginning and ending states, ignoring the bar's intermediate path of movement.

The most important illogical feature of preoperational thought is its **irreversibility.** Children of this stage cannot mentally go through a series of steps and then reverse direction, returning to the starting point. *Reversibility,* the opposite of this concept, is part of every logical operation. Notice how Jason cannot reverse after Priti spills her raisins. He does not think to himself, "I know that Priti doesn't have more raisins than I do. She just poured them out of that little red box, and if we put them back in again, her raisins and my raisins would look just the same."

TRANSDUCTIVE REASONING. Reversible thinking is flexible and well organized. Because preoperational children are not capable of it, Piaget concluded that their causal reasoning often consists of disconnected facts and contradictions. He called young children's incorrect explanations **transductive reasoning,** which means reasoning from particular to particular. In other words, preschoolers link together two events that occur close in time and space in a cause-and-effect fashion. Sometimes this leads to some fantastic connections, as in the following interview that Piaget conducted with a young child about why the clouds move:

> You have already seen the clouds moving along? What makes them move?—*When we move along, they move along too.*—Can you make them move?—*Everybody can, when they walk.*—When I walk and you are still, do they move?—*Yes.*—And at night, when everyone is asleep, do they move?—*Yes.*—But you tell me that they move when somebody walks.—*They always move. The cats, when they walk, and then the dogs, they make the clouds move along.* (Piaget, 1926/1929, p. 62)

Conservation
The understanding that certain physical characteristics of objects remain the same, even when their outward appearance changes.

Perception-bound
Being easily distracted by the concrete, perceptual appearance of objects.

Centration
The tendency to focus on one aspect of a situation and neglect other important features.

States versus transformations
The tendency to treat the initial and final states in a problem as completely unrelated.

Irreversibility
The inability to mentally go through a series of steps in a problem and then reverse direction, returning to the starting point.

Transductive reasoning
Reasoning from one particular event to another particular event, instead of from general to particular or particular to general.

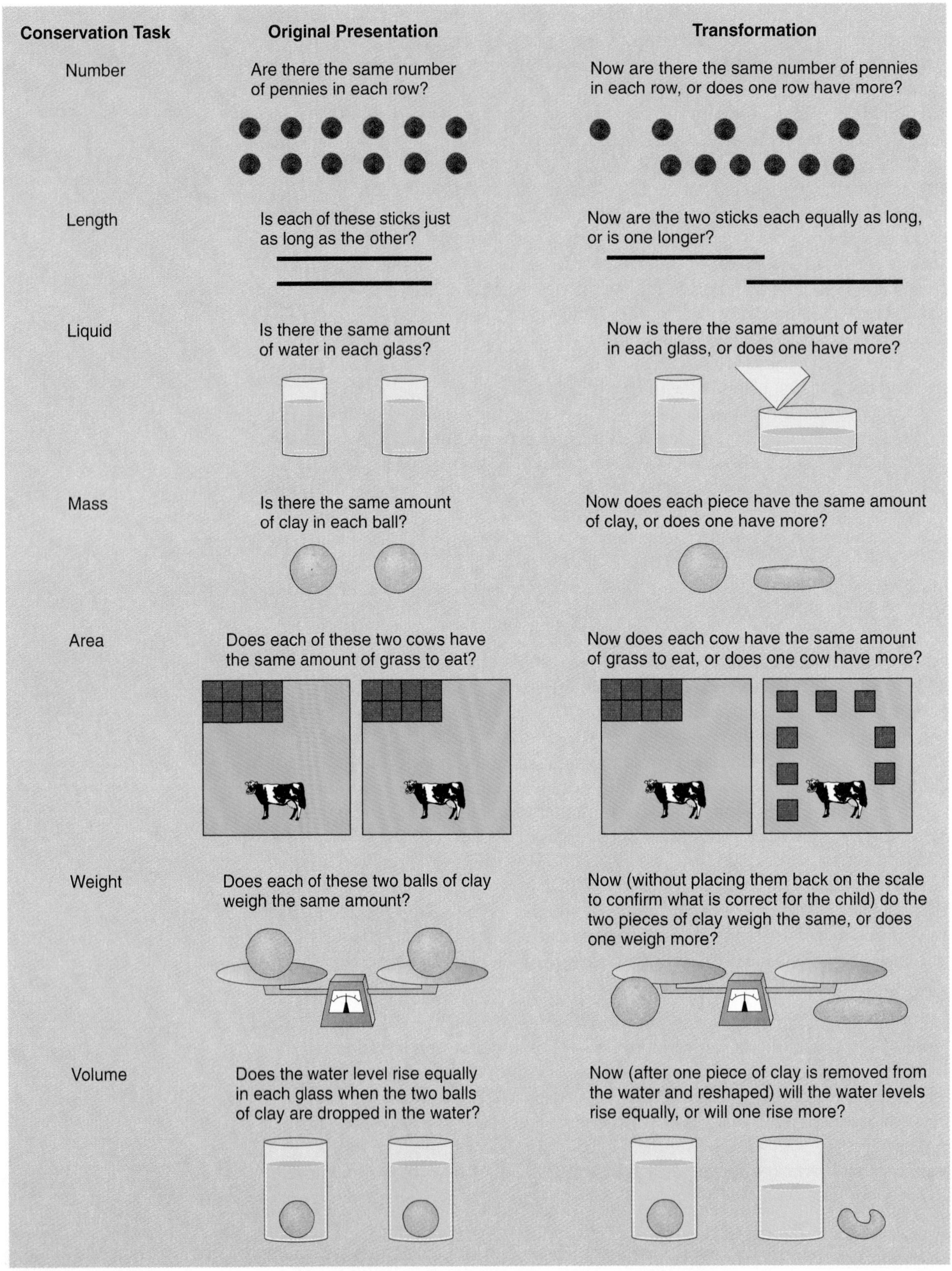
Conservation Task
Original Presentation
Transformation
Number
Are there the same number of pennies in each row?
Now are there the same number of pennies in each row, or does one row have more?
Length
Is each of these sticks just as long as the other?
Now are the two sticks each equally as long, or is one longer?
Liquid
Is there the same amount of water in each glass?
Now is there the same amount of water in each glass, or does one have more?
Mass
Is there the same amount of clay in each ball?
Now does each piece have the same amount of clay, or does one have more?
Area
Does each of these two cows have the same amount of grass to eat?
Now does each cow have the same amount of grass to eat, or does one cow have more?
Weight
Does each of these two balls of clay weigh the same amount?
Now (without placing them back on the scale to confirm what is correct for the child) do the two pieces of clay weigh the same, or does one weigh more?
Volume
Does the water level rise equally in each glass when the two balls of clay are dropped in the water?
Now (after one piece of clay is removed from the water and reshaped) will the water levels rise equally, or will one rise more?

FIGURE 9.2

Some Piagetian conservation tasks.
Children at the preoperational stage cannot yet conserve.

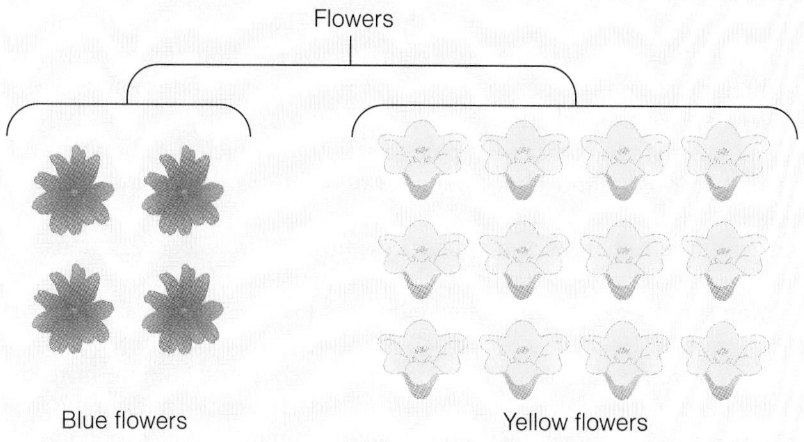

FIGURE 9.3

A Piagetian class inclusion problem.
Children are shown 16 flowers, 4 of which are blue and 12 of which are yellow. Asked whether there are more yellow flowers or more flowers, the preoperational child responds, "More yellow flowers," failing to realize that both yellow and blue flowers are included in the category of "flowers."

■ LACK OF HIERARCHICAL CLASSIFICATION. Because preoperational children are not yet capable of logical operations, they have difficulty with **hierarchical classification.** That is, they cannot yet organize objects into hierarchies of classes and subclasses on the basis of similarities and differences between the groups. Piaget illustrated this with his famous *class inclusion problem.* Children are shown a set of common objects, such as 16 flowers, most of which are yellow and a few of which are blue (see Figure 9.3). When asked whether there are more yellow flowers or more flowers, preoperational children respond confidently, "More yellow flowers!" Their approach to the problem shows a tendency to center on the overriding perceptual feature of yellow and an inability to think reversibly by moving from the whole class (flowers) to the parts (yellow and blue) and back again.

■ SUMMING UP PREOPERATIONAL THOUGHT. How can we combine the diverse characteristics of the preoperational stage into a unified description of what Piaget believed the young child's thought to be like? John Flavell, a well-known Piagetian scholar, suggests that Piaget viewed all these traits as expressions of a single, underlying cognitive orientation. Taken together, they reveal that preoperational thought

> bears the impress of its sensory-motor origins. . . . It is extremely concrete . . . concerned more with immobile, eye-catching configurations than with more subtle, less obvious components . . . it is unconcerned with proof or logical justification and, in general, unaware of the effect of its communication on others. In short, in more respects than not, it resembles sensory-motor action which has simply been transposed to a new (symbolic) arena of operation. (Flavell, 1963, p. 162)

RECENT RESEARCH ON PREOPERATIONAL THOUGHT

Over the past two decades, Piaget's account of a cognitively deficient preschool child has been seriously challenged. If researchers give his tasks in just the way that he originally designed them, indeed they find that preschoolers do perform poorly. But a close look at Piagetian problems reveals that many of them contain confusing or unfamiliar elements or too many pieces of information for young children to handle at once. As a result, preschoolers' responses do not reflect their true abilities. Piaget also missed many naturally occurring instances of preschoolers' effective reasoning. Let's look at some examples that illustrate these points.

Hierarchical classification
The organization of objects into classes and subclasses on the basis of similarities and differences between the groups.

EGOCENTRIC, ANIMISTIC, AND MAGICAL THINKING. Are young children really so egocentric that they believe a person standing in a different location in a room sees the same thing they see? Children's responses to Piaget's three-mountains task suggest that the answer is yes, but more recent studies say no. When researchers change the nature of the visual display to include familiar objects and use methods other than picture selection (which is difficult even for 10-year-olds), 4-year-olds show clear awareness of others' vantage points (Borke, 1975; Newcombe & Huttenlocher, 1992).

Nonegocentric responses also appear in young children's conversations. For example, preschoolers adapt their speech to fit the needs of their listeners. Jason uses shorter, simpler expressions when talking to his little brother Dwayne than to agemates or adults (Gelman & Shatz, 1978). Also, in describing objects, children do not use such words as "big" and "little" in a rigid, egocentric fashion. Instead, they *adjust* their descriptions, taking account of context. By age 3, children judge a 2-inch shoe as small when seen by itself (because it is much smaller than most shoes) but as big when asked about its appropriateness for a very tiny 5-inch doll (Ebeling & Gelman, 1994). These flexible communicative skills challenge Piaget's description of young children as strongly egocentric.

Recent studies also indicate that Piaget overestimated preschoolers' animistic beliefs because he asked children about objects with which they have little direct experience, such as the clouds, sun, and moon. Children as young as 3 rarely think that very familiar inanimate objects, like rocks and crayons, are alive. They do make errors when questioned about certain vehicles, such as trains and airplanes. But these objects appear to be self-moving, a characteristic of almost all living things. And they also have some lifelike features—for example, headlights that look like eyes (Dolgin & Behrend, 1984; Richards & Siegler, 1986). Children's animistic responses result from incomplete knowledge about objects, not from a rigid belief that inanimate objects are alive.

The same is true for other fantastic beliefs of the preschool years. Most 3- and 4-year olds believe in the supernatural powers of fairies, goblins, and other enchanted creatures that appear in storybooks, movies, and holiday legends. But they deny that magic can alter their everyday experiences—for example, turn a picture into a real object (Subbotsky, 1994). Instead, they think magic accounts for events that violate their expectations and that they cannot otherwise explain. Between 4 and 8 years, as familiarity with physical events and principles increases, children's magical beliefs decline (Phelps & Woolley, 1994). Most figure out who is really behind the activities of Santa Claus and the Tooth Fairy! The importance of knowledge and experience can be seen in preschoolers' grasp of other natural concepts, as the From Research to Practice box on the following page reveals.

ILLOGICAL CHARACTERISTICS OF THOUGHT. Many studies have re-examined the illogical characteristics that Piaget saw in the preoperational stage. Results show that when preschoolers are given tasks that are simplified and made relevant to their everyday lives, they do better than Piaget might have expected.

For example, when a conservation-of-number task is scaled down to include only three items instead of six or seven, preschoolers perform well (Gelman, 1972). And when preschoolers are asked carefully worded questions about what happens to substances (such as sugar) after they are dissolved in water, they give very accurate explanations. Most 3- to 5-year-olds know that the substance is conserved—that it continues to exist, can be tasted, and makes the liquid heavier, even though it is invisible in the water. And the majority of 5-year-olds reconcile the apparent contradiction between invisibility and continued existence by saying that particles too tiny to be seen are in the water (Au, Sidle, & Rollins, 1993; Rosen & Rozin, 1993). These findings indicate that preschoolers notice transformations, reverse their thinking, and understand causality in familiar contexts.

FROM RESEARCH TO PRACTICE

YOUNG CHILDREN'S UNDERSTANDING OF DEATH

Five-year-old Miriam arrived at preschool the day after her dog Pepper died. Instead of running to play with the other children, she stayed close by Leslie's side. Leslie noticed Miriam's discomfort and asked, "What's wrong?"

"Daddy said Pepper had a sick tummy. He fell asleep and died." For a moment, Miriam looked hopeful, "When I get home, Pepper might be up."

Leslie answered directly, "No, Pepper won't get up again. He's not asleep. He's dead, and that means he can't sleep, eat, run, or play anymore."

Miriam wandered off. Later, she returned to Leslie and confessed, "I chased Pepper too hard," tears streaming from her eyes.

Leslie put her arm around Miriam. "Pepper didn't die because you chased him. He was very old and very sick," she explained.

Over the next few days, Miriam asked many more questions: "When I go to sleep, will I die?" "Can a tummy ache make you die?" "Does Pepper feel better now?" "Will Mommy and Daddy die?"

As adults we understand death in terms of three basic ideas: (1) *permanence:* once a living thing dies, it cannot be brought back to life; (2) *universality:* all living things eventually die; and (3) *nonfunctionality:* all living functions, including thought, movement, and vital signs, cease at death.

Without clear explanations, young children rely on the egocentric and magical thinking of Piaget's preoperational stage to make sense of death. They may believe, as Miriam did, that they are responsible for a relative or pet's death. And they can easily arrive at incorrect conclusions—in Miriam's case, that sleeping or having a stomachache can cause someone to die.

Research shows that preschoolers master the three components of the death concept in a specific order, with most children arriving at an adultlike understanding by age 7. Permanence, the notion that death cannot be reversed, is the first and most easily understood idea. When Leslie explained that Pepper would not get up again, Miriam accepted this fact quickly, perhaps because she had seen it in other less emotionally charged situations, such as the dead butterflies and beetles that she picked up and inspected while playing outside (Furman, 1990). Appreciation of universality comes slightly later. At first, children think that certain people do not die, especially those with whom they have close emotional ties or who are like themselves—other children. Finally, nonfunctionality is the most difficult component of death for children to grasp. Many preschoolers view dead things as retaining living capacities. When they first comprehend nonfunctionality, they do so in terms of its most visible aspects, such as heart beat and breathing. Only later do they understand that thinking, feeling, and dreaming also cease (Lazar & Torney-Purta, 1991; Speece & Brent, 1992).

Although children usually arrive at a mature appreciation of death by the end of early childhood, there are wide individual differences. Experiences with death seem to exert a powerful influence. For example, terminally ill children under age 6 often have a well-developed concept of death (Bluebond-Langer, 1977). Also, most children find it more difficult to grasp plant death than human or animal death. They have seen wilted plants revive after watering, but they have not witnessed any similar event in the death of people or animals (Speece & Brent, 1992).

Preschoolers' incompletely formed ideas about death are important to keep in mind when the death of a pet or relative occurs. Simple, direct explanations help children understand. Although parents often worry that discussing death with children will fuel their fears, this is not the case. Instead, children who have a good grasp of the facts of death have an easier time accepting it (Essa & Murray, 1994). When preschoolers ask very difficult questions—"Will I die?" "Will you die?"—parents can be truthful as well as comforting by taking advantage of children's sense of time. They can say something like "Not for many, many years. First I'm going to enjoy you as a grown-up and be a grandparent." Open, honest discussions with children contribute not only to their cognitive appreciation of the concept, but also to their emotional well-being.

When children are puzzled or upset over the death of a loved one, an open, truthful conversation with a sympathetic adult helps them understand what has happened and accept the loss. *(Innervisions)*

Indeed, a close look at 3- and 4-year-olds' descriptions of the world reveals that they use causal terms, such as "if–then" and "because," with the same degree of accuracy as adults do (McCabe & Peterson, 1988). Transductive reasoning seems to occur only when preschoolers grapple with topics they know little about. Although young children cannot yet consider the complex interplay of forces that adolescents and adults can, they often analyze their experiences accurately in terms of basic cause-and-effect relations (Bullock, 1985).

■ HIERARCHICAL CLASSIFICATION. Even though preschoolers have difficulty with Piagetian class inclusion tasks, their everyday knowledge is organized into nested categories at an early age. By the second year, children have formed a variety of global categories consisting of objects that do not necessarily look alike but are the same kind of thing—kitchen utensils, bathroom objects, animals, vehicles, plants, and furniture (Bauer & Mandler, 1989; Mandler, Bauer, & McDonough, 1991). Consider these object groupings, and you will see that they challenge Piaget's assumption that young children's thinking is always perception-bound (Keil, 1989). For example, the category of "kitchen utensils" includes objects that differ widely in appearance but that go together because of their common function and place of use.

Over the preschool years, these global categories differentiate. Children form many *basic-level categories*—ones at an intermediate level of generality, such as "chairs," "tables," "dressers," and "beds." Performance on object-sorting tasks indicates that by age 3 or 4, children can easily move back and forth between basic-level categories and *general categories,* such as "furniture." They also break down the basic-level categories into *subcategories,* such as "rocking chairs" and "desk chairs" (Mervis, 1987; Mervis & Crisafi, 1982). Preschoolers' category systems are not yet very complex, and concrete operational reasoning facilitates their development (Ricco, 1989). But the capacity to classify hierarchically is present in early childhood.

■ APPEARANCE VERSUS REALITY. So far, we have seen that preschoolers show some remarkably advanced reasoning when presented with familiar situations and simplified problems. Yet new studies also reveal that in certain situations, young children are easily tricked by the outward appearance of things, just as Piaget suggested.

John Flavell and his colleagues took a close look at children's ability to distinguish appearance from reality. They presented children with objects that were disguised in various ways and asked what the items were "really and truly." At age 3, children had some ability to separate the way an object appeared to feel from the way it truly felt. For example, they understood that even though an ice cube did not feel cold to their gloved finger, it "really and truly" was cold (Flavell, Green, & Flavell, 1989). But preschoolers were easily tricked by sights and sounds. When asked whether a white piece of paper placed behind a blue filter is "really and truly blue" or whether a can that sounds like a baby crying when turned over is "really and truly a baby," they often responded, "Yes!" Not until 6 to 7 years did children do well on these tasks (Flavell, Green, & Flavell, 1987).

How do children go about mastering distinctions between appearance and reality? Make-believe play may be important. Children can tell the difference between pretend play and real experiences long before they answer many appearance–reality problems correctly (DiLalla & Watson, 1988; Woolley & Wellman, 1990). During early childhood, children integrate a wide variety of objects into their make-believe themes. Often we hear them say such things as "Pretend this block is a telephone" or "Let's use this box for a house." Experiencing the contrast between everyday and playful use of objects may help children refine their understanding of what is real and what is unreal in the surrounding world.

EVALUATION OF THE PREOPERATIONAL STAGE

How can we make sense of the contradictions between Piaget's conclusions and the findings of new research? The evidence as a whole indicates that Piaget was partly wrong and partly right about young children's cognitive capacities. When given simple tasks based on familiar experiences, preschoolers show the beginnings of logical operations long before the concrete operational stage. But their reasoning is not as well developed as that of school-age children, since they fail Piaget's three-mountains, conservation, and class inclusion tasks and have difficulty separating appearance from reality.

The fact that preschoolers have some logical understanding suggests that the attainment of logical operations is a gradual process. Operational thought is not absent at one point in time and suddenly present at another (Flavell, Miller, & Miller, 1993). Instead, children demonstrate mature reasoning at an early age, although it is fragile and incomplete. Evidence that preschool children can be trained to perform well on Piagetian problems, such as conservation and class inclusion, supports this idea (Beilin, 1978; McCabe & Siegel, 1987). It makes sense that children who possess partial capacity will benefit from training, unlike those with no understanding at all.

Still, the idea that logical operations develop gradually poses a serious challenge to Piaget's stage concept, which assumes sudden and abrupt change toward logical reasoning around 6 or 7 years of age. Does a preoperational stage of development really exist? Some researchers no longer think so. They believe that children work out their understanding of each type of task separately. Their thought processes are regarded as basically the same at all ages—just present to a greater or lesser extent (Gelman & Baillargeon, 1983). Recall from earlier chapters that the idea that cognitive development is continuous is the basis for an alternative approach: information processing, which we take up shortly.

Other experts think the stage concept is still valid, but it must be modified. For example, some theorists combine Piaget's stage approach with the information-processing emphasis on task-specific change (Case, 1992; Fischer & Farrar, 1987; Halford, 1993). They believe that Piaget's strict stage definition needs to be transformed into a less tightly knit concept, one in which a related set of competencies develops over an extended time period, depending on biological maturity and specific experiences. Flavell (1985) favors a flexible stage notion because it helps us appreciate the unique qualities of the young child's reasoning. In his words, "Perhaps what the field needs is another genius like Piaget to show us how, and to what extent, all those cognitive-developmental strands within the growing child are really knotted together" (p. 297).

PIAGET AND EDUCATION

Over the past 30 years, Piaget's theory has had a major impact on education, especially during early childhood. Leslie was greatly influenced by Piaget's work, which she studied in college. Three educational principles derived from his theory have become realities in her classroom:

1. *An emphasis on discovery learning.* Piaget believed that children learn best by acting directly on their world. In a Piagetian classroom, children are encouraged to discover for themselves through spontaneous interaction with the environment. Leslie has equipped her classroom with a rich variety of materials and play areas designed to promote exploration and discovery—art, puzzles, table games, dress-up clothing, building blocks, reading corner, woodworking, and more. For most of the morning, children choose freely among these activities.

2. *Sensitivity to children's readiness to learn.* A Piagetian classroom does not try to speed up development. Instead, Piaget believed that appropriate learning experiences build on children's current thinking. Leslie watches and listens to her pupils, introducing experiences that permit them to practice newly discovered cognitive schemes and that are likely to challenge their incorrect ways of viewing the world. But she does not impose new skills before children indicate they are interested and ready, since this leads to superficial acceptance of adult formulas rather than true understanding (Johnson & Hooper, 1982).

3. *Acceptance of individual differences.* Piaget's theory assumes that all children go through the same sequence of development, but they do so at different rates. Leslie makes a special effort to plan activities for individual children and small groups rather than for the total class (Ginsburg & Opper, 1988). In addition, since individual differences are expected, Leslie evaluates educational progress by comparing each child to his or her own previous course of development. She is less interested in how children measure up to normative standards or to the average performance of same-age peers (Gray, 1978).

In a Piagetian classroom, children are encouraged to act directly on the environment. Activities are designed for individuals and small groups rather than the total class. *(Tony Freeman/PhotoEdit)*

Educational applications of Piaget's theory, like his stages, have met with criticism. Perhaps the greatest challenge has to do with his insistence that young children learn only through acting on the environment. In the next section, we will see that they also use language-based routes to knowledge, which Piaget de-emphasized. In any case, Piaget's influence on education has been powerful and long-lasting. He gave teachers new ways to observe, understand, and enhance young children's development and offered strong theoretical justification for child-oriented approaches to classroom teaching and learning.

ASK YOURSELF . . .

- Recently, 2-year-old Brooke's father decided to shave off his thick beard and mustache. When Brooke saw him, she was very upset. Using Piaget's theory, explain why Brooke was distressed by her father's new appearance.
- One weekend, 4-year-old Will went fishing with his family. When his father asked, "Why do you think the river is flowing along?" Will responded, "Because it's alive and wants to." Yet at home, Will understands very well that his tricycle isn't alive and can't move by itself. What explains this contradiction in Will's reasoning?
- Jason returned to preschool after several days of illness due to the flu. Leslie said, "Jason, I'm so glad you're back. Why were you sick?" "I was sick because I threw up," replied Jason. What kind of reasoning is Jason demonstrating, and why did he reason this way in response to Leslie's question?

BRIEF REVIEW

During Piaget's preoperational stage, mental representation flourishes, as indicated by growth in language and make-believe play. Aside from representation, Piaget's theory emphasizes the young child's cognitive limitations. Egocentrism underlies a variety of illogical features of preoperational thought, including animism, an inability to pass conservation tasks, transductive reasoning, and lack of hierarchical classification. Recent research reveals that when tasks are simplified and made relevant to children's everyday experiences, preschoolers show the beginnings of logical reasoning. These findings indicate that operational thought is not absent during early childhood, and they challenge Piaget's notion of stage. Piaget's theory has had a powerful influence on education, promoting discovery learning, sensitivity to children's readiness to learn, and acceptance of individual differences.

VYGOTSKY'S SOCIOCULTURAL THEORY

Piaget's de-emphasis on language as an important source of cognitive development brought on yet another challenge, this time from Vygotsky's sociocultural theory. We have seen in earlier chapters that Vygotsky stressed the social context of cognitive development. During early childhood, rapid growth in language broadens children's ability to participate in social communication. Soon young children start to talk to themselves in much the same way that they converse with others, and this greatly enhances cognitive development. Let's see how this happens.

CHILDREN'S PRIVATE SPEECH

Watch preschoolers as they go about their daily activities, and you will see that they frequently talk out loud to themselves as they play and explore the environment. For example, as Jason worked a puzzle one day, I heard him say, "Where's the red piece? I need the red one. Now, a blue one. No, it doesn't fit. Try it here." On another occasion, while sitting next to another child, he blurted out, "It broke," without explaining what or when.

Piaget (1923/1926) called these utterances *egocentric speech,* a term expressing his belief that they reflect the preoperational child's inability to imagine the perspectives of others. For this reason, Piaget said, young children's talk is often "talk for self" in which they run off thoughts in whatever form they happen to occur, regardless of whether they are understandable to a listener. Piaget believed that cognitive maturity and certain social experiences—namely, disagreements with peers—eventually bring an end to egocentric speech. Through arguments with agemates, children repeatedly see that others hold viewpoints different from their own. As a result, egocentric speech gradually declines and is replaced by social speech, in which children adapt what they say to their listeners.

Vygotsky (1934/1987) voiced a powerful objection to Piaget's conclusion that young children's language is egocentric and nonsocial. He reasoned that children speak to themselves for self-guidance and self-direction. Because language helps children think about their own behavior and select courses of action, Vygotsky viewed it as the foundation for all higher cognitive processes, such as controlled, sustained attention; deliberate memorization and recall; categorization; planning; problem solving; and self-reflection. As children get older and tasks become easier, their self-directed speech declines and is internalized as silent, inner speech—the verbal dialogues we carry on with ourselves while thinking and acting in everyday situations.

Over the past two decades, researchers have carried out many studies to determine which of these two views—Piaget's or Vygotsky's—is correct. Almost all the findings have sided with Vygotsky. As a result, children's "speech to self" is now referred to as **private speech** instead of *egocentric speech.* Research shows that children use more of it when tasks are difficult, after they make errors, or when they are confused about how to proceed (Berk, 1992a). Also, just as Vygotsky predicted, with age private speech goes underground, changing from utterances spoken out loud into whispers and silent lip movements (Berk & Landau, 1993; Frauenglass &

During the preschool years, children frequently talk to themselves as they play and explore the environment. Research supports Vygotsky's theory that children use private speech to guide their behavior when faced with challenging tasks. With age, private speech is transformed into silent, inner speech, or verbal thought. *(Elizabeth Crews)*

Private speech
Self-directed speech that children use to plan and guide their own behavior.

Diaz, 1985). Finally, children who use private speech freely when faced with difficult tasks are more attentive and involved and show greater improvement in task performance than their less talkative agemates (Berk & Spuhl, 1995; Bivens & Berk, 1990).

If private speech is a central force in cognitive development, where does it come from? Vygotsky's answer to this question highlights the social origins of cognition, his main difference of opinion with Piaget.

SOCIAL ORIGINS OF EARLY CHILDHOOD COGNITION

Recall from Chapter 6 that Vygotsky stressed the role of social experience in cognitive development by conceiving of children's learning as taking place within the *zone of proximal development*—a range of tasks too difficult for the child to do alone but that can be accomplished with the help of others. During infancy, communication in the zone of proximal development is largely nonverbal. In early childhood, verbal dialogues are added as adults and more skilled peers help children master challenging activities. Consider the following example in which Jason's mother helped him put a difficult puzzle together:

Jason: "I can't get this one in." (tries to insert a piece in the wrong place)

Mother: "Which piece might go down here?" (points to the bottom of the puzzle)

Jason: "His shoes." (looks for a piece resembling the clown's shoes but tries the wrong one)

Mother: "Well, what piece looks like this shape?" (pointing again to the bottom of the puzzle)

Jason: "The brown one." (tries it, and it fits; then attempts another piece and looks at his mother)

Mother: "Try turning it just a little." (gestures to show him)

Jason: "There!" (puts in several more pieces. His mother watches.)

Eventually, children take the language of these dialogues, make it part of their private speech, and use this speech to organize their independent efforts in the same way.

To promote cognitive development, social interaction must have certain features. The first is **intersubjectivity.** It refers to the process whereby two participants who begin a task with different understandings arrive at a shared understanding (Newson & Newson, 1975). Intersubjectivity creates a common ground for communication as each partner adjusts to the perspective of the other. Adults try to promote it when they translate their own insights in ways that are within the child's grasp. As the child stretches to understand the interpretation, he is drawn into a more mature approach to the situation (Rogoff, 1990).

A second feature of social experience that fosters development is **scaffolding** (Bruner, 1983; Wood, 1989). It refers to a changing quality of social support over the course of a teaching session. Adults who offer an effective scaffold for children's independent mastery adjust the assistance they provide to fit the child's current level of performance. Jason's mother offers help at just the right moment and in the right amount. As Jason becomes better at the task, his mother permits him to take over her guiding role and apply it to his own activity.

Is there evidence to support Vygotsky's ideas on the social origins of cognitive development? In two studies, mothers who used patient, sensitive communication

Intersubjectivity
The process whereby two participants who begin a task with different understandings arrive at a shared understanding.

Scaffolding
A changing quality of support over the course of a teaching session in which the adult adjusts the assistance provided to fit the child's current level of performance. As competence increases, the adult permits the child to take over her guiding role and apply it to his own activity.

in teaching their preschoolers how to solve a challenging puzzle had children who used more private speech and were more successful when asked to do a similar puzzle by themselves (Behrend, Rosengren, & Perlmutter, 1992; Berk & Spuhl, 1995). Other research indicates that although young children benefit from working on tasks with same-age peers, their planning and problem solving show more improvement when their partner is either an "expert" peer (especially capable at the task) or an adult (Azmitia, 1988; Radziszewska & Rogoff, 1988). Also, conflict and disagreement (the feature of peer interaction emphasized by Piaget) does not seem to be as important in fostering cognitive development as the extent to which children resolve differences of opinion, cooperate, and share purposes and meanings (Cannella, 1993; Tudge, 1990).

VYGOTSKY AND EDUCATION

Today, educators are eager to use Vygotsky's ideas to enhance children's learning. Piagetian and Vygotskian classrooms clearly have features in common, such as opportunities for active participation and acceptance of individual differences in cognitive development. But a Vygotskian classroom goes beyond independent discovery learning. Instead, it promotes *assisted discovery*. Teachers guide children's learning with explanations, demonstrations, and verbal prompts, carefully tailoring their efforts to each child's zone of proximal development. Assisted discovery is also helped along by peer collaboration. Teachers arrange *cooperative learning* experiences, grouping together classmates whose abilities differ and encouraging them to teach and help one another (Forman, Minick, & Stone, 1993).

At this point, it is important to note that some of Vygotsky's ideas, like Piaget's, have been challenged. As Barbara Rogoff (1990) notes, verbal communication may not be the only means, or even the most important means, through which thought develops in some cultures. For example, the young child learning to sail a canoe in Micronesia or weave a garment on a foot loom in Guatemala may gain more from direct observation and practice accompanied by nonverbal communication (a gaze, a change in posture, or a sensitive touch) than from verbal guidance. New findings suggest that the kind of assistance offered to children varies from one culture to another, depending on the tasks that must be mastered to become a contributing member of society (Rogoff et al., 1993). Thus, we are reminded once again that children learn in a great many ways, and as yet, no single theory provides a complete account of cognitive development.

BRIEF REVIEW

Piaget and Vygotsky disagreed on the meaning of preschoolers' self-directed speech. Piaget regarded these utterances as egocentric and nonsocial. In contrast, Vygotsky viewed private speech as communication with the self for self-guidance and self-direction. According to Vygotsky, language provides the foundation for all higher cognitive processes. As adults and more skilled peers provide children with verbal guidance in the zone of proximal development, children incorporate these dialogues into their private speech and use them to guide their own behavior. Research supports Vygotsky's ideas. A Vygotskian classroom emphasizes assisted discovery. Verbal support from teachers and peer collaboration are important.

ASK YOURSELF . . .

- Tanisha sees her 5-year-old son Toby talking out loud to himself while he plays. She wonders whether she should discourage this behavior. Use Vygotsky's theory to explain why Toby talks to himself. How would you advise Tanisha?

INFORMATION PROCESSING IN EARLY CHILDHOOD

Return for a moment to the model of information processing discussed on page 221 of Chapter 6. Recall that information processing focuses on *control processes,* or *mental strategies,* that children use to transform stimuli flowing into their mental systems. During early childhood, advances in representation and children's ability to guide their own behavior lead to more efficient ways of manipulating information and solving problems. In the following sections, we look at how attention and memory change over the preschool years. We also examine children's growing awareness of their own mental life and its role in cognitive development. Finally, we see how young children begin to acquire academic skills that prepare them for learning in school.

ATTENTION

Parents and teachers are quick to notice that preschoolers spend only short times involved in tasks, have difficulty focusing on details, and are easily distracted. The capacity to sustain attention does improve during early childhood, and fortunately so, since children will rely on it greatly once they enter school. In one study, 1- to 4-year-olds were seated at a table with toys. Concentrated involvement rose steadily with age. After playing for a short time, toddlers lost interest. In contrast, preschoolers became increasingly attentive as the session progressed. Their capacity to engage in complex play seemed to support focused engagement with objects (Ruff & Lawson, 1990). However, even 5- and 6-year-olds do not remain attentive for very long. When observed during free play at preschool, the average time they spend in a single activity is about 7 minutes (Stodolsky, 1974).

By the end of early childhood, attention also becomes more *planful,* as children's visual search behavior in familiar environments indicates. In one study, researchers had 3- to 5-year-olds look for a lost object in their preschool play yard. Each child was taken though the setting by an experimenter, who stopped at eight locations along the way to play a game (see Figure 9.4). In the third location, the adult took the child's picture, but by the seventh, the camera was missing. After reaching the eighth location, the child was asked to search for the camera. When 3-year-olds could not find it at location 3, they gave up or searched outside the "critical area" (the path between location 3 where the picture was taken and location 7 where the camera was discovered missing). In contrast, older preschoolers were more likely to confine their search to the critical area and visit each possible location, searching systematically and exhaustively (Wellman, Somerville, & Haake, 1979).

Still, children's attentional strategies have a long way to go before they are very mature. When given detailed pictures or written materials, preschoolers fail to search thoroughly (Enns, 1990). As we will see in Chapter 12, attentional behavior on these tasks improves greatly during middle childhood.

MEMORY

Unlike infants and toddlers, preschoolers have the language skills to describe what they remember, and they can follow directions on simple memory tasks. As a result, several aspects of memory development—recognition and recall, memory for everyday events, and the capacity to use remembered information in new situations—become easier to study in early childhood.

■ **RECOGNITION AND RECALL.** Try showing a young child a set of 10 pictures or toys. Then mix them up with some unfamiliar items and ask the

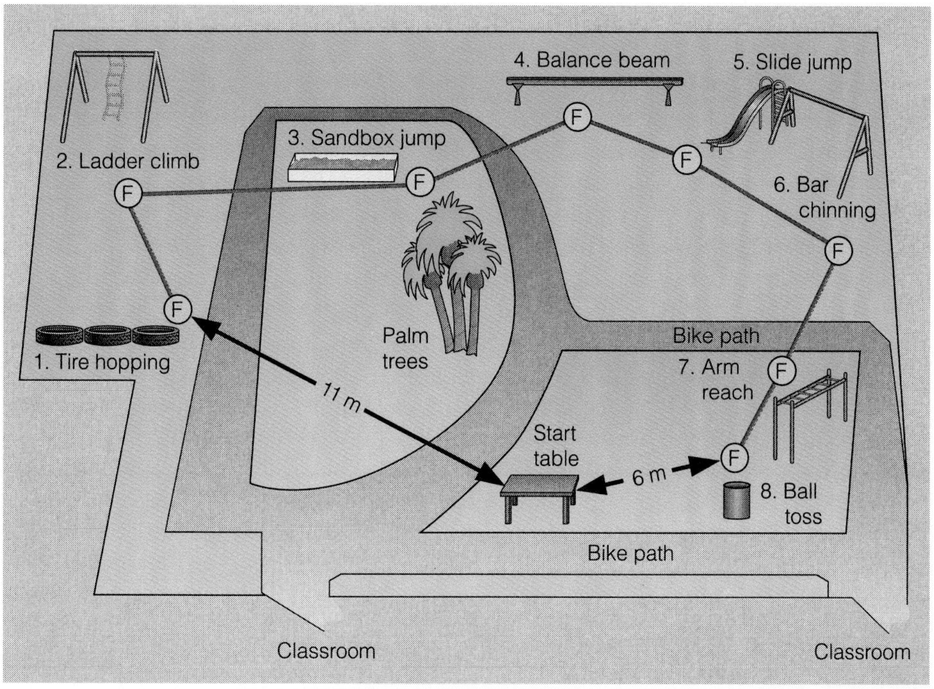

FIGURE 9.4

Layout of the playground in a study of children's visual search behavior. The children played games at eight locations. Each location was marked by a flag (F) displaying a picture of the game played there. Red yarn stretching between the flags defined the path from locations 1 to 8, so children could easily retrace their steps during the search phase of the study. *(From H. M. Wellman, S. C. Somerville, & R. J. Haake, 1979, "Development of search procedures in real-life spatial environments,"* Developmental Psychology, *15, p. 532. Copyright © 1979 by the American Psychological Associa-tion. Reprinted by permission of the publisher and author.)*

child to point to the ones in the original set. You will find that preschoolers' *recognition* memory (ability to tell whether a stimulus is the same as or similar to one they have seen before) is remarkably good. It becomes even more accurate by the end of early childhood. In fact, 4- and 5-year-olds perform nearly perfectly. Now, give the child a more demanding task. While keeping the items out of view, ask the child to name the ones she saw. This requires *recall*—that the child generate a mental image of an absent stimulus. One of the most obvious features of young children's memories is that their recall is much poorer than their recognition. At age 2, they can recall no more than one or two of the items, at age 4 only about three or four (Perlmutter, 1984).

Of course, recognition is much easier than recall for adults as well, but in comparison to adults, children's recall is quite deficient. The reason is that young children are less effective at using **memory strategies,** deliberate mental activities that improve our chances of remembering. For example, when you want to retain information, you might *rehearse,* or repeat the items over and over again. Or you might *organize* it, intentionally grouping together items that are alike so that you can easily retrieve them by thinking of their similar characteristics.

Preschoolers do show the beginnings of memory strategies. For example, when circumstances permit, they arrange items in space to aid their memories. In a study of 2- to 5-year-olds, an adult placed either an M&M or a wooden peg in each of 12 identical containers and handed them one by one to the child, who was asked to remember where the candy was hidden. By age 4, children put the candy containers in one place on the table and the peg containers in another, a strategy that almost always led to perfect recall (DeLoache & Todd, 1988). But preschoolers do not yet rehearse or organize items into categories (for example, all the vehicles together, all the animals together) when asked to recall a set of items. Even when trained to do so, their memory performance may not improve, and they rarely apply these strategies in new situations (Gathercole, Adams, & Hitch, 1994; Lange & Pierce, 1992).

Perhaps young children are not very strategic memorizers because they see little need to remember information for its own sake, when there is no clear reason to do so. In support of this explanation, the memory strategies that preschoolers do use are most effective when recall leads to a desired goal—for example, an M&M to eat, as in the research just described (Wellman, 1988a).

Memory strategies
Deliberate mental activities that improve the likelihood of remembering.

Like adults, young children remember familiar experiences in terms of scripts. After going to the grocery store with his father many times, this boy is unlikely to recall the details of a particular shopping trip. But he will be able to describe what typically happens when you go shopping, and his account will become more elaborate with age. Scripts help us organize and interpret our everyday experiences. (Tony Freeman/PhotoEdit)

MEMORY FOR EVERYDAY EXPERIENCES. Think about the difference in your recall of the listlike information discussed in the previous section and your memory for everyday experiences. In the former, you are asked to recall isolated pieces and bits of information, and you try to reproduce them exactly as you originally learned them. In the latter, you must recall complex, meaningful events. Remembering this kind of information involves selecting experiences, relating them to one another, and interpreting them on the basis of previous knowledge. Do children remember everyday experiences in these ways? The answer is clearly yes.

Like adults, preschoolers remember familiar experiences in terms of **scripts,** general descriptions of what occurs and when it occurs in a particular situation. For very young children, scripts begin as a general structure of main acts. For example, when asked to tell what happens when you go to a restaurant, a 3-year-old might say, "You go in, get the food, eat, and then pay." Children's first scripts contain only a few acts, but as long as events in a situation take place in logical order, they are almost always recalled in correct sequence (Fivush, Kuebli, & Clubb, 1992). This is true even for 1- and 2-year-olds, who cannot yet verbally describe events but who act them out with toys (Bauer & Hertsgaard, 1993; Bauer & Mandler, 1992). With age, children's scripts become more elaborate, as in the following restaurant account given by a 5-year-old child: "You go in. You can sit in the booths or at a table. Then you tell the waitress what you want. You eat. If you want dessert, you can have some. Then you pay and go home" (Fivush, 1984; Nelson & Gruendel, 1981).

Scripts seem to be a basic means through which children organize and interpret their everyday experiences. For example, young children rely on scripted knowledge when listening to and telling stories. They recall more events from stories that are based on familiar event sequences than on unfamiliar ones (Hudson & Nelson, 1983). Preschoolers also use script structures for the stories they act out in play. Listen carefully to preschoolers' make-believe. You will hear everyday scripts reflected in their dialogues as they pretend to put the baby to bed, go on a trip, or play school.

Parents and teachers can enhance preschoolers' memory for everyday events by the way they talk about them with children. Mothers who converse about the past often, ask many questions, and provide a great deal of elaborative information have children who recount past events and stories in a more organized fashion and in greater detail (Fivush, 1991; Hudson, 1990). In line with Vygotsky's ideas, these findings indicate that early social experiences play an important role in the development of memory skills.

GENERALIZING REMEMBERED INFORMATION TO NEW SITUATIONS. Once information is stored in memory, children must learn to use it flexibly, applying it in new situations similar to the ones in which it was originally learned. Without the ability to generalize remembered information in this way, everything children learn would be limited to the context in which it was first acquired. There would be no general skills or knowledge (DeLoache, 1990).

To what extent can preschoolers take their memory for something experienced in one context and apply it to a new context? In one study, children of two ages—2 1/2 and 3—watched as a small toy (Little Snoopy) was hidden in a scale model of a room. Then they were asked to find a larger toy (Big Snoopy) hidden in the room that the model represented. The findings were startling. Although children of both ages remembered where the original object was hidden equally well, 2 1/2-year-olds were unable to transfer this knowledge to the new situation. But by age 3, most children could find the toy in the larger room (DeLoache, 1987).

These findings show that the capacity to generalize remembered information from one context to another improves rapidly over the third year of life. Advances in representation may account for this change. Although very young preschoolers can represent their world, they are just beginning to *represent relations* between stimuli. Between ages 2 1/2 and 3, children realize that the model is not just a toy room; it is a symbol of another room. At first, this understanding is fragile. For

Scripts
General descriptions of what occurs and when it occurs in a particular situation. A basic means through which children organize and interpret their everyday experiences.

example, 3-year-olds' performance depends on a high degree of similarity between the model and the room, such as furniture in the same position and covered with the same fabric (DeLoache, Kolstad, & Anderson, 1991).

The more experience young children have with various forms of representation, the better they can generalize remembered information to new situations. For example, exposure to model–room relations helps 2 1/2-year-olds understand the function of simple maps (Marzolf & DeLoache, 1994). In everyday life, picture books and make-believe play may increase the flexibility of memory.

THE YOUNG CHILD'S THEORY OF MIND

As their representation of the world and ability to remember and solve problems improve, children start to reflect on their own thought processes. They begin to construct a *theory of mind,* or set of beliefs about mental activities. This understanding is often called **metacognition.** The prefix "meta-," meaning beyond or higher, is applied to the term because the central meaning of metacognition is "thinking about thought." As adults, we have a complex appreciation of our inner mental worlds. For example, you can tell the difference between a wide variety of cognitive activities, such as knowing, remembering, guessing, forgetting, and imagining, and you are aware of a great many factors that influence them. We rely on these understandings to interpret our own and others' behavior as well as to improve our performance on various tasks. How early are preschoolers aware of their mental lives, and how complete and accurate is their knowledge?

■ **AWARENESS OF AN INNER MENTAL LIFE.** Listen closely to the conversations of young children, and you will find evidence that awareness of mental activity emerges remarkably early. Such words as "think," "remember," and "pretend" are among the first verbs to appear in children's vocabularies. After age 2 1/2, they use them appropriately to refer to internal states (Wellman, 1985). For example, one day, while looking for crayons and paper, Jason said, "I *thought* they were in the drawer, 'cept they weren't."

More convincing evidence that preschoolers grasp the difference between an inner mental and outer physical world comes from games that involve misleading another person. Findings show that between ages 3 and 4, children begin to understand that belief and reality can differ—in other words, that people can hold *false beliefs* (Harris, 1991; Perner, 1991). In a recent study, preschoolers saw a story enacted with play people in which Mom and Jane put a bag of material in a red drawer and a different bag in a blue drawer. After Mom leaves the room, Jane switches the bags. Then Mom calls from another room, "Jane, I need some more material. It's the bag in the red drawer." When asked which bag Mom really wants, many 3-year-olds were aware of her false belief. They stated that she actually wants the one in the blue drawer (Robinson & Mitchell, 1994). Over the next year, children's understanding of false belief becomes more secure. They master more complex tasks involving deliberate deception in which they must trick another person about the location of an object by moving it, laying false tracks, or giving incorrect information (Ruffman et al., 1993a; Sodian et al., 1991).

Besides knowing that an internal cognitive system exists, preschoolers are aware of some factors that affect its functioning. For example, 3- and 4-year-olds realize that noise, lack of interest, and thinking about other things can interfere with attention to a task (Miller & Zalenski, 1982). And by age 4 to 5, children know that information briefly presented or that must be retained for a long time is more likely to be forgotten (Kreutzer, Leonard, & Flavell, 1975; Lyon & Flavell, 1993).

Is this early grasp of mentality unique to children growing up in industrialized nations, where adults frequently explain behavior in terms of inner beliefs and desires? A recent study of 2- to 6-year-olds among the Baka, a hunting and gathering people living in Cameroon, West Africa, addressed this question. The results showed that Baka children grasp the notion of false belief at about the age that it is

Metacognition
Thinking about thought; awareness of mental activities.

achieved in the United States (Avis & Harris, 1991). The fact that reasoning about the mind emerges around the same time in such different cultures strengthens the possibility that it is a universal feature of early childhood development.

■ **LIMITATIONS OF THE YOUNG CHILD'S THEORY OF MIND.** Although surprisingly advanced, preschoolers' awareness of inner cognitive activities is far from complete. When questioned about subtle distinctions between mental states, children below age 5 often express confusion. For example, they believe that if you get an answer right, then you "knew" and "remembered," but if you get it wrong, then you "guessed" or "forgot" (Miscione et al., 1978; Moore, Bryant, & Furrow, 1989). Preschoolers do not realize that the meaning of these terms depends on people's *certainty about their knowledge,* not on their objective performance. Furthermore, young children believe that all events must be directly observed to be known. They do not understand that *mental inferences* can be a source of knowledge (Sodian & Wimmer, 1987). Finally, preschoolers are unaware that people continue to think while they are waiting or otherwise not doing something. They conclude that mental activity stops when no obvious external cues exist to suggest that a person is thinking (Flavell, Green, & Flavell, 1993).

How, then, should we describe the difference between the young child's theory of mind and that of the older child? Preschoolers know that we have an internal mental life. But they seem to view the mind as a passive container of information. They believe that physical experience with the environment determines mental experience. In contrast, older children view the mind as an active, constructive agent that selects and transforms information and affects how the world is perceived (Pillow, 1988; Wellman, 1988b). We will consider this change further in Chapter 12 when we take up metacognition in middle childhood.

Preschoolers aquire a great deal of knowledge about literacy informally as they participate in everyday activities involving written symbols. They try to figure out how print conveys meaningful information, just as they strive to make sense of other aspects of their world. *(Sybil Shackman/Monkmeyer Press)*

EARLY LITERACY AND MATHEMATICAL DEVELOPMENT

Researchers have begun to study how children's information-processing capacities affect the development of basic reading, writing, and mathematical skills that prepare them for school. The study of how preschoolers start to master these complex activities provides us with additional information on their cognitive strengths and limitations. In addition, we can use this knowledge to find ways to foster early literacy and mathematical development.

■ **EARLY CHILDHOOD LITERACY.** One week, Leslie's pupils brought empty food boxes from home to place on special shelves in the classroom. Soon a make-believe grocery store opened. Children labeled items with prices, made shopping lists, and wrote checks at the cash register. A sign at the entrance announced the daily specials: "APLS BNS 5¢" ("apples bananas 5¢").

As their grocery store play reveals, preschoolers understand a great deal about written language long before they learn to read or write in conventional ways. This is not surprising when we consider that children in industrialized nations live in a world filled with written symbols. Each day, they observe and participate in activities involving storybooks, calendars, greeting cards, lists, and signs, to name just a few. As part of these experiences, children try to figure out how written symbols convey meaningful information, just as they strive to make sense of other aspects of their world.

Young preschoolers search for units of written language as they "read" memorized versions of stories and recognize familiar signs, such as "ON" and "OFF" on light switches and "PIZZA" at their favorite fast food counter. But their early ideas about how written language is related to meaning are quite different from our own. For example, many preschoolers think that a single letter stands for a whole word or that each letter in a person's signature represents a separate name. Often they believe that letters (just like pictures) look like the meanings they represent. One child explained that the word *deer* begins with the letter *O* because it is shaped like a deer; then he demonstrated by drawing an *O* and adding a set of antlers to it (Dyson, 1984). Another stated that the letter *R* belonged to Ruben, just like any other possession (Ferreiro, 1986). During the early period of literacy development, children view writing as a direct representation of objects and people (Sulzby, 1985).

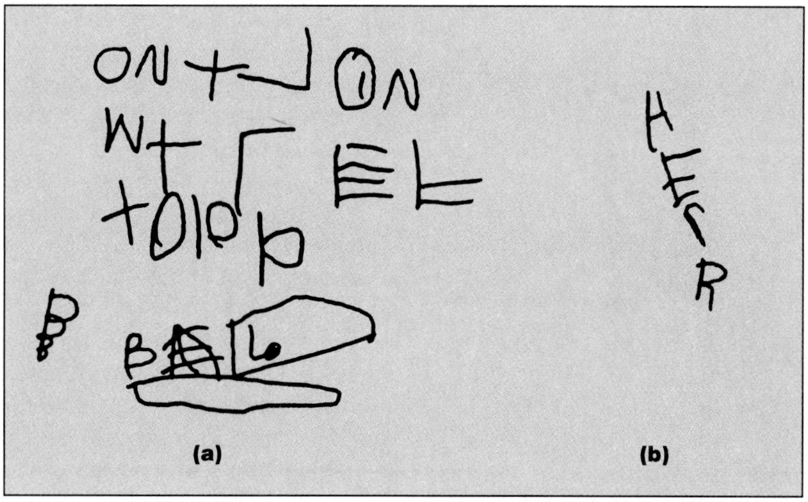

FIGURE 9.5

A story (a) and a grocery list (b) written by a 4-year-old.
This child's writing has many features of real print. It also reveals an awareness of different kinds of written expression. *(From L. M. McGee & D. J. Richgels, 1990,* Literacy's Beginnings, *Boston: Allyn and Bacon, p. 166. Reprinted by permission.)*

Gradually children revise these ideas as their perceptual and cognitive capacities improve, as they encounter writing in many different contexts, and as adults help them with various aspects of written communication. Soon preschoolers become aware of some general characteristics of written language. As a result, they create symbols in their own writing that have many features of real print. Figure 9.5 shows a story and grocery list written by a 4-year-old. This child understands that stories are written from left to right, that print appears in rows, that letters have certain features, and that stories look different from shopping lists. He has begun to pay attention to many features of written language (McGee & Richgels, 1990).

By the end of early childhood, children make other discoveries. In their own writing, they combine letters. However, their first ideas about how letters contribute to larger units are usually incorrect. Children often think that each letter represents a syllable. For example, a child named Santiago wrote his name with three letters ("SIO"), which he read, "San-tia-go." At the same time, he had clearly taken an important step in recognizing that letters are parts of words. Soon children realize that letters and sounds are linked in systematic ways. You can see this in the invented spellings that are typical between ages 5 and 7. At first, children rely heavily on the names of letters when deciding what to include in these spellings. A favorite example is "ADE LAFWTS KRMD NTU A LAVATR" ("eighty elephants crammed into a[n] elevator"). They do not use the standard spelling of adults, but their system is just as predictable. Over time, they will switch to conventional forms (Gentry, 1981; McGee & Richgels, 1989).

Literacy development builds on a broad foundation of spoken language and knowledge about the world. The more literacy-related experiences young children have in their everyday lives, the better prepared they are to tackle the complex tasks involved in becoming skilled readers and writers. Adults can provide literacy-rich physical environments and encourage literacy-related play (Roskos & Neuman, 1993; Snow, 1993). Storybook reading with caregivers is especially important. As we noted in Chapter 6, it is related to preschoolers' reading readiness scores and to later success in school. In early childhood, parents and teachers need not be overly concerned about the correctness of children's interpretations of written language. Instead, they can help most by accepting preschoolers' ideas and supporting their active efforts to revise and extend their knowledge.

YOUNG CHILDREN'S MATHEMATICAL REASONING. Mathematical reasoning, like literacy, builds on a foundation of informally acquired knowledge. In the early preschool period, children start to attach verbal labels (such as "lots," "little," "big," "small") to different amounts and sizes. And between ages 2 and 3, many begin to count. At first, counting is little more than a memorized routine. Often numbers are recited in an unbroken string like this: "Onetwothreefourfivesix!" Or children repeat a few number words while vaguely pointing toward objects they have seen others count (Fuson, 1988).

Very soon, however, counting strategies become more precise. By age 3, most children have established an accurate one-to-one correspondence between a short sequence of number words and the items they represent. Three-year-olds may not yet have memorized the appropriate number labels. For example, one child counted a sequence of three items by saying, "1, 6, 10." But her general method of counting was correct. She used only as many verbal tags as there were items to count (Gelman & Gallistel, 1986).

Sometime between ages 3 and 4, children grasp the vital **cardinality principle.** They understand that the last number in a counting sequence indicates the quantity of items in the set. If you return to the beginning of this chapter, you will see that Jason showed an appreciation of cardinality when he counted out milk cartons for his snack group. Mastery of cardinality helps children's counting become more flexible and efficient. By the late preschool years, children no longer need to start a counting sequence with the number "1." Instead, knowing that there are six items in one pile and some additional ones in another, they begin with the number "6" and *count on* to determine the total quantity. Eventually, they generalize this strategy and *count down* to find out how many items remain after some are taken away. Once they master these procedures, children start to manipulate numbers without requiring that countable objects be physically present (Fuson, 1988). At this point counting on fingers becomes an intermediate step on the way to automatically doing simple addition and subtraction.

Cross-cultural research suggests that the basic arithmetic knowledge just described emerges universally around the world (Resnick, 1989). However, children may acquire it at different rates, depending on the extent to which counting experiences are available in their everyday lives. In homes and preschool where adults provide many occasions and requests for counting, children construct these basic understandings sooner. Then they are solidly available as supports for the wide variety of mathematical skills they will be taught once they enter school.

In this preschool classroom, children have many opportunities to become familiar with written symbols in developmentally appropriate ways. Walls are colorfully decorated with pictures and printed labels, and children explore books with the encouragement and assistance of adults. These teachers seem to know that formal academic training is not for preschoolers. *(Paul Conklin/ Monkmeyer Press)*

A NOTE ON ACADEMICS IN EARLY CHILDHOOD

Does preschoolers' developing grasp of literacy and mathematical concepts mean that we should expose them to school-like instruction aimed at accelerating these skills? Experts in early childhood education agree that it would be a serious mistake to do so. Premature academic training, which requires young children to sit quietly for long periods of drill on reading, writing, and math facts does not fit with their developmental needs. These demands are likely to frustrate even the most patient of preschoolers and cause them to react negatively to school experiences. Formal academic training also takes time away from activities known to promote young children's cognitive and social development, including play, peer interaction, and rich, stimulating conversations between adult and child (Greenberg, 1990).

How can we provide young children with the academic foundation they need? We can best do so by embedding written language and number concepts in everyday experiences. For example, in Leslie's classroom, play activities (such as the grocery store) provided opportunities for children to discover and practice academic-related knowledge. Around the room, names of pupils, labels for objects, and numbers appeared in large print so that children could become familiar with written symbols. Books and writing materials were always handy. As children explored them, they often came up with projects, such as writing a letter to a friend or relative with the teacher's help. Special techniques are needed to acquaint young children with academics if we are to do no harm:

> These methods keep academic content meaningful, integrate it into larger goals, allow for high levels of child choice and initiation, and provide for exploration and play. They also provide for high levels of supportive and responsive adult interaction, in situations where children want to know about and do what's beyond their independent reach. (Schikedanz et al., 1990, p. 12)

Cardinality principle
A principle stating that the last number in a counting sequence indicates the quantity of items in the set.

BRIEF REVIEW

With age, preschoolers sustain attention for longer periods of time and search planfully for missing objects in familiar environments. By the end of early childhood, recognition memory is highly accurate. In contrast, recall improves slowly because preschoolers use memory strategies less effectively than older children and adults. Like adults, young children remember everyday experiences in terms of scripts, which become more elaborate with age. The capacity to generalize remembered information from one context to another improves rapidly during the third year. Around this time, children begin to construct a theory of mind. By age 4, it includes an understanding of false belief. Preschoolers also develop a basic understanding of written symbols and mathematical concepts through informal experiences.

ASK YOURSELF . . .

- Piaget believed that preschoolers' egocentrism prevents them from reflecting on their own mental activities. What evidence in the preceding sections would contradict this assumption?
- Lena notices that her 4-year-old son Gregor can recognize his name in print and count to twenty. She wonders why Gregor's preschool teacher permits him to spend so much time playing instead of teaching him academic skills. Gregor's teacher responds, "I *am* teaching him academics—through play." Explain how this is the case.

INDIVIDUAL DIFFERENCES IN MENTAL DEVELOPMENT DURING EARLY CHILDHOOD

So far in this chapter, we have not said much about individual differences. Preschoolers differ markedly in intellectual progress, just as they vary in physical growth and motor skills. Psychologists and educators typically measure how well preschoolers are developing cognitively by giving them intelligence tests. Scores are computed in the same way as they are for infants and toddlers (return to Chapter 6, page 228, to review). Test content, however, is markedly different than it was during the first 2 years of life. Instead of emphasizing perceptual and motor responses, tests for preschoolers sample a wide range of verbal and nonverbal cognitive abilities.

Child development specialists are interested in young children's mental test scores because by age 5 to 6, they become good predictors of later intelligence and academic achievement (Honzik, Macfarlane, & Allen, 1948; Siegler & Richards, 1982). In addition, understanding the link between early childhood experiences and test performance gives us ways to intervene in children's lives to support their cognitive growth. Let's look at how intelligence is measured in early childhood. Then we will consider the impact of home environment, preschool and day care, and television viewing on young children's mental development.

EARLY CHILDHOOD INTELLIGENCE TESTS

Five-year-old Hallie, whom we introduced in Chapter 8, sat in a small, strange testing room while Sarah, an adult he met only a short while ago, gave him an intelligence test. The questions Sarah asked were of many kinds. Some were *verbal.* For example, Sarah held out a picture of shovel and said, "Tell me what this shows?", an item measuring vocabulary. Then she tested his memory by asking him to repeat sentences and lists of numbers back to her. Hallie's quantitative knowledge was probed by seeing if he could count and solve simple addition and subtraction problems. Other tasks Sarah gave were *nonverbal* and largely assessed spatial reasoning. Hallie copied designs by arranging special blocks, figured out the pattern in a series of shapes, and indicated what a piece of paper folded and cut would look like when unfolded (Thorndike, Hagen, & Sattler, 1986).

Before Sarah began the test, she took special steps to ensure that Hallie's responses would accurately reflect his knowledge. Sarah was aware that Hallie came from an impoverished family background. When low-income and ethnic minority preschoolers are faced with an unfamiliar adult who bombards them with questions, they sometimes become anxious and afraid. Also, such children may not define the testing situation in achievement terms. Often they look for attention and approval from the examiner rather than focusing on the test questions themselves. As a result, they may settle for lower levels of performance than their abilities allow (Zigler & Seitz, 1982). Sarah spent time playing with Hallie before she began testing. In addition, she praised and encouraged him while the test was in progress. When testing conditions like these are used, low-income preschoolers improve in performance. In one study, they gained as much as 10 points, whereas middle-class children improved only slightly, about 3 points (Zigler, Abelson, & Seitz, 1973).

Perhaps you are wondering whether intelligence tests underestimate the abilities of minority children in other ways. The questions that Sarah asked Hallie tap knowledge and skills that not all children have had equal opportunity to learn. The issue of *cultural bias* in intelligence testing is a hotly debated topic that we will take up in Chapter 12. For now, keep in mind that intelligence tests do not sample the full range of human abilities, and performance is affected by cultural and situational factors. Nevertheless, test scores remain important because they predict school achievement, and this, in turn, is strongly related to vocational success in complex industrialized societies. Let's see how the environments in which children spend their days—home, preschool, and day care—affect mental test performance in early childhood.

HOME ENVIRONMENT AND MENTAL DEVELOPMENT

A special version of the *Home Observation for Measurement of the Environment (HOME),* covered in Chapter 6, assesses aspects of 3- to 6-year-olds' homelives that support intellectual growth (see Table 9.1). In agreement with the theories of both Piaget and Vygotsky, physical surroundings and child-rearing practices play important roles. Preschoolers who develop well intellectually have parents who provide a home rich in toys and books, who are warm and affectionate, who stimulate language and academic knowledge, and who arrange outings to places where there are interesting things to see and do. Such parents also make reasonable demands for socially mature behavior—for example, that the child perform simple chores and behave courteously toward others. And when conflicts arise, these parents use reasoning to resolve them instead of physical force and punishment (Bradley & Caldwell, 1979, 1982).

TABLE 9.1

Home Observation for the Measurement of the Environment (HOME): Early Childhood Subscales

SUBSCALE	SAMPLE ITEM
Stimulation through toys, games, and reading material	Home includes toys to learn colors, sizes, and shapes.
Language stimulation	Parent teaches child about animals through books, games, and puzzles.
Organization of the physical environment	All visible rooms are reasonably clean and minimally cluttered.
Pride, affection, and warmth	Parent spontaneously praises child's qualities or behavior twice during observer's visit.
Stimulation of academic behavior	Child is encouraged to learn colors.
Modeling and encouragement of social maturity	Parent introduces interviewer to child.
Variety in daily stimulation	Family member takes child on one outing at least every other week (picnic, shopping).
Avoidance of physical punishment	Parent neither slaps nor spanks child during observer's visit.

Source: Bradley & Caldwell, 1979.

Of course, relating to young children in these ways demands a great deal of time and patience. It also requires money—to provide children with the materials and experiences they need to develop at their best. As we saw in Chapter 2, the characteristics described here are less likely to be found in poverty-stricken families where parents lead highly stressful lives (Garrett, Ng'andu, & Ferron, 1994). In instances in which low-income parents manage, despite daily pressures, to obtain high HOME scores, their youngsters do substantially better on intelligence and achievement tests (Bradley & Caldwell, 1979, 1981). These findings, along with additional evidence we will discuss in Chapter 12, suggest that the home plays a major role in the generally poorer intellectual performance of low-income children in comparison to their middle-class peers.

PRESCHOOL AND DAY CARE

Even more than infants and toddlers, children between the ages of 2 and 6 spend considerable time away from their homes and parents attending preschools and day care programs. Over the last thirty years, the number of young children enrolled in preschool or day care has steadily increased, a trend that is largely due to the dramatic rise in women participating in the labor force. Currently, 64 percent of American preschool-age children have mothers who are employed (U.S. Bureau of the Census, 1994). Figure 9.6 shows the varied ways in which preschoolers spend their days while their parents are at work.

The term *preschool* refers to half-day programs with planned educational experiences aimed at enhancing the development of 2- to 5-year-olds. In contrast, *day care* identifies a variety of arrangements for supervising children of employed parents, ranging from care in someone else's or the child's own home to some type of center-based program. But the line between preschool and day care is a fuzzy one. As Figure 9.6 indicates, parents often select a preschool as a child-care option. Many preschools (and public school kindergartens as well) have increased their hours to full days in response to the needs of employed parents (National Center for Education Statistics, 1994). At the same time, today we know that good day care is not simply a matter of keeping children safe and adequately fed in their parents' absence. Day care should provide the same high-quality educational experiences that an effective preschool does, the only difference being that children attend for an extended day.

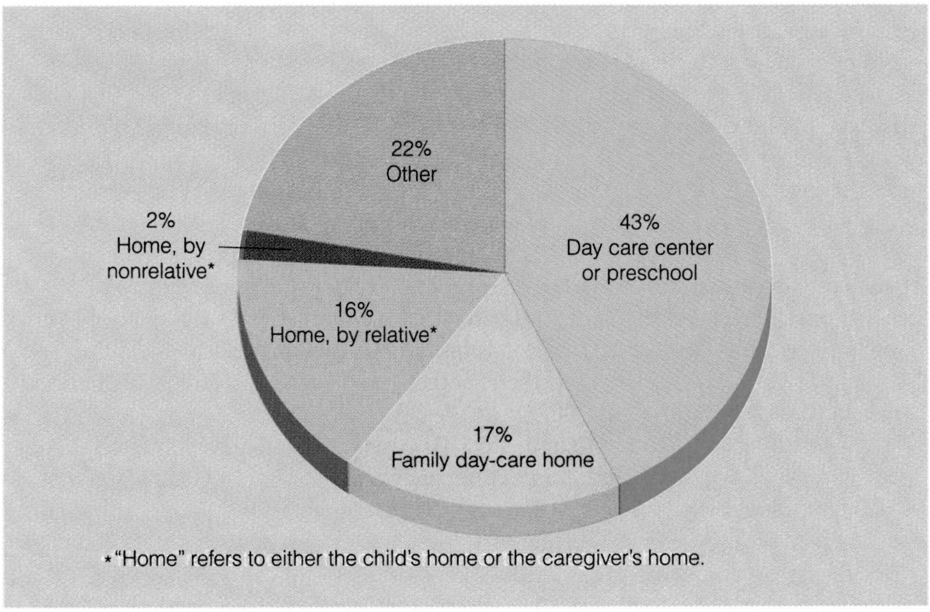

FIGURE 9.6

Who's minding America's preschoolers?

The chart refers to settings in which 3- and 4-year-olds spend most time while their mothers are at work. The "other" category consists mostly of children cared for by their mothers during working hours. Over one-fourth of 3- and 4-year-olds actually experience more than one type of child care, a fact not reflected in the chart. *(Adapted from B. Willer, S. L. Hofferth, E. E. Kisker, P. Divine-Hawkins, E. Farquhar, & F. B. Glantz, 1991,* The Demand and Supply of Child Care in 1990: Joint Findings from the National Child Care Survey 1990 and A Profile of Child Care Settings, *Washington, DC: National Association for the Education of Young Children. Reprinted by permission.)*

■ **TYPES OF PRESCHOOL.** Preschool programs come in great variety, ranging along a continuum from child-centered to teacher-directed. In **child-centered preschools,** teachers provide a wide variety of activities from which children select, and most of the day is devoted to free play. In contrast, **academic preschools** are ones in which teachers structure the program. Children are taught letters, numbers, colors, shapes, and other academic skills through repetition and drill, and play is de-emphasized. Despite grave concern about the appropriateness of this approach, preschool teachers have felt increased pressure to stress formal academic training. The trend is motivated by a widespread belief that providing academic instruction at earlier ages will improve the ultimate achievement of American youth. In contrast, in countries that outperform the United States in math and science achievement, such as Japan and Korea, children have a relaxed early childhood. They are not hurried into academic work during the preschool years (Song & Ginsburg, 1987).

Research on the consequences of preschool attendance indicates that overall, middle-class children experience no more than small gains in test scores. Although a good preschool provides these youngsters with many extra and pleasurable opportunities to explore, solve problems, and develop socially, it has little impact on mental development beyond the advantages provided by their privileged home lives (Zigler, 1987). But for low-income children, the benefits of preschool are considerable.

■ **EARLY INTERVENTION FOR AT-RISK PRESCHOOLERS.** In the 1960s, during a decade in which the United States launched a "war on poverty," a wide variety of intervention programs for economically disadvantaged preschoolers were initiated. They were based on the assumption that learning problems were best treated early, before the beginning of formal schooling.

Project Head Start, begun by the federal government in 1965, is the most extensive of these experiments. A typical Head Start program provides children with a year or two of preschool education before they enter school, along with nutritional and medical services. In addition, parent involvement is a central part of the Head Start philosophy. Parents serve on policy councils and contribute to program planning. They also work directly with children in classrooms, attend special programs on parenting and child development, and receive services directed at their own social, emotional, and vocational needs. Currently, over 1,300 Head Start centers located around the country enroll about 720,000 children each year (Kassebaum, 1994). Even so, Head Start reaches only one-third of eligible children.

Two decades of research establishing the long-term benefits of preschool intervention helped Head Start survive. The most important of these studies was coordinated by the Consortium for Longitudinal Studies, a group of investigators who combined data from seven university-based interventions. Results showed that children who attended the programs scored higher in IQ and school achievement than controls during the first 2 to 3 years of elementary school. After that time, differences in test scores declined. Nevertheless, children who received intervention remained ahead on measures of real-life school adjustment into adolescence. As Figure 9.7 shows, they were less likely to be placed in special education classes or retained in grade, and a greater number graduated from high school. There were also lasting benefits in attitudes and motivation. Children who attended the programs were more likely to give achievement-related reasons (such as school or job accomplishments) for being proud of themselves, and their mothers held higher vocational aspirations for them (Lazar & Darlington, 1982).

A separate report on one program suggests benefits lasting into young adulthood. It was associated with a reduction in delinquency and teenage pregnancy and a greater likelihood of employment (Berrueta-Clement et al., 1984). Considering educational and social outcomes together, the researchers estimated substantial savings to society from participation in preschool intervention—for every $1 spent, $7 saved due to reduced grade retention, crime, and welfare use (Schweinhart et al., 1984).

Child-centered preschools
Preschools in which teachers provide a wide variety of activities from which children select, and most of the day is devoted to free play.

Academic preschools
Preschools in which teachers structure the program, training children in academic skills through repetition and drill.

Project Head Start
A federal program that provides low-income children with a year or two of preschool education before school entry and that encourages parent involvement in children's development.

Do these findings on the impact of outstanding university-based programs generalize to Head Start centers located in American communities? As long as programs are of high quality, the outcomes are much the same (Zigler & Styfco, 1994). In fact, as the Social Issues box on page 342 indicates, mental test score gains are much greater for Head Start than for other types of preschool. This suggests that the Head Start model, which combines early childhood education with parental support, is especially advantageous (Collins, 1993).

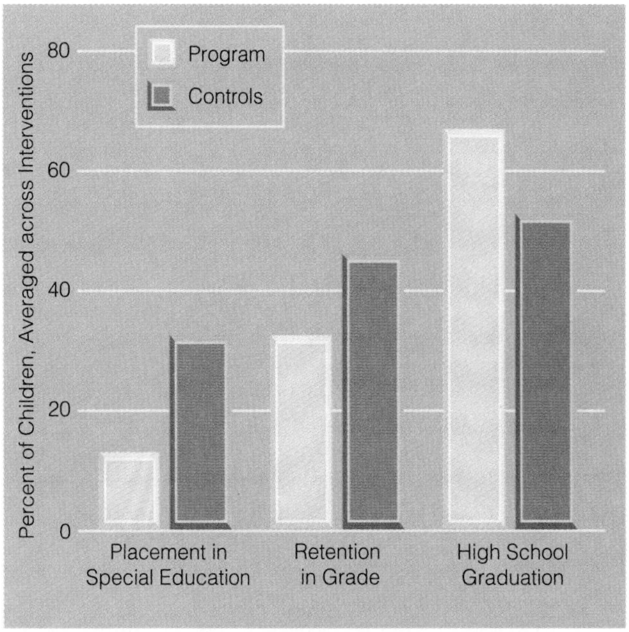

FIGURE 9.7

Benefits of preschool intervention programs.
Low-income children who received intervention fared better than controls on real-life indicators of school adjustment. *(Adapted from Royce, Darlington, & Murray, 1983.)*

■ RESEARCH ON DAY CARE. We have seen that high-quality early intervention can enhance the development of economically disadvantaged children. However, as we noted in Chapter 6, much day care in the United States is not of this high quality. Preschoolers exposed to poor-quality day care, regardless of whether they come from middle- or low-income homes, score lower on measures of cognitive and social skills (Howes, 1988b, 1990; Vandell & Powers, 1983). Inadequate day care can undermine the development of children from all walks of life. In contrast, good day care can reduce the negative impact of an underprivileged home life, and it sustains the benefits of growing up in an advantaged family (Phillips et al., 1994).

What are the ingredients of high-quality day care in early childhood? Large-scale studies of center- and home-based care reveal that the following factors are especially important: group size (number of children in a single space), caregiver–child ratio, caregiver's educational preparation, and caregiver's personal commitment to learning about and taking care of children. When these characteristics are favorable, adults are more verbally stimulating and sensitive to children's needs, and children perform especially well on measures of intelligence, language, and social development (Divine-Hawkins, 1981; Galinski et al., 1994; Ruopp et al., 1979; Howes, Phillips, & Whitebook, 1992). Other research shows that spacious, well-equipped

Among the characteristics of high-quality early childhood programs are frequent interaction between teachers and parents about children's behavior and development. *(David Young-Wolff/PhotoEdit)*

SOCIAL ISSUES

PROJECT HEAD START: A SOCIAL POLICY SUCCESS STORY

The impact of Project Head Start on the lives of preschoolers has been questioned many times since the program began. Yet research reporting only minimal benefits is often biased by one very important factor: Because not all poor children can be served, Head Start typically enrolls the most economically disadvantaged. Controls to whom they are compared often do not come from such extremely impoverished families. A study of Head Start programs in two large cities took this into account. It also looked carefully at the effectiveness of Head Start by comparing it to other preschool alternatives as well as to no preschool at all.

Results showed that Head Start children, compared to "other preschool" and "no preschool" groups, had less educated mothers, came from more crowded households, and were more likely to be growing up in single-parent homes. Before entering preschool, they scored well below the other groups on mental tests. Yet a year later, Head Start children showed *greater gains* than both comparison groups (Lee, Brooks-Gunn, & Schnur, 1988). Furthermore, when African-American children, who comprised a majority of the sample, were followed up one to two years after Head Start, gains on intellectual measures were sustained, although they were no longer as great as they had been immediately after the program (Lee et al., 1990).

These findings indicate that Head Start's unique model of combining high-quality education with efforts to help parents improve their own lives leads to impressive improvements in test scores. At the same time, we know that Head Start children do not emerge from the program with cognitive skills equal to those of children from advantaged backgrounds.

Yet we must keep in mind that it is unrealistic to expect a single year of Head Start to make up for the early experiences of these youngsters. And on completion of Head Start, most poverty-stricken children enter underfunded, poorer-quality schools that may cancel out earlier gains. This suggests that to be most effective, interventions need to be supplemented with high-quality educational supports through the school years (Ramey & Ramey, 1990). Yet the fact remains that a short-term Head Start experience can have lasting effects on children's ability to meet basic school requirements (refer to Figure 9.7). This provides ample justification for current plans to expand Head Start to reach all eligible 3- and 4-year-olds (Collins, 1993).

The success of Head Start has inspired another federal program that promises to dramatically improve the nation's early intervention services. By 1991, public schools were required to offer preschool intervention for 3- to 5-year-olds who either have or are at risk for serious developmental problems. In addition, each state has taken steps to extend intervention downward to infants with delays in development. Like Head Start, programs must ensure that parents participate in the education of their children (Richmond & Ayoub, 1993). Involving and supporting parents increases the likelihood that program effects will be sustained. When parents feel better about their own lives and realize how much their children can learn, they teach and stimulate their youngsters more and hold higher expectations for their performance. These changes help prevent school failure and translate into greater life success in adolescence and adulthood.

Economically disadvantaged preschoolers who experience the comprehensive early intervention of Head Start show greater short-term gains in IQ than do similar children who attend other types of preschools or no preschool at all. Although the IQ advantage washes out over time, early intervention has a lasting impact on children's ability to meet basic educational requirements during elementary and secondary school. *(J. Chenet/ Woodfin Camp & Associates)*

TRY THIS . . .

- Arrange to visit a Head Start program in your community. Ask the director what proportion of eligible children are served. Request information on how each component of this comprehensive early intervention is implemented: education, nutrition, health, social service, and parent involvement. If possible, talk to one or more Head Start parents to find out how the program has changed their lives.

TABLE 9.2

Signs of Developmentally Appropriate Early Childhood Programs

PROGRAM CHARACTERISTIC	SIGNS OF QUALITY
Physical setting	Indoor environment is clean, in good repair, and well ventilated. Classroom space is divided into richly equipped activity areas, including make-believe play, blocks, science, math, games and puzzles, books, art, and music. Fenced outdoor play space is equipped with swings, climbing equipment, tricycles, and sandbox.
Group size	In preschools and day care centers, group size is no greater than 18 to 20 children with two teachers.
Caregiver/child ratio	In day care centers, teacher is responsible for no more than 8 to 10 children. In family day care homes, caregiver is responsible for no more than 6 children.
Daily activities	Most of the time, children work individually or in small groups. Children select many of their own activities and learn through experiences relevant to their own lives. Teachers facilitate children's involvement, accept individual differences, and adjust expectations to children's developing capacities.
Interactions among adults and children	Teachers move among groups and individuals, asking questions, offering suggestions, and adding more complex ideas. They use positive guidance techniques, such as modeling and encouraging expected behavior and redirecting children to more acceptable activities.
Teacher qualifications	Teachers have college-level specialized preparation in early childhood development, early childhood education, or a related field.
Relationships with parents	Parents are encouraged to observe and participate. Teachers talk frequently with parents about children's behavior and development.
Licensing and accreditation	Program is licensed by the state. If a preschool or day care center, accreditation by the National Academy of Early Childhood Programs is evidence of an especially high-quality program. If a daycare home, accreditation by the National Association for Family Day Care is evidence of high-quality experiences for children.

Sources: Bredekamp, 1987; National Association for the Education of Young Children, 1991.

environments and a rich variety of activities that meet the needs and interests of preschool-age children also contribute to positive outcomes (Burchinal, Lee, & Ramey, 1989; Howes, 1988b).

Table 9.2 summarizes characteristics of high-quality early childhood programs, based on standards for developmentally appropriate practice devised by the National Association for the Education of Young Children. Taken together, they offer a set of worthy goals as our nation strives to expand and upgrade day care and educational services for young children.

EDUCATIONAL TELEVISION

Besides home and preschool, young children spend a great deal of time in another learning environment: television. The average 2- to 6-year-old watches TV from 2 to 3 hours a day—a very long time in the life of a young child (Liebert & Sprafkin, 1988). Each afternoon, Jason looked forward to watching certain educational programs. The well-known "Sesame Street" was his favorite.

Find a time to watch an episode of "Sesame Street" yourself. The program was originally designed for the same population served by Head Start—low-income children who enter school academically behind their middle-class peers. Its founders believed that using fast-paced action, lively sound effects, and humorous puppet characters to stress letter and number recognition, counting, vocabulary, and basic concepts might support children's academic development. Today, half of America's 2- to 5-year-olds regularly watch "Sesame Street," and it is broadcast in more than 40 countries around the world (Liebert & Sprafkin, 1988).

Research shows that "Sesame Street" works well as an academic tutor. The more children watch, the higher they score on tests designed to measure the program's learning goals (Bogatz & Ball, 1972; Rice et al., 1990). In other respects, however, the rapid-paced format of "Sesame Street" and other children's programs has been criticized. When different types of programs are compared, ones with slow-paced action and easy-to-follow story lines lead to more elaborate make-believe play. Those presenting quick, disconnected bits of information do not (Huston-Stein et al., 1981; Tower et al., 1979).

Some experts argue that because television presents such complete data to the senses, in heavy doses it encourages passive thinking. Too much television also takes up time children would otherwise spend reading, playing, and interacting with adults and peers (Singer & Singer, 1990). But television can support cognitive development as long as children's viewing is not excessive and programs meet their developmental needs. We will consider the impact of television on young children's emotional and social development in the next chapter.

ASK YOURSELF . . .

- Senator Smith heard that IQ gains resulting from Head Start do not last, so he plans to vote against funding for the program. Write a letter to Senator Smith explaining why he should support Head Start.

BRIEF REVIEW

By 5 to 6 years of age, IQ scores become good predictors of school achievement. A stimulating home environment, warm parenting, and reasonable demands for mature behavior are positively related to mental test scores. Project Head Start, an intervention for low-income children that combines preschool education with parental support, results in immediate gains in IQ and achievement. Although these decline over time, children show lasting benefits in real-life indicators of school adjustment. High-quality day care can serve as effective early intervention, whereas poor day care undermines the development of children from all social classes. Preschoolers who watch "Sesame Street" score higher on tests of academic knowledge, but too much TV watching takes time away from many cognitively stimulating, worthwhile activities.

LANGUAGE DEVELOPMENT IN EARLY CHILDHOOD

Language is intimately related to virtually all the cognitive changes we have discussed in this chapter. Through it, children express a wide variety of cognitive skills, and it also extends many aspects of cognitive development. Between the years of 2 and 6, advances in language are awesome and momentous. Preschoolers' remarkable achievements, as well as their mistakes along the way, indicate that they master their native tongue in an active, rule-oriented fashion.

VOCABULARY DEVELOPMENT

At age 2, Jason had a vocabulary of 200 words. By age 6, he will have acquired around 10,000 words. To accomplish this extraordinary feat, Jason will learn about 5 new words each day (Anglin, 1993). How do children build their vocabularies so quickly? Researchers have discovered that they can connect a new word with an underlying concept after only a brief encounter, a process called **fast mapping.** In one study, an adult presented preschoolers with a novel nonsense word, "koob," in a game in which the object for which it stood (an oddly shaped plastic ring) was labeled only once. Children as young as 2 picked up the meaning of the word (Dollaghan, 1985). Even toddlers comprehend new labels remarkably quickly, but

Fast mapping
Connecting a new word with an underlying concept after only a brief encounter.

they need more repetitions than preschoolers, who are better at remembering and categorizing speech-based information (Gathercole et al., 1992; Woodward, Markman, & Fitzsimmons, 1994).

Once children fast-map a word, they often have to refine their first guess about its meaning. For example, Jason heard Leslie announce to the children one day that they would soon take a field trip. He excitedly told his mother at noon, "We're going on a field trip!" When she asked where the class would go, Jason responded matter-of-factly, "To a field, of course."

Jason's error suggests that young children fast-map some words more easily than others, and, indeed, this is the case. Young preschoolers seem to acquire labels for objects especially rapidly because these refer to concrete items they already know a great deal about from exploring their world (Gentner, 1982). Words for actions are soon added in large numbers ("go," "run," "broke"), as well as modifiers that refer to noticeable features of objects and people ("red," "round" "sad"). If modifiers are related to one another in meaning, they take somewhat longer to learn. For example, 2-year-olds grasp the general distinction between "big" and "small," but not until age 3 to 5 are more refined differences between "tall" and "short," "high" and "low," and "long" and "short" understood. Similarly, children acquire "now–then" before "yesterday–today–tomorrow" (Clark, 1983; Stevenson & Pollitt, 1987).

Preschoolers seem to figure out the meanings of new words by contrasting them with ones they already know. But exactly how they discover which concept each word picks out is not yet fully understood. Ellen Markman (1989, 1992) believes that in the early phases of vocabulary growth, children adopt a principle of mutual exclusivity. They assume that words refer to entirely separate (nonoverlapping) categories. The **principle of mutual exclusivity** works well as long as available referents are perceptually very distinct. For example, when 2-year-olds are told the names of two very different novel objects (a clip and a horn), they assign each label correctly, to the whole object and not a part of it (Waxman & Senghas, 1992).

But mutual exclusivity cannot account for what young children do when adults call a single object by more than one name. Under these conditions, they look for cues in the adult's speech and behavior to determine whether the new word refers to a higher- or lower-order category or to particular features, such as a part of the object, its shape, or its color. For example, while manipulating the propeller of a toy airplane, Leslie remarked, "Look at this propeller!" Jason quickly understood that "airplane" refers to the whole object, the new label "propeller" to a special part of it (Tomasello & Barton, 1994; Waxman & Hatch, 1992). When no such cues are available, children as young as 2 demonstrate remarkable flexibility in their word learning strategies. They abandon the mutual exclusivity principle and treat the new word as a second name for the object (Mervis, Golinkoff, & Bertrand, 1994). Although these findings tell us something about how children master object labels, far less is known about the principles they use for other types of words (Bloom, Tinker, & Margulis, 1993).

Once preschoolers have a sufficient vocabulary, they use words creatively to fill in for ones they have not yet learned. As early as age 2, children coin new words, and they do so in systematic ways. For example, Jason said "plant-man" for gardener (created a compound word) and "crayoner" for a child using crayons (added the ending "-er") (Clark & Hecht, 1982). Children's ability to invent these expressions is evidence for a remarkable, rule-governed approach to language at an early age.

Yet another way that preschoolers extend language meanings is through metaphor. Some very clever ones appear in their everyday language. For example, one 3-year-old used the expression "fire engine in my tummy" to describe a recent stomachache (Winner, 1988). Not surprisingly, the metaphors preschoolers use and understand involve concrete, sensory comparisons, such as "clouds are pillows" and "leaves are dancers." Once their vocabulary and knowledge of the world expand, they start to appreciate ones based on nonsensory comparisons as well, such as

Principle of mutual exclusivity
The assumption by children in the early stages of vocabulary growth that words mark entirely separate (nonoverlapping) categories.

"Friends are like magnets" (Karadsheh, 1991; Keil, 1986). Metaphors permit young children to communicate in especially vivid and memorable ways. And sometimes they are the only means we have to convey what we want to say.

GRAMMATICAL DEVELOPMENT

Grammar refers to the way we combine words into meaningful phrases and sentences. Between ages 2 and 3, English-speaking children use simple sentences that follow a subject–verb–object word order. This shows that they have a beginning grasp of the grammar of their language (de Villiers & de Villiers, 1992).

As young children conform to rules about word order, they also begin to make the small additions and changes in words that enable us to express meanings flexibly and efficiently—for example, adding "-s" to express plural (as in "cats"), applying prepositions (such as "in" and "on"), and forming various tenses from the verb "to be" ("is," "are," "were," "has been," "will"). All English-speaking children master these grammatical markers in a regular sequence, starting with the ones that involve the simplest meanings and the fewest structural changes (Brown, 1973; de Villiers & de Villiers, 1973). For example, children master the plural form "-s" before they learn tenses of the verb "to be." Pluralization requires just one distinction, the difference between one and more than one. In contrast, using tenses of the verb "to be" requires that children understand both number and time, and they must make several grammatical changes in a sentence at once.

By age 3 1/2, children have acquired a great many of these rules, and they apply them so consistently that they overextend the rules to words that are exceptions, a type of error called **overregularization.** "My toy car *breaked,*" "I *runned* faster than you," and "We each got two *feets,*" are expressions that start to appear between 2 and 3 years of age. Overregularization occurs only occasionally, at a rate that remains constant into middle childhood. Therefore, it does not reflect a grammatical defect that must be unlearned. Instead, it shows that children apply grammatical rules creatively, since they do not hear mature speakers use these overregularized forms (Marcus et al., 1992).

Between 3 and 6 years, children master even more complex grammatical forms, although they make predictable errors along the way. In asking questions, preschoolers are reluctant to let go of the "subject–verb–object" structure that is so basic to the English language. At first, they form questions by using rising intonation and failing to invert the subject and verb, as in "Mommy baking cookies?" and "What you are doing, Daddy?" (Tyack & Ingram, 1977). Other errors also occur because children tend to cling to a consistent word order. For example, some passive sentences give them trouble. When told, "The car was pushed by the truck," preschoolers often make a toy car push a truck. By age 5, they understand expressions like these, but mastery of the passive form in its full range of possibilities is a long development that is not complete until the end of middle childhood (Horgan, 1978; Lempert, 1989).

Even though they make errors, preschoolers' grasp of grammar is impressive. By age 4 to 5, they form embedded sentences ("I think *he will come*"), tag questions ("Dad's going to be home soon, *isn't he?*"), and indirect objects ("He showed *his friend* the present"). As the preschool years draw to a close, children use most of the grammatical constructions of their language competently (Tager-Flusberg, 1989).

BECOMING AN EFFECTIVE CONVERSATIONALIST

Overregularization
Application of regular grammatical rules to words that are exceptions.

Besides acquiring vocabulary and grammar, children must learn to use language successfully in social contexts. For a conversation to go well, participants must take turns, stay on the same topic, state their messages clearly, and conform to cultural rules that govern how individuals are supposed to interact. This practical side of language is called **pragmatics**, and children make considerable headway in mastering it over the preschool years.

At the beginning of early childhood, children are already skilled conversationalists. In face-to-face interaction with peers, they take turns, respond appropriately to their partner's remarks, and maintain a topic over time (Garvey, 1975; Podrouzek & Furrow, 1988). The number of turns over which children can sustain interaction increases with age, but even 2-year-olds are capable of effective conversation. These surprisingly advanced abilities probably grow out of early interactive experiences with adults and siblings (see Chapter 7).

By age 4, children already know a great deal about culturally accepted ways of adjusting their speech to fit the age, sex, and social status of their listeners. In one study, 4- to 7-year-olds were asked to act out different roles with hand puppets. Children of all ages used more commands when playing high-status and "masculine" roles, such as teacher, doctor, and father. In contrast, they spoke more politely and used more indirect requests when acting out lower-status and "feminine" roles, such as pupil, patient, and mother (Anderson, 1984). Older preschoolers also adjust their speech on the basis of how well they know their conversational partner. They give fuller explanations to a stranger than to someone with whom they share common experiences, such as a family member or friend (Menig-Peterson, 1975).

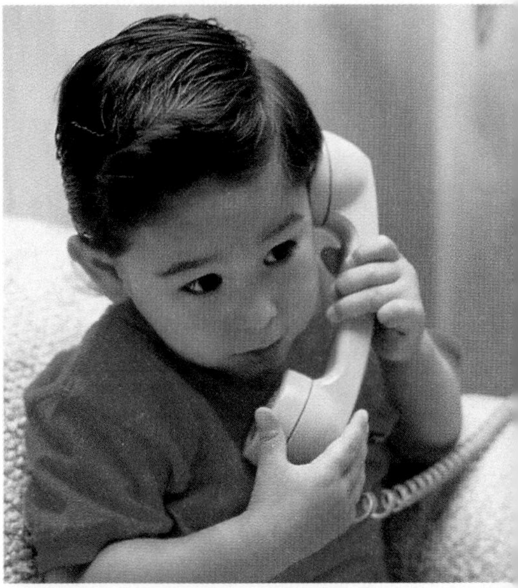

In highly demanding situations, preschool children's conversational skills can break down. This 3-year-old is likely to have trouble communicating clearly on the telephone because he lacks the supports available in face-to-face interaction, such as visual access to his partner's reaction and to objects that are topics of conversation. *(Tony Freeman/PhotoEdit)*

Preschoolers' conversational skills occasionally do break down. For example, have you tried talking on the telephone with a preschooler lately? Here is an excerpt of one 4-year-old's telephone conversation with his grandfather:

Grandfather:	"How old will you be?"
John:	"Dis many." (Holding up four fingers)
Grandfather:	"Huh?"
John:	"Dis many." (Again holding up four fingers)
Grandfather:	"How many is 'at?"
John:	"Four."
John:	"I'm gonna change ears, okay?"
Grandfather:	"Okay."
John:	"I'm back. I had ta change ears."
Grandfather:	"Okay. Was one of your ears gettin' tired?"
John:	"Yeah. This one is." (Points to his left ear) (Warren & Tate, 1992, pp. 259–260)

John used gestures that his grandfather could not see, and when his grandfather signaled that he could not understand ("Huh?"), John did not revise his message. In fact, John's communication resembles the egocentric speech identified by Piaget, discussed earlier in this chapter. But children rarely use egocentric speech in informal, face-to-face interaction. Their speech is most likely to become egocentric in highly demanding situations. While on the telephone, children cannot see their listeners' reactions or rely on typical conversational aids, such as toys and objects to talk about. Not until middle childhood do children interact effectively without these supports.

These findings indicate that preschoolers' communication does vary considerably across contexts. When talking face to face with familiar people about topics they know well, preschoolers make sophisticated language adjustments. Their conversations appear less mature when they cannot use gestures and other concrete props to help overcome the limits of their current knowledge, vocabulary, and

Pragmatics
The practical, social side of language that is concerned with how to engage in effective and appropriate communication with others.

memory (Warren-Leubecker & Bohannon, 1989). Recall the many examples we have seen in which preschoolers' cognitive capacities depend on the difficulty of the task. Research on children's conversational skills echoes this familiar theme.

Conversational give-and-take with adults, either at home or in preschool, promotes young children's language development. *(R. Sidney/The Image Works)*

SUPPORTING LANGUAGE LEARNING IN EARLY CHILDHOOD

From what you have learned so far, what experiences do you think would foster preschoolers' language growth? Perhaps you recall from Chapter 6 that interaction with more skilled speakers is especially important during toddlerhood. The same is true during the early childhood years. Opportunities for conversational give-and-take with adults, either at home or in preschool, are consistently related to general measures of language progress (Byrne & Hayden, 1980; McCartney, 1984).

Researchers have discovered that sensitive, caring adults use special techniques that promote language skills when talking to preschoolers. When children use words incorrectly or communicate unclearly, such adults give helpful, explicit feedback, such as "There are several balls over there, and I can't tell exactly which one you want. Do you mean a large or small one or a red or green one?" (Robinson, 1981). At the same time, they do not overcorrect, especially when children make grammatical mistakes, because criticism discourages children from actively experimenting with language rules in ways that lead to new skills.

Instead, adults provide subtle, indirect feedback about grammar by using two strategies, often in combination: **expansions** and **recasts** (Bohannon & Stanowicz, 1988). For example, a parent hearing a child say, "I gotted new red shoes," might respond, "Yes, you got a pair of new red shoes," *expanding* the complexity of the child's statement as well as *recasting* its incorrect features into appropriate form. Mothers who frequently reformulate children's utterances in these ways have preschoolers who make especially rapid language progress (Farrar, 1990; Nelson et al., 1984). Nevertheless, some investigators question whether expansions and recasts are as important in children's mastery of grammar as mere exposure to a rich language environment containing abundant examples of correct forms. Adults do not use these strategies very often, and they are not provided to children in all cultures (Marcus, 1993; Valian, 1993).

Do the findings just described remind you once again of Vygotsky's theory? In language as in other aspects of intellectual growth, parents and teachers seem to interact with young children in ways that gently prompt them to take the next developmental step forward. They respond to children's natural desire to become competent speakers by listening attentively, elaborating on what they say, modeling correct usage, and stimulating them to talk further. In the next chapter we will see that this special combination of warmth and encouragement of mature behavior is at the heart of early childhood emotional and social development as well.

ASK YOURSELF . . .

- One day, Jason's mother explained to him that the family would take a vacation in Miami. The next morning, Jason emerged from his room with belongings spilling out of a suitcase and remarked, "I gotted my bag packed. When are we going to Your-ami?" What do Jason's errors reveal about his approach to mastering language?

Expansions
Adult responses that elaborate on a child's utterance, increasing its complexity.

Recasts
Adult responses that restructure children's incorrect speech into a more mature form.

SUMMARY

PIAGET'S THEORY: THE PREOPERATIONAL STAGE

Describe advances in mental representation and limitations of thinking during the preoperational stage.

- Rapid advances in mental representation, notably language and make-believe play, mark the beginning of the **preoperational stage.** With age, make-believe becomes increasingly complex, evolving into **sociodramatic play** with others. Preschoolers' make-believe supports many aspects of cognitive development.

- Aside from representation, Piaget described the young child in terms of deficits rather than strengths. Preoperational children are **egocentric**—unable to imagine the perspectives of others and reflect on their own thinking. Egocentrism leads to a variety of illogical features of thought. According to Piaget, preschoolers engage in **animistic thinking,** and their cognitions are **perception-bound, centered,** focused on **states rather than transformations,** and **irreversible.** In addition, preoperational children engage in **transductive reasoning** rather than truly causal reasoning. Because of these difficulties, they fail **conservation** and **hierarchical classification** tasks.

What are the implications of recent research for the accuracy of the preoperational stage?

- When young children are given simplified problems relevant to their everyday lives, their performance appears more mature than Piaget assumed. Operational thinking develops gradually over the preschool years, a finding that challenges Piaget's concept of stage.

What educational principles can be derived from Piaget's theory?

- Piaget's theory has had a lasting impact on educational programs for young children. A Piagetian classroom promotes three educational principles: discovery learning, sensitivity to children's readiness to learn, and acceptance of individual differences.

VYGOTSKY'S SOCIOCULTURAL THEORY

Describe Vygotsky's perspective on the origins and significance of children's private speech.

- Whereas Piaget believed that language does not play a major role in cognitive development, Vygotsky regarded it as the foundation for all higher cognitive processes. According to Vygotsky, **private speech,** or self-directed language, emerges out of social communication as adults and more skilled peers help children master challenging tasks within the zone of proximal development. Eventually private speech is internalized as inner, verbal thought. **Intersubjectivity** and **scaffolding** are features of social interaction that promote transfer of cognitive processes to children.

Describe applications of Vygotsky's theory to education.

- A Vygotskian classroom emphasizes assisted discovery. Verbal guidance from teachers and peer collaboration are vitally important.

INFORMATION PROCESSING IN EARLY CHILDHOOD

How do attention and memory change during early childhood?

- Preschoolers spend only short times involved in tasks, have difficulty focusing on details, and are easily distracted. Attention gradually becomes more sustained and planful during early childhood.

- Young children's recognition memory is remarkably good and becomes even more accurate by the end of early childhood. In comparison to older children and adults, preschoolers' recall for list-like information is poor because they use **memory strategies** less effectively.

- Like adults, preschoolers remember familiar experiences in terms of **scripts,** which become more elaborate with age. The capacity to generalize remembered information from one situation to another improves rapidly around 3 years of age.

Describe the young child's theory of mind.

- Preschoolers begin to construct a theory of mind, indicating that they are capable of **metacognition,** or thinking about thought. Between ages 2 and 3, they distinguish between an inner mental and outer physical world. Between ages 3 and 4, they understand that people can hold false beliefs. However, young children regard the mind as a passive container of information rather than an active, constructive agent.

Summarize children's literacy and mathematical knowledge during early childhood.

- Children understand a great deal about literacy long before they read or write in conventional ways. Preschoolers gradually revise incorrect ideas about the meaning of written symbols as their perceptual and cognitive capacities improve, as they encounter writing in many different contexts, and as adults help them make sense of written information. Children also experiment with counting strategies and discover basic mathematical concepts, including the **cardinality principle,** during the preschool years.

INDIVIDUAL DIFFERENCES IN MENTAL DEVELOPMENT DURING EARLY CHILDHOOD

Describe the content of early childhood intelligence tests and testing conditions that affect children's performance.

- Intelligence tests in early childhood include a wide variety of verbal and nonverbal items that assess vocabulary, memory, quantitative knowledge, spatial reasoning, and other cognitive skills. When taking an intelligence test, low-income and ethnic minority children, especially, benefit from time to get to know the examiner and generous praise and encouragement.

Describe the impact of home, preschool and day care, and educational television on mental development in early childhood.

- Children growing up in warm, stimulating homes with parents who make reasonable demands for mature behavior score higher on mental tests. Home environment plays a major role in the poorer intellectual performance of low-income children in comparison to their middle-class peers.
- Preschool programs come in great variety. **Child-centered preschools** emphasize free play. In **academic preschools,** teachers train academic skills through repetition and drill. Formal academic instruction, however, is inconsistent with young children's developmental needs.
- **Project Head Start** is the largest federally funded preschool program for low-income children in the United States. High-quality preschool intervention results in immediate test score gains and long-term improvements in school adjustment for economically disadvantaged children. The Head Start model, which combines early childhood education with parental support, is especially effective. Good day care can also serve as effective early intervention. In contrast, poor-quality day care undermines the development of children from all walks of life.
- Children pick up many cognitive skills from educational television programs like "Sesame Street." Programs with slow-paced action and easy-to-follow story lines foster make-believe play.

LANGUAGE DEVELOPMENT IN EARLY CHILDHOOD

Trace the development of vocabulary, grammar, and conversational skills in early childhood.

- Supported by **fast mapping,** children's vocabularies grow dramatically during early childhood. Preschoolers figure out the meaning of new words by contrasting them with one they already know. The **principle of mutual exclusivity** explains children's acquisition of some, but not all, early words. Once preschoolers have a sufficient vocabulary, they extend language meanings, coining new words and creating metaphors.
- Between ages 2 and 3, children adopt the basic word order of their language. As they master additional grammatical constructions, they occasionally **overregularize,** or apply the rules to words that are exceptions. By the end of the preschool years, children have acquired a wide variety of complex grammatical forms.
- **Pragmatics** refers to the practical, social side of language. In face-to-face interaction with peers, young preschoolers are already skilled conversationalists. By age 4, they adapt their speech to their listeners in culturally accepted ways. Preschoolers' communicative skills appear less mature in highly demanding contexts.

Cite factors that support language learning in early childhood.

- Conversational give-and-take with more skilled speakers fosters preschoolers' language skills. When adults provide explicit feedback on the clarity of children's utterances and use **expansions** and **recasts,** preschoolers show especially rapid language progress. However, the impact of these strategies on grammatical development has been challenged. For this aspect of language, exposure to a rich language environment may be sufficient.

IMPORTANT TERMS AND CONCEPTS

preoperational stage (p. 314)
sociodramatic play (p. 316)
operations (p. 316)
egocentrism (p. 318)
animistic thinking (p. 318)
conservation (p. 319)
perception-bound (p. 319)
centration (p. 319)
states versus transformations (p. 319)
irreversibility (p. 319)
transductive reasoning (p. 319)
hierarchical classification (p. 321)
private speech (p. 327)
intersubjectivity (p. 328)
scaffolding (p. 328)
memory strategies (p. 331)
scripts (p. 332)
metacognition (p. 333)
cardinality principle (p. 336)
child-centered preschool (p. 340)
academic preschool (p. 340)
Project Head Start (p. 340)
fast mapping (p. 344)
principle of mutual exclusivity (p. 345)
overregularization (p. 346)
pragmatics (p. 347)
expansions (p. 348)
recasts (p. 348)

FYI...

FOR FURTHER INFORMATION AND SPECIAL HELP, CONSULT THE FOLLOWING ORGANIZATIONS:

EARLY CHILDHOOD DEVELOPMENT AND EDUCATION

Association for Childhood Education International (ACEI)
11561 Georgia Avenue, Suite 312
Wheaton, MD 20902
(301) 942-2443

Organization interested in promoting sound educational practice from infancy through early adolescence. Student membership is available and includes a subscription to Childhood Education, *a bimonthly journal covering research, practice, and public policy issues.*

National Association for the Education of Young Children (NAEYC)
1509 16th Street, N.W.
Washington, DC 20036-1426
(202) 232-8777 (800) 424-2460

Organization open to all individuals interested in acting on behalf of young children's needs, with primary focus on educational services. Student membership is available and includes a subscription to Young Children, *a bimonthly journal covering theory, research, and practice in infant and early childhood development and education.*

PRESCHOOL INTERVENTION

National Head Start Association
201 N. Union Street, Suite 320
Alexandria, VA 22314
(703) 739-0875

Association of Head Start directors, parents, staff, and others interested in the Head Start program. Works to upgrade the quantity and quality of Head Start services.

High/Scope Educational Research Foundation
600 N. River Street
Ypsilanti, MI 48198
(313) 485-2000

Devoted to improving development and education from infancy through adolescence. Conducts longitudinal research to determine the effects of early intervention on development.

DAY CARE

Child Care Resource and Referral, Inc.
2116 Campus Drive, S.E.
Rochester, MN 55904
(507) 287-2220

Represents more than 260 local agencies that work for high-quality day care and provide information on available services.

National Association for Family Day Care
725 15th Street, N.W., Suite 505
Washington, DC 20005
(202) 347-3356

Organization open to caregivers, parents, and other individuals involved or interested in family day care. Serves as a national voice that promotes high-quality day care.

"I listen to the birds singing under the tree"
Cui Tao Ren
7 years, China

This scene of young children engaged in joint outdoor play depicts the expanding peer activities and first friendships of early childhood. Chapter 10 describes these emotional and social capacities.

10

Emotional and Social Development in Early Childhood

ERIKSON'S THEORY: INITIATIVE VERSUS GUILT

SELF-DEVELOPMENT IN EARLY CHILDHOOD

Foundations of Self-Concept • Understanding Intentions • Emergence of Self-Esteem

EMOTIONAL DEVELOPMENT IN EARLY CHILDHOOD

Understanding Emotion • Improvements in Emotional Self-Regulation • Changes in Self-Conscious Emotions • Development of Empathy

PEER RELATIONS IN EARLY CHILDHOOD

Advances in Peer Sociability • First Friendships

FOUNDATIONS OF MORALITY IN EARLY CHILDHOOD

The Psychoanalytic Perspective • Behaviorism and Social Learning Theory • The Cognitive-Developmental Perspective • The Other Side of Morality: Development of Aggression

GENDER TYPING IN EARLY CHILDHOOD

Preschoolers' Gender-Stereotyped Beliefs and Behaviors • Genetic Influences on Gender Typing • Environmental Influences on Gender Typing • Gender-Role Identity • Reducing Gender Stereotyping in Young Children

CHILD REARING AND EMOTIONAL AND SOCIAL DEVELOPMENT IN EARLY CHILDHOOD

Styles of Child Rearing • What Makes Authoritative Child Rearing So Effective? • Cultural and Situational Influences on Child-Rearing Styles • Child Maltreatment

As the children in Leslie's classroom moved through the preschool years, their personalities took on clearer definition. By age 3, they voiced firm likes and dislikes as well as new ideas about themselves. "Stop bothering me," Jason said to Mark as he aimed a beanbag toward the mouth of a large clown face. "See, I'm great at this game," Jason announced with confidence, an attitude that kept him trying, even though he missed most of the throws.

The children's conversations also revealed their first notions about morality. Often they combined statements about right and wrong they had heard from adults with forceful attempts to defend their own desires. "You're 'posed to share," stated Mark while he grabbed a beanbag out of Jason's hand.

"I was here first! Gimme it back," demanded Jason, who pushed Mark while reaching for the beanbag. The two boys continued to struggle until Leslie intervened, provided an extra set of beanbags, and showed them how they could both play at once.

As Jason and Mark's interaction reveals, preschoolers are quickly becoming complex social beings. Although arguments and aggression take place among all young children, cooperative exchanges are far more frequent. Between the years of 2 and 6, first friendships emerge in which children converse, act out complementary roles, and learn that their own desires for companionship and toys are best met when they consider the needs and interests of others.

Individual differences in sociability are also evident, becoming a distinct part of preschoolers' personalities. Jason was an assertive, outgoing child who organized many episodes of make-believe play with his classmates. In contrast, Shirley spent so much time by herself working puzzles and painting pictures that one day her mother asked Leslie if this behavior was normal. Robbie's impulsive and distractible temperament made it difficult for him to make friends. He screamed and hit when he didn't get his way, and Leslie worked hard at showing him how to join play groups and settle conflicts successfully.

The children's play highlighted their developing understanding of their social world. Nowhere was this more apparent than in the attention they gave to the dividing line between male and female. While Lynette and Karen cared for a sick baby doll in the housekeeping area, Jason, Vance, and Mark transformed the block corner into a busy intersection. "Green light, go!" shouted police officer Jason as Vance and Mark pushed large wooden cars and trucks across the floor. Already, the children preferred to interact with same-sex peers, and their play themes mirrored the gender stereotypes of their cultural community.

This chapter is devoted to the many facets of emotional and social development in early childhood. We begin with the theory of Erik Erikson, which provides an overview of personality change during the preschool years. Then we consider children's concepts of themselves, their insights into their social and moral worlds, their increasing ability to manage their emotional and social behaviors, and the many factors that support these competencies. In the final sections of this chapter, we answer the question "What is effective child rearing?" We also consider the complex conditions that support good parenting or lead it to break down. Today, child abuse and neglect rank among America's most serious national problems.

ERIKSON'S THEORY: INITIATIVE VERSUS GUILT

Erikson (1950) described early childhood as a period of "vigorous unfolding" (p. 255). Once children have a sense of autonomy and feel secure about separating from parents, they become more relaxed and less contrary than they were as toddlers. Their energies are freed for tackling the critical psychological conflict of the preschool years: **initiative versus guilt.**

The word *initiative* means spirited, enterprising, and ambitious. It suggests that the young child has a new sense of purposefulness. Preschoolers are eager to tackle new tasks, join in activities with peers, and discover what they can do with the help of adults. At no time, commented Erikson, is the child "more ready to learn quickly and avidly . . . than during this period of his development" (p. 258).

Erikson regarded play as a central means through which young children find out about themselves and their social world. Play permits preschoolers to try out new skills with little risk of criticism and failure. It also creates a small social organization of children who must cooperate to achieve common goals. Make-believe, especially, offers unique opportunities for developing initiative. In cultures around the world, children act out family scenes and highly visible occupations—police officer, doctor, and nurse in our society, rabbit hunter and potter among the Hopi Indians, and hut builder and spear maker among the Baka of West Africa (Garvey, 1990). In this way, make-believe provides children with important insights into the link between self and wider society.

As you know from earlier chapters, Erikson's theory builds on Freud's psychosexual stages. Freud's **phallic stage** of early childhood is a time when sexual impulses transfer to the genital region of the body, and the well-known **Oedipus conflict** arises. The young boy wishes to have his mother all to himself and feels hostile and jealous of his father. Freud described a similar **Electra conflict** for girls, who want to possess their fathers and who envy their mothers. These feelings soon lead to intense anxiety, since children fear they will lose their parents' love and be punished for their unacceptable wishes. To master the anxiety, avoid punishment,

Initiative versus guilt
In Erikson's theory, the psychological conflict of early childhood, which is resolved positively through play experiences that foster a healthy sense of initiative and through development of a superego, or conscience, that is not overly strict and guilt ridden.

Phallic stage
Freud's psychosexual stage of early childhood, in which sexual impulses transfer to the genital region of the body and the Oedipus and Electra conflicts are resolved.

Oedipus conflict
The conflict of Freud's phallic stage, in which the boy desires to possess his mother and feels hostile toward his father. He resolves the conflict by becoming like his father and forming a superego.

Electra conflict
The conflict of Freud's phallic stage, in which the girl desires to possess her father and feels hostile toward her mother. She resolves the conflict by becoming like her mother and forming a superego.

and maintain the affection of parents, children form a **superego**, or conscience, through **identification** with the same-sex parent. They take the parent's characteristics into their personality, and as a result, adopt the moral and gender role standards of their society. In other words, they settle for the next best thing to replacing the envied parent: becoming *like* that parent. Finally, children turn the hostility previously aimed at the same-sex parent toward themselves, which leads to painful feelings of guilt each time the child disobeys the standards of conscience.

For Erikson, the negative outcome of early childhood is an overly strict superego, one that causes children to feel too much guilt because they have been threatened, criticized, and punished excessively by adults. When this happens, preschoolers' exuberant play and bold efforts to master new tasks break down. Their self-confidence is shattered, and they approach the world timidly and fearfully.

At this point, it is important to note that Freud's Oedipus and Electra conflicts are no longer regarded as satisfactory explanations of children's emotional, moral, and gender-role development. In later sections of this chapter, when we discuss these topics in detail, we will critically evaluate Freud's psychosexual ideas. At the same time, Erikson's image of initiative captures the diverse changes that take place in young children's emotional and social lives. The preschool years are, indeed, a time when children develop a confident self-image, more effective control over emotions, new social skills, the foundations of morality, and a clear sense of themselves as boy or girl. Now let's take a close look at each of these aspects of development.

According to Freud and Erikson, preschoolers form a superego by identifying with the same-sex parent and, thereby, adopting the moral and gender-role standards of their society. This young boy displays a sense of initiative when he joins his father in making home repairs. *(Ann Hagen Griffiths/OPC)*

SELF-DEVELOPMENT IN EARLY CHILDHOOD

Children emerge from toddlerhood with a firm awareness of their separateness from others. During the preschool years, new powers of representation permit them to reflect on themselves. Preschoolers start to develop a **self-concept**, a set of beliefs about their own characteristics.

FOUNDATIONS OF SELF-CONCEPT

Ask a 3- to 5-year-old to tell you about him- or herself, and you are likely to hear something like this:

> I'm Tommy. See, I got this new red T-shirt. I'm 4 years old. I can brush my teeth, and I can wash my hair all by myself. I have a new Tinkertoy set, and I made this big, big tower.

As these statements indicate, preschoolers' self-concepts, like other aspects of their thinking, are very concrete. Usually they mention observable characteristics, such as their name, physical appearance, possessions, and everyday behaviors (Keller, Ford, & Meecham, 1978).

However, young children's understanding of themselves is not limited to observable attributes. By age 3 1/2, they also describe themselves in terms of typical beliefs, emotions, and attitudes, as in "I'm happy when I play with my friends" or "I don't like being with grown-ups" (Eder, 1989). This indicates that they have a beginning understanding of their unique psychological characteristics. And when read statements and asked to tell whether they are true of themselves (a much easier task than producing a self-description), 3 1/2-year-olds often respond consistently. For example, a child who says that she "doesn't push in front of other people in line" is also likely to indicate that she "feels like being quiet when angry" and "usually does what Mommy or the teacher says," as if she recognizes that she is high in self-control (Eder, 1990). But preschoolers do not yet make explicit reference to internal dispositions, such as "I'm helpful," "I'm friendly," or I'm usually truthful."

Superego
In Freud's theory, conscience.

Identification
In Freud's theory, the process leading to formation of the superego in which children take the same-sex parent's characteristics into their personality.

Self-concept
A set of beliefs about one's own characteristics.

The capacity to do so must wait for the greater cognitive maturity of middle childhood.

In fact, very young preschoolers' concepts of themselves are so bound up with particular possessions and actions that they spend much time asserting their rights to objects, as Jason did in the beanbag incident at the beginning of this chapter. In a study of the relationship between self-awareness and social behavior, 2-year-olds' ability to distinguish self from other was assessed. For example, children were asked to perform actions that indicated they understood the difference between the personal pronouns "my" and "your," as in "Touch my nose" and "Tickle your stomach." Then the experimenter observed each child interacting with a peer in a laboratory playroom. The stronger the children's self-definition, the more possessive they were about objects, claiming them as "Mine!" This was despite the fact that the playroom contained duplicates of many toys (Levine, 1983). These observations suggest that young children's struggles over objects may not be a negative sign of selfishness. Instead, they seem to be a positive sign of developing selfhood, an effort to clearly mark off boundaries between self and others.

The ability to distinguish self from other underlies more than young children's disagreements. It also permits them to cooperate for the first time in resolving disputes over objects, playing games, and solving simple problems (Brownell & Carriger, 1990; Caplan et al., 1991). Adults might take both of these capacities into account when trying to promote friendly peer interaction. For example, teachers and parents can accept the young child's possessiveness as a sign of self-assertion ("Yes, that's your toy") and then encourage compromise ("but in a little while, can you give someone else a turn?"), rather than simply insisting on sharing.

UNDERSTANDING INTENTIONS

As children learn more about themselves by reflecting on their own behavior, they start to distinguish actions that are deliberate and intentional from those that are accidental. By age 2, preschoolers already have intentions on their minds. In everyday conversations, they say "gonna," "hafta," and "wanna" to announce actions they are about to perform (Brown, 1973). Soon they use this grasp of purposefulness to defend themselves. After being scolded for bumping into a playmate or spilling a glass of milk, preschoolers often exclaim, "It was an accident!" or "I didn't do it on purpose!" (Shultz, 1980).

By 2 1/2 to 3 years, this understanding extends to others. Preschoolers become sensitive to cues that help them tell if another person is acting intentionally. At first, they focus on the person's statements. If a person says he is going to do something and then does it, 3-year-olds judge the behavior as deliberate. If statements and actions do not match, then the behavior was not intended (Astington, 1991). By the end of the preschool years, children use a much wider range of information to judge intentionality. For example, 5-year-olds note whether a person is concentrating on what she is doing, whether her action leads to positive or negative outcomes (negative ones are usually not intended), and whether some external cause can account for the person's behavior (Smith, 1978).

Interpreting others' behavior and responding to it appropriately often depends on being able to separate deliberate acts from accidental ones. Older preschoolers who get along well with peers make these judgments accurately and easily. When a playmate appears to have knocked down their block tower on purpose, they become angry and retaliate, but they do not do so if the behavior seems to be accidental. In contrast, highly aggressive children (whom we will discuss in a later section) have difficulty diagnosing intentions. They perceive hostile motives where they do not exist and, as a result, strike out even when the behavior of others is unintentional (Dodge & Somberg, 1987; Quiggle et al., 1992). Such children require special help in learning how to interpret the behavior of others.

EMERGENCE OF SELF-ESTEEM

Another aspect of self-concept emerges in early childhood: **self-esteem,** the judgments we make about our own worth and the feelings associated with those judgments. Self-esteem ranks among the most important aspects of self-development, since evaluations of our own competencies affect emotional experiences, future behavior, and long-term psychological adjustment. Take a moment to think about your own self-esteem. Besides a global appraisal of your worth as a person, you have a variety of separate self-judgments. For example, you may regard yourself as well liked by others, very good at schoolwork, but only so-so at sports.

Preschoolers' sense of self-esteem is not as well defined as that of older children and adults. Young children distinguish how well others like them (social acceptance) from how "good" they are at doing things (competence). But before age 7, they do not discriminate competence at different activities. Also, when asked how well they can do something, they usually rate their own ability as extremely high and often underestimate task difficulty (Harter, 1983, 1990). Jason's announcement that he was great at beanbag throwing despite his many misses of the target is a typical self-evaluation during the preschool years.

Preschoolers' high sense of self-esteem is adaptive during a period in which so many new skills must be mastered, and it contributes greatly to their sense of initiative. Young children's belief in their own capacities is supported by the patience and encouragement of adults. Most parents realize that their preschool youngsters are developing rapidly in a great many ways. They know that a child who has trouble riding a tricycle or cutting with scissors at age 3 will be able to do so a short time later. Preschoolers, too, know that they are growing bigger and stronger, and they see that failure on one occasion often translates into success on another.

Most preschoolers have a high sense of self-esteem, a quality that encourages them to persist at tasks during a period in which many new skills must be mastered. *(Miro Vintoniv/Stock Boston)*

Still, even a little disapproval can undermine a young child's self-esteem and enthusiasm for learning. In one study, 5-year-olds were told stories about a child who works hard on a task (such as drawing a picture) but makes a small error and receives criticism from the teacher. To help children relate the stories to themselves, they were asked to act them out with toys and assume the role of the main character. Kindergartners who downgraded their products in response to criticism were more likely to view themselves as bad and deserving of criticism, to say they would no longer participate in the activity, and to generalize their negative feelings to new tasks. They were also more likely to report that their parents would berate them for making the mistake that happened in the story (Heyman, Dweck, & Cain, 1992).

In Chapter 13, we will see that once children enter school, they become even more aware of others' evaluations of their performance on various tasks. As a result, self-esteem declines and becomes more differentiated during middle childhood.

EMOTIONAL DEVELOPMENT IN EARLY CHILDHOOD

Gains in representation, language, and self-concept support emotional development in early childhood. Between the ages of 2 and 6, children achieve a better understanding of their own and others' feelings, and their ability to regulate the expression of emotion improves. Self-development also contributes to a rise in *self-conscious emotions*— shame, embarrassment, guilt, envy, and pride.

UNDERSTANDING EMOTION

Preschoolers' vocabulary for talking about emotion expands rapidly, and they use it skillfully to reflect on their own and others' behavior. Here are some excerpts

Self-esteem
An aspect of self-concept that involves judgments about one's own worth and the feelings associated with those judgments.

from everyday conversations in which 2-year-olds and 6-year-olds commented on emotionally charged experiences:

> *Two-year-old:* (After father shouted at child, she became angry, shouting back) "I'm mad at you, Daddy. I'm going away. Good-bye."
>
> *Two-year-old:* (Commenting on another child who refused to nap and cried) "Mom, Annie cry. Annie sad."
>
> *Six-year-old:* (In response to mother's comment, "It's hard to hear the baby crying") "Well, it's not as hard for me as it is for you." (When mother asked why) "Well, you like Johnny better than I do! I like him a little, and you like him a lot, so I think it's harder for you to hear him cry."
>
> *Six-year-old:* (Trying to comfort a small boy in church whose mother had gone up to communion) "Aw, that's all right. She'll be right back. Don't be afraid. I'm here." (Bretherton et al., 1986, pp. 536, 540, 541)

As these examples show, early in the preschool years, children refer to causes, consequences, and behavioral signs of emotion, and over time their understanding improves in accuracy and complexity. By age 4 to 5, children correctly judge the causes of many basic emotional reactions. When asked why a nearby playmate is happy, sad, or angry, they describe events similar to those identified by adults and that fit the emotion being expressed, such as "He's happy because he's swinging very high," "She's mad because he wouldn't share the toy," or "He's sad because he misses his mother." However, they are likely to emphasize external factors over internal states as explanations—a balance that changes with age (Fabes et al., 1991). Preschoolers are also good at predicting what a playmate expressing a certain emotion might do next. For example, they know that an angry child might hit someone or grab a toy back and that a happy child is more likely to share (Russell, 1990). They are even aware that a lingering mood can affect a person's behavior for some time in the future (Bretherton et al., 1986).

If you look carefully at the examples just given, you will see that young children use emotional language not only to comment on and explain the reactions of others, but also to guide and influence a companion's behavior. Preschoolers also come up with effective ways to relieve others' negative feelings. For example, they suggest physical comfort, such as hugging, to reduce sadness and giving a desired object to a playmate to reduce anger (Fabes et al., 1988). Overall, preschoolers have an impressive ability to interpret, predict, and change others' feelings—knowledge that is of great help in their efforts to get along with peers and adults.

At the same time, there are limits to young children's emotional understanding. They do not grasp abstract emotional terms, such as gratitude, envy, and pity. Also, in situations in which there are conflicting cues about how a person is feeling, preschoolers have difficulty making sense of what is going on. For example, when asked what might be happening in a picture showing a happy-faced child with a broken bicycle, 4- and 5-year-olds tended to rely only on the emotional expression ("He's happy because he likes to ride his bike"). Older children more often reconciled the two cues ("He's happy because his father promised to help fix his broken bike") (Gnepp, 1983). Much like their approach to Piagetian tasks, preschoolers focus on the most obvious aspect of a complex emotional situation to the neglect of other relevant information.

IMPROVEMENTS IN EMOTIONAL SELF-REGULATION

Language also contributes to preschoolers' improved *emotional self-regulation,* or ability to control the expression of emotion. By age 3 to 4, children verbalize a variety of strategies for adjusting their emotional arousal to a more comfortable level. For example, they know that emotions can be blunted by restricting sensory input (covering your eyes or ears to block out a scary sight or sound), talking to yourself ("Mommy said she'll be back soon"), or changing your goals (deciding that you don't want to play anyway after being excluded from a game) (Thompson, 1990a).

Children's increasing awareness and use of these strategies means that intense emotional outbursts become less frequent over the preschool years. In fact, by age 3 children can even pose an emotion they do not feel, although these emotional "masks" are largely limited to the positive feelings of happiness and surprise. Children of all ages (and adults as well) find it more difficult to act sad, angry, or disgusted than to seem pleased (Lewis, Sullivan, & Vasen, 1987). Undoubtedly this is because most cultures encourage their members to communicate positive feelings and inhibit unpleasant ones as a way of promoting good interpersonal relations, and young children try hard to conform to this rule. As early as the preschool years, children who have trouble coping with negative emotion respond with irritation to others' distress and get along poorly with peers (Eisenberg et al., 1993; Fabes et al., 1994).

By watching adults handle their own feelings, children pick up strategies for regulating emotion. When parents have difficulty controlling anger and hostility, children have problems as well (Gottman & Katz, 1989). Adults' conversations with and instructions to children also provide information about cultural expectations for emotional control and techniques for regulating feelings. Parents who prepare children for difficult experiences, such as a trip to the dentist's office or the first day of nursery school, by describing what to expect and ways to handle anxiety, offer coping strategies that children can later apply to themselves. The From Research to Practice box on page 360 discusses several ways that parents can help young children manage fears that are a normal part of early childhood.

CHANGES IN SELF-CONSCIOUS EMOTIONS

One morning in Leslie's classroom, a group of children crowded around for a bread-baking activity. Leslie asked them to wait patiently while she got a baking pan. In the meantime, Jason reached for the dough to feel it, but the bowl came too close to the edge of the table, and the entire contents tumbled over the side. A chorus of "Uh-ohs!" arose from the children. When Leslie returned, Jason looked at her for a moment, covered his eyes with his hands, and said, "I did something bad." He was feeling ashamed and guilty.

As children's self-concepts become better developed, they become increasingly sensitive to praise and blame or (in Jason's case) the possibility of such feedback. As a result, they experience self-conscious emotions more often—feelings that involve injury to or enhancement of their sense of self (see Chapter 7). By age 3, self-conscious emotions are clearly linked to self-evaluation (Lewis, Alessandri, & Sullivan, 1992).

As Jason's reaction indicates, preschoolers do not yet label self-conscious emotions precisely. And they experience them under somewhat different conditions than do older children and adults. For example, young children are likely to feel guilty for any act that can be described as wrongdoing, even if it was accidental. In contrast, elementary school children only report guilt for intentional misbehavior, such as ignoring chores, cheating, or lying (Graham, Doubleday, & Guarino, 1984). Also, the presence of an audience seems to be necessary for preschoolers to experience self-conscious emotions. In the case of pride, children depend on external recognition, such as a parent or teacher saying, "That's a great picture you drew" or "You did a good job picking up your toys today." And they are only likely to experience guilt and shame if their misdeeds are observed or detected by others (Harter & Whitesell, 1989).

Self-conscious emotions play an important role in children's achievement-related and moral behavior. Since preschoolers are still developing standards of excellence and conduct, they depend on instruction, feedback, and example from adults to know when to feel pride, guilt, and shame. As children develop guidelines for good

FROM RESEARCH TO PRACTICE

HELPING YOUNG CHILDREN MANAGE FEARS

Tonight was the third evening in a row that 5-year-old Hillary called from her bedroom after the lights had been turned out. "Mommy, Daddy, monsters are in my room again." Already, Hillary's parents had removed the animal pictures from her wall and the mobile that hung from the ceiling. Still, monsters lurked under the bed and in the closet.

Young children's vivid imaginations combined with their difficulty in separating appearance from reality (see Chapter 9) make fears common in early childhood. Preschoolers are likely to conjure up scary ghosts and bogeymen as shadows pass over the walls of their room at night, to fear the dark itself, and to express concern about being left alone. Other typical fears of this period include wariness of animals, anxiety about going to preschool or day care, resistance at getting into swimming pools, and apprehension of the doctor or dentist (Morris & Kratochwill, 1983).

Some fears are well founded and adaptive, and parents intentionally encourage them. Venturing into a busy street and going with strangers are examples. But Hillary's fear of monsters is unrealistic and irrational, causing her to avoid bedtime, lose sleep, and be irritable during the day. Hillary's parents wanted to ease her anxiety as quickly as possible.

Fortunately, most early childhood fears last no more than a few months. They are best dealt with through understanding and patience—acknowledging the child's feelings, encouraging the child to talk about them, offering reassurance, and waiting until the fear declines. Here are some techniques for handling specific fears:

- *Monsters, ghosts, and darkness.* Reduce exposure to frightening stories in books and on TV until the child is better able to sort out appearance from reality. Make a thorough search of the room for monsters, showing the child that none are there. Leave a night-light burning, sit by the child's bed until she falls asleep, and tuck in a favorite toy for protection.
- *Preschool or day care.* Find out if the child fears separation from the parent or dislikes preschool itself. If the child resists getting up and preparing to go but seems content once there, then the fear is probably separation. Under these circumstances, provide a sense of warmth and caring while gently encouraging independence. If the child fears being at preschool, try to find out what is frightening—the teacher, the children, or perhaps a crowded, noisy environment. Provide extra support by accompanying the child at the beginning and lessening the amount of time you are present.
- *Animals.* Do not force the child to approach a dog, cat, or other animal that arouses fear. Let the child move at his own pace. Demonstrate how to hold and pet the animal, showing the child that when treated gently, the animal reacts in a friendly way. If the child is bigger than the animal, emphasize this: "You're so big. That kitty is probably afraid of you!"
- *Swimming pools.* Expose the child to water bit by bit. Begin with a sprinkler and gradually work up to a wading pool. Then move to the shallow end of a swimming pool, holding and playing with the child until she is ready to stand in the water independently (Feiner & Subak-Sharpe, 1988).

If a child's fear is very intense, persists for a long time, interferes with daily activities, and cannot be reduced in any of the ways just suggested, it has reached the level of a **phobia.** Sometimes phobias are linked to family problems, and special counseling is needed to reduce them. At other times, phobias simply diminish over time without treatment (DuPont, 1983).

Parents need to keep in mind that fears are normal throughout childhood. As the anxieties of one age period decline, others arise that are related to new developmental challenges. In later chapters, we will see that the haunting monsters of the preschool years are eventually replaced by more realistic concerns having to do with peer acceptance, performance in school, and frightening world events (Morris & Kratochwill, 1983). Some fears—of the dark and of being alone—continue for many years and are common across cultures (Robinson, Robinson, & Whetsell, 1988). Older children and adolescents simply develop more effective ways of managing them.

Forcing a child to confront a fear-arousing situation is more likely to increase anxiety than reduce it. This young girl, who is afraid of cats, is allowed to move at her own pace in approaching the animal. Offering a kitten instead of a full-grown cat also helps reduce her apprehension. *(W. Hill, Jr./The Image Works)*

As young children's language skills expand and their ability to take the perspective of others improves, expressions of empathy become more common. *(Lora E. Askinazi/ The Picture Cube)*

behavior, the presence of others will no longer be necessary to evoke these emotions. In addition, they will be limited to situations in which children feel personally responsible for an outcome (Lewis, 1992; Stipek, Recchia, & McClintic, 1992).

Already you may have noticed that current research does not support Freud's view of guilt as hostility toward the same-sex parent that is redirected toward the self. Instead, guilt is an emotion that, in mature form, is experienced each time we deliberately violate our own personal standards for right action (Campos et al., 1983; Hoffman, 1988). Because these standards take a long time to develop, the circumstances under which children experience guilt change considerably with age.

DEVELOPMENT OF EMPATHY

Another emotion occurs more often in early childhood: *empathy.* During preschool years, the ability to recognize and respond sympathetically to the feelings of others is an important motivator of positive social behavior. Young children who react with empathy are more likely to share and help when they notice another person in distress (Eisenberg & Miller, 1987).

Recall from Chapter 7 that as toddlers become more self-aware, they display empathy for the first time. They offer comfort and reassurance when someone is sad or hurt. As language develops, children rely increasingly on words to console others, a change that indicates a more reflective level of empathy. A 6-year-old said this to his mother after noticing she was distressed at not being able to find a motel after a long day's travel: "You're pretty upset, aren't you, Mom. You're pretty sad. Well, I think, it's going to be all right. I think we'll find a nice place and it'll be all right" (Bretherton et al., 1986, p. 540). As children's ability to take the perspective of others gradually improves, empathic responding increases over early and middle childhood.

The development of empathy depends on cognitive and language development, but it is also supported by early experience. Parents who are warm and encouraging and who show a sensitive, empathic concern for their children have preschoolers who are likely to react in a concerned way to the distress of others (Radke-Yarrow & Zahn-Waxler, 1984). This is not true for children who are repeatedly scolded and punished. In one study, researchers observed physically abused preschoolers at a day care center to see how they reacted to other children's distress. Compared to nonabused youngsters, they rarely showed any signs of empathy. Instead, they responded with fear, anger, and physical attacks (Klimes-Dougan & Kistner, 1990). The children reacted to the suffering of others in the same way that their parents

Phobia
A fear that is very intense, persists for a long time, and cannot be reduced through reasoning and gentle encouragement.

responded to them. Harsh, punitive parenting disrupts the development of empathy at a very early age.

ASK YOURSELF . . .

- Reread the description of Jason and Mark's argument at the beginning of this chapter. On the basis of what you know about self-development, why was it a good idea for Leslie to resolve the dispute by providing an extra set of beanbags so that both boys could play at once?
- Four-year-old Tia had just gotten her face painted at a carnival. As she walked around with her mother, the heat of the afternoon caused her balloon to pop. When Tia started to cry, her mother said, "Oh, Tia, balloons aren't such a good idea when it's hot outside. We'll get another on a cooler day. If you cry, you'll mess up your beautiful face painting." What aspect of emotional development is Tia's mother trying to promote, and why is her intervention likely to be helpful to Tia?

BRIEF REVIEW

Erikson's stage of initiative versus guilt provides an overview of the personality changes that take place in early childhood. During the preschool years, children develop a self-concept made up of observable characteristics and typical beliefs, emotions, and attitudes. They also distinguish actions that are deliberate and intentional from those that are accidental. Preschoolers' high sense of self-esteem supports their enthusiasm for mastering new skills. Language for talking about emotion grows rapidly. Young children have an accurate grasp of the causes and consequences of basic emotional states, and they verbalize a variety of strategies for regulating the expression of emotion. As self-awareness increases, children become more sensitive to the praise and criticism of others, and they experience self-conscious emotions more often. Cognition, language, and warm, sensitive parenting support the development of empathy in early childhood.

PEER RELATIONS IN EARLY CHILDHOOD

As children become increasingly self-aware, more effective at communicating, and better at understanding the thoughts and feelings of others, their social skills improve rapidly. Nowhere is this more apparent than in their increasingly social play with peers.

Peer interaction provides young children with learning experiences that they can get in no other way. Because peers interact with one another on an equal footing, they must assume greater responsibility for keeping a conversation going, cooperating, planning, and setting goals for a play theme than when they associate with adults or older siblings. With peers, children form friendships—special relationships marked by attachment and common interests. In the following sections, we look at how peer interaction changes over the preschool years.

ADVANCES IN PEER SOCIABILITY

At 18 months, Jason's brother Dwayne interacted with peers, but he did so far less often than a preschool child. In a toddler play group, Dwayne spent much time standing and watching and orienting toward adults. When he did play with a peer, he usually imitated the other child's actions—jumping, chasing, or banging a toy after a playmate did so. By age 2 1/2, children use words to affect a peer's behavior, as when they say "Want to jump?" or "Let's play chase." They also do things that complement one another's actions, such as feeding a doll that another child is holding (Eckerman, Davis, & Didow, 1989).

In the early part of this century, Mildred Parten (1932) observed young children in nursery school and noticed a dramatic rise with age in joint, interactive play. She concluded that social development proceeds in a three-step sequence. It begins with **nonsocial activity**—unoccupied, onlooker behavior and solitary play. Then it shifts to a limited form of social participation called **parallel play,** in which a child plays near other children with similar materials but does not try to influence their behavior. At the highest level, preschoolers engage in two forms of true social interaction. The first is **associative play,** in which children engage in separate activities, but they interact by exchanging toys and commenting on one another's behavior. The

Nonsocial activity
Unoccupied, onlooker behavior and solitary play.

Parallel play
A form of limited social participation in which the child plays near other children with similar materials but does not interact with them.

Associative play
A form of true social participation in which children are engaged in separate activities, but they interact by exchanging toys and commenting on one another's behavior.

CONCEPT REVIEW TABLE

Parten's Social Play Categories

CONCEPT	IMPORTANT POINT	EXAMPLE
Nonsocial activity	The child is is unoccupied, watches others, or plays alone. Remains frequent throughout the preschool years, accounting for about 40 percent of 3- to 4-year-olds' play time and 35 percent of 5- to 6-year-olds' play time.	During free play at preschool, 3-year-old Jason spends much time wandering around, observing other children's activities, and working puzzles by himself.
Parallel play	Limited social participation: The child plays near other children with similar materials but does not try to influence their behavior. Accounts for about 20 percent of 3- to 6-year-olds' play time.	Jason sits next to Hallie at the art table, cutting and pasting colored paper. Each child works on his own picture and does not interact with the other.
Associative play	True social interaction: Although involved in separate activities, children talk, trade toys, and comment on one another's behavior. They do not engage in joint efforts directed toward a common goal.	Jason digs a tunnel at one end of the sand table, while Shirley makes cupcakes at the other. The children converse and pass sand tools back and forth as they play.
Cooperative play	True social interaction: Children play *with*, rather than *beside*, one another; their actions are directed toward a common goal. Along with associative play, accounts for about 40 percent of 3- to 4-year-olds' play time and 45 percent of 5- to 6-year-olds.'	"Let's play train," suggests Jason to Mark and Lynette. Together, the children line up several riding toys, climb aboard, and prepare to leave the station.

Sources: Occurrences of play categories are averages of those reported by Barnes (1971); Rubin, Maioni, & Hornung (1976); Rubin, Watson, & Jambor (1978); and Smith (1978).

second is **cooperative play**—a more advanced type of interaction in which children orient toward a common goal, such as acting out a make-believe theme or working on the same product, for example, a sand castle or painting (see the Concept Review Table above).

Find a time to observe young children of varying ages and note how long they spend in each of these types of play. You will probably discover that these play forms emerge in the order suggested by Parten, but they do not form a developmental sequence in which later-appearing ones replace earlier ones (Howes & Matheson, 1992). Instead, all types coexist during the preschool years. Furthermore, although nonsocial activity declines with age, it is still the most frequent form of behavior among 3- to 4-year-olds. Even among kindergartners it continues to take up as much as a third of children's free-play time (refer again to the Concept Review Table above). Also, solitary and parallel play remain fairly stable from 3 to 6 years, and together, these categories account for as much of the young child's play as highly social, cooperative interaction. Social development during the preschool years is not just a matter of eliminating nonsocial and partially social activity from the child's behavior.

We now understand that it is the *type*, rather than the amount, of solitary and parallel play that changes during early childhood. In a detailed study of preschoolers' play behavior, researchers rated the *cognitive maturity* of nonsocial, parallel, and cooperative play by applying the categories shown in the Concept Review Table on page 365. Within each of Parten's play types, 5-year-olds engaged in more cognitively mature behavior than did 4-year-olds (Rubin, Watson, & Jambor, 1978).

Cooperative play
A form of true social participation in which children's actions are directed toward a common goal.

These children are engaged in parallel play. Although they sit side by side and use similar materials, they do not try to influence one another's behavior. Parallel play remains frequent and stable over the preschool years, accounting for about one-fifth of children's play time. *(George Doodwin/ Monkmeyer Press)*

These findings are helpful in responding to the concerns of Shirley's mother, raised at the beginning this chapter. Often parents wonder if a preschooler who spends large amounts of time playing alone is developing normally. Only *certain types* of nonsocial activity—aimless wandering, hovering near peers, and functional play involving immature, repetitive motor action—are cause for concern during the preschool years (Coplan et al., 1994). Most nonsocial play of preschoolers is not of this kind. Instead, it is positive and constructive, and teachers encourage it when they set out art materials, puzzles, and building toys during free play. Children like Shirley, who spend much time in these activities, are not maladjusted. Instead, they are bright youngsters, who, when they do play with peers, show socially skilled behavior (Rubin, 1982).

As we noted in Chapter 9, *sociodramatic play* (or make-believe with peers) becomes especially common during the preschool years. It supports both cognitive and social development. In joint make-believe, preschoolers act out and respond to one another's pretend feelings. Their play is rich in references to emotional states. Young children also explore and gain control of fear-arousing experiences when they play doctor or dentist or pretend to search for monsters in a magical forest. As a result, they are better able to understand the feelings of others and regulate their own. Finally, to collectively create and manage complex plots, preschoolers must resolve their disputes through negotiation and compromise—experiences that contribute greatly to their ability to get along with others (Garvey, 1990; Singer & Singer, 1990).

As these preschoolers trade toys and comment on each other's activities at the sand table, they engage in a form of true social interaction called associative play. *(Mary Kate Denny/ PhotoEdit)*

In cooperative play, the most advanced form of social participation, children join in action directed toward a common goal. These boys develop an imaginative transportation scene in which one drives the vehicle while the other cooperates as passenger. By the end of early childhood, associative and cooperative play account for nearly half of children's play time. *(Arlene Collins/Monkmeyer Press)*

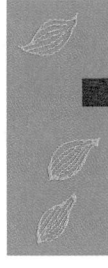

CONCEPT REVIEW TABLE

Developmental Sequence of Cognitive Play Categories

CONCEPT	IMPORTANT POINT	EXAMPLE
Functional play	Simple, repetitive motor movements with or without objects; especially common during the first two years of life	Running around a room, rolling a car back and forth, kneading clay with no intent to make something
Constructive play	Creating or constructing something; especially common between 3 and 6 years of age	Making a house out of toy blocks, drawing a picture, putting together a puzzle
Make-believe play	Acting out everyday and imaginary roles; especially common between 2 and 6 years of age	Playing house, school, or police officer; acting out fairytales or television characters

Sources: Rubin, Fein, & Vandenberg, 1983; Smilansky, 1968.

FIRST FRIENDSHIPS

As preschoolers interact, first friendships form that serve as important contexts for emotional and social development. Take a moment to jot down what the word *friendship* means to you. You probably thought of a mutual relationship involving companionship, sharing, understanding of thoughts and feelings, and caring for and comforting one another in times of need. In addition, mature friendships endure over time and survive occasional conflicts.

Interviews with preschoolers show that they already understand something about the uniqueness of friendship. They know that a friend is someone "who likes you" and with whom you spend a lot of time playing (Youniss, 1980). Yet their ideas about friendship are far from mature. We have already seen that in early childhood, children typically describe themselves in concrete, activity-based terms. Their notion of friendship is much the same. Four- to 7-year-olds regard friendship as pleasurable play and sharing of toys. As yet, friendship does not have a long-term, enduring quality based on mutual trust (Damon, 1977; Selman, 1980). Indeed, Jason could be heard declaring, "Mark's my best friend" on days when the boys got along well. But he would state just the opposite—"Mark, you're not my friend!"—when a dispute arose that was not quickly settled.

Although the meaning of friendship is quite different in early childhood than it will be later, interactions between friends already have a unique quality. Preschoolers give twice as much reinforcement, in the form of greetings, praise, and compliance, to children whom they identify as friends, and they also receive more from them. Friends are also more emotionally expressive, talking, laughing, and looking at each other more often than nonfriends (Hartup, 1983). Apparently, sensitivity, spontaneity, and intimacy characterize friendships very early, although children are not able to say that these qualities are essential to a good friendship until much later.

As early as the preschool years, some children have difficulty making friends (Hartup, 1989; Howes, 1988a). In Leslie's classroom, Robbie was one of them. His demanding, aggressive behavior caused other children to actively dislike him. Wherever he happened to be, such comments as "I don't want to sit next to Robbie," "Robbie ruined our block tower," and "Robbie hit me for no reason" could be heard. Robbie was, to begin with, a temperamentally difficult child, but he also experienced parenting practices that increased his hostility and aggressiveness. You will learn more about Robbie's problems as we take up the topic of moral development in the next section.

ASK YOURSELF . . .

- Three-year-old Bart lives in the country where there are no other preschoolers nearby. His parents wonder whether it is worth driving Bart into town once a week to play with his 3-year-old cousin. What advice would you give Bart's parents, and why?

BRIEF REVIEW

Beginning in early childhood, peer interaction provides an important context for the development of social skills. Over the preschool years, cooperative play becomes common, although solitary and parallel play are also frequent. Although preschoolers do not have a mature understanding of friendship, interactions between friends are already more positive, emotionally expressive, and rewarding.

FOUNDATIONS OF MORALITY IN EARLY CHILDHOOD

Preschoolers' first concepts of morality emerge in interactions with adults and peers. If you watch young children's behavior and listen in on their conversations, you will find many examples of their developing moral sense. By age 2, children show great concern with deviations from the way objects should be and people should act. They point to destroyed property, such as spots on furniture or broken toys, with an expression of discomfort, often exclaiming, "Uh-oh!" In addition, they typically react with alarm to behaviors that are aggressive or that might otherwise harm someone (Lamb, 1991). Soon they comment directly on their own and others' actions: "I naughty. I wrote on wall," or (after having been hit by another child) "Connie not nice to me."

Throughout the world, adults take note of this budding capacity to distinguish right from wrong. In some cultures, special terms are used to describe it. The Utku Indians of Hudson Bay say the child develops *ihuma* (reason). The Fijians believe that *vakayalo* (sense) appears. In response, parents hold children more responsible for their behavior (Kagan, 1989). By the end of early childhood, children can state a great many moral rules, such as "You're not supposed to take things without asking" or "Tell the truth!" In addition, they argue over matters of justice, as when they say, "You sat there last time, so it's my turn" or "It's not fair. He got more!"

All theories of moral development recognize that conscience begins to take shape during the preschool years. And most agree on the general direction of moral growth. At first, the child's morality is *externally controlled* by adults. Gradually, it becomes regulated by *inner standards.* Truly moral individuals do not just do the right thing when authority figures are around. Instead, they have developed *principles of good conduct,* which they follow in a wide variety of situations.

Although points of agreement exist among major theories, there are also important differences. Each emphasizes a different aspect of moral functioning. Psychoanalytic theory stresses the *emotional side* of conscience development—in particular, identification and guilt as motivators of good conduct. Social learning theory focuses on *moral behavior* and how it is learned through reinforcement and modeling. And the cognitive-developmental perspective emphasizes *thinking*—children's ability to reason about justice and fairness. In addition, theories differ in the extent to which they view children as actively contributing to their own moral development. Think back to Chapter 1 and see if you can predict ahead of time which perspective regards the child as an active moral being who wonders about right and wrong and searches for moral truth. Then refer to Table 10.1 for a summary of each approach before we consider them in the following sections.

TABLE 10.1

An Overview of Three Theoretical Perspectives on Moral Development

THEORETICAL PERSPECTIVE	DESCRIPTION
Psychoanalytic theory	To avoid punishment and loss of parental love, young children resolve Freud's Oedipus and Electra conflicts by forming a superego containing the same-sex parents' moral standards. Children obey the superego to avoid guilt.
Behaviorism and social learning theory	Modeling and reinforcement are powerful techniques for teaching young children to behave morally. When these experiences are positive and consistent, children internalize moral rules that guide their behavior in the absence of adults.
Cognitive-developmental theory	Young children actively think about right and wrong and construct their own principles of justice and fairness.

THE PSYCHOANALYTIC PERSPECTIVE

From our discussion of psychoanalytic theory earlier in this chapter, you already know something about this approach to moral development. To briefly review, in Freud's Oedipal and Electra conflicts, children desire to possess the opposite-sex parent, but they give up this wish because they fear punishment and loss of parental love. Instead, they form a *superego,* or conscience, by *identifying* with the same-sex parent, whose moral standards they take into their own personalities. Children obey the superego to avoid *guilt,* a painful emotion that arises each time they are tempted to misbehave. According to Freud, moral development is largely complete by 5 to 6 years of age, at the end of the phallic stage.

Although Freud's theory of conscience development is accepted by psychoanalysts, most child development researchers disagree with it. First, if you look carefully at the Oedipus and Electra conflicts, you will see that discipline promoting fear of punishment and loss of parental love should motivate young children to behave morally (Kochanska, 1993). Yet research shows that this is not the case. Children whose parents frequently use threats, commands, or physical force usually feel little guilt after harming others, and they show poor self-control. In the case of love withdrawal—for example, when a parent refuses to speak to or actually states a dislike for the child—children often respond with high levels of self-blame. They might think to themselves, "I'm no good, and nobody loves me." Eventually, these youngsters may protect themselves from overwhelming feelings of guilt by denying the emotion when they do something wrong. So they, too, develop a weak conscience (Kochanska, 1991; Zahn-Waxler et al., 1990).

In contrast to these techniques, a special type of discipline called **induction** does support conscience formation. It involves pointing out the effects of the child's misbehavior on others, by saying such things as "If you keep pushing him, he'll fall down and cry" or "She feels so sad because you won't give back her doll" (Hoffman, 1988). As long as the explanation matches the child's capacity to understand, induction is effective with children as early as 2 years of age. In one study, mothers who used inductive reasoning had children who were more likely to make up for their misdeeds. They also showed more **prosocial, or altruistic, behavior**—actions that benefit another person without any expected reward for the self. For example, they spontaneously gave hugs, toys, and verbal sympathy to others in distress (Zahn-Waxler, Radke-Yarrow, & King, 1979).

Why is induction so effective? The reason is that it tells children how to behave so they can call on this information in future situations. Also, by pointing out the impact of the child's actions on others, parents encourage preschoolers to empathize, which promotes prosocial behavior. In contrast, discipline that relies too heavily on threats of punishment or love withdrawal produces such high levels of

Induction
A type of discipline in which the effects of the child's misbehavior on others are communicated to the child.

Prosocial, or altruistic, behavior
Actions that benefit another person without any expected reward for the self.

fear and anxiety that children cannot think clearly enough to figure out what they should do. These practices may stop unacceptable behavior temporarily, but in the long run they do not get children to internalize moral rules.

Although there is little support for Freudian mechanisms of conscience development, Freud was correct that guilt is an important motivator of moral action. Around age 3, guilt reactions are clearly evident, and internalization of the parent's moral voice has begun, as this typical statement by a young preschooler reveals: "Didn't you hear my mommy? We better not play with these toys" (Emde & Buchsbaum, 1990). Furthermore, temperament influences early conscience development. Highly inhibited, nonimpulsive preschoolers are more likely to confess and make amends after a transgression and (if they are girls) to experience emotional discomfort and be concerned about restoring parental approval (Kochanska et al., 1994).

But contrary to what Freud believed, guilt is not the only force that compels us to act morally. And moral development is not an abrupt event that is virtually complete by the end of early childhood. Instead, it is a much more gradual process, beginning in the preschool years and extending into adulthood.

BEHAVIORISM AND SOCIAL LEARNING THEORY

According to the traditional behaviorist view, *operant conditioning* is regarded as an important way in which children pick up new responses. From this perspective, children start to behave in accord with adult moral standards because parents and teachers follow up "good behavior" with *positive reinforcement* in the form of approval, affection, and other rewards.

THE IMPORTANCE OF MODELING. Some social learning theorists point out that operant conditioning is not enough for children to acquire many moral responses. Recall from Chapter 5 that for a behavior to be reinforced, it must first occur spontaneously and then be rewarded. Yet many prosocial behaviors, such as sharing, helping, or comforting an unhappy playmate, do not occur often enough at first for reinforcement to explain their rapid development in early childhood. Instead, social learning theorists believe that children largely learn to act morally through *modeling*—by observing and imitating models who demonstrate appropriate behavior (Bandura, 1977; Grusec, 1988). Once children acquire a moral response, such as sharing or telling the truth, reinforcement in the form of praising the act ("That was a very nice thing to do") and the child's character ("You're a very kind and considerate boy") increases its frequency (Mills & Grusec, 1989).

Many studies show that models who behave helpfully or generously increase young children's prosocial responses. In fact, models exert their most powerful effect on prosocial development during the preschool years. At the end of early childhood, children who have a history of consistent exposure to caring adults tend to behave prosocially regardless of whether a model is present. By that time, they have internalized prosocial rules from repeated experiences in which they have seen others help and give and been encouraged to behave in a similar way themselves (Mussen & Eisenberg-Berg, 1977).

A model's characteristics have a major impact on children's willingness to imitate their behavior. First, preschoolers are more likely to copy the prosocial actions of an adult who is warm and responsive than one who is cold and distant (Yarrow, Scott, & Waxler, 1973). Warmth may make children more receptive to the model and therefore more attentive to the model's behavior. Also, warm, affectionate responding is an example of altruism, and part of what children may be imitating is this aspect of the model's behavior. Second, children tend to select competent, powerful models to imitate—the reason that they are especially willing to copy the behavior of older peers and adults. Powerful individuals serve as effective models because children want to acquire their prestige for themselves (Bandura, 1977). A final characteristic that affects children's willingness to imitate is whether adults "practice what they preach." When models say one thing and do another—for example, announce that "it's important to help others" but rarely engage in helpful acts—children generally choose the most lenient standard of behavior that adults demonstrate (Mischel & Liebert, 1966).

Is this mother using threats, commands, and physical force to discipline her young daughter? When parents rely on these techniques, they model aggressive behavior, induce high levels of anxiety in children, and encourage them to avoid the punitive adult. Frequent use of harsh punishment interferes with conscience development. *(D. Ogust The Image Works)*

■ **EFFECTS OF PUNISHMENT.** Undoubtedly you remember from earlier chapters that operant conditioning can involve *punishment*—scolding, criticism, spankings, and other outcomes that reduce the chances that an unacceptable behavior will occur again. The use of sharp reprimands or physical force to restrain or move a child from one place to another is justified when immediate obedience is necessary—for example, when a 3-year-old is about to run into the street. In fact, parents are most likely to use forceful techniques under these conditions. When they are interested in fostering long-term goals, such as acting kindly toward others, they tend to rely on warmth and reasoning (Kuczynski, 1984).

Most parents are aware that the usefulness of punishment is limited and that it should be applied sparingly. Indeed, a great deal of research shows that punishment only promotes momentary compliance, not lasting changes in children's behavior. For example, Robbie's parents punished often—spanking, shouting, and criticizing when he did something wrong. Robbie usually stopped misbehaving when his mother and father were around, but he displayed the behavior again as soon as they were out of sight and he thought he could get away with it. As a result, Robbie was especially unmanageable in settings away from home, such as preschool (Eron et al., 1974).

Harsh punishment also has undesirable side effects. First, it provides children with adult models of aggression. One reason that Robbie lashed out when he was frustrated was that he often saw his parents behaving this way (Emery, 1989). Second, children who are frequently punished soon learn to avoiding the punishing adult. When children avoid interacting with adults who are responsible for their upbringing, those adults have little opportunity to teach desirable behaviors to replace unacceptable responses (Redd, Morris, & Martin, 1975). Finally, as punishment "works" to stop children's misbehavior temporarily, it offers immediate relief to adults, and they are reinforced for using coercive discipline. For this reason, a punitive adult is likely to punish with greater frequency over time, a course of action that can spiral into serious abuse (Parke & Collmer, 1975).

■ **ALTERNATIVES TO HARSH PUNISHMENT.** Alternatives to criticism, slaps, and spankings can reduce the side effects of punishment. One technique is called **time out,** in which children are removed from the immediate setting—for example, by sending them to their rooms—until they are ready to act appropriately. Time out is useful when a child is out of control and other effective methods of discipline cannot be applied at the moment (Betz, 1994). It usually requires only a few minutes to change behavior, and it also offers a "cooling off" period for parents, who may be highly angered by the child's unacceptable acts. Another approach is *withdrawal of privileges,* such as playing outside or going to the movies.

Time out
A form of mild punishment in which children are removed from the immediate setting until they are ready to act appropriately.

Removing privileges often generates some resentment in children, but it allows parents to avoid harsh techniques that could easily intensify into violence (Parke, 1977).

When parents do decide to use punishment, its effectiveness can be increased in several ways. The first involves *consistency.* Punishment that is unpredictable is related to especially high rates of disobedience in children. When parents permit children to act inappropriately on some occasions but scold them on others, children are confused about how to behave, and the unacceptable act persists. Second, a *warm parent–child relationship* increases the effectiveness of an occasional punishment (Parke & Walters, 1967). Children of involved and caring parents find the interruption in parental affection that accompanies punishment to be especially unpleasant. As a result, they want to regain the warmth and approval of parents as quickly as possible. Third, punishment works best when it is accompanied by an *explanation* (Harter, 1983). Explanations increase the effectiveness of punishment because they help children recall the misdeed and relate it to expectations for future behavior (Walters & Andres, 1967).

Finally, parenting practices that do not wait for children to misbehave but that encourage and reward good conduct are the most effective forms of discipline. This means letting children know ahead of time how to act, serving as a good example, and praising children when they behave well. Adults can also reduce opportunities for misbehavior. For example, on a long car trip, parents can bring along back-seat activities that relieve children's restlessness and boredom. At the supermarket, where there are a great many exciting temptations, they can engage preschoolers in conversation and encourage them to help with the shopping rather than waiting for them to get into mischief before intervening (Holden, 1983; Holden & West, 1989). When adults help children acquire acceptable behaviors that they can use to replace forbidden acts, the need for punishment is greatly reduced.

THE COGNITIVE-DEVELOPMENTAL PERSPECTIVE

The psychoanalytic and behaviorist approaches to morality that we have just discussed have one feature in common: Both focus on how children acquire ready-made standards of good conduct held by adults. The cognitive-developmental perspective is different. It regards children as *active thinkers* about social rules. As early as the preschool years, children make moral judgments, deciding what is right or wrong on the basis of concepts they construct about justice and fairness (Gibbs, 1991).

Piaget's (1932/1965) work served as the original inspiration for the cognitive-developmental approach to morality. We will consider his theory of moral development in Chapter 16 because it has important implications for adolescent moral understanding. Today, we know that Piaget underestimated young children's moral reasoning, just as he overlooked their ability to think about many aspects of their physical world (see Chapter 9). Young children already have some well-developed ideas about morality. For example, 3-year-olds respond that a child who intentionally knocks a playmate off a swing is worse than one who does so accidentally while trying to chase a ball, even though (as we saw earlier in this chapter) they report guilt for both types of acts (Yuill & Perner, 1988). They are also aware that disobeying *moral rules,* such as being kind to others and not taking someone else's possessions, is much more serious than violating *social conventions,* such as not saying "please" or "thank you" or eating messy food with fingers (Smetana & Braeges, 1990; Turiel, 1983).

How do young children come to make these distinctions? According to cognitive-developmental theorists, not through direct teaching, modeling, and reinforcement, since adults insist that children conform to social conventions just as often as they press for obedience to moral rules. Instead, children *actively make sense* of their experiences in moral and social-conventional situations. They observe that people respond differently to violations of moral rules than to breaks with social convention. When a moral offense occurs, children react emotionally, describe their own injury or loss, tell another child to stop, or retaliate. And an adult who intervenes is likely to call attention to the rights and feelings of the victim. In contrast, children are less likely to react to violations of social convention. And in these situations, adults tend to demand obedience without explanation, as when they state, "Say the magic word!" or "Don't eat with your fingers" (Smetana, 1989; Turiel, Smetana, & Killen, 1991).

Young preschoolers are clearly off to a good start in appreciating that moral rules are important because they protect the rights and welfare of people. Their developing cognition and language supports this understanding. But children's social experiences also contribute. Disputes over rights, possessions, and property usually occur when children interact with peers and siblings, providing important opportunities to work out first ideas about justice and fairness. The way parents handle violations of rules and discuss moral issues with children also helps them reason about morality. Children who are advanced in moral thinking have parents who adapt their communications about fighting, honesty, and ownership to what their children can understand, respect the child's opinion, and gently stimulate the child to think further, without being hostile or critical (Walker & Taylor, 1991a).

Preschoolers who are disliked by peers because of their aggressive approach to resolving conflict show difficulties with moral reasoning. They have trouble distinguishing moral rules from social conventions, and they violate both kinds often (Sanderson & Siegal, 1988). Without special help, such children show long-term disruptions in moral development.

THE OTHER SIDE OF MORALITY: DEVELOPMENT OF AGGRESSION

Beginning in late infancy, all children display aggression from time to time as they become better at identifying sources of anger and frustration. By the early preschool years, two forms of aggression emerge. The most common is **instrumental aggression.** In this form, children are not deliberately hostile. Instead, they want an object, privilege, or space, and in trying to get it, they push, shout at, or otherwise attack a person who is in the way. The other type, **hostile aggression,** is meant to hurt, as when the child hits, insults, or tattles on a playmate to injure the other person.

For most preschoolers, instrumental aggression declines with age as they learn to compromise over possessions. In contrast, hostile aggression increases between 4 and 7, although it is rare compared to children's friendly interactions (Shantz, 1987). This slight rise in hostile encounters occurs during an age period in which children become better at detecting others' intentions. Older preschoolers are more likely to recognize when another child is being deliberately malicious and to try to get even by attacking in return (Hartup, 1983).

Although children of both sexes show this general pattern of development, on the average boys are more aggressive than girls, a trend that appears in many cultures (Whiting & Edwards, 1988b). The sex difference is, in part, due to biology—in particular, to male sex hormones, or androgens. In humans, androgens contribute to boys' higher rate of physical activity, which may increase their opportunities for aggressive encounters (Parsons, 1982). At the same time, the development of gender typing (a topic we will take up shortly) is also important. As soon as 2-year-olds become dimly aware of gender stereotypes—that males and females are expected to behave differently—aggression drops off in girls but is maintained in boys (Fagot & Leinbach, 1989). Then (as we will see in a moment) parents' tendency to discipline boys more harshly magnifies this effect.

Instrumental aggression
Aggression aimed at obtaining an object, privilege, or space with no deliberate intent to harm another person.

Hostile aggression
Aggression intended to harm another person.

An occasional expression of aggression is normal in early childhood. This preschooler displays instrumental aggression as he pushes a toddler aside to get to an attractive toy. Instrumental aggression declines with age as children learn how to compromise and share. *(Arlene Collins)*

An occasional aggressive exchange between young children is normal and to be expected. As we saw earlier in this chapter, preschoolers sometimes assert their developing sense of self through these encounters, which become important learning experiences as adults intervene and teach alternative ways of satisfying desires. But some preschoolers like Robbie show abnormally high rates of aggression. Researchers have traced their problems to strife-ridden families, poor parenting practices, and exposure to television violence—factors that often can be found together.

THE FAMILY AS TRAINING GROUND FOR AGGRESSIVE BEHAVIOR. "I can't control him, he's impossible," complained Nadine, Robbie's mother, at a conference with Leslie one day. When Leslie asked what might be going on at home that made it hard to handle Robbie, she discovered that Robbie's parents fought constantly. Their conflict led to high levels of family stress and a "spillover" of hostile communication into child rearing that stimulated and perpetuated Robbie's aggression (Miller et al., 1993).

Observations in families like Robbie's reveal that anger and punitiveness can quickly spread from one family member to another, creating a conflict-ridden family atmosphere and an "out of control" child. The pattern begins with forceful discipline, which is made more likely by stressful life experiences (such as economic hardship or an unhappy marriage), a parent's own personality, or a temperamentally difficult child (Dodge, Pettit, & Bates, 1994; Patterson, DeBaryshe, & Ramsey, 1989). Once the parent threatens, criticizes, and punishes, then the child whines, yells, and refuses until the parent finds the child's behavior to be too much and "gives in." As these cycles become more frequent, they generate anxiety and irritability among other family members, who soon join in the hostile interactions (Patterson, 1982). Aggressive children who are products of these family processes soon learn to view the world from a violent perspective. Because they expect others to react with anger and physical force, they see hostile intent where it does not exist. As a result, they make many unprovoked attacks, which contribute to the aggressive cycle.

For at least two reasons, boys are more likely than girls to become involved in family interactions that promote aggressive behavior. First, parents more often use commands and physical punishment with sons, which encourages them to adopt the same tactics (Lytton & Romney, 1991). Second, parents are less likely to interpret fighting as aggressive when it occurs among boys, so they may overlook it more than they do with girls (Condry & Ross, 1985). In line with this idea, by middle childhood boys expect less parental disapproval and report feeling less guilty over aggression than do girls (Perry, Perry, & Weiss, 1989).

Unfortunately, highly aggressive children often have serious adjustment problems. Because of their hostile style of responding and their poor self-control, they tend to be rejected by peers, to fail in school, and (by adolescence) to seek out deviant peer groups, which lead them toward delinquency and adult criminality (see Chapter 16). These children need treatment early, before their antisocial behavior becomes so well practiced that it is difficult to change.

HELPING CHILDREN AND PARENTS CONTROL AGGRESSION. Help for aggressive children must break the cycle of hostilities between family members, replacing it with effective interaction styles. Leslie suggested that Robbie's parents see a family therapist, who observed their inept practices, demonstrated alternatives, and had Nadine and her husband practice them. They learned not to give in to Robbie, to pair commands with reasons, and to replace verbal insults and spankings with more effective punishments, such as time out and withdrawal of privileges (Patterson, 1981).

At the same time, Leslie began teaching Robbie more successful ways of relating to peers. As opportunities arose, she encouraged Robbie to talk about a playmate's feelings and express his own. This helped Robbie take the perspective of others and empathize with them. Soon he showed greater willingness to share and cooperate (Feshbach & Feshbach, 1982). Robbie also participated in **social problem-solving training.** Over several months, he met with Leslie and a small group of preschoolers. The children used puppets to act out common conflicts, discussed effective and ineffective ways of resolving them, and tried out successful strategies in the classroom. Children who receive such training show gains in social competence that are still present a year after the intervention (Feis & Simons, 1985; Spivack & Shure, 1974). Besides improving peer relations, effective social problem solving can provide children with a sense of mastery and self-worth in the face of stressful life events. It reduces the risk of adjustment difficulties in children from low-income and troubled families (Downey & Walker, 1989).

Finally, Robbie's parents got help with their marital problems. This, in addition to their improved ability to manage Robbie's behavior, greatly reduced tension and conflict in the household.

TELEVISION, AGGRESSION, AND OTHER ASPECTS OF SOCIAL LEARNING. Televised violence also encourages childhood aggression. In the United States, 82 percent of programs broadcast contain at least some violence. In children's programming, the incidence is especially high: 32 violent acts per hour, a rate that is greater than that of adult prime-time shows. Of all TV fare, children's cartoons are the most violent (Waters, 1993).

Young children are especially likely to be influenced by television. One reason is that below the age of 8, children do not understand a great deal of what they see on TV. Because they have difficulty connecting separate scenes into a meaningful story line, they do not relate the actions of a TV character to motives or consequences (Collins et al., 1978). A villain who gets what he wants by punching, shooting, and killing may not be a "bad guy" to a preschooler, who fails to notice that the character was brought to justice in the end. Young children also find it hard to separate true-to-life from fantasized television content. They assume that TV reflects their world, unless extreme violations of reality occur, such as Superman dashing across the sky (Kelly, 1981). These misunderstandings increase young children's willingness to uncritically accept and imitate what they see on TV.

Reviewers of thousands of studies have concluded that television violence increases children's aggressive behavior (Liebert & Sprafkin, 1988). Violent programming not only creates short-term difficulties in parent and peer relations, but has long-term effects as well. Longitudinal research reveals that highly aggressive children have a greater appetite for violent TV. As they watch more, they become increasingly likely to resort to hostile ways of solving problems, a spiraling pattern of learning that contributes to serious antisocial acts by adolescence and young adulthood (Friedrich-Cofer & Huston, 1986; Huesmann, 1986). Television violence also "hardens" children to aggression, making them more willing to tolerate it in others. Heavy TV viewers begin to see the world as a mean and scary place where aggressive acts are a normal and acceptable means for solving problems (Parke & Slaby, 1983).

TV promotes conflict in a second way: through its advertising. Since preschoolers (and many older children as well) innocently believe that the promises of TV ads are true, they ask for products that they see. In the aisles of grocery and toy stores, adult refusals often lead to arguments between parents and children (Atkin, 1978). Commercials for sugary foods make up about 80 percent of advertising aimed at children. When parents give in to children's demands, young TV viewers come to prefer these snacks and are convinced by TV messages that they are healthy (Gorn & Goldberg, 1982).

Finally, television conveys ethnic and gender stereotypes that are common in American society. Although African-Americans are better represented on TV than

Social problem-solving training
Training in which children are taught how to resolve social conflicts through discussing and trying out successful strategies.

SOCIAL ISSUES

REGULATING CHILDREN'S TELEVISION

Exposure to television is almost universal in the United States and other Western industrialized nations. Ninety-eight percent of American homes have a least one television set, and a TV is switched on in a typical household for a total of 7.1 hours a day. TV enters the lives of children at an early age, becoming a major teacher of undesirable attitudes and behavior. Yet television has as much potential for good as it does for ill. If the content of television were changed, it could promote prosocial attitudes and behavior and convey information about nonviolent aspects of the world, such as history, science, literature, fine arts, and other cultures (Huston, Watkins, & Kunkel, 1989).

Since the early days of television, high-quality programming for children has dropped off while advertising has risen as commercial broadcasting stations have tried to reach larger audiences and boost profits. Public broadcasting and cable TV offer some excellent programs for children. But government funding for public television has declined over the past two decades, and cable (which depends on user fees) is less available to low-income families. Furthermore, there are fewer restrictions today than there once were on program content and advertising for children. For example, a decade ago, characters in children's programs were not permitted to sell products. Today they commonly do—a strategy that greatly increases children's desire to buy (Kunkel, 1993).

Professional organizations, citizens' groups, and public officials have pressed for government regulation of TV. Many would like to see networks required to provide a certain amount of educational programming for children. And some believe that it would be best to ban advertising directed at children. But the First Amendment right to free speech has made the federal government reluctant to place limits on television content. And broadcasters, whose profits are at risk, are certainly against restrictions (Auletta, 1993).

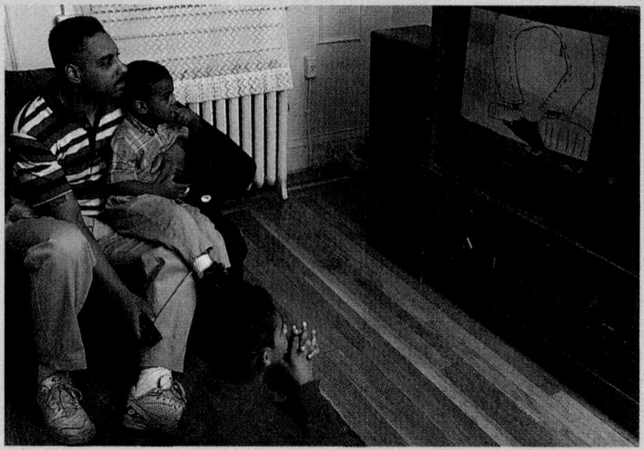

Parents who watch TV with their children can help them interpret and evaluate televised messages. They can also encourage children to build on TV content in constructive ways—for example, through active play or a trip to the library to gather more information. *(Laura Dwight/Omni-Photo Communications)*

Until television does improve, protecting children from the impact of harmful TV rests in the hands of parents. Here are some strategies that they can use:

- Avoid using TV as a baby-sitter. Provide children with clear rules that limit the amount of time they can watch—for example, an hour a day and only certain programs—and stick to the rules.
- Do not use television to reward or punish children, a practice that increases its attractiveness.
- Encourage children to watch programs that are child-appropriate and informative.
- As much as possible, watch with children, helping them understand what they see. When adults express disapproval of on-screen behavior, raise questions about the realism of televised information, and encourage children to discuss it, they teach children to evaluate TV content rather than accept it uncritically.
- Build on TV programs in constructive ways, encouraging children to move away from the set into active engagement with their surroundings. For example, a program on animals might spark a trip to the zoo, a visit to the library for books about animals, or new ways of observing and caring for the family pet.
- Avoid excess television viewing, especially violent programs, yourself. Parental viewing patterns influence children's viewing patterns.
- Respond to children with warmth and reasonable demands for mature behavior. Children who experience these parenting practices prefer programs with prosocial content and are less attracted to violent TV (Dorr, Kovaric, & Doubleday, 1989; St. Peters et al., 1991).

TRY THIS . . .

- Watch several Saturday morning cartoons, late-afternoon children's shows, and prime-time adult television programs. Count the number of prosocial and aggressive acts you see. Also note the roles that male and female characters play. How do the programs compare in terms of the social messages they send to children?

they once were, too often they are segregated from whites in child- and adult-oriented programs. Other minorities rarely appear, and when they do, they tend to be depicted negatively, as villains or victims of violence. Similarly, women appear less often than men as main characters, and they are usually cast in "feminine" roles, such as wife, mother, nurse, teacher, or secretary (Liebert & Sprafkin, 1988; Zillman, Bryant, & Huston, 1994).

The ease with which television can manipulate the beliefs and behavior of children has resulted in strong public pressures to improve its content. Unfortunately, as the Social Issues box on the opposite page indicates, these efforts have not been very successful. At present, it is up to parents to regulate their children's exposure—a heavy burden, given that children find TV so attractive.

BRIEF REVIEW

The young child's morality gradually shifts from externally controlled responses to internalized standards. Contrary to predictions from Freudian theory, power assertion and love withdrawal do not promote the development of conscience. Instead, induction is far more successful. Behaviorism and social learning theory have shown that modeling combined with reinforcement in the form of praise is effective in encouraging prosocial acts. In contrast, harsh punishment promotes temporary compliance, not lasting changes in children's behavior. According to cognitive-developmental theory, children actively think about justice and fairness. During the preschool years, they recognize that intentionally hurting someone is worse than doing so accidentally, and they distinguish moral rules from social conventions. Hostile family atmospheres, poor parenting practices, and heavy television viewing promote childhood aggression, which can spiral into serious antisocial activity. TV also fosters a naive belief in the truthfulness of advertising and ethnic and gender stereotypes.

ASK YOURSELF . . .

- Alice and Wayne want their two young children to develop a strong, internalized conscience and to become generous, caring individuals. List as many parenting practices as you can that would promote these goals.
- Nanette told her 3-year-old son Darren not to go into the front yard without asking, since the house faces a very busy street. Darren disobeyed several times, and now Nanette thinks it's time to punish him. How would you recommend that Nanette discipline Darren, and why?

GENDER TYPING IN EARLY CHILDHOOD

The process of developing *gender roles,* or gender-linked preferences and behaviors valued by the larger society, is called **gender typing.** Early in the preschool years, gender typing is well underway. In Leslie's classroom, children tended to play and form friendships with peers of their own sex. Girls spent more time in the housekeeping, art, and reading corners, whereas boys gathered more often in blocks, woodworking, and active play spaces. As we saw in the previous section, television plays an important role in children's gender-related learning. But gender typing occurs so rapidly in early childhood that other powerful influences are clearly involved.

The same three theories that provide accounts of morality have been used to explain gender-role development. According to *psychoanalytic theory,* gender-stereotyped beliefs and behaviors are adopted in the same way as other social standards—through identification with the same-sex parent as the Oedipus and Electra conflicts are resolved. Recall that Freud's ideas worked poorly in the area of morality. They also have difficulty accounting for gender typing. Research shows that the same-sex parent is only one of many influences in gender-role development. Opposite-sex parents, peers, teachers, and the broader social environment are important as well.

Social learning theory, with its emphasis on modeling and reinforcement, and *cognitive-developmental theory,* with its focus on children as active thinkers about their social world, are major current approaches to understanding children's gender typing. We will see that neither has proved entirely adequate by itself. Consequently,

Gender typing
The process of developing gender roles, or gender-linked preferences and behaviors valued by the larger society.

a new perspective that combines elements of both, called *gender schema theory,* has recently arisen. In the following sections, we consider the early development of gender typing, along with genetic and environmental factors that contribute to it.

PRESCHOOLERS' GENDER-STEREOTYPED BELIEFS AND BEHAVIORS

Recall from Chapter 7 that around age 2, children begin to label their own sex and that of other people. As soon as basic gender categories are established, children start to sort out what they mean in terms of activities and behaviors. A wide variety of gender stereotypes are quickly mastered.

Preschoolers associate many toys, articles of clothing, tools, household items, games, occupations, behaviors, and even colors (pink and blue) with one sex as opposed to the other (Huston, 1983; Picariello, Greenberg, & Pillemer, 1990). And their actions fall in line with their beliefs—not only in play preferences, but in personality traits as well. We have already seen that boys tend to be more active, assertive, and aggressive. In contrast, girls tend to be more fearful, dependent, compliant, and emotionally sensitive (Jacklin & Maccoby, 1983).

Over the preschool years, children's gender-stereotyped beliefs become stronger—so much so that they operate like blanket rules rather than flexible guidelines (Biernat, 1991a; Martin, 1989). Once, when Leslie showed the children a picture of a Scottish bagpiper wearing a kilt, they insisted, "Men don't wear skirts!" During free play, they often exclaimed that girls don't drive fire engines and can't be police officers and boys don't take care of babies and can't be the teacher. These one-sided judgments are a joint product of gender stereotyping in the environment, preschoolers' cognitive tendency to exaggerate differences they observe, and their limited understanding of the biological basis of male and female. As we will see later, concrete observable characteristics—activities, toys, occupations, hairstyles, and clothing—define gender for the majority of 3- to 5-year-olds. Most have not yet learned that genitals, hidden beneath clothing, determine a person's sex.

GENETIC INFLUENCES ON GENDER TYPING

The sex differences that we have just described appear in many cultures around the world (Whiting & Edwards, 1988a). Certain of them—the preference for same-sex playmates as well as male activity level and aggression—are widespread among animal species as well (Meany, Stewart, & Beatty, 1985). So it is reasonable to ask whether gender typing might be influenced by genetic factors. We have already indicated that there is good evidence that aggression is indirectly linked to sex hormones in human children. That is, androgens promote active play among boys, increasing the likelihood of hostile encounters.

Eleanor Maccoby (1990) argues that hormonal differences between males and females have important consequences for gender typing. Early on, hormones affect play styles, leading to rough, noisy movements among boys and calm, gentle actions among girls. Then, as children begin to interact with peers, they naturally choose same-sex partners whose interests and behaviors are compatible with their own. By age 2, girls already appear overwhelmed by boys' rambunctious behavior. When paired with a boy in a laboratory play session, the girl stands idly by while he explores the toys (Jacklin & Maccoby, 1978). Over the preschool years, girls increasingly seek out other girls and like to play in dyads because of a common preference for quieter activities. And boys come to prefer larger-group play with other boys, who respond positively to one another's desire to run, climb, play-fight, and build up and knock down. At age 4, children already spend three times as much time with same-sex as opposite-sex playmates. By age, 6, this ratio has climbed to 11 to 1 (Benenson, 1993; Maccoby & Jacklin, 1987).

Gender-stereotyped game and toy choices emerge early in the preschool years and increase with age. Already, these 3-year-olds play in highly gender-stereotyped ways. *(Left, Erika Stone/Photo Researchers; Right, Stephen Marks)*

However, we must be careful not to overemphasize the contribution of heredity to gender typing. Research shows that the components of gender stereotyping—activities, behaviors, occupations, and personality traits—do not correlate highly. A child's knowledge of one is only weakly related to knowledge of another (Serbin, Powlishta, & Gulko, 1993). This suggests that gender typing is not a unitary aspect of development. Instead, it is more like "an intricate puzzle that the child pieces together in a rather idiosyncratic way" (Hort, Leinbach, & Fagot, 1991, p. 196). As we will see in the next section, a wide variety of environmental forces build on hereditary influences to promote children's awareness of and conformity to gender roles.

ENVIRONMENTAL INFLUENCES ON GENDER TYPING

A wealth of evidence reveals that family influences, encouragement by teachers and peers, and examples in the broader social environment combine to promote the vigorous gender typing of early childhood.

THE FAMILY. Beginning at birth, parents hold different perceptions and expectations of their sons and daughters (see Chapter 7), a trend that continues into the preschool years. Many parents state that they want their children to play with "gender-appropriate" toys, and they also believe that boys and girls should be reared differently. When asked about their child-rearing values, parents are likely to describe achievement, competition, and control of emotion as important for sons and warmth, "ladylike" behavior, and close supervision of activities as important for daughters (Brooks-Gunn, 1986; McGuire, 1988).

These beliefs carry over into actual parenting practices. Mothers and fathers are far more likely to purchase guns, cars, and footballs for sons and dolls, tea sets, and jump ropes for daughters—toys that promote very different play styles. In addition, parents actively reinforce many gender-stereotyped behaviors. For example, they react more positively when a young son as opposed to a daughter plays with cars and trucks, demands attention, or tries to take toys from others, thereby rewarding his active and assertive behavior (Fagot & Hagan, 1991). In contrast, they more often direct play activities, provide help, and discuss emotions with a daughter, encouraging her dependency and emotional sensitivity (Kuebli & Fivush, 1992; Lytton & Romney, 1991).

These factors are major influences in gender-role learning, since parents who consciously avoid behaving in these ways have less gender-typed children (Weisner & Wilson-Mitchell, 1990). Besides parents, other family members contribute to gender typing. For example, preschoolers with older, opposite-sex siblings have many more opportunities to imitate and participate in "cross-gender" play (Stoneman, Brody, & MacKinnon, 1986). In any case, of the two sexes, boys are clearly the more gender typed. One reason is that parents—particularly fathers—are less tolerant of "cross-gender" behavior in their sons than daughters. They are more concerned if a boy acts like a sissy than if a girl acts like a tomboy (Lytton & Romney, 1991; Maccoby, 1980).

■ **TEACHERS.** Besides parents, teachers encourage children to conform to gender roles. Several times, Leslie caught herself responding in ways that furthered sex segregation and stereotyping in her classroom. One day when the class was preparing to leave for a field trip, she called out, "Will the girls line up on one side and the boys on the other?" Then, as the class became noisy with excitement, she pleaded, "Boys, I wish you'd quiet down like the girls!"

As in their experiences at home, girls get more encouragement to participate in adult-structured activities at preschool. They can frequently be seen clustered around the teacher, following directions in an activity. In contrast, boys more often choose areas of the classroom where teachers are minimally involved or entirely absent. As a result, boys and girls engage in very different social behaviors. Compliance and bids for help occur more often in adult-structured contexts, whereas assertiveness, leadership, and creative use of materials appear more often in unstructured pursuits (Carpenter, 1983).

■ **PEERS.** Once formed, children's same-sex peer relationships become powerful environments for strengthening stereotyped beliefs and behavior. By age 3, same-sex peers positively reinforce one another for gender-typed play by praising, imitating, or joining in the activity of an agemate who shows a "gender-appropriate" response (Fagot & Patterson, 1969). Similarly, when preschoolers engage in "gender-inappropriate" activities—for example, when boys play with dolls or girls with woodworking tools—they receive criticism from peers. Boys are especially intolerant of "cross-gender" play in their male companions (Fagot, 1977). A boy who frequently crosses gender lines is likely to be ignored by other boys even when he does engage in "masculine" activities!

Children also develop different styles of social influence in sex-segregated peer groups. To get their way with male peers, boys more often rely on commands, threats, and physical force. In contrast, girls learn to use polite requests and persuasion. These strategies succeed with other girls but not with boys, who start to ignore girls' gentle tactics by the end of early childhood (Borja-Alvarez, Zarbatany, & Pepper, 1991; Leaper, 1991). Consequently, an additional reason that girls may stop interacting with boys is that they do not find it very rewarding to communicate with an unresponsive social partner.

■ **THE BROADER SOCIAL ENVIRONMENT.** A wide variety of examples of gender-typed behavior are available in children's everyday environments. Although American society has changed to some degree, children come in contact with many real people who conform to traditional gender-role expectations. As one writer points out,

> The average child sees women cooking, cleaning, and sewing; working in "female" jobs such as clerical, secretarial, sales, teaching, nursing; choosing to dance, sew, or play bridge for recreation; and achieving in artistic or literary areas more often than in science and engineering. That same child sees men mowing the lawn, washing the car, or doing household repairs; working in "male" occupations . . . choosing team sports, fishing, and nights with "the boys" for recreation; and achieving in math, science, and technical areas more often than in poetry or art. In school, the teachers of young children are women; the teachers of older students and the administrators with power are

> usually men. . . . Hence, although there are some individual differences, most children are exposed continually in their own environments to models of [gender-stereotyped] activities, interests, and roles. (Huston, 1983, pp. 420–421)

As we will see in the next section, young children do not just imitate the many gender-linked responses they observe. They also start to view themselves and the surrounding world in gender-biased ways, a perspective that can seriously limit their interests and skills.

GENDER-ROLE IDENTITY

As adults, each of us has a **gender-role identity**—an image of oneself as relatively masculine or feminine in characteristics. By middle childhood, researchers can measure gender role identity by asking children to rate themselves on personality traits, since at that time self-concepts begin to emphasize psychological attributes over concrete behaviors.

Individuals differ considerably in the way that they respond to these questionnaires. A child or adult with a "masculine" identity scores high on traditionally masculine items (such as self-sufficient, ambitious, and forceful) and low on traditionally feminine ones (such as affectionate, soft-spoken, and cheerful). Someone with a "feminine" identity does just the reverse. Although the majority of individuals view themselves in gender-typed terms, a substantial minority (especially females) have a type of gender role identity called **androgyny.** They score high on both masculine and feminine personality characteristics (Bem, 1974; Boldizar, 1991).

Research indicates that gender-role identity is a good predictor of psychological adjustment. Masculine and androgynous children and adults have a higher sense of self-esteem, whereas feminine individuals often think poorly of themselves, perhaps because many feminine traits are not highly valued in our society (Alpert-Gillis & Connell, 1989; Boldizar, 1991). In line with their flexible self-definitions, androgynous individuals are more adaptable in behavior—for example, able to show masculine independence or feminine sensitivity, depending on the situation (Taylor & Hall, 1982). The concept of androgyny reveals that masculinity and femininity are not opposites, as many people believe. It is possible for children to acquire a mixture of positive qualities traditionally associated with each gender—an orientation that may best help them realize their potential.

■ EMERGENCE OF GENDER-ROLE IDENTITY. How do children develop gender-role identities that consist of varying mixtures of masculine and feminine characteristics? Both social learning and cognitive-developmental answers to this question exist. According to *social learning theory,* behavior comes before self-perceptions. Preschoolers first acquire gender-typed responses through modeling and reinforcement. Only later do they organize these behaviors into gender-linked ideas about themselves. In contrast, *cognitive-developmental theory* regards the direction of development as the other way around. Over the preschool years, children first acquire a cognitive appreciation of the permanence of their sex. They develop **gender constancy,** the understanding that sex remains the same even if clothing, hairstyle, and play activities change. Once formed, children use this idea to guide their behavior, and a preference for gender-typed activities appears (Kohlberg, 1966).

Research indicates that gender constancy is not present in most children until the end of the preschool years, when they pass Piagetian conservation tasks (De Lisi & Gallagher, 1991). Shown a doll whose hairstyle and clothing are transformed before their eyes, a child younger than age 6 is likely to insist that the doll's sex has changed as well (McConaghy, 1979). And when asked such questions as "When you (a girl) grow up, could you ever be a daddy?" or "Could you be a boy if you wanted to?" young children freely answer yes (Slaby & Frey, 1975).

Gender-role identity
An image of oneself as relatively masculine or feminine in characteristics.

Androgyny
A type of gender-role identity in which the person scores high on both masculine and feminine personality characteristics.

Gender constancy
The understanding that sex remains the same even if clothing, hairstyle, and play activities change.

Yet cognitive immaturity is not the only reason for preschoolers' poor performance on gender constancy tasks, as cognitive-developmental theory assumes. It also results from limited social experience—in particular, lack of opportunity to learn about genital differences between the sexes. In many households in Western societies, young children do not see members of the opposite sex naked. Therefore, they distinguish males and females using the only information they do have—the way each gender dresses and behaves. Children as young as 3 who are aware of genital differences usually answer gender constancy questions correctly (Bem, 1989).

Is cognitive-developmental theory correct that gender constancy is responsible for children's gender-typed behavior? Perhaps you have already concluded that evidence for this assumption is weak. Long before most preschoolers appreciate the permanence of their sex, they show many gender-typed responses. "Gender-appropriate" behavior appears so early in the preschool years that modeling and reinforcement must account for its initial appearance. At present, researchers disagree on just how gender constancy contributes to gender-role development (Bussey & Bandura, 1992; Frey & Ruble, 1992). But they do know that once children begin to reflect on gender roles, they form basic gender categories that strengthen gender-typed self-images and behavior. Yet another theoretical perspective shows how this happens.

■ GENDER SCHEMA THEORY: A NEW APPROACH TO GENDER-ROLE IDENTITY. **Gender schema theory** is an information-processing approach to gender typing that combines social learning and cognitive-developmental features, emphasizing that both environmental pressures and children's cognitions work together to shape gender-role development (Bem, 1984; Martin & Halverson, 1981, 1987). Beginning at an early age, children respond to instruction from others, picking up gender-stereotyped preferences and behaviors. At the same time, they start to organize their experiences into *gender schemas,* or masculine and feminine categories, that they use to interpret their world. A young child who says, "Only boys can be doctors" or "Cooking is a girl's job" already has some well-formed gender schemas. As soon as preschoolers can label their own sex, they start to select gender schemas that are consistent with it, applying those categories to themselves (Fagot & Leinbach, 1989; Martin & Little, 1990). As a result, their self-perceptions become gender typed and serve as additional gender schemas that children use to process information and guide their own behavior.

Let's look at the example in Figure 10.1 to see exactly how this network of gender schemas strengthens gender-typed preferences and behavior. Our 3-year-old girl, Mandy, has been taught that "dolls are for girls" and "trucks are for boys." She also knows that she is a girl. Mandy uses this information to make decisions about how to behave. Because her schemas lead her to conclude that "dolls are for me," when given a doll she approaches it, explores it, and learns more about it. In contrast, on seeing a truck, she uses her gender schemas to conclude that "trucks are not for me" and responds by avoiding the "gender-inappropriate" toy (Martin & Halverson, 1981). Gender schemas are so powerful that when children see others behaving in "gender-inconsistent" ways, they often cannot remember the information or distort it to make it "gender consistent" (Liben & Signorella, 1993; Signorella & Liben, 1984).

Gender schema theory
An information-processing approach to gender typing that combines social learning and cognitive-developmental features to explain how environmental pressures and children's cognitions work together to shape gender-role development.

REDUCING GENDER STEREOTYPING IN YOUNG CHILDREN

How can adults help young children avoid developing rigid gender schemas that restrict their behavior and learning opportunities? Sandra Bem (1984) points out that gender-linked associations are so common in our environment that parents and teachers must work especially hard to prevent young children from absorbing them.

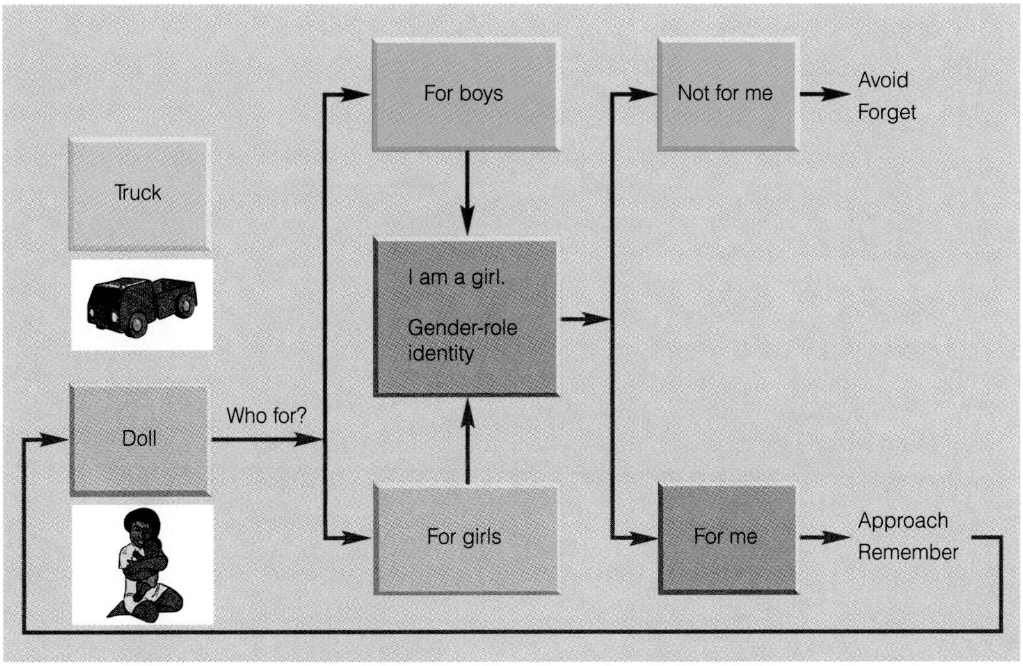

FIGURE 10.1

Effect of gender schemas on gender-stereotyped preferences and behavior.
Mandy's network of gender schemas leads her to approach and explore "feminine" toys, such as dolls, and to avoid "masculine" ones, such as trucks. *(From C. L. Martin & C. F. Halverson, 1981, "A Schematic Processing Model of Sex Typing and Stereotyping in Children,"* Child Development, *52, p. 1121. © The Society for Research in Child Development, Inc. Adapted by permission.)*

Adults can begin by eliminating gender stereotyping from their own behavior and from the alternatives they provide for children. For example, mothers and fathers can take turns making dinner, bathing children, and driving the family car. They can provide sons and daughters with both trucks and dolls and pink and blue clothing. And teachers can make sure that all children spend some time each day in adult-structured and unstructured activities.

At the same time, adults can teach young children that anatomy and reproduction are the only characteristics that determine a person's sex. Because many preschoolers do not understand this idea, they mistakenly assume that arbitrary cultural practices are the basis of gender. Then, to preserve their own identity as boy or girl, they insist that these must be strictly obeyed. Bem's son Jeremy, having been taught that boys have penises and girls have vaginas, argued with his peers about gender-typed conventions. When a playmate at his preschool announced that "only girls wear barrettes," Jeremy, who had put one in his hair that day, asserted that "wearing barrettes doesn't matter; being a boy means having a penis and testicles" (Bem, 1989, p. 662).

Finally, once children notice the vast array of gender stereotypes in their society, parents and teachers can point out exceptions. For example, they can arrange for children to see males and females pursuing nontraditional careers. And they can reason with children, explaining that interests and skills, not gender, should determine a person's occupation and activities. Recent evidence shows that such reasoning is very effective in reducing children's tendency to view the world in a gender-biased fashion (Bigler & Liben, 1990, 1992). And, as we will see in the next section, a rational approach to child rearing promotes healthy, adaptable functioning in many other areas as well.

ASK YOURSELF . . .

- Geraldine cut her 3-year-old daughter Fern's hair very short for the summer. When Fern looked in the mirror, she said, "I don't wanna be a boy," and began to cry. Why is Fern upset about her short hairstyle, and what can Geraldine do to help?
- When 4-year-old Roger was in the hospital, he was cared for by a male nurse named Jared. After Roger recovered, he told his friends about Dr. Jared. Using gender schema theory, explain why Roger remembered Jared as a doctor, not a nurse.

BRIEF REVIEW

During the preschool years, children develop a wide variety of gender-typed beliefs, personality traits, and behaviors. Although heredity contributes to several aspects of gender typing, environmental forces play an especially powerful role. Parents view and treat boys and girls differently, and traditional gender-role learning receives further support from teachers, same-sex peers, and the wider social environment. Children gradually develop a gender-role identity, a view of themselves as masculine, feminine, or androgynous in characteristics. Neither the cognitive-developmental nor the social learning account of gender role-identity provides a complete explanation. Gender schema theory is an information-processing approach that shows how environmental pressures and children's cognitions work together to sustain gender-typed preferences and behavior.

CHILD REARING AND EMOTIONAL AND SOCIAL DEVELOPMENT IN EARLY CHILDHOOD

Throughout this chapter and the previous one, we have discussed many ways in which parents can foster children's development—by serving as warm models and reinforcers of mature behavior, by using reasoning, explanation, and inductive discipline, by avoiding harsh punishment, and by encouraging children to master new skills. As we conclude our discussion of early childhood, let's put these elements together into an overall view of effective parenting.

STYLES OF CHILD REARING

In a series of landmark studies, Diana Baumrind gathered information on child-rearing practices by watching parents interact with their preschoolers in a variety of situations. Two broad dimensions of child rearing emerged from the observations. The first is *demandingness*. Some parents establish high standards for their children and insist that their youngsters meet those standards. Other parents demand very little and rarely try to influence their child's behavior. The second dimension is *responsiveness*. Some parents are accepting and responsive to their children. They frequently engage in open discussion and verbal give-and-take. Others are rejecting and unresponsive.

As Table 10.2 shows, the various combinations of control and responsiveness yield four styles of child rearing. Baumrind's research focused on three of them: authoritative, authoritarian, and permissive.

■ AUTHORITATIVE CHILD REARING. The **authoritative style** is the most adaptive approach to child rearing. Authoritative parents make reasonable demands for maturity, and they enforce them by setting limits and insisting that the child obey. At the same time, they express warmth and affection, listen patiently to their child's point of view, and encourage participation in family decision making. Authoritative child rearing is a rational, democratic approach that recognizes and respects the rights of both parents and children.

Baumrind's findings revealed that children of these parents were developing especially well. They were lively and happy in mood, self-confident in their mastery of new tasks, and self-controlled in their ability to resist engaging in disruptive behavior (Baumrind, 1967). These children also seemed less gender typed. Girls scored particularly high in independence and desire to master new tasks and boys in friendly, cooperative behavior (Baumrind & Black, 1967).

Authoritative style
A child-rearing style that is demanding and responsive. A rational, democratic approach in which parents' and children's rights are respected.

TABLE 10.2

A Two-Dimensional Classification of Child-Rearing Styles

	RESPONSIVE	UNRESPONSIVE
DEMANDING	Authoritative parent	Authoritarian parent
UNDEMANDING	Permissive parent	Uninvolved parent

Source: Adapted from E. E. Maccoby & J. A. Martin, 1983, "Socialization in the Context of the Family: Parent–Child Interaction," in E. M. Hetherington (Ed.), *Handbook of Child Psychology: Vol. 4. Socialization, Personality, and Social Development* (4th ed., p. 39). New York: Wiley. Copyright © 1983 by John Wiley & Sons. Reprinted by permission.

■ AUTHORITARIAN CHILD REARING. Parents who use an **authoritarian style** are also demanding, but they place such a high value on conformity that they are unresponsive—even outright rejecting—when children are unwilling to obey. "Do it because I said so!" is the attitude of these parents. As a result, they engage in very little give-and-take with children, who are expected to accept their parent's word for what is right in an unquestioning manner. If they do not, authoritarian parents resort to force and punishment.

Baumrind found that preschoolers with authoritarian parents were anxious, withdrawn, and unhappy. When interacting with peers, they tended to react with hostility when frustrated (Baumrind, 1967). Boys, especially, showed high rates of anger and defiance. Girls were dependent and lacking in exploration, and they retreated from challenging tasks (Baumrind, 1971).

■ PERMISSIVE CHILD REARING. The **permissive style** of child rearing is nurturant and accepting, but it avoids making demands or imposing controls of any kind. Permissive parents allow children to make many of their own decisions at an age when they are not yet capable of doing so. They can eat meals and go to bed when they feel like it and watch as much television as they want. They do not have to learn good manners or do any household chores. When visitors come to the home, these youngsters are allowed to interrupt and annoy others without any parental effort to stop their irritating behavior. Although some permissive parents truly believe this approach to child rearing is best, many others lack confidence in their ability to influence their youngster's behavior and are disorganized and ineffective in running their households.

Baumrind found that children of permissive parents were very immature. They had difficulty controlling their impulses and were disobedient and rebellious when asked to do something that conflicted with their momentary desires. They were also overly demanding and dependent on adults, and they showed less persistence on tasks at preschool than children of parents who exerted more control. The link between permissive parenting and dependent, nonachieving behavior was especially strong for boys (Baumrind, 1971).

WHAT MAKES AUTHORITATIVE CHILD REARING SO EFFECTIVE?

Since Baumrind's early work, a great many studies have confirmed her findings. Throughout childhood and adolescence, authoritative parenting is consistently associated with task persistence, social maturity, high self-esteem, internalized moral standards, and superior academic achievement (Denham, Renwick, & Holt, 1991; Maccoby & Martin, 1983; Steinberg, Elman, & Mounts, 1989).

Why does this approach to parenting work so well? There are several reasons. First, control that appears fair and reasonable to the child, not abrupt and arbitrary, is far more likely to be complied with and internalized. Second, nurturant parents

Authoritarian style
A child-rearing style that is demanding but low in responsiveness to children's rights and needs. Conformity and obedience are valued over open communication with the child.

Permissive style
A child-rearing style that is responsive but undemanding. An overly tolerant approach to child rearing.

who are secure in the standards they hold for their children provide models of caring concern as well as confident, assertive behavior. Finally, parents who are authoritative make demands that are reasonable in terms of their child's developing capacities. By adjusting expectations to fit children's ability to take responsibility for their own behavior, these parents let children know that they are competent individuals who can do things successfully for themselves. As a result, high self-esteem, and mature, independent behavior are fostered (Kuczynski et al., 1987).

CULTURAL AND SITUATIONAL INFLUENCES ON CHILD-REARING STYLES

Despite broad agreement about the impact of child-rearing styles on development, some subcultural groups show variations that are adaptive when viewed in light of cultural values and family living conditions. For example, compared to Caucasian-Americans, Chinese adults describe their parenting techniques as more demanding (Berndt et al., 1993). As Figure 10.2 shows, this greater emphasis on control continues to characterize Chinese parents who have immigrated to the United States. It seems to reflect deeply engrained Confucian beliefs in the importance of strict discipline, respect for elders, and teaching socially desirable behavior (Chao, 1994; Lin & Fu, 1990). In Hispanic families, insistence on deference to parental authority, particularly that of the father, is paired with unusually high maternal warmth. This combination is believed to promote compliance and strong family commitment in Hispanic children (Fracasso & Busch-Rossnagel, 1992). Although wide variation among African-Americans exists, some research suggests that black mothers (especially those who are younger, less educated, and single) often rely on an adult-centered approach in which they expect immediate obedience from children (Kelley, Power, & Wimbush, 1992). But when parents have few social supports and live in dangerous neighborhoods, forceful discipline may be necessary to protect children from becoming victims of crime or involved in antisocial activities (Ogbu, 1985).

If you turn back to Table 10.2, you will see that we have not yet considered one pattern of parenting: the *uninvolved* style, which combines undemanding with indifferent, rejecting behavior. Uninvolved parents show little commitment to their role as caregivers beyond the minimum effort required to feed and clothe the child. Often they are emotionally detached and depressed and so overwhelmed by the many stresses in their lives that they have little time and energy to spare for children (Maccoby & Martin, 1983).

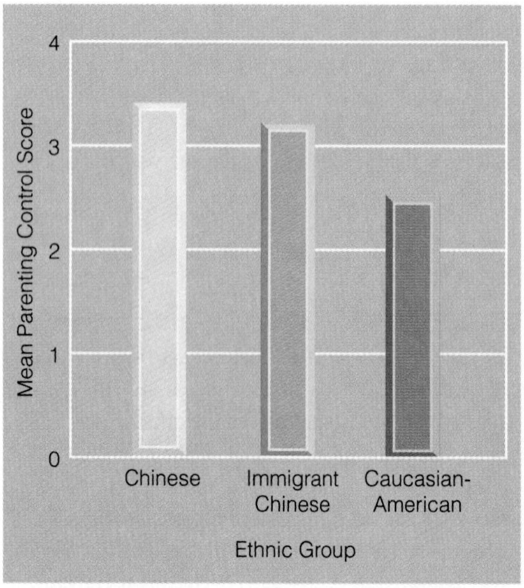

FIGURE 10.2

Self-reported emphasis on control in child rearing by Chinese, immigrant Chinese, and Caucasian-American parents.

In this study, mothers and fathers who were living in Taiwan, who had immigrated from Taiwan to the United States, and who were Caucasian-Americans were asked to rate their parenting styles. Both groups of Chinese parents emphasized control to a greater extent than did Caucasian-American parents. *(Adapted from Lin & Fu, 1990.)*

At its extreme, uninvolved parenting is a form of child maltreatment called *neglect.* Especially when it begins early, it disrupts virtually all aspects of development, including attachment, cognition, play, and social and emotional skills (Egeland & Sroufe, 1981; Radke-Yarrow et al., 1985). As we turn to the topic of child maltreatment in the final section of this chapter, we will see that effective child rearing is sustained not just by the desire of mothers and fathers to be good parents. Almost all want to be. A great many factors, both within and outside the family, contribute to parents' capacity to be warm, consistent, and appropriately demanding. Unfortunately, when these vital supports for good parenting break down, children as well as their parents can suffer terribly.

CHILD MALTREATMENT

Child abuse is as old as the history of humankind, but only recently has there been widespread acceptance that the problem exists, research aimed at understanding it, and programs directed at helping maltreated children and their families. Perhaps the increase in public concern is due to the fact that child maltreatment is especially common in large, industrialized nations (Gelles & Cornell, 1983). It occurs so often in the United States that a recent government committee called it "a national emergency." A total of 2.9 million cases were reported to juvenile authorities in 1992, an increase of 132 percent over the previous decade (Children's Defense Fund, 1994). The true figure is surely much higher, since most cases, including ones in which children suffer serious physical injury, go unreported.

Child maltreatment takes the following forms:

1. *Physical abuse*—assaults on children that produce pain, cuts, welts, bruises, burns, broken bones, and other injuries
2. *Sexual abuse*—sexual comments, fondling, intercourse, and other forms of exploitation
3. *Physical neglect*—living conditions in which children do not receive enough food, clothing, medical attention, or supervision
4. *Emotional neglect*—failure of caregivers to meet children's needs for affection and emotional support
5. *Psychological abuse*—actions that seriously damage children's emotional, social, or cognitive functioning

Although all experts recognize that these five types exist, they do not agree on how frequent and intense an adult's actions must be to be called maltreatment. Definitions of abuse and neglect vary a great deal. The greatest problems arise in the case of subtle, ambiguous behaviors. Whereas all of us can agree that broken bones, cigarette burns, and bite marks are abusive, the decision is harder to make in instances in which an adult touches or makes degrading comments to a child (Barnett, Manly, & Cicchetti, 1993). Yet some experts regard psychological and sexual abuse as the most destructive forms. The rate of psychological abuse may be the highest, since it accompanies most other types. Over 200,000 cases of child sexual abuse are reported each year. Yet this statistic greatly underestimates the actual number, since affected children may feel frightened, confused, and guilty and are usually pressured into silence (Hartman & Burgess, 1989). Although children of all ages are targets, the largest number of sexual abuse victims are identified in middle childhood. We will pay special attention to this form of maltreatment in Chapter 13.

ORIGINS OF CHILD MALTREATMENT. When child maltreatment first became a topic of research in the early 1960s, it was viewed as rooted in adult psychological disturbance. The first studies indicated that adults who abused or neglected their children usually had a history of maltreatment in their own childhoods, unrealistic expectations that children satisfy their own unmet emotional needs, and poor control of aggressive impulses (Kempe et al., 1962; Spinetta & Rigler, 1972).

It soon became clear that although child abuse was more common among disturbed parents, a single "abusive personality type" did not exist. Sometimes even "normal" parents harmed their children! Also, parents who were abused as children

TABLE 10.3

Factors Related to Child Maltreatment

FACTOR	DESCRIPTION
Parent characteristics	Psychological disturbance; substance abuse; history of abuse as a child; belief in harsh, physical discipline; desire to satisfy unmet emotional needs through the child; unreasonable expectations for child behavior; young age (most under 30); low educational level
Child characteristics	Premature or very sick baby; difficult temperament; inattentiveness and overactivity; and other developmental problems
Family characteristics	Low income; poverty; homelessness; marital instability; social isolation; physical abuse of mother by husband or boyfriend; frequent moves; large, closely spaced families; overcrowded living conditions; disorganized household; lack of steady employment; other signs of high life stress
Community	Characterized by social isolation; few parks, day care centers, preschool programs, recreation centers, and churches to serve as family supports
Culture	Approval of physical force and violence as ways to solve problems

Sources: Belsky, 1993; Pianta, Egeland, & Erickson, 1989; Simons et al., 1991.

did not always repeat the cycle with their own youngsters (Kaufman & Zigler, 1989; Simons et al., 1991).

For help in understanding child maltreatment, researchers turned to the *social systems perspective* on family functioning (see Chapter 2). They discovered that child abuse and neglect are affected by many interacting variables—at the family, community, and cultural levels (Belsky, 1993). Table 10.3 summarizes factors associated with child maltreatment. The more of these risks that are present, the greater the likelihood that it will occur. Let's examine each set of influences in turn.

The Family. Within the family, certain children—those whose characteristics make them more of a challenge to rear—have an increased likelihood of becoming targets of abuse. These include premature or very sick babies and children who are temperamentally difficult, inattentive and overactive, or who have other developmental problems. But whether such children actually are maltreated depends on characteristics of parents (Belsky, 1993). In one study, temperamentally difficult youngsters who were physically abused had mothers who believed that they could do little to control the child's behavior. Instead, they attributed the child's unruliness to a stubborn or bad disposition, a perspective that led them to move quickly toward physical force when the child misbehaved (Bugental, Blue, & Cruzcosa, 1989).

Once child abuse gets started, it quickly becomes part of a self-sustaining family relationship. The small irritations to which abusive parents react—a fussy baby, a preschooler who knocks over a glass of milk, or a child who will not mind immediately—soon become bigger ones. Then the harshness of parental behavior increases as well. By the preschool years, abusive and neglectful parents seldom interact with their children. When they do, they rarely express pleasure and affection; the communication is almost always negative (Trickett & Kuczynski, 1986; Trickett et al., 1991).

Most parents, however, have enough self-control not to respond to their children's misbehavior with abuse, and not all children with developmental problems are mistreated. Other factors must combine with these conditions to prompt an extreme parental response. Research reveals that unmanageable parental stress is strongly associated with all forms of maltreatment. Such factors as low income, unemployment, marital conflict, overcrowded living conditions, frequent moves, and extreme household disorganization are common in abusive homes. These conditions increase the chances that parents will be so overwhelmed that they cannot meet basic child-rearing responsibilities or will vent their frustrations by lashing out at their children (Pianta, Egeland, & Erickson, 1989).

The Community. The majority of abusive parents are isolated from both formal and informal social supports in their communities. There are at least two causes of this social isolation. First, because of their own life histories, many of these parents have learned to mistrust and avoid others. They do not have the skills necessary for establishing and maintaining positive relationships with friends and relatives (Polansky et al., 1985). Second, abusive parents are more likely to live in neighborhoods that provide few links between family and community, such as parks, day care centers, preschool programs, recreation centers, and churches (Garbarino & Kostelny, 1992). For these reasons, they lack "lifelines" to others and have no one to turn to for help during particularly stressful times.

The Larger Culture. One final factor—the values, laws, and customs of our culture—profoundly affects the chances that child maltreatment will occur when parents feel overburdened. Societies that view force and violence as appropriate ways to solve problems set the stage for child abuse. These conditions exist in the United States. Although all 50 states have laws designed to protect children from maltreatment, there is still strong support for the use of physical force in parent–child relations. For example, during the past quarter century, the United States Supreme Court has twice upheld the right of school officials to use corporal punishment to discipline children. Crime rates have risen in American cities, and television sets beam graphic displays of violence into family living rooms. In view of the widespread acceptance of violent behavior in American culture, it is not surprising that most parents use slaps and spankings at one time or another to discipline their children. In countries where physical punishment is not accepted, such as China, Japan, Luxembourg, and Sweden, child abuse is rare (Zigler & Hall, 1989).

■ **CONSEQUENCES OF CHILD MALTREATMENT.** The family circumstances of maltreated children impair the development of emotional self-regulation, self-concept, and social skills. Over time, these youngsters show serious learning and adjustment problems, including difficulties with peers, academic failure, severe depression, substance abuse, and delinquency (Hotaling et al., 1988; Simons, Conger, & Whitbeck, 1988).

How do these damaging consequences occur? Think back to our earlier discussion of the effects of hostile cycles of parent–child interaction, which are especially severe for abused children. Indeed, a family characteristic strongly associated with child abuse is domestic violence, in which mothers are repeatedly brutalized (physically and psychologically) by their partners (Salzinger et al., 1993). Clearly, the home lives of abused children overflow with opportunities to learn to use aggression as a way of solving problems. The low warmth and control to which neglected children are exposed also promotes aggressive, acting-out behavior (Miller et al., 1993).

Furthermore, demeaning parental messages, in which children are ridiculed, humiliated, rejected, or terrorized, result in low self-esteem, high anxiety, self-blame, and efforts to escape from extreme psychological pain—at times severe enough to lead to attempted suicide in adolescence (Briere, 1992; Sternberg et al., 1993). At school, maltreated children are serious discipline problems. Their noncompliance, poor motivation, and cognitive immaturity interfere with academic achievement—an outcome that further undermines their chances for life success (Eckenrode, Laird, & Doris, 1993).

■ **PREVENTING CHILD MALTREATMENT.** Since child maltreatment is embedded within families, communities, and society as a whole, efforts to prevent it must be directed at each of these levels. Many approaches have been sug-

you idiot!
you idiot!
you idiot!
you idiot!
you idiot!
you idiot!
you idiot!
Children learn by repetition.
You don't have to hit to hurt.
San Francisco Child Abuse Council
(415) 668-0494

Public service announcements help prevent child abuse by educating people about the problem and informing them of where to seek help. This poster reminds adults that degrading remarks can hit as hard as a fist. *(Courtesy San Francisco Child Abuse Council)*

gested. These include interventions that teach high-risk parents effective child-rearing and disciplinary strategies, high school child development courses that include direct experience with children, and broad social programs that have as their goal better economic conditions for low-income families.

In earlier parts of this book, we saw that providing social supports to families is very effective in easing parental stress. It is not surprising that this approach sharply reduces child maltreatment as well. Research indicates that a trusting relationship with another person is the most important factor in preventing mothers with childhood histories of abuse from repeating the cycle with their own youngsters (Caliso & Milner, 1992; Egeland, Jacobvitz, & Sroufe, 1988). Parents Anonymous, a national organization that has as its main goal helping child-abusing parents learn constructive parenting practices, does so largely through providing social supports to families. Each of its local chapters offers self-help group meetings, daily phone calls, and regular home visits to relieve social isolation and teach alternative child-rearing skills.

Other preventive approaches include announcements in newspapers, magazines, and on television and radio that are designed to educate people about child maltreatment and tell them where to seek help (Rosenberg & Reppucci, 1985). Besides these efforts, changes in the overall attitudes and practices of American culture are needed. Many experts believe that child maltreatment cannot be eliminated as long as violence is widespread and corporal punishment continues to be regarded as an acceptable child-rearing alternative (Gil, 1987; Zigler & Hall, 1989).

Although more cases reach the courts than in decades past, child maltreatment remains a crime that is difficult to prove. Most of the time, the only witnesses are the child victims themselves or other loyal family members. Even in court cases in which the evidence is strong, judges hesitate to impose the ultimate safeguard against further harm: permanent removal of the child from the family.

There are several reasons for this reluctant attitude. First, in American society, government intervention into family life is viewed as a last resort, to be used only when there is near certainty that a child will be denied basic care and protection. Second, despite destructive family relationships, maltreated children and their parents are usually attached to one another. Most of the time, neither desires separation. Finally, the American legal system tends to regard children as parental property rather than as human beings in their own right, and this has also stood in the way of court-ordered protection (Hart & Brassard, 1987).

Even with intensive treatment, some adults persist in their abusive acts. An estimated 1,500 American children die from maltreatment each year (Children's Defense Fund, 1994). In cases in which parents are unlikely to change their behavior, taking the drastic step of separating parent from child and legally terminating parental rights is the only reasonable course of action.

Child maltreatment is a distressing and horrifying topic—a sad note on which to end our discussion of a period of childhood that is so full of excitement, awakening, and discovery. But there is reason to be optimistic. Great strides have been made in understanding and preventing child maltreatment over the last several decades. Although we still have a long way to go, the situation for abused and neglected children is far better now than it has been at any time in history (Kempe & Kempe, 1984).

ASK YOURSELF . . .

- Earlier in this chapter, we discussed induction as an especially effective form of discipline. Of Baumrind's three child-rearing styles, which is most likely to be associated with use of induction, and why?
- Chandra heard a news report that ten severely neglected children, living in squalor in an inner-city tenement, were discovered by Chicago police. Chandra thought to herself, "What could possibly lead parents to mistreat their children so badly?" How would you answer Chandra's question?

SUMMARY

ERIKSON'S THEORY: INITIATIVE VERSUS GUILT

What personality changes take place during Erikson's stage of initiative versus guilt?

- According to Erikson, during early childhood children develop a new sense of purposefulness as they grapple with the psychological conflict of **initiative versus guilt.** A healthy sense of initiative depends on resolving the **Oedipus** and **Electra conflicts** of Freud's **phallic stage,** in which the **superego,** or conscience, is formed through **identification** with the same-sex parent. Although Freud's ideas are no longer widely accepted, Erikson's image of initiative captures the emotional and social changes that take place during this phase of development.

SELF-DEVELOPMENT IN EARLY CHILDHOOD

Describe preschoolers' self-concepts, understanding of intentions, and self-esteem.

- Preschoolers' **self-concepts** largely consist of observable characteristics and typical beliefs, emotions, and attitudes. Their increasing self-awareness underlies struggles over objects as well as first efforts to cooperate. Children become more skilled at distinguishing intentional from unintentional acts over the preschool years.
- During early childhood, **self-esteem** is not yet well differentiated. Preschoolers' high self-esteem contributes to their mastery-oriented approach to the environment. However, even a little adult disapproval can undermine a young child's self-esteem and enthusiasm for learning.

EMOTIONAL DEVELOPMENT IN EARLY CHILDHOOD

Cite changes in understanding and expression of emotion during early childhood.

- Young children have an impressive understanding of the causes and consequences of basic emotional reactions. By age 3 to 4, they are also aware of a variety of strategies that assist with emotional self-regulation. As a result, intense emotional outbursts become less frequent.
- Preschoolers experience self-conscious emotions more often as their self-concepts become better developed and they become increasingly sensitive to the praise and criticism of others. Empathy becomes more common over the preschool years.

PEER RELATIONS IN EARLY CHILDHOOD

Trace the development of peer sociability in early childhood.

- During early childhood, interactive play with peers increases. According to Parten, peer interaction begins with **nonsocial activity,** shifts to **parallel play,** and then moves to **associative** and **cooperative play.** However, preschoolers do not follow this straightforward developmental sequence. Solitary play and parallel play remain common throughout early childhood. Sociodramatic play becomes especially frequent and supports many aspects of emotional and social development.

Describe the quality of preschoolers' friendships.

- Preschoolers view friendship in concrete, activity-based terms. Already, their interactions with friends have a unique quality. Young children are especially positive and emotionally expressive toward their friends.

FOUNDATIONS OF MORALITY IN EARLY CHILDHOOD

What are the central features of psychoanalytic, behaviorist and social learning, and cognitive-developmental approaches to moral development?

- The psychoanalytic and behaviorist approaches to morality focus on how children acquire ready-made standards held by adults. In contrast to Freud's theory, discipline promoting fear of punishment and loss of parental love does not foster conscience development. Instead, **induction** is far more effective in encouraging self-control and **prosocial,** or **altruistic, behavior.**
- Behaviorism and social learning theory regard reinforcement and modeling as the basis for moral action. Effective adult models of morality are warm, powerful, and practice what they preach. Harsh punishment does not promote moral internalization and socially desirable behavior.
- The cognitive-developmental perspective views children as active thinkers about social rules. Preschoolers understand that disobeying moral rules is more serious than violating social conventions. Peer interaction provides children with important opportunities to work out their first ideas about justice and fairness. Parents who discuss moral issues with their children help them reason about morality.

Describe the development of aggression in early childhood, including family and television as major influences.

- All children display aggression from time to time. During early childhood, **instrumental**

aggression declines while **hostile aggression** increases. Boys tend to be more aggressive than girls, a difference that may be linked to boys' higher activity level.

- Ineffective discipline and a conflict-ridden family atmosphere promote and sustain aggression in children. Teaching parents effective child-rearing practices and providing children with **social problem-solving training** are ways of reducing aggressive behavior. Television promotes childhood aggression, belief in the truthfulness of advertising, and ethnic and gender stereotypes.

GENDER TYPING IN EARLY CHILDHOOD

Discuss genetic and environmental influences on preschoolers' gender-stereotyped beliefs and behavior.

- **Gender typing** is well underway in the preschool years. Young children display a wide range of gender-stereotyped beliefs and behaviors. Genetic factors are believed to play a role in boys' higher activity level and aggression and children's preference for same-sex playmates. At the same time, the environment provides powerful support for gender typing. Parents, teachers, peers, and the broader social environment encourage many gender-typed responses.

Describe and evaluate the accuracy of major theories of the emergence of gender role identity.

- **Gender-role identity** is measured by asking children and adults to rate themselves on gender-stereotyped personality traits. Although most people have traditional gender-role identities, some are **androgynous,** scoring high on both masculine and feminine characteristics.
- According to social learning theory, preschoolers first acquire gender-typed responses through modeling and reinforcement and then organize them into gender-linked ideas about themselves. Cognitive-developmental theory suggests that **gender constancy** must be mastered before children develop gender-typed behavior.
- In contrast to cognitive-developmental predictions, gender-role behavior is acquired long before gender constancy. **Gender schema theory** is an information-processing approach to gender typing that combines social learning and cognitive-developmental features. As children acquire gender-stereotyped preferences and behaviors, they form masculine and feminine categories, or gender schemas, that they apply to themselves and use to interpret their world.

CHILD REARING AND EMOTIONAL AND SOCIAL DEVELOPMENT IN EARLY CHILDHOOD

Describe the impact of child-rearing styles on children's development, and explain why authoritative parenting is so effective.

- Two broad dimensions, demandingness and responsiveness, describe differences in styles of child rearing. The **authoritative style,** which is both demanding and responsive, promotes cognitive, emotional, and social competence. The **authoritarian style,** which is high in demandingness but low in responsiveness, is associated with anxious, withdrawn behavior. The **permissive style** is responsive but undemanding; children who experience it typically show rebelliousness and poor self-control. Warmth, explanations, and reasonable demands for mature behavior account for the effectiveness of the authoritative style.

Discuss the multiple origins of child maltreatment and its consequences for development.

- Child maltreatment is related to factors within the family, community, and larger culture. Child and parent characteristics often feed on one another to produce abusive behavior. Unmanageable parental stress and social isolation greatly increase the chances that abuse and neglect will occur. When a society approves of force and violence as a means for solving problems, child abuse is promoted.

IMPORTANT TERMS AND CONCEPTS

initiative versus guilt (p. 354)
phallic stage (p. 354)
Oedipus conflict (p. 354)
Electra conflict (p. 354)
superego (p. 355)
identification (p. 355)
self-concept (p. 355)
self-esteem (p. 357)
phobia (p. 361)
nonsocial activity (p. 362)
parallel play (p. 362)
associative play (p. 362)
cooperative play (p. 363)
induction (p. 367)
prosocial, or altruistic, behavior (p. 367)
time out (p. 369)
instrumental aggression (p. 371)
hostile aggression (p. 371)
social problem-solving training (p. 373)
gender typing (p. 375)
gender-role identity (p. 379)
androgyny (p. 379)
gender constancy (p. 379)
gender schema theory (p. 380)
authoritative style (p. 382)
authoritarian style (p. 383)
permissive style (p. 383)

FYI...

FOR FURTHER INFORMATION AND SPECIAL HELP, CONSULT THE FOLLOWING ORGANIZATIONS:

CHILDREN'S TELEVISION

Council for Children's Television and Media
33290 W. 14 Mile Road, Suite 488
West Bloomfield, MI 48322
(313) 489-5499

An organization of parents, teachers, and concerned citizens that works for high-quality children's television programming and that seeks to improve viewing habits.

CHILD ABUSE AND NEGLECT

Child Help USA, Inc.
6463 Independence Avenue
Woodland Hills, CA 91370
(818) 347-7280

Promotes public awareness of child abuse through publications, media campaigns, and a speakers' bureau. Supports the National Child Abuse Hotline, (800) 4-A-CHILD. Callers may request information about child abuse or speak with a crisis counselor.

Parents Anonymous
520 S. Lafayette Park Place, Suite 316
Los Angeles, CA 90057
(213) 388-6685

Dedicated to prevention and treatment of child abuse. Local groups provide support to child-abusing parents and training in nonviolent child-rearing techniques.

National Center on Child Abuse and Neglect
P.O. Box 1182
Washington, DC 20013
(703) 385-7565

Provides information to states and communities wishing to develop programs and activities that identify, prevent, and treat child abuse and neglect.

MILESTONES OF DEVELOPMENT IN EARLY CHILDHOOD

AGE	PHYSICAL	COGNITIVE	LANGUAGE	EMOTIONAL/SOCIAL
2 years	■ Slower gains in height and weight than in toddlerhood. ■ Balance improves, walking becomes better coordinated. ■ Running, jumping, hopping, throwing, and catching appear. ■ Puts on and removes some items of clothing. ■ Uses spoon effectively.	■ Make-believe becomes less dependent on realistic toys, less self-centered, and more complex. ■ Can take the perspective of others in simple situations. ■ Recognition memory well developed. ■ Aware of the difference between inner mental and outer physical events.	■ Vocabulary increases rapidly. ■ Sentences follow basic word order of native language; grammatical markers are added. ■ Displays effective conversational skills, such as turn taking and topic maintenance.	■ Begins to develop self-concept and self-esteem. ■ Distinguishes intentional from unintentional acts. ■ Cooperation and instrumental aggression appear. ■ Understands causes and consequences of basic emotions. ■ Empathy increases. ■ Gender-stereotyped beliefs and behavior increase.
3–4 years	■ Running, jumping, hopping, throwing, and catching become better coordinated. ■ Galloping and one-foot skipping appear. ■ Rides tricycle. ■ Uses scissors, draws first picture of a person. ■ Can tell the difference between writing and nonwriting.	■ Notices transformations, reverses thinking, and has a basic understanding of causality in familiar situations. ■ Classifies familiar objects hierarchically. ■ Uses private speech to guide behavior when engaged in challenging tasks. ■ Remembers familiar experiences in terms of scripts. ■ Can generalize remembered information from one situation to another. ■ Understands that people can hold false beliefs. ■ Aware of some meaningful features of written language. ■ Counts small numbers of objects and grasps the cardinality principle.	■ Occasionally overextends grammatical rules to exceptions. ■ Understands many culturally accepted ways of adjusting speech to fit the age, sex, and social status of speakers and listeners.	■ Emotional self-regulation improves. ■ Self-conscious emotions (shame, embarrassment, guilt, envy, and pride) become more common. ■ Nonsocial activity declines and joint, interactive play increases. ■ Instrumental aggression declines and hostile aggression increases. ■ Forms first friendships. ■ Distinguishes moral rules from social conventions. ■ Preference for same-sex playmates increases.

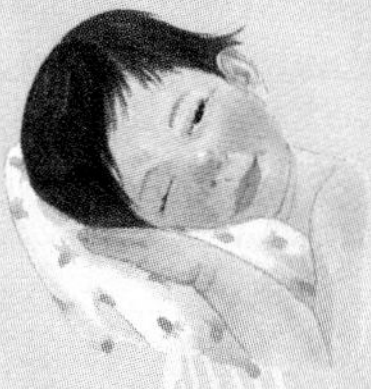

"Nose your touch!"
"That's backwards!"

AGE	PHYSICAL	COGNITIVE	LANGUAGE	EMOTIONAL/SOCIAL
5–6 years	■ Body is streamlined and longer-legged, with proportions similar to that of an adult. ■ First permanent tooth erupts. ■ Skipping appears. ■ Gross motor skills increase in speed and endurance. ■ Ties shoes, draws more elaborate pictures, writes name. ■ Can discriminate more fine-grained visual forms, such as letters of the alphabet.	■ Ability to distinguish appearance from reality improves. ■ Attention becomes more sustained and planful. ■ Recall and scripted memory improve. ■ Understands that letters and sounds are linked in systematic ways. ■ Counts on and counts down, engaging in simple addition and subtraction.	■ Vocabulary reaches about 10,000 words. ■ Has mastered many complex grammatical forms.	■ Bases understanding of people's intentions on a wider range of social cues. ■ Ability to interpret, predict, and influence others' emotional reactions improves. ■ Relies on language to express empathy. ■ Has acquired many morally relevant rules and behaviors. ■ Grasps the genital basis of sex differences and shows gender constancy.

"School medical checkup"
Ritsu Matsuoka
6 years, Japan

Middle childhood is accompanied by greater awareness of characteristics of the self and other people. Was this artist imagining how gains in size and strength will affect his everyday activities? Or was he reflecting on the consequences of wide individual differences in body size? Chapter 11 takes up these issues.

Reprinted by permission from The International Museum of Children's Art, Oslo, Norway.

11

Physical Development in Middle Childhood

I'm on my way, Mom!" hollered 10-year-old Joey as he stuffed the last bite of toast into his mouth, slung his book bag over his shoulder, dashed out the door, jumped on his bike, and headed down the street for school. Joey's 8-year-old sister Lizzie followed next, quickly kissing her mother good-bye and hurrying to catch up with Joey. Off she raced, peddling furiously, until soon she was side by side with her older brother. Rena, the children's mother and one of my colleagues at the university, watched from the front porch as her son and daughter disappeared in the distance.

"They're branching out," Rena remarked to me over lunch that day as she described the children's expanding activities and relationships. Homework, household chores, soccer teams, music lessons, scouting, friends at school and in the neighborhood, and Joey's new paper route were all part of the children's routine. Commenting on how life was different from the way it had been a few years earlier, Rena said, "It seems as if the basics are all there; I don't have to monitor Joey and Lizzie so constantly anymore. But being a parent is still very challenging. Now it's more a matter of refinements—helping them become independent, competent, and productive individuals."

Joey and Lizzie have entered the phase of development called middle childhood, which spans the years from 6 to 11. Around the world, children of this age are assigned new responsibilities as they begin the process of entering the adult world. Joey and Lizzie, like other youngsters growing up in industrialized nations, spend many long hours in school—an institution designed to assist parents in preparing the young for adult roles in complex societies. Indeed, middle childhood has often

BODY GROWTH IN MIDDLE CHILDHOOD

Changes in Body Size and Proportions • Secular Trends in Physical Growth • Skeletal Growth • Brain Development

COMMON HEALTH PROBLEMS IN MIDDLE CHILDHOOD

Vision and Hearing • Malnutrition • Obesity • Type A Behavior • Bedwetting • Illnesses • Unintentional Injuries

HEALTH EDUCATION IN MIDDLE CHILDHOOD

MOTOR DEVELOPMENT AND PLAY IN MIDDLE CHILDHOOD

Gross Motor Development • Fine Motor Development • Individual and Group Differences in Motor Development • Organized Games with Rules • Shadows of Our Evolutionary Past • Physical Education

been called the "school years," since its onset is marked by the start of formal schooling. In village and tribal cultures, the school may be a field or a jungle rather than a classroom. But universally, mature members of society guide children of this age period toward more realistic tasks that increasingly resemble those they will perform as adults (Erikson, 1950; Rogoff et al., 1975).

This chapter focuses on physical growth in middle childhood—changes that are less spectacular than those of the earlier years. By age 6, the brain has reached 95 percent of its adult size, and the body continues to grow slowly. In this way, nature grants school-age children the mental powers to master challenging tasks as well as added time to learn before reaching physical maturity. We begin our discussion by reviewing typical growth trends as well as special health concerns of middle childhood. Then we turn to children's rapid gains in motor abilities, which support practical everyday activities, athletic skills, and participation in organized games. We will see that each of these achievements is affected by and contributes to cognitive and social development. Our discussion will echo a familiar theme—that all areas of development are interrelated.

BODY GROWTH IN MIDDLE CHILDHOOD

During middle childhood, the lower portion of the body is growing fastest. These 8-year-old girls are taller and longer legged than they were as preschoolers. *(Arnie Katz/Stock South)*

CHANGES IN BODY SIZE AND PROPORTIONS

The rate of physical growth during the school years is an extension of the pattern that characterized early childhood. Compared to the rapid height and weight gain of the first 2 years of life, growth is slow and regular. At age 6, the average child weighs about 45 pounds and is 3 1/2 feet tall. As Figure 11.1 shows, children continue to add about 2 to 3 inches in height and 5 pounds in weight each year. However, when researchers carefully track individual cases, growth is not quite as steady as these age-related norms suggest. A longitudinal study of Scottish children, who were followed between ages 3 and 10, revealed slight spurts in height. Girls tended to forge ahead at ages 4 1/2, 6 1/2, 8 1/2, and 10, boys slightly later, at 4 1/2, 7, 9, and 10 1/2. In between these spurts were lulls in which growth was slower (Butler, McKie, & Ratcliffe, 1990).

Look again at Figure 11.1, and you will see that girls are slightly shorter and lighter than boys at ages 6 to 8. By age 9, this trend reverses. Already, Rena noticed, Lizzie was starting to catch up with Joey in physical size. For many girls, the 10-year-old height spurt overlaps with the much more dramatic adolescent growth spurt, which takes place 2 years earlier in girls than boys.

Because the lower portion of the body is growing fastest at this age period, Joey and Lizzie appeared longer-legged than they had in early childhood. Rena discovered that they grew out of their jeans more quickly than their jackets and frequently needed larger shoes. As in early childhood, during the school years girls have slightly more body fat and boys more muscle. After age 8, girls begin accumulating fat at a faster rate, and they will add even more during adolescence (Tanner, 1990).

A glance into any elementary school classroom reveals that individual differences in body growth remain great in middle childhood. The diversity among children in physical size is especially apparent when we travel to different nations. Measurements of 8-year-olds living in many parts of world reveal a 9-inch gap between the smallest and the largest youngsters. The shortest children tend to be found in South America, Asia, the Pacific Islands, and parts of Africa and include such ethnic groups as Colombian, Burmese, Thai, Vietnamese, Ethiopian, and Bantu. The tallest children reside in Australia, northern and central Europe, and the United States and consist of Czech, Dutch, Latvian, Norwegian, Swiss, and black and white American children (Meredith, 1978). These findings remind us that growth norms, such as those in Figure 11.1, need to be interpreted cautiously, espe-

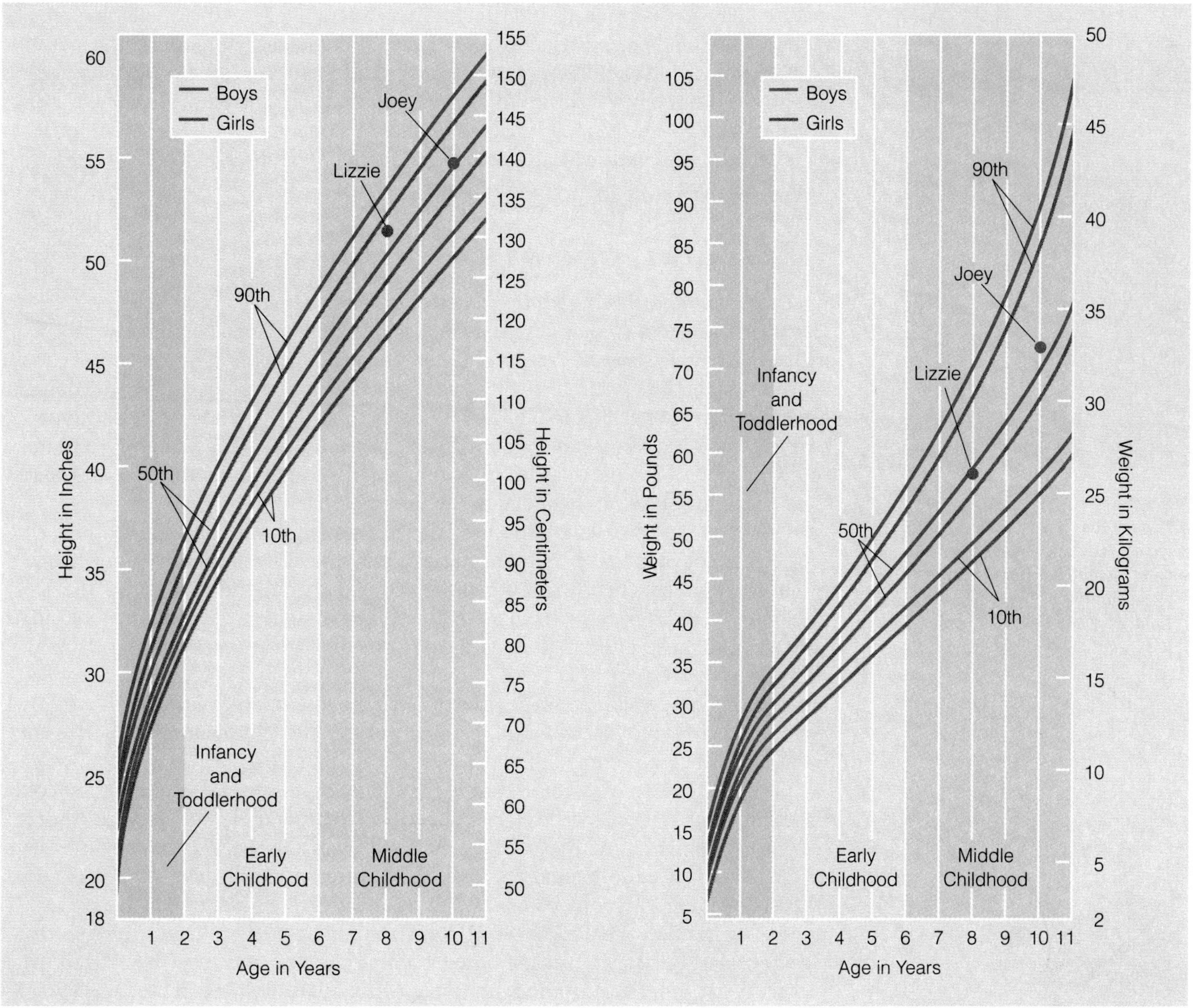

FIGURE 11.1

Gains in height and weight during middle childhood among American children.
The slow rate of growth established in early childhood extends into the school years. Girls are slightly shorter and lighter than boys until age 9, at which time this trend is reversed as girls approach the adolescent growth spurt. Eight-year-old Lizzie is beginning to catch up with 10-year-old Joey in physical size. Wide individual differences in body size continue to exist, as the percentiles on these charts reveal.

cially in countries like the United States, where so many racial and ethnic groups are represented.

What accounts for these vast differences in physical size? Both heredity and environment are involved. Body size is sometimes the result of evolutionary adaptations to a particular climate. For example, long, lean physiques are typical in hot, tropical regions and short, stocky ones in cold, arctic areas. At the same time, children who grow tallest usually reside in developed countries where food is plentiful and infectious diseases are largely controlled. In contrast, small children tend to live in less developed regions, where poverty, hunger, and disease are common (Tanner, 1990).

SECULAR TRENDS IN PHYSICAL GROWTH

Over the past century, **secular trends in physical growth**—changes in body size from one generation to the next—have taken place in industrialized nations. Joey and Lizzie are taller and heavier than their parents and grandparents were as children. These trends have been found in nearly all European nations, in Japan, and among black and white children in the United States. The difference appears early in life and becomes greater over childhood and early adolescence. Then, as

Secular trends in physical growth
Changes in body size from one generation to the next.

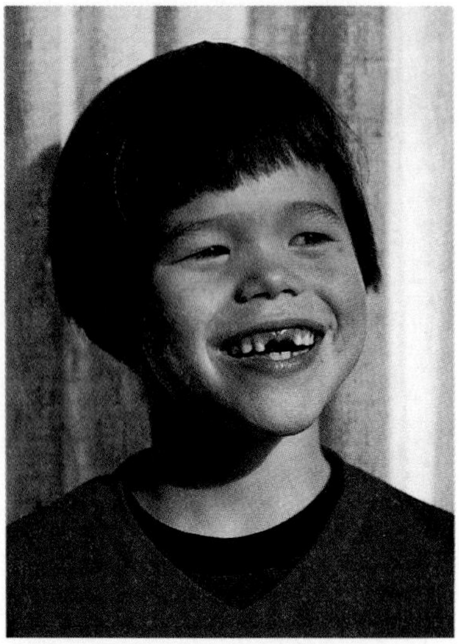

This boy has the "toothless" smile typical of 6- and 7-year-olds. Two permanent lower front teeth have already erupted. The large, upper front teeth will be next to emerge. *(L.L. Smith/Photo Researchers)*

mature body size is reached, it declines. This pattern suggests that the larger size of modern children is mostly due to a faster rate of physical maturation (Roche, 1979).

Why are so many children growing larger and maturing earlier than their ancestors? Once again, improved health and nutrition play major roles. The secular gain in height and weight is not as great among low-income groups, who have poorer diets. In countries with widespread poverty, famine, and disease, a secular decrease in body size has actually occurred (Tobias, 1975).

SKELETAL GROWTH

During middle childhood, the bones of the body lengthen and broaden. However, ligaments are not yet firmly attached to bones. This, combined with increasing muscle strength, grants children unusual flexibility of movement. School-age youngsters often seem like "physical contortionists," turning cartwheels, doing handstands, and engaging in fancy break-dance routines. As their bodies become stronger, many children experience a greater desire for physical exercise. Nighttime "growing pains"—stiffness, aches, and muscle pulls—are common as muscles adapt to an enlarging skeleton (Sheiman & Slomin, 1988).

One of the most striking aspects of skeletal growth in middle childhood is replacement of primary or "baby" teeth with permanent teeth. Recall from Chapter 8 that children lose their first tooth at the end of early childhood. Between the ages of 6 and 12, all 20 primary teeth are replaced by permanent ones, with girls losing their teeth slightly earlier than boys. The first teeth to go are the central incisors (lower and then upper front teeth), giving many first and second graders a "toothless" smile. For a while, permanent teeth seem much too large. Growth of facial bones, especially the jaw and chin, gradually causes the child's face to lengthen and mouth to widen, accommodating the newly erupting teeth.

Care of the teeth is essential during the school years, since dental health affects the child's appearance, speech, and ability to chew properly. Children often neglect to brush thoroughly, and they usually cannot floss by themselves until about 9 years of age. Parents need to remind and help them with these tasks. Regular trips to the dentist, avoiding sugary foods, and water fluoridation continue to be effective in preventing cavities (see Chapter 8). On one recent dental visit, Rena requested that *plastic sealants* be placed over the biting surfaces of Lizzie and Joey's back teeth to protect them from decay. Although plastic sealants have been available for 25 years and are highly effective in reducing cavities, less than 10 percent of American schoolchildren receive them (Seligmann & Namuth, 1991).

About one-third of school-age youngsters suffer from **malocclusion,** a condition in which the upper and lower teeth do not meet properly. In about 14 percent of cases, serious difficulties in biting and chewing result. Malocclusion can be caused by thumb and finger sucking after permanent teeth erupt. Children who were eager thumb suckers during infancy and early childhood may require gentle but persistent encouragement to give up the habit by school entry. A second cause of malocclusion is crowding of permanent teeth. In some children, this problem clears up as the jaw grows. Others need braces, a common sight by the end of elementary school (Kilman & Helpin, 1983).

Malocclusion
A condition in which the upper and lower teeth do not meet properly.

BRAIN DEVELOPMENT

During middle childhood, brain development largely involves more efficient functioning of various structures. The *frontal lobe* of the cortex (responsible for thought and consciousness) shows a slight increase in surface area between ages 5 and 7 due to continuing *myelinization* (Luria, 1973). In addition, *lateralization* of the cerebral hemispheres, already well established in early childhood, becomes stronger over the school years (Thatcher, Walker, & Giudice, 1987).

Little information is available on how the brain changes in other ways during this age period. One idea is that development occurs at the level of **neurotransmitters,** chemicals that permit *neurons* to communicate across small gaps, or *synapses,* between them (see Chapter 5, page 174). Over time, neurons become increasingly selective, responding only to certain chemical messages. This change may contribute to more efficient and flexible thinking and behavior during middle childhood. Secretions of particular neurotransmitters are related to cognitive performance, social and emotional adjustment, and ability to withstand stress in children and adults. Children may suffer serious developmental problems, such as inattention and overactivity, emotional disturbance, and epilepsy (an illness involving brain seizures and loss of motor control) when neurotransmitters are not present in appropriate balances (Shonkoff, 1984; Zametkin et al., 1990).

Researchers also believe that brain functioning may change during middle childhood because of the influence of hormones. Around age 7 to 8, an increase in *androgens* (male sex hormones), secreted by the adrenal glands located on top of the kidneys, occurs in children of both sexes. Androgens will rise further among boys at puberty, when the testes release them in large amounts. In many animal species, androgens affect brain organization and behavior, and they do so in humans as well (Hines & Green, 1991). Recall from Chapter 10 that androgens contribute to boys' higher activity level. They may also promote social dominance and play fighting, topics that we will take up at the end of this chapter (Maccoby, 1990).

BRIEF REVIEW

Body growth takes place slowly in middle childhood, at a pace similar to that of the preschool years. Gains in height occur in slight spurts followed by lulls; growth of the legs accounts for most of the increase. Large individual differences in body size result from both genetic and environmental factors. Children in industrialized nations are growing larger and reaching physical maturity earlier than they did in past generations because of better nutrition and health care. Between ages 6 and 12, all primary teeth are replaced by permanent ones. Brain development in middle childhood may involve neurotransmitter and hormonal influences.

ASK YOURSELF . . .

- How is body growth during the school years consistent with the cephalocaudal trend of development that you studied in Chapter 5?
- Joey complained to his mother one evening that it wasn't fair that his younger sister Lizzie was almost as tall as he was. He worried that he wasn't growing fast enough. How should Rena respond to Joey's concern?

COMMON HEALTH PROBLEMS IN MIDDLE CHILDHOOD

Children like Joey and Lizzie, who come from advantaged homes, appear to be at their healthiest during middle childhood, full of energy and play. The cumulative effects of good nutrition, combined with rapid development of the body's immune system, offer greater protection against disease. Infections occur less often now than they did during early childhood. At the same time, growth in lung size permits more air to be exchanged with each breath, so children are better able to exercise vigorously without tiring.

Nevertheless, a variety of health problems do occur during the school years. We will see that many of them are more prevalent among low-income than middle-income youngsters. Return to Chapter 8, page 298, to review the status of children's health care in the United States. Because economically disadvantaged families often lack health insurance and cannot afford to pay for medical visits on their own, many youngsters continue to be deprived of regular access to a doctor. And a

Neurotransmitters
Chemicals that permit neurons to communicate across synapses.

growing number also lack such basic necessities as a comfortable home and regular meals. Not surprisingly, poverty continues to be a powerful predictor of ill health during middle childhood.

VISION AND HEARING

The most common vision problem in middle childhood is **myopia**, or nearsightedness. By the end of the school years, nearly 25 percent of children are affected. The rate is slightly higher in girls than boys and about twice as great in white as black youngsters (Sperduto et al., 1983). Heredity contributes to myopia, since identical twins are more likely than fraternal twins to have the condition to a similar degree (Teikari et al., 1991). But myopia is also related to experience. Parents often warn their youngsters not to read in dim light or to sit too close to the TV set, exclaiming, "You'll ruin your eyes!" Their concern may be well founded. Myopia is one of the few health conditions that increases with family income and education, an association that is almost entirely explained by how people use their eyes. The more time people spend reading and doing other close-up work, the more likely they are to be myopic (Angle & Wissmann, 1980). Fortunately, for those youngsters who develop nearsightedness because they love reading, sewing, drawing, or model building, the condition can easily be corrected with glasses.

During middle childhood, the eustachian tube (canal that runs from the inner ear to the throat) becomes longer, narrower, and more slanted, preventing fluid and bacteria from traveling so easily from the mouth to the ear. As a result, ear infections become less frequent. Still, some children get ear infections that, if left untreated, can lead to permanent hearing defects. About 3 to 4 percent of the school-age population, and as many as 18 to 20 percent of low-income youngsters, develop some hearing loss for this reason (Mott, James, & Sperhac, 1990). Regular screening tests for both vision and hearing are important so that defects can be corrected before they lead to serious learning difficulties.

MALNUTRITION

School-age children need a well-balanced, plentiful diet to provide energy for successful learning in school and increased physical activity. Many youngsters are so focused on play, friendships, and new activities that they spend little time at the table. Joey's hurried breakfast, described at the beginning of this chapter, is a common event during middle childhood. Readily available, healthy between-meal snacks—cheese, fruit, raw vegetables, and peanut butter—help meet nutritional needs during the school years.

As long as parents encourage healthy eating, the mild nutritional deficits that result from the child's busy daily schedule have no impact on development. But as we have seen in earlier chapters, many poverty-stricken children in developing countries and in the United States suffer from serious and prolonged malnutrition. By middle childhood, the effects are apparent in retarded physical growth, low intelligence test scores, poor motor coordination, inattention, and distractibility. Research on animals reveals that diet affects the operation of neurotransmitters in the brain (Zeisel, 1986). The negative impact of malnutrition on learning and behavior may be extended during middle childhood in just this way.

Unfortunately, when malnutrition persists for many years, permanent damage is done. Prevention through government-sponsored food programs beginning in the early years and continuing throughout childhood and adolescence is necessary (Lozoff, 1989). Chronic hunger is painful and disabling. As one 10-year-old boy living with his family in a welfare hotel in New York City explained, "I just cannot

Myopia
Nearsightedness; inability to see distant objects clearly.

think in school when I am hungry. My mind just stops thinking and this cannot go on for ever . . . ." (Select Committee on Children, Youth, and Families, 1986, pp. 47–48).

OBESITY

Mona, a very overweight child in Lizzie's class, often stood on the side lines and watched during recess. When she did join in the children's games, she was slow and clumsy. On a daily basis, Mona was the target of unkind comments: "Move it, Tubs!" "Tree trunks for legs!" "No fatsoes allowed!" Although Mona was a good student, other children continued to reject her inside the classroom. When it was time to choose partners for a special activity, Mona was one of the last to be selected. On most afternoons, she walked home from school by herself while the other children gathered in groups, talking, laughing, and chasing. Once home and in the kitchen, Mona sought comfort in high-calorie snacks, which promoted further weight gain.

Mona is one of about 27 percent of American children who suffer from **obesity**, a greater than 20 percent increase over average body weight, based on the child's age, sex, and physical build (Gortmaker et al., 1987). Overweight and obesity are growing problems in affluent nations such as the United States. Childhood obesity has climbed steadily since the 1960s, with over 80 percent of youngsters like Mona retaining their overweight status as adults (Dietz, Bandini, & Gortmaker, 1990; Muecke et al., 1992).

Obese children have serious emotional and social difficulties and are at risk for lifelong health problems. High blood pressure and cholesterol levels along with respiratory abnormalities begin to appear in the early school years, symptoms that are powerful predictors of heart disease and early death (Taitz, 1983; Unger, Kreeger, & Christoffel, 1990). As you can see from Table 11.1, childhood obesity is a complex physical disorder with multiple causes.

TABLE 11.1

Factors Associated with Childhood Obesity

FACTOR	DESCRIPTION
Heredity	Obesity runs in families. Obese children are likely to have at least one obese parent.
Social class	Obesity is more common in low-income than middle-income groups.
Early growth pattern	Infants who gain weight rapidly during the first year are at slightly greater risk for obesity.
Family eating habits	When parents purchase high-calorie treats and junk food and use them to reward children and reduce anxiety, their youngsters are more likely to be obese.
Responsiveness to food cues	Obese children often decide when to eat on the basis of external cues, such as taste, smell, sight, and time of day, rather than hunger.
Physical activity	Obese children are less physically active than their normal-weight peers.
Television viewing	Children who spend many hours watching television are more likely to become obese.
Traumatic events	Traumatic events, such as divorce, death of a family member, or child abuse and neglect, can trigger obesity.

Obesity
A greater than 20 percent increase over average body weight, based on the child's age, sex, and physical build.

■ **CAUSES OF OBESITY.** All children are not equally at risk for becoming overweight. Fat children tend to have fat parents, and concordance for obesity is greater in identical than fraternal twins. (Return to Chapter 2, page 88, to review the concept of concordance.) But similarity among family members is not strong enough to imply that genetics accounts for any more than a tendency to gain weight (Dietz, Bandini, & Gortmaker, 1990). One indication that environment is powerfully important is the consistent relation between social class and obesity. Low-income youngsters in industrialized nations are not just at greater risk for malnutrition. They are also more likely to be overweight (Stunkard & Sørenson, 1993). Among factors responsible are lack of knowledge about healthy diet; a tendency to buy high-fat, low-cost foods; and family stress, which prompts overeating in some individuals.

Recall from Chapter 5 that a slight relationship exists between very rapid weight gain in infancy and fatness in childhood. Although some researchers believe that the high-protein, high-fat content of cows-milk formula contributes to the chances that a child will become overweight (Kramer et al., 1985), most bottle-fed and chubby babies do not become obese. Other influences must also be present for later weight problems to appear. Parental feeding practices seem to play important roles. Some mothers interpret almost all the cries of their infants as a desire for food. They anxiously overfeed their babies and fail to help them learn the difference between hunger and other physical and emotional discomforts (Weil, 1975). Parents of older obese children can be seen using food as a reward and as a way to relieve the child's anxiety (Bruch, 1970). When food is used to reinforce other behaviors, children start to value the treat itself as well as other similar foods (Birch, 1987). In families where these practices are common, high-calorie treats gradually come to symbolize warmth, comfort, and relief of tension.

Obesity is an emotionally painful and physically debilitating disorder. This boy has difficulty keeping up with his agemates in a gunnysack race. Because of peer rejection, fat children often lead lonely lives. *(Bob Daemmrich/Stock Boston)*

Perhaps because of these feeding experiences, obese children soon develop maladaptive eating habits. Research shows that they are more responsive to external stimuli associated with food—taste, sight, smell, and time of day—and less responsive to internal hunger cues than are normal-weight individuals. This difference is already present in middle childhood and may develop even earlier (Ballard et al., 1980; Constanzo & Woody, 1979). Overweight individuals also eat faster and chew their food less thoroughly, a behavior pattern that appears in overweight children as early as 18 months of age (Drabman et al., 1979).

Fat children do not just eat more; they are also less physically active than their normal-weight peers. This inactivity is both cause and consequence of their overweight condition. Recent evidence indicates that the rise in childhood obesity in the United States over the past 30 years is in part due to television viewing. Next to already existing obesity, time spent in front of the TV set is the best predictor of future obesity among school-age children. The rate of obesity increases by 2 percent for each additional hour of TV watched per day (Dietz & Gortmaker, 1985; Gortmaker, Dietz, & Cheung, 1990). Television greatly reduces the time that children devote to physical exercise. At the same time, TV ads encourage them to eat fattening, unhealthy snacks—soft drinks, sweets, and salty chips and popcorn (Carruth, Goldberg, & Skinner, 1991).

One final factor can trigger childhood obesity: traumatic events, such as divorce, death of a family member, or child abuse and neglect. When children experience a sense of personal loss or feel unloved, they seek other sources of emotional support, and some turn to food. In one recent study, 12 cases of severe childhood obesity were linked to extreme family disorganization. Parents had psychological and substance abuse problems, failed to supervise and discipline their children, and were hostile to professionals who tried to help. Once placed in foster homes, these children lost weight easily. Those who later returned to their disorganized home lives gained the weight back immediately (Christoffel & Forsyth, 1989).

CONSEQUENCES OF OBESITY. Unfortunately, physical attractiveness is a powerful predictor of social acceptance in our culture. Both children and adults rate obese youngsters as less likable than children with a wide range of physical disabilities (Brenner & Hinsdale, 1978; Lerner & Schroeder, 1971). By middle childhood, obese children have a low sense of self-esteem, report feeling more depressed, and display more behavior problems than their peers. A vicious cycle emerges in which unhappiness and overeating contribute to one another, and the child remains overweight (Banis et al., 1988).

The psychological consequences of obesity combine with continuing discrimination to result in reduced life chances. By young adulthood, overweight individuals have completed fewer years of schooling, have lower incomes, and marry less often than do individuals with other chronic health problems. These outcomes are particularly strong for females (Gortmaker et al., 1993).

TREATING OBESITY. Overweight and obesity are best treated in childhood, before harmful eating patterns become well established. Yet childhood obesity is difficult to treat because it is a family disorder. Parents, who encourage, model, and reinforce behaviors that lead to overeating, must be willing to help their children change.

In Mona's case, the school nurse suggested that Mona and her obese mother enter a weight loss program together. But Mona's mother, unhappily married for many years, had her own reasons for continuing to overeat. She rejected this idea, claiming that Mona would eventually decide to lose weight on her own. Although many obese youngsters do try to slim down in adolescence, they usually do not choose sensible ways of doing so. Often they try crash diets in which they deprive themselves of essential nutrients during a period of rapid growth. These efforts can actually make matters worse. Temporary starvation leads to physical stress, discomfort, and fatigue. Soon the child returns to old eating patterns, and weight rebounds to a higher level. Then, to protect itself, the body burns calories more slowly and becomes more resistant to future weight loss (Pinel, 1993).

When parents decide to seek treatment for an obese child, long-term changes in body weight do occur. A recent study found that the most effective interventions were family based and focused on changing behaviors. Both parent and child revised eating patterns, exercised daily, and reinforced each other with praise and points for progress, which they exchanged for special activities and times together (Epstein et al., 1987). A follow-up after 5 years showed that children maintained their weight loss more effectively than did adults. This finding underscores the importance of intervening with obese children at an early age (Epstein et al., 1990).

TYPE A BEHAVIOR

Besides obesity, another serious health problem also has roots in childhood and leads to later heart disease. Perhaps you have heard of the **Type A personality**—an adult who is overly competitive, impatient, restless, and time conscious. Both on the job and during leisure time activities, Type A people are so focused on success that they become irritated and angry if anyone or anything hinders them. Their tense and driven approach to daily life is associated with high blood pressure and cholesterol levels and a rate of heart disease that is twice as high as that of more easygoing Type B individuals (Friedman & Rosenman, 1959; Glass et al., 1980).

The Type A behavior pattern and its physical symptoms begin to emerge in early and middle childhood. Already, Joey's friend Terry showed signs of it. "Hurry up!" Terry complained as he waited for Joey to get his books from his locker after school one day. Terry paced, sighed, squirmed, and clicked his tongue with impatience until Joey was ready. Out on the playground, Terry constantly wanted to be first, challenged other children to competitive races, and became upset if he did not win.

Type A personality
A personality characterized by excessive competitiveness, impatience, restlessness, and irritability. Associated with high blood pressure and cholesterol levels as well as heart disease in adulthood.

During class, he frequently interrupted other children, squirmed in his seat, and looked annoyed (Matthews & Angulo, 1980; Vega-Lahr et al., 1988).

An intense, determined temperamental style probably contributes to the early appearance of Type A behavior. But not all Type A children become Type A adults. The Type A pattern is not very stable until adolescence (Steinberg, 1988b). Environmental forces combine with inherited dispositions to sustain Type A traits. Consistent with this idea, Type A children are more likely than their agemates to have Type A parents as well as a family history of heart disease (Räikkönen, Keltikangas-Järvinen, & Pietikäinen, 1991; Trieber et al., 1990). When parents model impatience, anger, and competitiveness and set unrealistically high goals, Type A behaviors may be encouraged in children who are prone to be hard driving and irritable in the first place.

Look carefully at the characteristics of the Type A personality, and you will see that it includes both prosocial and antisocial tendencies. On the positive side, Type A children display a special potential for leadership and achievement. On the negative side, they are impatient, hostile, and inconsiderate of others. Researchers hope to find ways to preserve the prosocial elements of the Type A personality while discouraging the antisocial ones as they experiment with ways to prevent this important cause of later heart disease.

BEDWETTING

One Friday afternoon, Terry called up Joey to see if he could sleep over, but Joey refused. "I can't," said Joey anxiously, without giving an explanation.

"Why not? We can take our sleeping bags out in the backyard. Come on, it'll be super!"

"My mom won't let me," Joey responded, unconvincingly. "I mean, well, I think we're busy, we're doing something tonight."

"Gosh, Joey, this is the third time you've said no. See if I'll ask *you* again!" snapped Terry as he hung up the phone.

Joey is one of 8 percent of American school-age children who suffer from **nocturnal enuresis,** or bedwetting during the night (Rappaport, 1993). Enuresis evokes considerable distress in children and parents alike. For children, it restricts social activities and embarrasses them in front of family members. Most parents say that they worry about the problem and find the frequent night wakings and bedding changes annoying (Foxman, Valdez, & Brook, 1986). In one large-scale study, 36 percent admitted they punished their children for wetting (Haque et al., 1981).

Although enuretic children show a slightly higher rate of psychological distress than their peers, this may be an outcome of the bedwetting itself. In the overwhelming majority of cases, the problem has biological roots. Heredity is a major contributing factor. Parents with a history of bedwetting are far more likely to have a child with the problem (McGuire & Savashino, 1984). Enuresis is unrelated to the depth of a child's sleep, and only rarely is it due to abnormalities in the urinary tract. Most often, it is caused by a failure of muscular responses that inhibit urination or a hormonal imbalance that permits too much urine to accumulate during the night (Houts, 1991). Punishing a school-age child for wetting is only likely to make matters worse.

To treat enuresis, doctors often prescribe antidepressant drugs, which reduce the amount of urine produced. But these gains are usually temporary. Once children stop taking the medication, they typically begin wetting again. Also, a small number of youngsters show side effects, such as anxiety, loss of sleep, and personality changes (Moffatt et al., 1993). The most effective treatment is a urine alarm that wakes the child at the first sign of dampness and works according to conditioning principles. Success rates of about 70 percent occur after 4 to 6 months of treatment. Most children who relapse achieve dryness after trying the alarm a second time

Nocturnal enuresis
Repeated bedwetting during the night.

(Rushton, 1989). Although many children outgrow enuresis without any form of intervention, it generally takes years for them to do so.

ILLNESSES

Children experience a somewhat higher rate of illness during the first 2 years of elementary school than they will later, due to exposure to sick children and the fact that their immune system is still developing. On the average, illness causes children to miss about 11 days of school per year, but most absences can be traced to a few students. These children tend to be low-income African-American and Hispanic youngsters with chronic health problems. Among children without diagnosed health difficulties, girls are more likely to miss school than boys. When a child shows symptoms of illness, gender stereotypes may cause parents to perceive their daughters as more vulnerable than their sons (Kornguth, 1990).

Allergies, colds, influenza, muscle sprains, and bone fractures are common reasons for missing school. But the most frequent cause of school absence and childhood hospitalization is **asthma,** a condition in which the bronchial tubes (passages that connect the throat and lungs) are highly sensitive. In response to a variety of stimuli, such as cold weather, infection, exercise, or allergies, they fill with mucus and contract, leading to coughing, wheezing, and serious breathing difficulties. The number of children with asthma has increased by 50 percent over the last decade. Today, 6 to 12 percent of American youngsters are affected, and asthma-related deaths have risen in recent years (Celano & Geller, 1993; Gergen, Mullally, & Evans, 1988). Although heredity contributes to asthma, researchers believe that environmental factors are necessary to spark the illness. Boys, African-American children, and children who were born underweight, whose parents smoke, and who live in poverty are at greatest risk (Chilmonczyk et al., 1993; Weitzman, Gortmaker, & Sobol, 1990). Perhaps black and poverty-stricken youngsters experience a higher rate of asthma because of pollution in inner-city areas (which triggers allergic reactions), stressful home lives, and lack of access to good health care.

About 2 percent of American children have chronic illnesses that are more severe than asthma, such as cystic fibrosis (see Table 2.3, pages 62–63), cancer, and acquired immune deficiency syndrome (AIDS). Painful medical treatments, physical discomfort, and changes in appearance often disrupt the sick child's daily life, making it difficult to concentrate in school and causing withdrawal from peers. As the illness worsens, family stress increases. Mothers, who typically bear the burden of caring for a very ill child, report more health problems of their own. For these reasons, chronically ill youngsters are at risk for academic, emotional, and social difficulties (Garrison & McQuiston, 1989). Many interventions have been found to improve their adjustment, including

- Family and health education, in which parents and children learn about the illness and get training in how to manage it
- Home visits by health professionals, who offer counseling and social support
- Disease-specific summer camps, which teach children self-help skills and grant parents time off from the demands of caring for an ill youngster
- Parent and peer support groups
- Individual and family therapy

Roller blading is a favorite pasttime for modern school-age children. Parents of these youngsters insist that they wear protective helmets and knee guards. Taking these precautions dramatically reduces the chances of serious injury. *(David Young-Wolff/ PhotoEdit)*

Asthma
An illness in which highly sensitive bronchial tubes fill with mucus and contract, leading to episodes of coughing, wheezing, and serious breathing difficulties.

UNINTENTIONAL INJURIES

As we conclude our discussion of threats to children's health during the school years, let's return for a moment to the topic of unintentional injuries (discussed in detail in Chapter 8). As Figure 11.2 shows, the frequency of injuries increases steadily over middle childhood into adolescence, with boys continuing to show a

FIGURE 11.2

Rates of unintentional injury by age and sex of child in a sample drawn from nearly 700 American families. Injuries increase steadily from 5 to 14 years, after which they decline. Boys experience more injuries than girls throughout childhood and adolescence. *(From E. L. Schor, 1987, "Unintentional Injuries,"* American Journal of Diseases of Children, *194, p. 1281. Reprinted by permission.)*

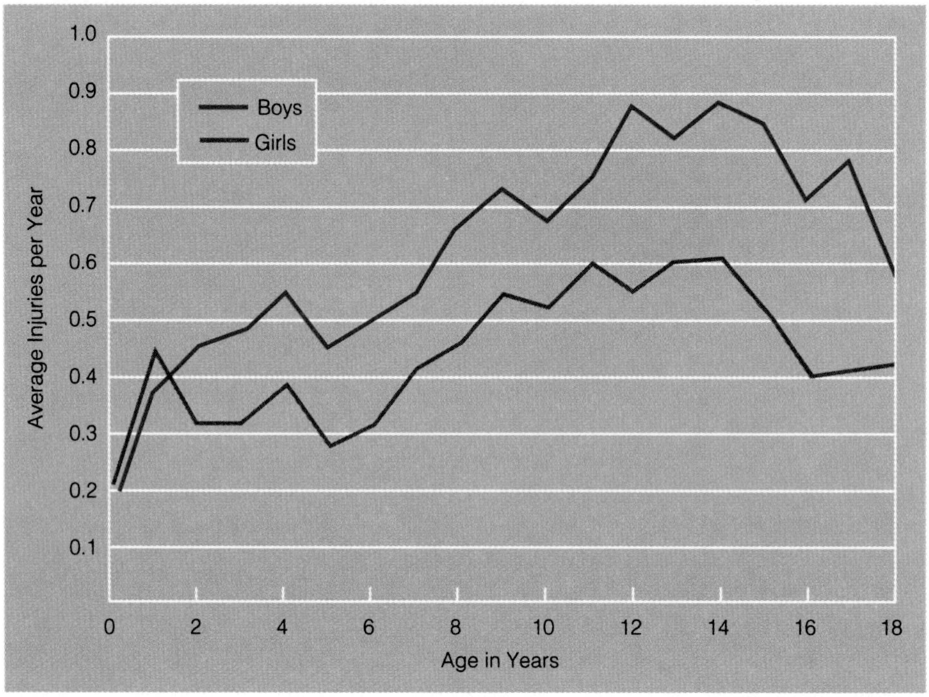

higher rate than girls. Auto and bicycle collisions account for most of this rise (Brooks & Roberts, 1990; Williams & Kotch, 1990).

As school-age children spend more time away from parents and range farther from home, safety education becomes especially important, along with incentives for following safety rules. Parents and teachers can enhance safety in middle childhood by continuing to make good use of the principles of behaviorism. For example, programs that reward children with prizes for arriving at school properly restrained in car seat belts are effective, just as they were in early childhood (Roberts & Fanurik, 1986). Insisting that children wear protective helmets while bicycling, roller skating, or skateboarding is also important. This simple safety precaution leads to an 85 percent reduction in the risk of head injury, a leading cause of permanent physical disability and death during the school years (Safe Kids, 1991).

Not all school-age children are likely to respond to efforts to increase their safety. By middle childhood, the greatest risk takers tend to have parents who do not act as safety-conscious models or who try to enforce rules by using punitive or inconsistent discipline (Roberts, Elkins, & Royal, 1984). These child-rearing techniques, as we saw in Chapter 10, spark defiance in children, reduce their willingness to comply, and may actually promote high-risk behavior. The greatest challenge for injury control programs is how to reach these "more difficult-to-reach" youngsters, alter their family contexts, and reduce the dangers to which they are exposed (Brooks & Roberts, 1990).

HEALTH EDUCATION IN MIDDLE CHILDHOOD

Child development specialists have become intensely interested in finding ways to help school-age youngsters understand how their bodies work, acquire mature conceptions of health and illness, and develop patterns of behavior that foster good health throughout life. Successfully targeting children for intervention on any health issue requires information on their current health-related knowledge. What information can they understand? What reasoning processes do they use? What factors influence what they know? The Cultural Influences box on page 408 summarizes findings on children's concepts of health and illness during middle childhood.

The school-age period may be an especially important time for fostering healthy life-styles because of the child's growing independence, increasing cognitive capacities, and rapidly developing self-concept, which includes perceptions of physical well-being (Harter, 1990). During middle childhood, children can learn a wide variety of health-related information—about the structure and functioning of their bodies, about good nutrition, and about the causes and consequences of physical injuries and diseases (Shannon & Chen, 1988; Trieber, Schramm, & Mabe, 1986; Vessey, 1988).

Yet in virtually every effort to impart health concepts to children, researchers have found that health habits show little change. Why is there such a gap between health knowledge and practice in middle childhood? There are several related reasons. First, health is not an important goal to children. They are far more concerned about schoolwork, friends, and play. Second, school-age youngsters, who feel good most of the time, do not perceive themselves as vulnerable to serious health problems. Third, children do not yet have an adultlike time perspective, which relates past, present, and future. Engaging in preventive behaviors is difficult when so much time intervenes between what children do now and its health consequences (Kalnins & Love, 1982). Finally, much health information that children get is contradicted by other sources, such as television advertising (see Chapter 10) and the examples of adults and peers.

This does not mean that teaching school-age children health-related facts is unimportant. But information must be supplemented by other efforts. As we saw in earlier chapters, one effective way to foster children's health is to reduce hazards, such as pollution, inadequate medical care, and non-nutritious foods that are widely available in homes as well as school cafeterias (Children's Defense Fund, 1992; Shapiro, 1991). At the same time, since environments will never be totally free of health risks, parents and teachers need to coach children in good health practices and model and reinforce these behaviors as much as possible (Friedman, Greene, & Stokes, 1991).

BRIEF REVIEW

Although many children are at their healthiest in middle childhood, a variety of health problems do occur. Most are more common among low-income youngsters, who are exposed to more health risks throughout development. Vision and hearing difficulties, malnutrition, overweight and obesity, Type A behavior, nighttime bedwetting, respiratory illnesses that result in school absences, and unintentional injuries are among the most frequent health concerns during the school years. Genetic and environmental factors combine to increase children's vulnerability to certain health problems, such as nearsightedness, obesity, Type A traits, and asthma. School-age children can learn a wide range of health information, but it has little impact on their everyday behavior. Interventions must also provide them with healthier environments and directly promote good health practices.

ASK YOURSELF . . .

- Rena discovered that Joey had stopped drinking milk in the school cafeteria because several of his friends no longer drank it. Also, he often skipped the main dish in favor of an extra dessert. Rena did not try to change Joey's eating practices at school. Instead, she encouraged him to eat a nutritious snack when he arrived home each day. What do you think about Rena's approach to handling this problem? What should Joey's school be doing to foster good nutrition?
- Nine-year-old Talia is afraid to hug and kiss her grandmother, who has cancer. What explains Talia's mistaken belief that the same behaviors that cause colds to spread might lead her to catch cancer?

CULTURAL INFLUENCES

CHILDREN'S UNDERSTANDING OF HEALTH AND ILLNESS

Lizzie lay on the living room sofa with a stuffy nose and sore throat, disappointed that she was missing her soccer team's final game and pizza party. "How'd I get this dumb cold anyhow?" she wondered aloud to Joey. "I probably did it to myself by playing outside without a hat the other day when it was freezing cold."

"No, no," Joey contradicted. "You can't get sick that way. Some creepy little viruses got into your bloodstream and attacked, just like an army."

"What're viruses? I didn't eat any viruses," answered Lizzie, puzzled.

"You don't eat them, silly, you breathe them in. Somebody probably sneezed them all over you at school. That's how you got sick!"

Lizzie and Joey are at different developmental levels in their understanding of health and illness—ideas that are influenced by cognitive development, exposure to biological knowledge, and cultural beliefs and practices. Researchers have asked 4- to 14-year-olds in Western cultures questions designed to tap what they know about the causes of health and certain illnesses, such as colds, AIDS, and cancer.

During the preschool and early school years, children do not have much biological knowledge to bring to bear on their understanding of health and illness. For example, if you ask 4- to 8-year-olds to tell you what is inside their bodies, you will find that they know little about their internal organs and how they work. As a result, young children fall back on their rich knowledge of people's behavior to account for health and illness (Carey, 1985). Children of this age regard health as a matter of engaging in specific practices (eating the right foods, getting enough exercise, and wearing warm clothing on cold days) and illness as a matter of failing to follow these rules or coming too close to a sick person. Because of their limited knowledge, they sometimes view illness in superstitious ways—for example, as transmitted by magic or as punishment for doing something bad (Bibace & Walsh, 1980; Natapoff, 1978; Perrin & Gerrity, 1981).

Over the course of middle childhood, children acquire more knowledge about their bodies and are cognitively better able to make sense of it. By age 9 or 10, they name a wide variety of internal organs and view them as interconnected, working as a system (Carey, 1985; Crider, 1981). Around this time, children's concepts of health and illness shift to biological explanations. Joey understands that illness can be caused by contagion—breathing in a harmful substance (a virus), which affects the operation of the body in some way.

By early adolescence, explanations become more elaborate and precise. Eleven- to 14-year-olds recognize health as a long-term condition that depends on the interaction of body, mind, and environmental influences (Hergenrather & Rabinowitz, 1991). And the adolescent's notions of illness involve clearly stated ideas about interference in normal body processes: "You get a cold when your sinuses fill up with mucus. Sometimes your lungs do, too, and you get a cough. Colds come from viruses. They get into the blood stream and make your platelet count go down" (Bibace & Walsh, 1980).

School-age children everywhere are capable of grasping basic biological ideas, but whether or not they do so depends on information in their everyday environments along with cultural beliefs about health and disease. Research reveals that children are likely to generalize their knowledge of familiar diseases to less familiar ones. As a result, they often conclude that risk factors for colds (sharing a Coke or sneezing on someone) can cause AIDS. And lacking much understanding of cancer, they assume that it (like colds and AIDS) is communicable (Sigelman et al., 1993). These incorrect ideas can lead to unnecessary anxiety about getting a serious disease as well as negative attitudes toward its victims. Furthermore, in Western society, a rational view of illness as disordered biological processes prevails, but the biological model is not accepted everywhere. A skin rash is likely to be understood very differently by a 10-year-old child growing up in a tribal society of believers in evil eyes and demons than in a middle-class family in the United States (Shonkoff, 1984).

The extent to which children in our own culture comprehend illness from a biological rather than magical point of view can be undermined by widely held attitudes in their social worlds. When certain diseases take on powerful symbolic meanings—for example, cancer as a malignant, destructive evil and AIDS as a sign of moral decay—even adults who have an accurate biological understanding of the illness irrationally expect bad things to happen from associating with affected people (Pryor et al., 1989). These beliefs are quickly picked up by children (Brown & Fritz, 1988), and they help explain the severe social rejection experienced by some youngsters with chronic diseases, such as AIDS and cancer.

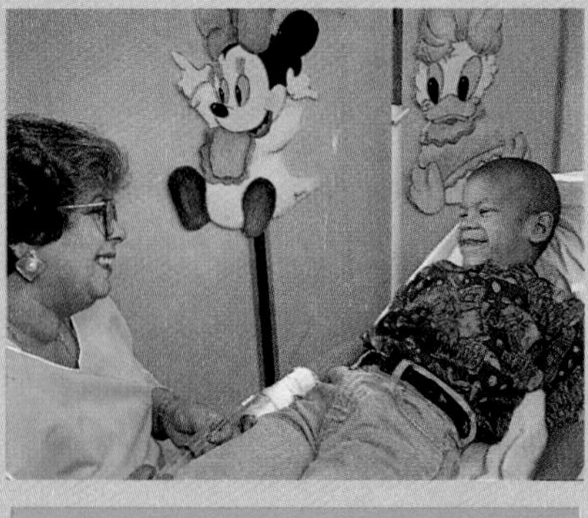

How will classmates of this 9-year-old cancer patient treat him after he is released from the hospital? Helping school-age children understand that cancer is not communicable can prevent them from developing negative attitudes toward its victims. *(Geoff Tomkinson/Science Photo Library)*

MOTOR DEVELOPMENT AND PLAY IN MIDDLE CHILDHOOD

Visit a city park on a pleasant weekend afternoon, watch several preschool and school-age children at play, and jot down their various physical activities. You will see that gains in body size and muscle strength support improved motor coordination during middle childhood. In addition, greater cognitive and social maturity permits older children to use their new motor skills in more complex ways. You are likely to notice a major change in children's play at this time.

GROSS MOTOR DEVELOPMENT

During middle childhood, running, jumping, hopping, and ball skills become more refined. At Joey and Lizzie's school one day, I watched during the third- to sixth-graders' recess. Children burst into sprints as they raced across the playground, jumped quickly over rotating ropes, engaged in intricate patterns of hopscotch, kicked and dribbled soccer balls, swung bats at balls pitched by their classmates, and balanced adeptly as they walked toe-to-toe across narrow ledges. Table 11.2 summarizes gross motor achievements between 6 and 12 years of age.

The diverse motor skills that improve during the school years reflect gains in four basic motor capacities. The first is *flexibility*. Compared to the movements of preschoolers, those of school-age children are more pliable and elastic, a difference that can be seen as children swing a bat, kick a ball, jump over a hurdle, or execute tumbling routines. Second, *balance* improves, both when the child is moving and when standing still. School-age children can walk a narrower balance beam than

TABLE 11.2

Changes in Gross Motor Skills During Middle Childhood

SKILL	DEVELOPMENTAL CHANGE
Running	Running speed increases from 12 feet per second at age 6 to over 18 feet per second at age 12.
Other gait variations	Skipping improves. Sideways stepping appears around age 6 and becomes more continuous and fluid with age.
Vertical jump	Height jumped increases from 4 inches at age 6 to 12 inches at age 12.
Standing broad jump	Distance jumped increases from 3 feet at age 6 to over 5 feet at age 12.
Precision jumping and hopping (on mat divided into squares)	By age 7 children can accurately move from square to square, a performance that improves until age 9 and then levels off.
Throwing	Throwing speed, distance, and accuracy increase for both sexes, but much more for boys than girls. At age 6, a ball thrown by a boy travels 39 feet per second, one by a girl 29 feet per second. At age 12, a ball thrown by a boy travels 78 feet per second, one by a girl 56 feet per second.
Catching	Ability to catch small balls thrown over greater distances improves with age.
Kicking	Kicking speed and accuracy improve, with boys considerably ahead of girls. At age 6, a ball kicked by a boy travels 21 feet per second, one by a girl 13 feet per second. At age 12, a ball kicked by a boy travels 34 feet per second, one by a girl 26 feet per second.
Batting	Batting motions become more effective with age, increasing in speed and accuracy and involving the entire body.
Dribbling	Style of hand dribbling gradually changes, from awkward slapping of the ball to continuous, relaxed, even stroking.

Sources: Cratty, 1986; Malina & Bouchard, 1991; Roberton, 1984.

During middle childhood, gross motor skills become more refined. Gains in flexibility, balance, agility, and force permit this girl to jump faster, higher, and with fancier footwork than she could as a younger child. *(Roswell Angier/Stock Boston)*

they could during early childhood, and their ability to remain in a one-foot stand increases. Improved balance supports advances in a great many athletic skills, including running, hopping, skipping, throwing, kicking, and the rapid changes of direction required in many team sports (Clark & Watkins, 1984). Third, children show marked gains in *agility,* or quickness and accuracy of movement. This change can be seen in the fancy footwork of jump rope and hopscotch, as well as in the forward, backward, and sideways motions older children use as they dodge opponents in tag and soccer. Finally, over the school years, children perform almost all movements with greater *force*. Older youngsters can throw and kick a ball harder and propel themselves further off the ground when running and jumping than they could at early ages (Cratty, 1986).

Although body growth contributes greatly to the improved motor performance of school-age children, more efficient information processing also plays an important role (Roberton, 1984). Steady improvements in *reaction time* occur during middle childhood, with 14-year-olds responding almost twice as quickly to a stimulus as 6-year-olds (Southard, 1985). As a result, younger children often have difficulty with skills that require immediate responding. When they dribble a ball, they often lose control, and when up at bat, they usually swing too late. Reaction time combines several cognitive skills that are crucial for effective motor performance—time to recognize a stimulus, time to formulate an appropriate response, and time for the plan of action to reach the muscles (Cratty, 1986). The fact that speed of reaction is not yet well developed in younger school-age children has practical implications for physical education. Since 6- and 7-year-olds are seldom successful at batting a thrown ball, T-ball is more appropriate for them than baseball. And handball, four-square, and kickball should precede instruction in tennis, basketball, and football (Thomas, 1984).

FINE MOTOR DEVELOPMENT

Fine motor development also improves steadily over the school years, a change that is apparent in the activities children of this age period enjoy. On rainy afternoons, Joey and Lizzie could be found experimenting with yo-yos, building model airplanes, weaving potholders on small looms, and working puzzles with hundreds of tiny pieces. Middle childhood is also the time when many children take up musical instruments, which demand considerable fine motor control.

Gains in fine motor skill are especially evident in children's writing and drawing, as Figure 11.3 reveals. By age 6, most children can print the alphabet, their first and last names, and the numbers from 1 to 10 with reasonable clarity. However, their writing tends to be quite large because they use the entire arm to make strokes rather than just the wrist and fingers. Children usually master uppercase letters first because these rely on horizontal and vertical motions, which are easier to control than the small curves of the lowercase alphabet. Legibility of writing gradually increases, not just because older children form letters more accurately, but also because they can produce letters of uniform height and spacing (Cratty, 1986). The letter reversals that often occur in early writing disappear as children become sensi-

Ted's Picture with Label

Ted's Space Trip Story

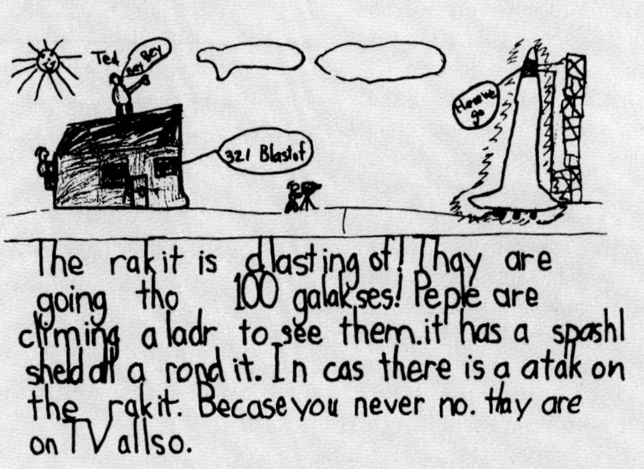

The rocket is blasting off! They are going through 100 galaxies! People are climbing a ladder to see them. It has a special shield all around it. In case there is an attack on the rocket. Because you never know. They are on TV also.

Ted's War of 1812 Essay

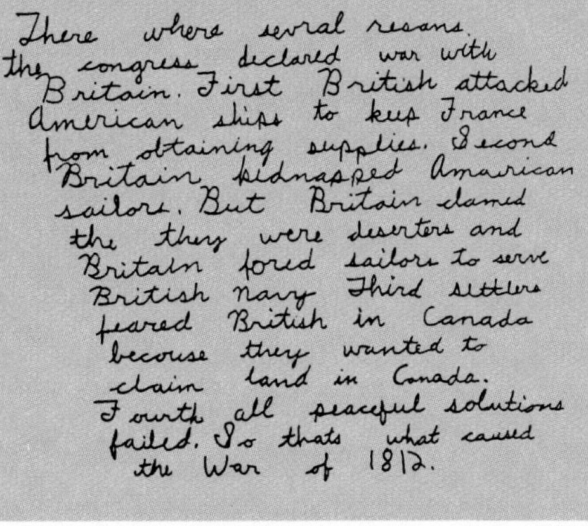

There were several reasons that Congress declared war with Britain. First, the British attacked American ships to keep France from obtaining supplies. Second, Britain kidnapped American sailors. But Britain claimed that there were deserters, and Britain forced sailors to serve the British Navy. Third, settlers feared the British in Canada because they wanted to claim land in Canada. Fourth, all peaceful solutions failed. So that's what caused the War of 1812.

FIGURE 11.3

Fine motor coordination improves over middle childhood, as these writing samples reveal.
At age 5, Ted printed in large, uppercase letters, asking for help in spelling the words. By age 7, he had mastered the lowercase alphabet, and his printing was small and evenly spaced. At age 9, he used cursive writing. Notice, also, how letter reversals and invented spellings decline with age. *(Ted's picture with label and space trip story from L. M. McGee & D. J. Richgels, 1990,* Literacy's Beginnings, *Boston: Allyn and Bacon, p. 312. Reprinted by permission of the authors. Ted's War of 1812 essay from D. J. Richgels, L. M. McGee, & E. A. Slaton, 1989, "Teaching Expository Text Structure in Reading and Writing," in K. D. Muth, Ed.,* Children's Comprehension of Text, *Newark, DE: International Reading Association, p. 180. Reprinted by permission.)*

tive to perceptual distinctions between mirror image forms (see Chapter 8). These improvements prepare children for mastering cursive writing by third grade.

Children's drawings show dramatic gains in organization, detail, and representation of depth during middle childhood. By the end of the preschool years, children can accurately copy many two-dimensional shapes, and they integrate these into their drawings. Some depth cues have also begun to appear, such as making distant objects smaller than near ones (Braine et al., 1993). Yet before age 9 or 10, most children have difficulty copying a three-dimensional form, such as a cube or cylinder. Around this time, the third dimension becomes clearly evident in children's drawings. Older school-age youngsters master *linear perspective,* Western culture's system for creating the illusion of depth on a two-dimensional surface (Winner, 1986).

At first, children's efforts at three-dimensional drawing contain predictable errors. In one study, 5- to 17-year-olds were seated in front of a table with objects on it and asked to draw what they saw. As you can see in Figure 11.4, the youngest children used horizontal and vertical arrangements of objects to depict depth. They drew the table as a straight line or surface with the objects sitting on and floating above it. By age 7 to 8, children used a front–behind arrangement. Around age 9 to 10, overlapping objects were drawn in diagonal relationship to one another. In addition, the tabletop was depicted as a rectangle or parallelogram. Not until adolescence did drawings accurately conform to the rules of perspective, with the sides of the table top represented as converging lines (Willats, 1977).

All children do not follow precisely the same sequence in mastering representation of the third dimension (Nicholls & Kennedy, 1992). Furthermore, use of depth cues appears more advanced when children are asked to put stickers of objects on paper, a less demanding task than drawing. Under these conditions, diagonal place-

FIGURE 11.4

Children ranging in age from 5 to 17 were asked to draw a table with objects on it.
Five- to 6-year-olds used horizontal and vertical arrangements of objects to depict depth; 7- to 8-year-olds used a front–behind organization. Around age 9 to 10, overlapping objects appeared in diagonal relationship to one another, but the tabletop was drawn as a rectangle or parallelogram. Not until adolescence did drawings accurately conform to the rules of linear perspective, with the sides of the tabletop represented as converging lines. *(From J. Willats, 1977, "How Children Learn to Represent Three-Dimensional Space in Drawings," in G. Butterworth, Ed.,* The Child's Representation of the World, *New York: Plenum, pp. 192–195. Reprinted by permission.)*

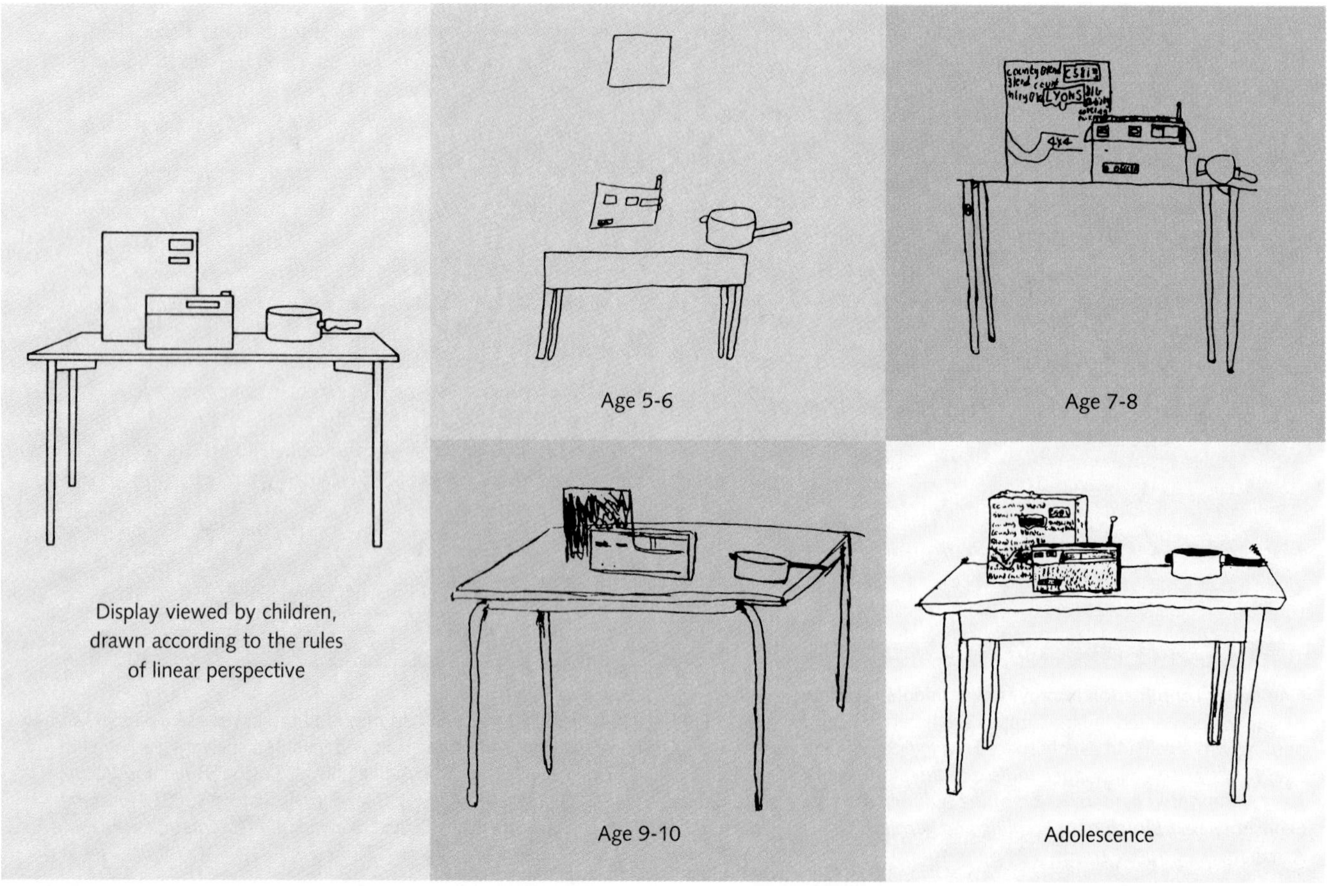

ment is common among first graders (Braine et al., 1993). Over the school years, children gradually solve the problem of how to include the third dimension in their artistic creations.

INDIVIDUAL AND GROUP DIFFERENCES IN MOTOR DEVELOPMENT

As was the case at younger ages, school-age children show marked individual differences in motor capacities that are influenced by both heredity and environment. Body build continues to affect gross motor performance, with the taller, more muscular child excelling on many tasks. At the same time, parents who encourage physical exercise tend to have youngsters who enjoy it more and who are also more skilled. Social class affects children's opportunities to develop a variety of physical abilities. Economically advantaged children are far more likely to have ballet, tennis, gymnastics, and music lessons than youngsters from low-income families.

Sex differences in motor skills that began to appear during the preschool years extend into middle childhood and, in some instances, become more pronounced. Girls remain ahead in the fine motor area, including handwriting and drawing. They also continue to have an edge in gross motor skills that depend on balance and precision of movement, such as skipping, jumping, and hopping. But on all other skills listed in Table 11.2, boys outperform girls, and in the case of throwing and kicking, the difference is large (Cratty, 1986; Roberton, 1984; Thomas & French, 1985).

School-age boys' genetic advantage in muscle mass is not great enough to account for their superiority in so many gross motor skills. Instead, environment plays a much larger role. Although women's participation in athletics has increased since the 1970s, it does not equal that of men (Coakley, 1990). Lizzie, for example, saw her father read magazines and watch TV programs about sports far more often than her mother. In addition, most participants in public sports events are men. Although Lizzie was encouraged to play in the city soccer league, both parents believed that Joey was better at athletics and that it was more critical for his development that he do well at sports.

A recent study of over 800 elementary school pupils found that parents hold higher expectations for boys' athletic performance, and children absorb these social messages at an early age. Kindergartners through third graders of both sexes viewed sports in a gender-stereotyped fashion—as much more important for boys. Boys were also more likely to indicate that it was important to their parents that they participate in athletics. These attitudes affected children's physical self-images as well as behavior. Girls saw themselves as having less talent at sports, and by sixth grade they devoted less time to athletics than did their male classmates (Eccles & Harold, 1991; Eccles, Jacobs, & Harold, 1990).

These findings indicate that special measures need to be taken to raise girls' confidence that they can do well at sports. Educating parents about the minimal differences in school-age boys' and girls' physical capacities and sensitizing them to unfair biases against girls' athletic ability may prove helpful. In addition, greater emphasis on skill training for girls along with increased attention to their athletic achievements in schools and communities is likely to improve their performance. Middle childhood may be a crucial time to take these steps, since during the school years children start to discover what they are good at and make some definite skill commitments.

ORGANIZED GAMES WITH RULES

The physical activities of school-age children reflect an important advance in the quality of their play: Organized games with rules become common in middle childhood. In cultures around the world, the variety of children's spontaneous rule-based games is enormous. Some are variants on popular sports, such as soccer, baseball, basketball, and football. Others are well-known childhood games, such as tag, jacks, and hopscotch. Children have also invented hundreds of less well-known games and passed them from one generation to the next. Observing the spontaneous play of children in England and Israel, researchers identified over 2,000 games in each country. You may remember some from your own childhood, such as red rover, statues, blind man's Buff, leapfrog, one-o-cat, kick the can, and prisoner's base (Eifermann, 1971; Opie & Opie, 1969).

Gains in perspective taking—in particular, children's ability to understand the roles of several players in a game—permit this transition to rule-oriented games. The contribution of these play experiences to development is great. Child-invented games usually rely on simple physical skills and a sizable element of luck. As a result, they rarely become contests of individual ability. Instead, they permit children to try out different styles of competing, winning, and losing with little personal risk. Also, in their efforts to organize a game, children discover why rules are necessary and which ones work well. Without rules that are fair and that keep things interesting for all participants, the game is likely to break apart. In fact, children often spend as much time working out the details of how a game should proceed as they do playing the game itself (Devereux, 1976). As we will see in Chapter 13, these experiences help children form more mature concepts of fairness and justice.

Because of their value for children's development, some researchers are concerned about the recent decline in child-organized games. Today, school-age youngsters spend less time gathering on sidewalks and playgrounds than they did in generations past. Children's attraction to television and video games accounts for some of this change. But adult-organized sports, such as Little League baseball and city soccer and hockey leagues, also fill many hours that children used to devote to spontaneous play. Are adult-structured athletics that mirror professional sports robbing children of critical learning experiences and endangering their development? For a look at this controversial issue, turn to the Social Issues box on the following page.

SHADOWS OF OUR EVOLUTIONARY PAST

Besides a new level of structure and organization, some additional qualities of physical play become common in middle childhood. While watching children at your city park, notice how they occasionally wrestle, roll, hit, and run after one another while smiling and laughing. This friendly chasing and play-fighting is called **rough-and-tumble play.** Research indicates that it is a good-natured, sociable activity that is quite distinct from aggressive fighting. Children in many cultures engage in it with peers whom they like especially well, and they continue interacting after a rough-and-tumble episode rather than separating, as they do at the end of an aggressive encounter. Sometimes parents and teachers mistake rough-and-tumble for real fighting and try to intervene. In these instances, children often respond, "It's all right, we're only playing!" School-age youngsters are quite good at telling the difference between playful wrestling and a true aggressive attack (Costabile et al., 1991; Smith & Boulton, 1990). Only those who have poor relations with peers sometimes confuse rough-and-tumble with hostility (Pellegrini, 1988).

Children's rough-and-tumble play is similar to the social behavior of young mammals of many species. Does it have some adaptive value? By age 11, children choose rough-and-tumble partners who are not only likable but similar in strength to themselves. In our evolutionary past, this form of interaction may have been important for the development of fighting skill (Humphreys & Smith, 1987). Rough-and-tumble play occurs more often among boys, but girls also display it. Girls' rough-and-tumble largely consists of running and chasing, whereas boys engage in more playful wrestling and hitting (Blurton Jones, 1972).

Rough-and-tumble play
A form of peer interaction involving friendly chasing and play-fighting that, in our evolutionary past, may have been important for the development of fighting skill.

SOCIAL ISSUES

ARE ADULT-ORGANIZED SPORTS GOOD FOR CHILDREN?

The last several decades have witnessed a tremendous expansion of adult-organized sports for children. Today, youth programs in baseball, football, basketball, soccer, and hockey exist in many American cities. Across the United States, there are nearly 50,000 Little League Baseball teams, with half a million players. The number of children involved in soccer has risen 15-fold since 1975 and now exceeds 1.5 million (Kolata, 1992). Perhaps you participated in one of these sports during your own childhood. If so, what were your experiences like?

Adult-organized athletics for children have both critics and supporters. Critics make the following points:

- When adults become involved in children's games, their focus becomes overly competitive—less on the process of playing and more on the product of winning. Children feel too much pressure from coaches and parents, who become overly critical when players make errors.
- In adult-organized sports, children learn little about leadership, decision making, and fair play because adults control the game.
- Assigning children to specific roles (for example, catcher, first base, or outfield) inhibits the experimentation and creativity common in child-organized games.
- Highly structured, competitive sports are less fun; they resemble "work" more than "play."

Supporters argue this way:

- Adult-structured athletics teaches children how to accept authority and prepares them for realistic competition—the kind they will one day face as adults.
- Regularly scheduled practices and games ensure that children get plenty of exercise. They also fill free time that might otherwise be devoted to less constructive pursuits, such as watching television or hanging out.
- Children get instruction in physical skills necessary for future success in athletics.
- Adult-controlled sports enable parents and children to share an activity that both enjoy.

Are these Little League coaches careful to encourage rather than criticize? To what extent do they emphasize teamwork, fair play, courtesy, and skill development over winning? These factors determine whether adult-organized sports are pleasurable, constructive experiences for children. *(Bob Daemmrich/Stock Boston)*

At present, the debate about the value of adult-organized sports is unresolved. Reviewing available research, one investigator concluded that there is little evidence that children's athletic leagues result in long-term psychological benefits or damage. Interviews with over fifty Little League Baseball players and a sampling of their parents revealed that most were satisfied with their experiences, even when they were associated with losing teams (Fine, 1987). But the arguments of critics are valid in some cases. Children who join teams so early that the skills demanded are beyond their current capabilities soon lose interest and want to drop out. And when parents and coaches criticize rather than encourage and do not let players who have lost a game forget about defeat, a few children react to competitive sports with intense anxiety. Eventually, these youngsters may avoid athletics entirely (Horn, 1987; Kolata, 1992).

TRY THIS . . .

- Observe a baseball, soccer, or other adult-organized sports event in your community, and take notes on the behavior of parents, coaches, and players during the game. How much pressure is placed on children to win? Do children seem to be enjoying the game?

Rough-and-tumble play can be distinguished from aggression by its good-natured quality. In our evolutionary past, it may have been important for the development of fighting skills. *(Nancy Sheehan/ The Picture Cube)*

Rough-and-tumble tends to occur among children who are alike in physical capacity, but as we have seen, children of the same age vary greatly in size and strength. When children gather in groups for physical activity, social structures emerge on the basis of toughness and assertiveness. A **dominance hierarchy** is a stable ordering of individuals that predicts who will win when conflict arises between group members. Dominance hierarchies exist in the social organization of many animal species, and they are a basic feature of human group interaction as well. Observations of arguments, threats, and physical attacks between children reveal a consistent lineup of winners and losers as early as the preschool years. This hierarchy becomes increasingly stable during middle childhood and adolescence, especially among boys (Pettit et al., 1990; Savin-Williams, 1979).

Like dominance relations among animals, those among human children serve the adaptive function of limiting aggression among group members. Once a dominance hierarchy is clearly established, hostility is rare. When it occurs, it is very restrained, often taking the form of playful verbal insults that can be accepted cheerfully by a partner (Fine, 1980). For example, Joey rarely challenges Sean, a child much larger than he, on the playground. But when he is unhappy about how things are going in a game, Joey is likely to tumble over humorously on the grass while saying something like "Hey, Sean, you've been up at bat so long you'll fall over dead if you swing at one more ball! Come on, give one of us a chance." This gradual replacement of direct hostility with friendly insults provides school-age children with an effective means of influencing their physically more powerful peers.

PHYSICAL EDUCATION

In the preceding sections, we have seen that physical activity supports many aspects of children's development—the health of their bodies, their sense of self-worth as physically active and capable beings, and the cognitive and social skills necessary for getting along well with others. Physical education classes that provide regularly scheduled opportunities for exercise and play help ensure that all children have access to these benefits.

Yet physical education is not taught often enough in American schools. Only one-third of elementary school pupils have a daily physical education class; the average school-age child gets only 20 minutes of physical education a week (Steinhardt, 1992). This means that children get most of their exercise outside of school. But on their own, American children often do not engage in enough vigorous physical activity. The growing fitness movement among adults has not yet filtered down to children, many of whom ride to and from school in buses and cars, sit in classrooms most of the day, and watch TV for 3 to 4 hours after they arrive home. The National Children and Youth Fitness Study, which tested thousands of schoolchildren on a variety of fitness items (such as pull-ups, sit-ups, and one-mile run), revealed that only two-thirds of 10- to 12-year-old boys and about half of 10- to 12-year-old girls met basic fitness standards for children their age (Looney & Plowman, 1990).

These findings indicate that American schools need to do a better job of providing physical education. Besides offering more frequent classes, many experts believe that schools should change the content of physical education programs. Training in competitive sports is often a high priority, but it is unlikely to reach the least physically fit youngsters, who draw back when an activity demands a high level of skill. Instead, programs should emphasize informal games that most children can perform well and individual exercise—walking, running, jumping, tumbling, and climbing. These athletic pursuits are also the ones most likely to last into later years.

Physical fitness builds on itself. Children who are in good physical condition have more energy, and they take great pleasure in their rapidly developing motor

Dominance heirarchy
A stable ordering of group members that predicts who will win under conditions of conflict..

skills and ability to control their own bodies. As a result, they seek out these activities in the future, developing rewarding interests in physical exercise that pave the way toward a lifelong commitment to an active and healthy lifestyle.

SUMMARY

BODY GROWTH IN MIDDLE CHILDHOOD

Describe changes in body size, proportions, and skeletal maturity during middle childhood.

- Gains in body size during middle childhood extend the pattern of growth established during the preschool period. On the average, children add about 5 pounds in weight and 2 to 3 inches in height each year. Growth is not steady; children show slight spurts in height followed by lulls over the school years. By age 9, girls overtake boys in physical size.
- Large individual differences in body growth exist, which are especially evident when children in different parts of the world are compared. **Secular trends in physical growth** have occurred in industrialized nations. Because of improved health and nutrition, many children are growing larger and reaching physical maturity earlier than their ancestors.
- During the middle childhood, bones continue to lengthen and broaden, and all 20 primary teeth are replaced by permanent ones. About one third of school-age children suffer from **malocclusion,** a condition in which the upper and lower teeth do not meet properly. Braces are common by the end of elementary school.

Describe brain development in middle childhood.

- Only a small increase in brain size occurs during middle childhood. Myelinization and lateralization of the cerebral hemispheres continue. Brain development during the school years is believed to involve **neurotransmitter** and hormonal influences.

COMMON HEALTH PROBLEMS IN MIDDLE CHILDHOOD

What vision and hearing problems are common during middle childhood?

- During middle childhood, children from advantaged homes are at their healthiest, due to the cumulative effects of good nutrition combined with rapid development of the body's immune system. At the same time, a variety of health problems do occur, many of which are more common among low-income children.
- The most common vision problem in middle childhood is **myopia,** or nearsightedness. It is influenced by heredity as well as the way children use their eyes. Myopia is one of the few health conditions that increases with family education and income. Because of untreated ear infections, many low-income children experience some hearing loss during the school years.

Describe the causes and consequences of serious nutritional problems in middle childhood, granting special attention to obesity.

- Poverty-stricken children in developing countries and in the United States continue to suffer from malnutrition during middle childhood. When malnutrition is allowed to persist for many years, its negative impact on physical growth, intellectual development, and motor performance is permanent.
- Overweight and **obesity** are growing problems in affluent nations such as the United States. Although heredity contributes to obesity, parental feeding practices, maladaptive eating habits, and lack of exercise also play important roles. Obese children are often rejected by their classmates and display serious adjustment and behavior problems. Family-based interventions in which both parents and children revise eating patterns, engage in regular daily exercise, and reinforce one another's progress are the most effective approaches to treating childhood obesity.

What factors contribute to the Type A behavior pattern, nocturnal enuresis, and asthma, and how can these health problems be reduced?

- Signs of the **Type A personality**—competitiveness, impatience, irritation, and anger—begin to emerge in some children by early and middle childhood. An intense, determined temperamental style probably contributes to Type A behavior. However, Type A traits do not become stable until adolescence. Parenting practices may lead the behavior pattern to continue in some children but not in others.
- **Nocturnal enuresis,** or bedwetting during the night, affects 8 percent of American school-age children. In the majority of cases, it has biological roots. The most effective treatment is a urine alarm that works according to conditioning principles.

- The most common cause of school absence and childhood hospitalization is **asthma.** It occurs more often among African-American and poverty-stricken children, perhaps because of pollution, stressful home lives, and lack of access to good health care. Children with severe chronic illnesses are at risk for academic, emotional, and social difficulties and benefit from a variety of interventions.

Describe changes in unintentional injuries during middle childhood.

- The rate of unintentional injuries increases over middle childhood and adolescence. Auto and bicycle collisions account for most of the rise. Safety education and incentives for following safety rules are especially important during the school years.

HEALTH EDUCATION IN MIDDLE CHILDHOOD

What can parents and teachers do to encourage good health practices in school-age children?

- School-age children can successfully acquire a wide range of health-related information, but it seldom changes their health-related behavior. Besides educating children about good health, adults need to reduce health hazards in children's environments and model and reinforce good health practices.

MOTOR DEVELOPMENT AND PLAY IN MIDDLE CHILDHOOD

Cite major changes in gross and fine motor development during early childhood.

- Gradual increases in body size and muscle strength support the refinement of many gross motor capacities in middle childhood. Gains in flexibility, balance, agility, and force occur. In addition, improvements in reaction time contribute to the athletic performance of school-age children.
- Fine motor development also improves during the school years. Children's writing becomes more legible, and their drawings show dramatic increases in organization, detail, and representation of depth.

Describe individual and group differences in motor performance during middle childhood.

- Children show wide individual differences in motor capacities that are influenced by both genetic and environmental factors. Body build, parental encouragement, and opportunities to take lessons support a variety of physical abilities. Gender stereotypes, which affect parental expectations for children's athletic performance, largely account for boys' superiority on a wide range of gross motor skills in middle childhood.

What qualities of children's play are evident in middle childhood?

- Organized games with rules become common during the school years. Children's spontaneous games support many aspects of development. Some features of children's physical activity reflect our evolutionary past. **Rough-and-tumble play** may have at one time been important for the development of fighting skill. **Dominance hierarchies** become increasingly stable in middle childhood and serve the adaptive function of limiting aggression among group members.

Why is high-quality physical education important during the school years?

- Physical education classes help ensure that all children have access to the benefits of regular exercise and play. Yet physical education does not take place often enough in American schools. Many school-age youngsters do not meet basic physical fitness standards for children their age. Both the quantity and quality of physical education needs to be improved.

IMPORTANT TERMS AND CONCEPTS

secular trends in physical growth (p. 397)
malocclusion (p. 398)
neurotransmitters (p. 399)
myopia (p. 400)
obesity (p. 401)
Type A personality (p. 403)
nocturnal enuresis (p. 404)
asthma (p. 405)
rough-and-tumble play (p. 414)
dominance hierarchy (p. 416)

FYI...

FOR FURTHER INFORMATION AND SPECIAL HELP, CONSULT THE FOLLOWING ORGANIZATIONS:

CHRONIC ILLNESS IN CHILDHOOD

Asthma and Allergy Foundation of America
1125 15th Street, N.W., Suite 502
Washington, DC 20005
(202) 466-7643

Devoted to solving health problems posed by allergic diseases, including asthma. Supports research and medical training and provides information to health professionals and the public.

Candlelighters Childhood Cancer Foundation
1312 18th Street N.W., Suite 200
Washington, DC 20036
(301) 657-8401

Increases public awareness of childhood cancer and provides information, guidance, and emotional support to parents with affected children. Has a crisis hot line, (800) 366-2223.

Cystic Fibrosis Foundation
6931 Arlington Road, No. 200
Bethesda, MD 20814
(301) 951-4422

Supports research, education, and care centers to benefit children and young adults with cystic fibrosis.

Ryan White National Fund
c/o Athletes and Entertainers for Kids
P.O. Box 191 Building B
Gardena, CA 90248-0191

Consists of corporations and individuals concerned about children with catastrophic illnesses, particularly AIDS. Provides assistance to children and families, including medical care and counseling. Operates Kids 'n AIDS National Program, which offers AIDS education in schools.

ADULT-ORGANIZED SPORTS FOR CHILDREN

Little League Baseball
P.O. Box 3485
Williamsport, PA 17701
(717) 326-1921

Organizes baseball and softball programs for children 6 to 18 years of age. Operates a special division for children with disabilities and sponsors an annual world series.

Soccer Association for Youth
4903 Vine Street
Cincinnati, OH 45217
(513) 242-4263

Supports soccer programs for children between 6 to 18 years of age throughout the United States. Seeks to encourage widespread participation and offer equal opportunity regardless of ability or sex. Distributes supplies and support necessary to form teams.

"Going to school"
He Si Nuo
5 years, China

Standing on the threshold of the school years, this artist seems to be wondering: What will school life bring? The bright red sun suggests new joys. The perspiration rolling off the biker's brow suggests new challenges. The tiny creature tagging along behind displays the eager, confident attitude that supports mastery of increasingly complex cognitive tasks, described in Chapter 12.

12

Cognitive Development in Middle Childhood

PIAGET'S THEORY: THE CONCRETE OPERATIONAL STAGE

Conservation • Classification • Seriation • Spatial Reasoning • Limitations of Concrete Operational Thought • Recent Research on Concrete Operational Thought • Evaluation of the Concrete Operational Stage

INFORMATION PROCESSING IN MIDDLE CHILDHOOD

Attention • Memory Strategies • The Knowledge Base and Memory Performance • Culture and Memory Strategies • The School-Age Child's Theory of Mind • Self-Regulation • Applications of Information Processing to Academic Learning

INDIVIDUAL DIFFERENCES IN MENTAL DEVELOPMENT DURING MIDDLE CHILDHOOD

Defining and Measuring Intelligence • Explaining Individual and Group Differences in IQ • Overcoming Cultural Bias in Intelligence Tests

LANGUAGE DEVELOPMENT IN MIDDLE CHILDHOOD

Vocabulary • Grammar • Pragmatics • Learning Two Languages at a Time

CHILDREN'S LEARNING IN SCHOOL

The Educational Philosophy • Teacher–Pupil Interaction • Computers in the Classroom • Teaching Children with Special Needs

HOW WELL EDUCATED ARE AMERICA'S CHILDREN?

"Finally!" Lizzie exclaimed the day she entered first grade. "Now I get to go to *real* school just like Joey!" Rena remembered how 6-year-old Lizzie had walked confidently into her classroom, pencils, crayons, and writing pad in hand, ready for a more disciplined approach to learning than she had experienced in early childhood. As a preschooler, Lizzie had loved playing school, giving assignments as the "teacher" and pretending to read and write as the "pupil." Now she was there in earnest, eager to master the tasks that had sparked her imagination as a 4- and 5-year-old.

Lizzie entered a whole new world of challenging mental activities. In a single morning, she and her classmates wrote in journals, met in reading groups, worked on addition and subtraction, and sorted leaves gathered on the playground for a special science project. As Lizzie and Joey moved through the elementary school grades, they tackled increasingly complex tasks and gradually became more accomplished at reading, writing, math skills, and general knowledge of the world.

Cognitive development had prepared Joey and Lizzie for this new phase. We begin this chapter by returning to Piaget's theory and the information-processing approach. Together, they provide us with an overview of cognitive change during the school years. Then we take an in-depth look at individual differences in mental development. We examine the genetic and environment roots of IQ scores, which often enter into important educational decisions. Next our attention turns to language. Vocabulary, grammar, and communication skills continue to blossom during middle childhood, even though changes are less dramatic than they were during the preschool years. Finally, we consider the importance of schools in children's learning and development.

PIAGET'S THEORY: THE CONCRETE OPERATIONAL STAGE

As a preschooler, Lizzie had once visited my child development class, where we watched her do several of Piaget's conservation problems (see Chapter 9, page 320). At age 4, Lizzie was easily confused by them. She was sure that after a row of six pennies had been placed in a pile, there were fewer of them. And when asked if the amount of water was still the same after it had been poured into a short, wide container, she insisted that it was not.

At age 8, when Lizzie returned to my class for a second session, these problems were easy. "Of course it's the same," she said after the water had been poured in conservation of liquid, somewhat annoyed by this obvious question. "The water's shorter but it's also wider. Pour it back," she instructed the college student who was interviewing her. "You'll see, it's the same amount!" Lizzie's response indicates that she has entered Piaget's **concrete operational stage,** which spans the years from 7 to 11. During this period, thought is far more logical, flexible, and organized than it was during the preschool period. The older child is better at distinguishing fantasy from reality and reasons correctly about many changes in objects and events in the everyday world. The Concept Review Table on the following page summarizes major characteristics of this stage, evident in the school-age child's performance on a wide variety of Piagetian tasks.

CONSERVATION

Piaget regarded *conservation* as the single most important achievement of the concrete operational stage. It provides clear evidence of *operations*—mental actions that obey logical rules. Notice how Lizzie coordinates several aspects of the task rather than *centering* on only one, as a preschooler would do. In other words, Lizzie is capable of **decentration;** she recognizes that a change in one aspect of the water (its height) is compensated for by a change in another aspect (its width). Lizzie also demonstrates **reversibility,** the capacity to mentally go through a series of steps in a problem and then reverse direction, returning to the starting point. Recall from Chapter 9 that reversibility is part of every logical operation. It is solidly achieved in middle childhood.

CLASSIFICATION

Operational thought permits school-age children to categorize more effectively. By the end of middle childhood, they pass Piaget's *class inclusion problem* (see page 321). They can group objects into hierarchies of classes and subclasses more effectively than they could at earlier ages (Achenbach & Weisz, 1975; Hodges & French, 1988). You can see this in children's play activities. Collections of all kinds of objects—stamps, coins, baseball cards, rocks, bottle caps, and more—become common in middle childhood. At age 10, Joey spent hours sorting and resorting his large box of baseball cards. At times he grouped them by league and team membership, at other times by playing position and batting average. He could separate the players into a variety of classes and subclasses and flexibly move back and forth between them. This understanding is beyond the grasp of preschoolers, who usually insist that a set of objects can be sorted in only one way.

Concrete operational stage
Piaget's third stage, during which thought is logical, flexible, and organized in its application to concrete information. However, the capacity for abstract thinking is not yet present. Spans the years from 7 to 11.

Decentration
The ability to focus on several aspects of problem at once and relate them.

Reversibility
The ability to mentally go through a series of steps in a problem and then reverse direction, returning to the starting point.

CONCEPT REVIEW TABLE

Major Characteristics of the Concrete Operational Stage

CONCEPT	IMPORTANT POINT	EXAMPLE
Conservation	Concrete operational children recognize that certain physical characteristics of objects remain the same even when their outward appearance changes.	After spilling 10 pennies stacked on her desk all over the floor, Lizzie bent down to search for them. "I know there have to be 10," she said to herself, "because that's how many I put in that little pile on my desk yesterday."
Decentration	Concrete operational children coordinate several important features of a task rather than centering only on the perceptually dominant one.	After getting two glasses of lemonade from the kitchen, one for Joey and one for herself, Lizzie remarked, "Don't worry, I gave you just as much. My glass is tall but thin. Yours is short but wide."
Reversibility	Concrete operational children can think through the steps in a problem and then go backward, returning to the starting point.	Lizzie understands that addition and subtraction are reversible operations. In other words, when you add 7 plus 8 to get 15, then this tells you that 15 minus 8 must be 7.
Hierarchical classification	Concrete operational children can flexibly group and regroup objects into hierarchies of classes and subclasses.	Lizzie discussed how to display her rock collection with her friend Marina. Marina suggested, "You could divide them up by size and then by color. Or you could use shape and color."
Seriation	Concrete operational children are guided by an overall plan when arranging items in a series.	Lizzie decided to arrange her rocks by size. She quickly lined up all 20 rocks in a row, selecting the smallest and then the next smallest from the pile, until the arrangement was complete.
Transitive inference	Concrete operational children can seriate mentally. After comparing A with B and B with C, they can infer the relationship between A and C.	"I saw Tina's new lunch box, and it's bigger than mine," Marina said while eating her sandwich with Lizzie one day. "Well, it must be bigger than mine, too, because look—my box isn't even as big as yours," said Lizzie.
Spatial reasoning	Concrete operational children conserve distance; understand the relations among distance, time, and speed; and can give clear, well-organized directions for how to get from one place to another.	Lizzie realizes that a truck blocking the sidewalk does not change the distance to the end of her street. She also knows that if she runs faster than Marina for the same amount of time, she will travel farther. And she can give clear directions for how to get from her own house to Marina's.
Horizontal décalage	Logical concepts are mastered gradually over the course of middle childhood.	Lizzie understood conservation of number and liquid before she mastered conservation of area and weight.

An improved ability to categorize underlies children's interest in collecting objects during middle childhood. This boy enjoys sorting his rock collection into an elaborate structure of classes and subclasses. *(Blair Seitz/ Photo Researchers)*

SERIATION

Seriation refers to the ability to order items along a quantitative dimension, such as length or weight. To test for it, Piaget asked children to arrange sticks of different lengths from shortest to longest. Older preschoolers can create the series, but they do so haphazardly. They put the sticks in a row but make many errors and take a long time to correct them. In contrast, 6- to 7-year-olds are guided by an orderly plan. They create the series efficiently by beginning with the smallest stick, then moving to the next smallest, and so on, until the ordering is complete.

The concrete operational child's improved grasp of quantitative arrangements is also evident in a more challenging seriation problem—one that requires children to seriate mentally. This ability is called **transitive inference.** In a well-known transitive inference problem, Piaget showed children pairings of differently colored sticks. From observing that stick A is longer than stick B and stick B is longer than stick C, children must make the mental inference that A is longer than C. Not until age 9 or 10 do children perform well on this task (Chapman & Lindenberger, 1988; Piaget, 1967).

SPATIAL REASONING

Piaget found that school-age youngsters have a more accurate understanding of space than they did during early childhood. For example, their comprehension of distance improves, as a special conservation task reveals. To give this problem, make two small trees out of modeling clay and place them apart on a table. Next, put a block or thick piece of cardboard between the trees. Then ask the child whether the trees are nearer together, farther apart, or still the same distance apart. Preschoolers say that the distance has become smaller. They do not understand that a filled-up space has the same value as an empty space (Piaget, Inhelder, & Szeminska, 1948/1960). By the early school years, children grasp this idea easily. Although 4-year-olds can conserve distance when questioned about objects that are very familiar to them, their understanding is not as solid and complete as that of the school-age child (Miller & Baillargeon, 1990).

According to Piaget (1946/1970), concrete operational thinking permits children to combine distance with other physical concepts, such as time and speed. He reported that children first master the positive relationships between speed and distance (the faster you travel, the farther you go) and time and distance (the longer you travel, the farther you go). Only later do they grasp the negative relationship between speed and time (the faster you travel, the less time it takes to get to your destination). More recent research confirms that children grasp these associations in the order predicted by Piaget between first and third grade (Acredolo, Adams, & Schmid, 1984).

School-age children's more advanced understanding of space can also be seen in their ability to give directions. Stand facing a 5- or 6-year-old, and ask the child to name an object on your left and one on your right. Children of this age answer incorrectly; they apply their own frame of reference to that of others. Between 7 and 8 years, children start to perform *mental rotations,* in which they align the self's frame to match that of a person in a different orientation. As a result, they can identify left and right for positions they do not occupy (Roberts & Aman, 1993). Around 8 to 10 years, children can give clear, well-organized directions for how to get from one place to another. Aided by their capacity for operational thinking, they use a "mental walk" strategy in which they imagine another person's movements along a route (Gauvain & Rogoff, 1989b). Six-year-olds give more organized directions after they walk the route themselves or are specially prompted. Otherwise, they focus on the end point without describing exactly how to get there (Plumert et al., 1994).

Seriation
The ability to order items along a quantitative dimension, such as length or weight.

Transitive inference
The ability to seriate—or order items along a quantitative dimension—mentally.

LIMITATIONS OF CONCRETE OPERATIONAL THOUGHT

Because of their improved ability to conserve, classify, seriate, and deal with spatial concepts, school-age children are far more capable problem solvers than they were during the preschool years. But concrete operational thinking suffers from one important limitation. Children think in an organized, logical fashion only when dealing with concrete information they can directly perceive. Their mental operations work poorly when applied to abstract ideas—ones not apparent in the real world.

Children's solutions to transitive inference problems provide a good illustration. When shown pairs of sticks of unequal length, Lizzie easily figured out that if stick A is longer than stick B and stick B is longer than stick C, then stick A is longer than stick C. But when given an entirely hypothetical version of this task, such as "Susan is taller than Sally and Sally is taller than Mary. Who is the tallest?" she had great difficulty. Not until age 11 or 12 can children solve this problem easily.

The fact that logical thought is at first tied to immediate situations helps account for a special feature of concrete operational reasoning. Perhaps you have already noticed that school-age children do not master all of Piaget's concrete operational tasks at once. Instead, they do so in a step-by-step fashion. For example, they usually grasp conservation problems in a certain order: first number; then length, mass, and liquid; and finally area and weight (Brainerd, 1978). Piaget used the term **horizontal décalage** (meaning development within a stage) to describe this gradual mastery of logical concepts. The horizontal décalage is another indication of the concrete operational child's difficulty with abstractions. School-age children do not come up with the general principle of conservation and then apply it to all relevant situations. Rather, they seem to work out the logic of each problem they encounter separately.

RECENT RESEARCH ON CONCRETE OPERATIONAL THOUGHT

From researchers' attempts to verify Piaget's assumptions about concrete operations, two themes emerge. The first has to do with the impact of specific experiences on the attainment of the concrete operational stage. The second deals with how best to explain children's sequential mastery of logical problems during middle childhood. Some theorists believe that the horizontal décalage can best be understood within an information-processing framework.

THE IMPACT OF CULTURE AND SCHOOLING. According to Piaget, brain maturation combined with experience in a rich and varied external world should lead children everywhere to reach the concrete operational stage. He did not believe that operational thinking depended on particular kinds of experiences. Yet recent evidence indicates that specific cultural practices have a great deal to do with children's mastery of Piagetian tasks (Rogoff, 1990).

A large body of evidence shows that conservation is often delayed in non-Western societies. For example, among the Hausa of Nigeria, who live in small agricultural settlements and rarely send their children to school, even the most basic conservation tasks—number, length, and liquid—are not understood until age 11 or later (Fahrmeier, 1978). This suggests that for children to master conservation and other Piagetian concepts, they must take part in everyday activities that promote this way of thinking (Light & Perrett-Clermont, 1989). Joey and Lizzie, for example, have learned to think of fairness in terms of equal distribution—a value emphasized in their culture. They have frequent opportunities to divide materials, such as crayons, Halloween treats, and lemonade, equally among themselves and their

Horizontal décalage
Development within a Piagetian stage. Gradual mastery of logical concepts during the concrete operational stage is an example.

In non-Western societies, conservation is often delayed. The everyday activities of this Nigerian girl may not promote the kind of reasoning required to pass Piagetian conservation tasks. Compared to her Western counterparts, she probably has fewer opportunities to see the same quantity arranged in different ways. *(M. Bertinetti/Photo Researchers)*

friends. Because they often see the same quantity arranged in different ways, they grasp conservation early. For children who grow up in societies where equal sharing of goods is not common, conservation is unlikely to appear at the expected age.

The very experience of going to school seems to promote concrete operational reasoning. Research shows that when children of the same age are tested, those who have been in school longer do better on transitive inference problems. In fact, among 9- to 12-year-olds, the impact of schooling on transitive inference is much larger than the impact of age (Artman & Cahan, 1993). How might schooling affect transitive inference? The many opportunities it affords for seriating objects, learning about order relations, and remembering the parts of a complex problem are probably responsible.

These findings may remind you of a challenge to Piaget's theory we have mentioned several times before. Some investigators believe that the forms of logic required by Piagetian tasks do not emerge spontaneously in all children. Instead, they regard these concepts as socially generated—as outcomes of practical activities in particular cultures. This approach to cognitive development is much like Vygotsky's sociocultural theory, which we discussed in earlier chapters.

■ **AN INFORMATION-PROCESSING VIEW OF THE HORIZONTAL DÉCALAGE.** If you think carefully about the horizontal décalage, you will see that it too raises a familiar question about Piaget's theory: Is an abrupt stagewise transition to logical thought the best way to describe cognitive development in middle childhood? In Chapter 9, we showed that the beginnings of logical thinking are evident during the preschool years on simplified and familiar tasks. The horizontal décalage suggests that logical understanding continues to improve over the school years.

Some theorists argue that the development of operational thinking can best be understood in terms of gains in information-processing capacity rather than a sudden shift to a new stage. For example, Robbie Case (1985, 1992) proposes that as children repeatedly use cognitive schemes, they demand less attention and become more automatic. This frees up space in *working memory* (see page 222) so that children can focus on combining old schemes and generating new ones. For instance, the child confronted with water poured from one container to another recognizes that the height of the liquid changes. As this understanding becomes routine, the child notices that width of the water changes as well. Soon the child coordinates both these observations, and conservation of liquid is achieved. Then, as this logical idea becomes well practiced, the child transfers it to more demanding situations, such as area and weight. A similar explanation of the horizontal décalage has been suggested by Kurt Fischer (1980; Fischer & Farrar, 1987), who believes that eventually school-age youngsters coordinate several context-specific skills into a general logical principle. At this point, thinking is highly efficient and abstract—the kind of change we will see when we discuss formal operational thought in Chapter 15.

Is there evidence to support an information-processing view of gains in operational thought? If you think back to the various Piagetian tasks we have discussed, you will see that those passed at older ages require that a greater number of items be held in working memory and combined to reach a correct solution. Children's mastery of more advanced conservation problems is correlated with their memory spans (how many digits they can recall when given a list of numbers to learn). This finding is consistent with the idea that combining schemes in more complex problem solving is accompanied by an expansion of working memory with development (Case, 1985).

EVALUATION OF THE CONCRETE OPERATIONAL STAGE

Piaget was indeed correct that school-age youngsters approach a great many problems in systematic and rational ways that were not possible just a few years before. But whether it is best to regard this period in terms of *continuous* improvement in logical skills or *discontinuous* restructuring of children's thinking (as Piaget's stage idea assumes) is still an issue about which there is little agreement. A growing number of researchers think that both types of change may be involved (Carey, 1985; Case, 1992; Fischer, 1980; Sternberg & Odagaki, 1989). From early to middle childhood, children apply logical schemes to a much wider range of tasks. Yet in the process, their thought seems to undergo qualitative change—toward a more comprehensive grasp of the underlying principles of logical thought. Piaget himself seems to have recognized this possibility in the very concept of the horizontal décalage. So perhaps some blend of Piagetian and information-processing ideas holds greatest promise for understanding cognitive development in middle childhood. With this thought in mind, let's take a closer look at what the information-processing perspective has to say about changes in thinking during the school years.

BRIEF REVIEW

During the concrete operational stage, thought is more logical, flexible, and organized than it was during the preschool years. The ability to conserve indicates that children can decenter and reverse their thinking. School-age children also have an improved grasp of classification, seriation, and spatial concepts. However, they cannot yet think abstractly. Cross-cultural findings raise questions about Piaget's assumption that mastery of concrete operational tasks emerges spontaneously in all children. In addition, the gradual development of operational concepts challenges Piaget's notion of an abrupt stagewise transition to logical thought. A blend of Piagetian and information-processing views may be the best way to understand cognitive change in middle childhood.

ASK YOURSELF . . .

- Mastery of the conservation problems provides one illustration of Piaget's horizontal décalage. Review the preceding sections. Then list as many additional examples as you can find that operational reasoning develops gradually over middle childhood.
- Nine-year-old Adrienne spends many hours helping her father build furniture in his woodworking shop. Explain how this experience may have contributed to Adrienne's advanced performance on Piagetian seriation problems.

INFORMATION PROCESSING IN MIDDLE CHILDHOOD

In contrast to Piaget's theory, which focuses on overall changes in children's approach to solving problems and interpreting their world, the information-processing perspective examines separate aspects of thinking. Attention and memory, which underlie every act of cognition, are central concerns in middle childhood, just as they were during infancy and the preschool years. In addition, researchers have been interested in finding out how children's growing knowledge of the world and awareness of their own mental activities affect these basic components of thinking. Finally, increased understanding of how children process information is being applied to their academic learning in school—in particular, to reading and mathematics.

ATTENTION

During middle childhood, attention changes in three ways. It becomes more controlled, adaptable, and planful.

CONTROL. As Joey and Lizzie moved through the elementary school years, they became better at deliberately attending to just those aspects of a situation that were relevant to their task goals, ignoring other sources of information. Researchers study this increasing control of attention by introducing irrelevant stimuli into a task. Then they see how well children attend to its central elements (Lane & Pearson, 1982). In a typical experiment of this kind, school-age children and adults were asked to sort decks of cards as fast as possible on the basis of shapes appearing on each card—for example, circles in one pile and squares in another. Some decks contained no irrelevant information. Others included irrelevant stimuli, such as lines running across the shapes or stars appearing above or below them. Children's ability to ignore unnecessary information was determined by seeing how much longer it took them to sort decks with irrelevant stimuli. Their ability to keep attention focused on central features of the task improved sharply between 6 and 9 years of age (Strutt, Anderson, & Well, 1975).

ADAPTABILITY. Older children are also more adaptable; they flexibly adjust their attention to the momentary requirements of situations. For example, in judging whether pairs of stimuli are the same or different, sixth graders quickly shift their basis of judgment (from size to shape to color) when asked to do so. Second graders have trouble with this type of task (Pick & Frankel, 1974).

Older children also adapt their attention to changes in their own learning. For example, when studying for a spelling test, 10-year-old Joey devoted most attention to the words he knew least well. Lizzie was much less likely do so (Masur, McIntyre, & Flavell, 1973).

PLANFULNESS. School-age children's attentional strategies become more planful. As Figure 12.1 shows, they scan detailed pictures and written materials for similarities and differences more thoroughly than do preschoolers (Vurpillot, 1968). And on complex tasks, school-age children make decisions about what to do first and what to do next in an orderly fashion. In one study, 5- to 9-year-olds were given lists of 25 items to obtain from a play grocery store. Older children more often took time to scan the store before starting on a shopping trip, and they also followed shorter routes through the aisles (Gauvain & Rogoff, 1989a). Over time, children become better at planning before acting, and this foresight results in more efficient attention to different parts of a task.

Why does attention improve from early to middle childhood? Brain maturation is partly responsible. Research indicates that the capacity of the information-processing system expands over middle childhood, permitting individuals to hold onto more information at once and scan it more rapidly and systematically (Kail, 1991). In addition, the attentional strategies we have discussed are crucial for success in school, and the demands of school tasks undoubtedly contribute to their development. Unfortunately, some children have great difficulty paying attention during the school years. See the From Research to Practice box on page 430 for a discussion of the serious learning and behavior problems of children with attention-deficit hyperactivity disorder.

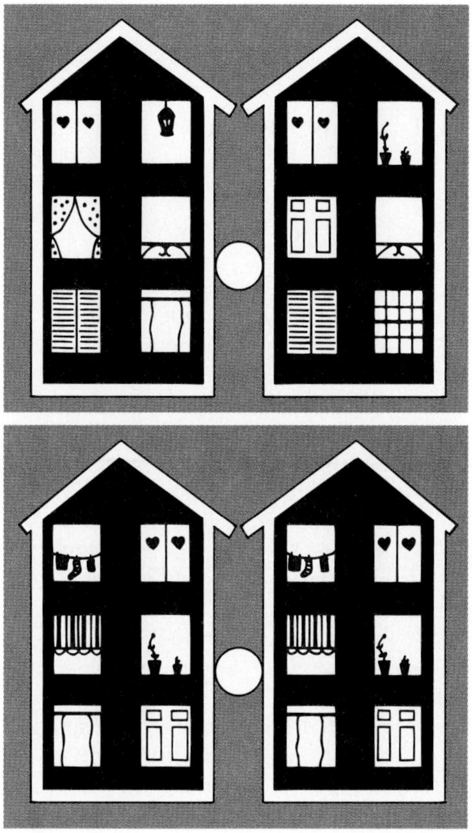

FIGURE 12.1

Pairs of houses children were asked to judge as the same or different. Preschoolers' eye movements showed that they did not examine all features systematically. As a result, they frequently judged different houses to be the same. In contrast, 6- to 9-year-olds used an exhaustive search strategy in which they compared the details of the houses window to window. *(From E. Vurpillot, 1968, "The Development of Scanning Strategies and Their Relation to Visual Differentiation,"* Journal of Experimental Child Psychology, *6, p. 634. Copyright © by Academic Press. Reprinted by permission.)*

MEMORY STRATEGIES

As attention improves with age, so do *memory strategies*, the deliberate mental activities we use to store and retain information (see the Concept Review Table on page 431). During the school years, these techniques for holding information in working memory and transferring it to our long-term knowledge base take a giant leap forward (Kail, 1990).

When Lizzie had a list of things to learn, such as a phone number, the capitals of the United States, or the names of geometric shapes, she immediately used **rehearsal,** repeating the information to herself over and over again. This memory strategy first appears in the early grade school years. Soon after, a second strategy becomes common: **organization.** Children group together related items (for example, all capitals in the same part of the country), an approach that improves recall dramatically (Bjorklund & Muir, 1988; Keeney, Canizzo, & Flavell, 1967).

Memory strategies require time and effort to perfect. At first, school-age children do not use them very effectively, and performance benefits are minimal. For example, 8-year-old Lizzie rehearsed in a piecemeal fashion. After being given the word *cat* in a list of items, she said, "Cat, cat, cat." In contrast, 10-year-old Joey combined previous words with each new item, saying, "Desk, man, yard, cat, cat" (Kunzinger, 1985; Ornstein, Naus, & Liberty, 1975). Joey also organized more skillfully, grouping items into fewer categories. In addition, he used organization in a wide range of memory tasks, whereas Lizzie used it only when categorical relations among items were very obvious. Not surprisingly, Joey retained much more information (Bjorklund et al., 1994). Experience with materials that form clear categories eventually helps younger children apply it to less related materials (Best, 1993).

Children start to use a third memory strategy, **elaboration,** by the end of middle childhood. It involves creating a relationship, or shared meaning, between two or more pieces of information that are not members of the same category. For example, suppose the words *fish* and *pipe* are among those you want to learn. If, in trying to remember them, you generate a mental image of a fish smoking a pipe or recite a sentence expressing this relationship ("The fish puffed the pipe"), you are using elaboration. Once children discover this memory technique, they find it so effective

Rehearsal
The memory strategy of repeating information.

Organization
The memory strategy of grouping together related items.

Elaboration
The memory strategy of creating a relation between two or more items that are not members of the same category.

FROM RESEARCH TO PRACTICE

CHILDREN WITH ATTENTION-DEFICIT HYPERACTIVITY DISORDER

While the other fifth graders worked quietly at their desks, Calvin squirmed in his seat, dropped his pencil, looked out the window, fiddled with his shoelaces, and talked out. "Hey Joey," he yelled over the top of several desks, "wanna play ball after school?" Joey didn't answer. He and the other children weren't eager to play with Calvin. Out on the playground, Calvin was a poor listener and failed to follow the rules of the game. When up at bat, he had difficulty taking turns. In the outfield, he tossed his mitt up in the air and looked elsewhere when the ball came his way. Calvin's desk at school and his room at home were a chaotic mess. He often lost pencils, books, and other materials necessary for completing assignments.

Calvin is one of 3 to 5 percent of school-age children with **attention-deficit hyperactivity disorder (ADHD)** (American Psychiatric Association, 1994). Although boys are diagnosed 5 to 10 times more often than girls, recent evidence suggests that just as many girls may suffer from the disorder. Girls are less likely to be identified because their symptoms are usually not as flagrant (Hynd et al., 1991).

Children with ADHD have great difficulty staying on task for more than a few minutes. In addition, they often act impulsively, ignoring social rules and lashing out with hostility when frustrated. Many (but not all) are *hyperactive.* They charge through their days with excessive motor activity, leaving parents and teachers frazzled and other children annoyed. ADHD youngsters have few friends; they are soundly rejected by their classmates (Henker & Whalen, 1989).

The intelligence of ADHD children is normal, and they show no signs of serious emotional disturbance. Instead, attentional difficulties are at the heart of their problems. They do poorly on laboratory tasks requiring sustained attention, and they find it hard to ignore irrelevant information (Douglas, 1983; Landau, Lorch, & Milich, 1992). Although some outgrow these difficulties, most ADHD youngsters continue to have problems concentrating and finding friends into adolescence and adulthood.

ADHD does not have one single cause. Heredity plays an important role, since the disorder runs in families, and identical twins share it more often than do fraternal twins. Also, an adopted child who is inattentive and hyperactive is likely to have a biological parent (but not an adoptive parent) with similar symptoms (Biederman et al., 1990).

At the same time, ADHD is associated with a variety of environmental factors. These children are somewhat more likely to come from homes in which marriages are unhappy and family stress is high (Bernier & Siegel, 1994). Also, recall from earlier chapters that prenatal teratogens as well as childhood lead exposure are linked to later attentional problems. Dietary causes, such as food additives and sugar, have been suggested, but there is little evidence that these play important roles (Hynd et al., 1991).

Calvin's doctor eventually prescribed stimulant medication, the most common treatment for ADHD. As long as dosage is carefully regulated, these drugs reduce activity level and improve attention, academic performance, and peer relations for 70 percent of children who take them (Barkley, 1990). Researchers do not know precisely why stimulants are helpful. Some speculate that they change the chemical balance in brain regions that inhibit impulsiveness and hyperactivity. Others believe that children with ADHD are chronically underaroused. That is, normal levels of stimulation do not engage their interest and attention, so they seek excitement anywhere and everywhere. Stimulant drugs may work because they have an alerting effect on the brain. As a result, they decrease the child's need to engage in off-task and self-stimulating behavior.

Although stimulant medication is relatively safe, its impact is only short term. Drugs cannot teach children ways of compensating for inattention and impulsivity (Whalen & Henker, 1991). Combining medication with interventions that model and reinforce appropriate academic and social behavior seems to be the most effective approach to treatment (Barkley, 1990). Teachers can also create conditions in classrooms that support these pupils' special learning needs. Short work periods followed by a chance to get up and move around help them concentrate. Finally, family intervention is particularly important. Inattentive, overactive children strain the patience of parents, who are likely to react punitively and inconsistently in return—a child-rearing style that strengthens inappropriate behavior. Breaking this cycle is as important for ADHD children as it is for the defiant, aggressive youngsters we discussed in Chapter 10. In fact, 50 percent of the time, these two sets of behavior problems occur together (Henker & Whalen, 1989).

CONCEPT REVIEW TABLE

Memory Strategies of Middle Childhood

CONCEPT	IMPORTANT POINT	EXAMPLE
Rehearsal	The first deliberate memory strategy to appear in middle childhood. Involves repeating information to oneself.	To memorize the the capitals of the United States, Lizzie recited their names over and over again.
Organization	A memory strategy that appears during the mid-elementary school years. Involves grouping together related items.	Joey memorized the names of the state capitals by organizing them into eastern, western, midwestern, and southern regions.
Elaboration	A cognitively demanding memory strategy that appears at the end of middle childhood. Involves creating a shared meaning between two previously unrelated items.	Joey played a memory game in which he had to remember pairs of words, such as "elephant, clock." To recall this pair, he imagined an elephant holding a clock in its trunk.

that it tends to replace other strategies. The very reason elaboration is so successful helps explain why it is late to develop. To use elaboration, we must translate items into images and think of a relationship between them. The capacity of children's working memories must expand before they can carry out these activities at once. Elaboration becomes increasingly common during adolescence and young adulthood (Schneider & Pressley, 1989).

Because the strategies of organization and elaboration combine items into *meaningful chunks*, they permit children to hold on to much more information. As a result, the strategies contribute further to the expansion of working memory. In addition, when children store a new item in long-term memory by linking it to information they already know, they can *retrieve* it easily by thinking of other items associated with it. As we will see in the next section, this is one reason that memory improves steadily during the school years.

THE KNOWLEDGE BASE AND MEMORY PERFORMANCE

During middle childhood, the long-term knowledge base grows larger and becomes better organized. Children arrange the vast amount of information in their memories into increasingly elaborate, hierarchically structured networks (Ford & Keating, 1981). Many researchers believe that this rapid growth of knowledge helps children use strategies and remember. In other words, knowing more about a particular topic makes new information more meaningful and familiar so it is easier to store and retrieve (Bjorklund & Muir, 1988; Chi & Ceci, 1987).

If children's growing knowledge base does account for better memory performance, then in areas in which children are more knowledgeable than adults, they should show better recall. To test this idea, Michelene Chi (1978) looked at how well third- through eighth-grade chess experts could remember complex chessboard arrangements. The children were compared to adults who knew how to play chess but were not especially knowledgeable. Just as expected, the children could reproduce the chessboard configurations considerably better than the adults could. These findings cannot be explained by the selection of very bright youngsters with exceptional memories. On a standard memory span task in which the participants had to recall a list of numbers, the adults did better than the children (see Figure 12.2).

Attention-deficit hyperactivity disorder (ADHD)
A childhood disorder involving inattentiveness, impulsivity, and excessive motor activity. Often leads to academic failure and social problems.

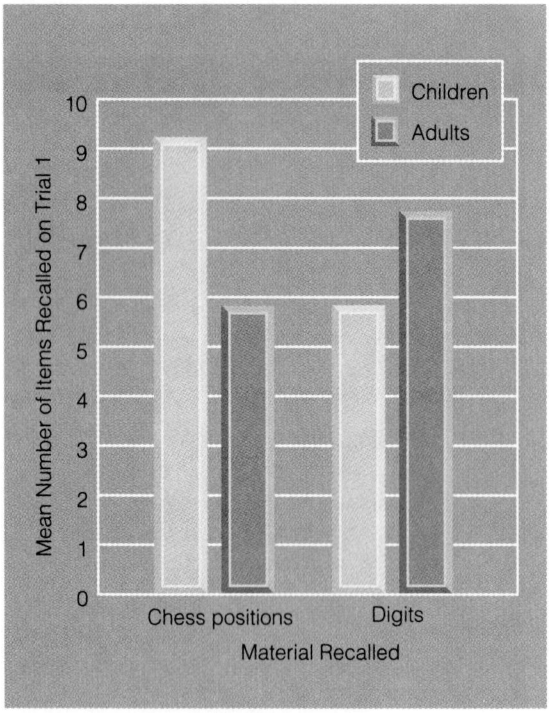

FIGURE 12.2

Performance of skilled child chess players and adults on two tasks: memory for complex chessboard arrangements and numerical digits. The child chess experts recalled more on the chess tasks, the adults on the digit task. These findings show that size of the knowledge base contributes to memory performance. *(Adapted from Chi, 1978).*

The children showed superior memory performance only in the domain of knowledge in which they were expert.

Although knowledge clearly plays an important role in memory development, it may have to be quite broad and well structured before it can facilitate the use of strategies and recall. A brief series of lessons designed to increase knowledge in a particular area (for example, short videotapes about various species of birds) does not affect children's ability to remember new information in that domain (DeMarie-Dreblow, 1991). Until children have enough knowledge and have had time to connect it into stable, well-formed hierarchies, they may not be able to apply it to new memory problems (Chi & Ceci, 1987).

Finally, we must keep in mind that knowledge is not the only important factor in children's strategic memory processing. Children who are expert in a particular area, whether it be chess, math, social studies, or spelling, are usually highly motivated. Faced with new material, they say to themselves, "What can I do to clarify the meaning of this information so I can learn it more easily?" As a result, they not only acquire knowledge more quickly, but they *actively use what they already know* to add more. Research indicates that academically successful and unsuccessful fifth graders differ in just this way. Poor students fail to approach memory tasks by asking how previously stored information can clarify new material. This, in turn, interferes with the development of a broad knowledge base (Bransford et al., 1981; Brown et al., 1983). So at least by the end of the school years, knowledge acquisition and use of memory strategies are intimately related and support one another.

CULTURE AND MEMORY STRATEGIES

Think, for a moment, about the kinds of situations in which the strategies of rehearsal, organization, and elaboration are useful. People usually employ these techniques when they need to remember information for its own sake. On many other occasions, they participate in daily activities that produce excellent memory as a natural by-product of the activity itself. For example, Joey can spout off a wealth of facts about baseball teams and players—information he picked up from watching the game, discussing it, and trading baseball cards with his friends. And without prior rehearsal, he can recount the story line of an exciting movie or novel, narrative material that is already meaningfully organized. (To review how children recall this kind of information, return to the discussion of scripts in Chapter 9, page 332.)

A repeated finding of cross-cultural research is that people in non-Western cultures who have no formal schooling do not use or benefit from instruction in memory strategies (Cole & Scribner, 1977; Rogoff, 1990). Tasks that require children to recall isolated bits of information are common in classrooms, and they provide children with a great deal of motivation to use memory strategies. In fact, Western children get so much practice with this type of learning that they do not refine other techniques for remembering that rely on spatial location and arrangement of objects, cues that are readily available in everyday life. Australian aboriginal and Guatemalan Mayan children are considerably better at these memory skills (Kearins, 1981; Rogoff, 1986). Looked at in this way, the development of memory strategies is not just a matter of a more competent information-processing system. It is also a product of task demands and cultural circumstances.

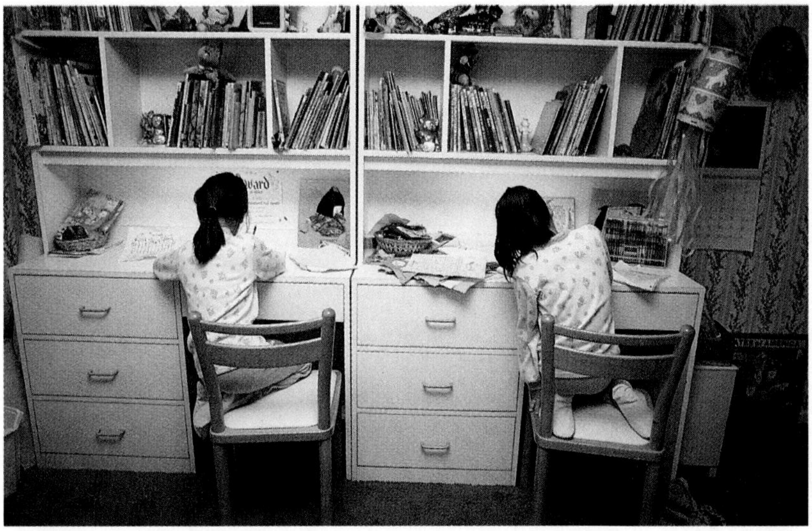

Culture affects use of memory strategies. These Western children are given homework assignments that often require them to learn isolated bits of information. Deliberate strategies are necessary for success on many school tasks. *(Comstock)*

THE SCHOOL-AGE CHILD'S THEORY OF MIND

During middle childhood, children's *theory of mind,* or set of beliefs about mental activities, becomes much more elaborate and refined. You may recall from Chapter 9 that this awareness of cognitive processes is often referred to as *metacognition.* School-age children's improved ability to reflect on their own mental life is another reason for the advances in thinking and problem solving that take place at this time.

Unlike preschoolers, who view the mind as a passive container of information, older children regard it as an active, constructive agent capable of selecting and transforming information (Pillow, 1988; Wellman, 1988b). Consequently, they have a much better understanding of the impact of psychological factors on cognitive performance. They know, for example, that mental inferences can be a source of knowledge and that doing well on a task depends on focusing attention—concentrating on it, wanting to do it, and not being tempted by anything else (Miller & Bigi, 1979; Sodian & Wimmer, 1987). They are also aware that in studying material for later recall, it is helpful to devote most effort to items that you know least well. And when asked, elementary school pupils show that they know quite a bit about effective memory strategies. Witness this 8-year-old's response to the question of what she would do to remember a phone number:

> Say the number is 663-8854. Then what I'd do is—say that my number is 663, so I won't have to remember that, really. And then I would think now I've got to remember 88. Now I'm 8 years old, so I can remember, say, my age two times. Then I say how old my brother is, and how old he was last year. And that's how I'd usually remember that phone number. [Is that how you would most often remember a phone number?] Well, usually I write it down. (Kreutzer, Leonard, & Flavell, 1975, p. 11)

This child clearly understands the importance of establishing connections between new information and existing knowledge. And she also recognizes that she can use external aids to enhance memory—in this case, writing the phone number down.

Once children become conscious of the many factors that influence mental activity, they combine these into an integrated understanding. School-age children take account of *interactions* among variables—how age and motivation of the learner, effective use of strategies, and nature and difficulty of the task work together to affect cognitive performance (Wellman, 1985). In this way, metacognition truly becomes a comprehensive theory during middle childhood.

School-age children have an improved ability to reflect on their own mental life. This child is aware that external aids to memory are often necessary to ensure that information will be retained. *(Frank Siteman/The Picture Cube)*

SELF-REGULATION

Although metacognition expands, school-age youngsters often have difficulty putting what they know about thinking into action. They are not yet good at **self-regulation,** the process of continuously monitoring progress toward a goal, checking outcomes, and redirecting unsuccessful efforts. For example, Lizzie is aware that she should group items together in a memory task and that she should read a complicated paragraph more than once to make sure she understands it. But she does not always do these things when working on an assignment (Beal, 1990; Brown et al., 1983).

It is not surprising that the capacity for self-regulation develops slowly. Monitoring learning outcomes is a cognitively demanding activity itself, requiring moment-by-moment evaluation of effort and progress. Self-regulation does not become well developed until adolescence. By then it is a strong predictor of academic success. Students who do well in school know when they possess a skill and when they do not. If they run up against obstacles, such as poor study conditions, a confusing text passage, or a class presentation that is unclear, they take steps to organize the learning environment, review the material, or seek other sources of support. This active, purposeful approach contrasts sharply with the passive orientation of students who do poorly (Borkowski et al., 1990; Zimmerman, 1990).

Parents and teachers can foster children's self-regulatory skills by pointing out the special demands of tasks, indicating how use of strategies will improve performance, and emphasizing the value of self-correction. Many studies show that providing children with instructions to check and monitor their progress toward a goal has a substantial impact on how well they do (Pressley & Ghatala, 1990).

Children who acquire effective self-regulatory skills succeed at challenging tasks. As a result, they develop confidence in their own ability—a belief that supports the use of self-regulation in the future (Paris & Newman, 1990; Schunk, 1990). Unfortunately, some children receive messages from parents and teachers that seriously undermine their academic self-esteem and self-regulatory skills. We will consider the special problems of these *learned helpless* youngsters, along with ways to help them, in Chapter 13.

APPLICATIONS OF INFORMATION PROCESSING TO ACADEMIC LEARNING

Joey entered first grade able to recognize only a handful of written words. By fifth grade, he was a proficient reader. His eyes moved quickly across the page, and his hand flew up when the teacher asked questions that probed how well the children understood an assignment. Similarly, at age 6, Joey had an informally acquired knowledge of number concepts. By age 10, he could add, subtract, multiply, and divide with ease, and he had begun to master fractions and percentages.

Over the past decade, fundamental discoveries about the development of information processing have been applied to children's learning of reading and mathematics. Researchers have begun to identify the cognitive ingredients of skilled performance, trace their development, and distinguish good from poor learners by pinpointing the cognitive skills in which they are deficient. They hope, as a result, to design teaching methods that will help children master these essential skills.

■ READING. While reading, we use a large number of skills at once, taxing all aspects of our information-processing systems. We must perceive single letters and letter combinations, translate them into speech sounds, hold chunks of text in working memory while interpreting their meaning, and combine the meanings of various parts of a text passage into an understandable whole. In fact, reading is such a demanding process that most or all of these skills must be done automatically. If one or more are poorly developed, they will compete for space in our limited work-

Self-regulation
The process of continuously monitoring progress toward a goal, checking outcomes, and redirecting unsuccessful efforts.

ing memories, and reading performance will decline (Frederiksen & Warren, 1987; Perfetti, 1988).

Researchers do not yet know how children manage to acquire and combine all these varied skills into fluent reading. Currently, psychologists and educators are engaged in a "great debate" about how to teach beginning reading. On one side are those who take a **whole-language approach** to reading instruction. They argue that reading should be taught in a way that parallels natural language learning. From the very beginning, children should be exposed to text in its complete form—stories, poems, letters, posters, and lists—so they can appreciate the communicative function of written language. According to these experts, as long as reading is kept whole and meaningful, children will be motivated to discover the specific skills they need as they gain experience with the printed word (Goodman, 1986; Watson, 1989). On the other side of the debate are those who advocate a **basic-skills approach.** According to this view, children should be given simplified text materials. At first, they should be coached on *phonics*—the basic rules for translating written symbols into sounds. Only later, after they have mastered these skills, should they get complex reading material (Rayner & Pollatsek, 1989; Samuels, 1985).

Researchers do not yet know how children acquire and combine a wide variety of cognitive skills into fluid reading. Recent evidence suggests that a balanced mixture of instruction in basic skills and emphasis on meaning is the best way to help school-age children learn to read. *(Will Faller)*

As yet, research does not show clear-cut superiority for either of these approaches (Stahl, McKenna, & Pagnucco, 1994). In fact, a third group of experts believes that children may learn best when they receive a balanced mixture of both (Pressley, 1994; Stahl, 1992). In a recent study, 7-year-old poor readers showed greater reading gains when assigned to a combined "phonics/meaningful reading" intervention than to either a "phonics alone" alone or a "reading alone" teaching condition (Hatcher, Hulme, & Ellis, 1994). Learning the basics—relationships between letters and sounds—enables children to decipher words they have never seen before. As this process becomes more automatic, it releases children's attention to the higher-level activities involved in comprehending the text's meaning. But if practice in basic skills is overemphasized, children may lose sight of the goal of reading—understanding. Many teachers report cases of pupils who can read aloud fluently but who register little or no meaning. These children might have been spared serious reading problems if they had been exposed to rich early childhood literacy experiences (see Chapter 9) followed by meaning-based instruction that includes attention to basic skills.

■ MATHEMATICS. Once children enter elementary school, they apply their rich informal knowledge of number concepts and counting to more complex mathematical skills (Resnick, 1989). For example, children first understand multiplication as a kind of repeated addition. When given the following problem, "Sue has 5 books. Joe has 3 times as many. How many books does Joe have?" Lizzie thought to herself, "What's 5 × 3?" When she had difficulty remembering the answer, she said, "Okay, it's got to be 5 books + 5 books + 5 books. I know, it's 15!" Lizzie's use of addition strengthened her understanding of multiplication. It also helped her recall a multiplication fact that she had been trying to memorize.

Mathematics as taught in many classrooms, however, does not make good use of children's basic grasp of number concepts. Children are given procedures for solving problems without linking these to their informally acquired understandings. Consequently, they often apply a rule that is close to what they have been taught but that yields a wrong answer. Their mistakes indicate that they have tried to memorize a method, but they do not comprehend the basis for it. For example, look at the following subtraction errors made by two of Lizzie's classmates:

$$\begin{array}{r} 427 \\ -138 \\ \hline 311 \end{array} \qquad \begin{array}{r} {}^{6}\not{7}00{}^{1}2 \\ 5445 \\ \hline 1447 \end{array}$$

Whole-language approach
An approach to beginning reading instruction that parallels children's natural language learning and keeps reading materials whole and meaningful.

Basic-skills approach
An approach to beginning reading instruction that emphasizes training in phonics—the basic rules for translating written symbols into sounds—and simplified reading materials.

In the first problem, the child consistently subtracts a smaller from a larger digit, regardless of which is on top. In the second, columns with zeros are skipped in a borrowing operation, and whenever there is a zero on top, the bottom digit is written as the answer. Researchers believe that drill-oriented math instruction that provides children with little information on the reasons behind procedures is at the heart of these difficulties (Fuson, 1990; Resnick, 1989).

Arguments about how to teach early mathematics closely resemble the positions we considered earlier in the area of reading. Drill in computational skills is pitted against "number sense" or understanding. Yet once again, a blend of the two is probably best. Research indicates that conceptual knowledge serves as a vital base for the development of accurate, efficient computation in middle childhood (Byrnes & Wasik, 1991).

Cross-cultural evidence suggests that in Asian countries, pupils receive a variety of supports for acquiring mathematical knowledge that are not broadly available in the United States. For example, use of the metric system, which presents ones, tens, hundreds, and thousands values in all areas of measurement, helps Asian children think in ways that foster a grasp of place value. The consistent structure of number words in Asian languages ("ten two" for 12, "ten three" for 13) also makes this idea clear (Fuson & Kwon, 1992). Furthermore, number words in Asian languages are shorter and more quickly pronounced, so more digits can be held in working memory at once. This eases the verbal counting strategies children use to solve math problems and increases the speed with which they can retrieve math facts from long-term memory (Geary et al., 1993; Jensen & Whang, 1994). Finally, as we will see later in this chapter, in Asian classrooms, much more time is spent exploring underlying math concepts and much less on drill and repetition.

ASK YOURSELF . . .

- One day, the children in Lizzie and Joey's school saw a slide show about endangered species. They were told to remember as many animal names as they could. Fifth and sixth graders recalled considerably more than second and third graders. What factors might account for this difference?
- Lizzie knows that if you have difficulty learning part of a task, you should devote most of your attention to that aspect. But she plays each of her piano pieces from beginning to end instead of picking out the hard parts for extra practice. What explains Lizzie's failure to apply what she knows?

BRIEF REVIEW

Over the school years, attention becomes more controlled, adaptable, and planful, and memory strategies become more effective. An expanding knowledge base contributes to improved memory performance. However, children's willingness to use what they know when learning new information is also important. Metacognition moves from a passive to an active view of mental functioning during middle childhood. Self-regulation develops slowly; school-age children do not always apply their metacognitive understanding, but they can be taught to improve their self-regulatory skills. Information processing has been applied to children's academic learning in school. Instruction that provides balanced attention to basic skills and understanding seems to be most effective in reading and mathematics.

INDIVIDUAL DIFFERENCES IN MENTAL DEVELOPMENT DURING MIDDLE CHILDHOOD

During middle childhood, intelligence tests become increasingly important for assessing individual differences in mental development. Around age 6, IQ becomes more stable than it was at earlier ages, and it correlates well with academic achievement, from .40 to .70 (Siegler & Richards, 1982). Because IQ predicts school performance, it plays an important role in educational decisions. Children with low IQs who do poorly in school are often assumed to have limited potential to learn. Consequently, these pupils (a great many of whom come from low-income ethnic minority homes) may be placed in slower educational tracks, assigned to remedial classrooms, or held back in grade.

Do intelligence tests provide an accurate indication of the school-age child's ability to profit from instruction? In the following sections, we take a close look at this controversial issue.

DEFINING AND MEASURING INTELLIGENCE

Take a moment to jot down a list of behaviors that you regard as typical of a highly intelligent school-age child. Did you come up with just one or two or a great many? Virtually all intelligence tests provide an overall score (the IQ), which is taken to represent *general intelligence* or reasoning ability. Yet a diverse array of tasks appear on most tests for children. Today, there is widespread agreement that intelligence is a collection of many mental capacities, not all of which are included on currently available tests.

Test designers use a complicated statistical technique called *factor analysis* to identify the various abilities measured by intelligence tests. This procedure determines which sets of items on the test correlate strongly with one another. Those that do are assumed to measure a similar ability and therefore are designated as a separate factor. To understand the types of intellectual factors measured in middle childhood, let's look at some representative intelligence tests and how they are administered.

■ SOME REPRESENTATIVE INTELLIGENCE TESTS.

Intelligence tests for children come in great variety. Those that Joey and Lizzie take every two or three years in school are *group-administered tests.* They permit large numbers of pupils to be tested at once and require very little training of teachers who give them. Group tests are useful for instructional planning and identifying children who require more extensive evaluation with *individually administered tests.* Unlike group tests, individually administered ones demand considerable training and experience to give well. The examiner not only considers the child's answers, but also carefully observes the child's behavior, noting such things as attentiveness to and interest in the tasks and wariness of the adult. These reactions provide insight into whether the test score is accurate or underestimates the child's abilities.

Two individual tests—the Stanford-Binet and the Wechsler—are most often used to identify highly intelligent children and diagnose those with learning problems. As we look at each, refer to Figure 12.3, which shows some of the items that typically appear on intelligence tests for children.

The Stanford-Binet Intelligence Scale. The modern descendent of Alfred Binet's first successful intelligence test is the **Stanford-Binet Intelligence Scale,** which is appropriate for individuals between 2 years of age and adulthood. Its latest version measures both general intelligence and four intellectual factors: verbal reasoning, quantitative reasoning, abstract/visual reasoning, and short-term memory (Thorndike, Hagen, & Sattler, 1986). Within these factors are 15 subtests that permit a detailed analysis of each child's mental abilities. The verbal and quantitative factors emphasize culturally loaded, fact oriented information, such as the child's knowledge of vocabulary and comprehension of sentences. In contrast, the abstract/visual reasoning factor is believed to be less culturally biased because it demands little in the way of specific information. Instead, it tests children's ability to see complex relationships, as illustrated by the spatial visualization item shown in Figure 12.3.

Like many current tests, the Stanford-Binet is designed to be sensitive to minority children and children with disabilities and to reduce gender bias. Pictures of children from different ethnic groups, a child in a wheelchair, and "unisex" figures that can be interpreted as male or female are included. One serious drawback is that the test takes an especially long time to give—up to two hours for some children (Sattler, 1988).

Stanford-Binet Intelligence Scale
An individually administered intelligence test that is the modern descendent of Alfred Binet's first successful test for children. Measures general intelligence and four factors: verbal reasoning, quantitative reasoning, spatial reasoning, and short-term memory.

FIGURE 12.3

Sample items similar to those that appear on common intelligence tests for children.
In contrast to verbal items, nonverbal items do not require reading or direct use of language. Performance items are also nonverbal, but they require the child to draw or construct something rather than merely give a correct answer. As a result, they appear only on individually administered intelligence tests. (*Logical reasoning, picture oddities, and spatial visualization examples are adapted with permission of The Free Press, a Division of Macmillan, Inc., from A. R. Jensen, 1980,* Bias in Mental Testing, *New York: The Free Press, pp. 150, 154, 157.)*

Item Type	Typical Verbal Items
Vocabulary	Tell me what "carpet" means.
General Information	How many ounces make a pound? What day of the week comes right after Thursday?
Verbal Comprehension	Why are police officers needed?
Verbal Analogies	A rock is hard; a pillow is ______ .
Logical Reasoning	Five girls are sitting side by side on a bench. Jane is in the middle and Betty sits next to her on the right. Alice is beside Betty, and Dale is beside Ellen, who sits next to Jane. Who are sitting on the ends?
Number Series	Which number comes next in the series? **4 8 6 12 10 __**

Typical Nonverbal Items

Picture Oddities

Which picture does not belong with the others?

Spatial Visualization

Which of the boxes on the right can be made from the pattern shown on the left?

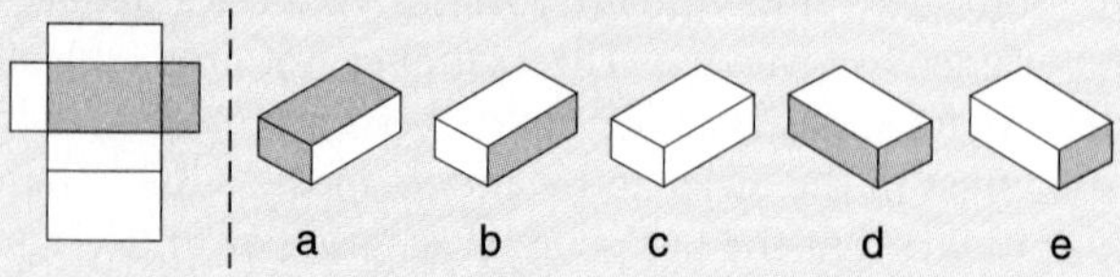

Typical Performance Items

Picture Series

Put the pictures in the right order so that what is happening makes sense.

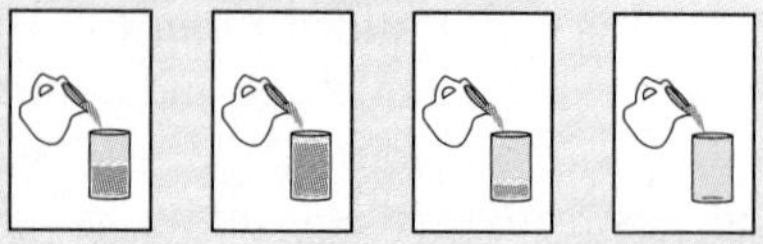

Puzzles

Put these pieces together so they make a wagon.

The Wechsler Intelligence Scale for Children–III. The **Wechsler Intelligence Scale for Children–III (WISC–III)** is the third edition of a widely used test for 6- through 16-year-olds. A downward extension of it—the *Wechsler Preschool and Primary Scale of Intelligence-Revised (WPPSI–R)*—is appropriate for children 3 through 8 (Wechsler, 1989, 1991). The Wechsler tests offered both a measure of general intelligence and a variety of factor scores long before the Stanford-Binet. As a result, over the past two decades, psychologists and educators have come to prefer the WISC and WPPSI.

Both the WISC–III and the WPPSI–R measure two broad intellectual factors: verbal and performance. Each contains six subtests, yielding 12 separate scores in all. Performance items (see examples in Figure 12.3) require the child to arrange materials rather than talk to the examiner. Consequently, these tests provided one of the first means through which non-English-speaking children and children with speech and language disorders could demonstrate their intellectual strengths.

The Wechsler tests were also the first to be standardized on samples representing the total population of the United States, including ethnic minorities. Their broadly representative standardization samples have served as models for many other tests, including the recent version of the Stanford-Binet.

Other Intelligence Tests. Although the Stanford-Binet and the Wechsler scales are the most well known intelligence tests, others based on alternative approaches do exist. For example, several Piagetian tests for school-age children include a variety of conservation and classification problems (Goldschmid & Bentler, 1968; Humphreys, Rich, & Davey, 1985). Performance on these measures correlates well with IQ and achievement. But Piagetian tests have not caught hold strongly, largely because they do not sample as many abilities as the Stanford-Binet and Wechsler scales.

Perhaps the most innovative effort to measure children's intelligence in recent years is the **Kaufman Assessment Battery for Children (K-ABC).** It is the first major test to be grounded in information-processing theory. Published in 1983, the K-ABC measures the intelligence of children from age 2 1/2 through 12 on the basis of two broad types of information-processing skills. The first, *simultaneous processing,* demands that children integrate a variety of stimuli at the same time, as when they recall the placement of objects on a page presented only briefly. The second, *sequential processing,* refers to problems that require children to think in a step-by-step fashion. Examples include repeating a series of digits or hand movements presented by the examiner. The K-ABC also makes a special effort to respond to the needs of culturally different children. If a child fails one of the first three items on any subtest, the examiner is permitted to "teach the task." The tester can use alternative wording and gestures and may even communicate in a language other than English (Kaufman & Kaufman, 1983).

The K-ABC is not without its critics. Some point out that the test samples a very narrow range of information-processing skills and that there is little research support for the simultaneous–sequential processing distinction (Goetz & Hall, 1984; Sternberg, 1984). Nevertheless, the K-ABC is responsive to a new trend to define intelligence in terms of cognitive processes, as we will see in the following section.

■ RECENT DEVELOPMENTS IN DEFINING INTELLIGENCE. As the K-ABC suggests, researchers have started to combine the factor analytic approach to defining intelligence with information processing. Those involved in this effort believe that factors on intelligence tests are of limited usefulness unless we can identify the cognitive processes responsible for them. Once we understand the underlying basis of IQ, we will know much more about why a particular child does well or poorly and what capacities must be worked on to improve performance. These researchers conduct *componential analyses* of children's IQ scores. This means that they look for relationships between aspects (or components) of information processing and intelligence test scores. Preliminary findings reveal that the

Wechsler Intelligence Scale for Children–III (WISC–III)
An individually administered intelligence test that includes both a measure of general intelligence and a variety of verbal and performance scores.

Kaufman Assessment Battery for Children (K-ABC)
An individually administered intelligence test that measures two broad types of information-processing skills: simultaneous and sequential processing. The first major test to be grounded in information-processing theory.

FIGURE 12.4

Sternberg's triarchic theory of intelligence.

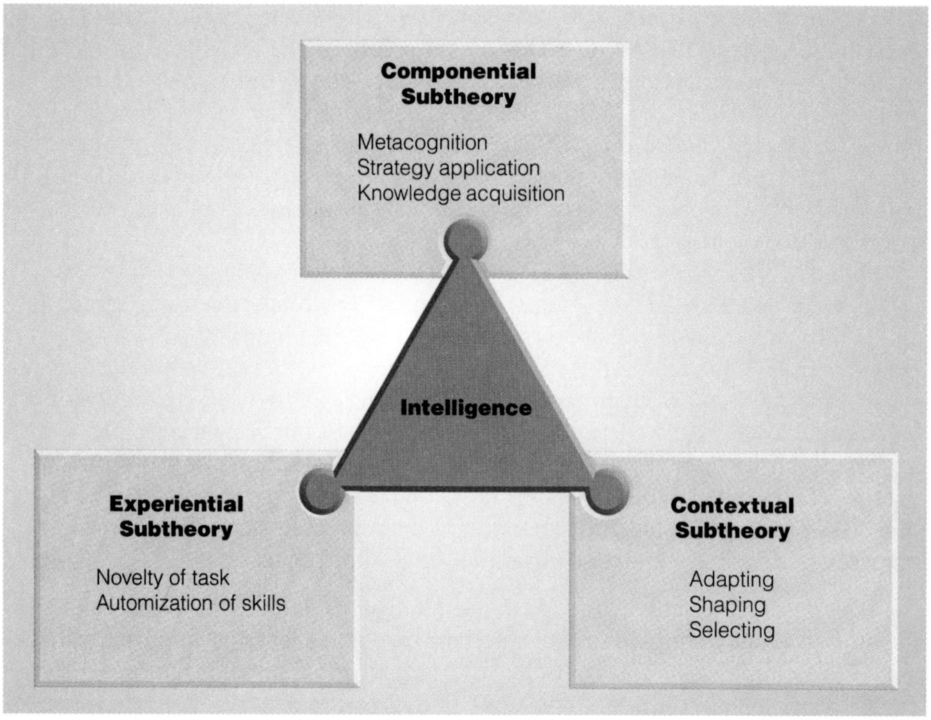

speed with which individuals perceive and manipulate information and the effectiveness with which they apply strategies to remember and solve problems are related to IQ (Geary & Burlingham-Dubree, 1989; Jensen, 1988; Larson, 1989).

The componential approach has one major shortcoming: It regards intelligence as entirely due to causes within the child. Yet throughout this book, we have seen how cultural and situational factors profoundly affect children's cognitive skills. Recently, Robert Sternberg expanded the componential approach into a comprehensive theory that regards intelligence as a product of both inner and outer forces.

■ STERNBERG'S TRIARCHIC THEORY. As Figure 12.4 shows, Sternberg's (1985, 1988) **triarchic theory of intelligence** is made up of three interacting subtheories. The first, the *componential subtheory,* spells out the information-processing skills that underlie intelligent behavior. You are already familiar with its main elements—strategy application, knowledge acquisition, metacognition, and self-regulation.

According to Sternberg, children's use of these components is not just a matter of internal capacity. It is also a function of the conditions under which intelligence is assessed. The *experiential subtheory* states that highly intelligent individuals, compared to less intelligent ones, process information more skillfully in novel situations. When given a relatively new task, the bright person learns rapidly, making strategies automatic so working memory is freed for more complex aspects of the situation.

Think, for a moment, about the implications of this idea for measuring children's intelligence. To accurately compare children in brightness—in ability to deal with novelty and learn efficiently—all children would need to be presented with equally unfamiliar test items. Otherwise, some children will appear more intelligent than others simply because of their past experiences, not because they are really more cognitively skilled. These children start with the unfair advantage of prior practice on the tasks.

This point brings us to the third part of Sternberg's model, the *contextual subtheory.* It proposes that intelligent people skillfully *adapt* their information-processing skills to fit their personal desires and the demands of their everyday worlds. When they cannot adapt to a situation, they try to *shape,* or change, it to meet their

Triarchic theory of intelligence
Sternberg's theory, which states that information-processing skills, prior experience with tasks, and contextual (or cultural) factors interact to determine intelligent behavior.

TABLE 12.1

Gardner's Multiple Intelligences

INTELLIGENCE	PROCESSING OPERATIONS	END-STATE PERFORMANCE POSSIBILITIES
Linguistic	Sensitivity to the sounds, rhythms, and meanings of words and the different functions of language	Poet, journalist
Logico-mathematical	Sensitivity to, and capacity to detect, logical or numerical patterns; ability to handle long chains of logical reasoning	Mathematician, scientist
Musical	Ability to produce and appreciate pitch, rhythm (or melody), and aesthetic-sounding tones; understanding of the forms of musical expressiveness	Violinist, composer
Spatial	Ability to perceive the visual-spatial world accurately, to perform transformations on those perceptions, and to recreate aspects of visual experience in the absence of relevant stimuli	Sculptor, navigator
Bodily-kinesthetic	Ability to use the body skillfully for expressive as well as goal-directed purposes; ability to handle objects skillfully	Dancer, athlete
Interpersonal	Ability to detect and respond appropriately to the moods, temperaments, motivations, and intentions of others	Therapist, salesperson
Intrapersonal	Ability to discriminate complex inner feelings and to use them to guide one's own behavior; knowledge of one's own strengths, weaknesses, desires, and intelligences	Person with detailed, accurate self-knowledge

Sources: Gardner, 1983; Gardner & Hatch, 1989.

needs. If they cannot shape it, they *select* new contexts that are consistent with their goals. The contextual subtheory emphasizes that intelligent behavior is never culture free. Because of their backgrounds, some children come to value behaviors required for success on intelligence tests, and they easily adapt to the tasks and testing conditions. Others with different life histories misinterpret the testing context or reject it entirely because it does not suit their needs. Yet such children may display very sophisticated abilities in daily life—for example, telling stories, engaging in complex artistic activities, or interacting skillfully with other people (Sternberg, 1988).

Sternberg's theory emphasizes the complexity of intelligent behavior and the wide variety of human mental skills. As you can already see, his ideas are relevant to the controversy surrounding cultural bias in IQ testing, which we will address shortly.

■ GARDNER'S THEORY OF MULTIPLE INTELLIGENCES. Howard Gardner's (1983) **theory of multiple intelligences** provides yet another view of how information-processing skills underlie intelligent behavior. But unlike the componential approach, it does not begin with existing mental tests and try to isolate the processing elements required to succeed on them. Instead, Gardner believes that intelligence should be defined in terms of distinct sets of processing operations that permit individuals to engage in a wide range of culturally valued activities. Therefore, Gardner dismisses the idea of general intelligence and proposes seven independent intelligences, which are described in Table 12.1.

Gardner argues that each intelligence has a unique biological basis, a distinct course of development, and different expert, or "end-state," performances. At the same time, he emphasizes that a lengthy process of education is required to transform any raw potential into a mature social role. This means that cultural values and learning opportunities have a great deal to do with the extent to which a child's intellectual strengths are realized and the ways in which they are expressed.

Gardner's list of abilities has yet to be firmly grounded in research. For example, biological evidence for the independence of his abilities is weak. Similarly, there are

Theory of multiple intelligences
Gardner's theory, which identifies seven independent intelligences on the basis of distinct sets of processing operations that permit individuals to engage in a wide range of culturally valued activities.

exceptionally gifted individuals whose abilities are broad rather than limited to a particular domain (Feldman, 1991). Finally, current mental tests do tap several of Gardner's intelligences (linguistic, logico-mathematical, and spatial), and evidence suggests that they have at least some common features. Nevertheless, Gardner's theory has been especially helpful in efforts to understand and nurture children's special talents, a topic we will discuss at the end of this chapter.

EXPLAINING INDIVIDUAL AND GROUP DIFFERENCES IN IQ

When we compare individuals in terms of academic achievement, years of education, and the status of their occupations, it quickly becomes clear that certain sectors of the population are advantaged over others. In trying to explain these differences, researchers have examined the intelligence test performance of children from different ethnic and social-class backgrounds. Many studies show that American black children score, on the average, 15 IQ points below American white children (Brody, 1992). Social-class differences in IQ also exist. The gap between middle-income and low-income children is about 9 points (Jensen & Figueroa, 1975). These figures are, of course, averages. There is considerable variation *within* each ethnic and social-class group. Still, ethnic and social-class differences in IQ are large enough and of serious enough consequence that they cannot be ignored.

In 1969, psychologist Arthur Jensen published a controversial article in the *Harvard Educational Review* entitled, "How Much Can We Boost IQ and Scholastic Achievement?" Jensen's answer to this question was "not much." He argued that heredity is largely responsible for individual, ethnic, and social-class differences in intelligence, a position he continues to maintain (Jensen, 1980, 1985a). Jensen's work received widespread public attention. It was followed by an outpouring of responses and research studies, leading to a heated nature–nurture debate on the origins of IQ. Recently, the controversy was rekindled in Richard Herrnstein and Charles Murray's (1994) *The Bell Curve*. Like Jensen, these authors concluded that the contribution of heredity to individual and social-class differences in IQ is substantial. At the same time, they stated that the relative role of heredity and environment in the black–white IQ gap remains unresolved. Let's look closely at some important evidence.

■ **NATURE VERSUS NURTURE.** In Chapter 2, we introduced the *heritability estimate*. Recall that heritabilities are obtained from *kinship studies*, which compare family members. The most powerful evidence regarding heritability of IQ involves twin comparisons. Identical twins (who share all their genes) have more similar IQ scores than do fraternal twins (who are genetically no more alike than ordinary siblings). On the basis of this and other kinship evidence, current researchers estimate the heritability of IQ to be about .50 (Loehlin, 1989). This means that about half the differences among children in IQ can be traced to their genetic makeup. However, if you return for a moment to our discussion of heritability in Chapter 2 (pages 87–89), you will see that these figures risk overestimating genetic influences and underestimating the importance of environment. Although heritability research offers convincing evidence that genetic factors contribute to IQ, disagreement persists over just how large the role of heredity really is (Ceci, 1990).

Furthermore, a widespread misconception exists that if a characteristic is heritable, then the environment can do little to affect it. A special type of kinship study, involving adopted children and their biological and adoptive relatives, shows that this assumption is incorrect. In one investigation of this kind, children of two extreme groups of biological mothers, those with IQs below 95 and those with IQs above 120, were chosen for special study. All the children were adopted at birth by parents who were well above average in income and education. When tested during the school years, children of the low-IQ biological mothers scored above average in IQ, indicating that test performance can be greatly improved by an advantaged home life! At the same time, they did not do as well as children of high IQ biological mothers placed in similar adoptive families. Adoption research confirms the balanced position that both heredity and environment affect IQ scores (Horn, 1983; Willerman, 1979).

Some intriguing adoption research also sheds light on the origins of the black–white IQ gap. Black children placed in well-to-do white homes during the first year of life also score high on intelligence tests. In two such studies, adopted black children attained mean IQs of 110 and 117 by middle childhood, well above average and 20 to 30 points higher than the typical scores of children growing up in low-income black communities (Scarr & Weinberg, 1983; Moore, 1986). However, a follow-up in one investigation revealed that test scores of black adoptees declined by adolesence; the customary black–white difference was again apparent (Weinberg, Scarr, & Waldman, 1992).

Adoption findings do not completely resolve questions about ethnic differences in IQ. Nevertheless, the IQ gains of adopted black children "raised in the culture of the tests and schools" are consistent with a wealth of evidence indicating that poverty severely depresses the intelligence of large numbers of ethnic minority youngsters (Scarr & Weinberg, 1983, p. 261). And in many other cases, unique cultural values and practices do not prepare these children for the kinds of tasks that are sampled by intelligence tests and valued in school.

■ CULTURAL INFLUENCES. Jermaine, a black child in Lizzie's third-grade class, participated actively in class discussion and wrote complex, imaginative stories. But he did not enter first grade feeling so comfortable with classroom life. At the beginning, Jermaine responded, "I don't know," to the simplest of questions, including "What's your name?" Fortunately, Jermaine's teacher understood his uneasiness. Slowly and gently, she helped him build a bridge between the learning style fostered by his cultural background and the style necessary for academic success. A growing body of evidence reveals that IQ scores are affected by specific learning experiences, including exposure to certain language customs and knowledge.

Language Customs. Ethnic minority subcultures often foster unique language skills that do not fit the expectations of most classrooms and testing situations. Shirley Brice Heath (1982, 1989), an anthropologist who has spent many hours observing in low-income black homes in a southeastern American city, found that adults asked black children very different kinds of questions than is typical in white middle-class families. From an early age, white parents ask knowledge-training questions, such as "What color is it?" and "What's this story about?" that resemble the questioning style of tests and classrooms. In contrast, the black parents asked only "real" questions—ones that they themselves did not know the answer to. Often these were analogy questions ("What's that like?") or story-starter questions ("Didja hear Miss Sally this morning?") that called for elaborate responses about whole events and no single right answer. The black children developed complex verbal skills at home, such as story telling and exchanging quick-witted remarks. But these worked poorly when they got to school. The children were confused by the questions in classrooms and often withdrew into silence.

Other minority youngsters also develop distinct language styles. For example, Navajo Indian children speak slowly and rhythmically, leaving much time between phrases and sentences. Teachers and testers often think these youngsters have finished responding when they have only paused. In contrast, Native Hawaiian children prefer rapid-fire, overlapping speech. Non-Hawaiian adults may interpret this style as rude interruption, although in Hawaiian society it signals interest and involvement (Tharp, 1989).

When faced with the strangeness of the testing situation, the minority child may look to the examiner for cues about how to respond. Yet most intelligence tests permit tasks to be presented in only one way, and they allow no feedback to children. Consequently, minority children may simply give the first answer that comes to mind, not one that truly represents what they know. For example, look at the following responses of a black child to a series of test questions:

Tester: "How are wood and coal alike? How are they the same?"

Child: "They're hard."

Tester: "An apple and a peach?"

Child: "They taste good."

Tester: "A ship and an automobile?"

Child: "They're hard."

Tester: "Iron and silver?"

Child: "They're hard." (Miller-Jones, 1989, p. 362)

Earlier in the testing session, this child asked whether she was doing all right but got no reply. She probably repeated her first answer because she had trouble figuring out the task's meaning, not because she was unable to classify objects. Had the tester prompted her to look at the questions in a different way, her performance might have been better.

Familiarity with Test Content. Many researchers argue that IQ scores are affected by specific information acquired as part of middle-class upbringing. Unfortunately, attempts to change tests by eliminating fact-oriented verbal tasks and relying only on spatial reasoning and performance items (believed to be less culturally loaded) have not raised the scores of low-income minority children very much (Kaplan, 1985).

Nevertheless, even these test items seem to depend on learning opportunities. In one study, children's performance on a spatial reasoning task was related to the extent to which they had played a popular but expensive game that (like the test items) required them to arrange blocks to duplicate a design as quickly as possible (Dirks, 1982). Low-income minority children, who often grow up in more "people-oriented" than "object-oriented" homes, may lack opportunities to use games and objects that promote certain intellectual skills. In line with this possibility, when ethnically diverse parents were asked for their idea of an intelligent first grader, Anglo-Americans valued cognitive traits over noncognitive ones. In contrast, ethnic minorities (Cambodian, Filipino, Vietnamese, and Mexican immigrants) saw noncognitive characteristics—motivation, self-management, and social skills—as equally or more important than cognitive skills (Okagaki & Sternberg, 1993).

That specific experiences affect performance on intelligence tests is also supported by evidence indicating that the amount of time a child spends in school is a strong predictor of IQ. When children of the same age who are in different grades are compared, those who have been in school longer score higher on intelligence tests. Similarly, dropping out of school leads to a decrease in IQ. The earlier children leave school, the greater their loss of IQ points. Taken together, these findings indicate that a more intelligent child may come to school with a greater ability to profit from instruction. But teaching children the factual knowledge and ways of thinking valued in classrooms has a sizable impact on their intelligence test performance (Ceci, 1990, 1991).

OVERCOMING CULTURAL BIAS IN INTELLIGENCE TESTS

Although not all experts agree, today there is greater acknowledgment than ever before that IQ scores can underestimate the intelligence of culturally different children. A special concern exists about incorrectly labeling minority children as slow learners and assigning them to remedial classes, which are far less stimulating than regular school experiences. Because of this danger, precautions should be taken when evaluating children for the purpose of educational placement. Besides test scores, assessments of children's adaptive behavior—their ability to cope with the demands of their everyday environments—should be obtained (Landesman & Ramey, 1989). The child who does poorly on an IQ test yet plays a complex game on the playground, figures out how to rewire a broken TV, or cares for younger siblings responsibly is unlikely to be mentally deficient. As we will see later, current definitions of mental retardation do include both IQ and adaptive behavior.

These children are taking an intelligence test. How accurately will the resulting scores represent the mental abilities of ethnic minority children in this class? The issue of cultural bias in intelligence testing continues to be hotly debated. *(Bob Daemmerich/ Stock Boston)*

A few experts believe intelligence tests are so biased that they should be banned entirely. Most regard this solution as unacceptable, since important educational decisions would be based only on subjective impressions. This policy actually increases the discriminatory placement of minority children. Intelligence tests are useful measures when interpreted carefully by examiners who are sensitive to the impact of culture on test performance (Reschly, 1981). And despite their limitations, IQ scores continue to be valid measures of school learning potential for the majority of Western children.

BRIEF REVIEW

Intelligence tests for children measure overall IQ as well as a variety of separate intellectual factors. The Stanford-Binet Intelligence Scale and the Wechsler Intelligence Scale for Children–III (WISC–III) are commonly used tests in middle childhood. The Kaufman Assessment Battery for Children (K-ABC) is the first major test to be grounded in information-processing theory.

Recently, researchers have combined the factor analytic approach to defining intelligence with information processing in an effort to discover the cognitive processes underlying IQ scores. Sternberg has expanded this componential approach into a triarchic theory of intelligence. It states that information-processing skills, prior experience with the tasks, and contextual factors (the child's cultural background and interpretation of the testing situation) interact to determine IQ. According to Gardner's theory of multiple intelligences, seven distinct abilities, each defined by unique processing operations, represent the diversity of human intelligence.

Heritability and adoption research shows that both genetic and environmental factors contribute to individual differences in intelligence. Because of different language customs and unfamiliar test content, the IQ scores of low-income minority children often do not reflect their true abilities.

ASK YOURSELF . . .

- Desiree, a low-income African-American child, was quiet and withdrawn while taking an intelligence test. Later she remarked to her mother, "I can't understand why that lady asked me all those questions, like what a ball and stove are for. She's a grownup. She *must* know what a ball and stove are for!" Using Sternberg's triarchic theory, explain Desiree's reaction to the testing situation. Why is Desiree's score likely to underestimate her intelligence?

LANGUAGE DEVELOPMENT IN MIDDLE CHILDHOOD

Language continues to develop in middle childhood, although changes are less obvious than those that occurred at earlier ages. Vocabulary, grammar, and pragmatics expand and become more refined. In addition, children's attitude toward language undergoes a fundamental shift. School-age children attend to language much more directly. They develop *language awareness.*

VOCABULARY

Because the average 6-year-old's vocabulary is already quite large (about 10,000 words), parents and teachers usually do not notice rapid gains during the school years. Between the start of elementary school and its completion, recognition vocabulary increases fourfold, eventually reaching about 40,000 words. On the average, about 20 new words are learned each day—a rate of growth that exceeds that of early childhood. In addition to the fast-mapping process we discussed in Chapter 9, school-age children enlarge their vocabularies through an increasingly powerful ability to analyze the structure of complex words. From "happy," "wise," and "decide," they quickly derive the meanings of "happiness," "wisdom," and "decision" (Anglin, 1993). Many more words are picked up from context, especially while reading (Miller, 1991).

As we saw earlier in this chapter, the conceptual knowledge underlying vocabulary becomes better organized during middle childhood. This change permits children to use and think about words more precisely. If you look carefully at children's word definitions, you will see examples of this change. Five- and 6-year-olds give very concrete descriptions that refer to functions or appearance—for example, knife: "when you're cutting carrots"; bicycle: "it's got wheels, a chain, and handlebars." By the end of elementary school, their definitions emphasize more general, socially shared information. Synonyms and explanations of categorical relationships appear—for example, knife: "something you could cut with. A saw is like a knife. It could also be a weapon" (Litowitz, 1977; Wehren, DeLisi, & Arnold, 1981). This advance reflects the older child's ability to deal with word meanings on an entirely verbal plane. Fifth and sixth graders no longer need to be shown what a word refers to in order to understand it. They can add new words to their vocabulary simply by being given a definition (Dickinson, 1984).

School-age children's more reflective and analytical approach to language permits them to appreciate the multiple meanings of words. For example, they recognize that a great many words, such as "sharp" or "cool," have psychological as well as physical meanings: "What a cool shirt!" or "That movie was really neat!" This grasp of double meanings permits 8- to 10-year-olds to comprehend more subtle metaphors than they could at earlier ages, such as "sharp as a tack," "spilling the beans," and "left high and dry" (Waggoner & Palermo, 1989; Winner, 1988). It also leads to a change in children's humor. In middle childhood, riddles and puns requiring children to go back and forth between different meanings of the same key word are common:

"Hey, did you take a bath?" "No! Why, is one missing?"

"Order! Order in the court!" "Ham and cheese on rye, your honor?"

"Why did the old man tiptoe past the medicine cabinet?" "Because he didn't want to wake up the sleeping pills."

Preschoolers may laugh at these statements because they are nonsensical. But they cannot tell a good riddle or pun, nor do they understand why these jokes are funny (McGhee, 1979).

GRAMMAR

Although children have mastered most of the grammar of their language by the time they enter school, use of complex grammatical constructions improves. The passive voice is one example. At all ages, children produce more abbreviated passives ("It got broken" or "They got lost") than full passives ("The glass was broken by Mary"). However, full passives are rarely used by 3- to 6-year-olds. They increase steadily over middle childhood (Horgan, 1978). Older children also apply their understanding of the passive voice to a wider range of nouns and verbs. Preschoolers comprehend the passive best when the subject of the sentence is an animate being and the verb is an action word ("The *boy* is *kissed* by the girl"). During the school years, inanimate subjects, such as "drum" or "hat," and experiential verbs, such as "like" or "know," are included (Lempert, 1989; Pinker, Lebeaux, & Frost, 1987).

Another grammatical achievement of middle childhood is the understanding of infinitive phrases, such as the difference between "John is eager to please" and "John is easy to please" (Chomsky, 1969). Like gains in vocabulary, appreciation of these subtle grammatical distinctions is supported by children's cognitive development and their improved ability to analyze and reflect on language. During middle childhood, children can judge the grammatical correctness of a sentence even if its meaning is false or senseless, whereas preschoolers cannot (Bialystok, 1986).

PRAGMATICS

Improvements in pragmatics, the communicative side of language, take place in middle childhood. One of the most obvious gains is the ability to adapt to the needs of listeners in challenging communicative situations. In one study, 3- to 10-year-olds were shown eight objects, which were similar in size, shape, and color. The children were asked to indicate which object they liked best as a birthday present for an imaginary friend. Preschoolers gave ambiguous descriptions, such as "the red one." In contrast, school-age youngsters referred to the objects in much more precise ways—for example, "the round red one with stripes on it" (Deutsch & Pechmann, 1982).

Conversational strategies also become more refined in middle childhood. For example, older children have a more advanced appreciation of how to phrase things to get their way. When faced with an adult who refuses to hand over a desired object, 9-year-olds, but not 5-year-olds, state their second requests more politely (Axia & Baroni, 1985). School-age children are also more sensitive than preschoolers to distinctions between the form and meaning of utterances. Even 3-year-olds know that a playmate who says, "I need a pencil," is not just making a statement. She is asking for a pencil. But 8-year-olds understand more unconventional expressions of meaning. For example, the day after she forgot to take the garbage out, Lizzie knew that her mother's statement "The garbage is beginning to smell," really meant "Take that garbage out!" Making subtle inferences about the relationship between an utterance and its context is beyond the ability of preschoolers (Ackerman, 1978).

LEARNING TWO LANGUAGES AT A TIME

Like most American children, Joey and Lizzie speak only one language, their native tongue of English. Yet throughout the United States and the world, many children grow up *bilingual.* They learn two languages, and sometimes more than two, during childhood. Current estimates indicate that 2.5 million American school-age children speak a language other than English at home. This figure is expected to double by the year 2000 (Hakuta & Garcia, 1989).

Children can become bilingual in two ways: (1) by acquiring both languages at the same time in early childhood, or (2) by learning a second language after mastering

Several million American school-age children speak a language other than English in their homes and neighborhoods. Research shows that bilingualism enhances many cognitive and linguistic skills. *(Chet Seymour/The Picture Cube)*

the first. Children of bilingual parents who teach them both languages in early childhood show no special problems with language development. For a time, they appear to develop more slowly because they mix the two languages. But this is not an indication of confusion, since bilingual parents do not maintain strict language separation either (Goodz, 1989). These bilingual children acquire normal native ability in the language of their surrounding community and good to native ability in the second language, depending on their exposure to it. When children acquire a second language after they already speak a first language, it generally takes them about a year to become as fluent in the second language as native-speaking age-mates (Reich, 1986).

A large body of research shows that bilingualism has a positive impact on cognitive development. Children who are fluent in two languages do better than others on tests of analytical reasoning, concept formation, and cognitive flexibility (Hakuta, Ferdman, & Diaz, 1987). In addition, bilingual children are advanced in their ability to reflect on language. They are more aware that words are arbitrary symbols, more conscious of language structure and detail, and better at noticing errors of grammar and meaning in spoken and written prose (Galambos & Goldin-Meadow, 1990; Ricciardelli, 1992). This sensitivity to language as a system is a strong predictor of other measures of cognitive, language, and literacy development.

The advantages of bilingualism provide strong justification for bilingual education programs in American schools. The Cultural Influences box on the following page describes the current controversy over bilingual education in the United States. As you will see, bilingual children rarely receive support for their native language in classrooms. Yet bilingualism provides one of the best examples of how language, once learned, becomes an important tool of the mind and fosters cognitive development. In fact, the goals of schooling could reasonably be broadened to include helping all children become bilingual, thereby fostering the cognitive, language, and cultural enrichment of the entire nation (Hakuta, 1986; Ruiz, 1988).

ASK YOURSELF . . .

- Ten-year-old Shana arrived home from school after a long day, sank into the livingroom sofa, and commented, "I'm totally wiped out!" Megan, her 5-year-old sister, looked puzzled and asked, "What did'ya wipe out, Shana?" Explain Shana and Megan's different understanding of the meaning of this expression.

BRIEF REVIEW

During the school years, vocabulary increases rapidly, and children develop a more precise and flexible understanding of word meanings. Mastery of complex grammatical constructions becomes more refined. School-age children express themselves well in challenging communicative situations, and they acquire more subtle conversational strategies. Bilingualism has a positive impact on cognitive development and language awareness.

CHILDREN'S LEARNING IN SCHOOL

Throughout this chapter, we have touched on evidence indicating that schools are vital forces in children's cognitive development, affecting their modes of remembering, reasoning, problem solving, and language skills. How do schools exert such a powerful impact? Research looking at schools as complex social systems—their educational philosophies, teacher–pupil interaction patterns, and the larger cultural context in which they are embedded—provides important insights into this question.

THE EDUCATIONAL PHILOSOPHY

Each teacher brings to the classroom an educational philosophy that plays a major role in children's learning experiences. Two philosophical approaches have been studied in American education. They differ in what children are taught, the way they are believed to learn, and how their progress is evaluated.

SOCIAL ISSUES

BILINGUAL EDUCATION IN THE UNITED STATES

Vincente, a 7-year-old boy who recently immigrated from Mexico to the United States, attends a bilingual education classroom in a large American city. His teacher, Serena, is fluent in both Spanish and English. At the beginning of the year, Serena instructed Vincente and his classmates in their native tongue. As the children mixed with English-speaking youngsters at school and in the community, they quickly picked up English phrases, such as "My name is . . .," "I wanna," and "Show me." Serena reinforced her pupil's first efforts to speak English, helping them feel confident about communicating in a second language. Gradually, she introduced more English into classroom learning experiences. At the same time, she continued to strengthen the children's native language and culture.

When bilingual education programs provide instruction in both the child's native language and in English, children are more involved in learning and are advanced in language development. *(Will Faller)*

Vincente is enrolled in one of many bilingual education programs serving the growing number of American children with limited proficiency in English. Although state and federal funding for bilingual education has increased in recent years, the question of how Vincente and his classmates should be taught continues to be hotly debated.

On one side of the controversy are those who believe that Vincente should be instructed only in English. According to this view, time spent communicating in the child's native tongue subtracts from English language achievement, which is crucial for success in the world of school and work. On the other side are educators like Serena, who are committed to truly *bilingual* education—developing Vincente's native language while fostering his mastery of English. Supporters of this view believe that providing instruction in the native tongue lets minority children know that their heritage is respected (McGroarty, 1992). In addition, by avoiding abrupt submersion in an English-speaking environment, bilingual education prevents *semilingualism,* or inadequate proficiency in both languages. When minority children experience a gradual loss of the first language as a result of being taught the second, they end up limited in both languages for a period of time, a circumstance that leads to serious academic difficulties. Semilingualism is one factor believed to contribute to the high rates of school failure and dropout among low-income Hispanic youngsters, who make up nearly 50 percent of the American language minority population (August & Garcia, 1988; Ruiz, 1988).

At present, public opinion sides with the first of these two viewpoints. Many states have passed laws declaring English to be their official language, creating conditions in which schools have no obligation to teach minority pupils in languages other than English. Yet research underscores the value of instruction in the child's native tongue. In classrooms where both languages are integrated into the curriculum, minority children are more involved in learning, participate more actively in class discussions, and acquire the second language more easily. In contrast, when teachers speak only in a language their pupils can barely understand, children display frustration, boredom, and withdrawal (Cazden, 1984; Wong-Fillmore et al., 1985).

TRY THIS . . .

- Ask several people you know for their opinion on the value of bilingual education for ethnic minority children. Which side does each take on the controversy described here? For those who think children should be taught only in English, describe research findings on the benefits of bilingualism. Did any change their minds?

■ TRADITIONAL VERSUS OPEN CLASSROOMS. In a **traditional classroom,** children are relatively passive in the learning process. The teacher is the sole authority for knowledge, rules, and decision making and does most of the talking. Pupils spend most of their time at their desks—listening, responding when called on, and completing teacher-assigned tasks. Their progress is evaluated by how well they keep pace with a uniform set of standards for all pupils in their grade.

In contrast, in an **open classroom,** children are viewed as active agents in their own development. The teacher assumes a flexible authority role, sharing decision making with pupils, who learn at their own pace. Pupils are evaluated by considering their progress in relation to their own prior development. How well they compare to same-age pupils is of lesser importance. A glance inside the door of an open classroom reveals richly equipped learning centers, small groups of pupils working on tasks they choose themselves, and a teacher who moves from one area to another, guiding and supporting in response to children's individual needs (Minuchin & Shapiro, 1983).

Over the past few decades, the pendulum in American education has swung back and forth between these two views. In the 1960s and early 1970s, open education gained in popularity, inspired by Piaget's vision of the child as an active, motivated learner. Then, as high school students' scores on the Scholastic Aptitude Test (SAT) dropped over the 1970s, a "back to basics" movement arose. Classrooms returned to traditional, teacher-directed instruction, which remains the dominant approach today.

The combined results of many studies reveal that children in traditional classrooms have a slight edge in terms of academic achievement. At the same time, open settings are associated with other benefits. Open-classroom pupils are more independent, and they value and respect individual differences in their classmates more. Pupils in open environments also like school better than those in traditional classrooms, and their attitudes toward school become increasingly positive as they spend more time there (Hedges, Giaconia, & Gage, 1981; Walberg, 1986). In contrast, the high teacher structure and lack of pupil autonomy in traditional classrooms seems to contribute to a general decline in pupil motivation throughout the school years (Eccles et al., 1993b; Skinner & Belmont, 1993).

■ NEW PHILOSOPHICAL DIRECTIONS. The philosophies of some teachers are neither traditional nor open. Instead, they fall somewhere in between. These teachers want to foster high achievement as well as independence, positive social relationships, and excitement about learning. New experiments in elementary education, grounded in Vygotsky's sociocultural theory, represent this intermediate point of view (Forman, Minick, & Stone, 1993). One that has received widespread attention is the Kamehameha Elementary Education Program (KEEP). Vygotsky's concept of the *zone of proximal development*—a range of challenging tasks that the child is ready to master with the help of a more skilled partner (see Chapter 6)—serves as the foundation for KEEP's theory of instruction. To promote development, KEEP combines a variety of strategies that have traditionally belonged to other theories:

- *Modeling,* to introduce children to unfamiliar skills
- *Instructing,* to direct children toward the next specific act they need to learn in order to move through the zone of proximal development
- *Verbal feedback* (or reinforcement), to let children know how well they are progressing in relation to reasonable standards of performance
- *Questioning,* to encourage children to think about the task
- *Explaining,* to provide strategies and knowledge necessary for thinking in new ways

Traditional classroom
An elementary school classroom based on the educational philosophy that children are passive learners who acquire information presented by teachers. Pupils are evaluated on the basis of how well they keep up with a uniform set of standards for all pupils in their grade.

Open classroom
An elementary school classroom based on the educational philosophy that children are active agents in their own development and learn at different rates. Teachers share decision making with pupils. Pupils are evaluated in relation to their own prior development.

These techniques are applied in activity settings specially designed to enhance opportunities for teacher–child and child–child dialogue. In each setting, children work on a project that ensures that their learning will be active and directed toward a meaningful goal. For example, they might read a story and discuss its meaning or draw a map of the playground to promote an understanding of geography. Once in a while, activity settings include the whole class. More often, they involve small groups that foster cooperative learning and permit teachers to stay in touch with how well each child is doing. The precise organization of each KEEP classroom is adjusted to fit the unique learning styles of its pupils, creating culturally responsive environments (Tharp, 1993; Tharp & Gallimore, 1988).

Thousands of low-income minority children have attended KEEP classrooms in the public schools of Hawaii, on a Navajo reservation in Arizona, and in Los Angeles. So far, research suggests that the approach is highly effective. In KEEP schools, minority pupils performed at their expected grade level in reading achievement, much better than children of the same background enrolled in traditional schools (see Figure 12.5). Classroom observations also showed that KEEP pupils participated actively in class discussion, used elaborate language structures, frequently supported one another's learning, and were more attentive and involved than were non-KEEP controls (Tharp & Gallimore, 1988). As the KEEP model becomes more widely applied, perhaps it will prove successful with all types of children because of its comprehensive goals and effort to meet the learning needs of a wide range of pupils.

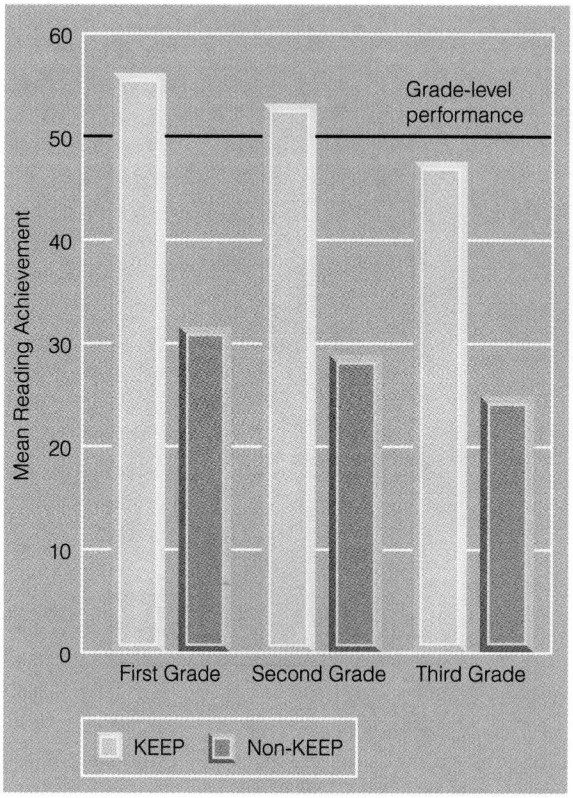

FIGURE 12.5

Reading achievement of KEEP-instructed and traditionally instructed first- through third-grade low-income minority pupils. The KEEP children performed at grade level; the non-KEEP pupils performed substantially below grade level. *(Adapted from R. G. Tharp and R. Gallimore, 1988,* Rousing Minds to Life: Teaching Learning, and Schooling in Social Context, *New York: Cambridge University Press, p. 116. Adapted by permission.)*

TEACHER–PUPIL INTERACTION

In all classrooms, teachers vary in the way they interact with children—differences that are consistently related to academic achievement. Lizzie's third-grade teacher, for example, organized the learning environment so that activities ran smoothly, transitions were brief and orderly, and there were few disruptions and discipline problems. Teachers who are effective classroom managers have pupils who spend more time learning, and this is reflected in higher achievement test scores (Brophy, 1986).

The quality of teachers' instructional messages also affects children's involvement and achievement. Although Lizzie's teacher was well organized and efficient, she usually emphasized factual knowledge. She seldom encouraged the children to think critically about what they had learned or apply their knowledge to new situations. Down the hall in Joey's class, higher-level questions were common. Joey's teacher asked, "Why is the main character in this story a hero?" and "Now that you are good at division, let's use what we know. How many teams should we have at recess? How many children on each team?" In an observational study of fifth-grade social studies and math lessons, students were far more attentive when teachers encouraged higher-level thinking rather than limiting instruction to simple memory exercises (Stodolsky, 1988).

Teachers do not interact in the same way with all children. Some get more attention and praise than others. Well-behaved, high-achieving pupils experience positive interactions with their teachers. In contrast, teachers especially dislike children who achieve poorly and are disruptive. These unruly pupils are often criticized and are rarely called on to contribute to class discussion. When they seek special help or permission, their requests are usually denied (Brophy & Good, 1974).

Unfortunately, once teachers' attitudes toward pupils are established, they are in danger of becoming more extreme than is warranted by children's behavior.

When teachers emphasize competition, make public evaluations of pupils, and are overly critical of those who do poorly, negative self-fulfilling prophecies can be set in motion that undermine children's self-esteem and achievement. *(MacDonald Photography/Envision)*

A special concern is that an **educational self-fulfilling prophecy** can be set in motion. In other words, children may adopt teachers' positive or negative views and start to live up to them. Over the past thirty years, many studies have found that school-age children become increasingly aware of teacher opinion, and it can influence their attitudes and performance (Harris & Rosenthal, 1985; Skinner & Belmont, 1993). This effect is especially strong in certain classrooms—those in which teachers emphasize competition and frequently make public comparisons among children (Weinstein et al., 1987).

In many schools, pupils are *ability grouped* into classes in which children of similar achievement levels are taught together. Some researchers believe that teachers' treatment of different ability groups may be an especially powerful source of self-fulfilling prophecies (Brophy, 1983; Corno & Snow, 1986). In low-ability groups, pupils get more drill on basic facts and skills, a slower learning pace, and less time on academic work. Gradually, children in low groups show a drop in self-esteem and are viewed by themselves and others as "not smart." Not surprisingly, ability grouping widens the gap between high and low achievers (Oakes, Gamoran, & Page, 1992).

COMPUTERS IN THE CLASSROOM

Besides teachers, another interactive aid to learning can be found in most modern classrooms. In each room in Joey and Lizzie's school, a computer sat in a quiet corner. Children took turns working on special assignments, sometimes by themselves and at other times with their classmates. By the early 1990s, over 97 percent of American public schools had integrated computers into their instructional programs (U.S. Bureau of the Census, 1994). A growing research literature reveals that computers can have rich educational benefits.

ADVANTAGES OF COMPUTERS. Computers are typically used in three different ways in classrooms. The first is **computer-assisted instruction (CAI),** in which specially designed educational software permits children to practice basic skills and acquire new knowledge. For example, Lizzie and her classmates often used the computer to practice multiplication and division. They could begin at their current level of mastery, and the computer provided immediate feedback and extra practice with problems they missed. Other programs contain gamelike activities that teach new concepts. In one, Lizzie operated a lemonade stand and learned about economic principles of cost, profit, supply, and demand in a familiar context. Gains in achievement occur when computer-assisted instruction is a regular part of children's school experiences. The benefits are greatest for younger pupils and those who are doing poorly in school (Clements & Nastasi, 1992; Lepper & Gurtner, 1989).

As soon as children begin to read and write, they can also use the computer for *word processing.* It permits them to write freely and experiment with letters and words without being slowed down by the fine motor task of handwriting. When children use the computer to write stories, letters, and other text material, they are less concerned about making mistakes because they can easily revise and polish their work. As a result, their written products are longer and of higher quality (Clements & Nastasi, 1992; Levin, Boruta, & Vasconcellos, 1983).

Finally, *programming* offers children the highest degree of control over the computer, since they must tell it what to do. Specially designed computer languages are available to introduce children to programming skills. As long as teachers encourage and support children's efforts, computer programming leads to improvements in concept formation, problem solving, and creativity (Clements & Nastasi, 1992; Degelman et al., 1986). Also, since children must detect errors in their programs to get them to work, programming helps them reflect on their own thought processes. Gains in metacognition and self-regulation result from programming experiences

Educational self-fulfilling prophecy
The idea that children may adopt teachers' positive or negative attitudes toward them and start to live up to these views.

Computer-assisted instruction (CAI)
Use of computers to transmit new knowledge and practice academic skills.

(Clements, 1990). Finally, children who know how to program are more aware of the uses of computers and how they function. They are better prepared to participate in a society in which computers are becoming increasingly important in everyday life.

Special steps are needed to ensure that girls have equal access to computers during the school years. When classrooms emphasize cooperative learning and software is designed with the interests of girls in mind, they become enthusiastic users. *(Stephen Marks)*

■ **CONCERNS ABOUT COMPUTERS.** Although computers provide children with many learning advantages, they raise serious concerns as well. Computers appear most often in the classrooms of economically well-off pupils. Parents of these children are far more likely to buy computers and extend their educational benefits into the home. As a result, some experts believe that computers are widening the intellectual performance gap between lower- and middle-income children (Laboratory of Comparative Human Cognition, 1989).

Furthermore, by the end of middle childhood boys spend much more time with computers than do girls, both in and out of school. Traditional gender-role expectations have led adults to encourage this difference. Parents of sons are twice as likely as parents of daughters to install a computer in the home. Even when girls have ready access to computers, much of the software available is unappealing to them because it emphasizes themes of war, violence, and male-dominated sports (Lepper, 1985). Girls' reduced involvement with computers may contribute to sex differences in mathematical achievement and interest in scientific careers that emerge by adolescence (see Chapter 15). Yet girls' tendency to retreat from computers can be overcome. When teachers present computers in the context of cooperative rather than competitive learning activities and software is designed with the interests of girls in mind, they become enthusiastic users (Hawkins & Sheingold, 1986; Linn, 1985).

Finally, computers are especially attractive to children because of their multiple communication modes. Color graphics, lively animation, voice, music, and text combine to sustain children's interest. Critics worry that children might become too dependent on this highly stimulating, entertaining format. Will children be able to generalize the academic skills they acquire from the computer to other contexts? At present, this unanswered question awaits further research.

TEACHING CHILDREN WITH SPECIAL NEEDS

So far, we have seen that effective teachers flexibly adjust their teaching strategies to accommodate pupils with a wide range of abilities and characteristics. But such adjustments are increasingly difficult to make at the very low and high ends of the ability distribution. How do schools serve children with special learning needs?

■ **MAINSTREAMING CHILDREN WITH LEARNING DIFFICULTIES.** The Individuals with Disabilities Education Act (Public Law 101-475), first passed by Congress in 1975 and revised in 1990, mandates that schools place children who require special supports for learning in the "least restrictive" environments that meet their educational needs. The law led to a rapid increase in **mainstreaming** of many pupils who otherwise would have been served in special education classes. Instead, they were integrated into regular classrooms for part or all of the school day, a practice designed to better prepare them for participation in society. Most mainstreamed pupils are mildly retarded or learning disabled. Let's take a brief look at the characteristics of these youngsters.

Mildly Mentally Retarded Children. About 1.5 percent of the child population suffers from **mental retardation,** or substantially below-average intellectual performance. Approximately 85 percent of these children are mildly mentally retarded—the highest functioning category (see Table 12.2). Their IQs fall between 55 and 70, and they also show problems in adaptive behavior (social and self-help skills in everyday life). Typically, a mildly mentally retarded child can be educated to the level of an average sixth grader. In adulthood, most can live independently and hold routine jobs, although they require extra guidance and support during times of stress (American Psychiatric Association, 1994; Grossman, 1983).

Mainstreaming
The integration of pupils with learning difficulties into regular classrooms for part or all of the school day.

Mental retardation
Substantially below-average intellectual functioning.

TABLE 12.2

Classification of Mental Retardation

LEVEL OF RETARDATION	APPROXIMATE IQ RANGE	DESCRIPTION
Mild	55 – 70	Can be educated to about the sixth-grade level by late adolescence. In adulthood, can live independently and hold a routine job. Requires extra support when under stress.
Moderate	40 – 54	Can be educated to about fourth-grade level by late adolescence. In adulthood, usually requires living arrangements with moderate supervision. Can be employed in a sheltered workshop or unskilled job.
Severe	25 – 39	Can learn to talk and be trained in basic health habits, but cannot acquire academic skills. In adulthood, requires extensive supervision.
Profound	Below 25	Develops only minimal speech and motor functioning. Little capacity to profit from training of any kind. Requires complete care and supervision.

Sources: Grossman, 1983; Sloan and Birch, 1955.

As you know from earlier chapters, the depressed intellectual functioning that characterizes mentally retarded children can develop in many ways. Hereditary defects, a faulty prenatal environment, birth complications, childhood injuries, a severely impoverished home life, or some combination of these factors are common causes.

Learning Disabled Children. The largest number of mainstreamed children have **learning disabilities.** About 5 to 10 percent of school-age children are affected. These youngsters obtain average or above-average IQ scores. Nevertheless, they have great difficulty with one or more aspects of learning. As a result, their achievement is considerably behind what would be expected on the basis of their IQ. The problems of these children cannot be traced to any obvious physical or emotional difficulty or to environmental disadvantage. Instead, faulty brain functioning is believed to be responsible (Hammill, 1990). Some of the disorders run in families, suggesting that they are at least partly genetic (Pennington & Smith, 1988). In most instances, the cause is unknown.

Learning disabled children display a wide variety of cognitive processing deficits. Usually, the basic area of difficulty is noted. A problem with reading is called *dyslexia,* one with arithmetic *dyscalculia,* and one with writing *dysgraphia.* But impairments are much more varied than these categories suggest. For example, one dyslexic child might have difficulty interpreting visual stimuli. The letters d, b, p, q, and g are confused, so that "dog" is read as "god" and "ball" as "gall." Another might have trouble tracking from left to right and as a result, read the same line twice, jump over words, or skip lines. Some children cannot integrate information appropriately. After reading a story, they mix up the sequence of events. In retelling it, they start in the middle, go to the beginning, and then shift to the end. Serious memory problems can contribute to spelling and math difficulties. A child might study a spelling list or math concept, know it well, but forget it completely an hour or two later. Finally, sometimes the muscles of the hand fail to work together, resulting in extremely slow, unclear handwriting (Silver, 1989a).

The learning problems of these children are so frustrating that they can lead to serious emotional, social, and family difficulties (Silver, 1989b). Yet those who are treated with patience and understanding and who receive appropriate educational intervention have a good chance of making a satisfactory adjustment in adulthood. Although the disability usually persists, these individuals find ways to compensate for it. Often they select college majors and careers that do not rely heavily on the skill in which they are deficient. For example, one youngster with a severe reading disability received a college scholarship in art. Another learned to play five musical instruments proficiently. The majority of learning disabled adults manage to equal

Learning disabilities Specific learning disorders that lead children to achieve poorly in school, despite an average or above-average IQ. Believed to be due to faulty brain functioning.

or exceed the average educational and occupational attainment of the general population (Horn, O'Donnell, & Vitulano, 1983).

How Effective Is Mainstreaming? Does mainstreaming accomplish its two goals—providing more appropriate academic experiences and integrated participation in classroom life? At present, research findings are not positive on either of these points. Achievement differences between mainstreamed pupils and those taught in self-contained classrooms are not great (MacMillan, Keogh, & Jones, 1986). Furthermore, mainstreamed children are often rejected by peers. Those who are mentally retarded are overwhelmed by the social skills of their classmates; they cannot interact quickly or adeptly in a conversation or game. And the processing deficits of some learning-disabled children lead to problems in social awareness and responsiveness (Rourke, 1988; Taylor, Asher, & Williams, 1987).

Does this mean that mainstreaming is not a good way to serve children with special learning needs? This extreme conclusion is not warranted. Many regular classroom teachers do not have the specialized training or the time to give these pupils all the help they need. Often these children do best when they receive instruction in a *resource room* for part of the day and in the regular classroom for the remainder. In the resource room, a special education teacher works with pupils individually and in small groups. Then, depending on their abilities, children are mainstreamed for different subjects and amounts of time. This flexible approach makes it more likely that the unique academic needs of each child will be served (Keogh, 1988; Lerner, 1989).

Once children enter the regular classroom, special steps must to be taken to promote peer acceptance. When instruction is carefully individualized and teachers minimize comparisons with higher-achieving classmates, mainstreamed pupils show gains in self-esteem and achievement (Madden & Slavin, 1983). Also, cooperative learning experiences in which a mainstreamed child and several normal peers work together on the same task have been found to promote friendly interaction and social acceptance (Nastasi & Clements, 1991). Finally, teachers can prepare children for the arrival of a special-needs pupil. Under these conditions, mainstreaming may lead to gains in emotional sensitivity and prosocial behavior among classmates. When carefully implemented, mainstreaming may very well break down social barriers and foster early integration of children with disabilities into the mainstream of American life.

■ GIFTED CHILDREN. In Joey and Lizzie's school, some children were **gifted.** They displayed exceptional intellectual strengths. As with mainstreamed pupils, their characteristics were diverse. In every grade were one or two pupils with IQ scores above 130, the standard definition of giftedness based on intelligence test performance (Horowitz & O'Brien, 1986). High-IQ children, as we have seen, are particularly quick at academic work. They have keen memories and an exceptional capacity to analyze a challenging problem and efficiently move toward a correct solution.

Yet earlier in this chapter, we noted that intelligence tests do not sample the entire range of human mental skills. Over the past two decades, recognition of this fact has led to an expanded conception of giftedness in schools.

Creativity. Besides general intelligence, high *creativity* can result in a child being designated as gifted. Tests that measure it tap a form of cognition called **divergent thinking**—the generation of multiple and unusual possibilities when faced with a task or problem. Divergent thinking contrasts sharply with **convergent thinking,** which involves arriving at a single correct answer—the type of cognition emphasized on intelligence tests (Guilford, 1985).

Highly creative children, like high-IQ youngsters, are often better at some types of tasks than others. Verbal, figural, and "real-world problem" measures of divergent thinking exist. A verbal measure might ask children to name as many uses for common objects (such as a newspaper) as they can. A figural measure might ask them to come up with as many drawings based on a circular motif as possible

Giftedness
Exceptional intellectual ability. Includes high IQ, creativity, and specialized talent.

Divergent thinking
The generation of multiple and unusual possibilities when faced with a task or problem. Associated with creativity.

Convergent thinking
The generation of a single correct answer to a problem. The type of cognition emphasized on intelligence tests.

(Torrance, 1980). A "real-world problem" measure either gives children everyday problems or requires them to think of such problems and then suggest solutions (Runco, 1992, 1993). Responses to all these tests can be scored for the number of ideas generated as well as their originality. For example, on a verbal test, saying that a newspaper can be used "as handgrips for a bicycle" would be more unusual than saying it can be used "to clean things." Figure 12.6 displays the responses of a highly creative 8-year-old in Lizzie's class to a figural creativity test.

Divergent thinking is only weakly related to intelligence test performance. Children who are both highly intelligent and highly creative are the exception rather than the rule (Kogan, 1983). Also, comparisons of identical and fraternal twins reveal that genetic influences on divergent thinking are extremely weak (Pezzullo, Thorsen, & Madaus, 1972). This suggests that creativity may be especially sensitive to encouragement by parents and teachers.

Research reveals that parents of creative children value nonconformity, emphasize intellectual curiosity and freedom of exploration, and are highly accepting of their youngster's individual characteristics. Creative children are, in turn, broad in their interests, attracted by complexity, and relatively unconcerned about conventional social norms (Wallach, 1985). Because of these characteristics, creative children are often not well liked by teachers—especially those with rigid expectations for how pupils should respond in class. Creative pupils often interpret assignments in novel and humorous ways, as you can see in the following autobiography written by a youngster who scored high in divergent thinking:

> I was transferred from another world or "hatched" as you might call it, at a very young age (0 for a fact). I called my mammy and she came runnin'. Den dat dok came an' he done took me and ah' squealed with fright. O' course I couldn' see anythin' anyhoo. . . . Den a grown up fur' three (3) yer' before my brudder was bornded. He is de' durndest critter ah' eveh' saw podnah'. At this time in my life you can see I played cowboy, with my mudder as injun. She never was the same cause ah used to hit her with a frin' pan . . . . (Getzels & Jackson, 1962, p. 100)

Unfortunately, many teachers are annoyed rather than intrigued by this inventive reformulation of a problem.

Talent. Correlations between divergent thinking and real-life creative accomplishment range from weak to moderate (Cramond, 1994; Wallach, 1985). Partly for this reason, definitions of giftedness have been extended to include *specialized talent.* There is clear evidence that outstanding performances in particular areas, such as mathematics, science, music, art, athletics, and leadership, have roots in specialized skills that first appear in childhood (Gardner, 1983; Gardner & Hatch, 1989).

At the same time, native ability is not enough for the development of talent. It must be nurtured in a favorable environment. Studies of highly accomplished musicians, mathematicians, and Olympic athletes show that they had deeply committed parents and inspiring teachers who encouraged them from an early age. In addition, as children these individuals displayed extraordinary dedication, devoting many long hours to practice—much more than they gave to any other activity (Bloom, 1985; Feldman, 1991). These findings suggest that the most effective way to foster creativity is to provide talented pupils with training aimed at helping them reach the limits of a particular field and then move beyond.

Educating the Gifted. Teaching gifted children with such a wide range of capacities is, indeed, a monumental task. Enrichment activities in regular classrooms and pull-out programs in which bright youngsters are gathered together for special instruction have been common ways of serving the gifted for decades. Yet these approaches are of limited value, since they usually provide the same experience to all pupils without considering each child's unique talents and skills.

FIGURE 12.6

Responses of a highly creative 8-year-old to a figural measure of creativity.
This child was asked to make as many pictures as she could from the circles on the page. The titles she gave her drawings, from left to right, are as follows: "Dracula," "one-eyed monster," "pumpkin," "Hula-Hoop," "poster," "wheelchair," "earth," "moon," "planet," "movie camera," "sad face," "picture," "stoplight," "beach ball," "the letter O," "car," "glasses." *(Test form copyright © 1980 by Scholastic Testing Service, Inc. Reprinted by permission of Scholastic Testing Service, Inc., from* The Torrance Tests of Creative Thinking *by E. P. Torrance.)*

Current trends in gifted education place greater emphasis on building each child's special abilities. Enrichment might include mentorship programs in which a highly skilled adult tutors the gifted pupil in a relevant field, such as art or public speaking (Kornhaber, Krechevsky, & Gardner, 1991). Another approach is to provide accelerated learning programs in which gifted pupils are given fast-paced instruction in a particular subject or are advanced to a higher grade. Acceleration is a controversial practice because of concerns that bright youngsters might suffer socially if they are placed with older pupils. Yet when children are carefully selected on the basis of their maturity, acceleration is highly successful. Longitudinal studies of accelerated students indicate that they continue to be socially well adjusted while demonstrating outstanding academic accomplishments (Brody & Benbow, 1987).

Today, the educational needs of gifted children are commanding greater attention, and other innovative techniques for teaching them are being tried. These include gifted resource rooms, cluster groups that bring children with similar talents together, and special after-school and Saturday programs. In some states, "governor's schools" provide advanced instruction in both academic and artistic fields. A promising outcome of these efforts is that practices designed to stimulate complex problem solving and creativity in the gifted are spilling over into regular classrooms, extending learning opportunities for all pupils. These efforts may eventually increase the identification of talented minority children, who are underrepresented in school programs for the gifted (Ford & Harris, 1990; Reis, 1989).

ASK YOURSELF . . .

- Saul, a third-grade teacher, places stars by the names of children who get A's on assignments. Children who earn at least 10 stars each week are called "all stars." What effect is this practice likely to have on children who achieve poorly, and why?
- Carrie is a mainstreamed first grader with a learning disability. What steps can her teacher take to make sure her academic and social needs are met in a regular classroom?

BRIEF REVIEW

Schools are powerful forces in children's cognitive development. Pupils who attend traditional classrooms are slightly advantaged in academic achievement; those in open classrooms are more independent, tolerant of individual differences, and excited about learning. The Kamehameha Elementary Education Program (KEEP), an approach grounded in Vygotsky's theory, has resulted in both academic and social benefits. Teachers who are effective classroom managers and who provide cognitively stimulating activities enhance children's involvement and learning. Self-fulfilling prophecies are likely to occur when teachers emphasize competition and make public comparisons among pupils. Computers lead to rich educational benefits in classrooms, but they reach affluent children and boys more effectively than low-income children and girls. To be effective, mainstreaming must be carefully tailored to meet the academic and social needs of children who are mildly retarded or learning disabled. Today, giftedness means more than high IQ; it includes creativity and specialized talent. Gifted children are best served by educational programs that build on their unique strengths.

HOW WELL EDUCATED ARE AMERICA'S CHILDREN?

Our discussion of schooling has largely focused on what teachers can do in classrooms to support the education of children. Yet a great many factors, both within and outside schools, affect children's learning. Societal values, school resources, quality of teaching, and parental encouragement all play important roles. Nowhere are these multiple influences more apparent than when schooling is examined in cross-cultural perspective.

Perhaps you are aware from recent news reports that American children fare poorly when their achievement is compared to that of children in other industrial-

Japanese children achieve considerably better than their American counterparts for a variety of reasons. Their culture stresses the importance of working hard to master academic skills. Their parents help more with homework and communicate more often with teachers. And a longer school day permits frequent alternation of academic instruction with pleasurable activity. This approach makes learning easier and more enjoyable. *(Eiji Miyazawa/Black Star Publishing Company)*

CULTURAL INFLUENCES

EDUCATION IN JAPAN, TAIWAN, AND THE UNITED STATES

Why do Asian children perform so well academically? Recent research examining societal, school, and family conditions in Japan, Taiwan, and United States provides some answers:

Cultural Valuing of Academic Achievement. In Japan and Taiwan, natural resources are limited. Progress in science and technology is essential for economic well-being. Because a well-educated work force is necessary to meet this goal, children's mastery of academic skills is vital. In the United States, attitudes toward academic achievement are far less unified. Many Americans believe that it is more important to encourage children to feel good about themselves and to explore various areas of knowledge than to perform well in school.

Emphasis on Effort. Japanese and Taiwanese parents and teachers believe that all children have the potential to master challenging academic tasks if they work hard enough. In contrast, many more of their American counterparts regard native ability as the key to academic success (Stevenson, 1992). These differences in attitude may contribute to the fact that American parents are less likely to encourage activities at home that might enhance school performance. Japanese and Taiwanese children spend more free time reading and playing academic-related games than do children in the United States (Stevenson & Lee, 1990).

Involvement of Parents in Education. Asian parents devote many hours to helping their children with homework. American parents spend very little and, at least while their children are in elementary school, do not regard homework as especially important. Overall, American parents are far more satisfied with the quality of their children's education, hold much lower standards for their children's academic performance, and are far less concerned about how well their youngsters are doing in school (Stevenson, Chen, & Lee, 1993; Stevenson & Lee, 1990).

High Quality Education for All. Unlike teachers in the United States, Japanese and Taiwanese teachers do not make early educational decisions on the basis of achievement. There are no separate ability groups in elementary schools. Instead, all pupils receive the same nationally mandated high-quality instruction. In the United States, wide variation in quality of schooling exists. Low-income, ethnic minority children have a much higher likelihood of attending underequipped schools offering poor quality instruction than do their middle-income counterparts.

Coherent Lessons that Actively Involve Children in Learning. Academic lessons in Japanese and Taiwanese classrooms are particularly well organized and presented in ways that capture children's attention and involve them actively in the learning process. Japanese and Taiwanese teachers assume the role of knowledge guide rather than dispenser of information. Each daily lesson begins with an engaging practical problem and, like a good story, has an introduction, conclusion, and consistent theme. Discussion is frequent as Asian teachers stimulate children to explain and evaluate their solutions. Compared to American classrooms, topics in mathematics are treated in greater depth, and there is less repetition of material taught the previous year (Stevenson & Lee, 1990).

More Time Devoted to Instruction. In Japan and Taiwan, the school year is over 50 days longer than in the United States, and much more time is devoted to academic pursuits, especially mathematics. Furthermore, time is used more effectively in Asian classrooms. In one cross-cultural comparison of elementary school academic lessons, the teacher was the leader of the child's activity 90 percent of the time in Taiwan, 74 percent in Japan, but only 46 percent in the United States. Most often, American children worked on their own at their desks—a circumstance that frequently resulted in loss of focus on the purpose of the activity. In contrast, Japanese and Taiwanese teachers alternated between short seatwork periods and group discussion of problems, thereby embedding independent work into the larger lesson and keeping children involved. Furthermore, Asian schools are not regimented places with a single-minded emphasis on academics, as many Americans believe. An 8-hour school day and effective use of class time permits extra recesses and a longer lunch period, with plenty of time for play, social interaction, field trips, and extracurricular activities (Stevenson, 1992, 1994).

Communication between Teachers and Parents. Japanese and Taiwanese teachers get to know their pupils especially well. They teach the same children for two or three years and make visits to the home once or twice a year. Continuous communication between teachers and parents takes place with the aid of small notebooks that children carry back and forth every day and in which messages about assignments, academic performance, and behavior are written. No such formalized system of frequent teacher–parent communication exists in the United States (Stevenson & Lee, 1990).

Do Japanese and Taiwanese children pay a price for the pressure placed on them to succeed? By high school, academic work often displaces other experiences, since Asian adolescents must pass a highly competitive entrance exam to gain admission to college. Yet the American approach seems to err in the other direction—by placing too little emphasis on diligence and excellence. Awareness of the ingredients of Asian success has prompted Americans to rethink current educational practices.

ized nations. In international studies of mathematics and science achievement, American students score no better than at the mean of participating countries, and often they fall at the bottom of the pack (International Education Association, 1988; McKnight et al., 1987). These trends emerge early in development. In a 1980 comparison of elementary school children in Japan, Taiwan, and the United States, large differences in mathematics achievement were present in kindergarten and became greater with increasing grade. Although less extreme gaps occurred in reading, a 1990 retest showed American children doing less well than both Asian groups in this area as well (Stevenson, Chen, & Lee, 1993; Stevenson & Lee, 1990). There is now clear evidence that too many American youngsters manage to complete their education with weak reading, writing, and mathematical skills (Mullis et al., 1991).

Why do American children fall behind in academic accomplishments? To find out, researchers have looked closely at learning environments in top-performing Asian nations. A common assumption is that Asian children are high achievers because they are "smarter," but this is not true. They do not do better on intelligence tests than their American agemates (Stevenson et al., 1985). Instead, as the Cultural Influences box on page 459 indicates, a variety of social forces combine to foster a much stronger commitment to learning in Asian families and schools.

Japan and Taiwan have established broad cultural climates for achievement. However, the educational system of one society cannot simply be transplanted to cure the ills of another. The United States faces challenges that are different from those in Asian countries—among them, the problem of how to educate children from a great many ethnic backgrounds for successful participation in a common culture (Leetsma et al., 1987). Yet members of diverse ethnic groups are in strong agreement about one thing: the importance of education and the need to improve it in the United States.

The Japanese and Taiwanese examples underscore that families, schools, and the larger society must work together to upgrade American education. Already, progress is being made. Throughout the country, academic standards and teacher certification requirements are being strengthened. Many schools are also making an effort to increase parent involvement in children's education. Parents who create stimulating learning environments at home, monitor their youngster's academic progress, help with homework, and communicate often with teachers have children who consistently show superior academic progress (Bradley, Caldwell, & Rock, 1988; Dossey et al., 1988; Stevenson & Baker, 1987). The current educational reform movement is an encouraging sign. It reflects the firm desire of many educators and concerned citizens to rebuild an educational system capable of guiding American children toward a prosperous and civilized adulthood in a complex, changing world.

SUMMARY

PIAGET'S THEORY: THE CONCRETE OPERATIONAL STAGE

What are the major characteristics of concrete operational thought?

- During the **concrete operational stage,** thought is far more logical and organized than it was during the preschool years. Conservation indicates that children can **decenter** and **reverse** their thinking. In addition, they are better at hierarchical classification, **seriation,** and **transitive inference.** School-age youngsters' spatial reasoning improves, as their understanding of distance and ability to give directions reveals.
- Concrete operational thought is limited in that children can reason logically only about concrete, tangible information; they have difficulty with abstractions. Piaget used the term **horizontal décalage** to describe the school-age child's gradual mastery of logical concepts such as conservation.

Discuss recent research on concrete operational thought.

- Recent evidence indicates that specific cultural practices, especially those associated with schooling, affect children's mastery of Piagetian tasks. Some researchers believe that the horizontal décalage can best be understood within an information processing framework.

INFORMATION PROCESSING IN MIDDLE CHILDHOOD

How do attention and memory change in middle childhood?

- During middle childhood, attention becomes much more controlled, adaptable, and planful. Children become better at ignoring irrelevant information, adjusting their attention to task demands and changes in their own learning, and scanning stimuli systematically.
- During the school years, children use memory strategies more often. **Rehearsal** appears first, followed by **organization** and then **elaboration.**
- Development of the long-term knowledge base facilitates strategic memory processing by making new information easier to store and retrieve. Children's motivation to use what they know also contributes to memory development. Memory strategies are promoted by learning activities in school.

Describe the school-age child's theory of mind and capacity to engage in self-regulation.

- Metacognition expands over middle childhood. School-age children regard the mind as an active, constructive agent, and they combine their metacognitive knowledge into an integrated theory of mind.
- School-age children are not yet good at **self-regulation**—putting what they know about thinking into action. Providing children with instructions to monitor their cognitive activity improves self-regulatory skills and task performance.

Discuss current controversies in teaching reading and mathematics to elementary school children.

- Skilled reading draws on all aspects of the information-processing system. Experts disagree on whether a **whole-language approach** or **basic-skills approach** should be used to teach beginning reading. A balanced mixture of both is probably most effective. As with reading, instruction that combines practice in basic skills with conceptual understanding seems best in mathematics.

INDIVIDUAL DIFFERENCES IN MENTAL DEVELOPMENT DURING MIDDLE CHILDHOOD

Cite commonly used intelligence tests in middle childhood, and describe major approaches to defining intelligence.

- During the school years, IQ becomes more stable, and it correlates strongly with academic achievement. Most intelligence tests yield an overall score representing general intelligence as well as scores for separate intellectual factors. Current widely used intelligence tests for children are the **Stanford-Binet Intelligence Scale,** the **Wechsler Intelligence Scale for Children–III (WISC–III),** and the **Kaufman Assessment Battery for Children (K–ABC).**
- To search for the precise mental processes underlying mental ability factors, researchers have combined the factor analytic approach to defining intelligence with information processing. Sternberg's **triarchic theory of intelligence** extends this effort. It views intelligence as a complex interaction of information processing skills, specific experiences, and contextual (or cultural) influences.
- According to Gardner's **theory of multiple intelligences,** mental abilities should be defined in terms of distinct sets of processing operations applied in culturally valued activities. His seven independent intelligences have been helpful in efforts to understand and nurture children's special talents.

Describe evidence indicating that both heredity and environment contribute to intelligence.

- Heritability estimates and adoption research reveal that intelligence is a product of heredity and environment. Studies of black children adopted into white middle-class homes indicate that the black–white IQ gap is substantially determined by environment.

- IQ scores are affected by specific learning experiences, including exposure to certain language customs and familiarity with the kind of knowledge sampled by the test. Cultural bias in intelligence tests can lead to overlabeling of low-income minority children as slow learners. Special precautions need to be taken when evaluating the mental abilities of these children.

LANGUAGE DEVELOPMENT IN MIDDLE CHILDHOOD

Describe changes in vocabulary, grammar, and pragmatics during middle childhood.

- During middle childhood, vocabulary continues to grow rapidly, and children have a more precise and flexible understanding of the meanings of words. Improvements in children's grasp of complex grammatical constructions also take place. School-age children can handle challenging communicative situations, and their conversational strategies become more refined.

What are the advantages of bilingualism in childhood?

- Research shows that bilingual children are advanced in cognitive development. They score higher on tests of analytical reasoning, concept formation, cognitive flexibility, and language awareness.

CHILDREN'S LEARNING IN SCHOOL

Describe the impact of educational philosophies on children's motivation and academic achievement.

- Schools exert powerful influences on children's cognitive development. Pupils in **traditional classrooms** are advantaged in terms of academic achievement. Those in **open classrooms** tend to be independent learners who respect individual differences and have more positive attitudes toward school. The Kamehameha Elementary Education Program (KEEP) uses a balanced philosophical viewpoint based on Vygotsky's theory. It promotes academic achievement and excitement about learning.

Discuss the role of teacher–pupil interaction in academic achievement.

- Patterns of teacher–pupil interaction affect children's academic progress. Teachers who are effective classroom managers have pupils who achieve especially well. Instruction that encourages higher-level thinking fosters children's interest and involvement. **Self-fulfilling prophecies,** in which children start to live up to the opinions of their teachers, are most likely to occur in classrooms that emphasize competition and public evaluation.

Describe advantages of and concerns about computers in classrooms.

- Computers can have rich educational benefits. Gains in academic performance result from **computer-assisted instruction (CAI)** and word processing. Programming promotes complex cognitive skills and knowledge of how computers function. However, computers may be widening intellectual gaps between the social classes and sexes.

Under what conditions is mainstreaming of mildly retarded and learning disabled children successful?

- Teachers face special challenges in meeting the needs of children at the very low and high ends of the ability distribution. Pupils with mild **mental retardation** and **learning disabilities** are often integrated into regular classrooms. The success of **mainstreaming** depends on efforts by teachers to provide individualized instruction and promote positive peer relations.

Describe the characteristics of gifted children and current efforts to meet their educational needs.

- **Giftedness** includes high IQ, high creativity, and exceptional talent. Gifted children are best served by educational programs that build on their special strengths. Academic acceleration is a controversial practice, but when carefully implemented, it is highly successful.

HOW WELL EDUCATED ARE AMERICA'S CHILDREN?

Why do American children fall behind children in other industrialized nations in academic accomplishments?

- American children fare poorly when their achievement is compared to that of children in other industrialized nations. In contrast, children from Japan and Taiwan are consistently among the top performers. A stronger commitment to learning in families and schools underlies the greater academic success of Asian over American pupils.

IMPORTANT TERMS AND CONCEPTS

concrete operational stage (p. 422)
decentration (p. 422)
reversibility (p. 422)
seriation (p. 424)
transitive inference (p. 424)
horizontal décalage (p. 425)
rehearsal (p. 429)
organization (p. 429)
elaboration (p. 429)
attention-deficit hyperactivity disorder (ADHD) (p. 431)
self-regulation (p. 434)
whole-language approach (p. 435)
basic-skills approach (p. 435)
Stanford-Binet Intelligence Scale (p. 437)
Wechsler Intelligence Scale for Children–III (WISC–III) (p. 439)
Kaufman Assessment Battery for Children (K-ABC) (p. 439)
triarchic theory of intelligence (p. 440)
theory of multiple intelligences (p. 441)
traditional classroom (p. 450)
open classroom (p. 450)
educational self-fulfilling prophecy (p. 452)
computer-assisted instruction (CAI) (p. 452)
mainstreaming (p. 453)
mental retardation (p. 453)
learning disabilities (p. 454)
giftedness (p. 455)
divergent thinking (p. 455)
convergent thinking (p. 455)

FYI...

FOR FURTHER INFORMATION AND SPECIAL HELP, CONSULT THE FOLLOWING ORGANIZATIONS:

ATTENTION-DEFICIT HYPERACTIVITY DISORDER

Children with Attention Deficit Disorders
499 N.W. 70th Avenue, Suite 308
Plantation, FL 33317
(305) 587-3700

Provides support and education to families of children with attention-deficit hyperactivity disorder. Encourages schools and health care professionals to be responsive to their needs.

BILINGUAL EDUCATION

National Association for Bilingual Education
Union Center Plaza
810 First Street, N.E., Third Floor
Washington, DC 20002
(202) 898-1829

An organization of educators, public citizens, and students aimed at increasing public understanding of the importance of bilingual education.

COMPUTERS

National Center for Computer Equity
99 Hudson Street
New York, NY 10013
(212) 925-6635

Works to resolve problems in equal access to computer education for girls. Sponsored by the National Organization for Women (NOW).

MENTAL RETARDATION

Division on Mental Retardation of the Council for Exceptional Children
245 Cedar Springs Drive
Athens, GA 30605
(404) 546-6132

An organization of teachers of the mentally retarded. Seeks to advance education, research, and public understanding. Publishes the journal Education and Training in Mental Retardation.

LEARNING DISABILITIES

Learning Disabilities Association of America
4156 Library Road
Pittsburgh, PA 15234
(412) 341-1515

A 60,000-member organization of parents of learning disabled children and interested professionals. Local groups provide parent support and education and sponsor recreational programs and summer camps for children.

GIFTEDNESS

The Association for the Gifted of the Council for Exceptional Children
1920 Association Drive
Reston, VA 22091
(703) 620-3660

An organization of educators and parents aimed at stimulating interest in program development for gifted children. Publishes the Journal for the Education of the Gifted.

National Association for Gifted Children
1155 15th Street N.W., No. 1002
Washington, DC 20005
(202) 785-4268

Association of scholars, educators, and librarians devoted to advancing education for gifted children. Distributes information and sponsors institutes. Publishes the journal Gifted Child Quarterly.

"Playing with Mum and Dad in the pool"
Ohmmar Coates
9 years, New Zealand

The link between the worlds of family and peers is exquisitely conveyed in this animated painting. As Chapter 13 reveals, children's relationships include a much wider social network during middle childhood than at younger ages. Nevertheless, parents remain powerful influences in children's lives.

13

Emotional and Social Development in Middle Childhood

ERIKSON'S THEORY: INDUSTRY VERSUS INFERIORITY

SELF-DEVELOPMENT IN MIDDLE CHILDHOOD

Changes in Self-Concept • Development of Self-Esteem • Influences on Self-Esteem

EMOTIONAL DEVELOPMENT IN MIDDLE CHILDHOOD

UNDERSTANDING OTHERS

Selman's Stages of Perspective Taking • Perspective Taking and Social Behavior

MORAL DEVELOPMENT IN MIDDLE CHILDHOOD

Learning About Justice Through Sharing • Changes in Moral and Social-Conventional Understanding

PEER RELATIONS IN MIDDLE CHILDHOOD

Changes in Peer Sociability • Peer Groups • Friendships • Peer Acceptance

GENDER TYPING IN MIDDLE CHILDHOOD

Gender-Stereotyped Beliefs • Gender-Role Identity and Behavior • Cultural Influences on Gender Typing

FAMILY INFLUENCES IN MIDDLE CHILDHOOD

Parent–Child Relationships • Siblings • Divorce • Remarriage • Maternal Employment

SOME COMMON PROBLEMS OF DEVELOPMENT

Fears and Anxieties • Child Sexual Abuse

STRESS AND COPING: THE RESILIENT CHILD

One late afternoon, Rena heard Joey dash through the front door, run upstairs, and call up his best friend Terry. "Terry, gotta talk to you," pleaded Joey, out of breath from running home. "Everything was going great until that word I got—*porcupine,*" remarked Joey, referring to the fifth-grade spelling bee at school that day. "Just my luck! *P-o-r-k,* that's how I spelled it! I can't believe it. Maybe I'm not so good at social studies," Joey confided, "but I *know* I'm better at spelling than that stuck-up Belinda Brown. Gosh, I knocked myself out studying those spelling lists. Then *she* got all the easy words. Did'ya see how snooty she acted after she won? If I *had* to lose, why couldn't it be to a nice person, anyhow!"

Joey's conversation reflects a whole new constellation of emotional and social capacities. First, Joey shows evidence of *industriousness.* By entering the spelling bee, he energetically pursued meaningful achievement in his culture—a major change of the middle childhood years. At the same time, Joey's social understanding has greatly expanded. He can size up himself and others in terms of strengths, weaknesses, and personality characteristics—a capacity that was beyond him during the preschool years. Furthermore, friendship means something quite different to Joey than it did at younger ages. Terry is not just a convenient playmate; he is a best friend whom Joey counts on for understanding and emotional support.

We begin this chapter by returning to Erikson's theory for an overview of the personality changes of middle childhood. Then we take a close look at a variety of aspects of emotional and social development. We will see how, as children reason more effectively and spend more time in school and with peers, their views of themselves, of others, and of social relationships become more complex.

Although school-age children spend less time with parents than they did at earlier ages, the family remains a powerful context for development. Joey and Lizzie,

When Joey and Belinda Brown competed in the spelling bee, they showed evidence of industriousness by pursuing meaningful achievement in their culture. Accoring to Erikson, developing a sense of industry is the critical psychosocial task of middle childhood. *(Charles Gupton/Stock Boston)*

along with many children of their generation, are growing up in homes profoundly affected by social change. Rena, unlike her own mother, has been employed since her children were preschoolers. In addition, Joey and Lizzie's home life has been disrupted by family discord; Rena is divorced. The children's personal experiences in adjusting to these departures from traditional family arrangements will help us appreciate the vital role of family relationships in all aspects of child development.

Finally, when stress is overwhelming and social support lacking, school-age children experience serious adjustment difficulties. Our chapter concludes with a discussion of some common emotional problems of middle childhood.

ERIKSON'S THEORY: INDUSTRY VERSUS INFERIORITY

According to Erikson (1950), the personality changes of the school years build on Freud's **latency stage**, a period in which the sexual instincts lie dormant after the Oedipus and Electra conflicts of early childhood are resolved. In Chapter 10, we noted that Freud's theory is no longer widely accepted. Yet when experiences with caregivers have been positive, children enter middle childhood with the calm confidence that Freud intended when he used the word *latency* to describe this stage. Their energies are redirected from the make-believe of early childhood into realistic accomplishment.

Erikson believed that the combination of adult expectations and children's drive toward mastery sets the stage for the psychological conflict of middle childhood: **industry versus inferiority.** Industry means developing competence at useful skills and tasks. In cultures everywhere, improved physical and cognitive capacities mean that adults impose new demands. Children, in turn, are ready to meet these challenges and benefit from them:

- Among the Baka hunters and gatherers of Cameroon, 5- to 7-year-olds begin to fetch and carry water, bathe and mind younger siblings, and accompany adults on food-gathering missions. Behind the main camp stands a miniature village. In this "school" of the Baka society, children practice the arts of hut building, spear shaping, and fire making (Avis & Harris, 1991).
- The Ngoni of Malawi, Central Africa, believe that when children shed their first teeth, they are ready for a different kind of life. Between ages 6 and 7, they stop their childish games and start skill training. Boys move out of the huts of family members into dormitories, where they enter a system of male domination and instruction. At that time, children are expected to show independence and are held personally accountable for irresponsible and disrespectful behavior (Read, 1968; Rogoff et al., 1975).

In industrialized nations, the transition to middle childhood is marked by the beginning of formal schooling. With it comes literacy training, which provides children with the widest possible preparation for the vast array of specialized careers in complex societies. In school, children engage in productive work beside and with other children. They become aware of their own and others' unique capacities, learn the value of division of labor, and develop a sense of moral commitment and responsibility. The danger at this stage is *inferiority,* reflected in the sad pessimism of some children who have come to believe they will never be good at anything. This profound sense of inadequacy can develop when family life has not prepared children for school life or when experiences with teachers and peers are so negative that they destroy children's feelings of competence and mastery.

Latency stage
Freud's psychosexual stage of middle childhood, in which the sexual instincts lie dormant.

Industry versus inferiority
In Erikson's theory, the psychological conflict of middle childhood, which is resolved positively when experiences lead children to develop a sense of competence at useful skills and tasks.

Erikson's sense of industry combines several developments of middle childhood: a positive but realistic self-concept, pride in doing things well, moral responsibility, and cooperative participation with agemates. Let's look at how these aspects of self and social relationships change over the school years.

SELF-DEVELOPMENT IN MIDDLE CHILDHOOD

In middle childhood, several transformations in self-understanding take place. First, children can describe themselves in terms of psychological traits. Second, they start to compare their own characteristics to those of their peers. Finally, they speculate about the causes of their strengths and weaknesses. These new capacities for thinking about the self have a major impact on children's developing sense of self-esteem.

CHANGES IN SELF-CONCEPT

During the school years, children organize their observations of behaviors and internal states into general dispositions that they can verbalize to others, with a major change taking place between ages 8 and 11. The following responses of two children, who were asked to tell about themselves, reflect this change:

> *A boy age 7:* I am 7 and I have hazel brown hair and my hobby is stamp collecting. I am good at football and I am quite good at sums and my favourite game is football and I love school and I like reading books and my favourite car is an Austin. (Livesley & Bromley, 1973, p. 237)

> *A girl age 11 1/2:* My name is A. I'm a human being. I'm a girl. I'm a truthful person. I'm not pretty. I do so-so in my studies. I'm a very good cellist. I'm a very good pianist. I'm a little bit tall for my age. I like several boys. I like several girls. I'm old-fashioned. I play tennis. I am a very good swimmer. I try to be helpful. I'm always ready to be friends with anybody. Mostly I'm good, but I lose my temper. I'm not well liked by some girls and boys. I don't know if I'm liked by boys or not. (Montemayor & Eisen, 1977, pp. 317–318)

Notice that instead of specific behaviors, school-age children emphasize competencies, as in "I am quite good at sums" or "I'm a very good cellist" (Damon & Hart, 1988). In addition, the younger of the two children does not refer to any psychological traits, whereas the older one clearly describes her personality. For example, she notes that she is truthful, old-fashioned, helpful, friendly, and short-tempered.

Another change in self-concept takes place in middle childhood: Children begin to make **social comparisons.** In other words, they judge their appearance, abilities, and behavior in relation to those of others. Return to Joey's comments about the spelling bee at the beginning of this chapter. You will see that he expressed some thoughts about how good he was compared to Belinda Brown—better at spelling but not so great at social studies. Children younger than 7 practically never include social comparison information in their self-descriptions (Ruble, 1988).

What factors are responsible for these revisions in self-concept? Cognitive development certainly affects the changing *structure* of the self. School-age children, as we saw in Chapter 12, are better at coordinating several aspects of a situation in reasoning about their physical world. They show an improved ability to relate separate observations in the social realm as well, combining typical experiences and behaviors into stable psychological dispositions (Harter, 1983; Paget & Kritt, 1986).

The *content* of the developing self-concept, however, comes largely from interactions with others. Early in this century, sociologist George Herbert Mead (1934)

Social comparisons
Judgments of abilities, behavior, appearance, and other characteristics in relation to those of others.

During the school years, children's self-concepts expand to include feedback from a wider range of people as they spend more time in settings beyond the home. Girl scouting and its associated qualities of friendliness, helpfulness, and kindness are probably important aspects of the self-definitions of these two girls.
(Joel Gordon)

described the self as a blend of what important people in our lives think of us. He believed that a well-organized psychological self emerges when children can imagine the attitude that others take toward them. In other words, *perspective-taking* skills emerging during middle childhood—in particular, the ability to imagine what other people are thinking—play a crucial role in the development of a psychological self. Indeed, as we will see later in this chapter, perspective taking improves greatly over the school years. Children become better at reading the messages they receive from others and incorporating these into their self-definitions (Rosenberg, 1979).

During middle childhood, children look to more people for information about themselves as they enter a wider range of settings in school and community. This is reflected in children's frequent reference to social groups in their self-descriptions (Livesley & Bromley, 1973). "I'm a Boy Scout, a paper boy, and a Prairie City soccer player," Joey remarked when asked to describe himself. Gradually, as children move toward adolescence, their sources of self-definition become more selective. Although parents remain influential, between ages 8 and 15 peers become more important. And over time, self-concept becomes increasingly vested in feedback from close friends (Rosenberg, 1979).

DEVELOPMENT OF SELF-ESTEEM

Self-esteem, the judgments children make about their own worth, is also reorganized in middle childhood. Recall from Chapter 10 that most preschoolers have extremely high self-esteem. As children move into middle childhood, they get much more feedback about their performance in different activities compared to that of their peers. Grades on papers and tests, report cards, and the comments of adults and other children are integrated into self-evaluations. As a result, self-esteem differentiates, and it also adjusts to a more realistic level (Stipek & Mac Iver, 1989).

A HIERARCHICALLY STRUCTURED SELF-ESTEEM. Susan Harter (1982, 1986) asked children to indicate the extent to which a variety of statements, such as "I am good at homework," "I'm usually the one chosen for games," and "Most kids like me," are true of themselves. Her findings, and those of other researchers, reveal that classrooms, playgrounds, and peer groups are key contexts in which children evaluate their own competence. By age 7 to 8, children have formed at least three separate self-esteems—academic, physical, and social—that become more refined with age. For example, academic self-worth divides into performance in different school subjects, social self-worth into peer and parental relationships (Marsh, 1990). Furthermore, school-age children combine their separate

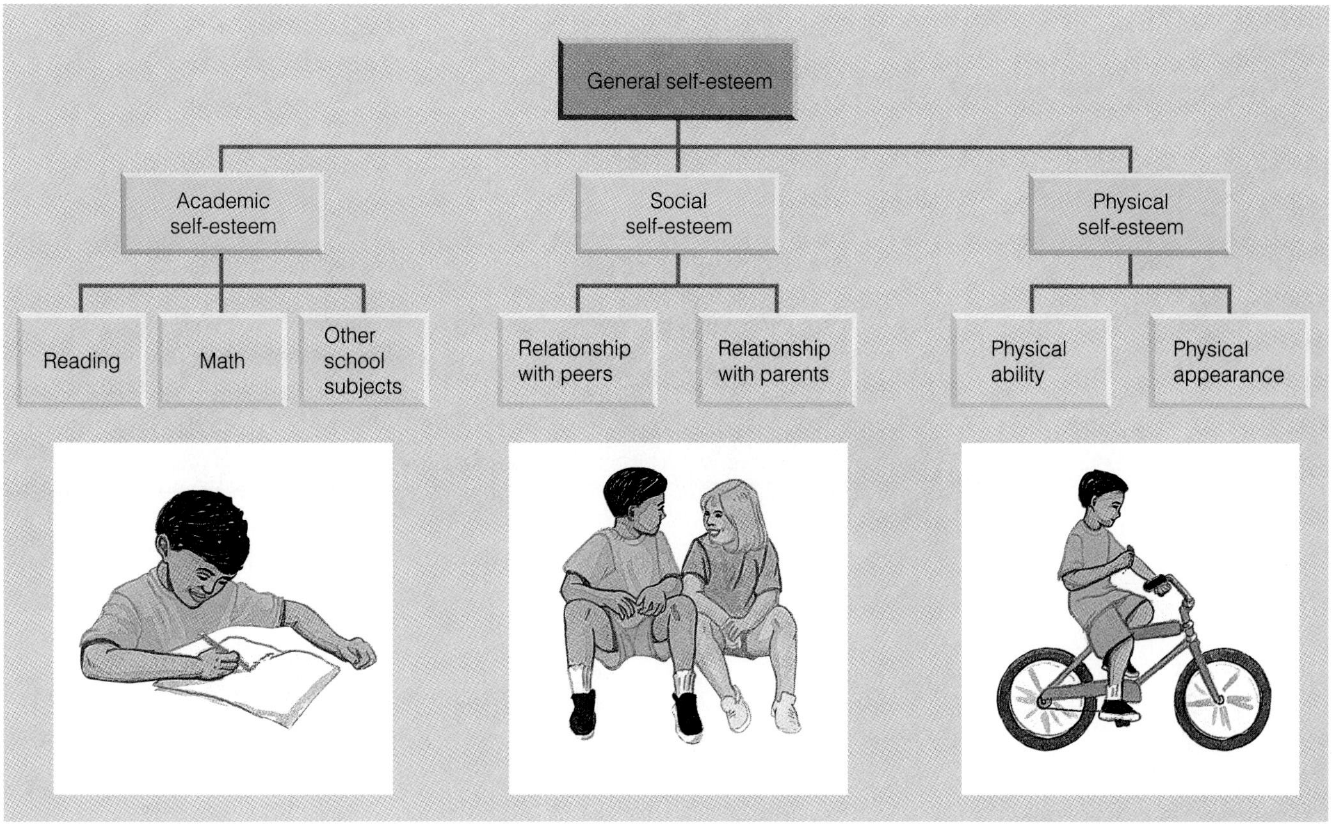

FIGURE 13.1

Hierarchical structure of self-esteem in the mid-elementary school years. From their experiences in different settings, children form at least three separate self-esteems—academic, social, and physical. These differentiate into additional self-evaluations and combine to form an overall sense of self-worth.

self-evaluations into a general psychological image of themselves—an overall sense of self-worth (Harter, 1990). Consequently, by the mid-elementary school years, self-esteem takes on the hierarchical structure shown in Figure 13.1.

■ CHANGES IN LEVEL OF SELF-ESTEEM. As children evaluate themselves in various areas, they lose the sunny optimism of early childhood. Self-esteem drops during the first few years of elementary school (Stipek & Mac Iver, 1989). This decline can be explained by the fact that children gradually adjust their self-judgments to fit the opinions of others as well as their objective performance. In one study, kindergartners through third graders were asked to rate their own and each of their classmates' "smartness" at school. Even the youngest children were able to judge their peers fairly accurately. But their own self-ratings were overly favorable; most kindergartners and first graders placed themselves at the top of the class! By second grade, children had figured out where they stood in relation to other pupils, and their self-esteem began to match the opinions of those around them (Stipek, 1981).

Typically, this drop in self-esteem is not great enough to be harmful. Most (but not all) children appraise their characteristics and competencies realistically while maintaining an attitude of self-acceptance and self-respect. In fact, from fourth to sixth grade, self-esteem rises for the majority of youngsters, who feel especially good about their athletic capabilities and peer relationships (Nottelmann, 1987; Wallace, Cunningham, & Del Monte, 1984). As we will see in Chapter 16, self-esteem will decline again, and more seriously so, when children enter junior high school and encounter many new experiences and expectations.

INFLUENCES ON SELF-ESTEEM

From middle childhood on, strong relationships exist between self-esteem and everyday behavior. For example, academic self-esteem predicts children's school achievement as well as their willingness to try hard at challenging tasks (Marsh,

CONCEPT REVIEW TABLE

An Attributional Approach to Success and Failure in Middle Childhood

CONCEPT	IMPORTANT POINT	EXAMPLE
Mastery-Oriented Attributions	Children with mastery-oriented attributions attribute success to ability and failure to effort. Because they regard outcomes as controllable, they approach challenging tasks with effort and enthusiasm.	Roy received a D on his recent math test. When his parents inquired about the low grade, Roy said, "I guess I wasn't really trying. I know I can do these problems." Roy reworked the ones he missed.
Learned Helplessness	Children with learned helplessness attribute failure to ability. When faced with challenging tasks, they experience an anxious loss of control and give up without really trying.	After Adrian did poorly on a math test, he said to his parents, "I just can't understand this stuff! No matter what I do, I keep getting bad grades. Let's face it, I'm stupid at math."

Smith, & Barnes, 1985). Children with high social self-esteem are consistently better liked by their peers (Harter, 1982). And as we saw in Chapter 11, boys come to believe they have more athletic talent than do girls, and they are also more advanced in a variety of physical skills.

Because self-esteem is so powerfully related to individual differences in behavior, researchers have been intensely interested in finding out exactly which social influences cause it to be high for some children and low for others. If ways can be found to improve children's sense of self-worth, then many aspects of child development might be enhanced as well.

■ CHILD-REARING PRACTICES. School-age children whose parents are warm and responsive and who provide firm but reasonable expectations for behavior—that is, who use an *authoritative* child-rearing style (see Chapter 10)—feel especially good about themselves (Bishop & Ingersoll, 1989; Coopersmith, 1967). If you think carefully about this finding, you will see that it makes perfect sense. Warm, positive parenting lets children know that they are accepted as competent, worthwhile human beings. And firm but appropriate expectations, backed up with explanations, seem to help children make sensible choices and evaluate their own behavior against reasonable standards.

Although parental acceptance and maturity demands are undoubtedly important ingredients of high self-esteem, we must keep in mind that these findings are correlational. We cannot really tell the extent to which child-rearing styles are causes of or reactions to children's characteristics and behavior. Research on the precise content of adults' messages to children has been far more successful at isolating factors that affect children's sense of self-worth. Let's see how these communicative forces mold children's evaluations of themselves in achievement contexts.

■ MAKING ACHIEVEMENT-RELATED ATTRIBUTIONS. **Attributions** are our common, everyday explanations for the causes of behavior—the answers we provide to the question, "Why did I (or another person) do that?" Look back at Joey's conversation about the spelling bee at the beginning of this chapter. Notice how he attributes his second-place performance to *luck* (Belinda got all the easy words) and his usual success at spelling to *ability* (he *knows* he's a better speller than Belinda). Joey also appreciates that *effort* makes a difference; he "knocked himself out studying those spelling words."

Attributions
Common, everyday explanations for the causes of behavior.

Cognitive development permits children to recognize and separate all these variables in explaining performance—something they could not do during the preschool years (Chapman & Skinner, 1989; Ruble, Eisenberg, & Higgins, 1994). Yet school-age children differ greatly in the extent to which they account for their successes and failures in healthy and adaptive ways. Children who are high in academic self-esteem develop **mastery-oriented attributions** (see the Concept Review Table on the opposite page). They believe their successes are due to ability—a characteristic they can count on in the future when faced with new challenges. And when failure occurs, they attribute it to factors about themselves or the environment that can be changed and controlled, such as insufficient effort or a very difficult task. So regardless of whether these children succeed or fail, they take an industrious, persistent, and enthusiastic approach to learning.

Unfortunately, other children, who develop **learned helplessness,** hold very discouraging explanations for their performance. They attribute their failures, not their successes, to ability. And on occasions when they do succeed, they are likely to conclude that external factors, such as luck, are responsible. Furthermore, unlike their mastery-oriented counterparts, learned-helpless children have come to believe that ability is a fixed characteristic of the self that cannot be changed. They do not think that competence can be improved by trying hard. So when a task is difficult, these children experience an anxious loss of control—in Erikson's terms, a pervasive sense of inferiority. They quickly give up, saying "I can't do this," before they have really tried (Dweck & Elliott, 1983; Dweck & Leggett, 1988).

Children who receive feedback from others that attributes their successes to high ability and their failures to insufficient effort are likely to be mastery-oriented youngsters who approach difficult tasks with enthusiasm. *(Dennis MacDonald/The Picture Cube)*

Over time, the ability of learned-helpless children no longer predicts their performance. Many are very bright pupils who have concluded that they are incompetent (Wagner & Phillips, 1992). Because they fail to make the connection between effort and success, learned-helpless children do not develop the metacognitive and self-regulatory skills that are necessary for high achievement (see Chapter 12). Lack of effective learning strategies, reduced persistence, and a sense of being controlled by external forces sustain one another in a vicious cycle (Heyman & Dweck, 1992).

■ INFLUENCES ON ACHIEVEMENT-RELATED ATTRIBUTIONS. What accounts for the very different attributions of mastery-oriented and learned-helpless children? The messages they receive from adults play a key role. Children with a learned-helpless style tend to have parents who set unusually high standards yet believe their child is not very capable and has to work harder to succeed (Parsons, Adler, & Kaczala, 1982; Phillips, 1987). In one study, researchers manipulated the feedback that fourth and fifth graders received after they failed at a task. Those receiving negative messages about their competence more often attributed failure to lack of ability than did children who were told that they had not tried hard enough (Dweck et al., 1978).

Some children are especially likely to have their performance undermined by adult feedback. Girls more often than boys blame their ability for poor performance. Girls also tend to receive messages from teachers and parents that their ability is at fault when they do not do well (Phillips & Zimmerman, 1990). Low-income ethnic minority children are also vulnerable to learned helplessness. In most studies comparing teacher communication with black and with white pupils, black children received less favorable treatment (Aaron & Powell, 1982; Hillman & Davenport, 1978; Irvine, 1986). Also, when ethnic minority children observe that adults in their own family are not rewarded by society for their achievement efforts, they may give up themselves. Many African-American children may come to believe that even if they do try in school, social prejudice will prevent them from succeeding in the end (Ogbu, 1988).

Finally, cultural values for achievement affect the likelihood that children will develop learned helplessness. Recall from Chapter 12 that compared to Americans, Japanese and Taiwanese parents and teachers believe that success in school depends much more on effort than innate ability. And Israeli children growing up on cooper-

Mastery-oriented attributions
Attributions that credit success to high ability and failure to insufficient effort. Leads to high self-esteem and a willingness to approach challenging tasks.

Learned helplessness
Attributions that credit success to luck and failure to low ability. Leads to anxious loss of control in the face of challenging tasks.

ative agricultural settlements called *kibbutzim* are shielded from learned helplessness by classrooms that emphasize mastery and cooperation rather than ability and competition. When asked why children look at each other's work at school, kibbutz third graders more often give a mastery-related reason ("You need to be sure what you're supposed to do, so you might check"). In contrast, urban Israeli third graders are likely to make a social comparison assessing ability ("You'd want to see if someone else's picture is better than yours") (Butler & Ruzany, 1993).

■ SUPPORTING CHILDREN'S SELF-ESTEEM. Attribution research suggests that even adults who are, on the whole, warm and supportive may send subtle messages to children that undermine their competence. **Attribution retraining** is an approach to intervention that encourages learned-helpless children to believe that they can overcome failure by exerting more effort. Most often, children are asked to work on tasks that are hard enough so that they will experience some failure. Then they get repeated feedback that helps them revise their attributions, such as "You can do it if you try harder." Children are also taught to view their successes as due to both ability and effort rather than chance factors, by giving them additional feedback after they succeed, such as "You're really good at this" or "You really tried hard on that one" (Dweck, 1975; Schunk, 1983). Another approach is to encourage these low-effort children to focus less on grades and more on mastering the task for its own sake (Stipek & Kowalski, 1989). Finally, learned-helpless children may need instruction in metacognition and self-regulation to make up for learning lost in this area because of their attributional styles (Borkowski et al., 1990).

To work well, attribution retraining is best begun in middle childhood, before children's views of themselves become hard to change. An even better approach is to prevent low self-esteem before it happens—by minimizing comparisons among children, helping them overcome failures, and designing school environments that accommodate individual differences in development and styles of learning. Finally, extra measures need to be taken to support the self-esteem of girls and ethnic minority children—by providing models of adult success, fostering ethnic pride, and ensuring equality of opportunity in society at large.

ASK YOURSELF . . .

- Return to page 413 of Chapter 11 and review the messages that parents send to girls about their athletic talent. On the basis of what you know about children's attributions for success and failure, why do school-age girls perform more poorly and spend less time at sports than do boys?
- In view of Joey's attributions for his spelling bee performance, is he likely to enter the next spelling bee and try hard to do well? Why or why not?

BRIEF REVIEW

Erikson's stage of industry versus inferiority indicates that when family, school, and peer experiences are positive, school-age children develop an industrious approach to productive work and feelings of competence and mastery. During middle childhood, psychological traits and social comparisons appear in children's self-descriptions. A differentiated, hierarchically organized self-esteem emerges, and children's sense of self-worth declines as they adjust their self-judgments to fit the opinions of others and objective performance. Parental warmth and reasonable maturity demands are related to high self-esteem. Attribution research has identified adult communication styles that affect children's explanations for success and failure and, in turn, their self-esteem and task performance.

Attribution retraining
An approach to intervention in which attributions of learned-helpless children are modified through feedback that encourages them to believe in themselves and persist in the face of task difficulty.

EMOTIONAL DEVELOPMENT IN MIDDLE CHILDHOOD

Greater self-awareness and social sensitivity support emotional development in middle childhood. Gains take place in children's experiencing of self-conscious emotions, awareness of emotional states, and emotional self-regulation.

In middle childhood, the self-conscious emotions of pride and guilt become clearly integrated with personal responsibility. Unlike preschoolers, 6- to 11-year-olds experience these feelings in the absence of adult monitoring. A teacher or parent does not have to be present for a new accomplishment to spark a glowing sense of pride or for a transgression to arouse painful pangs of guilt (Harter, Wright, & Bresnick, 1987). Also, school-age youngsters do not report guilt for any mishap, as they did at younger ages, but only for intentional wrongdoing, such as ignoring responsibilities, cheating, or lying (Graham, Doubleday, & Guarino, 1984; Ferguson, Stegge, & Damhuis, 1991). These changes reflect the older child's more mature sense of morality, a topic we will take up later in this chapter.

School-age children's understanding of psychological dispositions means that they are likely to explain emotion by making reference to internal states rather than physical events, as they did at younger ages (Strayer, 1993). They are also more aware of the diversity of emotional experiences. By age 8, children realize that they can experience more than one emotion at a time, each of which may differ in valence (positive versus negative) and intensity (Harter & Buddin, 1987; Wintre & Vallance, 1994). For example, recalling the birthday present he received from his grandmother, Joey reflected, "I was very happy I got something but a little sad that I didn't get just what I wanted." Similarly, Joey appreciates that emotional reactions need not reflect a person's true feelings. Consequently, he is much better at hiding his emotions when it is socially appropriate to do so. "I got all excited and told Grandma I liked that dumb plastic toy train," Joey said to Rena one day, "but I really don't. It's too babyish for a 10-year-old" (Saarni, 1989).

Rapid gains in emotional self-regulation occur in middle childhood as children come up with many more ways to handle emotionally arousing situations. In several studies, 5- to 11-year-olds were told stories about positive and negative events, such as having to wait before receiving an attractive prize or getting a bad grade on a test. Then they were asked what could be done to control emotions under these condi-

During the school years, children show gains in perspective taking. They are better able to detect the thoughts and feelings of others and imagine the self in another's place. Good perspective takers are more likely to display empathy and compassion. *(Susan Johns/Photo Researchers)*

In middle childhood, self-conscious emotions of pride and guilt become clearly linked to personal responsibility. This 9-year-old girl reacts with guilt to an intentional transgression. *(Stephen Marks)*

tions. With age, children were less likely to mention complete avoidance, such as leaving the scene or going to sleep—a form of coping that is usually counterproductive. And although children of all ages were aware that they could distract themselves with alternative behaviors, such as reading or watching TV, older children more often mentioned cognitive strategies for handling feelings. When an event could not be changed, they came up with ways of reinterpreting it that enabled them to accept current conditions (Altshuler & Ruble, 1989; Band & Weisz, 1988). For example, in response to the story about a bad grade, one child said, "Things could be worse. There'll be another test."

School-age children are not just better at recognizing and responding to their own feelings. They are also more aware of the thoughts and feelings of others, as we will see in the next section.

UNDERSTANDING OTHERS

By the mid-elementary school years, children discover consistencies in the behavior of people they know. As with their self-descriptions, they begin to describe other people in terms of psychological traits (Barenboim, 1977; Eder, 1989). This increases their awareness that others may react differently than they do to social situations. Middle childhood brings major advances in **perspective taking**—the capacity to imagine what other people may be thinking and feeling.

SELMAN'S STAGES OF PERSPECTIVE TAKING

Robert Selman developed a five-stage model describing changes in children's perspective-taking skill. He asked preschool through adolescent youngsters to respond to social dilemmas in which the characters have differing information and opinions about an event. Here is one example:

> Holly is an 8-year-old girl who likes to climb trees. She is the best tree climber in the neighborhood. One day while climbing down from a tall tree she falls off the bottom branch but does not hurt herself. Her father sees her fall. He is upset and asks her to promise not to climb the trees anymore. Holly promises.
>
> Later that day, Holly and her friends meet Sean. Sean's kitten is caught up in a tree and cannot get down. Something has to be done right away or the kitten may fall. Holly is the only one who climbs trees well enough to reach the kitten and get it down, but she remembers her promise to her father. (Selman & Byrne, 1974, p. 805)

After the dilemma is presented, children answer questions that highlight their ability to interpret the story from varying points of view, such as

> Does Sean know why Holly cannot decide whether or not to climb the tree?
>
> What will Holly's father think? Will he understand if she climbs the tree?
>
> Does Holly think she will be punished for climbing the tree? Should she be punished for doing so?

Table 13.1 summarizes Selman's five stages of perspective taking. As you can see, children gradually include a wider range of information in their understanding of others' viewpoints. At first, they have only a limited idea of what other people might be thinking and feeling. Over time, they become more conscious of the fact that people can interpret the same event in quite different ways. Soon they can "step in another person's shoes" and reflect on how that person might regard their own thoughts, feelings, and behavior. Finally, they can examine the relationship between

Perspective taking
The capacity to imagine what other people may be thinking and feeling.

TABLE 13.1

Selman's Stages of Perspective Taking

STAGE	APPROXIMATE AGE RANGE	DESCRIPTION	TYPICAL RESPONSE TO "HOLLY" DILEMMA
Level 0: Undifferentiated perspective taking	3–6	Children recognize that self and other can have different thoughts and feelings, but they frequently confuse the two.	The child predicts that Holly will save the kitten because she does not want it to get hurt and believes that Holly's father will feel just as she does about her climbing the tree: "Happy, he likes kittens."
Level 1: Social-informational perspective taking	4–9	Children understand that different perspectives may result because people have access to different information.	When asked how Holly's father will react when he finds out that she climbed the tree, the child responds, "If he didn't know anything about the kitten, he would be angry. But if Holly shows him the kitten, he might change his mind."
Level 2: Self-reflective perspective taking	7–12	Children can "step into another person's shoes" and view their own thoughts, feelings, and behavior from the other person's perspective. They also recognize that others can do the same.	When asked whether Holly thinks she will be punished, the child says, "No. Holly knows that her father will understand why she climbed the tree." This response assumes that Holly's point of view is influenced by her father being able to "step in her shoes" and understand why she saved the kitten.
Level 3: Third-party perspective taking	10–15	Children can step outside a two-person situation and imagine how the self and other are viewed from the viewpoint of a third, impartial party.	When asked whether Holly should be punished, the child says, "No, because Holly thought it was important to save the kitten. But she also knows that her father told her not to climb the tree. So she'd think she shouldn't be punished only if she could get her father to understand why she had to climb the tree." This response steps outside the immediate situation to view both Holly's and her father's perspectives simultaneously.
Level 4: Societal perspective taking	14–adult	Individuals understand that third-party perspective taking can be influenced by one or more systems of larger societal values.	When asked if Holly should be punished, the individual responds, "No. The value of humane treatment of animals justifies Holly's action. Her father's appreciation of this value will lead him not to punish her."

Sources: Selman, 1976; Selman & Byrne, 1974.

two peoples' perspectives simultaneously, at first from the vantage point of a disinterested spectator and, finally, by making reference to societal values.

Both cross-sectional and longitudinal research provides support for Selman's stages (Gurucharri & Selman, 1982; Selman, 1980). Even so, perspective-taking skill differs greatly among children of the same age. These individual differences are due to variations in cognitive maturity as well as everyday experiences in which adults and peers clarify their own viewpoints, encouraging children to look at situations from another's perspective (Dixon & Moore, 1990; Krebs & Gillmore, 1982).

PERSPECTIVE TAKING AND SOCIAL BEHAVIOR

Children's developing ability to appreciate the perspectives of others helps them get along with other people. When we anticipate another person's point of view, social relationships become more predictable. Each individual can plan actions with some knowledge of what the other person is likely to do in return.

In addition, when children recognize that other people may have thoughts and feelings different from their own, they can respond to the momentary needs of others more effectively.

It is not surprising that perspective taking is related to a wide variety of social skills in middle childhood. Good perspective takers are more likely to display empathy and compassion (Eisenberg et al., 1987). In addition, they are better at *social problem solving,* or thinking of effective ways to handle difficult social situations (Marsh, Serafica, & Barenboim, 1981). In fact, once children are capable of self-reflective perspective taking (see Table 13.1), they often rely on it to clear up everyday misunderstandings. For example, one day when Joey happened to tease Terry in a friendly way, Terry took offense. Joey made use of advanced perspective taking to patch up the situation. "Terry, I didn't mean it," he explained, "I *thought you would think* I was just kidding when I said that."

Although good perspective taking is a critical ingredient of mature social behavior, we must keep in mind that it does not always result in prosocial acts. How children apply their ability to imagine another person's viewpoint depends on the situation. In a competitive task, skilled perspective takers are often as good at defending their own viewpoint as they are at cooperating with other people. Also, even when children appreciate another person's feelings, additional factors, such as personality, influence whether they will act on their social awareness. For example, children who have learned to regulate their emotions effectively can avoid being overwhelmed by their own feelings and are therefore more likely to help others in distress (Fabes, Eisenberg, & Eisenbud, 1993).

Finally, children with very poor social skills—in particular, the angry, aggressive styles that we discussed in Chapter 10—have great difficulty imagining the thoughts and feelings of others. They often mistreat adults and peers without feeling the guilt and remorse that is engendered by awareness of another's point of view (MacQuiddy, Maise, & Hamilton, 1987). Interventions that provide these children with coaching and practice in perspective taking are helpful in reducing antisocial behavior and increasing empathy and prosocial responding (Chalmers & Townsend, 1990; Chandler, 1973).

MORAL DEVELOPMENT IN MIDDLE CHILDHOOD

Recall from Chapter 10 that preschoolers pick up a great many morally relevant behaviors through modeling and reinforcement. By middle childhood, they have had time to reflect on these experiences, putting them together into rules for good conduct, such as "It's good to help others in trouble" or "It's wrong to take something that doesn't belong to you." Consequently, school-age children are not as dependent on modeling and reinforcement as they were at younger ages. They can follow internalized standards, even when behaviors consistent with them are not being demonstrated or rewarded by others at the moment.

These changes lead children to become considerably more independent and trustworthy. During middle childhood, they can take on many more responsibilities, from running an errand at the supermarket to making sure a younger sibling does not wander into the street. Of course, these advances only take place when children have had much time to profit from the consistent guidance and example of caring adults in their lives.

In Chapter 10, we also saw that children do not just copy their morality from those around them. As the cognitive-developmental approach emphasizes, from an early age they actively think about right and wrong. Children's expanding social world and their increasing ability to take the perspective of others leads moral understanding to improve greatly in middle childhood.

LEARNING ABOUT JUSTICE THROUGH SHARING

These five school-age children have figured out how to divide up two pizzas fairly among themselves. Already, they have a well-developed sense of distributive justice. *(Will Faller)*

In everyday life, children frequently experience situations that involve **distributive justice**—beliefs about how to divide up material goods fairly. Heated discussions often take place over how much weekly allowance is to be given to siblings of different ages, who has to sit where in the family car on a long trip, and in what way an eight-slice pizza is to be shared by six hungry playmates. William Damon (1977, 1988) has studied children's changing concepts of distributive justice over early and middle childhood.

Even 4-year-olds recognize the importance of sharing, but their reasons for doing so often seem contradictory and self-serving. When asked why they gave some of their toys to a playmate, preschoolers typically say something like this: "I shared because if I didn't, she wouldn't play with me" or "I let her have some, but most are for me because I'm older."

As children enter middle childhood, they start to express more mature notions of distributive justice (see Table 13.2). At first, these ideas of fairness are based on *equality*. Children in the early school grades are intent on making sure that each person gets the same amount of a treasured resource, such as money, turns in a game, or a delicious treat.[1]

A short time later, children start to view fairness in terms of *merit*. Extra rewards should be given to someone who has worked especially hard or otherwise performed in an exceptional way. When asked if a child who made more paintings for a class art sale should get more of the money that is earned, first graders often say yes. Finally, around age 8, children can reason on the basis of *benevolence*. They recognize that special consideration should be given to those who are at a disadvantage, like the needy or the disabled. Older children indicate that an extra amount might be given to a child who cannot produce as much or who does not get any allowance from his parents. They also adapt their basis of fairness to fit the situation—for example, relying more on equality for allocating votes in an election and more on merit and benevolence when distributing material goods (Sigelman & Waitzman, 1991).

TABLE 13.2

Damon's Sequence of Distributive Justice Reasoning

BASIS OF REASONING	AGE	DESCRIPTION
Equality	5–6	Fairness involves strictly equal distribution of goods. Special considerations, such as merit and need, are not taken into account.
Merit	6–7	Fairness is based on deservingness. Children recognize that some people should get more because they have worked harder.
Benevolence	8	Fairness includes giving special consideration to those who are disadvantaged. More should be given to those who are in need.

[1]Recall from Chapter 12 that in some cultures, equal sharing of goods among children is not common, and conservation is greatly delayed (see page 425). It is possible that Damon's sequence of distributive justice reasoning does not represent children's concepts of fairness in all societies.

Distributive justice
Beliefs about how to divide up material goods fairly.

According to Damon (1988), parental advice and encouragement support these developing standards of justice, but the give-and-take of peer interaction is especially important. Peer disagreements, along with efforts to resolve them, make children more sensitive to others' perspectives, and this, in turn, supports their developing ideas of fairness (Kruger, 1992). Indeed, mature distributive justice reasoning shows many of the same relationships to everyday social behavior as perspective taking. For example, it is associated with more effective social problem solving and a greater willingness to help and share with others (Blotner & Bearison, 1984; McNamee & Peterson, 1986).

CHANGES IN MORAL AND SOCIAL-CONVENTIONAL UNDERSTANDING

As their ideas about justice advance, children clarify and create linkages between moral rules and social conventions. During middle childhood, they realize that situations do arise when the two overlap. Sometimes violations of social conventions are moral matters! For example, saying "thank you" after receiving a present is an arbitrary practice arrived at by social agreement. At the same time, not doing so can injure others by hurting their feelings (Turiel, 1983). School-age children are also aware that people whose knowledge differs may not be equally responsible for moral transgressions. They say that a parent who spanks a child in a country where everyone believes that corporal punishment scares away evil spirits that make children misbehave is less to blame than a parent who has not been taught this superstition (Wainryb, 1993).

As children think in more complex ways about social situations, they come to realize that certain conventions are far more arbitrary than they formerly believed. Gender stereotypes are an example. We will see later in this chapter that school-age children have a more flexible appreciation of the activities and occupations appropriate for males and females—a development that parallels their improved understanding of moral rules and social conventions (Carter & Patterson, 1982; Serbin, Powlishta, & Gulko, 1993).

At this point, you may be wondering: As children work out their ideas about morality, are their discoveries universal ones arrived at by children everywhere? The Cultural Influences box on the following page presents some intriguing evidence on this issue.

BRIEF REVIEW

In middle childhood, self-conscious emotions become clearly linked to personal responsibility. Children's awareness of emotional experience expands, and they become better at emotional self-regulation. Perspective taking undergoes major advances and is related to a wide variety of positive social skills. Moral understanding also improves. Children develop more advanced notions of distributive justice, and they clarify the distinction between moral rules and social conventions.

ASK YOURSELF . . .

- Return to Joey's description of Belinda Brown at the beginning of this chapter. How does it reflect changes in children's understanding of others during middle childhood?
- When given the Holly dilemma and asked, "Does Holly think she will be punished for climbing the tree?" Lizzie responded, "No, Holly knows that her father will understand how sad she would feel if she let that kitten fall out of the tree." Which of Selman's perspective-taking stages is Lizzie at?

CULTURAL INFLUENCES

CHILDREN'S MORAL CONCEPTS IN INDIA AND THE UNITED STATES

Are there universal moral imperatives, such as truth, justice, and the value of human life, that all children appreciate? Or does the understanding and acceptance of moral beliefs depend on cultural context? When American 10- to 16-year-olds of diverse religious backgrounds, including Amish-Mennonite, Dutch-Reform Calvinist, and Jewish, were interviewed, they separated moral from nonmoral rules in much the same way. All viewed morality as distinct from religious rituals and prescriptions for everyday living (Nucci & Turiel, 1993). But research comparing the United States with Hindu India, a culture that places much less emphasis on personal autonomy and freedom of choice, reveals that children's notions of morality are more diverse than researchers thought (Shweder, Mahapatra, & Miller, 1990).

For centuries, Hinduism has had a powerful influence on Indian thought. It regards a wide variety of moral and social rules as part of a natural world order, not as invented by human beings. Indians do not distinguish between moral rules and social conventions in the same way as Westerners. In India, for example, violations of certain food customs are treated just as seriously as some acts intended to do harm to others. These ideas permeate the moral reasoning of children.

When 8- to 10-year-olds were asked to rank a large number of social and moral concerns from most serious to least serious, Indian and American youngsters differed sharply in their moral beliefs. Indian children regarded certain food and politeness transgressions as more serious than selfish behavior or even family violence. For example, they thought that eating chicken a day after a father's death or calling parents by their first names was much worse than a man beating his wife or his son for misbehavior. American children, in contrast, condemned wife and child beating but thought eating forbidden foods and referring to parents on a first-name basis were perfectly all right.

These findings suggest that the Western tendency to separate morality from social conventions is not shared by all cultures. In India, as in many developing countries, cultural and religious practices have profound moral significance. For example, one Indian mother explained that not taking a bath and changing clothes before eating breakfast would be considered an unfavorable sign—an indication that something bad might happen to the family. In her opinion, wearing the proper clothes at the right time is not arbitrary. "It has something to do with respect for oneself, for others, for one's station in life, for God, and for the rhythms of nature" (Shweder, 1990, p. 2063).

Finally, Indian and American children did not differ with respect to all moral beliefs. Both agreed that it is wrong to ignore beggars, break promises, destroy another person's property, kick harmless animals, and steal flowers. These responses may reflect a common basis of morality—a sense of justice that will become increasingly abstract and rational during adolescence and young adulthood. Although American children grapple with the relationship between moral rules and social conventions, never are the two as closely linked as they are for Indian children. There seem to be both cultural universals and diversity in moral thought.

This Hindu Indian girl is likely to say that eating forbidden foods and calling parents by their first names are very serious transgressions. Moral rules and social conventions are more closely linked in her culture than in the United States. *(Renato Rotolo/The Gamma Liason Network)*

PEER RELATIONS IN MIDDLE CHILDHOOD

In Chapter 10, we saw how peer interaction expands during the preschool years, supported by cognitive and language development as well as parental encouragement and example. In middle childhood, the society of peers becomes an increasingly important context for development.

CHANGES IN PEER SOCIABILITY

When formal schooling begins, children are exposed to agemates who differ in many ways, including achievement, ethnicity, religion, interests, and personality. Peer contact, as we have seen, plays a major role in the school-age child's perspective taking and understanding of self and others. These developments, in turn, contribute to the quality of peer interaction.

During middle childhood, peer relations are increasingly influenced by social conventions that promote courteous, prosocial behavior. Older children share, help, and cooperate more often than do preschoolers, and they also go about providing support differently. Four- and 5-year-olds move right in and give assistance, regardless of whether it is desired or not. In contrast, older children offer to help and wait for a peer to accept it before behaving prosocially. In line with children's greater sensitivity to prosocial expectations, aggression declines in middle childhood, but the drop is greatest for physical attacks. As we will see, verbal insults among boys and social ostracism among girls occur often as school-age children form peer groups and start to distinguish "insiders" from "outsiders."

PEER GROUPS

If you watch children in the school yard or neighborhood, you will see that groups of three to a dozen or more often gather. The organization of these collectives changes greatly with age. By the end of middle childhood, children display a strong desire for group belongingness. Together, they generate unique values and standards for behavior. They also create a social structure of leaders and followers that ensures group goals will be met. When these characteristics are present, a **peer group** has formed (Hartup, 1983).

The practices of these informal groups lead to a "peer culture" that typically consists of a specialized vocabulary, dress code, and place to "hang out" during leisure hours. For example, Joey formed a club with three other boys. The children met in the treehouse in Joey's backyard, called each other by nicknames, and wore a "uniform" consisting of T-shirts, jeans, and tennis shoes. Calling themselves "the pack," the boys developed a secret handshake and chose Joey as their leader. Their activities included improving the clubhouse, trading baseball cards, making trips to the video arcade, and—just as important—keeping girls and adults out!

As children develop these exclusive associations, the codes of dress and behavior that grow out of them become more broadly influential. At school, children who deviate are often rebuffed by their peers. "Kissing up" to teachers, wearing the wrong kind of shirt or shoes, tattling on classmates, or carrying a strange-looking lunch box are grounds for critical glances and comments until a child's behavior is brought in line with group expectations.

These special customs bind peers together, creating a sense of group identity. In addition, by participating in peer groups, children acquire many valuable social skills. The group provides a context in which children practice cooperation, leadership, and followership and develop a sense of loyalty to collective goals. Through these experiences, children experiment with and learn much about social organizations.

Peer group
Peers who form a social unit by generating shared values and standards of behavior and a social structure of leaders and followers.

Peer groups first form in middle childhood. These boys have probably established a social structure of leaders and followers as they gather often for joint activities, such as bike riding and basketball. Their body language suggests that they feel a strong sense of group belonging. *(R. Sidney/The Image Works)*

The beginning of peer group ties is also a time in which some of the "nicest children begin to behave in the most awful way" (Redl, 1966, p. 395). During their 10-year-old daughter's slumber party, two parents I know listened in on a stream of petty, malicious remarks about several uninvited classmates. The parents vowed to never permit their daughter to have friends sleep over again! From fourth grade on, gossip, rumor spreading, and exclusion rise among girls, who (because of gender role expectations) express aggression in subtle, indirect ways (Cairns et al., 1989). Boys are more straightforward in their hostility toward the "outgroup." Prank playing, such as egging a house, making a funny phone call, or ringing a door bell and running away, often occurs among small groups of boys, who provide one another with temporary social support for these mildly antisocial behaviors (Fine, 1980).

The school-age child's desire for group belonging can also be satisfied through formal group ties—Girl Scouts, Boy Scouts, 4-H, church groups, and other associations. Adult involvement holds in check the negative behaviors associated with children's informal peer groups. In addition, children gain much from these memberships as they work on joint projects and help in their communities. Those who participate are advanced in social and moral understanding (Harris, Mussen, & Rutherford, 1976; Keasey, 1971).

FRIENDSHIPS

Whereas peer groups provide children with insight into larger social structures, close, one-to-one friendships contribute to the development of trust and sensitivity. During the school years, children's concepts of friendship become more complex and psychologically based. Compare the following answers of a 5-year-old and an 8-year-old to questions about what makes a best friend:

> (five-year-old). Why is Amy your best friend? *I like her. I knew her in. . . [preschool] and I knew her before I came to school.* How did you meet Amy? *We sat on the bus, we played together. . . .* Would you let Amy ride your bike? *Yes, if she came over to my house.* Why would Amy come over to your house? *Because I want her to. . . .* How do you make a friend? *You say, "Hi, what's your name," and that's all.*
>
> (eight-year-old). Who's your best friend? *Shelly.* Why is Shelly your best friend? *Because she helps me when I'm sad, and she shares. . . .* What makes Shelly so special? *I've known her longer, I sit next to her and got to know her better. . . .* How come you like Shelly better than anyone else? *She's done the most for me. She never disagrees, she never eats in front of me, she never walks away when I'm crying, and she helps me on my homework. . . .* How do you get someone to like you? . . . *If you're nice to [your friends], they'll be nice to you.* (Damon, 1988, pp. 80–81)

As these responses show, during middle childhood friendship is no longer just a matter of engaging in the same activities. Instead, it is a mutually agreed-on relationship in which children like each other's personal qualities and respond to one another's needs and desires. Since friendship is a matter of both children wanting to be together, getting it started takes more time and effort than it did at earlier ages.

During middle childhood, concepts of friendship become more psychologically based. Although these boys enjoy playing baseball, they want to spend time together because they like each other's personal qualities. Mutual trust is a defining feature of their friendship. Each child counts on the other to provide support and assistance. *(Richard Hutchings/Photo Researchers)*

And once a friendship forms *trust* becomes its defining feature. School-age children state that a good friendship is based on acts of kindness that signify each person can be counted on to support the other. Consequently, events that break up a friendship are quite different than they were during the preschool years. Older children regard violations of trust, such as not helping when others need help, breaking promises, and gossiping behind the other's back, as serious breaches of friendship (Damon, 1977; Selman, 1980).

Because of these features, school-age children are more selective about their friendships. Preschoolers say they have lots of friends—sometimes, everyone in their class! By age 8 or 9, children have only a handful of people they call friends and, very often, only one best friend. Girls, especially, are likely to be exclusive in their friendships because they demand greater closeness in the relationship than do boys (Berndt, 1986). In addition, throughout childhood friends tend to be of the same age, sex, race, and social class. Note, however, that characteristics of schools and neighborhoods affect friendships. For example, in integrated schools, as many as 50 percent of pupils report at least one close cross-race friend (DuBois & Hirsch, 1990).

Through friendship, children learn the importance of emotional commitment. They come to realize that close relationships can survive disagreements if both parties are secure in their liking for one another (Hartup et al., 1993; Nelson & Aboud, 1985). Friendships remain fairly stable over middle childhood. Most last for several years. But as children approach puberty, their varying rates of development and changing interests cause many friendships to break up and new ones to be established (Berndt, 1988). As we will see in Chapter 16, the basis of friendship will change further in adolescence.

PEER ACCEPTANCE

Sociometric techniques Self-report measures that ask peers to evaluate one another's likability.

Popular children Children who get many positive votes on sociometric measures of peer acceptance.

Rejected children Children who are actively disliked and get many negative votes on sociometric measures of peer acceptance.

Controversial children Children who get a large number of positive and negative votes on sociometric measures of peer acceptance.

Neglected children Children who are seldom chosen, either positively or negatively, on sociometric measures of peer acceptance.

As we all know from our own childhoods, some children make friends and enter peer groups far more easily than others. In Chapters 11 and 12, we saw that obese children and children with serious learning problems often have great difficulty with peer acceptance. Yet there are other children whose appearance and intellectual abilities are quite normal; still, their classmates despise them.

Researchers assess peer acceptance with **sociometric techniques.** These are self-report measures that ask peers to evaluate one another's likability. For example, children may be asked to nominate several peers in their class whom they especially like or dislike, to indicate for all possible pairs of classmates which one they prefer to play with, or to rate each peer on a scale from "like very much" to "like very little" (Asher & Hymel, 1981). Children's responses reveal four different categories of social acceptance: **popular children,** who get many positive votes; **rejected children,** who are actively disliked; **controversial children,** who get a large number of positive and negative votes; and **neglected children,** who are seldom chosen, either positively or negatively. About two-thirds of pupils in a typical elementary school classroom fit one of these categories. The remaining one-third are *average* in peer acceptance; they do not receive extreme scores (Coie, Dodge, & Coppotelli, 1982).

Peer acceptance is a powerful predictor of current as well as later psychological adjustment. Rejected children, especially, are unhappy, alienated, poorly achieving children with a low sense of self-esteem (French & Waas, 1985). Both teachers and parents rate them as having a wide range of emotional and social problems. Peer rejection in middle childhood is also strongly associated with poor school performance, dropping out, antisocial behavior, and delinquency in adolescence and criminality in young adulthood (Parker & Asher, 1987; Ollendick et al., 1992).

■ **DETERMINANTS OF PEER ACCEPTANCE.** What causes one child to be liked and another to be rejected? A wealth of research reveals that social behavior plays a powerful role. Popular children have very positive social skills. They communicate with peers in sensitive, friendly, and cooperative ways. When they do not understand another child's reaction, they ask for an explanation. If they disagree with a play partner in a game, they go beyond voicing their displeasure; they suggest what the other child could do instead. When they want to enter an ongoing play group, they adapt their behavior to the flow of the activity (Gottman, Gonso, & Rasmussen, 1975; Ladd & Price, 1987).

Rejected children, in contrast, display a wide range of negative social behaviors. But not all these disliked children look the same. At least two subtypes exist. **Rejected-aggressive children,** the largest subgroup, show severe conduct problems—high rates of conflict, hostility, and hyperactive, inattentive, and impulsive behavior. They are also deficient in social understanding. For example, they are more likely than other children to misinterpret the innocent behaviors of peers as hostile and to blame others for their social difficulties (Crick & Ladd, 1993; Waas, 1988). In contrast, **rejected-withdrawn children,** a smaller subgroup, are passive and socially awkward. These children, especially, feel lonely, hold negative expectations for how peers will treat them, and are very concerned about being scorned and attacked (Bierman, Smoot, & Aumiller, 1993; Parkhurst & Asher, 1992; Rabiner, Keane, & MacKinnon-Lewis, 1993). Because of their inept, submissive style of interaction, rejected-withdrawn children are at risk for abuse by bullies, who look for victims unlikely to retaliate (Schwartz, Dodge, & Coie, 1993).

Consistent with the mixed peer opinion they engender, controversial children display a blend of positive and negative social behaviors. Like rejected-aggressive children, they are hostile and disruptive, but they also engage in high rates of positive, prosocial acts. Even though they are disliked by some peers, controversial children have some qualities that protect them from social exclusion. As a result they are relatively happy and comfortable with their peer relationships (Newcomb, Bukowski, & Pattee, 1993; Parkhurst & Asher, 1992).

Finally, perhaps the most surprising finding on peer acceptance is that neglected children, once thought to be in need of treatment, are usually well adjusted. Although these youngsters engage in low rates of interaction and are considered shy by their classmates, they are not less socially skilled than average children. They do not report feeling especially lonely or unhappy about their social life, and when they want to, they can break away from their usual pattern of playing by themselves (Crick & Ladd, 1993; Newcomb, Bukowski, & Pattee, 1993). Neglected children remind us that there are other paths to emotional well-being besides the outgoing, gregarious personality style so highly valued in our culture.

■ **HELPING REJECTED CHILDREN.** A variety of interventions aimed at improving the rejected child's peer relations and psychological adjustment have been developed. Most involve coaching, modeling, and reinforcement of positive social skills, such as how to begin interacting with a peer, cooperate in play, and respond to another child with friendly emotion and approval. Several of these programs have produced lasting gains in social competence and peer acceptance (Bierman, 1986; Mize & Ladd, 1990).

Some researchers believe that these interventions might be even more effective when combined with other treatments. Often rejected children are poor students, and their low academic self-esteem magnifies their negative reactions to teachers and classmates. Intensive academic tutoring improves both their school achievement and social acceptance (Coie & Krehbiel, 1984). Other interventions focus on training in perspective taking and social problem solving (Ladd & Mize, 1983). Still

Rejected-aggressive children
A subgroup of rejected children who engage in high rates of conflict, hostility, and hyperactive, inattentive, and impulsive behavior.

Rejected-withdrawn children
A subgroup of rejected children who are passive and socially awkward.

another approach is to increase rejected children's expectations for social success. Many conclude, after repeated rebuffs from peers, that no matter how hard they try, they will never be liked. Rejected youngsters make better use of the social skills they do have when they believe peers will accept them (Rabiner & Coie, 1989).

GENDER TYPING IN MIDDLE CHILDHOOD

Children's understanding of gender roles broadens in middle childhood, and their gender-role identities (views of themselves as relatively masculine or feminine) change as well. We will see that the direction of development is different for boys and girls, and it can vary considerably across cultures.

GENDER-STEREOTYPED BELIEFS

During the school years, children extend the gender-stereotyped beliefs they acquired in early childhood. As children think more about people as personalities, they label some traits as more typical of one sex than the other. For example, they regard "tough," "aggressive," "rational," and "dominant" as masculine and "gentle," "sympathetic," "excitable," and "affectionate" as feminine, in much the same way adults do (Best et al., 1977; Serbin, Powlishta, & Gulko, 1993).

Shortly after entering elementary school, children figure out which academic subjects and skill areas are "masculine" and which are "feminine." Throughout the school years, they regard reading, art, and music as more for girls and mathematics, athletics, and mechanical skills as more for boys (Eccles, Jacobs, & Harold, 1990; Huston, 1983). This form of stereotyping influences children's preferences for certain subjects and, in turn, how well they do at them. In a study in which children in Japan, Taiwan, and the United States were asked to name the school subject they liked best, girls were more likely to choose reading and boys mathematics in all three cultures. Asked to predict their future performance, boys thought they would do better in math than did girls. In contrast, no sex difference in favor of girls emerged in predictions about reading (Lummis & Stevenson, 1990). As we will see in Chapter 15, these beliefs become realities in adolescence.

During middle childhood, girls feel freer than boys to engage in "opposite-gender" activities. These girls participate in a team sport typically reserved for boys and men. *(Tony Freeman/PhotoEdit)*

Of course, just because children are aware of stereotypes does not mean that they endorse them. Unlike preschoolers, school-age youngsters do not necessarily approve of gender-typed distinctions (Trautner et al., 1989). In middle childhood, children realize that boys and girls often do certain things because, as one child put it, "it is the way we have been brought up," not because of physical differences between the sexes. This view seems to be more common among girls than boys. A large body of research reveals that throughout childhood and adolescence, boys hold more gender-stereotyped beliefs, and they are also more likely to think sex differences are due to biological rather than social causes (Huston, 1983; Smith & Russell, 1984). However, in a few recent studies, boys and girls did not differ in these ways (Biernat, 1991b; Serbin, Powlishta, & Gulko, 1993). One heartening possibility is that boys' appreciation of gender-role possibilities is starting to become more flexible.

GENDER-ROLE IDENTITY AND BEHAVIOR

Boys' and girls' gender-role identities follow different paths of development in middle childhood. Self-ratings on personality traits reveal that from third to sixth grade, boys strengthen their identification with the "masculine" role. In contrast, girls' identification with "feminine" attributes declines. Although girls still lean toward the "feminine" side, they begin to describe themselves as having some "opposite-gender" characteristics (Boldizar, 1991; Serbin, Powlishta, & Gulko, 1993). This difference is also evident in the activities children choose in middle childhood. Whereas boys usually stick to "masculine" pursuits, girls feel free to experiment with a wider range of options. Besides cooking, sewing, and baby-sitting, they join organized sports teams, take up science projects, and build forts in the backyard (Huston-Stein & Higgins-Trenk, 1978).

In Chapter 10, we saw that parents encourage gender-typed activities and behaviors, and they are far less tolerant when sons as opposed to daughters cross gender lines. These child-rearing influences play important roles in the developmental trends just described. Peers are also influential. A tomboyish girl can make her way into boys' activities without losing status with her female peers, but a boy who hangs out with girls is likely to be ridiculed and rejected. Finally, perhaps school-age girls realize that society attaches greater prestige to "masculine" characteristics. As a result, they want to try some of the activities and behaviors associated with the more highly valued gender role (Ullian, 1976).

This Kenyan boy is often assigned "feminine" tasks, such as caring for infants and helping with household chores. Compared to boys in other cultures, he is likely to be less gender-stereotyped in personality characteristics. *(Paul Conklin/Monkmeyer Press)*

CULTURAL INFLUENCES ON GENDER TYPING

Although the sex differences just described are typical in Western nations, they do not apply to children everywhere. Girls are less likely to experiment with "masculine" activities in cultures and subcultures in which the gap between male and female roles is especially wide. And when social and economic conditions make it necessary for boys to take over "feminine" tasks, their personalities and behaviors become less stereotyped.

To clarify how cultures shape gender-typed behavior, Beatrice Whiting and Carolyn Edwards (1988a, 1988b) collected detailed information on the daily activities of children in 12 communities around the world. Their findings revealed that in most societies, boys were dominant and aggressive and girls were dependent, compliant, and nurturant. But striking exceptions emerged in communities in which children were given "cross-gender" assignments as part of their daily responsibilities.

One such community is Nyansongo, a small agricultural settlement in Kenya. Nyansongo mothers, who work 4 to 5 hours a day in the gardens, assign the care of young children, the tending of the cooking fire, and the washing of dishes to older siblings. Half the boys between ages 5 and 8 take care of infants, and half help with household chores. As a result, girls are relieved of total responsibility for "feminine" tasks and have more time to interact with agemates. Their greater freedom and independence leads them to score higher than girls of other village and tribal cultures in dominance, assertiveness, and playful roughhousing. In contrast, boys' caregiving responsibilities mean that they often display help giving and emotional support.

Although these findings might be taken to suggest that boys in Western cultures be assigned more "cross-gender" tasks, the consequences of doing so are not so straightforward. Recent evidence shows that when fathers hold traditional gender-role beliefs and their sons engage in "feminine" housework, boys experience strain in the father–child relationship, feel stressed by their responsibilities, and judge themselves as less competent (McHale et al., 1990). So parental values may need to be consistent with task assignments for children to benefit from them.

ASK YOURSELF . . .

- Apply your understanding of attributions to rejected children's social self-esteem. How are rejected children likely to explain their failure to gain peer acceptance? What impact on future efforts to get along with agemates are these attributions likely to have?
- Return to Chapter 10, page 379, and review the concept of androgyny. Which of the two sexes is more androgynous in middle childhood, and why?

BRIEF REVIEW

During middle childhood, children become members of peer groups, through which they learn much about the functioning of larger social structures. Friendships change, emphasizing mutual trust and assistance. Peer acceptance is a powerful predictor of current and future psychological adjustment. Popular children interact in a cooperative, friendly fashion; rejected children behave antisocially and ineptly; and controversial children display a mixture of positive and negative social behaviors. Although neglected children engage in low rates of peer interaction, they are usually competent and well adjusted. Interventions that train social skills, improve academic performance, and increase social understanding lead to improved peer acceptance of rejected children.

Over the school years, children extend their gender-typed beliefs to personality characteristics and achievement areas. Boys' "masculine" gender-role identities strengthen, whereas girls' identities become more flexible. However, cultural values and practices can modify these developmental trends.

FAMILY INFLUENCES IN MIDDLE CHILDHOOD

As children move into school, peer, and community contexts, the parent–child relationship changes. At the same time, the school-age child's developing sense of competence continues to depend on the quality of family interaction. We will see that recent changes in the American family—high rates of divorce, remarriage, and maternal employment—can have positive as well as negative effects on children.

PARENT–CHILD RELATIONSHIPS

During middle childhood, the amount of time children spend with parents declines dramatically. In a study in which parents were asked to keep diaries of family activities, they reported spending less than half as much time in caregiving, teaching, reading, and playing with 5- to 12-year-olds as they did with preschoolers (Hill & Stafford, 1980).

NEW CHILD-REARING ISSUES. The school-age child's growing independence means that parents must deal with new issues. "I've struggled with how many chores to demand of them, how much allowance for what kinds of work, and whether their friends are good influences," noted Rena. "And then there's the problem of how to keep track of them when they're out of the house or even when they're home and I'm not there to see what's going on." Rena worried, especially, about too much television viewing. Indeed, the amount of time children spend in front of the set rises over the school years, from 3 hours a day at age 6 to more than 4 hours at age 11 (Liebert & Sprafkin, 1988). Rena also became concerned over Joey's passion for video games, largely because of their highly violent content. Yet at present, we do not know if video games are as detrimental to children's well-being as televised violence (see Chapter 10, page 373) (Delphi Communication Sciences, 1990).

Besides wondering how to promote responsible behavior and constructive use of leisure time, parents must figure out how to deal with children's problems at school. This task is especially difficult for low-income and ethnic minority parents, who often feel alienated from the school environment. Finally, American parents worry about how much to become involved in their youngster's homework, although (as we saw in Chapter 12) their support plays an important role in children's school success (Maccoby, 1984a).

■ **PARENT–CHILD COMMUNICATION.** Although parents face a new set of concerns, child rearing actually becomes easier for those who established an authoritative style during the early years (Maccoby, 1984b). Reasoning works more effectively with school-age children because of their greater capacity for logical thinking. Of course, older children sometimes use their cognitive powers to bargain and negotiate—a circumstance that can try their parents' patience. "Mom," Joey pleaded for the third time, "if you let Terry and me go to the mall to see that car show tonight, I'll rake all the leaves in the yard, I promise."

Fortunately, parents can appeal to the child's better developed sense of self-esteem, humor, and morality to resolve these difficulties. "Joey, you know it's a school night, and you have a test tomorrow," Rena responded. "You'll be unhappy at the results if you stay out late and don't study. Come on, no more wheeler-dealering!" Perhaps because parents and children have, over time, learned how to resolve conflicts, coercive discipline declines over the school years (Maccoby, 1984a).

As children demonstrate that they can manage daily activities and responsibilities, effective parents gradually shift control from adult to child. This does not mean that they let go entirely. Effective parents of school-age children engage in **coregulation,** a transitional form of supervision in which they exercise general oversight, while permitting children to be in charge of moment-by-moment decision making. Coregulation supports and protects children, who are not yet ready for total independence. At the same time, it prepares them for adolescence, when they will need to make many important decisions themselves.

Coregulation grows out of a cooperative relationship between parent and child—one based on give-and-take and mutual respect. Here is a summary of its ingredients:

> The parental tasks . . . are threefold: First, [parents] must monitor, guide, and support their children at a distance—that is, when their children are out of their presence; second, they must effectively use the times when direct contact does occur; and third, they must strengthen in their children the abilities that will allow them to monitor their own behavior, to adopt acceptable standards of good (conduct), to avoid undue risks, and to know when they need parental support and guidance. Children must be willing to inform parents of their whereabouts, activities, and problems so that parents can mediate and guide when necessary. (Maccoby, 1984a, pp. 191–192)

Although school-age children often press for greater independence, they also know how much they need their parents' continuing support. In one study, fifth and sixth graders described parents as the most influential people in their lives.

Coregulation
A transitional form of supervision in which parents exercise general oversight while permitting children to be in charge of moment-by-moment decision making.

They often turned to mothers and fathers for affection, advice, enhancement of self-worth, and assistance with everyday problems (Furman & Buhrmester, 1992).

SIBLINGS

In addition to parents and friends, siblings are important sources of support to school-age youngsters. Siblings provide one another with companionship, help with difficult tasks, and comfort during times of emotional stress (Furman et al., 1989). Because of the uniqueness of the sibling relationship, older siblings provide an especially effective scaffold for children's learning. When researchers had either a sibling or a good friend of the sibling teach a younger school-age child a complex block-building task, siblings offered more explanations and encouragement and gave the child greater control over the task. In part, this occurred because younger children observed, imitated, consulted, and exerted pressure for task control more often with siblings. As a result, children taught by siblings performed much better on the task (Azmitia & Hesser, 1993).

Although sibling rivalry tends to increase in middle childhood, siblings also provide one another with emotional support and help with difficult tasks. *(Erika Stone)*

Yet as everyone with a brother or sister knows, sibling relationships are marked by conflict as well as caring. Over middle childhood, sibling rivalry tends to increase. As children participate in a wider range of activities, parents often compare siblings' traits, abilities, and accomplishments. The child who gets less parental attention, more disapproval, and fewer material resources is likely to express resentment toward a sibling who receives more favorable treatment (Boer, Goedhart, & Treffers, 1992; Hetherington, 1988).

When siblings are close in age and the same sex, parental comparisons take place more frequently, and more quarreling and antagonism results. This effect is particularly strong when fathers prefer one child. Perhaps because fathers spend less time with children, their favoritism is more noticeable, thereby triggering greater anger during sibling interactions (Brody, Stoneman, & McCoy, 1992; Brody et al., 1992).

Siblings often take steps to reduce this rivalry by striving to be different from one another (Huston, 1983). For example, two brothers I know deliberately selected different school subjects, athletic pursuits, and music lessons. At age 7, the younger one said, "What can I play that's *not* the piano (his brother's instrument)?" If the older one did especially well at an activity, the younger one did not want to try it. Of course, parents can reduce these effects by making an effort not to compare children. But some feedback about their competencies is inevitable, and as siblings strive to win recognition for their own uniqueness, they shape important aspects of each other's development.

Birth order clearly plays an important role in sibling experiences. For a time, oldest children have their parents' attention all to themselves. Even after brothers and sisters are born, they receive greater pressure for mature behavior from parents. For this reason, the oldest child is slightly advantaged in IQ and school achievement (Zajonc, Markus, & Markus, 1979; Paulhus & Shaffer, 1981). Younger siblings, in contrast, tend to be more popular with agemates (Miller & Maruyama, 1976). Perhaps as the result of learning to get along with larger, more powerful brothers and sisters, they become especially skilled at negotiating and compromising.

DIVORCE

Sibling interaction is affected by other aspects of family life. Joey and Lizzie's relationship, Rena told me, had been particularly negative a only few years before. Joey pushed, hit, taunted, and called Lizzie names. Although she tried to retaliate, she was little match for Joey's larger size. The arguments usually ended with Lizzie running in tears to her mother. Joey and Lizzie's fighting coincided with Rena and her husband's growing marital unhappiness. When Joey was 8 and Lizzie 5, their father Drake moved out.

The children were not alone in having to weather this traumatic event. Between 1960 and 1980, the divorce rate in the United States tripled and then stabilized. Currently, it is the highest in the world, nearly doubling that of the second-ranked country, Sweden. Over one million American children experience the separation and divorce of their parents each year. At any given time, about one-fourth of American youngsters live in single-parent households. Although the large majority (85 percent) reside with their mothers, the number in father-headed households has increased over the past decade, from 9 to 15 percent (Meyer & Garasky, 1993).

Children spend an average of 5 years in a single-parent home, or almost a third of their total childhood. For many, divorce eventually leads to new family relationships. About two-thirds of divorced parents marry a second time. Half of these children eventually experience a third major change—the end of their parent's second marriage (Furstenberg & Cherlin, 1991; Glick, 1990).

These figures reveal that divorce is not a single event in the lives of parents and children. Instead, it is a transition that leads to a variety of new living arrangements, accompanied by changes in housing, income, and family roles and responsibilities (Wallerstein, 1991). Since the 1960s, many studies have reported that marital breakup is quite stressful for children. But the research also reveals great individual differences in how children respond. Among factors that make a difference are the custodial parent's psychological well-being, the child's characteristics, and social supports within the family and surrounding community. As we look at evidence on the impact of divorce, you may find it helpful to refer to the summary in Table 13.3.

■ **IMMEDIATE CONSEQUENCES.** "Things were worst during the period in which Drake and I decided to separate," Rena reflected. "We fought over everything—from custody of the children to the living room furniture. I guess it was all an expression of our raging anger at one another, and the kids really suffered. Lizzie would burst into tears for what seemed like no reason. Once, sobbing, she told me she was 'sorry she made Daddy go away.' Joey kicked and threw things at home. At school, his teacher complained that he was distracted and often didn't do his work. In the midst of everything, I could hardly deal with their problems. We had to sell the house; there was no way I could afford it alone. And I needed a better-paying job. I had to change from teaching part-time to full-time at the university or start looking."

Rena's description captures conditions in many newly divorced households. Family conflict often rises as parents try to settle disputes over children and personal belongings. Once one parent moves out, additional events threaten supportive interactions between parents and children. Mother-headed households typically

TABLE 13.3

Factors Related to Children's Adjustment to Divorce

FACTOR	DESCRIPTION
Custodial parents' psychological health	A mature, well-adjusted parent is better able to handle stress, shield the child from conflict, and engage in authoritative parenting.
Child characteristics	
Age	Preschool and early elementary school children often blame themselves and show intense separation anxiety. Older children may also react strongly by engaging in disruptive, antisocial acts. However, some display unusually mature, responsible behavior.
Temperament	Children with difficult temperaments are less able to withstand stress and show longer-lasting difficulties.
Sex	Boys in mother-custody households experience more severe and longer-lasting problems than do girls.
Social supports	The ability of divorced parents to set aside their hostilities, contact with the noncustodial parent, and positive relationships with extended family members, teachers, and friends lead to improved outcomes for children.

The period surrounding parental separation is the most difficult for children of divorce. Family conflict, decreased contact with the noncustodial parent, and having to move to new housing for economic reasons produce painful emotional reactions. *(Richard Hutchings/PhotoEdit)*

experience a sharp drop in income. Many divorced women lack the education and experience needed for well-paid jobs. To make matters worse, three-fourths of those who are supposed to receive child support from the absent father get less than the full amount or none at all (Children's Defense Fund, 1994). Divorced mothers often have to move to new housing for economic reasons, reducing supportive ties to neighbors and friends. When those who were homemakers must find immediate employment, young children are likely to experience poor-quality child care while the mother is away and a distracted, unavailable parent while she is at home (Nelson, 1993).

These life circumstances often lead to a highly disorganized family situation called "minimal parenting" (Wallerstein & Kelly, 1980). "Meals and bedtimes were at all hours, the house didn't get cleaned, and I stopped taking Joey and Lizzie on weekend outings," said Rena. As children react with distress and anger to their less secure home lives, discipline may become harsh and inconsistent as mothers try to recapture control of their upset youngsters. Fathers usually spend more time with children immediately after divorce, but often this contact decreases over time. When fathers see their children only occasionally, they are inclined to be permissive and indulgent. This often conflicts with the mother's style of parenting and makes her task of managing the child on a day-to-day basis even more difficult (Furstenberg & Nord, 1985; Hetherington, Cox, & Cox, 1982).

In view of these changes, it is not surprising that children experience painful emotional reactions during the period surrounding divorce. But the intensity of their feelings and the way these are expressed varies with the child's age, temperament, and sex.

Children's Age. Five-year-old Lizzie's fear that she had caused her father to leave home is not unusual. The cognitive immaturity of preschool and early school-age children makes it difficult for them to grasp the reasons behind their parent's separation. Younger children often blame themselves and take the marital breakup as a sign that they could be abandoned by both parents. They may whine and cling, displaying intense separation anxiety. Preschoolers are especially likely to fantasize that their parents will get back together (Wallerstein, 1983; Wallerstein, Corbin, & Lewis, 1988). For example, when playing with her dolls, Lizzie made the mother and father hug and kiss. Then she said to Rena, "That's how I want it. You and Daddy love each other again."

Older children are better able to understand the reasons behind their parents' divorce. They recognize that strong differences of opinion, incompatible personalities, and lack of caring for one another are responsible (Neal, 1983). The ability to accurately assign blame may reduce some of the pain that children feel. Still, many school-age and adolescent youngsters react strongly to the end of their parents' marriage. Particularly when family conflict is high, they are likely to display adjustment difficulties (Borrine et al., 1991; Forehand et al., 1991). Undesirable peer activities that provide an escape from unpleasant home lives, such as running away, truancy, and delinquent behavior, are common (Doherty & Needle, 1991; Dornbusch et al., 1985).

However, not all older children react this way. For some—especially the oldest child in the family—divorce can trigger more mature behavior. These youngsters may willingly take on extra burdens, such as household tasks, care and protection of younger siblings, and emotional support of a depressed, anxious mother. But if these demands are too great, older children may eventually become resentful and withdraw from the family into some of the more destructive behavior patterns just described (Hetherington, Stanley-Hagan, & Anderson, 1989; Wallerstein & Kelly, 1980).

Children's Temperament and Sex. In Chapter 7, we noted that temperament can either increase or reduce children's risk for maladjustment. When temperamentally difficult children are exposed to stressful life events and inadequate parenting, their problems are magnified. In contrast, easy children are less often targets of parental anger and are also better able to cope with adversity when it hits (Rutter, 1987).

These findings help us understand sex differences in children's response to divorce. Girls sometimes respond as Lizzie did, with internalizing reactions, such as crying, self-criticism, and withdrawal. More often, they show some demanding, attention-getting behavior. But in mother-custody families, boys experience more serious adjustment problems. Recall from Chapter 10 that boys are more active and noncompliant than girls. These behaviors increase when boys encounter parental conflict and inconsistent discipline. Studies in Great Britain and the United States reveal that many sons of divorcing couples were impulsive and defiant long before the marital breakup—behaviors that may have contributed to as well as been caused by their parents' problems. As a result, these boys entered the period of turmoil surrounding divorce with a reduced capacity to cope with family stress (Cherlin et al., 1991; Hetherington, 1991).

Perhaps because their behavior is so unruly, boys of divorcing parents receive less emotional support from mothers, teachers, and peers. And as Joey's behavior toward Lizzie illustrates, the coercive cycles of interaction between boys and their divorced mothers soon spread to sibling relations (MacKinnon, 1989). These outcomes compound boys' difficulties. Children of both sexes show declines in school achievement during the aftermath of divorce, but school problems are greater for boys (Guidubaldi & Cleminshaw, 1985).

■ **LONG-TERM CONSEQUENCES.** Rena eventually found full-time work at the university and gained control over the daily operation of the household. Her own feelings of anger and rejection over the divorce also declined. And after several meetings with a counselor, Rena and Drake realized the harmful impact of their quarreling on Joey and Lizzie. They resolved to keep the children out of future disagreements. Drake visited regularly and handled Joey's disobedience with firmness and consistency. Soon Joey's school performance improved, his behavior problems subsided, and both children seemed calmer and happier.

Like Joey and Lizzie, the majority of children show improved adjustment by 2 years after divorce. Yet a significant number continue to have serious difficulties for many years. Boys and children with difficult temperaments are especially likely to experience lasting emotional problems (Hetherington & Clingempeel, 1992). Among girls, the major long-term effects involve heterosexual behavior—a rise in sexual activity at adolescence, short-lived sexual relationships in early adulthood, and lack of self-confidence in associations with men (Kalter et al., 1985; Wallerstein & Corbin, 1989).

The overriding factor in positive adjustment following divorce is effective parenting—in particular, how well the custodial parent handles stress, shields the child from family conflict, and engages in authoritative parenting (Amato, 1993; Hetherington, 1991). Contact with fathers is also important. For girls, a good father–child relationship appears to contribute to heterosexual development. For boys, it seems to affect overall psychological well-being. In fact, several studies indicate that outcomes for sons are better when the father is the custodial parent (Camara & Resnick, 1988; Santrock & Warshak, 1986). Fathers are more likely than mothers to praise a boy's good behavior and less likely to ignore his disruptiveness.

The father's image of greater power and authority may also help him obtain more compliance from a son.

Although divorce is painful for children, there is clear evidence that remaining in a stressed intact family is much worse than making the transition to a low-conflict, single-parent household (Block, Block, & Gjerde, 1988; Hetherington, Cox, & Cox, 1982). Children whose divorcing parents put aside their disagreements and support each other in their parenting roles have the best chance of growing up competent, stable, and happy. When parental cooperation is not possible, caring extended-family members, teachers, and friends can reduce the likelihood that divorce will result in long-term disruption (Hetherington, Stanley-Hagan, & Anderson, 1989).

DIVORCE MEDIATION, JOINT CUSTODY, AND CHILD SUPPORT. Awareness that divorce is highly stressful for children and families has led to community-based services aimed at helping them through this difficult time. One is **divorce mediation.** It consists of a series of meetings between divorcing adults and a trained professional, who tries to help them settle disputes, such as property division and child custody. Its purpose is to avoid legal battles that intensify family conflict. In some states, divorce mediation is voluntary. In others, it must be attempted before a case is heard by a judge. Research reveals that it increases out-of-court settlements, compliance with these agreements, and feelings of well-being among divorcing parents. By reducing family hostilities, it probably has great benefits for children (Emery & Wyer, 1987).

A relatively new child custody option tries to keep both parents involved with children. In **joint custody,** the court grants the mother and father equal say in important decisions about the child's upbringing. Yet many experts have raised questions about the practice. Joint custody results in a variety of living arrangements. In most instances, children reside with one parent and see the other on a fixed schedule, much like the typical sole-custody situation. But in other cases, parents share physical custody, and children must move between homes and sometimes schools and peers as well. These transitions introduce a new kind of instability that may be especially hard on some children (Johnston, Kline, & Tschann, 1989). The success of joint custody requires a cooperative relationship between divorcing parents. If they continue to quarrel, it prolongs children's exposure to a hostile family atmosphere (Furstenburg & Cherlin, 1991; Mirman, 1993).

Finally, many single-parent families depend on child support from the absent parent to relieve financial strain. In response to a recent federal law, all states have established procedures for withholding wages from parents who fail to make these court-ordered payments. Although child support is usually not enough to lift a single-parent family out of poverty, it can ease the burden substantially. An added benefit is that children are more likely to maintain contact with a noncustodial father if he pays child support (Stephen, Freedman, & Hess, 1993).

REMARRIAGE

"If you get married to Wendell and Daddy gets married to Carol," Lizzie wondered aloud to Rena, "then I'll have two sisters and one more brother. And let's see, how many grandmothers and grandfathers? Gosh, a lot!" exclaimed Lizzie. "But what will I call them all?" she asked, looking worried.

For many children, life in a single-parent family is temporary. Their parents remarry within a few years. As Lizzie's comments indicate, entry into these **blended, or reconstituted, families** leads to a complex set of new relationships. For some children, this expanded family network is a positive turn of events that brings with it greater adult attention. But for most, it presents difficult adjustments (Bray, 1988; Hetherington, Cox, & Cox, 1985). Stepparents often use different child-rearing practices than the child was used to, and having to switch to new rules and expec-

Divorce mediation
A series of meetings between divorcing adults and a trained professional, who tries to help them settle disputes. Aimed at avoiding legal battles that intensify family conflict.

Joint custody
A child custody arrangement following divorce in which the court grants both parents say in important decisions about the child's upbringing.

Blended, or reconstituted, family
A family structure resulting from remarriage of a divorced parent that includes parent, child, and new steprelatives.

tations can be stressful for children (Lutz, 1983). In addition, children often regard steprelatives as "intruders" into the family. Indeed, their arrival does change interaction with the natural parent. But how well children adapt is, once again, related to the overall quality of family functioning. This often depends on which parent remarries as well as the age and sex of the child. As we will see, older children and girls seem to have the hardest time (see Table 13.4).

■ MOTHER–STEPFATHER FAMILIES. The most frequent form of blended family is a mother–stepfather arrangement, since mothers generally retain custody of the child. Under these conditions, boys usually adjust quickly. They welcome a stepfather who is warm and responsive and who offers relief from the coercive cycles of interaction that tend to build with their divorced mothers. Mothers' friction with sons also declines for other reasons—greater economic security, another adult to share household tasks, and an end to loneliness. One study found that less than 2 years after remarriage, boys living in mother–stepfather households were doing almost as well as those living in nondivorced families (Hetherington, Cox, & Cox, 1985). In contrast, girls adapt less favorably when custodial mothers remarry. Stepfathers disrupt the close ties many girls established with mothers in a single-parent family, and girls often react to the new arrangement with "sulky, resistant, ignoring, critical behavior" (Hetherington, 1989, p. 7; Vuchinich et al., 1991).

Note, however, that age affects these findings. Older school-age and adolescent youngsters of both sexes find it harder to adjust to blended families (Hetherington & Clingempeel, 1992; Hobart, 1987). Perhaps because they are more aware of the impact of remarriage on their own lives, they challenge some aspects of it that younger children simply accept, creating more relationship issues with their steprelatives.

■ FATHER–STEPMOTHER FAMILIES. Although only a few studies have focused on father–stepmother families, research consistently reveals more confusion for children under these conditions. In the case of noncustodial fathers, remarriage often leads to reduced contact. They tend to withdraw from their "previous" families—more so if they have daughters rather than sons (Hetherington, Cox, & Cox, 1982). When fathers have custody, children typically react negatively to remarriage. One reason is that children living with fathers often start out with more problems. Perhaps the biological mother could no longer handle the unruly child (usually a boy), so the father and his new wife are faced with a youngster who has serious behavior problems. In other instances, the father is granted custody because of a very close relationship with the child, and his remarriage disrupts this bond (Brand, Clingempeel, & Bowen-Woodward, 1988).

Table 13.4

Factors Related to Children's Adjustment to Remarriage

FACTOR	DESCRIPTION
Form of blended family	Children living in father–stepmother families display more adjustment difficulties than those in mother–stepfather families, perhaps because father-custody children start out with more problems.
Child characteristics	
Age	Older children are more aware of the impact of remarriage on their own life circumstances and find it harder to adjust.
Sex	Girls display more severe reactions than do boys because of interruptions in close bonds with custodial parents and greater conflict with stepmothers.
Social supports	(See Table 13.3.)

Girls, especially, have a hard time getting along with their stepmothers (Hobart & Brown, 1988). Sometimes (as just mentioned) this occurs because the girl's relationship with her father is threatened by the remarriage. In addition, girls often become entangled in loyalty conflicts between their two mother figures. Noncustodial mothers (unlike fathers) are likely to maintain regular contact with children, but frequent visits by the mother are associated with less favorable stepmother–stepdaughter relations. The longer girls live in father–stepmother households, the more positive their interaction with stepmothers becomes. With time and patience they do adjust, and eventually girls benefit from the support of a second mother figure (Brand, Clingempeel, & Bowen-Woodward, 1988).

MATERNAL EMPLOYMENT

For many years, divorce has been associated with a high rate of maternal employment, due to financial strains experienced by mothers responsible for maintaining their own families. But as we have seen, women of all sectors of the population—not just those who are single and poor—have gone to work in increasing numbers. Today, single and married mothers are in the labor market in nearly equal proportions, and over 70 percent of those with school-age children are employed (U.S. Bureau of the Census, 1994).

■ MATERNAL EMPLOYMENT AND CHILD DEVELOPMENT. In Chapter 7, we saw that the impact of maternal employment on infant development depends on the quality of day care and the continuing parent–child relationship. This same conclusion applies during later years. In addition, many studies agree that a host of factors—the mother's work satisfaction, the support she receives from her husband, the child's sex, and the social class of the family—have a bearing on whether children show benefits or problems from growing up in an employed-mother family.

Children of mothers who enjoy their work and remain committed to parenting show especially positive adjustment—a higher sense of self-esteem, more positive family and peer relations, less gender-stereotyped beliefs, and better grades in school (Hoffman, 1989; Williams & Radin, 1993). These benefits undoubtedly result from parenting practices. Employed mothers who value their parenting role are more likely to use authoritative child rearing (Greenberger & Goldberg, 1989). They schedule special times to devote to their children and also encourage greater responsibility and independence. A modest increase in fathers' involvement in child care and household duties also accompanies maternal employment. More contact with the father is related to intelligence, achievement, mature social behavior, and flexible gender-role attitudes (Gottfried, 1991; Williams, Radin, & Allegro, 1992; Zaslow, Rabinovich, & Suwalsky, 1991).

But there are some qualifiers to these encouraging findings. Outcomes are more favorable for daughters than sons. Girls, especially, profit from the image of female competence. Daughters of employed mothers have higher educational aspirations and, in college, are more likely to choose nontraditional careers, such as law, medicine, and physics (Hoffman, 1974). In contrast, boys in low-income homes are sometimes adversely affected. They tend to admire their fathers less and to interact more negatively with them. These findings are probably due to a lingering belief in many lower-class homes that when a mother works, the father has failed in his provider role (Hoffman, 1989).

Futhermore, when employment places heavy demands on the mother's schedule, children are at risk for ineffective parenting. Working long hours and spending little time with school-age children are associated with less favorable outcomes, both cognitively and socially (Moorehouse, 1991). In contrast, part-time employment seems to have benefits for children of all ages, probably because it permits mothers to meet the needs of children with a wide range of characteristics (Lerner & Abrams, 1994; Williams & Radin, 1993).

CHILD CARE FOR SCHOOL-AGE CHILDREN. The impact of maternal employment is also related to quality of child care for school-age children. In recent years, much public concern has been voiced about the estimated 2.4 million 5- to 13-year-olds in the United States who regularly look after themselves during after-school hours (Cain & Hofferth, 1989). Although many return home to an empty house, others "hang out" with peers in the neighborhood or in nearby shopping malls during late afternoons and evenings.

Research on these **self-care children** reveals inconsistent findings. Some studies report that they suffer from low self-esteem, fearfulness, and low academic achievement, whereas others show no such effects (Padilla & Landreth, 1989). Why these contradictions? The way self-care children spend their time seems to be the critical factor. Children who have a history of authoritative child rearing, are monitored from a distance by telephone calls, and have regular after-school chores appear responsible and well adjusted. In contrast, those left to their own devices are more likely to bend to peer pressures and engage in antisocial behavior (Steinberg, 1986, 1988a). Children from single-parent, poverty-stricken homes who look after themselves are at special risk for antisocial involvement. Nevertheless, self-care for these children is no worse than returning home to an overwhelmed, psychologically unavailable mother who offers her child little emotional support (Vandell & Ramanan, 1991).

In the United States, millions of children care for themselves during after-school hours. A history of authoritative child rearing and parental monitoring from a distance help protect the safety and adjustment of these youngsters. *(Jeff Dunn/The Picture Cube)*

Parents need to consider children's maturity before deciding on self-care. Before age 8 or 9, children should not be left unsupervised because most are not yet competent to deal with emergencies (Galambos & Maggs, 1991). Unfortunately, when children express discomfort with self-care or are not mature enough to handle it, many employed parents have no alternative. After-school programs for 6- to 13-year-olds are rare in American communities. Enrolling children in poor-quality after-school care can undermine their academic and social competence (Vandell & Corasaniti, 1988). In contrast, when after-school programs support academic learning and offer enrichment activities (scouting, music lessons, and organized sports) unavailable to many low-income children, they show improved school performance, peer relations, and psychological adjustment (Posner & Vandell, 1994).

SUPPORT FOR EMPLOYED MOTHERS AND THEIR FAMILIES. The research we have reviewed indicates that as long as mothers have the necessary supports to engage in effective child rearing, maternal employment offers children many advantages. In a dual-earner family, the husband's willingness to share responsibilities is crucial. Although men assist to a greater extent than they did in decades past, women still shoulder most household and child care tasks (Robinson, 1988). If the father helps very little or not at all, the mother carries a double load, at home and at work, leading to fatigue, distress, and reduced time and energy for children.

Besides fathers, work settings and communities can help employed mothers in their child-rearing roles. Part-time employment and time off when children are ill would help many women juggle the demands of work and child rearing. Although these workplace supports are available in western Europe and Canada, at present only unpaid employment leave is mandated by U.S. federal law. Equal pay and equal employment opportunities for women are also important. Because they enhance financial status and morale, they improve the way mothers feel and behave when they arrive home. Finally, high-quality child care is vital for parents' peace of mind and children's well-being at all ages, even during the middle childhood years.

Self-care children
Children who look after themselves while their parents are at work.

ASK YOURSELF . . .

- "How come you don't study hard and get good grades like your sister?" a mother exclaimed in exasperation after seeing her son's poor report card. What impact do remarks like this have on sibling interaction, and why?
- What advice would you give divorcing parents of two school-age sons about how to help their children adapt to life in a single-parent family?
- Eight-year-old Bobby's mother has just found employment, so Bobby takes care of himself after school. What factors are likely to affect Bobby's adjustment to this arrangement?

BRIEF REVIEW

During the school years, child rearing shifts toward coregulation, a transitional form of supervision in which parents exercise general oversight while granting children more decision-making power. Sibling rivalry tends to increase, and children often take steps to reduce it by striving to be different from one another.

Large numbers of American children experience the divorce of their parents. Although many adjust well by 2 years after the divorce, boys and temperamentally difficult children are likely to experience lasting emotional problems. Effective parenting is the most important factor in helping children adapt to life in a single-parent family. When parents remarry, children living in father–stepmother families, and daughters especially, display more adjustment difficulties.

Maternal employment is related to high self-esteem, reduced gender stereotyping, and mature social behavior. However, these outcomes vary with children's sex and social class, the demands of the mother's job, and the father's participation in child rearing. The impact of self-care on school-age children varies with parenting practices and how children spend their time.

SOME COMMON PROBLEMS OF DEVELOPMENT

Throughout our discussion, we have considered a variety of stressful experiences that place children at risk for future problems. In the following sections, we touch on two more areas of concern: school-age children's fears and anxieties and the devastating consequences of child sexual abuse. Finally, we sum up factors that help children cope effectively with stress and those that predispose them to long-term psychological dysfunction.

FEARS AND ANXIETIES

Although fears of the dark, thunder and lightning, and supernatural beings (often stimulated by movies and television) persist into middle childhood, children's anxieties are also directed toward new concerns. As Table 13.5 shows, school-age youngsters worry about academic performance, physical appearance, staying alone, and physical injuries. In addition, as children begin to understand the realities of the wider world, media events often trouble them. During the Persian Gulf War, a major American newspaper ran a hot line for children. The majority of callers were 8- to 11-year-olds, who asked about the bruised faces of prisoners of war, whether bombs and terrorists might reach the United States, what might happen to relatives who were in the Middle East, and whether nuclear war was possible (DeAngelis, 1991).

Most children handle their fears constructively, by talking about them with parents, teachers, and friends and relying on the more sophisticated emotional self-regulation strategies that develop in middle childhood. But about 20 percent of children develop an intense, unmanageable anxiety of some kind (Beidel, 1991). **School phobia** is an example. Typically, children with this disorder are middle-class youngsters whose achievement is average or above. Still, they feel severe apprehension about attending school, often accompanied by physical complaints (dizziness, nausea, stomachaches, and vomiting) that disappear once they are allowed to

School phobia
Severe apprehension about attending school, often accompanied by physical complaints that disappear once the child is allowed to remain home.

TABLE 13.5

Common Fears in Middle Childhood

AGE	FEARS
6 years	Supernatural beings (ghosts, witches), physical injuries, thunder and lightning, dark, sleeping or staying alone, separation from parent
7–8 years	Supernatural beings, physical injuries, dark, staying alone, media events
9–12 years	Physical injuries, thunder and lightening, tests and grades in school, physical appearance, death, war

Sources: DeAngelis, 1991; Morris & Kratochwill, 1983.

remain home. About one-third are 5- to 7-year-olds, most of whom do not fear school so much as separation from their mother. The difficulty can often be traced to a troubled parent–child relationship in which the mother does not want to let go and encourages clinginess and dependency. Intensive family therapy is necessary to help these children (Leung, 1989; Pilkington & Piersel, 1991).

Most cases of school phobia appear later, around 11 to 13, during the transition from middle childhood to adolescence (Last et al., 1987; Rutter & Hersov, 1985). These older children usually do not suffer from separation anxiety, as was once believed. Instead, they find a particular aspect of school experience frightening—an overcritical teacher, a school bully, a threatening gang, being called on in class, the jeering remarks of insensitive peers, or too much parental pressure for school success. Treating this form of school phobia may require a change in school environment or parenting practices (Pilkington & Piersel, 1991). Firm insistence that the child return to school along with training in how to cope with difficult situations is also helpful (Klungness, 1990).

Severe childhood anxieties may also arise from harsh living conditions. A great many children live in midst of constant violence. In inner-city ghettos and in war-torn areas of the world, they learn to drop to the floor at the sound of gunfire, and they witness the wounding and killing of friends and relatives. As the Social Issues box on page 498 reveals, these youngsters often suffer from long-term emotional stress. Finally, as we saw in our discussion of child abuse in Chapter 10, too often violence and other destructive acts become part of adult–child relationships. During middle childhood, child sexual abuse increases, and the damage done to children can be profound and long-lasting.

CHILD SEXUAL ABUSE

Until very recently, child sexual abuse was viewed as a rare occurrence. When children came forward with it, adults often thought they had fantasized the experience and did not take their claims seriously. In the 1970s, efforts by professionals along with widespread media attention caused child sexual abuse to be recognized as a serious national problem. Several hundred thousand cases are reported each year (see Chapter 10).

CHARACTERISTICS OF ABUSERS AND VICTIMS. Sexual abuse is committed against children of both sexes, but more often against girls than boys. The most likely victims are between ages 9 and 11. However, sexual abuse also occurs at younger and older ages, and few children experience only a single incident. For some, the abuse begins early in life and continues for many years (Finkelhor, 1984; Gomez-Schwartz, Horowitz, & Cardarelli, 1990; Russell, 1983).

Generally, the abuser is a male—a parent or someone whom the parent knows well. Often it is a father, stepfather, or live-in boyfriend; somewhat less often an uncle or older brother. In a few instances, mothers are the offenders, more often

SOCIAL ISSUES

CHILDREN OF WAR

On May 27, 1992, Zlata Filipovic, a 10-year-old Bosnian girl, recorded the following reactions to the intensifying Serb attack on the city of Sarajevo in her diary:

> SLAUGHTER! MASSACRE! HORROR! CRIME! BLOOD! SCREAMS! TEARS! DESPAIR!
>
> That's what Vaso Miskin Street looks like today. Two shells exploded in the street and one in the market. Mommy was nearby at the time. She ran to Grandma and Granddad's. Daddy and I were beside ourselves because she hadn't come home. I saw some of it on TV but I still can't believe what I actually saw. It's unbelievable. I've got a lump in my throat and a knot in my tummy. HORRIBLE. They're taking the wounded to the hospital. It's a madhouse. We kept going to the window hoping to see Mommy, but she wasn't back. . . . Daddy and I were tearing our hair out. . . . I looked out the window one more time and . . . I SAW MOMMY RUNNING ACROSS THE BRIDGE. As she came into the house she started shaking and crying. Through her tears she told us how she had seen dismembered bodies. (Filipovic, 1994, p. 55)

Since World War II, almost all but one of the 150 conflicts around the globe have been internal civil wars. Besides being armed encounters, modern wars are usually social upheavals in which well-established ways of life are threatened or destroyed and women and children are frequent victims (Ressler, 1993).

Children's experiences under conditions of armed conflict are diverse. Some may participate in the fighting, either because they are forced or because they want to please adults. Others are kidnapped, terrorized, or tortured. Those who are bystanders often come under direct fire and may be killed or physically maimed for life. And, as Zlata's diary entry illustrates, many children of war watch in horror as family members, friends, and neighbors flee, are wounded, or die (Macksoud, 1994).

The initial reactions of most children to these experiences are similar. They include disturbed sleep, difficulty concentrating, decreased interest in pleasurable activities, emotional detachment from parents and friends, repetitive play with traumatic themes, and a heightened state of alertness in response to acute and constant danger (Garbarino, Kostelny, & Grady, 1993).

When war and social crises are temporary, most children are comforted by caregivers' reassuring messages and do not show long-term emotional difficulties (Garmezy & Rutter, 1985; Jensen & Shaw, 1993). But chronic danger requires children to make substantial adjustments, and their psychological functioning can be seriously impaired. Many children of war lose their sense of safety, acquire a high tolerance for violence, are haunted by terrifying memories, become suspicious of others, and build a pessimistic view of the future.

The extent to which children are negatively affected by war depends on mediating factors. Closeness to wartime events increases the chances of maladjustment. For example, an estimated 50 percent of traumatized 6- to 12-year-old Cambodian war refugees continued to show intense stress reactions when they reached young adulthood (Kinzie et al., 1989). The support and affection of parents is the best safeguard against lasting problems. Unfortunately, many children of war are separated from family members. Sometimes, the child's community can offer protection. For example, Israeli children who lost a parent in battle fared best when they lived on kibbutzim, cohesive agricultural settlements where many adults knew the child well and felt responsible for his or her welfare (Lifschitz et al., 1977).

This boy lives in a United Nations refugee camp in Zaire. Having experienced the trauma of war, he is likely to show lasting emotional problems without special support from caring adults. *(B. Press/Woodfin Camp & Associates)*

When wartime drains families and communities of resources, international organizations need to step in and help children. Until we know how to prevent war, efforts to preserve children's physical and psychological well-being may be the best way to stop transmission of violence to the next generation in some parts of the world (Macksoud, 1994).

TRY THIS . . .

- Obtain a copy of Zlata's Diary: A Child's Life In Sarajevo, from your library or bookstore. What factors helped Zlata cope with the extreme trauma of living in midst of armed conflict for 2 years?
- The United Nations Convention on the Rights of the Child is an international treaty designed to ensure children's basic rights, including protection from abuse, neglect, and involvement in warfare. Write to the United Nations, c/o UNICEF, 3 UN Plaza, New York, NY 10017, for a copy of the convention and a list of the nations that have agreed to abide by it.

with sons than daughters. If it is a nonrelative, it is usually someone the child has come to know and trust (Alter-Reid et al., 1986; Pierce & Pierce, 1985).

In the overwhelming majority of cases, the abuse is serious. Children are subjected to vaginal or anal intercourse, oral genital contact, fondling, and forced stimulation of the adult. Abusers make the child comply in a variety of distasteful ways, including deception, bribery, verbal intimidation, and aggressive acts, such as physical force and threats with weapons. Sexually abusing relatives are just as likely as nonrelatives to resort to violence to get the child to submit (Gomez-Schwartz, Horowitz, & Cardarelli, 1990).

At this point, you may be wondering how any adult—especially, a parent or close relative—could possibly violate a child sexually. Many offenders deny their own responsibility. They blame the abuse on the willing participation of a seductive youngster. Yet children are not capable of making a deliberate, informed decision to enter into a sexual relationship! Even at older ages, they are not free to say yes or no (Finkelhor, 1984). Instead, abusers tend to have characteristics that predispose them toward sexual exploitation of children. As Table 13.6 shows, they have great difficulty controlling their impulses, may suffer from psychological disorders, and are often addicted to alcohol or drugs. Often they pick out children who are unlikely to defend themselves—those who are physically weak, emotionally deprived, and socially isolated.

Reported cases of child sexual abuse are strongly linked to poverty, marital instability, and resulting weakening of family ties. Children who live in homes with a history of constantly changing characters—repeated marriages, separations, and new partners—are especially vulnerable. But community surveys reveal that middle-class children in relatively stable homes are also victims. Economically advantaged families are simply more likely to escape detection. Intense pressure toward secrecy and feelings of confusion and guilt prevent most children from seeking help (Gomez-Schwartz, Horowitz, & Cardarelli, 1990).

■ **CONSEQUENCES FOR CHILDREN.** Virtually all children are emotionally distressed at the time sexual abuse occurs. Long-term consequences can be prevented if the abuse is stopped after only a few instances and children are assured that caring, nonabusive adults will support and protect them (Goodman et al., 1992). Unfortunately, the outcomes for a great many youngsters are not so favorable. Sexually abused children often become known to authorities only after they have developed extreme behavioral symptoms. Perhaps a school official suspects abuse, or a parent observes the child's emotional difficulties and seeks professional help (Faller, 1990).

So there really was a monster in her bedroom.
For many kids, there's a real reason to be afraid of the dark.
Last year in Indiana, there were 6,912 substantiated cases of sexual abuse. The trauma can be devastating for the child and for the family. So listen closely to the children around you.
If you hear something you don't want to believe, perhaps you should. For helpful information on child abuse prevention, contact the LaPorte County Child Abuse Prevention Council, 7451 Johnson Road, Michigan City, IN 46360. (219) 874-0007
LaPorte County Child Abuse Prevention Council

This public service announcement reminds adults that child sexual abuse, until recently regarded as a product of children's vivid imaginations, is a devastating reality. Victims are in urgent need of protection and treatment. *(La Porte County Child Abuse Protection Council)*

TABLE 13.6

Factors Related to Child Sexual Abuse

FACTOR	DESCRIPTION
Abuser	Usually a male and a member of the child's family. Finds children sexually arousing, has difficulty controlling impulses, rationalizes that the victim wants sex and will enjoy it, and has learned to believe that sexual use of others is appropriate. May have a history of alcohol or drug addiction, serious psychological disturbance, or sexual abuse as a child.
Victim	More often female than male. Abusers tend to select children that seem like easy targets—ones who are physically weak, compliant in personality, emotionally needy, and socially isolated.
Family	Often associated with poverty and repeated marital breakup. However, also occurs in relatively stable, middle-class families.

Sources: Faller, 1990; Finkelhor, 1984.

The adjustment problems of child sexual abuse victims are often severe. Depression, low self-esteem, mistrust of adults, feelings of anger and hostility, and difficulties in getting along with peers are common. Younger children often react with sleep difficulties, loss of appetite, and generalized fearfulness and anxiety. Adolescents may show runaway and suicidal reactions, substance abuse, and delinquency (Haugaard & Reppucci, 1988; Kendall-Tackett, Williams, & Finkelhor, 1993).

Sexually abused children frequently display sexual knowledge and behavior beyond their years. They have learned from their abusers that sexual overtures are acceptable ways to get attention and rewards. As they move toward young adulthood, abused girls often enter into unhealthy relationships. Many become promiscuous, believing that their bodies are for the use of others. When they marry, they are likely to choose husbands who are abusive toward them and their children (Faller, 1990). And as mothers, they often show poor parenting skills, abusing and neglecting their youngsters (Pianta, Egeland, & Erickson, 1989). In these ways, the harmful impact of sexual abuse is transmitted to the next generation.

FROM RESEARCH TO PRACTICE

CHILDREN'S EYEWITNESS TESTIMONY

Renata, a physically abused and neglected 8-year-old, was taken from her parents and placed in foster care. There, she was seen engaging in sexually aggressive behavior toward other children, including grabbing their sex organs and using obscene language. Renata's foster mother suspected that sexual abuse had taken place in her natural home. She informed the child protective service worker, who met with Renata to gather information. But Renata appeared distraught and frightened. She did not want to answer any questions.

Increasingly, children are being called on to testify in court cases involving child abuse and neglect, child custody, and other matters. Having to provide such information can be difficult and traumatic. Almost always, children must report on highly stressful events. In doing so, they may have to speak against a parent or other relative to whom they feel a strong sense of loyalty. In some family disputes, they may fear punishment for telling the truth. In addition, child witnesses are faced with a strange and unfamiliar situation—at the very least an interview in the judge's chambers, and at most an open courtroom with judge, jury, spectators, and the possibility of unsympathetic cross-examination. Not surprisingly, there is considerable debate about the accuracy of children's recall under these conditions.

In most states, it is rare for children under age 5 to be asked to testify, whereas those age 6 and older often are. Children between ages 10 and 14 are generally assumed competent to testify (Saywitz, 1987). These guidelines make good sense in terms of what we know about memory development. Compared to preschoolers, school-age children are better able to give detailed descriptions of past experiences and make accurate inferences about others' motives and intentions. Also, older children are more resistant to misleading questions of the sort asked by attorneys when they probe for more information or, in cross-examination, try to influence the content of the child's response (Ceci & Bruck, 1993b; Goodman & Tobey, 1994).

Nevertheless, when properly questioned, even 3-year-olds can recall recent events accurately—including ones that were highly stressful (Baker-Ward et al., 1993; Goodman et al., 1991). But court testimony often involves repeated interviews in which children are asked suggestive questions. These circumstances increase the likelihood of incorrect reporting—even among school-age children, whose descriptions are usually elaborate and dependable (Ceci, Leichtman, & White, 1994; Leichtman & Ceci, 1995). By the time children come to court, it is weeks, months, or even years after the occurrence of the target events. When a long delay is combined with suggestions about what happened, children can easily be misled into giving false information (Ceci, Leichtman, & Bruck, 1994).

When children are interviewed in a frightening legal setting, their ability to report past events completely and accurately is reduced further (Goodman et al., 1992). To ease the task of providing testimony, special interviewing methods have been devised for children. In Renata's case,

■ **PREVENTION AND TREATMENT.** Treating child sexual abuse is difficult. Once it is revealed, the reactions of family members—anxiety about harm to the child, anger toward the abuser, and sometimes hostility toward the victim for telling—can increase children's distress. Sensitive work with parents is essential for helping the abused child. Since sexual abuse typically appears in midst of other serious family problems, long-term therapy with children and families is usually necessary (Briere, 1992; Gomez-Schwartz, Horowitz, & Cardarelli, 1990).

The best way to reduce the suffering of child sexual abuse victims is to prevent it from continuing. Today, courts are prosecuting abusers (especially nonrelatives) more rigorously. And, as the From Research to Practice box on page below indicates, children's testimony is being taken more seriously. New ways have been devised to help children tell about their experiences without suffering additional emotional harm. In schools, sex education programs can help children recognize inappropriate sexual advances and encourage them to report these actions. Finally, educating teachers, caregivers, and other adults who work with children about the signs and symptoms of sexual abuse can help ensure that victimized children are identified early and receive the help they need.

a professional used puppets to ask questions and had Renata respond through them. In many child sexual abuse cases, anatomically correct dolls have been used to prompt children's recall. However, serious concerns have been raised about this method. Research indicates that it does not improve the accuracy of young children's answers. And it can encourage them to report physical and sexual contact that, in fact, never happened (Berry & Skinner, 1993; Wolfner, Faust, & Dawes, 1993).

Child witnesses need to be prepared so that they understand the courtroom process and know what to expect. Below age 8, children have little grasp of the differing roles of judge, attorney, and police officer. Many regard the court negatively, as "a room you pass through on your way to jail" (Saywitz, 1989, p. 149). In some places, "court schools" exist in which children are taken through the setting and given an opportunity to role-play court activities. As part of this process, children can be encouraged to admit not knowing an answer rather than guessing or going along with what an adult expects (Cole & Loftus, 1987). At the same time, legal professionals need to take steps to lessen the risk of suggestibility—by limiting the number of times children are interviewed, asking questions in nonleading ways, and being warm and patient (Ceci & Bruck, 1993b).

If a child is likely to experience emotional trauma or later punishment (in a family dispute), then courtroom procedures can be adapted to protect them. For example, Renata eventually testified over closed-circuit TV so she would not have to face her abusive father. When it is not wise for a child to participate directly, expert witnesses can provide testimony that reports on the child's psychological condition and includes important elements of the child's story. But for such testimony to be worthwhile, witnesses need to be impartial and carefully trained in how to question children in ways that minimize false reporting (Ceci & Bruck, 1993a).

Will this 6-year-old boy recount events accurately and completely on the witness stand? The answer to this question depends on many factors—his cognitive maturity, the way he is questioned, how long ago the events occurred, whether adults in his life have tried to influence his responses, how the doll is used to prompt his recall, and his understanding of the courtroom process. *(Stacy Pick/Stock Boston)*

STRESS AND COPING: THE RESILIENT CHILD

Throughout middle childhood—and other phases of development as well—children are confronted with challenging and sometimes threatening situations that require them to cope with psychological stress. In this trio of chapters, we have considered such topics as chronic illness, learning disabilities, divorce, and child sexual abuse. Each taxes children's coping resources, creating serious risks for development.

At the same time, many studies indicate that only a modest relationship exists between stressful life experiences and psychological disturbance in childhood (Compas et al., 1989; Dubow et al., 1991; Rutter, 1979). If you recall our discussion of the consequences of birth complications in Chapter 4, we noted that some children manage to defy all the odds, overcoming the combined effects of birth trauma, poverty, and a deeply troubled family life. The same is true when we look at research on family transitions, school difficulties, and child maltreatment. What factors promote such remarkable resilience in the face of adversity? If we can identify aspects of individuals and environments that reduce the impact of stressful experiences, then we will be in a better position to help children cope with difficult life conditions.

Research on stress-resistant children highlights three broad factors that consistently protect against maladjustment (Garmezy, 1983):

- Personal characteristics of children—an easy temperament, high self-esteem, and a mastery-oriented approach to new situations
- A family environment that provides warmth, closeness, and order and organization to the child's life
- A person outside the immediate family—perhaps a grandparent, teacher, or close friend—who develops a special relationship with the child, offering a support system and a positive coping model

Any one of these ingredients can account for why one child fares well and another poorly when exposed to extreme hardship. Yet most of the time, personal and environmental resources are interconnected (Compas, 1987; Sorenson, 1993). Throughout this book, we have seen many examples of how unfavorable life experiences increase the chances that parents and children will act in ways that expose them to further hardship, magnifying stress and diminishing their ability to cope effectively. Children can usually handle one stressor in their lives, even if it is chronic. But when negative conditions pile up, such as marital discord, poverty, crowded living conditions, and parental psychological disorder, the rate of maladjustment is multiplied (Capaldi & Patterson, 1991; Rutter, 1979).

Social supports are especially important during periods of developmental transition—when children are more vulnerable because they are faced with many new tasks (Rutter, 1987). One such turning point is the beginning of middle childhood, a time of new challenges in academic work and peer relations. We have seen how families, schools, communities, and society as a whole can enhance or undermine the school-age child's developing sense of competence. Another major turning point is the transition to adolescence. As the next three chapters will reveal, young people whose experiences have helped them learn how to overcome obstacles and strive for self-direction meet the challenges of this new phase quite well.

SUMMARY

ERIKSON'S THEORY: INDUSTRY VERSUS INFERIORITY

What personality changes take place during Erikson's stage of industry versus inferiority?

- According to Erikson, the personality changes of the school years build on Freud's **latency stage.** Children who successfully resolve the critical psychological conflict of **industry versus inferiority** develop the capacity to engage in productive work, learn the value of division of labor, and develop a sense of moral commitment and responsibility.

SELF-DEVELOPMENT IN MIDDLE CHILDHOOD

Describe school-age children's self-concept and self-esteem, and discuss factors that affect their achievement-related attributions.

- During middle childhood, children's self-concepts include personality traits and **social comparisons.** Self-esteem becomes hierarchically organized and declines over the early school years as children adjust their self-judgments to feedback from the environment.
- Studies of children's **attributions** have identified adult communication styles that affect self-esteem. Children with **mastery-oriented attributions** credit their successes to high ability and their failures to insufficient effort. In contrast, those with **learned helplessness** attribute failures to low ability. Children who receive negative feedback about their ability develop the learned-helpless pattern. **Attribution retraining** encourages learned helpless children to revise their failure-related attributions, thereby improving self-esteem.

EMOTIONAL DEVELOPMENT IN MIDDLE CHILDHOOD

Cite changes in understanding and expression of emotion in middle childhood.

- In middle childhood, the complex emotions of pride and guilt become integrated with personal responsibility. School-age children also recognize that people can experience more than one emotion at a time. Emotional self-regulation improves as children use cognitive strategies for controlling feelings.

UNDERSTANDING OTHERS

How does perspective taking change in middle childhood?

- **Perspective taking** improves greatly over middle childhood, as Selman's five-stage sequence indicates. Cognitive maturity and experiences in which adults and peers encourage children to take note of another's viewpoint support school-age children's perspective-taking skill. Good perspective takers show more positive social skills.

MORAL DEVELOPMENT IN MIDDLE CHILDHOOD

Describe changes in moral understanding during middle childhood.

- By middle childhood, children have internalized a wide variety of moral rules. Consequently, they are less dependent on modeling and reinforcement for morally relevant behavior than they were at younger ages.
- Children's concepts of **distributive justice** change over middle childhood, from equality to merit to benevolence. School-age children also begin to grasp the linkage between moral rules and social conventions.

PEER RELATIONS IN MIDDLE CHILDHOOD

How do peer sociability and friendship change in middle childhood?

- In middle childhood, peer interaction becomes more positive and prosocial, and physical aggression declines. By the end of the school years, children organize themselves into **peer groups.** Friendships develop into mutual relationships based on trust.

Describe major categories of peer acceptance and ways to help rejected children.

- **Sociometric techniques** are used to distinguish four types of peer acceptance: (1) **popular children,** who are liked by many agemates; (2) **rejected children,** who are actively disliked; (3) **controversial children,** who are both liked and disliked; and (4) **neglected children,** who are seldom chosen, either positively or negatively. At least two subtypes of peer rejection exist: **rejected-aggressive children,** who show severe conduct problems, and **rejected-withdrawn children,** who are passive and socially awkward. Both subgroups often experience lasting adjustment difficulties. Interventions that provide coaching in social skills, academic tutoring, and training in social understanding have been used to help rejected youngsters.

GENDER TYPING IN MIDDLE CHILDHOOD

What changes in gender-stereotyped beliefs and gender-role identity take place during middle childhood?

- School-age children extend their awareness of gender stereotypes to personality characteristics and academic subjects. Boys strengthen their identification with the masculine role, whereas girls feel free to experiment with "opposite gender" activities. Cultures shape gender-typed behavior through the daily activities assigned to children.

FAMILY INFLUENCES IN MIDDLE CHILDHOOD

How do parent–child communication and sibling relationships change in middle childhood?

- Effective parents of school-age youngsters engage in **coregulation,** exerting general oversight while permitting children to be in charge of moment-by-moment decision making. Coregulation depends on a cooperative relationship between parent and child.
- During middle childhood, sibling rivalry increases as children participate in a wider range of activities and parents compare their abilities. Siblings often try to reduce this rivalry by striving to be different from one another. Older siblings tend to be advantaged in IQ and school achievement. Younger siblings are more popular.

What factors influence children's adjustment to divorce and remarriage?

- Divorce is common in the lives of American children. Although most experience painful emotional reactions, younger children and boys in mother-custody homes tend to react more strongly. Boys and children with difficult temperaments are more likely to show lasting psychological problems. The overriding factor in positive adjustment following divorce is good parenting. Contact with noncustodial fathers is also important. Because **divorce mediation** helps parents resolve their disputes, it can reduce children's exposure to conflict. **Joint custody** is a controversial practice that may create additional strains for children.
- Many divorced parents remarry, a transition that also creates difficulties for children. How well children do in these **blended, or reconstituted, families** depends on the age and sex of the child. Children in father–stepmother families, especially girls, display the greatest adjustment problems.

What factors influence the impact of maternal employment on school-age children?

- As long as mothers enjoy their work and remain committed to parenting, maternal employment is associated with positive outcomes for children, including a higher sense of self-esteem, more positive family and peer relations, less gender-stereotyped beliefs, and better grades in school. However, outcomes are more positive for daughters than sons, and boys in low-income homes sometimes show adverse effects.
- **Self-care children** who are monitored from a distance and experience authoritative parenting appear responsible and well adjusted. High-quality after-school child care, fathers' involvement in family responsibilities, and opportunities for part-time employment help mothers balance the multiple demands of work and child rearing.

SOME COMMON PROBLEMS OF DEVELOPMENT

Cite common fears and anxieties in middle childhood.

- During middle childhood, children's fears are directed toward new concerns having to do with achievement, physical appearance, physical safety, and media events. Some children develop intense, unmanageable fears, such as **school phobia.** Severe anxiety can also result from harsh living conditions.

Discuss factors related to child sexual abuse and its consequences for children's development.

- Child sexual abuse is generally committed by male family members, more often against girls than boys. Abusers have characteristics that predispose them toward sexual exploitation of children. Reported cases are strongly associated with poverty and marital instability. Adjustment problems of abused children are often severe. Common reactions are depression, low self-esteem, mistrust of adults, anger and hostility, difficulties with peer relations, and inappropriate sexual behavior.

STRESS AND COPING: THE RESILIENT CHILD

Cite factors that help children cope with stress and reduce the chances of maladjustment.

- Only a modest relationship exists between stressful life experiences and psychological disturbance in childhood. Personal characteristics of children, a warm, well-organized home life, and social supports outside the family are related to childhood resilience in the face of stress.

IMPORTANT TERMS AND CONCEPTS

latency stage (p. 466)
industry versus inferiority (p. 466)
social comparisons (p. 467)
attributions (p. 470)
mastery-oriented attributions (p. 471)
learned helplessness (p. 471)
attribution retraining (p. 472)
perspective taking (p. 474)
distributive justice (p. 477)
peer group (p. 480)
sociometric techniques (p. 482)
popular children (p. 482)
rejected children (p. 482)
controversial children (p. 482)
neglected children (p. 482)
rejected-aggressive children (p. 483)
rejected-withdrawn children (p. 483)
coregulation (p. 487)
divorce mediation (p. 492)
joint custody (p. 492)
blended, or reconstituted, family (p. 492)
self-care children (p. 495)
school phobia (p. 496)

FYI...

FOR FURTHER INFORMATION AND SPECIAL HELP, CONSULT THE FOLLOWING ORGANIZATIONS:

DIVORCE

Parents Without Partners
8807 Colesville Road
Silver Spring, MD 20910
(301) 588-9354

Organization of custodial and noncustodial single parents that provides support in the upbringing of children. Many local groups exist throughout the United States.

REMARRIAGE

Stepfamily Association of America
215 Centennial Mall South, Suite 212
Lincoln, NE 68508
(402) 477-7837

Association of families interested in stepfamily relationships. Organizes support groups and offers education and children's services.

Stepfamily Foundation
333 West End Avenue
New York, NY 10023
(212) 877-3244

Organization of remarried parents, interested professionals, and divorced individuals. Arranges group counseling sessions for stepfamilies and provides training for professionals.

CHILD SEXUAL ABUSE

Committee for Children
172 20th Avenue
Seattle, WA 98122
(206) 322-5050

Develops programs for preschool, elementary, and high school students that can be used in schools to help prevent child sexual abuse. Also conducts training programs for teachers. Supports legislation benefiting victims. Publishes the journal, Connections in the Prevention of Child Sexual Abuse.

Parents United International
232 Gish Road
San Jose, CA 95112
(408) 453-7616

Organization of individuals who have experienced child sexual abuse. Assists families affected by incest and other types of sexual abuse by providing information and arranging for medical and legal counseling.

Society's League Against Molestation
c/o Women Against Rape/Childwatch
P.O. Box 346
Collingswood, NJ 08108
(609) 858-7800

A 100,000-member organization that works to prevent child sexual abuse through public education. Offers counseling and assistance to victims and their families.

MILESTONES OF DEVELOPMENT IN MIDDLE CHILDHOOD

AGE	PHYSICAL	COGNITIVE	LANGUAGE	EMOTIONAL/SOCIAL
6–8 years	■ Slow gains in height and weight continue until adolescent growth spurt. ■ Gradual replacement of primary teeth by permanent teech throughout middle childhood. ■ Writing becomes smaller and more legible. Letter reversals decline. ■ Drawings become more organized and detailed and include some depth cues. ■ Organized games with rules and rough-and-tumble play become common. ■ Dominance hierarchies become more stable, especially among boys.	■ Thought becomes more logical, as shown by the ability to pass Piagetian conservation, class inclusion, and seriation problems. ■ Understanding of spatial concepts, including ability to integrate distance, time, and speed and to give directions, improve. ■ Attention becomes more focused, adaptable, and planful. ■ Uses memory strategies of rehearsal and organization. ■ Awareness of the importance of memory strategies and the impact of psychological factors (attention, motivation) in task performance improves.	■ Vocabulary increases rapidly throughout middle childhood. ■ Word definitions are concrete, referring to functions and appearance. ■ Language awareness improves over middle childhood.	■ Self-esteem differentiates, becomes hierarchically organized, and declines to a more realistic level. ■ Distinguishes ability, effort, and luck in attributions for success and failure. ■ Understands that access to different information often causes people to have different perspectives. ■ Becomes more responsible and independent. ■ Distributive justice reasoning changes from equality to merit to benevolence. ■ Peer interaction becomes more prosocial, and physical aggression declines. ■ Self-conscious emotions of pride and guilt are integrated with personal responsibility.

AGE	PHYSICAL	COGNITIVE	LANGUAGE	EMOTIONAL/SOCIAL
9–11 years	■ Adolescent growth spurt begins 2 years earlier for girls than boys. ■ Gross motor skills of running, jumping, throwing, catching, kicking, batting, and dribbling are executed more quickly and with better coordination. ■ Reaction time improves, contributing to motor skill development. ■ Representation of depth in drawings expands.	■ Logical thought remains tied to concrete situations until the end of middle childhood. ■ Piagetian tasks continue to be mastered in a step-by-step fashion. ■ Memory strategies of rehearsal and organization become more effective. Memory strategy of elaboration appears. ■ Long-term knowledge base grows larger and becomes better organized. ■ Self-regulation of cognitive performance improves.	■ Word definitions emphasize synonyms and categorical relations. ■ Understanding of complex grammatical forms improves. ■ Grasps double meanings of words, as reflected in comprehension of metaphors and humor. ■ Adapts messages to the needs of listeners in complex communicative situations. ■ Conversational strategies become more refined.	■ Self-concept includes personality traits and social comparisons. ■ Self-esteem tends to rise. ■ Recognizes that individuals can experience more than one emotion at a time, each of which may differ in valence and intensity. ■ Emotional self-regulation includes cognitive strategies. ■ Can "step into another's shoes" and view the self from that person's perspective. ■ Later, can view the relationship between self and other from the perspective of a third, impartial party. ■ Appreciates the linkage between moral rules and social conventions. ■ Peer groups emerge. ■ Friendships are based on mutual trust. ■ Academic subjects and personality traits become gender stereotyped, but school-age children (especially girls) view the capacities of males and females more flexibly. ■ Sibling rivalry tends to increase.

"Love, life and sorrow"
Maria Elena Nilsen
14 years, Norway

The arrival of puberty is accompanied by greater self-awareness as adolescents adjust to a transformed body and sexual maturity. This painting depicts the increased self-focusing of the adolescent years. A beautiful girl sits on top of the Earth, at the center of the universe, as other-worldly creatures look on.

Reprinted by permission from The International Museum of Children's Art, Oslo, Norway.

14

Physical Development in Adolescence

CONCEPTIONS OF ADOLESCENCE

Biologically Oriented Views • The Environmental Perspective • A Balanced Point of View

PUBERTY: THE PHYSICAL TRANSITION TO ADULTHOOD

Hormonal Changes • Changes in Body Size and Proportions • Muscle–Fat Makeup and Other Internal Changes • Sexual Maturation • Individual and Group Differences in Pubertal Growth • The Secular Trend

THE PSYCHOLOGICAL IMPACT OF PUBERTAL EVENTS

Reactions to Pubertal Changes • Pubertal Change, Emotion, and Social Behavior • Early Versus Late Maturation

HEALTH ISSUES DURING ADOLESCENCE

Nutritional Needs • Serious Eating Disturbances • Sexual Activity • Teenage Pregnancy and Childbearing • Sexually Transmitted Disease • Substance Use and Abuse • Unintentional Injuries

MOTOR DEVELOPMENT DURING ADOLESCENCE

On her eleventh birthday, Sabrina's friend Joyce gave a surprise party, but Sabrina seemed somber and withdrawn during the celebration. Although Sabrina and Joyce had been close friends since third grade, their relationship seemed to be faltering. The largest child in her sixth-grade class, Sabrina was a head taller and some 20 pounds heavier than most of the other girls. Her breasts were already well developed, her hips and thighs had broadened, and she had begun to menstruate. In contrast, Joyce still had the short, lean, angular, flat-chested body of a school-age child.

Sabrina hadn't told Joyce about her menstrual periods or talked about how she felt about her developing body. Since Joyce wasn't "there" yet, Sabrina was convinced she wouldn't understand. Ducking into the bathroom while Joyce and the other girls set the table for cake and ice cream, Sabrina looked herself over in the mirror, straightened her blouse, smoothed her skirt, and whispered, "Gosh, I feel so big and heavy." At church youth group on Sunday evenings, Sabrina broke away from Joyce and spent time with the eighth-grade girls, around whom she didn't feel so large and awkward.

Once every 2 weeks, parents gathered at Sabrina and Joyce's school for discussions about child-rearing concerns. Sabrina's Italian-American parents, Franca and Antonio, came whenever they could. At one meeting, they talked about their youngsters' changing bodies and behavior.

"How you know they are becoming teenagers is this," volunteered Antonio. "The bedroom door is closed, and they want to be alone. They leave makeup, deodorant, and hair gel all over the bathroom counter. They are always preening in front of the mirror. Also, they contradict and disagree. I tell Sabrina, 'Only three minutes in the shower—there has to be water for the rest of us.' Or I say, 'You have to go to Aunt Gina's on Saturday for dinner with the family.' The next thing I know, she is arguing with me."

"All our four children were early developers," Franca added. "The three boys, too, were tall by age 12 or 13, but it was easier for them. They felt big and important. Sabrina is moody and doesn't want to be with her old friends. She was skinny as a little girl, but now she says she is too fat and wants to diet. She thinks about boys and doesn't concentrate on her studies. I try to be patient and listen to her," reflected Franca sympathetically. "It's not so easy for her to adjust."

Sabrina has entered adolescence, a period of development in which she will cross the dividing line between childhood and adulthood. In modern societies, the skills young people must master are so complex and the choices confronting them so diverse that adolescence lasts for nearly a decade. But around the world, the basic tasks of this phase are much the same. Sabrina must accept her full-grown body, acquire adult ways of thinking, attain emotional and economic independence, develop more mature ways of relating to peers of both sexes, and construct an identity—a secure sense of who she is, sexually, morally, politically, and vocationally.

The beginning of adolescence is marked by **puberty**, a flood of biological events leading to an adult-sized body and sexual maturity. During no other period of life except infancy do so many physical changes take place in such a short time. As you can already tell from Sabrina's reactions, entry into adolescence can be a trying time, more so for some youngsters than for others. In this chapter, we trace the events of puberty and take up a variety of health concerns—nutrition, sexual activity, and serious health problems affecting teenagers who encounter difficulties on the path to maturity. We conclude with a discussion of adolescent motor development, which highlights the large sex differences that appear at this time. But before we delve into these specifics, let's begin with an overview of changing views of adolescence during this century.

Puberty
Biological changes at adolescence that lead to an adult-sized body and sexual maturity.

CONCEPTIONS OF ADOLESCENCE

BIOLOGICALLY ORIENTED VIEWS

When you next have a chance, ask several new parents what they expect their sons and daughters to be like as teenagers. You will probably get answers like these: "Rebellious and uncontrollable," "Full of rages and tempers," "Plagued by one crisis after another." This view, widespread in contemporary American society, dates back to the writings of eighteenth-century philosopher Jean-Jacques Rousseau, whom we introduced in Chapter 1. Rousseau believed that a natural outgrowth of the biological upheaval of puberty was heightened emotionality, conflict, and defiance of adults. Comparing adolescence to a violent storm, he cautioned parents,

> As the roaring of the waves precedes the tempest, so the murmur of rising passions . . . warns us of the approaching danger. A change of temper, frequent outbreaks of anger, a perpetual stirring of the mind, make the child almost ungovernable. . . . Keep your hand upon the helm or all is lost." (Rousseau, 1762/1955, pp. 172–173)

Although Rousseau had no scientific evidence for these impressions, they were nevertheless picked up and extended by twentieth-century theorists. The most influential of these was G. Stanley Hall, whose view of development was grounded in Darwin's theory of evolution (see Chapter 1, page 12). Hall (1904) described adolescence as a cascade of instinctual passions, a phase of growth so turbulent that it resembled the period in which human beings evolved from savages into civilized beings. Without efforts by adults to redirect this sexual fervor into socially useful activities, it could lead young people into a life of decadence and conflict with society.

Sigmund Freud, as well, emphasized the emotional storminess of the teenage years. He called adolescence the **genital stage,** a period in which instinctual drives reawaken and shift to the genital region of the body. According to Freud, adolescent sexual impulses are so powerful and urgent that they upset the delicate balance between id, ego, and superego established during middle childhood. As a result, the struggle of the earlier phallic period is renewed, resulting in psychological conflict and volatile, unpredictable behavior. But unlike preschool children, adolescents can find romantic partners outside the family. As they do so, inner forces gradually achieve a new, more mature harmony, and the stage concludes with marriage, birth, and the rearing of children. In this way, young people fulfill their biological destiny and the goal of development: sexual reproduction and the survival of the species.

THE ENVIRONMENTAL PERSPECTIVE

Recent research on large numbers of teenagers suggests that Rousseau, Hall, and Freud's image of adolescence as a biologically determined, inevitable period of storm and stress is greatly exaggerated. A number of problems, such as eating disorders, depression, suicide, and law breaking, occur more often in adolescence than earlier. But the overall rate of severe psychological disturbance rises only slightly (by 2 percent) from childhood to adolescence, when it is the same as in the adult population—about 15 to 20 percent (Powers, Hauser, & Kilner, 1989; Rutter et al., 1976). The serious difficulties some teenagers encounter should not be dismissed as unimportant. But emotional turbulence is not a routine feature of this phase of development.

The first researcher to point out the wide variability in adolescent adjustment was anthropologist Margaret Mead (1901–1978). In 1926, she traveled to the Pacific islands of Samoa, returning a short time later with a startling conclusion: Samoan adolescence was free of all those characteristics that made it hazardous for young people and dreaded by adults in more complex societies. Because of the culture's relaxed social relationships and openness toward sexuality, adolescence, Mead (1928) reported, "is perhaps the pleasantest time the Samoan girl (or boy) will ever know" (p. 308).

Mead offered an alternative view—one in which the social environment was judged to be entirely responsible for the range of teenage experiences, from erratic and agitated to calm and stress free. Yet this conclusion is just as extreme as the biological perspective it tried to replace! Later researchers, who looked more closely at Samoan society, found that adolescence was not as smooth and untroubled as Mead made it out to be (Freeman, 1983). Still, Mead's work had an enormous impact. She convinced researchers that (1) adolescence need not be a time of emotional turmoil, and (2) greater attention must be paid to social and cultural influences for this period of development to be understood.

Observations of anthropologist Margaret Mead in Samoa underscored the contribution of culture to the wide variation in adolescent adjustment. Today we know that biological and environmental pressures combine to affect adolescent well-being. Still, Mead's work overturned the commonly held belief that adolescence is an inevitable period of storm and stress. *(Dennis Black/Black Star)*

A BALANCED POINT OF VIEW

Today, we know that adolescence is neither biologically nor socially determined, but rather a product of the two. Biological changes are universal—found in all primates, in all cultures, throughout history. These internal stresses and the social expectations accompanying them—that the young person move away from childish ways of behaving, develop new interpersonal relationships, and take on greater responsibility—are likely to prompt moments of uncertainty, self-doubt, and disappointment in all teenagers.

At the same time, the length of adolescence and the number of hurdles a young person must overcome vary greatly from one culture to the next. In line with Mead's

Genital stage
Freud's psychosexual stage of adolescence, in which instinctual drives are reawakened and shift to the genital region, upsetting the delicate balance between id, ego, and superego established during middle childhood.

observations in Samoa, simpler societies have a shorter transition to adulthood (Whiting, Burbank, & Ratner, 1986). But most of the time, adolescence is not absent. A recent study of 186 tribal and village cultures revealed that almost all had an intervening phase, however brief, between childhood and full assumption of adult roles (Schlegel & Barry, 1991, p. 42).

In industrialized nations, successful participation in the economic life of society requires many years of education. Consequently, young people face extra years of dependence on parents and a long period in which they are expected to postpone sexual gratification while they master complex systems of knowledge essential to a productive work life. As a result, adolescence is greatly extended, and teenagers confront a wider array of psychological challenges. Adolescence is so drawn out in modern industrialized nations that researchers commonly divide it into three phases:

1. *Early adolescence,* from 11 or 12 to 14 years of age, a period of rapid pubertal change
2. *Middle adolescence,* from 14 to 18 years, when pubertal changes are nearly complete
3. *Late adolescence* (sometimes called *youth*), from 18 to 21 years, when the young person achieves full adult appearance and faces more complete assumption of adult roles

Girls reach puberty, on the average, two years earlier than boys. Although these early adolescents are the same age, the girl is much taller and more mature looking. *(J. Gerard Smith/Monk-meyer Press)*

These divisions also correspond to the way industrialized societies commonly group adolescents—into middle or junior high school, high school, and college (Steinberg, 1993).

Throughout our discussion, we will see that the extent to which the social environment supports young people in achieving adult responsibilities has much to do with how well they fare. For all the biological tensions and uncertainties about the future that modern teenagers feel, most are surprisingly good at negotiating the twists and turns of this period of life. With this idea in mind, let's look closely at puberty, the dawning of adolescent development.

PUBERTY: THE PHYSICAL TRANSITION TO ADULTHOOD

The changes of puberty are dramatic and momentous. Within a few years, the childish appearance of the school-age youngster is transformed into that of a full-grown adult. The various aspects of pubertal growth are regulated by genetically influenced hormonal processes. Girls, who have been advanced in physical maturity since the prenatal period, reach puberty, on the average, 2 years earlier than boys.

HORMONAL CHANGES

To young adolescents and their parents, major signs of puberty often seem to appear quite suddenly. But the complex hormonal changes that underlie them are actually very gradual, already underway by age 8 or 9 (see Figure 14.1). Recall from Chapter 8 that the *pituitary gland,* located at the base of the brain, plays a vital role in physical growth. It releases *growth hormone (GH)* and stimulates other glands to produce hormones that act on body tissues, causing them to mature. GH and *thyroxine* (a hormone released by the thyroid gland) contribute to the tremendous gains in body size and completion of skeletal maturation during puberty. If the quantity of either hormone is too low or entirely absent, adolescent growth will be reduced.

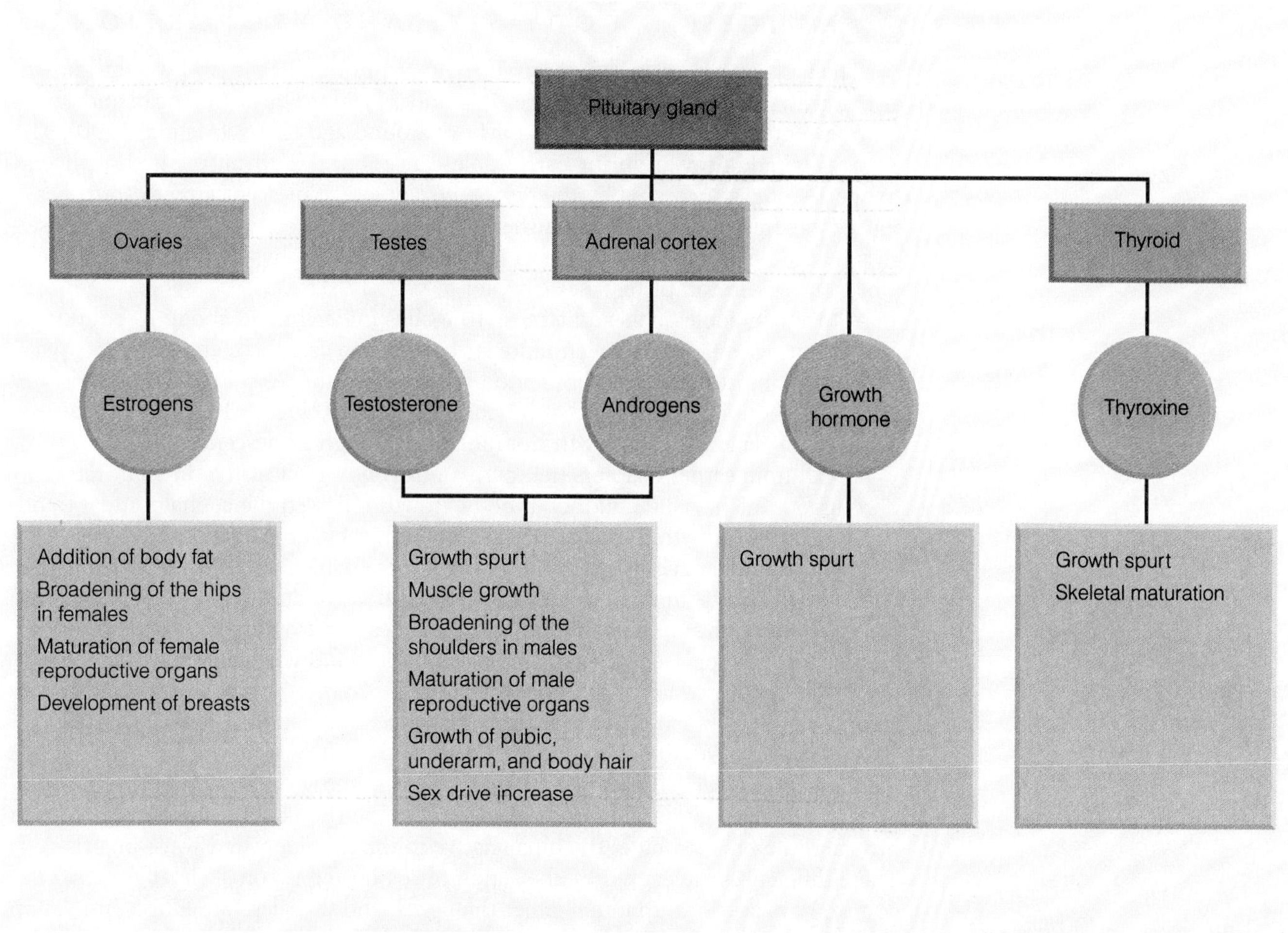

FIGURE 14.1

Hormonal influences on the body at puberty.

Sexual maturation is controlled by the sex hormones. Although *estrogens* are thought of as female hormones and *androgens* as male hormones, both types are present in each sex, but in different amounts. The boy's testes release large quantities of the androgen *testosterone,* which leads to muscle growth, body and facial hair, and other male sex characteristics. Testosterone also contributes to gains in body size. Estrogens released by the girl's ovaries cause the breasts, uterus, and vagina to mature, the body to take on feminine proportions, and fat to accumulate. In addition, estrogens contribute to regulation of the menstrual cycle. Girls' changing bodies are also affected by the release of androgens from the adrenal glands, located on top of each kidney. *Adrenal androgens* influence the girl's height spurt and stimulate growth of underarm and pubic hair. They have little impact on boys, whose physical characteristics are mainly influenced by androgen secretions from the testes.

As you can tell from our discussion so far, pubertal changes can be divided into two broad types: (1) overall body growth, which includes changes in size, proportion, and muscle–fat makeup, and (2) maturation of sex characteristics (Malina, 1990). We will take up each of these sets of changes separately, but keep in mind that they are interrelated. We have already seen that the hormones responsible for sexual changes also affect body growth; boys and girls differ in both aspects. In fact, puberty is the time of greatest sexual differentiation since prenatal life.

CHANGES IN BODY SIZE AND PROPORTIONS

The first outward sign of puberty is the rapid gain in height and weight known as the **growth spurt.** On the average, it is underway for North American and European girls shortly after age 10, for boys around age 12 1/2 (Malina, 1990). The girl is taller and heavier during early adolescence, but this advantage is short-lived. At age 14, she is surpassed by the typical boy, whose adolescent growth spurt has started, whereas hers is almost finished. Growth in body size is complete for most girls by age 16 and for boys by age 17 1/2, when the epiphyses at the ends of the long bones close completely (see Chapter 5, page 173).

Altogether, adolescents add almost 10 inches in height and about 40 pounds in weight during puberty. But even more striking is how fast these changes takes place. When growing at their peak, boys add over 4 inches and 26 pounds in a single year, girls about 3.5 inches and as much as 20 pounds. Figure 14.2 provides an overview of general body growth from infancy through adolescence.

Recall from earlier chapters that parts of the body grow at the different rates. Throughout infancy and childhood, body growth followed the cephalocaudal trend. In adolescence, growth actually proceeds in the reverse direction. At first, the hands, legs, and feet accelerate, and then the torso, which accounts for most of the adolescent height gain (Wheeler, 1991). This pattern of development explains why young adolescents stop growing out of their shoes and trousers before they stop growing out of their jackets. It also helps us understand why early adolescence is regarded as an awkward phase. Because growth is uneven, many young teenagers appear out of proportion—long-legged and with giant feet and hands (Malina, 1990; Tanner, 1990).

During adolescence, major differences in boys' and girls' body proportions appear. The most obvious are the broadening of the shoulders relative to the hips in boys and the broadening of the hips relative to the shoulders and waist in girls. These differences are caused by the action of sex hormones on skeletal growth. Of course, boys also end up much larger than girls, and their legs are longer in relation to the rest of the body. The major reason is that boys benefit from 2 extra years of preadolescent growth, when the legs are growing the fastest (Tanner, 1990).

Preoccupation with physical appearance is typical during the adolescent years. Teenage girls are the largest consumers of cosmetic products in the United States. *(Stephen Marks)*

Growth spurt
Rapid gain in height and weight during adolescence.

MUSCLE–FAT MAKEUP AND OTHER INTERNAL CHANGES

One reason that 11-year-old Sabrina became very concerned about her weight is that compared to her later-developing girlfriends, her more mature body had accumulated much more fat. Around age 8, girls start to add more fat than boys on their arms, legs, and trunk, and they continue to do so throughout puberty. In contrast, the arm and leg fat of adolescent boys decreases. Although both sexes gain in muscle at puberty, this increase is much greater for boys, who develop larger skeletal muscles, hearts, and lung capacity. Also, the number of red blood cells, and therefore the ability to carry oxygen from the lungs to the muscles, increases in boys but not in girls (Katchadourian, 1977). The combined result of these changes is that boys gain far more muscle strength than do girls, a difference that contributes to boys' superior athletic performance during the teenage years.

During puberty, the sex hormones stimulate glandular secretions. Consequently, perspiration, body odor, and oiliness of the skin and hair increase. Sabrina, who often resisted taking a shower as a school-age child, started to monopolize the bathroom. And like other adolescents, she began to use a variety of cosmetics, from deodorants and colognes to special shampoos and skin cleansers. Cosmetic sales to American teenage girls total $5 billion a year—the highest of any age group (Graham & Hamdan, 1987). Increased activity of the sebaceous glands of the skin leads to the most common medical disorder of adolescence—acne. About 80 to 90 percent of teenage boys and girls are affected. Usually acne is mild and clears up on

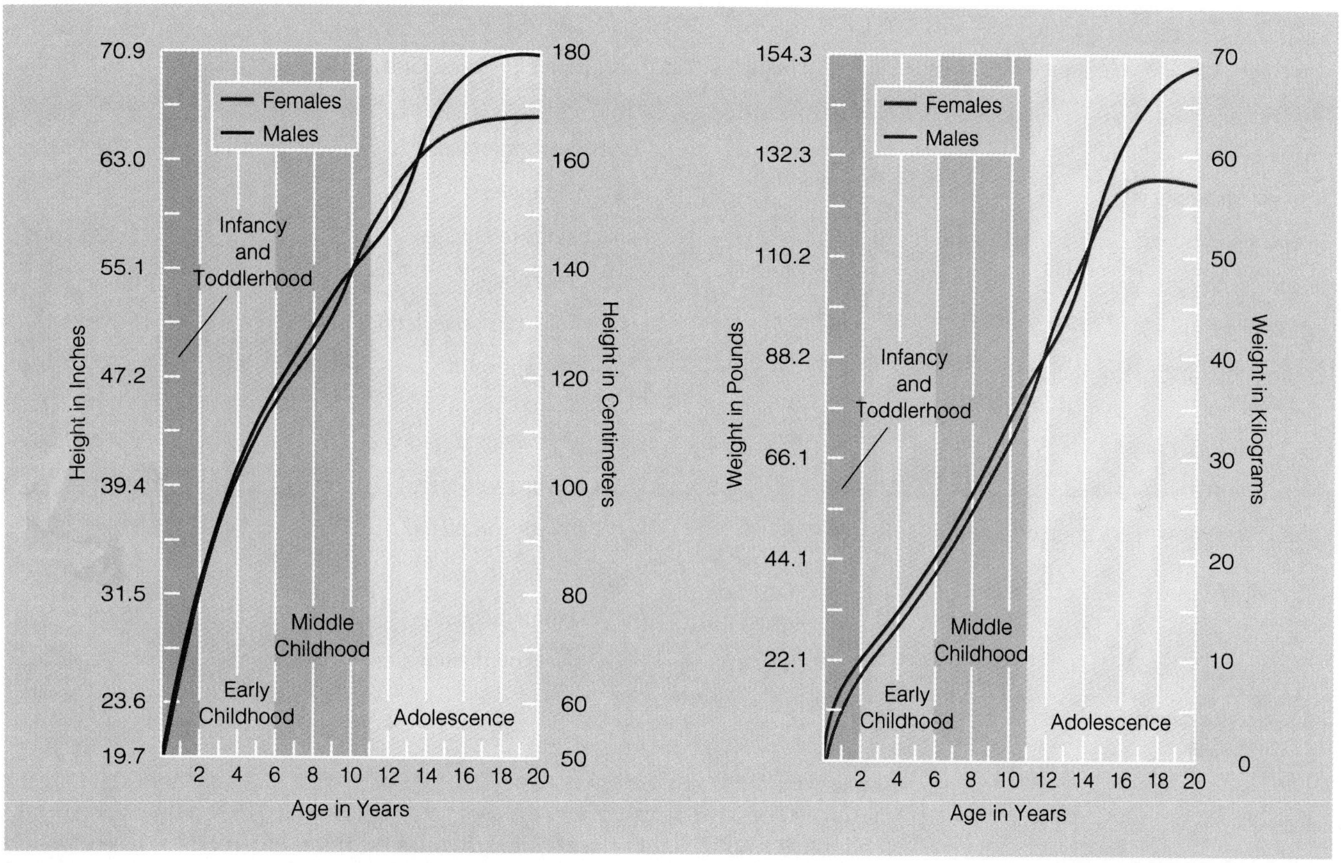

FIGURE 14.2

Average height and weight from infancy through adolescence by sex. Note that the adolescent growth spurt takes place earlier for girls than boys. *(From R. M. Malina, 1975,* Growth and Development: The First Twenty Years in Man, *Minneapolis: Burgess Publishing Company, p. 19. Adapted by permission.)*

its own by the end of puberty. In the few severe cases, it can be physically disfiguring and psychologically damaging. Fortunately, new medical treatments are remarkably successful in controlling it (Sykes, 1994).

SEXUAL MATURATION

Accompanying the rapid increase in body size are changes in physical features related to sexual functioning. Some, called **primary sexual characteristics,** involve the reproductive organs directly (ovaries, uterus, and vagina in females; penis, scrotum, and testes in males). Others, called **secondary sexual characteristics,** are visible on the outside of the body and serve as additional signs of sexual maturity (for example, breast development in females, appearance of underarm and pubic hair in both sexes). As you can see in Table 14.1, these characteristics develop in a fairly standard sequence, but the age at which each begins and is completed varies greatly (Brooks-Gunn & Reiter, 1990).

Primary sexual characteristics
Physical features that involve the reproductive organs directly (ovaries, uterus, and vagina in females; penis, scrotum, and testes in males).

Secondary sexual characteristics
Features visible on the outside of the body that serve as signs of sexual maturity but do not involve the reproductive organs (for example, breast development in females, appearance of underarm and pubic hair in both sexes).

Menarche
First menstruation.

■ SEXUAL MATURATION IN GIRLS. **Menarche** (from the Greek word *arche,* meaning "beginning") is the scientific name for first menstruation. Because most people view it as the major sign that puberty has arrived in girls, you may be surprised to learn that menarche actually occurs late in the sequence of pubertal events. Female puberty usually begins with the budding of the breasts and the growth spurt. (For about 15 percent of girls, pubic hair is present before breast development.) Menarche typically happens around 12 1/2 years for North American girls, around 13 for Europeans. But the age range is wide, extending from 10 1/2 to 15 1/2 years. Following menarche, pubic hair and breast development are completed, and underarm hair appears. Most girls take 3 to 4 years to complete this sequence. Some mature more rapidly, in as little as a year and a half. Others take longer, perhaps as much as 5 years (Tanner, 1990; Wheeler, 1991).

TABLE 14.1

Average Age and Age Range of of Major Pubertal Changes in North American Boys and Girls

GIRLS	AVERAGE	RANGE	BOYS	AVERAGE	RANGE
Breasts begin to "bud"	10	(8–13)	Testes begin to enlarge	11.5	(9.5–13.5)
Height spurt begins	10	(8–13)	Pubic hair appears	12	(10–15)
Pubic hair appears	10.5	(8–14)	Penis begins to enlarge	12	(10.5–14.5)
Peak of strength spurt	11.6	(9.5–14)	Height spurt begins	12.5	(10.5–16)
Peak of height spurt	11.7	(10–13.5)	Spermarche (first ejaculation) occurs	13	(12–16)
Menarche (first menstruation) occurs	12.8	(10.5–15.5)	Peak of height spurt	14	(12.5–15.5)
Adult stature reached	13	(10–16)	Facial hair begins to grow	14	(12.5–15.5)
Breast growth completed	14	(10–16)	Voice begins to deepen	14	(12.5–15.5)
Pubic hair growth completed	14.5	(14–15)	Penis growth completed	14.5	(12.5–16)
			Peak of strength spurt	15.3	(13–17)
			Adult stature reached	15.5	(13.5–17.5)
			Pubic hair growth completed	15.5	(14–17)

Sources: Malina and Bouchard, 1991; Tanner, 1990.

Table 14.1 shows that all girls experience menarche after the peak in the height spurt, once they have nearly reached their mature body size. This sequence has clear adaptive value. Nature delays menstruation until the girl's body is large enough for successful childbearing. As an extra measure of security, for 12 to 18 months following menarche, the menstrual cycle often takes place without an ovum being released from the ovaries. However, this temporary period of sterility does not apply to all girls, and it cannot be counted on for protection against pregnancy (Tanner, 1990).

■ SEXUAL MATURATION IN BOYS. The first sign of puberty in boys is the enlargement of the testes (glands that manufacture sperm), accompanied by changes in the texture and color of the scrotum. Pubic hair emerges a short time later, about the same time the penis begins to enlarge (Wheeler, 1991).

Refer again to Table 14.1, and you will see that the growth spurt occurs much later in the sequence of pubertal events for boys than girls. When it reaches its peak (at about age 14), enlargement of the testes and penis is nearly complete, and underarm hair appears soon after. Facial and body hair also emerges just after the peak in body growth, but it increases slowly, continuing to develop for several years after puberty. Another landmark of male physical maturity is the deepening of the voice as the larynx enlarges and the vocal cords lengthen. (Girls' voices also deepen slightly.) Voice change usually takes place at the peak of the male growth spurt and is often not complete until puberty is over. When it first occurs, many boys have difficulty with voice control. Occasionally their newly acquired baritone breaks into a high-pitched sound (Katchadourian, 1977).

While the penis is growing, the prostate gland and seminal vesicles (which together produce semen, the fluid in which sperm are bathed) enlarge. (To see where these organs are located, return to Chapter 2, page 57.) Then, around age 13, **spermarche,** or first ejaculation, occurs (Jorgensen & Keiding, 1991). For a while, the semen contains few living sperm. So, like girls, boys have an initial period of reduced fertility. Spermarche may be as psychologically significant for boys as menarche is for girls, an issue we will take up shortly.

Spermarche
First ejaculation of seminal fluid.

INDIVIDUAL AND GROUP DIFFERENCES IN PUBERTAL GROWTH

We have already noted wide individual differences in the timing and speed of pubertal maturation. Heredity is partly responsible. For example, identical twins generally reach menarche within a month or two of each other, whereas fraternal twins differ by about 12 months (Tanner, 1990). At the same time, nutrition and exercise contribute. In females, a sharp rise in body weight and fat may trigger sexual maturation. Girls who begin serious athletic training at young ages or who eat very little (both of which reduce the percentage of body fat) often show greatly delayed menstruation. In contrast, overweight girls typically start menstruating early (Post & Kemper, 1993; Rees, 1993).

Group differences in pubertal growth also exist, among regions of the world and social classes. Heredity probably plays little role in these variations, since groups with very different genetic origins living under similarly advantaged conditions resemble one another in pubertal timing. For example, in Japan, the United States, and Western Europe, menarche occurs at approximately the same age—between 12 1/2 and 13 1/2 years (Eveleth & Tanner, 1976). Overall physical health appears to be largely responsible for these differences. In poverty-stricken regions where malnutrition and infectious disease are widespread, menarche is greatly delayed. In many parts of Africa, it does not occur until age 14 to 17. And within countries, girls from higher-income families consistently reach menarche 6 to 18 months earlier than those living in economically disadvantaged homes.

THE SECULAR TREND

In Chapter 11, we saw that children in industrialized nations are growing faster and larger than in generations past. This *secular trend* is also apparent in age of menarche. As Figure 14.3 shows, it has declined steadily from 1860 to 1970, by about 3 to 4 months per decade. This secular trend in pubertal timing lends added support to the role of overall physical well-being in adolescent growth. Nutrition, health care, sanitation, and control of infectious disease have improved greatly over the past century (Eveleth & Tanner, 1976).

Of course, humans cannot keep growing larger and maturing earlier indefinitely, since we cannot exceed the genetic limitations of our species. Secular gains have slowed or stopped entirely in some developed countries, such as England, Sweden, Norway, Japan, and the United States (McAnarney et al., 1992; Roche, 1979). Consequently, modern young people reared under good nutritional and social conditions are likely to resemble their parents in physical growth more than at any time during the previous 130 years.

In girls, a sharp rise in body weight and fat may trigger sexual maturation. Girls who begin serious athletic training early often retain a prepubertal body shape and experience delayed menarche. *(Bob Daemmrich/Stock Boston)*

FIGURE 14.3

Secular trend in age of first menstruation (menarche) from 1860 to 1970 in industrialized nations.
Data for Norway, which extend to 1980, suggest that secular change has recently leveled off. *(Reprinted by permission of the publisher from J. M. Tanner, 1990,* Foetus into Man *(2nd ed., p. 160), Cambridge, MA: Harvard University Press. Copyright © 1990 by J. M. Tanner. All rights reserved.)*

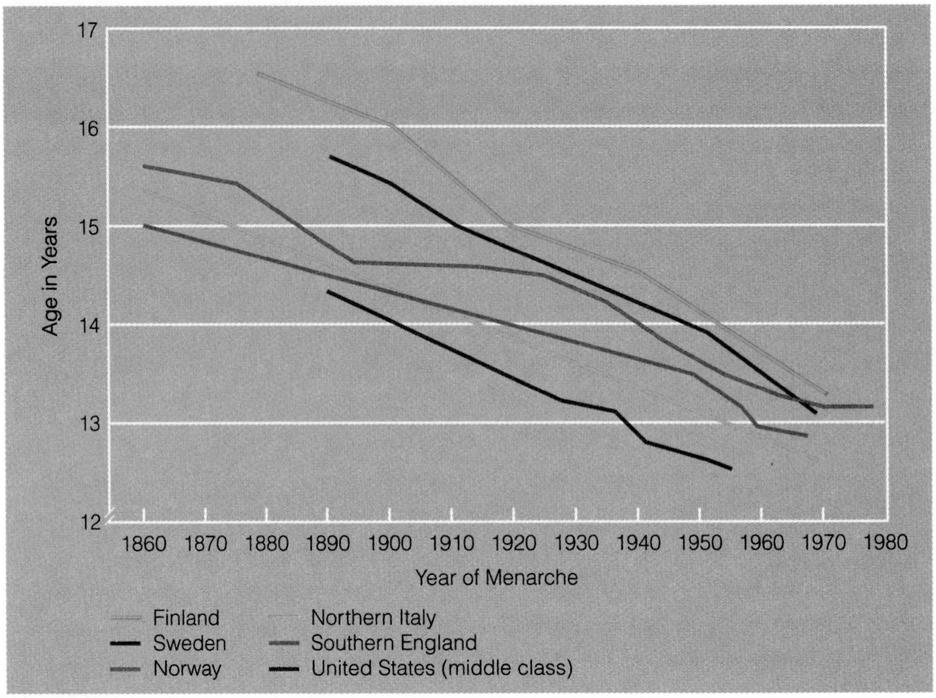

ASK YOURSELF . . .

- Millie, mother of an 11-year-old son, is convinced that the rising sexual passions of puberty cause rebelliousness in all adolescents. Where did this belief originate? Explain why it is incorrect.
- Sabrina, who reached menarche before age 11, was already much taller and heavier than her classmates. She worried that she was going to keep on growing larger and larger. How would you respond to Sabrina's concern?

BRIEF REVIEW

Adolescence is the transitional period between childhood and adulthood, a time of dramatic physical change leading to an adult-sized body and sexual maturity. Early biologically oriented theories viewed puberty as an inevitable period of storm and stress. This perspective was challenged by evidence that serious psychological disturbance is not a common feature of the teenage years. Modern researchers recognize that adolescent development and adjustment are a product of both biological and social forces. Adolescence is greatly extended in complex societies that require a long period of education for a productive work life.

Puberty is the time of greatest sexual differentiation since the prenatal period—in body size, proportions, muscle–fat makeup, and primary and secondary sexual characteristics. The physical changes of adolescence are regulated by growth and sex hormones. On the average, girls experience puberty 2 years earlier than boys. However, wide individual differences exist, to which both heredity and environment contribute. Nutrition and health account for regional and social-class differences in pubertal timing and the secular trend in industrialized nations.

THE PSYCHOLOGICAL IMPACT OF PUBERTAL EVENTS

Think back to your late elementary school and junior high school days. Were you early, late, or about on time in physical maturation with respect to your peers? How did your feelings about yourself and your relationships with others change? A large body of research reveals that puberty affects the adolescent's self-image, mood, and interaction with parents and peers. Some of these outcomes are a response to dramatic physical change, regardless of when it occurs. Others have to do with the timing of pubertal maturation.

REACTIONS TO PUBERTAL CHANGES

How do girls and boys react to the massive physical changes of puberty? Most research aimed at answering this question has focused on girls' feelings about menarche.

GIRLS' REACTIONS TO MENARCHE. Research of a generation or two ago indicated that menarche was often traumatic and disturbing. For example, one woman, who reached puberty in the 1950s, reported,

> I had no information whatsoever, no hint that anything was going to happen to me. . . . I thought I was on the point of death from internal hemorrhage. . . . What did my highly educated mother do? She read me a furious lecture about what a bad, evil, immoral thing I was to start menstruating at the age of eleven! So young and so vile! Even after thirty years, I can feel the shock of hearing her condemn me for "doing" something I had no idea occurred. (Weideger, 1976, cited in Brooks-Gunn & Reiter, 1990, p. 37)

Recent findings show that girls' reactions to menarche are rarely so unfavorable today. The most common response is "surprise," undoubtedly caused by the sudden nature of the event. Girls often report a mixture of positive and negative emotions—"excited and pleased" as well as "scared and upset." But there are wide individual differences. Some, like this girl, react with joy and elation:

> When I discovered it, I called my mother and she showed me what to do. Then she did something I'll never forget. She told me to come with her and we went to the living room to tell my father. She just looked at me and then at him and said, 'Well, your little girl is a young lady now!' My dad gave me a hug and congratulated me and I felt grown-up and proud that I was really a lady at last. That was one of the most exciting days of my life. (Shipman, 1971, p. 331)

As these two accounts suggest, girls' feelings about menarche depend on prior knowledge and support from family members. Both are influenced by social and cultural attitudes toward puberty and sexuality (Greif & Ulman, 1982).

For girls who have no advance information about sexuality, menarche can be shocking and disturbing. Fortunately, the number of girls with no advance preparation is much smaller today than it was several decades ago. In the 1950s, up to 50 percent were given no prior warning (Shainess, 1961). Today, no more than 10 to 15 percent are uninformed (Brooks-Gunn, 1988b). This shift is probably due to modern parents' greater willingness to discuss sexual matters with their youngsters. Currently, almost all girls get some information from their mothers (Brooks-Gunn & Ruble, 1983). And girls whose fathers are told about pubertal changes adjust especially well. Perhaps a father's involvement reflects a family atmosphere that is highly understanding and accepting of physical and sexual matters (Brooks-Gunn & Ruble, 1980).

BOYS' REACTIONS TO SPERMARCHE. Spermarche is the male pubertal event that is most similar to menarche, but we have much less information about its psychological impact. Available research indicates that like girls' reactions to menarche, boys' responses to spermarche are not intensely negative. Most reported mixed feelings. Virtually all boys know about ejaculation ahead of time, but few get any information from parents. Usually they obtain it from reading material (Gaddis & Brooks-Gunn, 1985). In addition, although at first girls keep menarche secret from their peers, within 6 months almost all tell a friend that they are menstruating. In contrast, far fewer boys ever tell anyone about spermarche (Brooks-Gunn et al., 1986). Overall, boys seem to get much less social support for the physical changes of puberty than do girls. This suggests that boys might benefit, especially, from opportunities to ask questions and discuss feelings with a sympathetic male teacher at school.

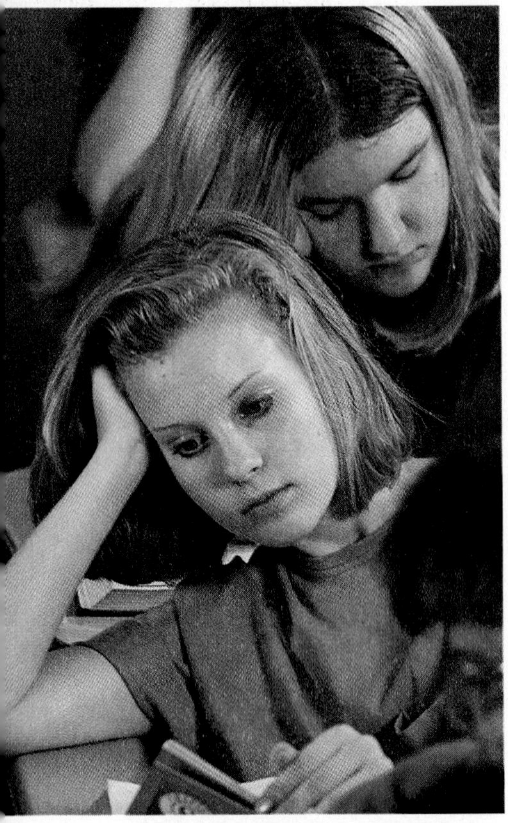

Compared to children and adults, adolescents often seem like moody creatures. But teenagers also move from one situation to another more often, and their mood swings are associated with these changes. Low points tend to occur in adult-structured settings, such as class and school library. *(Will & Deni McIntyre/Photo Researchers)*

THE FUNCTION OF ADOLESCENT INITIATION CEREMONIES. The experience of puberty is affected by the larger cultural context in which boys and girls live. Many tribal and village societies celebrate puberty with a *rite of passage*—a community-wide event that marks an important change in privilege and responsibility. Consequently, all young people know that pubertal changes are honored and valued in their culture (see the Cultural Influences box on the following page). In contrast, Western societies grant little formal recognition to movement from childhood to adolescence or from adolescence to adulthood. Certain religious ceremonies, such as confirmation and the Jewish bar or bat mitzvah, do resemble a rite of passage. But not all young people take part in these rituals, and they usually do not lead to any meaningful change in social status.

Instead, modern adolescents are confronted with many ages at which they are granted partial adult status—for example, an age for starting employment, for driving, for leaving high school, for voting, and for drinking. In some contexts (on the highway and at their place of work), they may be treated like adults. In others (at school and at home), they may still be regarded as children. The absence of a widely accepted marker of physical and social maturity makes the process of becoming an adult especially confusing. Perhaps modern adolescents would benefit from a socially and culturally appropriate substitute to serve the function that simpler societies meet with adolescent initiation rituals (Whisnant & Zegans, 1975).

Adolescent initiation ceremony
A ritual, or rite of passage, announcing to the community that a young person is making the transition into adolesence or full adulthood.

PUBERTAL CHANGE, EMOTION, AND SOCIAL BEHAVIOR

In the preceding sections, we considered adolescents' reactions to their sexually maturing bodies. Puberty can also affect the young person's emotional state and social behavior. A common belief is that pubertal change has something to do with adolescent moodiness and the desire for greater physical and psychological separation from parents.

ADOLESCENT MOODINESS. Recently, researchers have explored the role of sex hormones in adolescents' emotional reactions. Indeed, higher hormone levels are related to greater moodiness, in the form of anger and irritability for males and anger and depression for females, between 9 and 14 years of age (Brooks-Gunn & Warren, 1989; Nottelmann et al., 1990). But these links are not strong, and we cannot really be sure that a rise in pubertal hormones causes adolescent moodiness.

What else might contribute to the common observation that adolescents are moody creatures? In several studies, the mood fluctuations of children, adolescents, and adults were tracked over a week by having them carry electronic pagers. At random intervals, they were beeped and asked to write down what they were doing, whom they were with, and how they felt.

As expected, adolescents reported somewhat lower moods than did school-age children or adults (Csikszentmihalyi & Larson, 1984; Larson & Lampman-Petraitis, 1989). But young people whose moods were especially negative were experiencing a greater number of negative life events, such as difficulties in getting along with parents, disciplinary actions at school, and breaking up with a boyfriend or girlfriend. Negative events increased steadily from childhood to adolescence, and teenagers also seemed to react to them with greater emotion than did children (Larson & Ham, 1993).

Furthermore, compared to the moods of adults, adolescents' feelings were less stable. They often varied from cheerful to sad and back again. But teenagers also moved from one situation to another more often, and their mood swings were strongly related to these changes. For example, consider one particular Wednesday and Thursday in the lives of two very different young people—Katherine Tennison, a goal-oriented high school musician, and Gregory Stone, a boy who rejected the

CULTURAL INFLUENCES

ADOLESCENT INITIATION CEREMONIES

An **adolescent initiation ceremony** is a ritualized announcement to the community that a young person is ready to make the transition from childhood into adolescence or full adulthood. These special rites of passage reach their fullest expression in small tribal and village societies. Besides celebration, they often include such features as teaching of sexual techniques, fertility rituals, genital operations, and training in cultural customs and adult work roles.

Among the !Kung hunters and gatherers of Botswana, Africa, a girl menstruating for the first time is carried by an old woman to a special isolated shelter. There, the woman stays with the girl and holds her during urination and defecation, since there is a taboo on the girl's feet touching the ground during these functions. While the girl remains in the shelter, women and old men dance and sing the First Menstruation music, which is full of sexual symbolism. When the menstrual flow stops, a red design is painted on the girl's face, and she is washed and rubbed with oil. Although she need not go into isolation again during her periods, she must observe special taboos during this time. If she has sex with her husband or touches hunting implements, she will rob him of his capacity to hunt successfully (Fried & Fried, 1980).

The Tikopians of Melanesia, a culture of small farming and fishing villages, take the pubertal boy on a special fishing expedition. For the first time, he participates as a member of the crew, an event that warrants celebration. The parents of several boys who are ready to be initiated prepare for a great feast. As each boy visits the houses of relatives, he is anointed with turmeric (a special spice) mixed with coconut oil. The boy appears "drenched in blood," a symbol of the injury he will soon suffer in the superincision ceremony. When it is time for this ritual, the mother's brother (who has formed a special bond with the boy) grabs him and carries him to a place where coconut leaves have been strewn on the ground. There, while community members look on, another man holds the boy as the uncle makes a swift cut in the foreskin of his penis. An elaborate meal and exchange of gifts takes place after the operation. When healing is complete, the boy is considered an adult and may participate fully in Tikopian society. Boys who undergo superincision together retain a close relationship throughout their lives (Fried & Fried, 1980).

In this adolescent initiation ceremony, an Apache community celebrates the arrival of puberty in a young girl with an elaborate ritual. *(Bill Gillette/ Stock Boston)*

Research on adolescent initiation ceremonies reveals that their forms and features have special adaptive value. Ceremonial themes always reflect central aspects of adult roles, such as sexuality, fertility, responsibility, wisdom, and bravery. The event helps ensure that important cultural and practical information is transmitted to the young and that they will become productive members of their community. Adolescent initiation ceremonies also foster group unity, in much the same way that college fraternity and sorority initiations do. The bonding that typically takes place between agemates who undergo challenging and painful experiences together provides a measure of social solidarity extending beyond family ties.

In most initiation ceremonies, the appearance of initiates is changed so all members of the community can identify and treat them differently. Sometimes physical markers of increased status involve temporary body decorations, such as painting and jewelry. At other times, the changes are permanent, consisting of new types of clothing or scars engraved on some part of the body—usually the face, back, chest, or penis.

Ceremonies for girls are more common than those for boys in the simplest societies. In small bands of hunters and gatherers, females are in short supply. The loss of any woman of childbearing age can threaten the survival of the social group. In these cultures, female initiation rites typically last for several weeks and are especially elaborate, designed to provide the girl with both social recognition and magical protection. As cultures move from simple foraging to farming communities, rituals for boys increase in frequency. Initiation rites in farming villages typically recognize young people of both sexes for their distinct reproductive and economic roles. In more complex cultures, adolescent initiation ceremonies recede in importance and disappear (Schlegel & Barry, 1980).

values of school and community (Figure 14.4). Their profiles illustrate mood changes common to most adolescents. High points of their days were times spent with friends and in self-chosen leisure and hobby activities. Low points tended to occur in adult-structured settings—class, job, school halls, school library, and church. Taken together, these findings suggest that situational factors may combine with hormonal influences to affect teenagers' moodiness—an explanation consistent with the balanced view of biological and social forces described earlier in this chapter.

■ PARENT–CHILD RELATIONSHIPS. Sabrina's father noticed that as his children entered adolescence, their bedroom doors started to close, they resisted spending time with the family, and they became more argumentative. Within a two-day period, Sabrina and her mother squabbled over Sabrina's messy room ("Mom, it's *my* room. You don't have to live in it!") and her clothing purchases ("Sabrina, if you *buy* it, then *wear* it. Otherwise, you are wasting money!"). And Sabrina resisted the family's regular weekend visit to Aunt Gina's ("Why do I have to go *every* week? There's nothing to do there!"). Many studies show that puberty is related to a rise in parent–child conflict. Bickering and standoffs increase as adolescents move toward the peak of pubertal growth. During this time, both parents and teenagers report feeling less close to one another (Hill, 1988; Paikoff & Brooks-Gunn, 1991).

Why should a youngster's more adultlike appearance trigger these petty disputes between parent and child? Researchers believe the association may have some adaptive value. Among nonhuman primates, the young typically leave the family group around the time of puberty. The same is true in many nonindustrialized cultures (Caine, 1986; Schlegel & Barry, 1991). Departure of young people from the family discourages sexual relations among close blood relatives. But because children in industrialized societies remain economically dependent on parents long after they reach puberty, they cannot leave the family. Consequently, a modern substitute for physical departure seems to have emerged—psychological distancing between parents and children (Steinberg, 1987).

In later chapters, we will see that adolescents' new powers of reasoning may also contribute to a rise in family tensions. Also, the need for families to redefine relationships as children become physically mature and demand to be treated in adultlike ways may produce a temporary period of conflict. The quarreling that does take place is generally mild. Only a small minority of families experience a serious break in parent–child relationships. In reality, parents and children display both conflict and affection toward one another throughout adolescence. This also makes sense from an evolutionary perspective. Although separation from parents is adaptive, both generations benefit from warm, protective family bonds that last for many years to come (Steinberg, 1990).

EARLY VERSUS LATE MATURATION

Recall that Sabrina's mother reported that all her children matured early, but her daughter reacted quite differently from her sons. Maturational timing influences adolescent adjustment, in opposite directions for girls than boys.

■ EFFECTS OF MATURATIONAL TIMING. Sabrina was self-conscious about her well-developed body, felt awkward and unsure of herself, and withdrew from her peers. In contrast, her brothers were confident and proud of their large, muscular physiques.

Several longitudinal studies report findings that match the experiences of Sabrina and her brothers. Early maturing boys appeared advantaged in many aspects of emotional and social functioning. Both adults and peers viewed them as

Katherine Tennison

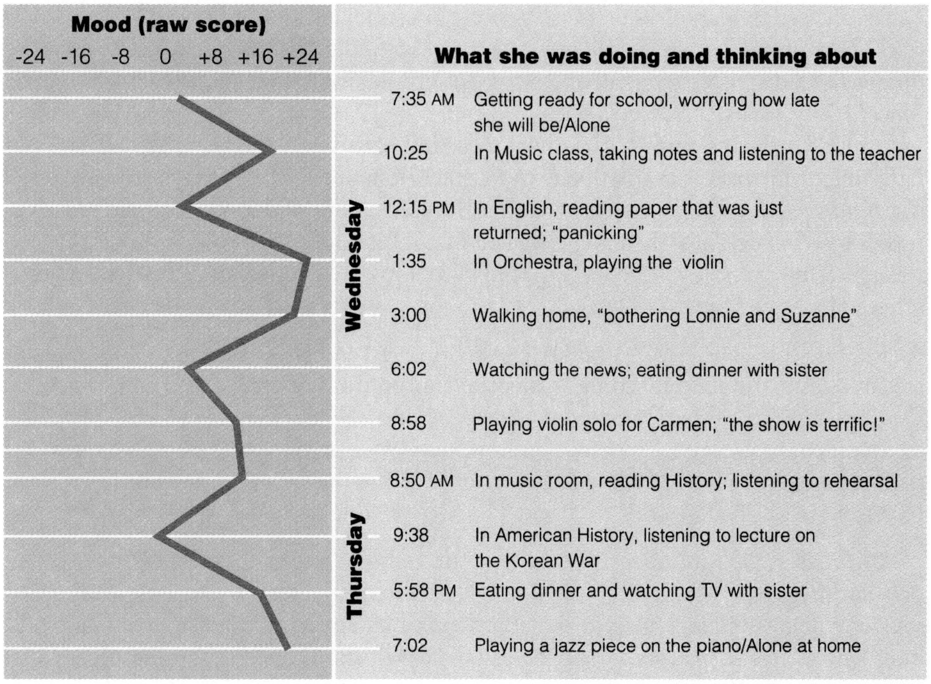
Mood (raw score)
-24 -16 -8 0 +8 +16 +24
What she was doing and thinking about
Wednesday
7:35 AM Getting ready for school, worrying how late she will be/Alone
10:25 In Music class, taking notes and listening to the teacher
12:15 PM In English, reading paper that was just returned; "panicking"
1:35 In Orchestra, playing the violin
3:00 Walking home, "bothering Lonnie and Suzanne"
6:02 Watching the news; eating dinner with sister
8:58 Playing violin solo for Carmen; "the show is terrific!"
Thursday
8:50 AM In music room, reading History; listening to rehearsal
9:38 In American History, listening to lecture on the Korean War
5:58 PM Eating dinner and watching TV with sister
7:02 Playing a jazz piece on the piano/Alone at home

Gregory Stone

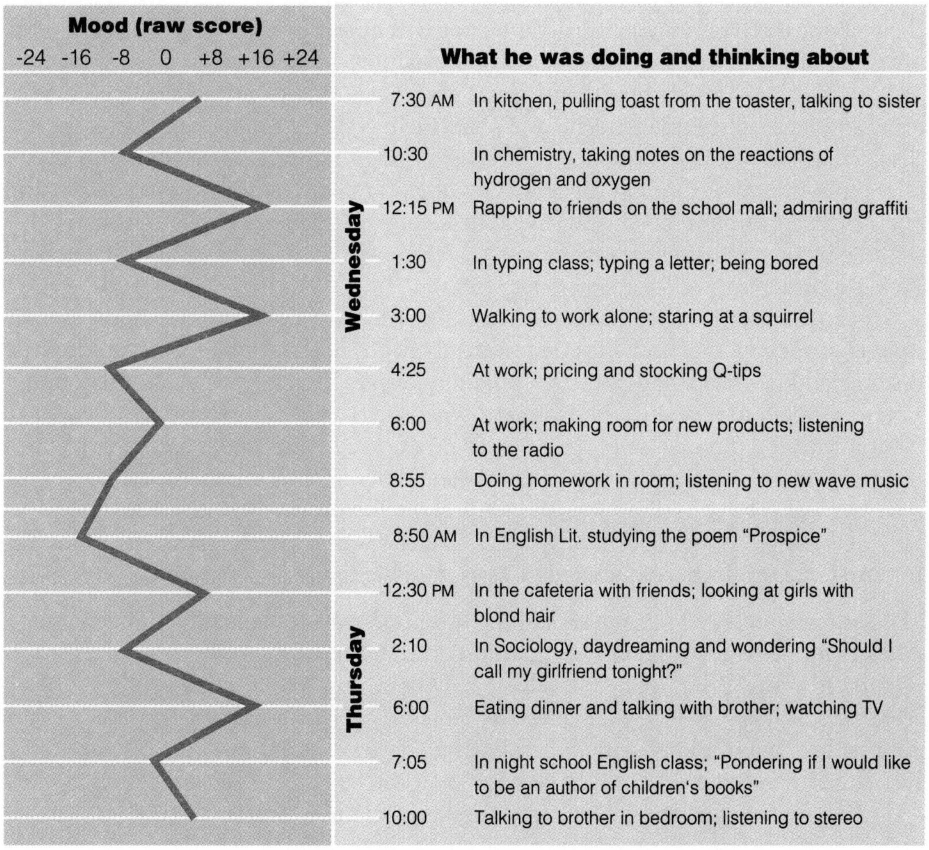
Mood (raw score)
-24 -16 -8 0 +8 +16 +24
What he was doing and thinking about
Wednesday
7:30 AM In kitchen, pulling toast from the toaster, talking to sister
10:30 In chemistry, taking notes on the reactions of hydrogen and oxygen
12:15 PM Rapping to friends on the school mall; admiring graffiti
1:30 In typing class; typing a letter; being bored
3:00 Walking to work alone; staring at a squirrel
4:25 At work; pricing and stocking Q-tips
6:00 At work; making room for new products; listening to the radio
8:55 Doing homework in room; listening to new wave music
Thursday
8:50 AM In English Lit. studying the poem "Prospice"
12:30 PM In the cafeteria with friends; looking at girls with blond hair
2:10 In Sociology, daydreaming and wondering "Should I call my girlfriend tonight?"
6:00 Eating dinner and talking with brother; watching TV
7:05 In night school English class; "Pondering if I would like to be an author of children's books"
10:00 Talking to brother in bedroom; listening to stereo

FIGURE 14.4

Mood changes over a typical Wednesday and Thursday for Katherine Tennison and Gregory Stone.
The chart shows self-reported mood scores for each random interval in which the two teenagers were paged. *(From M. Csikszentmihalyi & R. Larson, 1984,* Being Adolescent: Conflict and Growth in the Teenage Years, *New York: Basic Books, pp. 111, 117. Adapted by permisson.)*

relaxed, independent, self-confident, and physically attractive. Popular with agemates, they held many leadership positions in school and tended to be athletic stars. In contrast, late maturing boys were not well liked. Peers and adults viewed them as anxious, overly talkative, and attention seeking in behavior (Clausen, 1975; Jones, 1965; Jones & Bayley, 1950).

Among girls, the impact of early versus late maturation was just the reverse. Early maturing girls had emotional and social difficulties. They were below average in popularity, appeared withdrawn and lacking in self-confidence, and held few positions of leadership. Instead, their late maturing counterparts were especially well off. They were regarded as physically attractive, lively, sociable, and leaders at school (Jones & Mussen, 1958).

EXPLAINING MATURATIONAL TIMING EFFECTS. Most research on maturational timing was completed in the 1950s and 1960s, but new studies show the same trends today (Brooks-Gunn, 1988a; Petersen, 1985). Two factors seem to account for them: (1) how closely the adolescent's body matches cultural ideals of physical attractiveness, and (2) how well young people "fit in" physically with their peers.

The Role of Physical Attractiveness. Flip through the pages of your favorite popular magazine, and look at the figures of men and women in the ads. You will see convincing evidence for our society's view of an attractive female as thin and long-legged and a good-looking male as tall, broad-shouldered, and muscular. The female image is a girlish shape that favors the late developer. The male image is consistent with that of the early maturing boy.

As their bodies change, adolescents of both sexes become preoccupied with their physical selves, unable to pass a mirror without inspecting what they see. Girls are especially likely to analyze all their body features—whether their eyebrows and lips are too thick or too thin, their breasts and hips too large or too small, and their arms and legs sufficiently graceful and shapely. In addition, adolescents get a great deal of feedback from others—both directly, through remarks about their appearance, and indirectly, through the tendency of children and adults to treat physically attractive people more positively. The conclusions that young people draw about their appearance strongly affect their satisfaction with their bodies and, ultimately, their psychological well-being (Lerner, 1985).

A consistent finding is that early maturing girls have a less positive **body image**—conception of and attitude toward their physical appearance—than do their on-time and late-maturing agemates. Among boys, the opposite is true: early maturation is linked to a positive body image, whereas late maturation predicts dissatisfaction with the physical self (Simmons & Blyth, 1987). Both boys and girls who have physical characteristics regarded by themselves and others as less attractive have a lower sense of self-esteem and are less well liked by agemates (Langlois & Stephan, 1981). The adoption of society's "beauty is best" stereotype seems to be an important factor in the adjustment of early and late maturing boys and girls.

The Importance of Fitting In with Peers. A second way of explaining differences in adjustment between early and late maturers is in terms of their physical status in relation to peers. From this perspective, early maturing girls and late maturing boys have difficulty because they fall at the extremes of physical development. Recall that Sabrina felt "out of place" and embarrassed when with her agemates. She was not just larger than the girls; she also towered over the boys. Late maturing boys are self-conscious about their childish appearance, and many harbor doubts and fears about whether they will grow larger. Not surprisingly, adolescents feel most com-

Body image
Conception of and attitude toward one's physical appearance.

fortable with peers who match their own level of biological maturity (Brooks-Gunn et al., 1986; Stattin & Magnusson, 1990).

Because few agemates of the same biological status are available, early maturing adolescents of both sexes seek out older companions—a tendency that can lead to some unfavorable consequences. Older peers often encourage early maturing youngsters into activities that they find difficult to resist and are not yet ready to handle emotionally, including sexual activity, drug and alcohol use, and minor delinquent acts. For example, the eighth graders that Sabrina met at church introduced her to several high school boys, who were quite unconcerned that she was just a sixth grader! Sabrina welcomed their attentions, which gratified her desire to feel socially accepted and physically attractive. Perhaps because of involvements like these, the academic performance of early maturers tends to suffer (Duncan et al., 1985; Stattin & Magnusson, 1990).

Interestingly, school contexts can modify these maturational timing effects. In one study, early maturing sixth grade girls felt better about themselves when they attended kindergarten through sixth grade (K–6) rather than kindergarten through eighth-grade (K–8) schools, where they could mix with older adolescents. In the K–6 settings, they were relieved of pressures to adopt behaviors for which they were not ready (Blyth, Simmons, & Zakin, 1985). Similarly, a New Zealand study found that delinquency among early maturing girls was greatly reduced in all-girl schools, which limit opportunities to associate with norm-violating peers (most of whom are older boys) (Caspi et al., 1993).

LONG-TERM CONSEQUENCES. Do the effects of early and late maturation persist into adulthood? Longitudinal research reveals some unexpected findings. Among boys, several aspects of adolescent adjustment were still evident well into middle adulthood. At age 38, the social prestige of early maturing males could still be detected in greater social ease and responsible, self-controlled, cooperative behavior. Similarly, late maturing males, who as adolescents often tried to compensate for their small size through clowning and other antics, remained more impulsive and assertive over the years (Livson & Peskin, 1980).

Beyond these few consistencies, long-term follow-ups show some striking turnabouts in overall well-being. Many early maturing boys and late maturing girls, who had been the focus of admiration in adolescence, became rigid, inflexible, conforming, and somewhat discontented adults. In contrast, late maturing boys and early maturing girls, who were stress-ridden as teenagers, often developed into adults who were independent, flexible, cognitively competent, and satisfied with the direction of their lives (Macfarlane, 1971). How can we explain these remarkable reversals? Perhaps the confidence-inducing adolescence of early maturing boys and late maturing girls does not promote the coping skills needed to solve life's later problems. In contrast, the painful experiences associated with off-time pubertal growth may, in time, contribute to sharpened awareness, clarified goals, and greater stability.

Finally, it is important to note that these long-term outcomes may not hold completely in all cultures. In a Swedish study, achievement difficulties of early maturing girls persisted into young adulthood. They were twice as likely to leave high school after completing the minimum years of compulsory education as their on-time and later maturing counterparts (Stattin & Magnusson, 1990). In countries with highly selective college entrance systems, perhaps it is harder for early maturers to recover from declines in school performance. Clearly, the effects of maturational timing involve a complex blend of biological, immediate social setting, and cultural factors.

ASK YOURSELF . . .

- Sasha remembers menarche as a traumatic experience. When she discovered she was bleeding, she thought she had a deadly illness and didn't tell anyone for 2 days. What is the likely cause of Sasha's negative reaction?
- How might adolescent moodiness contribute to the psychological distancing between parents and children that accompanies puberty? (*Hint:* Think about bidirectional influences in parent–child relationships discussed in previous chapters.)
- Return to the beginning of this chapter and review Sabrina's feelings about her well-developed body and her behavior toward peers. How are they typical of an early maturing girl?

BRIEF REVIEW

Puberty has important psychological and social consequences. Typically, girls' reactions to menarche and boys' reactions to spermarche are mixed, although prior knowledge and social support affect their responses. Adolescent moodiness is related to both sex hormones and changes in the social environment. Puberty prompts increased conflict and psychological distancing between parent and child. These reactions appear to be modern substitutes for physical departure from the family in our evolutionary history. Standards and expectations of the culture and peer group lead early maturing boys and late maturing girls to be advantaged in emotional and social adjustment. In contrast, late maturing boys and early maturing girls have adjustment difficulties. The stresses associated with off-time pubertal growth may eventually spark more effective coping skills.

HEALTH ISSUES DURING ADOLESCENCE

As young people move into adolescence, they begin to view physical health in a broader way—as more than just the absence of illness. To teenagers, being healthy means functioning physically, mentally, and socially at their best (Millstein & Irwin, 1987). Consistent with this new view, the arrival of puberty is accompanied by new health concerns related to the young person's striving to meet physical and psychological needs. As the body grows and takes on mature proportions, eating disturbances appear in many young people who worry about falling short of their idealized image of attractiveness and fitness. Sexual activity brings with it the risk of early pregnancy and sexually transmitted disease. Substance abuse and certain unintentional injuries also increase. (We will take up suicide—another serious adolescent health problem—in Chapter 16.)

Perhaps you can already tell from this list of health issues that the young person's own behavior, or *lifestyle,* plays a much larger role than it did at earlier ages. As adolescents are granted greater autonomy, personal decision making becomes important, in health as well as other areas (Millstein & Litt, 1990). Yet none of the health difficulties we are about to discuss can be traced to a single cause within the individual. Throughout development, physical, psychological, family, and cultural factors jointly contribute to health and well-being.

NUTRITIONAL NEEDS

When their sons reached puberty, Franca and Antonio reported a "vacuum cleaner effect" in the kitchen. The boys routinely emptied the refrigerator of whatever happened to be in it. Rapid body growth during adolescence leads to a dramatic rise in food intake. During the growth spurt, boys require about 2,700 calories a day and much more protein, girls about 2,200 calories and somewhat less protein than boys because of their smaller size and muscle mass. Calcium is especially important for skeletal growth. Extra iron is needed to support gains in muscle mass and blood volume in boys and to make up for the loss of blood in the menstrual flow of girls (Mott, James, & Sperhac, 1990).

This increase in nutritional requirements comes at a time when the eating habits of many young people are the poorest. Of all age groups, adolescents are the most likely to consume empty calories. Often they eat on the run—whatever happens to be handy. Fast-food restaurants, which are favorite teenage gathering places, have started to offer more healthful menu options. But adolescents need to know how to select these alternatives—baked foods and salads instead of fried foods, milk and fruit juice instead of soft drinks and high-calorie shakes. The eating habits of teenagers are particularly harmful if they extend a lifelong pattern of poor nutrition, less serious if they are just a temporary response to peer influences and a busy schedule.

The most common nutritional problem of adolescence is iron deficiency, affecting about 75 percent of American teenagers (McWilliams, 1986). A tired, listless, irritable adolescent may be suffering from anemia rather than unhappiness and should have a medical checkup. Most adolescents do not get enough calcium, and they are also deficient in riboflavin (vitamin B_2) and magnesium, both of which support metabolism. And contrary to what many parents believe, obese children rarely outgrow their weight problem when they become teenagers. Instead, the difficulty usually worsens (Malina, 1990).

Adolescents, especially girls who are concerned about their weight, tend to be attracted to the latest fad diets. Unfortunately, most are too limited in nutrients and calories to be healthy for fast-growing, active teenagers. The adolescent years are also a time when many young people choose to become vegetarians. As they begin to formulate a philosophy of life, some find the killing of animals distasteful. Others claim that meats are sources of impurities and toxins. Still others cannot yet explain their reasons. A properly planned vegetarian diet can be very healthy, but one that is not well chosen can be dangerous. When a youngster insists on trying a special diet, parents should, in turn, insist that they first consult with a doctor or dietitian (McWilliams, 1986).

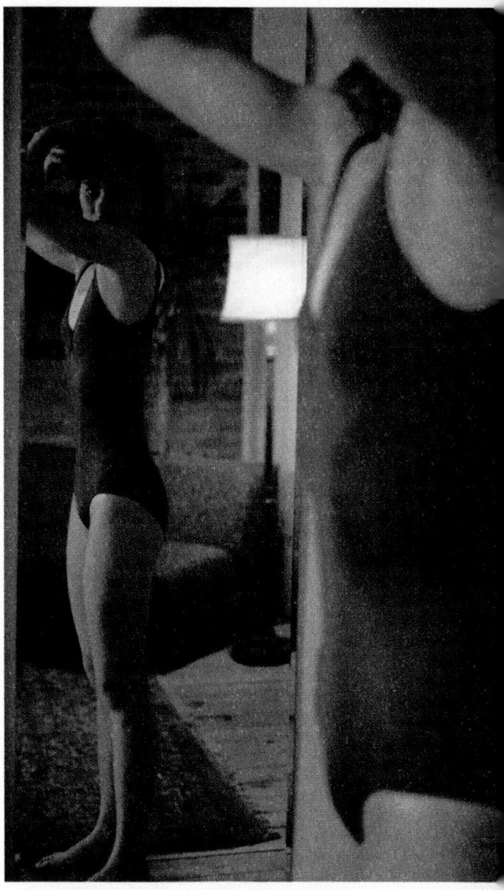

Adolescents with anorexia nervosa have an unrealistic image of their physical appearance. Even after they have become painfully thin, they refuse food and engage in strenuous physical exercise. *(George S. Zimbell/ Monkmeyer Press)*

SERIOUS EATING DISTURBANCES

Franca worried about Sabrina's desire to lose weight at such an early age, explained to her that she was really quite average in build for an adolescent girl, and reminded Sabrina that her Italian ancestors thought a plump female body was more beautiful than a thin one. Girls who reach puberty early, who are very dissatisfied with their body image, and who grow up in economically advantaged homes where a cultural concern with weight and thinness is especially strong are at risk for developing eating problems. And despite the fact that these disturbances are viewed as "female conditions," we will see that males also suffer from them. The two most serious eating disorders of adolescence are anorexia nervosa and bulimia.

■ ANOREXIA NERVOSA. **Anorexia nervosa** is a tragic eating disturbance in which young people starve themselves because of a compulsive fear of getting fat. About 90 percent of cases are females between ages 12 and 25. Currently, more males are being diagnosed, due either to new cases or to better recognition. However, far less is known about development of the disorder in males. In all, about 1 million Americans are affected (Garner, 1993; Seligmann, 1994). It is ironic that in industrialized nations, malnutrition severe enough to interfere with normal adolescent growth occurs most often in affluent homes where food is plentiful, not in poverty-stricken families.

Anorexics have an extremely distorted body image. Even after they have become severely underweight, they conclude that they are fat. Most lose weight by going on a self-imposed diet so strict that they struggle to avoid eating in response to hunger. Although anorexics avoid food, they think about it constantly. At times, their hunger becomes so overwhelming that they go on eating binges, which are usually followed by self-induced vomiting. To enhance weight loss, anorexics engage in strenuous physical exercise. If family members try to stop them, they seek other ways, such as pacing back and forth in their rooms or getting up in the middle of the night for an energetic work-out (Gilbert & DeBlassie, 1984).

Anorexia nervosa
An eating disorder in which individuals (usually females) starve themselves because of a compulsive fear of getting fat.

The physical consequences of this attempt to reach "perfect" slimness are severe. Anorexics lose between 25 and 50 percent of their body weight and appear painfully thin. Because a normal menstrual cycle requires about 15 percent body fat, either menarche does not occur or menstrual periods stop. Malnutrition causes additional physical symptoms—pale skin; brittle, discolored nails; fine dark hairs all over the body; and extreme sensitivity to cold. If allowed to continue, anorexia nervosa can result in shrinking of the heart muscle and kidney failure. About 5 percent die of the disorder (Harris, 1991).

Anorexia nervosa is the combined result of forces within the individual, the family, and the larger culture. We have already seen that the societal image of "thin is beautiful" contributes to the poorer body image of early maturing girls, who are at greatest risk for anorexia (Attie & Brooks-Gunn, 1989). But though almost all adolescent girls go on diets at one time or another, anorexics persist in weight loss to an extreme. Many are perfectionists who have high standards for their own behavior and performance. Typically, these girls are excellent students who are responsible and well behaved—ideal daughters in many respects.

Yet researchers who have studied the family interaction of parents and anorexic daughters have identified problems related to adolescent autonomy that may trigger the compulsive dieting. Often these parents have high expectations for achievement and social acceptance and are overprotective and controlling. Although the daughter tries to meet these demands, inside she is angry at not being recognized as an individual in her own right. Instead of rebelling openly, the anorexic girl expresses her feelings through dieting. Without saying so directly, she tells her parents, "I am a separate person from you, and I can do what I want with my own body!" At the same time, this youngster, who has been so used to having parents make decisions for her, meets the challenges of adolescence with little self-confidence. Starving herself is also a way of avoiding new expectations by returning to a much younger, preadolescent image (Halmi, 1987; Maloney & Kranz, 1991).

Anorexic girls typically deny that any problem exists, so treating the disorder is difficult. Hospitalization is often a first step. Since malnutrition affects brain and cognitive functioning, usually the girl's diet must be improved before she can gain insight into her problems. Because the roots of anorexia nervosa are in individual and family problems, family therapy, in which efforts are made to change parent–child interaction and expectations, is the most successful treatment. As a supplementary approach, applied behavior analysis, in which hospitalized anorexics are rewarded for gaining weight with praise, social contact, and opportunities for exercise, is helpful (Gilbert & DeBlassie, 1984). Still, only 30 percent of anorexics fully recover. For many others, eating problems continue in less extreme form. One-third of anorexics show signs of a less severe disorder—bulimia—that is still physically and psychologically damaging (Kreipe, Churchill, & Strauss, 1989).

BULIMIA. When Sabrina's 16-year-old brother Louis brought his girlfriend Cassie to the house, Sabrina admired her good figure. "Cassie hardly touches any food when she's with Louis," Sabrina thought to herself. "What willpower! That must be how she keeps her weight down. But what in the world is wrong with Cassie's teeth?"

Willpower was not the secret of Cassie's slender shape. When it came to food, she actually had great difficulty controlling herself. Cassie suffered from **bulimia,** an eating disorder in which young people (again, mainly girls) engage in binge eating followed by deliberate vomiting, purging with laxatives, and strict dieting. When by herself, Cassie had periods of feeling lonely, unhappy, and anxious. In response, she went on eating rampages, consuming thousands of calories in an hour or two. The vomiting that followed eroded the enamel on Cassie's teeth. In some cases, life-threatening damage to the throat and stomach also results (Halmi, 1987).

Bulimia
An eating disorder in which individuals (mainly females) go on eating binges followed by deliberate vomiting, other purging techniques such as heavy doses of laxatives, and strict dieting.

Bulimia is much more common than anorexia nervosa. Only 5 percent of bulimic girls have previously been anorexic (Johnson et al., 1983). Although bulimics share with anorexics a pathological fear of getting fat and a middle-class family background with high expectations, most have quite different personality characteristics. Typically, bulimics are not just impulsive eaters; they also lack self-control in other areas of their lives. Although they tend to be good students and liked by peers, many engage in petty shoplifting and alcohol abuse. Bulimics also differ from anorexics in that they are aware of their abnormal eating habits, feel depressed and guilty about them, and are usually desperate to get help. As a result, bulimia is usually easier to treat through individual and family therapy, support groups, and nutrition education (Harris, 1991; Thackwray et al., 1993).

We have seen that young people with certain physical, psychological, and family characteristics are prone to develop serious eating disorders. Yet anorexia nervosa and bulimia, like so many aspects of adolescent development, cannot be understood apart from the cultural context in which they occur—a world in which an ultrathin body form is elevated to high importance and impossible for most women to achieve.

SEXUAL ACTIVITY

Louis and Cassie hadn't planned to have intercourse after taking a ride in Louis's car one Friday night. It "just happened." But before and after, a lot of things passed through Cassie and Louis's minds. Cassie had been dating Louis for 3 months, and she began to think, "Will he think I'm normal if I don't have sex with him? If he wants to and I say no, will I lose him?" Both young people knew their parents wouldn't approve. In fact, when Franca and Antonio noticed how attached Louis was to Cassie, they talked to him about the importance of waiting and the dangers of pregnancy. Still, Louis was sure he loved Cassie, and that Friday evening, his feelings for her seemed overwhelming. As things went farther and father, Louis thought, "She wouldn't be doing this if she wasn't prepared." And Cassie convinced herself she'd be okay. She'd heard from one of her girlfriends that you couldn't get pregnant the first time. Besides, if she brought up the subject of contraception, it would be like admitting she *wanted* to have sex. In reality, she wasn't so sure about it.

Virtually all theorists agree that adolescence is an especially important time for the development of sexuality. With the arrival of puberty, hormonal changes—in particular, the production of androgens in young people of both sexes—lead to an increase in sex drive (Udry, 1990). As Louis and Cassie's inner thoughts reveal, adolescents become very concerned about how to manage sexuality in social relationships. New cognitive capacities involving perspective taking and self-reflection affect their efforts to do so. Yet like the eating behaviors we have just discussed, adolescent sexuality is heavily influenced by the social context in which the young person is growing up.

THE IMPACT OF CULTURE. Think, for a moment, about when you first learned about the facts of life and how you found out about them. In your family, was sex discussed openly or treated with secrecy? Cross-cultural research reveals that exposure to sex, education about it, and efforts to restrict the sexual curiosity of children and adolescents vary widely around the world. At one extreme are a number of Middle Eastern peoples, who are known to kill girls who dishonor their families by losing their virginity before marriage. At the other extreme are several Asian and Pacific Island groups with very permissive sexual attitudes and practices. For example, among the Trobriand Islanders of Melanesia, older companions provide children with explicit instruction in sexual practices. Bachelor houses are maintained, where adolescents are expected to engage in sexual experimentation with a variety of partners (Benedict, 1934a; Ford & Beach, 1951).

Adolescence is an especially important time for the development of sexuality. American teenagers receive contradictory and confusing messages from the social environment about the appropriateness of sex. Although the rate of premarital sex has risen among adolescents, most engage in low levels of sexual activity and have only a single partner. *(Nancy Sheehan/The Picture Cube)*

For all the publicity granted to the image of a sexually free and sophisticated modern adolescent, you may be surprised to learn that American society falls on the restrictive side of this cultural continuum. Typically, American parents give children little information about sex, discourage them from engaging in sex play, and rarely talk about sex in their presence. When young people become interested in sex, they seek information elsewhere, turning to friends, books, magazines, movies, and television. On prime-time television shows, which adolescents watch the most, premarital sex occurs two to three times each hour and is spontaneous and passionate. Characters are rarely shown taking steps to avoid pregnancy or sexually transmitted disease (Braverman & Strasburger, 1994; Strasburger, 1989).

Think about the messages delivered by these two sets of sources, and you will see that they are contradictory and confusing. On the one hand, adults emphasize that sex at a young age and outside of marriage is wrong. On the other hand, adolescents encounter much in the broader social environment that extols the excitement and romanticism of sex. These mixed messages leave many American teenagers bewildered, poorly informed about sexual facts, and with little sound advice on how to conduct their sex lives responsibly (Gordon & Gilgun, 1987).

ADOLESCENT SEXUAL ATTITUDES AND BEHAVIOR. Although differences exist among subcultural groups, over the past 30 years the sexual attitudes of American adolescents and adults have become more liberal. Compared to a generation ago, more people believe that sexual intercourse before marriage is all right, as long as two people are emotionally committed to one another (Beeghley & Sellers, 1986). At the end of the 1980s, a slight swing back in the direction of conservative sexual beliefs occurred. A growing number of young people said they were opposed to premarital sex, largely due to the risk of sexually transmitted disease (especially AIDS) (Roper Starch Worldwide, 1994).

A second change in sexual attitudes is that the *double standard* has declined. In the 1950s and 1960s, sexual freedom was far more acceptable for males than females. Today, most adolescents and young adults think men and women should be held to the same standards for sexual behavior (Miller & Olson, 1988). However, adolescents do not endorse promiscuity on the part of either sex, and (as we will see in a moment) they do not typically engage in it.

Trends in the sexual behavior of adolescents are quite consistent with their attitudes. The rate of premarital sex among young people has risen over time. For example, among unmarried 15- to 19-year-olds, females claiming to have had sexual intercourse grew from 28 percent in 1971 to 48 percent in 1990 (Braverman & Strasburger, 1993; Forrest & Singh, 1990). As Table 14.2 reveals, a substantial minority of boys and girls are sexually active quite early, by ninth grade. The table also indicates that males tend to have their first intercourse earlier than females, and sexual activity is especially high among black adolescents—particularly boys.

Yet timing of first intercourse provides only a limited picture of adolescent sexual behavior. Most teenagers engage in relatively low levels of sexual activity. The typical 15- to 19-year-old sexually active male—white, black, or Hispanic—has relations with only one girl at a time and spends half the year with no partner at all (Sonenstein, Pleck, & Ku, 1991). Contrary to popular belief, a runaway sexual revolution does not characterize American young people. In fact, the rate of teenage sexual activity in the United States is about the same as in western European nations (Jones et al., 1988).

CHARACTERISTICS OF SEXUALLY ACTIVE ADOLESCENTS. Teenage sexual activity is linked to a wide range of personal, family, peer, and educational variables. These include early physical maturation, parental separation and divorce, large family size, sexually active friends and older siblings, poor school performance, and lower educational aspirations (Braverman &

TABLE 14.2

Teenage Sexual Activity Rates by Sex, Ethnic Group, and Grade

	ETHNIC GROUP			GRADE				
SEX	WHITE	BLACK	HISPANIC	9	10	11	12	TOTAL
Male	56.4	87.8	63.0	48.7	52.5	62.6	76.3	60.8
Female	47.0	60.0	45.0	31.9	42.9	52.7	66.6	48.0
Total	51.6	72.3	53.4	39.6	47.6	57.3	71.9	54.2

Note: Data reflect the percentage of high school students who report ever having had sexual intercourse.
Source: U.S. Centers for Disease Control, 1992.

Strasburger, 1994; Ku, Sonenstein, & Pleck, 1993). Since many of these factors are associated with growing up in a low-income family, it is not surprising that early sexual activity is more common among young people from economically disadvantaged homes. In fact, the high rate of premarital intercourse among black teenagers can largely be accounted for by widespread poverty in the black population (Sullivan, 1993).

At one time researchers thought that all adolescents who engaged in premarital sex suffered from serious adjustment difficulties (Dreyer, 1982). Recent evidence shows that this is not true for all sexually active teenagers—only for some of them. Adolescents who feel inadequate and inferior, who are without the rewards of meaningful education and work, and who feel compelled to prove something to themselves or others through sex are especially likely to engage in irresponsible sexual behavior. Often they have several casual partners, and their sex acts tend to be exploitative, as when boys misrepresent their feelings to persuade a girl to have sex or force her to do so. Girls who become involved in these unhealthy relationships generally have serious family, peer, and school difficulties (Gordon & Gilgun, 1987).

CONTRACEPTIVE USE. Unfortunately, nearly half of sexually active American teenagers are at risk for unplanned pregnancy because they do not use contraception at all or use it only occasionally (Braverman & Strasburger, 1993; Santelli & Beilenson, 1992). Why do so many teenagers fail to take precautions? In Chapter 15, we will see that compared to school-age children, adolescents can consider many more possibilities when faced with a problem. But at first, they fail to apply this reasoning to everyday situations. As a result, they do not do the kind of planning and decision making necessary to protect themselves from harmful outcomes. In several studies, teenagers were asked to explain why they did not use birth control. Here are some typical answers:

> You don't say, "Well, I'm going to his house, and he's probably going to try to get to bed with me, so I better make sure I'm prepared." I mean, you don't know it's coming, so how are you to be prepared?
>
> I wouldn't [use contraception] if I was going . . . to have sex casually, you know, like once a month or once every two months. It's more for somebody who has a steady boyfriend. (Kisker, 1985, p. 84)

One reason for responses like these is that advances in perspective taking lead teenagers, for a time, to be extremely concerned about others' opinion of them. Recall how Cassie worried about what Louis would think if she decided not to have sex. And she was convinced, as many American girls are, that if she brought up the subject of birth control, her boyfriend would conclude that she was "sex crazed" or "an easy take" (Gordon & Gilgun, 1987). Another reason for lack of planning before sex is that intense self-reflection may encourage adolescents to view themselves as unique and invulnerable to danger. Recent evidence indicates that teenagers and adults differ very little on questionnaires asking about consequences of engaging in risky behaviors; both report similar levels of vulnerability (Beyth-Marom et al., 1993; Quadrel, Fischhoff, & Davis, 1993). Still, in midst of everyday social pressures, adolescents often seem to conclude that pregnancy happens to others, not to themselves (Jaskiewicz & McAnarney, 1994; Voydanoff & Donnelly, 1990).

Although adolescent cognition may have something to do with teenagers' reluctance to use contraception, the social environment also contributes to it. Teenagers who talk openly with their parents about sex are not less sexually active, but they are more likely to use birth control (Brooks-Gunn, 1988b; Moore, Peterson, & Furstenberg, 1986). Unfortunately, many adolescents say that they are too scared or embarrassed to ask parents questions about sex or contraception. When a sexual encounter does occur, they are ambivalent about whether to go ahead, and many leap into the experience without much forethought. Although most get some sex education at school, teenagers' knowledge about sex and contraception is often incomplete or just plain wrong. Many do not know where to get birth control counseling and devices (Hayes, 1987). When they do, they tend to be just as uncomfortable about going to a doctor or family planning clinic as they are about seeking advice from parents (Kisker, 1985).

■ **SEXUAL ORIENTATION.** Up to this point, our discussion has focused only on heterosexual behavior. About 1 to 4 percent of young people discover they are lesbian or gay. Adolescence is an equally crucial time for the sexual development of these individuals, and societal attitudes, once again, loom large in how well they fare.

Cultures vary as much in their acceptance of homosexuality as they do in their approval of premarital sex. In the United States, homosexuals are stigmatized, as shown by the degrading language often used to describe them (Sturdevant & Ramafedi, 1992). Yet research indicates that homosexuals have no more choice in their sexual orientation than do their heterosexual counterparts.

Although the extent to which homosexuality is due to genetic versus environmental forces remains highly controversial, new evidence indicates that heredity makes an important contribution. Identical twins of both sexes are much more likely than fraternal twins to share a homosexual orientation; the same is true for biological as opposed to adoptive relatives (Bailey & Pillard, 1991; Bailey et al., 1993). Furthermore, male homosexuality tends to be more common on the maternal than paternal side of families. This suggests that it might be X-linked (see Chapter 2). Indeed, a recent gene-mapping study found that among 40 pairs of homosexual brothers, 33 (85.5 percent) had an identical segment of DNA on the X chromosome. One or several genes in that region might predispose males to become homosexual (Hamer et al., 1993).

Yet these findings do not apply to all gay men, since some do not have the genetic marker just described. Family factors are also associated with homosexuality. Looking back at their childhoods, both male and female homosexuals tend to view their same-sex parent as cold and distant (Bell, Weinberg, & Hammersmith, 1981). This does not mean that parents cause their youngsters to become homosexual. Rather, for some children, an early genetic bias away from traditional gender-role behavior may lead them to feel alienated from same-sex parents and peers. A strong desire for affection from people of their own sex may join with biology to push these youngsters in a homosexual direction (Green, 1987). Once again, however, homosexuality does not always develop in this way, since some homosexuals are very comfortable with their gender role and have warm relationships with parents. Homosexuality probably results from a variety of biological and environmental combinations that are not well understood.

A passing attraction to members of the same sex is common during adolescence. About 18 percent of boys and 6 percent of girls have participated in at least one homosexual act by age 19 (Braverman & Strasburger, 1993). In some tribal and village cultures, homosexual behavior among young males is encouraged, as a way of learning about sex and discharging the sex drive (Savin-Williams, 1990). But adolescents in industrialized nations who discover that they have a compelling interest in same-sex partners often experience intense inner conflict. They get little approval for their sexual orientation and feel a profound sense of isolation and loneliness. Almost always, their parents are very upset. Even very open-minded parents respond with considerable pain because they know that their youngster will encounter limited acceptance by the larger society. Homosexual adolescents have a special need for caring adults and peers who can help them establish a positive sexual identity and find social acceptance (Sturdevant & Ramafedi, 1992).

Sexually active adolescents, both heterosexual and homosexual, face serious health risks. In the following sections, we examine the high rates of pregnancy, childbirth, and sexually transmitted disease among American teenagers.

TEENAGE PREGNANCY AND CHILDBEARING

Cassie was lucky not to get pregnant after having sex with Louis, but some of her high school classmates weren't so fortunate. She'd heard about Veronica, who missed several periods, pretended nothing was wrong for as long as she could, and didn't go to a doctor until a month before she gave birth. Veronica lived at home until she became pregnant a second time. At that point, her parents told her there wasn't room in the house for a second baby. So Veronica dropped out of school and moved in with her 17-year-old boyfriend Todd, who worked in a fast-food restaurant. A few months later, Todd left Veronica because he couldn't stand being tied down with the babies. Veronica had to apply for public aid to support herself and the two infants.

Each year, more than a million American teenagers become pregnant, 30,000 under the age of 15. As Figure 14.5 shows, the adolescent pregnancy rate in the United States is twice that of England, Canada, and France, three times that of Sweden, and six times that of the Netherlands. The United States differs from these nations in three important ways: (1) effective sex education reaches fewer teenagers; (2) convenient, low-cost contraceptive services for adolescents are scarce; and (3) many more families live in poverty, which encourages young people to take risks without considering the future implications of their behavior (Jones et al., 1988).

Not all adolescents who conceive give birth to a baby. About 40 percent choose to have an abortion, and 13 percent of teenage pregnancies end in miscarriage (Chase-Lansdale & Brooks-Gunn, 1994; Jaskiewicz & McAnarney, 1994). Because the United States has one of the highest adolescent abortion rates of any developed country, the total number of teenage births is actually lower than it was 30 years ago (Vinovskis, 1988). But teenage parenthood is a much greater problem today because modern adolescents are far less likely to marry before childbirth. In 1960, only 15 percent of teenage births were to unmarried females, whereas today nearly 70 percent are (Children's Defense Fund, 1994). Increased social acceptance of a young single mother raising a child, along with the belief of many teenage girls that a baby might fill a void in their lives, has meant that only a small number give their infants

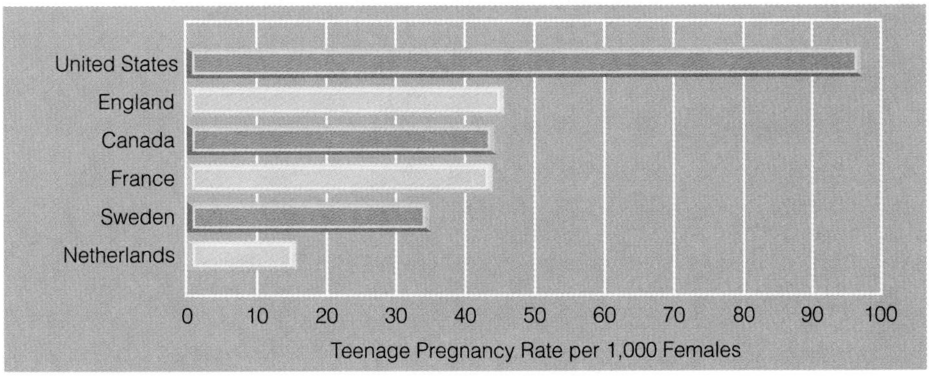

FIGURE 14.5

Teenage pregnancy rate in six industrialized nations.
(Adapted from Jones et al., 1985.)

up for adoption. Each year, about 320,000 unmarried adolescent girls take on the responsibilities of parenthood before they are psychologically mature.

CORRELATES AND CONSEQUENCES OF TEENAGE PARENTHOOD. Becoming a parent is challenging and stressful for any person, but it is especially difficult for adolescents. Teenage parents have not yet established a clear sense of direction for their own lives. As we have seen, adolescent sexual activity is linked to economic disadvantage. Teenage mothers are many times more likely to be poor than are women who postpone childbearing. A high percentage of out-of-wedlock births are to members of low-income minorities, especially African-American, Native-American, and Hispanic teenagers (see Figure 14.6). Many of these young people seem to turn to early parenthood as a way to move into adulthood when educational and career avenues are unavailable (Caldas, 1993; Murry, 1992).

Think about these characteristics of teenage parents, and you will quickly see why early childbirth imposes lasting hardships on two generations—adolescent and newborn baby. The lives of pregnant teenagers are often troubled in many ways, and after the baby is born, their circumstances worsen. We have already mentioned that academic achievement and educational aspirations of sexually active young people tend to be low. Early parenthood further reduces their life chances. Only 50 percent of girls who give birth before age 18 finish high school, compared to 96 percent of those who wait to become parents. Both teenage mothers and fathers are likely to be on welfare. If they are employed, their limited education restricts them to unsatisfying, low-paid jobs (Furstenberg, Brooks-Gunn, & Chase-Lansdale, 1989; Mott & Marsiglio, 1985).

In Chapter 4, we saw that poverty-stricken pregnant women are more likely to have inadequate diets and to expose their unborn babies to harmful environmental influences, such as illegal drugs. And many do not receive early prenatal care. These conditions are widespread among pregnant teenagers. As a result, adolescent mothers often experience prenatal and birth complications, and their infants are likely to be born underweight and premature (Makinson, 1985).

Children of teenagers are also at risk for poor parenting. Compared to adult mothers, adolescent mothers know less about child development, feel less positively about the parenting role, and interact less effectively with their infants (Sommer et al., 1993). As they get older, many children of adolescent mothers score low on intelligence tests, achieve poorly in school, and engage in disruptive social behavior.

FIGURE 14.6

Births per 1,000 females ages 15 to 19 by ethnic group.
Poverty and weak academic skills are key reasons birth rates are much higher among African-American, Hispanic, and Native-American teenagers than among whites and Asian-Americans. *(From U.S. Bureau of the Census, 1994.)*

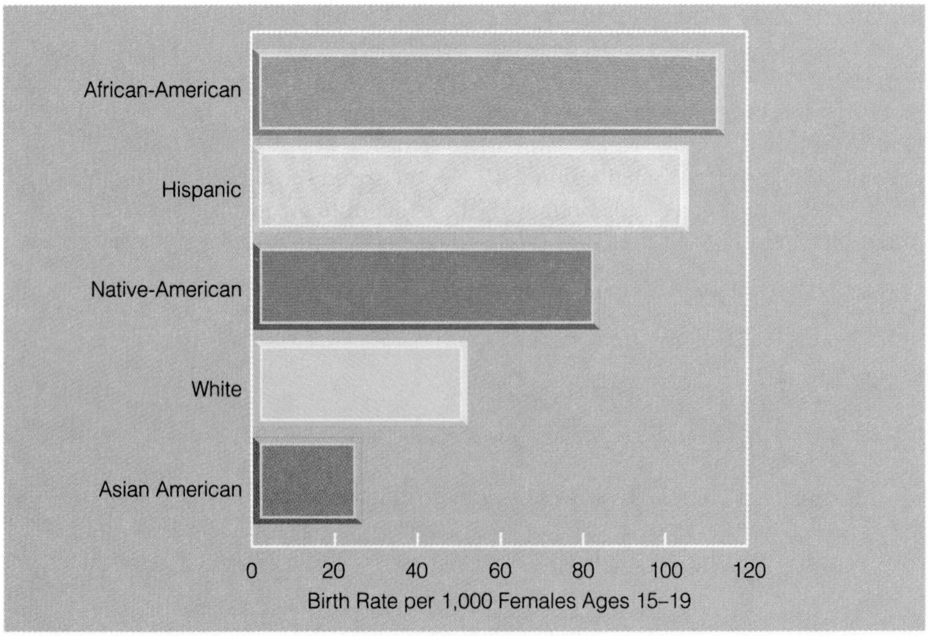

Too often, the cycle of adolescent pregnancy is repeated in the next generation. About one-third of girls who have a baby before age 19 were born to teenage mothers (Furstenberg, Levine, & Brooks-Gunn, 1990).

Still, how well adolescent parents and their children fare varies a great deal. Outcomes are more favorable when mothers return to school after giving birth and continue to live in their parents' homes, where child care can be shared with experienced adults. If the teenage mother finishes high school, avoids additional births, and finds a stable marriage partner, long-term disruptions in her own and her child's development are less severe. The small minority of young mothers who fail in all three of these ways face a life of continuing misfortune (Furstenberg, Brooks-Gunn, & Morgan, 1987).

■ **PREVENTION STRATEGIES.** Preventing teenage pregnancy requires strategies addressing the many factors that underlie early sexual activity and lack of contraceptive use. Informing adolescents about sex and contraception is crucial. Almost all junior high and high school students receive some sex education in the public schools, but its content and quality vary widely. Too often, courses are given late in high school (after sexual activity has begun), last no more than a few sessions, and are limited to a catalogue of facts about anatomy and reproduction. Sex education that goes beyond this bare minimum does not encourage early sex, as some opponents claim. It does improve awareness of sexual facts—knowledge that is necessary for responsible sexual behavior (Katchadourian, 1990).

Knowledge, however, is not sufficient to convince adolescents of the importance of postponing sexual activity and practicing contraception. To change teenagers' behavior, sex education must help them build a bridge between what they know and what they do in their everyday lives. Today, a new wave of sex education programs has emerged in which creative discussion and role-playing techniques are being used to teach adolescents the decision-making and social skills they need to resist early and unprotected sex (Kirby, 1992). One such program is described in the From Research to Practice box on page 536.

The most controversial aspect of adolescent pregnancy prevention is a growing movement to provide teenagers with easy access to contraceptives. In some large cities, school-based health clinics offering contraceptive services have been established. Many Americans argue that placing birth control pills or condoms in the hands of teenagers is equivalent to saying that early sex is okay. Yet in western Europe, where these clinics are common, teenage sexual activity is no higher than it is in the United States, but pregnancy, childbirth, and abortion rates are much lower (Hayes, 1987; Zabin & Hayward, 1993).

Efforts to prevent adolescent pregnancy and parenthood must go beyond improving sex education and access to contraception. Teenagers who look forward to a promising future are far less likely to engage in early and irresponsible sex. Society can provide young people with good reasons to postpone early childbearing by expanding their educational, vocational, and employment opportunities. We will take up these issues in Chapter 15.

■ **INTERVENING WITH TEENAGE PARENTS.** The most difficult and costly way to deal with adolescent parenthood is to wait until after it has happened. Young single mothers need health care for themselves and their children, encouragement to stay in school, job training, instruction in parenting and life management techniques, and high-quality, affordable day care. New programs that focus on fathers are attempting to increase their financial and emotional commitment to the baby and strengthen the bond between teenage parents (Children's Defense Fund, 1991a). But fathers are very difficult to reach because most either do not admit their paternity or abandon the young mother and baby after a short time. At present, the majority of adolescent parents of both sexes do not receive the help they need.

FROM RESEARCH TO PRACTICE

A NEW APPROACH TO SEX EDUCATION

In Atlanta, Georgia, a select group of high school seniors begins an intensive, 20-hour series of training sessions that will prepare them to serve as sex educators of younger students. They are part of Postponing Sexual Involvement, a special program designed to promote attitudes and skills that early adolescents can use to delay intercourse until they are mature enough to manage their sexuality responsibly. Postponing Sexual Involvement is based on three assumptions:

1. Most young teenagers do not yet have the cognitive maturity to consider the future implications of their sexual behavior.
2. The needs that early adolescents try to meet through sexual activity—desire for social acceptance and affection, confirmation of masculinity or femininity, and escape from loneliness and boredom—can be satisfied in other ways.
3. Young people often do not want to engage in sexual intercourse but are pressured into it by peers and glamorous media images.

Recognizing that merely conveying facts about sexuality will not change teenagers' behavior, Postponing Sexual Involvement translates the facts into active learning experiences. A "social inoculation" approach is used in which eighth graders, through discussion and role playing, confront sexual situations similar to those they will encounter in everyday life. Specific activities help students identify the sources of pressures to have sex, analyze why they are tempted to give in, and develop skills to resist. Delaying sex became a major goal of the program after one survey of more than 1,000 sexually active teenage girls revealed that the overwhelming majority wanted more information on how to "say no" without hurting another person's feelings. Older peers serve as teachers because of their effectiveness as models for younger students and their ability to demonstrate that there are many ways to win social admiration other than through sexual activity.

Postponing Sexual Involvement has produced remarkable results among teenagers who were not yet sexually active. A follow-up more than year after the program ended revealed that many more nonparticipants than participants had begun sexual activity (61 versus 39 percent for boys; 27 versus 17 percent for girls). Program students who did engage in intercourse were more likely than controls to use contraceptives and to experiment with sex only once or twice (Howard & McCabe, 1990).

Perhaps because of its theme of abstinence, Postponing Sexual Involvement did not change the behavior of adolescents who were already sexually experienced. But other research shows that learning activities relevant to the situations of these young people are effective. Sexually active teenagers who are encouraged to relate sexual information to their own values, to personalize that information ("Each time Ann and I have unprotected intercourse, we risk pregnancy"), and to use it in decision making ("Since neither of us wants her to get pregnant, we had better start using birth control") do practice more effective contraception (Barth, Petro, & Leland, 1992; Schinke, Blythe, & Gilchrist, 1981).

DON'T LET A HOT DATE
TURN INTO A DUE DATE.
Just a reminder that one night with your girlfriend could last a lifetime.
THE CHILDREN'S DEFENSE FUND

Convincing teenagers of the consequences of early sexual activity and helping them acquire social skills to resist it can help reduce the high rate of teenage pregnancy and childbearing in the United States. This public service poster is distributed to American communities by the Children's Defense Fund as part of its adolescent pregnancy prevention program. (See Chapter 2, page 95, for the address and phone number of the Children's Defense Fund.) *(The Children's Defense Fund)*

SEXUALLY TRANSMITTED DISEASE

Early sexual activity and inconsistent contraceptive use lead to another health problem that is widespread among teenagers: sexually transmitted disease (STD) (see Table 14.3). Adolescents have the highest rates of STD of any age group. One out of six sexually active teenagers—2.5 million young people—contract one of these illnesses each year. If left untreated, sterility and life-threatening complications can result (Braverman & Strasburger, 1994). Teenagers in greatest danger of STD are the same ones who tend to engage in irresponsible sexual behavior—poverty-stricken young people who feel a sense of inferiority and hopelessness about their lives (Holmbeck, Waters, & Brookman, 1990).

By far the most serious STD is AIDS. Although not many adolescents have AIDS, over one-fifth of cases in the United States occur between ages 20 and 29.

TABLE 14.3

Most Common Sexually Transmitted Diseases of Adolescence

DISEASE	INCIDENCE (RATE PER 100,000)	CAUSE	SYMPTOMS AND CONSEQUENCES	TREATMENT
AIDS	17[a]	Virus	Fever, weight loss, severe fatigue, swollen glands, and diarrhea. As the immune system weakens, severe pneumonias and cancers, especially on the skin, appear. Death due to other diseases usually occurs.	No cure; experimental drug AZT prolongs life
Chlamydia	215	Bacteria	Discharge from the penis in males; painful itching and burning, vaginal discharge, and dull pelvic pain in females. Often no symptoms. If left untreated, can lead to inflammation of the pelvic region, infertility, and sterility.	Antibiotic drugs
Cytomegalovirus	Unknown[b]	Virus of the herpes family	No symptoms in most cases. Sometimes, a mild flu-like reaction. In a pregnant woman, can spread to the embryo or fetus and cause miscarriage or serious birth defects (see Table 3.4, page 117).	None. Usually disappears on its own.
Genital warts	451	Virus	Warts that grow near the vaginal opening in females, on the penis or scrotum in males. Can cause severe itching. Related to cancer of the cervix.	Removal of warts
Gonorrhea	300	Bacteria	Discharge from the penis or vagina, painful urination. Sometimes no symptoms. If left untreated, can spread to other regions of the body, resulting in such complications as infertility, sterility, blood poisoning, arthritis, and inflammation of the heart.	Antibiotic drugs
Herpes simplex 2 (genital herpes)	167	Virus	Fluid-filled blisters on the genitals; high fever, severe headache, and muscle aches and tenderness. No symptoms in a few people. In a pregnant woman, can spread to the embryo or fetus and cause birth defects (see Table 3.4, page 117).	No cure. Can be controlled with drug treatment
Syphillis	75	Bacteria	Painless chancre (sore) at site of entry of germ and swollen glands, followed by rash, patchy hair loss, and sore throat within 1 week to 6 months. These symptoms disappear without treatment. Latent syphilis varies from no symptoms to damage to the brain, heart, and other organs after 5 to 20 years. In pregnant women, can spread to the embryo and fetus and cause birth defects (see Table 3.4, page 117).	Antibiotic drugs

[a]This figure includes both adolescents and young adults. For most of these cases, the virus is contracted in adolescence, and symptoms appear in early adulthood.
[b]Cytomegalovirus is the most common STD. Because there are no symptoms in most cases, its precise rate of occurrence is unknown. Half of the population or more may have had the virus sometime during their lives.
Sources: U.S. Department of Heath and Human Services, 1994a.

Nearly all of these originate in adolescence, since AIDS symptoms take several years to emerge in a person carrying the virus. AIDS seems to be on the rise among teenagers and young adults. During the late 1980s, it moved from the seventh to sixth leading cause of death for 15- to 25-year-olds. Drug-abusing and homosexual adolescents account for most cases, but heterosexual spread of the disease is increasing rapidly, especially among females (Braverman & Strasburger, 1994; U.S. Centers for Disease Control, 1995).

The epidemic of STD among American adolescents is particularly tragic because these illnesses are preventable. Besides helping teenagers understand sex, pregnancy, and contraception, another important goal of sex education is to help them avoid STD. As the result of school courses and media campaigns, over 90 percent of high school students are aware of basic facts about AIDS. But a considerable number hold false beliefs that put them at risk—for example, that birth control pills provide some protection or that it is possible to tell whether people have AIDS by looking at them (Anderson et al., 1990; DiClemente, 1993). Almost all parents favor AIDS education in the public schools, and most states now require it.

SUBSTANCE USE AND ABUSE

Just as they experimented with sex, so Louis and Cassie tried several forbidden substances during their teenage years. When he was 14, Louis took a couple of cigarettes out of his uncle's pack, waited until he was alone in the house, and smoked them. At an unchaperoned party, he and Cassie drank several cans of beer, largely because everyone else was doing it. One summer at a beach gathering, someone pulled out a handful of marijuana joints, and Louis and his friends lit up. Louis got little physical charge out of these experiences. He was a good student, was well liked by peers, and got along well with his parents. He had no need for drugs as an escape valve from daily life. But he knew of others at his school for whom things were different—students who started with alcohol and cigarettes, increased their consumption, moved to harder substances, and eventually were hooked.

In the United States, teenage alcohol and drug use is pervasive—higher than in any other industrialized nation (Newcomb & Bentler, 1989). By age 14, 56 percent of young people have already tried smoking, 81 percent drinking, and 39 percent at least one illegal drug (usually marijuana). By the end of high school, 15 percent are regular cigarette users, 32 percent have engaged in heavy drinking at least once, and over 43 percent have experimented with illegal drugs. Of these, about one-third have tried at least one highly addictive and toxic substance, such as amphetamines, cocaine, phencyclidine (PCP), inhalants, or heroin (National Institute on Drug Abuse, 1991; U.S. Department of Health and Human Services, 1994b).

Modern adolescents observe adults using drugs to help themselves through their daily lives and relieve many common symptoms. So it is not surprising that most teenagers experiment with drugs at one time or another. Those who make the transition from use to abuse are seriously troubled young people who are inclined to express their unhappiness through impulsive, antisocial behavior. *(Michaud/Photo Researchers)*

Surprisingly, these high figures actually represent an overall decline in adolescent alcohol and drug use during the past decade, a period in which the media gave greater attention to the potential hazards of these substances (see Figure 14.7). Why do so many young people continue to subject themselves to health risks associated with these substances? Part of the reason is cultural. Modern adolescents live in a drug-dependent society. They see adults using caffeine to wake up in the morning, cigarettes to cope with daily hassles, a drink to calm down in the evening, and other remedies to relieve stress, headaches, depression, and physical illness (Horan & Straus, 1987).

For most young people, drug use simply reflects their intense curiosity about "adultlike" behaviors. A recent longitudinal study revealed that the majority of teenagers dabbled in alcohol as well as tobacco and marijuana. These *experimenters* were not headed for a life of decadence and addiction, as many adults believe. Instead, they were psychologically healthy, sociable, inquisitive young people who were actually better adjusted throughout their childhoods than *abstainers*—teenagers who never used drugs at all (Shedler & Block, 1990). In a society in which substance use is commonplace, some involvement with drugs is normal and to be expected.

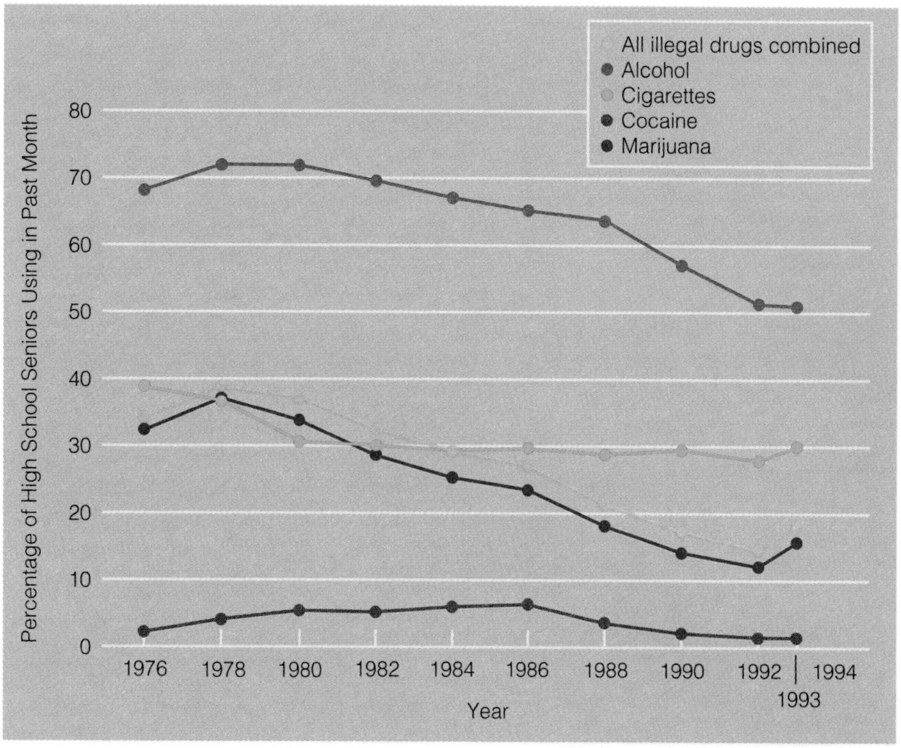

FIGURE 14.7

Percentages of high school seniors reporting use of alcohol, cigarettes, and illegal drugs in the past month, 1976–1993.

Substance use continues to be widespread among adolescents, although overall it has declined during the past decade. However, the sharp increase from 1992 to 1993—largely accounted for by marijuana and cigarette smoking—has sounded a note of alarm. (From U.S. Department of Health and Human Services, 1994b.)

Yet adolescent drug experimentation should not be taken lightly. Because most drugs impair perception and thought processes, a single heavy dose can lead to permanent injury or death. And a worrisome minority of teenagers move from substance *use* to *abuse*—taking drugs regularly, requiring increasing amounts to achieve the same effect, and finding themselves unable to stop (Kandel & Yamaguchi, 1993). Four percent of high school seniors are daily drinkers, and almost as many indicate that they took an illegal drug on a daily basis over the past month (U.S. Department of Health and Human Services, 1991, 1994b).

CORRELATES AND CONSEQUENCES OF ADOLESCENT SUBSTANCE ABUSE. In contrast to experimenters, drug abusers are seriously troubled adolescents who are inclined to express their unhappiness through impulsive, antisocial behavior. Peer encouragement—friends who use drugs, urge the adolescent to do so, and provide access to illegal substances—is the most consistent predictor of early abuse, but it does not occur in isolation. Other predisposing factors include a low-income background, family mental health problems, parental drug use, poor school performance, and such psychological traits as low self-esteem, anxiety, depression, lack of close social relationships, and attraction to deviant behaviors. The more of these risk factors that are present at once, the more likely an adolescent is to become a heavy user of alcohol, cigarettes, and marijuana and to move in the direction of addiction to hard drugs (Pentz, 1994).

Teenage substance abuse is a devastating turn of events that often has lifelong consequences. When adolescents depend on alcohol and hard drugs to deal with daily stresses, they fail to learn responsible decision-making skills and alternative coping techniques—crucial lessons during this time of transition to adulthood. Longitudinal research shows that these young people enter into marriage, childbearing, and the work world prematurely and fail at them readily. Adolescent drug addiction is associated with high rates of divorce and job loss—painful outcomes that encourage further addictive behavior (Newcomb & Bentler, 1988).

Of all drug habits, teenage cigarette smoking has received the least attention because its short-term effects are minimal. Yet it may be the deadliest substance in the long run. The relationship of tobacco use to heart and lung disease and cancer is well established.

PREVENTION STRATEGIES. As with sex education, school-based programs that go beyond conveying information to teach skills for resisting peer pressure reduce experimentation to some degree (Pentz, 1994). But this approach is effective only if adults do not "pathologize" adolescents' tendency to try drugs from time to time. When teenagers are labeled as sick, screwed up, or "druggies" for having taken a sip or puff of an illegal substance, they are likely to rebel against the source of these alarmist and insulting messages. Under these conditions, the frequency of drug use often rises. Scare tactics, in which teenagers are shown graphic films of the dire consequences of addiction, also work poorly (Newcomb & Bentler, 1989; Shedler & Block, 1990).

Adults are better off accepting the idea that some drug taking is inevitable during the teenage years. Programs that provide substitute activities and that prevent adolescents from endangering themselves and others when they do experiment may be the best way to handle the risks of teenage use. For example, some communities provide weekend on-call transportation services that any young person can contact for a safe ride home from parties or other events, with no questions asked. Others offer appealing recreational and service pursuits, such as drug-free video arcades, dances, sports activities, and social and environmental projects. Efforts like these may be partly responsible for the gradual decline in teenage substance use in recent years.

Drug abuse, as we have seen, occurs for quite different reasons than does occasional use. Therefore, different strategies are required to deal with it. Hospitalization is often a necessary and even life-saving first step. Once the young person is weaned from the drug, long-term therapy to treat low self-esteem, anxiety, and impulsivity and academic and vocational training to improve life success and satisfaction are generally needed. Not much is known about the best way to treat adolescent drug abuse. Even the most comprehensive programs have relapse rates that are alarmingly high—from 35 to 70 percent (Newcomb & Bentler, 1989).

UNINTENTIONAL INJURIES

Adolescent risk taking, fueled by sensation seeking and a tendency to act without forethought, results in a rise in certain kinds of unintentional injuries. As we saw in Chapter 11, the total rate of injuries increases through the early teenage years and then declines (see page 406). But one type—automobile injuries—becomes more common. Motor vehicle collisions are the leading killer of adolescents, accounting for almost 40 percent of deaths between ages 15 and 24. Many result from driving at high speeds and while intoxicated (Children's Defense Fund, 1991; Arnett & Balle-Jensen, 1993). Insurance companies that charge steep rates for teenage males, especially those who are poor students, are well aware of young people at greatest risk. Parents need to set firm limits on their teenager's car use, particularly with respect to drinking and driving. These efforts are most likely to be successful when there is a history of good parent–child communication—a powerful preventive of adolescent injury (Millstein & Irwin, 1988).

Other unintentional injuries account for an additional 11 percent of adolescent deaths. The majority are caused by firearms. Recently, in my own community, a 16-year-old boy boasted to a friend about possession of a sawed-off shotgun. When his companion asked to see it, the boy got the gun and, thinking it was unloaded, playfully pointed it at his friend's chest and pulled the trigger. In countries where gun sales are banned (Canada, all of western Europe, and Japan), such needless deaths almost never happen. The rate of disability and death caused by firearms (both unintentional and homicidal) is especially high among low-income minority youths, particularly black males living in inner-city ghettos (Children's Defense Fund, 1994).

A third form of adolescent injury—less serious but still largely avoidable—is sports related. By high school, 15 percent of students involved in athletics experience injuries that require medical treatment. Most are mild, involving muscle strains and bruises, but an occasional serious injury (generally from playing football) does occur (Micheli & Klein, 1991). Errors by coaches are an important source of athletic injuries. In their drive to win, they sometimes make unreasonable demands of players. Early adolescents are especially vulnerable. Many coaches match competitors on the basis of age and weight without considering physical maturity. Too often, this allows "(120 pounds) of mature muscle and mustache to compete against (120 pounds) of peach fuzz and baby fat" (Stanitski, 1989, p. 35). The safest athletic activities during the period of rapid pubertal growth are noncontact team sports, such as volleyball and softball, and individual sports, such as track, swimming, and tennis.

BRIEF REVIEW

The arrival of puberty is accompanied by new health concerns. Greater nutritional requirements of a rapidly growing body come at a time when the eating habits of many young people are the poorest. For some teenagers, the cultural ideal of thinness combines with family and psychological problems to produce the serious eating disturbances of anorexia nervosa and bulimia.

Hormonal changes of puberty lead to an increase in the sex drive, but how young people manage their sexuality is affected by social contexts. American adolescents receive mixed messages from adults and the larger culture about sexual activity. The percentage of sexually active teenagers has increased over time. Homosexual young people face special challenges in establishing a positive sexual identity. Adolescent cognitive processes along with lack of social supports for responsible sexual behavior contribute to high rates of teenage pregnancy, abortion, and premarital childbirth in the United States. Adolescent parenthood is linked to low education and poverty, conditions that risk the development of both teenagers and their children. Sexually transmitted disease is an additional danger of early sexual activity and lack of contraceptive use.

Although most adolescents experiment with alcohol and drugs, a worrisome minority make the transition from use to abuse. Teenage substance abuse is linked to a variety of family, peer, and psychological problems, and treatment is difficult. Motor vehicle, firearm, and sports-related injuries increase during adolescence.

ASK YOURSELF . . .

- Fourteen-year-old Lindsay says she couldn't possibly get pregnant because her boyfriend told her he would never do anything to "mess her up." What factors might account for Lindsay's unrealistic reasoning?
- Return to page 533 and review Veronica's life circumstances after becoming a teenage mother. Why is it likely that Veronica and her children will experience long-term hardships?
- Explain how adolescent substance abuse follows the pattern of other teenage health problems in being a product of both social and psychological forces.

MOTOR DEVELOPMENT DURING ADOLESCENCE

Puberty is accompanied by steady improvement in motor performance, but the pattern of change is quite different for boys and girls. Girls' gains are slow and gradual, leveling off by age 14. In contrast, boys show a dramatic spurt in strength, speed, and endurance that continues through the end of the teenage years. Figure 14.8 illustrates this sex difference for running speed, broad jump, and vertical jump. Notice how the gender gap in physical skill widens over time. By mid-adolescence, very few girls perform as well as the average boy, and practically no boys score as low as the average girl (Malina & Bouchard, 1991).

Because girls and boys are no longer well matched physically, sex-segregated physical education usually begins in junior high school. At the same time, athletic options for both sexes expand. Many new sports are added to the curriculum—track and field, wrestling, tackle football, weight lifting, floor hockey, archery, tennis, and golf, to name just a few.

Since competence at sports is strongly related to peer admiration among adolescent boys, it becomes even more important in boys' self-esteem than it was at earlier ages. Some adolescent males become so obsessed with physical prowess that they try to increase their skill artificially. A growing problem among professional and amateur athletes is the use of anabolic steroids to boost muscle size and strength. In the United States, about 6.6 percent of high school males take these illegal drugs, ignoring their serious side effects (Yesalis et al., 1989). These include damage to the liver, circulatory system, and reproductive organs as well as an increase in mood swings and aggressive behavior (American College of Sports Medicine, 1984; Committee on Sports Medicine, 1989;).

In 1972, the federal government required schools receiving public funds to provide equal opportunities for males and females in all educational programs, including athletics. The law sparked a dramatic rise in girls' sports participation. Still, it falls far short of boys'. According one recent estimate, about 64 percent of males but only 41 percent of females are active in high school sports (Berk, 1992b). In Chapter 11, we saw that beginning at an early age, girls get less encouragement and recognition for athletic achievement. This pattern continues into the teenage years. Look in your local newspaper, and note the much greater attention given to boys' school sports than girls'. Girls' athletic events rarely attract more than a handful of spectators (Eder & Parker, 1987).

Sports do not just improve motor performance. They influence cognitive and social development as well. Interschool and intramural athletics provide important lessons in competition, assertiveness, problem solving, and teamwork. These experiences are less available to females because of the lower status of girls' sports. A positive sign is that the sex difference in high school athletic participation is becoming smaller. Although we still have a long way to go, we are closer today than ever before to equality of opportunity for the sexes in sports as well as other areas of human skill.

FIGURE 14.8

Age changes in running speed, broad jump, and throwing distance for boys and girls.
The gender gap in athletic performance widens during adolescence. *(From A. Espenschade & H. Eckert, 1974, "Motor Development," in W. R. Warren & E. R. Buskirk, Eds.,* Science and Medicine of Exercise and Sport, *pp. 329–330, New York: Harper & Row. Adapted by permission of HarperCollins Publishers, Inc.)*

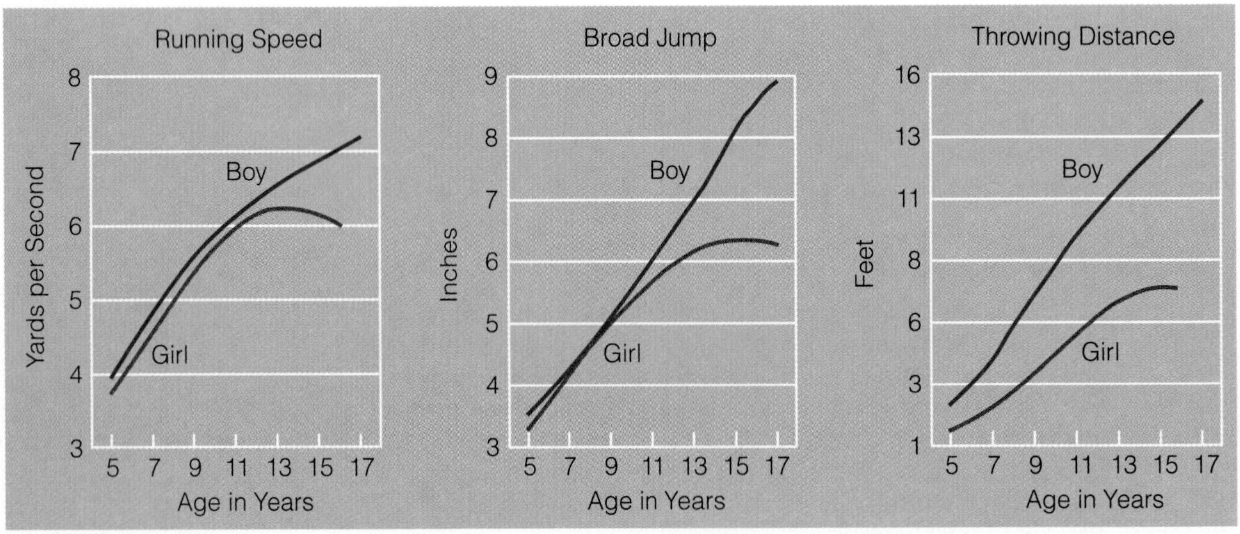

SUMMARY

CONCEPTIONS OF ADOLESCENCE

How have conceptions of adolescence changed over the twentieth century?

- Early biologically oriented theories viewed **puberty** as an inevitable period of storm and stress. An alternative perspective regarded the social environment as entirely responsible for the wide variability in adolescent adjustment. Modern research shows that adolescence is neither biologically nor socially determined, but a product of the two. In cultures where many years of education are required for successful participation in the work life of the community, adolescence is greatly extended.

PUBERTY: THE PHYSICAL TRANSITION TO ADULTHOOD

Describe pubertal changes in body size, proportions, and sexual maturity.

- Hormonal changes beginning in middle childhood initiate puberty, which begins, on the average, 2 years earlier for girls than boys. The first outward sign of puberty is the rapid gain in height and weight known as the **growth spurt.** In early adolescence, the cephalocaudal trend of body growth reverses. Lengthening of the torso accounts for most of the adolescent height gain. As the body enlarges, girls' hips and boys' shoulders broaden. Girls add more fat, boys more muscle.
- Sex hormones regulate changes in **primary** and **secondary sexual characteristics. Menarche** occurs relatively late in the girl's sequence of pubertal events, following the rapid increase in body size. After menarche, growth of the breasts and pubic and underarm hair are completed. Among boys, as the sex organs and body enlarge and pubic and underarm hair appear, **spermarche** (first ejaculation) takes place. This is followed by growth of facial and body hair and deepening of the voice.

What factors influence the timing of puberty?

- In addition to heredity, nutrition and overall physical health contribute to the timing of puberty. Menarche is delayed in poverty-stricken regions of the world and among young people from low-income families. A secular trend toward an earlier age of puberty has occurred in industrialized nations.

THE PSYCHOLOGICAL IMPACT OF PUBERTAL EVENTS

What factors influence adolescents' reactions to the physical changes of puberty?

- Girls generally react to menarche with surprise and mixed emotions, but whether their feelings lean in a positive or negative direction depends on advance information and support from family members. Boys usually know ahead of time about spermarche, but they receive less support for the physical changes of puberty than do girls. The absence of a widely accepted rite of passage for physical and social maturity in contemporary society makes the process of becoming an adult especially confusing.
- Besides higher hormone levels, negative life events and situational changes are associated with adolescent moodiness. Puberty is accompanied by psychological distancing between parent and child. The reaction may be a modern substitute for physical departure from the family, which typically occurs at sexual maturity in primate species.

Describe the impact of maturational timing on adolescent adjustment, noting sex differences.

- Timing of puberty influences adolescent psychological adjustment. Early maturing boys and late maturing girls, whose appearance closely matches cultural standards of physical attractiveness, have a more positive **body image,** feel more self-confident, and hold more positions of leadership. In contrast, early maturing girls and late maturing boys, who fit in least well physically with peers, experience emotional and social difficulties. Long-term follow-ups show that these trends are reversed in adulthood. However, maturational timing effects may persist in some cultures.

HEALTH ISSUES DURING ADOLESCENCE

Describe nutritional needs, and cite factors related to serious eating disturbances during adolescence.

- As the body grows, nutritional requirements increase, at a time when the eating habits of young people are the poorest. Many adolescents suffer from iron, vitamin, and mineral deficiencies.
- Girls who reach puberty early, who are very dissatisfied with their body images, and who grow up in economically advantaged homes where thinness is idealized are at risk for eating disorders. **Anorexia nervosa** tends to appear in girls who have perfectionist personalities and overprotective and controlling parents. The impulsive eating and purging of **bulimia** is associated with lack of self-control in other areas of life.

Discuss social and cultural influences on adolescent sexual attitudes and behavior.

- The hormonal changes of puberty lead to an increase in sex drive, but social factors affect how teenagers manage their sexuality. Compared to most other cultures, the United States is fairly restrictive in its attitude toward adolescent sex. Young people receive contradictory messages from the larger social environment. Sexual attitudes of adults and adolescents have become somewhat more liberal in recent years, and the rate of teenage sexual activity has risen.

- Early sexual activity is linked to a variety of factors associated with economic disadvantage. About half of sexually active American teenagers do not practice contraception regularly. Adolescent cognitive processes and a lack of social support for responsible sexual behavior underlie the failure of so many young people to protect themselves against pregnancy. Teenagers who talk openly with their parents about sex are more likely to use birth control.

Describe factors related to the development of homosexuality.

- About 1 to 4 percent of young people discover that they are lesbian or gay. Although heredity makes an important contribution, homosexuality probably results from a variety of biological and environmental combinations that are not yet well understood. Lesbian and gay teenagers face special problems in establishing a positive sexual identity.

Discuss factors related to teenage pregnancy, childbearing, and sexually transmitted disease.

- Adolescent pregnancy, abortion, and childbearing are higher in the United States than in many industrialized nations. Teenage parenthood is often associated with dropping out of school and poverty, circumstances that risk the well-being of both adolescent and newborn child. Improved sex education and contraceptive services for adolescents reduce teenage pregnancy and childbearing.

- A high rate of sexually transmitted disease (STD) among American adolescents is another consequence of early sexual activity and inconsistent contraceptive use. Many individuals contract the AIDS virus as teenagers. Drug-abusing and homosexual adolescents account for most cases, but heterosexual spread of the disease is increasing.

What personal and social factors are related to adolescent substance use and abuse?

- Teenage alcohol and drug use is widespread in the United States. Adolescents who experiment with drugs are well-adjusted young people who are curious about these forbidden substances. The minority who move from use to abuse have family, school, and psychological problems.

Cite common unintentional injuries in adolescence.

- Motor vehicle collisions are the leading cause of adolescent injury and death. The rate of disability and death caused by firearms is also high. A third, less serious type of injury is sports related.

MOTOR DEVELOPMENT DURING ADOLESCENCE

Describe sex differences in motor development during adolescence.

- Pubertal changes lead both sexes to improve in gross motor performance during adolescence, although boys show much larger gains than girls. Girls continue to receive less encouragement and recognition for developing athletic skill, although their involvement in high school sports has increased in recent years.

IMPORTANT TERMS AND CONCEPTS

puberty (p. 510)
genital stage (p. 511)
growth spurt (p. 514)
primary sexual characteristics (p. 515)
secondary sexual characteristics (p. 515)
menarche (p. 515)
spermarche (p. 516)
adolescent initiation ceremony (p. 520)
body image (p. 524)
anorexia nervosa (p. 527)
bulimia (p. 528)

FYI...

FOR FURTHER INFORMATION AND SPECIAL HELP, CONSULT THE FOLLOWING ORGANIZATIONS:

EATING DISORDERS

Anorexia Nervosa and Related Eating Disorders
P.O. Box 5102
Eugene, OR 97405
(503) 344-1144

An association of anorexics and bulimics, their families and friends, and concerned professionals that provides information, support, medical referrals, and counseling.

SEXUAL BEHAVIOR

Alan Guttmacher Institute
111 Fifth Avenue
New York, NY 10003
(212) 254-5656

Compiles statistics on sexual behavior and fertility and promotes public policy related to birth control. Publishes the journal Family Planning Perspectives, *which includes articles on teenage sexual behavior, pregnancy, and childbearing.*

SEXUALLY TRANSMITTED DISEASE (STD)

American Social Health Association
P.O. Box 13827
Research Triangle Park, NC 27709
(919) 361-8400

A national health agency that works to expand research, provide information to communities, and improve public health policy related to STD. Operates the Herpes Resource Center, a support program for sufferers of incurable genital herpes.

National AIDS Information Clearinghouse
P.O. Box 6003
Rockville, MD 20849-6003
(800) 458-5231

Government-sponsored agency that provides information about AIDS and AIDS-related health services. Operates toll-free AIDS information hotline, (800) 342-AIDS.

Teens Teaching AIDS Prevention
3030 Walnut
Kansas City, MO 64108
(816) 561-8784

Provides teenagers with information on AIDS through peer counseling. Operates a toll-free hot line staffed by trained high school students and adult advisers, (800) 234-TEEN.

SUBSTANCE ABUSE

Do It Now Foundation
P.O. Box 27568
Tempe, AZ 85285
(602) 491-0393

Works to provide factual information to adolescents and adults about alcohol, drugs, and related health issues. Assists organizations engaged in drug education.

Drugs Anonymous
P.O. Box 772
Bronx, NY 10451
(212) 874-0700

An organization devoted to helping people recover from addiction to mood-altering drugs that follows the methods used by Alcoholics Anonymous.

(See page 131 for additional organizations related to alcohol abuse.)

TEENAGE PREGNANCY

National Organization of Adolescent Pregnancy and Parenting
4421A East–West Highway
Bethesda, MD 20814
(301) 913-0378

An association that promotes community services designed to treat problems associated with adolescent pregnancy and childbearing.

"The greenhouse effect"
Kimiko Shimada
13 years, Japan

During adolescence, cognition moves beyond the real to the possible. This 13-year-old's fantastic vision of the devastation that humankind can wreak on its earthly habitat is a product of new abstract reasoning powers discussed in Chapter 15.

15

Cognitive Development in Adolescence

PIAGET'S THEORY: THE FORMAL OPERATIONAL STAGE

Hypothetico-Deductive Reasoning • Propositional Thought • Recent Research on Formal Operational Thought

AN INFORMATION-PROCESSING VIEW OF ADOLESCENT COGNITIVE DEVELOPMENT

Siegler's Rule-Assessment Approach • Gradual Mastery of Formal Operational Abilities

CONSEQUENCES OF ABSTRACT THOUGHT

Argumentativeness • Self-Consciousness and Self-Focusing • Idealism and Criticism • Planning and Decision Making

SEX DIFFERENCES IN MENTAL ABILITIES

LANGUAGE DEVELOPMENT IN ADOLESCENCE

Vocabulary and Grammar • Pragmatics • Second-Language Learning

LEARNING IN SCHOOL

School Transitions • Academic Achievement • Dropping Out

VOCATIONAL DEVELOPMENT

Selecting a Vocation • Making the Transition from School to Work

One mid-December evening, a knock at the front door announced the arrival of Franca and Antonio's oldest son, Jules, home for vacation after the fall semester of his sophomore year at college. "He's here!" Franca shouted upstairs to Antonio, hugging 19-year-old Jules and guiding him into the kitchen.

Moments later, the family gathered around the kitchen table. "How did it all go, Jules?" inquired Antonio while passing out pieces of apple pie.

"Well, math was only so-so. But physics and philosophy were awesome. The last few weeks, our physics prof introduced us to Einstein's relativity theory. Boggles my mind, it's so incredibly counterintuitive."

"Counter-what?" asked 11-year-old Sabrina, trying hard to follow the conversation.

"Counterintuitive. Unlike what you'd normally expect," explained Jules. "Imagine this. You're on a train, going unbelievably fast, like 160,000 miles a second. The faster you go approaching the speed of light, the slower time passes and the denser and heavier things get relative to on the ground. The theory revolutionized the way we think about time, space, matter—the entire universe."

Sabrina wrinkled her forehead in a puzzled expression, unable to comprehend Jules's other-worldly reasoning. "Time slows down when I'm bored, like right now, not on a train when I'm going somewhere exciting. No speeding train ever made me denser and heavier, but this apple pie will if I eat any more of it," Sabrina announced with finality, getting up and leaving the table.

Louis, several years older than Sabrina, reacted differently. "Totally cool, Jules. So what'd you do in philosophy?"

"It was a course in philosophy of technology. One of the things we studied was the ethics of futuristic methods in human reproduction. For example, we argued the pros and cons of a world in which all embryos develop in artificial wombs."

"What do you mean?" asked Louis. "You order your kid at the lab?"

"That's right. I wrote my term paper on it. I had to evaluate it in terms of principles of justice and freedom. I can see some advantages but also lots of dangers. . . ."

As this conversation illustrates, adolescence brings with it vastly expanded powers of reasoning. At age 11, Sabrina's logic is still concrete, tied to the here-and-now. She finds it difficult to move beyond her own firsthand experiences into a world of possibilities. Over the next few years, her thinking will take on the abstract qualities that characterize the cognition of her older brothers. Jules juggles variables in complex combinations and thinks about situations not easily detected in the real world or that do not exist at all. His adultlike thinking makes him a far better problem solver than he was at earlier ages. It also opens up whole new realms of learning. Adolescents can grasp complex scientific and mathematical principles, grapple with puzzling social and political issues, detect the hidden meaning of a poem or story, and deal with language in increasingly flexible, creative ways. Compared to school-age children's thinking, adolescent thought is more enlightened, imaginative, and rational.

The first part of this chapter traces these extraordinary changes, from both Piaget's and the information-processing point of view. Next, we take a close look at a set of research findings that has attracted a great deal of public attention: sex differences in mental abilities. We also discuss important gains in language that reflect as well as contribute to the advanced thinking of the teenage years. The middle portion of this chapter is devoted to the primary setting in which adolescent thought takes shape: the school. Then, in late adolescence and young adulthood, schooling gives way to work and career. We conclude with a consideration of vocational development during the teenage years.

PIAGET'S THEORY: THE FORMAL OPERATIONAL STAGE

According to Piaget, the capacity for abstract thinking begins around age 11. At the **formal operational stage,** the adolescent reasons much like a scientist searching for solutions in the laboratory. Concrete operational children can only "operate on reality," but formal operational adolescents can "operate on operations." In other words, concrete things and events are no longer required as objects of thought. Instead, adolescents can come up with new, more general logical rules through internal reflection (Brainerd, 1978; Inhelder & Piaget, 1955/1958). The Concept Review Table on page 550 summarizes two major features of formal operational reasoning.

Formal operational stage
Piaget's final stage, in which adolescents develop the capacity for abstract, scientific thinking. Begins around 11 years of age.

Hypothetico-deductive reasoning
A formal operational problem-solving strategy in which adolescents begin with a general theory of all possible factors that could affect an outcome in a problem and deduce specific hypotheses, which they test in an orderly fashion.

HYPOTHETICO-DEDUCTIVE REASONING

At adolescence, young people first become capable of **hypothetico-deductive reasoning.** When faced with a problem, they start with a *general theory* of all possible factors that might affect the outcome and *deduce* from it specific *hypotheses* (or predictions) about what might happen. Then they test these hypotheses in an orderly fashion to see which ones work in the real world. Notice how this form of problem solving begins with possibility and proceeds to reality. In contrast, concrete operational children start with reality—with the most obvious predictions about a

During the formal operational stage, adolescents solve problems by thinking of all possible hypotheses that could occur in a situation. Then they test these predictions systematically to see which ones apply in the real world. *(Will Faller)*

situation. When these are not confirmed, they cannot think of alternatives and fail to solve the problem.

Adolescents' performance on Piaget's famous *pendulum problem* illustrates this new hypothetico-deductive approach. Suppose we present several school-age children and adolescents with strings of different lengths, objects of different weights to attach to the strings, and a bar from which to hang the strings. Then we ask each of them to figure out what influences the speed with which a pendulum swings through its arc.

Formal operational adolescents come up with four hypotheses: (1) the length of the string; (2) the weight of the object hung on it; (3) how high the object is raised before it is released; and (4) how forcefully the object is pushed. Then, by varying one factor at a time while holding all the others constant, they try out each of these possibilities. Eventually they discover that only string length makes a difference.

In contrast, concrete operational children's experimentation is unsystematic. They cannot separate out the effects of each variable. For example, they may test for the effect of string length without holding weight constant by comparing a short, light pendulum with a long, heavy one. Also, school-age youngsters fail to notice variables that are not immediately suggested by the concrete materials of the task—the height and forcefulness with which the pendulum is released.

PROPOSITIONAL THOUGHT

A second important characteristic of the formal operational stage is **propositional thought.** Adolescents can evaluate the logic of propositions (verbal statements) without referring to real-world circumstances. In contrast, concrete operational children can evaluate the logic of statements only by considering them against concrete evidence in the real world.

In one study of propositional reasoning, an experimenter showed children and adolescents a pile of poker chips and indicated that some statements would be made about them. Each participant was asked to tell whether each statement was true, false, or uncertain. In one condition, the experimenter hid a chip in her hand and then asked the young person to evaluate the following propositions:

Propositional thought
A type of formal operational reasoning in which adolescents evaluate the logic of verbal statements without referring to real-world circumstances.

CONCEPT REVIEW TABLE

Major Characteristics of Formal Operational Thought

CONCEPT	IMPORTANT POINT	EXAMPLE
Hypothetico-deductive reasoning	When faced with a problem, formal operational adolescents think of all possible factors that could affect the outcome, even those not immediately suggested by concrete features of the situation. Then they try them out in step-by-step fashion to find out which ones work in the real world.	In biology class, Louis had to determine which of two fertilizers was best for growing African violets. Louis thought, "The kind of fertilizer might not be the only factor that's important. Its concentration and how often the plant is fed might also make a difference." So Louis planned an experiment in which each fertilizer would be applied in several strengths and according to different feeding schedules. He made sure to design the experiment so he could determine the separate effects of each factor, and their combined effects, on plant growth.
Propositional thought	Formal operational adolescents can evaluate the logic of statements by reflecting on the statements themselves. They do not need to consider them against real-world circumstances.	Louis was given the following propositional task and asked to indicate whether the conclusion was true, false, or uncertain: Premise 1: All animals are purple. Premise 2: A frobe is purple. Conclusion: A frobe is an animal. Louis concluded, correctly, that whether a frobe is an animal is uncertain. "A frobe might be an animal," he answered, "but it might also be a purple thing that is not an animal."

"*Either* the chip in my hand is green *or* it is not green."

"The chip in my hand is green *and* it is not green."

In another condition, the experimenter held either a red or a green chip in full view and made the same statements.

School-age children focused on the concrete properties of the poker chips rather than on the logic of the statements. As a result, they replied that they were uncertain to both statements when the chip was hidden from view. When it was visible, they judged both statements to be true if the chip was green and false if it was red. In contrast, adolescents analyzed the logic of the statements as propositions. They understood that the "either–or" statement is always true and the "and" statement is always false, regardless of the poker chip's color (Osherson & Markman, 1975).

Although Piaget did not believe that language plays a central role in cognitive development (see Chapter 9), he acknowledged that it is more important during adolescence. Abstract thought requires language-based systems of representation that do not stand for real things, such as those that exist in higher mathematics. Around age 14 or 15, high school students start to use these systems in algebra and geometry. Formal operational thought also involves verbal reasoning about abstract concepts (Brainerd, 1978). Jules showed that he could think in this way when he pondered the relationships among time, space, and matter in physics and wondered about justice and freedom in philosophy.

RECENT RESEARCH ON FORMAL OPERATIONAL THOUGHT

Many researchers have conducted follow-up studies of formal operational thought, asking questions similar to those we discussed with respect to Piaget's earlier stages: Is there evidence that abstract thinking appears earlier than Piaget expected? Do all individuals reach formal operations during their teenage years?

ARE YOUNG CHILDREN CAPABLE OF ABSTRACT THINKING? School-age children show the glimmerings of hypothetico-deductive reasoning, but they are not as competent as adolescents and adults. For example, in simplified situations—ones involving no more than two possible causal variables—6-year-olds understand that hypotheses must be confirmed by appropriate evidence. They also realize that once supported, a hypothesis shapes predictions about what might happen in the future (Ruffman et al., 1993b). But unlike adolescents, children cannot sort out evidence that bears on three or more variables at once. And they have difficulty explaining why a pattern of observations supports a hypothesis, even when they recognize the connection between the two (Kuhn, Amsel, & O'Loughlin, 1988; Schauble, 1990). Clearly, adolescents are capable of a deeper grasp of scientific principles than are their younger counterparts. Consistent with this idea, training improves performance on hypothetico-deductive tasks like the pendulum problem for both children and adolescents. But the effects of training last longer and generalize more easily to new tasks with a high school or college student than with a school-age child (Greenbowe et al., 1981; Kuhn, Ho, & Adams, 1979).

School-age children's capacity for propositional thought is also limited. For example, they have great difficulty reasoning from premises that contradict reality or their own beliefs. Consider the following set of statements: "If dogs are bigger than elephants and elephants are bigger than mice, then dogs are bigger than mice." Children younger than 10 judge this reasoning to be false, since all the relations specified do not occur in real life (Moshman & Franks, 1986).

Furthermore, in instances in which school-age children respond correctly to propositional tasks, their success seems to be due to an "atmosphere effect." Positive statements are always answered yes and negative statements are always answered no, even though this strategy often violates the most basic rules of logic (Markovits,

Adolescents' ability to evaluate the logic of propositions without referring to real-world circumstances provides them with access to new realms of knowledge, such as higher mathematics. These girls explore the abstract representational principles of geometry. *(Susan Lapides/Design Conceptions)*

Schleifer, & Fortier, 1989). For example, when given the following premises (one of which is negative), school-age children usually draw an incorrect conclusion:

Premise 1: If there is a knife, then there is a fork.

Premise 2: There is not a knife.

Question: Is there a fork?

Wrong Conclusion: No, there is not a fork. (Kodroff & Roberge, 1975)

Around age 11, young people can analyze the logic of a series of propositions, regardless of whether statements are positive, negative, or consistent with reality or their own values. As Piaget's theory indicates, propositional thought improves steadily over the adolescent years (Markovits & Vachon, 1989, 1990).

DO ALL INDIVIDUALS REACH THE FORMAL OPERATIONAL STAGE? Try giving the knife-and-fork task to some of your friends and see how well they do. You are likely to find that even well-educated adults have difficulty with abstract thinking! About 40 to 60 percent of college students fail Piaget's formal operational problems (Keating, 1979).

Why is it that so many college students, and adults in general, are not fully formal operational? The reason is that people are most likely to think abstractly in situations in which they have had extensive experience. This is supported by the finding that adolescents and adults can be trained to a high level of performance on formal operational tasks. Other evidence indicates that taking college courses leads to improvements in formal reasoning related to course content (Lehman & Nisbett, 1990). The physics student grasps Piaget's pendulum problem with ease. The English enthusiast excels at analyzing the themes of a Shakespeare play, whereas the history buff skillfully evaluates the causes and consequences of the Vietnam War. Because of differences in training and experience, the person who does well at one of these tasks may not be especially good at the others.

Consider these findings carefully, and you will see that formal operations, like the concrete reasoning that preceded it, seems to be a gradual rather than abrupt development. And rather than emerging in all contexts at once, it is specific to situation and task. All normal adults are capable of abstract thought, but they are likely to demonstrate it only in areas in which they have achieved considerable mastery.

Finally, you may recall from Chapter 13 that the development of concrete operations is greatly delayed in some village and tribal societies. In many of these cultures, formal operational reasoning does not appear at all (Cole, 1990; Gellatly, 1987). Piaget acknowledged that because of lack of opportunity to solve hypothetical problems, abstract thought might not appear in some societies. Still, these findings raise further questions about the universal nature of Piaget's stage sequence. Is the highest stage really an outgrowth of children's independent efforts to make sense of their world? Or is it a culturally transmitted way of reasoning that is specific to literate societies and taught in school? These issues have prompted some investigators to turn toward an information-processing view.

AN INFORMATION-PROCESSING VIEW OF ADOLESCENT COGNITIVE DEVELOPMENT

Information-processing theorists agree with the broad outlines of Piaget's description of adolescent cognition. Compared to children, teenagers are much better at abstract reasoning because of gains in an underlying capacity to attend to information, hold it in memory, and combine it into more efficient and effective representations (Case, 1985, 1992; Demetriou et al., 1993; Fischer, 1980). But unlike Piaget, who thought that formal operations emerge out of self-discovery, information-processing researchers believe that abstract reasoning can and often needs to be directly taught.

SIEGLER'S RULE-ASSESSMENT APPROACH

During a free moment in science class, Sabrina wandered to the back of the room and experimented with a balance scale. "What makes it work?" she thought to herself. "If I put equal weights in the same place on both sides, it balances. If I put them in different places, it doesn't. If I add more weight to one side, I can make it balance again. So both weight and distance make a difference. But how do they work together?" she wondered while hanging weights in different places on the arms of the scale.

The balance scale problem that Sabrina posed is yet another Piagetian formal operational task. As an early adolescent, Sabrina has a far more sophisticated understanding of how the scale works than a younger child. Yet her grasp of the underlying principle is still imprecise. Robert Siegler (1981, 1983a, 1983b) restudied Piagetian tasks in an effort to trace the development of children's problem solving from an information-processing perspective.

Siegler believes that cognitive development involves acquiring increasingly powerful rules, or cognitive procedures, for solving problems. For example, he gave 3- to 17-year-olds the various balance scale problems shown in Figure 15.1 and asked them to predict what would happen. Three-year-olds answered randomly, using no systematic procedures at all. But from the late preschool period on, children used four developmentally ordered rules, each of which led to a particular pattern of responses on the balance scale tasks (refer to the columns in Figure 15.1):

Rule I. Four- to 6-year-olds took into account only the weight on each side, ignoring distance from the center. If the number of weights was equal, they predicted that the scale would balance. If it was not equal, they predicted it would not balance.

Rule II. By middle childhood, many children had modified Rule I slightly. They continued to focus only on weight, except when the weights on both sides were equal. When this occurred, they predicted that the scale would balance if the two distances were equal. If they were not, children predicted that the scale would not balance.

Rule III. Adolescents considered both weight and distance. If one dimension was equal and the other was not, they based their decision on the unequal dimension and said the scale would not balance. If both dimensions were unequal, they had no rule for handling the situation and simply guessed.

Rule IV. Very few young people used this rule. It involves realizing that only when the product of weight × distance on both sides of the scale is equal will the scale balance.

Further research by Siegler showed that providing children and adolescents with information that addresses specific flaws in their reasoning encourages them to use more advanced rules. For example, when preschoolers who used no rule were trained to notice weight, they advanced to Rule I. When those who used Rule I were trained to notice distance, they moved to Rule II. Similarly, adolescents grasped Rule IV when given aids designed to help them discover the weight × distance principle. In each case, the most effective instruction provided information just beyond the child's current performance. As children used this information to revise their rule for solving the problem, they noticed a dimension of the task they had not taken into account before. Consequently, they moved to the next level of understanding (Siegler, 1976, 1978, 1991).

Problem Type	Rule I	Rule II	Rule III	Rule IV
1. Equal weight–equal distance 	100%	100%	100%	100%
2. Unequal weight–equal distance 	100%	100%	100%	100%
3. Unequal distance–equal weight 	0% should say "Balance"	100%	100%	100%
4. Conflict–weight (more weight on one side, more distance on the other, configuration arranged so side with more weight goes down) 	100%	100%	33% (chance responding)	100%
5. Conflict–distance (similar to conflict–weight, but side with greater distance goes down) 	0% should say "Right side down"	0% should say "Right side down"	33% (chance responding)	100%
6. Conflict–balance (like the above two problems, except the scale remains balanced) 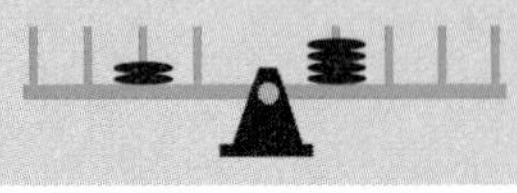	0% should say "Right side down"	0% should say "Right side down"	33% (chance responding)	100%

FIGURE 15.1

Percentage of correct responses expected on Siegler's balance scale problems for children and adolescents using different rules. For each problem type, subjects are asked to indicate whether they think the scale will balance or whether the right or left side will go down. *(From R. S. Siegler, "The Origins of Scientific Reasoning," in R. S. Siegler, Ed.,* Children's Thinking: What Develops? *Hillsdale, NJ: Erlbaum, pp. 104–149. Copyright 1978 by Lawrence Erlbaum Associates. Adapted by permission.)*

GRADUAL MASTERY OF FORMAL OPERATIONAL ABILITIES

Siegler believes that extending his rule-assessment approach to other domains of learning could lead to a general model of how individuals of different ages solve problems. Can all types of problem solving be captured in this way? Some critics believe that the approach may apply only to highly structured tasks (Strauss & Levin, 1981). Although this may be true, recent evidence suggests that *on different kinds* of structured problems, adolescents grasp formal operational abilities in a similar, step-by-step fashion.

In one series of studies, 10- to 20-year-olds were given sets of problems graded in difficulty. For example, one set consisted of quantitative-relational tasks like the balance scale problems shown in Figure 15.1. Another set contained verbal propositional tasks like the poker chip problem on page 550. And in still another set were causal-experimental tasks such as the fertilizer problem described in the Concept Review Table on page 550. In each of these task domains, adolescents mastered component skills in sequential order, with simpler abilities providing the foundation for more complex ones. For example, on causal-experimental problems, they first became aware of the many possibilities that could influence an outcome and combined them systematically. This enabled them to formulate and test hypotheses. Over time, adolescents combined separate skills into a smoothly functioning system. They constructed a general model that could be applied to many instances of a given type of problem (Demetriou, Efklides, & Platsidou, 1993, Demetriou et al., 1993).

What factors support adolescents' progress through this sequence? Greater information-processing capacity, exposure to increasingly complex problems, and instruction that highlights critical features of tasks and effective strategies are believed to be important (Kuhn, Amsel, & O'Loughlin, 1988; Siegler, 1991). Since adolescents often have more experience with certain kinds of problems than others, their level of development can vary considerably across task domains.

Return for a moment to Siegler's four developmentally ordered rules for solving the balance scale problems on page 553. Notice how each successive rule requires awareness of more variables. In addition, note the similarity of Siegler's rules to Piaget's stages. Rule I reflects the preoperational child's tendency to focus on a single element to the neglect of other important features of the task. Rules II and III resemble the concrete operational child's ability to coordinate two dimensions in a problem. And Rule IV displays the formal operational adolescent's capacity to come up with a general model that covers a wide range of similar situations. Although Piaget and information-processing theorists agree on the general direction of cognitive development, Piaget neglected the importance of a long history of effective teaching in paving the way toward abstract thought. Information processing is currently offering the field a more precise description of cognitive change than provided by Piaget's broad concepts of assimilation and accommodation (Klahr, 1992; Kuhn, 1992). In doing so, it is stimulating new methods of instruction that enhance the thinking abilities of children and adolescents.

CONSEQUENCES OF ABSTRACT THOUGHT

The development of formal operations results in dramatic revisions in the way adolescents see themselves, others, and the world in general. Adjusting to thinking on a higher plane presents as many challenges as coming to terms with the physical changes of puberty. Just as adolescents are occasionally awkward in the use of their transformed bodies, they are sometimes faltering and clumsy in the use of abstract thought. As we will see in the following sections, parents and teachers must be careful not to mistake the many typical reactions of the teenage years—argumentativeness, self-concern, insensitive remarks, and indecisiveness—for anything other than inexperience with new reasoning powers.

ARGUMENTATIVENESS

As adolescents acquire formal operations, they are motivated to use them. As a result, the once pliable school-age child becomes a feisty, argumentative teenager who can marshal facts and ideas to build a case (Elkind, 1984). "A simple, straightforward explanation used to be good enough to get Louis to obey," complained Antonio. "Now, he wants a thousand reasons. And worse yet, he finds a way to contradict them all!" Antonio was reflecting on the previous evening, when he had taken a strong stand in forbidding Louis to go to a movie with Cassie. Here is what happened:

Antonio: "Louis, no going out tonight. It's a school night, and you have homework."

Louis: "Dad, I've done most of my homework. I can do the rest before class in the morning. Besides, I fell asleep this afternoon. There's no way I'll be able to go to bed early."

Antonio: "You fell asleep because you didn't get enough rest the night before. You've been out several evenings in a row. You need to stay home."

Louis: "You never made Jules stay in on school nights when he was my age. How come you don't treat me equally?"

Antonio: "I did just the same thing with Jules. Homework is one of your responsibilities. It comes before going out on school nights."

Louis: "If it's my responsibility, then I'll take care of it. You don't need to worry about it."

Antonio: "But you're not taking care of it unless you stay home and do it."

Louis: "Dad, you're unfair! You treat Jules like an adult. You treat me like a child!"

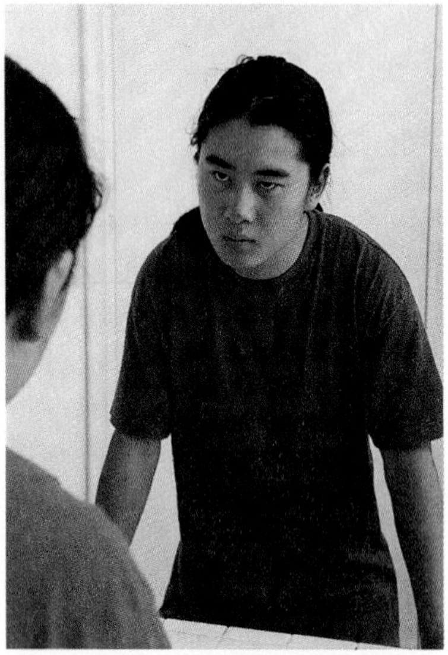

This teenager is probably wondering how she could possibly appear in public with a pimple on her nose. The imaginary audience of early adolescence has convinced her that she is the focus of everyone else's attention and concern. *(Michael Newman/PhotoEdit)*

Parents often comment that teenagers "argue for the sake of arguing," and this is very much the case. As long as parent–child disagreements remain focused on principles and do not deteriorate into meaningless battles, they can promote development. Through discussions of family rules and practices, adolescents become more aware of their parents' values and the reasons behind them. Gradually, they come to see the validity of parental beliefs and adopt many as their own (Alessandri & Wozniak, 1987).

Teenagers' capacity for effective argument opens the door to intellectually stimulating pastimes. Debate teams provide high school students with practice in reasoning effectively about both sides of controversial issues. And endless bull sessions with friends over moral, ethical, and political concerns are common during the adolescent years.

SELF-CONSCIOUSNESS AND SELF-FOCUSING

Adolescents' ability to reflect on their own thoughts, combined with the physical and psychological changes they are undergoing, means that they start to think more about themselves. Piaget believed that the arrival of formal operations is accompanied by a new form of egocentrism: the inability to distinguish the abstract perspectives of self and others (Inhelder & Piaget, 1955/1958). For a time, teenagers become very wrapped up in the importance of their own thoughts, appearance, and behavior. As they imagine what others must be thinking, two distorted images of the relation between self and other appear (see the Concept Review Table on the following page).

The first is called the **imaginary audience.** Young teenagers regard themselves as always on stage. They are convinced that they are the focus of everyone else's attention and concern (Elkind & Bowen, 1979). As a result, they become extremely self-conscious, often going to great lengths to avoid embarrassment. Sabrina, for example, woke up one Sunday morning with a large pimple on her chin. "I can't possibly go to church!" she cried. "*Everyone* will notice how ugly I look." The notion of the imaginary audience helps us understand the long hours adolescents spend in the bathroom inspecting every detail of their appearance as they envision the response of the rest of the world. It also accounts for their extreme sensitivity to public criticism. To teenagers, who believe that everyone is monitoring their performance, a critical remark from a parent or teacher can be mortifying. Adults need to

Imaginary audience
Adolescents' belief that they are the focus of everyone else's attention and concern.

CONCEPT REVIEW TABLE

Two Aspects of Adolescent Self-Consciousness

CONCEPT	IMPORTANT POINT	EXAMPLE
Imaginary audience	Adolescents' greater self-reflective capacity causes them to become overly self-conscious. They imagine themselves as always on stage, as the center of everyone's else's attention and concern.	Sabrina passed Joyce and Luella in the hallway at school, huddled together and whispering. Sabrina thought to herself, "They must be talking about me—my hair, my clothes, maybe the way I walk." She ducked into the restroom for a reassuring look at herself in the mirror.
Personal fable	Adolescents' self-consciousness leads them to develop an exaggerated view of their own importance. They regard their thoughts and feelings as special and unique. They also believe that they are invulnerable to the same dangers as others.	Louis convinced himself that he didn't need to spend much time preparing his oral report for English class. "I'll cruise through it, get inspiration on the spot. I don't have to write out and memorize this stuff," he thought. The next day, Louis was surprised to find himself stumbling over his words and groping for things to say.

be careful not to engage in faultfinding in front of others. Instead, they should wait until they can speak to the teenager alone.

A second cognitive distortion is the **personal fable.** Because teenagers are so sure that others are observing and thinking about them, they develop an inflated opinion of their own importance. They start to feel that they are special and unique. Many adolescents view themselves as reaching great heights of glory as well as sinking to unusual depths of despair—experiences that others could not possibly understand (Elkind, 1985). Sabrina, for example, wrote in her diary one day, "My parents' lives seem so ordinary, so stuck in a rut. Mine will be different. I'll realize all my hopes and ambitions." On another occasion, she had a crush on a boy who failed to return her affections. As she lay on the sofa feeling depressed, Franca tried to assure her that there would be other boys. "Mom," Sabrina snapped. "You don't know what it's like to be in love!" The personal fable may also contribute to adolescent risk taking. Teenagers who have sex without contraceptives or weave in and out of traffic at 80 miles an hour seem, at least for the moment, to be convinced of their uniqueness and invulnerability (see Chapter 14, page 531).

The imaginary audience and personal fable are strongest during the transition from concrete to formal operations. They gradually decline over the adolescent years as abstract thinking becomes better established (Enright, Lapsley, & Shukla, 1979; Lapsley et al., 1988). Some experts believe these distorted visions of the self may not represent a return to egocentrism, as Piaget's theory suggests. Instead, they may be an outgrowth of advances in perspective taking, which cause young teenagers to be very concerned with what others think (Lapsley, 1985; Lapsley et al., 1986). Take a moment to look back at Selman's stages of perspective taking on page 475 of Chapter 13. The *self-reflective* approach of late childhood and early adolescence could account for the imaginary audience and personal fable. The more objective *third-party* approach could explain their decline. Adolescents may also cling to the idea that others are preoccupied with their thoughts and feelings for emotional reasons. Doing so helps them maintain a hold on important relationships as they struggle to separate from parents and establish an independent sense of self (Lapsley, 1990, 1993).

Personal fable
Adolescents' belief that they are special and unique. Leads them to conclude that others cannot possibly understand their thoughts and feelings. May promote a sense of invulnerability to danger.

Adolescents' newfound capacity for abstraction leads them to veiw themselves and world in new ways. The blissful smile on this teenager's face suggests that he may be thinking about his own specialness or imagining a perfect world of beauty and harmony. *(Kathleen Mary Menke/Crystal Images/Monkmeyer Press)*

IDEALISM AND CRITICISM

Because abstract thinking permits adolescents to go beyond the real to the possible, it opens up the world of the ideal and of perfection. Teenagers can imagine alternative family, religious, political, and moral systems, and they want to explore them. Doing so is part of investigating new realms of experience, developing larger social commitments, and defining their own values, tastes, and preferences.

The idealism of teenagers leads them to construct grand visions of a perfect world—with no injustice, discrimination, oppression, or tasteless behavior. Then they insist that reality submit itself completely to their ideals. They do not make room for the shortcomings of everyday life. Adults, with their longer life experience, have a more jaded, realistic outlook. The disparity between adults' and teenagers' world views is often called the "generation gap," and it creates tension between parent and child. Adolescents, aware of the perfect family against which their real parents and siblings do not measure up, become fault-finding critics. Recall the research in Chapter 14, in which teenagers were paged periodically during the day. When adolescents interacted with family members, their negative moods outnumbered positive ones by 10 to 1. Here is a sample of what different adolescents were thinking about when they were beeped:

> "Why my mother manipulates the conversation to get me to hate her."
>
> "Why my brother was scraping the breading off a perfectly good veal Parmesan."
>
> "How ugly my mom's taste is."
>
> "How pig-headed my mom and dad are."
>
> "How much I really don't like my sister's hair." (Csikszentmihalyi & Larson, 1984, p. 139)

When voiced directly, these remarks make adolescents seem insensitive, unloving, and demanding. Yet teenage idealism and criticism have benefits in the long run. Once adolescents learn to see other people as having both strengths and weaknesses, they have a much greater capacity to work constructively for social change and to form positive and lasting relationships. Parents can help teenagers forge a better balance between the ideal and the real by being tolerant of their criticism while reminding the young person that all people, including adolescents themselves, are blends of virtues and imperfections (Elkind, 1984).

PLANNING AND DECISION MAKING

Adolescents, who think more analytically, handle cognitive tasks more effectively than they did at younger ages. Given a homework assignment, they are far better at *self-regulation*—planning what to do first and what to do next, monitoring progress toward a goal, and redirecting actions that prove unsuccessful (Brown et al., 1983; Piaget, 1978). For this reason, study skills improve from middle childhood into adolescence. In addition, adolescents are better at **comprehension monitoring.** While reading or listening, they continually evaluate how well they understand. Compared to younger pupils, 12- and 13-year-olds more often notice when a passage does not make sense. Rather than just moving ahead, they slow down and look back to see if they missed some important information (Garner, 1990). Their greater sensitivity to text errors means that they are more likely to revise their written work (Beal, 1990).

But when it comes to planning and decision making in everyday life, teenagers (especially young ones) often feel overwhelmed by the many possibilities before them. As a result, their efforts to choose among alternatives frequently break down.

Comprehension monitoring
Sensitivity to how well one understands a spoken or written message.

They may resort to habit, act on impulse, or not make a decision at all (Elkind, 1984). On many mornings, for example, Sabrina tried on five or six outfits before leaving for school. Her entire closet was strewn across the floor. Often she shouted from the bedroom, "Mom, what shall I wear?" Then, when Franca made a suggestion, Sabrina rejected it, opting for one of the two or three sweaters she had worn for weeks. Similarly, Louis procrastinated about registering for college entrance tests. When Franca mentioned that he was about to miss the deadline, Louis sat over the forms, unable to decide when or where he wanted to take the test. Parents may have to help with patient reminders and diplomatic suggestions until the young person gathers more experience and can make choices with greater confidence and certainty.

BRIEF REVIEW

In Piaget's formal operational stage, adolescents become capable of abstraction, as indicated by hypothetico-deductive reasoning and propositional thought. Recent research shows that the glimmerings of abstract reasoning are present in childhood, but it is not well developed until after age 11. Adolescents and adults are most likely to think abstractly in areas in which they have had extensive experience. In village and tribal cultures, formal thought often does not appear at all. These findings challenge Piaget's view of formal operations as a broad change in cognition that results from independent discovery. According to the information-processing perspective, abstract reasoning develops gradually, is specific to situation and task, and often must be directly taught.

The dramatic cognitive changes of adolescence are reflected in many aspects of everyday behavior. The ability to think in more sophisticated ways leads teenagers to become more argumentative, self-conscious and self-focused, and idealistic and critical. Because of gains in self-regulation, study skills improve. Yet in everyday life, adolescents are often overwhelmed by possibilities, and they may react impulsively and indecisively.

ASK YOURSELF . . .

- Given a problem in which weight and distance were unequal on the two sides of the balance scale, 14-year-old Andrew realized that both factors made a difference in whether the scale would balance. But he could not predict what would happen. Explain Andrew's difficulty with this problem.
- Cassie insisted that she had to have high heels to go with her prom dress. "No way I can wear those low heels, Mom. They'll make me look way too short next to Louis, and the whole evening will be ruined!" Why is Cassie so concerned about a detail of her appearance that most people would be unlikely to notice?
- Return to page 556 and review Antonio's argument with Louis over going out on a school night. What aspects of Antonio's response probably contributed to his success in getting Louis to stay home?

SEX DIFFERENCES IN MENTAL ABILITIES

Sex differences in intellectual performance have been studied since the beginning of this century, and they have sparked almost as much controversy as the racial and social-class differences in IQ that we discussed in Chapter 12. Although boys and girls do not differ in general intelligence, they do vary in specific mental abilities. Girls, as we saw in Chapter 6, are ahead in early language development. Throughout the school years, girls attain higher scores on reading achievement tests and account for a lower percentage of children referred for remedial reading instruction (Halpern, 1986; Lummis & Stevenson, 1990; Mullis et al., 1991). Girls' advantage on tests of general verbal ability is still present in adolescence. However, it is so slight that it is not really meaningful (Feingold, 1988; Hyde and Linn, 1988).

Sex differences in mathematics do not exist in the early years, but by adolescence boys start to do better than girls (Feingold, 1988; Linn & Hyde, 1989; Mullis et al., 1991). The gender gap is largest among gifted youngsters. In some widely publicized research on bright seventh and eighth graders who were invited to take the Scholastic Aptitude Test (SAT) long before they needed to do so for college admission, boys outscored girls on the mathematics subtest year after year. Twice as many boys as girls had scores above 500; 13 times as many scored over 700 (Benbow & Stanley, 1980, 1983). Sex differences in mathematics do not occur on all kinds of test items. Boys and girls do equally well on tests of basic math knowledge, and girls do better in computational skills. The difference appears on tests of mathematical reasoning, primarily in solving complex word problems (Friedman, 1989; Hyde, Fenema, & Lamon, 1990).

Some researchers believe that the gender gap in mathematics, especially the tendency for many more boys to be extremely talented in math, is genetically based. Although several hypotheses about the biological factors involved exist (including sex differences in hormones and brain lateralization), none have been confirmed by research (Benbow, 1988; Finegan, Niccols, & Sitarenios, 1992). One common assumption is that sex differences in mathematical ability are rooted in boys' superior spatial skills. But boys score higher than girls only on certain kinds of spatial tasks, and their better spatial performance is not a good predictor of mathematics achievement (Linn & Petersen, 1985).

Although evidence for the role of heredity is weak, support for the importance of environment has become increasingly strong. The mathematics gender gap is related to pupil attitudes and self-esteem. Beginning in elementary school, long before sex differences in math achievement are present, both boys and girls view math as a "male domain" (see Chapter 13, page 484). In addition, girls regard math as less useful for their future lives, perceive themselves as having to work harder at it to do well, and more often blame their errors on lack of ability. These beliefs, in turn, lead girls to take fewer math courses in high school and college. The end result of this chain of events is that girls—even those who are highly talented academically—are handicapped in developing abstract mathematical concepts and effective problem-solving strategies (Byrnes & Takahira, 1993; Linn & Hyde, 1989; Marsh, 1989).

A positive sign is that sex differences in cognitive abilities of all kinds have declined steadily over the past several decades. Today, boys are ahead of girls in mathematical reasoning by a much smaller margin than in the 1940s and 1960s. Paralleling this change is an increase in girls' enrollment in advanced high school math and science courses, a critical factor in eliminating sex differences in knowledge and skill (Mullis et al., 1991). Also, test designers are being much more careful about creating tests that are gender fair, in much the same way that they have been concerned with culture-fair testing practices in recent years (see Chapter 12).

Still, extra steps need to be taken to promote girls' interest in and confidence at doing math and science. By the end of high school, sex differences in attitudes are much larger than the gap in test performance. Clearly, many more girls have the capacity to study advanced math and science than choose to do so. Experts point out that junior and senior high school teachers need to do a better job of demonstrating the relevance of math and science to everyday life. In addition, all students benefit from encouragement and constructive feedback rather than criticism when engaged in problem solving. Finally, exposure to role models of successful women is likely to improve girls' belief in their capacity to do well at math and science.

LANGUAGE DEVELOPMENT IN ADOLESCENCE

Although language development is largely complete by the end of childhood, subtle but important changes take place during adolescence. These gains are largely influenced by cognitive changes —in particular, adolescents' improved capacity for reflective thought and abstraction.

VOCABULARY AND GRAMMAR

In Chapter 12, we saw that school-age children's vocabulary grows rapidly, and they use words more precisely and define them more clearly than they did at earlier ages. During adolescence, these trends are extended. As vocabulary expands, a wide variety of abstract words are added. Return for a moment to Jules's conversation at the beginning of this chapter. "Counterintuitive," "incredible," "revolutionized," "philosophy," "reproduction," and "justice" were among the complex words he used. Jules can define them easily and accurately. As a 9- or 10-year-old, he rarely used such words, and he had difficulty grasping their meaning.

Recall from Chapter 12 that school-age youngsters can move beyond the literal interpretation of words. They understand many metaphors (such as "spilling the beans") and other figures of speech. Formal operations permits adolescents to go further. Teenagers become masters of irony and sarcasm (Winner, 1988). "Don't have a major brain explosion," Louis commented to Sabrina when she complained about having to work on an essay for school one evening. And on another occasion, when Franca fixed a dish for dinner that Louis disliked, he quipped, " Oh boy, my favorite!" Young children sometimes realize that a sarcastic remark is insincere if it is said in a very exaggerated, mocking tone of voice. But adolescents and adults need only notice the discrepancy between the statement and its context to grasp the intended meaning (Capelli, Nakagawa, & Madden, 1990). Increased sensitivity to the nuances of language enables teenagers to read and understand adult literary works.

Adolescents also use more elaborate grammatical constructions. Their sentences are longer and consist of a greater number of subordinate clauses than those of children. In addition, they are much more effective at analyzing and reflecting on the grammar of their language. Not surprisingly, diagramming sentences is a skill reserved for the junior high and high school years.

PRAGMATICS

Perhaps the most obvious change in language at adolescence is an improved capacity to vary language style according to the situation. Teenagers talk differently depending on where they are and whom they are with—at home with their parents, out with friends, at work with the boss, or in the classroom with teachers. And they are much more aware of what should and should not be said in each of these contexts. For example, they know that in some situations (such as a job interview) it is appropriate to boast about your accomplishments, but doing so in others can lead to ridicule and rejection (Obler, 1989).

Adolescents' capacity to make subtle adjustments in speech style is partly the result of opportunities to enter many more situations in which there is pressure to do so. To be successful on the debate team, Louis had to speak in a rapid-fire, well-organized manner. In theater class, he worked on reciting memorized lines as if they were natural. At work, his boss insisted that he respond to customers cheerfully and courteously. The ability to reflect on the features of language and engage in self-regulation also supports effective use of language styles. Teenagers are far more likely than school-age children to practice what they want to say in an expected situation, review what they did say, and figure out how they could say it better (Romaine, 1984).

Adolescents' mastery of language styles is particularly apparent in their use of teen slang. Listen closely to a group of adolescents talk, and you will hear expressions like this: "That's awesome!" "She's a real airhead." "That music's really bad" (meaning it's good). "I'm completely bummed out." "She was pretty snooty 'til we all put the chill on her" (Spears, 1991). Teenagers use their slang as a sign of group belonging and as a way of distinguishing themselves from adults. Doing so is part of the process of separating from parents and seeking a temporary self-definition in the peer group. We will discuss these developments further in Chapter 16.

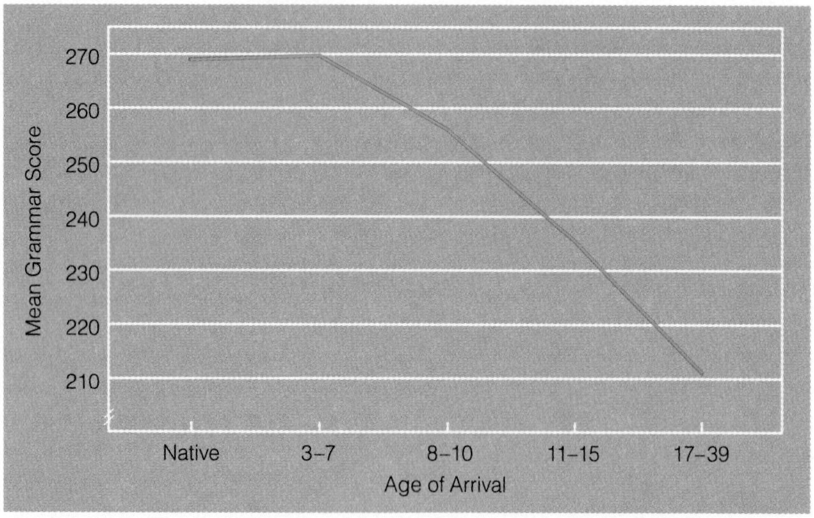

FIGURE 15.2

Relationship between age of arrival of Chinese and Korean immigrants in the United States and performance on a test of English grammar.
Individuals who began learning English in childhood attained the competence of native speakers. With increasing age through adolescence, scores declined. *(From J. S. Johnson & E. L. Newport, 1989, "Critical Period Effects in Second Language Learning: The Influence of Maturational State on the Acquisition of English as a Second Language,"* Cognitive Psychology, *21, p. 79. Copyright © 1989 by Academic Press. Reprinted by permission.)*

SECOND-LANGUAGE LEARNING

Many people assume that the best time to become bilingual is in childhood—that picking up a second language is harder during adolescence and adulthood. Research supports this widely held idea. Compared to children, adolescents and adults make faster initial progress when they move to a foreign country and must learn a new language (Snow & Hoefnagel-Höhle, 1978). But their ultimate attainment is not as high. For example, in a study of Chinese and Korean adults who had immigrated to the United States at varying ages, those who began mastering English between 3 and 7 years scored as well as native speakers on a test of grammatical knowledge. Figure 15.2 shows that as age of arrival in the United States increased through adolescence, test scores gradually declined (Johnson & Newport, 1989). The ability to pronounce a second language without an accent also decreases with age—gradually during childhood and sharply at adolescence (Anderson & Graham, 1994; Flege & Fletcher, 1992).

Research on children deprived of early language stimulation shows that there is a *sensitive period* for first-language development. That is, mastery of a native tongue must begin sometime in childhood for full development to occur (Curtiss, 1977; Mayberry, 1993). This same principle seems to apply to second-language learning. Because biological readiness for language is greatest in childhood, bilingual development is best begun at an early age. Still, adolescents can become quite competent speakers of a second language. In fact, most aspects of language continue to improve with use, well into mature adulthood (Obler, 1989).

ASK YOURSELF . . .

- Research shows that girls perform more poorly than do boys on certain formal operational tasks, such as the pendulum and balance scale problems (Meehan, 1984). On the basis of what you know about the development of formal operational thought and sex differences in mental abilities, how would you account for this finding?
- At home, Louis often created humorous parodies of the way his teachers spoke at school. Sabrina tried to do the same, but her imitations were less accurate and effective. What accounts for the skill of older adolescents in mimicking the speech mannerisms of people they know?

BRIEF REVIEW

Although girls score better than boys on tests of general verbal ability, the difference is so slight that it is not meaningful. By adolescence, boys are ahead of girls in mathematical performance, a difference related to attitudes toward math, self-perceptions of ability, enrollment in advanced mathematics courses, and use of effective problem-solving strategies. Sex differences in mathematical reasoning have declined over the past several decades, while girls' enrollment in advanced high school math and science courses has increased.

During adolescence, language continues to develop in subtle but important ways. Teenagers add many abstract words to their vocabularies. The ability to move beyond the literal meaning of words improves, and the grammatical structure of speech becomes more complex. Adolescents are better than children at modifying their language style to fit different situations. They also make faster initial progress in learning a second language, although their ultimate attainment is not as high.

LEARNING IN SCHOOL

In complex societies, adolescence coincides with entry into secondary school. Most young people move into either a middle or junior high school and then into a high school. With each change, academic achievement becomes more serious business, affecting college choices and job opportunities. In the following sections, we take up a variety of aspects of secondary school life. We also consider the serious problem of high school dropout and how well prepared American high school graduates are for life in a technologically advanced, rapidly changing world.

SCHOOL TRANSITIONS

The months after Sabrina started junior high brought a period of increased stress and strain. She left a small, intimate, self-contained sixth-grade classroom for a much larger, impersonal school. "I don't know most of the kids in my classes," Sabrina complained to her mother at the end of the first week. "Monday I have to decide where I'm going to sit at lunchtime in the cafeteria for the rest of the year, but I haven't had a chance to make any friends yet. Besides, there's just too much homework. I get assignments in all my classes at once. I can't do all this!" shouted Sabrina, bursting into tears.

IMPACT OF SCHOOL TRANSITIONS. As Sabrina's reactions suggest, school transitions can drastically alter academic and social experiences, creating new adjustment problems. With each school change—from elementary to middle or junior high and then to high school—adolescents' course grades decline. The drop is partly due to tighter academic standards. At the same time, going to a new school often causes students to readjust their feelings of self-confidence and self-worth as friendships break up, school environments become more impersonal and competitive, and academic expectations are revised (Eccles et al., 1993a). A large-scale study showed that the earlier the school transition, the more powerful and longer lasting its consequences, especially for girls (Simmons & Blyth, 1987).

Many adolescents find it stressful to move from a small, self-contained elementary school classroom to a large, impersonal secondary school. *(Will Faller)*

The researchers followed over 300 adolescents living in a large Midwestern city from sixth to tenth grade. Some were enrolled in school districts with a 6–3–3 grade organization (a K–6 elementary school, a 3-year junior high, and a 3-year high school). These students made two school changes, one to junior high and one to high school. A comparison group attended schools with an 8–4 grade organization. They made only one school transition, from a K–8 elementary school to high school.

For the sample as a whole, grade-point average dropped and feelings of anonymity increased after each school transition. Participation in extracurricular activities declined more in the 6–3–3 than in the 8–4 arrangement, although the drop was greater for girls. Sex differences in self-esteem were even more striking. As Figure 15.3 shows, boys' self-esteem increased throughout junior high and high school, except for those in 6–3–3 schools, who leveled off after entering high school. Girls in the 6–3–3 arrangement fared especially poorly. Their self-esteem declined with each school change. In contrast, their 8–4 counterparts gained steadily in feelings of self-worth throughout the secondary school years.

These findings show that any school transition is likely to temporarily depress adolescents' psychological well-being, but the earlier it occurs, the more dramatic and long lasting its impact. Girls in 6–3–3 schools fared poorest, the researchers argued, because movement to junior high tended to coincide with other life changes—namely, the onset of puberty and dating. Adolescents who must cope with added stresses, such as family disruption or a shift in residence around the time they change schools, are at greatest risk for academic and emotional difficulties (Simmons et al., 1987). Poorly achieving and poverty-stricken young people show an especially sharp drop in school performance after the transition to junior high school. These pupils are likely to turn to peers, whose values they describe as becoming increasingly antisocial, for the support they lack in other spheres of school life (Seidman et al., 1994). For some, school transition initiates a downward spiral in academic performance and school involvement that eventually leads to failure and dropping out (Eccles, 1990; Simmons, Black, & Zhou, 1991).

FIGURE 15.3

Self-esteem from sixth to tenth grade by school type for boys and girls.
In this longitudinal study of over 300 adolescents, self-esteem increased steadily for both sexes in the 8–4 school arrangement. Girls in 6–3–3 schools fared especially poorly. Their self-esteem dropped sharply after each school change. *(Adapted from Simmons & Blyth, 1987.)*

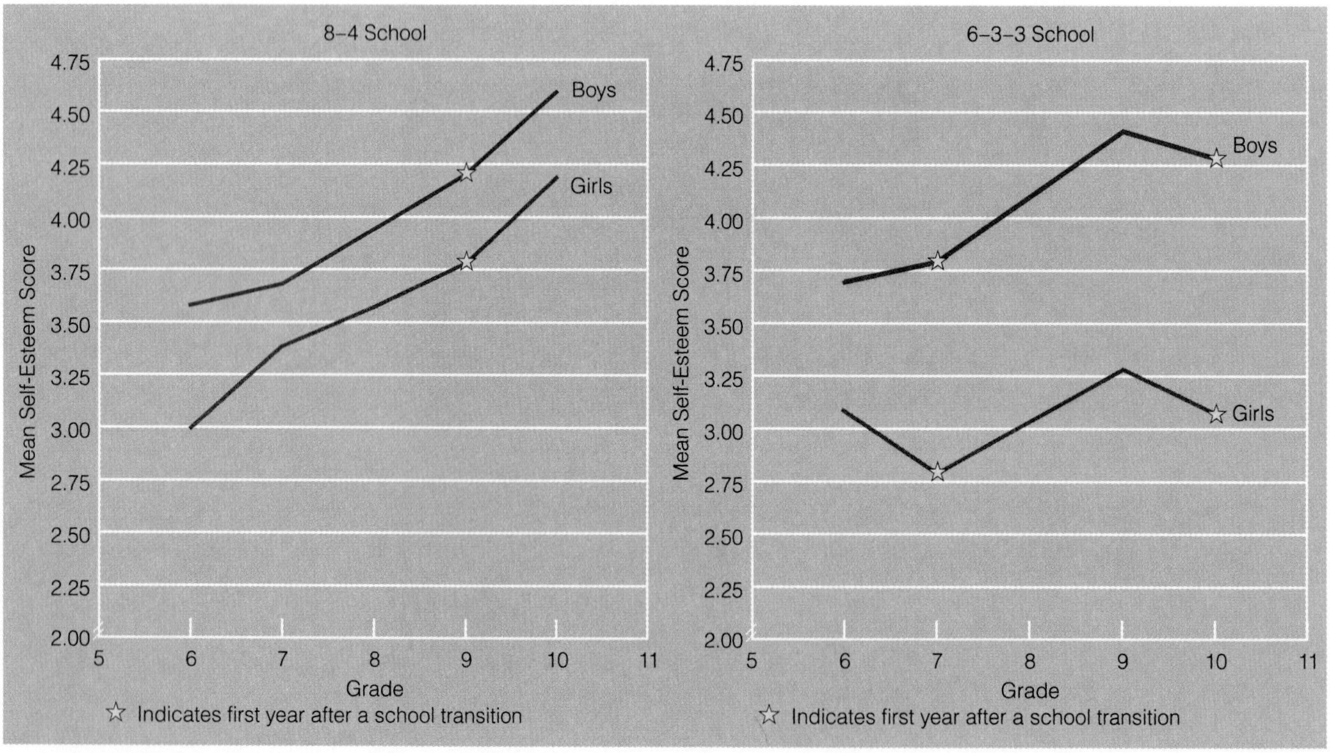

HELPING ADOLESCENTS ADJUST TO SCHOOL TRANSITIONS. Fortunately, there are ways to ease the strain of going from elementary to secondary school. Since most students do better in an 8–4 school arrangement, school districts thinking about reorganization might give serious thought to this plan.[1] When early school transitions cannot be avoided, smaller social units can be formed within large schools to relieve students' feelings of anonymity. Some schools use a "team" or "house" approach that reduces the size of the young person's reference group, permitting closer relations with teachers and peers and greater extracurricular involvement (Berk, 1992b; Eccles et al., 1993a).

Other less extensive changes in the school environment are also helpful. During the first year after a school transition, homerooms can be provided in which teachers offer academic and personal counseling and work closely with parents to promote favorable school adjustment. Students can also be assigned to classes with several familiar peers or a constant group of new peers—arrangements that promote emotional security and social support. In one study, high school freshmen experiencing these interventions showed much better academic performance and psychological adjustment at the end of the school year than did controls. These benefits were long lasting. A follow-up after 4 years revealed that only half as many students in the intervention group had dropped out of school (Felner & Adan, 1988).

Finally, successful transitions are most likely to occur in schools that foster adolescents' growing capacity for autonomy, responsibility, and control over their everyday lives. Yet entry into secondary school often means stricter control as teachers try to manage large numbers of students. Rigid school rules that strike young people as unfair and punitive frustrate their developmental needs, contributing to long-term dissatisfaction with school life (Eccles et al., 1993a; Fenzel, Blyth, & Simmons, 1990).

ACADEMIC ACHIEVEMENT

The extent to which teenagers are successful in school and, in turn, prepared for the world of work is the result of a complex array of personal and environmental forces. Generally, these factors go hand in hand and show continuity with previous development. Early on, positive educational environments, both family and school, lead to personal traits that support achievement—intelligence, confidence in one's own abilities, the desire to succeed, and high educational aspirations. In contrast, living in an environment that provides little encouragement or opportunity for success results in a decline in ability and the belief that trying hard is futile.

Table 15.1 summarizes environmental factors that enhance achievement during the teenage years. Although adolescent achievement is the result of a long history of cumulative effects, improving an unfavorable environment can help a poorly performing young person bounce back and open the door to a more satisfying adult life.

CHILD-REARING PRACTICES. Authoritative parenting (which combines warmth with reasonable demands for maturity) is linked to achievement in adolescence, just as it predicts mastery-oriented behavior during the childhood years. In research involving thousands of adolescents, the authoritative style predicted higher grades, whereas authoritarian and permissive styles were associated with lower grades. Of all parenting approaches, an inconsistent style (one that mixed authoritarian and permissive techniques) predicted the poorest school performance (Dornbusch et al., 1987).

[1]Recall from Chapter 14 (page 525) that girls who reach puberty early fare better in K–6 schools, where they are relieved of pressures from older adolescents to become involved in dating, sexual activity, and drug experimentation before they are ready. Although the 8–4 organization is best for the majority of adolescents, early maturing girls require special support under these conditions.

This parent is involved with her adolescent's school career. Besides keeping tabs on his progress, she is probably in frequent contact with the school. She sends a message to her son about the importance of education and teaches him how to solve academic problems and make wise educational decisions. *(Erika Stone)*

Why does authoritative parenting promote intellectual persistence during the adolescent years? Recall from Chapter 10 that authoritative parents carefully adjust their expectations to children's capacity to take responsibility for their own behavior. Parents who engage in joint decision making with adolescents, gradually permitting more autonomy with age, have youngsters who achieve especially well (Dornbusch et al., 1990). Open discussion accompanied by warmth and firmness makes adolescents feel competent and valued, encourages constructive thinking and self-control, and increases awareness of the importance of doing well in school. These factors, in turn, are related to independent effort and achievement among high school students (Baumrind, 1991; Carlson, Hsu, & Cooper, 1990; Wentzel & Feldman, 1993).

■ **PARENT–SCHOOL INVOLVEMENT.** Besides authoritative child rearing, parents' involvement in the adolescent's secondary school career fosters academic success. High-achieving young people typically have parents who keep tabs on their child's progress, communicate with teachers, and make sure that their child is enrolled in classes that are challenging and well taught. These efforts are just as important during junior and senior high school as they were earlier. Parents who are in frequent contact with the school send a message to their child about the importance of education, promote wise educational decisions, and model constructive solutions to academic problems. Involved parents can also prevent school personnel from placing a bright student not working up to potential in unstimulating learning situations (Grolnick & Slowiaczck, 1994; Stevenson & Baker, 1987).

When we look at these findings as a whole, they help us understand why middle-class youngsters score higher on achievement tests, earn better grades, and complete more years of schooling than their less advantaged counterparts. Teenagers from economically advantaged families are more likely to grow up in stimulating homes where parents use authoritative techniques and feel comfortable about contacting the school. But note that *within each social class,* parents who engage in these practices tend to have teenagers who perform very well (Dornbusch et al., 1990; Lamborn et al., 1991; Steinberg et al., 1992).

Secondary schools need to do a better job of increasing parent involvement during adolescence. They can do so by fostering personal relationships between parents and teachers, by showing parents how to support their adolescent's education at home, and by developing assignments that give parents a meaningful role to play (such as finding out about cultural heritage, parents' experiences while growing up, or community history). Schools can also include parents in basic planning and governance to ensure that they are invested in school goals (Eccles & Harold, 1993).

TABLE 15.1

Factors That Support High Achievement During Adolescence

FACTOR	DESCRIPTION
Child-rearing practices	Authoritative parenting
	Joint parent–adolescent decision making
	Parent involvement in the adolescent's education
Peer influences	Peer valuing of and support for high achievement
School characteristics	Teachers who are warm and supportive
	Learning activities that encourage high-level thinking

■ PEER INFLUENCES. Peers also play an important role in achievement during adolescence, in a way that is related to both family and school (Delgado-Gaitan, 1986). Adolescents whose parents value achievement are likely to choose friends who share those values (Epstein, 1983a; Kinderman, 1993). For example, when Sabrina began to make new friends in junior high, she often studied with her girlfriends and called them to check answers to homework assignments. Each girl wanted to do well in school and reinforced the same desire in the others.

Peer support for high achievement also depends on the overall climate of the school. High schools differ in the extent to which the peer culture emphasizes academic success as a route toward status and popularity. When achievement is not highly valued, students are less likely to work up to their ability (Coleman, 1961). In some schools, ethnic minority students react against working hard, convinced that getting good grades will have little payoff in the future and regarding it as a threat to their ethnic identity. In one case study of an inner-city high school, black students who did achieve were labeled as "brainiacs" and had to cope with the "burden of acting white." Many capable adolescents felt caught between achievement and peer approval and resolved the dilemma by "putting the brakes" on academic effort (Fordham & Ogbu, 1986).

When the peer culture of the high school emphasizes academic success as a route toward status and popularity, adolescents encourage high achievement in one another. *(Will Faller)*

■ SCHOOL CHARACTERISTICS. Adolescents need school environments that are responsive to their expanding powers of reasoning. Without appropriate learning experiences, the potential for abstract thought is unlikely to be realized.

Classroom Learning Experiences. Unfortunately, the transition to secondary school often brings with it less individualized attention, more whole-class instruction, and less chance to participate in classroom decision making. As a result, students report that their junior high teachers care less about them, are less friendly, and grade less fairly than did their elementary school teachers (Eccles et al., 1993b; Feldlaufer, Midgley, & Eccles, 1988). In a study focusing on math classes, researchers found that students moving from an elementary school classroom high in support to a junior high classroom low in support showed a sharp decline in their liking for and personal sense of competence in the subject. When the direction of change was reversed—that is, when students moved from classrooms low in support to ones high in support—their evaluations of themselves and attitudes toward the subject improved (Midgley, Feldlaufer, & Eccles, 1989).

The perception of many adolescents that their classes lack warmth and supportiveness is the result of a large, departmentalized school organization that makes it difficult for teachers and students to get to know each other well. Adolescents, like children, need opportunities to form close relationships with teachers. As they begin to develop an identity beyond the family, they seek out adult models other than their parents (Eccles et al., 1993a). Of course, one important reason for separate classes in each subject is that adolescents can be taught by experts, who are more likely to encourage high-level thinking. But the classroom experiences of many junior and senior high school students do not work out this way. In a study of seventh- through tenth-grade English, social studies, and science teachers with reputations for excellence, students were not equally or consistently given assignments that stimulated abstract thought (Sanford, 1985).

Because of the uneven quality of instruction in American schools, a great many seniors graduate from high school poorly equipped with basic academic skills (see the Social Issues box on page 568). Mastery of reading, writing, mathematics, and science by low-income ethnic minority students is particularly disappointing. Many attend underfunded schools with run-down buildings, outdated equipment, and textbook shortages. In some, crime and discipline have become so overwhelming that attention to these problems has taken the lead over learning and instruction (Kozol, 1991). By junior high, large numbers of poverty-stricken minority students have been placed in low academic tracks, compounding their learning difficulties.

SOCIAL ISSUES

THE NATION'S REPORT CARD: HOW ACADEMICALLY COMPETENT ARE AMERICAN ADOLESCENTS?

Over the past several decades, serious concerns have been raised about the academic competence of American youths. The scores of high school seniors on the Scholastic Aptitude Test (SAT) dropped steadily from 1963 to 1980. Over the 1980s, SAT performance showed a slow recovery, but the verbal score declined again in the early 1990s (U.S. Department of Education, 1994). Many studies indicate that low-income minority students are severely deficient in basic academic skills. And international comparisons reveal that the math and science achievement of American students falls behind that of young people in most other industrialized nations (see Chapter 12).

In response to these alarming trends, Congress mandated continuous monitoring of the performance of young Americans in various learning areas. The Nation's Report Card includes national assessments of reading, writing, mathematics, and science achievement from the early 1970s to the early 1990s. Large samples of 9-, 13-, and 17-year-olds were tested every 4 years. Although the findings point to some hopeful signs, they reveal a worrisome overall picture.

On the positive side, the Nation's Report Card shows that over 90 percent of students master basic literacy and mathematics skills by age 13. Also, the gap separating African-American and Hispanic students from white students has declined since the 1970s, due to gradual gains in achievement of ethnic minorities (Wolf, 1993). Nevertheless, accomplishments at the end of high school are disappointing. For example, in the most recent assessment, the average performance of 17-year-olds did not reach a level in reading that permitted them to understand and explain moderately complicated information. In math, it did not move beyond an intermediate level of skill required to read simple graphs and solve basic algebraic equations. Results on writing and scientific reasoning were least encouraging. Only 68 percent of 17-year-olds could prepare a clear paragraph for a job application. Only 43 percent showed some specialized knowledge of scientific principles and an understanding of experimental design (Mullis et al., 1991).

Additional information in the Nation's Report Card highlights several causes of these disappointing outcomes. Consistent with findings we have discussed in previous chapters, a stimulating home environment was related to better academic performance. But schooling also played a major role, since quality of classroom instruction was clearly associated with achievement. For example, amount of homework assigned was positively correlated with performance. By the 1980s, teachers were giving more homework than they had in previous years. Still, as many as 30 percent of high school students reported less than one hour per night, and 6 percent had none. In math, the cognitive level of most classroom teaching matched the low level of pupil performance. Math instruction rarely moved beyond memorizing basic facts and rules (Dossey et al., 1988).

By the turn of the twenty-first century, many more jobs in the United States will demand high levels of literacy and technical knowledge. American young people are clearly capable of keeping pace with their agemates in other industrialized nations. For example, when tested on material they have been taught, the academically top 20 percent of American eighth graders do just as well as their Japanese counterparts (Westbury, 1992). School reforms are currently underway, aimed at helping young people master the language, math, and science necessary to meet modern work force needs.

Effective educational change, however, must take into account the life background and future goals of students. Toughening academic standards in secondary schools will improve the competence of teenagers from economically advantaged homes. But it is likely to further discourage many low-income, poorly achieving young people, who can only fall further behind under these conditions (Parrish, 1991). In short, not all adolescents can be successfully educated for adulthood in just the same way. We will discuss this issue further in later sections of this chapter.

TRY THIS . . .

- When you next have a chance, ask several high school students to describe their previous week's assignments in English, mathematics, and science as well as the number of hours they spent on homework. Does their schoolwork seem to be appropriately stimulating and challenging?

Tracking. Ability grouping, as we saw in Chapter 12, is detrimental during the elementary school years. Students in low groups generally get poor-quality instruction. Soon they view themselves as failures, and their peers label them this way as well. Students in the same ability group typically stick together, forming separate subcultures that result in a split in the student body of the school. High-group students often feel superior, and low-group students respond with hostility and resentment. These influences severely undermine the motivation and academic progress of low-group students. At least into the early years of secondary school, mixed-ability classes are desirable. Research suggests that they do not stifle the more able students, and they have intellectual and social benefits for poorly performing youngsters (Oakes, Gamoran, & Page, 1992).

By high school, some grouping is unavoidable because certain aspects of education must dovetail with the young person's future educational and career plans. In the United States, high school students are counseled into college preparatory, vocational, or general education tracks. Unfortunately, this sorting tends to perpetuate educational inequalities of earlier years. Low-income minority students are assigned in large numbers to noncollege tracks. One study found that a good student from an economically disadvantaged family had only half as much chance of ending up in an academically oriented program as a student of equal ability from a middle-class background (Vanfossen, Jones, & Spade, 1987).

High school students are separated into academic and vocational tracks in virtually all industrialized nations. But the American system differs from those of western Europe, Japan, and China in important respects. In most of those countries, students take a national examination to determine their placement in high school. The outcome usually fixes future possibilities for the young person. In the United States, educational decisions are more fluid. Students who are not assigned to a college preparatory track or who do poorly in high school can still get a college education. But by the adolescent years, social-class differences in quality of education and academic achievement have already sorted American students more drastically than is the case in other countries. In the end, many young people do not benefit from this more open system. Compared to other developed nations, the United States has a higher percentage of high school dropouts and adolescents with very limited academic skills (Hamilton, 1990; Rohlen, 1983).

DROPPING OUT

Across the aisle from Louis in math class sat Norman, who daydreamed, crumpled his notes into his pocket after class, and rarely did his homework. On test days, he twirled a rabbit's foot for good luck but left most of the questions blank. Louis had been in school with Norman since fourth grade, but the two boys had little to do with one another. To Louis, who was quick at schoolwork, Norman seemed to live in another world.

Once or twice each week, Norman cut class, and one spring day, he stopped coming altogether. Several months later, Louis ran into Norman at the supermarket, where he had a part-time job stocking shelves.

"Norm, where ya' been? Haven't seen you at school lately," remarked Louis.

"Come on, Louis, you oughta know. There wasn't nothin' for me there. Got to the point where I just couldn't go back. I'd go to those classes, and the minute I got there I'd wanna get out. My mind just turned off, I felt so ashamed and stupid."

Norman is one of 14 percent of American young people who, by 18 years of age, leave high school without a diploma (Children's Defense Fund, 1993, 1994). The dropout rate is particularly high among low-income ethnic minority youths, especially Hispanic teenagers (see Figure 15.4). The decision to leave school has dire consequences. As Figure 15.5 shows, dropouts are far less likely to be

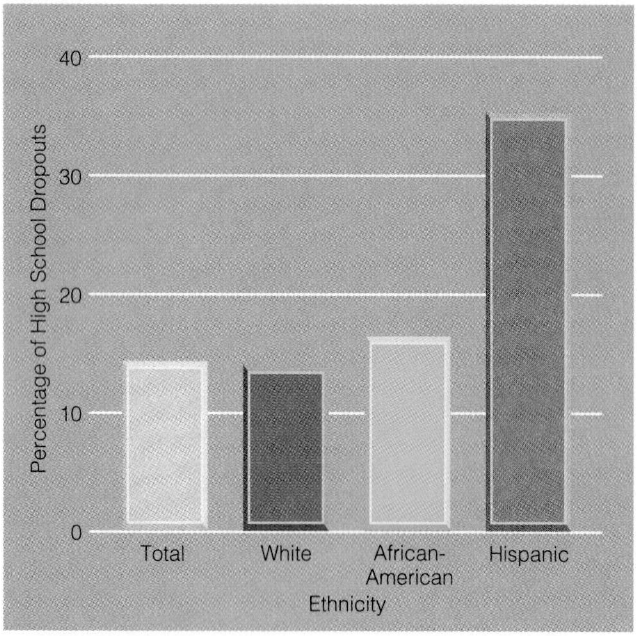

FIGURE 15.4

Percentage of high school dropouts by ethnicity.
Because African-American and Hispanic teenagers are more likely to come from low-income and poverty-stricken families, their dropout rates are above the national average. The rate for Hispanic young people is especially high. *(From U.S. Department of Education, 1994.)*

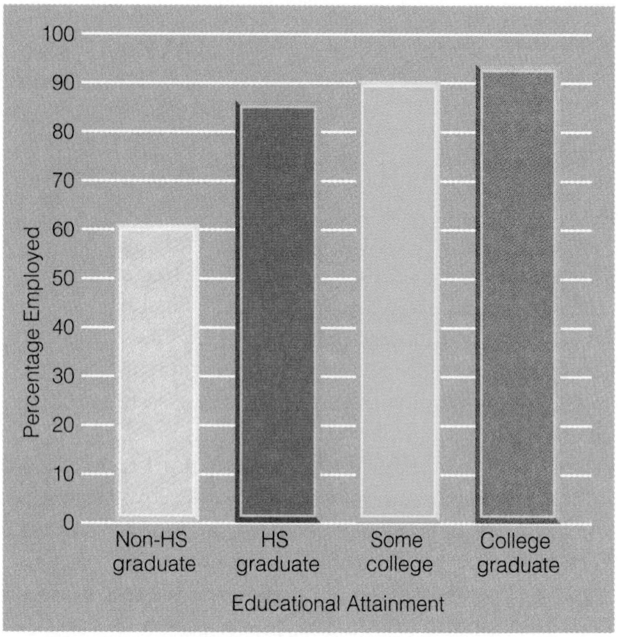

FIGURE 15.5

Employment rates of 16- to 24-year-olds by educational attainment.
Those who do not graduate from high school are much less likely to get jobs than are their counterparts with high school diplomas. Employment rates increase with years of schooling completed. *(From U.S. Department of Education, 1994.)*

employed than are high school graduates who do not go to college. And even when they are employed, they have a much greater chance of remaining in menial, low-paying jobs and of being out of work from time to time (Eccles, 1990).

■ FACTORS RELATED TO DROPPING OUT. Table 15.2 lists the many factors related to leaving school early. The more that are present at once, the greater the risk that an adolescent will drop out. Norman showed many of these signs. Because of a long history of poor school performance, his perception of his own ability was extremely low. He gave up on tasks that presented the least bit of challenge and counted on luck—his rabbit's foot—to get him by. As Norman got older, he attended class less regularly, failed to pay attention when he was there, rarely did his homework, and was a discipline problem. He didn't join any school clubs or participate in athletics. Because he was uninvolved in activities within and outside the classroom, few teachers or students got to know him well. The day Norman left, he felt alienated from all aspects of school life.

As with other dropouts, Norman's family background contributed to his problems. Compared to other students, even those with the same social class and grade profile, dropouts are more likely to have parents who are less involved in their youngster's education. Many did not finish high school themselves and are unemployed, on welfare, or coping with the aftermath of divorce. When their youngsters bring home poor report cards, these parents are more likely to respond with punishment and anger—reactions that cause adolescents to rebel further against academic work (Rumberger et al., 1990). In some instances, family members need the adolescent's assistance for health, emotional, or economic reasons and encourage the young person to leave school (Fine, 1986).

Academically marginal students who drop out often have school experiences that undermine their chances for success. Recent reports indicate that over 60 percent of adolescents enrolled in some inner-city high schools do not graduate.

TABLE 15.2

Factors Related to Dropping Out of High School

STUDENT CHARACTERISTICS	FAMILY CHARACTERISTICS	SCHOOL CHARACTERISTICS
Poor school attendance	Parents who do not support or emphasize achievement	Unstimulating classes
Inattentiveness in class	Parents who were high school dropouts	Lack of opportunity to form personal relationships with teachers
School discipline problems, especially aggressive behavior	Parents who are uninvolved in the adolescent's education	Curriculum irrelevant to student interests and needs
Inability to get along with teachers	Parents who react with anger and punishment to the adolescent's low grades	School authority structure that emphasizes the teacher; student input is discouraged
1 to 2 years behind in grade level	Single-parent household	Large student body
Low academic achievement	Low income	
A sharp drop in achievement after school transition		
Dislike of school		
Enrollment in a general education or vocational track		
Low educational aspirations		
Low self-esteem, especially academic self-esteem		
Friendships with peers who have left school		
Low involvement in extracurricular activities		
Drug use		
Law-breaking behavior		
Teenage childbearing		

Sources: Cairns, Cairns, & Neckerman, 1989; Eckstrom et al., 1986; Roderick, 1994; Rumberger, 1990; West, 1991.

These institutions are unresponsive, crime ridden, and rejecting (Kozol, 1991). Students in general education and vocational tracks, where teaching tends to be the least stimulating, are three times more likely to drop out as those in a college preparatory track (Office of Educational Research and Improvement, 1993). Some young people leave with a powerful critique of their school experiences, claiming that what happens in the classroom is unrelated to their cultural background and everyday lives. As one African-American student who dropped out of school reflected,

> I'm not smart, but I'm wise. I understand people and situations. Don't take much for me to know what's going on. I know what people be thinkin'. But I don't know what they be talkin' about in history class. (Fine, 1986, p. 402)

■ PREVENTION STRATEGIES. Many programs have been developed to help teenagers who are at risk for leaving school early. The strategies used are diverse, but several common themes are related to success:

- *High-quality vocational training.* At-risk young people often benefit from special school programs that emphasize high-quality vocational training. For many marginal students, the real-life nature of vocational education is more comfortable and effective than purely academic work. But to work well, it must carefully integrate academic and job-related instruction so students can see the relevance of what happens in the classroom to their future goals (Hamilton, 1993).
- *Remedial instruction and counseling that offer personalized attention.* Most potential dropouts need intensive remedial instruction in small classes that permit warm, caring teacher–student relationships to form. To overcome the negative psychological effects of repeated school failure, good academic assistance must be combined with social support and special counseling (Rumberger, 1990).

- *Efforts to address the many factors in students' lives related to leaving school early.* Programs that strengthen parent involvement, offer flexible work–study arrangements, and provide on-site child care for teenage mothers can make it easier for at-risk adolescents to stay in school (Comer, 1986).
- *Participation in extracurricular activities.* Another way of helping marginal students is to draw them into the community life of the school. The most powerful influence on extracurricular involvement is small school size. In smaller high schools (500 to 700 students or less), a greater proportion of the student body is needed to staff and operate activities. As a result, potential dropouts are far more likely to participate, feel needed, gain recognition for their abilities, and remain until graduation. "House" plans, which create smaller units within large schools, can have the same effect (Berk, 1992b).

These drama club members find rehearsing for a school play involving and pleasurable. Each club member contributes to a successful production. When students at risk for dropping out are drawn into the extracurricular life of the school, they feel needed, gain recognition for their abilities, and are more likely to remain until graduation. *(Will Faller)*

As we conclude our discussion of academic achievement, let's place the school dropout problem in historical perspective. Over the last half century, the percentage of American adolescents completing high school has risen dramatically—from 39 percent in 1940 to 86 percent in the 1990s. During that same period, college attendance also increased. Today, nearly 40 percent of 18- to 24-year-old high school graduates are working toward college degrees—the highest rate in the world. Finally, about one-third of all high school dropouts return on their own to finish their education within a few years, and some extend their schooling further (Children's Defense Fund, 1993). Although early school leaving is still a very serious problem, as the end of adolescence approaches, many young people realize how essential education is for a rewarding job and career.

ASK YOURSELF . . .

- Tanisha is finishing sixth grade. She could either continue in her current school through eighth grade or switch to a much larger junior high school in town. What would you suggest she do, and why?
- In a workshop for parents of adolescents, one father asks what he might do to encourage his teenage children to do well in school. Provide a list of suggestions along with the reasons they are effective.

BRIEF REVIEW

School transitions create new adjustment problems for adolescents, especially when they coincide with other life stresses. Academic achievement is the result of a complex blend of personal and environmental forces. Authoritative child rearing, joint parent–child decision making, and parent involvement in the young person's secondary school career support achievement during adolescence. Peers who value achievement and classroom environments that encourage warm teacher–student relations and high-level thinking also promote academic success. Quality of instruction is often poorest in general education and vocational tracks, which enroll a large number of low-income, ethnic minority students. Disengagement from school and dropping out are particularly high among these adolescents. For many teenagers, family background and school experiences combine to either promote or undermine academic success.

VOCATIONAL DEVELOPMENT

During late adolescence, young people face a major life decision: the choice of a suitable work role. As we will see in Chapter 16, the selection of a career is a central part of identity development for modern adolescents. This is not surprising, since paid employment and economic independence are hallmarks of adulthood in contemporary society.

Being a productive worker calls for many of the same qualities needed to be an active citizen and nurturant family member—good judgment, responsibility, dedication, and cooperation. An adolescent well prepared for work is better able to fulfill other adult roles. How do young people make decisions about careers, and what influences their choices? What is the transition from school to work like, and what factors make it easy or difficult?

SELECTING A VOCATION

In societies with an abundance of career possibilities, occupational choice is a gradual process, beginning long before adolescence. Major theorists view the young person as moving through several phases of vocational development (Ginzberg, 1972, 1988; Super, 1980, 1984).

PHASES OF VOCATIONAL DEVELOPMENT. Sabrina, Louis, and Jules are each at different points in the development of occupational plans. All three began to toy with career possibilities during early and middle childhood. Louis is further along than Sabrina in selecting a vocational direction. Jules is close to crystallizing his career choice.

1. The **fantasy period** (early and middle childhood). As we saw in Chapter 10, young children fantasize about career options through make-believe play. However, their preferences bear little relation to the decisions they will eventually make. When Sabrina announced at age 8 that she wanted to be an astronaut, a dancer, or a news reporter, her choices were determined by familiarity, glamour, and excitement. They did not include a realistic appraisal of her strengths, weaknesses, and special talents.

2. The **tentative period** (early and middle adolescence). Between the ages of 11 and 17, young people start to think about careers in more complex ways. During early adolescence, they evaluate vocational options in terms of *interests*. For example, Sabrina wrote a paper on the pyramids of Egypt and was fascinated by what she learned. For a time, she wanted to be an archeologist. One summer, she visited a national park, learned to ride horseback, and thought it would be fun to be a forest ranger.

   By mid-adolescence, young people become more aware of personal and educational requirements for different vocations. Louis weighed possibilities not just against his interests, but also against his *abilities and values*. "I like business and selling things," he said one day to Jules. "I won a prize for raising the most money for our class trip. Trouble is, I'm not a very exacting person. I'm good with people, though, and I'd like to do something to help others. So maybe social work or teaching would fit my needs."

3. The **realistic period** (late adolescence and young adulthood). By the end of the teenage years, the economic and practical realities of adulthood are just around the corner, and adolescents start to narrow their options. At first, many do so through further *exploration,* gathering more information about a set of possibilities that blends with their personal characteristics. Then they enter a final phase of *crystallization* in which they focus on a general vocational category. Within it, they experiment for a period of time before settling on a single occupation. As a college sophomore, Jules plans to enter a scientific field, but he is not sure whether he prefers chemistry, math, or physics. Within the next few months, he will decide on a major. Then he will consider whether he wants to work for a company following graduation or study further to become a doctor or research scientist.

FACTORS INFLUENCING CAREER CHOICE. Although most adolescents follow this general pattern of vocational development, there are exceptions in both timing and sequence. A few know from an early age just what they want to be and pursue a direct path to a career goal. Others keep their options open

Fantasy period
The period of vocational development in which young children fantasize about career options through make-believe play. Spans early and middle childhood.

Tentative period
The period of vocational development in which adolescents weigh vocational options against their interests, abilities, and values. Spans early and middle adolescence.

Realistic period
The period of vocational development in which adolescents focus on a general career category and, slightly later, settle on a single occupation. Spans late adolescence and young adulthood.

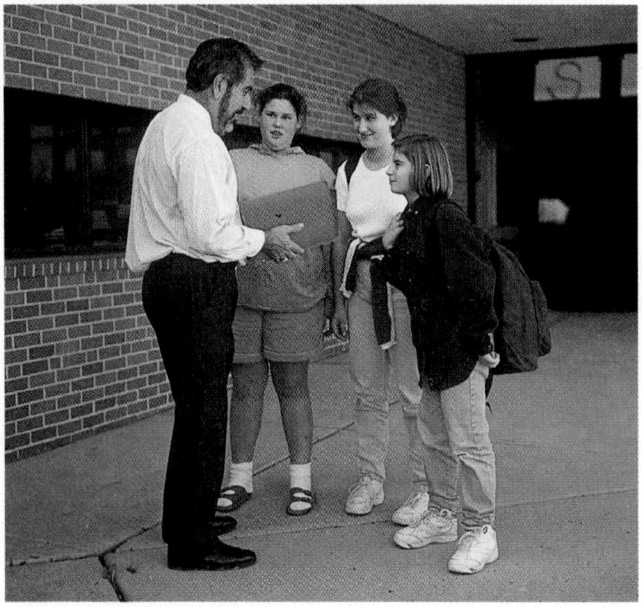

Adolescents benefit when schools encourage warm, supportive teacher–student relationships. Under these conditions, teachers serve as influential models of character and accomplishment. *(© Will Faller 1994)*

for an extended period. College students are granted added time to explore and decide. In contrast, the life conditions of low-income minority youths prevent them from having the range of choices that economically advantaged young people do.

Consider for a moment how an occupational choice is made, and you will see that vocational choice is not just a rational process in which young people match abilities, interests, and values against career options. Like other adolescent milestones, it is the result of a dynamic interaction between person and environment. A great many social influences feed into the adolescent's decision.

Family Influences. Adolescent vocational aspirations are strongly correlated with the jobs of their parents. Teenagers from middle-class homes are more likely to select high-status, white-collar occupations, such as doctor, lawyer, scientist, and engineer. In contrast, low-income adolescents tend to choose low-status and blue-collar careers—for example, plumber, construction worker, food service employee, and secretary. Parent–child similarity is partly a function of educational attainment. The single best predictor of occupational status is number of years of schooling completed (Featherman, 1980).

Family resemblance in occupational choice also comes about for other reasons. Middle-class parents are more likely to give their children important information about the world of work and to have connections with people who can help the young person obtain a high-status position (Grotevant & Cooper, 1988). Parenting practices also shape the young person's work-related values. Recall from Chapter 2 (pages 76–77) that middle-class parents tend to promote curiosity and independence, which are required for success in many high-status careers. Lower-class parents, in contrast, emphasize conformity and obedience. At work, they are used to following the directives of others (Kohn, 1977). Eventually, young people choose careers that are compatible with these values. The jobs that appeal to them tend to be like those of their parents.

Teachers. Teachers also play a powerful role in adolescents' career decisions. Jules regards his high school chemistry teacher as the most important influence on his choice of a scientific vocation. "Mr. Garvin showed me how to think about chemistry—and science in general. If I hadn't taken his class my junior year, I probably wouldn't have considered a career in science."

In one study, college freshmen were asked who had the greatest impact on their choice of a field of study. The people most often mentioned (by 39 percent of the sample) were high school teachers (Johnson, 1967, as cited by Rice, 1993). College-bound adolescents are likely to have closer relations with teachers than are other students, whose parents are more influential. These findings provide yet another reason for promoting positive teacher–student relations, especially for low-income adolescents. The power of teachers as role models could serve as an important source of upward mobility for these young people.

Cultural Stereotypes: Sex Differences in Vocational Development. Over the past two decades, high school boys' career preferences have remained strongly gender stereotyped, whereas girls have expressed increasing interest in occupations largely held by men (Sandberg et al., 1991). Changes in gender-role attitudes along with the dramatic rise in employed mothers, who serve as career-oriented models for their daughters (see Chapter 13), are common explanations for girls' interest in nontraditional careers.

At the same time, women's progress in entering and excelling at male-dominated professions has been slow. As Table 15.3 shows, the percentage of women engineers, lawyers, and doctors increased between 1972 and 1993 in the United States, but it falls far short of equal representation. Women remain heavily concentrated in the less well-paid, traditionally feminine professions of literature, social work, education, and nursing (U.S. Bureau of the Census, 1994). In virtually all fields, their achievements lag behind those of men, who write more books, make more discoveries, hold more positions of leadership, and produce more works of art (Reis, 1991).

Ability cannot account for these dramatic sex differences. As we have seen, the gender gap in cognitive performance of all kinds is small and is declining. Instead, gender-stereotyped messages from the social environment play a key role. Although girls' grades are higher than boys', girls reach secondary school less confident of their ability and more likely to underestimate their achievement (Bornholt, Goodnow, & Cooney, 1994). Between tenth and twelfth grade, the proportion of girls in gifted programs declines. Those who remain do not develop their talents to the same degree as boys, either educationally or vocationally (Read, 1991; Reis, 1991).

When high school students were asked what discouraged them from continuing in gifted programs, parental and peer pressures and attitudes of teachers and counselors ranked high on girls' lists (Read, 1991). Some parents still regard vocational accomplishment as unnecessary for girls and as risking their chances for marriage and motherhood. At times, counselors advise girls not to enroll in advanced math and science courses for similar reasons. And there is evidence that high school teachers tend to view bright male students as more capable than their female coun-

TABLE 15.3

Percentage of Females in Various Professions, 1972, 1983, 1993

PROFESSION	1972	1983	1993
Engineering	0.8%	5.8%	8.5%
Law	3.8	15.8	21.4
Medicine	9.3	15.8	20.4
Writing, art, entertainment	31.7	42.7	47.2
Social work	55.1	64.3	68.9
Elementary and secondary education	70.0	70.9	74.8
Higher education	28.0	36.3	40.9
Library, museum curatorship	81.6	84.4	83.6
Nursing	92.6	95.8	94.3

Source: U.S. Bureau of the Census, 1994.

terparts (Blaubergs, 1980; Grau, 1985). Once communicated, these beliefs can be reinforced by peers.

During college, the career aspirations of academically talented females decline further. In one longitudinal study, high school valedictorians were followed over a 10-year period—through college and into the work world. By their sophomore year, young women shifted their expectations toward less demanding careers because of concerns about combining work with child rearing and unresolved questions about their ability. Even though female valedictorians outperformed their male counterparts in college courses, they achieved at lower levels after career entry (Arnold & Denny, 1985). Another study reported similar findings. Educational aspirations of mathematically talented females declined considerably during college, as did the number majoring in the sciences (Benbow & Arjmand, 1990).

These findings reveal a pressing need for programs that sensitize parents, teachers, and school counselors to the special problems girls face in developing and maintaining high career aspirations. Research shows that academically talented girls' aspirations rise in response to career guidance that encourages them to set goals that match their abilities, interests, and values (Kerr, 1983). Models of accomplished women who combine work with motherhood are also important. Many girls are surprised to learn that married women scientists with children achieve just as much professionally as their single female colleagues do (Cole & Zuckerman, 1987).

Access to Vocational Information. Finally, all adolescents could profit from greater access to career information. In thinking about business, teaching, and social work, Louis had little notion of just what he would have to do to enter these careers. This is true for many high school students. In one study of over 6,000 high school seniors, more than one-third had only sketchy knowledge of their preferred vocation. Only about half planned to get the appropriate amount of education to reach their goals, and many selected occupations that were not compatible with their interests (Grotevant & Durrett, 1980). As we will see in the next section, the limited work knowledge and experience of American adolescents—especially those who terminate their education with a high school diploma—complicates the transition from school to career.

MAKING THE TRANSITION FROM SCHOOL TO WORK

Franca and Antonio's middle son, 18-year-old Martin, graduated from high school in a vocational track. Like 25 percent of young people with a high school diploma, he had no plans to go to college. While in school, Martin held a part-time job selling candy at the local shopping mall. He hoped to work in data processing after graduation, but 6 months later he was still a part-time sales clerk at the candy store. Although Martin had filled out many job applications, he got no interviews or offers.

Martin's inability to find a job other than the one he held as a student is typical for American non-college-bound high school graduates. His brother Jules, as a college student, will have a much easier time. Jules will emerge from school as a young adult, having profited from the advice of faculty in his major field of study, access to a wide variety of career services, and perhaps an internship in his chosen vocation.

Although high school graduates are more likely to find employment than those who drop out, they have fewer work opportunities than they did several decades ago. More than one-fourth of high school graduates younger than 20 who do not continue their education are unemployed (U.S. Department of Education, 1994). When they do find work, most are limited to low-paid, unskilled jobs. In addition, they have few alternatives to turn to for vocational counseling and job placement as they make the transition from school to work (Bailey, 1993; Hamilton, 1990).

CULTURAL INFLUENCES

WORK-STUDY APPRENTICESHIPS IN GERMANY

Rolf, an 18-year-old German vocational student, is an apprentice at Brandt, a large industrial firm known worldwide for its high-quality products. Like many German companies, Brandt has a well-developed apprenticeship program that includes a full-time professional training staff, a suite of classrooms, and a lab equipped with the latest learning aids. Apprentices move through more than 10 major divisions in the company that are carefully selected to meet their learning needs. Rolf has worked in purchasing, inventory, production, personnel, marketing, sales, and finance. Now in cost accounting, he assists Herr Stein, his supervisor, in designing a computerized inventory control system. Rolf draws a flowchart of the new system under the direction of Herr Stein, who explains that each part of the diagram will contain a set of procedures to be built into a computer program.

Rolf is involved in complex and challenging projects, guided by caring mentors who love their work and want to teach it to others. Two days a week, he attends the *Berufsschule,* a part-time vocational school. On the job, Rolf applies a wide range of academic skills, including reading, writing, problem solving, and logical thinking. His classroom learning is directly relevant to his daily life (Hamilton, 1990).

Germany has the most successful apprenticeship system in the world for preparing young people to enter modern business and industry. More than 60 percent of adolescents participate in it, making it the most common form of secondary education. German adolescents who do not go to the *Gymnasium* (college preparatory high school) usually complete full-time schooling by age 15 or 16, but education remains compulsory until age 18. They fill the 2-year gap with part-time vocational schooling combined with apprenticeship. Students are trained for a wide range of occupations—more than 400 leading to over 20,000 specialized careers. Each apprenticeship is jointly planned by educators and employers. Apprentices who complete training and pass a qualifying examination are certified as skilled workers and earn union-set wages for that occupation. Businesses provide financial support for the program because they know it guarantees a competent, dedicated work force (Hamilton, 1990, 1993).

The German apprenticeship system offers a smooth and rewarding path from school to career for young people who do not enter higher education. Many apprentices are hired by the firms in which they were trained. Most others find jobs in the same occupation. For those who change careers, the apprentice certificate is a powerful credential. Employers view successful apprentices as responsible and capable workers. They are willing to invest in further training to adapt the individual's skills to other occupations. As a result, between the ages of 18 and 20, German young people establish themselves in well-paid careers with security and advancement possibilities (Hamilton, 1990).

The success of the German system suggests that some kind of national apprenticeship program would improve the transition from school to work for young people in the United States. Nevertheless, implementing an American apprenticeship system poses major challenges. Among these are overcoming the reluctance of employers to assume part of the responsibility for youth vocational training; creating institutional structures that ensure cooperation between schools and businesses; and finding ways to prevent low-income youths from being concentrated in the lowest-skilled apprenticeship placements, which would perpetuate current social inequalities (Bailey, 1993; Hamilton, 1993). Pilot apprenticeship projects are currently under way, in an effort to solve these problems and build a bridge between learning and working in the United States.

High-quality vocational training combined with apprenticeship enables West German youths who do not go to college to enter well-paid careers around age 18. In this vocational class, academic skills are integrated with practical activities to ensure that students become competent at both. *(Owen Franken/ German Information Center)*

Most work experiences available to American teenagers consist of low-level, repetitive tasks. They do not help prepare non-college-bound young people for highly skilled, well-paid occupations. Although this adolescent receives instruction from an adult supervisor, contact between adults and teenage employees is usually rare. *(Will Faller)*

American employers prefer to hire young adults, regarding the recent high school graduate as poorly prepared for a demanding, skilled occupation. Indeed, there is some truth to this conclusion. During high school, almost half of American adolescents are employed—a greater percentage than in any other developed country. But most of these are middle-class students in pursuit of spending money rather than vocational training. Low-income teenagers who need to contribute to family income find it harder to get jobs (Children's Defense Fund, 1994).

Furthermore, the jobs adolescents hold are limited to low-level repetitive tasks that provide little contact with adult supervisors and that do not prepare them for well-paid careers. A heavy commitment to such jobs is actually harmful. High school students who work more than 15 hours per week have poorer school attendance, lower grades, and less time for extracurricular activities. They also report more drug and alcohol use and feel more distant from their parents. And perhaps because of the menial nature of their jobs, employed teenagers tend to become cynical about work life. Many admit to having stolen from their employers (Greenberger & Steinberg, 1986; Steinberg & Dornbusch, 1991).

When work experiences are specially designed to meet educational and vocational goals, outcomes are very different. Work–study programs are related to positive school and work attitudes, improved achievement, and lower dropout rates among teenagers whose low-income backgrounds and weak academic skills make them especially vulnerable to unemployment (Owens, 1982; Steinberg, 1984). Yet high-quality vocational preparation for American adolescents who do not go to college is scarce. Unlike western European nations, the United States has no widespread training system to prepare its youths for skilled business and industrial occupations and manual trades. The federal government does support some job-training programs, and funding for them has recently increased. But most are too short to make a difference in the lives of poorly skilled adolescents, who need intensive training and academic remediation before they are ready to enter the job market. And at present, these programs serve only a small minority of young people who need assistance (Children's Defense Fund, 1994).

Inspired by successful programs in western Europe, youth apprenticeship strategies that coordinate on-the-job training with classroom instruction are being considered as an important dimension of educational reform in the United States. The Cultural Influences box on page 577 describes Germany's highly successful apprenticeship system. Bringing together the worlds of schooling and work offers many benefits. These include helping non-college-bound adolescents establish productive lives right after graduation, motivating at-risk youths to stay in school, and contributing to the nation's economic growth (Bailey, 1993; Hamilton, 1993).

Although vocational development is a lifelong process, the most important period in it is adolescence. Young people well prepared for an economically and personally satisfying career are much more likely to become productive citizens, devoted family members, and contented adults. The support of families, schools, communities, and society as a whole can contribute greatly to a positive outcome.

ASK YOURSELF . . .

- What steps can schools take to help ensure that adolescents' occupational choices match their interests, abilities, values, and personal aspirations?
- In high school, Valerie wanted to become an astronomer. By her second year of college, she continued to excell in physics classes, but she gave up her dream of becoming a research scientist. What factors might have led Valerie to change her mind?

SUMMARY

PIAGET'S THEORY: THE FORMAL OPERATIONAL STAGE

What are the major characteristics of formal operational thought?

- During Piaget's **formal operational stage,** abstract thinking appears. Adolescents engage in **hypothetico-deductive reasoning.** When faced with a problem, they think of all possibilities, including ones that are not obvious, and test them against reality in an orderly fashion. **Propositional thought** also develops. Young people can evaluate the logic of verbal statements without considering them against real-world circumstances.

Discuss recent research on formal operational thought and its implications for the accuracy of Piaget's formal operational stage.

- Recent research reveals that school-age children display the beginnings of abstract reasoning, but they are not as cognitively competent as adolescents and adults. In addition, many college students and adults think abstractly only in situations in which they have had extensive experience, and formal thought does not appear in many village and tribal cultures. These findings indicate that Piaget's highest stage is reached gradually rather than abruptly and is affected by specific learning opportunities.

AN INFORMATION-PROCESSING VIEW OF ADOLESCENT COGNITIVE DEVELOPMENT

How do information-processing researchers account for the development of abstract reasoning?

- Information-processing researchers believe that gains in information-processing capacity and opportunities to acquire knowledge and cognitive strategies account for the development of abstract reasoning. According to Robert Siegler, cognitive development involves the use of increasingly powerful rules for solving problems. Providing children and adolescents with information that addresses specific flaws in their reasoning encourages them to use more advanced rules. On different kinds of structured problems, adolescents grasp formal operational abilities in a similar, step-by-step fashion.

CONSEQUENCES OF ABSTRACT THOUGHT

Describe typical reactions of adolescents that result from new abstract reasoning powers.

- Adolescents' new cognitive powers are reflected in many aspects of their daily behavior. Teenagers become more argumentative, idealistic, and critical. As they think more about themselves, two distorted images of the relation between self and other appear—the **imaginary audience** and **personal fable.** Adolescents show gains in self-regulation and **comprehension monitoring** on cognitive tasks. However, they often have difficulty making decisions in everyday life.

SEX DIFFERENCES IN MENTAL ABILITIES

Describe sex differences in mental abilities at adolescence, along with factors that influence them.

- Boys and girls do not differ in general intelligence, but they do vary in specific mental abilities. During adolescence, the female advantage in general verbal ability is very slight. Boys do better in mathematical reasoning, especially in solving complex word problems. A variety of environmental factors, including pupil attitudes, self-esteem, and problem-solving strategies, contribute to the gender gap. They stem from gender stereotyping of math as a "male domain."

LANGUAGE DEVELOPMENT IN ADOLESCENCE

Describe changes in vocabulary, grammar, and pragmatics during adolescence.

- Teenagers add many abstract words to their vocabulary and use more elaborate grammatical constructions. The capacity to think flexibly about word meanings permits adolescents to understand irony and sarcasm and interpret adult literary works. The most obvious change in language at adolescence is the ability to make subtle adjustments in language style, depending on the situation.

Compare adolescents' capacity for second-language learning to that of children.

- Compared to young children, adolescents make faster initial progress when learning a second language. However, their ultimate attainment is not as high. Biological readiness for language learning is greatest in childhood.

LEARNING IN SCHOOL

Discuss the impact of school transitions on adolescent adjustment.

- School transitions in adolescence can be stressful. With each school change, grades decline and feelings of anonymity increase. Girls experience more adjustment difficulties after the elementary to junior high transition, since other life changes (puberty and the beginning of dating) tend to occur at the same time. Adolescents who have to cope with added stresses around the time they change schools—especially poorly achieving and poverty-stricken young people—are at greatest risk for academic and emotional difficulties.

Discuss family, peer, and school influences on academic achievement during adolescence.

- A variety of interrelated environmental factors affect academic performance during adolescence. Authoritative parenting, joint parent–child decision making, and parents' involvement in the adolescent's secondary school career promote high achievement. Teenagers with parents who encourage achievement are likely to choose friends who do the same. Warm, supportive learning environments with activities that emphasize high-level thinking enable adolescents to reach their cognitive potential.
- By high school, separate educational tracks that dovetail with adolescents' future plans are necessary. Unfortunately, high school tracking in the United States usually extends the educational inequalities of earlier years.

What factors are related to dropping out of school?

- Fourteen percent of American young people leave high school without a diploma, many of whom are low-income, ethnic minority youths. Dropping out is the result of a slow, cumulative process of disengagement from school. Family and school influences combine to undermine the young person's chances for success.

VOCATIONAL DEVELOPMENT

Trace the development of vocational choice.

- During late adolescence, young people face a major life decision: the choice of a career. Vocational development moves through three phases: a **fantasy period,** in which children explore career options through play; a **tentative period,** in which teenagers weigh different careers against their interests, abilities, and values; and a **realistic period,** in which older adolescents settle on a vocational category and, finally, a specific career.

What social factors influence adolescents' vocations decisions?

- Many social influences feed into adolescents' vocational decisions. Teenagers' career aspirations are strongly correlated with the jobs of their parents. The resemblance is due to educational opportunities, modeling of vocational roles, and teaching of work-related values. Teachers often have a powerful impact on adolescents' choice of a vocation. Today, more girls express interest in occupations dominated by men. However, gender-stereotyped messages prevent many girls from reaching their career potential. Girls' vocational aspirations decline from high school into college.

What problems do American non-college-bound youths face in making the transition from school to work?

- The United States needs to help its non-college-bound high school graduates make an effective transition from school to work. Unlike western European young people, American adolescents have no widespread vocational training system to assist them in preparing for challenging, well-paid careers in business, industry, and manual trades. Of those who do find work, most are limited to low-paid, unskilled jobs.

IMPORTANT TERMS AND CONCEPTS

formal operational stage (p. 548)
hypothetico-deductive reasoning (p. 548)
propositional thought (p. 550)
imaginary audience (p. 556)
personal fable (p. 557)
comprehension monitoring (p. 558)
fantasy period (p. 573)
tentative period (p. 573)
realistic period (p. 573)

FYI...

FOR FURTHER INFORMATION AND SPECIAL HELP, CONSULT THE FOLLOWING ORGANIZATIONS:

ACADEMIC ACHIEVEMENT

The Nation's Report Card
National Assessment of Educational Progress
Education Information Branch
Office of Educational Research and Improvement
United States Department of Education
P.O. Box 6710
Princeton, NJ 08541
(800) 233-0267

A nationally representative and continuing assessment of the achievement of American students in various subject areas. Distributes reports of recent findings.

DROPOUT PREVENTION

National Dropout Prevention Center
Clemson University
205 Martin Street
Clemson, SC 29634-5111
(803) 656-2599

A center offering information on school dropout prevention and identifying high-risk youth. Provides consultation and referral services to school systems, agencies, and associations dealing with the dropout problem.

YOUTH EMPLOYMENT

Job Corps
Employment Training Administration
607 14th St. NW, Suite 610
Washington, DC 20005
(202) 537-0996

A nationwide, federally sponsored training program offering education, vocational training, and work experience to economically disadvantaged young people between 16 and 21 years of age. Serves about 3 percent of the nation's unemployed teenagers.

"The handicapped girl's dream"
Katarina Jackovic
16 years, Yugoslavia

In this painting, a teenage girl "dreams the impossible dream." Her image of a perfect, harmonious world suggests an optimistic commitment to a better reality. As adolescents search for values to have faith in, they bring a sense of idealism and hopefulness to society. Chapter 16 considers young people's efforts to define themselves and the directions they will pursue in life.

16

Emotional and Social Development in Adolescence

ERIKSON'S THEORY: IDENTITY VERSUS IDENTITY DIFFUSION

SELF-DEVELOPMENT IN ADOLESCENCE

Changes in Self-Concept • Changes in Self-Esteem • Paths to Identity • Identity Status and Personality Characteristics • Factors That Affect Identity Development

MORAL DEVELOPMENT IN ADOLESCENCE

Piaget's Theory of Moral Development • Kohlberg's Extension of Piaget's Theory • Environmental Influences on Moral Reasoning • Are There Sex Differences in Moral Reasoning? • Moral Reasoning and Behavior

GENDER TYPING IN ADOLESCENCE

THE FAMILY IN ADOLESCENCE

Parent–Child Relationships • Siblings

PEER RELATIONS IN ADOLESCENCE

Adolescent Friendships • Cliques and Crowds • Dating • Peer Pressure and Conformity

PROBLEMS OF DEVELOPMENT

Depression • Suicide • Delinquency

AT THE THRESHOLD

Louis sat on the grassy hillside overlooking the high school, waiting for his best friend Darryl to arrive from his fourth-period class. The two boys often met at noontime and then crossed the street to have lunch together at a nearby hamburger stand.

Watching as hundreds of students poured onto the school grounds, Louis reflected on what Mrs. Kemp had said in government class that day. "Suppose by chance I *had* been born in the People's Republic of China. I'd be sitting here, wearing different clothes, speaking a different language, being called by a different name, going home to different parents, and thinking about the world in different ways. Mrs. Kemp said I wouldn't have to worry about what I was going to do in life. I'd get assigned a job according to my abilities and where I was needed. Gosh, I am who I am through some quirk of fate," Louis pondered, looking around as the crowd of students picnicking on the grass grew denser.

Louis awoke from his thoughts with a start. Darryl was standing in front of him. "Hey, dreamer! I've been shouting and waving from the bottom of the hill for 5 minutes."

"Sorry," Louis responded, jumping up and joining his friend.

As they walked off, Darryl asked, "How come you're so spaced out lately, Louis?"

"Oh, just wondering about stuff—like what I want, what I believe in. My older brother Jules—I envy him. He seems to know just where he's going. Most of the time, I'm up in the air about it. You ever feel that way?"

"Yeah, a lot," admitted Darryl, looking at Louis seriously as they approached the hamburger stand. "I often think—What am I really like? Who will I become?"

Louis and Darryl's introspective remarks are signs of a major reorganization of the self that takes place at adolescence: the development of identity. Both young people are attempting to formulate who they are—their personal values and the directions they will pursue in life. As you know from earlier chapters, important changes in self-concept take place throughout childhood. But the restructuring of the self that happens at adolescence is profound. The rapid physical changes of puberty taking place on the outside prompt teenagers to reconsider what they are like as persons on the inside. And for the first time, adolescents have the capacity to think hypothetically and, therefore, to project themselves into the distant future. They start to realize how important their choice of values and goals is for their later lives.

We begin this chapter with Erikson's account of identity development and the research it has stimulated on teenagers' thoughts and feelings about themselves. The quest for identity extends to many aspects of development. Tremendous strides in moral understanding occur as teenagers imagine social systems different from their own and search for personally meaningful ideals. We will also see how adolescents' sense of cultural belonging and masculine and feminine self-images are refined during the teenage years. And as parent–child relationships are revised and young people become increasingly independent of the family, friendships and peer networks become critical contexts for bridging the gap between childhood and adulthood. Our chapter concludes with a discussion of several serious adjustment problems of adolescence—depression, suicide, and delinquency.

ERIKSON'S THEORY: IDENTITY VERSUS IDENTITY DIFFUSION

Erikson (1950, 1968) was the first to recognize **identity** as the major personality achievement of adolescence and as a crucial step toward becoming a productive, happy adult. Constructing an identity involves defining who you are, what you value, and the directions you choose to pursue in life. This search for self is the driving force behind many new commitments—to a sexual orientation (see Chapter 14), to a vocation (see Chapter 15), and to ethical, political, religious, and cultural ideals.

Identity formation actually begins long before the teenage years. Erikson regarded successful outcomes of earlier stages as paving the way toward a positive resolution of the adolescent psychological conflict, which he called **identity versus identity diffusion.** Young people who reach adolescence with a weak sense of *trust* have trouble finding ideals to have faith in. Those with little *autonomy* or *initiative* do not engage in the active exploration required to choose among alternatives. And those who lack a sense of *industry* fail to select a vocation that matches their interests and skills.

Although the seeds of identity formation are planted early, not until adolescence do young people become absorbed in this task. According to Erikson, in complex societies, teenagers experience an *identity crisis*—a temporary period of confusion and distress as they experiment with alternatives before settling on a set of values and goals. During this period, what adolescents once took for granted they question. "I've gone to church every Sunday morning since I was a little kid," Louis confided in Darryl. "Now I'm not so sure I can accept my parents' way of thinking about God." Teenagers who go through a process of inner soul-searching eventually arrive at a mature identity. They sift through characteristics that defined the self in childhood and combine them with new commitments. Then they mold these into a solid inner core that provides a sense of sameness as they move through different roles in daily life. Once formed, identity continues to be refined in adulthood as individuals re-evaluate earlier commitments and choices.

Current theorists agree with Erikson that questioning of the self's values, plans, and priorities is necessary for a mature identity, but they no longer refer to this process as a "crisis" (Baumeister, 1990). The term suggests a sudden, intense

Identity
A well-organized conception of the self made up of values, beliefs, and goals to which the individual is solidly committed.

Identity versus identity diffusion
In Erikson's theory, the psychological conflict of adolescence, which is resolved positively when adolescents attain an identity after a period of exploration and inner soul-searching.

upheaval of the self. For some young people, identity development is traumatic and disturbing, but for most it is not. "Exploration" better describes the typical adolescent's experience. Identity formation usually proceeds in a very gradual, uneventful way. The many daily choices that teenagers make—"whom to date, whether or not to break up, having intercourse, taking drugs, going to college or working, which college, what major, studying or playing, being politically active"—and the reasons for them are gradually put together into an organized self-structure (Marcia, 1980, p. 161).

The negative outcome of Erikson's fifth stage is *identity diffusion.* Some adolescents appear shallow and directionless, either because earlier conflicts have been resolved negatively or society restricts their choices to ones that do not match their abilities and desires. As a result, they are unprepared for the psychological challenges of adulthood. For example, Erikson's young adult stage centers on the development of *intimacy* (see Chapter 1, page 18). Individuals find it difficult to risk the self-sharing involved in intimacy if they are not certain that there is a firm sense of self (an identity) to which they can return.

Is there research to support Erikson's ideas about identity development? In the following sections, we will see that adolescents go about the task of defining the self in ways that closely match Erikson's description.

Accoding to Erikson, young people are best prepared for the challenges of adulthood when they have established a firm sense of identity. Is this marriage between two 15-year-olds at risk for future problems because the bride and groom have not yet had a chance to formulate their personal values and goals? *(Jeff Greenberg/The Picture Cube)*

SELF-DEVELOPMENT IN ADOLESCENCE

During adolescence, cognitive changes transform the young person's vision of the self into a more complex, well-organized, and consistent picture. Changes in self-concept and self-esteem set the stage for development of a unified personal identity.

CHANGES IN SELF-CONCEPT

Recall from Chapter 13 that by the end of middle childhood, children describe themselves in terms of personality traits, such as "I'm smart," "I'm shy," or "I'm honest." This change permits young people to establish links between their past, present, and future selves. But the self-statements of early adolescents are not interconnected, and sometimes they even include contradictory descriptions. For example, 12-year-olds might mention such opposing traits as "smart" and "dumb" or "shy" and "outgoing." When the inconsistency is pointed out, they are disturbed by it, but they cannot yet explain or resolve it (Damon & Hart, 1988).

By middle to late adolescence, teenagers combine their various traits into an organized system. In describing themselves, they begin to use qualifiers ("I have a *fairly* quick temper," "I'm *not thoroughly* honest"), which reveal their awareness that psychological qualities often change from one situation to the next (Barenboim, 1977). Older adolescents also add integrating principles, which make sense out of apparent contradictions. For example, one young person remarked, "I'm very adaptable. When I'm around my friends, who think that what I say is important, I'm very talkative; but around my family I'm quiet because they're never interested enough to really listen to me" (Damon, 1990, p. 88).

Compared to school-age children, teenagers also place more emphasis on social virtues, such as being friendly, considerate, kind, and cooperative. Adolescents, as we have seen, are very preoccupied with being liked and viewed positively by others, and their statements about themselves reflect this concern (Rosenberg, 1979). In addition, personal and moral values appear as key themes in older adolescents' self-concepts. For example, here is how one 16-year-old boy named Ben described himself in terms of honesty to himself and others:

Recognise opposing traits

qualifiers

emphasis on social virtues

Personal & moral values appear.

> I like being honest like with yourself and with everyone. . . . [A person] could be, in the eyes of everyone else the best person in the world, but if I knew they were lying or cheating, in my eyes they wouldn't be. . . . When I'm friendly, it's more to tell people that it's all right to be yourself. Not necessarily don't conform, but just whatever you are, you know, be happy with that. . . . So I'm not an overly bubbly person that goes around, "Hi, how are you?" . . . But if someone wants to talk to me, you know, sure. I wouldn't like, not talk to someone. (Damon & Hart, 1988, pp. 120–121)

Ben's well-integrated account of his personal traits and values is quite different from the fragmented, listlike self-descriptions of children (see Chapter 13, page 467). As adolescents' views of themselves are revised to include enduring beliefs and plans, they move toward the kind of unity of self that Erikson described in his theory of identity development.

CHANGES IN SELF-ESTEEM

Self-esteem, the evaluative side of self-concept, is also modified during the teenage years. In Chapter 13, we showed that during middle childhood, children form separate self-evaluations—academic competence, physical ability, and social self-worth—and combine them into an overall opinion of themselves. During adolescence, self-esteem differentiates further. Several new dimensions are added—close friendship, romantic appeal, and job competence—that reflect important concerns of this new period (Harter, 1990).

Level of self-esteem changes as well. Turn back to Figure 15.4 on page 570, and you will see that except for a temporary decline associated with school transition, self-esteem is on the rise for most adolescents (Nottelmann, 1987). This steady increase is yet another reason that modern researchers question the assumption that adolescence is a time of emotional turmoil. To the contrary, the rise in self-worth suggests that for most young people, becoming an adolescent leads to feelings of pride and self-confidence (Powers, Hauser, & Kilner, 1989). This is true not just in the United States, but around the world. A study of self-esteem in 10 industrialized countries showed that the majority of teenagers had an optimistic outlook on life, a positive attitude toward school and work, and faith in their ability to cope with life's problems (Offer, 1988).

+ attitude

Of course, as we already saw in Chapters 14 and 15, adolescents vary widely in self-esteem. Those who are off time in pubertal development, who are heavy drug users, and who fail in school feel poorly about themselves. Look back at Figure 15.4 once more, and you will see that girls score lower than boys in overall sense of self-worth. In addition, of those young people whose self-esteem drops during adolescence, most are girls (Block & Robins, 1994). Recall that teenage girls worry more about their physical appearance and feel more insecure about their abilities. Another factor related to self-esteem is social class. Economically advantaged teenagers evaluate themselves more positively than do low-income adolescents for several reasons—because they are more likely to experience authoritative parenting, to receive positive feedback from teachers, and to perform well academically (Rosenberg, Schooler, & Schoenbach, 1989).

At the same time, the context in which adolescents find themselves can modify these group differences. Adolescents who attend schools or live in neighborhoods where their social class or ethnic group is well represented have fewer self-esteem problems. For example, the self-esteem of African-American, Jewish, and Catholic teenagers is higher in schools where there are many students of the same background than in those where there are just a few (Rosenberg, 1975). Schools and communities that are accepting of the young person's cultural heritage support a positive sense of self-worth. And as we will see shortly, they foster the development of a solid and secure personal identity as well.

CONCEPT REVIEW TABLE

The Four Identity Statuses

CONCEPT	IMPORTANT POINT	EXAMPLE
Identity achievement	Having already explored alternatives, identity-achieved individuals are committed to a clearly formulated set of self-chosen values and goals. They feel a sense of psychological well-being, of sameness through time, and of knowing where they are going.	When asked how willing she would be to give up going into her chosen occupation if something better came along, Darla responded, "Well, I might, but I doubt it. I've thought long and hard about law as a career. I'm pretty certain it's for me."
Moratorium	The word moratorium means delay or holding pattern. These individuals have not yet made definite commitments. They are in the process of exploration—gathering information and trying out activities, with the desire to find values and goals to guide their life.	When asked if he had ever had doubts about his religious beliefs, Ramon said, "Yes, I guess I'm going through that right now. I just don't see how there can be a god and yet so much evil in the world."
Identity foreclosure	Identity-foreclosed individuals have committed themselves to values and goals without taking time to explore alternatives. Instead, they accept a ready-made identity that authority figures (usually parents but sometimes teachers, religious leaders, or romantic partners) have chosen for them.	When asked if she had ever reconsidered her political beliefs, Hillary answered, "No, not really, our family is pretty much in agreement on these things."
Identity diffusion	Identity-diffused individuals lack clear direction. They are not committed to values and goals, nor are they actively trying to reach them. They may have never explored alternatives, or they may have tried to do so but found the task too threatening and overwhelming.	When asked about his attitude toward nontraditional gender roles, Joel responded, "Oh, I don't know. It doesn't make much difference to me. I can take it or leave it."

PATHS TO IDENTITY

Adolescents' well-organized self-descriptions and expanded sense of self-esteem provide the cognitive foundation for forming an identity. Still, young people need to make further choices and harmonize them with other aspects of the self. Using a clinical interviewing procedure, researchers have grouped adolescents into four categories, called *identity statuses,* which show the progress they have made toward formulating a mature identity (Marcia, 1980). The Concept Review Table above summarizes these identity statuses: **identity achievement, moratorium, identity foreclosure**, and **identity diffusion.**

Adolescents often shift from one status to another until identity is achieved. For example, in junior high school, Louis accepted his parents' religious beliefs (foreclosure) and gave only passing thought to a vocational direction (diffusion). In high school, he started to actively explore these identity issues. Research shows that many young people follow this pattern. They start out as identity foreclosed and diffused, but by late adolescence they have moved toward moratorium and identity achievement (Archer, 1982; Meilman, 1979). College triggers increased exploration as young people are exposed to new career options and lifestyles. Most teenagers who go to work after high school graduation settle on a self-definition earlier than do college-bound youths (Munro & Adams, 1977). But those who find it difficult to realize their occupational goals because of lack of training or vocational choices (see Chapter 15) are at risk for identity diffusion (Archer, 1989b).

Identity achievement
The identity status of individuals who have explored and committed themselves to self-chosen values and occupational goals.

Moratorium
The identity status of individuals who are exploring alternatives in an effort to find values and goals to guide their life.

Identity foreclosure
The identity status of individuals who have accepted ready-made values and goals that authority figures have chosen for them.

Identity diffusion
The identity status of individuals who do not have firm commitments to values and goals and are not actively trying to reach them.

At one time, researchers thought that adolescent girls postponed the task of establishing an identity and, instead, focused their energies on Erikson's sixth stage, intimacy development. We now know that this is not the case. Girls do show more sophisticated reasoning in identity areas related to intimacy, such as sexuality and family–career priorities. In this respect, they are actually ahead of boys in identity development. Otherwise, the process and timing of identity formation is the same for boys and girls (Archer, 1989a; Archer & Waterman, 1994; Streitmatter, 1993).

IDENTITY STATUS AND PERSONALITY CHARACTERISTICS

According to Erikson, identity achievement and moratorium are psychologically healthy routes to a mature self-definition, whereas foreclosure and diffusion are maladaptive. Studies of personality characteristics associated with the four identity statuses support this conclusion. Young people who are identity achieved or actively exploring have a higher sense of self-esteem, are more likely to engage in abstract and critical thinking, report greater similarity between their ideal self (what they hoped to become) and their real self, and are more advanced in moral reasoning (Dellas & Jernigan, 1990; Marcia, 1980, p. 81). Also, identity-achieved individuals are less self-conscious and self-focused and more secure about revealing their true selves to others (Adams, Abraham, & Markstrom, 1987).

+ aspects of identity achievement & moratorium. *

Adolescents who get stuck in either foreclosure or diffusion have adjustment

CULTURAL INFLUENCES

IDENTITY DEVELOPMENT AMONG ETHNIC MINORITY ADOLESCENTS

Although Franca and Antonio's four children were aware of their Italian ancestry, it was not a matter of intense concern for them. The values of their home life were consistent with those of mainstream American culture, and Sabrina, Louis, Martin, and Jules blended easily into classroom and peer life. In this respect, they resemble the majority of American white adolescents, for whom ethnicity does not prompt intense identity exploration (Phinney, 1993).

But for teenagers who are members of minority groups, ethnicity is a central part of the quest for identity, and it presents difficult, sometimes overwhelming challenges. Different skin colors, native languages, and neighborhoods set minority youths apart from the majority and increase the prejudices to which they are exposed. As they develop cognitively and become more sensitive to feedback from the social environment, they become painfully aware that they are targets of discrimination and inequality. The discovery complicates their efforts to develop a sense of cultural belonging and personally meaningful life goals. One African-American journalist, looking back on his own adolescence, remarked, "If you were black, you didn't quite measure up . . . . you didn't see any black people doing certain things, and you couldn't rationalize it. I mean, you don't think it out but you say, 'Well, it must mean that white people are better than we are. Smarter, brighter—whatever' " (Monroe, Goldman, & Smith, 1988, pp. 98–99).

Minority youths often feel caught between the standards of the larger society and the traditions of their culture of origin. Some respond by rejecting aspects of their ethnic background. In one study, Asian-American 15- to 17-year-olds were more likely than blacks and Hispanics to hold negative attitudes toward their subcultural group. Perhaps the absence of a social movement stressing ethnic pride of the kind available to black and Hispanic teenagers underlies this finding. Asian-American young people in this study had trouble naming well-known personalities who might serve as ethnic role models (Phinney, 1989). Some Asian parents are overly restrictive of their teenagers out of fear that assimilation into the larger society will undermine cultural traditions, and their youngsters rebel. One Southeast Asian refugee described his daughter's behavior, "She complains about going to the Lao temple on the weekend and instead joined a youth group in a neighborhood Christian Church. She refused to wear traditional dress on the Lao New Year. The girl is setting a very bad example for her younger sisters and brothers" (Nidorf, 1985, pp. 422–423).

Other minority teenagers react to years of shattered self-esteem, school failure, and barriers to success in the American mainstream by defining themselves in contrast to majority values. A Mexican-American teenager who had given up on school commented, "Mexicans don't have a chance to go on to college and make something of themselves." Another, difficulties. Foreclosed individuals tend to be dogmatic, inflexible, and intolerant. Some use their commitments in a defensive way, regarding any difference of opinion as a threat (Frank, Pirsch, & Wright, 1990). Most are afraid of rejection by people on whom they depend for affection and self-esteem. A few foreclosed teenagers who are alienated from their families and society may join cults or other extremist groups, uncritically adopting a way of life that is different from their past.

Long-term diffused teenagers are the least mature in identity development. They typically entrust themselves to luck or fate, have an "I don't care" attitude, and tend to go along with whatever the "crowd" is doing at the moment. As a result, they are most likely to use and abuse drugs. At the heart of their apathy and impulsiveness is often a sense of hopelessness about the future (Archer & Waterman, 1990). Racial, ethnic, and religious prejudices are typical of both foreclosed and diffused young people. The foreclosed teenager tends to pick them up from authority figures, the diffused young person from peers (Streitmatter & Pate, 1989).

FACTORS THAT AFFECT IDENTITY DEVELOPMENT

Adolescent identity is the beginning of a lifelong process of refinement in personal commitments. In a fast-paced, changing world, individuals need to retain the capacity to engage in moratorium–achievement cycles throughout life (Archer, 1989b). A wide variety of factors influence identity development.

responding to the question of what it takes to be a successful adult, mentioned "being on the streets" and "knowing what's happening." He pointed to his uncle, leader of a local gang, as an example (Matute-Bianche, 1986, p. 250–251).

The challenges minority youths face in blending mainstream with ethnic-group values are also apparent in the experiences of academically successful African-American adolescents. To avoid being labeled white by their peers, they frequently try to conceal their abilities and accomplishments (Clark, 1991). Because it is painful and confusing, many minority high school students dodge the task of forming an ethnic identity. As many as 50 percent are diffused or foreclosed on ethnic identity issues (Phinney, 1989).

How can society help minority adolescents resolve identity conflicts constructively? A variety of efforts are relevant, including reducing poverty, promoting effective parenting, and ensuring that schools respect minority youths' ethnic heritage and unique learning styles. Minority adolescents who are ethnic-identity achieved—who have explored and adopted values from both their primary culture and the dominant culture—tend to be achieved in other areas of identity as well. They also have a higher sense of self-esteem, a greater sense of mastery over the environment, and more positive family and peer relations (Phinney, 1989; Phinney & Alipuria, 1990). These findings support the notion that promoting the ethnic identity of minority youths enhances many aspects of emotional and social adjustment.

Finally, lack of concern by many white adolescents with their own ethnic origins (other than American) implies a view of the social world that is out of touch with the pluralistic nature of American society. The racial and ethnic distinctions with which most of us are familiar (African-American, Asian-American, Caucasian, Hispanic, and Native-American) oversimplify the rich cultural diversity of the American populace (Spencer & Dornbusch, 1990). Interventions that increase the multicultural sensitivity of white teenagers lead to greater awareness of their own ethnic heritage. And majority adolescents who are secure in their own ethnic identity are less likely to hold negative stereotypes of their minority peers (Rosenthal, 1987; Rotheram-Borus, 1993).

These Mexican-American girls dress in traditional costume and perform traditional Mexican dances at a fiesta in a large Texas city. When minority youths encounter respect for their cultural heritage in schools and communities, they are more likely to retain ethnic values and customs as an important part of their identities. *(Bob Daemmrich/The Image Works)*

1. Cognitive processes
2. School + communities which offer opportunity
3. Culture + time.

Cognitive processes play an important role. Although the attainment of formal operations is not related to identity status, how adolescents grapple with competing beliefs and values makes a difference. Those who assume that absolute truth is always attainable tend to be foreclosed, whereas those who lack confidence in the prospect of ever knowing anything with certainty are more often identity diffused or in a state of moratorium. Adolescents who have come to appreciate that rational criteria can be used to choose among alternative visions are likely to have joined the ranks of the identity achieved (Boyes & Chandler, 1992).

Recall from Chapter 7 that toddlers with a healthy sense of self have mothers who provide both emotional support and freedom to explore. A similar link between parenting and identity exists at adolescence. When the family serves as a "secure base" from which teenagers can confidently move out into the wider world, identity development is enhanced. Adolescents who feel attached to their parents but who are also free to voice their own opinions tend to be identity achieved or in a state of moratorium (Grotevant & Cooper, 1985; Lapsley, Rice, & FitzGerald, 1990). Foreclosed teenagers usually have close bonds with parents, but they lack opportunities for healthy separation. And diffused young people report the lowest levels of warm, open communication at home (Papini, Micka, & Barnett, 1989).

Identity development also depends on schools and communities that provide young people with rich and varied opportunities for exploration. Erikson (1968, p. 132) noted that it is "the inability to settle on an occupational identity which most disturbs young people." Classrooms that promote high-level thinking, extracurricular and community activities that enable teenagers to take on responsible roles, and vocational training programs that immerse adolescents in the real world of adult work foster identity achievement. A chance to talk with adults and older peers who have worked through identity questions can also help young people resolve doubts about identity-related matters (Waterman, 1989).

Finally, the larger cultural context and historical time period affect identity development. Among modern adolescents, exploration and commitment take place earlier in the identity domains of vocational choice and gender-role preference than in religious and political values. Yet a generation ago, when the Vietnam War divided Americans and disrupted the lives of thousands of young people, the political beliefs of American youths took shape sooner (Archer, 1989b; Waterman, 1985). Societal forces are also responsible for the special problems that ethnic minority adolescents face in forming a secure personal identity, as the Cultural Influences box on pages 588–589 describes.

ASK YOURSELF . . .

- Return to the opening section of this chapter, and review the conversation between Louis and Darryl. What identity status best characterizes the two boys? Explain your answer.
- Jules is an identity-achieved young person, secure in his self-chosen values and future goals. What have you learned about Franca and Antonio's parenting style in previous chapters that helps explain Jules's adaptive approach to identity formation?

BRIEF REVIEW

Erikson's stage of identity versus identity diffusion recognizes the formation of a coherent set of values and life plans as the major personality achievement of adolescence. An organized self-concept and more differentiated sense of self-esteem prepare the young person for constructing an identity. For most teenagers, self-worth rises over the adolescent years, and the identity task does not spark a serious emotional crisis. Four identity statuses describe the degree of progress adolescents have made toward forming a mature identity. Identity achievement and moratorium are adaptive statuses associated with positive personality characteristics. Teenagers in a long-term state of identity foreclosure or diffusion tend to have adjustment difficulties. Identity development is fostered by the young person's realization that rational procedures can be used to choose among competing beliefs and values, by parents who provide emotional support and freedom to explore, by schools and communities that are rich in opportunities, and by societies that permit people from all backgrounds to realize their personal goals.

MORAL DEVELOPMENT IN ADOLESCENCE

Sabrina sat at the kitchen table reading the Sunday newspaper, her face wide-eyed with interest. "You gotta see this," she said to Louis, who sat munching cereal across from her. Sabrina held up a page of large photos, which showed a 70-year-old woman standing in the center of her home. The floor and furniture were piled with belongings, including stacks of newspapers, cardboard boxes, tin cans, glass containers, food, clothing, and other items. A bare lightbulb with exposed wiring hung from the ceiling. The plaster on the walls was crumbling, the pipes in the house were frozen, and the sinks, toilet, and furnace no longer worked. The headline read: "Loretta Perry: My Life Is None of Their Business."

"Look what they're trying to do to this poor lady," exclaimed Sabrina. "They wanna throw her out of her house and tear it down! Those city inspectors must not care about anyone. Here it says, 'Mrs. Perry has devoted much of her life to helping veterans and doing favors for people.' Why doesn't someone help *her?*"

"Sabrina, you missed the point," Louis responded. "Mrs. Perry is in violation of 30 building code standards. The law says you're supposed to keep your house clean and in good repair."

"But Louis, she's old and she needs help. She says her life will be over if they destroy her home."

"The building inspectors aren't being mean, Sabrina. Mrs. Perry is stubborn. She refuses to obey the law. By not taking care of her house, she's not just a threat to herself. She's a danger to her neighbors, too. Suppose her house caught on fire. You can't live around other people and say your life is nobody's business."

"You don't just knock someone's home down," Sabrina replied angrily. "Where're her friends and neighbors in all this? Why aren't they over there fixing up that house? You're like those building inspectors, Louis. You've got no feeling!"

Louis and Sabrina's disagreement over Mrs. Perry's plight illustrates the tremendous advances in moral understanding during adolescence. Changes in cognition and social experience permit young people to better understand larger social structures—societal institutions and lawmaking systems—that govern moral responsibilities. As their grasp of social arrangements expands, adolescents' ideas about what ought to be done when the needs and desires of people are in conflict also change, toward increasingly just, fair, and balanced solutions to moral problems (Rest, 1983).

PIAGET'S THEORY OF MORAL DEVELOPMENT

The most influential approach to moral development is Lawrence Kohlberg's cognitive-developmental perspective, which was inspired by Piaget's early work on the moral judgment of the child. Piaget (1932/1965) saw children as moving through two broad stages of moral understanding (see Table 16.1 for a summary).

Piaget's first stage is **heteronomous morality,** which extends from about 5 to 10 years of age. The word *heteronomous* means under the authority of another. As the term suggests, children of this stage view rules as handed down by authorities (God, parents, and teachers), as having a permanent existence, as unchangeable, and as requiring strict obedience. Also, in judging an act's wrongness, they focus on objective consequences rather than intent to do harm. When asked to decide which child is naughtier—John, who accidentally breaks 15 cups while on his way to dinner or Henry, who breaks 1 cup while stealing some jam—a 6- or 7-year-old chooses John.

According to Piaget, around age 10 children make the transition to **autonomous morality.** They realize that people can have different perspectives on moral matters and that the intentions of others, not just the outcomes of their actions, should serve as the basis for judging behavior. Piaget believed that improvements in per-

Heteronomous morality
Piaget's first stage of moral development, in which children view moral rules as permanent features of the external world that are handed down by authorities and cannot be changed. Extends from about 5 to 10 years of age.

Autonomous morality
Piaget's second stage of moral development, in which children view rules as flexible, socially agreed-on principles that can be revised when there is a need to do so. Begins around age 10.

TABLE 16.1

Piaget's Stages of Moral Understanding

STAGE	AGE RANGE	DESCRIPTION
Heteronomous	5–10	Younger children view rules as fixed, external features of the world that are handed down by authority figures and that should be unquestioningly obeyed. They judge acts as bad on the basis of physical consequences rather than intentions.
Autonomous	10–adult	Older children and adolescents view rules as socially agreed-on principles than can be changed, based on the standard of reciprocity. They take into account intentions when judging moral action.

spective taking, which result from cognitive development and opportunities to interact with peers, are responsible for this change. Autonomous individuals no longer view rules as fixed. Instead, they regard them as socially agreed-on principles that can be revised when there is a need to do so. In creating and changing rules, older children and adolescents use a standard of fairness called *reciprocity.* They express the same concern for the welfare of others as they do for themselves. Most of us are familiar with reciprocity in the form of the Golden Rule: "Do unto others as you would have them do unto you."

Take a moment to consider Piaget's theory in light of what you learned about moral development in earlier chapters. You will see that his account of young children as rigid, external, and focused on physical consequences underestimates their moral capacities. Even preschoolers do not view all rules of authority figures with equal reverence and respect. They believe that moral matters are more important than social conventions (see Chapter 10), and they regard an authority's power as legitimate only in certain situations (Laupa, 1994). In middle childhood, children work out remarkably sophisticated ideas about distributive justice (how to divide up goods fairly) that are based on reciprocity (see Chapter 13). And when questioned about moral issues in a way that makes a person's intentions stand out as strongly as the harm they do, preschool and early school-age children are quite capable of judging ill-intentioned people as naughtier than well-intentioned ones (Nelson-Le Gall, 1985; Yuill & Perner, 1988).

Nevertheless, Piaget's account of morality, like his cognitive theory, does describe the general direction of moral development. Although children are less rigid moral thinkers than Piaget made them out to be, they are not as advanced as adolescents and adults. Over the past two decades, Piaget's groundbreaking work has been replaced by Kohlberg's more comprehensive theory, which regards moral development as extending beyond childhood into adolescence and adulthood in a six-stage sequence.

KOHLBERG'S EXTENSION OF PIAGET'S THEORY

Kohlberg used a clinical interviewing procedure to study the development of moral understanding. He gave children, adolescents, and adults **moral dilemmas**—stories that present a genuine conflict between two moral values. Participants were asked to indicate what the main actor should do and why. The best known of these is the "Heinz dilemma," which presents a choice between the value of obeying the law (not stealing) and the value of human life (saving a dying person):

Moral dilemma
A conflict situation presented to individuals who are asked to decide both what the main actor should do and why. Used to assess the development of moral reasoning.

> In Europe a woman was near death from cancer. There was one drug that the doctors thought might save her. A druggist in the same town had discovered it, but he was charging ten times what the drug cost him to make. The sick woman's husband, Heinz, went to everyone he knew to borrow the money, but

he could only get together half of what it cost. The druggist refused to sell it cheaper or let Heinz pay later. So Heinz got desperate and broke into the man's store to steal the drug for his wife. Should Heinz have done that? Why? (paraphrased from Colby et al., 1983, p. 77)

Kohlberg emphasized that it is *the way an individual reasons* about the dilemma, not *the content of the response* (whether to steal or not to steal), that determines moral maturity. Individuals who believe Heinz should take the drug and those who think he should not can be found at each of Kohlberg's first four stages. At the highest two stages, moral reasoning and content come together. Given a choice between obeying the law and preserving individual rights, the most advanced moral thinkers support individual rights (in the Heinz dilemma, stealing the drug to save a life). As we look at development in Kohlberg's scheme, we will see that moral reasoning and content are at first independent, but eventually they are integrated into a coherent ethical system (Kohlberg, Levine, & Hewer, 1983). Does this remind you of adolescents' effort to formulate a sound, well-organized set of personal values in identity development? According to some theorists, the development of identity and moral understanding are part of the same process (Davidson & Youniss, 1991; Marcia, 1988).

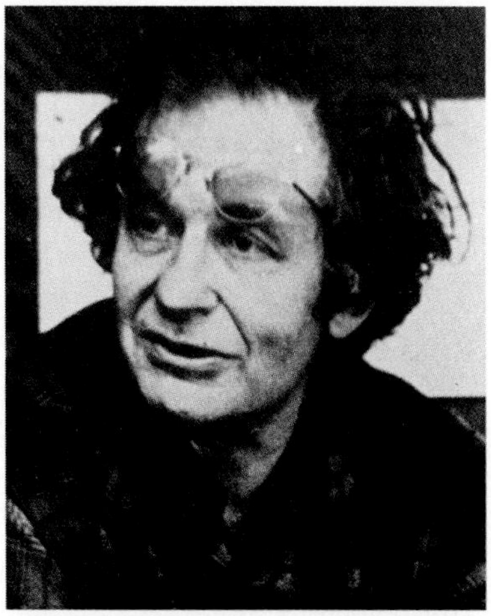

Lawrence Kolhberg's stage sequence of moral development extends Piaget's theory by providing a more complete description of changes in moral reasoning from childhood into adolescence and adulthood.

■ KOHLBERG'S STAGES OF MORAL UNDERSTANDING. Kohlberg organized his six stages into three general levels of moral development. He believed that moral understanding is promoted by the same factors that Piaget thought were important for cognitive growth: (1) actively grappling with moral issues and noticing weaknesses in one's current thinking, and (2) advances in perspective taking, which permit individuals to resolve moral conflicts in more complex and effective ways. As Table 16.2 shows, Kohlberg's moral stages are related to Piaget's cognitive and Selman's perspective-taking stages. As we examine Kohlberg's developmental sequence and illustrate it with responses to the Heinz dilemma, look for changes in perspective taking that each stage assumes.

The Preconventional Level. At the **preconventional level,** morality is externally controlled. As in Piaget's heteronomous stage, children accept the rules of authority figures and judge actions by their consequences. Behaviors that result in punishment are viewed as bad, and those that lead to rewards are seen as good.

Stage 1: The punishment and obedience orientation. Children at this stage find it difficult to consider two points of view in a moral dilemma. As a result, they ignore peoples' intentions and, instead, focus on fear of authority and avoidance of punishment as reasons for behaving morally. (Self)

Prostealing: "If you let your wife die, you will get in trouble. You'll be blamed for not spending the money to help her and there'll be an investigation of you and the druggist for your wife's death." (Kohlberg, 1969, p. 381)

Antistealing: "You shouldn't steal the drug because you'll be caught and sent to jail if you do. If you do get away, your conscience would bother you thinking how the police would catch up with you any minute." (Kohlberg, 1969, p. 381)

Stage 2: The instrumental purpose orientation. Awareness that people can have different perspectives in a moral dilemma appears, but this understanding is, at first, very concrete. Individuals view right action as what satisfies their personal needs, and they believe others also act out of self-interest. Reciprocity is understood as equal exchange of favors—"You do this for me and I'll do that for you."

Prostealing: "The druggist can do what he wants and Heinz can do what he wants to do. . . . But if Heinz decides to risk jail to save his wife, it's his life he's risking; he can do what he wants with it. And the same goes for the druggist; it's up to him to decide what he wants to do." (Rest, 1979, p. 26)

Preconventional level Kohlberg's first level of moral development, in which moral understanding is based on rewards, punishments, and the power of authority figures.

TABLE 16.2

The Relation Between Kohlberg's Moral, Piaget's Cognitive, and Selman's Perspective-Taking Stages

KOHLBERG'S MORAL STAGE	DESCRIPTION	PIAGET'S COGNITIVE STAGE	SELMAN'S PERSPECTIVE-TAKING STAGE[a]
Punishment and obedience orientation	Fear of authority and avoidance of punishment are reasons for behaving morally.	Preoperational, early concrete operational	Social-informational
Instrumental purpose orientation	Satisfying personal needs determines moral choice.	Concrete operational	Self-reflective
"Good boy–good girl" orientation	Maintaining the affection and approval of friends and relatives motivates good behavior.	Early formal operational	Third-party
Social-order-maintaining orientation	A duty to uphold laws and rules for their own sake justifies moral conformity.	Formal operational	Societal
Social contract orientation	Fair procedures for changing laws to protect individual rights and the needs of the majority are emphasized.		
Universal ethical principle orientation	Abstract universal principles that are valid for all humanity guide moral decision making.		

[a]To review these stages, return to Chapter 13, page 475.

> *Antistealing:* "(Heinz) is running more risk than it's worth unless he's so crazy about her he can't live without her. Neither of them will enjoy life if she's an invalid." (Rest, 1979, p. 27)

The Conventional Level. At the **conventional level,** individuals continue to regard conformity to social rules as necessary, but not for reasons of self-interest. They believe that actively maintaining the current social system is important for ensuring positive human relationships and societal order.

Stage 3: The "good boy–good girl" orientation, or the morality of interpersonal cooperation. The desire to obey rules because they promote social harmony first appears in the context of close personal ties. Stage 3 individuals want to maintain the affection and approval of friends and relatives by being a "good person"—trustworthy, loyal, respectful, helpful, and nice. The capacity to view a two-person relationship from the vantage point of an impartial, outside observer supports this new approach to morality. At this stage, the individual understands reciprocity in terms of the Golden Rule.

> *Prostealing:* "No one will think you're bad if you steal the drug, but your family will think you're an inhuman husband if you don't. If you let your wife die, you'll never be able to look anyone in the face again." (Kohlberg, 1969, p. 381)
>
> *Antistealing:* "It isn't just the druggist who will think you're a criminal, everyone else will too. After you steal it, you'll feel bad thinking how you've brought dishonor on your family and yourself; you won't be able to face anyone again." (Kohlberg, 1969, p. 381)

Conventional level
Kohlberg's second level of moral development, in which moral understanding is based on conforming to social rules to ensure positive human relationships and societal order.

Stage 4: The social-order-maintaining orientation. At this stage, the individual takes into account a larger perspective—that of societal laws. Moral choices no longer depend on close ties to others. Instead, rules must be enforced in the same even-handed fashion for everyone, and each member of society has a personal duty to uphold them. The Stage 4 individual believes that laws cannot be disobeyed under any circumstances because they are vital for ensuring societal order.

> *Prostealing:* "He should steal it. Heinz has a duty to protect his wife's life; it's a vow he took in marriage. But it's wrong to steal, so he would have to take the drug with the idea of paying the druggist for it and accepting the penalty for breaking the law later."

> *Antistealing:* "It's a natural thing for Heinz to want to save his wife, but it's still always wrong to steal. You have to follow the rules regardless of how you feel or regardless of the special circumstances. Even if his wife is dying, it's still his duty as a citizen to obey the law. No one else is allowed to steal, why should he be? If everyone starts breaking the law in a jam, there'd be no civilization, just crime and violence." (Rest, 1979, p. 30)

The Postconventional or Principled Level. Individuals at the **postconventional level** move beyond unquestioning support for the laws and rules of their own society. They define morality in terms of abstract principles and values that apply to all situations and societies.

(society)

Stage 5: The social contract orientation. At Stage 5, individuals regard laws and rules as flexible instruments for furthering human purposes. They can imagine alternatives to their social order, and they emphasize fair procedures for interpreting and changing the law when there is a good reason to do so. When laws are consistent with individual rights and the interests of the majority, each person follows them because of a *social contract orientation*—free and willing participation in the system because it brings about more good for people than if it did not exist.

> *Prostealing:* "Although there is a law against stealing, the law wasn't meant to violate a person's right to life. Taking the drug does violate the law, but Heinz is justified in stealing in this instance. If Heinz is prosecuted for stealing, the law needs to be reinterpreted to take into account situations in which it goes against people's natural right to keep on living."

Stage 6: The universal ethical principle orientation. At this highest stage, right action is defined by self-chosen ethical principles of conscience that are valid for all humanity, regardless of law and social agreement. These values are abstract, not concrete moral rules like the Ten Commandments. Stage 6 individuals typically mention such principles as equal consideration of the claims of all human beings and respect for the worth and dignity of each person.

> *Prostealing:* "If Heinz does not do everything he can to save his wife, then he is putting some value higher than the value of life. It doesn't make sense to put respect for property above respect for life itself. [People] could live together without private property at all. Respect for human life and personality is absolute and accordingly [people] have a mutual duty to save one another from dying. "(Rest, 1979, p. 37)

■ RESEARCH ON KOHLBERG'S STAGE SEQUENCE. Is there support for Kohlberg's stage sequence? Longitudinal studies provide the most convincing evidence. With few exceptions, individuals move through the stages in the order that Kohlberg expected (Colby et al., 1983; Walker, 1989; Walker & Taylor, 1991b). A striking finding is that moral development is very slow and gradual. Stages 1 and 2 decrease in early adolescence, whereas Stage 3 increases through mid-adolescence and then declines. Stage 4 rises over the teenage years until, by early adulthood, it is the typical response. Few people move beyond it to Stage 5. In fact, postconventional morality is so rare that there is no clear evidence that Kohlberg's Stage 6 actually follows Stage 5. The highest stage of moral development is still a matter of speculation.

Postconventional level
Kohlberg's highest level of moral development, in which individuals define morality in terms of abstract principles and values that apply to all situations and societies.

As you read the Heinz dilemma, you probably came up with your own solution to it. Now try to think of a moral dilemma you recently faced in everyday life. How did you solve it, and did your reasoning fall at the same stage as your thinking about Heinz and his dying wife? When people generate real-life moral problems of their own, they tend to fall at a lower stage than on hypothetical dilemmas (Trevethan & Walker, 1989). Perhaps real-life problems elicit moral reasoning below a person's actual capacity because they bring out the many practical considerations involved in an actual moral conflict. Consistent with this idea, moral responses also become less mature when dilemmas point out the possibility of punishment for the main actor—for example, stating that if Heinz decides to steal the drug, he will "be caught for sure and sent to prison" (Sobesky, 1983, p. 578). Emphasizing punishment increases concern with self-interest, a major preconventional basis of morality.

The influence of situational factors on moral judgments suggests that like Piaget's cognitive stages, Kohlberg's moral stages are best viewed in terms of a loose rather than strict concept of stage. Rather than developing in a neat stepwise fashion, each individual draws on a range of moral responses that vary with context. With age, this range shifts upward as less mature moral reasoning is gradually replaced by more advanced moral thought (Rest, 1979).

ENVIRONMENTAL INFLUENCES ON MORAL REASONING

Earlier we noted Kohlberg's belief that actively grappling with moral issues leads to gains in moral understanding. Many environmental factors have been found to promote stage change, including child-rearing practices, schooling, peer interaction, and aspects of culture. Growing evidence suggests that the way these experiences work is to present young people with cognitive challenges, which stimulate them to think about moral problems in more complex ways.

■ **CHILD-REARING PRACTICES.** In Chapter 10, we saw that in childhood, parents who are warm and consistent and who discuss moral concerns have children who are advanced in moral understanding. The same is true in adolescence. Teenagers who gain most in moral development have parents who encourage moral discussions and who create a supportive atmosphere by listening sensitively, asking clarifying questions, presenting higher-level reasoning, and using praise and humor. In contrast, parents who lecture, use threats, or make sarcastic remarks have youngsters who change little or not at all (Walker & Taylor, 1991a). In sum, the kind of parent who facilitates moral reasoning uses an authoritative approach that is verbal, rational, and affectionate and that promotes a cooperative style of family life (Boyes & Allen, 1993; Edwards, 1981).

■ **SCHOOLING.** Years of schooling completed is one of the most powerful predictors of moral development. In one study, adolescents who were at the same level of moral reasoning when they graduated from high school were followed over a 10-year period. Some did not go to college (the "low" education group), others went for a short time (the "moderate" education group), and still others graduated from college (the "high" education group). As Figure 16.1 shows, college graduates continued to gain in moral maturity, those with some college leveled off after they left college, and those with no college education declined (Rest & Narvaez, 1991). Other research also indicates that moral reasoning advances in late adolescence and young adulthood only as long as a person remains in school (Speicher, 1994).

Why does schooling make such a difference in moral maturity? There could be many reasons, including exposure to morally relevant subject matter and opportunities to interact with teachers and peers about moral concerns. Kohlberg (1984) suggested that higher education has a strong impact on moral development because it

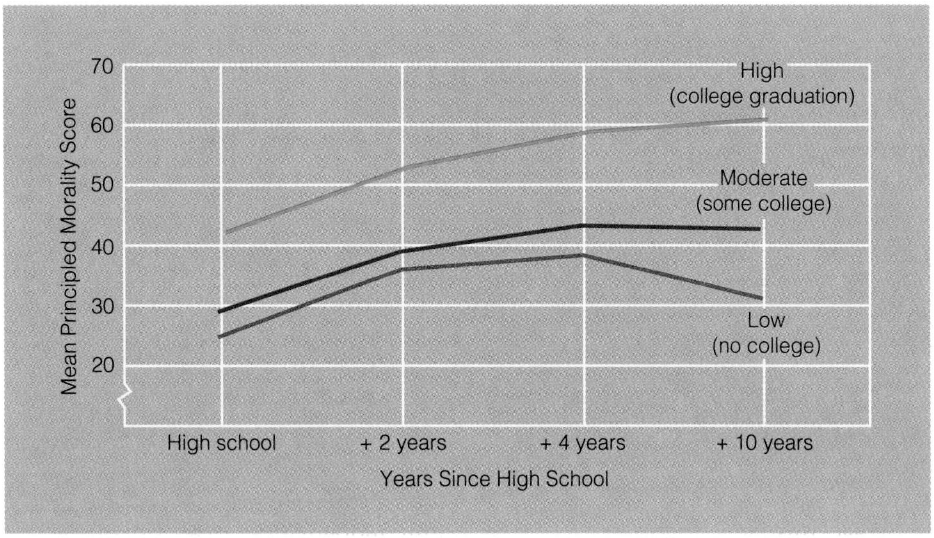

FIGURE 16.1

Relationship of level of schooling completed to moral reasoning in a study that followed young people over a 10-year period after high school graduation.
College graduates continued to gain in moral maturity. Those with some college leveled off, whereas those with no college declined. *(From J. R. Rest & D. Narvaez, 1991, "The College Experience and Moral Development," in W. M. Kurtines & J. L. Gewirtz, Eds.,* Handbook of Moral Behavior and Development, *Vol. 2, Hillsdale, NJ: Lawrence Erlbaum Associates, p. 235. Adapted by permission.)*

introduces young people to social issues that extend beyond personal relationships to entire political and cultural groups. Consistent with this idea, college students who report more academic perspective-taking opportunities (for example, classes that emphasize open discussion of opinions) and who indicate that they have become more aware of social diversity tend to be advanced in moral reasoning (Mason & Gibbs, 1993).

The question of how best to foster moral development in schools has been the focus of much recent research and debate. To find out more about Kohlberg's approach to moral education, turn to the From Research to Practice box on the following page.

■ PEER INTERACTION. Recall that Piaget believed that interaction among peers, who confront one another with differing viewpoints, promotes moral understanding. Many studies show that, indeed, this is the case. When researchers bring young people together to discuss moral issues, they often advance to higher stages. But peer interaction must have certain features to be effective. Look back at Sabrina and Louis's argument over the plight of Loretta Perry on page 591. Each teenager directly confronts and criticizes the other's statements, and emotionally intense expressions of disagreement occur. Peer discussions like this lead to much greater stage change than those in which adolescents state their opinions in a disorganized, uninvolved way (Berkowitz & Gibbs, 1983; Haan, Aerts, & Cooper, 1985). Also, note that Sabrina and Louis do not revise their ways of thinking after just one discussion. Because moral development is a gradual process, it takes many peer interaction sessions over weeks or months to produce moral change.

■ CULTURE. Cross-cultural research reveals that individuals in industrialized nations move through Kohlberg's stages more quickly and advance to higher levels than do individuals in simpler societies, who rarely move beyond Stage 3. In tribal and village cultures, moral cooperation is based on direct relations between people. Laws and governmental institutions do not exist to regulate it. Yet Stage 4 to 6 reasoning depends on an understanding of the role of larger societal structures in resolving moral conflict (Snarey & Keljo, 1991).

In cultures where young people begin to participate in the institutions of their society at early ages, moral development is advanced. For example, on *kibbutzim,* small but technologically complex agricultural settlements in Israel, children receive training in the governance of their community in middle childhood. By third grade, they mention more concerns about societal laws and rules when discussing moral

FROM RESEARCH TO PRACTICE

MORAL EDUCATION: THE JUST COMMUNITY

Kohlberg's theory has been the dominant force in moral education for the past quarter century (Sockett, 1992). His ideas changed over the course of his career, reflecting the tension between two major approaches to moral education. At first, Kohlberg rejected teaching moral content, or a ready-made "bag of virtues." Instead, he stressed improving moral reasoning through discussion of moral dilemmas. Many studies show that teacher-led peer dialogues about hypothetical moral problems (such as the Heinz dilemma) do lead to more mature moral reasoning. But Kohlberg came to question the ability of these interventions to change moral thinking and behavior in everyday life. Eventually he concluded that teaching moral content—kindness, honesty, fairness, and truthfulness—is necessary and compatible with his theory, as long as educators use a rational approach to rule making (Power, Higgins, & Kohlberg, 1989).

Kohlberg enlarged his concept of moral education to include training in moral content, reasoning, and behavior through the **just community,** a small society within a school in which teachers and students practice a democratic way of life. A central feature of the program is the weekly community meeting, in which the entire group gathers to create and refine school policy. Once rules are made, teachers do not stand back; they help students build a commitment to them. For example, at one meeting in a just community school, the group agreed not to allow smoking during a field trip to a movie. Yet as soon as the lights dimmed, several students lit up. The teachers stopped the film and led a short discussion about the importance of upholding agreements. Morality is also fostered through the teaching of subject matter. Students identify moral dilemmas in literature and evaluate courses of action. In social studies, they consider questions of human rights and good citizenship. And in science, they address such moral problems as environmental pollution and nuclear arms.

Do just community programs make a difference in the moral lives of students? When effectively implemented, they can be highly successful. As the moral atmosphere of the school takes shape, students usually express strong commitment to it. Here is a typical comment of a just community participant: "(Our school) is a real community. People have rights and can bring up issues of concern . . . and people listen to what you have to say, and therefore make you feel like a real person" (Power, Higgins, & Kohlberg, 1989, p. 190). Preliminary research indicates that advances in moral maturity from one year to the next were much greater in just community settings than in traditional or other alternative high schools. And adolescents who felt the strongest sense of community showed the greatest moral stage gains (Higgins, 1991).

According to Kohlberg, to understand and feel justice, adolescents have to be both justly treated and called on to act justly. This requires an educational democracy—a school in which everyone has a voice and in which the worth of rules is judged by their fairness to all involved (Sockett, 1992).

In a just community, teachers and students practice a democratic way of life. During weekly meetings, they jointly establish school policy. When students participate in creating the moral atmosphere of their school, they are more likely to be strongly committed to it. *(Will Faller)*

conflicts than do Israeli city-reared or American children (Fuchs et al., 1986). During adolescence and young adulthood, a greater percentage of kibbutz than American individuals reach Kohlberg's Stages 4 and 5 (Snarey, Reimer, & Kohlberg, 1985).

Taken together, these cultural differences raise an important question about Kohlberg's theory: Are the highest moral stages culturally universal, or do they emerge only in Western societies? By studying cultures just as complex as Western nations but guided by very different religious and philosophical traditions, researchers have tried to answer this question. In one investigation, adolescents and adults in India showed the same pattern of movement through Kohlberg's stages as Americans, and just as many or more reached the postconventional level. Still, the Indians often dealt with moral conflicts in ways that did not fit neatly into Kohlberg's scheme. For example, many resisted choosing a course of action in the Heinz dilemma, stating that moral problems cannot be solved at the level of a single individual's conscience (such as Heinz's). Instead, their resolution is the responsibility of the entire society (Vasudev & Hummel, 1987). Kohlberg's theory does seem to tap an important universal dimension of morality. At the same time, it does not capture all aspects of moral thinking in every culture.

This adolescent girl, who lives on an Israeli kibbutz, started to receive training in governance of her community in middle childhood. She is likely to be advanced in moral reasoning. *(Porterfield/Chickering)*

ARE THERE SEX DIFFERENCES IN MORAL REASONING?

The debate over the universality of Kohlberg's stages has also been extended to gender. Return once again to Sabrina and Louis's moral discussion at the beginning of this section. Sabrina's argument focuses on caring and commitment to others. Louis's approach is more impersonal. He looks at the dilemma of Loretta Perry in terms of competing rights and justice. Do Sabrina and Louis's moral approaches reflect a sex difference in moral understanding?

Carol Gilligan (1982) is the most well-known figure among those who have argued that Kohlberg's theory does not adequately represent the morality of girls and women. She believes that feminine morality emphasizes an "ethic of care" that is devalued in Kohlberg's system. Notice how Sabrina's reasoning falls at Stage 3, whereas Louis's is at Stage 4.[1] According to Gilligan, a concern for others is a *different,* not less valid, basis for moral judgment than a focus on impersonal rights.

Many studies have tested Gilligan's claim that Kohlberg's approach underestimates the moral maturity of females, and most do not support it (Walker, 1991). On hypothetical dilemmas as well as everyday moral problems, adolescent and adult females do not fall behind males in development. To the contrary, in some studies girls are ahead of boys in moral maturity! Also, themes of justice and caring appear in the responses of both sexes, and when girls do raise interpersonal concerns, they are not downscored in Kohlberg's system (Kahn, 1992; Thoma, 1986; Walker, 1989). These findings suggest that although Kohlberg emphasized justice rather than caring as the highest of moral ideals, his theory does tap both sets of values.

Still, Gilligan's claim that the study of moral development has been limited by too much attention to rights and justice (a "masculine" ideal) and too little attention to care and responsiveness (a "feminine" ideal) is a powerful one. Some evidence shows that although the morality of males and females taps both orientations, females do tend to stress care, or empathic perspective taking, whereas males either stress justice or use justice and care equally (Galotti, Kozberg, & Farmer, 1991; Gilligan & Attanucci, 1989). The difference in emphasis appears most often when people discuss real-life rather than hypothetical moral problems. Consequently, it may be largely a function of males' and females' daily lives. For example, in a study

Just community
Kohlberg's approach to moral education, in which a small society of teachers and students practice a democratic way of life.

[1]Sabrina's reasoning focuses on the importance of mutual trust and affection between people, a Stage 3 theme. Louis is at Stage 4 because he emphasizes the value of obeying the law to ensure societal order.

in which adolescents were asked to describe events that made them feel guilty, girls more often mentioned violating norms of compassion and trust (inconsiderate behavior, lying). In contrast, boys more often mentioned acting-out behaviors (fighting, damaging property, harming animals) (Williams & Bybee, 1994).

These findings suggest that like her older brother Louis, Sabrina will one day reason at Stage 4 or higher, but her justifications for moral action will continue to include concern for others. Although current evidence indicates that justice and caring are not gender-specific moralities, Gilligan's work has had the effect of broadening conceptions of the highly moral person. When Gilligan's and Kohlberg's theories are considered together,

> the moral person is seen as one whose moral choices reflect reasoned and deliberate judgments that ensure justice be accorded each person while maintaining a passionate concern for the well-being and care of each individual. Justice and care are then joined . . . in an enlarged and more adequate conception of morality. (Brabeck, 1983, p. 289)

MORAL REASONING AND BEHAVIOR

A final question about moral development concerns the relation between moral reasoning and behavior. If individuals do not act in accord with their principles, then their morality must be questioned. Kohlberg believed that moral thought and action are related in a very specific way: They should come closer together at the higher levels of moral understanding. Mature moral thinkers realize that behaving in line with their beliefs is an important part of creating a just social world (Blasi, 1990).

Consistent with this idea, advanced moral reasoning is related to many aspects of social behavior. Higher-stage individuals more often engage in prosocial acts, such as helping, sharing, and defending victims of injustice. They are also more honest. For example, they are less likely to cheat on assignments and tests school (Harris, Mussen, & Rutherford, 1976).

Yet even though a clear connection between moral thought and action exists, it is important to keep in mind that it is only moderate. As we saw in earlier chapters, moral behavior is influenced by a great many factors besides cognition, including the emotions of empathy and guilt and a long history of experiences that affect moral choice and decision making. Researchers have yet to discover how all these complex facets of morality work together (Blasi, 1983).

ASK YOURSELF . . .

- In our discussion of Kohlberg's theory, why were examples of both prostealing and antistealing responses to the Heinz dilemma presented for Stages 1 through 4 but only prostealing responses for Stages 5 and 6?
- Tam grew up in a small, isolated village culture. Lydia was raised in a large industrial city. At age 15, Tam reasons at Kohlberg's Stage 2, Lydia at Stage 4. What factors might account for the difference?

BRIEF REVIEW

According to Piaget, children move from an authority-focused, heteronomous morality to an autonomous morality based on reciprocity by the end of childhood. Lawrence Kohlberg's three-level, six-stage theory was inspired by Piaget's work. From late childhood into adulthood, morality changes from concrete, externally controlled reasoning to more abstract, principled justifications for moral choices. Like Piaget's cognitive stages, Kohlberg's moral stages fit a loose rather than strict concept of stage. A broad range of experiences fosters moral development, including moral discussions with parents and peers, years of schooling, and contact with larger social structures in complex societies. Although Kohlberg's theory emphasizes a "masculine" morality of justice rather than a "feminine" morality of care, it does not underestimate the moral maturity of females. As individuals advance through Kohlberg's stages, moral reasoning becomes better related to behavior.

GENDER TYPING IN ADOLESCENCE

As Sabrina entered adolescence, some aspects of her thinking and behavior became more gender typed. For example, she began to place more emphasis on excelling in traditionally feminine subjects of language, art, and music than in math and science. She also doubted her own abilities more than her older brothers did at the same age. And when with peers, Sabrina worried a great deal about how she should walk, talk, eat, dress, laugh, and compete, judged according to accepted social standards for maleness and femaleness.

Stronger for girls.

Research suggests that early adolescence is period of **gender intensification**—increased gender stereotyping of attitudes and behavior (Hill & Lynch, 1983). Although it occurs in both sexes, gender intensification is stronger for girls. Recall from earlier chapters that girls are less gender typed than boys during childhood, a difference that extends into the teenage years. But early adolescent girls feel less free to experiment with "opposite-gender" activities and behavior than they did in middle childhood (Huston & Alvarez, 1990).

What accounts for gender intensification? Biological, social, and cognitive factors are involved. Puberty magnifies sex differences in appearance, causing teenagers to spend more time thinking about themselves in gender-linked ways. Pubertal changes also prompt gender-typed pressures from others. Parents encourage competitiveness in boys and try to restrict the freedom of girls to a greater extent in early adolescence than they did in middle childhood (Block, 1984; Hill, 1988). And when adolescents start to date, they often become more gender typed as a way of increasing their attractiveness to opposite-sex peers (Crockett, 1990). Finally, cognitive changes—in particular, greater concern with what others think—make young teenagers more responsive to gender-role expectations.

Gender intensification seems to decline by middle to late adolescence, but not all young people move beyond it to the same degree. The social environment is a primary force in promoting gender-role flexibility, just as it was at earlier ages. Teenagers who are encouraged to explore non-gender-typed options and to question the value of gender stereotypes for themselves and society at large are more likely to build an androgynous gender-role identity, selecting "masculine" and "feminine" traits that suit their personally chosen goals (Eccles, 1987). Overall, androgynous adolescents tend to be psychologically healthier—more self-confident, better liked by peers, and identity achieved (Dusek, 1987; Massad, 1981; Ziegler, Dusek, & Carter, 1984).

Now let's turn to two aspects of adolescent social experience that play powerful roles in the identity, moral, and gender-role processes we have considered: family and peer relations.

THE FAMILY IN ADOLESCENCE

Franca works as a chemist in large drug company. Antonio owns and operates a downtown hardware store. Both parents remember Louis's freshman year of high school as a difficult time. Because of a demanding project at work, Franca was away from home many evenings and weekends. Antonio took over in her absence, but when business declined at the store, he, too, had less energy to devote to family life. Franca and Antonio began to argue over household responsibilities and expenses.

That year, Louis became involved in some unfavorable peer activities. He and two friends used their computer know-how to crack the code of a long-distance telephone service. From the family basement, they made calls around the country.

Gender intensification
Increased gender stereotyping of attitudes and behavior. Occurs in early adolescence.

Louis's grades fell, and he often left the house without saying where he was going. Franca and Antonio began to feel uncomfortable about the long hours Louis spent in the basement and their lack of contact with him. Finally, when the telephone company traced the illegally made calls to family's phone number, Franca and Antonio knew they had cause for concern.

Development at adolescence involves striving for **autonomy** on a much higher plane than during the second year of life, when independence first became a major issue for the child. Teenagers seek to establish themselves as separate, self-governing individuals. This means relying more on oneself and less on parents for direction and guidance. It also means making decisions independently by carefully weighing one's own judgment and the suggestions of others to arrive at a well-reasoned course of action (Hill & Holmbeck, 1986; Steinberg & Silverberg, 1986). A major way that teenagers seek greater self-directedness is to shift away from family to peers, with whom they explore courses of action that depart from earlier, more secure and stable patterns. Nevertheless, parent–child relationships remain vital for assisting adolescents in becoming autonomous, responsible individuals.

PARENT–CHILD RELATIONSHIPS

Throughout our discussion, we have emphasized that adolescents require freedom to experiment. Yet, as Franca and Antonio's episode with Louis reveals, they also need parental involvement and, at times, protection from situations that are dangerous. Think back to what we said earlier about parent–child relationships that foster academic achievement (Chapter 15), identity formation, and moral maturity. You will find a common thread. Effective parenting of adolescents strikes a balance between connection and separation. Recent research reveals that parental warmth and acceptance combined with firm (but not overly restrictive) monitoring of teenagers' activities is strongly related to many aspects of adolescent competence (Baumrind, 1991; Kurdek & Fine, 1994; Steinberg et al., 1994). Note that these parenting features make up the authoritative style that was so adaptive in childhood as well.

warmth + firm acceptance + monitoring

Maintaining an authoritative style during adolescence involves special challenges and adjustments. In Chapters 14 and 15, we showed that puberty brings increased

Parent–child conflict rises during adolescence. In Chapter 14, we noted that puberty prompts increased psychological distancing between teenagers and parents. Also, adolescents' improved ability to reason means that they are more likely to disagree. *(Richard Hutchings/Photo Researchers)*

Autonomy
At adolescence, a sense of oneself as a separate, self-governing individual. Involves relying more on oneself and less on parents for direction and guidance and engaging in careful, well-reasoned decision making.

parent–child conflict, for both biological and cognitive reasons. Teenagers' improved ability to reason about social relationships adds to family tensions. Perhaps you can recall a time during your own adolescence when you stopped viewing your parents as all-knowing and perfect and saw them as "just people" (Steinberg & Silverberg, 1986). Once teenagers *de-idealize* their parents, they no longer bend as easily to parental authority as they did at earlier ages. One outcome of this shift is that adolescents regard many matters (such as cleaning up their rooms, coming and going from the household, and doing their schoolwork) as their own personal business, whereas parents continue to think of these as shared concerns (Smetana, 1988; Smetana & Asquith, 1994). Disagreements are harder to settle when parents and teenagers approach situations from such different perspectives.

In Chapter 2, we described the family as a *system* that must adapt to changes in its members. But when development is very rapid, the process of adjustment is harder. Adolescents are not the only family members undergoing a major life transition. Many parents who have reached their forties (a period often called the "mid-life crisis") are changing as well. While teenagers face a boundless future and a wide array of choices, their parents must come to terms with the fact that half their life is over and possibilities are narrowing. The pressures experienced by each generation act in opposition to one another (Hill & Holmbeck, 1987). For example, parents often can't understand why the adolescent wants to skip family activities to be with peers. And teenagers fail to appreciate that parents want the family to be together as often as possible because an important stage in adult life—parenthood—will soon be over.

Parental activity & relationships effect adolescent development.

Finally, as Franca and Antonio's experience with Louis reminds us, family interaction at adolescence continues to be embedded in a larger context. Parents' difficulties at work as well as other life stresses can interfere with marital happiness, with nurturant, involved parenting, and (in turn) with adolescent adjustment (Conger et al., 1993, 1994). However, we must keep in mind that maternal employment by itself does not reduce parental time spent with teenagers, nor is it harmful to adolescent development (Richards & Duckett, 1994). To the contrary, parents who are financially secure, invested in their work, and content with their marriages usually have fewer mid-life difficulties and find it easier to grant teenagers an appropriate degree of autonomy (Silverberg & Steinberg, 1990). When Franca and Antonio's work and financial stresses eased and they realized Louis's need for more support and guidance, his problems subsided.

As teenagers move closer to adulthood, the task for parents and children is not one of just separating. They must establish a blend of togetherness and independence—a relationship in which parental control gradually relaxes without breaking the parent–child bond. In healthy families, teenagers remain attached to parents and continue to seek their advice, but they do so in a context of greater freedom (Allen et al., 1994; Lamborn & Steinberg, 1993). By middle to late adolescence, most parents and children achieve this more mature, mutual relationship. The mild conflict that occurs along the way facilitates the development of adolescent identity and autonomy by helping family members learn to express and tolerate disagreement (Steinberg, 1990).

SIBLINGS

Earlier in this chapter, we saw that Sabrina and Louis disagreed over a moral dilemma they read about in the newspaper. Had Sabrina been younger, she probably would not have taken on her older brother in such a debate. Instead, she would have given in to his greater status and power. Like parent–child relationships, sibling interactions adapt to change at adolescence. Teenage siblings relate to one another on a more equal footing than they did earlier. This is understandable, if you consider that the gap in competence between an older and younger child shrinks over time. As younger siblings mature and become more self-sufficient, they are no longer willing to accept as much direction from their older brothers and sisters (Stocker & Dunn, 1990).

As siblings become more evenly matched in ability, does quarreling between them increase? Usually not. Sibling interaction often becomes less intense during adolescence, in both positive and negative feelings. As teenagers become more involved in friendships and romantic relationships, they invest less time and energy in siblings. Also, adolescents may not want to interact as much with siblings, who are part of the family from which they are trying to establish autonomy (Buhrmester & Furman, 1990; Furman & Buhrmester, 1992).

Despite a drop in companionship, attachment between siblings, like closeness to parents, remains strong for most young people. One large survey found that 77 percent of high school students regarded siblings as major influences in their lives (Blyth, Hill, & Thiel, 1982). Quality of sibling relationships is quite stable over time. Brothers and sisters who established a positive bond in early childhood are more likely to display affection and caring during the teenage years (Dunn, Slomkowski, & Beardsall, 1994). In addition, sibling interaction at adolescence continues to be affected by other relationships, both within and outside the family. Teenagers whose parents are warm and supportive have more positive sibling ties (Brody et al., 1992). And for those who have difficulty making friends at school, siblings can provide compensating emotional supports (East & Rook, 1992).

PEER RELATIONS IN ADOLESCENCE

As adolescents spend less time with family members, peers become increasingly important. Recall the study in which teenagers were paged at random intervals, described in Chapter 14. Figure 16.2 shows that these young people were in the company of age-mates for over half their waking hours. In contrast, they spent only about one-fifth of their time with families (Csikszentmihalyi & Larson, 1984).

Contact among adolescents is common in all cultures, but it is much higher in industrialized countries than simpler societies. In modern nations, young people spend most of each weekday with agemates in school. Adolescents also spend considerable out-of-class time together, especially in the United States. American teenagers average 20 hours per week with peers outside the classroom, compared to 2 to 3 hours reported in Japan and Russia (Savin-Williams & Berndt, 1990). High rates of maternal employment, less demanding academic standards, and communities that provide special gathering places (such as video arcades and fast-food restaurants) probably account for this difference.

Is the large amount of time American teenagers spend together beneficial or harmful? This question has sparked much debate. We will see that adolescent peer relations can be both positive and negative. At their best, peers serve as bridges between the family and adult social roles. Rewarding friendships as well as larger peer group ties influence attitudes and behavior, foster psychological growth and social skills, and provide emotional support as teenagers advance toward maturity.

ADOLESCENT FRIENDSHIPS

When together, best friends Louis and Darryl relaxed, joked, watched TV, listened to tapes, or just talked about themselves, their classmates, and events in the wider world. During these times, the two boys felt they were understood and could

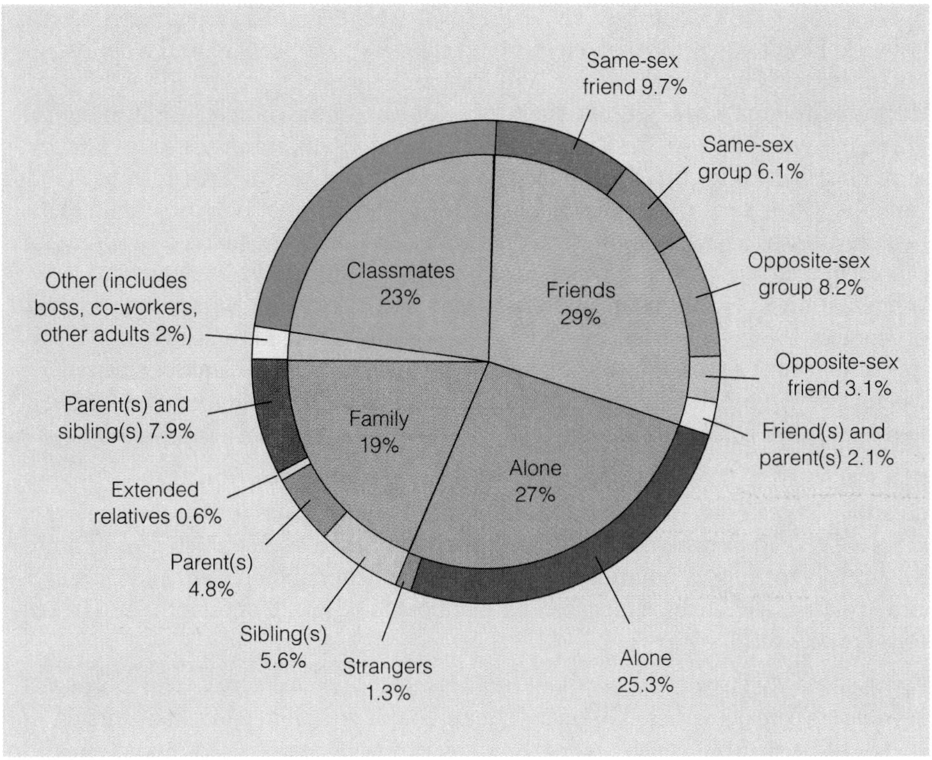

FIGURE 16.2

With whom do high school students spend their time? Students carrying electronic pagers were beeped periodically and asked to write down what they were doing, how they felt, and whom they were with. The chart shows that they spent over half their time in the company of agemates. They spent only about one-fifth with family members, and of this time, very little was spent exclusively with adults. *(From M. Csikszentmihalyi & R. Larson, 1984,* Being Adolescent: Conflict and Growth in the Teenage Years, *New York: Basic Books, p. 71. Reprinted by permission.)*

fully be themselves. It is not surprising that adolescents report that they enjoy being with friends more than any other activity (Csikszentmihalyi & Larson, 1984).

■ CHARACTERISTICS OF ADOLESCENT FRIENDSHIPS. The number of individuals young people call best friends declines from about four to six in early adolescence to one or two in adulthood. At the same time, the nature of the relationship changes. When asked to comment on the meaning of friendship, teenagers stress two characteristics. The first, and most important, is *intimacy*. Adolescents seek psychological closeness, trust, and mutual understanding from their friends. Second, more than younger children, teenagers want their friends to be *loyal*—to stick up for them and not to leave them for somebody else (Berndt & Perry, 1990).

1. Intimacy
2. Loyalty > Friendship

As frankness and faithfulness increase in friendships, teenagers get to know each other better as personalities. With age, best friends can describe one another's psychological traits with greater accuracy and completeness (Diaz & Berndt, 1982). Adolescent friends also cooperate more and compete less than do younger children. This change may reflect greater effort and skill at preserving the relationship as well as increased sensitivity to a friend's needs and desires (Berndt & Perry, 1990).

With whom do adolescents share their innermost thoughts and feelings? In Chapter 13, we noted that school-age friends are similar in age, sex, race, and social class. The same is true in adolescence. Teenage friends are also alike in attitudes and values, such as educational aspirations, political beliefs, and willingness to try drugs and engage in minor lawbreaking acts (Epstein, 1983a). The resemblance is partly due to the way the social world of adolescents is organized. Most teenagers live in neighborhoods that are segregated by income, race, and belief systems. And schools sort them through tracking. Adolescents may also choose companions like themselves to increase the supportiveness of friendship. Once they do so, adolescent friends influence each other. They become more alike in attitudes and values over time (Kandel, 1978).

SEX DIFFERENCES IN FRIENDSHIPS. Ask several adolescent girls and boys to describe their close friendships. You are likely to find a consistent sex difference. Emotional closeness and trust are more common in girls' talk about friends than boys'. Girls also rate their friendships as more intimate (Buhrmester & Furman, 1987; Bukowski & Kramer, 1986). This does not mean that boys rarely form close friendship ties. They often do, but the quality of their friendships is more variable. In one survey of high school students, 45 percent of boys described their best friendships as highly intimate; 35 percent said they were guarded in communication. In contrast, 65 percent of girls reported very intimate best friendships, whereas only 5 percent had relationships that were distant and superficial (Youniss & Smollar, 1986). The intimacy of boys' friendships is related to gender-role identity. Androgynous boys are just as likely as girls to form intimate same-sex ties, whereas boys who identify strongly with the traditional masculine role are less likely to do so (Jones & Dembo, 1989).

BENEFITS OF ADOLESCENT FRIENDSHIPS. What benefits do adolescents derive from their friends? Close friendship ties during the teenage years are related to many aspects of psychological health and competence. Although teenagers who are well adjusted to begin with are better able to form and sustain close peer ties, friendships further their emotional and social development. The reasons are several:

- *Close friendships provide opportunities to explore the self and develop a deep understanding of another.* Through open, honest communication, adolescent friends become sensitive to each other's strengths and weaknesses, needs and desires. They get to know themselves and their friend especially well, a process that supports the development of self-concept, perspective taking, identity, and intimate ties beyond the family (Sullivan, 1953).
- *Close friendships help young people deal with the stresses of adolescence.* Because friendship enhances sensitivity to and concern for another, it increases the likelihood of empathy and prosocial behavior. Teenagers with supportive friendships report fewer daily hassles and more "uplifts" than do others (Kanner et al., 1987). As a result, anxiety and loneliness are reduced while self-esteem and sense of well-being are fostered.
- *Close friendships can improve adolescents' attitudes toward school.* Teenagers with satisfying friendships tend to do well in school. The link between friendship and academic performance depends, of course, on the extent to which each friend values achievement (Epstein, 1983b). But overall, close friendship ties promote good school adjustment in both middle- and low-income students. When teenagers enjoy interacting with friends at school, perhaps they begin to view all aspects of school life more positively (Savin-Williams & Berndt, 1990).

CLIQUES AND CROWDS

Friends do not just spend time in pairs. They also gather in *peer groups* (see Chapter 13), which become increasingly common during adolescence. The peer groups of the teenage years are more tightly structured and exclusive than those of middle childhood. Adolescent peer groups are organized around **cliques,** small groups of about five to seven members who are good friends and, therefore, usually alike in age, race, and social class. In early adolescence, cliques are limited to same-sex members, but by the mid-adolescent years, mixed-sex groups become common. The cliques within a typical high school can be identified by their interests. Once formed, they often develop dress codes, ways of speaking, and behaviors that separate them from one another and from the adult world.

Clique
A small group of about five to seven members who are either close or good friends.

These teenage girls have a unique dress code, speak to each other in distinct ways, and engage in behaviors that separate them from other cliques and the adult world. Cliques serve as the main context for peer interaction during adolescence, permitting young people to acquire new social skills and experiment with values and roles in the absence of adult monitoring. *(Roger Dollarhide/Monkmeyer Press)*

Sometimes several cliques with similar norms form a larger, more loosely organized group called a **crowd.** Unlike the more intimate clique, membership in a crowd is based on reputation and stereotype. Whereas the clique serves as the main context for direct interaction, the crowd grants the adolescent an identity within the larger social structure of the school. For example, Louis and Darryl hung out with members of the debate team, who wore identical sweatshirts to practices, tournaments, and informal weekend gatherings. Both boys were well aware of other crowds at their school. The "jocks" were very involved in athletics, the "brains" worried about their grades, and the "workers" had part-time jobs and lots of spending money. The "druggies" used drugs on more than a one-time basis, while the "greasers" wore leather jackets, crossed the street to smoke cigarettes, and felt alienated from most aspects of school life (Hartup, 1983).

In early adolescence, as interest in dating increases, boys' and girls' cliques come together. The merger takes place slowly. At junior high school dances and parties, clusters of boys and girls can be seen standing on opposite sides of the room, watching but seldom interacting. As mixed-sex cliques form and "hang out" together, they provide a supportive context for boys and girls to get to know each other. Cliques offer models for how to interact with the opposite sex and a chance to do so without having to be intimate. In addition, members can check with one another to find out if their attraction to someone is likely to be returned. Gradually, the larger group divides into couples, several of whom spend time together, going to parties and movies. By late adolescence, boys and girls feel comfortable enough about approaching each other directly that the mixed-sex clique is no longer needed and disappears (Dunphy, 1963; Padgham & Blyth, 1990).

Just as cliques gradually decline in importance, so do crowds. As adolescents formulate their own personal values and goals, they no longer feel a strong need to wear a "badge" that broadcasts, through dress, language, and preferred activities, who they are. Nevertheless, both cliques and crowds serve vital functions during the teenage years. The clique provides a context for acquiring new social skills and for experimenting with values and roles in the absence of adult monitoring. The crowd offers adolescents the security of a temporary identity as they separate from the family and begin to construct a coherent sense of self (Brown, 1990).

Crowd
A large, loosely organized group consisting of several cliques. Membership is based on reputation and sterotype.

DATING

Within a few months, Louis, Cassie, and four other friends split off from a crowd of high school debate and drama students, went out for cokes and burgers, and arranged to go bowling on Saturday afternoons. Once Louis felt reasonably certain that Cassie liked him, he asked her out. They went to the movies, shared a soda, kissed, and held hands—a typical first date for a young teenager (Spreadbury, 1982). On the average, adolescent girls in the United States start to date around age 13 or 14, boys at 14 or 15. By age 16, most teenagers have had at least one date. About 75 percent become involved in a steady relationship before the end of high school (Dickenson, 1975).

Although sexual interest is affected by the hormonal changes of puberty (see Chapter 14), the beginning of dating is regulated by social expectations of the peer group (Dornbusch et al., 1981). In one study, early, middle, and late adolescents were asked about their reasons for dating. Younger teenagers were more likely to say that they dated for recreation and to achieve status with agemates. In choosing a partner, they often focused on the person's external characteristics and approval by peers. By late adolescence, these factors were less important. As young people become ready for and capable of greater psychological intimacy in a dating relationship, they look for other qualities—someone who shares their interests, who has clear goals for the future, and who is likely to make a good permanent partner (Roscoe, Diana, & Brooks, 1987).

The achievement of intimacy in dating relationships typically lags behind that of same-sex friendships. By the end of high school, teenagers' interaction with a boyfriend or girlfriend shows gains in mutual sharing, but it is still less intimate than their same-sex best friendship (Buhrmester & Furman, 1987). Perhaps because communication between boys and girls remains stereotyped and shallow through mid-adolescence, early dating has a negative rather than positive impact on social maturity (Douvan & Adelson, 1966). It also carries with it a higher risk of premarital pregnancy. Sticking with mixed-sex group activities, such as parties and dances, before becoming involved with a steady boyfriend or girlfriend is best for young teenagers.

As long as dating does not begin too soon, romantic involvements extend the benefits of adolescents' same-sex friendships. Besides fun and enjoyment, dating provides lessons in cooperation, etiquette, and how to deal with people in a wider range of situations. As teenagers relate to someone whose needs are different from their own, sensitivity, empathy, and identity development are enhanced (Zani, 1993). First romances usually serve as practice for later, more mature bonds. About half do not survive high school graduation and entry into college, and those that do become less satisfying (Shaver, Furman, & Buhrmester, 1985). Because young people are still forming their identities, those who like each other at one point in time often find that they do not have much in common later.

PEER PRESSURE AND CONFORMITY

Earlier in this chapter, we saw that Louis became involved in a delinquent act during his freshman year of high school. When Franca and Antonio discovered it, they began to worry (as many parents do) about the negative side of adolescent peer networks. Louis's lawbreaking, however, was an isolated event. As we will see in a later section, most young people engage in mild illegal activity during adolescence, but it does not last. Teenagers who join peer groups committed to antisocial behavior generally have a long history of family, peer, and school difficulties.

Conformity to peer pressure is greater during adolescence than in childhood or young adulthood—a finding that is not surprising, when we consider how much time teenagers spend together. But contrary to popular belief, adolescence is not a period in which young people blindly do what their peers ask. Peer conformity is actually a complex process that varies with the adolescent's age and need for social approval and with the situation.

In one study of nearly 400 junior and senior high school students, adolescents felt greatest pressure to conform to the most obvious aspects of the peer culture—dressing and grooming like everyone else and participating in social activities, such as dating and going to parties and school dances (see Figure 16.3). Peer pressure to engage in pro-adult behavior, such as getting good grades and cooperating with parents, was also strong. Although pressure toward misconduct rose in early adolescence, compared to other areas it was low. Many teenagers said that their friends actively discouraged antisocial acts. These findings show that peers and parents often act in concert with one another, toward desirable ends! Finally, peer pressures were only modestly related to teenagers' actual values and behaviors. Clearly, these young people did not always follow the dictates of peers (Brown, Lohr, & McClenahan, 1986).

Perhaps because of their greater concern with what their friends think of them, early adolescents are more likely than younger or older individuals to give in to peer pressure, especially when it comes to antisocial behavior (Brown, Clasen, & Eicher, 1986). Yet when parents and peers disagree, even young teenagers do not consistently rebel against the family. Instead, parents and peers differ in their spheres of greatest influence. Parents have more impact on teenagers' basic life values and educational plans (Kandel & Lesser, 1972; Sebald, 1986). Peers are more influential in short-term, day-to-day matters, such as dress, music, and choice of friends. Adolescents' personal characteristics also make a difference. Young people who feel competent and worthwhile are less likely to fall in line behind peers.

Finally, authoritative child rearing, which fosters high self-esteem, social and moral maturity, and a positive view of parents, is related to resistance to unfavorable peer pressure (Baumrind, 1991). In contrast, adolescents who experience extremes of parental behavior—either too much restrictiveness or too little monitoring—tend to be highly peer oriented. They more often rely on friends for advice about their personal lives and future and are more willing to break their parents' rules, ignore their schoolwork, and hide their talents to be popular with agemates (Fuligni & Eccles, 1993).

Conformity to peer pressure is greater during adolescence than in childhood or adulthood. These teenagers wear similar clothing and probably like the same music. Nevertheless, their parents remain powerful sources of influence on their basic life values and educational plans. *(Bill Bachman/Photo Researchers)*

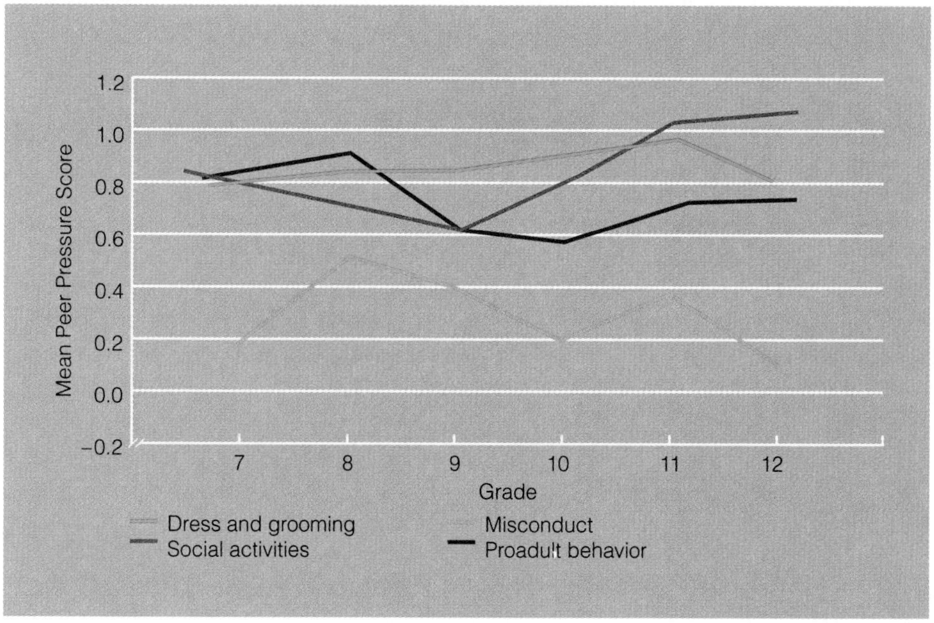

FIGURE 16.3

Grade changes in perceived peer pressure for four areas of behavior in a cross-sectional study of junior and senior high school students. Overall, teenagers felt greatest pressure to conform to dress and grooming styles and social activities. Pressure to engage in proadult behavior was also high. Although peer pressure toward misconduct peaked in early adolescence, it was relatively low. *(From B. B. Brown, M. J. Lohr, & E. L. McClenahan, 1986, "Early Adolescents' Perceptions of Peer Pressure,"* Journal of Early Adolescence, 6, *p. 147. Reprinted by permission.)*

ASK YOURSELF . . .

- How does Louis and Darryl's lunchtime conversation at the beginning of this chapter reflect the special characteristics of adolescent friendship?
- Phyllis likes her 14-year-old daughter Farrah's friends, but she wonders what Farrah gets out of hanging out at Jake's Pizza Parlor with them on Friday and Saturday evenings. Explain to Phyllis what Farrah is learning.
- How might gender intensification contribute to the shallow quality of early adolescent dating relationships?

BRIEF REVIEW

Biological, social, and cognitive factors combine to make early adolescence a period of gender intensification. Within the family, parents who strike a balance between connection and separation through authoritative child rearing assist teenagers in achieving autonomy. Sibling relationships become less intense as adolescents increase their independence from the family and spend more time with peers.

Intimacy and loyalty are central features of friendship during the teenage years. Close friendship ties are related to many aspects of psychological health and competence. Adolescent peer groups are organized around cliques (small groups of good friends) and crowds (large, loosely organized groups based on reputation and stereotype). The clique provides a setting in which adolescents learn social skills and try out new values and roles. The crowd offers a temporary identity as teenagers work on constructing their own. As adolescents become interested in dating, mixed-sex cliques form, which divide into couples. Although dating relationships increase in intimacy with age, they lag behind same-sex friendships. Conformity to peer pressure rises in early adolescence, but teenagers do not mindlessly "follow the crowd." Peers are more powerful influences on dress, music, and social activities, parents on life values and educational plans.

PROBLEMS OF DEVELOPMENT

Although most young people move through adolescence with little difficulty, we have seen in previous chapters that some encounter major disruptions in development, such as premature parenthood, substance abuse, and school failure. Our discussion has also shown that psychological and behavior problems cannot be accounted for by any single factor. Instead, healthy as well as problematic development is the combined result of several levels of influence. Biological and psychological change, families, schools, peers, communities, and society act together to produce a particular outcome. This theme is apparent in three additional problems of the teenage years: depression, suicide, and delinquency.

DEPRESSION

Depression—feeling sad, frustrated, and hopeless about life—is the most common psychological problem of adolescence. Although depressive feelings are not absent in childhood, they increase dramatically around the time of puberty. This change is understandable, if we stop and think about the many challenges adolescents face and their greater capacity for focusing on themselves. About 20 to 35 percent of teenagers experience mild feelings of depression, but they bounce back after a short period. Others display a more worrisome picture. About 12 to 15 percent are moderately depressed, and 5 percent severely so (Brooks-Gunn & Petersen, 1991). These teenagers are gloomy and self-critical for weeks at a time. They withdraw from pleasurable activities and show a loss of energy, a change in appetite, and disturbed sleep.

Depression prevents young people from mastering important developmental tasks. Without treatment, depressed teenagers have a high likelihood of becoming depressed adults. Adolescent depression is also associated with drug abuse, lawbreaking, and car accidents, and it predicts future problems in school performance, employment, and marriage (Lewinsohn et al., 1993). Unfortunately, depressive symptoms tend to be overlooked by parents and teachers alike. Because of the popular stereotype of adolescence as a period of storm and stress, many adults interpret depressive reactions as "normal" and just a passing phase (Strober, McCracken, & Hanna, 1990). Depression is also hard to recognize in teenagers because they manifest it in such a wide variety of ways. Some translate their pessimistic outlook into excessive worries about their health, difficulties in concentrating, and restless, undirected behavior. Others act it out by running away or behaving rebelliously (Rutter & Garmezy, 1983).

Both biological and environmental factors are related to severe depression (see Table 16.3). As we saw in Chapter 2, kinship studies reveal that heredity plays an important role. Genes promote depression by affecting the balance of biochemical substances in the brain. Perhaps depression rises at adolescence because the hormonal changes of puberty trigger it in susceptible young people, who tend to be withdrawn and lacking in social skills (Kennedy, 1993). But environmental events can also activate depression. Sometimes it follows a profound loss, such as parental divorce or the end of a close friendship or dating relationship. At other times, failing at something important sets it off. Still other cases are related to long-term psychological stress. Both poverty and ethnic minority status place teenagers at higher risk for depressive symptoms (Garrison et al., 1989; Sadler, 1991).

Another consistent finding is that depression occurs twice as often in girls as in boys (Rutter, 1986). On the basis of what you know about sex differences in adolescent development, perhaps you can think of several explanations. Pubertal hormones might contribute. In Chapter 14, we noted that higher hormone levels are linked to anger and irritability in boys and anger and depression in girls. In addition, adolescents who experience puberty and school transition at the same time (most of whom are girls) are more vulnerable to depression (Petersen, Sarigiani, & Kennedy, 1991). But gender-typed coping styles seem to be a critical link in these relationships. The gender intensification girls experience in early adolescence promotes passivity and dependency—an approach to the world that results in anxiety and helplessness in the face of stress and challenge. Consistent with this idea, one study found that girls with either an androgynous or masculine gender-role identity showed a much lower rate of depressive symptoms—one no different from that of masculine-identified boys (Wilson & Cairns, 1988).

TABLE 16.3

Factors Related to Adolescent Depression

FACTOR	DESCRIPTION
Heredity	Depression is moderately heritable and runs in families.
Precipitating events	Disruption of a relationship or failure at an important event can trigger depression.
Stress	Depression is higher among teenagers subjected to constant daily stress due to living in poverty. It is also higher among adolescents who experience puberty and school transition at the same time.
Sex	The rate of depression is twice as high in girls as in boys.
Gender-role identity	Adolescents with a feminine gender-role identity are more likely to experience depression than those with a masculine or androgynous identity.
Thoughts about the self	Learned helplessness, the belief that trying hard will not improve negative life conditions, is related to depression.

Profound depression often leads to suicidal thoughts, which all too often are translated into action. When a teenager tries to take, or succeeds at taking, his or her own life, depression is one of the factors that precedes it.

SUICIDE

Compared to his sister, who was an outstanding student, 17-year-old Brad just couldn't measure up. His high school grades were mediocre, and by his senior year he still had no idea what he wanted. Brad's parents had been critical of his school performance for years. Now, with adulthood just around the corner, they berated him for being so undirected. "At your age, you oughta know where you're going!" Brad's father shouted one day. "Pick a college or get a trade. But for heaven's sake, stop sitting around."

Throughout high school, Brad had been a loner. Although he excelled in art class, his parents never showed much interest in his drawings, which were piled in a corner of his room. There, Brad spent hours by himself, sketching and reading science fiction books. It bothered Brad's parents that he seemed unhappy and didn't have many friends. But at least he wasn't getting into much trouble like some other kids.

One day, Brad got up enough nerve to ask out a girl at school. His father, encouraged by Brad's interest in dating, gave him permission to use the family car. Brad planned the evening carefully, consulting his sister about where to go, what to do, and how to behave. But when Brad arrived to pick the girl up, she wasn't home. Several hours later, Brad's parents got a call from the police. He had been picked up for speeding, "driving under the influence," and evading the police. The chase through city streets finally ended when Brad drove off the road into a ditch. Although he wasn't injured, the car was totaled. A terrible argument followed between Brad and his parents.

Over the next 2 days, Brad was somber and withdrawn. Then, after dinner one night, he seemed resolved to make things better. "I've taken care of things, I won't be any more trouble to you," he remarked to his parents. Handing several of his favorite drawings to his sister, he said, "Here, I want you to have these—for keeps, to think of me." Early the next morning, Brad's parents found him hanging from a rope in his room.

■ **FACTORS RELATED TO ADOLESCENT SUICIDE.** The suicide rate increases over the life span. Although it is lowest in childhood and highest in old age, it jumps sharply from middle childhood into adolescence, as Figure 16.4 shows. Currently, suicide is the third leading cause of death among young people, after motor vehicle collisions and homicides. It is a growing national problem, having tripled over the past 30 years, perhaps because modern teenagers face more stresses and have fewer supports than they did in past decades (U.S. Department of Health and Human Services, 1994c).

Striking sex differences in suicidal behavior exist. The number of boys who kill themselves exceeds the number of girls by four or five to one. This may surprise you, since girls show a higher rate of depression. Yet these findings are not inconsistent. Girls make more unsuccessful suicide attempts and use methods with a greater likelihood of revival, such as a sleeping pill overdose. In contrast, boys tend to select more active techniques that lead to instant death, such as firearms or hanging. Once again, gender-role expectations may be responsible. There is less tolerance for feelings of helplessness and failed efforts in males than females (Garland & Zigler, 1993).

Suicide tends to occur in two types of young people. In the first group are adolescents much like Brad—highly intelligent but solitary, withdrawn, and unable to meet their own standards or those of important people in their lives. A second, larger group shows antisocial tendencies. These young people express their despondency

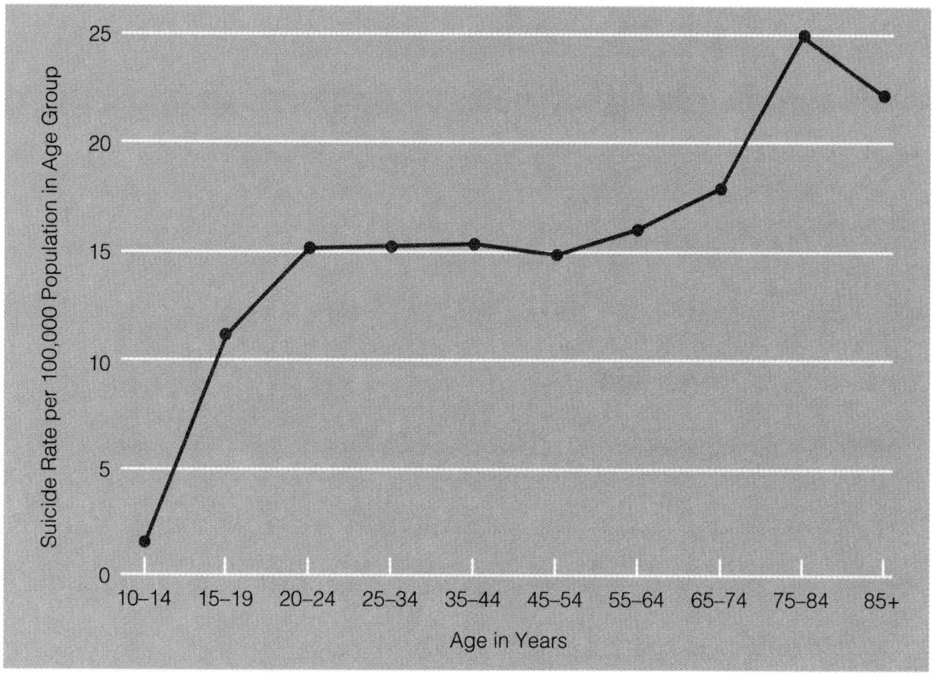

FIGURE 16.4

Suicide rate over the life span. Although teenagers do not commit suicide as often as adults and the aged, suicide rises sharply from childhood to adolescence. *(From U.S. Department of Health and Human Services, 1994c.)*

through bullying, fighting, stealing, and increased risk taking and drug use (Adcock, Nagy, & Simpson, 1991; Kandel, Raveis, & Davies, 1991). Besides turning their anger and disappointment inward, they are hostile and destructive toward others.

Family turmoil, parental emotional problems, and marital breakup are common in the backgrounds of suicidal teenagers, who typically feel distant from parents and peers (Shagle & Barber, 1993; Spirito et al., 1989). Their fragile self-esteem disintegrates in the face of stressful life events. Common circumstances just before a suicide include the breakup of an important peer relationship or the humiliation of having been caught engaging in irresponsible, antisocial acts.

Why is suicide rare in childhood but on the rise in adolescence? Teenagers' improved ability to plan ahead seems to be involved. Few successful suicides are sudden and impulsive. Instead, young people at risk usually take purposeful steps toward killing themselves. Warning signs, some of which are intended as calls for help, are listed in Table 16.4. Other cognitive changes also contribute to the age-related increase in suicide. Belief in the personal fable leads many depressed young people to conclude that no one could possibly understand the intense pain they feel. As a result, it deepens the hopelessness, isolation, and despair of vulnerable teenagers (Shaffer, 1985).

■ PREVENTION AND TREATMENT. Picking up on the signals that a troubled teenager sends is a crucial first step in preventing suicide. Parents and teachers need to be trained in warning signs. Schools can help by providing sympathetic counselors, peer support groups, and information about telephone hot lines that adolescents can call in an emergency. Once a teenager takes steps toward suicide, staying with the young person, listening, and expressing sympathy and concern until professional help can be obtained is essential (Pallikkathayil & Flood, 1991).

Intervention with depressed and suicidal adolescents takes many forms, from antidepressant medication to individual, family, and group therapy. Sometimes, hospitalization is necessary to ensure the teenager's safety and swift entry into treatment. Until the adolescent improves, parents are usually advised to remove weapons, knives, razors, scissors, and drugs from the home. On a broader scale, gun control legislation that limits adolescents' access to the most frequent and

TABLE 16.4

Warning Signs of Suicide

Efforts to put personal affairs in order—smoothing over troubled relationships, giving away treasured possessions
Verbal cues—saying goodbye to family members and friends, making direct or indirect references to suicide ("I won't have to worry about these problems much longer." "I wish I were dead." "I wonder what dying is like.")
Feelings of sadness, despondency, "not caring" anymore
Extreme fatigue, lack of energy, and boredom
No desire to socialize; withdrawal from friends
Easily frustrated
Emotional outbursts—spells of crying or laughing, bursts of energy
Inability to concentrate, distractible
Decline in grades, absence from school, discipline problems
Neglect of personal appearance
Sleep change—loss of sleep or excessive sleepiness
Appetite change—eating more or less than usual
Physical complaints—stomachaches, backaches, headaches

Source: Capuzzi, 1989.

deadly suicide method would greatly reduce both the number of suicides and the high teenage homicide rate (Shaffer et al., 1988).

After a suicide, family and peer survivors need support to assist them in coping with grief, anger, and guilt for not having been able to help the victim. Teenage suicides often take place in clusters. When one occurs, it increases the likelihood of others among peers who knew the young person or heard about the death through the media (Gould, 1990; Lewinsohn, Rohde, & Seeley, 1994). In view of this trend, an especially watchful eye needs to be kept on vulnerable adolescents after a suicide happens. Restraint by journalists in reporting teenage suicides on television or in newspapers can also aid in preventing them (Eisenberg, 1984).

DELINQUENCY

Juvenile delinquents are children or adolescents who engage in illegal acts. Young people under the age of 21 account for a large proportion of police arrests in the United States—about 30 percent (U.S. Department of Justice, 1994). Yet this official estimate of delinquency is misleading. It does not tell us how many teenagers have committed offenses but not been caught, how serious their crimes are, and whether many or just a few young people are responsible for them (Henggeler, 1989).

When teenagers are asked directly, and confidentially, about lawbreaking, almost all admit that they are guilty of an offense of one sort or another (Farrington, 1987). But most of the time, adolescents do not commit major crimes. Instead, they engage in petty stealing, disorderly conduct, and acts that are illegal only for minors, such as underage drinking, violating curfews, and running away from home. Both police arrests and self-reports show that delinquency rises over the early teenage years, remains high during middle adolescence, and then declines into young adulthood (see Figure 16.5). What is responsible for this trend? Recall that the desire for peer approval increases antisocial behavior among young teenagers. Over time, peers become less influential, moral reasoning matures, and young people enter social contexts (such as marriage, work, and career) that are less conducive to lawbreaking.

For most adolescents, a brush with the law does not forecast long-term antisocial behavior. But repeated arrests are cause for concern. Teenagers who have many encounters with the police are usually serious offenders, according to their own self-reports (Dunford & Elliott, 1984). About 12 percent of violent crimes (homicide, rape, robbery, and assault) and 22 percent of property crimes (burglary and theft) are committed by adolescents (U.S. Department of Justice, 1994). A small percentage of young people are responsible. Their antisocial tendencies are usually present early in development and remain stable over time. In one longitudinal study that spanned two generations, highly aggressive 8-year-olds became adults who were more likely to use physical aggression with other family members and to be convicted of serious criminal offenses. Their children also showed signs of repeating the cycle of violence and criminality (Huesmann et al., 1984).

Although an occasional brush with the law is common during adolescence, teenagers who repeatedly commit antisocial acts are in danger of becoming serious adult offenders. These young people usually have a long history of family, school, and peer difficulties. *(Bachman/Photo Reaearchers)*

intelligence
school performance
peer rejection.

■ FACTORS RELATED TO DELINQUENCY. Many factors are related to chronic delinquency. Depending on the estimate, about three to seven times as many boys as girls commit major offenses. Although social class and race are strong predictors of arrest records, they are only mildly related to teenagers' self-reports of antisocial acts. This is probably due to biases in the juvenile justice system—in particular, the tendency to arrest, charge, and punish low-income, ethnic minority youths more often than their middle-class white and Asian counterparts (Fagan, Slaughter, & Hartstone, 1987).

Low verbal intelligence, poor school performance, peer rejection in childhood, and entry into antisocial peer groups are also linked to delinquency. How do these factors fit together? Think back to what you learned about the development of

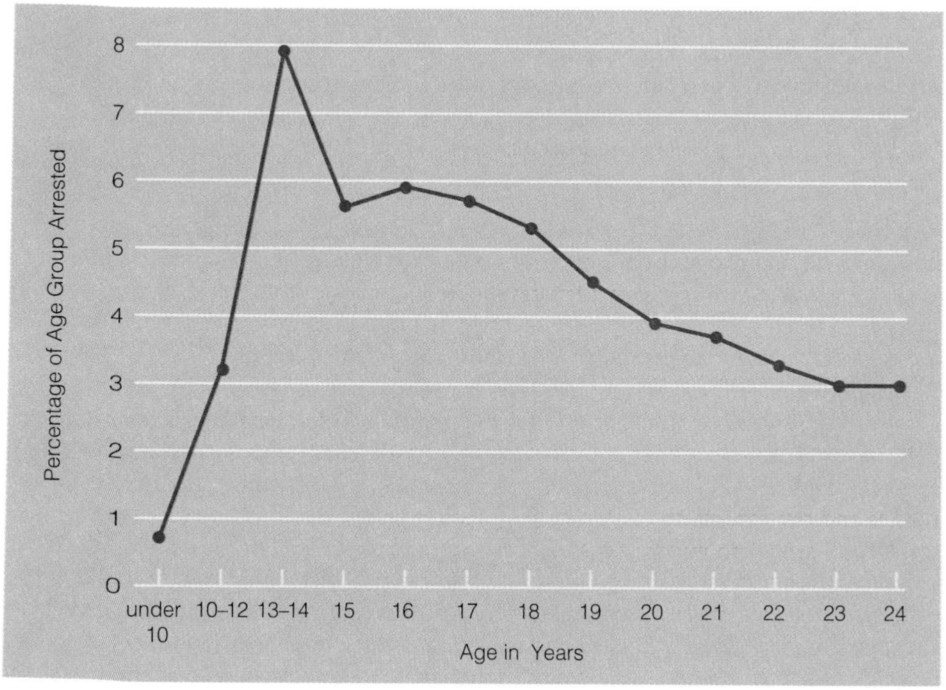

FIGURE 16.5

Age changes in delinquency, based on police arrests.
Delinquency rises during the early teenage years, remains high in middle adolescence, and then declines. Adolescents' self-reported lawbreaking shows a similar trend. (From U.S. Department of Justice, 1994.)

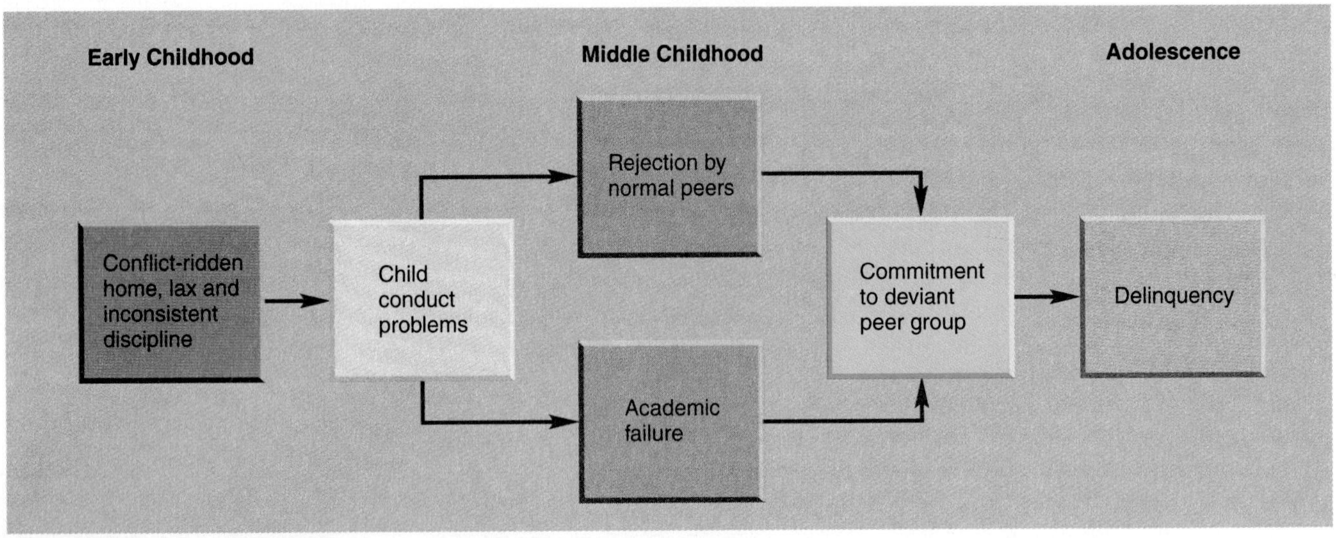

FIGURE 16.6

Developmental path to chronic delinquency.
(From G. R. Patterson, B. D. DeBaryshe, & E. Ramsey, 1989, "A Developmental Perspective on Antisocial Behavior," American Psychologist, *44, p. 331. Copyright 1989 by the American Psychological Association. Reprinted by permission.)*

cognitive and social competence in earlier chapters. One of the most consistent findings about delinquent youths is that their family environments are low in warmth, high in conflict, and characterized by lax and inconsistent discipline. Beginning in early childhood, these forms of child rearing breed antisocial behavior (Feldman & Weinberger, 1994; Miller et al., 1993). Research suggests that the path to chronic delinquency unfolds through the series of steps shown in Figure 16.6.

Return for a moment to our discussion of the development of aggression on pages 371–375 in Chapter 10. It explains just how ineffective parenting can promote and sustain hostile responding in all family members. Boys are more likely than girls to be targets of angry, inconsistent discipline because they are more active and impulsive and therefore harder to control. When boys with attention deficits, who are extreme in these characteristics, are exposed to inept parenting, aggression rises during childhood, is transformed into criminality by adolescence, and persists into adulthood (Farrington, Loeber, & van Kammen, 1990; Moffitt, 1990).

Factors beyond the family and peer group also contribute to delinquency. Students enrolled in schools that fail to meet their developmental needs—those with large classes, poor-quality instruction, and rigid rules—show higher rates of lawbreaking, even after other influences are controlled (Hawkins & Lam, 1987). And in poverty-stricken neighborhoods with fragmented community ties and adult criminal subcultures, teenagers have few constructive alternatives to antisocial behavior. Youth gangs often originate in these environments (see the Social Issues box on the following page).

■ **PREVENTION AND TREATMENT.** Because delinquency has roots in childhood and results from events in several contexts, prevention must start early and take place at multiple levels. Helping parents to use authoritative parenting, schools to teach children more effectively, and communities to provide the economic and social conditions necessary for healthy development would go a long way toward reducing adolescent criminality.

Treating serious offenders also requires an approach that recognizes the multiple determinants of delinquency. When interventions address only one aspect, they are generally ineffective. So far as possible, adolescents are best kept in their own homes and communities to increase the possibility that treatment changes will transfer to their daily lives. Many treatment models exist, including individual therapies and community-based interventions involving halfway houses, day treatment centers, special classrooms, work experience programs, and summer camps. Those that work best are lengthy and intensive and use problem-focused methods that teach cognitive and social skills needed to overcome family, peer, and school difficulties (Goldstein, 1990; Mulvey, Arthur, & Reppucci, 1993).

SOCIAL ISSUES

YOUTH GANGS

National surveys report a steady increase in youth gangs over the past two decades in the United States. Serious gang problems exist in 90 percent of the 80 largest American cities (Curry, 1994). Although most gangs operate in inner-city areas, a growing number are springing up in places where once there was little or no trouble—in working-class neighborhoods, well-to-do suburbs, medium-size cities, and even small towns. The large majority of members are males, ranging in age from preteen to the mid-twenties. Although a few female gangs exist, girls are usually attracted to gangs through their friendships with boys. Adolescents in the same gang are generally alike in social-class and ethnic background and come from the same neighborhood, which serves as their "turf."

Why have gangs risen in number? Experts offer several explanations. First, the gang problem, although spreading, is concentrated in poverty-stricken areas. Today, there are many more poor urban youths who face a life of hopelessness. Second, young people with stressful home lives are particularly likely to join gangs. Consider Zeke, the oldest of eight children growing up in a Detroit ghetto. When he was 10, his parents began to fight, and his father left home. Zeke's mother worked for a time but soon became severely depressed over her husband's departure. When she could no longer provide her children with financial or emotional support, they turned to the streets. Zeke joined a gang, where his desire for recognition and belonging could be satisfied and where he learned to steal the things he did not have at home. Although 16-year-old Patrice came from an affluent home, some of her experiences resembled Zeke's. Her parents were preoccupied with their own lives and seemed uninterested in her. When she began to date a gang member, for the first time, she reported, "I felt like I had a family." She finally joined (Dolan & Finney, 1984).

In addition to being more widespread, gangs are far more violent than they used to be. Their illegal activities include everything from vandalism and muggings to auto theft, armed robbery, drug trafficking, and murder. Some crimes are directed at rival gangs, others at the public—most often, residents of the gang's neighborhood. What explains this increased criminality? Many of today's gangs are led by young adults who did not leave the group for employment in late adolescence. Some could not find jobs; others chose to remain with the gang instead of risking a return to their former unhappy life. Instead, they became hardened criminals. Often gang violence seems undirected, aimed at anyone and anything. It appears to stem from intense anger, sparked by personal problems or unrelenting poverty. In addition, many gang members believe that the only way to avoid being victims themselves is to commit acts of brutality that display their power and "guts." When used against other gangs, these hostilities become part of a vicious cycle (Dolan & Finney, 1984).

How can gang activity be reduced and controlled? Multifaceted interventions tailored for each community work best. Jailing leaders often helps in suburban areas where gangs are held together by only a few highly committed individuals. But in the inner city, gangs have been in existence too long to be wiped out this way. Redirecting the energies of members and potential members is crucial. New educational, employment, and leisure-time opportunities need to be created in fragmented neighborhoods that breed gang violence. Until these are in place, caring and committed streetworkers can provide counseling for troubled youths and discourage young people from joining. Social agencies can help parents of difficult youths understand teenagers' needs and teach them how to monitor and set limits on their activities (Hagedorn, 1991).

Curbing the gang problem is especially challenging. Members have established strong emotional bonds and are accustomed to an exciting life in which illegal activities pay off more quickly and at a higher rate than going to school or engaging in routine, regular work.

TRY THIS . . .

- Young people join gangs for many reasons, including stressful home lives, low self-esteem, poor academic performance, peer pressure, lack of support from important adults, and feelings of hopelessness. How many ways can you think of—in families, schools, and communities—to offer children and adolescents positive alternatives to gang membership before they join?

Youth gangs are a growing problem in the United States. These teenagers probably joined a gang to escape from stressful homelives and a future that looks bleak. In the gang, they satisfy their desire for recognition and belonging. *(Alon Reininger/Unicorn Stock)*

ASK YOURSELF . . .

- Return to Chapter 11 and reread the sections on teenage pregnancy and substance abuse. What factors do these problems have in common with adolescent suicide and delinquency? How would you explain the finding that teenagers who experience one of these difficulties are likely to display others?

The hard-core delinquent for whom other efforts have failed may have to be removed from the community and placed in an institution. Overall, the success of institutional programs has not been encouraging. Positive behavior changes typically do not last once young people return to the everyday settings that contributed to their difficulties (Quay, 1987). Recently, boot camps, which use military procedures to rehabilitate youth offenders, have become common in the United States. Some studies indicate that boot camp graduates are less likely to repeat their lawbreaking than are delinquents who attended other institutional programs (Polsky & Fast, 1993). However, close monitoring (sometimes electronic) of youths after release rather than the camp experience itself may explain this outcome. In addition, many experts regard the boot camp experience, which uses verbal insults and other forms of harassment to induce compliance, as inhumane and as modeling dangerous lessons about how to treat other people (James, 1993). When the evidence is considered as a whole, we are reminded that the best way to combat adjustment problems in adolescence is through prevention, beginning early in life.

AT THE THRESHOLD

Because some of the most complex and rapid changes of development take place during adolescence, teenagers are vulnerable to certain problems, but most do not show serious depression, suicidal tendencies, or persistent antisocial behavior. As we look back on the demands and expectations, the dangers and temptations of the adolescent period, the strength and vitality of young people are all the more remarkable. We have seen that teenagers in industrialized nations confront challenges that are far more numerous and complex than those of adolescents in other cultures and at previous times during history. On a daily basis, young people must decide how vigorously to apply themselves in school, what kinds of friends to make, and whether to adopt risky behaviors, such as premarital sex and drug experimentation. These short-term choices can have a major impact on long-term options—length and type of formal education, career direction, and values and moral ideals. Yet as influential as the teenage years are, they occur within the context of an overall life course. Children enter adolescence having been shaped by heredity and a myriad of prior experiences. The paths adolescents choose and the contexts that affect their choices, in turn, shape many aspects of their future lives.

Society has good reason to treasure its youth as a rich national resource. Adolescents' ability to think seriously and deeply about possibilities, to commit themselves to idealistic causes, to be loyal to one another, and to experiment and take risks, while sometimes hazardous to themselves, energizes progress. Each new generation arrives at the threshold of adulthood with the capacity to benefit from the past while charting new, more fruitful directions. As individuals, as communities, and as a nation, we can do much to enhance adolescence as a final period of preparation for adulthood and a gateway to a better life for all. As we invest in the next generation, we invest in ourselves and the future of humankind. To our youth will be entrusted the task of taking care of us and our world.

SUMMARY

ERIKSON'S THEORY: IDENTITY VERSUS IDENTITY DIFFUSION

According to Erikson, what is the major personality achievement of adolescence?

- Erikson's theory emphasizes **identity** as the major personality achievement of adolescence. Young people who successfully resolve the psychological conflict of **identity versus identity diffusion** construct a solid self-definition consisting of self-chosen values and goals.

SELF-DEVELOPMENT IN ADOLESCENCE

Describe changes in self-concept and self-esteem during adolescence.

- Changes in self-concept and self-esteem set the stage for identity formation. Adolescents' self-descriptions become more organized and consistent, and personal and moral values appear as key themes. New dimensions of self-esteem are also added. For most adolescents, self-esteem rises. Boys and middle-class adolescents are advantaged in self-esteem, although school and community contexts can modify these group differences.

Describe the four identity statuses, along with factors that promote identity development.

- In complex societies, a period of exploration is necessary to form a personally meaningful identity. **Identity achievement** and **moratorium** are psychologically healthy identity statuses. **Identity foreclosure** and **identity diffusion** are related to adjustment difficulties.
- Adolescents who recognize that rational criteria can be used to choose among beliefs and values and who feel attached to parents but free to disagree are likely to be advanced in identity development. Schools and communities that provide young people with rich and varied options for exploration support the search for identity.

MORAL DEVELOPMENT IN ADOLESCENCE

Describe Piaget's theory of moral development, and evaluate its accuracy.

- Piaget's cognitive-developmental approach to moral development inspired Kohlberg's expanded stage theory. Piaget identified two stages of moral understanding: (1) **heteronomous morality,** in which moral rules are viewed as fixed dictates of authority figures; and (2) **autonomous morality,** in which rules are seen as flexible, socially agreed-on principles that can be changed when there is a need to do so. Although Piaget's theory describes the general direction of moral development, it underestimates young children's moral capacities.

Describe Kohlberg's extension of Piaget's theory, and evaluate its accuracy.

- According to Kohlberg, moral development is a gradual process that extends beyond childhood into adolescence and adulthood. By examining responses to **moral dilemmas,** Kohlberg found that moral reasoning advances through three levels, each of which contains two stages: (1) the **preconventional level,** in which morality is viewed as controlled by rewards, punishments, and the power of authority figures; (2) the **conventional level,** in which conformity to laws and rules is regarded as necessary to preserve positive human relationships and societal order; and (3) the **postconventional level,** in which individuals define morality in terms of abstract, universal principles of justice. Because situational factors affect moral judgments, Kohlberg's moral stages are best viewed in terms of a loose rather than strict concept of stage.

What environmental factors affect moral reasoning?

- Many experiences contribute to moral maturity, including warm, rational child-rearing practices, years of schooling, and peer discussion of moral issues. Young people in industrialized nations advance to higher moral levels than do those in simpler societies. Kohlberg's theory does not capture all aspects of moral thinking in every culture.

Evaluate claims that Kohlberg's theory does not adequately represent the morality of females, and describe the relationship of moral reasoning to behavior.

- Although Kohlberg's theory does not underestimate the moral maturity of females, it emphasizes justice rather than caring as a moral ideal. As individuals advance to higher stages, moral reasoning and behavior come closer together.

GENDER TYPING IN ADOLESCENCE

Why is early adolescence a period of gender intensification?

- **Gender intensification** occurs in early adolescence for several reasons. Physical and cognitive changes prompt young teenagers to view themselves in gender-linked ways, and gender-typed pressures from parents and peers increase. Teenagers who eventually build an androgynous gender-role identity show better psychological adjustment.

THE FAMILY IN ADOLESCENCE

Discuss changes in parent–child relationships during adolescence.

- Effective parenting of adolescents requires an authoritative style that strikes a balance between connection and separation. Adapting family interaction to meet adolescents' need for **autonomy** is especially challenging. As teenagers de-idealize their parents, they often question parental authority. Because both adolescents and parents are undergoing major life transitions, they approach situations from very different perspectives.

How do sibling relationships change during adolescence?

- Sibling relationships become less intense as adolescents separate from the family and turn toward peers. Still, attachment to siblings remains strong for most young people.

PEER RELATIONS IN ADOLESCENCE

Describe adolescent friendships and their consequences for development.

- Teenagers in industrialized nations spend many hours in the company of agemates. The nature of friendship changes, toward greater intimacy and loyalty. Intimate sharing is greater in girls' than boys' friendships. Close friendship ties promote self-concept, perspective taking, identity, the capacity for romantic involvements, and improved academic performance.

Describe peer groups and dating relationships in adolescence.

- Adolescent peer groups are organized around **cliques,** small groups of friends with common interests, dress styles, and behavior. Sometimes several cliques form a larger, more loosely organized group called a **crowd** that grants the adolescent an identity within the larger social structure of the school. Mixed-sex cliques provide a supportive context for boys and girls to acquire social skills and get to know one another.
- Intimacy in dating relationships lags behind that of same-sex friendships. First romances serve as practice for later, more mature bonds. They generally dissolve or become less satisfying after graduation from high school.

Discuss conformity to peer pressure in adolescence.

- Peer conformity is greater during adolescence than at younger or older ages. Young teenagers are most likely to give in to peer pressure for antisocial behavior. At the same time, most peer pressures are not in conflict with important adult values. Peers have greatest influence on short-term, day-to-day matters. Adults have more impact on long-term values and educational plans. Authoritative child rearing is related to resistance to unfavorable peer pressure.

PROBLEMS OF DEVELOPMENT

What factors are related to adolescent depression and suicide?

- Depression is the most common psychological problem of the teenage years. Adolescents who are severely depressed are likely to remain so as adults. Heredity contributes to depression, but stressful life events are necessary to trigger it. Depression is more common in girls than boys.
- Profound depression often leads to suicidal thoughts. The suicide rate increases dramatically at adolescence. Boys account for most suicides because their efforts usually succeed. Girls make more unsuccessful attempts at suicide. Family stress is common in the backgrounds of suicidal adolescents, who react intensely to loss, failure, or humiliation.

Discuss factors related to delinquency.

- Almost all teenagers become involved in some delinquent activity, but only a few are serious and repeat offenders. Most of these are boys with a childhood history of antisocial behavior. Although many factors are related to delinquency, one of the most consistent is a family environment low in warmth, high in conflict, and characterized by lax and inconsistent discipline. Schools that fail to meet adolescents' developmental needs and poverty-stricken neighborhoods with high crime rates also contribute to delinquency.

IMPORTANT TERMS AND CONCEPTS

identity (p. 584)
identity versus identity diffusion (p. 584)
identity achievement (p. 587)
moratorium (p. 587)
identity foreclosure (p. 587)
identity diffusion (p. 587)
heteronomous morality (p. 591)
autonomous morality (p. 591)
moral dilemma (p. 592)
preconventional level (p. 593)
conventional level (p. 594)
postconventional level (p. 595)
just community (p. 599)
gender intensification (p. 601)
autonomy (p. 602)
clique (p. 606)
crowd (p. 607)

FYI...

FOR FURTHER INFORMATION AND SPECIAL HELP, CONSULT THE FOLLOWING ORGANIZATIONS:

SUICIDE

National Committee on Youth Suicide Prevention
65 Essex Road
Chestnut Hill, MA 02167
(617) 738-0700

A volunteer network of parents and professionals that works to increase public awareness of youth suicide, publicize warning signs, and develop prevention programs in schools and communities.

DELINQUENCY

National Council on Crime and Delinquency
685 Market Street, No. 620
San Francisco, CA 94105
(415) 896-6223

An 11,000-member organization of professionals and other concerned individuals interested in the development of programs that prevent and treat crime and delinquency. Publishes the journal Crime and Delinquency.

MILESTONES OF DEVELOPMENT IN ADOLESCENCE

AGE	PHYSICAL	COGNITIVE	LANGUAGE	EMOTIONAL/SOCIAL
Early adolescence 11–14 years	■ If a girl, reaches peak of growth spurt. ■ If a girl, adds more body fat than muscle. ■ If a girl, starts to menstruate. ■ If a boy, starts to ejaculate seminal fluid. ■ If a girl, motor performance gradually increases and then levels off. ■ If a boy, begins growth spurt.	■ Becomes capable of formal operational thought. ■ Can argue more effectively. ■ Becomes more self-conscious and self-focused. ■ Becomes more idealistic and critical. ■ Self-regulation of cognitive performance continues to improve. ■ Evaluates vocational options in terms of interests.	■ Vocabulary continues to increase as abstract words are added. ■ Grasps irony and sarcasm. ■ Understanding of complex grammatical forms continues to improve. ■ Can make subtle adjustments in speech style, depending on the situation.	■ Moodiness and parent–child conflict increase. ■ Spends less time with parents and siblings. ■ Spends more time with peers. ■ Friendships are defined by intimacy and loyalty. ■ Peer groups become organized around cliques. ■ Several cliques form a crowd, based on reputation and stereotype. ■ Peer pressure to conform increases.

AGE	PHYSICAL	COGNITIVE	LANGUAGE	EMOTIONAL/SOCIAL
Middle adolescence 14–18 years	■ If a girl, completes growth spurt. ■ If a boy, reaches peak and then completes growth spurt. ■ If a boy, voice deepens. ■ If a boy, adds muscle while body fat declines. ■ May have had sexual intercourse. ■ If a boy, motor performance increases dramatically. 	■ Is likely to show formal operational reasoning on familiar tasks. ■ Long-term knowledge base continues to expand. ■ Develops more complex rules for solving problems. ■ Masters the components of formal operational reasoning in sequential order. ■ Becomes less self-conscious and self-focused. ■ Becomes better at everyday planning and decision making. ■ Evaluates vocational options in terms of interests, abilities, and values.	■ Can read and interpret adult literary works. 	■ Combines features of the self into an organized self-concept. ■ Self-esteem differentiates further. ■ Self-esteem tends to rise. ■ Is likely to be searching for an identity. ■ Is likely to engage in societal perspective taking. ■ Is likely to have a conventional moral orientation. ■ Has probably started dating.
Late adolescence 18–21 years	■ If a boy, gains in motor performance continue.	■ Narrows vocational options and settles on a specific career.		■ Is likely to be identity achieved. ■ May develop a postconventional moral orientation. ■ Is likely to move away from home.

GLOSSARY

A

AB search error The error made by 8- to 12-month-olds after an object is moved from hiding place A to hiding place B. Infants in Piaget's Substage 4 search for it only in the first hiding place (A).

Academic preschools Preschools in which teachers structure the program, training children in academic skills through repetition and drill. Distinguished from *child-centered preschools.*

Accommodation That part of adaptation in which new schemes are created and old ones adjusted to produce a better fit with the environment. Distinguished from *assimilation.*

Acquired immune deficiency syndrome (AIDS) A relatively new viral infection that destroys the immune system and is spread through transfer of body fluids from one person to another. It can be transmitted prenatally.

Adaptation In Piaget's theory, the process of building schemes through direct interaction with the environment. Made up of two complementary processes: *assimilation* and *accommodation.*

Adolescent initiation ceremony A ritual, or rite of passage, announcing to the community that a young person is making the transition into adolescence or full adulthood.

Age of viability The age at which the fetus can first survive if born early. Occurs sometime between 22 and 26 weeks.

Allele Each of two forms of a gene located at the same place on the autosomes.

Amnion The inner membrane that forms a protective covering around the prenatal organism.

Amniotic fluid The fluid that fills the amnion, helping to keep temperature constant and to provide a cushion against jolts caused by the mother's movement.

Anal stage Freud's second psychosexual stage, in which toddlers take pleasure in retaining and releasing urine and feces at will.

Analgesic A mild pain-relieving drug.

Androgyny A type of gender-role identity in which the person scores high on both masculine and feminine personality characteristics.

Anesthetic A strong pain-killing drug that blocks sensation.

Animistic thinking The belief that inanimate objects have lifelike qualities, such as thoughts, wishes, feelings, and intentions. A characteristic of Piaget's preoperational stage.

Anorexia nervosa An eating disorder in which individuals (usually females) starve themselves because of a compulsive fear of getting fat.

Anoxia Inadequate oxygen supply.

Apgar scale A rating used to assess the newborn baby's physical condition immediately after birth.

Applied behavior analysis A set of practical procedures that combine reinforcement, modeling, and the manipulation of situational cues to change behavior.

Assimilation That part of adaptation in which the external world is interpreted in terms of current schemes. Distinguished from *accommodation.*

Associative play A form of true social participation in which children are engaged in separate activities, but they interact by exchanging toys and commenting on one another's behavior. Distinguished from *nonsocial activity, parallel play,* and *cooperative play.*

Asthma An illness in which highly sensitive bronchial tubes fill with mucus and contract, leading to episodes of coughing, wheezing, and serious breathing difficulties.

Attachment The strong, affectional tie that humans feel toward special people in their lives.

Attention-deficit hyperactivity disorder (ADHD) A childhood disorder involving inattentiveness, impulsivity, and excessive motor activity. Often leads to academic failure and social problems.

Attribution retraining An approach to intervention in which attributions of learned-helpless children are modified through feedback that encourages them to believe in themselves and persist in the face of task difficulty.

Attributions Common, everyday explanations for the causes of behavior.

Authoritarian style A child-rearing style that is demanding but low in responsiveness to children's rights and needs. Conformity and obedience are valued over open communication with the child. Distinguished from *authoritative* and *permissive styles.*

Authoritative style A child-rearing style that is demanding and responsive. A rational, democratic approach in which parents' and children's rights are respected. Distinguished from *authoritarian* and *permissive* styles.

Autonomous morality Piaget's second stage of moral development, in which children view rules as flexible, socially agreed-on principles that can be revised when there is a need to do so. Begins around age 10.

Autonomy At adolescence, a sense of oneself as a separate, self-governing individual. Involves relying more on oneself and less on parents for direction and guidance and engaging in careful, well-reasoned decision making.

Autonomy versus shame and doubt In Erikson's theory, the psychological conflict of toddlerhood, which is resolved positively if parents provide young children with suitable guidance and appropriate choices.

Autosomes The 22 matching chromosome pairs in each human cell.

Avoidant attachment The quality of insecure attachment characterizing infants who are usually not distressed by parental separation and who avoid the parent when she returns. Distinguished from *secure, resistant,* and *disorganized/disoriented attachment.*

B

Babbling Repetition of consonant–vowel combinations in long strings, beginning around 6 months of age.

Basic emotions Emotions that can be directly inferred from facial expressions, such as happiness, interest, surprise, fear, anger, sadness, and disgust.

Basic-skills approach An approach to beginning reading instruction that emphasizes training in phonics—the basic rules for translating written symbols into sounds—and simplified reading materials. Distinguished from *whole-language approach.*

Basic trust versus mistrust In Erikson's theory, the psychological conflict of infancy, which is resolved positively if caregiving, especially during feeding, is sympathetic and loving.

Behaviorism An approach that views directly observable events—stimuli and responses—as the appropriate focus of study and the development of behavior as taking place through classical and operant conditioning.

Blastocyst The zygote 4 days after fertilization, when the tiny mass of cells forms a hollow, fluid-filled ball.

Blended, or reconstituted, family A family structure resulting from remarriage of a divorced parent that includes parent, child, and new steprelatives.

Body image Conception of and attitude toward one's physical appearance.

Bonding Parents' feelings of affection and concern for the newborn baby.

Brain plasticity The ability of other parts of the brain to take over functions of damaged regions.

Breech position A position of the baby in the uterus that would cause the buttocks or feet to be delivered first.

Bulimia An eating disorder in which individuals (mainly females) go on eating binges followed by deliberate vomiting, other purging techniques such as heavy doses of laxatives, and strict dieting.

C

Canalization The tendency of heredity to restrict the development of some characteristics to just one or a few outcomes.

Cardinality principle A principle stating that the last number in a counting sequence indicates the quantity of items in the set.

Carrier A heterozygous individual who can pass a recessive gene to his or her children.

Catch-up growth Physical growth that returns to its genetically determined path after being delayed by environmental factors.

Centration The tendency to focus on one aspect of a situation and neglect other important features. Distinguished from *decentration.*

Cephalocaudal trend An organized pattern of physical growth and motor control that proceeds from head to tail.

Cerebellum A brain structure that aids in balance and control of body movements.

Cerebral cortex The largest structure of the human brain that accounts for the highly developed intelligence of the human species. Surrounds the rest of the brain, much like a half-shelled walnut.

Cerebral palsy A general term for a variety of problems, all of which involve muscle coordination, that result from brain damage before, during, or just after birth.

Cesarean delivery A surgical delivery in which the doctor makes an incision in the mother's abdomen and lifts the baby out of the uterus.

Child-centered preschools Preschools in which teachers provide a wide variety of activities from which children select, and most of the day is devoted to free play. Distinguished from *academic preschools.*

Child development A field of study devoted to understanding all aspects of human growth from conception through adolescence.

Chorion The outer membrane that forms a protective covering around the prenatal organism. It sends out tiny, fingerlike villi, from which the placenta begins to emerge.

Chromosomes Rodlike structures in the cell nucleus that store and transmit genetic information.

Circular reaction In Piaget's theory, a means of building schemes in which infants try to repeat a chance event caused by their own motor activity.

Classical conditioning A form of learning that involves associating a neutral stimulus with a stimulus that leads to a reflexive response.

Clinical interview A method in which the researcher uses a flexible, conversational style to probe for the participant's point of view.

Clinical method A method in which the researcher attempts to understand the unique individual child by combining interview data, observations, and sometimes test scores.

Clique A small group of about five to seven members who are either close or good friends.

Codominance A pattern of inheritance in which both alleles, in a heterozygous combination, are expressed.

Cognitive-developmental theory An approach introduced by Piaget that views the child as actively building mental structures and cognitive development as taking place in stages.

Cohort effects The effects of cultural-historical change on the accuracy of findings: Children born in one period of time are influenced by particular cultural and historical conditions.

Compliance Voluntary obedience to adult requests and commands.

Comprehension In language development, the words and word combinations that children understand. Distinguished from *production.*

Comprehension monitoring Sensitivity to how well one understands a spoken or written message.

Computer-assisted instruction (CAI) Use of computers to transmit new knowledge and practice academic skills.

Concordance rate The percentage of instances in which both members of a twin pair show a trait when it is present in one pair member. Used to study the role of heredity in emotional and behavior disorders, which can be judged as either present or absent.

Concrete operational stage Piaget's third stage, during which thought is logical, flexible, and organized in its application to concrete information. However, the capacity for abstract thinking is not yet present. Spans the years from 7 to 11.

Conditioned response (CR) In classical conditioning, an originally reflexive response that is produced by a conditioned stimulus (CS).

Conditioned stimulus (CS) In classical conditioning, a neutral stimulus that through pairing with an unconditioned stimulus (UCS) leads to a new response (CR).

Conservation In Piaget's theory, the understanding that certain physical characteristics of objects remain the same, even when their outward appearance changes.

Continuous development A view that regards development as a cumulative process of adding on more of the same types of skills that were there to begin with. Distinguished from *discontinuous development.*

Contrast sensitivity A general principle accounting for early pattern preferences, which states that if babies can detect a difference in contrast between two patterns, they will prefer the one with more contrast.

Control processes, or mental strategies In information processing, procedures that operate on and transform information, increasing the efficiency of thinking as well as the chances that information will be retained.

Controversial children Children who get a large number of positive and negative votes on sociometric measures of peer acceptance. Distinguished from *popular, neglected,* and *rejected children.*

Conventional level Kohlberg's second level of moral development, in which moral understanding is based on conforming to social rules to ensure positive human relationships and societal order.

Convergent thinking The generation of a single correct answer to a problem. The type of cognition emphasized on intelligence tests. Distinguished from *divergent thinking.*

Cooing Pleasant vowel-like noises made by infants beginning around 2 months of age.

Cooperative play A form of true social participation in which children's actions are directed toward a common goal. Distinguished from *nonsocial activity, parallel play,* and *associative play.*

Coregulation A transitional form of supervision in which parents exercise general oversight while permitting children to be in charge of moment-by-moment decision making.

Corpus callosum The large bundle of fibers that connects the two hemispheres of the brain.

Correlation coefficient A number, ranging from +1.00 to –1.00, that describes the strength and direction of the relationship between two variables.

Correlational design A research design in which the researcher gathers information without altering participants' experiences and examines relationships between variables. Does not permit inferences about cause and effect.

Crossing over Exchange of genes between chromosomes next to each other during meiosis.

Cross-sectional design A research design in which groups of participants of different ages are studied at the same point in time. Distinguished from *longitudinal design.*

Crowd A large, loosely organized group consisting of several cliques. Membership is based on reputation and stereotype.

D

Decentration The ability to focus on several aspects of problem at once and relate them. Distinguished from *centration.*

Deferred imitation The ability to remember and copy the behavior of models who are not immediately present.

Deoxyribonucleic acid (DNA) Long, double-stranded molecules that make up chromosomes.

Dependent variable The variable the researcher expects to be influenced by the independent variable in an experiment.

Deprivation dwarfism A growth disorder observed between 2 and 15 years of age. Characterized by very short stature, weight that is usually appropriate for height, immature skeletal age, and decreased GH secretion. Caused by emotional deprivation.

Developmental psychology A branch of psychology devoted to understanding all changes that human beings experience throughout the life span.

Developmental quotient, or DQ A score on an infant intelligence test, based primarily on perceptual and motor responses. Computed in the same manner as an IQ.

Developmentally appropriate practice A set of standards devised by the National Association for the Education of Young Children that specify program characteristics that meet the developmental and individual needs of young children of varying ages, based on current research and the consensus of experts.

Diethylstilbestrol (DES) A synthetic hormone widely used between 1945 and 1970 to prevent miscarriage. It increases the chances of genital tract abnormalities and cancer of the vagina and testes in adolescence and young adulthood.

Differentiation theory The view that perceptual development involves the detection of increasingly fine-grained, invariant features in the environment.

Difficult child A child whose temperament is such that he or she is irregular in daily routines, is slow to accept new experiences, and tends to react negatively and intensely. Distinguished from *easy child* and *slow-to-warm-up child.*

Dilation and effacement of the cervix Widening and thinning of the cervix during the first stage of labor.

Discontinuous development A view in which new and different ways of interpreting and responding to the world emerge at particular time periods. Assumes that development takes place in stages. Distinguished from *continuous development.*

Dishabituation Increase in responsiveness after stimulation changes.

Disorganized/disoriented attachment The quality of insecure attachment characterizing infants who respond in a confused, contradictory fashion when reunited with the parent. Distinguished from *secure, avoidant,* and *resistant attachment.*

Distributive justice Beliefs about how to divide up material goods fairly.

Divergent thinking The generation of multiple and unusual possibilities when faced with a task or problem. Associated with creativity. Distinguished from *convergent thinking.*

Divorce mediation A series of meetings between divorcing adults and a trained professional, who tries to help them settle disputes. Aimed at avoiding legal battles that intensify family conflict.

Dominance hierarchy A stable ordering of group members that predicts who will win under conditions of conflict.

Dominant cerebral hemisphere The hemisphere of the brain responsible for skilled motor action. The left hemisphere is dominant in right-handed individuals. In left-handed individuals, the right hemisphere may be dominant, or motor and language skills may be shared between the hemispheres.

Dominant–recessive inheritance A pattern of inheritance in which, under heterozygous conditions, the influence of only one allele is apparent.

Drive reduction explanation of attachment A behaviorist view that regards the mother's satisfaction of the baby's hunger (primary drive) as the basis for the infant's preference for her (secondary drive).

E

Easy child A child whose temperament is such that he or she quickly establishes regular routines in infancy, is generally cheerful, and adapts easily to new experiences. Distinguished from *difficult child* and *slow-to-warm-up child.*

Ecological systems theory Bronfenbrenner's approach, which views the child as developing within a complex system of relationships affected by multiple levels of the environment, from immediate settings of family and school to broad cultural values and programs.

Educational self-fulfilling prophecy The idea that children may adopt teachers' positive or negative attitudes toward them and start to live up to these views.

Ego In Freud's theory, the rational part of personality that reconciles the demands of the id, the external world, and the conscience.

Egocentrism The inability to distinguish the symbolic viewpoints of others from one's own.

Elaboration The memory strategy of creating a relation between two or more items that are not members of the same category.

Electra conflict The conflict of Freud's phallic stage in which the girl desires to possess her father and feels hostile toward her mother. She resolves the conflict by becoming like her mother and forming a superego.

Embryo The prenatal organism from 2 to 8 weeks after conception, during which time the foundations of all body structures and internal organs are laid down.

Embryonic disk A small cluster of cells on the inside of the blastocyst, from which the embryo will develop.

Emotional self-regulation Strategies for adjusting our emotional state to a comfortable level of intensity.

Empathy The ability to understand and respond sympathetically to the feelings of others.

Epiphyses Growth centers in the bones where new cartilage cells are produced and gradually harden.

Episiotomy A small incision made during childbirth to increase the size of the vaginal opening.

Equilibration In Piaget's theory, back-and-forth movement between cognitive equilibrium and disequilibrium throughout development, which leads to more effective schemes.

Ethnography A method in which the researcher attempts to understand the unique values and social processes of a culture or a distinct social group by living with its members and taking field notes for an extended period of time.

Ethological theory of attachment A theory formulated by Bowlby, which views the infant's emotional tie to the mother as an evolved response that promotes survival.

Ethology An approach concerned with the adaptive, or survival, value of behavior and its evolutionary history.

Expansions Adult responses that elaborate on a child's utterance, increasing its complexity.

Experimental design A research design in which the investigator randomly assigns paticipants to treatment conditions. Since the researcher directly manipulates changes in an independent variable and observes their effects on a dependent variable, the design permits inferences about cause and effect.

Expressive style A style of early language learning in which toddlers use language mainly to talk about the feelings and needs of themselves and other people. Initial vocabulary emphasizes pronouns and social formulas. Distinguished from *referential style.*

Extended-family household A household in which parent and child live with one or more adult relatives.

Extinction In classical conditioning, decline of the conditioned response (CR) as a result of presenting the conditioned stimulus (CS) enough times without the unconditioned stimulus (UCS).

F

Fantasy period The period of vocational development in which young children fantasize about career options through make-believe play. Spans early and middle childhood.

Fast-mapping Connecting a new word with an underlying concept after only a brief encounter. Explains how children manage to add new words to their vocabularies at such a rapid rate.

Fetal alcohol effects (FAE) The condition of children who display some but not all the defects of fetal alcohol syndrome. Usually their mothers drank alcohol in smaller quantities during pregnancy.

Fetal alcohol syndrome (FAS) A set of defects that results when women consume large amounts of alcohol during most or all of pregnancy. Includes mental retardation, slow physical growth, and facial abnormalities.

Fetal monitors Electronic instruments that track the baby's heart rate during labor.

Fetus The prenatal organism from the beginning of the third month to the end of pregnancy, during which time completion of body structures and dramatic growth in size takes place.

Fontanels Six soft spots that separate the bones of the skull at birth.

Forceps Metal clamps placed around the baby's head, used to pull the infant from the birth canal.

Formal operational stage Piaget's final stage, in which adolescents develop the capacity for abstract, scientific thinking. Begins around 11 years of age.

Fraternal, or dizygotic, twins Twins resulting from the release and fertilization of two ova. They are genetically no more alike than ordinary siblings. Distinguished from *identical,* or *monozygotic, twins.*

Functional play A type of play involving pleasurable motor activity with or without objects. Enables infants and toddlers to practice sensorimotor schemes.

G

Gametes Human sperm and ova, which contain half as many chromosomes as a regular body cell.

Gender constancy The understanding that sex remains the same even if clothing, hairstyle, and play activities change.

Gender intensification Increased gender stereotyping of attitudes and behavior. Occurs in early adolescence.

Gender-role identity An image of oneself as relatively masculine or feminine in characteristics.

Gender schema theory An information-processing approach to gender typing that combines social learning and cognitive-developmental features to explain how environmental pressures and children's cognitions work together to shape gender-role development.

Gender typing The process of developing gender roles, or gender-linked preferences and behaviors valued by the larger society.

Gene A segment of a DNA molecule that contains hereditary instructions.

General growth curve A curve that represents overall changes in body size—rapid growth during infancy, slower gains in early and middle childhood, and rapid growth once more during adolescence.

Genetic counseling Counseling that helps couples assess the likelihood of giving birth to a baby with a hereditary disorder.

Genetic–environmental correlation The idea that heredity influences the environments to which individuals are exposed.

Genetic imprinting A pattern of inheritance in which alleles are imprinted, or chemically marked, in such a way that one pair member is activated, regardless of its makeup.

Genital stage Freud's psychosexual stage of adolescence, in which instinctual drives are reawakened and shift to the genital region, upsetting the delicate balance between id, ego, and superego established during middle childhood.

Genotype The genetic makeup of the individual.

Giftedness Exceptional intellectual ability. Includes high IQ, creativity, and specialized talent.

Glial cells Cells serving the function of myelinization.

Goodness of fit An effective match between child-rearing practices and a child's temperament, leading to favorable adjustment.

Growth hormone (GH) A pituitary hormone that affects the development of almost all body tissues, except the central nervous system and the genitals.

Growth spurt Rapid gain in height and weight during adolescence.

H

Habituation A gradual reduction in the strength of a response as the result of repetitive stimulation.

Heritability estimate A statistic that measures the extent to which individual differences in complex traits, such as intelligence or personality, are due to genetic factors.

Heteronomous morality Piaget's first stage of moral development, in which children view moral rules as permanent features of the external world that are handed down by authorities and cannot be changed. Extends from about 5 to 10 years of age.

Heterozygous Having two different alleles at the same place on a pair of chromosomes. Distinguished from *homozygous.*

Hierarchical classification The organization of objects into classes and subclasses on the basis of similarities and differences between the groups.

Home Observation for Measurement of the Environment (HOME) A checklist for gathering information about the quality of children's home lives through observation and parental interview.

Homozygous Having two identical alleles at the same place on a pair of chromosomes. Distinguished from *heterozygous.*

Horizontal décalage Development within a Piagetian stage. Gradual mastery of logical concepts during the concrete operational stage is an example.

Hostile aggression Aggression intended to harm another person. Distinguished from *instrumental aggression.*

Human development An interdisciplinary field of study devoted to understanding all changes that human beings experience throughout the life span.

Hypothetico-deductive reasoning A formal operational problem-solving strategy in which adolescents begin with a general theory of all possible factors that could affect an outcome in a problem and deduce specific hypotheses, which they test in an orderly fashion.

I

Id In Freud's theory, the part of personality that is the source of basic biological needs and desires.

Identical, or monozygotic, twins Pairs of twins that result when a zygote, during the early stages of cell duplication, divides in two. They have the same genetic makeup. Distinguished from *fraternal, or dizygotic, twins.*

Identification In Freud's theory, the process leading to formation of the superego in which children take the same-sex parent's characteristics into their personality.

Identity A well-organized conception of the self made up of values, beliefs, and goals to which the individual is solidly committed.

Identity achievement The identity status of individuals who have explored and committed themselves to self-chosen values and occupational goals. Distinguished from *moratorium, identity foreclosure,* and *identity diffusion.*

Identity diffusion The identity status of individuals who do not have firm commitments to values and goals and are not actively trying to reach them. Distinguished from *identity achievement, moratorium,* and *identity foreclosure.*

Identity foreclosure The identity status of individuals who have accepted ready-made values and goals that authority figures have chosen for them. Distinguished from *identity achievement, moratorium,* and *identity diffusion.*

Identity versus identity diffusion In Erikson's theory, the psychological conflict of adolescence, which is resolved positively when adolescents attain an identity after a period of exploration and inner soul-searching.

Imaginary audience Adolescents' belief that they are the focus of everyone else's attention and concern.

Imitation Learning by copying the behavior of another person. Also called *modeling* or *observational learning.*

Implantation Attachment of the blastocyst to the uterine lining 7 to 9 days after fertilization.

Independent variable The variable manipulated by the researcher in an experiment.

Induced labor A labor started artificially by breaking the amnion and giving the mother a hormone that stimulates contractions.

Induction A type of discipline in which the effects of the child's misbehavior on others are communicated to the child.

Industry versus inferiority In Erikson's theory, the psychological conflict of middle childhood, which is resolved positively when experiences lead children to develop a sense of competence at useful skills and tasks.

Infant mortality The number of deaths in the first year of life per 1,000 live births.

Information processing An approach that views the human mind as a symbol-manipulating system through which information flows and regards cognitive development as a continuous process.

Initiative versus guilt In Erikson's theory, the psychological conflict of early childhood, which is resolved positively through play experiences that foster a healthy sense of initiative and through development of a superego, or conscience, that is not overly strict and guilt ridden.

Instrumental aggression Aggression aimed at obtaining an object, privilege, or space with no deliberate intent to harm another person. Distinguished from *hostile aggression.*

Intelligence quotient, or IQ A score that permits an individual's performance on an intelligence test to be compared to the performances of other individuals of the same age.

Intentional, or goal-directed, behavior A sequence of actions in which schemes are deliberately combined to solve a problem.

Interactional synchrony A sensitively tuned "emotional dance," in which the caregiver responds to infant signals in a well-timed, appropriate fashion and both partners match emotional states, especially the positive ones.

Intermodal perception Perception that combines information from more than one sensory system.

Internal working model A set of expectations derived from early caregiving experiences concerning the availability of attachment figures and their likelihood of providing support during times of stress. Becomes a model, or guide, for all future close relationships.

Intersubjectivity The process whereby two participants who begin a task with different understandings arrive at a shared understanding.

Invariant features In differentiation theory of perceptual development, features that remain stable in a constantly changing perceptual world.

Irreversibility The inability to mentally go through a series of steps in a problem and then reverse direction, returning to the starting point. Distinguished from *reversibility.*

J

Joint custody A child custody arrangement following divorce in which the court grants both parents say in important decisions about the child's upbringing.

Just community Kohlberg's approach to moral education, in which a small society of teachers and students practice a democratic way of life.

K

Kaufman Assessment Battery for Children (K-ABC) An individually administered intelligence test that measures two broad types of information-processing skills: simultaneous and sequential processing. The first major test to be grounded in information-processing theory.

Kinship studies Studies comparing the characteristics of family members to determine the importance of heredity in complex human characteristics.

Kwashiorkor A disease usually appearing between 1 and 3 years of age that is caused by a diet low in protein. Symptoms include an enlarged belly, swollen feet, hair loss, skin rash, and irritable, listless behavior.

L

Language acquisition device (LAD) In Chomsky's theory, a biologically based innate system for picking up language that permits children, as soon as they have learned enough words, to combine them into grammatically consistent expressions and to understand the meaning of sentences they hear.

Lanugo A white, downy hair that covers the entire body of the fetus, helping the vernix stick to the skin.

Latency stage Freud's psychosexual stage of middle childhood, in which the sexual instincts lie dormant.

Lateralization Specialization of functions of the two hemispheres of the cortex.

Learned helplessness Attributions that credit success to luck and failure to low ability. Leads to anxious loss of control in the face of challenging tasks. Distinguished from *mastery-oriented attributions.*

Learning disabilities Specific learning disorders that lead children to achieve poorly in school, despite an average or above-average IQ. A problem with reading is called *dyslexia,* one with arithmetic *dyscalculia,* and one with writing *dysgraphia.* Believed to be due to faulty brain functioning.

Longitudinal design A research design in which in which one group of participants is studied repeatedly at different ages. Distinguished from *cross-sectional design.*

Longitudinal-sequential design A research design with both longitudinal and cross-sectional components in which groups of participants born in different years are followed over time.

Long-term memory In information processing, the part of the mental system that contains our permanent knowledge base.

M

Mainstreaming The integration of pupils with learning difficulties into regular classrooms for part or all of the school day.

Make-believe play A type of play in which children pretend, acting out everyday and imaginary activities.

Malocclusion A condition in which the upper and lower teeth do not meet properly.

Marasmus A disease usually appearing in the first year of life that is caused by a diet low in all essential nutrients. Leads to a wasted condition of the body.

Mastery-oriented attributions Attributions that credit success to high ability and failure to insufficient effort. Leads to high self-esteem and a willingness to approach challenging tasks. Distinguished from *learned helplessness.*

Maturation A genetically determined, naturally unfolding course of growth.

Mechanistic theories Theories that regard the child as a passive reactor to environmental inputs. Distinguished from *organismic theories.*

Meiosis The process of cell division through which gametes are formed and in which the number of chromosomes in each cell is halved.

Memory strategies Deliberate mental activities that improve the likelihood of remembering.

Menarche First menstruation.

Mental representation An internal image of an absent object or a past event.

Mental retardation Substantially below-average intellectual functioning.

Metacognition Thinking about thought; awareness of mental activities.

Mitosis The process of cell duplication, in which each new cell receives an exact copy of the original chromosomes.

Moral dilemma A conflict situation presented to individuals, who are asked to decide both what the main actor should do and why. Used to assess the development of moral reasoning.

Moratorium The identity status of individuals who are exploring alternatives in an effort to find values and goals to guide their life. Distinguished from *identity achievement, identity foreclosure,* and *identity diffusion.*

Motherese A form of language used by adults to speak to infants and toddlers that consists of short sentences with exaggerated expression and very clear pronunciation.

Mutation A sudden but permanent change in a segment of DNA.

Myelinization A process in which neural fibers are coated with an insulating fatty sheath (called *myelin*) that improves the efficiency of message transfer.

Myopia Nearsightedness; inability to see distant objects clearly.

N

Natural, or prepared, childbirth An approach designed to reduce pain and medical intervention and to make childbirth a rewarding experience for parents.

Naturalistic observation A method in which the researcher goes into the natural environment to observe the behavior of interest. Distinguished from *structured observation.*

Nature–nurture controversy Disagreement among theorists about whether genetic or environmental factors are the most important determinants of development and behavior.

Neglected children Children who are seldom chosen, either positively or negatively, on sociometric measures of peer acceptance. Distinguished from *popular, rejected,* and *controversial children.*

Neonatal Behavioral Assessment Scale (NBAS) A test developed to assess the behavior of the infant during the newborn period. Considers reflexes, state changes, responsiveness to physical and social stimuli, motor abilities, and other reactions.

Neonatal mortality The number of deaths in the first month of life per 1,000 live births.

Neural tube The primitive spinal cord that develops from the ectoderm, the top of which swells to form the brain.

Neurons Nerve cells that store and transmit information.

Neurotransmitters Chemicals that permit neurons to communicate across synapses.

Niche-picking A type of genetic–environmental correlation in which individuals actively choose environments that complement their heredity.

Noble savage Rousseau's view of the child as naturally endowed with an innate plan for orderly, healthy growth.

Nocturnal enuresis Repeated bedwetting during the night.

Nonorganic failure to thrive A growth disorder usually present by 18 months of age that is caused by lack of affection and stimulation.

Nonsocial activity Unoccupied, onlooker behavior and solitary play. Distinguished from *parallel, associative,* and *cooperative play.*

Non-rapid-eye-movement (NREM) sleep A "regular" sleep state in which the body is quiet and heart rate, breathing, and brain wave activity are slow and regular. Distinguished from *rapid-eye-movement (REM) sleep.*

Normative approach An approach in which age-related averages are computed to represent the typical child's development.

O

Obesity A greater than 20 percent increase over average body weight, based on the child's age, sex, and physical build.

Object permanence The understanding that objects continue to exist when they are out of sight.

Oedipus conflict The conflict of Freud's phallic stage in which the boy desires to possess his mother and feels hostile toward his father. He resolves the conflict by becoming like his father and forming a superego.

Open classroom An elementary school classroom based on the educational philosophy that children are active agents in their own development and learn at different rates. Teachers share decision making with pupils. Pupils are evaluated in relation to their own prior development. Distinguished from *traditional classroom.*

Operant conditioning A form of learning in which a spontaneous behavior is followed by a stimulus that changes the probability that the behavior will occur again.

Operations In Piaget's theory, mental representations of actions that obey logical rules.

Oral stage Freud's first psychosexual stage, during which infants obtain pleasure through the mouth.

Organismic theories Theories that assume the existence of psychological structures inside the child that underlie and control development. Distinguished from *mechanistic theories.*

Organization In Piaget's theory, the internal rearrangement and linking together of schemes so that they form a strongly interconnected cognitive system. In information processing, the memory strategy of grouping together related items.

Overextension An early vocabulary error in which a word is applied too broadly, to a wider collection of objects and events than is appropriate. Distinguished from *underextension.*

Overregularization Application of regular grammatical rules to words that are exceptions. For example, saying "mouses" instead of "mice."

P

Parallel play A form of limited social participation in which the child plays near other children with similar materials but does not interact with them. Distinguished from *nonsocial, associative,* and *cooperative play.*

Peer group Peers who form a social unit by generating shared values and standards of behavior and a social structure of leaders and followers.

Perception bound Being easily distracted by the concrete, perceptual appearance of objects. A characteristic of Piaget's preoperational stage.

Permissive style A child-rearing style that is responsive but undemanding. An overly tolerant approach to child rearing. Distinguished from *authoritative* and *authoritarian styles.*

Personal fable Adolescents' belief that they are special and unique. Leads them to conclude that others cannot possibly understand their thoughts and feelings. May promote a sense of invulnerability to danger.

Perspective taking The capacity to imagine what other people may be thinking and feeling.

Phallic stage Freud's psychosexual stage of early childhood, in which sexual impulses transfer to the genital region of the body and the Oedipus and Electra conflicts are resolved.

Phenotype The individual's physical and behavioral characteristics, which are determined by both genetic and environmental factors.

Phobia A fear that is very intense, persists for a long time, and cannot be reduced through reasoning and gentle encouragement.

Pincer grasp The well-coordinated grasp emerging at the end of the first year, involving thumb and forefinger opposition.

Pituitary gland A gland located near the base of the brain that releases hormones affecting physical growth.

Placenta The organ that separates the mother's bloodstream from the embryo or fetal bloodstream but permits exchange of nutrients and waste products.

Polygenic inheritance A pattern of inheritance in which many genes determine a characteristic.

Popular children Children who get many positive votes on sociometric measures of peer acceptance. Distinguished from *rejected, controversial,* and *neglected children.*

Postconventional level Kohlberg's highest level of moral development, in which individuals define morality in terms of abstract principles and values that apply to all situations and societies.

Postpartum depression Feelings of sadness and withdrawal that appear shortly after childbirth and that continue for weeks or months.

Postterm Infants who spend a longer than average time period in the uterus—more than 42 weeks.

Pragmatics The practical, social side of language that is concerned with how to engage in effective and appropriate communication with others.

Preconventional level Kohlberg's first level of moral development, in which moral understanding is based on rewards, punishments, and the power of authority figures.

Preformationism Medieval view of the child as a miniature adult.

Prenatal diagnostic methods Medical procedures that permit detection of developmental problems before birth. Includes amniocentesis, chorionic villi biopsy, ultrasound, fetoscopy, and maternal blood analysis.

Preoperational stage Piaget's second stage, in which rapid growth in representation takes place. However, thought is not yet logical. Spans the years from 2 to 7.

Prereaching The poorly coordinated, primitive reaching movements of newborn babies.

Preterm Infants born several weeks or more before their due date. Although small in size, their weight may still be appropriate for the time they spent in the uterus.

Primary sexual characteristics Physical features that involve the reproductive organs directly (ovaries, uterus, and vagina in females; penis, scrotum, and testes in males). Distinguished from *secondary sexual characteristics.*

Principle of mutual exclusivity The assumption by children in the early stages of vocabulary growth that words mark entirely separate (nonoverlapping) categories.

Private speech Self-directed speech that children use to plan and guide their own behavior.

Production In language development, the words and word combinations that children use. Distinguished from *comprehension.*

Project Head Start A federal program that provides low-income children with a year or two of preschool education before school entry and that encourages parent involvement in children's development.

Propositional thought A type of formal operational reasoning in which adolescents evaluate the logic of verbal statements without referring to real-world circumstances.

Prosocial, or altruistic, behavior Actions that benefit another person without any expected reward for the self.

Proximo-distal trend An organized pattern of physical growth and motor control that proceeds from the center of the body outward.

Psychoanalytic perspective An approach to personality development introduced by Freud that assumes children move through a series of stages in which they confront conflicts between biological drives and social expectations. The way these conflicts are resolved determines psychological adjustment.

Psychosexual theory Freud's theory, which emphasizes that how parents manage children's sexual and aggressive drives during the first few years is crucial for healthy personality development.

Psychosocial theory Erikson's theory, which emphasizes that the demands of society at each Freudian stage not only promote the development of a unique personality, but also ensure that individuals acquire attitudes and skills that help them become active, contributing members of their society.

Puberty Biological changes at adolescence that lead to an adult-sized body and sexual maturity.

Public policies Laws and government programs designed to improve current conditions.

Punishment In operant conditioning, removing a desirable stimulus or presenting an unpleasant one to decrease the occurrence of a response.

R

Range of reaction Each person's unique, genetically determined response to a range of environmental conditions.

Rapid-eye-movement (REM) sleep An "irregular" sleep state in which brain wave activity is similar to that of the waking state; eyes dart beneath the lids, heart rate, blood pressure, and breathing are uneven, and slight body movements occur. Distinguished from *non-rapid-eye-movement (NREM) sleep.*

Realistic period Period of vocational development in which adolescents focus on a general career category and, slightly later, settle on a single occupation. Spans late adolescence and young adulthood.

Recall A type of memory that involves remembering a stimulus that is not present.

Recasts Adult responses that restructure children's incorrect speech into a more mature form.

Recognition A type of memory that involves noticing whether a stimulus is identical or similar to one previously experienced.

Referential style A style of early language learning in which toddlers use language mainly to label objects. Distinguished from *expressive style.*

Reflex An inborn, automatic response to a particular form of stimulation.

Rehearsal The memory strategy of repeating information.

Reinforcer In operant conditioning, a stimulus that increases the occurrence of a response.

Rejected-aggressive children A subgroup of rejected children who engage in high rates of conflict, hostility, and hyperactive, inattentive, and impulsive behavior. Distinguished from *rejected-withdrawn children.*

Rejected children Children who are actively disliked and get many negative votes on sociometric measures of peer acceptance. Distinguished from *popular, controversial,* and *neglected children.*

Rejected-withdrawn children A subgroup of rejected children who are passive and socially awkward. Distinguished from *rejected-aggressive children.*

Resistant attachment The quality of insecure attachment characterizing infants who remain close to the parent before departure and display angry, resistive behavior when she returns. Distinguished from *secure, avoidant,* and *disorganized/disoriented attachment.*

Respiratory distress syndrome A disorder of preterm infants in which the lungs are so immature that the air sacs collapse, causing serious breathing difficulties.

Reticular formation A brain structure that maintains alertness and consciousness.

Reversibility The ability to mentally go through a series of steps in a problem and then reverse direction, returning to the starting point. Distinguished from *irreversibility.*

Rh factor A protein that, when present in the fetus's blood but not in the mother's, can cause the mother to build up antibodies. If these return to the fetus's system, they destroy red blood cells, reducing the oxygen supply to organs and tissues.

Rooming in An arrangement in which the newborn baby stays in the mother's hospital room all or most of the time.

Rough-and-tumble play A form of peer interaction involving friendly chasing and play-fighting that, in our evolutionary past, may have been important for the development of fighting skill.

Rubella Three-day German measles. Causes a wide variety of prenatal abnormalities, especially when it strikes during the embryonic period.

S

Scaffolding A changing quality of support over the course of a teaching session in which the adult adjusts the assistance provided to fit the child's current level of performance. As competence increases, the adult permits the child to take over her guiding role and apply it to his own activity.

Scheme In Piaget's theory, a specific structure, or organized way of making sense of experience, that changes with age.

School phobia Severe apprehension about attending school, often accompanied by physical complaints that disappear once the child is allowed to remain home.

Scripts General descriptions of what occurs and when it occurs in a particular situation. A basic means through which children organize and interpret their everyday experiences.

Secondary sexual characteristics Features visible on the outside of the body that serve as signs of sexual maturity but do not involve the reproductive organs (for example, breast development in females, appearance of underarm and pubic hair in both sexes). Distinguished from *primary sexual characteristics.*

Secular trends in physical growth Changes in body size from one generation to the next.

Secure attachment The quality of attachment characterizing infants who are distressed by parental separation and easily comforted by the parent when she returns. Distinguished from *secure, avoidant,* and *disorganized/disoriented attachment.*

Secure base The use of the familiar caregiver as a base from which the infant confidently explores the environment and returns for emotional support.

Self-care children Children who look after themselves while their parents are at work.

Self-concept A set of beliefs about one's own characteristics.

Self-conscious emotions Emotions that involve injury to or enhancement of the sense of self. Examples are shame, embarrassment, guilt, envy, and pride.

Self-control The capacity to resist a momentary impulse to engage in socially disapproved behavior.

Self-esteem An aspect of self-concept that involves judgments about one's own worth and the feelings associated with those judgments.

Self-regulation The process of continuously monitoring progress toward a goal, checking outcomes, and redirecting unsuccessful efforts.

Sensitive period A time span that is optimal for certain capacities to emerge and in which the individual is especially responsive to environmental influences.

Sensorimotor stage Piaget's first stage, during which infants and toddlers "think" with their eyes, ears, hands, and other sensorimotor equipment. Spans the first 2 years of life.

Sensory register In information processing, that part of the mental system in which sights and sounds are held briefly before they decay or are transferred to working, or short-term, memory.

Separation anxiety An infant's distressed reaction to the departure of the familiar caregiver.

Separation–individuation In Mahler's theory, the process of separating from the mother and becoming aware of the self, which is triggered by crawling and walking.

Seriation The ability to order items along a quantitative dimension, such as length or weight.

Sex chromosomes The twenty-third pair of chromosomes, which determines the sex of the child. In females, called XX; in males, called XY.

Skeletal age An estimate of physical maturity based on development of the bones of the body.

Slow-to-warm-up child A child whose temperament is such that he or she is inactive, shows mild, low-key reactions to environmental stimuli, is negative in mood, and adjusts slowly when faced with new experiences. Distinguished from *easy child* and *difficult child.*

Small for date Infants whose birth weight is below normal when length of pregnancy is taken into account.

Social comparisons Judgments of abilities, behavior, appearance, and other characteristics in relation to those of others.

Social learning theory An approach that emphasizes the role of modeling, or observational learning, in the development of behavior.

Social problem-solving training Training in which children are taught how to resolve social conflicts through discussing and trying out successful strategies.

Social referencing Relying on a trusted person's emotional reaction to decide how to respond to an uncertain situation.

Social smile The smile evoked by the stimulus of the human face. First appears between 6 and 10 weeks.

Social systems perspective A view of the family as a complex system in which the behaviors of each family member affect those of others.

Sociocultural theory Vygotsky's theory, in which children acquire the ways of thinking and behaving that make up a community's culture through cooperative dialogues with more knowledgeable members of society.

Sociodramatic play The make-believe play with peers that first appears around age 2 1/2 and increases rapidly until 4 to 5 years.

Sociometric techniques Self-report measures that ask peers to evaluate one another's likability.

Spermarche First ejaculation of seminal fluid.

Stage A qualitative change in thinking, feeling, and behaving that characterizes a particular time period of development.

Stanford-Binet Intelligence Scale An individually administered intelligence test that is the modern descendent of Alfred Binet's first successful test for children. Measures general intelligence and four factors: verbal reasoning, quantitative reasoning, spatial reasoning, and short-term memory.

States of arousal Different degrees of sleep and wakefulness.

States versus transformations The tendency to treat the initial and final states in a problem as completely unrelated. A characteristic of Piaget's preoperational stage.

Strange Situation A procedure involving short separations from and reunions with the parent that assesses the quality of the attachment bond.

Stranger anxiety The infant's expression of fear in response to unfamiliar adults. Appears in many babies after 7 months of age.

Structured interview A method in which each participant is asked the same questions in the same way.

Structured observation A method in which the investigator sets up a situation that evokes the behavior of interest and observes it in a laboratory. Distinguished from *naturalistic observation.*

Subculture A group of people with beliefs and customs that differ from those of the larger culture.

Sudden infant death syndrome (SIDS) Death of a seemingly healthy baby, who stops breathing, usually during the night, without apparent cause.

Superego In Freud's theory, the part of personality that is the seat of conscience and is often in conflict with the id's desires.

Symbiosis In Mahler's theory, the baby's intimate sense of oneness with the mother, encouraged by warm, physical closeness and gentle handling.

Synapses The gaps between neurons, across which chemical messages are sent.

Systems of action In motor development, combinations of previously acquired skills that lead to more advanced ways of exploring and controlling the environment.

T

Tabula rasa Locke's view of the child as a blank slate whose character is shaped by experience.

Telegraphic speech Toddlers' two-word utterances that, like a telegram, leave out smaller and less important words.

Temperament Stable individual differences in quality and intensity of emotional reaction.

Tentative period Period of vocational development in which adolescents weigh vocational options against their interests, abilities, and values. Spans early and middle adolescence.

Teratogen Any environmental agent that causes damage during the prenatal period.

Thalidomide A sedative widely available in Europe, Canada, and South America in the early 1960s. When taken by mothers between the fourth to sixth week after conception, it produced gross deformities of the embryo's arms and legs.

Theory An orderly, integrated set of statements that describes, explains, and predicts behavior.

Theory of multiple intelligences Gardner's theory, which identifies seven independent intelligences on the basis of distinct sets of processing operations that permit individuals to engage in a wide range of culturally valued activities (linguistic, logico-mathematical, musical, spatial, bodily-kinesthetic, interpersonal, and intrapersonal).

Thyroid-stimulating hormone (TSH) A pituitary hormone that stimulates the thyroid gland to release thyroxine, which is necessary for normal brain development and body growth.

Time out A form of mild punishment in which children are removed from the immediate setting until they are ready to act appropriately.

Toxemia An illness of the last half of pregnancy in which the mother's blood pressure increases sharply and her face, hands, and feet swell. If untreated, it can cause convulsions in the mother and death of the fetus.

Toxoplasmosis A parasitic disease caused by eating raw or undercooked meat or contact with the feces of infected cats. During the first trimester, it leads to eye and brain damage.

Traditional classroom An elementary school classroom based on the educational philosophy that children are passive learners who acquire information presented by teachers. Pupils are evaluated on the basis of how well they keep up with a uniform set of standards for all pupils in their grade. Distinguished from *open classroom.*

Transductive reasoning Reasoning from one particular event to another particular event, instead of from general to particular or particular to general. A characteristic of Piaget's preoperational stage.

Transition Climax of the first stage of labor, in which the frequency and strength of contractions are at their peak and the cervix opens completely.

Transitive inference The ability to seriate—or order items along a quantitative dimension—mentally.

Triarchic theory of intelligence Sternberg's theory, which states that information processing skills, prior experience with tasks, and contextual (or cultural) factors interact to determine intelligent behavior.

Trimesters Three equal time periods in prenatal development, each of which lasts 3 months.

Type A personality A personality characterized by excessive competitiveness, impatience, restlessness, and irritability. Associated with high blood pressure and cholesterol levels as well as heart disease in adulthood.

U

Ulnar grasp The clumsy grasp of the young infant, in which the fingers close against the palm.

Umbilical cord The long cord connecting the prenatal organism to the placenta that delivers nutrients and removes waste products.

Unconditioned response (UCR) In classical conditioning, a reflexive response that is produced by an unconditioned stimulus (UCS).

Unconditioned stimulus (UCS) In classical conditioning, a stimulus that leads to a reflexive response.

Underextension An early vocabulary error in which a word is applied too narrowly, to a smaller number of objects and events than is appropriate. Distinguished from *overextension*.

V

Vacuum extractor A plastic cup attached to a suction tube, used to deliver the baby.

Vernix A white, cheeselike substance covering the fetus and preventing the skin from chapping due to constant exposure to the amniotic fluid.

Visual acuity Fineness of visual discrimination.

W

Wechsler Intelligence Scale for Children–III (WISC–III) An individually administered intelligence test that includes both a measure of general intelligence and a variety of verbal and performance scores.

Whole-language approach An approach to beginning reading instruction that parallels children's natural language learning and keeps reading materials whole and meaningful. Distinguished from *basic-skills approach*.

Working, or short-term, memory In information processing, the conscious part of the mental system, where we actively "work" on a limited amount of information to ensure that it will be retained.

X

X-linked inheritance A pattern of inheritance in which a recessive gene is carried on the X chromosome. Males are more likely to be affected.

Z

Zone of proximal development In Vygotsky's theory, a range of tasks that the child cannot yet handle alone but can do with the help of more skilled partners.

Zygote The newly fertilized cell formed by the union of sperm and ovum at conception.

REFERENCES

Aaron, R., & Powell, G. (1982). Feedback practices as a function of teacher and pupil race during reading groups instruction. *Journal of Negro Education, 51,* 50–59.

Aaronson, L. S., & MacNee, C. L. (1989). Tobacco, alcohol, and caffeine use during pregnancy. *Journal of Obstetrics, Gynecology, and Neonatal Nursing, 18,* 279–287.

Abbott, S. (1992). Holding on and pushing away: Comparative perspectives on an eastern Kentucky child-rearing practice. *Ethos, 20,* 33–65.

Abbotts, B., & Osborn, L. M. (1993). Immunization status and reasons for immunization delay among children using public health immunization clinics. *American Journal of Diseases of Children, 147,* 965–968.

Abel, E. L. (1988). Fetal alcohol syndrome in families. *Neurotoxicology and Teratology, 10,* 1–2.

Abramovitch, R., Freedman, J. L., Thoden, K., & Nikolich, C. (1991). Children's capacity to consent to participation in psychological research: Some empirical findings. *Child Development, 62,* 1100–1109.

Abravanel, E., & Sigafoos, A. D. (1984). Exploring the presence of imitation during early infancy. *Child Development, 55,* 381–392.

Achenbach, T. M., Phares, V., Howell, C. T., Rauh, V. A., & Nurcombe, B. (1990). Seven-year outcome of the Vermont program for low-birthweight infants. *Child Development, 61,* 1672–1681.

Achenbach, T. M., & Weisz, J. R. (1975). A longitudinal study of developmental synchrony between conceptual identity, seriation, and transitivity of color, number, and length. *Child Development, 46,* 840–848.

Ackerman, B. P. (1978). Children's understanding of speech acts in unconventional frames. *Child Development, 49,* 311–318.

Acredolo, C., Adams, A., & Schmid, J. (1984). On the understanding of the relationships between speed, duration, and distance. *Child Development, 55,* 2151–2159.

Adams, G. R., Abraham, K. G., & Markstrom, C. A. (1987). The relations among identity development, self-consciousness, and self-focusing during middle and late adolescence. *Developmental Psychology, 23,* 292–297.

Adams, R. J. (1987). An evaluation of color preference in early infancy. *Infant Behavior and Development, 10,* 143–150.

Adcock, A. G., Nagy, S. N., & Simpson, J. A. (1991). Selected risk factors in adolescent suicide attempts. *Adolescence, 26,* 817–828.

Adolph, K. E., Eppler, M. A., & Gibson, E. J. (1993). Development of perception of affordances. In C. Rovee-Collier & L. P. Lipsitt (Eds.), *Advances in infancy research* (Vol. 8, pp. 51–98). Norwood, NJ: Ablex.

Ahlsten, G., Cnattingius, S., & Lindmark, G. (1993). Cessation of smoking during pregnancy improves fetal growth and reduces infant morbidity in the neonatal period: A population-based prospective study. *Acta Paediatrica, 82,* 177–181.

Ainsworth, M. D. S., Blehar, M. C., Waters, E., & Wall, S. (1978). *Patterns of attachment.* Hillsdale, NJ: Erlbaum.

Albright, A. (1993). Postpartum depression: An overview. *Journal of Counseling & Development, 71,* 316–319.

Ales, K. L., Druzin, M. L., & Santini, D. L. (1990). Impact of advanced maternal age on the outcome of pregnancy. *Surgery, Gynecology & Obstetrics, 171,* 209–216.

Alessandri, S. M., & Wozniak, R. H. (1987). The child's awareness of parental beliefs concerning the child: A developmental study. *Child Development, 58,* 316–323.

Alessandri, S. M., Sullivan, M. W., Imaizumi, S., & Lewis, M. (1993). Learning and emotional responsivity in cocaine-exposed infants. *Developmental Psychology, 29,* 989–997.

Allen, J. P., Hauser, S. T., Bell, K. L., & O'Connor, T. G. (1994). Longitudinal assessment of autonomy and relatedness in adolescent–family interactions as predictors of adolescent ego development and self-esteem. *Child Development, 65,* 179–194.

Allen, L. F., Palomares, R. S., DeForest, P., Sprinkle, B., & Reynolds, C. R. (1991). The effects of intrauterine cocaine exposure: Transient or teratogenic? *Archives of Clinical Neurospsychology, 6,* 133–146.

Alpert-Gillis, L. J., & Connell, J. P. (1989). Gender and sex-role influences on children's self-esteem. *Journal of Personality, 57,* 97–114.

Altemeier, W. A., O'Connor, S. M., Sherrod, K. B., & Vietze, P. M. (1984). Prospective study of antecedents for nonorganic failure to thrive. *Journal of Pediatrics, 106,* 360–365.

Alter-Reid, K., Gibbs, M. S., Lachenmeyer, J. R., Sigal, J., & Massoth, N. A. (1986). Sexual abuse of children: A review of empirical findings. *Clinical Psychology Review, 6,* 249–266.

Altshuler, J. L., & Ruble, D. N. (1989). Developmental changes in children's awareness of strategies for coping with uncontrollable stress. *Child Development, 60,* 1337–1349.

Amato, P. R. (1993). Children's adjustment to divorce: Theories, hypotheses, and empirical support. *Journal of Marriage and the Family, 55,* 23–38.

American Academy of Pediatrics (1984). Report of the task force on the assessment of the scientific evidence relating to infant-feeding practices and infant health. *Pediatrics, 74,* 579-762.

American College of Sports Medicine. (1984). Position stand on the use of anabolic-androgenic steroids in sports. *Medical Science and Sports, 19,* 534–539.

American Psychiatric Association. (1994). *Diagnostic and statistical manual of mental disorders* (4th ed.). Washington, DC: Author.

American Psychological Association. (1992). Ethical principles of psychologists and code of conduct. *American Psychologist, 44,* 1597–1611.

Anand, K. J. S., Phil, D., & Hickey, P. R. (1987). Pain and its effects in the human neonate and fetus. *New England Journal of Medicine, 317,* 1321–1329.

Anderson, E. S. (1984). The acquisition of sociolinguistic knowledge: Some evidence from children's verbal role play. *Western Journal of Speech Communication, 48,* 125–144.

Anderson, G. C. (1991). Current knowledge about skin-to-skin (kangaroo) care for preterm infants. *Journal of Perinatology, 11,* 216–226.

Anderson, J. E., Kann, L., Holtzman, D., Arday, S., Truman, B., & Kolbe, L. (1990). HIV/AIDS knowledge and sexual behavior among high school students. *Family Planning Perspectives, 22,* 252–255.

Anderson, P. J., & Graham, S. M. (1994). Issues in second-language phonological acquisition among children and adults. *Topics in Language Disorders, 14,* 84–100.

Andersson, B-E. (1989). Effects of public day care—A longitudinal study. *Child Development, 60,* 857–866.

Andersson, B-E. (1992). Effects of day care on cognitive and socioemotional competence of thirteen-year-old Swedish schoolchildren. *Child Development, 63,* 20–36.

Angle, J., & Wissmann, D. A. (1980). The epidemiology of myopia. *American Journal of Epidemiology, 111,* 220–228.

Anglin, J. M. (1993). Vocabulary development: A morphological analysis. *Monographs of the Society for Research in Child Development, 58*(10, Serial No. 238).

Antonarakis, S. E. (1992). The meiotic stage of nondisjunction in trisomy 21: Determination by using DNA polymorphisms. *American Journal of Human Genetics, 50,* 544–550.

Apgar, V. (1953). A proposal for a new method of evaluation in the newborn infant. *Current Research in Anesthesia and Analgesia, 32,* 260–267.

Appleton, T., Clifton, R. K., & Goldberg, S. (1975). The development of behavioral competence in infancy. In F. D. Horowitz (Ed.), *Review of child development research* (Vol. 4, pp. 101–186). Chicago: University of Chicago Press.

Archer, S. L. (1982). The lower age boundaries of identity development. *Child Development, 53,* 1551–1556.

Archer, S. L. (1989a). Gender differences in identity development: Issues of process, domain, and timing. *Journal of Adolescence, 2,* 117–138.

Archer, S. L. (1989b). The status of identity: Reflections on the need for intervention. *Journal of Adolescence, 12,* 345–359.

Archer, S. L., & Waterman, A. S. (1990). Varieties of identity diffusions and foreclosures: An exploration of subcategories of the identity statuses. *Journal of Adolescent Research, 5,* 96–111.

Archer, S. L., & Waterman, A. S. (1994). Adolescent identity development: Contextual perspectives. In C. B. Fisher & R. M. Lerner (Eds.), *Applied developmental psychology* (pp. 76–100). New York: McGraw-Hill.

Ariès, P. (1962). *Centuries of childhood.* New York: Random House.

Arnett, J., & Balle-Jensen, L. (1993). Cultural bases of risk behavior: Danish adolescents. *Child Development, 64,* 1842–1859.

Arnold, K., & Denny, T. (1985). *The lives of academic achievers: The career aspirations of male and female high school valedictorians and salutatorians.* Paper presented at the annual meeting of the American Educational Research Association, Chicago.

Arterberry, M. E., & Yonas, A. (1988). Infants' sensitivity to kinetic information for three-dimensional object shape. *Perception and Psychophysics, 44,* 1–6.

Artman, L., & Cahan, S. (1993). Schooling and the development of transitive inference. *Developmental Psychology, 29,* 753–759.

Asher, S. R., & Hymel, S. (1981). Children's social competence in peer relations: sociometric and behavioral assessment. In J. D. Wine & W. D. Smye (Eds.), *Social competence* (pp. 125–157). New York: Guilford Press.

Ashmead, D. H., & Perlmutter, M. (1980). Infant memory in everyday life. In M. Perlmutter (Ed.), *New directions for child development* (Vol. 10, pp. 1–16). San Francisco: Jossey-Bass.

Ashmead, D. H., Davis, D. L., Whalen, T., & Odom, R. D. (1991). Sound localization and sensitivity to interaural time differences in human infants. *Child Development, 62,* 1211–1226.

Ashmead, D. H., McCarty, M. E., Lucas, L. S., & Belvedere, M. C. (1993). Visual guidance in infants' reaching toward suddenly displaced targets. *Child Development, 64,* 1111–1127.

Aslin, R. N. (1987). Visual and auditory development in infancy. In J. D. Osofsky (Ed.), *Handbook of infant development* (2nd ed., pp. 5–97). New York: Wiley.

Aslin, R. N., Pisoni, D. B., & Jusczyk, P. W. (1983). Auditory development and speech perception in infancy. In M. M. Haith & J. J. Campos (Eds.), *Handbook of child psychology: Vol. 2. Infancy and developmental psychobiology* (4th ed., pp. 573–687). New York: Wiley.

Astington, J. W. (1991). Intention in the child's theory of mind. In C. Moore & D. Frye (Eds.), *Children's theories of mind* (pp. 157–172). Hillsdale, NJ: Erlbaum.

Astley, S. J., Clarren, S. K., Little, R. E., Sampson, P. D., & Daling, J. R. (1992). Analysis of facial shape in children gestationally exposed to marijuana, alcohol, and/or cocaine. *Pediatrics, 89,* 67–77.

Atkin, C. (1978). Observation of parent–child interaction in supermarket decision making. *Journal of Marketing, 42,* 41–45.

Atkinson, R. C., & Shiffrin, R. M. (1968). Human memory: A proposed system and its control processes. In K. W. Spence & J. T. Spence (Eds.), *Advances in the psychology of learning and motivation* (Vol. 2, pp. 90–195). New York: Academic Press.

Attie, I., & Brooks-Gunn, J. (1989). Development of eating problems in adolescent girls: A longitudinal study. *Developmental Psychology, 25,* 70–79.

Au, T. K., Sidle, A. L., & Rollins, K. B. (1993). Developing an intuitive understanding of conservation and contamination: Invisible particles as a plausible mechanism. *Developmental Psychology, 29,* 286–299.

August, D., & Garcia, E. E. (1988). *Language minority education in the United States.* Springfield, IL: Thomas.

Auletta, K. (1993, November 8). The electronic parent. *The New Yorker,* pp. 68–75.

Avis, J., & Harris, P. L. (1991). Belief–desire reasoning among Baka children: Evidence for a universal conception of mind. *Child Development, 62,* 460–467.

Axia, G., & Baroni, R. (1985). Linguistic politeness at different age levels. *Child Development, 56,* 918–927.

Azmitia, M. (1988). Peer interaction and problem solving: When are two heads better than one? *Child Development, 59,* 87–96.

Azmitia, M., & Hesser, J. (1993). Why siblings are important agents of cognitive development: A comparison of siblings and peers. *Child Development, 64,* 430–444.

Bahrick, L. E. (1983). Infants' perception of substance and temporal synchrony in multimodal events. *Infant Behavior and Development, 6,* 429–451.

Bahrick, L. E. (1988). Intermodal learning in infancy: Learning on the basis of two kinds of invariant relations in audible and visible events. *Child Development, 59,* 197–209.

Bahrick, L. E. (1992). Infants' perceptual differentiation of amodal and modality-specific audio-visual relations. *Journal of Experimental Child Psychology, 53,* 180–199.

Bai, D. L., & Bertenthal, B. I. (1992). Locomotor status and the development of spatial search skills. *Child Development, 63,* 215–226.

Bailey, J. M., & Pillard, R. C. (1991). A genetic study of male sexual orientation. *Archives of General Psychology, 43,* 808–812.

Bailey, J. M., Pillard, R. C., Neale, M. C., & Agyei, Y. (1993). Heritable factors influence sexual orientation in women. *Archives of General Psychiatry, 50,* 217–223.

Bailey, R. C. (1990). Growth of African pygmies in early childhood. *New England Journal of Medicine, 323,* 1146.

Bailey, T. (1993). Can youth apprenticeship thrive in the United States? *Educational Researcher, 22*(3), 4–10.

Baillargeon, R. (1987). Object permanence in 3 1/2- and 4 1/2-month-old infants. *Developmental Psychology, 23,* 655–664.

Baillargeon, R. (1993). The object concept revisited: New directions. In C. Granrud (Ed.), *Visual perception and cognition in infancy* (pp. 265–315). New York: Academic Press.

Baillargeon, R., & DeVos, J. (1991). Object permanence in young infants: Further evidence. *Child Development, 62,* 1227–1246.

Baillargeon, R., Graber, M., DeVos, J., & Black, J. (1990). Why do young infants fail to search for hidden objects? *Cognition, 36,* 255–284.

Baird, P. A., & Sadovnick, A. D. (1987). Maternal age-specific rates for Down syndrome: Changes over time. *American Journal of Medical Genetics, 29,* 917–927.

Baker-Ward, L., Gordon, B. N., Ornstein, P. A., Larus, D. M., & Clubb, P. A. (1993). Young children's long-term retention of a pediatric examination. *Child Development, 64,* 1519–1533.

Ballard, B. D., Gipson, M. T., Guttenberg, W., & Ramsey, K. (1980). Palatability of food as a factor influencing obese and normal-weight children's eating habits. *Behavior Research and Therapy, 18,* 598–600.

Bancroft, J., Axworthy, D., & Ratcliffe, S. (1982). The personality and psycho-sexual development of boys with 47 XXY chromosome constitution. *Journal of Child Psychology and Psychiatry, 23,* 169–180.

Band, E. B., & Weisz, J. R. (1988). How to feel better when it feels bad: Children's perspectives on coping with everyday stress. *Developmental Psychology, 24,* 247–253.

Bandura, A. (1977). *Social learning theory.* Englewood Cliffs, NJ: Prentice Hall.

Bandura, A. (1986). *Social foundations of thought and action: A social cognitive theory.* Englewood Cliffs, NJ: Prentice Hall.

Bandura, A. (1989). Social cognitive theory. In R. Vasta (Ed.), *Annals of child development* (Vol. 6, pp. 1–60). Greenwich, CT: JAI Press.

Banis, H. T., Varni, J. W., Wallander, J. L., Korsch, B. M., Jay, S. M., Adler, R., Garcia-Temple, E., & Negrete, V. (1988). Psychological and social adjustment of obese children and their families: *Child: Care, Health, and Development, 14,* 157–173.

Banks, M. S. (1980). The development of visual accommodation during early infancy. *Child Development, 51,* 157–173.

Banks, M. S., & Ginsburg, A. P. (1985). Early visual preferences: A review and new theoretical treatment. In H. W. Reese (Ed.), *Advances in child development and behavior* (Vol. 19, pp. 207–246). New York: Academic Press.

Banks, M. S., & Salapatek, P. (1981). Infant pattern vision: A new approach based on the contrast sensitivity function. *Journal of Experimental Child Psychology, 31,* 1–45.

Banks, M. S., & Salapatek, P. (1983). Infant visual perception. In M. M. Haith & J. J. Campos (Eds.), *Handbook of child psychology: Vol. 2. Infancy and developmental psychobiology* (pp. 435–571). New York: Wiley.

Barenboim, C. (1977). Developmental changes in the interpersonal cognitive system from middle childhood to adolescence. *Child Development, 48,* 1467–1474.

Barker, D. J. P., Gluckman, P. D., Godfrey, K. M., Harding, J. E., Owens, J. A., & Robinson, J. S. (1993). Fetal nutrition and cardiovascular disease in adult life. *Lancet, 341,* 938–941.

Barker, R. G. (1955). *Midwest and its children.* Stanford, CA: Stanford University Press.

Barkley, R. A. (1990). *Attention deficit hyperactivity disorder: A handbook for diagnosis and treatment.* New York: Guilford.

Barnes, K. E. (1971). Preschool play norms: A replication. *Developmental Psychology, 5,* 99–103.

Barnes, S., Gutfreund, M., Satterly, D., & Wells, D. (1983). Characteristics of adult speech which predict children's language development. *Journal of Child Language, 10,* 65–84.

Barnett, D., Manly, J., & Cicchetti, D. (1993). Defining child maltreatment: The interface between policy and research. In D. Cicchetti & S. Toth (Eds.), *Child abuse, child development, and social policy* (pp. 7–73). Norwood, NJ: Ablex.

Barnett, M. (1982). Infant outcome in relation to second stage labor pushing method. *Birth, 9,* 221–228.

Barnett, W. S. (1993). New wine in old bottles: Increasing the coherence of early childhood care and educational policy. *Early Childhood Research Quarterly, 8,* 519–558.

Barol, B. (1986, July 28). Cocaine babies: Hooked at birth. *Newsweek, 58*(4), 56–57.

Barr, H. M., Streissguth, A. P., Darby, B. L., & Sampson, P. D. (1990). Prenatal exposure to alcohol, caffeine, tobacco, and aspirin: Effects on fine and gross motor performance in 4-year-old children. *Developmental Psychology, 26,* 339–348.

Barr, R. (1991, May). Toward a balanced perspective on beginning reading. *Educational Researcher, 20*(4), 30–32.

Barrera, M. E., & Maurer, D. (1981a). Discrimination of strangers by the three-month-old. *Child Development, 52,* 559–563.

Barrera, M. E., & Maurer, D. (1981b). Recognition of mother's photographed face by the three-month-old infant. *Child Development, 52,* 714–716.

Barrett, D. E., & Yarrow, M. R. (1977). Prosocial behavior, social inferential ability, and assertiveness in children. *Child Development, 48,* 475–481.

Barrett, K. C., & Campos, J. J. (1987). Perspectives on emotional development: II. A functionalist approach to emotion. In J. D. Osofsky (Ed.), *Handbook of infant development* (2nd ed., pp. 1101–1149). New York: Wiley.

Barth, R. P., Petro, J. V., & Leland, N. (1992). Preventing adolescent pregnancy with social and cognitive skills. *Journal of Adolescent Research, 7,* 208–222.

Bastian, H. (1993). Personal beliefs and alternative childbirth choices: A survey of 552 women who planned to give birth at home. *Birth, 20,* 186–192.

Bates, E. (1979). *The emergence of symbols: Cognition and communication in infancy.* New York: Academic Press.

Bates, E., Bretherton, I., & Snyder, L. (1988). *From first words to grammar.* Cambridge, England: Cambridge University Press.

Bates, J. E. (1987). Temperament in infancy. In J. D. Osofsky (Ed.), *Handbook of infant development* (2nd ed., pp. 1101–1149). New York: Wiley.

Bates, J. E., & Bayles, K. (1988). Attachment and the development of behavior problems. In J. Belsky & T. Nexworski (Eds.), *Clinical implications of attachment* (pp. 253–294). Hillsdale, NJ: Erlbaum.

Bauer, P. J., & Hertsgaard, L. A. (1993). Increasing steps in recall of events: Factors facilitating immediate and long-term memory in 13.5- and 16.5-month-old children. *Child Development, 64,* 1204–1223.

Bauer, P. J., & Mandler, J. M. (1989). One thing follows another: Effects of temporal structure on 1- to 2-year-olds' recall of events. *Developmental Psychology, 25,* 197–206.

Bauer, P. J., & Mandler, J. M. (1992). Putting the horse before the cart: The use of temporal order in recall of events by one-year-old children. *Developmental Psychology, 28,* 441–452.

Baumeister, R. F. (1990). Identity crisis. In R. M. Lerner, A. C. Petersen, & J. Brooks-Gunn (Eds.), *The encyclopedia of adolescence* (Vol. 1, pp. 518–521). New York: Garland.

Baumrind, D. (1967). Child care practices anteceding three patterns of preschool behavior. *Genetic Psychology Monographs, 75,* 43–88.

Baumrind, D. (1971). Current patterns of parental authority. *Developmental Psychology Monograph, 4*(No. 1, Pt. 2).

Baumrind, D. (1983). Rejoinder to Lewis's reinterpretation of parental firm control effects: Are authoritative families really harmonious? *Psychological Bulletin, 94,* 132–142.

Baumrind, D. (1991). The influence of parenting style on adolescent competence and substance use. *Journal of Early Adolescence, 11,* 56–95.

Baumrind, D., & Black, A. E. (1967). Socialization practices associated with dimension of competence in preschool boys and girls. *Child Development, 38,* 291–327.

Bayley, N. (1969). *Bayley Scales of Infant Development.* New York: Psychological Corporation.

Bayley, N. (1993). *Bayley Scales of Infant Development* (2nd ed.). New York: Psychological Corporation.

Beal, C. R. (1990). The development of text evaluation and revision skills. *Child Development, 61,* 247–258.

Beautrais, A. L., Fergusson, D. M., & Shannon, F. T. (1982). Life events and childhood morbidity: A prospective study. *Pediatrics, 70,* 935–940.

Beck, M. (1994, January 17). How far should we push mother nature? *Newsweek,* pp. 54–57.

Beeghley, L., & Sellers, C. (1986). Adolescents and sex: A structural theory of premarital sex in the United States. *Deviant Behavior, 7,* 313–336.

Behrend, D. (1988). Overextensions in early language comprehension: Evidence from a signal detection approach. *Journal of Child Language, 15,* 63–75.

Behrend, D. A., Rosengren, K. S., & Perlmutter, M. (1992). The relation between private speech and parental interactive style. In R. M. Diaz & L. E. Berk (Eds.), *Private speech: From social interaction to self-regulation* (pp. 85–100). Hillsdale, NJ: Erlbaum.

Behrman, R. E., & Vaughan, V. C. (1987). *Nelson textbook of pediatrics* (13th ed.). Philadelphia: Saunders.

Beidel, D. (1991). Social phobia and overanxious disorder in school-age children. *Journal of the American Academy of Child and Adolescent Psychiatry, 30,* 545–552.

Beilin, H. (1978). Inducing conservation through training. In G. Steiner (Ed.), *Psychology of the twentieth century* (Vol. 7, pp. 260–289). Munich: Kindler.

Beilin, H. (1992). Piaget's enduring contribution to developmental psychology. *Developmental Psychology, 28,* 191–204.

Belkin, L. (1992, July 28). Childless couples hang on to last hope, despite law. *The New York Times,* pp. B1–B2.

Bell, A., Weinberg, M., & Hammersmith, S. (1981). *Sexual preference: Its development in men and women.* Blooming-ton, IN: Indiana University Press.

Bell, M. A., & Fox, N. A. (1992). The relations between frontal brain electrical activity and cognitive development during infancy. *Child Development, 63,* 1142–1163.

Bellinger, D., Leviton, A., Waternaux, C., Needleman, H., & Rabinowitz, M. (1987). Longitudinal analysis of prenatal and postnatal lead exposure and early cognitive development. *New England Journal of Medicine, 316,* 1037–1043.

Belsky, J. (1993). Etiology of child maltreatment: A developmental-ecological analysis. *Psychological Bulletin, 114,* 413–434.

Belsky, J., & Braungart, J. M. (1991). Are insecure-avoidant infants with extensive day-care experience less stressed by and more independent in the Strange Situation? *Child Development, 62,* 567–571.

Belsky, J., Fish, M., & Isabella, R. (1991). Continuity and discontinuity in infant negative and positive emotionality: Family antecedents and attachment consequences. *Developmental Psychology, 27,* 421–431.

Belsky, J., Goode, M. K., & Most, R. K. (1980). Maternal stimulation and infant exploratory competence: Cross-sectional, correlational, and experimental analyses. *Child Development, 51,* 1163–1178.

Belsky, J., Rovine, M., & Taylor, D. G. (1984). The Pennsylvania Infant and Family Development Project: III. The origins of individual differences in infant–mother attachment: Maternal and infant contributions. *Child Development, 55,* 718–728.

Belsky, J., Spanier, G. B., & Rovine, M. (1983). Stability and change in marriage across the transition to parenthood. *Journal of Marriage and the Family, 45,* 567–577.

Bem, S. L. (1974). The measurement of psychological androgyny. *Journal of Consulting and Clinical Psychology, 42,* 155–162.

Bem, S. L. (1984). Androgyny and gender schema theory: A conceptual and empirical integration. In R. A. Dienstbier & T. B. Sondregger (Eds.), *Nebraska Symposia on Motivation* (Vol. 34, pp. 179–226). Lincoln: University of Nebraska Press.

Bem, S. L. (1989). Genital knowledge and gender constancy in preschool children. *Child Development, 60,* 649–662.

Benacerraf, B. R., Green, M. F., Saltzman, D. H., Barss, V. A., Penso, C. A., Nadel, A. S., Heffner, L. J., Stryker, J. M., Sandstrom, M. M., & Frigoletto, F. D., Jr. (1988). Early amniocentesis for prenatal cytogenetic evaluation. *Radiology, 169,* 709–710.

Benbow, C. P. (1986). Physiological correlates of extreme intellectual precocity. *Neuropsychologia, 24,* 719–725.

Benbow, C. P. (1988). Sex differences in mathematical reasoning ability in intellectually talented preadolescents: Their nature, effects, and possible causes. *Behavioral and Brain Sciences, 11,* 169–232.

Benbow, C. P., & Arjmand, O. (1990). Predictors of high academic achievement in mathematics and science by mathematically talented students: A longitudinal study. *Journal of Educational Psychology,* 82, 430–441.

Benbow, C. P., & Stanley, J. C. (1980). Sex differences in mathematical ability: Fact or artifact? *Science, 210,* 1262–1264.

Benbow, C. P., & Stanley, J. C. (1983). Sex differences in mathematical reasoning: More facts. *Science, 222,* 1029–1031.

Bench, R. J., Collyer, Y., Mentz, L., & Wilson, I. (1976). Studies in infant behavioural audiometry: I. Neonates. *Audiology, 15,* 85–105.

Benedict, R. (1934a). Anthropology and the abnormal. *Journal of Genetic Psychology, 10,* 59–82.

Benedict, R. (1934b). *Patterns of culture.* Boston: Houghton Mifflin.

Benenson, J. F. (1993). Greater preference among females than males for dyadic interaction in early childhood. *Child Development, 64,* 544–555.

Berezin, J. (1990). *The complete guide to choosing child care.* New York: Random House.

Berg, M., & Medrich, E. A. (1980). Children in four neighborhoods: The physical environment and its effects on play and play patterns. *Environment and Behavior, 12,* 320–348.

Berg, W. K., & Berg, K. M. (1987). Psychophysiological development in infancy: State, startle, and attention. In J. Osofsky (Ed.), *Handbook of infant development* (2nd ed., pp. 238–317). New York: Wiley.

Berk, L. E. (1985). Relationship of caregiver education to child-oriented attitudes, job satisfaction, and behaviors toward children. *Child Care Quarterly, 14,* 103–129.

Berk, L. E. (1992a). Children's private speech: An overview of theory and the status of research. In R. M. Diaz & L. E. Berk (Eds.), *Private speech: From social interaction to self-regulation* (pp. 17–53). Hillsdale, NJ: Erlbaum.

Berk, L. E. (1992b). The extracurriculum. In P. W. Jackson (Ed.), *Handbook of research on curriculum* (pp. 1002–1043). New York: Macmillan.

Berk, L. E., & Landau, S. (1993). Private speech of learning disabled and normally achieving children in classroom academic and laboratory contexts. *Child Development, 64,* 556–571.

Berk, L. E., & Spuhl, S T. (1995). Maternal interaction, private speech, and task performance in preschool children. *Early Childhood Research Quarterly, 10,* 145–169.

Berko Gleason, J. (1989). Studying language development. In J. Berko Gleason (Ed.), *The development of language* (pp. 1–34). Columbus, OH: Merrill.

Berkowitz, M. W., & Gibbs, J. C. (1983). Measuring the developmental features of moral discussion. *Merrill-Palmer Quarterly, 29,* 399–410.

Berman, P. W. (1980). Are women more responsive than men to the young? A review of developmental and situational variables. *Psychological Bulletin, 88,* 668–695.

Berman, P. W., & Pedersen, F. A. (Eds.). (1987). *Men's transition to parenthood: Longitudinal studies and early family experience.* Hillsdale, NJ: Erlbaum.

Berndt, T. J. (1986). Children's comments about their friendships. In M. Perlmutter (Ed.), *Cognitive perspectives on children's social and behavioral development* (pp. 189–212). Hillsdale, NJ: Erlbaum.

Berndt, T. J. (1988). The nature and significance of children's friendships. In R. Vasta (Ed.), *Annals of child development* (Vol. 5, pp. 155–186). Greenwich, CT: JAI Press.

Berndt, T. J., & Perry, T. B. (1990). Distinctive features and effects of early adolescent friendships. In R. Montemayor, G. R. Adams, & T. P. Gullotta (Eds.), *From childhood to adolescence: A transitional period?* (pp. 269–287). Newbury Park, CA: Sage.

Berndt, T. J., Cheung, P. C., Lau, S., Hau, K-T., & Lew, W. J. F. (1993). Perceptions of parenting in mainland China, Taiwan, and Hong Kong: Sex differences and societal differences. *Developmental Psychology, 29,* 156–164.

Bernier, J. C., & Siegel, D. H. (1994). Attention-deficit hyperactivity disorder: A family ecological systems perspective. *Families in Society, 75,* 142–150.

Berry, K., & Skinner, L. G. (1993). Anatomically detailed dolls and the evaluations of child sexual abuse allegations: Psychometric considerations. *Law and Human Behavior, 17,* 399–422.

Bertenthal, B. I., & Campos, J. J. (1987). New directions in the study of early experience. *Child Development, 58,* 560–567.

Bertenthal, B. I., Campos, J. J., & Barrett, K. (1984). Self-produced locomotion: An organizer of emotional, cognitive, and social development in infancy. In R. Emde & R. Harmon (Eds.), *Continuities and discontinuities in development* (pp. 174–210). New York: Plenum.

Bertenthal, B. I., Campos, J. J., & Haith, M. (1980). Development of visual organization: The perception of subjective contours. *Child Development, 51,* 1077–1080.

Bertenthal, B. I., Proffitt, D. R., Kramer, S. J., & Spetner, N. B. (1987). Infants' encoding of kinetic displays varying in relative coherence. *Developmental Psychology, 23,* 171–178.

Bertenthal, B. I., Proffitt, D. R., Spetner, N. B., & Thomas, M. A. (1985). The development of infant sensitivity to biomechanical motions. *Child Development, 56,* 531–543.

Best, D. L. (1993). Inducing children to generate mnemonic organizational strategies: An examination of long-term retention and materials. *Developmental Psychology, 29,* 324–336.

Best, D. L., Williams, J. E., Cloud, J. M., Davis, S. W., Robertson, L. S., Edwards, J. R., Giles, H., & Fowles, J. (1977). Development of sex-trait stereotypes among young children in the United States, England, and Ireland. *Child Development, 48,* 1375–1384.

Betz, C. (1994, March). Beyond time-out: Tips from a teacher. *Young Children, 49*(3), 10–14.

Beyth-Marom, R., Austin, L., Fischhoff, B., Palmgren, C., & Jacobs-Quadrel, M. (1993). Perceived consequences of risky behaviors: Adults and adolescents. *Developmental Psychology, 29,* 549–563.

Bialystok, E. (1986). Factors in the growth of linguistic awareness. *Child Development, 57,* 498–510.

Bibace, R., & Walsh, M. E. (1980). Development of children's concepts of illness. *Pediatrics, 66,* 912–917.

Biederman, J., Faraone, S. V., Keenan, K., Knee, D., & Tsuang, M. T. (1990). Family-genetic and psychosocial risk factors in DSM–III attention deficit disorder. *Journal of the American Academy of Child and Adolescent Psychiatry, 29,* 526–533.

Bierman, K. L. (1986). Process of change during social skills training with preadolescents and its relation to treatment outcome. *Child Development, 57,* 230–240.

Bierman, K. L., Smoot, D. L., & Aumiller, K. (1993). Characteristics of aggressive-rejected, aggressive (nonrejected), and rejected (nonaggressive) boys. *Child Development, 64,* 139–151.

Biernat, M. (1991a). Gender stereotypes and the relationship between masculinity and femininity: A developmental analysis. *Journal of Personality and Social Psychology, 61,* 351–365.

Biernat, M. (1991b). A multi-component, developmental analysis of sex-typing. *Sex Roles, 24,* 567–586.

Bigler, R. S., & Liben, L. S. (1990). The role of attitudes and interventions in gender-schematic processing. *Child Development, 61,* 1440–1452.

Bigler, R. S., & Liben, L. S. (1992). Cognitive mechanisms in children's gender stereotyping: Theoretical and educational implications of a cognitive-based intervention. *Child Development, 63,* 1351–1363.

Bijeljac-Babic, R., Bertoncini, J., & Mehler, J. (1993). How do 4-day-old infants categorize multisyllable utterances? *Developmental Psychology, 29,* 711–721.

Birch, L. L. (1987). Children's food preferences: Developmental patterns and environmental influences. In G. Whitehurst & R. Vasta (Eds.), *Annals of child development* (Vol. 4, pp. 171–208). Greenwich, CT: JAI Press.

Birch, L. L. (1990). Development of food acceptance patterns. *Developmental Psychology, 26,* 515–519.

Birch, L. L., Johnson, S. L., & Fisher, J. A. (1995, January). Children's eating: The development of food acceptance patterns. *Young Children, 50*(2), 71–78.

Birch, L. L., Johnson, S. L., Andresen, G., Peters, J. C., & Schulte, M. C. (1991). The variability of young children's energy intake. *New England Journal of Medicine, 324,* 232–235.

Birch, L. L., McPhee, L., Shoba, B. C., Steinberg, L., & Krehbiel, R. (1987). "Clean up your plate": Effects of child feeding practices on the development of intake regulation. *Learning and Motivation, 18,* 301–317.

Birch, L. L., Zimmerman, S., & Hind, H. (1980). The influence of social-affective context on preschool children's food preferences. *Child Development, 51,* 856–861.

Birnholz, J. C., & Benacerraf, B. R. (1983). The development of human fetal hearing. *Science, 222,* 516–518.

Bishop, S. M., & Ingersoll, G. M. (1989). Effects of marital conflict and family structure on the self-concepts of pre- and early adolescents. *Journal of Youth and Adolescence, 18,* 25–38.

Bivens, J. A., & Berk, L. E. (1990). A longitudinal study of the development of elementary school children's private speech. *Merrill-Palmer Quarterly, 36,* 443–463.

Bjorklund, D. F., & Muir, J. E. (1988). Children's development of free recall: Remembering on their own. In R. Vasta (Ed.), *Annals of child development* (Vol. 5, pp. 79–123). Greenwich, CT: JAI Press.

Bjorklund, D. F., Schneider, W., Cassel, W. S., & Ashley, E. (1994). Training and extension of a memory strategy: Evidence for utilization deficiencies in the acquisition of an organizational strategy in high- and low-IQ children. *Child Development, 65,* 951–965.

Black, M. (1993). *Girls and women: A UNICEF development priority.* New York: United Nations Children's Fund.

Blake, J. (1989). *Family size and achievement.* Berkeley: University of California Press.

Blanchard, M., & Main, M. (1979). Avoidance of the attachment figure and social-emotional adjustment in day-care infants. *Developmental Psychology, 15,* 445–446.

Blasi, A. (1983). Moral cognition and moral action: A theoretical perspective. *Developmental Review, 3,* 178–210.

Blasi, A. (1990). Kohlberg's theory and moral motivation. In D. Schrader (Ed.), *New directions for child development* (No. 47, pp. 51–57). San Francisco: Jossey-Bass.

Blass, E. M., & Ciaramitaro,V. (1994). A new look at some old mechanisms in human newborns: Taste and tactile determinants of state, affect, and action. *Monographs of the Society for Research in Child Development, 59*(1, Serial No. 239).

Blass, E. M., Ganchrow, J. R., & Steiner, J. E. (1984). Classical conditioning in newborn humans 2–48 hours of age. *Infant Behavior and Development, 7,* 223–235.

Blaubergs, M. S. (1980, March). Sex-role stereotyping and gifted girls' experience and education. *Roeper Review, 2(3),* 13–15.

Block, J., & Robins, R. W. (1994). A longitudinal study of consistency and change in self-esteem from early adolescence to early adulthood. *Child Development, 64,* 909–923.

Block, J., Block, J. H., & Gjerde, P. F. (1988). Parental functioning and home environment in families of divorce: Prospective and concurrent analyses. *Journal of the American Academy of Child and Adolescent Psychiatry, 27,* 207–213.

Block, J. H. (1984). *Sex role identity and ego development.* San Francisco: Jossey-Bass.

Bloom, B. S. (Ed.). (1985). *Developing talent in young people.* New York: Ballantine Books.

Bloom, L., Tinker, E., & Margulis, C. (1993). The words children learn: Evidence against a noun bias in early vocabularies. *Cognitive Development, 8,* 431–450.

Blotner, R., & Bearison, D. J. (1984). Developmental consistencies in socio-moral knowledge: Justice reasoning and altruistic behavior. *Merrill-Palmer Quarterly, 30,* 349–367.

Bluebond-Langer, M. (1977). Meanings of death to children. In H. Feifel (Ed.), *New meanings of death* (pp. 47–66). New York: McGraw-Hill.

Blurton Jones, N. (1972). Categories of child–child interaction. In N. Blurton Jones (Ed.), *Ethological studies of child behaviour* (pp. 97–127). Cambridge, England: Cambridge University Press.

Blyth, D. A., Hill, J. A., & Thiel, K. (1982). Early adolescents' significant others: Grade and gender differences in perceived relationships with familial and nonfamilial adults and young people. *Journal of Youth and Adolescence, 11,* 425–450.

Blyth, D. A., Simmons, R. G., & Zakin, D. F. (1985). Satisfaction with body image for early adolescent females: The impact of pubertal timing within different school environments. *Journal of Youth and Adolescence, 14,* 207–225.

Bobak, I. M., Jensen, M. D., & Zalar, M. K. (1989). *Maternity and gynecologic care.* St. Louis: Mosby.

Bodurtha, J., Tams, L., & Jackson-Cook, C. (1992). Prenatal genetic counseling: What is fragile X? *Virginia Medical Quarterly, 119,* 97–98.

Boer, F., Goedhart, A. W., & Treffers, P. D. A. (1992). Siblings and their parents. In F. Boer & J. Dunn (Eds.), *Children's sibling relationships* (pp. 41–54). Hillsdale, NJ: Erlbaum.

Bogatz, G. A., & Ball, S. (1972). *The second year of Sesame Street: A continuing evaluation.* Princeton, NJ: Educational Testing Service.

Bohannon, J. N., III, & Stanowicz, L. (1988). The issue of negative evidence: Adult responses to children's language errors. *Developmental Psychology, 24,* 684–689.

Bohannon, J. N., III, & Warren-Leubecker, A. (1989). Theoretical approaches to language acquisition. In J. Berko Gleason (Ed.), *The development of language* (pp. 167–223). Columbus, OH: Merrill.

Boldizar, J. P. (1991). Assessing sex typing and androgyny in children: The children's sex role inventory. *Developmental Psychology, 27,* 505–515.

Borghraef, M., Fryns, J. P., Dielkens, A., Pyck, K., & van den Berghe, H. (1987). Fragile (X) syndrome: A study of the psychological profile of 23 prepubertal patients. *Clinical Genetics, 32,* 179–186.

Borja-Alvarez, T., Zarbatany, L., & Pepper, S. (1991). Contributions of male and female guests and hosts to peer group entry. *Child Development, 62,* 1079–1090.

Borke, H. (1975). Piaget's mountains revisited: Changes in the egocentric landscape. *Developmental Psychology, 11,* 240–243.

Borkowski, J. G., Carr, M., Rellinger, E., & Pressley, M. (1990). Self-regulated cognition: Interdependence of metacognition, attributions, and self-esteem. In B. Jones & L. Idol (Eds.), *Developmental psychology: An advanced textbook* (pp. 151–204). Hillsdale, NJ: Erlbaum.

Bornholt, L. J., Goodnow, J. J., & Cooney, G. H. (1994). Influences of gender stereotypes on adolescents' perceptions of their own achievement. *American Educational Research Journal, 31,* 675–692.

Bornstein, M. H. (1989). Sensitive periods in development: Structural characteristics and causal interpretations. *Psychological Bulletin, 105,* 179–197.

Bornstein, M. H. (1992). Perception across the life cycle. In M. H. Bornstein & M. E. Lamb (Eds.), *Developmental psychology: An advanced textbook* (3rd ed., pp. 155–209). Hillsdale, NJ: Erlbaum.

Bornstein, M. H., & Lamb, M. E. (1992). *Development in infancy: An introduction* (3rd ed.). New York: McGraw-Hill.

Bornstein, M. H., & Sigman, M. D. (1986). Continuity in mental development from infancy. *Child Development, 57,* 251–274.

Borrine, M. L., Handal, P. J., Brown, N. Y., & Searight, H. R. (1991). Family conflict and adolescent adjustment in intact, divorced, and blended families. *Journal of Consulting and Clinical Psychology, 59,* 753–755.

Borstelmann, L. J. (1983). Children before psychology: Ideas about children from antiquity to the late 1800s. In W. Kessen (Ed.), *Handbook of child psychology: Vol. 1. History, theory, and methods* (pp. 1–40). New York: Wiley.

Bossard, J. S. S., & Boll, E. S. (1956). *The large family system.* Philadelphia: University of Pennsylvania Press.

Bouchard, T. J., Jr., Lykken, D. T., McGue, M., Segal, N. L., & Tellegen, A. (1990). Sources of human psychological differences: The Minnesota Study of Twins Reared Apart. *Science, 250,* 223–228.

Bouchard, T. J., Jr., & McGue, M. (1981). Familial studies of intelligence: A review. *Science, 212,* 1055–1058.

Boukydis, C. F. Z. (1985). Perception of infant crying as an interpersonal event. In B. M. Lester & C. F. Z. Boukydis (Eds.), *Infant crying* (pp. 187–215). New York: Plenum.

Boukydis, C. F. Z., & Burgess, R. L. (1982). Adult physiological response to infant cries: Effects of temperament of infant, parental status and gender. *Child Development, 53,* 1291–1298.

Bowlby, J. (1969). *Attachment and loss: Vol. 1. Attachment.* New York: Basic Books.

Bowlby, J. (1980). *Attachment and loss: Vol. 3.* Loss. New York: Basic Books.

Boyes, M. C., & Allen, S. G. (1993). Styles of parent–child interaction and moral reasoning in adolescence. *Merrill-Palmer Quarterly, 39,* 551–570.

Boyes, M. C., & Chandler, M. (1992). Cognitive development, epistemic doubt, and identity formation in adolescence. *Journal of Youth and Adolescence, 21,* 277–304.

Boysson-Bardies, B. de, & Vihman, M. M. (1991). Adaptation to language: Evidence from babbling and first words in four languages. *Language, 67,* 297–319.

Brabeck, M. (1983). Moral judgment: Theory and research on differences between males and females. *Developmental Review, 3,* 274–291.

Brackbill, Y., McManus, K., & Woodward, L. (1985). *Medication in maternity: Infant exposure and maternal information.* Ann Arbor: University of Michigan Press.

Bradley, R. H., & Caldwell, B. M. (1979). Home Observation for Measurement of the Environment: A revision of the preschool scale. *American Journal of Mental Deficiency, 84,* 235–244.

Bradley, R. H., & Caldwell, B. M. (1981). The HOME Inventory: A validation of the preschool scale for black children. *Child Development, 52,* 708–710.

Bradley, R. H., & Caldwell, B. M. (1982). The consistency of the home environment and its relation to child development. *International Journal of Behavioral Development, 5,* 445–465.

Bradley, R. H., Caldwell, B. M., & Rock, S. L. (1988). Home environment and school performance: A ten-year follow-up and examination of three models of environmental action. *Child Development, 59,* 852–867.

Bradley, R. H., Caldwell, B. M., Rock, S. L., Ramey, C. T., Barnard, D. E., Gray, C., Hammond, M. A., Mitchell, S., Gottfried, A., Siegel, L., & Johnson, D. L. (1989). Home environment and cognitive development in the first 3 years of life: A collaborative study involving six sites and three ethnic groups in North America. *Developmental Psychology, 25,* 217–235.

Braine, L. G., Schauble, L., Kugelmass, S., & Winter, A. (1993). Representation of depth by children: Spatial strategies and lateral biases. *Developmental Psychology, 29,* 466–479.

Braine, M. D. S. (1976). Children's first word combinations. *Monographs of the Society for Research in Child Development, 41*(1, Serial No. 164).

Brainerd, C. J. (1978). *Piaget's theory of intelligence.* Englewood Cliffs, NJ: Prentice Hall.

Brand, E., Clingempeel, W. G., & Bowen-Woodward, K. (1988). Family relationships and children's psychological adjustment in stepmother and stepfather families: Findings and conclusions from the Philadelphia Stepfamily Research Project. In E. M. Hetherington & J. D. Arasteh (Eds.), *Impact of divorce, single-parenting, and stepparenting on children* (pp. 299–324). Hillsdale, NJ: Erlbaum.

Bransford, J. D., Stein, B. S., Shelton, T. S., & Owings, R. A. (1981). Cognition and adaptation: The importance of learning to learn. In J. Harvey (Ed.), *Cognition, social behavior, and the environment* (pp. 93–110). Hillsdale, NJ: Erlbaum.

Braungart, J. M., Plomin, R., DeFries, J. C., & Fulker, D. W. (1992). Genetic influence on tester-rated infant temperament as assessed by Bayley's Infant Behavior Record: Nonadoptive and adoptive siblings and twins. *Developmental Psychology, 28,* 40–47.

Braverman, P. K., & Strasburger, V. C. (1993). Adolescent sexual activity. *Clinical Pediatrics, 32,* 658–668.

Braverman, P. K., & Strasburger, V. C. (1994). Sexually transmitted diseases. *Clinical Pediatrics, 33,* 26–37.

Bray, J. H. (1988). Children's development during early remarriage. In E. M. Hetherington & J. D. Arasteh (Eds.), *Impact of divorce, single parenting, and stepparenting on children* (pp. 279–298). Hillsdale, NJ: Erlbaum.

Brazelton, T. B. (1962). A child-oriented approach to toilet-training. *Pediatrics, 29,* 121–128.

Brazelton, T. B. (1984). *Neonatal Behavioral Assessment Scale.* Philadelphia: Lippincott.

Brazelton, T. B. (1989). Culture and newborn behavior: Uses of the NBAS in different cultural settings. In J. K. Nugent, B. M. Lester, & T. B. Brazelton (Eds.), *Biology, culture, and development* (Vol. 1, pp. 367–381). Norwood, NJ: Ablex.

Brazelton, T. B., Koslowski, B., & Tronick, E. (1976). Neonatal behavior among urban Zambians and Americans. *Journal of the American Academy of Child Psychiatry, 15,* 97–107.

Brazelton, T. B., Nugent, J. K., & Lester, B. M. (1987). Neonatal Behavioral Assessment Scale. In J. D. Osofsky (Ed.), *Handbook of infant development* (2nd ed., pp. 780–817). New York: Wiley.

Bread for the World Institute. (1994). *Hunger 1994.* Silver Spring, MD: Author.

Bredekamp, S. (Ed.). (1987). *Developmentally appropriate practice in early childhood programs serving children from birth through age 8* (expanded ed.). Washington, DC: National Association for the Education of Young Children.

Brennan, W. M., Ames, E. W., & Moore, R. W. (1966). Age differences in infants' attention to patterns of different complexities. *Science, 151,* 354–356.

Brenner, D., & Hinsdale, G. (1978). Body build stereotypes and self-identification in three age groups of females. *Adolescence, 13,* 551–562.

Bretherton, I. (1992). The origins of attachment theory: John Bowlby and Mary Ainsworth. *Developmental Psychology, 28,* 759–775.

Bretherton, I., Fritz, J., Zahn-Waxler, C., & Ridgeway, D. (1986). Learning to talk about emotions: A functionalist perspective. *Child Development, 57,* 529–548.

Bretherton, I., O'Connell, B., Shore, C., & Bates, E. (1984). The effect of contextual variation on symbolic play: Development from 20 to 28 months. In I. Bretherton (Ed.), *Symbolic play and the development of social understanding* (pp. 271–298). New York: Academic Press.

Briere, J. N. (1992). *Child abuse trauma.* Newbury Park, CA: Sage.

Brindley, B. A., & Sokol, R. J. (1988). Induction and augmentation of labor: Basis and methods for current practice. *Obstetrics and Gynecology Survey, 43,* 730–743.

Brody, G. H., Stoneman, Z., & Burke, M. (1987). Child temperaments, maternal differential behavior, and sibling relationships. *Developmental Psychology, 23,* 354–362.

Brody, G. H., Stoneman, Z., & McCoy, J. K. (1992). Associations of maternal and paternal direct and differential behavior with sibling relationships: Contemporaneous and longitudinal analyses. *Child Development, 63,* 82–92.

Brody, G. H., Stoneman, Z., McCoy, J. K., & Forehand, R. (1992). Contemporaneous and longitudinal associations of sibling conflict with family relationship assessments and family discussions about sibling problems. *Child Development, 63,* 391–400.

Brody, L. E., & Benbow, C. P. (1987). Accelerative strategies: How effective are they for the gifted? *Gifted Child Quarterly, 3,* 105–110.

Brody, N. (1992). *Intelligence* (2nd ed.). San Diego: Academic Press.

Broman, S. H. (1983). Obstetric medications. In C. C. Brown (Ed.), *Childhood learning disabilities and prenatal risk* (pp. 56–64). New York: Johnson & Johnson.

Bronfenbrenner, U. (1979). *The ecology of human development: Experiments by nature and design.* Cambridge, MA: Harvard University Press.

Bronfenbrenner, U. (1989). Ecological systems theory. In R. Vasta (Ed.), *Annals of child development* (Vol. 6, pp. 187–251). Greenwich, CT: JAI Press.

Bronfenbrenner, U., & Crouter, A. C. (1983). The evolution of environmental models in developmental research. In W. Kessen (Ed.), *Handbook of child psychology: Vol. 1. History, theory and methods* (Vol. 1, pp. 357–476). New York: Wiley.

Bronson, G. W. (1991). Infant differences in rate of visual encoding. *Child Development, 62,* 44–54.

Brooks, P. H., & Roberts, M. C. (1990, Spring). Social science and the prevention of children's injuries. *Social Policy Report of the Society for Research in Child Development,* 4(1).

Brooks-Gunn, J. (1986). The relationship of maternal beliefs about sex typing to maternal and young children's behavior. *Sex Roles, 14,* 21–35.

Brooks-Gunn, J. (1988a). Antecedents and consequences of variations in girls' maturational timing. *Journal of Adolescent Health Care, 9,* 365–373.

Brooks-Gunn, J. (1988b). The impact of puberty and sexual activity upon the health and education of adolescent girls and boys. *Peabody Journal of Education, 64,* 88–113.

Brooks-Gunn, J., Klebanov, P. K., Liaw, F., & Spiker, D. (1993). Enhancing the development of low-birthweight, premature infants: Changes in cognition and behavior over the first three years. *Child Development, 64,* 736–753.

Brooks-Gunn, J., & Petersen, A. C. (1991). Studying the emergence of depression and depressive symptoms during adolescence. *Journal of Youth and Adolescence, 20,* 115–119.

Brooks-Gunn, J., & Reiter, E. O. (1990). The role of pubertal processes in the early adolescent transition. In S. Feldman & G. Elliott (Eds.), *At the threshold: The developing adolescent* (pp. 16–53). Cambridge, MA: Harvard University Press.

Brooks-Gunn, J., & Ruble, D. N. (1980). Menarche: The interaction of physiology, cultural, and social factors. In A. J. Dan, E. A. Graham, & C. P. Beecher (Eds.), *The menstrual cycle: A synthesis of interdisciplinary research* (pp. 141–159). New York: Springer-Verlag.

Brooks-Gunn, J., & Ruble, D. N. (1983). The experience of menarche from a developmental perspective. In J. Brooks-Gunn & A. C. Peterson (Eds.), *Girls at puberty* (pp. 155–177). New York: Plenum.

Brooks-Gunn, J., & Warren, M. P. (1989). Biological and social contributions to negative affect in young adolescent girls. *Child Development, 60,* 40–55.

Brooks-Gunn, J., Warren, M. P., Samelson, M., & Fox, R. (1986). Physical similarity of and disclosure of menarcheal status to friends: Effects of grade and pubertal status. *Journal of Early Adolescence, 6,* 3–14.

Brophy, J. E. (1983). Research on the self-fulfilling prophecy and teacher expectations. *Journal of Educational Psychology, 75,* 631–661.

Brophy, J. E. (1986). Teacher influences on student achievement. *American Psychologist, 41,* 1069–1077.

Brophy, J. E., & Good, T. L. (1974). *Teacher–student relationships: Causes and consequences.* New York: Holt, Rinehart and Winston.

Brown, A. L., Bransford, J. D., Ferrara, R. A., & Campione, J. C. (1983). Learning, remembering, and understanding. In J. H. Flavell & E. M. Markman (Eds.), *Handbook of child psychology: Vol. 3. Cognitive development* (4th ed., pp. 77–166). New York: Wiley.

Brown, B. B. (1990). Peer groups. In S. Feldman & G. Elliott (Eds.), *At the threshold: The developing adolescent* (pp. 171–196). Cambridge, England: Cambridge University Press.

Brown, B. B., Lohr, M. J., & McClenahan, E. L. (1986). Early adolescents' perceptions of peer pressure. *Journal of Early Adolescence, 6,* 139–154.

Brown, B., Clasen, D., & Eicher, S. (1986). Perceptions of peer pressure, peer conformity dispositions, and self-reported behavior among adolescents. *Developmental Psychology, 22,* 521–530.

Brown, L. K., & Fritz, G. K. (1988). Children's knowledge and attitudes about AIDS. *Journal of the American Academy of Child and Adolescent Psychiatry, 27,* 504–508.

Brown, R. W. (1973). *A first language: The early stages.* Cambridge, MA: Harvard University Press.

Brownell, C. A., & Carriger, M. S. (1990). Changes in cooperation and self–other differentiation during the second year. *Child Development, 61,* 1164–1174.

Bruch, H. (1970). Juvenile obesity: Its courses and outcome. In C. V. Rowlan (Ed.), *Anorexia and obesity* (pp. 231–254). Boston: Little Brown.

Bruner, J. S. (1990). *Acts of meaning.* Cambridge, MA: Harvard University Press.

Bruner, J. S. (1983). *Child's talk: Learning to use language.* Oxford: Oxford University Press.

Bryant, B. K. (1985). The neighborhood walk: Sources of support in middle childhood. *Monographs for the Society for Research in Child Development, 50*(3, Serial No. 210).

Bryant, D. M., & Ramey, C. T. (1987). An analysis of the effectiveness of early intervention programs for environmentally at-risk children. In M. J. Guralnick & F. C. Bennett (Eds.), *The effectiveness of early intervention for at-risk handicapped children* (pp. 33–78). Orlando, FL: Academic Press.

Buck, G. M., Cookfair, D. L., Michalek, A. M., Nasca, P. C., Standfast, S. J., Sever, L. E., & Kramer, A. A. (1989). Intrauterine growth retardation and risk of sudden infant death syndrome (SIDS). *American Journal of Epidemiology, 129,* 874–884.

Buekens, P., Kotelchuck, M., Blondel, B., Kristensen, F. B., Chen, J-H., & Masuy-Stroobant, G. (1993). A comparison of prenatal care use in the United States and Europe. *American Journal of Public Health, 83,* 31–36.

Bugental, D. B., Blue, J., & Cruzcosa, M. (1989). Perceived control over caregiving outcomes: Implications for child abuse. *Developmental Psychology, 25,* 532–539.

Buhrmester, D., & Furman, W. (1987). The development of companionship and intimacy. *Child Development, 58,* 1101–1115.

Buhrmester, D., & Furman, W. (1990). Perceptions of sibling relationships during middle childhood and adolescence. *Child Development, 61,* 1387–1398.

Bukowski, W. M., & Kramer, T. L. (1986). Judgments of the features of friendship among early adolescent boys and girls. *Journal of Early Adolescence, 6,* 331–338.

Bulatao, R. A., & Arnold, F. (1977). *Relationships between the value and cost of children and fertility: Cross-cultural evidence.* Paper presented at the General Conference of the International Union for the Scientific Study of Population, Mexico City.

Bullock, M. (1985). Causal reasoning and developmental change over the preschool years. *Human Development, 28,* 169–191.

Bullock, M., & Lutkenhaus, P. (1990). Who am I? The development of self-understanding in toddlers. *Merrill-Palmer Quarterly, 36,* 217–238.

Burchinal, M., Lee, M., & Ramey, C T. (1989). Type of day care and preschool intellectual development in disadvantaged children. *Child Development, 60,* 128–137.

Burke, B. S., Beal, V. A., Kirkwood, S. B., & Stuart, H. C. (1943). The influence of nutrition during pregnancy upon the conditions of the infant at birth. *Journal of Nutrition, 26,* 569–583.

Burns, S. M., & Brainerd, C. J. (1979). Effects of constructive and dramatic play on perspective taking in very young children. *Developmental Psychology, 15,* 512–521.

Burton, B. K. (1992). Limb anomalies associated with chorionic villus sampling. *Obstetrics and Gynecology, 79*(Pt. 1), 726–730.

Bushnell, E. W. (1985). The decline of visually guided reaching during infancy. *Infant Behavior and Development, 8,* 139–155.

Bushnell, E. W., & Boudreau, J. P. (1993). Motor development and the mind: The potential role of motor abilities as a determinant of aspects of perceptual development. *Child Development, 64,* 1005–1021.

Buss, A. H., & Plomin, R. (1984). *Temperament: Early developing personality traits.* Hillsdale, NJ: Erlbaum.

Bussey, K., & Bandura, A. (1992). Self-regulatory mechanisms governing gender development. *Child Development, 63,* 1236–1250.

Butler, G. E., McKie, M., & Ratcliffe, S. G. (1990). The cyclical nature of prepubertal growth. *Annals of Human Biology, 17,* 177–198.

Butler, R., & Ruzany, N. (1993). Age and socialization effects on the development of social comparison motives and normative ability assessment in kibbutz and urban children. *Child Development, 64,* 532–543.

Byrne, M. C., & Hayden, E. (1980). *Topic maintenance and topic establishment in mother–child dialogue.* Paper presented at the meeting of the American Speech and Hearing Association, Detroit, MI.

Byrnes, J. P., & Takahira, S. (1993). Explaining gender differences on SAT-math items. *Developmental Psychology, 29,* 805–810.

Byrnes, J. P., & Wasik, B. A. (1991). Role of conceptual knowledge in mathematical procedural learning. *Developmental Psychology, 27,* 777–786.

Cain, V. S., & Hofferth, S. L. (1989). Parental choice of self-care for school-age children. *Journal of Marriage and the Family, 51,* 65–77.

Caine, N. (1986). Behavior during puberty and adolescence. In G. Mitchell & J. Erwin (Eds.), *Comparative primate biology: Vol. 2A. Behavior, conservation, and ecology* (pp. 327–361). New York: Liss.

Cairns, R. B. (1983). The emergence of developmental psychology. In W. Kessen (Ed.), *Handbook of child psychology: Vol. 1. History, theory, and methods* (4th ed., pp. 41–102). New York: Wiley.

Cairns, R. B., Cairns, B. D., & Neckerman, H. J. (1989). Early school dropout: Configurations and determinants. *Child Development, 60,* 1437–1452.

Cairns, R. B., Cairns, B. D., Neckerman, H. J., Ferguson, L. L., & Gariépy, J-L. (1989). Growth and aggression: 1. Childhood to early adolescence. *Developmental Psychology, 25,* 320–330.

Caldas, S. J. (1993). Current theoretical perspectives on adolescent pregnancy and childbearing in the United States. *Journal of Adolescent Research, 8,* 4–20.

Caliso, J., & Milner, J. (1992). Childhood history of abuse and child abuse screening. *Child Abuse and Neglect, 16,* 647–659.

Camara, K. A., & Resnick, G. (1988). Interparental conflict and cooperation: Factors moderating children's post-divorce adjustment. In E. M. Hetherington & J. D. Arasteh (Eds.), *Impact of divorce, single parenting, and stepparenting on children* (pp. 169–195). Hillsdale, NJ: Erlbaum.

Campbell, F. A., & Ramey, C. T. (1991). *The Carolina Abecedarian Project.* Paper presented at the biennial meeting of the Society for Research in Child Development, Seattle, WA.

Campbell, F. A., & Ramey, C. T. (1994). Effects of early intervention on intellectual and academic achievement: A follow-up study of children from low-income families. *Child Development, 65,* 684–698.

Campos, J. J., & Bertenthal, B. I. (1989). Locomotion and psychological development. In F. Morrison, K. Lord, & D. Keating (Eds.), Applied developmental psychology (Vol. 3, pp. 229–258). New York: Academic Press.

Campos, J. J., Caplovitz, K. B., Lamb, M. E., Goldsmith, H. H., & Stenberg, C. (1983). Socioemotional development. In M. M. Haith & J. J. Campos (Eds.), *Handbook of child psychology: Vol. 2. Infancy and developmental psychobiology* (4th ed., pp. 783–915). New York: Wiley.

Campos, R. G. (1989). Soothing pain-elicited distress in infants with swaddling and pacifiers. *Child Development, 60,* 781–792.

Camras, L. A., Oster, H., Campos, J. J., Miyake, K., & Bradshaw, D. (1992). Japanese and American infants' responses to arm restraint. *Developmental Psychology, 28,* 578–583.

Canick, J. A., & Saller, D. N., Jr. (1993). Maternal serum screening for aneuploidy and open fetal defects. *Obstetrics and Gynecology Clinics of North America, 20,* 443–454.

Cannella, G. S. (1993). Learning through social interaction: Shared cognitive experience, negotiation strategies, and joint concept construction for young children. *Early Childhood Research Quarterly, 8,* 427–444.

Capaldi, D. M., & Patterson, G. R. (1991). Relation of parental transitions to boys' adjustment problems: I. A linear hypothesis. II. Mothers at risk for transitions and unskilled parenting. *Developmental Psychology, 27,* 489–504.

Capelli, C. A., Nakagawa, N., & Madden, C. M. (1990). How children understand sarcasm: The role of context and intonation. *Child Development, 61,* 1824–1841.

Caplan, M., Vespo, J., Pedersen, J., & Hay, D. F. (1991). Conflict and its resolution in small groups of one- and two-year-olds. *Child Development, 62,* 1513–1524.

Capuzzi, D. (1989). *Adolescent suicide prevention.* Ann Arbor, MI: ERIC Counseling and Personnel Services Clearinghouse.

Carey, S. (1985). *Conceptual change in childhood.* Cambridge, MA: MIT Press.

Carle, E. (1969). *The very hungry caterpillar.* New York: Philomel.

Carlson, C., Hsu, J., & Cooper, C. R. (1990, March). *Predicting school achievement in early adolescence: The role of family process.* Paper presented at the Conference on Human Development, Atlanta, GA.

Carlson, V., Cicchetti, D., Barnett, D., & Braunwald, K. (1989). Disorganized/disoriented attachment relationship in maltreated infants. *Child Development, 25,* 525–531.

Carpenter, C. J. (1983). Activity structure and play: Implications for socialization. In M. Liss (Eds.), *Social and cognitive skills: Sex roles and children's play* (pp. 117–145). New York: Academic Press.

Carruth, B. R., Goldberg, D. L., & Skinner, J. D. (1991). Do parents and peers mediate the influence of television advertising on food-related purchases? *Journal of Adolescent Research, 6,* 253–271.

Carter, D. B., & Patterson, C. J. (1982). Sex roles as social conventions: The development of children's conceptions of sex-role stereotypes. *Developmental Psychology, 18,* 812–824.

Case, R. (1985). *Intellectual development: A systematic reinterpretation.* New York: Academic Press.

Case, R. (1991). Stages in the development of the young child's first sense of self. *Developmental Review, 11,* 210–230.

Case, R. (1992). *The mind's staircase: Exploring the conceptual underpinnings of children's thought and knowledge.* Hillsdale, NJ: Erlbaum.

Casey, M. B. (1986). Individual differences in selective attention among prereaders: A key to mirror-image confusions. *Developmental Psychology, 22,* 824–831.

Caspi, A., Elder, G. H., Jr., & Bem, D. J. (1987). Moving against the world: Life-course patterns of explosive children. *Developmental Psychology, 23,* 308–313.

Caspi, A., Elder, G. H., Jr., & Bem, D. J. (1988). Moving away from the world: Life-course patterns of shy children. *Developmental Psychology, 24,* 824–831.

Caspi, A., Lynam, D., Moffitt, T. E., & Silva, P. A. (1993). Unraveling girls' delinquency: Biological, dispositional, and contextual contributions to adolescent misbehavior. *Developmental Psychology, 29,* 19–30.

Cassidy, J., & Berlin, L. J. (1994). The insecure/ambivalent pattern of attachment: Theory and research. *Child Development, 65,* 971–991.

Caudill, W. (1973). Psychiatry and anthropology: The individual and his nexus. In L. Nader & T. W. Maretzki (Eds.), *Cultural illness and health: Essays in human adaptation* (Anthropological Studies 9, pp. 67–77). Washington, DC: American Anthropological Association.

Cazden, C. (1984). *Effective instructional practices in bilingual education.* Washington, DC: National Institute of Education.

Ceci, S. J. (1990). *On intelligence . . . More or less.* Englewood Cliffs, NJ: Prentice Hall.

Ceci, S. J. (1991). How much does schooling influence general intelligence and its cognitive components? A reassessment of the evidence. *Developmental Psychology, 27,* 703–722.

Ceci, S. J., & Bruck, M. (1993a). Child witnesses: Translating research into policy. *Social Policy Report of the Society for Research in Child Development, 7*(3).

Ceci, S. J., & Bruck, M. (1993b). Suggestibility of the child witness: A historical review and synthesis. *Psychological Bulletin, 113,* 403–439.

Ceci, S. J., Leichtman, M. D., & Bruck, M. (1994). The suggestibility of children's eyewitness reports: Methodological issues. In F. Weinert & W. Schneider (Eds.), *Memory development: State of the art and future directions.* Hillsdale, NJ: Erlbaum.

Ceci, S. J., Leichtman, M. D., & White, T. (1994). Interviewing preschoolers: Remembrance of things planted. In D. P. Peters (Ed.), *The child witness in context: Cognitive, social, and legal perspectives.* Amsterdam: Kluwer.

Celano, M. P., & Geller, R. J. (1993). Learning, school performance, and children with asthma: How much risk? *Journal of Learning Disabilities, 26,* 23–32.

Cernoch, J. M., & Porter, R. H. (1985). Recognition of maternal axillary odors by infants. *Child Development, 56,* 1593–1598.

Chalmers, J. B., & Townsend, M. A. R. (1990). The effects of training in social perspective taking on socially maladjusted girls. *Child Development, 61,* 178–190.

Chamberlain, M. C., Nichols, S. L., & Chase, C. H. (1991). Pediatric AIDS: Comparative cranial MRI and CT scans. *Pediatric Neurology, 7,* 357–362.

Chandler, M. J. (1973). Egocentrism and antisocial behavior: The assessment and training of social perspective-taking skills. *Developmental Psychology, 9,* 326–332.

Chandra, R. K. (1991). Interactions between early nutrition and the immune system. In *Ciba Foundation Symposium No. 156* (pp. 77–92). Chichester, England: Wiley.

Chang, H. (1992). *Adolescent life and ethos: An ethnography of a U.S. high school.* Washington, DC: Falmer.

Chao, R. K. (1994). Beyond parental control and authoritarian parenting style: Understanding Chinese parenting through the cultural notion of training. *Child Development, 65,* 1111–1119.

Chapman, M., & Lindenberger, U. (1988). Functions, operations, and décalage in the development of transitivity. *Developmental Psychology, 24,* 542–551.

Chapman, M., & Skinner, E. A. (1989). Children's agency beliefs, cognitive performance, and conceptions of effort and ability: Individual and developmental differences. *Child Development, 60,* 1229–1238.

Charo, R. A. (1994). USA: New York surrogacy law. *Lancet, 440,* 361.

Chase-Lansdale, P. L., & Brooks-Gunn, J. (1994). Correlates of adolescent pregnancy and parenthood. In C. B. Fisher & R. M. Lerner (Eds.), *Applied developmental psychology* (pp. 207–236). New York: McGraw-Hill.

Chase-Lansdale, P. L., & Brooks-Gunn, J. (Eds.). (1994). *Escape from poverty: What makes a difference for children?* New York: Cambridge University Press.

Chase-Lansdale, P. L., Brooks-Gunn, J., & Zamsky, E. S. (1994). Young African-American multigenerational families in poverty: Quality of mothering and grandmothering. *Child Development, 65,* 373–393.

Chasnoff, I. J., Griffith, D. R., MacGregor, S., Dirkes, K., & Burns, K. S. (1989). Temporal patterns of cocaine use in pregnancy: Perinatal outcome. *Journal of the American Medical Association, 261,* 1741–1744.

Chatkupt, S., Mintz, M., Epstein, L. G., Bhansali, D., & Koenigsberger, M. R. (1989). Neuroimaging studies in children with human immunodeficiency virus type 1 infection. *Annals of Neurology, 26,* 453.

Cheng, M., & Hannah, M. (1993). Breech delivery at term: A critical review of the literature. *Obstetrics & Gynecology, 82,* 605–618.

Cherlin, A. J., & Furstenberg, F. F., Jr. (1986). *The new American grandparent.* New York: Basic Books.

Cherlin, A. J., & Furstenberg, F. F., Jr., Chase-Lansdale, P.L., Kiernan, K. E., Robins, P. K., Morrison, D. R., & Teitler, J. O. (1991). Longitudinal studies of effects of divorce on children in Great Britain and the United States. *Science, 252,* 1386-1389.

Chess, S., & Thomas, A. (1984). *Origins and evolution of behavior disorders.* New York: Brunner/Mazel.

Chi, M. T. H. (1978). Knowledge structures and memory development. In R. S. Siegler (Ed.), *Children's thinking: What develops?* (pp. 73–96). Hillsdale, NJ: Erlbaum.

Chi, M. T. H., & Ceci, S. J. (1987). Content knowledge: Its role, representation, and restructuring in memory development. In H. W. Reese (Ed.), *Advances in child development and behavior* (Vol. 20, pp. 91–142). Orlando, FL: Academic Press.

Children's Defense Fund. (1991a). *The adolescent and young adult fact book.* Washington, DC: Author.

Children's Defense Fund. (1991b, April). Hunger in America. *CDF Reports, 12(7),* 4–5.

Children's Defense Fund. (1991c, May). Vaccine shortages causing immunization crisis. *CDF Reports, 12*(8), 3, 12.

Children's Defense Fund. (1992). *The health of America's children.* Washington, DC: Author.

Children's Defense Fund. (1993). *Progress and peril: Black children in America.* Washington, DC: Author.

Children's Defense Fund. (1994). *The state of America's children: Yearbook 1994.* Washington, DC: Author.

Childs, C. P., & Greenfield, P. M. (1982). Informal modes of learning and teaching: The case of Zinacanteco weaving. In N. Warren (Ed.), *Advances in cross-cultural psychology* (Vol. 2, pp. 269–316). London: Academic Press.

Chilmonczyk, B. A., Salmun, L. M., Megathlin, K. N., Neveus, L. M., Palomaki, G. E., Knight, G. J., Pulkkinen, A. J., & Haddow, J. E. (1993). Association between exposure to environmental tobacco smoke and exacerbations of asthma in children. *New England Journal of Medicine, 328,* 1665–1669.

Chisholm, J. S. (1989). Biology, culture, and the development of temperament: A Navajo example. In J. K. Nugent, B. M. Lester, & T. B. Brazelton (Eds.), *Biology, culture, and development* (Vol. 1, pp. 341–364). Norwood, NJ: Ablex.

Chomsky, C. (1969). *The acquisition of syntax in children from five to ten.* Cambridge, MA: MIT Press.

Chomsky, N. (1957). *Syntactic structures.* The Hague: Mouton.

Christoffel, K. K., & Forsyth, B. W. (1989). Mirror image of environmental deprivation: Severe childhood obesity of psychosocial origin. *Child Abuse and Neglect, 13,* 249–256.

Christophersen, E. R. (1989). Injury control. *American Psychologist, 44,* 237–241.

Churchill, S. R. (1984). Disruption: A risk in adoption. In P. Sachdev (Ed.), *Adoption: Current issues and trends* (pp. 115–127). Toronto: Butterworth.

Cicchetti, D., & Aber, J. L. (1986). Early precursors of later depression: An organizational perspective. In L. P. Lipsitt & C. Rovee-Collier (Eds.), *Advances in infancy research* (Vol. 4, pp. 87–137). Norwood, NJ: Ablex.

Clark, E. V. (1983). Meanings and concepts. In J. H. Flavell & E. M. Markman (Eds.), *Handbook of child psychology: Vol. 3. Cognitive development* (pp. 787–840). New York: Wiley.

Clark, E. V., & Hecht, B. F. (1982). Learning to coin agent and instrument nouns. *Cognition, 12,* 1–24.

Clark, J. E., Phillips, S., & Petersen, R. (1989). Developmental stability in jumping. *Developmental Psychology, 25,* 929–935.

Clark, J. E., & Watkins, D. L. (1984). Static balance in young children. *Child Development, 55,* 133–139.

Clark, M. L. (1991). Social identity, peer relations, and academic competence of African-American adolescents. *Education and Urban Society, 24,* 41–52.

Clarke-Stewart, K. A. (1973). Interactions between mothers and their young children: Characteristics and consequences. *Monographs of the Society for Research in Child Development, 38*(6–7, Serial No. 153).

Clarke-Stewart, K. A. (1989). Infant day care: Maligned or malignant? *American Psychologist, 44,* 266–273.

Claudy, J. G. (1984). The only child as a young adult: Results from Project Talent. In T. Falbo (Ed.), *The single-child family* (pp. 211–252). New York: Guilford Press.

Clausen, J. A. (1975). The social meaning of differential physical and sexual maturation. In S. E. Dragastin & G. H. Elder (Eds.), *Adolescence in the life cycle: Psychological change and the social context* (pp. 25–47). New York: Halsted.

Clavadetscher, J. E., Brown, A. M., Ankrum, C., & Teller, D. Y. (1988). Spectral sensitivity and chromatic discriminations in 3- and 7-week-old human infants. *Journal of the Optical Society of America, 5,* 2093–2105.

Clements, D. H. (1990). Metacomponential development in a Logo programming environment. *Journal of Educational Psychology, 82,* 141–149.

Clements, D. H., & Nastasi, B. K. (1992). Computers and early childhood education. In M. Gettinger, S. N. Elliott, & T. R. Kratochwill (Eds.), *Advances in school psychology: preschool and early childhood treatment directions* (pp. 187–246). Hillsdale, NJ: Erlbaum.

Clifton, R. K., Muir, D. W., Ashmead, D. H., & Clarkson, M. G. (1993). Is visually guided reaching in early infancy a myth? *Child Development, 64,* 1099–1110.

Coakley, J. (1990). *Sport and society: Issues and controversies* (4th ed.). St. Louis: Mosby.

Cohen, F. L. (1984). *Clinical genetics in nursing practice.* Philadelphia: Lippincott.

Cohen, F. L. (1993a). Epidemiology of HIV infection and AIDS in children. In F. L. Cohen & J. D. Durham (Eds.), *Women, children, and HIV/AIDS* (pp. 137–155). New York: Springer.

Cohen, F. L. (1993b). HIV infection and AIDS: An overview. In F. L. Cohen & J. D. Durham (Eds.), *Women, children, and HIV/AIDS* (pp. 3–30). New York: Springer.

Cohen-Overbeek, W. C. J., Hop, M., Ouden, M. den, Pipers, L., Jahoda, M. G. J., &

Wladimiroff, J. W. (1990). Spontaneous abortion rate and advanced maternal age: Consequences for prenatal diagnosis. *Lancet, 336,* 27–29.

Cohn, J. F., Campbell, S. B., Matias, R., & Hopkins, J. (1990). Face-to-face interactions of postpartum depressed and nondepressed mother–infant pairs at 2 months. *Developmental Psychology, 26,* 15–23.

Coie, J. D., Dodge, K. A., & Coppotelli, H. (1982). Dimensions and types of social status: A cross-age perspective. *Developmental Psychology, 18,* 557–570.

Coie, J. D., & Krehbiel, G. (1984). Effects of academic tutoring on the social status of low-achieving, socially rejected children. *Child Development, 55,* 1465–1478.

Colby, A., Kohlberg, L., Gibbs, J., & Lieberman, M. (1983). A longitudinal study of moral judgment. *Monographs of the Society for Research in Child Development, 48*(1–2, Serial No. 200).

Cole, C. B., & Loftus, E. F. (1987). The memory of children. In S. J., Ceci, M. P. Toglia, & D. F. Ross (Eds.), *Children's eyewitness memory* (pp. 178–208). New York: Springer-Verlag.

Cole, J. R., & Zuckerman, H. (1987, February). Marriage, motherhood, and research performance in science. *Scientific American, 256*(2), 119–125.

Cole, M. (1990). Cognitive development and formal schooling: The evidence from cross-cultural research. In L. C. Moll (Ed.), *Vygotsky and education* (pp. 89–110). New York: Cambridge University Press.

Cole, M., & Scribner, S. (1977). Cross-cultural studies of memory and cognition. In R. V. Kail, Jr. & J. W. Hagen (Eds.), Perspectives on the development of memory and cognition (pp. 239–271). Hillsdale, NJ: Erlbaum.

Coleman, J. (1961). *The adolescent society.* Glencoe, IL: Free Press.

Collea, J. V., Chein, C., & Quilligan, E. J. (1980). The randomized management of term frank breech presentations: A study of 208 cases. *American Journal of Obstetrics and Gynecology, 137,* 235–244.

Collins, W. A. (1993, January). Head Start: Steps toward a two-generation program strategy. *Young Children, 48*(2), 25–33.

Collins, W. A., Wellman, H., Keniston, A. H., & Westby, S. D. (1978). Age-related aspects of comprehension and inference from a televised dramatic narrative. *Child Development, 49,* 389–399.

Colman, L. L., & Colman, A. D. (1991). *Pregnancy: The psychological experience.* Noonday Press.

Comer, J. P. (1986). Parent participation in the schools. *Phi Delta Kappan, 67,* 442–444.

Committee on Sports Medicine, American Academy of Pediatrics. (1989). Anabolic steroids and the adolescent athlete. *Pediatrics, 83,* 127–128.

Compas, B. E. (1987). Stress and life events during childhood and adolescence. *Clinical Psychology Review, 7,* 275–302.

Compas, B. E., Howell, D. C., Phares, V., Williams, R. A., & Giunta, C. T. (1989). Risk factors for emotional/behavioral problems in young adolescents: A prospective analysis of adolescent and parental stress and symptoms. *Journal of Consulting and Clinical Psychology, 57,* 732–740.

Condry, J., & Ross, D. F. (1985). Sex and aggression: The influence of gender label on the perceptions of aggression in children. *Child Development, 56,* 225–233.

Conel, J. L. *The postnatal development of the human cerebral cortex.* Cambridge, MA: Harvard University Press, 1959.

Conger, R. D., Conger, K. J., Elder, G. H., Jr., Lorenz, F. O., Simons, R. L., & Whitbeck, L. B. (1992). A family process model of economic hardship and adjustment of early adolescent boys. *Child Development, 63,* 527–541.

Conger, R. D., Conger, K. J., Elder, G. H., Jr., Lorenz, F. O., Simons, R. L., & Whitbeck, L. B. (1993). Family economic stress and adjustment of early adolescent girls. *Developmental Psychology, 29,* 206–219.

Conger, R. D., Ge, X., Elder, G. H., Jr., Lorenz, F. O., & Simons, R. L. (1994). Economic stress, coercive family process, and developmental problems of adolescents. *Child Development, 65,* 541–561.

Connolly, J. A., & Doyle, A. B. (1984). Relations of social fantasy play to social competence in preschoolers. *Developmental Psychology, 20,* 797–806.

Connolly, J. A., Doyle, A. B., & Reznick, E. (1988). Social pretend play and social interaction in preschoolers. *Journal of Applied Developmental Psychology, 9,* 301–313.

Connolly, K., & Dagleish, M. (1989). The emergence of tool-using skill in infancy. *Developmental Psychology, 25,* 894–912.

Constanzo, P. R., & Woody, E. Z. (1979). Externality as a function of obesity in children: Pervasive style or eating-specific attribute? *Journal of Personality and Social Psychology, 37,* 2286–2296.

Cooke, R. A. (1982). The ethics and regulation of research involving children. In B. B. Wolman (Ed.), *Handbook of developmental psychology* (pp. 149–172). Englewood Cliffs, NJ: Prentice Hall.

Cooper, R. P., & Aslin, R. N. (1990). Preference for infant-directed speech in the first month after birth. *Child Development, 61,* 1584–1595.

Coopersmith, S. (1967). *The antecedents of self-esteem.* San Francisco: Freeman.

Coplan, R. J., Rubin, K. H., Fox, N. A., Calkins, S. D., & Stewart, S. L. (1994). Being alone, playing alone, and acting alone: Distinguishing among reticence and passive and active solitude in young children. *Child Development, 65,* 129–137.

Copper, R. L., Goldenberg, R. L., Creasy, R. K., DuBard, M. B., Davis, R. O., Entman, S. S., Iams, J. D., & Cliver, S. P. (1993). A multicenter study of preterm birth weight and gestational age-specific neonatal mortality. *American Journal of Obstetrics and Gynecology, 168,* 78–84.

Corah, N. L., Anthony, E. J., Painter, P., Stern, J. A., & Thurston, D. L. (1965). Effects of perinatal anoxia after seven years. *Psychological Monographs 79*(3, Whole No. 596).

Coren, S., & Halpern, D. F. (1991). Left-handedness: A marker for decreased survival fitness. *Psychological Bulletin, 109,* 90–106.

Corman, H. H., & Escalona, S. K. (1969). Stages of sensorimotor development: A replication study. *Merrill-Palmer Quarterly, 15,* 351–360.

Cornell, E. H., & Gottfried, A. W. (1976). Intervention with premature human infants. *Child Development, 47,* 32–39.

Corno, L., & Snow, R. E. (1986). Adapting teaching to individual differences among learners. In M. C. Wittrock (Ed.), *Handbook of research on teaching* (3rd ed., pp. 214–229). New York: Macmillan.

Corrigan, R. (1987). A developmental sequence of actor–object pretend play in young children. *Merrill-Palmer Quarterly, 33,* 87–106.

Costabile, A., Smith, P. K., Matheson, L., Aston, J., Hunter, T., & Boulton, M. (1991). Cross-national comparison of how children distinguish serious and playful fighting. *Developmental Psychology, 27,* 881–887.

Cotton, P. (1990). Sudden infant death syndrome: Another hypothesis offered but doubts remain. *Journal of the American Medical Association, 263,* 2865, 2869.

Courage, M. L., & Adams, R. J. (1990). Visual acuity assessment from birth to three years using the acuity card procedures: Cross-sectional and longitudinal samples. *Optometry and Vision Science, 67,* 713–718.

Cowan, C. P., & Cowan, P. A. (1988). Changes in marriage during the transition to parenthood: Must we blame the baby? In G. Y. Michaels & W. A. Goldberg (Eds.), *The transition to parenthood* (pp. 114–154). New York: Cambridge University Press.

Cowan, C. P., Cowan, P. A., Heming, G., Garrett, E., Coysh, W. S., Curtis-Boles, H., & Boles, A. J. (1985). Transition to parenthood: His, hers, and theirs. *Journal of Family Issues, 6,* 461–481.

Cox, K., & Schwartz, J. D. (1990). *The well-informed patient's guide to caesarean births.* New York: Dell.

Cox, M. J., Owen, M., Henderson, V. K., & Margand, N. A. (1992). Prediction of infant–father and infant–mother attachment. *Developmental Psychology, 28,* 474–483.

Cox, M. J., Owen, M., Lewis, J. M., & Henderson, V. K. (1989). Marriage, adult adjustment, and early parenting. *Child Development, 60,* 1015–1024.

Craik, F. I. M., & Lockhart, R. S. (1972). Levels of processing: A framework for memory research. *Journal of Verbal Learning and Verbal Behavior, 11,* 671–684.

Crain-Thoreson, C., & Dale, P. S. (1992). Do early talkers become early readers? Linguistic precocity, preschool language, and emergent literacy. *Developmental Psychology, 28,* 421–429.

Cramond, B. (1994). The Torrance Tests of Creative Thinking: From design through establishment of predictive validity. In R. F. Subotnik & K. D. Arnold (Eds.), *Beyond*

Terman: Contemporary longitudinal studies of giftedness and talent (pp. 229–254). Norwood, NJ: Ablex.
Cratty, B. J. (1986). *Perceptual and motor development in infants and children* (3rd ed.). Englewood Cliffs, NJ: Prentice Hall.
Crick, N. R., & Ladd, G. W. (1993). Children's perceptions of their peer experiences: Attributions, loneliness, social anxiety, and social avoidance. *Developmental Psychology, 29,* 244–254.
Crider, C. (1981). Children's conceptions of the body interior. In R. Bibace & M. Walsh (Eds.), *New directions in child development* (No. 14, pp. 49–65). San Francisco: Jossey-Bass.
Crockenberg, S. B. (1981). Infant irritability, mother responsiveness, and social support influences on the security of mother–infant attachment. *Child Development, 52,* 857–865.
Crockenberg, S. B. (1986). Are temperamental differences in babies associated with predictable differences in care-giving? In J. V. Lerner & R. M. Lerner (Eds.), *New directions for child development* (No. 30, pp. 75–88). San Francisco: Jossey-Bass.
Crockenberg, S. B., & Litman, C. (1990). Autonomy as competence in 2-year-olds: Maternal correlates of child defiance, compliance, and self-assertion. *Developmental Psychology, 26,* 961–971.
Crockett, L. J. (1990). Sex role and sex-typing in adolescence. In R. M. Lerner, A. C. Petersen, & J. Brooks-Gunn (Eds.), *The encyclopedia of adolescence* (Vol. 2, pp. 1007–1017). New York: Garland.
Crook, C. K. (1978). Taste perception in the newborn infant. *Infant Behavior and Development, 1,* 52–69.
Crook, C. K., & Lipsitt, L. P. (1976). Neonatal nutritive sucking: Effects of taste stimulation upon sucking rhythm and heart rate. *Child Development, 47,* 518–522.
Crowell, J. A., & Feldman, S. S. (1991). Mothers' working models of attachment relationships and mother and child behavior during separation and reunion. *Developmental Psychology, 27,* 597–605.
Csikszentmihalyi, M., & Larson, R. (1984). *Being adolescent.* New York: Basic Books.
Cummings, E. M., Iannotti, R. J., & Zahn-Waxler, C. (1985). Influence of conflict between adults on the emotions and aggression of young children. *Developmental Psychology, 21,* 495–507.
Curry, G. D. (1994). Gang-related violence. *Clearinghouse Review, 28,* 443–451.
Curtiss, S. (1977). *Genie: a psycholinguistic study of a modern-day "wild child."* New York: Academic Press.
Cytryn, L., McKnew, D. H., Zahn-Waxler, C., & Gershon, E. S. (1986). Developmental issues in risk research: The offspring of affectively ill parents. In M. Rutter, C. E. Izard, & P. B. Read (Eds.), *Depression in young people: Developmental and clinical perspectives* (pp. 163–188). New York: Guilford.
Damon, W. (1977). *The social world of the child.* San Francisco: Jossey-Bass.
Damon, W. (1988). *The moral child.* New York: Free Press.
Damon, W. (1990). Self-concept, adolescent. In R. M. Lerner, A. C. Petersen, & J. Brooks-Gunn (Eds.), *The encyclopedia of adolescence* (Vol. 2, pp. 87–91). New York: Garland.
Damon, W., & Hart, D. (1988). *Self-understanding in childhood and adolescence.* New York: Cambridge University Press.
Dannemiller, J. L., & Stephens, B. R. (1988). A critical test of infant pattern preference models. *Child Development, 59,* 210–216.
Darwin, C. (1877). Biographical sketch of an infant. *Mind, 2,* 285–294.
Darwin, C. (1936). *On the origin of species by means of natural selection.* New York: Modern Library. (Original work published 1859)
David, H. P., Dytrych, Z., Matejcek, Z., & Schüller, V. (1988). *Born unwanted.* New York: Springer-Verlag.
Davidson, E., Levine, M., Malvern, J., Niebyl, J., & Tobin, M. (1993, May). A rebirth of obstetrical care. *Medical World News, 34*(5), 42–47.
Davidson, P., & Youniss, J. (1991). Which comes first, morality or identity? In W. M. Kurtines & J. L. Gewirtz (Eds.), *Handbook of moral behavior and development* (Vol. 1, pp. 105–121). Hillsdale, NJ: Erlbaum.
Day, S. (1993, May). Why genes have a gender. *New Scientist, 138*(1874), 34–38.
De Lisi, R., & Gallagher, A. M. (1991). Understanding gender stability and constancy in Argentinean children. *Merrill-Palmer Quarterly, 37,* 483–502.
de Villiers, J. G., & de Villiers, P. A. (1973). A cross-sectional study of the acquisition of grammatical morphemes in child speech. *Journal of Psycholinguistic Research, 2,* 267–278.
de Villiers, P. A., & de Villiers, J. G. (1992). Language development. In M. H. Bornstein & M. E. Lamb (Eds.), *Developmental psychology: An advanced textbook* (3rd ed., pp. 337–418). Hillsdale, NJ: Erlbaum.
DeAngelis, T. (1991, March). Psychologists take calls from kids about the war. *APA Monitor, 22(11),* 8.
DeCasper, A. J., & Spence, M. J. (1986). Prenatal maternal speech influences newborns' perception of speech sounds. *Infant Behavior and Development, 9,* 133–150.
Declercq, E. R. (1992). The transformation of American midwifery: 1975 to 1988. *American Journal of Public Health, 82,* 680–684.
DeFrain, J., Ernst, L., & Jakub, D. (1991). *Sudden infant death: Enduring the loss.* Lexington, MA: Heath.
Degelman, D., Free, J. U., Scarlato, M., Blackburn, J. M., & Golden, T. (1986). Concept learning in preschool children: Effects of a short-term Logo experience. *Journal of Educational Computing Research, 2,* 199–205.
Delgado-Gaitan, C. (1986). Adolescent peer influence and differential school performance. *Journal of Adolescent Research, 1,* 449–462.
Delgado-Gaitan, C. (1992). School matters in the Mexican-American home: Socializing children to education. *American Educational Research Journal, 29,* 495–515.
Dellas, M., & Jernigan, L. P. (1990). Affective personality characteristics associated with undergraduate ego identity formation. *Journal of Adolescent Research, 5,* 306–324.
DeLoache, J. S. (1987). Rapid change in symbolic functioning of very young children. *Science, 238,* 1556–1557.
DeLoache, J. S. (1990). Young children's understanding of models. In R. Fivush & J. Hudson (Eds.), *Knowing and remembering in young children* (pp. 94–126). New York: Cambridge University Press.
DeLoache, J. S., Kolstad, V., & Anderson, K. N. (1991). Physical similarity and young children's understanding of scale models. *Child Development, 62,* 111–126.
DeLoache, J. S., & Todd, C. M. (1988). Young children's use of spatial categorization as a mnemonic strategy. *Journal of Experimental Child Psychology, 46,* 1–20.
Delphi Communication Sciences. (1990). *Video game use symposium.* Los Angeles, CA: Author.
DeMarie-Dreblow, D. (1991). Relation between knowledge and memory: A reminder that correlation does not imply causality. *Child Development, 62,* 484–498.
Demetriou, A., Efklides, A., & Platsidou, M. (1993). The architecture and dynamics of developing mind. *Monographs of the Society for Research in Child Development, 58*(No. 5–6, Serial No. 234).
Demetriou, A., Efklides, A., Papadaki, M., Papantoniou, G., & Economou, A. (1993). Structure and development of causal–experimental thought: From early adolescence to youth. *Developmental Psychology, 29,* 480–497.
Denham, S. A., Renwick, S. M., & Holt, R. W. (1991). Working and playing together: Prediction of preschool social-emotional competence from mother–child interaction. *Child Development, 62,* 242–249.
Dennis, W. (1960). Causes of retardation among institutionalized children: Iran. *Journal of Genetic Psychology, 96,* 47–59.
Dennis, W., & Dennis, M. G. (1940). The effect of cradling practices upon the onset of walking in Hopi children. *Journal of Genetic Psychology, 56,* 77–86.
Deutsch, F. M., Ruble, D. N., Fleming, A., Brooks-Gunn, J., & Stangor, C. (1988). Information-seeking and maternal self-definition during the transition to motherhood. *Journal of Personality and Social Psychology, 55,* 420–431.
Deutsch, W., & Pechmann, T. (1982). Social interaction and the development of definite descriptions. *Cognition, 11,* 159–184.
Devereux, E. C. (1976). Backyard versus Little League Baseball: The impoverishment of children's games. In D. M. Landers (Ed.), *Social problems in athletics* (pp. 37–56). Urbana: University of Illinois Press.
Diamond, A. (1991). Neuropsychological insights into the meaning of object concept development. In S. Carey & R. Gelman

(Eds.), *The epigenesis of mind: Essays on biology and knowledge* (pp. 67–110). Hillsdale, NJ: Erlbaum.

Diamond, A., Cruttenden, L., & Neiderman, D. (1994). AB with multiple wells: 1. Why are multiple wells sometimes easier than two wells? 2. Memory or memory + inhibition. *Developmental Psychology, 30,* 192–205.

Dias, M. G., & Harris, P. L. (1990). The influence of imagination on reasoning by young children. *British Journal of Developmental Psychology, 8,* 305–318.

Diaz, R. M., & Berndt, T. J. (1982). Children's knowledge of a best friend: Fact or fancy. *Developmental Psychology, 18,* 787–794.

Dick-Read, G. (1959). *Childbirth without fear.* New York: Harper & Brothers.

Dickenson, G. (1975). Dating behavior of black and white adolescents before and after desegregation. *Journal of Marriage and the Family, 37,* 602–608.

Dickinson, D. K. (1984). First impressions: Children's knowledge of words gained from a single exposure. *Applied Psycholinguistics, 5,* 359–373.

DiClemente, R. J. (1993). Preventing HIV/AIDS among adolescents. *Journal of the American Medical Association, 270,* 760–762.

Dietz, W. H., Jr., & Gortmaker, S. L. (1985). Do we fatten our children at the television set? Obesity and television viewing in children and adolescents. *Pediatrics, 75,* 807–812.

Dietz, W. H., Jr., Bandini, L. G., & Gortmaker, S. L. (1990). Epidemiologic and metabolic risk factors for childhood obesity. *Klinische Pädiatrie, 202,* 69–72.

DiLalla, L. F., & Watson, M. W. (1988). Differentiation of fantasy and reality: Preschoolers' reactions to interruptions in their play. *Developmental Psychology, 24,* 286–291.

Dirks, J. (1982). The effect of a commercial game on children's Block Design scores on the WISC–R test. *Intelligence, 6,* 109–123.

Dittrichova, J., Brichacek, V., Paul, K., & Tautermannova, M. (1982). The structure of infant behavior: An analysis of sleep and waking in the first months of life. In W. W. Hartup (Ed.), *Review of child development research* (Vol. 6, pp. 73–100). Chicago: University of Chicago Press.

Divine-Hawkins, P. (1981). *Family day care in the United States: National Day Care Home Study final report, executive summary.* Washington, DC: U.S. Government Printing Office.

Dixon, J. A., & Moore, C. F. (1990). The development of perspective taking: Understanding differences in information and weighting. *Child Development, 61,* 1502–1513.

Dixon, R. A., & Lerner, R. M. (1992). A history of systems in developmental psychology. In M. H. Bornstein & M. E. Lamb (Eds.), *Developmental psychology: An advanced textbook* (3rd ed., pp. 3–58). Hillsdale, NJ: Erlbaum.

Dlugosz, L., & Bracken, M. B. (1992). Reproductive effects of caffeine: A review and theoretical analysis. *Epidemiological Review, 14,* 83–100.

Dodge, K. A. (1989). Coordinating responses to aversive stimuli: Introduction to a special section on the development of emotional regulation. *Developmental Psychology, 25,* 339–342.

Dodge, K. A., & Somberg, D. R. (1987). Hostile attributional biases among aggressive boys are exacerbated under conditions of threats to the self. *Child Development, 58,* 213–224.

Dodge, K. A., Pettit, G. S., & Bates, J. E. (1994). Socialization mediators of the relation between socioeconomic status and child conduct problems. *Child Development, 65,* 649–665.

Dodwell, P. C., Humphrey, G. K., & Muir, D. W. (1987). Shape and pattern perception. In P. Salapatek & L. Cohen (Eds.), *Handbook of infant perception* (Vol. 2, pp. 1–77). Orlando, FL: Academic Press.

Doherty, W. J., & Needle, R. H. (1991). Psychological adjustment and substance use among adolescents before and after parental divorce. *Child Development, 62,* 328–337.

Doi, L. T. (1973). *The anatomy of dependence* (J. Bester, Trans.). Tokyo: Kadansha International.

Dolan, E. F., Jr., & Finney, S. (1984). *Youth gangs.* New York: Messner.

Dolgin, K. G., & Behrend, D. A. (1984). Children's knowledge about animates and inanimates. *Child Development, 55,* 1646–1650.

Dollaghan, C. (1985). Child meets word: "Fast mapping" in preschool children. *Journal of Speech and Hearing Research, 28,* 449–454.

Dontas, C., Maratsos, O., Fafoutis, M., & Karangelis, A. (1985). Early social development in institutionally reared Greek infants: Attachment and peer interaction. In I. Bretherton & E. Waters (Eds.), Growing points of attachment theory and research. *Monographs of the Society for Research in Child Development, 50*(1–2, Serial No. 209).

Dornbusch, S. M., Carlsmith, J., Gross, R., Martin, J., Jennings, D., Rosenberg, A., & Duke, P. (1981). Sexual development, age, and dating: A comparison of biological and social influences upon one set of behaviors. *Child Development, 52,* 179–185.

Dornbusch, S. M., Carlsmith, J. M., Bushwall, S. J., Ritter, P. L., Leiderman, H., Hastorf, A. H., & Gross, R. T. (1985). Single parents, extended households, and the control of adolescents. *Child Development, 56,* 326–341.

Dornbusch, S. M., Ritter, P. L., Liederman, P. H., Roberts, D. F., & Fraleigh, M. J. (1987). The relation of parenting style to adolescent school performance. *Child Development, 58,* 1244–1257.

Dornbusch, S. M., Ritter, P. L., Mont-Reynaud, R., & Chen, Z. (1990). Family decision making and academic performance in a diverse high school population. *Journal of Adolescent Research, 5,* 143–160.

Dorr, A., Kovaric, P., & Doubleday, C. (1989). Parent–child coviewing of television. *Journal of Broadcasting and Electronic Media, 33,* 35–51.

Dorris, M. (1989). *The broken cord.* New York: Harper & Row.

Dossey, J. A., Mullis, I. V. S., Lindquist, M. M., & Cambers, D. L. (1988). *The Mathematics Report Card: Are we measuring up?* Princeton, NJ: Educational Testing Service.

Douglas, V. I. (1983). Attentional and cognitive problems. In M. Rutter (Ed.), *Developmental neuropsychiatry* (pp. 280–329). New York: Guilford.

Douvan, E., & Adelson, J. (1966). *The adolescent experience.* New York: Wiley.

Downey, G., & Walker, E. (1989). Social cognition and adjustment in children at risk for psychopathology. *Developmental Psychology, 25,* 835–845.

Drabman, R. S., Cordua, G. D., Hammer, D., Jarvie, G. J., & Horton, W. (1979). Developmental trends in eating rates of normal and overweight preschool children. *Child Development, 50,* 211–216.

Draper, P., & Cashdan, E. (1988). Technological change and child behavior among the !Kung. *Ethnology, 27,* 339–365.

Dreyer, P. (1982). Sexuality during adolescence. In B. Wolman (Ed.), *Handbook of developmental psychology* (pp. 559–601). Englewood Cliffs, NJ: Prentice Hall.

Drotar, D., & Sturm, L. (1988). Prediction of intellectual development in young children with early histories of nonorganic failure-to-thrive. *Journal of Pediatric Psychology, 13,* 281–296.

DuBois, D. L., & Hirsch, B. J. (1990). School and neighborhood friendship patterns of black and whites in early adolescence. *Child Development, 61,* 524–536.

Dubow, E. F., Tisak, J., Causey, D., Hryshko, A., & Reid, G. (1991). A two-year longitudinal study of stressful life events, social support, and social problem-solving skills: Contributions to children's behavioral and academic adjustment. *Child Development, 62,* 583–599.

Duncan, G. J., Brooks-Gunn, J., & Klebanov, P. K. (1994). Economic deprivation and early childhood development. *Child Development, 65,* 296–318.

Duncan, P., Ritter, P., Dornbusch, S., Gross, R., & Carlsmith, J. (1985). The effects of pubertal timing on body image, school behavior, and deviance. *Journal of Youth and Adolescence, 14,* 227–236.

Duncan, S. W., & Markman, H. J. (1988). Intervention programs: Prevention perspective. In G. Y. Michaels & W. A. Goldberg (Eds.), *The transition to parenthood* (pp. 270–310). New York: Cambridge University Press.

Dunford, F. W., & Elliott, D. S. (1984). Identifying career offenders using self-reported data. *Journal of Research in Crime and Delinquency, 21,* 57–86.

Dunham, P. J., & Dunham, F. (1992). Lexical development during middle infancy: A mutually driven infant–caregiver process. *Developmental Psychology, 28,* 414–420.

Dunham, P. J., Dunham, F., & Curwin, A.

(1993). Joint-attentional states and lexical acquisition at 18 months. *Developmental Psychology, 29,* 827–831.
Dunn, J. (1989). Siblings and the development of social understanding in early childhood. In P. G. Zukow (Ed.), *Sibling interaction across cultures* (pp. 106–116). New York: Springer-Verlag.
Dunn, J. (1992). Sisters and brothers: Current issues in developmental research. In F. Boer & J. Dunn (Eds.), *Children's sibling relationships* (pp. 1–17). Hillsdale, NJ: Erlbaum.
Dunn, J., & Kendrick, C. (1982). *Siblings: Love, envy and understanding.* Cambridge, MA: Harvard University Press.
Dunn, J., Bretherton, I., & Munn, P. (1987). Conversations about feeling states between mothers and their young children. *Developmental Psychology, 23,* 132–139.
Dunn, J., Slomkowski, C., & Beardsall, L. (1994). Sibling relationships from the preschool period through middle childhood and early adolescence. *Developmental Psychology, 30,* 315–324.
Dunphy, D. C. (1963). The social structure of urban adolescent peer groups. *Sociometry, 26,* 230–246.
DuPont, R. L. (1983). Phobias in children. *Journal of Pediatrics, 102,* 999–1002.
Dusek, J. B. (1987). Sex roles and adjustment. In D. B. Carter (Ed.), *Current conceptions of sex roles and sex typing* (pp. 211–222). New York: Praeger.
Dweck, C. S. (1975). The role of expectations and attributions in the alleviation of learned helplessness. *Journal of Personality and Social Psychology, 31,* 674–685.
Dweck, C. S., & Elliott, E. S. (1983). Achievement motivation. In E. M. Hetherington (Ed.), *Handbook of child psychology: Vol. 4. Socialization, personality, and social development* (pp. 643–691). New York: Wiley.
Dweck, C. S., & Leggett, E. L. (1988). A social-cognitive approach to motivation and personality. *Psychological Review, 95,* 256–273.
Dweck, C. S., Davidson, W., Nelson, S., & Enna, B. (1978). Sex differences in learned helplessness: III. An experimental analysis. *Developmental Psychology, 14,* 268–276.
Dye-White, E. (1986). Environmental hazards in the work setting: Their effect on women of child-bearing age. *American Association of Occupational Health and Nursing Journal, 34,* 76–78.
Dyson, A. H. (1984). Emerging alphabetic literacy in school contexts: Toward defining the gap between school curriculum and child mind. *Written Communication, 1,* 5–55.
East, P. L., & Rook, K. S. (1992). Compensatory patterns of support among children's peer relationships: A test using school friends, nonschool friends, and siblings. *Developmental Psychology, 28,* 168–172.
Easterbrooks, M. A. (1989). Quality of attachment to mother and to father: Effects of perinatal risk status. *Child Development, 60,* 831–837.
Ebeling, K. S., & Gelman, S. A. (1994). Children's use of context in interpreting "big" and "little." *Child Development, 65,* 1178–1192.
Eberhart-Phillips, J. E., Frederick, P. D., & Baron, R. C. (1993). Measles in pregnancy: A descriptive study of 58 cases. *Obstetrics and Gynecology, 82,* 797–801.
Eccles, J. S. (1987). Adolescence: Gateway to gender-role transcendence. In D. B. Carter (Ed.), *Current conceptions of sex roles and sex typing: Theory and research* (pp. 225–241). New York: Praeger.
Eccles, J. S. (1990). Academic achievement. In R. M. Lerner, A. C. Petersen, & J. Brooks-Gunn (Eds.), *The encyclopedia of adolescence* (pp. 1–5). New York: Garland.
Eccles, J. S., & Harold, R. D. (1991). Gender differences in sport involvement: Applying the Eccles' expectancy-value model. *Journal of Applied Sport Psychology, 3,* 7–35.
Eccles, J. S., & Harold, R. D. (1993). Parent–school involvement during the early adolescent years. *Teachers College Record, 94,* 568–587.
Eccles, J. S., Jacobs, J., & Harold, R. D. (1990). Gender-role stereotypes, expectancy effects, and parents' role in the socialization of gender differences in self-perceptions and skill acquisition. *Journal of Social Issues, 46,* 183–201.
Eccles, J. S., Midgley, C., Wigfield, A., Buchanan, C. M., Reuman, D., Flanagan, C., & Mac Iver, D. (1993a). Development during adolescence: The impact of stage–environment fit on young adolescents' experiences in schools and in families. *American Psychologist, 48,* 90–101.
Eccles, J. S., Wigfield, A., Midgley, C., Reuman, D., Mac Iver, D., & Feldlaufer, H. (1993b). Negative effects of traditional middle schools on students' motivation. *Elementary School Journal, 93,* 553–574.
Eckenrode, J., Laird, M., & Doris, J. (1993). School performance and disciplinary problems among abused and neglected children. *Developmental Psychology, 29,* 53–62.
Eckerman, C. O., Davis, C. C., & Didow, S. M. (1989). Coordination of size standards by young children. *Child Development, 59,* 888–896.
Eckstrom, R. B., Goertz, M. E., Pollack, J. M., & Rock, D. A. (1986). Who drops out of school and why? Findings from a national study. *Teachers College Record, 87,* 356–373.
Eder, D., & Parker, S. (1987). The cultural production and reproduction of gender: The effect of extracurricular activities on peer-group culture. *Sociology of Education 60,* 200–213.
Eder, R. A. (1989). The emergent personologist: The structure and content of 3 1/2-, 5 1/2-, and 7 1/2-year-olds' concepts of themselves and other persons. *Child Development, 60,* 1218–1228.
Eder, R. A. (1990). Uncovering young children's psychological selves: Individual and developmental differences. *Child Development, 61,* 849–863.
Edwards, C. P. (1981). The comparative study of the development of moral judgment and reasoning. In R. L. Munroe, R. Munroe, & B. B. Whiting (Eds.), *Handbook of cross-cultural human development* (pp. 501-528). New York: Garland.
Edwards, J. N. (1991). New conceptions: Biosocial innovations and the family. *Journal of Marriage and the Family, 53,* 349–360.
Egeland, B., Jacobvitz, D., & Sroufe, L. A. (1988). Breaking the cycle of abuse. *Child Development, 59,* 1080–1088.
Egeland, B., & Sroufe, L. A. (1981). Developmental sequelae of maltreatment in infancy. In R. Rizley & D. Cicchetti (Eds.), *New directions for child development* (No. 11, pp. 77–92). San Francisco: Jossey-Bass.
Eifermann, R. R. (1971). Social play in childhood. In R. E. Herron & B. Sutton-Smith (Eds.), *Child's play* (pp. 270–297). New York: Wiley.
Eisenberg, L. (1984). The epidemiology of suicide in adolescents. *Pediatric Annals, 13,* 47–54.
Eisenberg, N., & Miller, P. A. (1987). The relation of empathy to prosocial and related behaviors. *Psychological Bulletin, 101,* 91–119.
Eisenberg, N., Fabes, R. A., Bernzweig, J., Karbon, M., Poulin, R., & Hanish, L. (1993). The relations of emotionality and regulation to preschoolers' social skills and sociometric status. *Child Development, 64,* 1418–1438.
Eisenberg, N., Shell, R., Pasternack, J., Lennon, R., Beller, R., & Mathy, R. M. (1987). Prosocial development in middle childhood: A longitudinal study. *Developmental Psychology, 23,* 712–718.
Ekman, P., & Friesen, W. (1972). Constants across culture in the face and emotion. *Journal of Personality and Social Psychology, 17,* 124–129.
Elardo, R., & Bradley, R. H. (1981). The Home Observation for Measurement of the Environment (HOME) Scale: A review of research. *Developmental Review, 1,* 113–145.
Elicker, J., Englund, M., & Sroufe, L. A. (1992). Predicting peer competence and peer relationships in childhood from early parent–child relationships. In R. D. Parke & G. W. Ladd (Eds.), *Family–peer relationships: Modes of linkage* (pp. 77–106). Hillsdale, NJ: Erlbaum.
Elkind, D. (1984). *All grown up and no place to go: Teenagers in crisis.* Reading, MA: Addison-Wesley.
Elkind, D. (1985). Egocentrism redux. *Developmental Review, 5,* 218–226.
Elkind, D., & Bowen, R. (1979). Imaginary audience behavior in children and adolescents. *Developmental Psychology, 15,* 33–44.
Ellsworth, C. P., Muir, D. W., & Hains, S. M. J. (1993). Social competence and person–object differentiation: An analysis of the still-face effect. *Developmental Psychology, 29,* 63–73.
Emde, R. N. (1992). Individual meaning and increasing complexity: Contributions of Sigmund Freud and René Spitz to developmental psychology. *Developmental Psychology, 28,* 347–359.

Emde, R. N., & Buchsbaum, H. K. (1990). "Didn't you hear my mommy?" Autonomy with connectedness in moral self-emergence. In D. Cicchetti & M. Beeghly (Eds.), *Development of the self through transition* (pp. 35–60). Chicago: University of Chicago Press.

Emde, R. N., Gaensbauer, T. J., & Harmon, R. J. (1976). Emotional expression in infancy: A biobehavioral study. *Psychological Issues, 10*(No. 37). New York: International Universities Press.

Emde, R. N., & Koenig, K. L. (1969). Neonatal smiling and rapid eye movement states. *American Academy of Child Psychiatry, 8,* 57–67.

Emde, R. N., Plomin, R., Robinson, J., Corley, R., DeFries, J., Fulker, D. W., Reznick, J. S., Campos, J., Kagan, J., & Zahn-Waxler, C. (1992). Temperament, emotion, and cognition at fourteen months: The MacArthur Longitudinal Twin Study. *Child Development, 63,* 1437–1455.

Emery, R. E. (1989). Family violence. *American Psychologist, 44,* 321–328.

Emery, R. E., & Wyer, M. M. (1987). Divorce mediation. *American Psychologist, 42,* 472–480.

Emory, E. K., & Toomey, K. A. (1988). Environmental stimulation and human fetal responsibility in late pregnancy. In W. P. Smotherman & S. R. Robinson (Eds.), *Behavior of the fetus* (pp. 141–161). Caldwell, NJ: Telford.

Engel, N. (1989). An American experience of pregnancy and childbirth in Japan. *Birth, 16,* 81–86.

Enns, J. T. (Ed.). (1990). *The development of attention: Research and theory.* Amsterdam: North-Holland.

Enright, R. D., Lapsley, D. K., & Shukla, D. (1979). Adolescent egocentrism in early and late adolescence. *Adolescence, 14,* 687–695.

Epstein, J. L. (1983). Selection of friends in differently organized schools and classrooms. In J. L. Epstein & N. L. Karweit (Eds.), *Friends in school* (pp. 73–92). New York: Academic Press.

Epstein, J. L. (1983b). The influence of friends on achievement and affective outcomes. In J. L. Epstein & N. L. Karweit (Eds.), *Friends in school* (pp. 177–200). New York: Academic Press.

Epstein, L. H., McCurley, J., Wing, R. R., & Valoski, A. (1990). Five-year follow-up of family-based treatments for childhood obesity. *Journal of Consulting and Clinical Psychology, 58,* 661–664.

Epstein, L. H., Wing, R. R., Koeske, R., & Valoski, A. (1987). Long-term effects of family-based treatment of childhood obesity. *Journal of Consulting and Clinical Psychology, 55,* 91–95.

Erikson, E. H. (1950). *Childhood and society.* New York: Norton.

Erikson, E. H. (1968). *Identity, youth, and crisis.* New York: Norton.

Ernhart, C. B., Wolf, A. W., Filipovich, H. F., Kennard, M. J., Erhard, P., & Sokol, R. J. (1985). Intrauterine lead exposure. *Teratology, 31,* 7B–8B.

Eron, L. D., Walder, L. O., Huesmann, L. R., & Lefkowitz, N. M. (1974). The convergence of laboratory and field studies of the development of aggression. In J. deWit & W. W. Hartup (Eds.), *Determinants of the origins of aggressive behavior* (pp. 347–380). The Hague: Mouton.

Ervin-Tripp, S. (1991). Play in language development. In B. Scales, M. Almy, A. Nicolopoulou, & S. Ervin-Tripp (Eds.), *Play and the social context of development in early care and education* (pp. 84–97). New York: Teachers College Press.

Escalona, S. K., & Corman, H. H. (1969). *Albert Einstein Scales of Sensorimotor Development.* New York: Albert Einstein College of Medicine, Yeshiva University.

Espenschade, A., & Eckert, H. (1974). Motor development. In W. R. Johnson & E. R. Buskirk (Eds.), *Science and medicine of exercise and sport* (pp. 322–333). New York: Harper & Row.

Espenschade, A., & Eckert, H. (1980). *Motor development.* Columbus, OH: Merrill.

Essa, E. L., & Murray, C. I. (1994, May). Young children's understanding and experience with death. *Young Children, 49*(4), 74–81.

Eveleth, P. B., & Tanner, J. M. (1976). *Worldwide variation in human growth.* Cambridge, England: Cambridge University Press.

Eyer, D. E. (1992). *Mother–infant bonding: A scientific fiction.* New Haven, CT: Yale University Press.

Fabes, R. A., Eisenberg, N., & Eisenbud, L. (1993). Behavioral and physiological correlates of children's reactions to others in distress. *Developmental Psychology, 29,* 655–663.

Fabes, R. A., Eisenberg, N., McCormick, S. E., & Wilson, M. S. (1988). Preschoolers' attributions of the situational determinants of others' naturally occurring emotions. *Developmental Psychology, 24,* 376–385.

Fabes, R. A., Eisenberg, N., Karbon, M., Troyer, D., & Switzer, G. (1994). The relations of children's emotion regulation to their vicarious emotional responses and comforting behaviors. *Child Development, 65,* 1678–1693.

Fabes, R. A., Eisenberg, N., Nyman, M., & Michealieu, Q. (1991). Young children's appraisals of others' spontaneous emotional reactions. *Developmental Psychology, 27,* 858–866.

Fackelmann, K. A. (1992, November 28). Finding Marfan syndrome in the womb. *Science News, 142*(22), 382.

Fagan, J. F., III. (1971). Infants' recognition memory for a series of visual stimuli. *Journal of Experimental Child Psychology, 11,* 244–250.

Fagan, J. F., III. (1973). Infants' delayed recognition memory and forgetting. *Journal of Experimental Child Psychology, 16,* 424–450.

Fagan, J. F., III. (1977). Infant recognition memory: Studies in forgetting. *Child Development, 45,* 351–356.

Fagan, J. F., III, & Montie, J. E. (1988). The behavioral assessment of cognitive well-being in the infant. In J. Kavanagh (Ed.), *Understanding mental retardation* (pp. 207–221). Baltimore: Brookes.

Fagan, J. F., III, Shepherd, P. A., & Knevel, C. R. (1991). *Predictive validity of the Fagan Test of Infant Intelligence.* Paper presented at the biennial meeting of the Society for Research in Child Development, Seattle, WA.

Fagan, J., Slaughter, E., & Hartstone, E. (1987). Blind justice? The impact of race on the juvenile justice process. *Crime & Delinquency, 33,* 224–258.

Fagot, B. I. (1977). Consequences of moderate cross-gender behavior in preschool children. *Child Development, 48,* 902–907.

Fagot, B. I. (1978). The influence of sex of child on parental reactions to toddler children. *Child Development, 49,* 459–465.

Fagot, B. I., & Hagan, R. I. (1991). Observations of parent reactions to sex-stereotyped behaviors: Age and sex effects. *Child Development, 62,* 617–628.

Fagot, B. I., & Kavanaugh, K. (1990). The prediction of antisocial behavior from avoidant attachment classifications. *Child Development, 61,* 864–873.

Fagot, B. I., & Leinbach, M. D. (1989). The young child's gender schema: Environmental input, internal organization. *Child Development, 60,* 663–672.

Fagot, B. I., Leinbach, M. D., & O'Boyle, C. (1992). Gender labeling, gender stereotyping, and parenting behaviors. *Developmental Psychology, 28,* 225–230.

Fagot, B. I., & Patterson, G. R. (1969). An in vivo analysis of reinforcing contingencies for sex-role behaviors in the preschool child. *Developmental Psychology, 1,* 563–568.

Fahrmeier, E. D. (1978). The development of concrete operations among the Hausa. *Journal of Cross-Cultural Psychology, 9,* 23–44.

Falbo, T., & Polit, D. (1986). A quantitative review of the only child literature: Research evidence and theory development. *Psychological Bulletin, 100,* 176–189.

Falbo, T., & Poston, D. L., Jr. (1993). The academic, personality, and physical outcomes of only children in China. *Child Development, 64,* 18–35.

Faller, K. C. (1990). *Understanding child sexual maltreatment.* Newbury Park, CA: Sage.

Fantz, R. L. (1961, May). The origin of form perception. *Scientific American, 204*(5), 66–72.

Fantz, R. L. (1963). Pattern vision in newborn infants. *Science, 140,* 296–297.

Farrar, M. J. (1990). Discourse and the acquisition of grammatical morphemes. *Journal of Child Language, 17,* 607–624.

Farrington, D. P. (1987). Epidemiology. In H. C. Quay (Ed.), *Handbook of juvenile delinquency* (pp. 33–61). New York: Wiley.

Farrington, D. P., Loeber, R., & van Kammen, W. B. (1990). Long-term criminal outcomes of hyperactivity-impulsivity-attention deficit and conduct problems in childhood. In L. N. Robins & M. R. Rutter (Eds.), *Straight and devious pathways to adulthood* (pp. 62–81). New York: Cambridge University Press.

Fawcett, S. B., Seekins, T., & Jason, L. A. (1987). Policy research and child passenger safety legislation: A case study and experimental evaluation. *Journal of Social Issues, 43,* 133–148.

Feagans, L. V., Kipp, E., & Blood, I. (1994). The effects of otitis media on the attention skills of day-care-attending toddlers. *Developmental Psychology, 30,* 701–708.

Featherman, D. (1980). Schooling and occupational careers: Constancy and change in worldly success. In O. Brim, Jr., & J. Kagan (Eds.), *Constancy and change in human development* (pp. 675–738). Cambridge, MA: Harvard University Press.

Fedele, N. M., Golding, E. R., Grossman, F. K., & Pollack, W. S. (1988). Psychological issues in adjustment to first parenthood. In G. Y. Michaels & W. A. Goldberg (Eds.), *The transition to parenthood* (pp. 85–113). New York: Cambridge University Press.

Fee, E. (1990). Public health in practice: An early confrontation with the "silent epidemic" of childhood lead paint poisoning. *Journal of the History of Medicine and Allied Sciences, 45,* 570–606.

Fein, G. G., Gariboldi, A., & Boni, R. (1993). The adjustment of infants and toddlers to group care: The first six months. *Early Childhood Research Quarterly, 8,* 1–14.

Feiner, J., & Subak-Sharpe, G. (1988, November). Understanding children's fears. *Parents,* pp. 101–105.

Feingold, A. (1988). Cognitive gender differences are disappearing. *American Psychologist, 43,* 95–103.

Feis, C. L., & Simons, C. (1985). Training preschool children in interpersonal cognitive problem-solving skills: A replication. *Prevention in Human Services, 3,* 59–70.

Feldlaufer, H., Midgley, C., & Eccles, J. S. (1988). Student, teacher, and observer perceptions of the classroom environment before and after the transition to junior high school. *Journal of Early Adolescence, 8,* 133–156.

Feldman, D. H. (1991). *Nature's gambit.* New York: Teacher's College Press.

Feldman, S. S., & Weinberger, D. A. (1994). Self-restraint as a mediator of family influences on boys' delinquent behavior: A longitudinal study. *Child Development, 65,* 195–211.

Felner, R. D., & Adan, A. M. (1988). The School Transitional Environment Project: An ecological intervention and evaluation. In R. H. Price, E. L. Cowan, R. P. Lorion, & J. Ramos-McKay (Eds.), *14 ounces of prevention: A casebook for practitioners* (pp. 111–122). Washington, DC: American Psychological Association.

Fenson, L., Dale, P. S., Reznick, J. S., Bates, E., Thal, D. J., & Pethick, S. J. (1994). Variability in early communicative development. *Monographs of the Society for Research in Childhood Development, 59* (5, Serial No. 242).

Fenzel, L. M., Blyth, D. A., & Simmons, R. G. (1990). School transitions: Secondary. In R. M. Lerner, A. C. Petersen, & J. Brooks-Gunn (Eds.), *The encyclopedia of adolescence* (pp. 970–973). New York: Garland.

Ferguson, L. R. (1978). The competence and freedom of children to make choices regarding participation in research: A statement. *Journal of Social Issues, 34,* 114–121.

Ferguson, T. J., Stegge, H., & Damhuis, I. (1991). Children's understanding of guilt and shame. *Child Development, 62,* 827–839.

Fergusson, D. M., Horwood, L. J., & Lynskey, M. T. (1993). Maternal smoking before and after pregnancy: Effects on behavioral outcomes in middle childhood. *Pediatrics, 92,* 815–822.

Fergusson, D. M., Horwood, L. J., & Shanon, F. T. (1987). Breast-feeding and subsequent social adjustment in six- to eight-year-old children. *Journal of Child Psychology and Psychiatry, 28,* 378–386.

Fernald, A. (1993). Approval and disapproval: Infant responsiveness to vocal affect in familiar and unfamiliar languages. *Child Development, 64,* 657–674.

Fernald, A., & Morikawa, H. (1993). Common themes and cultural variations in Japanese and American mothers' speech to infants. *Child Development, 64,* 637–656.

Fernald, A., Taeschner, T., Dunn, J., Papousek, M., Boyssen-Bardies, B., & Fukui, I. (1989). A cross-language study of prosodic modifications in mothers' and fathers' speech to preverbal infants. *Journal of Child Language, 16,* 477–502.

Ferrazin, A., De Maria, A., & Gotta, C. (1993). Zidovudine therapy of HIV-1 infection during pregnancy: Assessment of the effect on newborns. *Journal of Acquired Immune Deficiency Syndrome, 6,* 376–379.

Ferreiro, E. (1986). The interplay between information and assimilation in beginning literacy. In W. H. Teale & E. Sulzby (Eds.), *Emergent literacy: Writing and reading* (pp. 15–49). Norwood, NJ: Ablex.

Feshbach, N. D., & Feshbach, S. (1982). Empathy training and the regulation of aggression: Potentialities and limitations. *Academic Psychology Bulletin, 4,* 399–413.

Field, T. M., Schanberg, S. M., Scafidi, F., Bauer, C. R., Vega-Lahr, N., Garcia, R., Nystrom, J., & Kuhn, C. M. (1986). Effects of tactile/kinesthetic stimulation on preterm neonates. *Pediatrics, 77,* 654–658.

Field, T. M., Woodson, R., Greenberg, R., & Cohen, D. (1982). Discrimination and imitation of facial expressions by neonates. *Science, 218,* 179–181.

Fiese, B. (1990). Playful relationships: A contextual analysis of mother–toddler interaction and symbolic play. *Child Development, 61,* 1648–1656.

Filipovic, Z. (1994). *Zlata's diary: A child's life in Sarajevo.* New York: Penguin.

Fine, G. A. (1980). The natural history of preadolescent male friendship groups. In H. C. Foot, A. J. Chapman, & J. R. Smith (Eds.), *Friendship and social relations in children* (pp. 293–320). Chichester, England: Wiley.

Fine, G. A. (1987). *With the boys: Little League Baseball and preadolescent culture.* Chicago: University of Chicago Press.

Fine, M. (1986). Why urban adolescents drop into and out of public high school. *Teacher's College Record, 87,* 393–409.

Finegan, J. K., Niccols, G. A., & Sitarenios, G. (1992). Relations between prenatal testosterone levels and cognitive abilities at 4 years. *Developmental Psychology, 28,* 1075–1089.

Finkelhor, D. (1984). *Child sexual abuse: New theory and research.* New York: Free Press.

Fischer, K. W. (1980). A theory of cognitive development: The control and construction of hierarchies of skills. *Psychological Review, 87,* 477–531.

Fischer, K. W., & Farrar, M. J. (1987). Generalizations about generalizations: How a theory of skill development explains both generality and specificity. *International Journal of Psychology, 22,* 643–677.

Fischer, K. W., & Pipp, S. L. (1984). Processes of cognitive development: Optimal level and skill acquisition. In R. J. Sternberg (Ed.), *Mechanisms of cognitive development* (pp. 45–80). New York: Freeman.

Fisher, C. B. (1993, Winter). Integrating science and ethics in research with high-risk children and youth. *Social Policy Report of the Society for Research in Child Development, 4*(4).

Fisher, C. B., Bornstein, M. H., & Gross, G. G. (1985). Left–right coding skills related to beginning reading. *Journal of Developmental and Behavioral Pediatrics, 6,* 279–283.

Fivush, R. (1984). Learning about school: The development of kindergartners' school scripts. *Child Development, 55,* 1697–1709.

Fivush, R. (1991). The social construction of personal narratives. *Merrill-Palmer Quarterly, 37,* 59–81.

Fivush, R., Kuebli, J., & Clubb, P. A. (1992). The structure of events and event representations: A developmental analysis. *Child Development, 63,* 188–201.

Flavell, J. H. (1963). *The developmental psychology of Jean Piaget.* New York: Van Nostrand.

Flavell, J. H. (1985). *Cognitive development* (2nd ed.). Englewood Cliffs, NJ: Prentice Hall.

Flavell, J. H., Green, F. L., & Flavell, E. R. (1987). Development of knowledge about the appearance–reality distinction. *Monographs of the Society for Research in Child Development, 51*(1, Serial No. 212).

Flavell, J. H., Green, F. L., & Flavell, E. R. (1989). Young children's ability to differentiate appearance–reality and level 2 perspectives in the tactile modality. *Child Development, 60,* 201–213.

Flavell, J. H., Green, F. L., & Flavell, E. R. (1993). Children's understanding of the stream of consciousness. *Child Development, 64,* 387–398.

Flavell, J. H., Miller, P. H., & Miller, S. A. (1993). *Cognitive development* (3rd ed.). Englewood Cliffs, NJ: Prentice Hall.

Flege, J. E., & Fletcher, K. L. (1992). Talker and listener effects on the perception of degree of foreign accent. *Journal of the Acoustical Society of America, 91,* 370–389.

Fleming, P. J., Gilbert, R., Azaz, Y., Berry, P. J., Rudd, P. T., Stewart, A., & Hall, E. (1990). Interaction between bedding and sleep position in sudden infant death syndrome: A population based-control study. *British Medical Journal, 301,* 85–89.

Fogel, A., Toda, S., & Kawai, M. (1988). Mother–infant face-to-face interaction in Japan and the United States: A laboratory comparison using 3-month-old infants. *Developmental Psychology, 24,* 398–406.

Fonagy, P., Steele, H., & Steele, M. (1991). Maternal representations of attachment during pregnancy predict the organization of infant–mother attachment at one year of age. *Child Development, 62,* 891–905.

Food Research and Action Center (1991). *Community Childhood Hunger Identification Project.* Washington, DC: Author.

Ford, C., & Beach, F. (1951). *Patterns of sexual behavior.* New York: Harper & Row.

Ford, D. Y., & Harris, J. J., III. (1990). On discovering the hidden treasure of gifted and talented black children. *Roeper Review, 13,* 27–32.

Ford, K., & Labbok, M. (1993). Breast-feeding and child health in the United States. *Journal of Biosocial Science, 25,* 187–194.

Ford, M. E., & Keating, D. P. (1981). Development and individual differences in long-term memory retrieval: Process and organization. *Child Development, 52,* 234–241.

Fordham, S., & Ogbu, J. U. (1986). Black students' school success: Coping with the "burden of 'acting white'." *Urban Review, 18,* 176–206.

Forehand, R., Wierson, M., Thomas, A. M., Fauber, R., Armistead, L., Kempton, T., & Long, N. (1991). A short-term longitudinal examination of young adolescent functioning following divorce: The role of family factors. *Journal of Abnormal Child Psychology, 19,* 97–111.

Forman, E. A., Minick, N., & Stone, C. A. (Eds.). (1993). *Contexts for learning.* New York: Oxford University Press.

Forrest, J. D., & Singh, S. (1990). The sexual and reproductive behavior of American women, 1982–1988. *Family Planning Perspectives, 22,* 206–214.

Fox, N. A. (1991). If it's not left, it's right: Electroencephalograph asymmetry and the development of emotion. *American Psychologist, 46,* 863–872.

Fox, N. A., Bell, M. A., & Jones, N. A. (1992). Individual differences in response to stress and cerebral asymmetry. *Developmental Neuropsychology, 8,* 161–184.

Fox, N. A., & Davidson, R. J. (1986). Taste-elicited changes in facial signs of emotion and the asymmetry of brain electrical activity in newborn infants. *Neuropsychologia, 24,* 417–422.

Foxman, B., Valdez, R. B., & Brook, R. H. (1986). Childhood enuresis: Prevalence, perceived impact, and prescribed treatments. *Pediatrics, 77,* 482–487.

Fracasso, M. P., & Busch-Rossnagel, N. A. (1992). Parents and children of Hispanic origin. In M. E. Procidano & C. B. Fisher (Eds.), *Contemporary families* (pp. 83–98). New York: Teachers College Press.

Francis, P. L., & McCroy, G. (1983). *Bimodal recognition of human stimulus configurations.* Paper presented at the biennial meeting of the Society for Research in Child Development, Detroit.

Frank, S. J., Pirsch, L. A., & Wright, V. C. (1990). Late adolescents' perceptions of their relationships with their parents: Relationships among deidealization, autonomy, relatedness, and insecurity and implications for adolescent adjustment and ego identity status. *Journal of Youth and Adolescence, 19,* 571–588.

Frankel, K. A., & Bates, J. E. (1990). Mother–toddler problem solving: Antecedents in attachment, home behavior, and temperament. *Child Development, 61,* 810–819.

Frauenglass, M. H., & Diaz, R. M. (1985). Self-regulatory functions of children's private speech: A critical analysis of recent challenges to Vygotsky's theory. *Developmental Psychology, 21,* 357–364.

Frederiksen, J. R., & Warren, B. M. (1987). A cognitive framework for developing expertise in reading. In R. Glaser (Ed.), *Advances in instructional psychology* (Vol. 3, pp. 1–39). Hillsdale, NJ: Erlbaum.

Freedman, D. G., & Freedman, N. (1969). Behavioral differences between Chinese-American and European-American newborns. *Nature, 224,* 1227.

Freeman, D. (1983). *Margaret Mead and Samoa: The making and unmaking of an anthropological myth.* Cambridge, MA: Harvard University Press.

French, D. C., & Waas, G. A. (1985). Behavior problems of peer-neglected and peer rejected elementary age children: Parent and teacher perspectives. *Child Development, 56,* 246–252.

Freud, S. (1973). *An outline of psychoanalysis.* London: Hogarth. (Original work published 1938)

Freud, S. (1974). *The ego and the id.* London: Hogarth. (Original work published 1923)

Frey, K. S., & Ruble, D. N. (1992). Gender constancy and the "cost" of sex-typed behavior: A test of the conflict hypothesis. *Developmental Psychology, 28,* 714–721.

Fried, M. N., & Fried, M. H. (1980). *Transitions: Four rituals in eight cultures.* New York: Norton.

Fried, P. A., & Makin, J. E. (1987). Neonatal behavioral correlates of prenatal exposure to marijuana, cigarettes, and alcohol in a low risk population. *Neurobehavioral Toxicology and Teratology, 9,* 1–7.

Fried, P. A., & O'Connell, C. M. (1987). A comparison of the effects of prenatal exposure to tobacco, alcohol, cannabis, and caffeine on birth size and subsequent growth. *Neurobehavioral Toxicology and Teratology, 9,* 79–85.

Fried, P. A., & Watkinson, B. (1990). 36- and 48-month neurobehavioral follow-up of children prenatally exposed to marijuana, cigarettes, and alcohol. *Journal of Developmental and Behavioral Pediatrics, 11,* 49–58.

Friedman, A. G., Greene, P. G., & Stokes, T. (1991). Improving dietary habits of children: Effects of nutrition education and correspondence training. *Behavior Therapy and Experimental Psychiatry, 21,* 263–268.

Friedman, J. A., & Weinberger, H. L. (1990). Six children with lead poisoning. *American Journal of Diseases of Children, 144,* 1039–1044.

Friedman, L. (1989). Mathematics and the gender gap: A meta-analysis of recent studies on sex differences in mathematical tasks. *Review of Educational Research, 59,* 185–214.

Friedman, M., & Rosenman, R. H. (1959). Association of specific overt behavior patterns with blood and cardiovascular findings. *Journal of the American Medical Association, 169,* 1286–1296.

Friedman, M., & Weiss, E. (1993, December). America's vaccine crisis. *Parents,* Vol. 68, No. 2, pp. 39–43.

Friedrich-Cofer, L., & Huston, A. C. (1986). Television violence and aggression: The debate continues. *Psychological Bulletin, 100,* 364–371.

Frisch, R. E., Gotz-Welbergen, A., McArthur, J. W., Albright, T., Witschi, J., Bullen, B., Birnholz, J., Reed, R. B., & Hermann, H. (1981). Delayed menarche and amenorrhea of college athletes in relation to age of onset of training. *Journal of the American Medical Association, 246,* 1559–1563.

Frodi, A. (1985). When empathy fails: Aversive infant crying and child abuse. In B. M. Lester & C. F. Z. Boukydis (Eds.), *Infant crying: Theoretical and research perspectives* (pp. 263–277). New York: Plenum.

Froggatt, P., Beckwith, J. B., Schwartz, P. J., Valdes-Dapena, M., & Southall, D. P. (1988). Cardiac and respiratory mechanisms that might be responsible for sudden infant death syndrome. In P. J. Schwartz, D. P. Southall, & M. Valdes-Dapena (Eds.), *The sudden infant death syndrome* (Annals of the New York Academy of Sciences, Vol. 533, pp. 421–426). New York: New York Academy of Sciences.

Fuchs, I., Eisenberg, N., Hertz-Lazarowitz, R., & Sharabany, R. (1986). Kibbutz, Israeli city, and American children's moral reasoning about prosocial moral conflicts. *Merrill-Palmer Quarterly, 32,* 37–50.

Fuligni, A. J., & Eccles, J. S. (1993). Perceived parent–child relationships and early adolescents' orientation toward peers. *Developmental Psychology, 29,* 622–632.

Furman, E. (1990, November). Plant a potato—learn about life (and death). *Young Children, 46*(1), 15–20.

Furman, W., & Buhrmester, D. (1992). Age and sex differences in perceptions of networks of personal relationships. *Child Development, 63,* 103–115.

Furman, W., Jones, L., Buhrmester, D., & Adler, T. (1989). Children's, parents', and observers' perspectives on sibling relationships. In P. G. Zukow (Ed.), *Sibling interaction across cultures* (pp. 165–183). New York: Springer-Verlag.

Furrow, D., & Nelson, K. (1984). Environmental correlates of individual differences in language acquisition. *Journal of Child Language, 11,* 523–534.

Furstenberg, F. F., Jr., Brooks-Gunn, J., & Morgan, S. P. (1987). *Adolescent mothers and their children in later life.* Cambridge, England: Cambridge University Press.

Furstenberg, F. F., Jr., & Cherlin, A. J. (1991). *Divided families.* Cambridge, MA: Harvard University Press.

Furstenberg, F. F., Jr., Brooks-Gunn, J., & Chase-Lansdale, L. (1989). Teenaged pregnancy and childbearing. *American Psychologist, 44,* 313–320.

Furstenberg, F. F., Jr., & Crawford, D. B. (1978). Family support: Helping teenagers to cope. *Family Planning Perspectives, 10,* 322–333.

Furstenberg, F. F., Jr., Levine, J. A., & Brooks-Gunn, J. (1990). The children of teenage mothers: Patterns of early childbearing in two generations. *Family Planning Perspectives, 22,* 54–61.

Furstenberg, F. F., Jr., & Nord, C. W. (1985). Parenting apart: Patterns of childrearing after marital disruption. *Journal of Marriage and the Family, 47,* 893–904.

Furuno, S., O'Reilly, K., Inatsuka, T., Hosaka, C., Allman, T., & Zeisloft-Falbey, B. (1987). *Hawaii Early Learning Profile.* Palo Alto, CA: VORT Corporation.

Fuson, K. C. (1988). *Children's counting and concepts of number.* New York: Springer-Verlag.

Fuson, K. C. (1990). Issues in place-value and multidigit addition and subtraction learning and teaching. *Journal for Research in Mathematics Education, 21,* 273–280.

Fuson, K. C., & Kwon, Y. (1992). Korean children's understanding of multidigit addition and subtraction. *Child Development, 63,* 491–506.

Gaddis, A., & Brooks-Gunn, J. (1985). The male experience of pubertal change. *Journal of Youth and Adolescence, 14,* 61–69.

Galambos, S. J., & Goldin-Meadow, S. (1990). The effects of learning two languages on levels of metalinguistic awareness. *Cognition, 34,* 1–56.

Galambos, S. J., & Maggs, J. L. (1991). Children in self-care: Figures, facts and fiction. In J. V. Lerner & N. L. Galambos (Eds.), *Employed mothers and their children* (pp. 131–157). New York: Garland.

Galin, D., Johnstone, J., Nakell, L., & Herron, J. (1979). Development of the capacity for tactile information transfer between hemispheres in normal children. *Science, 204,* 1330–1332.

Galinsky, E., Howes, C., Kontos, S., & Shinn, M. (1994). *The study of children in family child care and relative care: Highlights of finding selective initiatives to improve the quality of family child care.* New York: Families and Work Institute.

Galler, J. R., Ramsey, C. F., Morley, D. S., Archer, E., & Salt, P. (1990). The long-term effects of early kwashiorkor compared with marasmus. IV. Performance on the National High School Entrance Examination. *Pediatric Research, 28,* 235–239.

Galler, J. R., Ramsey, F., & Solimano, G. (1985a). A follow-up study of the effects of early malnutrition on subsequent development: I. Physical growth and sexual maturation during adolescence. *Pediatric Research, 19,* 518–523.

Galler, J. R., Ramsey, F., & Solimano, G. (1985b). A follow-up study of the effects of early malnutrition on subsequent development: II. Fine motor skills in adolescence. *Pediatric Research, 19,* 524–527.

Galler, J. R., Ramsey, F., Solimano, G., Kucharski, L. T., & Harrison, R. (1984). The influence of early malnutrition on subsequent behavioral development: IV. Soft neurological signs. *Pediatric Research, 18,* 826–832.

Galotti, K. M., Kozberg, S. F., & Farmer, M. C. (1991). Gender and developmental differences in adolescents' conceptions of moral reasoning. *Journal of Youth and Adolescence, 20,* 13–30.

Gandour, M. J. (1989). Activity level as a dimension of temperament in toddlers: Its relevance for the organismic specificity hypothesis. *Child Development, 60,* 1092–1098.

Garbarino, J., & Kostelny, K. (1992). Child maltreatment as a community problem. *Child Abuse and Neglect, 16,* 455–464.

Garbarino, J., Kostelny, K., & Grady, J. (1993). Children in dangerous environments: Child maltreatment in the context of community violence. In D. Cicchetti & S. L. Toth (Eds.), *Advances in applied developmental psychology* (Vol. 8, pp. 167–189). Norwood, NJ: Ablex.

Gardner, H. (1980). *Artful scribbles: The significance of children's drawings.* New York: Basic Books.

Gardner, H. (1983). *Frames of mind: The theory of multiple intelligences.* New York: Basic Books.

Gardner, H., & Hatch, T. (1989, November). Multiple intelligences go to school. *Educational Researcher, 18*(8), 4–10.

Gardner, M. J., Snee, M. P., Hall, A. J., Powell, C. A., Downes, S., & Terrell, J. D. (1990). Leukemia cases linked to fathers' radiation dose. *Nature, 343,* 423–429.

Garland, A. F., & Zigler, E. (1993). Adolescent suicide prevention: Current research and social policy implications. *American Psychologist, 48,* 169–182.

Garmezy, N. (1983). Stressors of childhood. In N. Garmezy & M. Rutter (Eds.), *Stress, coping, and development in children* (pp. 43–84). New York: McGraw-Hill.

Garmezy, N., & Rutter, M. (1985). Acute reactions to stress. In M. Rutter & L. Hersov (Eds.), *Child and adolescent psychiatry: Modern approaches* (2nd ed., pp. 152–176). Oxford, England: Blackwell.

Garner, D. M. (1993). Pathogenesis of anorexia nervosa. *Lancet, 341,* 1631–1635.

Garner, R. (1990). Children's use of strategies in reading. In D. F. Bjorklund (Ed.), *Children's strategies: Contemporary views of cognitive development* (pp. 245–268). Hillsdale, NJ: Erlbaum.

Garrett, P., Ng'andu, N., & Ferron, J. (1994). Poverty experiences of young children and the quality of their home environments. *Child Development, 65,* 331–345.

Garrison, C., Schluchter, M., Schoenbach, V., & Kaplan, B. (1989). Epidemiology of depressive symptoms in young adolescents. *Journal of the American Academy of Child and Adolescent Psychiatry, 28,* 343–351.

Garrison, W. T., & McQuiston, S. (1989). *Chronic illness during childhood and adolescence.* Newbury Park, CA: Sage.

Garvey, C. (1975). Requests and responses in children's speech. *Journal of Child Language, 2,* 41–63.

Garvey, C. (1990). *Play.* Cambridge, MA: Harvard University Press.

Garwood, S. G., Phillips, D., Hartman, A., & Zigler, E. F. (1989). As the pendulum swings: Federal agency programs for children. *American Psychologist, 44,* 434–440.

Gathercole, S. E., Adams, A-M., & Hitch, G. (1994). Do young children rehearse? An individual-differences analysis. *Memory & Cognition, 22,* 201–207.

Gathercole, S. E., Willis, C. S., Emslie, H., & Baddeley, A. D. (1992). Phonological memory and vocabulary development during the early school years: A longitudinal study. *Developmental Psychology, 28,* 887–898.

Gauvain, M., & Rogoff, B. (1989a). Collaborative problem solving and children's planning skills. *Developmental Psychology, 25,* 139–151.

Gauvain, M., & Rogoff, B. (1989b). Ways of speaking about space: The development of children's skill in communicating spatial knowledge. *Cognitive Development, 4,* 295–307.

Geary, D. C., Bow-Thomas, C. C., Fan, L., & Siegler, R. S. (1993). Even before formal instruction, Chinese children outperform American children in mental addition. *Cognitive Development, 8,* 517–529.

Geary, D. C., & Burlingham-Dubree, M. (1989). External validation of the strategy choice model for addition. *Journal of Experimental Child Psychology, 47,* 175–192.

Gellatly, A. R. H. (1987). Acquisition of a concept of logical necessity. *Human Development, 30,* 32–47.

Gelles, R. J., & Cornell, C. P. (1983). International perspectives on child abuse. *Child Abuse & Neglect, 7,* 375–386.

Gelman, R. (1972). Logical capacity of very young children: Number invariance rules. *Child Development, 43,* 75–90.

Gelman, R., & Baillargeon, R. (1983). A review of some Piagetian concepts. In J. H. Flavell & E. M. Markman (Eds.), *Handbook of child psychology: Vol. 3. Cognitive Development* (4th ed., pp. 167–230). New York: Wiley.

Gelman, R., & Gallistel, C. R. (1986). *The child's understanding of number.* Cambridge, MA: Harvard University Press.

Gelman, R., & Shatz, M. (1978). Appropriate speech adjustments: The operation of conversational constraints on talk to two-year-olds. In M. Lewis & L. A. Rosenblum (Eds.), *Interaction, conversation, and the development of language* (pp. 27–61). New York: Wiley.

Gelman, S. A., & Ebeling, K. S. (1989). Children's use of nonegocentric standards in judgments of functional size. *Child Development, 60,* 920–932.

Gentner, D. (1982). Why nouns are learned before verbs: Linguistic relativity versus natural partitioning. In S. A. Kuczaj, II (Ed.), *Language development: Vol. 2. Language, thought, and culture* (pp. 301–322). Hillsdale, NJ: Erlbaum.

Gentry, J. R. (1981, January). Learning to spell developmentally. *The Reading Teacher, 35*(2), 378–381.

George, C., Kaplan, N., & Main, M. (1985). The adult attachment interview. Unpublished manuscript, University of California at Berkeley.

Gergen, P. J., Mullally, D. I., & Evans, R. (1988). National survey of prevalence of asthma among children in the United States, 1976–1980. *Pediatrics, 81,* 1–7.

Gershon, E. S., Targum, S. D., Kessler, L. R., Mazure, C. M., & Bunney, W. E., Jr. (1977). Genetics studies and biologic strategies in affective disorders. *Progress in Medical Genetics, 2,* 103–164.

Gesell, A. (1933). Maturation and patterning of behavior. In C. Murchison (Ed.), *A handbook of child psychology.* Worcester, MA: Clark University Press.

Gesell, A., & Ilg, F. L. (1949). The child from five to ten. In A. Gesell & F. L. Ilg (Eds.), *Child development* (pp. 394–454). New York: Harper & Row. (Original work published 1946)

Gesell, A., & Ilg, F. L. (1949). The infant and child in the culture of today. In A. Gesell & F. L. Ilg (Eds.), *Child development* (pp. 1–393). New York: Harper & Row. (Original work published 1943)

Getchell, N., & Roberton, M. A. (1989). Whole body stiffness as a function of developmental level in children's hopping. *Developmental Psychology, 25,* 920–928.

Getzels, J. W., & Jackson, P. W. (1962). *Creativity and intelligence.* New York: Wiley.

Gibbs, J. C. (1991). Toward an integration of Kohlberg's and Hoffman's theories of morality. In W. M. Kurtines & J. L. Gewirtz (Eds.), *Handbook of moral behavior and development* (Vol. 1, pp. 183–222). Hillsdale, NJ: Erlbaum.

Gibson, E. J. (1970). The development of perception as an adaptive process. *American Scientist, 58,* 98–107.

Gibson, E. J., & Walk, R. D. (1960). The "visual cliff." *Scientific American, 202,* 64–71.

Gibson, J. J. (1979). *The ecological approach to visual perception.* Boston: Houghton Mifflin.

Giebink, G. S. (1993). Care of the ill child in day-care settings. *Pediatrics, 91,* 229–233.

Gil, D. G. (1987). Maltreatment as a function of the structure of social systems. In M. R. Brassard, R. Germain, & S. N. Hart (Eds.), *Psychological maltreatment of children and youth* (pp. 159–170). New York: Pergamon Press.

Gilbert, E. H., & DeBlassie, R. R. (1984). Anorexia nervosa: Adolescent starvation by choice. *Adolescence, 76,* 839–846.

Gilfillan, M. C., Curtis, L., Liston, W. A., Pullen, I., Whyte, D. A., & Brock, J. J. H. (1992). Prenatal screening for cystic fibrosis. *Lancet, 340,* 214–216.

Gilligan, C. F. (1982). *In a different voice.* Cambridge, MA: Harvard University Press.

Gilligan, C., & Attanucci, J. (1989). Two moral orientations: Gender differences and similarities. *Merrill-Palmer Quarterly, 34,* 223–237.

Ginsburg, H. P., & Opper, S. (1988). *Piaget's theory of intellectual development* (3rd ed.). Englewood Cliffs, NJ: Prentice Hall.

Ginzberg, E. (1972). Toward a theory of occupational choice: A restatement. *Vocational Guidance Quarterly, 20,* 169–176.

Ginzberg, E. (1988). Toward a theory of occupational choice. *Career Development Quarterly, 36,* 358–363.

Glass, D. C., Krakoff, L. R., Contrada, R., Hilton, W. F., Kehoe, K., Mannucci, E. G., Collins, C., Snow, B., & Elting, E. (1980). Effect of harassment and competition upon cardiovascular and plasma catecholamine responses in Type A and Type B individuals. *Psychophysiology, 17,* 453–463.

Glick, P. C. (1990). American families: As they are and were. *Sociology and Social Research, 74,* 139–145.

Glidden, L. M., & Pursley, J. T. (1989). Longitudinal comparisons of families who have adopted children with mental retardation. *American Journal on Mental Retardation, 94,* 272–277.

Gnepp, J. (1983). Children's social sensitivity: Inferring emotions from conflicting cues. *Developmental Psychology, 19,* 805–814.

Goetz, E. T., & Hall, R. J. (1984). A critical analysis of the psychometric properties of the K-ABC. *Journal of Special Education, 18,* 281–296.

Goffin, S. G. (1988, March). Putting our advocacy efforts into a new context. *Young Children, 43*(3), 52–56.

Goldfield, B. A. (1987). Contributions of child and caregiver to referential and expressive language. *Applied Psycholinguistics, 8,* 267–280.

Goldin-Meadow, S., & Morford, M. (1985). Gesture in early language: Studies of deaf and hearing children. *Merrill-Palmer Quarterly, 31,* 145–176.

Goldschmid, M. L., & Bentler, P. M. (1968). *Manual: Concept Assessment Kit—Conservation.* San Diego, CA: Educational and Industrial Testing Service.

Goldsmith, H. H. (1987). Roundtable: What is temperament? Four approaches. *Child Development, 58,* 505–529.

Goldsmith, H. H., & Gottesman, I. I. (1981). Origins of variation in behavioral style: A longitudinal study of temperament in young twins. *Child Development, 52,* 91–103.

Goldstein, A. P. (1990). *Delinquents on delinquency.* Champaign, IL: Research Press.

Gomez-Schwartz, B., Horowitz, J. M., & Cardarelli, A. P. (1990). *Child sexual abuse: Initial effects.* Newbury Park, CA: Sage.

Gonzalez, N. M., & Campbell, M. (1994). Cocaine babies: Does prenatal exposure to cocaine affect development? *Journal of the American Academy of Child and Adolescent Psychiatry, 33,* 16–19.

Goodlad, J. I. (1984). *A place called school.* New York: McGraw-Hill.

Goodman, G. S., & Tobey, A. E. (1994). Memory development within the context of child sexual abuse investigations. In C. B. Fisher & R. M. Lerner (Eds.), *Applied developmental psychology* (pp. 46–75). New York: McGraw-Hill.

Goodman, G. S., Hirschman, J. E., Hepps, D., & Rudy, L. (1991). Children's memory for stressful events. *Merrill-Palmer Quarterly, 37,* 109–158.

Goodman, G. S., Taub, E. P., Jones, D. P. H., England, P., Port, L. K., Rudy, L., & Prado, L. (1992). Testifying in criminal court: Emotional effects on child sexual assault victims. *Monographs of the Society for Research in Child Development, 57*(No. 5, Serial No. 229).

Goodman, K. S. (1986). *What's whole in whole language?* Portsmouth, NH: Heinemann.

Goodman, R. A., & Whitaker, H. A. (1985). Hemispherectomy: A review (1928–1981) with special reference to the linguistic abilities and disabilities of the residual right hemisphere. In R. A. Goodman & H. A. Whitaker (Eds.), *Hemispheric functions and collaboration in the child* (pp. 121–155). New York: Academic Press.

Goodwyn, S. W., & Acredolo, L. P. (1993). Symbolic gesture versus word: Is there a modality advantage for onset of symbol use? *Child Development, 64,* 688–701.

Goodz, N. S. (1989). Parental language mixing in bilingual families. *Infant Mental Health Journal, 10,* 25–44.

Goossens, F. A., & van IJzendoorn, M. H. (1990). Quality of infants' attachments to professional caregivers: Relation to infant–parent attachment and day-care characteristics. *Child Development, 61,* 832–837.

Gopnik, A., & Choi, S. (1990). Do linguistic differences lead to cognitive differences? A cross-linguistic study of semantic and cognitive development. *First Language, 11,* 199–215.

Gopnik, A., & Meltzoff, A. N. (1986). Relations between semantic and cognitive development in the one-word stage: The specificity hypothesis. *Child Development, 57,* 1040–1053.

Gopnik, A., & Meltzoff, A. N. (1987). The development of categorization in the second year and its relation to other cognitive and linguistic developments. *Child Development, 58,* 1523–1531.

Gopnik, A., & Meltzoff, A. N. (1992). Categorization and naming: Basic-level sorting in eighteen-month-olds and its relation to language. *Child Development, 63,* 1091–1103.

Gordon, S., & Gilgun, J. F. (1987). Adolescent sexuality. In V. B. Van Hasselt & M. Hersen (Eds.), *Handbook of adolescent psychology* (pp. 147–167). New York: Pergamon Press.

Gorman, J., Leifer, M., & Grossman, G. (1993). Nonorganic failure to thrive: Maternal history and current maternal functioning. *Journal of Clinical Child Psychology, 22,* 327–336.

Gorn, G. J., & Goldberg, M. E. (1982). Behavioral evidence of the effects of televised food messages on children. *Journal of Consumer Research, 9,* 200–205.

Gortmaker, S. L., Dietz, W. H., Jr., & Cheung, L. W. Y. (1990). Inactivity, diet, and the fattening of America. *Journal of the American Dietetic Association, 90,* 1247–1252.

Gortmaker, S. L., Dietz, W. H., Jr., Sobol, A. M., & Wehler, C. A. (1987). Increasing pediatric obesity in the United States. *American Journal of Diseases of Children, 141,* 535–540.

Gortmaker, S. L., Must, A., Perrin, J. M., Sobol, A. M., & Dietz, W. H., Jr. (1993). Social and economic consequences of overweight in adolescence and young adulthood. *New England Journal of Medicine, 329,* 1008–1012.

Gotlib, I. H., Whiffen, V. E., Mount, J. H., Milne, K., & Cordy, N. I. (1989). Prevalence rates and demographic characteristics associated with depression in pregnancy and postpartum. *Journal of Consulting and Clinical Psychology, 57,* 269–274.

Gottesman, I. I. (1963). Genetic aspects of intelligent behavior. In N. Ellis (Ed.), *Handbook of mental deficiency* (pp. 253–296). New York: McGraw-Hill.

Gottfried, A. E. (1991). Maternal employment in the family setting: Developmental and environmental issues. In J. V. Lerner & N. L. Galambos (Eds.), *Employed mothers and their children* (pp. 63–84). New York: Garland.

Gottlieb, G. (1991). Experiential canalization of behavioral development: Theory. *Developmental Psychology, 27,* 4–13.

Gottman, J. M., Gonso, J., & Rasmussen, B. (1975). Social interaction, social competence, and friendship in children. *Child Development, 46,* 709–718.

Gottman, J. M., & Katz, L. F. (1989). Effects of marital discord on young children's peer interaction and health. *Developmental Psychology, 25,* 373–381.

Gould, M. S. (1990). Cluster suicides. In R. M. Lerner, A. C. Petersen, & J. Brooks-Gunn (Eds.), *The encyclopedia of adolescence* (Vol. 2, pp. 1117–1122). New York: Garland.

Graham, C. J., Dick, R., Rickert, V. I., & Glenn, R. (1993). Left-handedness as a risk factor for unintentional injury in children. *Pediatrics, 92,* 823–826.

Graham, F. K., Ernhart, C. B., Thurston, D. L., & Craft, M. (1962). Development three years after perinatal anoxia and other potentially damaging newborn experiences. *Psychological Monographs, 76*(3, Whole No. 522).

Graham, L., & Hamdan, L. (1987). *Youth trends: Capturing the $200 billion youth market.* New York: St. Martin's Press.

Graham, S., Doubleday, C., & Guarino, P. A. (1984). The development of relations between perceived controllability and the emotions of pity, anger, and guilt. *Child Development, 55,* 561–565.

Gralinski, J. H., & Kopp, C. B. (1993). Everyday rules for behavior: Mothers' requests to young children. *Developmental Psychology, 29,* 573–584.

Grant, J. P. (1992). *The state of the world's children.* New York: Oxford University Press (in cooperation with UNICEF).

Grant, J. P. (1993). *The state of the world's children.* New York: Oxford University Press (in cooperation with UNICEF).

Grant, J. P. (1994). *The state of the world's children.* New York: Oxford University Press (in cooperation with UNICEF).

Grantham-McGregor, S., Powell, C., Walker, S., Chang, S., & Fletcher, P. (1994). The long-term follow-up of severely malnourished children who participated in an intervention program. *Child Development, 65,* 428–439.

Grantham-McGregor, S., Schofield, W., & Powell, C. (1987). Development of severely malnourished children who received psychosocial stimulation: Six-year follow-up. *Pediatrics, 79,* 247–254.

Grattan, M. P., De Vos, E., Levy, J., & McClintock, M. K. (1992). Asymmetric action in the human newborn: Sex differences in patterns of organization. *Child Development, 63,* 273–289.

Grau, P. N. (1985). Counseling the gifted girl. *Gifted Child Today, 38,* 8–11.

Gravel, J. S., & Wallace, I. F. (1994). Listening and language at 4 years of age: Effects of early otitis media. *Journal of Speech and Hearing Research, 35,* 588–595.

Gray, W. M. (1978). A comparison of Piagetian theory and criterion-referenced measurement. *Review of Educational Research, 48,* 223–250.

Green, J. A., Gustafson, G. E., & West, M. J. (1980). Effects of infant development on mother–infant interactions. *Child Development, 51,* 199–207.

Green, J. A., Jones, L. E., & Gustafson, G. E. (1987). Perception of cries by parents and nonparents: Relation to cry acoustics. *Developmental Psychology, 23,* 370–382.

Green, R. (1987). *The "sissy boy" syndrome and the development of homosexuality.* New Haven, CT: Yale University Press.

Greenberg, M., & Morris, N. (1974). Engrossment: the newborn's impact upon the father. *American Journal of Orthopsychiatry, 44,* 520–531.

Greenberg, P. (1990, February). Why not academic preschool? *Young Children, 45(2),* 70–80.

Greenberger, E., & Goldberg, W. A. (1989). Work, parenting, and the socialization of children. *Developmental Psychology, 25,* 22–35.

Greenberger, E., & Steinberg, L. (1986). *When teenagers work.* New York: Basic Books.

Greenbowe, T., Herron, J. D., Lucas, C., Nurrenbern, S., Staver, J. R., & Ward, C. R. (1981). Teaching preadolescents to act as scientists: Replication and extension of an earlier study. *Journal of Educational Psychology, 73,* 705–711.

Greenfield, P. M. (1992, June). *Notes and references for developmental psychology.* Conference on Making Basic Texts in Psychology More Culture-Inclusive and Culture-Sensitive, Western Washington University, Bellingham, WA.

Greeno, J. G. (1989). A perspective on thinking. *American Psychologist, 44,* 134–141.

Greenough, W. T., Black, J. E., & Wallace, C. S. (1987). Experience and brain development. *Child Development, 58,* 539–559.

Greif, E. B., & Ulman, K. (1982). The psychological impact of menarche on early adolescent females: A review. *Child Development, 53,* 1413–1430.

Grimes, D. A., & Mishell, D. R., Jr. (1988). Congenital limb reduction deformities and oral contraceptives [letter]. *American Journal of Obstetrics and Gynecology, 158,* 439–440.

Grolnick, W. S., & Slowiaczek, M. L. (1994). Parents' involvement in children's schooling: A multidimensional conceptualization and motivational model. *Child Development, 65,* 237–252.

Gross, S. J., Geller, J., & Tomarelli, R. M. (1981). Composition of breast milk from mothers of preterm infants. *Pediatrics, 68,* 480–493.

Grossman, H. D. (Ed.). (1983). *Classification in mental retardation.* Washington, DC: American Association on Mental Deficiency.

Grossmann, K., Grossmann, K. E., Spangler, G., Suess, G., & Unzner, L. (1985). Maternal sensitivity and newborns' orientation responses as related to quality of attachment in Northern Germany. In I. Bretherton & E. Waters (Eds.), Growing points of attachment theory and research. *Monographs of the Society for Research in Child Development, 50*(1–2, Serial No. 209).

Grotevant, H. D., & Cooper, C. R. (1985). Patterns of interaction in family relationships and the development of identity exploration in adolescence. *Child Development, 56,* 415–428.

Grotevant, H. D., & Cooper, C. R. (1988). The role of family experience in career exploration during adolescence. In P. Baltes, D. Featherman, & R. Lerner (Eds.), *Life-span development and behavior* (Vol. 8, pp. 231–258). Hillsdale, NJ: Erlbaum.

Grotevant, H. D., & Durrett, M. (1980). Occupational knowledge and career development in adolescence. *Journal of Vocational Behavior, 17,* 171–182.

Grusec, J. E. (1988). *Social development: History, theory, and research.* New York: Springer-Verlag.

Grusec, J. E. (1992). Social learning theory and developmental psychology: The legacies of Robert Sears and Albert Bandura. *Developmental Psychology, 28,* 776–786.

Guidubaldi, J., & Cleminshaw, H. K. (1985). Divorce, family health and child adjustment. *Family Relations, 34,* 35–41.

Guilford, J. P. (1985). The structure-of-intellect model. In B. B. Wolman (Ed.), *Handbook of intelligence* (pp. 225–266). New York: Wiley.

Gunnar, M. R., & Nelson, C. A. (1994). Event-related potentials in year-old infants: Relations with emotionality and cortisol. *Child Development, 65,* 80–94.

Gurucharri, C., & Selman, F. L. (1982). The development of interpersonal understanding during childhood, preadolescence, and adolescence: A longitudinal follow-up study. *Child Development, 53,* 924–927.

Gustafson, G. E., & Harris, K. L. (1990). Women's responses to young infants' cries. *Developmental Psychology, 26,* 144–152.

Haan, N., Aerts, E., & Cooper, B. (1985). *On moral grounds: The search for practical morality.* New York: New York University Press.

Hack, M., B., Taylor, H. G., Klein, N., Eiben, R., Schatschneider, C., & Mercuri-Minich, N. (1994). School-age outcomes in children with birth weights under 750 g. *New England Journal of Medicine, 331,* 753–759.

Hagedorn, J. M. (1991). Gangs, neighborhoods, and public policy. *Social Problems, 38,* 529–542.

Hagerman, R. J. (1991). Physical and behavioral phenotype. In R. J. Hagerman & A. Cronister-Silverman (Eds.), *Fragile X syndrome: Diagnosis, treatment, and research* (pp. 3–68). Baltimore: Johns Hopkins University Press.

Hahn, W. K. (1987). Cerebral lateralization of function: From infancy through childhood. *Psychological Bulletin, 101,* 376–392.

Haight, W. L., & Miller, P. J. (1993). *Pretending at home: Early development in a sociocultural context.* Albany: State University of New York Press.

Hainline, L. (1985). Oculomotor control in human infants. In R. Groner, G. W., McConkie, & C. Menz (Eds.), *Eye movements and human information processing* (pp. 71–84). Amsterdam: Elsevier.

Hakuta, K. (1986). *Mirror of language.* New York: Basic Books.

Hakuta, K., & Garcia, E. E. (1989). Bilingualism and education. *American Psychologist, 44,* 374–379.

Hakuta, K., Ferdman, B. M., & Diaz, R. M. (1987). Bilingualism and cognitive development: Three perspectives. In S. Rosenberg (Ed.), *Advances in applied psycholinguistics: Vol. 2. Reading, writing, and language learning* (pp. 284–319). New York: Cambridge University Press.

Halford, G. S. (1993). *Children's understanding: The development of mental models.* Hillsdale, NJ: Erlbaum.

Hall, G. S. (1904). *Adolescence.* New York: Appleton-Century-Crofts.

Hall, J. G., Sybert, V. P., Williamson, R. A., Fisher, N. L., & Reed, S. D. (1982). Turner's syndrome. *West Journal of Medicine, 137,* 32–44.

Hall, W. S. (1989). Reading comprehension. *American Psychologist, 44,* 157–161.

Halmi, K. A. (1987). Anorexia nervosa and bulimia. In V. B. Van Hasselt & M. Hersen (Eds.), *Handbook of adolescent psychology* (pp. 265–287). New York: Pergamon.

Halpern, D. F. (1986). *Sex differences in cognitive abilities.* Hillsdale, NJ: Erlbaum.

Halpern, D. F., & Coren, S. (1991). Hand preference and life span. *New England Journal of Medicine, 325,* 998.

Halpern, D. F., & Coren, S. (1993). Left-handedness and life span: A reply to Harris. *Psychological Bulletin, 114,* 235–241.

Halverson, H. M. (1931). An experimental study of prehension in infants by means of systematic cinema records. *Genetic Psychology Monographs, 10,* 107–286.

Hamelin, K., & Ramachandran, C. (1993, June). Kangaroo care. *Canadian Nurse, 89*(6), 15–17.

Hamer, D. H., Hu, S., Magnuson, V. L., Hu, N., & Pattatucci, A. M. L. (1993). A linkage between DNA markers on the X chromosome and male sexual orientation. *Science, 261,* 321–327.

Hamilton, S. F. (1990). *Apprenticeship for adulthood: Preparing youth for the future.* New York: Free Press.

Hamilton, S. F. (1993). Prospects for an American-style youth apprenticeship system. *Educational Researcher, 22*(3), 11–16.

Hammersley, M. (1992). *What's wrong with ethnography?* New York: Routledge.

Hammill, D. D. (1990). On defining learning disabilities: An emerging consensus. *Journal of Learning Disabilities, 23,* 74–84.

Hanigan, W. C., Morgan, A. M., Stahlberg, L. K., & Hiller, J. L. (1990). Tentorial hemorrhage associated with vacuum extraction. *Pediatrics, 85,* 534–539.

Hanna, E., & Meltzoff, A. N. (1993). Peer imitation by toddlers in laboratory, home, and day-care contexts: Implications for social learning and memory. *Developmental Psychology, 29,* 701–710.

Haque, M., Ellerstein, N. S., Gundy, J. H., Shelov, S. P., Weiss, J. C., McIntire, M. S., Olness, K. N., Jones, D. J., Heagarty, M. C., & Starfield, B. H. (1981). Parental perceptions of enuresis. *American Journal of Diseases of Children, 135,* 809–811.

Harlow, H. F., & Zimmerman, R. (1959). Affectional responses in the infant monkey. *Science, 130,* 421–432.

Harris, G., & Booth, A. (1987). Infants' preference for salt in food: Its dependence upon recent dietary experience. *Journal of Reproductive and Infant Psychology, 5,* 97–104.

Harris, L. J. (1993). Do left-handers die sooner than right-handers? Commentary on Coren and Halpern's (1991) "Left-handedness: A marker for decreased survival fitness." *Psychological Bulletin, 114,* 203–234.

Harris, M. J., & Rosenthal, R. (1985). Mediation of interpersonal expectancy effects: 31 meta-analyses. *Psychological Bulletin, 97,* 363–386.

Harris, P. L. (1983). Infant cognition. In M. M. Haith & J. J. Campos (Eds.), *Handbook of child psychology: Vol. 2. Infancy and developmental psychobiology* (pp. 689–782). New York: Wiley.

Harris, P. L. (1991). The work of the imagination. In A. Whiten (Ed.), *Natural theories of mind* (pp. 283–304). Oxford: Blackwell.

Harris, R. T. (1991, March–April). Anorexia nervosa and bulimia nervosa in female adolescents. *Nutrition Today, 26*(2), 30–34.

Harris, S., Mussen, P. H., & Rutherford, E. (1976). Some cognitive, behavioral, and personality correlates of maturity of moral judgment. *Journal of Genetic Psychology, 128,* 123–135.

Harrison, A. O., Wilson, M. N., Pine, C. J., Can, S. Q., & Buriel, R. (1990). Family ecologies of ethnic minority children. *Child Development, 61,* 127–137.

Harrison, M. R. (1993). Fetal surgery. *Western Journal of Medicine, 159,* 341–349.

Hart, S. N., & Brassard, M. R. (1987). A major threat to children's mental health. *American Psychologist, 42,* 160–165.

Harter, S. (1982). The perceived competence scale for children. *Child Development, 53,* 87–97.

Harter, S. (1983). Developmental perspectives on the self-system. In E. M. Hetherington (Ed.), *Handbook of child psychology: Vol. 4. Socialization, personality, and social development* (4th ed., pp. 275–385). New York: Wiley.

Harter, S. (1986). Processes underlying the construction, maintenance, and enhancement of self-concept in children. In S. Suhls & A. Greenwald (Eds.), *Psychological perspectives of the self* (Vol. 3, pp. 136–182). Hillsdale, NJ: Erlbaum.

Harter, S. (1990). Issues in the assessment of the self-concept of children and adolescents. In A. LaGreca (Ed.), *Through the eyes of a child* (pp. 292–325). Boston: Allyn and Bacon.

Harter, S., & Buddin, B. J. (1987). Children's understanding of the simultaneity of two emotions: A five-stage developmental acquisition sequence. *Developmental Psychology, 23,* 388–399.

Harter, S., & Whitesell, N. (1989). Developmental changes in children's understanding of simple, multiple, and blended emotion concepts. In C. Saarni & P. Harris (Eds.), *Children's understanding of emotion* (pp. 81–116). Cambridge, England: Cambridge University Press.

Harter, S., Wright, K., & Bresnick, S. (1987). A developmental sequence of the emergence of self affects. Paper presented at the biennial meeting of the Society for Research in Child Development, Baltimore.

Hartman, C. R., & Burgess, A. W. (1989). Sexual abuse of children: Causes and consequences. In D. Cicchetti & V. Carlson (Eds.), *Child maltreatment* (pp. 95–128). New York: Cambridge University Press.

Hartup, W. W. (1983). Peer relations. In E. M. Hetherington (Ed.), *Handbook of child psychology: Vol. 4. Socialization, personality, and social development* (4th ed., pp. 103–196). New York: Wiley.

Hartup, W. W. (1989). Social relationships and their developmental significance. *American Psychologist, 44,* 120–126.

Hartup, W. W., French, D. C., Laursen, B., Johnston, M. K., & Ogawa, J. R. (1993). Conflict and friendship relations in middle childhood: Behavior in a closed-field situation. *Child Development, 64,* 445–454.

Hashimoto, K., Noguchi, M., & Nakatsuji, N. (1992). Mouse offspring derived from fetal ovaries or reaggregates which were cultured and transplanted into adult females. *Development: Growth & Differentiation, 34,* 233–238.

Hatch, M. C., Shu, X-O., McLean, D. E., Levin, B., Begg, M., Reuss, L., & Susser, M. (1993). Maternal exercise during pregnancy, physical fitness, and fetal growth. *American Journal of Epidemiology, 137,* 1105–1114.

Hatcher, P. J., Hulme, C., & Ellis, A. W. (1994). Ameliorating early reading failure by integrating the teaching of reading and phonological skills: The phonological linkage hypothesis. *Child Development, 65,* 41–57.

Haugaard, J. J., & Reppucci, N. D. (1988). *The sexual abuse of children.* San Francisco: Jossey-Bass.

Haviland, J. M., & Lelwica, M. (1987). The induced affect response: 10-week-old infants' responses to three emotion expressions. *Developmental Psychology, 23,* 97–104.

Hawke, S., & Knox, D. (1978). The one-child family: A new life-style. *The Family Coordinator, 27,* 215–219.

Hawkins, D. J., & Lam, T. (1987). Teacher practices, social development, and delinquency. In J. D. Burchard & S. N. Burchard (Eds.), *Prevention of delinquent behavior* (pp. 241–274). Newbury Park, CA: Sage.

Hawkins, J., & Sheingold, K. (1986). The beginnings of a story: Computers and the organization of learning in classrooms. In J. A. Culbertson & L. L. Cunningham (Eds.), *Microcomputers and education* (85th Yearbook of the National Society for the Study of Education, pp. 40–58). Chicago: University of Chicago Press.

Hayes, C. (Ed.). (1987). *Risking the future: Adolescent sexuality, pregnancy, and childbearing* (Vol. 1). Washington, DC: National Academy Press.

Hayghe, H. V. (1990, March). Family members in the work force. *Monthly Labor Review.* Washington, DC: U.S. Government Printing Office.

Hayne, H., Rovee-Collier, C., & Perris, E. E. (1987). Categorization and memory retrieval by three-month-olds. *Child Development, 58,* 750–767.

Haynes, C. F., Cutler, C., Gray, J., O'Keefe, K., & Kempe, R. S. (1983). Nonorganic failure to thrive: Implications of placement through analysis of videotaped interactions. *Child Abuse and Neglect, 7,* 321–328.

Heath, S. B. (1982). Questioning at home and at school: A comparative study. In G. Spindler (Ed.), *Doing the ethnography of schooling: Educational anthropology in action* (pp. 102–127). New York: Holt.

Heath, S. B. (1989). Oral and literate traditions among black Americans living in poverty. *American Psychologist, 44,* 367–373.

Heath, S. B. (1990). The children of Trackton's children: Spoken and written language in social change. In J. Stigler, G. Herdt, & R. A. Shweder (Eds.), *Cultural psychology: Essays on comparative human development* (pp. 496–519). New York: Cambridge University Press.

Hedges, L. V., Giaconia, R. M., & Gage, N. L. (1981). *Meta-analysis of the effects of open and traditional instruction.* Stanford, CA: Program on Teaching Effectiveness, Stanford University.

Heinl, T. (1983). *The baby massage book.* London: Coventure.

Heinonen, O. P., Slone, D., & Shapiro, S. (1977). *Birth defects and drugs in pregnancy.* Littleton, MA: PSG Publishing.

Henggeler, S. W. (1989). *Delinquency in adolescence.* Newbury Park, CA: Sage.

Henker, B., & Whalen, C. K. (1989). Hyperactivity and attention deficits. *American Psychologist, 44,* 216–223.

Henshaw, S. K. (1993). Teenage abortion, birth and pregnancy statistics by state, 1988. *Family Planning Perspectives, 25,* 122–126.

Hergenrather, J. R., & Rabinowitz, M. (1991). Age-related differences in the organization of children's knowledge of illness. *Developmental Psychology, 27,* 952–959.

Herkowitz, J. (1984). Developmentally engineered equipment and playgrounds. In J. R. Thomas (Ed.), *Motor development during childhood and adolescence* (pp. 139–173). Minneapolis: MN: Burgess.

Herrnstein, R. J., & Murray, C. (1994). *The bell curve.* New York: Free Press.

Hetherington, E. M. (1988). Parents, children, and siblings: Six years after divorce. In R. A. Hinde & J. Stevenson-Hinde (Eds.), *Relationships within families* (pp. 311–331). Oxford, England: Oxford University Press.

Hetherington, E. M. (1989). Coping with family transitions: Winners, losers, and survivors. *Child Development, 60,* 1–14.

Hetherington, E. M. (1991). The role of individual differences and family relationships in children's coping with divorce and remarriage. In P. A. Cowan & E. M. Hetherington (Eds.), *Family transitions* (pp. 165–194). Hillsdale, NJ: Erlbaum.

Hetherington, E. M., & Clingempeel, W. G. (1992). Coping with marital transitions: A family systems perspective. *Monographs of the Society for Research in Child Development, 57*(2–3, Serial No. 227).

Hetherington, E. M., Cox, M., & Cox, R. (1982). Effects of divorce on parents and children. In M. E. Lamb (Ed.), *Nontraditional families: Parenting and child development* (pp. 233–288). Hillsdale, NJ: Erlbaum.

Hetherington, E. M., Cox, M., & Cox, R. (1985). Long-term effects of divorce and remarriage on the adjustment of children. *Journal of the American Academy of Child Psychiatry, 24,* 518–530.

Hetherington, E. M., Stanley-Hagan, M., & Anderson, E. R. (1989). Marital transitions: A child's perspective. *American Psychologist, 44,* 303–312.

Hetherington, S. E. (1990). A controlled study of the effect of prepared childbirth classes on obstetric outcomes. *Birth, 17,* 86–90.

Hewlett, B. S. (1992). Husband–wife reciprocity and the father–infant relationship among Aka pygmies. In B. S. Hewlett (Ed.), *Father–child relations: Cultural and biosocial contexts* (pp. 153–176). New York: Aldine de Gruyter.

Heyman, G. D., & Dweck, C. S. (1992). Achievement goals and intrinsic motivation: Their relation and their role in adaptive motivation. *Motivation and Emotion, 16,* 231–247.

Heyman, G. D., Dweck, C. S., & Cain, K. M. (1992). Young children's vulnerability to self-blame and helplessness: Relationship to beliefs about goodness. *Child Development, 63,* 401–415.

Higgins, A. (1991). The just community approach to moral education: Evolution of the idea and recent findings. In W. M. Kurtines & J. L. Gewirtz (Eds.), *Handbook of moral behavior and development* (Vol. 3, pp. 111–141). Hillsdale, NJ: Erlbaum.

Hill, C. R., & Stafford, F. P. (1980). Parental care of children: Time diary estimate of quantity, predictability, and variety. *Journal of Human Resources, 15,* 219–239.

Hill, J. P. (1988). Adapting to menarche: Familial control and conflict. In M. Gunnar & W. A. Collins (Eds.), Development during the transition to adolescence. *Minnesota Symposia on Child Psychology* (Vol. 21, pp. 43–77). Hillsdale, NJ: Erlbaum.

Hill, J. P., & Holmbeck, G. N. (1986). Attachment and autonomy during adolescence. In G. Whitehurst (Ed.), *Annals of child development* (Vol. 3, pp. 145–189). Greenwich, CT: JAI Press.

Hill, J. P., & Holmbeck, G. N. (1987). Family adaptation to biological change during adolescence. In R. M. Lerner & T. T. Foch (Eds.), *Biological-psychosocial interactions in early adolescence* (pp. 207–224). Hillsdale, NJ: Erlbaum.

Hill, J. P., & Lynch, M. E. (1983). The intensification of gender-related role expectations during early adolescence. In J. Brooks-Gunn & A. C. Petersen (Eds.), *Girls at puberty: Biological and psychological perspectives* (pp. 201–228). New York: Plenum.

Hill, P. M., & Humphrey, P. (1982). *Human growth and development throughout life: A nursing perspective.* New York: Delmar.

Hillier, L., Hewitt, K. L., & Morrongiello, B. A. (1992). Infants' perception of illusions in sound localization: Reaching to sounds in the dark. *Journal of Experimental Child Psychology, 53,* 159–179.

Hillman, S. B., & Davenport, G. G. (1978). Teacher–student interactions in desegregated schools. *Journal of Educational Psychology, 70,* 545–553.

Hills-Banczyk, S. G., Avery, M. D., Savik, K., Potter, S., & Duckett, L. J. (1993). Women's experiences with combining breast-feeding and employment. *Journal of Nurse-Midwifery, 38,* 257–266.

Hinde, R. A. (1989). Ethological and relationships approaches. In R. Vasta (Ed.), *Annals of child development* (Vol. 6, pp. 251–285). Greenwich, CT: JAI Press.

Hines, M., & Green, R. (1991). Human hormonal and neural correlates of sex-typed behaviors. *Review of Psychiatry, 10,* 536–555.

Hinman, A. R. (1987). Vaccine-preventable diseases and child day care. In M. T. Osterholm, J. O. Klein, S. S. Aronson, & L.

K. Pickering (Eds.), *Infectious diseases in child day care* (pp. 61–71). Chicago: University of Chicago Press.

Hirsh-Pasek, K., Kemler Nelson, D. G., Jusczyk, P. W., Cassidy, K. W., Druss, B., & Kennedy, L. (1987). Clauses are perceptual units for young infants. *Cognition, 26,* 269–286.

Hiscock, M., & Kinsbourne, M. (1987). Specialization of the cerebral hemispheres: Implications for learning. *Journal of Learning Disabilities, 20,* 130–143.

Ho, H., Glahn, T. J., & Ho, J. (1988). The fragile-X syndrome. *Developmental Medicine and Child Neurology, 30,* 257–261.

Hobart, C. (1987). Parent–child relations in remarried families. *Journal of Family Issues, 8,* 259–277.

Hobart, C., & Brown, D. (1988). Effects of prior marriage children on adjustment in remarriages: A Canadian study. *Journal of Comparative Family Studies, 19,* 381–396.

Hock, E., & DeMeis, D. (1987). *Depression in mothers of infants: The role of maternal employment.* Paper presented at the biennial meeting of the Society for Research in Child Development, Baltimore, MD.

Hodges, J., & Tizard, B. (1989). Social and family relationships of ex-institutional adolescents. *Journal of Child Psychology and Psychiatry, 30,* 77–97.

Hodges, R. M., & French, L. A. (1988). The effect of class and collection labels on cardinality, class-inclusion, and number conservation tasks. *Child Development, 59,* 1387–1396.

Hoff-Ginsburg, E. (1986). Function and structure in maternal speech: Their relation to the child's development of syntax. *Developmental Psychology, 22,* 155–163.

Hoffman, L. W. (1974). Effects of maternal employment on the child—A review of the research. *Developmental Psychology, 10,* 204–228.

Hoffman, L. W. (1984). Work, family, and the socialization of the child. In R. D. Parke (Ed.), *Review of child development research* (Vol. 7, pp. 223–282). Chicago: University of Chicago Press.

Hoffman, L. W. (1989). Effects of maternal employment in the two-parent family. *American Psychologist, 44,* 283–292.

Hoffman, L. W., Thornton, A., & Manis, J. D. (1978). The value of children to parents in the United States. *Journal of Population, 1,* 91–131.

Hoffman, M. L. (1984). Interaction of affect and cognition in empathy. In C. E. Izard, J. Kagan, & R. B. Zajonc (Eds.), *Emotions, cognition, and behavior* (pp. 103–131). Cambridge, England: Cambridge University Press.

Hoffman, M. L. (1988). Moral development. In M. H. Bornstein & M. E. Lamb (Eds.), *Developmental psychology: An advanced textbook* (2nd ed., pp. 497–548). Hillsdale, NJ: Erlbaum.

Hofsten, C. von (1984). Developmental changes in the organization of prereaching movements. *Developmental Psychology, 20,* 378–388.

Hofsten, C. von (1989). Motor development as the development of systems: Comments on the special section. *Developmental Psychology, 25,* 950–953.

Holden, G. W. (1983). Avoiding conflict: Mothers as tacticians in the supermarket. *Child Development, 54,* 233–240.

Holden, G. W., & West, M. J. (1989). Proximate regulation by mothers: A demonstration of how differing styles affect young children's behavior. *Child Development, 60,* 64–69.

Holmbeck, G. N., Waters, K. A., & Brookman, R. R. (1990). Psychosocial correlates of sexually transmitted diseases and sexual activity in black adolescent females. *Journal of Adolescent Research, 5,* 431–448.

Holmes, L. B. (1993). Report on the National Institute of Child Health and Human Development workshop on chorionic villus sampling and limb and other defects. *Teratology, 48,* 7–13.

Hong, K., & Townes, B. (1976). Infants' attachment to inanimate objects. *Journal of the American Academy of Child Psychiatry, 15,* 49–61.

Honzik, M. P. (1983). Measuring mental abilities in infancy: The value and limitations. In M. Lewis (Ed.), *Origins of intelligence* (2nd ed., pp. 67–105). New York: Plenum.

Honzik, M. P., Macfarlane, J. W., & Allen, L. (1948). The stability of mental test performance between two and eighteen years. *Journal of Experimental Education, 17,* 309–329.

Hook, E. B. (1982). Epidemiology of Down syndrome. In S. M. Pueschel & J. E. Rynders (Eds.), *Down syndrome: Advances in biomedicine and the behavioral sciences* (pp. 21–43). Cambridge, MA: Ware Press.

Hook, E. B. (1988). Evaluation and projection of rates of chromosome abnormalities in chorionic villus studies (c.v.s.). *American Journal of Human Genetics Supplement, 43,* A108.

Hopkins, B., & Westra, T. (1988). Maternal handling and motor development: An intracultural study. *Genetic, Social and General Psychology Monographs, 14,* 377–420.

Horan, J. J., & Straus, L. K. (1987). Substance abuse in adolescence. In V. B. Ban Hasselt & M. Hersen (Eds.), *Handbook of adolescent psychology* (pp. 313–331). New York: Pergamon Press.

Horgan, D. (1978). The development of the full passive. *Journal of Child Language, 5,* 65–80.

Horn, J. M. (1983). The Texas Adoption Project: Adopted children and their intellectual resemblance to biological and adoptive parents. *Child Development, 54,* 268–275.

Horn, T. S. (1987). The influence of teacher-coach behavior on the psychological development of children. In D. Gould & M. R. Weiss (Eds.), *Advances in pediatric sport sciences* (Vol. 2, pp. 121–142). Champaign, IL: Human Kinetics.

Horn, W. F., O'Donnell, J. P., & Vitulano, L. A. (1983). Long-term follow-up studies of learning disabled persons. *Journal of Learning Disabilities, 16,* 542–555.

Horner, T. M. (1980). Two methods of studying stranger reactivity in infants: A review. *Journal of Child Psychology and Psychiatry, 21,* 203–219.

Horowitz, F. D. (1987). *Exploring developmental theories: Toward a structural/behavioral model of child development.* Hillsdale, NJ: Erlbaum.

Horowitz, F. D. (1992). John B. Watson's legacy: Learning and environment. *Developmental Psychology, 28,* 360–367.

Horowitz, F. D., & O'Brien, M. (1986). Gifted and talented children: State of knowledge and directions for research. *American Psychologist, 41,* 1147–1152.

Hort, B. E., Leinbach, M. D., & Fagot, B. I. (1991). Is there coherence among the cognitive components of gender acquisition? *Sex Roles, 24,* 195–207.

Hotaling, G. T., Finkelhor, D., Kirkpatrick, J. T., & Strauss, M. A. (Eds.). (1988). *Family abuse and its consequences: New directions in research.* Newbury Park, CA: Sage.

Houts, A. C. (1991). Nocturnal enuresis as a biobehavioral problem. *Behavior Therapy, 22,* 133–151.

Howard, M., & McCabe, J. B. (1990). Helping teenagers postpone sexual involvement. *Family Planning Perspectives, 22,* 21–26.

Howe, N., & Ross, H. S. (1990). Socialization, perspective-taking, and the sibling relationship. *Developmental Psychology, 26,* 160–165.

Howes, C. (1988a). Peer interaction of young children. Monographs of the Society for Research in *Child Development, 53*(1, Serial No. 217).

Howes, C. (1988b). Relations between early child care and schooling. *Developmental Psychology, 24,* 53–57.

Howes, C. (1990). Can the age of entry into child care and the quality of child care predict adjustment in kindergarten? *Developmental Psychology, 26,* 292–303.

Howes, C., Hamilton, C. E., & Matheson, C. C. (1994). Children's relationships with peers: Differential associations with aspects of the teacher–child relationship. *Child Development, 65,* 253–263.

Howes, C., & Matheson, C. C. (1992). Sequences in the development of competent play with peers: Social and social pretend play. *Developmental Psychology, 28,* 961–974.

Howes, C., Phillips, D. A., & Whitebook, M. (1992). Thresholds of quality: Implications for the social development of children in center-based child care. *Child Development, 63,* 449–460.

Howes, C., Rodning, C., Galluzzo, D. C., & Myers, L. (1988). Attachment and child care: Relationships with mother and caregiver. *Early Childhood Research Quarterly, 3,* 403–416.

Howes, P., & Markman, H. J. (1989). Marital quality and child functioning: A longitudinal investigation. *Child Development, 60,* 1044–1051.

Hoyseth, K. S., & Jones, P. J. H. (1989). Ethanol induced teratogenesis: Characterization, mechanisms, and diagnostic approaches. *Life Sciences, 44,* 643–649.

Hubel, D. H., & Wiesel, T. N. (1970). The period of susceptibility to the physiological effects of unilateral eye closure in kittens. *Journal of Physiology, 206,* 419–436.

Hudson, J. A. (1990). The emergence of autobiographic memory in mother–child conversations. In R. Fivush & J. A. Hudson (Eds.), *Knowing and remembering in young children* (pp. 166–196). New York: Cambridge University Press.

Hudson, J. A., & Nelson, K. (1983). Effects of script structure on children's story recall. *Developmental Psychology, 19,* 625–635.

Huesmann, L. R. (1986). Psychological processes promoting the relation between exposure to media violence and aggressive behavior by the viewer. *Journal of Social Issues, 42,* 125–139.

Huesmann, L. R., Lefkowitz, M. M., Eron, L. D., & Walder, L. O. (1984). Stability of aggression over time and generations. *Developmental Psychology, 20,* 1120–1134.

Humphrey, T. (1978). Function of the nervous system during prenatal life. In U. Stave (Ed.), *Perinatal physiology* (pp. 651–683). New York: Plenum.

Humphreys, A. P., & Smith, P. K. (1987). Rough and tumble, friendship, and dominance in schoolchildren: Evidence for continuity and change with age. *Child Development, 58,* 201–212.

Humphreys, L. G., Rich, S. A., & Davey, T. C. (1985). A Piagetian test of general intelligence. *Developmental Psychology, 21,* 871–877.

Huntington, L., Hans, S. L., & Zeskind, P. S. (1990). The relations among cry characteristics, demographic variables, and developmental test scores in infants prenatally exposed to methadone. *Infant Behavior and Development, 13,* 533–538.

Huston, A. C. (1983). Sex-typing. In E. M. Hetherington (Ed.), *Handbook of child psychology: Vol. 4. Socialization, personality, and social development* (4th ed., pp. 387–467). New York: Wiley.

Huston, A. C., & Alvarez, M. M. (1990). The socialization context of gender role development in early adolescence. In R. Montemayor, G. R. Adams, & T. P. Gullotta (Eds.), *From childhood to adolescence: A transitional period?* (pp. 156–179). Newbury Park, CA: Sage.

Huston, A. C., Watkins, B. A., & Kunkel, D. (1989). Public policy and children's television. *American Psychologist, 44,* 424–433.

Huston-Stein, A., & Higgins-Trenk, A. (1978). Development of females from childhood through adulthood: Career and feminine role orientations. In P. B. Baltes (Ed.), *Life-span development and behavior* (Vol. 1, pp. 257–296). New York: Academic Press.

Huston-Stein, A., Fox, S., Greer, D., Watkins, B. A., & Whitaker, J. (1981). The effects of TV action and violence on children's social behavior. *Journal of Genetic Psychology, 138,* 183–191.

Huttenlocher, J., Haight, W., Bryk, A., Seltzer, M., & Lyons, T. (1991). Early vocabulary growth: Relation to language input and gender. *Developmental Psychology, 27,* 236–248.

Huttenlocher, P. R. (1994). Synaptogenesis in human cerebral cortex. In G. Dawson & K. W. Fischer (Eds.), *Human behavior and the developing brain* (pp. 137–152). New York: Guilford.

Hyde, J. S., & Linn, M. C. (1988). Gender differences in verbal ability: A metaanalysis. *Psychological Bulletin, 104,* 53–69.

Hyde, J. S., Fenema, E., & Lamon, S. J. (1990). Gender differences in mathematics performance: A meta-analysis. *Psychological Bulletin, 107,* 139–155.

Hynd, G. W., Horn, K. L., Voeller, K. K., & Marshall, R. M. (1991). Neurobiological basis of attention-deficit hyperactivity disorder (ADHD). *School Psychology Review, 20,* 174–186.

Inhelder, B., & Piaget, J. (1958). *The growth of logical thinking from childhood to adolescence: An essay on the construction of formal operational structures.* New York: Basic Books. (Original work published 1955)

Institute of Medicine. (1990). *Nutrition in pregnancy.* Washington, DC: National Academy Press.

International Education Association. (1988). *Science achievement in seventeen countries: A preliminary report.* Oxford, England: Pergamon Press.

Irvine, J. J. (1986). Teacher-student interactions: Effects of student race, sex, and grade level. *Journal of Educational Psychology, 78,* 14–21.

Isabella, R. (1993). Origins of attachment: Maternal interactive behavior across the first year. *Child Development, 64,* 605–621.

Isabella, R., & Belsky, J. (1991). Interactional synchrony and the origins of infant–mother attachment: A replication study. *Child Development, 62,* 373–384.

Istvan, J. (1986). Stress, anxiety, and birth outcomes: A critical review of the evidence. *Psychological Bulletin, 100,* 331–348.

Izard, C. E. (1979). *The maximally discriminative facial movement scoring system.* Unpublished manuscript, University of Delware.

Izard, C. E. (1991). *The psychology of emotions.* New York: Plenum.

Izard, C. E., Haynes, O. M., Chisholm, G., & Baak, K. (1991). Emotional determinants of infant–mother attachment. *Child Development, 62,* 906–917.

Jacklin, C. N., & Maccoby, E. E. (1978). Issues of gender differentiation in normal development. In M. D. Levine, W. B. Carey, A. C. Crocker, & R. T. Gross (Eds.), *Developmental-behavioral pediatrics* (pp. 174–184). Philadelphia: Saunders.

Jacklin, C. N., & Maccoby, E. E. (1983). Issues of gender differentiation in normal development. In M. D. Levine, W. B. Carey, A. C. Crocker, & R. T. Gross (Eds.), *Developmental-behavioral pediatrics* (pp. 175–184). Philadelphia: Saunders.

Jacklin, C. N., Snow, M. E., Gahart, M., & Maccoby, E. E. (1980). Sleep pattern development from 6 to 33 months. *Journal of Pediatric Psychology, 5,* 295–303.

Jacobs, F. H., & Davies, M. W. (1991). Rhetoric or reality? Child and family policy in the United States. *Social Policy Report of the Society for Research in Child Development, 5(4).*

Jacobson, J. L., Jacobson, S. W., Fein, G., Schwartz, P. M., & Dowler, J. (1984). Prenatal exposure to an environmental toxin: A test of the multiple effects model. *Developmental Psychology, 20,* 523–532.

Jacobson, J. L., Jacobson, S. W., & Humphrey, H. E. B. (1990). Effects of in utero exposure to polychlorinated biphenyls on cognitive functioning in young children. *Journal of Pediatrics, 116,* 38–45.

Jacobson, J. L., Jacobson, S. W., Padgett, R. J., Brumitt, G. A., & Billings, R. L. (1992). Effects of prenatal PCB exposure on cognitive processing efficiency and sustained attention. *Developmental Psychology, 28,* 297–306.

Jacobson, S. W., Fein, G. G., Jacobson, J. L., Schwartz, P. M., & Dowler, J. (1985). The effect of intrauterine PCB exposure on visual recognition memory. *Child Development, 56,* 853–860.

Jacobson, S. W., Jacobson, J. L., Sokol, R. J., Martier, S. S., & Ager, J. W. (1993). Prenatal alcohol exposure and infant information processing ability. *Child Development, 64,* 1706–1721.

Jakobi, P., Weissman, A., Peretz, B. A., & Hocherman, I. (1993). Evaluation of prognostic factors for vaginal delivery after cesarean section. *Journal of Reproductive Medicine, 38,* 729–733.

James, C. (1993). Comment on Polsky and Fast: Humane and effective—Do boot camps meet the test? *Child & Youth Care Forum, 22,* 417–419.

Jaskiewicz, J. A., & McAnarney, E. R. (1994). Pregnancy during adolescence. *Pediatrics in Review, 15,* 32–38.

Jeans, P. C., Smith, M. B., & Stearns, G. (1955). Incidence of prematurity in relation to maternal nutrition. *Journal of the American Dietetic Association, 31,* 576–581.

Jensen, A. R. (1969). How much can we boost IQ and scholastic achievement? *Harvard Educational Review, 39,* 1–123.

Jensen, A. R. (1980). *Bias in mental testing.* New York: Free Press.

Jensen, A. R. (1985a). Methodological and statistical techniques for the chronometric study of mental abilities. In C. R. Reynolds & V. L. Willson (Eds.), *Methodological and statistical advances in the study of individual difference* (pp. 51–116). New York: Plenum.

Jensen, A. R. (1985b). The nature of the black–white difference on various psychometric tests: Spearman's hypothesis. *Behavioral and Brain Sciences, 8,* 193–219.

Jensen, A. R. (1988). Speed of information processing and population differences. In S. H. Irvine & J. W. Berry (Eds.), *Human abilities in cultural context* (pp. 105–145). New York: Cambridge University Press.

Jensen, A. R., & Figueroa, R. A. (1975). Forward and backward digit-span interaction with race and IQ: Predictions from Jensen's theory. *Journal of Educational Psychology, 67,* 882–893.

Jensen, A. R., & Whang, P. A. (1994). Speed of accessing arithmetic facts in long-term memory: A comparison of Chinese-American and Anglo-American children. *Contemporary Educational Psychology, 19,* 1–12.

Jensen, P. S., & Shaw, J. (1993). Children as victims of war: Current knowledge and future research needs. *Journal of the American Academy of Child and Adolescent Psychiatry, 32,* 679–708.

Johanson, R. B., Rice, C., Coyle, M., Arthur, J., Anyanwu, L., Ibrahim, J., Warwick, A., Redman, C. W. E., & O'Brien, P. M. S. (1993). A randomised prospective study comparing the new vacuum extractor policy with forceps delivery. *British Journal of Obstetrics and Gynaecology, 100,* 524–530.

Johnson, C. L., Stuckey, M. K., Lewis, L. D., & Schwartz, D. M. (1983). A survey of 509 cases of self-reported bulimia. In P. L. Darby (Ed.), *Anorexia nervosa: Recent developments in research* (pp. 159–171). New York: Liss.

Johnson, E. G. (1967). *The impact of high school teachers on the educational plans of college freshmen.* Testing and Counseling Service, Report No. 32. Orono: University of Maine.

Johnson, J. E., & Hooper, F. E. (1982). Piagetian structuralism and learning: Two decades of educational application. *Contemporary Educational Psychology, 7,* 217–237.

Johnson, J. S., & Newport, E. L. (1989). Critical period effects in second language learning: The influence of maturational state on the acquisition of English as a second language. *Cognitive Psychology, 21,* 60–99.

Johnston, J. R., Kline, M., & Tschann, J. M. (1989). Ongoing post-divorce conflict. *American Journal of Orthopsychiatry, 57,* 587–600.

Jones, C. P., & Adamson, L. B. (1987). Language use in mother–child and mother–child–sibling interactions. *Child Development, 58,* 356–366.

Jones, E. F., Forrest, J. D., Goldman, N., Henshaw, S. K., Lincoln, R., Rosoff, J. I., Westoff, C. F., & Wulf, D. (1985). Teenage pregnancy in developed countries: Determinants and policy implications. *Family Planning Perspectives, 17,* 53–63.

Jones, E. F., Forrest, J. D., Henshaw, S. K., Silverman, J., & Torres, A. (1988). Unintended pregnancy, contraceptive practice and family planning services in developed countries. *Family Planning Perspectives, 20,* 53–67.

Jones, G. P., & Dembo, M. H. (1989). Age and sex role differences in intimate friendships during childhood and adolescence. *Merrill-Palmer Quarterly, 35,* 445–462.

Jones, M. C. (1965). Psychological correlates of somatic development. *Child Development, 36,* 899–911.

Jones, M. C., & Bayley, N. (1950). Physical maturing among boys as related to behavior. *Journal of Educational Psychology, 41,* 129–148.

Jones, M. C., & Mussen, P. H. (1958). Self-conceptions, motivations, and interpersonal attitudes of early- and late-maturing girls. *Child Development, 29,* 491–501.

Jones, S. S., & Raag, T. (1989). Smile production in older infants: The importance of a social recipient for the facial signal. *Child Development, 60,* 811–818.

Jordan, A. E. (1987). The unresolved child care dilemma: Care for the acutely ill child. In M. T. Osterholm, J. O. Klein, S. S. Aronson, & L. K. Pickering (Eds.), *Infectious diseases in child day care* (pp. 114–118). Chicago: University of Chicago Press.

Jordan, B. (1993). *Birth in four cultures.* Prospect Heights, IL: Waveland.

Jordan, P. (1990). Laboring for relevance: The male experience of expectant and new parenthood. *Nursing Research, 39,* 15–19.

Jorgensen, M., & Keiding, N. (1991). Estimation of spermarche from longitudinal spermaturia data. *Biometrics, 47,* 177–193.

Jusczyk, P. W., Cutler, A., & Redanz, N. J. (1993). Infants' preference for the predominant stress patterns of English words. *Child Development, 64,* 675–687.

Kagan, J. (1989). *Unstable ideas: Temperament, cognition, and self.* Cambridge, MA: Harvard University Press.

Kagan, J. (1992). Behavior, biology, and the meanings of temperamental constructs. *Pediatrics, 90,* 510–513.

Kagan, J., Arcus, D., Snidman, N., Feng, W. Y., Hendler, J., & Greene, S. (1994). Reactivity in infants: A cross-national comparison. *Developmental Psychology, 30,* 342–345.

Kagan, J., Kearsley, R. B., & Zelazo, P. R. (1978). *Infancy: Its place in human development.* Cambridge, MA; Harvard University Press.

Kagan, J., Reznick, J. S., & Snidman, N. (1988). Biological bases of childhood shyness. *Science, 240,* 167–171.

Kagan, J., & Snidman, N. (1991). Temperamental factors in human development. *American Psychologist, 46,* 856–862.

Kahn, P. H., Jr. (1992). Children's obligatory and discretionary moral judgments. *Child Development, 63,* 416–430.

Kail, R. (1990). *The development of memory in children* (3rd ed.). New York: Freeman.

Kail, R. (1991). Processing time declines exponentially during childhood and adolescence. *Developmental Psychology, 27,* 259–266.

Kaitz, M., Good, A., Rokem, A. M., & Eidelman, A. I. (1987). Mothers' recognition of their newborns by olfactory cues. *Developmental Psychobiology, 20,* 587–591.

Kaitz, M., Good, A., Rokem, A. M., & Eidelman, A. I. (1988). Mothers' and fathers' recognition of their newborns' photographs during the postpartum period. *Journal of Developmental and Behavioral Pediatrics, 9,* 223–226.

Kaitz, M., Lapidot, P., Bronner, R., & Eidelman, A. I. (1992). Parturient women can recognize their infants by touch. *Developmental Psychology, 28,* 35–39.

Kaitz, M., Meschulach-Sarfaty, O., Auerbach, J., & Eidelman, A. (1988). A reexamination of newborns' ability to imitate facial expressions. *Developmental Psychology, 24,* 3–7.

Kaler, S. R., & Kopp, C. B. (1990). Compliance and comprehension in very young toddlers. *Child Development, 61,* 1997–2003.

Kalnins, I., & Love, R. (1982). Children's concepts of health and illness—and implications for health education: An overview. *Health Education Quarterly, 9,* 104–115.

Kalter, N., Riemer, B., Brickman, A., & Chen, J. W. (1985). Implications of parental divorce for female development. *Journal of the American Academy of Child Psychiatry, 24,* 538–544.

Kamerman, S. B. (1993). International perspectives on child care policies and programs. *Pediatrics, 91,* 248–252.

Kandel, D. B. (1978). Homophily, selection, and socialization in adolescent friendships. *American Journal of Sociology, 84,* 427–436.

Kandel, D. B., & Davies, M. (1986). Adult sequelae of adolescent depressive symptoms. *Archives of General Psychiatry, 43,* 255–262.

Kandel, D. B., & Lesser, G. S. (1972). *Youth in two worlds.* San Francisco: Jossey-Bass.

Kandel, D. B., Raveis, V. H., & Davies, M. (1991). Suicidal ideation in adolescence: Depression, substance use, and other risk factors. *Journal of Youth and Adolescence, 20,* 289–309.

Kandel, D. B., & Yamaguchi, K. (1993). From beer to crack: Developmental patterns of drug involvement. *American Journal of Public Health, 83,* 851–855.

Kanner, A. D., Feldman, S. S., Weinberger, D. A., & Ford, M. E. (1987). Uplifts, hassles, and adaptational outcomes in early adolescents. *Journal of Early Adolescence, 7,* 371–394.

Kantor, D., & Lehr, W. (1975). *Inside the family.* San Francisco: Jossey-Bass.

Kaplan, B. J. (1972). Malnutrition and mental deficiency. *Psychological Bulletin, 78,* 321–334.

Kaplan, R. M. (1985). The controversy related to the use of psychological tests. In B. B. Wolman (Ed.), *Handbook of intelligence* (pp. 465–504). New York: Wiley.

Karadsheh, R. (1991). *This room is a junkyard!: Children's comprehension of metaphorical language.* Paper presented at the biennial meeting of the Society for Research in Child Development, Seattle, WA.

Kassebaum, N. L. (1994). Head Start: Only the best for America's children. *American Psychologist, 49,* 123–126.

Katchadourian, H. (1977). *The biology of adolescence.* San Francisco: Freeman.

Katchadourian, H. (1990). Sexuality. In S. S. Feldman & G. R. Elliott (Eds.), *At the threshold: The developing adolescent* (pp. 330–351). Cambridge, MA: Harvard University Press.

Kaufman, A. S., & Kaufman, N. L. (1983). *Kaufman Assessment Battery for Children: Administration and scoring manual.* Circle Pines, MN: American Guidance Service.

Kaufman, J., & Zigler, E. (1989). The intergenerational transmission of child abuse. In D. Cicchetti & V. Carlson (Eds.), *Child maltreat-*

ment: Theory and research on the causes and consequences of child abuse and neglect (pp. 129–150). Cambridge, MA: Cambridge University Press.

Kavale, K. (1982). Meta-analysis of the relationship between visual perceptual skills and reading achievement. *Journal of Learning Disabilities, 15,* 42–51.

Kaye, K., Elkind, L., Goldberg, D., & Tytun, A. (1989). Birth outcomes for infants of drug abusing mothers. *New York State Journal of Medicine, 89,* 256–261.

Kaye, K., & Marcus, J. (1981). Infant imitation: The sensory-motor agenda. *Developmental Psychology, 17,* 258–265.

Kaye, K., & Wells, A. J. (1980). Mothers' jiggling and the burst–pause pattern in neonatal feeding. *Infant Behavior and Development, 3,* 29–46.

Kearins, J. M. (1981). Visual spatial memory in Australian aboriginal children of desert regions. *Cognitive Psychology, 13,* 434–460.

Keasey, C. B. (1971). Social participation as a factor in the moral development of preadolescents. *Developmental Psychology, 5,* 216–220.

Keating, D. (1979). Adolescent thinking. In J. Adelson (Ed.), *Handbook of adolescent psychology* (pp. 211–246). New York: Wiley.

Keeney, T. J., Canizzo, S. R., & Flavell, J. H. (1967). Spontaneous and induced verbal rehearsal in a recall task. *Child Development, 38,* 953–966.

Keens, T. G., & Ward, S. L. D. (1993). Apnea spells, sudden death, and the role of the apnea monitor. In J. R. Hageman (Ed.), *The pediatric clinics of North America* (Vol. 40, pp. 897–911). Philadelphia: Saunders.

Keil, F. C. (1986). Conceptual domains and the acquisition of metaphor. *Cognitive Development, 1,* 73–96.

Keil, F. C. (1989). *Concepts, kinds, and cognitive development.* Cambridge, MA: MIT Press.

Keller, A., Ford, L. H., & Meacham, J. A. (1978). Dimensions of self-concept in preschool children. *Developmental Psychology, 14,* 483–489.

Kelley, M. L., Power, T. G., & Wimbush, D. D. (1992). Determinants of disciplinary practices in low-income black mothers. *Child Development, 63,* 573–582.

Kelly, H. (1981). Viewing children through television. In H. Kelly & H. Gardner (Eds.), *New directions for child development* (No. 13, pp. 59–71). San Francisco: Jossey-Bass.

Kemp, J. S., & Thach, B. T. (1993). A sleep position-dependent mechanism for infant death on sheepskins. *American Journal of Diseases of Children, 147,* 642–646.

Kempe, C. H., Silverman, B. F., Steele, P. W., Droegemueller, P. W., & Silver, H. K. (1962). The battered-child syndrome. *Journal of the American Medical Association, 181,* 17–24.

Kempe, R. S., & Kempe, C. H. (1984). *The common secret: Sexual abuse of children and adolescents.* New York: Freeman.

Kendall-Tackett, K. A., Williams, L. M., & Finkelhor, D. (1993). Impact of sexual abuse on children: A review and synthesis of recent empirical studies. *Psychological Bulletin, 113,* 164–180.

Kendler, K. S., & Robinette, C. D. (1983). Schizophrenia in the National Academy of Sciences–National Research Council twin registry: A 16-year update. *American Journal of Psychiatry, 140,* 1551–1563.

Kendrick, A. S., Kaufman, R., & Messenger, K. P. (1991). *Healthy young children: A manual for programs.* Washington, DC: National Association for the Education of Young Children.

Kennedy, R. E. (1993). Depression as a disorder of social relationships: Implications for school policy and prevention. In R. M. Lerner (Ed.), *Early adolescence: Perspectives on research, policy, and intervention* (pp. 383–398). Hillsdale, NJ: Erlbaum.

Kennell, J. H., Klaus, M., McGrath, S., Robertson, S., & Hinkley, C. (1991). Continuous emotional support during labor in a U.S. hospital. *Journal of the American Medical Association, 265,* 2197–2201.

Keogh, B. K. (1988). Improving services for problem learners. *Journal of Learning Disabilities, 21,* 6–11.

Kermoian, R., & Campos, J. J. (1988). Locomotor experience: A facilitator of spatial cognitive development. *Child Development, 59,* 908–917.

Kerr, B. A. (1983). Raising the career aspirations of gifted girls. *Vocational Guidance Quarterly, 32,* 37–43.

Kerr, M., Lambert, W. W., Stattin, H., & Klackenberg-Larsson, I. (1994). Stability of inhibition in a Swedish longitudinal sample. *Child Development, 65,* 138–146.

Kessen, W. (1967). Sucking and looking: Two organized congenital patterns of behavior in the human newborn. In H. W. Stevenson, E. H. Hess, & H. L. Rheingold (Eds.), *Early behavior: Comparative and developmental approaches* (pp. 147–179). New York: Wiley.

Ketterlinus, R. D., Henderson, S. H., & Lamb, M. E. (1990). Maternal age, sociodemographics, prenatal health and behavior: Influences on neonatal risk status. *Journal of Adolescent Health Care, 11,* 423–431.

Kilbride, J. E., & Kilbride, P. L. (1975). Sitting and smiling behavior of Baganda infants. *Journal of Cross-Cultural Psychology, 6,* 88–107.

Kilman, C., & Helpin, M. L. (1983). Recognizing dental malocclusion in children. *Pediatric Nursing, 9,* 204–208.

Kinderman, T. A. (1993). Natural peer groups as contexts for individual development: The case of children's motivation in school. *Developmental Psychology, 29,* 970–977.

Kinzie, J. D., Sack, W., Angell, R., Clarke, G., & Ben, R. (1989). A three-year follow-up of Cambodian young people traumatized as children. *Journal of the American Academy of Child and Adolescent Psychiatry, 28,* 501–504.

Kirby, D. (1992). School-based programs to reduce sexual risk taking. *Journal of School Health, 62,* 280–287.

Kiser, L. J., Bates, J. E., Maslin, C. A., & Bayles, K. (1986). Mother–infant play at six months as a predictor of attachment security at thirteen months. *Journal of the American Academy of Child Psychiatry, 25,* 68–75.

Kisker, E. E. (1985). Teenagers talk about sex, pregnancy, and contraception. *Family Planning Perspectives, 17,* 83–90.

Klahr, D. (1989). Information-processing approaches. In R. Vasta (Ed.), *Annals of child development* (Vol. 6, pp. 133–185). Greenwich, CT: JAI Press.

Klahr, D. (1992). Information-processing approaches in cognitive development. In M. H. Bornstein & M. E. Lamb (Eds.), *Developmental psychology: An advanced textbook* (3rd ed., pp. 273–335). Hillsdale, NJ: Erlbaum.

Klaus, M. H., & Kennell, J. H. (1982). *Parent–infant bonding.* St. Louis: Mosby.

Klimes-Dougan, B., & Kistner, J. (1990). Physically abused preschoolers' responses to peers' distress. *Developmental Psychology, 26,* 599–602.

Klungness, L. (1990). Diagnosis and behavioral treatment of children who refuse to attend school. In P. A. Keller & S. R. Heyman (Eds.), *Innovations in clinical practice: A source book* (Vol. 9, pp. 107–118). Sarasota, FL: Professional Resource Exchange.

Kneisl, C. R. (1993). Psychosocial and economic concerns of women affected by HIV infection. In F. L. Cohen & J. D. Durham (Eds.), *Women, children, and HIV/AIDS* (pp. 137–155). New York: Springer.

Knittle, J. L., & Hirsch, J. (1968). Effect of early nutrition on the development of rat epididymal fat pads: Cellularity and metabolism. *Journal of Clinical Investigation, 47,* 2091–2098.

Knobloch, H., & Pasamanick, B. (Eds.). (1974). *Gesell and Amatruda's Developmental Diagnosis.* Hagerstown, MD: Harper & Row.

Knobloch, H., Stevens, F., & Malone, A. F. (1980). *Manual of developmental diagnosis.* Hagerstown, MD: Harper & Row.

Kochanska, G. (1991). Socialization and temperament in the development of guilt and conscience. *Child Development, 62,* 1379–1392.

Kochanska, G. (1993). Toward a synthesis of parental socialization and child temperament in early development of conscience. *Child Development, 64,* 325–347.

Kochanska, G., DeVet, K., Goldman, M., Murray, K., & Putnam, S. P. (1994). Maternal reports of conscience development and temperament in young children. *Child Development, 65,* 852–868.

Kochanska, G., & Radke-Yarrow, M. (1992). Inhibition in toddlerhood and the dynamics of the child's interaction with an unfamiliar peer at age five. *Child Development, 63,* 325–335.

Kodroff, J. K., & Roberge, J. J. (1975). Developmental analysis of the conditional reasoning abilities of primary-grade children. *Developmental Psychology, 11,* 21–28.

Kogan, N. (1983). Stylistic variation in childhood and adolescence: Creativity, metaphor, and cognitive style. In J. H. Flavell & E. M. Markman (Eds.), *Handbook of child psychology: Vol. 3. Cognitive development* (pp. 630–708). New York: Wiley.

Kohlberg, L. (1966). A cognitive-developmental analysis of children's sex-role concepts and attitudes. In E. E. Maccoby (Ed.), *The development of sex differences* (pp. 82–173). Stanford, CA: Stanford University Press.

Kohlberg, L. (1969). Stage and sequence: The cognitive-developmental approach to socialization. In D. A. Goslin (Ed.), *Handbook of socialization theory and research* (pp. 347–480). Chicago: Rand McNally.

Kohlberg, L. (1984). *Essays on moral development. Vol. 2: The psychology of moral development.* San Francisco: Harper & Row.

Kohlberg, L., Levine, C., & Hewer, A. (1983). *Moral stages: A current formulation and a response to critics.* Basel, Switzerland: Karger.

Kohn, M. L. (1977). *Class and conformity: A study in values* (rev. ed.). Chicago: University of Chicago Press.

Kohn, M. L. (1979). The effects of social class on parental values and practices. In D. Reiss & H. A. Hoffman (Eds.), *The American family: Dying or developing* (pp. 45–68). New York: Plenum.

Kojima, H. (1986). Childrearing concepts as a belief–value system of the society and the individual. In H. Stevenson, H. Azuma, & K. Hakuta (Eds.), *Child development and education in Japan* (pp. 39–54). New York: Freeman.

Kolata, G. (1992, April 26). A parents' guide to kids' sports. *New York Times Magazine,* pp. 12–15, 40, 44, 46.

Kolberg, R. (1993). Human embryo cloning reported. *Science, 262,* 652–653.

Kopp, C. B. (1983). Risk factors in development. In M. M. Haith & J. J. Campos (Eds.), *Handbook of child psychology: Vol. 2. Infancy and developmental psychobiology* (pp. 1081–1188). New York: Wiley.

Kopp, C. B. (1987). The growth of self-regulation: Caregivers and children. In N. Eisenberg (Ed.), *Contemporary topics in developmental psychology* (pp. 34–55). New York: Wiley.

Kopp, C. B. (1989). Regulation of distress and negative emotions: A developmental view. *Developmental Psychology, 25,* 343–354.

Kopp, C. B. (1994). Infant assessment. In C. B. Fisher & R. M. Lerner (Eds.), *Applied developmental psychology* (pp. 265–293). New York: McGraw-Hill.

Kopp, C. B., & Kaler, S. R. (1989). Risk in infancy. *American Psychologist, 44,* 224–230.

Kopp, C. B., & Krakow, J. B. (1982). *The child: Development in a social context.* Reading, MA: Addison-Wesley.

Korner, A. F. (1987). Infant stimulation: Issues of theory and research. In N. Gunzenhauser (Ed.), *Infant stimulation: For whom, what kind, and how much?* (pp. 88–97). New York: Johnson & Johnson.

Kornguth, M. L. (1990). School illnesses: Who's absent and why? *Pediatric Nursing, 16,* 95–99.

Kornhaber, M., Krechesvsky, M., & Gardner, H. (1991). Engaging intelligence. *Educational Psychologist, 25,* 177–199.

Korte, D., & Scaer, R. (1990). *A good birth, a safe birth.* New York: Bantam.

Kozol, J. (1991). *Savage inequalities.* New York: Crown.

Kramer, M. D., Taylor, V., Hickok, D. E., Caling, J. R., Vaughan, T. L., & Hollenbach, K. A. (1991). Maternal smoking and placenta previa. *Epidemiology, 2,* 221–223.

Kramer, M. S. (1993). Effects of energy and protein intakes on pregnancy outcome: An overview of the research evidence from controlled clinical trials. *American Journal of Clinical Nutrition, 58,* 627–635.

Kramer, M. S., Barr, R. G., Leduc, D. G., Biosjoly, C., & Pless, I. B. (1985). Infant determinants of childhood weight and adiposity. *Journal of Pediatrics, 107,* 104–107.

Krebs, D., & Gillmore, J. (1982). The relationship among the first stages of cognitive development, role-taking abilities, and moral development. *Child Development, 53,* 877–886.

Kreipe, R. E., Churchill, B. H., & Strauss, J. (1989). Long-term outcome of adolescents with anorexia nervosa. *American Journal of Diseases of Children, 143,* 1322–1327.

Kreminitzer, T. P., Vaughan, H. G., Kurtzberg, D., & Dowling, K. (1979). Smooth-pursuit eye movements in the newborn infant. *Child Development, 50,* 441–448.

Kreutzer, M. A., Leonard, C., & Flavell, J. H. (1975). An interview study of children's knowledge about memory. *Monographs of the Society for Research in Child Development, 40*(1, Serial No. 159).

Kricker, A., Elliott, J. W., Forrest, J. M., & McCredie, J. (1986). Congenital limb reduction deformities and use of oral contraceptives. *American Journal of Obstetrics and Gynecology, 155,* 1072–1078.

Kruger, A. C. (1992). The effect of peer and adult–child transactive discussions on moral reasoning. *Merrill-Palmer Quarterly, 38,* 191–211.

Ku, L. C., Sonenstein, F. L., & Pleck, J. H., (1993). Factors influencing first intercourse for teenage men. *Public Health Reports, 108,* 680–694.

Kuczaj, S. A., II. (1986). Thoughts on the intentional basis of early object word extension: Evidence from comprehension and production. In S. A. Kuczaj, II, & M. D. Barrett (Eds.), *The development of word meaning* (pp. 99–120). New York: Springer-Verlag.

Kuczynski, L. (1984). Socialization goals and mother–child interaction: Strategies for long-term and short-term compliance. *Developmental Psychology, 20,* 1061–1073.

Kuczynski, L., Kochanska, G., Radke-Yarrow, M., & Girnius-Brown, O. (1987). A developmental interpretation of young children's noncompliance. *Developmental Psychology, 23,* 799–806.

Kuebli, J., & Fivush, R. (1992). Gender differences in parent–child conversations about past emotions. *Sex Roles, 27,* 683–698.

Kuhl, P. K., & Meltzoff, A. N. (1984). The intermodal representation of speech in infants. *Infant Behavior and Development, 7,* 361–381.

Kuhl, P. K., Williams, K. A., Lacerda, F., Stevens, K. N., & Lindblom, B. (1992). Linguistic experience alters phonetic perception in infants by 6 months of age. *Science, 255,* 606–608.

Kuhn, D. (1992). Cognitive development. In M. H. Bornstein & M. E. Lamb (Eds.), *Developmental psychology: An advanced textbook* (3rd ed., pp. 211–272). Hillsdale, NJ: Erlbaum.

Kuhn, D., Amsel, E., & O'Loughlin, M. (1988). *The development of scientific thinking skills.* Orlando, FL: Academic Press.

Kuhn, D., Ho, V., & Adams, C. (1979). Formal reasoning among pre- and late adolescents. *Child Development, 50,* 1128–1135.

Kunkel, D. (1993). Policy and the future of children's television. In G. L. Berry & J. K. Asamen (Eds.), *Children & television* (pp. 273–290). Newbury Park, CA: Sage.

Kunzinger, E. L., III. (1985). A short-term longitudinal study of memorial development during early grade school. *Developmental Psychology, 21,* 642–646.

Kurdek, L. A., & Fine, M. A. (1994). Family acceptance and family control as predictors of adjustment in young adolescents: Linear, curvilinear, or interactive effects? *Child Development, 65,* 1137–1146.

Kurth, A. (1993). Reproductive issues, pregnancy, and childbearing in HIV-infected women. In F. L. Cohen & J. D. Durham (Eds.), *Women, children, and HIV/AIDS* (pp. 137–155). New York: Springer.

Kutner, L. (1993, June). Getting physical. *Parents,* Vol. 68, N. 6, pp. 96–98.

Laboratory of Comparative Human Cognition. (1989). Kids and computers: A positive vision of the future. *Harvard Educational Review, 59,* 73–86.

Ladd, G. W., & Mize, J. (1983). A cognitive-social learning model of social skill training. *Psychological Review, 90,* 127–157.

Ladd, G. W., & Price, J. M. (1987). Predicting children's social and school adjustment following the transition from preschool to kindergarten. *Child Development, 58,* 1168–1189.

Lagercrantz, H., & Slotkin, T. A. (1986). The "stress" of being born. *Scientific American, 254,* 100–107.

Lamaze, F. (1958). *Painless childbirth.* London: Burke.

Lamb, M. (1994). Infant care practices and the application of knowledge. In C. B. Fisher & R. M. Lerner (Eds.), *Applied developmental psychology* (pp. 23–45). New York: McGraw-Hill.

Lamb, M. E. (1976). Interaction between eight-month-old children and their fathers and mothers. In M. E. Lamb (Ed.), *The role of the father in child development* (pp. 307–327). New York: Wiley.

Lamb, M. E. (1987). *The father's role: Cross-cultural perspectives.* Hillsdale, NJ: Erlbaum.

Lamb, M. E., & Oppenheim, D. (1989). Fatherhood and father–child relationships: Five years of research. In S. H. Cath, A. Gurwitt, & L. Gunsberg (Eds.), *Fathers and their families* (pp. 11–26). Hillsdale, NJ: Erlbaum.

Lamb, M. E., Sternberg, K. J., & Prodromidis, M. (1992). Nonmaternal care and the security of infant–mother attachment: A reanalysis of the data. *Infant Behavior and Development, 15,* 71–83.

Lamb, M. E., Thompson, R. A., Gardner, W., Charnov, E. L., & Connell, J. P. (1985). Infant–mother attachment: The origins and developmental significance of individual differences in the Strange Situation: Its study and biological interpretation. *Behavioral and Brain Sciences, 7,* 127–147.

Lamb, S. (1991). First moral sense: Aspects of and contributors to a beginning morality in the second year of life. In W. M. Kurtines & J. L. Gewirtz (Eds.), *Handbook of moral behavior and development* (Vol. 2, pp. 171–189). Hillsdale, NJ: Erlbaum.

Lamborn, S. D., & Steinberg, L. (1993). Emotional autonomy redux: Revisiting Ryan and Lynch. *Child Development, 64,* 483–499.

Lamborn, S. D., Mounts, N. S., Steinberg, L., & Dornbusch, S. M. (1991). Patterns of competence and adjustment among adolescents from authoritative, authoritarian, indulgent, and neglectful families. *Child Development, 62,* 1049–1065.

Lampl, M. (1993). Evidence of saltatory growth in infancy. *American Journal of Human Biology, 5,* 641–652.

Lampl, M., Veldhuis, J. D., & Johnson, M. L. (1992). Saltation and stasis: A model of human growth. *Science, 258,* 801–803.

Landau, E. (1986). *Sexually transmitted diseases.* Hillside, NJ: Enslow.

Landau, S., Lorch, E. P., & Milich, R. (1992). Visual attention to and comprehension of television in attention-deficit hyperactivity disordered and normal boys. *Child Development, 63,* 828–937.

Landesman, S., & Ramey, C. (1989). Developmental psychology and mental retardation: Integrating scientific principles with treatment practices. *American Psychologist, 44,* 409–415.

Lane, D. M., & Pearson, D. A. (1982). The development of selective attention. *Merrill-Palmer Quarterly, 28,* 317–337.

Lange, G., & Pierce, S. H. (1992). Memory-strategy learning and maintenance in preschool children. *Developmental Psychology, 28,* 453–462.

Langlois, J. H., & Stephan, C. W. (1981). Beauty and the beast: The role of physical attractiveness in peer relationships and social behavior. In S. S. Brehm, S. M. Kassin, & S. X. Gibbons (Eds.), *Developmental social psychology: Theory and research* (pp. 152–168). New York: Oxford University Press.

Laosa, L. M. (1981). Maternal behavior: Sociocultural diversity in modes of family interaction. In R. W. Henderson (Ed.), *Parent–child interaction: Theory, research, and prospects* (pp. 125–167). New York: Academic Press.

Lapsley, D. K. (1985). Elkind on egocentrism. *Developmental Review, 5,* 227–236.

Lapsley, D. K. (1990). Egocentrism theory and the "new look" at the imaginary audience and personal fable in adolescence. In R. M. Lerner, A. C. Petersen, & J. Brooks-Gunn (Eds.), *The encyclopedia of adolescence* (pp. 281–286). New York: Garland.

Lapsley, D. K. (1993). Toward an integrated theory of adolescent ego development: The "new look" at adolescent egocentrism. *American Journal of Orthopsychiatry, 63,* 562–571.

Lapsley, D. K., Enright, R., & Serlin, R. (1989). Moral and social education. In F. Danner & J. Worell (Eds.), *The adolescent as a decision-maker: Applications to development and education* (pp. 111–141). New York: Academic Press.

Lapsley, D. K., Jackson, S., Rice, K., & Shadid, G. (1988). Self-monitoring and the "new look" at the imaginary audience and personal fable: An ego-developmental analysis. *Journal of Adolescent Research, 3,* 17–31.

Lapsley, D. K., Milstead, M., Quintana, S., Flannery, D., & Buss, R. (1986). Adolescent egocentrism and formal operations: Tests of a theoretical assumption. *Developmental Psychology, 22,* 800–807.

Lapsley, D. K., Rice, K. G., & FitzGerald, D. P. (1990). Adolescent attachment, identity, and adjustment to college: Implications for the continuity of adaptation hypothesis. *Journal of Counseling and Development, 68,* 561–565.

LaRossa, R., & LaRossa, M. M. (1981). *Transition to parenthood: How infants change families.* Beverly Hills, CA: Sage.

Larson, G. (1989). Cognitive correlates of general intelligence: Toward a process theory of G. *Intelligence, 13,* 5–31.

Larson, R., & Ham, M. (1993). Stress and "storm and stress" in early adolescence: The relationship of negative events with dysphoric affect. *Developmental Psychology, 29,* 130–140.

Larson, R., & Lampman-Petraitis, C. (1989). Daily emotional states as reported by children and adolescents. *Child Development, 60,* 1250–1260.

Last, C. G., Francis, G., Hersen, M., Kazdin, A. E., & Strauss, C. C. (1987). Separation anxiety and school phobia: A comparison using DSM-III criteria. *American Journal of Psychiatry, 144,* 653–657.

Laupa, M. (1994). "Who's in charge?" Preschool children's concepts of authority. *Early Childhood Research Quarterly, 9,* 1–7.

Lazar, A., & Torney-Purta, J. (1991). The development of the subconcepts of death in young children: A short-term longitudinal study. *Child Development, 62,* 1321–1333.

Lazar, I., & Darlington, R. (1982). Lasting effects of early education: a report from the Consortium for Longitudinal Studies. *Monographs of the Society for Research in Child Development, 47*(2–3, Serial No. 195).

Leach, P. (1989). *Babyhood* (2nd ed.). New York: Knopf.

Leaper, C. (1991). Influence and involvement in children's discourse. *Child Development, 62,* 797–811.

Lee, A. M. (1980). Child-rearing practices and motor performance of black and white children. *Research Quarterly for Exercise and Sport, 51,* 494–500.

Lee, C. L., & Bates, J. E. (1985). Mother–child interaction at age two years and perceived difficult temperament. *Child Development, 56,* 1314–1325.

Lee, S. H., Ewert, D. P., Frederick, P. D., & Mascola, L. (1992). Resurgence of congenital rubella syndrome in the 1990s. *Journal of the American Medical Association, 267,* 2616–2620.

Lee, V. E., Brooks-Gunn, J., & Schnur, E. (1988). Does Head Start work? A 1-year follow-up of disadvantaged children attending Head Start, no preschool. *Developmental Psychology, 24,* 210–222.

Lee, V. E., Brooks-Gunn, J., Schnur, E., & Liaw, F. (1990). Are Head Start effects sustained? A longitudinal follow-up comparison of disadvantaged children attending Head Start, no preschool, and other preschool programs. *Child Development, 61,* 495–507.

Leetsma, R., August, R. L., George, B., & Peak, L. (1987). *Japanese education today: A report from the U.S. Study of Education in Japan.* Washington, DC: U.S. Government Printing Office.

Lehman, D. R., & Nisbett, R. E. (1990). A longitudinal study of the effects of undergraduate training on reasoning. *Developmental Psychology, 26,* 952–960.

Leichtman, M. D., & Ceci, S. J. (1995). The effect of stereotypes and suggestions on preschoolers' reports. *Developmental Psychology, 31.*

Leifer, M. (1980). *Psychological aspects of motherhood: A study of first pregnancy.* New York: Praeger.

Lemire, R. J., Loeser, J. D., Leech, R. W., & Alvord, E. C. (1975). *Normal and abnormal development of the human nervous system.* New York: Harper & Row.

Lempert, H. (1989). Animacy constraints on preschoolers' acquisition of syntax. *Child Development, 60,* 237–245.

Lenneberg, E. H. (1967). *Biological foundations of language.* New York: Wiley.

Leonard, M. F., Rhymes, J. P., & Solnit, A. J. (1986). Failure to thrive in infants: A family problem. *American Journal of Diseases of Children, 111,* 600–612.

Lepper, M. R. (1985). Microcomputers in education: Motivational and social issues. *American Psychologist, 40,* 1–18.

Lepper, M. R., & Gurtner, J-L. (1989). Children and computers: Approaching the twenty-first century. *American Psychologist, 44,* 170–178.

Lerner, J. V., & Abrams, A. (1994). Developmental correlates of maternal employment influences on children. In C. B. Fisher & R. M. Lerner (Eds.), *Applied developmental psychology* (pp. 174–206). New York: McGraw-Hill.

Lerner, J. W. (1989). Educational interventions in learning disabilities. *Journal of the American Academy of Child and Adolescent Psychiatry, 28,* 326–331.

Lerner, M. R. (1985). Adolescent maturational changes and psychosocial development: A dynamic interactional perspective. *Journal of Youth and Adolescence, 14,* 355–372.

Lerner, R. M., & Schroeder, C. (1971). Physique identification, preference, and aversion in kindergarten children. *Developmental Psychology, 5,* 538.

Lester, B. M. (1985). Introduction: There's more to crying than meets the ear. In B. M. Lester & C. F. Z. Boukydis (Eds.), *Infant crying* (pp. 1–27). New York: Plenum.

Lester, B. M. (1987). Developmental outcome prediction from acoustic cry analysis in term and preterm infants. *Pediatrics, 80,* 529–534.

Lester, B. M., & Dreher, M. (1989). Effects of marijuana use during pregnancy on newborn cry. *Child Development, 60,* 765–771.

Lester, B. M., Kotelchuck, M., Spelke, E., Sellers, M. J., & Klein, R. E. (1974). Separation protest in Guatemalan infants: Cross-cultural and cognitive findings. *Developmental Psychology, 10,* 79–85.

Leung, A. K. C. (1989). School phobia: Sometimes a child or teenager has a good reason. *Postgraduate Medicine, 85,* 281–289.

Levin, J. A., Boruta, M. J., & Vasconellos, M. T. (1983). Microcomputer-based environments for writing: A writer's assistant. In A. C. Wilkinson (Ed.), *Classroom computers and cognitive science* (pp. 219–232). New York: Academic Press.

Levine, L. E. (1983). Mine: Self-definition in 2-year-old boys. *Developmental Psychology, 19,* 544–549.

LeVine, R. A., & LeVine, S. E. (1988). Parental strategies among the Gusii of Kenya. In R. A. LeVine, P. M. Miller, & M. M. West (Eds.), *Parental behavior in diverse societies* (pp. 27–35). San Francisco: Jossey-Bass.

Levitt, A. G., & Wang, Q. (1991). Evidence for language-specific rhythmic influences in the reduplicative babbling of French- and English-learning infants. *Language and Speech, 34,* 235–249.

Levy-Shiff, R., & Israelashvili, R. (1988). Antecedents of fathering: Some further exploration. *Developmental Psychology, 24,* 434–440.

Lewinsohn, P. M., Hops, H., Roberts, R. E., Seeley, J. R., & Andrews, J. A. (1993). Adolescent psychopathology: I. Prevalence and incidence of depression and other DSM–III–R disorders in high school students. *Journal of Abnormal Psychology, 102,* 133–144.

Lewinsohn, P. M., Rohde, P., & Seeley, J. R. (1994). Psychosocial risk factors for future suicide attempts. *Journal of Consulting and Clinical Psychology, 62,* 297–305.

Lewis, C. C. (1981). The effects of parental firm control: A reinterpretation of findings. *Psychological Bulletin, 90,* 547–563.

Lewis, M. (1991). Ways of knowing: Objective self-awareness or consciousness. *Developmental Review, 11,* 231–243.

Lewis, M. (1992a). *Shame: The exposed self.* New York: Free Press.

Lewis, M. (1992b). The self in self-conscious emotions (commentary on self-evaluation in young children. *Monographs of the Society for Research in Child Development, 57*(Serial No. 226, No. 1).

Lewis, M., Alessandri, S. M., & Sullivan, M. W. (1992). Differences in shame and pride as a function of children's gender and task difficulty. *Child Development, 63,* 630–638.

Lewis, M., & Brooks-Gunn, J. (1979). *Social cognition and the acquisition of self.* New York: Plenum.

Lewis, M., & McGurk, H. (1972). Evaluation of infant intelligence. *Science, 178,* 1174–1177.

Lewis, M., Ramsay, D. S., & Kawakami, K. (1993). Differences between Japanese infants and Caucasian American infants in behavioral and cortisol response to inoculation. *Child Development, 64,* 1722–1731.

Lewis, M., Sullivan, M. W., Stanger, C., & Weiss, M. (1989). Self development and self-conscious emotions. *Child Development, 60,* 146–156.

Lewis, M., Sullivan, M. W., & Vasen, A. (1987). Making faces: Age and emotion differences in the posing of emotional expressions. *Developmental Psychology, 23,* 690–697.

Li, C. Q., Windsor, R. A., & Perkins, L. (1993). The impact on infant birth weight and gestational age of cotinine-validated smoking reduction during pregnancy. *Journal of the American Medical Association, 269,* 1519–1524.

Liaw, F., & Brooks-Gunn, J. (1993). Patterns of low-birth-weight children's cognitive development. *Developmental Psychology, 29,* 1024–1035.

Liben, L. S., & Signorella, M. L. (1993). Gender-schematic processing in children: The role of initial interpretations of stimuli. *Developmental Psychology, 29,* 141–149.

Lie, S. O. (1990). Children in the Norwegian health care system. *Pediatrics, 86*(6, Pt. 2), 1048–1052.

Liebert, R. M., & Sprafkin, J. (1988). *The early window: Effects of television on children and youth* (3rd ed.). New York: Pergamon Press.

Lifschitz, M., Berman, D., Galili, A., & Gilad, D. (1977). Bereaved children: The effects of mother's perception and social system organization on their short range adjustment. *Journal of Child Psychiatry, 16,* 272–284.

Light, P., & Perret-Clermont, A-N. (1989). Social context effects in learning and testing. In A. Gellatly, D. Rogers, & J. Sloboda (Eds.), *Cognition and social worlds* (pp. 99–112). Oxford, England: Clarendon Press.

Lin, C. C., & Fu, V. R. (1990). A comparison of child-rearing practices among Chinese, immigrant Chinese, and Caucasian-American parents. *Child Development, 61,* 429–433.

Linde, E. V., Morrongiello, B. A., & Rovee-Collier, C. (1985). Determinants of retention in 8-week-old infants. *Developmental Psychology, 21,* 601–613.

Lindell, S. G. (1988). Education for childbirth: A time for change. *Journal of Obstetrics, Gynecology, and Neonatal Nursing, 17,* 108–112.

Lindgren, G. (1976). Height, weight, and menarche in Swedish urban school children in relation to socio-economic and regional factors. *Annals of Human Biology, 3,* 501–528.

Linn, M. C. (1985). Fostering equitable consequences from computer learning environments. *Sex Roles, 13,* 229–240.

Linn, M. C., & Hyde, J. S. (1989). Gender, mathematics, and science. *Educational Researcher, 18,* 17–27.

Linn, M. C., & Petersen, A. C. (1985). Emergence and characterization of sex differences in spatial ability: A meta-analysis. *Child Development, 56,* 1479–1498.

Linn, S., Lieberman, E., Schoenbaum, S. C., Monson, R. R., Stubblefield, P. G., & Ryan, K. J. (1988). Adverse outcomes of pregnancy in women exposed to diethylstilbestrol in utero. *Journal of Reproductive Medicine, 33,* 3–7.

Lipsitt, L. P. (1986). Learning in infancy: Cognitive development in babies. *Journal of Pediatrics, 109,* 172–182.

Lipsitt, L. P. (1990). Learning and memory in infants. *Merrill-Palmer Quarterly, 36,* 53–66.

Lipsitt, L. P., Sturner, W. Q., & Burke, P. (1979). Perinatal indicators and subsequent crib death. *Infant Behavior and Development, 2,* 325–328.

Litowitz, B. (1977). Learning to make definitions. *Journal of Child Language, 8,* 165–175.

Little, B. B., Snell, L. M., Klein, V. R., & Gilstrap, L. C., III (1989). Cocaine abuse during pregnancy: Maternal and fetal implications. *Obstetrics and Gynecology, 73,* 157–160.

Livesley, W. J., & Bromley, D. B. (1973). *Person perception in childhood and adolescence.* London: Wiley.

Livson, N., & Peskin, H. (1980). Perspectives on adolescence from longitudinal research. In J. Adelson (Ed.), *Handbook of adolescent psychology* (pp. 47–98). New York: Wiley.

Locke, J. (1892). Some thoughts concerning education. In R. H. Quick (Ed.), *Locke on education* (pp. 1–236). Cambridge, England: Cambridge University Press. (Original work published 1690)

Loehlin, J. C. (1989). Partitioning environmental and genetic contributions to behavioral development. *American Psychologist, 44,* 1285–1292.

Loehlin, J. C., Willerman, L., & Horn, J. M. (1988). Human behavior genetics. *Annual Review of Psychology, 38,* 101–133.

Looney, M. A., & Plowman, S. A. (1990). Passing rates of American children and youth on the FITNESSGRAM criterion-referenced physical fitness standards. *Research Quarterly of Exercise and Sport, 61,* 215–223.

Lorenz, K. Z. (1943). Die angeborenen Formen möglicher Erfahrung. *Zeitschrift für Tierpsychologie, 5,* 235–409.

Lorenz, K. Z. (1952). *King Solomon's ring.* New York: Crowell.

Louie, R., Brunelle, J. A., Maggiore, E. D., & Beck, R. W. (1990). Caries prevalence in Head Start children. *Journal of Public Health Dentistry, 50,* 299–305.

Lozoff, B. (1989). Nutrition and behavior. *American Psychologist, 44,* 231–236.

Lozoff, B., Wolf, A., & Davis, N. (1984). Cosleeping in urban families with young children in the United States. *Pediatrics, 74,* 171–182.

Ludemann, P. M. (1991). Generalized discrimination of positive facial expressions by seven- and ten-month-old infants. *Child Development, 62,* 55–67.

Lummis, M., & Stevenson, H. W. (1990). Gender differences in beliefs about achievement: A cross-cultural study. *Developmental Psychology, 26,* 254–263.

Luria, A. R. (1973). *The working brain.* New York: Basic Books.

Luster, T., Rhoades, K., & Haas, B. (1989). The relation between parental values and parenting behavior. *Journal of Marriage and the Family, 51,* 139–147.

Lutz, P. (1983). The stepfamily: An adolescent perspective. *Family Relations, 32,* 367–375.

Lyon, T. D., & Flavell, J. H. (1993). Young children's understanding of forgetting. *Child Development, 64,* 789–900.

Lyons-Ruth, K., Alpern, L., & Repacholi, B. (1993). Disorganized infant attachment classification and maternal psychosocial problems as predictors of hostile–aggressive behavior in the preschool classroom. *Child Development, 64,* 572–585.

Lyons-Ruth, K., Connell, D. B., Grunebaum, H. U., & Botein, S. (1990). Infants at social risk: Maternal depression and family support services as mediators of infant development and security of attachment. *Child Development, 61,* 85–98.

Lytton, H., & Romney, D. M. (1991). Parents' sex-related differential socialization of boys and girls: A meta-analysis. *Psychological Bulletin, 109,* 267–296.

Maccoby, E. E. (1980). Sex differences and sex typing. In E. Maccoby (Ed.), *Social development: Psychological growth and the parent–child relationship* (pp. 203–250). San Diego: Harcourt Brace Jovanovich.

Maccoby, E. E. (1984a). Middle childhood in the context of the family. In W. A. Collins (Ed.), *Development during middle childhood* (pp. 184–239). Washington, DC: National Academy Press.

Maccoby, E. E. (1984b). Socialization and developmental change. *Child Development, 55,* 317–328.

Maccoby, E. E. (1990). Gender and relationships. *American Psychologist, 45,* 513–520.

Maccoby, E. E., & Jacklin, C. N. (1987). Gender segregation in childhood. In E. H. Reese (Ed.), *Advances in child development and behavior* (Vol. 20, pp. 239–287). New York: Academic Press.

Maccoby, E. E., & Martin, J. A. (1983). Socialization in the context of the family: Parent–child interaction. In E. M. Hetherington (Ed.), *Handbook of child psychology: Vol. 4. Socialization, personality, and social development* (4th ed., pp. 1–101). New York: Wiley.

MacDonald, K. (1992). Warmth as a developmental construct: An evolutionary analysis. *Child Development, 63,* 753–773.

Macfarlane, J. W. (1971). From infancy to adulthood. In M. C. Jones, N. Bayley, J. W. Macfarlane, & M. P. Honzik (Eds.), *The course of human development* (pp. 406–410). Waltham, MA: Xerox College Publishing.

MacFarlane, J. (1975). Olfaction in the development of social preferences in the human neonate. In *Parent–infant interaction* (Ciba Foundation Symposium No. 33, pp. 103–117). Amsterdam: Elsevier.

MacFarlane, J., Smith, D. M., & Garrow, D. H. (1978). The relationship between mother and neonate. In S. Kitzinger (Ed.), *The place of birth* (pp. 185–200). New York: Oxford University Press.

MacKinnon, C. E. (1989). An observational investigation of sibling interactions in married and divorced families. *Developmental Psychology, 25,* 36–44.

Macksoud, M. (1994, March–April). Children in war. *World Health, 47*(2), pp. 21–23.

MacMillan, D. L., Keogh, B. K., & Jones, R. L. (1986). Special educational research on mildly handicapped learners. In M. C. Wittrock (Ed.), *Handbook of research on teaching* (3rd ed., pp. 686–724). New York: Macmillan.

MacQuiddy, S. L., Maise, S. J., & Hamilton, S. B. (1987). Empathy and affective perspective taking skills in parent identified conduct disordered boys. *Journal of Clinical Child Psychology, 16,* 260–268.

Madden, N., & Slavin, R. (1983). Mainstreaming students with mild handicaps: Academic and social outcomes. *Review of Educational Research, 53,* 519–659.

Mahalski, P. A., Silva, P. A., & Spears, G. F. S. (1985). Children's attachment to soft objects at bedtime, child rearing, and child development. *Journal of the American Academy of Child Psychiatry, 24,* 442–446.

Mahler, M. S., Pine, F., & Bergman, A. (1975). *The psychological birth of the human infant.* New York: Basic Books.

Main, M., & Goldwyn, R. (1994). *Interview-based adult attachment classifications: Related to infant–mother and infant–father attachment.* Unpublished manuscript, University of California, Berkeley.

Main, M., Kaplan, N., & Cassidy, J. (1985). Security in infancy, childhood, and adulthood: A move to the level of representation. *Monographs of the Society for Research in Child Development, 50*(1–2, Serial No. 209).

Main, M., & Solomon, J. (1990). Procedures for identifying infants as disorganized/disoriented during the Ainsworth Strange Situation. In M. Greenberg, D. Cicchetti, & M. Cummings (Eds.), *Attachment in the preschool years: Theory, research, and intervention* (pp. 121–160). Chicago: University of Chicago Press.

Makin, J. E., Fried, P. A., & Watkinson, B. (1991). A comparison of active and passive smoking during pregnancy: Long-term effects. *Neurotoxicology and Teratology, 13,* 5–12.

Makin, J. W., & Porter, R. H. (1989). Attractiveness of lactating females' breast odors to neonates. *Child Development, 60,* 803–810.

Makinson, C. (1985). The health consequences of teenage fertility. *Family Planning Perspectives, 17,* 132–139.

Malatesta, C. Z., Culver, C., Tesman, J. R., & Shepard, B. (1989). The development of emotion expression during the first two years of life. *Monographs of the Society for Research in Child Development, 54*(1–2, Serial No. 219).

Malatesta, C. Z., & Haviland, J. M. (1982). Learning display rules: The socialization of emotion expression in infancy. *Child Development, 53,* 991–1003.

Malatesta, C. Z., Grigoryev, P., Lamb, C., Albin, M., & Culver, C. (1986). Emotion socialization and expressive development in preterm and full-term infants. *Child Development, 57,* 316–330.

Malatesta-Magai, C. Z., Izard, C. E., & Camras, L. A. (1991). Conceptualizing early infant affect: Emotions as fact, fiction or artifact? In K. Strongman (Ed.), *International review of studies on emotion* (pp. 1–36). New York: Wiley.

Malina, R. M. (1975). *Growth and development: The first twenty years in man.* Minneapolis: Burgess.

Malina, R. M. (1990). Physical growth and performance during the transitional years (9–16). In R. Montemayor, G. R. Adams, & T. P. Gullotta (Eds.), *From childhood to adolescence: A transitional period?* (pp. 41–62). Newbury Park, CA: Sage.

Malina, R. M., & Bouchard, C. (1991). *Growth, maturation, and physical activity.* Champaign, IL: Human Kinetics.

Maloney, M., & Kranz, R. (1991). *Straight talk about eating disorders.* New York: Facts on File.

Manchester, D. (1988). Prehensile development: A contrast of mature and immature patterns. In J. E. Clark & J. H. Humphrey (Eds.), *Advances in motor development research* (pp. 165–199). New York: AMS Press.

Mandler, J. M. (1992a). The foundations of conceptual thought in infancy. *Cognitive Development, 7,* 273–285.

Mandler, J. M. (1992b). How to build a baby: II. Conceptual primitives.

Mandler, J. M., Bauer, P. J., & McDonough, L. (1991). Separating the sheep from the goats: Differentiating global categories. *Cognitive Psychology, 23,* 263–298.

Mandler, J. M., & McDonough, L. (1993). Concept formation in infancy. *Cognitive Development, 8,* 291–318.

Mangelsdorf, S., Gunnar, M., Kestenbaum, R., Lang, S., & Andreas, D. (1990). Infant proneness-to-distress temperament, maternal personality, and mother–infant attachment: Associations and goodness of fit. *Child Development, 61,* 820–831.

Maratsos, M. P., & Chalkley, M. A. (1980). The internal language of children's syntax: The ontogenesis and representation of syntactic categories. In K. Nelson (Ed.), *Children's language* (Vol. 2, pp. 127–214). New York: Gardner Press.

Marcella, S., & McDonald, B. (1990). The infant walker: An unappreciated household hazard. *Connecticut Medicine, 54,* 127–129.

Marcia, J. E. (1980). Identity in adolescence. In J. Adelson (Ed.), *Handbook of adolescent psychology* (pp. 159–187). New York: Wiley.

Marcia, J. E. (1988). Common processes

underlying ego identity, cognitive/moral development, and individuation. In D. K. Lapsley & F. P. Clark (Eds.), *Self, ego, and identity* (pp. 211–225). New York: Springer-Verlag.

Marcus, G. F. (1993). Negative evidence in language acquisition. *Cognition, 46,* 53–85.

Marcus, G. F., Pinker, S., Ullman, M., Hollander, M., Rosen, T. J., & Xu, F. (1992). Overregularization in language acquisition. *Monographs of the Society for Research in Child Development, 57*(4, Serial No. 228).

Margolis, M. Q., Hunt, R. J., & Vann, W. F., Jr. (1994). Distribution of primary tooth caries in first-grade children from two nonfluoridated U.S. communities. *Pediatric Dentistry, 16,* 200–205.

Markman, E. M. (1989). *Categorization and naming in children.* Cambridge, MA: MIT Press.

Markman, E. M. (1992). Constraints on word learning: Speculations about their nature, origins, and domain specificity. In M. R. Gunnar & M. P. Maratsos (Eds.), *Minnesota Symposia on Child Psychology* (Vol. 25, pp. 59–101). Hillsdale, NJ: Erlbaum.

Markovits, H., Schleifer, M., & Fortier, L. (1989). Development of elementary deductive reasoning in young children. *Developmental Psychology, 25,* 787–793.

Markovits, H., & Vachon, R. (1989). Reasoning with contrary-to-fact propositions. *Journal of Experimental Child Psychology, 47,* 398–412.

Markovits, H., & Vachon, R. (1990). Conditional reasoning, representation, and level of abstraction. *Developmental Psychology, 26,* 942–951.

Marsh, D. T., Serafica, F. C., & Barenboim, C. (1981). Interrelationships among perspective taking, interpersonal problem solving, and interpersonal functioning. *Journal of Genetic Psychology, 138,* 37–48.

Marsh, H. W. (1989). Sex differences in the development of verbal and mathematics constructs: The high school and beyond study. *American Educational Research Journal, 26,* 191–225.

Marsh, H. W. (1990). The structure of academic self-concept: The Marsh/Shavelson model. *Journal of Educational Psychology, 82,* 623–636.

Marsh, H. W., Smith, I. D., & Barnes, J. (1985). Multidimensional self-concepts: Relations with sex and academic achievement. *Journal of Educational Psychology, 77,* 581–596.

Martin, C. L. (1989). Children's use of gender-related information in making social judgments. *Developmental Psychology, 25,* 80–88.

Martin, C. L., & Halverson, C. F. (1981). A schematic processing model of sex typing and stereotyping in children. *Child Development, 52,* 1119–1134.

Martin, C. L., & Halverson, C. F. (1987). The role of cognition in sex role acquisition. In D. B. Carter (Ed.), *Current conceptions of sex roles and sex typing: Theory and research* (pp. 123–137). New York: Praeger.

Martin, C. L., & Little, J. K. (1990). The relation of gender understanding to children's sex-typed preferences and gender stereotypes. *Child Development, 61,* 1427–1439.

Martin, G. B., & Clark, R. D., III (1982). Distress crying in neonates: Species and peer specificity. *Developmental Psychology, 18,* 3–9.

Martin, J. A. (1981). A longitudinal study of the consequences of early mother–infant interaction: A microanalytic approach. *Monographs of the Society for Research in Child Development, 46*(3, Serial No. 190).

Martin, J. B. (1987). Molecular genetics: Applications to the clinical neurosciences. *Science, 298,* 765–772.

Martin, R. M. (1975). Effects of familiar and complex stimuli on infant attention. *Developmental Psychology, 11,* 178–185.

Martin, S. L., Ramey, C. T., & Ramey, S. (1990). The prevention of intellectual impairment in children of impoverished families: Findings of a randomized trial of educational day care. *American Journal of Public Health, 80,* 844–847.

Martorell, R. (1980). Interrelationships between diet, infectious disease, and nutritional status. In L. S. Greene & F. E. Johnston (Eds.), *Social and biological predictors of nutritional status, physical growth, and neurological development* (pp. 81–106). New York: Academic Press.

Marzolf, D. P., & DeLoache, J. S. (1994). Transfer in young children's understanding of spatial representations. *Child Development, 65,* 1–15.

Mason, M. G., & Gibbs, J. C. (1993). Social perspective taking and moral judgment among college students. *Journal of Adolescent Research, 8,* 109–123.

Massad, C. M. (1981). Sex role identity and adjustment during adolescence. *Child Development, 52,* 1290–1298.

Masur, E. F., McIntyre, C. W., & Flavell, J. H. (1973). Developmental changes in apportionment of study time among items in a multi-trial free recall task. *Journal of Experimental Child Psychology, 15,* 237–246.

Matas, L., Arend, R., & Sroufe, L. A. (1978). Continuity of adaptation in the second year: The relationship between quality of attachment and later competence. *Child Development, 49,* 547–556.

Matheny, A. P., Jr. (1987). Psychological characteristics of childhood accidents. *Journal of Social Issues, 43,* 45–60.

Matheny, A. P., Jr. (1991). Children's unintentional injuries and gender: Differentiation and psychosocial aspects. *Children's Environment Quarterly, 8,* 51–61.

Matias, R., & Cohn, J. F. (1993). Are MAX-specified infant facial expressions during face-to-face interaction consistent with differential emotions theory? *Developmental Psychology, 29,* 524–531.

Matthews, K. A., & Angulo, J. (1980). Measurement of the Type A behavior pattern in children: Assessment of children's competitiveness, impatience, anger, and aggression. *Child Development, 51,* 466–475.

Matute-Bianchi, M. E. (1986). Ethnic identities and patterns of school success and failure among Mexican-descent and Japanese-American students in a California high school: An ethnographic analysis. *American Journal of Education, 95,* 233–255.

Maurer, D. (1985). Infants' perception of facedness. In T. Fields & N. Fox (Eds.), *Social perception in infants* (pp. 73–100). Norwood, NJ: Ablex.

Mayberry, R. I. (1993). First-language acquisition after childhood differs from second-language acquisition: The case of American Sign Language. *Journal of Speech and Hearing Research, 36,* 1258–1270.

Mayers, M. M., Davenny, K., Schoenbaum, E. E., Feingold, A. R., Selwyn, P. A., Robertson, V., Ou, C. Y., Rogers, M. F., & Naccarato, M. (1991). A prospective study of infants of human immunodeficiency virus seropositive and seronegative women with a history of intravenous drug use or of intravenous drug-using sex partners, in the Bronx, New York City. *Pediatrics, 88,* 1248–1256.

Mayes, L. C., & Zigler, E. (1992). An observational study of the affective concomitants of mastery in infants. *Journal of Child Psychology and Psychiatry, 33,* 659–667.

McAnarney, E. R., Kreipe, R. E., Orr, D. P., & Comerci, G. D. (1992). *Textbook of adolescent development.* Philadelphia: Saunders.

McCabe, A. E., & Peterson, C. (1988). A comparison of adults' versus children's spontaneous use of *because* and *so. Journal of Genetic Psychology, 149,* 257–268.

McCabe, A. E., & Siegel, L. S. (1987). The stability of training effects in young children's class inclusion reasoning. *Merrill-Palmer Quarterly, 33,* 187–194.

McCall, R. B., Appelbaum, M. I., & Hogarty, P. S. (1973). Developmental changes in mental performance. *Monographs of the Society for Research in Child Development, 42*(3, Serial No. 171).

McCall, R. B., & Carriger, M. S. (1993). A meta-analysis of infant habituation and recognition memory performance as predictors of later IQ. *Child Development, 64,* 57–79.

McCartney, K. (1984). The effect of quality of day care environment upon children's language development. *Developmental Psychology, 20,* 244–260.

McCartney, K., Scarr, S., Phillips, D., & Grajek, S. (1985). Day care as intervention: Comparisons of varying quality programs. *Journal of Applied Developmental Psychology, 6,* 247–260.

McConaghy, M. J. (1979). Gender permanence and the genital basis of gender: Stages in the development of constancy of gender identity. *Child Development, 50,* 1223–1226.

McCormick, M. C., Gortmaker, S. L., & Sobol, A. M. (1990). Very low birth weight children: Behavior problems and school difficulty in a national sample. *Journal of Pediatrics, 117,* 687–693.

McCune, L. (1993). The development of play as the development of consciousness. In M. H. Bornstein & A. O'Reilly (Eds.), *New directions for child development* (No. 59, pp. 67–79). San Francisco: Jossey-Bass.

McGee, L. M., & Richgels, D. J. (1989, December). "K is Kristen's": Learning the alphabet from a child's perspective. *The Reading Teacher, 43*(3), 216–225.
McGee, L. M., & Richgels, D. J. (1990). *Literacy's beginnings: Supporting young readers and writers.* Boston: Allyn and Bacon.
McGhee, P. E. (1979). *Humor: Its origin and development.* San Francisco: Freeman.
McGinty, M. J., & Zafran, E. I. (1988). *Surrogacy: Constitutional and legal issues.* Cleveland: The Ohio Academy of Trial Lawyers.
McGroarty, M. (1992, March). The societal context of bilingual education. *Educational Researcher, 21*(2), 7–9.
McGuinness, D., & Pribram, K. H. (1980). The neuropsychology of attention: Emotional and motivational controls. In M. C. Wittcock (Ed.), *The brain and psychology* (pp. 95–139). New York: Academic Press.
McGuire, E. J., & Savashino, J. A. (1984). Urodynamic studies in enuresis and the nonneurogenic-neurogenic bladder. *Journal of Neurology, 132,* 299–302.
McGuire, J. (1988). Gender stereotypes of parents with two-year-olds and beliefs about gender differences in behavior. *Sex Roles, 19,* 233–240.
McHale, S. M., Bartko, W. T., Crouter, A. C., & Perry-Jenkins, M. (1990). Children's housework and psychosocial functioning: The mediating effects of parents' sex-role behaviors and attitudes. *Child Development, 61,* 1413–1426.
McKenna, M. C., Robinson, R. D., & Miller, J. W. (1990, November). Whole language: A research agenda for the nineties. *Educational Researcher, 19(8),* 3–6.
McKnight, C. C., Crosswhite, F. J., Dossey, J. A., Kifer, E., Swafford, J. O., Travers, K. J., & Cooney, T. J. (1987). *The underachieving curriculum: Assessing U.S. school mathematics from an international perspective.* Champaign, IL: Stipes.
McKusick, V. A. (1992). *Mendelian inheritance in man: Catalogs of autosomal dominant, autosomal recessive, and X-linked phenotypes* (10th ed.). Baltimore: Johns Hopkins University Press.
McLoyd, V. C. (1990). The impact of economic hardship on black families and children: Psychological distress, parenting, and socioemotional development. *Child Development, 61,* 311–346.
McManus, I. C., Sik, G., Cole, D. R., Mellon, A. F., Wong, J., & Kloss, J. (1988). The development of handedness in children. *British Journal of Developmental Psychology, 6,* 257–273.
McNamee, S., & Peterson, J. (1986). Young children's distributive justice reasoning, behavior, and role taking: Their consistency and relationship. *Journal of Genetic Psychology, 146,* 399–404.
McRae, M. J. (1993). Litigation, electronic fetal monitoring, and the obstetric nurse. *Journal of Obstetric, Gynecologic, and Neonatal Nursing, 22,* 410–419.
McWilliams, M. (1986). *The parents' nutrition book.* New York: Wiley.
Mead, G. H. (1934). *Mind, self, and society.* Chicago: University of Chicago Press.
Mead, M. (1928). *Coming of age in Samoa.* Ann Arbor, MI: Morrow.
Mead, M., & Newton, N. (1967). Cultural patterning of perinatal behavior. In S. Richardson & A. Guttmacher (Eds.), *Childbearing: Its social and psychological aspects* (pp. 142–244). Baltimore: Williams & Wilkins.
Meany, M. J., Stewart, J., & Beatty, W. W. (1985). Sex differences in social play: The socialization of sex roles. In J. S. Rosenblatt, C. Bear, C. M. Busnell, & P. Slater (Eds.), *Advances in the study of behavior* (Vol. 15, pp. 1–58). New York: Academic Press.
Medrich, E. A., Rosen, J., Rubin, V., & Buckley, S. (1982). *The serious business of growing up.* Berkeley: University of California Press.
Meehan, A. M. (1984). A meta-analysis of sex differences in formal operational thought. *Child Development, 55,* 1110–1124.
Mehler, J., Jusczyk, P. W., Lambertz, G., Halsted, N., Bertoncini, J., & Amiel-Tison, C. (1988). A precursor of language acquisition in young infants. *Cognition, 29,* 143–178.
Meilman, P. W. (1979). Cross-sectional age changes in ego identity status during adolescence. *Developmental Psychology, 15,* 230–231.
Melnikow, J., & Alemagno, S. (1993). Adequacy of prenatal care among inner-city women. *Journal of Family Practice, 37,* 575–582.
Meltzoff, A. N. (1988a). Infant imitation after a 1-week delay: Long-term memory for novel acts and multiple stimuli. *Developmental Psychology, 24,* 470–476.
Meltzoff, A. N. (1988b). Infant imitation and memory: Nine-month-olds in immediate and deferred tests. *Child Development, 59,* 217–255.
Meltzoff, A. N. (1990). Towards a developmental cognitive science. *Annals of the New York Academy of Sciences, 608,* 1–37.
Meltzoff, A. N. (1995). Apprehending the intentions of others: Re-enactment of intended acts by 18-month-old children. *Developmental Psychology, 31.*
Meltzoff, A. N., & Borton, R. W. (1979). Intermodal matching by human neonates. *Nature, 282,* 403–404.
Meltzoff, A. N., & Moore, M. K. (1977). Imitation of facial and manual gestures by human neonates. *Science, 198,* 75–78.
Meltzoff, A. N., & Moore, M. K. (1989). Imitation in newborn infants: Exploring the range of gestures imitated and the underlying mechanisms. *Developmental Psychology, 25,* 954–962.
Meltzoff, A. N., & Moore, M. K. (1992). Early imitation within a functional framework: The importance of person identity, movement, and development. *Infant Behavior and Development, 15,* 479–505.
Meltzoff, A. N., & Moore, M. K. (1994). Imitation, memory, and the representation of persons. *Infant Behavior and Development, 17,* 83–99.
Menig-Peterson, C. L. (1975). The modification of communicative behavior in preschool-aged children as a function of the listener's perspective. *Child Development, 46,* 1015–1018.
Menyuk, P. (1977). *Language and maturation.* Cambridge, MA: MIT Press.
Meredith, N. V. (1978). *Human body growth in the first ten years of life.* Columbia, SC: State Printing.
Mervis, C. B. (1985). On the existence of prelinguistic categories: A case study. *Infant Behavior and Development, 8,* 293–300.
Mervis, C. B. (1987). Child-basic object categories and early lexical development. In U. Neisser (Ed.), *Concepts and conceptual development: Ecological and intellectual factors in categorization* (pp. 201–233). Cambridge, England: Cambridge University Press.
Mervis, C. B., & Crisafi, M. A. (1982). Order of acquisition of subordinate-, basic-, and superordinate-level categories. *Child Development, 53,* 258–266.
Mervis, C. B., Golinkoff, R. M., & Bertrand, J. (1994). Two-year-olds readily learn multiple labels for the same basic-level category. *Child Development, 65,* 1163–1177.
Meyer, D. R., & Garasky, S. (1993). Custodial fathers: Myths, realities, and child support policy. *Journal of Marriage and the Family, 55,* 73–79.
Michaels, G. Y. (1988). Motivational factors in the decision and timing of pregnancy. In G. Y. Michaels & W. A. Goldberg (Eds.), *The transition to parenthood: Current theory and research* (pp. 23–61). New York: Cambridge University Press.
Michel, C. (1989). Radiation embryology. *Experientia, 45,* 69–77.
Micheli, L. J., & Klein, J. D. (1991). Sports injuries in children and adolescents. *British Journal of Sports Medicine, 25,* 6–9.
Midgley, C., Feldlaufer, H., & Eccles, J. S. (1989). Student/teacher relations and attitudes toward mathematics before and after the transition to junior high school. *Child Development, 60,* 981–992.
Milburn, N., & D'Ercole, A. (1991). Homeless women, children, and families. *American Psychologist, 46,* 1159–1160.
Miller, B. C., & Olson, T. D. (1988). Sexual attitudes and behavior of high school students in relation to background and contextual factors. *Journal of Sex Research, 24,* 194–200.
Miller, G. A. (1991). *The science of words.* New York: Scientific American Library.
Miller, K. F., & Baillargeon, R. (1990). Length and distance: Do preschoolers think that occlusion brings things together? *Developmental Psychology, 26,* 103–114.
Miller, N., & Maruyama, G. (1976). Ordinal position and peer popularity. *Journal of Personality and Social Psychology, 33,* 123–131.
Miller, N. B., Cowan, P. A., Cowan, C. P., Hetherington, E. M., & Clingempeel, W. G. (1993). Externalizing in preschoolers and early adolescents: A cross-study replication of a family model. *Developmental Psychology, 29,* 3–16.

Miller, P., & Sperry, L. L. (1987). The socialization of anger and aggression. *Merrill-Palmer Quarterly, 33,* 1–31.

Miller, P. H. (1993). *Theories of developmental psychology* (3rd ed.). New York: Freeman.

Miller, P. H., & Bigi, L. (1979). The development of children's understanding of attention. *Merrill-Palmer Quarterly, 25,* 235–250.

Miller, P. H., & Zalenski, R. (1982). Preschoolers' knowledge about attention. *Developmental Psychology, 18,* 871–875.

Miller, S. A. (1987). *Developmental research methods.* Englewood Cliffs, NJ: Prentice Hall.

Miller-Jones, D. (1989). Culture and testing. *American Psychologist, 44,* 360–366.

Mills, J., Harlap, S., & Harley, E. E. (1981). Should coitus late in pregnancy be discouraged? *Lancet, 2,* 136–138.

Mills, R., & Grusec, J. E. (1989). Cognitive, affective, and behavioral consequences of praising altruism. *Merrill-Palmer Quarterly, 35,* 299–326.

Millstein, S. G., & Irwin, C. E. (1987). Concepts of health and illness: Different constructs or variations on a theme? *Health Psychology, 6,* 515–524.

Millstein, S. G., & Irwin, C. E. (1988). Accident-related behaviors in adolescents: A biosocial view. *Alcohol, Drugs, and Driving, 4,* 21–29.

Millstein, S. G., & Litt, I. F. (1990). Adolescent health. In S. S. Feldman & G. R. Elliott (Eds.), *At the threshold: The developing adolescent* (pp. 431–456). Cambridge, MA: Harvard University Press.

Minuchin, P. P. (1988). Relationships within the family: A systems perspective on development. In R. A. Hinde & J. Stevenson-Hinde (Eds.), *Relationships within families: Mutual influences* (pp. 7–26). New York: Oxford University Press.

Minuchin, P. P., & Shapiro, E. K. (1983). The school as a context for social development. In E. M. Hetherington (Ed.), *Handbook of child psychology: Vol. 4. Socialization, personality, and social development* (4th ed., pp. 197–274). New York: Wiley.

Mirman, J. H. (1993, June). Father knows best? Male parent issues in custody cases. *Trial, 29*(6), 16–21.

Mischel, W., & Liebert, R. M. (1966). Effects of discrepancies between observed and imposed reward criteria on their acquisition and transmission. *Journal of Personality and Social Psychology, 3,* 45–53.

Miscione, J. L., Marvin, R. S., O'Brien, R. G., & Greenburg, M. T. (1978). A developmental study of preschool children's understanding of the words "know" and "guess." *Child Development, 48,* 1107–1113.

Miyake, K., Chen, S., & Campos, J. J. (1985). Infant temperament, mother's mode of interaction, and attachment in Japan: An interim report. In I. Bretherton & E. Waters (Eds.), Growing points of attachment theory and research. *Monographs of the Society for Research in Child Development, 50*(1–2, Serial No. 209).

Mize, J., & Ladd, G. W. (1990). A cognitive–social learning approach to social skill training with low-status preschool children. *Developmental Psychology, 26,* 388–397.

Moerk, E. L. (1989). The LAD was a lady and the tasks were ill-defined. *Developmental Review, 9,* 21–57.

Moffatt, M. E. K., Harlos, S., Kirshen, A. J., Burd, L. (1993). DDAVP and nocturnal enuresis: How much do we know? *Pediatrics, 92,* 420–425.

Moffitt, T. E. (1990). Juvenile delinquency and attention deficit disorder: Boys' developmental trajectories from age 3 to age 15. *Child Development, 61,* 893–910.

Moffitt, T. E., Caspi, A., Belsky, J., & Silva, P. A. (1992). Childhood experience and the onset of menarche: A test of a sociobiological model. *Child Development, 63,* 47–58.

Moilanen, I. (1989). The growth, development, and education of Finnish twins: A longitudinal follow-up study in a birth cohort from pregnancy to nineteen years of age. *Growth, Development and Aging, 18,* 302–306.

Monroe, S., Goldman, P., & Smith, V. E. (1988). *Brothers: Black and poor—a true story of courage and survival.* New York: Morrow.

Montemayor, R., & Eisen, M. (1977). The development of self-conceptions from childhood to adolescence. *Developmental Psychology, 13,* 314–319.

Moore, C., Bryant, D., & Furrow, D. (1989). Mental terms and the development of certainty. *Child Development, 60,* 167–171.

Moore, E. G. J. (1986). Family socialization and the IQ test performance of traditionally and transracially adopted black children. *Developmental Psychology, 22,* 317–326.

Moore, K., Peterson, J., & Furstenberg, F. F., Jr. (1986). Parental attitudes and the occurrence of early sexual activity. *Journal of Marriage and the Family, 48,* 777–782.

Moore, K. L., & Persaud, T. V. N. (1993). *Before we are born* (4th ed.). Philadelphia: Saunders.

Moorehouse, M. J. (1991). Linking maternal employment patterns to mother–child activities and children's school competence. *Developmental Psychology, 27,* 295–303.

Moran, G. F., & Vinovskis, M. A. (1986). The great care of godly parents: Early childhood in Puritan New England. *Monographs of the Society for Research in Child Development, 50*(4–5, Serial No. 211).

Morelli, G., Rogoff, B., Oppenheim, D., & Goldsmith, D. (1992). Cultural variation in infants' sleeping arrangements: Questions of independence. *Developmental Psychology, 28,* 604–613.

Morgane, P. J., Austin-LaFrance, R., Bronzino, J., Tonkiss, J., Diaz-Cintra, S., Cintra, L., Kemper, T., & Galler, J. R. (1993). Prenatal malnutrition and development of the brain. *Neuroscience and Biobehavioral Reviews, 17,* 91–128.

Morris, R., & Kratochwill, T. (1983). *Treating children's fears and phobias: A behavioral approach.* Elmsford, NY: Pergamon.

Morrongiello, B. A. (1986). Infants' perception of multiple-group auditory patterns. *Infant Behavior and Development, 9,* 307–319.

Moshman, D., & Franks, B. A. (1986). Development of the concept of inferential validity. *Child Development, 57,* 153–165.

Moss, M., Colombo, J., Mitchell, D. W., & Horowitz, F. D. (1988). Neonatal behavioral organization and visual processing at three months. *Child Development, 59,* 1211–1220.

Mott, F. L., & Marsiglio, W. (1985). Early childbearing and completion of high school. *Family Planning Perspectives, 17,* 234–237.

Mott, S. R., James, S. R., & Sperhac, A. M. (1990). *Nursing care of children and families.* Redwood City, CA: Addison-Wesley.

Muecke, L., Simons-Morton, B., Huang, I. W., & Parcel, G. (1992). Is childhood obesity associated with high-fat foods and low physical activity? *Journal of School Health, 62,* 19–23.

Mullis, I. V. S., Dossey, J. A., Foertsch, M. A., Jones, L. R., & Gentile, C. A. (1991). *Trends in academic progress.* Washington, DC: U.S. Government Printing Office.

Mullis, I. V. S., Dossey, J. A., Owen, E. H., & Phillips, G. W. (1991). *The state of mathematics achievement: Executive summary* (NAEP's 1990 assessment of the nation and the trial assessment of the states). Princeton, NJ: Educational Testing Service.

Mulvey, E. P., Arthur, M. W., & Reppucci, N. D. (1993). The prevention and treatment of juvenile delinquency: A review of the research. *Clinical Psychology Review, 13,* 133–167.

Munro, G., & Adams, G. R. (1977). Ego identity formation in college students and working youth. *Developmental Psychology, 13,* 523–524.

Murray, A. D. (1985). Aversiveness is in the mind of the beholder. In B. M. Lester & C. F. Z. Boukydis (Eds.), *Infant crying* (pp. 217–239). New York: Plenum.

Murray, A. D., Dolby, R. M., Nation, R. L., & Thomas, D. B. (1981). Effects of epidural anesthesia on newborns and their mothers. *Child Development, 52,* 71–82.

Murrett-Wagstaff, S., & Moore, S. G. (1989). The Hmong in America: Infant behavior and rearing practices. In J. K. Nugent, B. M. Lester, & T. B. Brazelton (Eds.), *Biology, culture, and development* (Vol. 1, pp. 319–339). Norwood, NJ: Ablex.

Murry, V. M. (1992). Incidence of first pregnancy among black adolescent females over three decades. *Youth & Society, 23,* 478–506.

Mussen, P., & Eisenberg-Berg, N. (1977). *Roots of caring, sharing, and helping.* San Francisco: Freeman.

Nachtigall, R. D. (1993). Secrecy: An unresolved issue in the practice of donor insemination. *American Journal of Obstetrics and Gynecology, 168,* 1846–1851.

Nanez, J. (1987). Perception of impending collision in 3- to 6-week-old infants. *Infant Behavior and Development, 11,* 447–463.

Nash, J. E., & Persaud, T. V. N. (1988). Embryopathic risks of cigarette smoking. *Experimental Pathology, 33,* 65–73.

Nastasi, B. K., & Clements, D. H. (1991). Research on cooperative learning: Implications for practice. *School Psychology Review, 20,* 110–131.

Natapoff, J. (1978). Children's views of health: A developmental study. *American Journal of Public Health, 68,* 995–1000.
National Association for the Education of Young Children. (1991). *Accreditation criteria and procedures of the National Academy of Early Childhood Programs* (rev. ed.) Washington, DC: Author.
National Center for Education Statistics, U.S. Department of Education. (1994). *Digest of Education Statistics 1993.* Washington, DC: U.S. Government Printing Office.
National Center for Health Statistics. (1994). *Advance Report of Final Natality Statistics* (Vol. 42). Washington, DC: U.S. Government Printing Office.
National Institute on Drug Abuse, U.S. Department of Health and Human Services. (1990). *Drug abuse among youth: Findings from the 1988 national household survey on drug abuse.* Washington, DC: U.S. Government Printing Office.
National Institute on Drug Abuse, U.S. Department of Health and Human Services. (1991). *Drug use among American high school seniors, college students and young adults, 1975–1990* (Vol. 1). Washington, DC: U.S. Government Printing Office.
Neal, J. H. (1983). Children's understanding of their parents' divorces. In L. A. Kurdek (Ed.), *New directions for child development* (Vol. 19, pp. 3–14). San Francisco: Jossey-Bass.
Needleman, H. L., Gunnoe, C., Leviton, A., Reed, R., Peresie, H., Maher, C., & Barrett, B. S. (1979). Deficits in psychologic and classroom performance of children with elevated dentine lead levels. *New England Journal of Medicine, 300,* 689–695.
Needleman, H. L., Schell, A., Bellinger, D., Leviton, A., & Allred, E. N. (1990). The long-term effects of exposure to low doses of lead in childhood. *New England Journal of Medicine, 322,* 83–88.
Nelson, G. (1993). Risk, resistance, and self-esteem: A longitudinal study of elementary school-aged children from mother-custody and two-parent families. *Journal of Divorce and Remarriage, 19,* 99–119.
Nelson, J., & Aboud, F. E. (1985). The resolution of social conflict between friends. *Child Development, 56,* 1009–1017.
Nelson, K. (1973). Structure and strategy in learning to talk. *Monographs of the Society for Research in Child Development, 38*(1–2, Serial No. 149).
Nelson, K. (1981). Individual differences in language development: Implications for development and language. *Developmental Psychology, 17,* 170–187.
Nelson, K., & Gruendel, J. (1981). Generalized event representations: Basic building blocks of cognitive development. In M. Lamb & A. Brown (Eds.), *Advances in developmental psychology* (Vol. 1, pp. 131–158). Hillsdale, NJ: Erlbaum.
Nelson, K., & Ross, G. S. (1980). The generalities and specifics of long-term memory in infants and young children. In M. Perlmutter (Ed.), *New Directions in Child Development* (Vol. 10, pp. 87–101). San Francisco: Jossey-Bass.
Nelson, K. E., Dinninger, M., Bonvillian, J., Kaplan, B., & Baker, N. (1984). Maternal adjustments and non-adjustments as related to children's linguistic advances and language acquisition theories. In A. Pelligrini & T. Yawkey (Eds.), *The development of oral and written languages: Readings in developmental and applied linguistics* (pp. 31–56). Norwood, NJ: Ablex.
Nelson-Le Gall, S. A. (1985). Motive–outcome matching and outcome foreseeability: Effects on attribution of intentionality and moral judgments. *Developmental Psychology, 21,* 332–337.
Netley, C. T. (1986). Summary overview of behavioural development in individuals with neonatally identified X and Y aneuploidy. *Birth Defects, 22,* 293–306.
Newacheck, P. W., & Starfield, B. (1988). Morbidity and use of ambulatory care services among poor and nonpoor children. *American Journal of Public Health, 78,* 927–933.
Newborg, J., Stock, J. R., & Wnek, L. (1984). *Battelle Developmental Inventory.* Allen, TX: LINC Associates.
Newcomb, A. F., Bukowski, W. M., & Pattee, L. (1993). Children's peer relations: A meta-analytic review of popular, rejected, neglected, controversial, and average sociometric status. *Psychological Bulletin, 113,* 99–128.
Newcomb, M. D., & Bentler, P. M. (1988). Consequences of adolescent substance use on young adult health status and utilization of health services: A structural equation model over four years. *Social Science and Medicine, 24,* 71–82.
Newcomb, M. D., & Bentler, P. M. (1989). Substance use and abuse among children and teenagers. *American Psychologist, 44,* 242–248.
Newcombe, N., & Huttenlocher, J. (1992). Children's early ability to solve perspective-taking problems. *Developmental Psychology, 28,* 635–643.
Newman, L. S. (1990). Intentional versus unintentional memory in young children: Remembering versus playing. *Journal of Experimental Child Psychology, 50,* 243–258.
Newport, E. L., Gleitman, H., & Gleitman, L. R. (1977). Mother, I'd rather do it myself: Some effects and non-effects of maternal speech style. In C. A. Ferguson & C. E. Snow (Eds.), *Talking to children* (pp. 109–149). New York: Cambridge University Press.
Newson, J., & Newson, E. (1975). Intersubjectivity and the transmission of culture: On the social origins of symbolic functioning. *Bulletin of the British Psychological Society, 28,* 437–446.
Nicholls, A. L., & Kennedy, J. M. (1992). Drawing development: From similarity of features to direction. *Child Development, 63,* 227–241.
Nichols, M. R. (1993). Paternal perspectives of the childbirth experience. *Maternal–Child Nursing Journal, 21,* 99–108.
Nidorf, J. F. (1985). Mental health and refugee youths: A model for diagnostic training. In T. C. Owen (Ed.), *Southeast Asian mental health: Treatment, prevention, services, training, and research* (pp. 391–427). Washington, DC: National Institute of Mental Health.
NIH/CEPH Collaborative Mapping Group. (1992). A comprehensive genetic linkage map of the human genome. *Science, 258,* 67–86.
Nilsson, L., & Hamberger, L. (1990). *A child is born.* New York: Delacorte.
Norbeck, J. S., & Tilden, V. P. (1983). Life stress, social support, and emotional disequilibrium in complications of pregnancy: A prospective, multivariate study. *Journal of Health and Social Behavior, 24,* 30–46.
Nottelmann, E. D. (1987). Competence and self-esteem during transition from childhood to adolescence. *Developmental Psychology, 23,* 441–450.
Nottelmann, E. D., Inoff-Germain, G., Susman, E. J., & Chrousos, G. P. (1990). Hormones and behavior at puberty. In J. Bancroft & J. M. Reinisch (Eds.), *Adolescence and puberty* (pp. 88–123). New York: Oxford University Press.
Notzon, F. C. (1990). International differences in the use of obstetric interventions. *Journal of the American Medical Association, 263,* 3286–3291.
Nowakowski, R. S. (1987). Basic concepts of CNS development. *Child Development, 58,* 568–595.
Nucci, L., & Turiel, E. (1993). God's word, religious rules, and their relation to Christian and Jewish children's concepts of morality. *Child Development, 64,* 1475–1491.
Nuckolls, K. B., Cassel, J., & Kaplan, B. H. (1972). Psychosocial assets, life crisis, and the prognosis of pregnancy. *American Journal of Epidemiology, 95,* 431–441.
O'Reilly, A. W., & Bornstein, M. H. (1993). Caregiver–child interaction in play. In M. H. Bornstein & A. W. O'Reilly (Eds.), *New directions for child development* (No. 59, pp. 55–66). San Francisco: Jossey-Bass.
Oakes, J., Gamoran, A., & Page, R. N. (1992). Curriculum differentiation: Opportunities, outcomes, and meanings. In P. W. Jackson (Ed.), *Handbook of research on curriculum* (pp. 570–608). New York: Macmillan.
Oakes, L. M., Madole, K. L., & Cohen, L. B. (1991). Infants' object examining: Habituation and categorization. *Cognitive Development, 6,* 377–392.
Oates, R. K. (1984). Similarities and differences between nonorganic failure to thrive and deprivation dwarfism. *Child Abuse and Neglect, 8,* 438–445.
Oates, R. K., Peacock, A., & Forrest, D. (1985). Long-term effects of nonorganic failure to thrive. *Pediatrics, 75,* 36–40.
Obler, L. K. (1989). Language beyond childhood. In J. Berko Gleason (Ed.), *The development of language* (pp. 275–301). Columbus, OH: Merrill.
Offer, D. (1988). *The teenage world: Adolescents' self-image in ten countries.* New York: Plenum.

Office of Educational Research and Improvement. (1993). *Youth indicators 1993: Trends in the well-being of American youth.* Washington, DC: U.S. Government Printing Office.

Ogbu, J. U. (1985). A cultural ecology of competence among inner-city blacks. In M. B. Spencer, G. K. Brookins, & W. R. Allen (Eds.), *Beginnings: The social and affective development of black children* (pp. 45–66). Hillsdale, NJ: Erlbaum.

Ogbu, J. U. (1988). Black education: A cultural-ecological perspective. In H. P. McAdoo (ed.), *Black families* (pp. 169–186). Beverly Hills, CA: Sage.

Okagaki, L., & Sternberg, R. J. (1993). Parental beliefs and children's school performance. *Child Development, 64,* 36–56.

Ollendick, T. H., Weist, M. D., Borden, M. C., & Greene, R. W. (1992). Sociometric status and academic, behavioral, and psychological adjustment: A five-year longitudinal study. *Journal of Consulting and Clinical Psychology, 60,* 80–87.

Oller, D. K., & Eilers, R. E. (1988). The role of audition in infant babbling. *Child Development, 59,* 441–449.

Omer, H., & Everly, G. S. (1988). Psychological factors in preterm labor: Critical review and theoretical synthesis. *American Journal of Psychiatry, 145,* 1507–1513.

Opie, I., & Opie, P. (1969). *Children's games in street and playground.* Oxford: Clarendon Press.

Ornstein, P. A., Naus, M. J., & Liberty, C. (1975). Rehearsal and organizational processes in children's memory. *Child Development, 46,* 818–830.

Osherson, D. N., & Markman, E. M. (1975). Language and the ability to evaluate contradictions and tautologies. *Cognition, 2,* 213–226.

Oster, H., Hegley, D., & Nagel, L. (1992). Adult judgments and fine-grained analysis of infant facial expressions: Testing the validity of a priori coding formulas. *Developmental Psychology, 28,* 1115–1131.

Otaki, M., Durrett, M., Richards, P., Nyquist, L., & Pennebaker, J. (1986). Maternal and infant behavior in Japan and America: A partial replication. *Journal of Cross-Cultural Psychology, 17,* 251–268.

Owen, M. T., & Cox, M. J. (1988). Maternal employment and the transition to parenthood. In A. E. Gottfried & A. W. Gottfried (Eds.), Maternal employment and children's development: *Longitudinal research* (pp. 85–119). New York: Plenum.

Owens, T. (1982). Experience-based career education: Summary and implications of research and evaluation findings. *Child and Youth Services Journal, 4,* 77–91.

Padgham, J. J., & Blyth, D. A. (1990). Dating during adolescence. In R. M. Lerner, A. C. Petersen, & J. Brooks-Gunn (Eds.), *The encyclopedia of adolescence* (Vol. 1, pp. 196–198). New York: Garland.

Padilla, M. L., & Landreth, G. L. (1989). Latchkey children: A review of the literature. *Child Welfare, 68,* 445–454.

Page, D. C., Mosher, R., Simpson, E. M., Fisher, E. M. C., Mardon, G., Pollack, J., McGillivray, B., de la Chapelle, A., & Brown, L. G. (1987). The sex-determining region of the human Y chromosome encodes a finger protein. *Cell, 51,* 1091–1104.

Paget, K. F., & Kritt, D. (1986). The development of the conceptual organization of self. *Journal of Genetic Psychology, 146,* 333–341.

Paikoff, R. L., & Brooks-Gunn, J. (1991). Do parent–child relationships change during puberty? *Psychological Bulletin, 110,* 47–66.

Palkovitz, R., & Copes, M. (1988). Changes in attitudes, beliefs and expectations associated with the transition to parenthood. *Marriage and Family Review, 6,* 183–199.

Pallikkathayil, L., & Flood, M. (1991). Adolescent suicide: Prevention, intervention, and postvention. *Nursing Clinics of North America, 26,* 623–634.

Papini, D. R., Micka, J. C., & Barnett, J. K. (1989). Perceptions of intrapsychic and extrapsychic functioning as bases of adolescent ego identity statuses. *Journal of Adolescent Research, 4,* 462–482.

Parekh, U. C., Pherwani, A., Udani, P. M., & Mukherjee, S. (1970). Brain weight and head circumference in fetus, infant and children of different nutritional and socio-economic groups. *Indian Pediatrics, 7,* 347–358.

Paris, S. G., & Newman, R. S. (1990). Developmental aspects of self-regulated learning. *Educational Psychologist, 25,* 87–102.

Parke, R. D. (1977). Punishment in children: Effects, side effects, and alternative control strategies. In H. Hom, Jr., & A. Robinson (Eds.), *Early childhood education: A psychological perspective* (pp. 71–97). New York: Academic Press.

Parke, R. D., & Collmer, C. W. (1975). Child abuse: An interdisciplinary analysis. In E. M. Hetherington (Ed.), *Review of child development research* (Vol. 5, pp. 264–283). Chicago: University of Chicago Press.

Parke, R. D., & Slaby, R. G. (1983). The development of aggression. In E. M. Hetherington (Ed.), *Handbook of child psychology: Vol. 4. Socialization, personality, and social development* (Vol. 4, pp. 547–641). New York: Wiley.

Parke, R. D., & Tinsley, B. R. (1981). The father's role in infancy: Determinants of involvement in caregiving and play. In M. E. Lamb (Ed.), *The role of the father in child development* (pp. 429–458). New York: Wiley.

Parke, R. D., & Walters, R. H. (1967). Some factors determining the efficacy of punishment for inducing response inhibition. *Monographs of the Society for Research in Child Development, 32*(1, Serial No. 109).

Parker, J. G., & Asher, S. R. (1987). Peer relations and later personal adjustment: Are low-accepted children at risk? *Psychological Bulletin, 102,* 357–389.

Parkhurst, J. T., & Asher, S. R. (1992). Peer relations and later personal adjustment: Are low-accepted children at risk? *Psychological Bulletin, 102,* 357–389.

Parmelee, A., Wenner, W., Akiyama, Y., Stern, E., & Flescher, J. (1967). Electroencephalography and brain maturation. In A. Minkowski (Ed.), *Symposium on regional development of the brain in early life.* Philadelphia: Davis.

Parmelee, A. H., Jr. (1986). Children's illnesses: Their beneficial effects on behavioral development. *Child Development, 57,* 1–10.

Parrish, L. H. (1991). Community resources and dropout prevention. In L. L. West (Ed.), *Effective strategies for dropout prevention of at-risk youth* (pp. 217–232). Gaithersburg, MD: Aspen.

Parsons, J. E. (1982). Biology, experience, and sex-dimorphic behaviors. In W. R. Gove & G. R. Carpenter (Eds.), *The fundamental connection between nature and nurture* (pp. 137–170). Lexington, MA: Lexington Books.

Parsons, J. E., Adler, T. F., & Kaczala, C. M. (1982). Socialization of achievement attitudes and beliefs: Parental influences. *Child Development, 53,* 310–321.

Parten, M. (1932). Social participation among preschool children. *Journal of Abnormal and Social Psychology, 27,* 243–269.

Passman, R. H. (1976). Arousal reducing properties of attachment objects: Testing the functional limits of the security blanket relative to the mother. *Developmental Psychology, 12,* 468–469.

Passman, R. H. (1987). Attachment to inanimate objects: Are children who have security blankets insecure? *Journal of Consulting and Clinical Psychology, 55,* 825–830.

Patterson, G. R. (1981). Mothers: the unacknowledged victims. *Monographs of the Society for Research in Child Development, 45*(5, Serial No. 186).

Patterson, G. R. (1982). *Coercive family processes.* Eugene, OR: Castilia Press.

Patterson, G. R., DeBaryshe, B. D., & Ramsey, E. (1989). A developmental perspective on antisocial behavior. *American Psychologist, 44,* 329–335.

Patteson, D. M., & Barnard, K. E. (1990). Parenting of low birth weight infants: A review of issues and interventions. *Infant Mental Health Journal, 11,* 37–56.

Paulhus, D., & Shaffer, D. R. (1981). Sex differences in the impact of number of older and number of younger siblings on scholastic aptitude. *Social Psychology Quarterly, 44,* 363–368.

Pearson, J. L., Hunter, A. G. Ensminger, M. E., & Kellam, S. G. (1990). Black grandmothers in multigenerational households: Diversity in family structure and parenting involvement in the Woodlawn community. *Child Development, 61,* 434–442.

Peckham, C. S., & Logan, S. (1993). Screening for toxoplasmosis during pregnancy. *Archives of Disease in Childhood, 68,* 3–5.

Pedlow, R., Sanson, A., Prior, M., & Oberklaid, F. (1993). Stability of maternally reported temperament from infancy to 8 years. *Developmental Psychology, 29,* 998–1007.

Pelchat, M. L., & Pliner, P. (1986). Antecedents and correlates of feeding problems in young children. *Journal of Nutrition Education, 18,* 23–29.

Pellegrini, A. D. (1988). Elementary-school children's rough-and-tumble play and social competence. *Developmental Psychology, 24,* 802–806.

Pennington, B. F., Bender, B., Puck, M., Salbenblatt, J., & Robinson, A. (1982). Learning disabilities in children with sex chromosome abnormalities. *Child Development, 53,* 1182–1192.

Pennington, B. F., & Smith, S. D. (1988). Genetic influences on learning disabilities: An update. *Journal of Consulting and Clinical Psychology, 56,* 817–823.

Pentz, M. A. (1994). Primary prevention of adolescent drug abuse. In C. B. Fisher & R. M. Lerner (Eds.), *Applied developmental psychology* (pp. 435–474). New York: McGraw-Hill.

Pepler, D. J., & Ross, H. S. (1981). The effects of play on convergent and divergent problem solving. *Child Development, 52,* 1202–1210.

Perfetti, C. A. (1988). Verbal efficiency in reading ability. In M. Daneman, G. E. MacKinnon, & T. G. Waller (Eds.), *Reading research: Advances in theory and practice* (Vol. 6, pp. 109–143). San Diego, CA: Academic Press.

Perlmutter, M. (1984). Continuities and discontinuities in early human memory: Paradigms, processes, and performances. In R. V. Kail, Jr., & N. R. Spear (Eds.), *Comparative perspectives on the development of memory* (pp. 253–287). Hillsdale, NJ: Erlbaum.

Perner, J. (1991). *Understanding the representational mind.* Cambridge, MA: Bradford/MIT Press.

Perrin, E. C., & Gerrity, P. S. (1981). There's a demon in your belly: Children's understanding of illness. *Pediatrics, 67,* 841–849.

Perry, D. G., Perry, L. C., & Weiss, R. J. (1989). Sex differences in the consequences that children anticipate for aggression. *Developmental Psychology, 25,* 312–319.

Peshkin, A. (1978). *Growing up American: Schooling and the survival of the community.* Chicago: University of Chicago Press.

Petersen, A. (1985). Pubertal development as a cause of disturbance: Myths, realities, and unanswered questions. *Genetic, Social, and General Psychology Monographs, 111,* 205–232.

Petersen, A. C., Sarigiani, P. A., & Kennedy, R. E. (1991). Adolescent depression: Why more girls? *Journal of Youth and Adolescence, 20,* 247–271.

Petitto, L. A., & Marentette, P. F. (1991). Babbling in the manual mode: Evidence for the ontogeny of language. *Science, 251,* 1493–1496.

Pettit, G. S., Bakshi, A., Dodge, K. A., & Coie, J. D. (1990). The emergence of social dominance in young boys' play groups: Developmental differences and behavioral correlates. *Developmental Psychology, 26,* 1017–1025.

Pezzullo, T. R., Thorsen, E. E., & Madaus, G. F. (1972). The heritability of Jensen's Level I and II and divergent thinking. *American Educational Research Journal, 9,* 539–546.

Phelps, K. E., & Woolley, J. D. (1994). The form and function of young children's magical beliefs. *Developmental Psychology, 30,* 385–394.

Philipps, C., & Johnson, N. E. (1977). The impact of quality of diet and other factors on birth weight of infants. *American Journal of Clinical Nutrition, 30,* 215–225.

Phillips, D. A. (1987). Socialization of perceived academic competence among highly competent children. *Child Development, 58,* 1308–1320.

Phillips, D. A., & Zimmerman, M. (1990). The developmental course of perceived competence and incompetence among competent children. In R. Sternberg, & J. Kolligian (Eds.), *Competence considered* (pp. 41–66). New Haven, CT: Yale University Press.

Phillips, D. A., McCartney, K., & Scarr, S. (1987). Child-care quality and children's social development. *Developmental Psychology, 23,* 537–543.

Phillips, D. A., Voran, M., Kisker, E., Howes, C., & Whitebook, M. (1994). Child care for children in poverty: Opportunity or inequity? *Child Development, 65,* 472–492.

Phillips, O. P., & Elias, S. (1993). Prenatal genetic counseling issues in women of advanced reproductive age. *Journal of Women's Health, 2,* 1–5.

Phinney, J., & Alipuria, L. (1990). Ethnic identity in college students from four ethnic groups. *Journal of Adolescence, 13,* 171–183.

Phinney, J. S. (1989). Stages of ethnic identity development in minority group adolescents. *Journal of Early Adolescence, 9,* 34–49.

Phinney, J. S. (1993). Multiple group identities: Differentiation, conflict, and integration. In J. Kroger (Ed.), *Discussions on ego identity* (pp. 47–73). Hillsdale, NJ: Erlbaum.

Piaget, J. (1926). *The language and thought of the child.* New York: Harcourt, Brace & World. (Original work published 1923)

Piaget, J. (1929). *The child's conception of physical causality.* New York: Harcourt, Brace & World. (Original work published 1926)

Piaget, J. (1930). The child's conception of the world. New York: Harcourt, Brace, & World. (Original work published 1926)

Piaget, J. (1950). *The psychology of intelligence.* New York: International Universities Press.

Piaget, J. (1951). *Play, dreams, and imitation in childhood.* New York: Norton. (Original work published 1945)

Piaget, J. (1952). *The origins of intelligence in children.* New York: International Universities Press. (Original work published 1936)

Piaget, J. (1965). *The moral judgment of the child.* New York: Free Press. (Original work published 1932)

Piaget, J. (1967). *Six psychological studies.* New York: Vintage.

Piaget, J. (1970). *The child's conception of movement and speed.* London: Routledge & Kegan Paul. (Original work published 1946)

Piaget, J. (1971). *Biology and knowledge.* Chicago: University of Chicago Press.

Piaget, J. (1978). *Success and understanding.* Cambridge, MA: Harvard University Press.

Piaget, J. (1985). *The equilibration of cognitive structures: The central problem of intellectual development.* Chicago: University of Chicago Press.

Piaget, J., & Inhelder, B. (1956). *The child's conception of space.* London: Routledge & Kegan Paul. (Original work published 1948)

Piaget, J., Inhelder, B., & Szeminska, A. (1960). *The child's conception of geometry.* New York: Basic Books. (Original work published 1948)

Pianta, R., Egeland, B., & Erickson, M. F. (1989). The antecedents of maltreatment: Results of the Mother–Child Interaction Research Project. In D. Cicchetti & V. Carlson (Eds.), *Child maltreatment* (pp. 203–253). New York: Cambridge University Press.

Picariello, M. L., Greenberg, D. N., & Pillemer, D. B. (1990). Children's sex-related stereotyping of colors. *Child Development, 61,* 1453–1460.

Pick, A. D., & Frankel, G. W. (1974). A developmental study of strategies of visual selectivity. *Child Development, 45,* 1162–1165.

Pick, H. L., Jr. (1989). Motor development: The control of action. *Developmental Psychology, 25,* 867–870.

Pickens, J., & Field, T. M. (1993). Facial expressivity in infants of depressed mothers. *Developmental Psychology, 29,* 986–988.

Pierce, R., & Pierce, L. H. (1985). The sexually abused child: A comparison of male and female victims. *Child Abuse and Neglect, 9,* 191–199.

Pilkington, C. L., & Piersel, W. C. (1991). School phobia: A critical analysis of the separation anxiety theory and an alternative conceptualization. *Psychology in the Schools, 28,* 290–303.

Pillow, B. H. (1988). The development of children's beliefs about the mental world. *Merrill-Palmer Quarterly, 34,* 1–32.

Pinel, J. P. J. (1993). *Biopsychology* (2nd ed.) Boston: Allyn and Bacon.

Pinker, S., Lebeaux, D. S., & Frost, L. A. (1987). Productivity and constraints in the acquisition of the passive. *Cognition, 26,* 195–267.

Pipes, P. L. (1989). *Nutrition in infancy and childhood* (4th ed.). St. Louis: Mosby.

Pless, I. B., & Arsenault, L. (1987). The role of health education in the prevention of injuries to children. *Journal of Social Issues, 43,* 87–104.

Plomin, R. (1989). Environment and genes: Determinants of behavior. *American Psychologist, 44,* 105–111.

Plomin, R. (1994). *Genetics and experience: The interplay between nature and nurture in development.* Newbury Park, CA: Sage.

Plomin, R., Chipuer, H. M., & Loehlin, J. C. (1990). Behavior genetics and personality. In L. A. Pervin (Ed.), *Handbook of personality theory and research* (pp. 225–243). New York: Guilford.

Plomin, R., Reiss, D., Hetherington, E. M., & Howe, G. W. (1994). Nature and nurture: Genetic contributions to measures of the family environment. *Developmental Psychology, 30,* 32–43.

Plumert, J. M., Pick, H. L., Jr., Marks, R. A., Kintsch, A. S., & Wegesin, D. (1994).

Locating objects and communicating about locations: Organizational differences in children's searching and direction-giving. *Developmental Psychology, 30,* 443–453.

Podrouzek, W., & Furrow, D. (1988). Preschoolers' use of eye contact while speaking: The influence of sex, age, and conversational partner. *Journal of Psycholinguistic Research, 17,* 89–93.

Poindron, P., & Le Neindre, P. (1980). Endocrine and sensory regulation of maternal behavior in the ewe. In J. S. Rosenblatt , R. A. Hinde, C. Beer, & M. Busnel (Eds.), *Advances in the study of behavior* (pp. 76–119). New York: Academic Press.

Polansky, N. A., Gaudin, J. M., Ammons, P. W., & Davis, K. B. (1985). The psychological ecology of the neglectful mother. *Child Abuse & Neglect, 9,* 265–275.

Pollitt, E., Gorman, K. S., Engle, P. L., Martorell, R., & Rivera, J. (1993). Early supplementary feeding and cognition. *Monographs of the Society for Research in Child Development, 58*(7, Serial No. 235).

Pollock, L. (1987). *A lasting relationship: Parents and children over three centuries.* Hanover, NH: University Press of New England.

Polsky, H. W., & Fast, J. (1993). Boot camps, juvenile offenders, and culture shock. *Child & Youth Care Forum, 22,* 403–415.

Porter, F. L., Porges, S. W., & Marshall, R. E. (1988). Newborn pain cries and vagal tone: Parallel changes in response to circumcision. *Child Development, 59,* 495–505.

Porter, R. H., Makin, J. W., Davis, L. B., & Christensen, K. M. (1992). An assessment of the salient olfactory environment of formula-fed infants. *Physiology & Behavior, 50,* 907–911.

Posner, J. K., & Vandell, D. L. (1994). Low-income children's after-school care: Are there beneficial effects of after-school programs? *Child Development, 64,* 440–456.

Post, G. B., & Kemper, H. C. G. (1993). Nutrient intake and biological maturation during adolescence. The Amsterdam growth and health longitudinal study. *European Journal of Clinical Nutrition, 47,* 400–408.

Poulin-Dubois, D., Serbin, L. A., Kenyon, B., & Derbyshire, A. (1994). Infants' intermodal knowledge about gender. *Developmental Psychology, 30,* 436–442.

Powell, B., & Steelman, L. C. (1993). The educational benefits of being spaced out: Sibship density and educational progress. *American Sociological Review, 58,* 367–381.

Power, F. C., Higgins, A., & Kohlberg, L. (1989). *Lawrence Kohlberg's approach to moral education.* New York: Columbia University Press.

Powers, S. I., Hauser, S. T., & Kilner, L. A. (1989). Adolescent mental health. *American Psychologist, 44,* 200–208.

Prechtl, H. F. R. (1958). Problems of behavioral studies in the newborn infant. In D. S. Lehrmann, R. A. Hinde, & E. Shaw (Eds.), *Advances in the study of behavior* (Vol. 1, pp. 75–98). New York: Academic Press.

Prechtl, H. F. R., & Beintema, D. (1965). *The neurological examination of the full-term newborn infant.* London: Heinemann Medical.

Prentice, A., & Lind, T. (1987). Fetal heart rate monitoring during labor—too frequent intervention, too little benefit? *Lancet, 2,* 1375–1377.

Pressley, M. (1979). Increasing children's self-control through cognitive interventions. *Review of Educational Research, 49,* 319–370.

Pressley, M. (1994). State-of-the-science primary-grades reading instruction or whole language? *Educational Psychologist, 29,* 211–215.

Pressley, M., & Ghatala, E. S. (1990). Self-regulated learning: Monitoring learning from text. *Educational Psychologist, 25,* 19–34.

Previc, F. H. (1991). A general theory concerning the prenatal origins of cerebral lateralization. *Psychological Review, 98,* 299–334.

Preyer, W. (1888). *The mind of the child* (2 vols.). New York: Appleton. (Original work published 1882)

Pryor, J. B., Reeder, G. D., Vinacco, R. J., & Kott, T. L. (1989). The instrumental and symbolic functions of attitudes toward persons with AIDS. *Journal of Applied Social Psychology, 19,* 377–404.

Qazi, Q. H., Sheikh, T. M., Fikrig, S., & Menikoff, H. (1988). Lack of evidence for craniofacial dysmorphism in perinatal human immunodeficiency virus infection. *Journal of Pediatrics, 11,* 7–11.

Quadrel, M. J., Fischhoff, B., & Davis, W. (1993). Adolescent (in)vulnerability. *American Psychologist, 48,* 102–116.

Quay, H. C. (1987). Institutional treatment. In H. C. Quay (Ed.), *Handbook of juvenile delinquency* (pp. 244–265). New York: Wiley.

Quiggle, N. L., Garber, J., Panak, W. F., & Dodge, K. A. (1992). Social information processing in aggressive and depressed children. *Child Development, 63,* 1305–1320.

Quintero, R. A., Puder, K. S., & Cotton, D. B. (1993). Embryoscopy and fetoscopy. *Obstetrics and Gynecology Clinics of North America, 20,* 563–581.

Rabiner, D. L., & Coie, J. D. (1989). Effect of expectancy inductions on rejected children's acceptance by unfamiliar peers. *Developmental Psychology, 25,* 450–457.

Rabiner, D. L., Keane, S. P., & MacKinnon-Lewis, C. (1993). Children's beliefs about familiar and unfamiliar peers in relation to their sociometric status. *Developmental Psychology, 29,* 236–243.

Radford, A. (1988). Small children's small clauses. *Transactions of the Philological Society, 86,* 1–46.

Radke-Yarrow, M., Cummings, E. M., Kuczynski, I., & Chapman, M. (1985). Patterns of attachment in two- and three-year-olds in normal families with parental depression. *Child Development, 56,* 884–893.

Radke-Yarrow, M., & Zahn-Waxler, C. (1984). Roots, motives, and patterns in children's prosocial behavior. In J. Reykowski, J. Karylowski, D. Bar-Tel, & E. Staub (Eds.), *The development and maintenance of prosocial behaviors: International perspectives on positive morality* (pp. 81–99). New York: Plenum.

Radziszewska, B., & Rogoff, B. (1988). Influence of adult and peer collaboration on the development of children's planning skills. *Developmental Psychology, 24,* 840–848.

Rafferty, Y., & Shinn, M. (1991). The impact of homelessness on children. *American Psychologist, 46,* 1170–1179.

Ragozin, A. S., Basham, R. B., Crnic, K. A., Greenberg, M. T., & Robinson, N. M. (1982). Effects of maternal age on parenting role. *Developmental Psychology, 18,* 627–634.

Räikkönen, K., Keltikangas-Järvinen, L. & Pietikäinen, M. (1991). Type A behavior and its determinants in children, adolescents and young adults with and without parental coronary heart disease: A case-control study. *Journal of Psychosomatic Research, 35,* 273–280.

Ramey, C. T., & Campbell, F. A. (1984). Preventive education for high-risk children: Cognitive consequences of the Carolina Abecedarian Project. *American Journal of Mental Deficiency, 88,* 515–523.

Ramey, C. T., & Ramey, S. L. (1990). Intensive educational intervention for children of poverty. *Intelligence, 14,* 1–9.

Ramsay, M., Gisel, E. G., & Boutry, M. (1993). Non-organic failure to thrive: Growth failure secondary to feeding-skills disorder. *Developmental Medicine and Child Neurology, 35,* 285–297.

Rappaport, L. (1993). The treatment of nocturnal enuresis—where are we now? *Pediatrics, 92,* 465–466.

Ratner, N., & Bruner, J. S. (1978). Social exchange and the acquisition of language. *Journal of Child Language, 5,* 391–402.

Rayner, K., & Pollatsek, A. (1989). *The psychology of reading.* Englewood Cliffs, NJ: Prentice Hall.

Read, C. R. (1991). Achievement and career choices: Comparisons of males and females. *Roeper Review, 13,* 188–193.

Read, M. (1968). *Children of their fathers: Growing up among the Ngoni of Malawi.* New York: Holt, Rinehart & Winston.

Redd, W. H., Morris, E. K., & Martin, J. A. (1975). Effects of positive and negative adult–child interaction on children's social preferences. *Journal of Experimental Child Psychology, 19,* 153–164.

Redl, F. (1966). *When we deal with children.* New York: Free Press.

Rees, M. (1993). Menarche when and why? *Lancet, 342,* 1375–1376.

Reich, P. A. (1986). *Language development.* Englewood Cliffs, NJ: Prentice Hall.

Reich, T., Van Eerdewegh, P., Riche, J., Jullaney, J., Endicott, J., & Klerman, G. L. (1987). The familial transmission of primary major depressive disorder. *Archives of General Psychology, 41,* 441–447.

Reik, W. (1992). Imprinting in leukaemia. *Nature, 359,* 362–363.

Reis, S. M. (1989). Reflections on policy affecting the education of gifted and talented students: Past and future perspectives. *American Psychologist, 44,* 399–408.

Reis, S. M. (1991). The need for clarification in

research designed to examine gender differences in achievement and accomplishment. *Roeper Review, 13,* 193–198.

Reiser, J., Yonas, A., & Wikner, K. (1976). Radial localization of odors by human neonates. *Child Development, 47,* 856–859.

Reisman, J. E. (1987). Touch, motion, and proprioception. In P. Salapatek & L. Cohen (Eds.), *Handbook of infant perception: Vol. 1. From sensation to perception* (pp. 265–303). Orlando, FL: Academic Press.

Reissland, N. (1988). Neonatal imitation in the first hour of life: Observations in rural Nepal. *Developmental Psychology, 24,* 464–469.

Reschly, D. J. (1981). Psychological testing in educational classification and placement. *American Psychologist, 36,* 1094–1102.

Resnick, L. B. (1989). Developing mathematical knowledge. *American Psychologist, 44,* 162–169.

Resnick, R. (1988). Introduction to Postterm Gestation: A symposium. *Journal of Reproductive Medicine, 33,* 249–251.

Ressler, E. M. (1993). *Children in war.* New York: United Nations Children's Fund.

Rest, J. R. (1979). *Development in judging moral issues.* Minneapolis: University of Minnesota Press.

Rest, J. R. (1983). Morality. In J. H. Flavell & E. M. Markman (Eds.), *Handbook of child psychology: Vol. 3. Cognitive development* (4th ed., pp. 556–629). New York: Wiley.

Rest, J. R., & Narvaez, D. (1991). The college experience and moral development. In W. M. Kurtines & J. L. Gewirtz (Eds.), *Handbook of moral behavior and development* (Vol. 2, pp. 229–245). Hillsdale, NJ: Erlbaum.

Reznick, J. S., & Goldfield, B. A. (1992). Rapid change in lexical development in comprehension and production. *Developmental Psychology, 28,* 406–413.

Ricciardelli, L. A. (1992). Bilingualism and cognitive development: Relation to threshold theory. *Journal of Psycholinguistic Research, 21,* 301–316.

Ricco, R. B. (1989). Operational thought and the acquisition of taxonomic relations involving figurative dissimilarity. *Developmental Psychology, 25,* 996–1003.

Rice, F. P. (1993). *The adolescent: Development, relationships, and culture* (7th ed.). Boston: Allyn and Bacon.

Rice, M. L., Huston, A. C., Truglio, R., & Wright, J. (1990). Words from "Sesame Street": Learning vocabulary while viewing. *Developmental Psychology, 26,* 421–428.

Richards, D. D., & Siegler, R. S. (1986). Children's understandings of the attributes of life. *Journal of Experimental Child Psychology, 42,* 1–22.

Richards, M. H., & Duckett, E. (1994). The relationship of maternal employment to early adolescent daily experience with and without parents. *Child Development, 65,* 225–236.

Richardson, P. (1983). Women's perceptions of change in relationships shared with their husbands during pregnancy. *Maternal-Child Nursing Journal, 12,* 1–19.

Richardson, S. A., Koller, H., & Katz, M. (1986). Factors leading to differences in the school performance of boys and girls. *Developmental and Behavioral Pediatrics, 7,* 49–55.

Richgels, D. J., McGee, L. M., & Slaton, E. A. (1989). Teaching expository text structure in reading and writing. In K. D. Muth (Ed.), *Children's comprehension of text* (pp. 167–184). Newark, DE: International Reading Association.

Richman, A. L., Miller, P. M., & LeVine, R. A. (1992). Cultural and educational variations in maternal responsiveness. *Developmental Psychology, 28,* 614–621.

Richmond, J., & Ayoub, C. C. (1993). Evolution of early intervention philosophy. In D. M. Bryant & M. A. Graham (Eds.), *Implementing early intervention* (pp. 1–17). New York: Guilford.

Riese, M. L. (1987). Temperament stability between the neonatal period and 24 months. *Developmental Psychology, 23,* 216–222.

Rivara, F. P., & Barber, M. (1985). Demographic analysis of childhood pedestrian injuries. *Pediatrics, 76,* 375–381.

Roberton, M. A. (1984). Changing motor patterns during childhood. In J. R. Thomas (Ed.), *Motor development during childhood and adolescence* (pp. 48–90). Minneapolis, MN: Burgess.

Roberton, M. A., & Halverson, L. E. (1988). The development of locomotor coordination: Longitudinal change and invariance. *Journal of Motor Behavior, 20,* 197–241.

Roberts, M. C., Alexander, K., & Knapp, L. G. (1990). Motivating children to use safety belts: A program combining rewards and "flash for life." *Journal of Community Psychology, 18,* 110–119.

Roberts, M. C., Elkins, P. D., & Royal, G. P. (1984). Psychological applications to the prevention of accidents and injuries. In M. C. Roberts & L. Peterson (Eds.), *Prevention of problems in childhood: Psychological research and applications* (pp. 173–199). New York: Wiley.

Roberts, M. C., & Fanurik, D. (1986). Rewarding elementary schoolchildren for their use of safety belts. *Health Psychology, 5,* 185–196.

Roberts, M. C., Fanurik, D., & Wilson, D. R. (1988). A community program to reward children's use of seat belts. *American Journal of Community Psychology, 16,* 395–407.

Roberts, R. J., Jr., & Aman, C. J. (1993). Developmental differences in giving directions: Spatial frames of reference and mental rotation. *Child Development, 64,* 1258–1270.

Robinson, E. H., III, Robinson, S. L., & Whetsell, M. V. (1988). A study of children's fears. *Journal of Humanistic Education and Development, 27,* 84–95.

Robinson, E. J. (1981). The child's understanding of inadequate messages and communication failure: A problem of ignorance or egocentrism? In W. P. Dickson (Ed.), *Children's oral communication skills* (pp. 167–188). New York: Academic Press.

Robinson, E. J., & Mitchell, P. (1994). Young children's false-belief reasoning: Interpretation of messages is not easier than the classic task. *Developmental Psychology, 30,* 67–72.

Robinson, J. L., Kagan, J., Reznick, J. S., & Corley, R. (1992). The heritability of inhibited and uninhibited behavior: A twin study. *Developmental Psychology, 28,* 1030–1037.

Robinson, J. P. (1988). Who's doing the housework? *American Demographics, 10,* 24–63.

Rochat, P. (1989). Object manipulation and exploration in 2- to 5-month-old infants. *Developmental Psychology, 25,* 871–884.

Roche, A. F. (1979). Secular trends in stature, weight, and maturation. In A. F. Roche (Ed.), Secular trends in human growth, maturation, and development. *Monographs of the Society for Research in Child Development, 44*(3–4, Serial No. 179).

Roche, A. F. (1981). The adipocyte-number hypothesis. *Child Development, 52,* 31–43.

Roderick, M. (1994). Grade retention and school dropout: Investigating the association. *American Educational Research Journal, 31,* 729–759.

Roffwarg, H. P., Muzio, J. N., & Dement, W. C. (1966). Ontogenetic development of the human sleep–dream cycle. *Science, 152,* 604–619.

Rogoff, B. (1986). The development of strategic use of context in spatial memory. In M. Perlmutter (Ed.), *Perspectives on intellectual development* (pp. 107–123). Hillsdale, NJ: Erlbaum.

Rogoff, B. (1990). *Apprenticeship in thinking.* New York: Oxford University Press.

Rogoff, B., & Morelli, G. (1989). Culture and American children: Section introduction. *American Psychologist, 44,* 341–342.

Rogoff, B., Malkin, C., & Gilbride, K. (1984). Interaction with babies as guidance in development. In B. Rogoff & J. V. Wertsch (Eds.), *New directions for child development* (No. 23, pp. 31–44). San Francisco: Jossey-Bass.

Rogoff, B., Mosier, C., Mistry, J., & Göncü, A. (1993). Toddlers' guided participation with their caregivers in cultural activity. In E. A. Forman, N. Minick, & C. A. Stone (Eds.), *Contexts for learning* (pp. 230–253). New York: Oxford University Press.

Rogoff, B., Sellers, M., Pirrotta, S., Fox, N., & White, S. (1975). Age of assignment of roles and responsibilities in children: A cross-cultural survey. *Human Development, 18,* 353–369.

Rohlen, T. P. (1983). *Japan's high schools.* Berkeley: University of California Press.

Rohner, R. P., & Rohner, E. C. (1981). Parental acceptance–rejection and parental control: Cross-cultural codes. *Ethnology, 20,* 245–260.

Romaine, S. (1984). *The language of children and adolescents: The acquisition of communicative competence.* Oxford, England: Blackwell.

Roopnarine, J. L., Talukder, E., Jain, D., Joshi, P., & Srivastav, P. (1990). Characteristics of holding, patterns of play, and social behaviors between parents and infants in New Delhi, India. *Developmental Psychology, 26,* 667–673.

Roosa, M. W. (1984). Maternal age, social class, and the obstetric performance of teenagers. *Journal of Youth and Adolescence, 13,* 365–374.

Roper Starch Worldwide (1994). *A national survey of 252 males and 251 females.* New York: Author.

Roscoe, B., Diana, M. S., & Brooks, R. H. (1987). Early, middle, and late adolescents' views on dating and factors influencing partner selection. *Adolescence, 22,* 59–68.

Rose, S. A. (1980). Enhancing visual recognition memory in preterm infants. *Developmental Psychology, 16,* 85–92.

Rosen, A. B., & Rozin, P. (1993). Now you see it, now you don't: The preschool child's conception of invisible particles in the context of dissolving. *Developmental Psychology, 29,* 300–311.

Rosen, M. G., & Dickinson, J. C. (1992). Management of post-term pregnancy. *New England Journal of Medicine, 326,* 1628–1629.

Rosen, W. D., Adamson, L. B., & Bakeman, R. (1992). An experimental investigation of infant social referencing: Mothers' messages and gender differences. *Developmental Psychology, 28,* 1172–1178.

Rosenberg, M. (1975). The dissonant context and the adolescent self-concept. In S. Dragastin & G. Elder, Jr. (Eds.), *Adolescence in the life cycle* (pp. 97–116). Washington, DC: Hemisphere.

Rosenberg, M. (1979). *Conceiving the self.* New York: Basic Books.

Rosenberg, M., Schooler, C., & Schoenbach, C. (1989). Self-esteem and adolescent problems: Modeling reciprocal effects. *American Sociological Review, 54,* 1004–1018.

Rosenberg, M. S., & Reppucci, N. D. (1985). Primary prevention of child abuse. *Journal of Consulting and Clinical Psychology, 53,* 576–585.

Rosenberg, R. N., & Pettigrew, J. W. (1983). Genetic neurologic diseases. In R. N. Rosenberg (Ed.), *The clinical neurosciences* (pp. 33–165). New York: Churchill Livingstone.

Rosenblatt, J. S., & Lehrman, D. (1963). Maternal behavior of the laboratory rat. In H. R. Rheingold (Ed.). *Maternal behavior in mammals* (pp. 8–57). New York: Wiley.

Rosenthal, D. A. (1987). Ethnic identity development in adolescents. In J. S. Phinney & M. J. Rotheram (Eds.), *Children's ethnic socialization* (pp. 156–179). Newbury Park, CA: Sage.

Roskos, K., & Neuman, S. B. (1993). Descriptive observations of adults' facilitation of literacy in young children's play. *Early Childhood Research Quarterly, 8,* 77–98.

Ross, G. S. (1980). Categorization in 1- to 2-year-olds. *Developmental Psychology, 16,* 391–396.

Rothbart, M. K. (1981). Measurement of temperament in infancy. *Child Development, 52,* 569–578.

Rotheram-Borus, M. J. (1993). Biculturalism among adolescents. In M. Bernal & G. Knight (Eds.), *Ethnic identity* (pp. 81–102). Albany, NY: State University of New York Press.

Rourke, B. P. (1988). Socioemotional disturbances of learning disabled children. *Journal of Consulting and Clinical Psychology, 56,* 801–810.

Rousseau, J. J. (1955). *Emile.* New York: Dutton. (Original work published 1762)

Rovee-Collier, C. K. (1984). The ontogeny of learning and memory in human infancy. In R. Kail & N. E. Spear (Eds.), *Comparative perspectives on the development of memory* (pp. 103–134). Hillsdale, NJ: Erlbaum.

Rovee-Collier, C. K. (1987). Learning and memory. In J. D. Osofsky (Ed.), *Handbook of infant development* (2nd ed., pp. 98–148). New York: Wiley.

Rovee-Collier, C. K. (1991). The "memory system" of prelinguistic infants. In A. Diamond (Ed.), *Annals of the New York Academy of Sciences* (Vol. 608, pp. 517–536). New York: New York Academy of Sciences.

Rovee-Collier, C. K., Patterson, J., & Hayne, H. (1985). Specificity in the reactivation of infant memory. *Developmental Psychobiology, 18,* 559–574.

Royce, J. M., Darlington, R. B., & Murray, H. W. (1983). Pooled analyses: Findings across studies. In Consortium for Longitudinal Studies (Ed.), *As the twig is bent: Lasting effects of preschool programs* (pp. 411–459). Hillsdale, NJ: Erlbaum.

Rozin, P. (1990). Development in the food domain. *Developmental Psychology, 26,* 555–562.

Rozin, P., & Schiller, D. (1980). The nature and acquisition of a preference for chili pepper by humans. *Motivation and Emotion, 4,* 77–101.

Rubin, J. Z., Provenzano, F. J., & Luria, Z. (1974). The eye of the beholder: Parents' views on sex of newborns. *American Journal of Orthopsychiatry, 44,* 512–519.

Rubin, K. H. (1982). Nonsocial play in preschoolers: Necessarily evil? *Child Development, 53,* 651–657.

Rubin, K. H., Fein, G. G., & Vandenberg, B. (1983). Play. In E. M. Hetherington (Ed.), *Handbook of child psychology: Vol. 4. Socialization, personality, and social development* (4th ed., pp. 693–744). New York: Wiley.

Rubin, K. H., Maioni, T. L., & Hornung, M. (1976). Free play behaviors in middle- and lower-class preschoolers: Parent and Piaget revisited. *Child Development, 47,* 414–419.

Rubin, K. H., Watson, K. S., & Jambor, T. W. (1978). Free-play behaviors in preschool and kindergarten children. *Child Development, 49,* 539–536.

Ruble, D. N. (1988). Sex-role development. In M. H. Bornstein & M. E. Lamb (Eds.), *Developmental psychology: An advanced textbook* (2nd ed., pp. 411–460). Hillsdale, NJ: Erlbaum.

Ruble, D. N., Eisenberg, R., & Higgins, E. T. (1994). Developmental changes in achievement evaluation: Motivational implications of self-other differences. *Child Development, 65,* 1095–1110.

Ruff, H. A., & Lawson, K. R. (1990). Development of sustained, focused attention in young children during free play. *Developmental Psychology, 26,* 85–93.

Ruff, H. A., Bijur, P. E., Markowitz, M., Ma, Y-C., & Rosen, J. F. (1993). Declining blood lead levels and cognitive changes in moderately lead-poisoned children. *Journal of the American Medical Association, 269,* 1641–1646.

Ruff, H. A., Lawson, K. R., Parrinello, R., & Weissberg, R. (1990). Long-term stability of individual differences in sustained attention in the early years. *Child Development, 61,* 60–75.

Ruffman, T., Olson, D. R., Ash, T., & Keenan, T. (1993a). The ABCs of deception: Do young children understand deception in the same way as adults? *Developmental Psychology, 27,* 74–87.

Ruffman, T., Perner, J., Olson, D. R., & Doherty, M. (1993b). Reflecting on scientific thinking: Children's understanding of the hypothesis–evidence relation. *Child Development, 64,* 1617–1636.

Ruiz, R. (1988). Bilingualism and bilingual education in the United States. In C. B. Paulston (Ed.), *International handbook of bilingualism and bilingual education* (pp. 539–560). New York: Greenwood Press.

Rumberger, R. W. (1990). Second chance for high school dropouts: Dropout recovery programs in the United States. In D. Inbar (Ed.), *Second chance in education: An interdisciplinary and international perspective* (pp. 227–250). Philadelphia: Falmer.

Rumberger, R. W., Ghatak, R., Poulos, G., Ritter, P. L., & Dornbusch, S. M. (1990). Family influences on dropout behavior in one California high school. *Sociology of Education, 63,* 283–299.

Runco, M. A. (1992). Children's divergent thinking and creative ideation. *Developmental Review, 12,* 233–264.

Runco, M. A. (1993). Divergent thinking, creativity, and giftedness. *Gifted Child Quarterly, 37,* 16–22.

Ruopp, R., Travers, J., Glantz, F., & Coelen, C. (1979). Children at the center: Final report of the National Day Care Study. Cambridge, MA: Abt Books.

Rushton, H. G. (1989). Nocturnal enuresis: Epidemiology, evaluation, and currently available treatment options. *Journal of Pediatrics, 114,* 691–696.

Russell, D. E. H. (1983). The incidence and prevalence of intrafamilial and extrafamilial sexual abuse of female children. *Child Abuse and Neglect, 7,* 133–146.

Russell, J. A. (1990). The preschooler's understanding of the causes and consequences of emotion. *Child Development, 61,* 1872–1881.

Rutter, M. (1979). Protective factors in children's responses to stress and disadvantage. In M. W. Kent & J. Rolf (Eds.), *Primary prevention of psychopathology: Vol 3. Social competence in children* (pp. 49–74). Hanover, NH: University Press of New England.

Rutter, M. (1986). The developmental psychology of depression: Issues and perspectives. In M. Rutter, C. E. Izard, & P. B. Read

(Eds.), *Depression in young people: Clinical and developmental perspectives* (pp. 3–30). New York: Guilford.

Rutter, M. (1987). Psychosocial resilience and protective mechanisms. *American Journal of Orthopsychiatry, 57,* 316–331.

Rutter, M., & Garmezy, N. (1983). Developmental psychopathology. In E. M. Hetherington (Ed.), *Handbook of child psychology: Vol. 4. Socialization, personality, and social development* (pp. 775–911). New York: Wiley.

Rutter, M., & Hersov, L. (Eds.). (1985). *Child and adolescent psychiatry: Modern approaches* (2nd ed.). London: Blackwell Press.

Rutter, M., & Madge, N. (1976). *Cycles of disadvantage.* London: Heinemann.

Rutter, M., Graham, P., Chadwick, O. F. D., & Yule, W. (1976). Adolescent turmoil: Fact or fiction. *Journal of Child Psychology and Psychiatry, 17,* 35–56.

Ryan, K. J. (1989). Ethical issues in reproductive endocrinology and infertility. *American Journal of Obstetrics and Gynecology, 160,* 1415–1417.

Saarni, C. (1989). Children's understanding of strategic control of emotional expression in social transactions. In C. Saarni & P. L. Harris (Eds.), *Children's understanding of emotion* (pp. 181–208). Cambridge, England: Cambridge University Press.

Sadler, L. S. (1991). Depression in adolescents: Context, manifestations, and clinical management. *Nursing Clinics of North America, 26,* 559–572.

Sadler, T. W. (1990). *Langman's medical embryology* (6th ed.). Baltimore: Williams & Wilkins.

Safe Kids. (1991). *National Safe Kids Campaign: 1991 Public Policy Priorities.* Washington, DC: Author.

Salapatek, P. (1975). Pattern perception in early infancy. In L. B. Cohen & P. Salapatek (Eds.), *Infant perception: From sensation to cognition* (pp. 133–248). New York: Academic Press.

Salapatek, P., & Cohen, L. B. (Eds.). (1987). *Handbook of infant perception: Vol. 2. From perception to cognition.* Orlando, FL: Academic Press.

Salzinger, S., Feldman, R. S., Hammer, M., & Rosario, M. (1993). The effects of physical abuse on children's social relationships. *Child Development, 64,* 169–187.

Samson, L. F. (1988). Perinatal viral infections and neonates. *Journal of Perinatal Neonatal Nursing, 1,* 56–65.

Samuels, M., & Samuels, N. (1986). *The well pregnancy book.* New York: Summit.

Samuels, S. J. (1985). Toward a theory of automatic information processing in reading: Updated. In H. Singer & R. B. Ruddell (Eds.), *Theoretical models and processes of reading* (3rd ed., pp. 719–721). Newark, DE: International Reading Association.

Sandberg, D. E., Ehrhardt, A. A., Ince, S. E., & Meyer-Bahlberg, H. F. L. (1991). Gender differences in children's and adolescents' career aspirations. *Journal of Adolescent Research, 6,* 371–386.

Sanderson, J. A., & Siegal, M. (1988). Conceptions of moral and social rules in rejected and nonrejected preschoolers. *Journal of Clinical Child Psychology, 17,* 66–72.

Sanford, J. P. (1985). *Comprehension-level tasks in secondary classrooms.* Austin: Research and Development Center for Teacher Education, University of Texas at Austin.

Santelli, J. S., & Beilenson, P. (1992). Risk factors for adolescent sexual behavior, fertility, and sexually transmitted diseases. *Journal of School Health, 62,* 271–279.

Santrock, J. W., & Warshak, R. A. (1986). Development of father custody relationships and legal/clinical considerations in father-custody families. In M. E. Lamb (Ed.), *The father's role: Applied perspectives* (pp. 135–166). New York: Wiley.

Sapienza, C. (1990, October). Parental imprinting of genes. *Scientific American, 263*(4), 52–60.

Sattler, J. M. (1988). *Assessment of children's intelligence and special abilities* (3rd ed.). San Diego: Author.

Saudino, K., & Eaton, W. O. (1991). Infant temperament and genetics: An objective twin study. *Child Development, 62,* 1167–1174.

Savin-Williams, R. C. (1979). Dominance hierarchies in groups of early adolescents. *Child development, 50,* 923–935.

Savin-Williams, R. C. (1990). *Gay and lesbian youth: Expressions of identity.* New York: Hemisphere.

Savin-Williams, R. C., & Berndt, T. J. (1990). Friendship and peer relations. In S. S. Feldman & G. R. Elliott (Eds.), *At the threshold: The developing adolescent* (pp. 277–307). Cambridge, MA: Harvard University Press.

Saxe, G. B. (1988, August–September). Candy selling and math learning. *Educational Researcher, 17*(6), 14–21.

Saywitz, K. J. (1987). Children's testimony: Age-related patterns of memory errors. In S. J. Ceci, M. P. Toglia, & D. F. Ross (Eds.), *Children's eyewitness memory* (pp. 36–52). New York: Springer-Verlag.

Saywitz, K. J. (1989). Children's conceptions of the legal system: "Court is a place to play basketball." In M. P. Toglia (Eds.), *Perspectives on children's testimony* (pp. 131–157). New York: Springer-Verlag.

Scarr, S. (1985). Constructing psychology: Making facts and fables for our times. *American Psychologist, 40,* 499–512.

Scarr, S. (1988). How genotypes and environments combine: Development and individual differences. In N. Bolger, A. Caspi, G. Downey, & M. Moorehouse (Eds.), *Persons in context: Developmental processes* (pp. 217–244). Cambridge, England: Cambridge University Press.

Scarr, S., & Kidd, K. K. (1983). Developmental behavior genetics. In M. M. Haith & J. J. Campos (Eds.), *Handbook of child psychology: Vol. 2. Infancy and developmental psychobiology* (pp. 345–433). New York: Wiley.

Scarr, S., & McCartney, K. (1983). How people make their own environments: A theory of genotype Æ environment effects. *Child Development, 54,* 424–435.

Scarr, S., Phillips, D. A., & McCartney, K. (1990). Facts, fantasies, and the future of child care in America. *Psychological Science, 1,* 26–35.

Scarr, S., & Weinberg, R. A. (1983). The Minnesota adoption studies: Genetic differences and malleability. *Child Development, 54,* 260–267.

Schachter, F. F., & Stone, R. K. (1985). Difficult sibling–easy sibling: Temperament and the within-family environment. *Child Development, 56,* 1335–1344.

Schaefer, M., Hatcher, R. P., & Bargelow, P. D. (1980). Prematurity and infant stimulation. *Child Psychiatry and Human Development, 10,* 199–212.

Schaffer, H. R., & Emerson, P. E. (1964). The development of social attachments in infancy. *Monographs of the Society for Research in Child Development, 29*(3, Serial No. 94).

Schanberg, S., & Field, T. M. (1987). Sensory deprivation stress and supplemental stimulation in the rat pup and preterm human neonate. *Child Development, 58,* 1431–1447.

Schauble, L. (1990). Belief revision in children: The role of prior knowledge and strategies for generating evidence. *Journal of Experimental Child Psychology, 49,* 31–57.

Schickedanz, J. A., Chay, S., Gopin, P., Sheng, L. L., Song, S., & Wild, N. (1990, November). Preschoolers and academics: Some thoughts. *Young Children, 46*(1), 4–13.

Schinke, S. P., Blythe, B. J., & Gilchrist, D. (1981). Cognitive-behavioral prevention of adolescent pregnancy. *Journal of Counseling Psychology, 28,* 451–454.

Schiavi, R. C., Theilgaard, A., Owen, D., & White, D. (1984). Sex chromosome anomalies, hormones, and aggressivity. *Archives of General Psychiatry, 41,* 93–99.

Schlegel, A., & Barry, H., III. (1980). The evolutionary significance of adolescent initiation ceremonies. *American Ethnologist, 7,* 696–715.

Schlegel, A., & Barry, H., III. (1991). *Adolescence: An anthropological inquiry.* New York: Free Press.

Schneider, W., & Pressley, M. (1989). *Memory development between 2 and 20.* New York: Springer-Verlag.

Schneirla, T. C., Rosenblatt, J. S., & Tobach, E. (1963). Maternal behavior in the cat. In H. R. Rheingold (Ed.), *Maternal behavior in mammals* (pp. 122–168). New York: Wiley.

Schoendorf, K. C., & Kiely, J. L. (1992). Relationship of sudden infant death syndrome to maternal smoking during and after pregnancy. *Pediatrics, 90,* 905–908.

Schor, E. L. (1987). Unintentional injuries. *American Journal of Diseases of Children, 141,* 1280–1284.

Schramm, W., Barnes, D., & Bakewell, J. (1987). Neonatal mortality in Missouri home births. *American Journal of Public Health, 77,* 930–935.

Schunk, D. H. (1983). Ability versus effort attributional feedback: Differential effects on

self-efficacy and achievement. *Journal of Educational Psychology, 75,* 848–856.
Schunk, D. H. (1990). Goal setting and self-efficacy during self-regulated learning. *Educational Psychologist, 25,* 71–86.
Schwartz, D., Dodge, K. A., & Coie, J. D. (1993). The emergence of chronic peer victimization in boys' play groups. *Child Development, 64,* 1755–1772.
Schwartz-Bickenbach, D., Schulte-Hobein, B., Abt, S., Plum, C., & Nau, H. (1987). Smoking and passive smoking during pregnancy and early infancy: Effects on birth weight, lactation period, and cotinine concentrations in mother's milk and infant's urine. *Toxicology Letters, 35,* 73–81.
Schweinhart, L. J., Barnes, H. V., & Weikart, D. P. (1993). Significant benefits: The High/Scope Perry Preschool Study through age 27. Monographs of the High/Scope Educational Research Foundation (No. 10). Ypsilanti, MI: High/Scope Press.
Sears, R. R., Maccoby, E. E., & Levin, H. (1957). *Patterns of child rearing.* New York: Harper & Row.
Sebald, H. (1986). Adolescents' shifting orientation toward parents and peers: A curvilinear trend over recent decades. *Journal of Marriage and the Family, 48,* 5–13.
Seidman, D. S., Laor, A., Gale, R., Stevenson, D. K., Mashiach, S., & Danon, Y. L. (1991). Long-term effects of vacuum and forceps deliveries. *Epidemiology, 337,* 1583–1585.
Seidman, E., Allen, L., Aber, J. L., Mitchell, C., & Feinman, J. (1994). The impact of school transitions in early adolescence on the self-system and perceived social context of poor urban youth. *Child Development, 65,* 507–522.
Select Committee on Children, Youth, and Families, House of Representatives. (1986). Testimony of David Bright. *Hearing on Hunger.* Washington, DC: U.S. Government Printing Office.
Seligman, M. E. P. (1975). *Helplessness: On depression, development, and death.* San Francisco: Freeman.
Seligmann, J. (1994, May 2). The pressure to lose. *Newsweek,* pp. 60–61.
Seligmann, J., & Namuth, T. (1991, Summer). How to baby your teeth. *Newsweek (special edition), 167*(26), 54, 57.
Selman, R. L. (1976). Social-cognitive understanding: A guide to educational and clinical practice. In T. Lickona (Ed.), *Moral development and behavior: Theory, research, and social issues* (pp. 299–316). New York: Holt, Rinehart, & Winston.
Selman, R. L. (1980). *The growth of interpersonal understanding.* New York: Academic Press.
Selman, R. L., & Byrne, D. F. (1974). A structural-developmental analysis of levels of role taking in middle childhood. *Child Development, 45,* 803–806.
Seltzer, V., & Benjamin, F. (1990). Breastfeeding and the potential for human immunodeficiency virus transmission. *Obstetrics and Gynecology, 75,* 713–715.
Serbin, L. A., Powlishta, K. K., & Gulko, J. (1993). The development of sex typing in middle childhood. *Monographs of the Society for Research in Child Development, 58*(2, Serial No. 232).
Sever, J. L. (1983). Maternal infections. In C. C. Brown (Ed.), *Childhood learning disabilities and prenatal risk* (pp. 31–38). New York: Johnson & Johnson.
Shaffer, D. (1985). Depression, mania, and suicidal acts. In M. Rutter & L. Hersov (Eds.), *Child and adolescent psychiatry: Modern approaches* (pp. 698–719). New York: Guilford Press.
Shaffer, D., Garland, A., Gould, M., Fisher, P., & Trautman, P. (1988). Preventing teenage suicide: A critical review. *Journal of the American Academy of Child and Adolescent Psychiatry, 27,* 675–687.
Shagle, S. C., & Barber, B. K. (1993). Effects of family, marital, and parent–child conflict on adolescent self-derogation and suicidal ideation. *Journal of Marriage and the Family, 55,* 964–974.
Shahar, S. (1990). *Childhood in the Middle Ages.* London: Routledge & Kegan Paul.
Shainess, N. (1961). A re-evaluation of some aspects of femininity through a study of menstruation: A preliminary report. *Comparative Psychiatry, 2,* 20–26.
Shalala, D. E. (1993). Giving pediatric immunizations the priority they deserve. *Journal of the American Medical Association, 269,* 1844–1845.
Shannon, B., & Chen, A. W. (1988). A three-year school based nutrition education study. *Journal of Nutrition Education, 20,* 114–123.
Shannon, D. C., Kelly, D. H., Akselrod, S., & Kilborn, K. M. (1987). Increased respiratory frequency and variability in high risk babies who die of sudden infant death syndrome. *Pediatric Research, 22,* 158–162.
Shantz, C. U. (1987). Conflicts between children. *Child Development, 58,* 283–305.
Shapiro, L. R. (1991, Summer). What's in a lunch? *Newsweek* (special issue), *117*(26), 66–68.
Shapiro, L. R., Crawford, P. B., Clark, M. J., Pearson, D. L., Raz, J., & Huenemann, R. (1984). Obesity prognosis: A longitudinal study of children from the age of 6 months to 9 years. *American Journal of Public Health, 74,* 968–972.
Shaver, P., Furman, W., & Buhrmester, D. (1985). Transition to college: Network changes, social skills, and loneliness. In S. Duck & D. Perlman (Eds.), *Understanding personal relationships: An interdisciplinary approach* (pp. 193–219). London: Sage.
Shedler, J., & Block, J. (1990). Adolescent drug use and psychological health: A longitudinal inquiry. *American Psychologist, 45,* 612–630.
Sherman, A. (1994). *Wasting America's future: The Children's Defense Fund report on the costs of child poverty.* Boston: Beacon Press.
Sheiman, D. L., & Slomin, M. (1988). *Resources for middle childhood.* New York: Garland.
Shettles, L. B., & Rorvik, D. M. (1984). *How to choose the sex of your baby.* New York: Doubleday.
Shiffrin, R. M., & Atkinson, R. C. (1969). Storage and retrieval processes in long-term memory. *Psychological Review, 76,* 179–193.
Shime, J. (1988). Influence of prolonged pregnancy on infant development. *Journal of Reproductive Medicine, 33,* 277–284.
Shinn, M. W. (1900). *The biography of a baby.* Boston: Houghton Mifflin.
Shipman, G. (1971). The psychodynamics of sex education. In R. Muuss (Ed.), *Adolescent behavior and society* (pp. 326–339). New York: Random House.
Shonkoff, J. P. (1984). The biological substrate and physical health in middle childhood. In W. A. Collins (Ed.), *Development during middle childhood* (pp. 24–69). Washington, DC: National Academy Press.
Shultz, T. R. (1980). Development of the concept of intention. In W. A. Collins (Ed.), *Minnesota Symposia on Child Psychology* (Vol. 13, pp. 131–164). Hillsdale, NJ: Erlbaum.
Shweder, R. A. (1990). In defense of moral realism: Reply to Gabennesch. *Child Development, 61,* 2060–2067.
Shweder, R. A., Mahapatra, M., & Miller, J. G. (1990). Culture and moral development. In J. Stigler, R. A. Shweder, & G. Herdt (Eds.), *Cultural psychology: Essays on comparative human development* (pp. 130–204). New York: Cambridge University Press.
Siebert, J. M., Garcia, A., Kaplan, M., & Septimus, A. (1989). Three model pediatric AIDS programs: Meeting the needs of children, families, and communities. In J. M. Siebert & R. A. Olson (Eds.), *Children, adolescents, and AIDS* (pp. 25–60). Lincoln: University of Nebraska Press.
Siegler, R. S. (1976). Three aspects of cognitive development. *Cognitive Psychology, 8,* 481–520.
Siegler, R. S. (1978). The origins of scientific reasoning. In R. S. Siegler (Ed.), *Children's thinking: What develops?* (pp. 109–149). Hillsdale, NJ: Erlbaum.
Siegler, R. S. (1981). Developmental sequences within and between concepts. *Monographs of the Society for Research in Child Development, 46*(2, Serial No. 189).
Siegler, R. S. (1983a). Five generalizations about cognitive development. *American Psychologist, 38,* 263–277.
Siegler, R. S. (1983b). Information processing approaches to development. In W. Kessen (Ed.), *Handbook of child psychology: Vol. 1. History, theory, and methods* (pp. 129–212). New York: Wiley.
Siegler, R. S. (1991). *Children's thinking* (2nd ed.). Englewood Cliffs, NJ: Prentice Hall.
Siegler, R. S. (1992). The other Alfred Binet. *Developmental Psychology, 28,* 179–190.
Siegler, R. S., & Richards, D. D. (1982). The development of intelligence. In R. J. Sternberg (Ed.), *Handbook of human intelligence* (pp. 897–971). Cambridge, England: Cambridge University Press.
Sigelman, C. K., Maddock, A., Epstein, J., & Carpenter, W. (1993). Age differences in understandings of disease causality: AIDS, colds, and cancer. *Child Development, 64,* 272–284.

Sigelman, C. K., & Waitzman, K. A. (1991). The development of distributive justice orientations: Contextual influences on children's resource allocations. *Child Development, 62,* 1367–1378.

Signorella, M. L., & Liben, L. S. (1984). Recall and reconstruction of gender-related pictures: Effects of attitude, task difficulty, and age. *Child Development, 55,* 393–405.

Silver, L. B. (1989a). Learning disabilities. *Journal of the American Academy of Child and Adolescent Psychiatry, 28,* 309–313.

Silver, L. B. (1989b). Psychological and family problems associated with learning disabilities: Assessment and intervention. *Journal of the American Academy of Child and Adolescent Psychiatry, 28,* 319–325.

Silver, M., & Wolfe, S. (1989). *Unnecessary cesarean sections: How to cure a national epidemic.* Washington, DC: Citizen's Health Research Group.

Silverberg, S. B., & Steinberg, L. (1990). Psychological well-being of parents with early adolescent children. *Developmental Psychology, 26,* 658–666.

Simkin, P., Whalley, J., & Keppler, A. (1984). *Pregnancy, childbirth, and the newborn.* New York: Meadowbrook.

Simmons, R. G., Black, A., & Zhou, Y. (1991). African-American versus white children and the transition to junior high school. *American Journal of Education, 99,* 481–520.

Simmons, R. G., & Blyth, D. A. (1987). *Moving into adolescence.* New York: Aldine de Gruyter.

Simmons, R. G., Burgeson, R., Carlton-Ford, S., & Blyth, D. A. (1987). The impact of cumulative change in early adolescence. *Child Development, 58,* 1220–1234.

Simons, R. L., Conger, R. D., & Whitbeck, L. B. (1988). A multistage social learning model of the influences of family and peers upon adolescent substance use. *Journal of Drug Issues, 18,* 293–316.

Simons, R. L., Lorenz, R. O., Conger, R. D., & Wu, C–I. (1992). Support from spouse as a mediator and moderator of the disruptive influence of economic strain on parenting. *Child Development, 63,* 1282–1301.

Simons, R. L., Whitbeck, L. B., Conger, R. D., & Chyi-In, W. (1991). Intergenerational transmission of harsh parenting. *Developmental Psychology, 27,* 159–171.

Simpson, S. A., & Harding, A. E. (1993). Predictive testing for Huntington's disease after the gene. *Journal of Medical Genetics, 30,* 1036–1038.

Singer, D. G., & Singer, J. L. (1990). *The house of make-believe.* Cambridge, MA: Harvard University Press.

Sirignano, S. W., & Lachman, M. E. (1985). Personality change during the transition to parenthood: The role of perceived infant temperament. *Developmental Psychology, 21,* 558–567.

Sivard, R. L. (1993). *World military and social expenditures* (15th ed.). Leesburg, VA: WMSE Publications.

Skinner, B. F. (1957). *Verbal behavior.* New York: Appleton-Century-Crofts.

Skinner, E. A., & Belmont, M. J. (1993). Motivation in the classroom: Reciprocal effects of teacher behavior and student engagement across the school year. *Journal of Educational Psychology, 85,* 571–581.

Slaby, R. G., & Frey, K. S. (1975). Development of gender constancy and selective attention to same-sex models. *Child Development, 46,* 849–856.

Slade, A. (1987). A longitudinal study of maternal involvement and symbolic play during the toddler period. *Child Development, 58,* 367–375.

Sloan, W., & Birch, J. W. (1955). A rationale for degrees of retardation. *American Journal of Mental Deficiency, 60,* 258–264.

Smeeding, T., Torrey, B. B., & Rein, M. (1988). Patterns of income and poverty: Economic status of children and the elderly in eight countries. In J. L. Palmer & I. V. Sawhill (Eds.), *The vulnerable* (pp. 89–119). Washington, DC: The Urban Institute Press.

Smetana, J. G. (1988). Concepts of self and social convention: Adolescents' and parents' reasoning about hypothetical and actual family conflicts. In M. Gunnar & W. A. Collins (Eds.), *Minnesota Symposia on Child Psychology* (Vol. 21, pp. 79–122). Hillsdale, NJ: Erlbaum.

Smetana, J. G. (1989). Toddlers' social interactions in the context of moral and conventional transgressions in the home. *Developmental Psychology, 25,* 499–508.

Smetana, J. G., & Asquith, P. (1994). Adolescents' and parents' conceptions of parental authority and personal autonomy. *Child Development, 65,* 1147–1162.

Smetana, J. G., & Braeges, J. L. (1990). The development of toddlers' moral and conventional judgments. *Merrill-Palmer Quarterly, 36,* 329–346.

Smilansky, S. (1968). *The effects of sociodramatic play on disadvantaged children: Preschool children.* New York: Wiley.

Smith, C., & Lloyd, B. (1978). Maternal behavior and perceived sex of infant: Revisited. *Child Development, 49,* 1263–1266.

Smith, H. (1992). The detrimental health effects of ionizing radiation. *Nuclear Medicine Communications, 13,* 4–10.

Smith, J., & Russell, G. (1984). Why do males and females differ? Children's beliefs about sex differences. *Sex Roles, 11,* 1111–1119.

Smith, M. C. (1978). Cognizing the behavior stream: The recognition of intentional action. *Child Development, 49,* 736–743.

Smith, P. K. (1978). A longitudinal study of social participation in preschool children: Solitary and parallel play reexamined. *Developmental Psychology, 14,* 517–523.

Smith, P. K., & Boulton, M. (1990). Rough-and-tumble play, aggression and dominance: Perception and behavior in children's encounters. *Human Development, 33,* 271–282.

Smolucha, F. (1992). Social origins of private speech in pretend play. In R. M. Diaz & L. E. Berk (Eds.), *Private speech: From social interaction to self-regulation.* Hillsdale, NJ: Erlbaum.

Snarey, J. R., & Keljo, K. (1991). In a gemeinschaft voice: The cross-cultural expansion of moral development theory. In W. M. Kurtines & J. L. Gewirtz (Eds.), *Handbook of moral behavior and development* (Vol. 1, pp. 395–424). Hillsdale, NJ: Erlbaum.

Snarey, J. R., Reimer, J., & Kohlberg, L. (1985). The development of social–moral reasoning among kibbutz adolescents: A longitudinal cross-cultural study. *Developmental Psychology, 21,* 3–17.

Snow, C. E. (1993). Families as social contexts for literacy development. In C. Daiute (Ed.), *New directions for child development* (No. 61, pp. 11–24). San Francisco: Jossey-Bass.

Snow, C. E., & Hoefnagel-Höhle, M. (1978). The critical period for language acquisition: Evidence from second language learning. *Child Development, 49,* 1114–1128.

Snowden, L. R., Schott, T. L., Awalt, S. J., & Gillis-Knox, J. (1988). Marital satisfaction in pregnancy: Stability and change. *Journal of Marriage and the Family, 50,* 325–333.

Sobesky, W. E. (1983). The effects of situational factors on moral judgments. *Child Development, 54,* 575–584.

Society for Research in Child Development. (1993). Ethical standards for research with children. In *Directory of Members* (pp. 337–339). Ann Arbor, MI: Author.

Sockett, H. (1992). The moral aspects of the curriculum. In P. W. Jackson (Ed.), *Handbook of research on curriculum* (pp. 543–569). New York: Macmillan.

Sodian, B., Taylor, C., Harris, P. L., & Perner, J. (1991). Early deception and the child's theory of mind: False trails and genuine markers. *Child Development, 62,* 468–483.

Sodian, B., & Wimmer, H. (1987). Children's understanding of inference as a source of knowledge. *Child Development, 58,* 424–433.

Soken, H. H., & Pick, A. D. (1992). Intermodal perception of happy and angry expressive behaviors by seven-month-old infants. *Child Development, 63,* 787–795.

Sommer, K., Whitman, T. L., Borkowski, J. G., Schellenbach, C., Maxwell, S., & Keogh, D. (1993). Cognitive readiness and adolescent parenting. *Developmental Psychology, 29,* 389–398.

Sommerville, J. (1982). *The rise and fall of childhood.* Beverly Hills, CA: Sage.

Sonenstein, F. L., Pleck, J. H., & Ku, L. C. (1991). Levels of sexual activity among adolescent males in the United States. *Family Planning Perspectives, 23,* 162–167.

Song, M., & Ginsburg, H. P. (1987). The development of informal and formal mathematical thinking in Korean and U.S. children. *Child Development, 58,* 1286–1296.

Sontag, C. W., Baker, C. T., & Nelson, V. L. (1958). Mental growth and personality development: A longitudinal study. *Monographs of the Society for Research in Child Development, 23*(2, Serial No. 68).

Sorce, J., Emde, R., Campos, J., & Klinnert, M. (1985). Maternal emotional signaling: Its effect on the visual cliff behavior of 1-year-olds. *Developmental Psychology, 21,* 195–200.

Sorenson, E. S. (1993). *Children's stress and coping.* New York: Guilford.

Sosa, R., Kennell, J., Klaus, M., Robertson, S., & Urrutia, J. (1980). The effect of a supportive companion on perinatal problems, length of labor, and mother–infant interaction. *New England Journal of Medicine, 303,* 597–600.

Southard, B. (1985). Interlimb movement control and coordination in children. In J. E. Clark & J. E. Humphrey (Eds.), *Motor development* (Vol. 1, pp. 55–66). Princeton, NJ: Princeton Books.

Spears, R. A. (1991). *Contemporary American slang.* Lincolnwood, IL: National Textbook Company.

Speece, M. W., & Brent, S. B. (1992). The acquisition of a mature understanding of three components of the concept of death. *Death Studies, 16,* 211–229.

Speicher, B. (1994). Family patterns of moral judgment during adolescence and early adulthood. *Developmental Psychology, 30,* 624–632.

Spelke, E. S. (1987). The development of intermodal perception. In P. Salapatek & L. Cohen (Eds.), *Handbook of infant perception: Vol. 2. From perception to cognition* (pp. 233–273). Orlando, FL: Academic Press.

Spelke, E. S. (1991). Physical knowledge in infancy: Reflections on Piaget's theory. In S. Carey & R. Gelman (Eds.), *The epigenesis of mind: Essays on biology and cognition* (pp. 133–169). Hillsdale, NJ: Erlbaum.

Spellacy, W. N., Miller, S. J., & Winegar, A. (1986). Pregnancy after 40 years of age. *Obstetrics and Gynecology, 68,* 452–454.

Spence, M. J., & DeCasper, A. J. (1987). Prenatal experience with low-frequency maternal voice sounds influences neonatal perception of maternal voice samples. *Infant Behavior and Development, 10,* 133–142.

Spencer, M. B., & Dornbusch, S. M. (1990). Challenges in studying minority youth. In S. Feldman & G. R. Elliott (Eds.), *At the threshold: The developing adolescent* (pp. 123–146). Cambridge, MA: Harvard University Press.

Sperduto, R. D., Seigel, D., Roberts, J., & Rowland, M. (1983). Prevalence of myopia in the United States. *Archives of Ophthalmology, 101,* 405–407.

Spinetta, J., & Rigler, D. (1972). The child-abusing parent: A psychological review. *Psychological Bulletin, 77,* 296–304.

Spirito, A., Brown, L., Overholser, J., & Fritz, G. (1989). Attempted suicide in adolescence: A review and critique of the literature. *Child Psychology Review, 9,* 336–363.

Spitz, R. A. (1945). Hospitalism: An inquiry into the genesis of psychiatric conditions in early childhood. *Psychoanalytic Study of the Child, 1,* 113–117.

Spitz, R. A. (1946). Anaclitic depression. *Psychoanalytic Study of the Child, 2,* 313–342.

Spivack, G., & Shure, M. B. (1974). *Social adjustment of young children: A cognitive approach to solving real life problems.* San Francisco: Jossey-Bass.

Spock, B., & Rothenberg, M. B. (1992). *Dr. Spock's baby and child care.* New York: Pocket Books.

Spreadbury, C. L. (1982). First date. *Journal of Early Adolescence, 2,* 83–89.

Spreen, O., Tupper, D., Risser, A., Tuokko, H., & Edgell, D. (1984). *Human developmental neuropsychology.* New York: Oxford University Press.

Sroufe, L. A. (1979). Socioemotional development. In J. D. Osofsky (Ed.), *Handbook of infant development* (pp. 462–516). New York: Wiley.

Sroufe, L. A. (1985). Attachment classification from the perspective of infant–caregiver relationships and infant temperament. *Child Development, 56,* 1–14.

Sroufe, L. A. (1988). A developmental perspective on day care. *Early Childhood Research Quarterly, 3,* 283–292.

Sroufe, L. A., & Waters, E. (1976). The ontogenesis of smiling and laughter: A perspective on the organization of development in infancy. *Psychological Review, 83,* 173–189.

Sroufe, L. A., & Wunsch, J. P. (1972). The development of laughter in the first year of life. *Child Development, 43,* 1324–1344.

St. Peters, M., Fitch, M., Huston, A. C., Wright, J. C., & Eakins, D. J. (1991). Television and families: What do young children watch with their parents? *Child Development, 62,* 1409–1423.

Stahl, S. A., (1992). Saying the "P" word: Nine guidelines for effective phonics instruction. *The Reading Teacher, 45,* 618–625.

Stahl, S. A., McKenna, M. C., & Pagnucco, J. R. (1994). The effects of whole-language instruction: An update and a reappraisal. *Educational Psychologist, 29,* 175–185.

Stamler, J. (1993). Epidemic obesity in the United States. *Archives of Internal Medicine, 153,* 1040–1044.

Stanhope, L., Bell, R. Q., & Parker-Cohen, N. Y. (1987). Temperament and helping behavior in preschool children. *Developmental Psychology, 23,* 347–353.

Stanitski, C. L. (1989). Common injuries in preadolescent and adolescent athletes. *Sports Medicine, 7,* 32–41.

Stark, L. J., Allen, K. D., Hurst, M., Nash, D. A., Rigney, B., & Stokes, T. F. (1989). Distraction: Its utilization and efficacy with children undergoing dental treatment. *Journal of Applied Behavior Analysis, 22,* 297–307.

Stattin, H., & Magnusson, D. (1990). *Pubertal maturation in female development.* Hillsdale, NJ: Erlbaum.

Stechler, G., & Halton, A. (1982). Prenatal influences on human development. In B. B. Wolman (Ed.), *Handbook of developmental psychology* (pp. 175–189). Englewood Cliffs, NJ: Prentice Hall.

Stein, Z., Susser, M., Saenger, G., & Marolla, F. (1975). *Famine and human development: The Dutch hunger winter of 1944–1945.* New York: Oxford.

Steinberg, L. (1984). The varieties and effects of work during adolescence. In M. Lamb, A. Brown, & B. Rogoff (Eds.), *Advances in developmental psychology* (pp. 1–37). Hillsdale, NJ: Erlbaum.

Steinberg, L. (1986). Latchkey children and susceptibility to peer pressure: An ecological analysis. *Developmental Psychology, 22,* 433–439.

Steinberg, L. (1987). The impact of puberty on family relations: Effects of pubertal status and pubertal timing. *Developmental Psychology, 23,* 451–460.

Steinberg, L. (1988a). Simple solutions to a complex problem: A response to Rodman, Pratto, & Nelson. *Developmental Psychology, 24,* 295–296.

Steinberg, L. (1988b). Stability of Type A behavior from early childhood to young adulthood. In P. B. Baltes, D. L. Featherman, & R. M. Lerner (Eds.), *Life-span development and behavior* (Vol. 8, pp. 129–161). Hillsdale, NJ: Erlbaum.

Steinberg, L. (1990). Interdependence in the family: Autonomy, conflict, and harmony in the parent–adolescent relationship. In S. S. Feldman & G. R. Elliott (Eds.), *At the threshold: The developing adolescent* (pp. 255–276). Cambridge, MA: Harvard University Press.

Steinberg, L. (1993). *Adolescence* (3rd ed.). New York: McGraw-Hill.

Steinberg, L., & Dornbusch, S. M. (1991). Negative correlates of part-time employment during adolescence: Replication and elaboration. *Developmental Psychology, 27,* 304–313.

Steinberg, L., Elman, J. D., & Mounts, N. S. (1989). Authoritative parenting, psychosocial maturity, and academic success among adolescents. *Child Development, 60,* 1424–1436.

Steinberg, L., Lamborn, S. D., Dornbusch, S. M., & Darling, N. (1992). Impact of parenting practices on adolescent achievement: Authoritative parenting, school involvement, and encouragement to succeed. *Child Development, 63,* 1266–1281.

Steinberg, L., Lamborn, S. D., Mounts, N. S., & Dornbusch, S. M. (1994). Over-time changes in adjustment and competence among adolescents from authoritative, authoritarian, indulgent, and neglectful families. *Child Development, 65,* 754–770.

Steinberg, L., & Silverberg, S. B. (1986). The vicissitudes of autonomy in early adolescence. *Child Development, 57,* 841–851.

Steiner, J. E. (1979). Human facial expression in response to taste and smell stimulation. In H. W. Reese & L. P. Lipsitt (Eds.), *Advances in child development and behavior* (Vol. 13, pp. 257–295). New York: Academic Press.

Steiner, M. (1990). Postpartum psychiatric disorders. *Canadian Journal of Psychiatry, 35,* 89–95.

Steinhardt, M. A. (1992). Physical education. In P. W. Jackson (Ed.), *Handbook of research on curriculum* (pp. 964–1001). New York: Macmillan.

Steinhausen, H. C., Willms, J., & Sphor, H-L. (1993). Long-term psychopathological and cognitive outcome of children with fetal alcohol syndrome. *Journal of the American Academy of Child and Adolescent Psychiatry, 32,* 990–994.

Stenberg, C., & Campos, J. (1990). The development of anger expressions in infancy. In

N. Stein, B. Leventhal, & T. Trabasso (Eds.), *Psychological and biological approaches to emotion* (pp. 247–282). Hillsdale, NJ: Erlbaum.

Stephen, E. H., Freedman, V. A., & Hess, J. (1993). Near and far: Contact of children with their non-residential fathers. *Journal of Divorce & Remarriage, 20,* 171–191.

Stern, D. N. (1985). *The interpersonal world of the infant: A view from psychoanalysis and developmental psychology.* New York: Basic Books.

Stern, M., & Karraker, K. H. (1989). Sex stereotyping of infants: A review of gender labeling studies. *Sex Roles, 20,* 501–522.

Sternberg, K. J., Lamb, M. E., Greenbaum, C., Cicchetti, D., Dawaud, S., Cortes, R. M., Krispin, O., & Lorey, F. (1993). Effects of domestic violence on children's behavior problems and depression. *Developmental Psychology, 29,* 44–52.

Sternberg, R. J. (1984). Evaluation of the Kaufman Assessment Battery for Children from an information processing perspective. *Journal of Special Education, 18,* 269–279.

Sternberg, R. J. (1985). *Beyond IQ: A triarchic theory of human intelligence.* New York: Cambridge University Press.

Sternberg, R. J. (1988). A triarchic view of intelligence in cross-cultural perspective. In S. H. Irvine & J. W. Berry (Eds.), *Human abilities in cultural context* (pp. 60–85). New York: Cambridge University Press.

Sternberg, R. J., & Odagaki, L. (1989). Continuity and discontinuity in intellectual development are not a matter of "either–or." *Human Development, 32,* 159–166.

Stevens, J. H. (1984). Black grandmothers' and black adolescent mothers' knowledge about parenting. *Developmental Psychology, 20,* 1017–1025.

Stevenson, D. L., & Baker, D. P. (1987). The family–school relation and the child's school performance. *Child Development, 58,* 1348–1357.

Stevenson, H. W. (1992, December). Learning from Asian schools. *Scientific American, 267*(6), 32–38.

Stevenson, H. W. (1994). Extracurricular programs in East Asian schools. *Teachers College Record, 95,* 389–407.

Stevenson, H. W., & Baker, D. P. (1987). The family–school relation and the child's school performance. *Child Development, 58,* 1348–1357.

Stevenson, H. W., & Lee, S-Y. (1990). Contexts of achievement: A study of American, Chinese, and Japanese children. *Monographs of the Society for Research in Child Development, 55*(1–2, Serial No. 221).

Stevenson, H. W., Chen, C., & Lee, S-Y. (1993). Mathematics achievement of Chinese, Japanese, and American children: Ten years later. *Science, 259,* 53–58.

Stevenson, H. W., Stigler, J. W., Lee, S–Y., Lucker, G. W., Litamura, S., & Hsu, C. (1985). Cognitive performance and academic achievement of Japanese, Chinese, and American children. *Child Development, 56,* 718–734.

Stevenson, R., & Pollitt, C. (1987). The acquisition of temporal terms. *Journal of Child Language, 14,* 533–545.

Stewart, D. A. (1982). *Children with sex chromosome aneuploidy: Follow-up studies.* New York: Liss.

Stewart, R. B. (1983). Sibling attachment relationships: Child–infant interactions in the Strange Situation. *Developmental Psychology, 19,* 192–199.

Stigler, J. W., & Stevenson, H. W. (1991, Spring). How Asian teachers polish each lesson to perfection. *American Educator, 15*(1), 12–20, 43–47.

Stillman, R. J. (1982). In utero exposure to diethylstilbestrol: Adverse effects on the reproductive tract and reproductive performance in male and female offspring. *American Journal of Obstetrics and Gynecology, 142,* 905–921.

Stipek, D. J. (1981). Children's perceptions of their own and their classmates' ability. *Journal of Educational Psychology, 73,* 404–410.

Stipek, D. J., Gralinski, J. H., & Kopp, C. B. (1990). Self-concept development in the toddler years. *Developmental Psychology, 26,* 972–977.

Stipek, D. J., & Kowalski, P. S. (1989). Learned helplessness in task-orienting versus performance-orienting testing conditions. *Journal of Educational Psychology, 81,* 384–391.

Stipek, D. J., & Mac Iver, D. (1989). Developmental change in children's assessment of intellectual competence. *Child Development, 60,* 531–538.

Stipek, D. J., Recchia, S., & McClintic, S. (1992). Self-evaluation in young children. *Monographs of the Society for Research in Child Development, 57*(Serial No. 226, No. 1).

Stoch, M. B., Smythe, P. M., Moodie, A. D., & Bradshaw, D. (1982). Psychosocial outcome and CT findings after growth undernourishment during infancy: A 20-year developmental study. *Developmental Medicine and Child Neurology, 24,* 419–436.

Stocker, C., & Dunn, J. (1990). Sibling relationships in adolescence. In R. M. Lerner, A. C. Petersen, & J. Brooks-Gunn (Eds.), *The encyclopedia of adolescence* (Vol. 2, pp. 1046–1048). New York: Garland.

Stocker, C., Dunn, J., & Plomin, R. (1989). Sibling relationships: Links with child temperament, maternal behavior, and family structure. *Child Development, 60,* 715–727.

Stodolsky, S. S. (1974). How children find something to do in preschools. *Genetic Psychology Monographs, 90,* 245–303.

Stodolsky, S. S. (1988). *The subject matters.* Chicago: University of Chicago Press.

Stoel-Gammon, C., & Otomo, K. (1986). Babbling development of hearing-impaired and normal hearing subjects. *Journal of Speech and Hearing Disorders, 51,* 33–41.

Stone, L. (1977). *The family, sex, and marriage in England, 1500–1800.* New York: Harper & Row.

Stoneman, Z., Brody, G. H., & MacKinnon, C. E. (1986). Same-sex and cross-sex siblings: Activity choices, roles, behavior, and gender stereotypes. *Sex Roles, 15,* 495–511.

Strasburger, V. C. (1989). Adolescent sexuality and the media. *Adolescent Gynecology, 36,* 747–773.

Strauss, S., & Levin, I. (1981). Commentary on Siegler's "Developmental sequences within and between concepts." *Monographs of the Society for Research in Child Development, 46*(2, Serial No. 189).

Strayer, J. (1993). Children's concordant emotions and cognitions in response to observed emotions. *Child Development, 64,* 188–201.

Streissguth, A. P., Barr, H. M., Sampson, P. D., Darby, B. L., & Martin, D. C. (1989). IQ at age 4 in relation to maternal alcohol use and smoking during pregnancy. *Developmental Psychology, 25,* 3–11.

Streissguth, A. P., Treder, R., Barr, H. M., Shepard, T., Bleyer, W. A., Sampson, P. D., & Martin, D. (1987). Aspirin and acetaminophen use by pregnant women and subsequent child IQ and attention decrements. *Teratology, 35,* 211–219.

Streitmatter, J. L. (1993). Gender differences in identity development: An examination of longitudinal data. *Adolescence, 28,* 55–66.

Streitmatter, J. L., & Pate, G. S. (1989). Identity status development and cognitive prejudice in early adolescents. *Journal of Early Adolescence, 9,* 142–152.

Strober, M., McCracken, J., & Hanna, G. (1990). Affective disorders. In R. M. Lerner, A. C. Petersen, & J. Brooks-Gunn (Eds.), *The encyclopedia of adolescence* (Vol. 1, pp. 18–25). New York: Garland.

Strutt, G. F., Anderson, D. R., & Well, A. D. (1975). A developmental study of the effects of irrelevant information on speeded classification. *Journal of Experimental Child Psychology, 20,* 127–135.

Stunkard, A. J., & Sørensen, T. I. A. (1993). Obesity and socioeconomic status—a complex relation. *New England Journal of Medicine, 329,* 1036–1037.

Stunkard, A. J., Sørenson, T. I. A., Hanis, C., Teasdale, T. W., Chakraborty, R., Schull, W. J., & Schulsinger, F. (1986). An adoption study of human obesity. *New England Journal of Medicine, 314,* 193–198.

Sturdevant, M. S., & Ramafedi, G. (1992). Special health needs of homosexual youth. *Adolescent Medicine State of the Art Reviews, 3,* 359–372.

Subbotsky, E. V. (1994). Early rationality and magical thinking in preschoolers: Space and time. *British Journal of Developmental Psychology, 12,* 97–108.

Suess, G. J., Grossmann, K. E., & Sroufe, L. A. (1992). Effects of infant attachment to mother and father on quality of adaptation in preschool: From dyadic to individual organisation of self. *International Journal of Behavioral Development, 15,* 43–65.

Sullivan, H. S. (1953). *The interpersonal theory of psychiatry.* New York: Norton.

Sullivan, J. W., & Horowitz, F. D. (1983). The effects of intonation on infant attention: The role of the rising intonation contour. *Journal of Child Language, 10,* 521–534.

Sullivan, L. W. (1987). The risks of the sickle-cell trait: Caution and common sense.

New England Journal of Medicine, 317, 830–831.
Sullivan, M. L. (1993). Culture and class as determinants of out-of-wedlock childbearing and poverty during late adolescence. *Journal of Research on Adolescence, 3,* 295–316.
Sullivan, S. A., & Birch, L. L. (1990). Pass the sugar, pass the salt: Experience dictates preference. *Developmental Psychology, 26,* 546–551.
Sulzby, E. (1985). Children's emergent reading of favorite books: A developmental study. *Reading Research Quarterly, 20,* 458–481.
Suomi, S. (1982). Biological foundations and developmental psychobiology. In C. B. Kopp & J. B. Krakow (Eds.), *The child: Development in a social context* (pp. 42–91). Reading, MA: Addison-Wesley.
Super, C. M. (1980). Cognitive development: Looking across at growing up. In C. Super & M. Harkness (Eds.), *New directions for child development* (No. 8, pp. 59–69). San Francisco: Jossey-Bass.
Super, C. M., & Harkness, S. (1982). The infant's niche in rural Kenya and metropolitan America. In L. L. Adler (Ed.), *Cross-cultural research at issue* (pp. 247–255). New York: Academic Press.
Super, D. (1980). A life-span, life-space approach to career development. *Journal of Vocational Behavior, 16,* 282–298.
Super, D. (1984). Career and life development. In D. Brown & L. Brooks (Eds.), *Career choice and development* (pp. 192–234). San Francisco: Jossey-Bass.
Swanson, H. S. W. (1993). Donor anonymity in artificial insemination: Is it still necessary? *Columbia Journal of Law and Social Problems, 27,* 151–190.
Sykes, N. L., Jr. (1994). Acne: A review of optimum treatment drugs. *Drugs, 48,* 59–70.
Tager-Flusberg, H. (1989). Putting words together: Morphology and syntax in the preschool years. In J. Berko Gleason (Ed.), *The development of language* (pp. 135–165). Columbus, OH: Merrill.
Taitz, L. S. (1983). *The obese child.* Boston: Blackwell.
Takahashi, K. (1990). Are the key assumptions of the "Strange Situation" procedure universal? A view from Japanese research. *Human Development, 33,* 23–30.
Tamis-LeMonda, C. S., & Bornstein, M. H. (1989). Habituation and maternal encouragement of attention in infancy as predictors of toddler language, play, and representational competence. *Child Development, 60,* 738–751.
Tanner, J. M. (1990). *Foetus into man* (2nd ed.). Cambridge, MA: Harvard University Press.
Tanner, J. M., Whitehouse, R. H., Cameron, N., Marshall, W. A., Healey, M. J. R., & Goldstein, H. (1983). *Assessment of skeletal maturity and prediction of adult height* (TW2 method) (2nd ed.). New York: Academic Press.
Taylor, A. R., Asher, S. R., & Williams, G. A. (1987). The social adaptation of mainstreamed mildly retarded children. *Child Development, 58,* 1321–1334.
Taylor, B. J. (1991). A review of epidemiological studies of sudden infant death syndrome in southern New Zealand. *Journal of Paediatric Child Health, 27,* 344–348.
Taylor, M. C., & Hall, J. A. (1982). Psychological androgyny: Theories, methods, and conclusions. *Psychological Bulletin, 92,* 347–366.
Taylor, R. D., Casten, R., & Flickinger, S. M. (1993). Influence of kinship social support on the parenting experiences and psychosocial adjustment of African-American adolescents. *Developmental Psychology, 29,* 382–388.
Teberg, A. J., Walther, F. J., & Pena, I. C. (1988). Mortality, morbidity, and outcome of the small-for-gestational-age infant. *Seminar in Perinatology, 12,* 84–94.
Tedder, J. L. (1991). Using the Brazelton Neonatal Assessment Scale to facilitate the parent–infant relationship in a primary care setting. *Nurse Practitioner, 16,* 27–36.
Teikari, J. M., O'Donnell, J. O., Kaprio, J., & Koskenvuo, M. (1991). Impact of heredity in myopia. *Human Heredity, 41,* 151–156.
Tertinger, D. A., Greene, B. F., & Lutzker, J. R. (1984). Home safety: Development and validation of one component of an ecobehavioral treatment program for abused and neglected children. *Journal of Applied Behavior Analysis, 17,* 159–174.
Tesman, J. R., & Hills, A. (1994). Developmental effects of lead exposure in children. *Social Policy Report of the Society for Research in Child Development, 8* (No. 3).
Thacker, S. B., Addiss, D. G., Goodman, R. A., Holloway, B. R., & Spencer, H. C. (1992). Infectious diseases and injuries in child day care. *Journal of the American Medical Association, 268,* 1720–1726.
Thackwray, D. E., Smith, M. C., Bodfish, J. W., & Meyers, A. W. (1993). A comparison of behavioral and cognitive-behavioral interventions for bulimia nervosa. *Journal of Consulting and Clinical Psychology, 61,* 639–645.
Tharp, R. G. (1989). Psychocultural variables and constants: Effects on teaching and learning in schools. *American Psychologist, 44,* 349–359.
Tharp, R. G. (1993). Institutional and social context of educational practice and reform. In E. A. Forman, N. Minick, & C. A. Stone (Eds.), *Contexts for learning* (pp. 269–282). New York: Oxford University Press.
Tharp, R. G., & Gallimore, R. (1988). *Rousing minds to life: Teaching, learning, and schooling in social context.* Cambridge, England: Cambridge University Press.
Thatcher, R. W., Walker, R. A., & Giudice, S. (1987). Human cerebral hemispheres develop at different rates and ages. *Science, 236,* 1110–1113.
Thelen, E. (1989). The (re)discovery of motor development: Learning new things from an old field. *Developmental Psychology, 25,* 946–949.
Thelen, E., & Adolph, K. E. (1992). Arnold Gesell: The paradox of nature and nurture. *Developmental Psychology, 28,* 368–380.
Thelen, E., Corbetta, D., Kamm, K., Spencer, J. P., Schneider, K., & Zernicke, R. F. (1993). The transition to reaching: Mapping intention and intrinsic dynamics. *Child Development, 64,* 1058–1098.
Thelen, E., Fisher, D. M., & Ridley-Johnson, R. (1984). The relationship between physical growth and a newborn reflex. *Infant Behavior and Development, 7,* 479–493.
Theorell, K., Prechtl, H. F. R., & Vos, J. (1974). A polygraphic study of normal and abnormal newborn infants. *Neuropaediatrie, 5,* 279–317.
Thoma, S. J. (1986). Estimating gender differences in the comprehension and preference of moral issues. *Developmental Review, 6,* 165–180.
Thoman, E., & Ingersoll, E. W. (1993). Learning in premature infants. *Developmental Psychology, 29,* 692–700.
Thomas, A., & Chess, S. (1977). *Temperament and development.* New York: Brunner/Mazel.
Thomas, A., Chess, S., & Birch, H. G. (1970, August). The origins of personality. *Scientific American, 223*(2), 102–109.
Thomas, A., Chess, S., & Korn, S. J. (1982). The reality of difficult temperament. *Merrill-Palmer Quarterly, 28,* 1–20.
Thomas, J. R. (1984). Children's motor skill development. In J. R. Thomas (Ed.), *Motor development during childhood and adolescence* (pp. 91–104). Minneapolis, MN: Burgess.
Thomas, J. R., & French, K. E. (1985). Gender differences across age in motor performance: A meta-analysis. *Psychological Bulletin, 98,* 260–282.
Thompson, R. A. (1990). On emotion and self-regulation. In R. A. Thompson (Ed.), *Nebraska Symposia on Motivation* (Vol. 36, pp. 383–483). Lincoln: University of Nebraska Press.
Thompson, R. A. (1990). Vulnerability in research: A developmental perspective on research risk. *Child Development, 61,* 1–16.
Thompson, R. A. (1994). Emotion regulation: A theme in search of definition. In N. A. Fox (Ed.), The development of emotion regulation. *Monographs of the Society for Research in Child Development, 59* (2–3, Serial No. 240).
Thompson, R. A., Lamb, M. E., & Estes, D. (1982). Stability of infant–mother attachment and its relationship to changing life circumstances in an unselected middle-class sample. *Child Development, 53,* 144–148.
Thompson, R. A., & Limber, S. (1991). "Social anxiety" in infancy: Stranger wariness and separation distress. In H. Leitenberg (Ed.), *Handbook of social and evaluation anxiety* (pp. 85–137). New York: Plenum.
Thompson, R. A., Tinsley, B. R., Scalora, M. J., & Parke, R. D. (1989). Grandparents' visitation rights: Legalizing the ties that bind. *American Psychologist, 44,* 1217–1222.
Thorndike, R. L., Hagen, E. P., & Sattler, J. M. (1986). *The Stanford-Binet Intelligence Scale.* Chicago: Riverside Publishing.
Tizard, B., & Hodges, J. (1978). The effect of early institutional rearing on the development of eight year old children. *Journal of Child Psychology and Psychiatry, 19,* 99–118.

Tizard, B., & Rees, J. (1975). The effect of early institutional rearing on the behaviour problems and affectional relationships of four-year-old children. *Journal of Child Psychology and Psychiatry, 16,* 61–73.

Tobias, P. V. (1975). Anthropometry among disadvantaged people: Studies in Southern Africa. In E. S. Watts, F. E. Johnston, & G. W. Lasker (Eds.), *Biosocial interrelations in population adaptation: World anthropology series* (pp. 287–305). The Hague: Mouton.

Toda, S., & Fogel, A. (1993). Infant response to the still-face situation at 3 and 6 months. *Developmental Psychology, 29,* 532–538.

Tolson, T. F. J., & Wilson, M. N. (1990). The impact of two- and three-generational black family structure on perceived family climate. *Child Development, 61,* 416–428.

Tomasello, M., & Barton, M. (1994). Learning words in nonostensive contexts. *Developmental Psychology, 30,* 639–650.

Tomasello, M., Mannle, S., & Kruger, A. C. (1986). Linguistic environment of 1- to 2-year-old twins. *Developmental Psychology, 22,* 169–176.

Torfs, C. P., Berg, B. van den, Oechsli, F. W., & Cummins, S. (1990). Prenatal and perinatal factors in the etiology of cerebral palsy. *Journal of Pediatrics, 116,* 615–619.

Torrance, E. P. (1980). *Torrance Tests of Creative Thinking.* New York: Scholastic Testing Service.

Tortorici, J. M., & Marcelino, A. (1993). *Children in war.* New York: United Nation's Children's Fund.

Touwen, B. C. L. (1984). Primitive reflexes—Conceptual or semantic problem? In H. F. R. Prechtl (Ed.), *Continuity of neural functions from prenatal to postnatal life* (Clinics in Developmental Medicine No. 94, pp. 115–125). Philadelphia: Lippincott.

Tower, R. B., Singer, D. G., Singer, J. L., & Biggs, A. (1979). Differential effects of television programming on preschoolers' cognition, imagination, and social play. *American Journal of Orthopsychiatry, 49,* 265–281.

Trautner, H. M., Helbing, N., Sahm, W. B., & Lohaus, A. (1989, April). *Beginning awareness–rigidity–flexibility: A longitudinal analysis of sex-role stereotyping in 4- to 10-year-old children.* Paper presented at the biennial meeting of the Society for Research in Child Development, Kansas City.

Trevethan, S. D., & Walker, L. J. (1989). Hypothetical versus real-life moral reasoning among psychopathic and delinquent youth. *Development and Psychopathology, 1,* 91–103.

Trickett, P. K., Aber, J. L., Carlson, V., & Cicchetti, D. (1991). Relationship of socioeconomic status to the etiology and developmental sequelae of physical child abuse. *Developmental Psychology, 27,* 148–158.

Trickett, P. K., & Kuczynski, L. (1986). Children's misbehaviors and parental discipline strategies in abusive and nonabusive families. *Developmental Psychology, 22,* 115–123.

Trieber, F. A., Mabe, P. A., Riley, W. T., McDuffie, M., Strong, W. B., & Levy, M. (1990). Children's Type A behavior: The role of parental hostility and family history of cardiovascular disease. *Journal of Social Behavior and Personality, 5,* 183–189.

Trieber, F. A., Schramm, L., & Mabe, P. A. (1986). Children's knowledge and concerns toward a peer with cancer: A workshop intervention approach. *Child Psychiatry and Human Development, 16,* 249–260.

Trinkoff, A., & Parks, P. L. (1993). Prevention strategies for infant walker-related injuries. *Public Health Reports, 108,* 784–788.

Tronick, E. Z. (1989). Emotions and emotional communication in infants. *American Psychologist, 44,* 112–119.

Tudge, J. (1990). Vygotsky, the zone of proximal development, and peer collaboration: Implications for classroom practice. In L. C. Moll (Ed.), *Vygotsky and education* (pp. 155–172). New York: Cambridge University Press.

Turiel, E. (1983). *The development of social knowledge: Morality and convention.* New York: Cambridge University Press.

Turiel, E., Smetana, J. G., & Killen, M. (1991). Social contexts in social cognitive development. In W. M. Kurtines & J. L. Gewirtz (Eds.), *Handbook of moral behavior and development* (Vol. 2, pp. 307–332). Hillsdale, NJ: Erlbaum.

Turiel, J. (1991a, February 3). At the survival borderline. *San Francisco Examiner,* pp. D13–D14.

Turiel, J. (1991b, February 10). Life-and-death battle. *San Francisco Examiner,* pp. D13–D14.

Turkheimer, E., & Gottesman, I. I. (1991). Individual differences and the canalization of human behavior. *Developmental Psychology, 27,* 18–22.

Tyack, D., & Ingram, D. (1977). Children's production and comprehension of questions. *Journal of Child Language, 4,* 211–224.

U.S. Bureau of the Census. (1994). *Statistical abstract of the United States* (114th ed.) Washington, DC: U.S. Government Printing Office.

U.S. Centers for Disease Control. (1992, January 3). Sexual behavior among high school students—United States, 1990. *Morbidity and Mortality Weekly Report, 40,* 885–888.

U.S. Centers for Disease Control. (1995, January). *HIV/AIDS surveillance.* Atlanta, GA: Author.

U.S. Department of Education. (1994). *Digest of educational statistics* (31st ed.). Washington, DC: U.S. Government Printing Office.

U.S. Department of Health and Human Services. (1988). *The Surgeon General's report on nutrition and health.* Washington, DC: U.S. Government Printing Office.

U.S. Department of Health and Human Services. (1994a). *Healthy people 2000.* Washington, DC: U.S. Government Printing Office.

U.S. Department of Health and Human Services, National Institute on Drug Abuse (1994b). *National survey results on drug use from Monitoring the Future study: Vol. 1. Secondary school students.* Washington, DC: U. S. Government Printing Office.

U.S. Department of Health and Human Services. (1994c). *Vital Statistics of the United States, 1991.* Washington, DC: U.S. Government Printing Office.

U.S. Department of Justice. (1994). *Crime in the United States.* Washington, DC: U.S. Government Printing Office.

U.S. Department of Labor. (1994). *Consumer Price Index: Detailed report.* Washington, DC: U.S. Government Printing Office.

Udry, J. R. (1990). Hormonal and social determinants of adolescent sexual initiation. In J. Bancroft & J. M. Reinisch (Eds.), *Adolescence and puberty* (pp. 70–87). New York: Oxford University Press.

Ullian, D. Z. (1976). The development of conceptions of masculinity and femininity. In B. Loyd & J. Archer (Eds.), *Exploring sex differences* (pp. 25–47). London: Academic Press.

Ulrich, B. D., & Ulrich, D. A. (1985). The role of balancing in performance of fundamental motor skills in 3-, 4-, and 5-year-old children. In J. E. Clark & J. H. Humphrey (Eds.), *Motor development* (Vol. 1, pp. 87–98). Princeton, NJ: Princeton Books.

Unger, R., Kreeger, L., & Christoffel, K. K. (1990). Childhood obesity: Medical and familial correlates and age of onset. *Clinical Pediatrics, 29,* 368–372.

United Nations. (1994). *Demographic yearbook: 1992.* New York: Author.

Uzgiris, I. C., & Hunt, J. McV. (1975). *Assessment in infancy: Ordinal scales of psychological development.* Urbana: University of Illinois Press.

Valdez-Menchaca, M. C., & Whitehurst, G. J. (1992). Accelerating language development through picture book reading: A systematic extension to Mexican day care. *Developmental Psychology, 28,* 1106–1114.

Valian, V. V. (1993). *Parental replies: Linguistic status and didactic role.* Cambridge, MA: MIT Press.

Van de Perre, P., Simonon, A., Hitimana, D., Davis, F., Msellati, P., Mukamabano, J., Van Goethem, C., Karita, E., & Lepage, P. (1993). Infective and anti-infective properties of breastmilk from HIV-1-infected women. *Lancet, 341,* 914–918.

van IJzendoorn, M. H., Goldberg, S., Kroonenberg, P. M. & Frenkel, O. J. (1992). The relative effects of maternal and child problems on the quality of attachment: A meta-analysis of attachment in clinical samples. *Child Development, 63,* 840–858.

van IJzendoorn, M. H., & Kroonenberg, P. M. (1988). Cross-cultural patterns of attachment: A meta-analysis of the Strange Situation. *Child Development, 59,* 147–156.

van IJzendoorn, M. H., Kranenburg, M. J., Zwart-Woudstra, A., van Busschbach, A. M., & Lambermon, M. W. E. (1991). Parental attachment and children's socio-emotional development: Some findings on the validity of the adult attachment interview in the Netherlands. *International Journal of Behavioral Development, 14,* 375–394.

Vandell, D. L., & Corasaniti, M. A. (1988). The relation between third graders' after-school care and social, academic, and emotional functioning. *Child Development, 59,* 868–875.

Vandell, D. L., & Powers, C. (1983). Day care quality and children's free play activities. *American Journal of Orthopsychiatry, 53,* 293–300.

Vandell, D. L., & Ramanan, J. (1991). Children of the National Longitudinal Survey of Youth: Choices in after-school care and child development. *Developmental Psychology, 27,* 637–643.

Vanfossen, B., Jones, J., & Spade, J. (1987). Curriculum tracking and status maintenance. *Sociology of Education, 60,* 104–122.

Vasudev, J., & Hummel, R. C. (1987). Moral stage sequence and principled reasoning in an Indian sample. *Human Development, 30,* 103–118.

Vaughn, B. E., & Waters, E. (1990). Attachment behavior at home and in the lab: Q-sort observations and Strange Situation classifications of one-year-olds. *Child Development, 61,* 1965–1973.

Vaughn, B. E., Kopp, C. B., & Krakow, J. B. (1984). The emergence and consolidation of self-control from eighteen to thirty months of age: Normative trends and individual differences. *Child Development, 55,* 990–1004.

Vaughn, B. E., Lefever, B. G., Seifer, R., & Barglow, P. (1989). Attachment behavior, attachment security, and temperament during infancy. *Child Development, 60,* 728–737.

Vaughn, B. E., Stevenson-Hinde, J., Waters, E., Kotsaftis, A., Lefever, G. B., Shouldice, A., Trudel, M., & Belsky, J. (1992). Attachment security and temperament in infancy and early childhood: Some conceptual clarifications. *Developmental Psychology, 28,* 463–473.

Veerula, G. R., & Noah, P. K. (1990). Clinical manifestations of childhood lead poisoning. *Journal of Tropical Medicine and Hygiene, 93,* 170–177.

Vega-Lahr, N., Field, T., Goldstein, S., & Carran, D. (1988). Type A behavior in preschool children. In T. M. Field, P. M. McCabe, & N. Schneiderman (Eds.), *Stress and coping across development* (pp. 89–107). Hillsdale, NJ: Erlbaum.

Ventura, S. J. (1989). Trends and variations in first births to older women in the United States, 1970–86. *Vital and Health Statistics* (Series 21). Hyattsville, MD: U.S. Department of Health and Human Services.

Verbrugge, H. P. (1990a). The national immunization program of the Netherlands. *Pediatrics, 86* (6, Pt. 2), 1060–1063.

Verbrugge, H. P. (1990b). Youth health care in the Netherlands: A bird's eye view. *Pediatrics, 86* (6, Pt. 2), 1044–1047.

Verhulst, F. C., Althaus, M., & Versluis-Den Bieman, H. J. M. (1990). Problem behavior in international adoptees: I. An epidemiological study. *Journal of the American Academy of Child and Adolescent Psychiatry, 29,* 94–103.

Vessey, J. A. (1988). Comparison of two teaching methods on children's knowledge of their internal bodies. *Nursing Research, 37,* 262–267.

Vinovskis, M. A. (1988). *An "epidemic" of adolescent pregnancy?* New York: Oxford University Press.

Vohr, B. R., & Garcia-Coll, C. T. (1988). Follow-up studies of high-risk low-birth-weight infants: Changing trends. In H. E. Fitzgerald, B. M. Lester, & M. W. Yogman (Eds.), *Theory and research in behavioral pediatrics* (pp. 1–65). New York: Plenum.

Volling, B. L., & Belsky, J. (1992). Contribution of mother–child and father–child relationships to the quality of sibling interaction: A longitudinal study. *Child Development, 63,* 1209–1222.

Vorhees, C. V. (1986). Principles of behavioral teratology. In E. P. Riley & C. V. Vorhees (Eds.), *Handbook of behavioral teratology* (pp. 23–48). New York: Plenum.

Vorhees, C. V., & Mollnow, E. (1987). Behavioral teratogenesis: Long-term influences on behavior from early exposure to environmental agents. In J. D. Osofsky (Ed.), *Handbook of infant development* (2nd ed., pp. 913–971). New York: Wiley.

Voydanoff, P., & Donnelly, B. W. (1990). *Adolescent sexuality and pregnancy.* Newbury Park, CA: Sage.

Vuchinich, S., Hetherington, E. M., Vuchinich, R. A., & Clingempeel, W. G. (1991). Parent–child interaction and gender differences in early adolescents' adaptation to stepfamilies. *Developmental Psychology, 27,* 618–626.

Vurpillot, E. (1968). The development of scanning strategies and their relation to visual differentiation. *Journal of Experimental Psychology, 6,* 632–650.

Vygotsky, L. S. (1978). *Mind in society: The development of higher psychological processes.* Cambridge, MA: Harvard University Press. (Original works published 1930, 1933, and 1935)

Vygotsky, L. S. (1987). Thinking and speech. In R. W. Rieber, A. S. Carton (Eds.), & N. Minick (Trans.), *The collected works of L. S. Vygotsky: Vol. 1. Problems of general psychology* (pp. 37–285). New York: Plenum. (Original work published 1934)

Waas, G. A. (1988). Social attributional biases of peer-rejected and aggressive children. *Child Development, 59,* 969–975.

Wachs, T. D. (1975). Relation of infants' performance on Piagetian scales between twelve and twenty-four months and their Stanford-Binet performance at thirty-one months. *Child Development, 46,* 929–935.

Waddington, C. H. (1957). *The strategy of the genes.* London: Allen & Unwin.

Waggoner, J. E., & Palermo, D. S. (1989). Betty is a bouncing bubble: Children's comprehension of emotion-descriptive metaphors. *Developmental Psychology, 25,* 152–163.

Wagner, B. M., & Phillips, D. A. (1992). Beyond beliefs: Parent and child behaviors and children's perceived academic competence. *Child Development, 63,* 1380–1391.

Wainryb, C. (1993). The application of moral judgments to other cultures: Relativism and universality. *Child Development, 64,* 924–933.

Wakat, D. K. (1978). Physiological factors of race and sex in sport. In L. K. Bunker & R. J. Rotella (Eds.), *Sport psychology: From theory to practice* (pp. 194–209). Charlotte, VA: University of Virginia. (Proceedings of the 1978 Sport Psychology Institute)

Walberg, H. J. (1986). Synthesis of research on teaching. In M. C. Wittrock (Ed.), *Handbook of research on teaching* (3rd ed., pp. 214–229). New York: Macmillan.

Wald, E. R., Guerra, N., & Byers, C. (1991). Frequency and severity of infections in day care: Three-year follow-up. *Journal of Pediatrics, 118,* 509–514.

Walden, T. A., & Ogan, T. A. (1988). The development of social referencing. *Child Development, 59,* 1230–1240.

Walk, R. D., & Gibson, E. J. (1961). A comparative and analytic study of visual depth perception. *Psychological Monographs, 75*(15, Whole No. 519).

Walker, D., Greenwood, C., Hart, B., & Carta, J. (1994). Prediction of school outcomes based on early language production and socioeconomic factors. *Child Development, 65,* 606–621.

Walker, L. J. (1989). A longitudinal study of moral reasoning. *Child Development, 60,* 157–166.

Walker, L. J. (1991). Sex differences in moral reasoning. In W. M. Kurtines & J. L. Gewirtz (Eds.), *Handbook of moral behavior and development* (Vol. 2, pp. 333–364). Hillsdale, NJ: Erlbaum.

Walker, L. J., & Taylor, J. H. (1991a). Family interactions and the development of moral reasoning. *Child Development, 62,* 264–283.

Walker, L. J., & Taylor, J. H. (1991b). Stage transitions in moral reasoning: A longitudinal study of developmental processes. *Developmental Psychology, 27,* 330–337.

Wallace, J. R., Cunningham, T. F., & Del Monte, V. (1984). Change and stability in self-esteem between late childhood and early adolescence. *Journal of Early Adolescence, 4,* 253–257.

Wallach, M. A. (1985). Creativity testing and giftedness. In F. D. Horowitz & M. O'Brien (Eds.), *The gifted and talented: Developmental perspectives* (pp. 99–123). Washington, DC: American Psychological Association.

Waller, M. B. (1993, January). Helping crack-affected children succeed. *Educational Leadership, 50*(4), 57–60.

Wallerstein, J. S. (1983). Children of divorce: The psychological tasks of the child. *American Journal of Orthopsychiatry, 53,* 230–243.

Wallerstein, J. S. (1991). The long-term effects of divorce on children: A review. *Journal of the American Academy of Child and Adolescent Psychiatry, 30,* 349–360.

Wallerstein, J. S., & Corbin, S. B. (1989). Daughters of divorce: Report from a ten-year follow-up. *American Journal of Orthopsychiatry, 59,* 593–604.

Wallerstein, J. S., & Kelly, J. B. (1980). *Surviving the break-up: How children and parents cope with divorce.* New York: Basic Books.

Wallerstein, J. S., Corbin, S. B., & Lewis, J. M. (1988). Children of divorce: A ten-year study. In E. M. Hetherington & J. Arasteh (Eds.), *Impact of divorce, single parenting, and stepparenting on children* (pp. 198–214). Hillsdale, NJ: Erlbaum.

Walters, R. H., & Andres, D. (1967). *Punishment procedures and self-control.* Paper presented at the annual meeting of the American Psychological Association, Washington, DC.

Warren, A. R., & Tate, C. S. (1992). Egocentrism in children's telephone conversations. In R. M. Diaz & L. E. Berk (Eds.), *Private speech: From social interaction to self-regulation* (pp. 245–264). Hillsdale, NJ: Erlbaum.

Warren, S. F., & Kaiser, A. P. (1988). Research in early language intervention. In S. L. Odom & M. B. Karnes (Eds.), *Early intervention for infants and children with handicaps* (pp. 89–108). Baltimore, MD: Paul H. Brookes.

Warren-Leubecker, A., & Bohannon, J. N., III (1989). Pragmatics: Language in social contexts. In J. Berko Gleason (Ed.), *The development of language* (pp. 327–368). Columbus, OH: Merrill.

Waterman, A. S. (1985). Identity in context of adolescent psychology. In A. S. Waterman (Ed.), *New Directions for Child Development* (No. 30, pp. 5–24). San Francisco: Jossey-Bass.

Waterman, A. S. (1989). Curricula interventions for identity change: Substantive and ethical considerations. *Journal of Adolescence, 12,* 389–400.

Waters, H. F. (1993, July 12). Networks under the gun. *Newsweek,* pp. 64–66.

Watson, D. J. (1989). Defining and describing whole language. *Elementary School Journal, 90,* 129–141.

Watson, J. B., & Raynor, R. (1920). Conditioned emotional reactions. *Journal of Experimental Psychology, 3,* 1–14.

Watson, J. D., & Crick, R. H. C. (1953). Molecular structure of nucleic acids. *Nature, 171,* 737–738.

Waxman, S. R., & Hall, D. G. (1993). The development of a linkage between count nouns and object categories: Evidence from fifteen- to twenty-one-month-old infants. *Child Development, 64,* 1224–1241.

Waxman, S. R., & Hatch, T. (1992). Beyond the basics: Preschool children label objects flexibly at multiple hierarchical levels. *Journal of Child Language, 19,* 153–166.

Waxman, S. R., & Senghas, A. (1992). Relations among word meanings in early lexical development. *Developmental Psychology, 28,* 862–873.

Wechsler, D. (1989). *Manual for the Wechsler Preschool and Primary Scale of Intelligence–Revised.* New York: Psychological Corporation.

Wechsler, D. (1991). *Manual for the Wechsler Intelligence Test for Children—III.* New York: Psychological Corporation.

Wegman, M. E. (1994). Annual summary of vital statistics—1993. *Pediatrics, 94,* 792–803.

Wehren, A., DeLisi, R., & Arnold, M. (1981). The development of noun definition. *Journal of Child Language, 8,* 165–175.

Weideger, P. (1976). *Menstruation and menopause.* New York: Knopf.

Weil, W. B. (1975). Infant obesity. In M. Winick (Ed.), *Childhood obesity* (pp. 61–72). New York: Wiley.

Weinberg, R. A., Scarr, S., & Waldman, I. D. (1992). The Minnesota transracial adoption study: A follow-up of IQ test performance at adolescence. *Intelligence, 16,* 117–135.

Weinstein, R. S., Marshall, H. H., Sharp, L., & Botkin, M. (1987). Pygmalion and the student: Age and classroom differences in children's awareness of teacher expectations. *Child Development, 58,* 1079–1093.

Weisner, T., & Gallimore, R. (1977). My brother's keeper: Child and sibling caretaking. *Current Anthropology, 18,* 169–190.

Weisner, T. S., & Wilson-Mitchell, J. E. (1990). Nonconventional family life-styles and sex typing in six-year-olds. *Child Development, 61,* 1915–1933.

Weitzman, M., Gortmaker, S., & Sobol, A. (1990). Racial, social, and environmental risks for childhood asthma. *American Journal of Diseases of Children, 144,* 1189–1194.

Wellman, H. M. (1985). The child's theory of mind: The development of conceptions of cognition. In S. R. Yussen (Ed.), *The growth of reflection in children* (pp. 169–206). San Diego, CA: Academic Press.

Wellman, H. M. (1988a). The early development of memory strategies. In F. F. Weinert & M. Perlmutter (Eds.), *Memory development: Universal changes and individual differences* (pp. 3–29). Hillsdale, NJ: Erlbaum.

Wellman, H. M. (1988b). First steps in the child's theorizing about mind. In J. W. Astington, P. L. Harris, & D. R. Olson (Eds.), *Developing theories of mind* (pp. 64–92). Cambridge, England: Cambridge University Press.

Wellman, H. M., Somerville, S. C., & Haake, R. J. (1979). Development of search procedures in real-life spatial environments. *Developmental Psychology, 15,* 530–542.

Welsh, M. C., Pennington, B. F., Ozonoff, S., Rouse, B., & McCabe, E. R. B. (1990). Neuropsychology of early-treated phenylketonuria: Specific executive function deficits. *Child Development, 61,* 1697–1713.

Wentzel, K., & Feldman, S. S. (1993). Parental predictors of boys' self-restraint and motivation to achieve at school: A longitudinal study. *Journal of Early Adolescence, 13,* 183–203.

Werner, E. E. (1989, April). Children of the garden island. *Scientific American, 260(4),* 106–111.

Werner, E. E., & Smith, R. S. (1982). *Vulnerable but invincible: A study of resilient children.* New York: McGraw-Hill.

Werner, E. E., & Smith, R. S. (1992). *Overcoming the odds: High risk children from birth to adulthood.* Ithaca, NY: Cornell University Press.

Werner, J. S., & Siqueland, E. R. (1978). Visual recognition memory in the preterm infant. *Infant Behavior and Development, 1,* 79–94.

Wertsch, J. V., & Tulviste, P. (1992). L. S. Vygotsky and contemporary developmental psychology. *Developmental Psychology, 28,* 548–557.

Wesley, B. D., van den Berg, B. J., & Reece, E. A. (1993). The effect of forceps delivery on cognitive development. *American Journal of Obstetrics and Gynecology, 169,* 1091–1095.

West, L. L. (1991). Introduction. In L. L. West (Ed.), *Effective strategies for dropout prevention of at-risk youth* (pp. 1–42). Gaithersburg, MD: Aspen.

Westbury, I. (1992, June–July). Comparing American and Japanese Achievement: Is the United States really a low achiever? *Educational Researcher, 21*(3), 18–24.

Whalen, C. K., & Henker, B. (1991). Therapies for hyperactive children: Comparisons, combinations, and compromises. *Journal of Consulting and Clinical Psychology, 59,* 126–137.

Wheeler, M. D. (1991). Physical changes of puberty. *Endocrinology and Metabolism Clinics of North America, 20,* 1–14.

Whiffen, V. E., & Gotlib, I. H. (1989). Infants of postpartum depressed mothers: Temperament and cognitive status. *Journal of Abnormal Psychology, 98,* 274–279.

Whisnant, L., & Zegans, L. (1975). A study of attitudes toward menarche in white middle-class American adolescent girls. *American Journal of Psychiatry, 132,* 809–814.

White, B., & Held, R. (1966). Plasticity of sensorimotor development in the human infant. In J. F. Rosenblith & W. Allinsmith (Eds.), *The causes of behavior* (pp. 60–70). Boston: Allyn and Bacon.

White, S. H. (1992). G. Stanley Hall: From philosophy to developmental psychology. *Developmental Psychology, 28,* 25–34.

Whitehurst, G. J. (1982). Language development. In B. B. Wolman (Ed.), *Handbook of developmental psychology* (pp. 367–386). New York: Wiley.

Whitehurst, G. J., Arnold, D. S., Epstein, J. N., Angell, A. L., Smith, M., & Fischel, J. E. (1994). A picture book reading intervention in day care and home for children from low-income families. *Developmental Psychology, 30,* 679–689.

Whitehurst, G. J., Fischel, J. E., Caulfield, M. B., DeBaryshe, B. D., & Valdez-Menchaca, M. C. (1989). Assessment and treatment of early expressive language delay. In P. R. Zelazo & R. Barr (Eds.), *Challenges to developmental paradigms: Implications for assessment and treatment* (pp. 113–135). Hillsdale, NJ: Erlbaum.

Whitehurst, G. J., & Vasta, R. (1975). Is language acquired through imitation? *Journal of Psycholinguistic Research, 4,* 37–59.

Whiting, B., & Edwards, C. P. (1988a). *Children in different worlds.* Cambridge, MA: Harvard University Press.

Whiting, B., & Edwards, C. P. (1988b). A cross-cultural analysis of sex differences in the behavior of children aged 3 through 11.

In G. Handel (Ed.), *Childhood socialization* (pp. 281–297). New York: Aldine de Gruyter.

Whiting, J. W. M., Burbank, V. K., & Ratner, M. S. (1986). The duration of maidenhood across cultures. In J. B. Lancaster & B. Hamburg (Eds.), *School-age pregnancy and parenthood: Biosocial dimensions* (pp. 273–302). New York: Aldine de Gruyter.

Wigfield, R. E., Fleming, P. J., Berry, P. J., Rudd, P. T., & Golding, J. (1992). Can the fall in Avon's sudden infant death rate be explained by changes in sleeping position? *British Medical Journal, 304,* 282–283.

Wilensky, H. L. (1983). Evaluating research and politics: Political legitimacy and consensus as missing variables in the assessment of social policy. In E. Spiro & E. Yuchtman-Yaar (Eds.), *Evaluating the welfare state: Social and political perspectives* (pp. 51–74). New York: Academic Press.

Willats, J. (1977). How children learn to represent three-dimensional space in drawings. In G. Butterworth (Ed.), *The child's representation of the world* (pp. 189–202). New York: Plenum.

Wille, D. E. (1991). Relation of preterm birth with quality of infant–mother attachment at one year. *Infant Behavior and Development, 14,* 227–240.

Willer, B., Hofferth, S. L., Kisker, E. E., Divine-Hawkins, P., Farquhar, E., & Glantz, F. B. (1991). *The demand and supply of child care in 1990: Joint findings from the National Child Care Survey 1990 and A Profile of Child Care Settings.* Washington, DC: National Association for the Education of Young Children.

Willerman, L. (1979). Effects of families on intellectual development. *American Psychologist, 34,* 923–929.

Williams, B. C. (1990). Immunization coverage among preschool children: The United States and selected countries. *Pediatrics, 86*(6, Pt. 2), 1052–1055.

Williams, B. C., & Kotch, J. B. (1990). Excess injury mortality among children in the United States: Comparison of recent international statistics. *Pediatrics, 86*(6, Pt. 2), 1067–1073.

Williams, C., & Bybee, J. (1994). What do children feel guilty about? Development and gender differences. *Developmental Psychology, 30,* 617–623.

Williams, C. S., Buss, K. A., & Eskenazi, B. (1992). Infant resuscitation is associated with an increased risk of left-handedness. *American Journal of Epidemiology, 136,* 277–286.

Williams, E., & Radin, N. (1993). Paternal involvement, maternal employment, and adolescents' academic achievement: An 11-year follow-up. *American Journal of Orthopsychiatry, 63,* 306–312.

Williams, E., Radin, N., & Allegro, T. (1992). Sex-role attitudes of adolescents reared primarily by their fathers: An 11-year follow-up. *Merrill-Palmer Quarterly, 38,* 457–476.

Wilson, A. L., & Neidich, G. (1991). Infant mortality and public policy. *Social Policy Report of the Society for Research in Child Development, 5*(2).

Wilson, M., & Baker, S. (1987). Structural approach to injury control. *Journal of Social Issues, 43,* 73–86.

Wilson, M. N. (1986). The black extended family: An analytical consideration. *Developmental Psychology, 22,* 246–258.

Wilson, R., & Cairns, E. (1988). Sex-role attributes, perceived competence and the development of depression in adolescence. *Journal of Child Psychology and Psychiatry, 29,* 635–650.

Wilson, R. S. (1976). Concordance in physical growth for monozygotic and dizygotic twins. *Annals of Human Biology, 3,* 1–10.

Wilson, R. S. (1983). The Louisville Twin Study: Developmental synchronies in behavior. *Child Development, 54,* 298–316.

Wilson, W. J. (1991). Studying inner-city social dislocations: The challenge of public agenda research. *American Sociological Review, 56,* 1–14.

Winick, M., & Noble, A. (1966). Cellular response in rats during malnutrition at various ages. *Journal of Nutrition, 89,* 300–306.

Winick, M., Rosso, P., & Waterlow, J. (1970). Cellular growth of cerebrum, cerebellum, and brain stem in normal and marasmic children. *Experimental Neurology, 26,* 393–400.

Winn, S., Tronick, E. Z., & Morelli, G. A. (1989). The infant and the group: A look at Efe caretaking. In J. K. Nugent, B. M. Lester, & T. B. Brazelton (Eds.), *Biology, culture, and development* (Vol. 1, pp. 87–109). Norwood, NJ: Ablex.

Winner, E. (1986, August). Where pelicans kiss seals. *Psychology Today, 20(8),* 25–35.

Winner, E. (1988). *The point of words: Children's understanding of metaphor and irony.* Cambridge, MA: Harvard University Press.

Winthrop, R. H. (1991). *Dictionary of concepts in cultural anthropology.* New York: Greenwood Press.

Wintre, M. G., & Vallance, D. D. (1994). A developmental sequence in the comprehension of emotions: Intensity, multiple emotions, and valence. *Developmental Psychology, 30,* 509–514.

Witelson, S. F., & Kigar, D. L. (1988). Anatomical development of the corpus callosum in humans: A review with reference to sex and cognition. In D. L. Molfese & S. J. Segalowitz (Eds.), *Brain lateralization in children* (pp. 35–57). New York: Guilford Press.

Wolf, R. M. (1993, November). The National Assessment of Educational Progress: The Nation's Report Card. *NASSP Bulletin, 77(556),* 36–45.

Wolff, P. H. (1966). The causes, controls and organization of behavior in the neonate. *Psychological Issues, 5*(1, Serial No. 17).

Wolfner, G., Faust, D., & Dawes, R. (1993). The use of anatomical dolls in sexual abuse evaluations: The state of the science. *Applied and Preventive Psychology, 2,* 1–11.

Wong-Fillmore, L., Ammon, P., McLaughlin, B., & Ammon, M. S. (1985). *Learning English through bilingual instruction.* Rosslyn, VA: National Clearinghouse for Bilingual Education.

Wood, D. J. (1989). Social interaction as tutoring. In M. H. Bornstein & J. S. Bruner (Eds.), *Interaction in human development* (pp. 59–80). Hillsdale, NJ: Erlbaum.

Woodward, A. L., Markman, E. M., & Fitzsimmons, C. M. (1994). Rapid word learning in 13- and 18-month-olds. *Developmental Psychology, 30,* 553–566.

Woolley, J. D., & Wellman, H. M. (1990). Young children's understanding of realities, nonrealities, and appearances. *Child Development, 61,* 946–961.

World Bank (1992). *World development report.* New York: Author.

Worobey, J., & Blajda, V. M. (1989). Temperament ratings at 2 weeks, 2 months, and 1 year: Differential stability of activity and emotionality. *Developmental Psychology, 25,* 257–263.

Wright, J. (1991). Poverty, homelessness, health, nutrition, and children. In J. H. Kryder-Coe, L. M. Salamon, & J. M. Molnar (Eds.), *Homeless children and youth: A new American dilemma* (pp. 71–104). New Brunswick, NJ: Transaction.

Yarrow, A. L. (1991). *Latecomers: Children of parents over 35.* New York: Free Press.

Yarrow, M. R., Scott, P. M., & Waxler, C. Z. (1973). Learning concern for others. *Developmental Psychology, 8,* 240–260.

Yazigi, R. A., Odem, R. R., & Polakoski, K. L. (1991). Demonstration of specific binding of cocaine to human spermatozoa. *Journal of the American Medical Association, 266,* 1956–1959.

Yesalis, C. E., Streit, A. L., Vicary, J. R., Friedl, K. E., Brannon, D., & Buckley, W. (1989). Anabolic steroid use: Indications of habituation among adolescents. *Journal of Drug Education, 19,* 103–116.

Yip, R., Scanlon, K., & Trowbridge, F. (1993). Trends and patterns in height and weight status of low-income U.S. children. *Critical Reviews in Food Science and Nutrition, 33,* 409–421.

Yogman, M. W. (1981). Development of the father–infant relationship. In H. Fitzgerald, B. Lester, & M. W. Yogman (Eds.), *Theory and research in behavioral pediatrics* (Vol. 1, pp. 221–279). New York: Plenum.

Yonas, A., Granrud, E. C., Arterberry, M. E., & Hanson, B. L. (1986). Infants' distance perception from linear perspective and texture gradients. *Infant Behavior and Development, 9,* 247–256.

Yonas, A., & Hartman, B. (1993). Perceiving the affordance of contact in four- and five-month-old infants. *Child Development, 64,* 298–308.

Young, C., McMahon, J. E., Bowman, V., & Thompson, D. (1989). Maternal reasons for delayed prenatal care. *Nursing Research, 38,* 242–243.

Young, K. T. (1990). American conceptions of infant development from 1955 to 1984: What the experts are telling parents. *Child Development, 61,* 17–28.

Younger, B. A. (1985). The segregation of items into categories by ten-month-old infants. *Child Development, 56,* 1574–1583.

Younger, B. A. (1993). Understanding category members as "the same sort of thing": Explicit categorization in ten-month infants. *Child Development, 64,* 309–320.

Youniss, J. (1980). *Parents and peers in social development: A Piagetian-Sullivan perspective.* Chicago: University of Chicago Press.

Youniss, J., & Smollar, J. (1986). *Adolescent relations with mothers, fathers, and friends.* Chicago: University of Chicago Press.

Yuill, N., & Perner, J. (1988). Intentionality and knowledge in children's judgments of actor's responsibility and recipient's emotional reaction. *Developmental Psychology, 24,* 358–365.

Zabin, L. S., & Hayward, S. C. (1993). *Adolescent sexual behavior and childbearing.* Newbury Park, CA: Sage.

Zahn-Waxler, C., Kochanska, G., Krupnick, J., & McKnew, D. (1990). Patterns of guilt in children of depressed and well mothers. *Developmental Psychology, 26,* 51–59.

Zahn-Waxler, C., Radke-Yarrow, M., & King, R. M. (1979). Child-rearing and children's prosocial initiations toward victims of distress. *Child Development, 50,* 319–330.

Zahn-Waxler, C., Radke-Yarrow, M., Wagner, E., & Chapman, M. (1992). Development of concern for others. *Developmental Psychology, 28,* 126–136.

Zajonc, R. B., Markus, H., & Markus, G. B. (1979). The birth order puzzle. *Journal of Personality and Social Psychology, 37,* 1325–1341.

Zametkin, A. J., Nordahl, T. E., Gross, M., King, A. C., Semple, W. E., Rumsey, J., Hamburger, S., & Cohen, R. M. (1990). Cerebral glucose metabolism in adults with hyperactivity of childhood onset. *New England Journal of Medicine, 323,* 1413–1415.

Zani, B. (1993). Dating and interpersonal relationships in adolescence. In S. Jackson & H. Rodriguez-Tomé (Eds.), *Adolescence and its social worlds* (pp. 95–119). Hillsdale, NJ: Erlbaum.

Zaslow, M. J., Rabinovich, B. A., & Suwalsky, J. T. (1991). From maternal employment to child outcomes: Preexisting group differences and moderating variables. In J. V. Lerner & N. L. Galambos (Eds.), *Employed mothers and their children* (pp. 237–282). New York: Garland.

Zeisel, S. H. (1986). Dietary influences on neurotransmission. *Advances in Pediatrics, 33,* 23–48.

Zelazo, N. A., Zelazo, P. R., Cohen, K. M., & Zelazo, P. D. (1993). Specificity of practice effects on elementary neuromotor patterns. *Developmental Psychology, 29,* 686–691.

Zelazo, P. R. (1983). The development of walking: New findings on old assumptions. *Journal of Motor Behavior, 2,* 99–137.

Zeskind, P. S., & Ramey, C. T. (1978). Fetal malnutrition: An experimental study of its consequences on infant development in two caregiving environments. *Child Development, 49,* 1155–1162.

Zeskind, P. S., & Ramey, C. T. (1981). Preventing intellectual and interactional sequelae of fetal malnutrition: A longitudinal, transactional, and synergistic approach to development. *Child Development, 52,* 213–218.

Zhang, J., Cai, W., & Lee, D. J. (1992). Occupational hazards and pregnancy outcomes. *American Journal of Industrial Medicine, 21,* 397–408.

Ziegler, C. B., Dusek, J. B., & Carter, D. B. (1984). Self-concept and sex-role orientation: An investigation of multidimensional aspects of personality development in adolescence. *Journal of Early Adolescence, 4,* 25–39.

Zigler, E., Abelson, W. D., & Seitz, V. (1973). Motivational factors in the performance of economically disadvantaged children on the Peabody Picture Vocabulary Test. *Child Development, 44,* 294–303.

Zigler, E., & Hall, N. W. (1989). Physical child abuse in America: Past, present, and future. In D. Cicchetti & V. Carlson (Eds.), *Child maltreatment* (pp. 203–253). New York: Cambridge University Press.

Zigler, E., & Seitz, V. (1982). Social policy and intelligence. In R. J. Sternberg (Ed.), *Handbook of human intelligence* (pp. 586–641). Cambridge, England: Cambridge University Press.

Zigler, E., & Styfco, S. J. (1994). Head Start: Criticisms in a constructive context. *American Psychologist, 49,* 127–132.

Zigler, E. F. (1987). Formal schooling for four-year-olds? No. *American Psychologist, 42,* 254–260.

Zigler, E. F., & Finn-Stevenson, M. E. (1992). Applied developmental psychology. In M. H. Bornstein & M. E. Lamb (Eds.), *Developmental psychology: An advanced textbook* (2nd ed., pp. 677–729). Hillsdale, NJ: Erlbaum.

Zigler, E. F., & Gilman, E. (1993). Day care in America: What is needed? *Pediatrics, 91,* 175–178.

Zillman, D., Bryant, J., & Huston, A. C. (1994). *Media, family, and children.* Hillsdale, NJ: Erlbaum.

Zimmerman, B. J. (1990). Self-regulation learning and academic achievement: An overview. *Educational Psychologist, 25,* 3–18.

Ziporyn, T. (1992, February). Postpartum depression: True blue? *Harvard Health Letter, 17*(4), 1–3.

Zuckerman, B., Frank, D. A., & Hingson, R. (1989). Effects of maternal marijuana and cocaine use on fetal growth. *New England Journal of Medicine, 320,* 762–768.

Zukow, P. G. (1986). The relationship between interaction with the caregiver and the emergence of play activities during the one-word period. *British Journal of Developmental Psychology, 4,* 223–234.

Zukow, P. G. (1989). Siblings as effective socializing agents: Evidence from central Mexico. In P. G. Zukow (Ed.), *Sibling interaction across cultures* (pp. 79–105). New York: Springer-Verlag.

NAME INDEX

Aaron, R., 471
Aaronson, L. S., 112, 114, 115
Abbott, S., 183
Abbotts, B., 297
Abel, E. L., 124
Abelson, W. D., 338
Aber, J. L., 193
Aboud, F. E., 482
Abraham, K. G., 588
Abramovitch, R., 46
Abrams, A., 495
Abravanel, E., 195
Achenbach, T. M., 149, 422
Ackerman, B. P., 447
Acredolo, C., 424
Acredolo, L. P., 238
Adams, Anne, 424
Adams, Anne-Marie., 331
Adams, C., 551
Adams, G. R., 587, 588
Adams, R. J., 158, 159, 198
Adamson, L. B., 242, 254
Adan, A. M., 565
Adcock, A. G., 613
Adelson, J., 608
Adler, T. F., 471
Adolf, K. E., 205
Adolph, K. E., 13
Aerts, E., 597
Ahlsten, G., 114
Ainsworth, M. D. S., 267, 268*n*, 270
Albright, A., 164
Alemagno, S., 125
Ales, K. L., 123
Alessandri, S. M., 113, 359, 556
Alexander, K., 301
Alipuria, L., 589
Allegro, T., 494
Allen, J. P., 603
Allen, Loretta F., 113
Allen, Lucile, 229, 337
Allen, S. G., 596
Alpern, L., 276
Alpert-Gillis, L. J., 379
Altemeier, W. A., 181
Alter-Reid, K., 498
Althaus, M., 72
Altshuler, J. L., 474
Alvarez, M. M., 601
Alvord, E. C., 176*n*
Amato, P. R., 491
American Academy of Pediatrics, 179*n*
American College of Sports Medicine, 542
American Psychiatric Association, 430, 453
American Psychological Association, 44, 45*n*
Ames, E. W., 201
Amsel, E., 551, 555
Anand, K. J. S., 157
Anderson, D. R., 428
Anderson, Edward R., 491, 492
Anderson, Elaine S., 347
Anderson, G. C., 149
Anderson, J. E., 538
Anderson, K. N., 333
Anderson, P. J., 562
Andersson, B-E., 231
Andres, D., 369
Angle, J., 400
Anglin, J. M., 344, 446
Angulo, J., 404
Antonarakis, S. E., 65
Apgar, V., 137, 138*n*
Appelbaum, M. I., 229
Appleton, T., 158
Archer, S. L., 587, 588, 589, 590
Arend, R., 275
Ariès, P., 9, 10
Arjmand, O., 576
Arnett, J., 540
Arnold, F., 274
Arnold, K., 576
Arnold, M., 446
Arsenault, L., 301
Arterberry, M. E., 199
Arthur, M. W., 616
Artman, L., 426
Asher, S. R., 455, 482, 483
Ashmead, D. H., 158, 189, 223
Aslin, R. N., 158, 242
Asquith, P., 603
Astington, J. W., 356
Astley, S. J., 115
Atkin, C., 373
Atkinson, R. C., 24, 221, 221*n*, 222
Attanucci, J., 599
Attie, I., 528
Au, T. K., 322
August, D., 449
Auletta, K., 374
Aumiller, K., 483
Avis, J., 334, 466
Axia, G., 447
Axworthy, D., 66*n*
Ayoub, C. C., 342
Azmitia, M., 329, 488

Bahrick, L. E., 203, 204
Bai, D. L., 200
Bailey, J. M., 532
Bailey, R. C., 287
Bailey, T., 576, 577, 578
Baillargeon, R., 23, 217, 218*n*, 219, 325, 424
Baird, P. A., 65
Bakeman, R., 254
Baker, C. T., 229
Baker, D. P., 80, 460, 566
Baker, S., 301
Baker-Ward, L., 500
Bakewell, J., 142
Ball, S., 344
Ballard, B. D., 402
Balle-Jensen, L., 540
Bancroft, J., 66*n*
Band, E. B., 474
Bandini, L. G., 401, 402
Bandura, A., 20, 368, 369, 380
Banis, H. T., 403
Banks, M. S., 158, 198, 199, 201, 201*n*
Barber, B. K., 613
Barber, M., 300
Barenboim, C., 474, 476, 585
Barett, K., 200
Bargelow, P. D., 149
Barker, D. J. P., 120
Barker, R. G., 80
Barkley, R. A., 430
Barnard, K. E., 148, 149
Barnes, D., 142
Barnes, J., 470
Barnes, K. E., 363*n*
Barnes, S., 242
Barnett, D., 385
Barnett, J. K., 590
Barnett, M., 141
Barnett, W. S., 232
Barol, B., 113
Baroni, R., 447
Barr, H. M., 112, 114, 115
Barrera, M. E., 202
Barrett, D. E., 33
Barrett, K. C., 251
Barry, H., III., 512, 521, 522
Barth, R. P., 536
Barton, M., 345
Bastian, H., 142
Bates, E., 237, 240
Bates, J. E., 76, 257, 262, 275, 276, 372
Bauer, P. J., 324, 332
Baumeister, R. F., 584
Baumrind, D., 75, 76, 382, 383, 566, 602, 609
Bayles, K., 276
Bayley, N., 185*n*, 188*n*, 195, 228, 229, 524
Beach, F., 529
Beal, C. R., 434, 558
Beardsall, L., 604
Bearison, D. J., 478
Beatty, W. W., 376
Beautrais, A. L., 293
Beck, M., 71
Beeghley, L., 530
Behrend, D. A., 239, 322, 329
Behrman, R. E., 63*n*
Beidel, D., 496
Beilenson, P., 531
Beilin, H., 21, 22, 325
Beintema, D., 154*n*
Belkin, L., 71
Bell, A., 532
Bell, M. A., 218, 257
Bell, R. Q., 34
Bellinger, D., 116
Belmont, M. J., 450, 452
Belsky, J., 128, 227, 262, 270, 273, 275, 386, 386*n*
Bem, D. J., 41, 259
Bem, S. L., 379, 380, 381
Benacerraf, B. R., 68*n*, 108
Benbow, C. P., 291, 457, 560, 576
Bench, R. J., 157
Benedict, R., 255, 529
Beneson, J. F., 376
Benjamin, F., 179
Bentler, P. M., 439, 538, 539, 540
Berezin, J., 231*n*
Berg, K. M., 182
Berg, M., 79
Berg, W. K., 182
Bergman, A., 250
Berk, L. E., 30, 35, 327, 328, 329, 542, 565, 572
Berko Gleason, J., 241
Berkowitz, M. W., 597
Berman, P. W., 137, 163
Berndt, T. J., 384, 482, 604, 605, 606
Bernier, J. C., 430
Berrueta-Clement, J. R., 340
Berry, K., 501
Bertenthal, B. I., 200, 201, 202
Bertoncini, J., 157
Bertrand, J., 345
Best, D. L., 429, 484
Betz, C., 369
Beyth-Marom, R., 532
Bialystok, E., 447
Bibace, R., 408
Biederman, J., 430
Bierman, K. L., 483
Biernat, M., 376, 485
Bigi, L., 433
Bigler, R. S., 381
Bijeljac-Babic, R., 157
Birch, H. G., 258*n*
Birch, J. W., 454*n*
Birch, L. L., 180, 293, 295, 296*n*, 402
Birnholz, J. C., 108
Bishop, S. M., 470
Bivens, J. A., 328
Bjorklund, D. F., 429, 431
Black, Allen E., 382
Black, Ann, 564
Black, J. E., 174
Black, M., 100
Blajda, V. M., 258
Blake, J., 101
Blanchard, M., 268
Blasi, A., 600
Blass, E. M., 157, 191
Blaubergs, M. S., 576
Block, Jack, 492, 539, 540, 586
Block, Jeanne H., 492, 601
Bloom, B. S., 456
Bloom, L., 345
Blotner, R., 478
Blue, J., 386
Bluebond-Langer, M., 323
Blurton Jones, N., 414
Blyth, D. A., 524, 563, 564*n*, 565, 604, 607
Blythe, B. J., 536
Bobak, I. M., 118, 141
Bodurtha, J., 64
Boer, F., 488
Bogatz, G. A., 344
Bohannon, J. N., III, 236, 348
Boldizar, J. P., 379, 485
Boll, E. S., 275
Boni, R., 273
Booth, A., 180
Borghraef, M., 66*n*
Borja-Alvarez, T., 378
Borke, H., 322
Borkowski, J. G., 434, 472
Bornholt, L. J., 575
Bornstein, M. H., 27, 223, 226, 227, 254, 309
Borrine, M. L., 490
Borstelmann, L. J., 10
Borton, R. W., 203
Boruta, M. J., 452
Bossard, J. S. S., 275
Bouchard, C., 172, 173, 289, 292, 302, 409, 516*n*, 542
Bouchard, T. J., 88, 92
Boudreau, J. P., 200
Boukydis, C. F. Z., 161, 162
Boulton, M., 414
Boutry, M., 181
Bowen, R., 556
Bowen-Woodward, K., 493, 494
Bowlby, J., 27, 266, 267, 272
Boyes, M. C., 590, 596
Boysson-Bardies, B. de., 237
Brabeck, M., 600
Brackbill, Y., 143
Bracken, M. B., 112
Bradley, R. H., 230, 230*n*, 338, 338*n*, 339, 460
Braeges, J. L., 370
Braine, L. G., 412, 413
Braine, M. D. S., 239
Brainerd, C. J., 316, 425, 548, 550
Brand, E., 493, 494
Bransford, J. D., 432
Brassard, M. R., 388
Braungart, J. M., 88, 273
Braverman, P. K., 530, 531, 532, 537, 538
Bray, J. H., 492
Brazelton, T. B., 81, 143, 162, 190
Bread for the World Institute, 180
Bredekamp, S., 231*n*, 232, 343*n*
Brennan, W. M., 201
Brenner, D., 403
Brent, S. B., 323
Bresnick, S., 473
Bretherton, I., 27, 240, 256, 267, 315, 358, 361
Briere, J. N., 387, 501
Brindley, B. A., 144
Brody, G. H., 275, 378, 488, 604

Brody, L. E., 457
Brody, N., 77, 232, 442
Broman, S. H., 143
Bromley, D. B., 467, 468
Bronfenbrenner, U., 27, 29, 74, 89
Bronson, G. W., 201
Brook, R. H., 404
Brookman, R. R., 537
Brooks, P. H., 299, 406
Brooks, R. H., 608
Brooks-Gunn, J., 78, 83, 147, 148, 150, 277, 342, 377, 515, 519, 520, 522, 524, 525, 528, 532, 533. 534, 535, 610
Brophy, J. E., 451, 452
Brown, A. L., 432, 434, 558
Brown, B. B., 607, 609, 609*n*
Brown, D., 494
Brown, L. K., 408
Brown, R. W., 239, 239*n*, 346, 356
Brownell, C. A., 356
Bruch, H., 402
Bruck, M., 500, 501
Bruner, J. S., 225, 237, 328
Bryant, B. K., 79
Bryant, Dana, 334
Bryant, Donna M., 232
Bryant, J., 375
Buchsbaum, H. K., 368
Buck, G. M., 194
Buddin, B. J., 473
Buekens, P., 124
Bugental, D. B., 386
Buhrmester, D., 43, 488, 604, 606, 608
Bukowski, W. M., 483, 606
Bulatao, R. A., 274
Bullock, M., 277, 324
Burbank, V. K., 512
Burchinal, M., 343
Burgess, A. W., 385
Burgess, R. L., 161
Burke, B. S., 118
Burke, M., 275
Burke, P., 194
Burlingham-Dubree, M., 440
Burns, S. M., 316
Burton, B. K., 68*n*
Busch-Rossnagel, N. A., 384
Bushnell, E. W., 188, 200
Buss, A. H., 258
Buss, K. A., 290
Bussey, K., 380
Butler, G. E., 396
Butler, R., 472
Bybee, J., 600
Byers, C., 300
Byrne, D. F., 474, 475*n*
Byrne, M. C., 348
Byrnes, J. P., 436, 560

Cahan, S., 426
Cai, W., 61
Cain, K. M., 357
Cain, V. S., 495
Caine, N., 522
Cairns, B. D., 571*n*
Cairns, E., 611
Cairns, R. B., 12, 481, 571*n*
Caldas, S. J., 534
Caldwell, B. M., 230, 338, 338*n*, 339, 460
Caliso, J., 388
Camara, K. A., 491
Cameron, N., 288*n*
Campbell, F. A., 233, 233*n*
Campbell, M., 113
Campos, J. J., 200, 201, 251, 252, 253, 255, 269, 361
Campos, R. G., 161*n*
Camras, L. A., 252, 253
Canick, J. A., 68*n*
Canizzo, S. R., 429
Cannella, G. S., 329
Capaldi, D. M., 502
Capelli, C. A., 561
Caplan, M., 356
Capuzzi, D., 614*n*
Cardarelli, A. P., 497, 498, 501
Carey, S., 408, 427
Carle, E., 313
Carlson, C., 566
Carlson, V., 271
Carpenter, C. J., 378
Carriger, M. S., 229, 356
Carruth, B. R., 402
Carter, D. B., 478, 601
Case, R., 23, 222, 224, 225, 277, 325, 426, 427, 552
Casey, M. B., 309
Cashdan, E., 82
Caspi, A., 41, 259, 525
Cassel, J., 122
Cassidy, J., 127
Casten, R., 83
Caudill, W., 186
Cazden, C., 449
Ceci, S. J., 431, 432, 442, 444, 500, 501
Celano, M. P., 405
Cernoch, J. M., 157
Chalkley, M. A., 236, 239
Chalmers, J. B., 476
Chamberlain, M. C., 119
Chandler, M. J., 476, 590
Chandra, R. K., 120
Chang, H., 37
Chao, R. K., 384
Chapman, M., 424, 471
Charo, R. A., 71
Chase, C. H., 119
Chase-Lansdale, L., 534
Chase-Lansdale, P. L., 78, 83, 533
Chasnoff, I. J., 113
Chatkupt, S., 117*n*, 119
Chein, C., 145
Chen, A. W., 407
Chen, C., 82, 458, 459
Chen, S., 269
Cheng, M., 145
Cherlin, A. J., 75, 489, 491, 492
Chess, S., 257, 258*n*, 259, 261, 262
Cheung, L. W. Y., 402
Chi, M. T. H., 431, 432, 432*n*
Children's Defense Fund, 29, 78, 84*n*, 85, 121, 124, 148, 151, 232, 295, 297, 298, 385, 388, 407, 490, 533, 535, 540, 541, 569, 572, 578
Childs, C. P., 30
Chilmonczyk, B. A., 405
Chipuer, H. M., 260
Chisholm, J. S., 162
Choi, S., 224
Chomsky, C., 447
Chomsky, N., 235
Christoffel, K. K., 401, 402
Christophersen, E. R., 299
Churchill, B. H., 528
Churchill, S. R., 72
Ciaramitare, V., 157
Cicchetti, D., 193, 385
Clark, E. V., 239, 345
Clark, J. E., 302, 410
Clark, M. L., 589
Clark, R. D. III., 160
Clarke-Stewart, K. A., 39, 273
Clasen, D., 609
Claudy, J. G., 101
Clausen, J. A., 524
Clavadetscher, J. E., 159, 198
Clements, D. H., 452, 453, 455
Cleminshaw, H. K., 491
Clifton, R. K., 158, 189
Clingempeel, W. G., 491, 493, 494
Clubb, P. A., 332
Cnattingius, S., 114
Coakley, J., 413
Cohen, F. L., 58*n*, 61, 63*n*, 66*n*, 117*n*, 119
Cohen, L. B., 205, 224
Cohen-Overbeek, W. C. J., 102
Cohn, J. F., 164, 252
Coie, J. D., 482, 483, 484
Colby, A., 593, 595
Cole, C. B., 501
Cole, J. R., 576
Cole, M., 432, 552
Coleman, J., 567
Collea, J. V., 145
Collins, W. A., 341, 342, 373
Collmer, C. W., 369
Colman, A. D., 126, 127, 164
Colman, L. L., 126, 127, 164
Comer, J. P., 572
Committee on Sports Medicine, 542
Compas, B. E., 502
Condry, J., 372
Conel, J. L., 175*n*
Conger, R. D., 78, 387, 603
Connell, J. P., 379
Connolly, J. A., 316
Connolly, K., 184
Constanzo, P. R., 402
Cooke, R. A., 46
Cooney, G. H., 575
Cooper, B., 597
Cooper, C. R., 566, 574, 590
Cooper, R. P., 242
Coopersmith, S., 470
Copes, M., 163
Coplan, R. J., 364
Copper, R. L., 148
Coppotelli, H., 482
Corah, N. L., 147
Corasaniti, M. A., 495
Corbin, S. B., 490, 491
Coren, S., 290
Corman, H. H., 219, 229
Cornell, C. P., 385
Cornell, E. H., 149
Corno, L., 452
Corrigan, R., 315, 316
Costabile, A., 414
Cotton, D. B., 68*n*
Cotton, P., 194
Courage, M. L., 158, 198
Cowan, C. P., 128, 163
Cowan, P. A., 163
Cox, K., 145
Cox, M. J., 75, 272, 273, 274, 490, 492, 493
Cox, R., 490, 492, 493
Craik, F. I. M., 24
Crain-Thoreson, C., 242
Cramond, B., 456
Cratty, B. J., 302, 303*n*, 409*n*, 410, 411, 413
Crawford, D. B., 83
Crick, F. H. C., 52
Crick, N. R., 483
Crider, C., 408
Crisafi, M. A., 324
Crockenberg, S. B., 262, 272, 279
Crockett, L. J., 601
Crook, C. K., 157
Crouter, A. C., 89
Crowell, J. A., 272
Cruttenden, L., 218
Cruzcosa, M., 386
Csikszentmihalyi, M., 520, 523*n*, 558, 604, 605, 605*n*
Cummings, E. M., 40
Cunningham, T. F., 469
Curry, G. D., 617
Curtiss, S., 562
Curwin, A., 237
Cutler, A., 198
Cytryn, L., 164

D'Ercole, A., 78
Dagleish, M., 184
Dale, P. S., 242
Damhuis, I., 473
Damon, W., 365, 467, 477, 478, 481, 482, 585, 586
Dannemiller, J. L., 202
Darlington, R., 340
Darwin, C., 11, 12
Davenport, G. G., 471
Davey, T. C., 439
David, H. P., 72
Davidson, E., 141
Davidson, P., 593
Davidson, R. J., 177
Davies, M. W., 84
Davies, Mark, 613
Davis, C. C., 362
Davis, N., 183
Davis, W., 532
Dawes, R., 501
Day, S., 63, 64
De Lisi, R., 379
de Villiers, J. G., 346
de Villiers, P. A., 346
DeAngelis, T., 496, 497*n*
DeBaryshe, B. D., 75, 372, 616*n*
DeBlassie, R. R., 527, 528
DeCasper, A. J., 108, 158
Declercq, E. R., 142
DeFrain, J., 194
Degelman, D., 452
Del Monte, V., 469
Delgado-Gaitan, C., 38, 80, 567
DeLisi, R., 446
Dellas, M., 588
DeLoache, J. S., 331, 332, 333
Delphi Communication Sciences, 487
DeMaria, A., 119
DeMarie-Dreblow, D., 432
Dembo, M. H., 606
DeMeis, D., 273
Dement, W. C., 160
Demetriou, A., 552, 555
Denham, S. A., 383
Dennis, M. G., 186
Dennis, W., 186
Denny, T., 576
Deutsch, F. M., 126, 127
Deutsch, W., 447
Devereux, E. C., 414
DeVos, J., 217, 218*n*
Diamond, A., 218
Diana, M. S., 608
Dias, M. G., 316
Diaz, R. M., 328, 448, 605
Dick-Read, G., 140
Dickenson, G., 608
Dickinson, D. K., 446
Dickinson, J. C., 143, 150
DiClemente, R. J., 538
Didow, S. M., 362
Dietz, W. H., Jr., 401, 402
DiLalla, L. F., 324
Dirks, J., 444
Dittrichova, J., 159
Divine-Hawkins, P., 339, 341
Dixon, J. A., 475
Dixon, R. A., 12
Dlugosz, L., 112
Dodge, K. A., 255, 356, 372, 482, 483
Dodwell, P. C., 201
Doherty,W. J., 490
Doi, L. T., 260
Dolan, E. F., Jr., 617
Dolgin, K. G., 322
Dollaghan, C., 344
Donnelly, B. W., 532
Dontas, C., 153
Doris, J., 387
Dornbusch, S. M., 490, 565, 566, 578, 589, 608
Dorr, A., 374
Dorris, M., 114, 124
Dossey, J. A., 460, 568
Doubleday, C., 359, 374, 473
Douglas, V. I., 430
Douvan, E., 608
Downey, G., 373
Doyle, A. B., 316
Drabman, R. S., 402
Draper, P., 82
Dreher, M., 113
Dreyer, P., 531
Drotar, D., 181
Druzin, M. L., 123
DuBois, D. L., 482
Dubow, E. F., 502
Duckett, E., 603
Duncan, G. J., 78
Duncan, P., 525
Duncan, S. W., 126, 127
Dunford, F. W., 615
Dunham, F., 237
Dunham, P. J., 237
Dunn, J., 256, 274, 275, 275*n*, 278, 604
Dunphy, D. C., 607
DuPont, R. L., 360
Durrett, M., 576
Dusek, J. B., 601
Dweck, C. S., 357, 471, 472
Dye-White, E., 116
Dyson, A. H., 335

East, P. L., 604
Easterbrooks, M. A., 271
Eaton, W. O., 260
Ebeling, K. S., 322
Eberhart-Phillips, J. E., 117
Eccles, J. S., 413, 450, 484, 563, 564, 565, 566, 567, 570, 601, 609
Eckenrode, J., 387
Eckerman, C. O., 362
Eckert, H., 307, 542*n*
Eckstrom, R. B., 571*n*
Eder, D., 542
Eder, R. A., 355, 474

Edwards, C. P., 371, 376, 485, 596
Edwards, J. N., 70
Efklides, A., 555
Egeland, B., 384, 386*n*, 387, 388, 500
Eicher, S., 609
Eifermann, R. R., 414
Eilers, R. E., 236
Eisen, M., 467
Eisenberg, L., 614
Eisenberg, N., 359, 361, 476
Eisenberg, R., 471
Eisenberg-Berg, N., 368
Eisenbud, L., 476
Ekman, P., 252
Elardo, R., 230*n*
Elder, G. H., Jr., 41, 259
Elias, S., 65, 102
Elicker, J., 275
Elkind, D., 555, 556, 557, 558, 559
Elkins, P. D., 406
Elliott, D. S., 615
Elliott, E. S., 471
Ellis, A. W., 435
Ellsworth, C. P., 252
Elman, J. D., 383
Emde, R. N., 18, 252, 253, 260, 368
Emerson, P. E., 264
Emery, R. E., 29, 369, 492
Emory, E. K., 137
Engel, N., 127
Englund, M., 275
Enns, J. T., 330
Enright, R. D., 557
Eppler, M. A., 205
Epstein, J. L., 567, 605, 606
Epstein, L. H., 403
Erickson, M. F., 386*n*, 387, 500
Erikson, E. H., 17, 248, 354, 396, 466, 584, 590
Ernhart, C. B., 116
Ernst, L., 194
Eron, L. D., 369
Ervin-Tripp, S., 316
Escalona, S. K., 219, 229
Eskenazi, B., 290
Espenschade, A., 307, 542*n*
Essa, E. L., 323
Estes, D., 272
Evans, R., 405
Eveleth, P. B., 517
Everly, G. S., 122
Eyer, D. E., 153

Fabes, R. A., 358, 359, 476
Fackelmann, K. A., 63*n*
Fagan, Jeffrey, 615
Fagan, Joseph F. III., 223, 229
Fagot, B. I., 261, 276, 278, 371, 377, 378, 380
Fahrmeier, E. D., 425
Falbo, T., 101
Faller, K. C., 498, 498*n*, 500
Fantz, R. L., 201, 202
Fanurik, D., 301, 406
Farmer, M. C., 599
Farquhar, E., 339
Farrar, M. J., 325, 348, 427
Farrington, D. P., 614, 616
Fast, J., 618
Faust, D., 501
Fawcett, S. B., 299
Featherman, D., 574
Fedele, N. M., 128
Fee, E., 294
Fein, G. G., 273, 365*n*
Feiner, J., 360
Feingold, A., 559
Feis, C. L., 373
Feldlaufer, H., 567
Feldman, D. H., 36, 442, 456
Feldman, S. S., 272, 566, 616
Felner, R. D., 565
Fenema, E., 560
Fenson, L., 237, 239, 240
Fenzel, L. M., 565
Ferdman, B. M., 448
Ferguson, L. R., 46
Ferguson, T. J., 473
Fergusson, D. M., 114, 179, 293
Fernald, A., 241, 242
Ferrazin, A., 119
Ferreiro, E., 335
Ferron, J., 78, 339
Ferstenberg, R. F., 75
Feshbach, N. D., 373
Feshbach, S., 373
Field, T. M., 149, 164, 195, 196*n*
Fiese, B., 226, 230
Figueroa, R. A., 442
Filipovic, Z., 499
Fine, G. A., 415, 416, 481
Fine, Mark A., 602
Fine, Michelle, 570, 571
Finegan, J. K., 560
Finkelhor, D., 497, 498, 498*n*, 500
Finn-Stevenson, M. E., 84
Finney, S., 617
Fischer, K. W., 23, 225, 325, 427, 552
Fischhoff, B., 532
Fish, M., 262
Fisher, C. B., 46, 309
Fisher, D. M., 155
Fisher, J. A., 295, 296*n*
FitzGerald, D. P., 590
Fitzsimmons, C. M., 345
Fivush, R., 332, 377
Flavell, E. R., 324, 334
Flavell, J. H., 212, 217, 321, 324, 325, 333, 334, 428, 429, 433
Flege, J. E., 562
Fleming, P. J., 194
Fletcher, K. L., 562
Flickinger, S. M., 83
Flood, M., 613
Fogel, A., 254, 260
Fonagy, P., 127
Food Research and Action Center, 181
Ford, C., 529
Ford, D. Y., 457
Ford, K., 179*n*
Ford, L. H., 355
Ford, M. E., 431
Forehand, R., 490
Forham, S., 567
Forman, E. A., 329, 450
Forrest, D., 293
Forrest, J. D., 530
Forsyth, B. W., 402
Fortier, L., 552
Fox, N. A., 177, 218, 252, 257
Foxman, B., 404
Fracasso, M. P., 384
Francis, P. L., 224
Frank, D. A., 113
Frank, S. J., 589
Frankel, G. W., 428
Frankel, K. A., 76, 275
Franks, B. A., 551
Frauenglass, M. H., 327
Frederiksen, J. R., 435
Freedman, D. G., 162
Freedman, N., 162
Freedman, V. A., 492
Freeman, D., 511
French, D. C., 482
French, K. E., 307, 413
French, L. A., 422
Freud, S., 16,17
Frey, K. S., 379, 380
Fried, Martha Nemes, 521
Fried, Morton H., 521
Fried, P. A., 113, 114
Friedman, A. G., 407
Friedman, J. A., 294
Friedman, L., 560
Friedman, M., 297, 403
Friedrich-Cofer, L., 373
Friesen, W., 252
Fritz, G. K., 408
Frodi, A., 162
Froggatt, P., 194
Frost, L. A., 447
Fu, V. R., 384, 384*n*
Fuchs, I., 599
Fuligni, A. J., 609
Furman, E., 323
Furman, W., 43, 488, 604, 606, 608
Furrow, D., 240, 334, 347
Furstenberg, F. F., Jr., 83, 489, 490, 492, 532, 534, 535
Furuno, S., 303*n*
Fuson, K. C., 335, 336, 436

Gaddis, A., 519
Gaensbauer, T. J., 253
Gage, N. L., 450
Galambos, S. J., 448, 495
Galin, D., 291
Galinski, E., 341
Gallagher, A. M., 379
Galler, J. R., 180, 181
Gallimore, R., 81, 451, 451*n*
Gallistel, C. R., 336
Galotti, K. M., 599
Gamoran, A., 452, 568
Ganchrow, J. R., 191
Gandour, M. J., 261
Garasky, S., 489
Garbarino, J., 79, 387, 499
Garcia, E. E., 447, 449
Garcia-Coll, C. T., 147, 148
Gardner, H., 305, 306*n*,, 441, 441*n*, 456, 457
Gardner, M. J., 61
Gariboldi, A., 273
Garland, A. F., 612
Garmezy, N., 499, 502, 611
Garner, D. M., 527
Garner, R., 558
Garrett, P., 78, 339
Garrison, C., 611
Garrison, W. T., 405
Garrow, D. H., 153
Garvey, C., 226, 347, 354, 364
Garwood, S. G., 82
Gathercole, S. E., 331, 345
Gauvain, M., 424, 428
Geary, D. C., 436, 440
Gellatly, A. R. H., 552
Geller, J., 179
Geller, R. J., 405
Gelles, R. J., 385
Gelman, R., 23, 322, 325, 336
Gelman, S. A., 322
Gentner, D., 345
Gentry, J. R., 335
George, C., 272
Gergen, P. J., 405
Gerrity, P. S., 408
Gershon, E. S., 88
Gesell, A., 12, 13
Getzels, J. W., 456
Ghatala, E. S., 434
Giaconia, R. M., 450
Gibbs, J. C., 370, 597
Gibson, E. J., 198, 204, 205, 308
Gibson, J. J., 204
Giebink, G. S., 300
Gil, D. G., 388
Gilbert, E. H., 527, 528
Gilchrist, D., 536
Gilfillan, M. C., 63*n*
Gilgun, J. F., 530, 531
Gilligan, C. F., 599
Gillmore, J., 475
Gilman, E., 231
Ginsburg, A. P., 201
Ginsburg, H. P., 211, 326, 340
Ginzberg, E., 573
Gisel, E. G., 181
Giudice, S., 289
Gjerde, P. F., 492
Glahn, T. J., 66*n*
Glantz, F. B., 339
Glass, D. C., 403
Gleitman, H., 241
Gleitman, L. R., 241
Glick, P. C., 98*n*, 489
Glidden, L. M., 72
Gnepp, J., 358
Goedhart, A. W., 488
Goez, E. T., 439
Goffin, S. G., 81
Goldberg, D. L., 402
Goldberg, M. E., 373
Goldberg, S., 158
Goldberg, W. A., 494
Goldfield, B. A., 239, 240
Goldin-Meadow, S., 237, 448
Goldman, P., 588
Goldschmid, M. L., 439
Goldsmith, H. H., 257, 259
Goldstein, A. P., 616
Goldstein, H., 288*n*
Goldwyn, R., 272
Golinkoff, R. M., 345
Gomez-Schwartz, B., 497, 498, 501
Gonso, J., 483
Gonzalez, N. M., 113
Good, T. L., 452
Goode, M. K., 227
Goodlad, J. I., 80
Goodman, G. S., 498, 500
Goodman, K. S., 435
Goodman, R. A., 177
Goodnow, J. J., 575
Goodwyn, S. W., 238
Goodz, N. S., 448
Goossens, F. A., 273
Gopnik, A., 224, 238
Gordon, S., 530, 531
Gorman, J., 181
Gorn, G. J., 373
Gortmaker, S. L., 147, 401, 402, 403, 405
Gotlib, I. H., 164
Gotta, C., 119
Gottesman, I. I., 89, 90, 91*n*, 259
Gottfried, Adele E., 494
Gottfried, Allen W., 149
Gottlieb, G., 90
Gottman, J. M., 359, 483
Gould, M. S., 614
Grady, J., 499
Graham, C. J., 290
Graham, F. K., 147
Graham, L., 514
Graham, Sandra, 359, 473
Graham, Suzanne M., 562
Gralinski, J. H., 278, 279
Grant, J. P., 82, 84*n*, 100, 101, 119, 128, 178, 296
Grantham-McGragor, S., 121
Grattan, M. P., 177
Grau, P. N., 576
Gray, W. M., 326
Green, F. L., 324, 334
Green, J. A., 76, 161
Green, R., 399, 532
Greenberg, D. N., 376
Greenberg, M., 152
Greenberg, P., 336
Greenberger, E., 494, 578
Greene, B. F., 301
Greene, P. G., 407
Greenebowe, T., 551
Greenfield, P. M., 30, 186
Greeno, J. G., 26
Greenough, W. T., 174
Greif, E. B., 519
Gretchell, N., 303, 303*n*
Grimes, D. A., 115
Grolnick, W. S., 566
Gross, G. G., 309
Gross, S. J., 179
Grossman, G., 181
Grossman, H. D., 453, 454*n*
Grossman, K., 269
Grossmann, K. E., 76
Grotevant, H. D., 574, 576, 590
Gruendel, J., 332
Grusec, J. E., 20, 368
Guarino, P. A., 359, 473
Guerra, N., 300
Guidice, S., 398
Guidubaldi, J., 491
Guilford, J. P., 455
Gulko, J., 377, 478, 484, 485
Gunnar, M. R., 257
Gurtner, J-L., 452
Gurucharri, C., 475
Gustafson, G. E., 76, 160, 161

Haake, R. J., 330, 331*n*
Haan, N., 597
Hack, M. B., 147
Haden, E., 348
Hagan, R. I., 377
Hagedorn, J. M., 617
Hagen, E. P., 337, 437
Hagerman, R. J., 64
Hahn, W. K., 177
Haight, W. L., 226, 316
Hainline, L., 198
Hains, S. M. J., 252
Haith, M., 202
Hakuta, K., 447, 448
Halford, G. S., 222, 325
Hall, D. G., 224
Hall, G. S., 12, 510
Hall, J. G., 66, 66*n*
Hall, Judith A., 379
Hall, N. W., 387, 388
Hall, R. J., 439
Hall, W. S., 26
Halmie, K. A., 528
Halpern, D. F., 290, 559
Halton, A., 146
Halverson, C. F., 25, 380, 381*n*

Halverson, H. M., 189
Halverson, L. E., 303
Ham, M., 520
Hamberger, L., 104*n*, 106, 107, 118
Hamdan, L., 514
Hamelin, K., 149
Hamer, D. H., 532
Hamilton, C. E., 273
Hamilton, Scott B., 476
Hamilton, Stephen F., 569, 571, 576, 577, 578
Hammersley, M., 37
Hammersmith, S., 532
Hammill, D. D., 454
Hanberger, L.,56
Hanigan, W. C., 144
Hanna, E., 218
Hanna, G., 611
Hannah, M., 145
Hans, S. L., 161
Haque, M., 404
Harding, A. E., 63*n*
Harkness, S., 182
Harlap, S., 127
Harley, E. E., 127
Harlow, H. F., 264
Harmon, R. J., 253
Harold, R. D., 413, 484, 566
Harris, G., 180
Harris, J. J., III., 457
Harris, K. L., 160
Harris, L. J., 290
Harris, M. J., 452
Harris, P. L., 219, 316, 333, 334, 466
Harris, R. T., 528, 529
Harris, S., 481, 600
Harrison, A. O., 82, 83
Harrison, M. R., 68
Hart, D., 467, 585, 586
Hart, S. N., 388
Harter, S., 357, 359, 370, 407, 467, 468, 469, 470, 473, 586
Hartman, B., 189
Hartman, C. R., 385
Hartstone, E., 615
Hartup, W. W., 365, 371, 480, 482, 607
Hashimoto, K., 71
Hatch, M. C., 118
Hatch, T., 345, 441*n*, 456
Hatcher, P. J., 435
Hatcher, R. P., 149
Haugaard, J. J., 500
Hauser, S. T., 511, 586
Haviland, J. M., 254, 256
Hawke, S., 101*n*
Hawkins, D. J., 616
Hawkins, J., 453
Hayes, C., 532, 535
Hayghe, H. V., 81
Hayne, H., 223
Haynes, C. F., 181
Hayward, S. C., 535
Healey, M. J. R., 288*n*
Heath, S. B., 77, 80, 443
Hecht, B. F., 345
Hedges, L. V., 450
Hegley, D., 252
Heinl, T., 161*n*
Heinonen, O. P., 123
Held, R., 189
Helpkin, M. L., 398
Henderson, S. H., 123
Henggeler, S. W, 614
Henker, B., 430
Henshaw, S. K., 69
Hergenrather, J. R., 408
Herkowitz, J., 307
Herrnstein, R. J., 442
Hersov, L., 497
Hertsgaard, L. A., 332
Hess, J., 492
Hesser, J., 488
Hetherington, E. M., 488, 490, 491, 492, 493
Hetherington, S. E., 141
Hewer, A., 593
Hewitt, K. L., 158
Hewlett, B. S., 274
Heyman, G. D., 357, 471
Hickey, P. R., 157
Higgins, A., 598
Higgins, E. T., 471
Higgins-Trenk, A., 485
Hill, C. R., 486
Hill, J. P., 522, 601, 602, 603, 604
Hill, P. M., 174*n*
Hillier, L., 158
Hillman, S. B., 471
Hills, A., 294
Hills-Banczyk, S. G., 179
Hind, H., 295
Hinde, R. A., 26, 27
Hines, M., 399
Hingson, R., 113
Hinman, A. R., 300
Hinsdale, G., 403
Hirsch, B. J., 482
Hirsch, J., 180
Hirsh-Pasek, K., 198
Hiscock, M., 290
Hitch, G., 331
Ho, H., 66*n*
Ho, J., 66*n*
Ho, V., 551
Hobart, C., 493, 494
Hock,E., 273
Hodges, J., 153 , 270
Hodges, R. M., 422
Hoefnagel-Höhle, M., 562
Hoff-Ginsburg, E., 242
Hofferth, S. L., 339, 495
Hoffman, L. W., 77, 98, 278, 494
Hoffman, M. L., 160, 361, 278
Hofsten, C. von., 184, 188
Hogarty, P. S., 229
Holden, G. W., 370
Holmbeck, G. N., 537, 602, 603
Holmes, L. B., 68*n*
Holt, R. W., 383
Hong, K., 265
Honzik, M. P., 229, 337
Hook, E. B., 65*n*, 67
Hooper, F. E., 326
Hopkins, B., 186, 187*n*
Horan, J. J., 539
Horgan, D., 346, 447
Horn, J. M., 88, 443
Horn, T. S., 415
Horn, W. F., 455
Horner, T. M., 253
Hornung, M., 363*n*
Horowitz, F. D., 19, 21, 158, 455
Horowitz, J. M., 497, 498, 501
Hort, B. E., 377
Horwood, L. J., 114, 179
Hotaling, G. T., 387
Houts, A. C., 404
Howard, M., 536
Howe, N., 275, 275*n*
Howes, C., 231, 273, 341, 343, 363, 365
Howes, P., 75
Hoyseth, K. S., 115
Hsu, J., 566
Hubel, D. H., 175
Hudson, J. A., 332
Huesmann, L. R., 373, 615
Hulme, C., 435
Hummel, R. C., 599
Humphrey, G. K., 201
Humphrey, H. E. B., 116
Humphrey, P., 174*n*
Humphrey, T., 156, 157
Humphreys, A. P., 414
Humphreys, L. G., 439
Hunt, J. McV., 219, 229
Hunt, R. J., 288
Huntington, L., 161
Huston, A. C., 373, 374, 375, 376, 379, 484, 485, 488, 601
Huston-Stein, A., 344, 485
Huttenlocher, J., 242, 322
Huttenlocher, P. R., 174, 177
Hyde, J. S., 559, 560
Hymel, S., 482
Hynd, G. W., 430

Iannotti, R. J., 40
Ilg, F. L., 13
Ingersoll, E. W., 193
Ingersoll, G. M., 470
Ingram, D., 346
Inhelder, B., 318, 424, 548, 556
Institute of Medicine, 121
International Education Association, 458
Irvine, J. J., 471
Irwin, C. E., 540
Isabella, R., 262, 270
Israelashvili, R., 274
Istvan, J., 122
Izard, C. E., 252, 253*n*, 271

Jacklin, C. N., 182, 240, 260, 376
Jackson, P. W., 456
Jackson-Cook, C., 64
Jacobs, F. H., 84
Jacobs, J., 413, 484
Jacobson, J. L., 116
Jacobson, S. W., 115, 116
Jacobvitz, D., 388
Jakobi, P., 145
Jakub, D., 194
Jambor, T. W., 363, 363*n*
James, C., 618
James, S. R., 173, 180, 286, 288, 400, 526
Jaskiewicz, J. A., 532, 533
Jason, L. A., 299
Jeans, P. C., 118
Jensen, A. R., 89, 436, 438*n*, 440, 442
Jensen, M. D., 118, 141
Jensen, P. S., 499
Jernigan, L. P., 588
Johanson, R. B., 144
Johnson, C. L., 529
Johnson, E. G., 575
Johnson, Jacqueline S., 562, 562*n*
Johnson, James E., 326
Johnson, M. L., 170
Johnson, N. E., 118
Johnson, S. L., 295, 296*n*
Johnston, J. R., 492
Jones, C. P., 242
Jones, E. F., 530, 533, 533*n*
Jones, G. P., 606
Jones, J., 569
Jones, L. E., 161
Jones, M. C., 524
Jones, N. A., 257
Jones, P. J. H., 115
Jones, R. L., 455
Jones, S. S., 253
Jordan, A. E., 300
Jordan, B., 139
Jordan, P., 142, 163
Jorgensen, M., 516
Jusczyk, P. W., 158, 198

Kaczala, C. M., 471
Kagan, J., 257, 260, 267*n*, 271, 366
Kahn, P. H., Jr., 599
Kail, R., 429
Kaiser, A. P., 241
Kaitz, M., 153, 195
Kaler, S. R., 111, 279
Kalnins, I., 407
Kalter, N., 491
Kamerman, S. B., 151
Kandel, D. B., 539, 605, 609, 613
Kanner, A. D., 606
Kantor, D., 74
Kaplan, B. H., 122
Kaplan, Bonnie J., 118
Kaplan, N., 127, 272
Kaplan, R. M., 444
Karadsheh, R., 346
Karraker, K. H., 261
Kassebaum, N. L., 340
Katchadourian, H., 514, 516, 535
Katz, L. F., 359
Katz, M., 61, 260
Kaufman, A. S., 439
Kaufman, J., 386
Kaufman, N. L., 439
Kaufmann, R., 294, 296*n*
Kavale, K., 309
Kavanaugh, K., 276
Kawai, M., 260
Kawakami, K., 260
Kaye, K., 113, 155, 214
Keane, S. P., 483
Kearins, J. M., 432
Kearsley, R. B., 267*n*
Keasey, C. B., 481
Keating, Daniel P., 431, 552
Keeney, T. J., 429
Keens, T. G., 194
Keiding, N., 516
Keil, F. C., 324, 346
Keljo, K., 597
Keller, A., 355
Kelley, M. L., 384
Kelly, H., 373
Kelly, J. B., 490, 491
Keltikangas-Järvinen, L., 404
Kemp, J. S., 194
Kempe, C. H., 385, 388
Kempe, R. S., 388
Kemper, H. C. G., 517
Kendall-Tackett, K. A., 500
Kendler, K. S., 88
Kendrick, A. S., 294, 296*n*
Kendrick, C., 274, 275, 275*n*
Kennedy, J. M., 412
Kennedy, R. E., 611
Kennell, J. H., 141, 152
Keogh, B. K,. 455
Keppler, A., 123
Kermoian, R., 200
Kerr, B. A., 576
Kerr, M., 259
Kessen, W., 154
Ketterlinus, R. D., 123
Kidd, K. K., 89
Kiely, J. L., 194
Kigar, D. L., 291
Kilbride, J. E., 186
Kilbride, P. L., 186
Killen, M., 271
Kilman, C., 398
Kilner, L. A., 511, 586
Kinderman, T. A., 567
King, R. M., 367
Kinsbourne, M., 290
Kinzie, J. D., 499
Kirby, D., 535
Kiser, L. J., 270
Kisker, E. E., 339, 531, 532
Kistner, J., 361
Klahr, D., 24, 25, 221, 555
Klaus, M. H., 152
Klebanov, P. K., 78
Klein, J. D., 541
Klimes-Dougan, B., 361
Kline, M., 492
Klungness, L., 497
Knapp, L. G., 301
Kneisl, C. R., 119
Knevel, C. R., 229
Knittle, J. L., 180
Knobloch, H., 13*n*, 154*n*, 155
Knox, D., 101*n*
Kochanska, G., 259, 279, 367, 368
Kodroff, J. K., 552
Koenig, K. L., 252
Kogan, N., 456
Kohlberg, L., 379, 593, 594, 596, 598, 599
Kohn, M. L., 77, 574
Kojima, H., 260
Kolata, G., 415
Kolberg, R., 71
Koller, H., 61, 260
Kolstad, V., 333
Kopp, C. B., 28*n*, 65, 111, 229, 256, 278, 279
Korn, S. J., 259
Korner, A. F., 149
Kornguth, M. L., 405
Kornhaber, M., 457
Korte, D., 144, 145*n*
Koslowski, B., 162
Kostelny, K., 79, 387, 499
Kotch, J. B., 299*n*, 300, 301, 406
Kovaric, P., 374
Kowalski, P. S., 472
Kozberg, S. F., 599
Kozol, J., 567, 571
Krakow, J. B., 28*n*, 279
Kramer, M. D., 146
Kramer, Michael S., 121, 402
Kramer, T. L., 606
Kranz, R., 528
Kratochwill, T., 360, 497*n*
Krebs, D., 475
Krechevsky, M., 457
Kreeger, L., 401
Krehbiel, G., 483
Kreipe, R. E., 528
Kreminitzer, T. P., 158
Kreutzer, M. A., 333, 433
Kricker, A., 115
Kritt, D., 467
Kroonenberg, P. M., 269, 269*n*
Kruger, A. C., 242, 478

Ku, L. C., 530, 531
Kuczaj, S. A. II., 240
Kuczynski, L., 369, 384, 386
Kuebli, J., 332
Landau, S., 327
Kuebli, J., 377
Kuhl, P. K., 197, 203
Kuhn, D., 22, 221, 551, 555
Kunkel, D., 374
Kunzinger, E. L., III., 429
Kurdek, L. A., 602
Kurth, A., 119
Kutner, L., 307
Kwon, Y., 436

Labbok, M., 179*n*
Laboratory of Comparative Human Cognition, 453
Lachman, M. E., 258
Ladd, G. W., 483
Lagercrantz, H., 137
Laird, M., 387
Lam, T., 616
Lamaze, F., 140
Lamb, M., 153
Lamb, Michael E., 123, 254, 272, 273, 274, 276
Lamb, S., 366
Lamborn, S. D., 566, 603
Lamon, S. J., 560
Lampl, M., 170
Lampman-Petraitis, C., 520
Landau, S., 430
Landreth, G. L., 495
Landsman, S., 445
Lane, D. M., 428
Lange, G., 331
Langlois, J. H., 524
Laosa, L. M., 77
Lapsley, D. K., 557, 590
LaRossa, M. M., 164
LaRossa, R., 164
Larson, G., 440
Larson, R., 520, 523*n*, 558, 604, 605, 605*n*
Last, C. G., 497
Laupa, M., 592
Lawson, K. R., 330
Lazar, A., 323
Lazar, I., 340
Le Neindre, P., 152
Leach, P., 190
Leaper, C., 378
Lebeaux, D. S., 447
Lee, A. M., 307
Lee, C. L., 262
Lee, D. J., 61
Lee, M., 343
Lee, S. H., 117
Lee, Shin-ying, 82, 458, 459
Lee, V. E., 342
Leech, R. W., 176*n*
Leetsma, R., 460
Leggett, E. L., 471
Lehman, D. R., 552
Lehr, W., 74
Lehrman, D., 152
Leichtman, M. D., 500
Leifer, M., 126, 181
Leinbach, M. D., 278, 371, 377, 380
Leland, N., 536
Lelwica, M., 254
Lemire, R. J., 176*n*
Lempert, H., 346, 447
Lenneberg, E. H., 177
Leonard, C., 333, 433
Leonard, M. F., 181
Lepper, M. R., 452, 453
Lerner, Jacqueline V., 495
Lerner, Janet W., 455
Lerner, M. R., 524
Lerner, R. M., 12, 403
Lesser, G. S., 609
Lester, B. M., 113, 143, 161, 161*n*, 162, 266
Leung, A. K. C., 497
Levin, H., 264
Levin, I., 554
Levin, J. A., 452
LeVine, R. A., 77, 270
LeVine, S. E., 270
Levine, C., 593
Levine, J. A., 535
Levine, L. E., 356
Levitt, A. G., 237
Levy-Shiff, R., 274
Lewinsohn, P. M., 611, 614
Lewis, C. C., 75
Lewis, J. M., 490
Lewis, M., 229, 255, 260, 277, 359, 361
Li, C. Q., 114
Liaw, F., 147, 148
Liben, L. S., 380, 381
Liberty, C., 429
Lie, S. O., 298
Liebert, R. M., 343, 369, 373, 375, 487
Lifschitz, M., 499
Light, P., 425
Limber, S., 253
Lin, C. C., 384, 384*n*
Lind, T., 143
Linde, E. V., 223
Lindell, S. G., 138, 141
Lindenberger, U., 424
Lindgren, G., 295
Lindmark, G., 114
Linn, M. C., 453, 559, 560
Linn, S., 115
Lipsitt, L. P., 157, 194, 195, 223
Litman, C., 279
Litowitz, B., 446
Litt, I. F., 526
Little, B. B., 113
Little, J. K., 380
Livesley, W. J., 467, 468
Livson, N., 525
Lloyd, B., 261
Locke, J., 10
Lockhart, R. S., 24
Loeber, R., 616
Loehlin, J. C., 88, 260, 442
Loeser, J. D., 176*n*
Loftus, E. F., 501
Logan, S., 117*n*, 118
Lohr, M. J., 609, 609*n*
Looney, M. A., 416
Lorch, E. P., 430
Lorenz, K. Z., 26, 137
Louie, R., 288
Love, R., 407
Lozoff, B., 120, 183, 400
Ludemann, P. M., 202, 224
Lummis, M., 484, 559
Luria, A. R., 398
Luria, Z., 261
Luster, T., 76
Lutkenhaus, P., 277
Lutz, P., 493
Lutzker, J. R., 301
Lynch, M. E., 601
Lynskey, M. T., 114
Lyon, T. D., 333
Lyons-Ruth, K., 271, 276
Lytton, H., 372, 377, 378

Mabe, P. A., 407
Mac Iver, D., 468, 469
Maccoby, E. E., 240, 260, 264, 376, 378, 383, 383*n*, 384, 399, 487
MacDonald, K., 270
MacFarlane, J., 153, 157
Macfarlane, J. W., 229, 337, 525
MacKinnon, C. E., 378, 491
MacKinnon-Lewis, C., 483
Macksoud, M., 499
MacMillan, D. L., 455
MacNee, C. L., 112, 114, 115
MacQuiddy, S. L., 476
Madaus, G. F., 456
Madden, C. M., 561
Madden, N., 455
Madge, N., 101
Madole, K. L., 224
Maggs, J. L., 495
Magnusson, D., 525
Mahalski, P. A., 265
Mahapatra, M., 479
Mahler, M. S., 250
Main, M., 127, 267, 268, 272
Maioni, T. L., 363*n*
Maise, S. J., 476
Makin, J. E., 113, 114
Makin, Jennifer W., 157
Makinson, C., 534
Malatesta, C. Z., 256, 270
Malatesta-Magai, C. Z., 252
Malina, R. M., 172, 173, 289, 292, 302, 409, 513, 514, 515*n*, 516*n*, 527, 542
Malone, A. F., 13*n*
Maloney, M., 528
Manchester, D., 184
Mandler, J. M., 205, 219, 224, 324, 332
Mangelsdorf, S., 271
Manis, J. D., 98
Manly, J., 385
Mannle, S., 242
Maratsos, M. P., 236, 239
Marcella, S., 200
Marcia, J. E., 585, 587, 588
Marcus, G. F., 346, 348
Marcus, J., 214
Marentette, P. F., 236
Margolis, M. Q., 288
Margulis, C., 345
Markman, E. M., 345, 550
Markman, H. J., 75, 126, 127
Markstrom, C. A., 588
Markus, G. B., 488
Markus, H., 488
Marovits, H., 551, 552
Marsh, D. T., 476
Marsh, H. W., 468, 469, 560
Marshall, R. E., 157
Marshall, W. A., 288*n*
Marsiglio, W., 534
Martin, C. L., 25, 376, 380, 381*n*
Martin, G. B., 160
Martin, John A., 39, 369, 383, 383*n*, 384
Martin, Joseph B., 63*n*
Martin, R. M., 223
Martin, S. L., 233
Martorell, R., 296
Maruyama, G., 488
Marzolf, D. P, 333
Mason, M. G., 597
Massad, C. M., 601
Masur, E. F., 428
Matas, L., 275
Matheny, A. P., Jr., 299, 300
Matheson, C. C., 273, 363
Matias, R., 252
Matthews, K. A., 404
Matute-Bianche, M. E., 589
Maurer, D., 202
Mayberry, R. I., 562
Mayers, M. M., 119
Mayes, L. C., 184
McAnarney, E. R., 517, 532, 533
McCabe, A. E., 324, 325
McCabe, J. B., 536
McCall, R. B., 229
McCartney, K., 91, 231, 273, 348
McClenahan, E. L., 609, 609*n*
McClintic, S., 361
McConaghy, M. J., 379
McCormick, M. C., 147
McCoy, J. K., 488
McCracken, J., 611
McCroy, G., 224
McCune, L., 316
McDonald, B., 200
McDonough, L., 224, 324
McGee, L. M., 335, 335*n*, 411*n*
McGhee, P. E., 446
McGinty, M. J., 71
McGroarty, M., 449
McGue, M., 88
McGuinness, D., 291
McGuire, E. J., 404
McGuire, J., 377
McGurk, H., 229
McHale, S. M., 486
McIntyre, C. W., 428
McKenna, M. C., 435
McKie, M., 396
McKnight, C. C., 84*n*, 458
McKusick, V. A., 60*n*, 61, 63*n*
McLoyd, V. C., 78, 83
McManus, I. C., 290
McManus, K., 143
McNamee, S., 478
McQuiston, S., 405
McRae, M. J., 143
McWilliams, M., 527
Mead, G. H., 467
Mead, M., 139, 511
Meany, M. J., 376
Medrich, E. A., 79
Meecham, J. A., 355
Meehan, A. M., 562
Mehler, J., 157, 158
Meilman, P. W., 587
Melnikow, J., 125
Meltzoff, A. N., 195, 196, 196*n*, 203, 218, 219, 224, 238
Menig-Peterson, C. L., 347
Menyuk, P., 236
Meredith, N. V., 396
Mervis, C. B., 223, 324, 345
Messenger, K. P., 294, 296*n*
Meyer, D. R., 489
Michaels, G. Y., 98, 99, 99*n*
Michel, C., 116
Micheli, L. J., 541
Micka, J. C., 590
Midgley, C., 567
Milburn, N., 78
Milich, R., 430
Miller, B. C., 530
Miller, G. A., 446
Miller, J. G., 479
Miller, K. F., 424
Miller, Nancy B., 372, 387, 616
Miller, Norman, 488
Miller, Patrice M., 77
Miller, Patricia H., 6, 19, 27, 217, 314, 325, 333, 433
Miller, Paul A., 361
Miller, Peggy J., 37, 226, 316
Miller, Scott A., 33, 217, 325
Miller, Stephen J., 123
Miller-Jones, D., 444
Mills, J., 127
Mills, R., 368
Millstein, S. G., 526, 540
Milner, J., 388
Minick, N., 329, 450
Minuchin, P. P., 74, 80, 450
Mirman, J. H., 492
Mischel, W., 369
Miscione, J. L., 334
Mishell, D. R. Jr., 115
Mitchell, P., 333
Miyake, K., 269
Mize, J., 483
Moerk, E. L., 236
Moffatt, M. E. K., 404
Moffitt, T. E., 616
Moilanen, I., 57
Mollnow, E., 111, 112, 113, 115, 116
Monroe, S., 588
Montemayor, R., 467
Montie, J. E., 229
Moore, C. F., 334, 475
Moore, E. G. J., 443
Moore, Keith L., 54, 56*n*, 69*n*, 103, 104, 104*n*, 105*n*, 106, 106*n*, 107*n*, 108, 111*n*, 112, 174
Moore, Kristin, 532
Moore, M. K., 195, 196, 196*n*, 218
Moore, R. W., 201
Moore, S. G., 162
Moorehouse, M. J., 494
Moran, G. F., 10
Morelli, G., 81, 183, 265
Morford, M., 237
Morgan, S. P., 535
Morgane, P. J., 120
Morikawa, H., 241
Morris, E. K., 369
Morris, N., 152
Morris, R., 360, 497*n*
Morrongiello, B. A., 157, 158, 197, 223
Moshman, D., 551
Moss, M., 159
Most, R. K., 227
Mott, F. L., 534
Mott, S. R., 173, 180, 286, 288, 400, 526
Mounts, N. S., 383
Muecke, L., 401, 402
Muir, D. W., 201, 252
Muir, J. E., 429, 431
Mullally, D. I., 405
Mullis, I. V. S., 458, 559, 560, 568
Mulvey, E. P., 616
Munn, P., 256
Munro, G., 587
Murray, A. D., 143, 161
Murray, Charles, 442

Murray, Colleen I., 323
Murray, V. M., 534
Murrett-Wagstaff, S., 162
Mussen, P. H., 368, 481, 524, 600
Muzio, J. N., 160

Nachtigall, R. D., 70
Nagel, L., 252
Nagy, S. N., 613
Nakagawa, N., 561
Nakatsuji, N., 71
Namuth, T., 398
Nanez, J., 199
Nash, J. E., 114
Nastasi, B. K., 452, 455
Natapoff, J., 408
National Association for the Education of Young Children, 231*n*, 343*n*
National Center for Education Statistics, 339
National Center for Health Statistics, 178
National Institute on Drug Abuse, 538
Naus, M. J., 429
Navaez, D., 596, 597*n*
Neal, J. H., 490
Neckerman, H. J., 571*n*
Needle, R. H., 490
Needleman, H. L., 294
Neiderman, D., 218
Neidich, G., 194
Nelson, C. A., 257
Nelson, G., 490
Nelson, J., 482
Nelson, Katherine, 223, 238, 240, 242, 332
Nelson, Keith E., 348
Nelson, V. L., 229
Nelson-Le Gall, S. A., 592
Netley, C. T., 66, 66*n*
Neuman, S. B., 335
Newborg, J., 303*n*, 304*n*
Newcomb, A. F., 483
Newcomb, M. D., 538, 539, 540
Newcombe, N., 322
Newman, L. S., 316
Newman, R. S., 434
Newport, E. L., 241, 562, 562*n*
Newson, E., 328
Newson, J., 328
Newton, N., 139
Ng'andu, N., 78, 339
Niccols, G. A., 560
Nicholls, A. L., 412
Nichols, M. R., 152
Nichols, S. L., 119
Nidorf, J. F., 588
NIH/CEPH Collaborative Mapping Group, 69
Nilsson, L., 56, 104*n*, 106, 107, 118
Nisbett, R. E., 552
Noah, P. K., 294
Noble, A., 180
Noguchi, M., 71
Norbeck, J. S., 122
Nord, C. W., 490
Nottelmann, E. D., 469, 520, 586
Notzon, F. C., 142
Nowakowski, R. S., 106, 107, 115
Nucci, L., 479
Nuckolls, K. B., 122
Nugent, J. K., 143, 162

O'Boyle, C., 278
O'Brien, M., 455
O'Connell, C. M., 113
O'Donnell, J. P., 455
O'Loughlin, M., 551, 555
O'Reilly, A. W., 226
Oakes, J., 452, 569
Oakes, L. M., 224
Oates, R. K., 181, 293
Obler, L. K., 561, 562
Odagaki, L., 427
Odem, R. R., 113
Offer, D., 586
Office of Educational Research and Improvement, 571
Ogan, T. A., 254
Ogbu, J. U., 384, 471, 567
Okagaki, L., 444
Ollendick, T. H., 483
Oller, D. K., 236
Olson, T. D., 530
Omer, H., 122
Opie, I., 414
Opie, P., 414
Oppenheim, D., 274
Opper, S., 211, 326
Ornstein, P. A., 429
Osborn, L. M., 297
Osherson, D. N., 550
Oster, H., 252
Otaki, M., 260
Otomo, K., 236
Owen, M. T., 273
Owens, T., 578

Padgham, J. J., 607
Padilla, M. L., 495
Page, D. C., 57
Page, R. N., 452, 569
Paget, K. F., 467
Pagnucco, J. R., 435
Paikoff, R. L., 522
Palermo, D. S., 446
Palkovitz, R., 163
Pallikkathayil, L., 613
Papini, D. R., 590
Parekh, U. C., 120
Paris, S. G., 434
Parke, R. D., 152, 369, 370, 373
Parker, D., 542
Parker, J. G., 483
Parker-Cohen, N. Y., 34
Parkhurst, J. T., 483
Parks, P. L., 201
Parmelee, A., 160
Parrish, L. H., 568
Parsons, J. E., 371, 471
Parten, M., 362
Pasamanick, B., 154*n*, 155
Passman, R. H., 265
Pate, G. S., 589
Pattee, L., 483
Patterson, C. J., 478
Patterson, G. R., 21, 75, 372, 378, 502, 616*n*
Patterson, J., 223
Patteson, D. M., 148, 149
Paulhus, D., 488
Peacock, A., 293
Pearson, D. A., 428
Pearson, J. L., 83
Pechmann, T., 447
Peckham, C. S., 117*n*, 118
Pedersen, F. A., 163
Pedlow, R., 259
Pelchat, M. L., 293
Pellegini, A. D., 414
Pena, I. C., 148
Pennington, B. F., 66, 66*n*, 454
Pentz, M. A., 539, 540
Pepler, D. J., 316
Pepper, S., 378
Perfetti, C. A., 435
Perkins, L., 114
Perlmutter, M., 223, 329, 331
Perner, J., 333, 370, 592
Perrett-Clermont, A-N., 425
Perrin, E. C., 408
Perris, E. E., 223
Perry, D. G., 372
Perry, L. C., 372
Perry, T. B., 605
Persaud, T. V. N., 54, 56*n*, 69*n*, 103, 104, 104*n*, 105*n*, 106, 106*n*, 107*n*, 108, 111*n*, 112, 114, 174
Peshkin, A., 37, 80
Peskin, H., 525
Petersen, A. C., 524, 560, 610, 611
Petersen, R., 302
Peterson, C., 324
Peterson, J., 478, 532
Petitto, L. A., 236
Petro, J. V., 536
Pettigrew, J. W., 65
Pettit, G. S., 372, 416
Pezzullo, T. R., 456
Phelps, K. E., 322
Phil, D., 157
Philipps, C., 118
Phillips, D. A., 231, 273, 341, 471
Phillips, O. P., 65, 102
Phillips, S., 302
Phinney, J. S., 588, 589
Piaget, J., 21, 35, 188, 195, 211, 212, 214, 215, 216, 318, 319, 327, 370, 424, 548, 556, 558, 591
Pianta, R., 386*n*, 387, 500
Picariello, M. L., 376
Pick, A. D., 203, 254, 428
Pick, H. L., Jr., 184
Pickens, J., 164
Pierce, L. H., 498
Pierce, R., 498
Pierce, S. H., 331
Piersel, W. C., 491
Pietikäinen, M., 404
Pilkington, C. L., 497
Pillard, R. C., 532
Pillemer, D. B., 376
Pillow, B. H., 334, 433
Pine, F., 250
Pinel, J. P. J., 403
Pinker, S., 447
Pipes, P. L., 178
Pipp, S. L., 23, 225
Pirsch, L. A., 589
Pisoni, D. B., 158
Platsidou, M., 555
Pleck, J. H., 530, 531
Pless, I. B., 301
Pliner, P., 293
Plomin, R., 88, 91, 92, 258, 260, 261, 275
Plowman, S. A., 416
Plumert, J. M., 424
Podrouzek, W., 347
Poindron, P., 152
Polakoski, K. L., 113
Polansky, N. A., 387
Polit, D., 101
Pollatsek, A., 435
Pollitt, C., 345
Pollitt, E., 121
Pollock, L., 10
Polsky, H. W., 618
Porges, S. W., 157
Porter, F. L., 157
Porter, R. H., 157
Posner, J. K., 495
Post, G. B., 517
Poston, D. L., Jr., 101
Poulin-DuBois, D., 224
Powell, B., 101
Powell, C., 121
Powell, G., 471
Power, F. C., 598
Power, T. G., 384
Powers, C., 341
Powers, S. I., 511, 586
Powlishta, K. K., 377, 478, 484, 485
Prechtl, H. F. R., 154, 154*n*, 160
Prentice, A., 143
Pressley, M., 279, 431, 434, 435
Previc, F. H., 290
Preyer, W., 12
Pribram, K. H., 291
Price, J. M., 483
Prodromidis, M., 273
Provenzano, F. J., 261
Pryor, J. B., 408
Puder, K. S., 68*n*
Pursley, J. T., 72

Quadrel, M. J., 532
Quay, H. C., 618
Quazi, Q. H., 117*n*
Quiggle, N. L., 356
Quilligan, E. J., 145
Quintero, R. A., 68*n*

Raag, T., 253
Rabiner, D. L., 483, 484
Rabinovich, B. A., 494
Rabinowitz, M., 408
Radford, A., 236
Radin, N., 494, 495
Radke-Yarrow, M., 259, 271, 361, 367, 384
Radziszewska, B., 329
Rafferty, Y., 78
Ragozin, A. S., 102
Räikkönen, K., 404
Ramachandran, C., 149
Ramafedi, G., 532, 533
Ramanan, J., 495
Ramey, C. T., 121, 232, 233, 233*n*, 342, 343, 445
Ramey, S. L., 233, 342
Ramsay, D. S., 260
Ramsay, M., 181
Ramsey, E., 372, 616*n*
Ramsey, F., 180, 181
Ramsey, R., 75
Rappaport, L., 404
Rasmussen, B., 483
Ratcliffe, S. G., 66*n*, 396
Ratner, M. S., 512
Ratner, N., 237
Raveis, V. H., 613
Rayner, K., 435
Raynor, R., 19
Read, C. R., 575
Read, M., 466
Recchia, S. 361
Redanz, N. J., 198
Redd, W. H., 369
Redl, F. M., 481
Reece, E. A., 144
Rees, J., 270
Rees, M., 517
Reich, P. A., 448
Reich, T., 88
Reik, W., 63
Reimer, J., 599
Rein, M., 84*n*
Reis, S. M., 457, 575
Reiser, J., 157
Reisman, J. E., 161, 161*n*
Reissland, N., 196
Reiter, E. O., 515, 519
Renwick, S. M., 383
Repacholi, B., 276
Reppucci, N. D., 388, 500, 616
Reschly, D. J., 445
Resnick, G., 491
Resnick, L. B., 26, 336, 435, 436
Resnick, R., 150
Ressler, E. M., 499
Rest, J. R., 591, 593, 594, 595, 596, 597*n*
Reznick, E., 316
Reznick, J. S., 239, 260
Rhymes, J. P., 181
Ricciardelli, L. A., 448
Ricco, R. B., 324
Rice, F. P., 575
Rice, K. G., 590
Rice, M. L., 344
Rich, S. A., 439
Richards, D. D., 322, 337, 436
Richards, M. H., 603
Richardson, P., 128
Richardson, S. A., 61, 260
Richgels, D. J., 335, 335*n*, 411*n*
Richman, A. L., 77
Richmond, J., 342
Ridley-Johnson, R., 155
Riese, M. L., 259
Rigler, D., 385
Rivara, F. P., 300
Roberge, J. J., 552
Roberton, M. A., 303, 303*n*, 304, 307, 409*n*, 410, 413
Roberts, M. C., 299, 301, 406
Robinette, C. D., 88
Robins, R. W., 586
Robinson, E. J., 333, 348
Robinson, Edward H., III, 360
Robinson, JoAnn L., 259, 260
Robinson, John P., 495
Robinson, S. L., 360
Rochat, P., 188*n*, 189
Roche, A. F., 180, 398, 517
Rock, S. L., 460
Roderick, M., 571*n*
Roffwarg, H. P., 160
Rogoff, B., 81, 225, 328, 329, 396, 424, 425, 428, 432, 466
Rohde, P., 614
Rohlen, T. P., 569
Rohner, E. C., 76
Rohner, R. P., 76
Rollins, K. B., 322
Romaine, S., 561
Romney, D. M., 372, 377, 378
Rook, K. S., 604
Roopnarine, J. L., 274
Roosa, M. W., 123
Roper Starch Worldwide, 530

Rorvik, D. M., 61
Roscoe, B., 608
Rose, S. A., 195
Rosen, A. B., 322
Rosen, M. G., 143, 150
Rosen, W. D., 254
Rosenberg, Mindy S., 388
Rosenberg, Morris, 468, 585, 586
Rosenberg, R. N., 65
Rosenblatt, J. S., 152
Rosengren, K. S., 329
Rosenman, R. H., 403
Rosenthal, D. A., 589
Rosenthal, R., 452
Roskos, K., 335
Ross, D. F., 372
Ross, G. S., 223, 224
Ross, H. S., 275, 275*n*, 316
Rothbart, M. K., 258
Rothenberg, M. B., 183
Rotheram-Borus, M. J., 589
Rourke, B. P., 455
Rousseau, J. J., 11, 510
Rovee-Collier, C. K., 190, 193, 223
Rovine, M., 128, 270
Royal, G. P., 406
Rozin, P., 293, 295, 322
Rubin, J. Z., 261
Rubin, K. H., 363, 363*n*, 364, 365*n*
Ruble, D. N., 380, 467, 471, 474, 519
Ruff, H. A., 259, 294, 330
Ruffman, T., 333 , 551
Ruiz, R., 448, 449
Rumberger, R. W., 570, 571, 571*n*
Runco, M. A., 456
Ruopp, R., 341
Rushton, H. G., 405
Russell, D. E. H., 497
Russell, G., 485
Russell, J. A., 358
Russo, P., 120
Rutherford, E., 481, 600
Rutter, M., 101, 491, 497, 499, 502, 511, 611
Ruzany, N., 472
Ryan, K. J., 70, 71

Saarni, C., 473
Sadler, L. S. 611
Sadler, T. W., 103
Sadovnick, A. D., 65
Safe Kids, 406
Salapatek, P., 199, 201, 201*n*, 202*n*,205
Saller, D. N., Jr., 68*n*
Salzinger, S., 387
Samson, L. F., 117, 117*n*
Samuels, M., 116, 118, 124, 127, 134
Samuels, N., 116, 118, 124, 127, 134
Samuels, S. J., 435
Sandberg, D. E., 575
Sanderson, J. A., 371
Sanford, J. P., 567
Santelli, J. S., 531
Santini, D. L., 123
Santrock, J. W., 491
Sapienza, C., 63
Sarigiani, P. A., 611
Sattler, J. M., 337, 437
Saudino, K., 260
Savashino, J. A., 404
Savin-Williams, R. C., 416, 533, 604, 606
Saxe, G. B., 30
Saywitz, K. J., 500, 501
Scaer, R., 144, 145*n*
Scanlon, K., 295
Scarr, S., 5, 86, 88, 89, 91, 92, 231, 273, 443
Schachter, F. F., 261
Schaefer, M., 149
Schaffer, H. R., 264
Schaivi, R. C., 66*n*
Schanberg, S., 149
Schauble, L., 551
Schikedanz, J. A., 336
Schiller, D., 295
Schinke, S. P., 536
Schlegel, A., 512, 521, 522
Schleifer, M., 552
Schmid, J., 424
Schneider, W., 431
Schneirla, T. C., 152
Schnur, E., 342
Schoenbach, C., 586
Schoendorf, K. C., 194
Schofield, W., 121
Schooler, C., 586
Schor, E. L., 406*n*
Schramm, L., 407
Schramm, W., 142
Schroeder, C., 403
Schunk, D. H., 434, 472
Schwartz, D., 483
Schwartz, J. D., 145
Schwartz-Bickenbach, D., 114
Schweinhart, L. J., 340
Scott, P. M., 41, 41*n*, 368
Scribner, S., 432
Sears, R. R., 264
Sebald, H., 609
Seekins, T., 299
Seeley, J. R., 614
Seidman, D. S., 144
Seidman, E., 564
Seitz, V., 338
Select Committee on Children, Youth, and Families, 401
Seligman, M. E. P., 193
Seligmann, J., 398, 527
Sellers, C., 530
Selman, F. L., 475
Selman, R. L., 365, 474, 475*n*, 482
Seltzer, V., 179
Senghas, A., 345
Serafica, F. C., 476
Serbin, L. A., 377, 478, 484, 485
Sever, J. L., 117*n*
Shaffer, David R., 488
Shaffer, David, 613, 614
Shagle, S. C., 613
Shahar, S., 10
Shainess, N., 519
Shalala, D. E., 297
Shannon, B., 407
Shannon, D. C., 194
Shannon, F. T., 293
Shanon, F. T., 179
Shantz, C. U., 371
Shapiro, E. K., 80, 450
Shapiro, L. R., 180, 407
Shapiro, S., 123
Shatz, M., 322
Shaver, P., 608
Shaw, J., 499
Shedler, J., 539, 540
Sheiman, D. L., 398
Sheingold, K., 453
Shepherd, P. H., 229
Sherman, A., 85
Shettles, L. B., 61
Shiffrin, R. M., 24, 221, 221*n*, 222
Shime, J., 150
Shinn, Marybeth, 78
Shinn, Milicent Washburn, 12
Shipman, G., 519
Shonkoff, J. P., 399, 408
Shukla, D., 557
Shultz, T. R., 356
Shure, M. B., 373
Shweder, R. A., 479
Sidle, A. L., 322
Siebert, J. M., 119
Siegal, M., 371
Siegel, D. H., 430
Siegel, L. S., 325
Siegler, R. S., 14, 26, 221, 322, 337, 436, 553, 554*n*, 555
Sigafoos, A. D., 195
Sigelman, C. K., 408, 477
Sigman, M. D., 223
Signorella, M. L., 380
Silva, P. A., 265
Silver, L. B., 454
Silver, M., 145
Silverberg, S. B., 602, 603
Simkin, P., 123
Simmons, R. G., 524, 563, 564, 564*n*, 565
Simons, C., 373
Simons, R. L., 75, 386, 386*n*, 387
Simpson, J. A., 613
Simpson, S. A., 63*n*
Singer, D. G., 315, 316, 344, 364
Singer, J. L., 315, 316, 344, 364
Singh, S., 530
Siqueland, E. R., 195, 222
Sirignano, S. W., 258
Sitarenios, G., 560
Sivard, R. L., 84*n*
Skinner, B. F., 235
Skinner, E. A., 450, 452, 471
Skinner, J. D., 402
Skinner, L. G., 501
Slaby, R. G., 373, 379
Slade, A., 226
Slaughter, E., 615
Slavin, R., 455
Sloan, D., 123
Sloan, W., 454*n*
Slomin, M., 398
Slomkowski, C., 604
Slotkin, T. A., 137
Slowiaczck, M. L., 566
Smeeding, T., 84*n*
Smetana, J. G., 370, 371, 603
Smilansky, S., 365*n*
Smith, C., 261
Smith, D. M., 153
Smith, H., 116
Smith, I. D., 470
Smith, J., 485
Smith, M. B., 118
Smith, Michael C., 356
Smith, P. K., 363*n*, 414
Smith, R. S., 79, 152
Smith, S. D., 454
Smith, V. E., 588
Smollar, J., 606
Smolucha, F., 226
Smoot, D. L., 483
Snarey, J. R., 597, 599
Snidman, N., 257, 260
Snow, C. E., 335, 562
Snow, R. E., 452
Snowden, L. R., 128
Snyder, L., 240
Sobesky, W. E., 596
Sobol, A. M., 147, 405
Society for Research in Child Development, 44, 45*n*
Sockett, H., 598
Sodian, B., 333, 334, 433
Soken, H. H., 203, 254
Sokol, R. J., 144
Solimano, G., 180, 181
Solnit, A. J., 181
Soloman, J., 267
Somberg, D. R., 356
Somerville, S. C., 330, 331*n*
Sommer, K., 534
Sommerville, J., 10
Sonenstein, F. L., 530, 531
Song, M., 340
Sontag, C. W., 229
Sorce, J., 254
Sorenson, E. S., 502
Sorenson, T. I. A., 402
Sosa, R., 141
Southard, B., 410
Spade, J., 569
Spanier, G. B., 128
Spears, G. F. S., 265
Spears, R. A., 561
Speece, M. W., 323
Speicher, B., 596
Spelke, E. S., 203, 204
Spellacy, W. N., 123
Spence, M. J., 108, 158
Spencer, M. B., 589
Sperduto, R. D., 400
Sperhac, A. M., 173, 180, 286, 288, 400, 526
Sperry, L. L., 37
Spinetta, J., 385
Spirito, A., 613
Spitz, R. A., 269
Spivack, G., 373
Spock, B., 183
Spohr, H-L., 114
Sprafkin, J., 343, 373, 375, 487
Spreadbury, C. L., 608
Spreen, O., 175, 176, 291
Spuhl, S. T., 328, 329
Sroufe, L. A., 76, 252, 253, 255, 271, 273, 275, 384, 388
St. Peters, M., 374
Stafford, F. P., 486
Stahl, S. A., 435
Stamler, J., 179
Stanhope, L., 34
Stanitski, C. L., 541
Stanley, J. C., 560
Stanley-Hagan, M., 491, 492
Stanowicz, L., 348
Stark, L. J., 21
Stattin, H., 525
Stearns, G., 118
Stechler, G., 146
Steele, H., 127
Steele, M., 127
Steelmen, L. C., 101
Stegge, H., 473
Stein, Z., 120
Steinberg, L., 383, 404, 495, 512, 522, 566, 578, 602, 603
Steiner, J. E., 157, 191
Steiner, M., 164
Steinhardt, M. A., 416
Steinhausen, H. C., 114
Stenberg, C., 253
Stephan, C. W., 524
Stephen, E. H., 492
Stephens, B. R., 202
Stern, D. N., 270
Stern, M., 261
Sternberg, K. J., 273, 387
Sternberg, R. J., 427, 439, 440, 441, 444
Stevens, F., 13*n*
Stevens, J. H., 83
Stevenson, D. L., 460
Stevenson, H. W., 80, 82, 458, 459, 484, 559, 566
Stevenson, R., 345
Stewart, D. A., 66
Stewart, J., 376
Stewart, R. B., 274
Stigler, J. W., 459
Stillman, R. J., 115
Stipek, D. J., 278, 361, 468, 469, 472
Stoch, M. B., 181
Stock, J. R., 303*n*, 304*n*
Stocker, C., 275, 604
Stodolsky, S. S., 330, 451
Stoel-Gammon, C., 236
Stokes, T., 407
Stone, C. A., 329, 450
Stone, L., 10
Stone, R. K., 261
Stoneman, Z., 275, 378, 488
Strasburger, V. C., 530, 531, 532, 537, 538
Straus, L. K., 539
Strauss, J., 528
Strauss, S., 554
Strayer, J., 473
Streissguth, A. P., 112, 114, 115
Streitmatter, J. L., 588, 589
Strober, M., 611
Strutt, G. F., 428
Stunkard, A. J., 178, 402
Sturdevant, M. S., 532, 533
Sturm, L., 181
Sturner, W. Q., 194
Styfco, S. J., 341
Subak-Sharpe, G., 360
Subbotsky, E. V., 322
Suess, G. J., 76
Sullivan, H. S., 606
Sullivan, J. W., 158
Sullivan, L. W., 60
Sullivan, Margaret W., 359
Sullivan, Mercer L., 531
Sullivan, S. A., 295
Sulzby, E., 335
Suomi, S., 175
Super, C. M., 82, 182
Super, D., 573
Suwalsky, J. T., 494
Swanson, H. S. W., 70
Sykes, N. L., Jr., 515
Szeminska, A., 424

Tager-Flusberg, H., 346
Taitz, L. S., 401
Takahashi, K., 183, 269
Takahira, S., 560
Tamis-LeModa, C. S., 227
Tams, L., 64
Tanner, J. M., 170, 172, 173, 173*n*, 286, 288*n*, 289, 289*n*, 291, 292, 293, 296, 396, 397, 514, 515, 516, 516*n*, 517, 518*n*
Tate, C. S., 347

Taylor, A. R., 455
Taylor, B. J., 194
Taylor, D. G., 270
Taylor, J. H., 371, 595, 596
Taylor, M. C., 379
Taylor, R. D., 83
Teberg, A. J., 148
Tedder, J. L., 162
Teikari, J. M., 400
Tertinger, D. A., 301
Tesman, J. R., 294
Thach, B. T., 194
Thacker, S. B., 300
Thackwray, D. E., 529
Tharp, R. G., 443, 451, 451*n*
Thatcher, R. W., 289, 398
Thelen, E., 13, 155, 184, 189
Theorell, K., 160
Thiel, K., 604
Thoma, S. J., 599
Thoman, E., 193
Thomas, A., 257, 258*n*, 259, 261, 262
Thomas, J. R., 307, 410, 413
Thompson, R. A., 46, 81, 253, 255, 256, 272, 359
Thorndike, R. L., 337, 437
Thornton, A., 98
Thorsen, E. E., 456
Tilden, V. P., 122
Tinker, E., 345
Tinsley, B. R., 152
Tizard, B., 153, 270
Tobey, A. E., 500
Tobias, P. V., 398
Toda, S., 254, 260
Todd, C. M., 331
Tolson, T. F. G., 83
Tomarelli, R. M., 179
Tomasello, M., 242, 345
Toomey, K. A., 137
Torfs, C. P., 146
Torney-Purta, J., 323
Torrance, E. P., 456, 457
Torrey, B. B., 84*n*
Touwen, B. C. L., 155
Tower, R. B., 344
Townes, B., 265
Townsend, M. A. R., 476
Trautner, H. M., 485
Treffers, P. D. A., 488
Trevethan, S. D., 596
Trickett, P. K., 386
Trieber, F. A., 404, 407
Trinkoff, A., 201
Tronick, E. Z., 81, 162, 270
Trowbridge, F., 295
Trudge, J., 329
Tschann, J. M., 492
Tulviste, P., 30
Turiel, E., 370, 371, 478, 479
Turiel, J., 147, 150
Turkheimer, E., 90
Tyack, D., 346

U.S. Bureau of the Census, 99, 113, 145, 230, 339, 452, 494, 534*n*, 575, 575*n*
U.S. Centers for Disease Control, 531*n*, 538
U.S. Department of Education, 568, 570*n*, 576
U.S. Department of Health and Human Services, 294, 537*n*, 538, 539, 539*n*, 612, 613*n*
U.S. Department of Justice, 614, 615, 615*n*
U.S. Department of Labor, 98*n*
Udry, J. R., 529
Ullian, D. Z., 485
Ulman, K., 519
Ulrich, B. D., 302
Ulrich, D. A., 302
Unger, R., 401
United Nations, 151*n*
Užgiris, I. C., 219, 229

Vachon, R., 552
Valdez, R. B., 404
Valdez-Menchaca, M. C., 242
Valian, V. V., 348
Vallance, D. D., 473
Van de Perre, P., 179
van den Berg, B. J., 144
van IJzendoorn, M. H., 127, 269, 269*n*, 271, 271*n*, 273
van Kammen, W. B., 616
Vandell, D. L., 341, 495
Vandenberg, B., 365*n*
Vanfossen, B., 569
Vann, W. F., Jr., 288
Vasconcellos, M. T., 452
Vasen, A., 359
Vasta, R., 235
Vasudev, J., 599
Vaughn, B. E., 268, 271, 272, 279
Vaughn, V. C., 63*n*
Veerula, G. R., 294
Vega-Lahr, N., 404
Veldhuis, J. D., 170
Ventura, S. J., 102
Verbrugge, H. P., 298
Verhulst, F. C., 72
Versluis-Den Bieman, H. J. M., 72
Vessey, J. A., 407
Vihman, M. M., 237
Vinovskis, M. A., 10, 533
Vitulano, L. A., 455
Vohr, B. R., 147, 148
Volling, B. L., 275
Vorhees, C. V., 111, 112, 113, 115, 116, 117*n*
Vos, J., 160
Voydanoff, P., 532
Vuchinich, S., 493
Vurpillot, E., 428, 429*n*
Vygotsky, L. S., 30, 225, 327

Waas, G. A., 482, 483
Wachs, T. D., 229
Waddington, C. H., 90
Waggoner, J. E., 446
Wagner, B. M., 471
Wainryb, C., 478
Waitzman, K. A., 477
Wakat, D. K., 307
Walberg, H. J., 450
Wald, E. R., 300
Walden, T. A., 254
Waldman, I. D., 443
Walk, R. D., 198
Walker, D., 77, 242
Walker, E., 373
Walker, L. J., 371, 595, 596, 599
Walker, R. A., 289, 398
Wallace, C. S., 174
Wallace, J. R., 469
Wallach, M. A., 456
Waller, M. B., 113
Wallerstein, J. S., 489, 490, 491
Walsh, M. E., 408
Walters, R. H., 369, 370
Walther, F. J., 148
Wang, Q., 237
Ward, S. L. D., 194
Warren, A. R., 347
Warren, B. M., 435
Warren, M. P., 520
Warren, S. F., 241
Warren-Leubecker, A., 236, 348
Warshak, R. A., 491
Wasik, B. A., 436
Waterlow, J., 120
Waterman, A. S., 588, 589, 590
Waters, E., 252, 268
Waters, H. F., 373
Waters, K. A., 537
Watkins, B. A., 374
Watkins, D. L., 410
Watkinson, B., 114
Watson, D. J., 435
Watson, J. B., 19
Watson, J. D., 52
Watson, K. S., 363, 363*n*
Watson, M. W., 324
Waxler, C. Z., 41, 41*n*, 368
Waxman, S. R., 224, 345
Wechsler, D., 439
Wegman, M. E., 84*n*, 151, 151*n*
Wehren, A., 446
Weideger, P., 519
Weil, W. B., 402
Weinberg, M., 532
Weinberg, R. A., 88, 92, 443
Weinberger, D. A., 616
Weinberger, H. L., 294
Weinstein, R. S., 452
Weisner, T. S., 81, 377
Weiss, E., 297
Weiss, R. J., 372
Weisz, J. R., 422, 474
Weitzman, M., 405
Well, A. D., 428
Wellman, H. M., 324, 330, 331, 331*n*, 333, 334, 433
Wells, A. J., 155
Welsh, M. C., 59
Wentzel, K., 566
Werner, E. E., 79, 152
Werner, J. S., 195, 222
Wertsch, J. V., 30
Wesley, B. D., 144
West, L. L., 571*n*
West, M. J., 76, 370
Westbury, I., 568
Westra, T., 186, 187*n*
Whalen, C. K., 430
Whalley, J., 123
Whang, P. A., 436
Wheeler, M. D., 514, 515, 516
Whetsell, M. V., 360
Whiffen, V. E., 164
Whisnant, L., 520
Whitaker, H. A., 177
Whitbeck, L. B., 387
White, B., 189
White, S. H., 13
White, T., 500
Whitebrook, M., 341
Whitehouse, R. H., 288*n*
Whitehurst, G. J., 21, 234, 235, 242
Whitesell, N., 359
Whiting, B., 371, 376, 485
Whiting, J. W. M., 512
Wiesel, T. N., 175
Wigfield, R. E., 194
Wikner, K., 157
Wilensky, H. L., 82
Willats, J., 412, 412*n*
Wille, D. E., 271
Willer, B., 339
Willerman, L., 88, 443
Williams, B. C., 297*n*, 298, 299*n*, 300, 301, 406
Williams, Christopher, 600
Williams, Cristianna S., 290
Williams, E., 494, 495
Williams, G. A., 455
Williams, L. M., 500
Willms, J., 114
Wilson, A. L., 194
Wilson, D. R., 301
Wilson, Melvin N., 83
Wilson, Modena, 301
Wilson, Ronald S., 92, 178
Wilson, Ronnie, 611
Wilson, W. J., 78
Wilson-Mitchell, J. E., 377
Wimbush, D. D., 384
Wimmer, H., 334, 433
Windsor, R. A., 114
Winegar, A., 123
Winick, M., 120, 180
Winn, S., 81
Winner, E., 305, 345, 412, 446, 561
Winthrop, R. H., 36
Wintre, M. G., 473
Wissmann, D. A., 400
Witelson, S. F., 291
Wnek, L., 303*n*, 304*n*
Wolf, A., 183
Wolf, R. M., 568
Wolfe, S., 145
Wolff, P. H., 160*n*
Wolfner, G., 501
Wong-Fillmore, L., 449
Wood, D. J., 328
Woodward, A. L., 345
Woodward, L., 143
Woody, E. Z., 402
Woolley, J. D., 322, 324
World Bank, 100
Worobey, J., 258
Wozniak, R. H., 556
Wright, J., 78
Wright, K., 473
Wright, V. C., 589
Wunsch, J. P., 253
Wyer, M. M., 492

Yamaguchi, K., 539
Yarrow, A. L., 102
Yarrow, M. R., 33, 41, 41*n*, 368
Yazigi, R. A., 113
Yesalis, C. E., 542
Yip, R., 295
Yogman, M. W., 274
Yonas, A., 157, 189, 199
Young, C., 125
Young, K. T., 14
Younger, B. A., 224
Youniss, J., 365, 593, 606
Yuill, N., 370, 592

Zabin, L. S., 535
Zafran, E. I., 71
Zahn-Waxler, C., 40, 278, 361, 367
Zajonc, R. B., 488
Zakin, D. F., 525
Zalar, M. K., 118, 141
Zalenski, R., 333
Zametkin, A. J., 399
Zamsky, E. S., 83
Zani, B., 608
Zarbatany, L., 378
Zaslow, M. J., 494
Zegans, L., 520
Zeisel, S. H., 400
Zelazo, N. A., 155
Zelazo, P. R., 155, 267*n*
Zeskind, P. S., 121, 161
Zhang, J., 61
Zhou, Y., 564
Ziegler, C. B., 601
Zigler, E. F., 84, 184, 231, 338, 340, 341, 386, 387, 388, 612
Zillman, D., 375
Zimmerman, B. J., 434
Zimmerman, M., 471
Zimmerman, R., 264
Zimmerman, S., 295
Ziporyn, T., 164
Zuckerman, B., 113
Zuckerman, H., 576
Zukow, P. G., 226

Subject Index

AB search error, 215, 218–219
Ability grouping in schools, 452
Abortion, 69, 72, 533
Abstract reasoning, 548–552
Abuse of children. *See* Child maltreatment; Child sexual abuse
Academic achievement, 450–452
  and academic self-esteem, 469
  in adolescence, 564–569
  and bilingualism, 449
  and birth order, 488
  and child-rearing practices, 565–566
  cross-cultural study of, 458–460, 568
  and culture, 436, 458–460, 471–472, 568
  and divorce, 491
  of learning disabled children, 454
  and pubertal timing, 525
  and school characteristics, 450–452
  and school mainstreaming, 455
  and school transitions, 564
  sex differences in, 559–560
  and sexual activity in adolescence, 534
  and social class, 566, 569
Academic learning. *See* Education; Educational *entries;* School(s), learning in
Academic preschools, 340
Academic self-esteem, 469–470
Academic training, in early childhood 336, 340, 343–344. *See also* Education
Accelerated learning programs, 457
Accommodation in cognitive development, 211, 212, 318
Achievement-related attributions, 470–472
Acne, 514–515
Acquired immune deficiency syndrome (AIDS), 117–119, 405, 408, 537–538
  information about, sources of, 131, 419, 545
Active genetic–environmental correlation, 91–92
Activity levels and child-rearing practices, 261
Adaptation in cognitive-developmental theory, 21–22, 211, 212
ADHD (attention-deficit hyperactivity disorder), 430, 431, 463, 616
Adolescence
  abortion in, 69, 533
  academic achievement in, 564–569
  adopted children in, 270
  argumentativeness in, 555–556
  biological changes in. *See* hormonal changes in, *below;* Puberty; Sexual maturation
  body growth in, 170, 513–518, 526
  body image in, 524, 527–529, 556–557. *See also* physical attractiveness in, *below*
  childbearing in, 533–534
  cognitive development in, 22, 23, 547–548, 601, 622–623
  cognitive impairment from lead poisoning in, 294
  conceptions of, 510–512
  death in, 299. *See also* suicide in, *below*
  delinquency in, 614–618, 621
  depression in, 610–612
  developmental milestones in, 622–623
  developmental problems in, 610–618
  dieting in, 403, 527. *See also* Eating disorders
  divorce of parents during, 490–491, 613
  eating habits in, 403, 526–529
  education in, 563–572
  emotional and social behavior during, 520, 522–524
  emotional and social development in, 583–618, 622–623
  employment in, 576–578, 581
  families in, 601–604
  friendships in, 604–609
  gender stereotypes in, 484, 485, 601
  gender typing in, 601
  grammatical development in, 561
  health issues in, 408, 526–541
  hormonal changes in, 512–515, 520, 611
  hypothetico-deductive reasoning in, 548–551
  idealism and criticism in, 558
  information processing in, 552–555
  initiation ceremonies in, 520, 521
  injuries in, 299, 405–406, 540–541
  language development in, 559–562, 622–623
  malnutrition in, 527–529
  memory strategies during, 431
  mental ability in, 559–560
  mood swings during, 520, 522, 523
  moral development in, 591–600
  motor development in, 412, 541–542
  muscle–fat makeup in, 172
  nutrition in, 526–529, 534
  obesity in, 527
  parent–child relationships in, 522, 602–603
  parenthood in, 83, 533–535
  peer relations in, 524–525, 561, 566, 567, 604–610
  perspective taking in, 475, 531, 557, 591–596, 599–600
  phases of, 512
  physical attractiveness in, 524–525
  physical development in, 289, 509–542, 622–623
  physical transition to adulthood in. *See* Puberty
  planning and decision making in, 558–559
  pragmatics in, 561
  pregnancy in, 123, 124, 340, 532–536, 545. *See also* childbearing in, *above*
  propositional thought in, 549–552
  psychosexual development in, 16, 18, 511
  psychosocial development in, 584–585
  remarriage of parent during, 493
  and school phobias, 497
  self-concept in, 585–586
  self-consciousness and self-focusing in, 556–557
  self-development in, 585–590
  self-esteem in, 586–589
  self-regulation in, 434, 558–559, 561
  sex education in, 529, 532, 533, 535, 536, 538
  sex hormones in, 513–515, 520, 611
  sexual abuse problems in, 500
  sexual activity in, 529–534
  sexual attitudes in, 530, 531
  sexual maturation in. *See* Puberty; Sexual maturation
  sexually transmitted diseases in, 537–538
  skeletal growth in, 514
  substance use and abuse in, 538–540, 578
  suicide in, 612–614, 621
  vocabulary development in, 561
  vocational (career) development in, 572–578
Adopted children
  attachment security of, 269–270
  intelligence of, 88
  problems of, 72
Adoption, 72–73, 95, 534
Adoption studies, 88, 442–443
Adrenal androgens, 513
Adult-organized sports, 414, 415, 419
Adulthood
  childbearing in, 102
  physical transition to. *See* Puberty
  suicide in, 612, 613, 621
Advertising on television, 373, 374
Affection and physical growth, 181
African-Americans
  academic achievement of, 567, 568
  adolescent sexual activity of, 530, 531
  body build of, 307
  body growth of, 170, 171
  child-rearing practices of, 384
  dental development of, 173
  dropping out of school by, 570
  extended families of, 81–83
  gun injuries and deaths of, 541
  in Head Start programs, 342
  health problems of children of, 405
  identity development among, 588, 589
  infant mortality among, 151
  infant sleeping arrangements of, 183
  intelligence testing of, 442–445
  learned helplessness among, 471
  premarital childbirth among, 534
  self-esteem of, 586
  sickle cell anemia in, 60, 62
  skeletal age of, 173
  television portrayals of, 373, 375
African societies. *See also specific entries, e.g.:* Aka (Central Africa) infant caregiving; Zambian infant behavior
  child rearing in, 81
  extended families in, 82, 83
  family size and education in, 100
  menarche timing in, 517
After-school child care, 495
Age
  birthrates by, 102
  and development, in medieval times, 9–10
  and fraternal twinning, 58
  in longitudinal research design, 41
  maternal. *See* Maternal age
  for motor development, 184, 185
  skeletal, 173, 288
  of viability of fetus, 108
Agency, sense of, 277
Aggression. *See also* Antisocial behavior; Difficult children; Rejected-aggressive children; Violence
  and attention-deficit hyperactivity disorder, 430
  controlling, 372–373
  development of, 371–375, 616
  and friendship, 365
  hostile, 371, 416
  instrumental, 371
  and intention diagnosis, 356
  in middle childhood, 480
  and moral reasoning, 371
  and punishment, 369, 372
  versus rough-and-tumble play, 414, 416
  sex differences in, 371
  and violence on television, 373–375
Agility in motor development, 410
AIDS (acquired immune deficiency syndrome), 117–119, 405, 408, 537–538
  information about, sources of, 131, 419, 545
Aka (Central Africa) infant caregiving, 274
Alcohol
  adolescent use of, 538–540, 578
  during pregnancy, 114–115, 124
Alcohol abuse, 114–115, 124, 131
Alleles, 58–60
  genetic imprinting of, 61, 63–64
Altruistic (prosocial) behavior, 367–369, 404, 476, 480
Amniocentesis, 68, 69
Amnion, 103

Amniotic fluid, 103
Anal stage of development, 16–18, 248, 249
Analgesics during childbirth, 143
Androgens, 371, 399, 513
Androgyny, 379, 601, 606, 611
Anemia, 527
  Cooley's, 62
  sickle cell, 60, 62, 95
Anesthetics during childbirth, 143
Anger in infants, 253–254
Animals, fear of, 360
Animistic thinking, 317, 318, 322
Anorexia nervosa, 527–529, 545
Anoxia (oxygen deprivation), 146–147, 150
Antibodies in fetal development, 108
Antidepressant drugs, 404
Antisocial behavior, 404. *See also* Delinquency
  in middle childhood, 476, 481
  and peer pressure, 608, 609
  and suicide, 612–613
Anxiety
  in middle childhood, 496–497, 499
  separation, 266–268, 490
  stranger, 253
Apache initiation ceremony, 521
Apgar Scale, 137–138
Appalachian sleeping arrangements for children, 183
Appearance versus reality, 324, 325
Appetite in early childhood, 293, 294
Applied behavior analysis, 21
Apprenticeships, work-study, 577, 578
Argumentativeness in adolescence, 555–556
Arousal states, 159–162, 181, 183
Asian Americans
  extended families of, 82
  identity development among, 588, 589
Asian countries
  academic achievement in, 436, 459, 460, 471
  child-rearing practices in, 260
  education in, 100, 484
  infant behavior in, 162
  mathematics achievement in, 436
  sexual attitudes in, 529
Aspirin during pregnancy, 112
Assimilation in cognitive development, 211, 212
Assisted discovery, 329
Associative play, 362–364
Asthma, 405
At-risk infants, 232, 233, 245, 271, 342
At-risk preschoolers, 340–342
Athletic achievement, 541–542. *See also* Sports
Attachment(s)
  avoidant, 268–270, 273
  defined, 263
  disorganized/disoriented, 268, 271
  drive reduction explanation of, 263–264
  in early childhood, 275
  early theories of, 263–267
  in infancy and toddlerhood, 27, 263–276
  and later development, 275–276
  multiple, 272, 274–275
  to objects, 264, 265
  resistant, 268–270
  secure, 268–271
  sibling, 604
Attachment security, 267–272, 590
Attention
  in early childhood, 330, 331, 333
  in infancy and toddlerhood, 222–223
  in middle childhood, 428–430
Attention-deficit hyperactivity disorder (ADHD), 430, 431, 463, 616
Attribution retraining, 472
Attributions, 470–472
Australian aborigine memory skills, 432
Authoritarian child rearing, 383, 565
Authoritative child rearing
  in adolescence, 565–566, 596, 602–603, 609, 616
  in early childhood, 382–384
  in middle childhood, 470, 487, 491, 494, 495
Autism, 64
Autonomous morality, 591–592
Autonomy
  in adolescence, 584, 602
  in infancy and toddlerhood, 18, 249–251, 279
Autosomal diseases, 62–63, 65
Autosomes, 56, 63
Avoidant attachment, 268–270, 273

Babbling by infants, 236–237
Babinski reflex, 154, 156
Baby biographies, 12
Bacterial diseases during pregnancy, 117, 118
Baganda (Uganda) infant motor skills, 186
Baka of Cameroon
  false belief reasoning of, 333–334
  industry stage of development in, 466
Balance in motor development, 409–410
Balance scale problem, 553–554
Ball skills and motor development, 303–305
Bandura's modeling theory, 20–21, 32, 368–369, 476
Bases in DNA, 52, 54
Basic-level categories, 324
Basic-skills approach to reading instruction, 435
Batting and motor development, 409, 410
Bayley Scales of Infant Development, 228, 229
Bedwetting (nocturnal enuresis), 404–405
Behavior, types of. *See specific entries, e.g.*: Antisocial behavior; Intentional (goal-directed) behavior
Behavior disorders, 88
Behaviorism, 19–21, 32, 193
  as attachment theory, 263–264
  forerunner of, 10
  in injury prevention, 301
  language development in, 235
  moral development in, 366–370
  and safety enhancement, 406
Bell-shaped (normal) curves, 228
Beneficial treatments as research right, 45
Benevolence in distributive justice, 477
Bermuda, day care in, 231
Bidirectional relationships, 28, 32, 74, 111
Bilingual education, 448, 449, 463
Bilingualism, 447–449, 562
Binocular depth cues, 199, 200, 204
Biological view of adolescence, 510–512
Birth centers, 140, 167
Birth complications, 271
Birth control pills, 115. *See also* Contraceptives
Birth defects, 95, 112, 113, 123–124, 131
Birth order in sibling experiences, 488
Birth weight, 112–117, 122, 147–151, 405
Birthrates, 100, 102
Births. *See also* Childbearing, timing of; Childbirth,
  multiple, 57–58. *See also* Twin *entries*
  number of, 58, 123–124
Bladder control, 189–190, 249
Blastocyst, 103–105, 108
Blended (reconstituted) families, 492–494
Blood analysis, maternal, 68
Blood type (Rh factor), 122–123
Bloody show in childbirth, 134
Bodily-kinesthetic intelligence, 441
Body build. *See* Body proportions
Body growth. *See also* Sexual maturation
  in adolescence, 170, 513–518, 526
  disorders of, diagnosing, 288
  in early childhood, 286–289, 306–307, 515
  in infancy and toddlerhood, 170–174, 515
  in middle childhood, 170, 396–399, 413, 515
Body image in adolescence, 524, 527–529, 556–557
Body proportions
  in adolescence, 513, 514
  in early childhood, 286–287, 306–307
  in infancy and toddlerhood, 170–172
  in middle childhood, 396, 397, 413
Body size. *See also* Obesity; Weight *entries*
  in adolescence, 170, 513–518
  in early childhood, 286–289
  in infancy and toddlerhood, 170, 171
  in middle childhood, 170, 396–398
Bonding of parents and infants, 153. *See also* Mother–infant relationships; Parent–infant relationships
Bone development, 173, 287. *See also* Skeletal growth
Boot camps, 618
Bottle-feeding of infants, 178–179, 402
Bowel control, 189–190, 249
Brain
  parts of. *See specific entries, e.g.*: Cerebral cortex; Reticular formation
  stimulation of, 174–175
Brain damage
  in childbirth, 146
  and handedness, 290
  in infancy, 177
  from lead poisoning, 294
  and newborn crying, 161
  and newborn reflexes, 155
Brain development
  in early childhood, 289–291, 308
  in infancy and toddlerhood, 174–177, 180–181, 289
  in middle childhood, 398–399, 428–429
  prenatal, 106–108
Brain lateralization, 176–177, 289–291, 398
Brain plasticity, 176–177
Breast development, 515, 516
Breast-feeding of infants, 178–179, 207
Breathing techniques in childbirth, 140
Breech position in childbirth, 145
Bulimia, 528–529, 545

Caffeine during pregnancy, 112
CAI (computer-assisted instruction), 452
Canalization, 90
Cancer, 405, 408, 419
Cardinality principle, 336
Careers, choosing, 572–578
Caregiving, 81, 270–271, 274, 276. *See also* Mother–infant relationships; Parent–infant relationships
Caring in moral development, 599–600
Carolina Abecedarian Project, 232, 233
Carriers of traits, 59
Cartilage, 173
Case study approach. *See* Clinical method of research
Catch-up growth, 178, 292
Catching and motor development, 303–305, 409
Categorization
  of information, 222–224
  in preoperational stage of cognitive development, 324
Cavities, 288, 398
Cells
  defined, 52
  division of (meiosis), 53–55
  duplication of (mitosis), 53, 54
  nuclei of, 52
  types of, 53–57. *See also* Neurons (nerve cells)
Centration in cognitive development, 317, 319, 422
Cephalocaudal trend, 170–172, 184
Cerebellum, 291
Cerebral cortex. *See also* Brain *entries*
  defined, 175
  development of, 108, 175–177, 255, 398
  hemispheres of, 176–177, 289, 290, 398
  lateralization of, 176–177, 289–291, 398
Cerebral palsy, 146, 167
Certainty about knowledge, 334
Cervix, 56
  dilation and effacement of, 135–136
Cesarean delivery, 144–145, 167
Child abuse and neglect. *See* Child maltreatment
Child care and maternal employment, 495. *See also* Day care; Preschools
Child-centered preschools, 340
Child custody after divorce, 492, 493
Child development. *See also* Developmental *entries; specific entries, e.g.*: Cognitive development; Physical development
  continuous versus discontinuous, 6–7, 11, 32, 427
  defined, 4
  field of, 4–5
  historical foundations of, 9–15
  scientific foundations of, 11–15
  themes and issues in, 5–8
Child development theories, 6–32. *See also specific entries, e.g.*: Ecological systems theory of development; Psychosocial theory of development (Erikson)
Child maltreatment, 384–388. *See also* Child sexual abuse
  and attachment insecurity, 271
  and community ties, 78–79
  consequences of, 387, 389
  court testimony of, 500–501
  of infants, 148, 161–162, 271

information about, sources of, 391
origins of, 385–387
preventing, 387–388
and punishment, 369
Child rearing
costs of, 98–99
styles of, 382–385, 565. *See also* Authoritative child rearing
Child-rearing practices, 76. *See also* Families; Family systems; Mother–infant relationships; Parent–child relationships; Parent–infant relationships
and academic achievement, 565–566
and activity levels, 261
culture in, 14, 17–18, 81–84, 182, 183, 384
and delinquency, 615–616
after divorce, 490–492, 505
in ecological systems theory, 27–29
and emotional and social development, 382–388, 486–487
in Enlightenment, 10–11
and gender-role identity, 485
and gender typing, 377–378, 382
and maternal employment, 494–495
and moral development, 596
and poverty, 77–78, 82, 83
of Puritans, 10
after remarriage, 492–494
and safety, 406
and self-esteem, 470
and social change, 14
and social class, 76–78
teaching, to stop maltreatment, 388
and television, 374
and temperament, 257, 260–263, 271
and values, 81
Child sexual abuse, 385, 497–498, 500–501, 505
Child study. *See specific entries, e.g.*: Child development, scientific foundations of; Research *entries*
Child support, 490, 492
Childbearing, timing of, 102, 533–534
Childbirth. *See also* Birth *entries*
approaches to, 138–142
complications during, 142, 145–152
and culture, 139, 142
delivery in, 136, 139, 141–146, 167
depression after, 164
drugs during, 141, 143–145
information about, sources of, 167
information-seeking about, 126
labor in, 134–137, 143–145
medical interventions during, 142–146
natural (prepared), 138, 140–141, 167
places of, 138–142, 167
positions for, 139–141
stages of, 134–138. *See also* delivery in, *above;* labor in, *above*
Childhood
adopted children in, 270
research rights in, 44–46
stages of. *See* Adolescence; Early childhood; Infancy and toddlerhood; Middle childhood
Children. *See specific entries, e.g.*: Adopted children; Difficult children; Parent–child relationships
Children's Defense Fund, 84, 85, 95, 536
Children's television, 374, 391
China
family size and education in, 101
infant temperament in, 260
school tracking in, 569
Chinese immigrants, second-language learning by, 562
Chlamydia, 537
Chorion, 103–104
Chorionic villus sampling, 68, 69, 103n
Chromosomal abnormalities, 65–66
Chromosomes, 52–55
crossing over of, 53–55
mapping, 69
pairs of, 52, 53
sex, 56–57, 65–66
Circular reactions in cognitive development, 213–216
City impact on development, 80–81
Class inclusion problem, 321, 324, 325, 422
Classical conditioning, 19, 190–193
Classrooms, traditional versus open, 450
Clinical interviews, 22, 34, 35, 592–593
Clinical method of research, 34, 36
in cognitive-developmental theory, 22
in personality development theories, 251
in psychoanalytic theory, 18
Cliques in adolescence, 606–607
Cloning, 69, 71
Cocaine during pregnancy, 112–113
Codominance in heredity, 60
Cognition
and language, 314
meta-, 333–334, 433, 471, 472
and social experience, 328–329
in social learning theory, 20–21
Cognitive development
in adolescence, 22, 23, 547–548, 601, 622–623
and attachment, 275–276
and attributions, 471
and bilingualism, 448
circular reactions in, 213–216
in early childhood, 289, 291, 305, 313–348, 361, 392–393
and empathy, 361
and health and illness understanding, 408
in infancy and toddlerhood, 22, 23, 195, 209–242, 245, 254, 282–283
information processing in. *See* Information processing
language development in. *See* Language development
lead poisoning impairing, 294
mental development in. *See* Intelligence *entries;* Mental development
mental representation in, 216, 314, 316
in middle childhood, 399, 422–460, 467, 471, 476, 506–507
and moral development, 366, 367, 370–371, 476, 592
and neurotransmitters, 399
rule-assessment approach to (Siegler), 553–555
schemes in, 210–214, 316, 426–427
and self-development, 467
sex differences in, 560
and social interaction, 363–365
sociocultural theory of. *See* Sociocultural theory of cognitive development (Vygotsky)
and sports, 542
stages of. *See* Concrete operational stage of cognitive development; Formal operational stage of cognitive development; Preoperational stage of cognitive development; Sensorimotor stage of cognitive development
Cognitive-developmental theory (Piaget), 21–23, 32, 210–220, 225–227
challenges to, 426
concepts in, 210–212
educational principles derived from, 325–326
and gender-role identity, 379–380
gender typing in, 375–376
intelligence tests based on, 439
moral development in, 366, 367, 370–371, 476
stages in. *See* Concrete operational stage of cognitive development; Formal operational stage of cognitive development; Preoperational stage of cognitive development; Sensorimotor stage of cognitive development
Cognitive equilibrium and disequilibrium, 211, 212
Cognitive rules for problem solving, 553–555
Cohort effects, 42–43, 290
Collective caregiving, 81
Color blindness, 61
Comanche childbirth practices, 139
Communication
parent–child, 487
parent–teacher, 459
verbal, 328–329
Communities
and family systems, 78–81, 387
in identity development, 590
just, in moral education, 598, 599
Compliance in infancy and toddlerhood, 279
Componential analyses of intelligence quotients, 439–441
Componential subtheory of triarchic theory of intelligence, 440
Comprehension
in language development, 240
monitoring, 558
Computer-assisted instruction (CAI), 452
Computers in schools, 452–453, 463
Conception, 55–56, 70–71
Concordance rates, 87–89
Concrete operational stage of cognitive development, 22, 23, 422–427
and culture, 552
evaluation of, 427
limitations in, 425
and moral development, 594
recent research on, 425–427
transition from, 557
Conditioned response (CR), 191, 192
Conditioned stimulus (CS), 191, 192
Conditioning
classical, 19, 190–193
operant, 19–20, 192–193, 235, 368
Conformity and peer pressure, 608–609
Conscience. *See* Moral *entries;* Superego
Consent in research, 45, 46
Conservation
in concrete operational stage of cognitive development, 422–427
and gender-role identity, 379
in preoperational stage of cognitive development, 319, 320, 322, 325
Constructive play, 365
Contexts for development, 26–31, 73–84
Contextual subtheory of triarchic theory of intelligence, 440
Continuous child development, 6–7, 11, 32, 427
Contraceptives
access to, 535
in adolescence, 531–533, 536
during pregnancy, 115
public policy on, 545
Contrast, defined, 201
Contrast sensitivity, 201
Control processes, 221–222
Controversial children, 482, 483
Conventional level of moral development, 594–595
Convergent thinking, 455
Conversational skills, 346–348, 447
Cooing by infants, 236, 237
Cooley's anemia, 62
Cooperation
in early childhood, 356
in moral development, 594, 595
Cooperative family systems, 81–83
Cooperative learning, 329, 455
Cooperative play, 363, 364
Coregulation, 487
Corporal punishment, 387, 478
Corpus callosum, 291
Corpus luteum, 55–56
Correlation, genetic–environmental, 90–92
Correlation coefficient, 39
Correlational research design, 37, 39, 42
Cortex. *See* Cerebral cortex
Cortisol, 257
Cosleeping, 183
Counting strategies, 335–336
CR (conditioned response), 191, 192
Crack (cocaine), 112, 113
Crawling, 200, 250
Creativity in giftedness, 455–457
Critical period of development, 26–27
Cross-cultural research and sociocultural theory, 29–31. *See also* Culture
Cross-sectional research design, 42–44
Crossing over of chromosomes, 53–55
Crowds in adolescence, 606, 607
Crowning in childbirth, 136
Crying by newborns, 160–162
CS (conditioned stimulus), 191, 192
Cultural bias in intelligence tests, 338, 437, 441, 444–445
Cultural deficits, 38
Cultural-historical change, 42–43
Cultural stereotypes, 575–576
Culturally specific practices, 30
Culture. *See also* Cross-cultural research and sociocultural theory; Ethnicity and race; Subcultures; *specific entries, e.g.*: African societies; Yurok Indian infant feeding
and academic achievement, 436, 458–460, 471–472, 568
and academic training, 340
and adolescent period, 511–512, 529–530, 534
and attachment, 265, 268–270

Culture *(continued)*
and child maltreatment, 387
in child-rearing practices, 14, 17–18, 81–84, 182, 183, 384
and childbirth, 139, 142, 534
and childhood injuries, 300–301
and cognitive development stages, 425–426, 552
and contraceptive access, 535
and conversational skills, 346–347
and corporal punishment, 478
and day care, 231
and drug use, 538–539
in ecological systems theory, 29
and education, 38, 82, 484, 577, 578
and emotions, 252, 255, 359
ethnographic research into, 34, 36–38
and food choices, 294–295
and games, 414
and gender typing, 376, 381, 485–486
and handedness, 290
and health and illness understanding, 408
and health care, 298
and homosexuality, 532–533
and identity development, 588–590
and industry stage of development, 466
and infant facial expressions, 252
and infant–parent relationships, 274
and infant sleeping arrangements, 182, 183
and inner mental life, 333–334
and intelligence quotients, 443–445
and intelligence tests, 441
and language learning, 240–241
and memory strategies, 432, 433
and moral concepts, 478, 479
and moral development, 366, 597, 599
and motor development, 186, 187
peer, 480
and peer relations, 604
and play, 226, 354, 414
and pregnancy, 127–128
and school tracking, 569
and separation anxiety, 266, 267
and sexual activity, 529–530
and sexual maturation, 520, 521, 525
and skeletal growth, 288
in sociocultural theory, 29–32
and temperament, 260
and work–study apprenticeships, 577, 578
Cuna Indian childbirth practices, 139
Custody of children after divorce, 492, 493
Cystic fibrosis, 62, 69, 405, 419
Cytomegalovirus, 117–118, 537
Cytoplasm, 53

Darkness, fear of, 360
Darwin's theory of evolution, 11
Dating, 608
Day care
for children of adolescent mothers, 535
in early childhood, 297, 300, 341, 343, 360
fear of, 360
field experiments in, 40–41
health and safety issues of, 297, 300, 311
for infants, 14, 230–233, 273, 300, 494
information about, sources of, 245, 351
and mental development, 230–233, 339, 341, 343
quality of, 273, 341, 343, 494
Deafness in infants, 236
Death
in adolescence, 538, 540–541, 612–614
from AIDS, 538
asthma-related, 405
from child maltreatment, 388
in infancy, 150, 151, 193, 194, 300
from suicide, 612–614
understanding, 323
from unintentional injuries, 299–301, 540–541
Debriefing as research right, 46
Decentration in cognitive development, 422, 423
Decision making in adolescence, 558–559
Deferred imitation, 216, 218–219
Delinquency, 340, 614–618, 621
Demandingness in child rearing, 382
Dental development, 173–174, 288, 398
Dental health, 288, 398
Deoxyribonucleic acid (DNA), 52–54, 61
Dependent variables, 39
Depression
in adolescence, 610–612. *See also* Suicide in adolescence
and concordance rates, 88
maternal, and attachment insecurity, 271
postpartum, 164
Deprivation dwarfism, 293
Depth cues in drawings, 412–413
Depth perception, 198–201
DES (diethylstilbestrol), 115, 131
Development. *See specific entries, e.g.:* Child development *entries;* Language development; Physical development
Developmental psychology, 4
Developmental quotients (DQs), 229
Developmental research designs, 41–44
Developmentally appropriate practice standards, 232
Diabetes (during pregnancy), 124
Diabetes insipidus, 63
Diet. *See* Eating *entries;* Food *entries;* Malnutrition; Nutrition
Diethylstilbestrol (DES), 115, 131
Dieting in adolescence, 403, 527. *See also* Eating disorders
Differentiation theory of perceptual development, 204–205, 308, 309
Difficult children, 258, 259, 262. *See also* Aggression
abuse of, 386
and divorce, 489, 491
and friendship, 365
Dilation and effacement of cervix, 135–136
Disabilities
and intelligence tests, 437
learning, and education, 454–455
students with, educating, 453–457
Discipline in moral development, 367–370
Discontinuous child development, 6–7, 11, 32, 427
Discovery, assisted, 329
Discovery learning, 325
Dishabituation, 195. *See also* Habituation–dishabituation response
Disorganized/disoriented attachment, 268, 271
Distributive justice, 477–478, 592
Divergent thinking, 455–456
Divorce, 488–492, 505, 613
Divorce mediation, 492
Divorce rates, 489
Dizygotic (fraternal) twins, 57, 58. *See also* Twin studies
DNA (deoxyribonucleic acid), 52–54, 61
Dominance hierarchy, 416
Dominant cerebral hemisphere, 290
Dominant–recessive inheritance, 58–64
Donor insemination, 70, 71
Double standard in sexual attitudes, 530
Down syndrome, 65, 95
DQs (developmental quotients), 229
Drawing and motor development, 304–306, 411–413
Dressing and motor development, 304–305
Dribbling and motor development, 409, 410
Drive reduction theory, 19, 263–264
Drives
primary, 19, 263–264
secondary (learned), 19, 263, 264
Dropping out of school, 569–572, 581
Drug addiction in infants, 113
Drug use and abuse, 112–113, 538–540, 545, 578
Drugs. *See also specific entries, e.g.:* Alcohol *entries;* Marijuana
during adolescence, 538–540, 578
in breast milk, 178–179
during childbirth, 141, 143–145
during pregnancy, 111–113, 534
Duchenne muscular dystrophy, 63, 69
Dwarfism, 293
Dyscalculia, 454
Dysgraphia, 454
Dyslexia, 454

Ear infections, 400
Early adolescence, 512, 622
Early childhood
academic training in, 336
attachment in, 275
attention in, 330, 331, 333
body growth in, 286–289, 306–307, 515
brain development in, 289–291, 308
child-rearing practices in, 382–388
cognitive development in, 289, 291, 305, 313–348, 361, 392–393
conversational skills in, 346–348
cooperation in, 356
day care in, 297, 300, 341, 343, 360
death understanding in, 323
delinquency in, 615, 616
developmental milestones in, 392–393
divorce during, 489, 490
education in, 339–344, 351
emotional development in, 355, 357–362, 382–388, 392–393
empathy development in, 361–362
fantasy period of vocational development in, 573
friendships in, 365
gender typing in, 278, 355, 371, 375–381
grammatical development in, 346, 348
health and illness understanding in, 408
health in, 292–301
infectious diseases in, 296–298
information processing in, 325, 330–336
injuries in, 297, 299–301
intelligence tests in, 337–339
intervention programs in, 340–342
language development in, 289, 290, 334–336, 344–348, 357–358, 361, 392–393, 562
lead poisoning in, 294
malnutrition in, 295
mathematical reasoning in, 335–336
memory in, 330–333, 500
mental development in, 337–344
metacognition in, 333–334
moral development in, 355, 366–375, 592
motor development in, 291, 302–307
nutrition in, 293–296
peer relations in, 275, 362–365, 372–373, 378
perceptual development in, 305, 306, 308–309
personality development in, 354–355
perspective taking in, 475
physical development in, 285–309, 392–393
preoperational stage in. *See* Preoperational stage of cognitive development
psychosexual development in, 354–355, 367, 368
psychosocial theory of development in, 354–355
remarriage of parent during, 493
self-development in, 355–357
sleep in, 182, 183
social development in, 353–357, 362–388, 392–393
vocabulary development in, 344–346, 357–358
Early sexual maturation, 522, 524–525
Easy children, 258, 259, 262, 491
Eating. *See* Food *entries;* Nutrition
Eating disorders, 527–529, 545
Eating habits in adolescence, 403, 526–529
Eclampsia (toxemia), 124
Ecological systems theory of development, 27–29, 32
Ectoderm, 105
Education. *See also* Academic achievement; Academic training; School *entries*
in adolescence, 563–572
bilingual, 448, 449, 463
and child maltreatment, 388
cognitive-developmental principles of, 325–326, 329
and concrete operational reasoning, 426
and culture, 38, 82, 484, 577, 578
in early childhood, 339–344, 351
elementary, 450–451
and family size, 100, 101
and gender stereotypes, 484
of gifted children, 455–457, 463
about health, 406–408
in infancy and toddlerhood, 245

in middle childhood, 406–408, 416–417, 448, 450–460
moral, 598, 599. *See also* Moral development
parent involvement in, 38, 459, 460
physical, 416–417
and poverty, 78
quality of, 458–460
about safety, 406
sex, 501
and social class, 77
and special learning needs, 453–457, 463
years of, number of, 444, 570, 596–597
Educational philosophies, 448, 450–451
Educational placement, 445
Educational self-fulfilling prophecies, 452
Educational television, 343–344
Efe of Zaire
body size of, 287
caregiving among, 81
Ego, 16–17, 32, 511
Ego integrity versus despair as stage, 18
Egocentric speech, 327, 347
Egocentrism, 317, 318, 322, 323
Ejaculation, 519
first (spermarche), 516, 519
Elaboration of information, 429, 431, 432. *See also* Memory strategies
Electra conflict, 16, 354–355, 367, 375
Elementary education, 450–451
Embryo, 105
period of the, 104–106, 108–111, 117
Embryonic disk, 103, 105
Emotion(s)
basic, 181, 252–254
and eating habits, 295
expressing, and culture, 252, 359
infant responses to, 254
mother–child matching of, 270
and physical development, 293
and play, 364
self-conscious. *See* Self-conscious emotions
understanding, 357–358
Emotional deprivation, 293
Emotional development. *See also* Social development; Temperament
in adolescence, 583–618, 622–623
in early childhood, 355, 357–362, 382–388, 392–393
in infancy and toddlerhood, 179, 251–276, 282–283
in middle childhood, 473–474, 506–507
Emotional difficulties
of institutionalized infants, 269–270
and war, 497, 499
Emotional disorders, 88. *See also specific entries, e.g.:* Depression; Schizophrenia
Emotional language, 357–359
Emotional neglect, 385. *See also* Child maltreatment
Emotional self-regulation
in early childhood, 358–360, 387
in infancy and toddlerhood, 255–256
in middle childhood, 473–474, 496
Emotional stress. *See* Stress
Emotional styles. *See* Temperament
Empathic perspective taking, 599–600
Empathy development, 278, 361–362
Employment
maternal, 494–495
and preschool intervention, 340
training programs for, 557, 578, 581
transition from school to, 576–578
Endoderm, 105
Enlightenment philosophies, 10–11
Enuresis (bedwetting), 404–405
Environment
and academic achievement, 560, 564–569
and adolescent depression, 611
in adolescent mood swings, 522
and attention-deficit hyperactivity disorder, 430
and body size, 397
in child development, 26–31, 73–84, 86–92
and child maltreatment, 386–387
in ecological systems theory, 27–29
in ethology, 27
and gender typing, 377–380
and genetics, relationship between, 86–92, 260–261. *See also* Nature–nurture controversy
and giftedness, 456
harmful, in child development, 90
home. *See* Home environment
in homosexuality, 532
in identity development, 590
infant exploration of, 277
and injuries, 299–301
and intelligence quotients, 442–443
invariant features of, 204–205
in language development, 235–236
in language learning, 240–241
and mental development, 229–233, 338–339
in moral development, 596–599
in motor development, 413
and mutations, 61
and myopia, 400
natural, in research, 33–35
and obesity, 401–403
pollution of, 116. *See also* Lead *entries*
in prenatal development, 110–125, 534
school, 567–569
and skeletal growth, 288
social. *See* Social environment
and temperament, 260–263
in Type A behavior, 404
and weight, 178
Environmental view of adolescence, 511
Epiphyses of bone, 173, 287
Episiotomies, 136, 141
Equality in distributive justice, 477
Equilibrium in cognitive-developmental theory, 22
and disequilibrium, 211, 212
Erikson's theory. *See* Psychosocial theory of development (Erikson)
Estrogens, 513
Ethic of care, 599–600
Ethics
of reproductive technologies, 71
in research, 44–46
Ethnicity and race. *See also* Culture; *specific entries, e.g.:* African Americans; Hispanics
and academic achievement, 567, 568
and adolescent depression, 611
and adolescent sexual attitudes, 530, 531
and bilingualism, 447–449, 562
and body size, 170, 171, 286–287, 396–397
and child-rearing practices, 384
and delinquency, 615
developmental influence of, 81–83
and dropping out of school, 569–570
and education, 38, 82, 460
and fraternal twinning, 58
and friendships, 482
and giftedness, 457
and gun injuries and deaths, 541
and identity development, 588–590
and infant mortality, 151
and intelligence and genetics, 89
and intelligence quotients, 436–437, 442–444
and intelligence tests, 337–338, 437, 439
and KEEP schools, 451
and learned helplessness, 471, 472
and low birth weight, 148
and menarche timing, 517
and poverty, 78
and school contact by families, 80
and school problems, 487
and self-esteem, 586
on television, 373, 375
and temperament, 260
Ethnography, 34, 36–38
Ethological theory of attachment (Bowlby), 263–267
Ethology, 26–27, 32
Europe, child health care in, 297, 298
Eustachian tube, 400
Evocative genetic–environmental correlation, 91
Evolution, Darwin's theory of, 11
Exercise
in menarche timing, 517
and obesity, 401, 402
during pregnancy, 118, 120
Exosystem of environment, 28, 29
Expansions in grammar development, 348
Experiential subtheory of triarchic theory of intelligence, 440
Experimental research designs, 39–42
Experiments
field, 40–42
laboratory, 39–40, 42
natural, 41
Explosive personality style, 41–42
Expressive style of language learning, 240
Extended-family households, 81–83
Extinction in classical conditioning, 191
Extracurricular activities, 572
Eye blink reflex, 154

Face perception, 202–204
Facial expressions, 252–254
Factor analysis in intelligence tests, 437, 439
FAE (fetal alcohol effects), 115
Fagan Test of Infant Intelligence, 229
Failure to thrive, 181
Fairness, 477–478, 592–596. *See also* Justice
Fallopian tubes, 55, 56, 70
False belief reasoning, 333–334
False labor, 134
Families. *See also* Home environment
in adolescence, 601–604
in aggression development, 372–373
and attachment security, 271–273
blended (reconstituted), 492–494
and career choices, 574
and delinquency, 615–617
developmental influences of, 73–76, 486–495
divorce affecting, 488–492
and dropping out of school, 570–571
in ecological systems theory of development, 27–29
extended, 81–83
father–stepmother, 493–494
functioning of, and social class, 76–78
and gender typing, 377–378
genetic studies of (kinship studies), 87–88, 442. *See also* Twin studies
and homosexuality, 532
mother–stepfather, 493
and obesity, 401, 402
stress in, 271, 293, 386–388, 613
in wartime, 499
Family planning, need for, 100, 101
Family size, 99–101
Family systems, 74–76
in adolescence, 603
and child maltreatment, 386–387
and community ties, 78–81, 387
cooperative, 81–83
Fantasy period of vocational development, 573
FAS (fetal alcohol syndrome), 114–115, 124
Fast-mapping, 344–345
Father–child relationships after divorce, 491–492
Father–stepmother families, 493–494
Fathers
infant caregiving by, 274
financial and emotional commitment after divorce, 535
and gender-role development of boys, 486
Fear
conditioning of, 19, 191–192
in early childhood, 359, 360
in infancy, 253–254
in middle childhood, 496–497, 499
Feeding
of infants, 178–180, 207, 263–266, 402
and motor development, 304
and obesity, 179–180, 401, 402
Female reproductive organs, 55–56
Fertility and age, 102
Fertility drugs, 57, 58
Fetal alcohol effects (FAE), 115
Fetal alcohol syndrome (FAS), 114–115, 124
Fetal medicine, 68–69
Fetal monitors, 142–143
Fetoscopy, 68, 107
Fetus
defined, 106
period of the, 104, 106–111, 117
Field experiments, 40–42
Fijian moral development, 366
Fine motor development
in adolescence, 412
in early childhood, 304–306
in infancy and toddlerhood, 184, 185, 188–189
in middle childhood, 410–413
Firearm injuries and death, 540–541

Fitness, 416–417
Fixation concept (Freud), 17
Flexibility in motor development, 409, 410
Fontanels (soft spots) of skull, 173, 174
Food
adolescent intake of, 526
early childhood intake of, 293–296
infant and toddler intake of, 180
middle childhood intake of, 400
as reward, 401, 402
Food programs, government-sponsored, 121, 400–401
Food supplements, 121, 181
Force in motor development, 410
Forceps in childbirth, 143–144
Formal operational stage of cognitive development, 22, 23, 548–555
and culture, 552
hypothetico-deductive reasoning in, 548–551
and identity development, 590
information-processing view of, 552–555
and moral development, 594
propositional thought in, 549–552
recent research on, 551–552
transition to, 557
Fragile X syndrome, 63–64
Fraternal (dizygotic) twins, 57, 58. *See also* Twin studies
Freestanding birth centers, 140
Freud's theory
of personality development, 16–17, 32, 248–249, 466. *See also* Psychosexual theory of development (Freud)
Friendships
in adolescence, 604–609
in early childhood, 365
in middle childhood, 481–482
Frontal lobe of cerebral cortex, 398
Functional play, 216, 365

Games, rule-oriented, 413–414. *See also* Play
Gametes (sex cells), 53–57. *See also* Ova; Sperm
Gangs, 616, 617
Gender bias in intelligence tests, 437
Gender constancy, 379–380
Gender differences. *See* Sex differences
Gender intensification, 601, 611
Gender-role expectations, 453, 481
Gender-role identity, 379–381, 484, 485, 606, 611
Gender roles, development of. *See* Gender typing
Gender schema theory, 380–381
Gender stereotypes. *See also* Gender typing
and aggression, 371
in adolescence, 484, 485, 601
in early childhood, 376
and illness symptoms, 405
in middle childhood, 484–485
and motor development, 413
reducing, 380–381
on television, 373, 375
Gender typing
in adolescence, 601
in career choices, 575–576
and child-rearing practices, 377–378, 382
in cognitive-developmental theory, 375–376
and culture, 376, 381, 485–486
in early childhood, 278, 355, 371, 375–381
and environment, 377–380
in gender schema theory, 380–381
and genetics, 376–377
in middle childhood, 478, 484–486
in psychoanalytic theory, 375
in social learning theory, 375–376
Gene splicing, 69
General anesthesia during childbirth, 143
General growth curve, 288–289
General intelligence, 437
General theories in hypothetico-deductive reasoning, 548
Generalizing of remembered information, 332–333
Generativity versus stagnation as stage, 18
Genes, 52–53. *See also* Alleles
cloning, 69, 71
modifier, 59
Genetic code, 52–53
Genetic counseling, 67–68, 73
Genetic disorders, 59–73, 95
Genetic engineering, 69
Genetic–environmental correlation, 90–92
Genetic imprinting, 61, 63–64
Genetics. *See also* Chromosomal abnormalities; Chromosomes; Heritability estimates; Inheritance
and adolescent depression, 611
and asthma, 405
and attention-deficit hyperactivity disorder, 430
in bedwetting, 404
and body size, 287, 397
in child development, 86–92
and environment, relationship between, 86–92, 260–261. *See also* Nature–nurture controversy
family studies of (kinship studies), 87–88, 442. *See also* Twin studies
and gender typing, 376–377
and giftedness, 456
and handedness, 290
in homosexuality, 532
and intelligence, 88, 89, 442–443
in language development, 235, 240–241
and learning disabilities, 454
in menarche timing, 517
in motor development, 186, 413
and myopia, 400
and obesity, 401, 402
patterns in, 58–64
and physical development, 178, 292–293
principles of, 52–64
and rough-and-tumble play, 414, 416
and sex differences in mathematics achievement, 560
and temperament, 259–260
in Type A behavior, 404
and weight, 178
Genital herpes (herpes simplex 2), 117–118, 537
Genital stage of development, 16–18, 511
Genital warts, 537
Genitals, 289, 380
Genotypes, 52
German or three-day measles (rubella), 117
Germany
attachment security in, 268–269
work–study apprenticeships in, 577, 578
Gestures, preverbal, 237, 238
GH (growth hormone), 292, 293, 512, 513
Giftedness and education, 455–457, 463
Glands
pituitary, 291–293, 512, 513
prostate, 516
sebaceous, 514–515
thyroid, 293, 512, 513
Glandular secretions, 514–515
Glial cells, 107, 175, 176
Goal-directed (intentional) behavior, 214–215, 254
Golden Rule, 592
Gonorrhea, 537
Good boy–good girl orientation, 594, 595
Goodness-of-fit model, 261–263, 271
Governor's schools, 457
Grammar, defined, 346
Grammatical development
in adolescence, 561
in early childhood, 346, 348
in middle childhood, 447
Grammatical rules, 235, 236
Grandparents as developmental influences, 75
Grasp reflex, 154, 155, 188, 189
Grasping, development of, 188, 189
Gross motor development
in early childhood, 302–304, 307
in infancy and toddlerhood, 184, 185, 188
in middle childhood, 409–410, 413
Group-administered intelligence tests, 437
Growth hormone (GH), 292, 293, 512, 513
Growth spurt in adolescence, 514–516
Guatemala
childbirth in, 141
children's health research in, 296
Mayans of, 183, 432
Guidance Study, 41
Guilt
in early childhood, 354–355, 359–360, 367, 368
mental stage, 18, 354–355
in middle childhood, 473, 474
in moral development, 367, 368
Gulf War, 496
Gun injuries and death, 540–541
Gusii (Kenya) attachment, 270

Habituation–dishabituation response, 193, 195
and infant attention and memory, 222–224
and intelligence, 229
in sensorimotor development research, 217–218
Handedness and brain lateralization, 289–291
Happiness in infants, 252–253
Harm, protection from, as research right, 45
Hausa (Nigeria) conservation development, 425
Hawaiians, Native, language styles of, 443
Head Start, 340–342, 351
Health
country rankings of, 82, 84
dental, 288, 398
information about, sources of, 207
and safety, in day care, 297, 300, 311
understanding, and development, 408
Health care
for adolescent mothers, 535
prenatal, 124–125, 131, 151, 534
in U.S. and Europe, 297, 298
Health education, 406–408
Health insurance, 298
Health issues
in adolescence, 408, 526–541
in early childhood, 292–301
in middle childhood, 399–406
Hearing
in infants, 156–158, 197–198, 203, 236, 241
in newborns, 156–158
Hearing impairments, 236, 241, 400
Heavy metal dangers, 116
Height. *See* Body size
Heinz dilemma, 592–596, 598, 599
Hemispheres of cerebral cortex, 176–177, 289, 290
Hemophilia, 61, 63
Heredity. *See* Genetic *entries*
Heritability estimates, 87–89, 260, 442. *See also* Inheritance
Heroin during pregnancy, 113
Herpes simplex 2 (genital herpes), 117–118, 537
Herpes viruses, 117–118
Heteronomous morality, 591, 592
Heterozygous pairings of alleles, 58–60
Hierarchical classification in cognitive development, 317, 321, 324, 422–424
Hierarchy, dominance, 416
High blood pressure during pregnancy, 124
Hinduism, moral concepts in, 479
Hispanics. *See also* Mexican-American families and education; Mexico
academic achievement of, 568
adolescent sexual activity among, 530, 531
child-rearing practices of, 384
dropping out of school by, 569–570
extended families of, 82
family size and education of, 100
health problems of children of, 405
identity development among, 588, 589
premarital childbirth among, 534
semilingualism among, 449
Home births, 138–142, 167
Home environment. *See also* Families; Family systems
and academic achievement, 568
and attention-deficit hyperactivity disorder, 430
and divorce, 490
lead poisoning in, 294
and mental development, 230, 338–339
Home Observation for Measurement of the Environment (HOME), 230, 338–339
Homelessness, 77, 78
Homosexuality, 532–533, 538
Homozygous pairings of alleles, 58–59
Hopi Indian motor development, 186
Hopping and motor development, 303, 409, 410
Horizontal décalage, 423, 425–427
Hormones
in adolescence, 512–513
in bedwetting, 404
and brain development, 399
during childbirth, 137, 144, 145
in conception, 55–56
and gender typing, 376

in in vitro fertilization, 70, 71
and physical development, 291–293
during pregnancy, 115, 122
types of. *See specific entries, e.g.:* Androgens; Stress hormones
Hostile aggression, 371, 416
Human development, defined, 4
Hunger, chronic, 400–401
Huntington disease, 60, 62, 63, 69
Hyaline membrane disease, 147
Hyperactivity, 430. *See also* Attention-deficit hyperactivity disorder
Hypotheses, 33, 548
Hypothetico-deductive reasoning, 548–551

Id, 16–17, 32, 511
Idealism in adolescence, 558
Identical (monozygotic) twins, 57, 58. *See also* Twin studies
Identification (in psychosexual theory), 355, 367
Identity
defined, 584
gender-role, 379–381, 484, 485, 606, 611
versus identity diffusion, as stage, 18, 584–585
peer-group, 480
Identity achievement, 587, 589, 590, 601
Identity crisis in adolescence, 584–585
Identity development, 584–590. *See also* Self-development
Identity diffusion, 587–590
Identity foreclosure, 587–590
Identity statuses, 587–590, 601
Illnesses. *See also* Health *entries;* Infectious diseases; *specific entries, e.g.:* Cancer; Schizophrenia
biological model of, 408
chronic, 405, 419
in middle childhood, 405, 419
understanding, and development, 408
Imaginary audiences, 556–557
Imitation. *See also* Modeling *entries*
deferred, 216, 218–219
by infants, 195–196, 219
in language development, 235
Immunizations, 296–298, 300
Implantation of blastocysts, 103, 105
Imprinting, 26, 27, 266
genetic, 61, 63–64
In vitro fertilization, 70, 71
Independent movement and depth perception, 200–201
Independent variables, 39
India
Hindu moral concepts in, 479
moral development in, 599
Individual differences
in cognitive development, 326, 329
in intelligence quotients, 442–444
in language development, 240–241
in mental development, 337–344, 436–445
in motor development, 413
in pubertal development, 517
Individually administered intelligence tests, 437
Individuals with Disabilities Education Act, 453
Individuation. *See* Self-awareness; Separation–individuation theory of development (Mahler)
Induction in moral development, 367–368
Industry
in adolescence, 584
versus inferiority, as stage, 18, 466–467
Infancy and toddlerhood. *See also* Infant *entries;* Newborns
abuse in, 148, 161–162, 271
adoption in, 534
attachment in, 27, 263–276
attachment security in, 271–272
attention and memory in, 222–223
body growth in, 170–174, 515
bowel and bladder control in, 189–190
brain development in, 174–177, 180–181, 289
brain functioning problems in, 193, 194
classical conditioning in, 190–193
cognitive development in, 22, 23, 195, 209–242, 245, 254, 282–283
day care in, 14, 230–233, 273, 300, 494
death in, 150, 151, 193, 194, 300
developmental milestones of, 282–283
drug addiction in, 113
education in, information sources for, 245
emotion responses in, 254
emotional development in, 179, 251–276, 282–283
environment exploring in, 277
facial expressions in, 252, 253
hearing in, 156–158, 197–198, 203, 236, 241
imitation in, 195–196, 219
information processing in, 220–225
institutionalization in, 269–270
intelligence tests in, 227–229, 233
intervention programs in, 232, 233, 245, 342
language development in, 224, 234–242, 282–283
learning mechanisms in, 190–196
malnutrition in, 120, 121, 178–181
mental testing in, 227–234
motor development in, 155, 169–172, 183–190, 302, 303
nutrition in, 178–180
operant conditioning in, 192–193
parental bonding in, 153. *See also* Mother–infant relationship; Parent–infant relationship
perceptual development in, 195, 197–205, 308
personality development in, 248–251
physical development in, 169–205, 282–283, 289
self-awareness in, 250, 276–279
self-categorization in, 278
self-control in, 279
self-development in, 276–279
self-recognition in, 277–278
sensorimotor stage in. *See* Sensorimotor stage of cognitive development
sleeping in, 182, 183
social development in, 248–251, 276–279, 282–283
states of arousal in, 181, 183
teething in, 174
temperament development in, 257–263, 271
thyroxine deficiency in, 293
visual development in, 198–203, 308. *See also* Visual acuity of newborns
vocabulary development in, 238–239
weight gain in, 402
Infant mortality, 150, 151, 193, 194, 300
Infant–parent relationships. *See* Mother–infant relationships; Parent–infant relationships
Infantile autism, 64
Infants. *See also* Infancy and toddlerhood
with AIDS, 119
at-risk, 232, 233, 245, 271, 342
birth weight of, 112–117, 122, 147–151, 405
feeding of, 178–180, 207, 263–266, 402
postterm, 150
premature. *See* Premature (preterm) infants
sick, abuse of, 161–162
small-for-date, 148
underweight, 147–148, 405
Infections
ear, 400
intestinal, 296
Infectious diseases. *See also specific entries, e.g.:* Acquired immune deficiency syndrome; Viral diseases during pregnancy
immunizations against, 296–298, 300
information about, sources of, 311
maternal. *See* Maternal diseases
and physical development, 296–298
Inferences
mental, 334, 433
transitive, 423–426
Infertility information sources, 95
Information. *See also* Memory *entries*
categorization of, 222–224
elaboration of, 429, 431, 432
organization of, 222, 331, 429, 431, 432
rehearsal of, 331, 429, 431, 432
remembered, generalizing, 332–333
retrieval of, 222, 431
Information processing
in adolescence, 552–555
approaches to, 24–26, 32
Atkinson and Shiffrin model of, 221–222
in cognitive-developmental stages, 426–427, 552–555
in early childhood, 325, 330–336
and gender schema theory, 380–381
in infancy and toddlerhood, 220–225
as intelligence testing approach, 439–441
and mental development, 229
in middle childhood, 410, 426–436
in motor development, 410
research about, evaluation of, 224–225
skills in, in intelligence tests, 439
Informed consent for research, 45, 46
Inheritance. *See also* Genetic *entries;* Heritability estimates
codominance in, 60
dominant–recessive, 58–64
polygenic, 64
X-linked, 61, 63, 64, 532
Initiation ceremonies, 520, 521
Initiative
in adolescence, 584
versus guilt, as developmental stage, 18, 354–355
Injuries
in adolescence, 299, 405–406, 540–541
in early childhood, 297, 299–301
information about, sources of, 311
in middle childhood, 405–406
sports-related, 541
Inner mental life, 333–334
Institutionalized infants, 269–270
Instrumental aggression, 371
Instrumental purpose orientation in moral development, 593–595
Instruments in childbirth, 143–144
Intelligence
and attention-deficit hyperactivity disorder, 430
defining and measuring, 437–442. *See also* Intelligence quotients; Intelligence tests
and genetics, 88, 89, 442–443
kinship studies of, 88
and malnutrition, 121
and sex chromosome disorders, 66
triarchic theory of (Sternberg), 440–441
types of, 66, 437, 441–442
Intelligence quotients (IQs)
and academic achievement, 436–437
of at-risk infants, 233
and birth order, 488
componential analyses of, 439–441
and computer use, 453
defined, 228
and giftedness, 455, 456
individual and group differences in, 442–444
and lead poisoning, 294
of learning disabled children, 454
of mentally retarded children, 453
and preschools, 340, 342
sex differences in, 559
in twin studies, 88–89
Intelligence tests. *See also* Scholastic Aptitude Test
cultural bias in, 338, 437, 441, 444–445
examples of, 437–439
for infants, 227–229, 233
group-administered versus individually administered, 437
history of, 13–15
in early childhood, 337–339
in middle childhood, 436–442
scores on, 228. *See also* Intelligence quotients
Intentional (goal-directed) behavior, 214–215, 254
Intentions in early childhood, 356
Interactional synchrony, 270
Interactionist perspective on language development, 236, 241–242
Intermodal perception, 203–204
Internal working model of attachment, 267
Interpersonal intelligence, 441
Intersubjectivity, 328
Intervention programs. *See also* Food programs
for at-risk infants and toddlers, 232, 233, 245, 342
for at-risk preschoolers, 340–342
for attention-deficit hyperactivity disorder, 430
in child maltreatment prevention, 388

Intervention programs (*continued*)
for chronic illness, 405
for delinquency treatment, 616–618
for eating disorders, 528, 529
information about, sources of, 245, 351
for obesity, 403
for rejected children, 483–484
in suicide prevention, 613–614
Interviews
clinical, 22, 34, 35, 592–593
structured, 34–36
Intimacy
in adolescent friendship, 605, 606
in dating relationships, 608
development of, 585
versus isolation, as stage, 18
Intrapersonal intelligence, 441
Inuit infant contact, 162
Invariant features of environment, 204–205
Iranian institutions, infants raised in, 186
Iron deficiency, 527
Irreversibility in cognitive development, 317, 319, 322
Isolettes, 149
Israeli children. *See also* Kibbutzim
and achievement-related attributions, 471–472
in wartime, 499

Japanese
academic achievement of, 459, 460, 471, 568
academic training of, 340
attachment security of, 269
child-rearing practices of, 182, 183, 186, 260
education of, gender stereotypes in, 484
infants of, 260, 269
language learning among, 240–241
menarche timing for, 517
peer relations of, 604
school tracking of, 569
self-conscious emotions among, 255
temperament of, 260
Japanese-Americans, body growth of, 170, 171
Jarara childbirth practices, 139
Jewish adolescents. *See also* Israeli children; Kibbutzim
initiation ceremony for, 520
self-esteem of, 586
Jobs. *See* Employment
Joint custody, 492
Jumping and motor development, 303, 307, 409, 410
Just communities in moral education, 598, 599
Justice. *See also* Fairness
distributive, 477–478, 592
in moral development, 599–600
Juvenile delinquency, 614–618

K-ABC (Kaufman Assessment Battery for Children), 439
Kamehameha Elementary Education Program (KEEP), 450–451
Kangaroo baby care, 149
Kauai study of birth complications, 150, 152
Kaufman Assessment Battery for Children (K-ABC), 439
KEEP (Kamehameha Elementary Education Program), 450–451
Kibbutzim, 472, 499, 597, 599
Kicking and motor development, 409, 410
Kinship studies, 87–88, 442. *See also* Twin studies
Klinefelter syndrome, 66
Knowledge
certainty about, 334
of results, as research right, 45
Knowledge base, 429, 431–432
Kohlberg's theory of moral development, 592–600
Korean immigrants, second-language learning by, 562
Koreans
academic training of, 340
language development of, 224
!Kung
childbirth practices of, 139
children's environments of, 82
menarche ceremony among, 521
Kwashiorkor, 180, 181

Labor, 134–137, 143–145
Labor coaches, 140
Laboratory experiments, 39–40, 42
LAD (language acquisition device), 235, 236
Language(s)
and cognition, 314
emotional, 357–359
in formal operational thought, 550
multiple, 447–449, 463, 562
sign, 236
social use of (conversational skills), 346–348, 447
whole, as reading instruction approach, 435
written. *See* Writing
Language acquisition device (LAD), 235, 236
Language awareness, 446
Language customs and intelligence quotients, 442–445
Language development. *See also* Grammatical development; Vocabulary development
in adolescence, 559–562, 622–623
in early childhood, 289, 290, 334–336, 344–348, 357–358, 361, 392–393, 562
and emotional self-regulation, 256
and empathy, 361
and handedness, 290
individual differences in, 240–241
in infancy and toddlerhood, 224, 234–242, 282–283
in middle childhood, 434–435, 446–448, 506–507, 562
milestones of, 236–240, 282–283
promoting, 241–242, 348
sensitive period for, 562
styles of, 240
theories of, 235–236, 241–242
Language styles, 561
Lanugo, 107
Laotian childbirth practices, 139
Late adolescence (youth), 512, 623
Late sexual maturation, 522, 524–525
Latency stage of development, 16, 18, 466
Lateralization of cerebral cortex, 176–177, 289–291, 398
Latin Americans. *See* Hispanics
Laughter in infants, 252–253
Lead, exposure to, and prenatal development, 116
Lead poisoning, 294, 430
Learned (secondary) drives, 19, 263, 264
Learned helplessness, 434, 470–472
Learning
academic. *See* Academic achievement; Academic training; Education; Educational *entries;* School *entries*
cooperative, 329, 455
discovery, 325
observational. *See* Modeling *entries*
readiness for, 326
in schools. *See* Academic achievement; Academic training; Education; Educational *entries;* School(s), learning in
social. *See* Social learning theory
Learning difficulties, 453–455
Learning disabilities, 454–455, 463
Learning mechanisms, 190–196. *See also* Classical conditioning; Operant conditioning
Lens (of eye), 158
Letters
combining, 335
formation of, 411
reversal of, 306, 308–309, 411–412
and sounds, 435
Lightening in childbirth, 134
Linear perspective in drawings, 412
Linguistic intelligence, 441, 442
Literacy development, 334–336
Little League baseball, 414, 415, 419
Locke's philosophy, 10–11
Logical operations, 316–325, 422
Logico-mathematical intelligence, 441, 442
Long-term knowledge base, 429, 431–432
Long-term memory, 222
Longitudinal research design, 41–43. *See also* New York Longitudinal Study
Longitudinal-sequential research design, 42–44
Low birth weight, 112–117, 122, 147–151
Loyalty in friendship, 605, 606
Lymph system development, 289

Macrosystem of environment, 28, 29
Magical thinking, 318, 322, 323, 408
Mahler's separation–individuation theory, 249–251
Mainstreaming of pupils with learning difficulties, 453–455
Make-believe play
in early childhood, 354, 363–365
in infancy and toddlerhood, 217, 226
and memory flexibility, 333
in preoperational stage of cognitive development, 315–316, 324
Malaria and sickle cell trait, 60
Male reproductive organs, 56, 57
Male sex hormones (androgens), 371, 399, 513
Malnutrition
in adolescence, 527–529
in early childhood, 288, 295
in infancy and toddlerhood, 120, 121, 178–181
and infectious disease, 296
information about, sources of, 207
in middle childhood, 400–401
and poverty, 295, 400–401
and prenatal development, 120, 121
and skeletal growth, 288
Malocclusion, 398
Marasmus, 180–181
Marfan syndrome, 63
Marijuana, 113, 538, 539
Marital relationship during pregnancy, 128
Mastery-oriented attributions, 470–472
Matching in experimental designs, 40
Maternal age
and Down syndrome risk, 65
and fertility, 102
and miscarriages, 102
and prenatal development, 123
Maternal blood analysis, 68
Maternal depression, 271
Maternal deprivation, 269–270
Maternal diseases
and breast-feeding, 179
during pregnancy, 117–119, 124
Maternal employment, 494–495, 603
Mathematical reasoning, 335–336
Mathematics. *See also* Logico-mathematical intelligence
learning disabilities involving, 454
teaching, 435–436
Mathematics achievement, 436, 460, 559–560, 568
Maturation
and babbling, 236
of brain. *See* Brain development
in motor development, 186, 187
sexual. *See* Puberty; Sexual maturation
Maturation concept, 11
MAX (Maximally Discriminative Facial Movement) System, 253
Mayans
of Guatemala, 183, 432
of the Yucatán, 139
Measles, 117
Mechanistic theories, 6, 11, 32
Meiosis, 53–55
Memory
for everyday experiences, 332
in court testimony, 500
in early childhood, 330–333, 500
in infancy and toddlerhood, 222–223
in middle childhood, 429, 431–433, 500
long-term, 222
recognition and recall in, 223, 330–331
scripts in, 332
working (short-term), 222, 426–427, 429, 437, 438
Memory performance, 429, 431–432
Memory span, 427, 431–432
Memory strategies, 222, 331, 429, 431–433
Menarche, 515–519, 521. *See also* Menstruation
Menopause, childbearing after, 71
Menstruation, 513, 515–519, 521, 528
Mental development. *See also* Cognitive development
in adolescence, 559–560
and day care, 230–233, 339, 341, 343
in early childhood, 337–344
and environment, 229–233, 338–339
sex differences in, 559–560
and information processing, 229
in middle childhood, 436–445
testing, 13–15, 227–234. *See also* Intelligence quotients; Intelligence tests
Mental illness. *See specific entries, e.g.:* Depression; Schizophrenia

Mental inferences, 334, 433
Mental life, awareness of inner, 333–334
Mental representation, 216, 314, 316
Mental retardation
and education, 453–455, 463
and genetic disorders, 63–65
and handedness, 290
and Rh factor, 122
and teratogens, 114–117
and thyroxine deficiency, 293
Mental rotations, in spatial reasoning 424
Mental states, 334
Mental strategies, 221–222
Mental testing, 13–15, 227–234. *See also* Intelligence quotients; Intelligence tests
Mercury, exposure to, and prenatal development, 116
Merit in distributive justice, 477
Mesoderm, 105
Mesosystem of environment, 28, 29
Metacognition, 333–334, 433, 471, 472
Metaphors, 345–346, 561
Methadone during pregnancy, 113
Mexican-American families and education, 38
Mexico
children's food choices in, 294–295
education of females in, 77
Microsystem of environment, 28–29
Middle adolescence, 512, 623
Middle childhood
attention in, 428–430
body growth in, 170, 396–399, 413, 515
brain development in, 398–399, 428–429
cognitive development in, 399, 422–460, 467, 471, 476, 506–507
concrete operational stage in. *See* Concrete operational stage of cognitive development
conversational skills in, 447
death in, 299, 612, 613
delinquency in, 615, 616
developmental milestones in, 506–507
divorce during, 489–491
education in, 406–408, 416–417, 448, 450–460
emotional development in, 473–474, 506–507
emotional self-regulation in, 473–474, 496
family influences in, 486–495
fantasy period of vocational development in, 573
fears and anxieties in, 496–497, 499
formal operational thought in, 551–552
friendships in, 481–482
gender typing in, 478, 484–486
grammatical development in, 447
health and illness understanding in, 408
health education in, 406–408
health problems in, 399–406, 419
information processing in, 410, 426–436
injuries in, 299
language development in, 434–435, 446–448, 506–507, 562
memory in, 429, 431–433, 500
mental development in, 436–445
metacognition in, 433, 452, 471, 472
moral development in, 476–479, 592
motor development in, 409–417
muscle–fat makeup in, 172
parent–child relationships in, 486–488
peer relations in, 275, 478, 480–485
perspective taking in, 468, 474–475
physical development in, 395–417, 506
psychosexual development in, 466–467
remarriage of parent during, 493
self-concept in, 467–468
self-development in, 467–472
self-esteem in, 468–472
self-regulation in, 434, 452, 471–474, 496
sexual abuse in, 497–498, 500–501
social development in, 465–502, 506–507
stress in, coping with, 502
suicide in, 612, 613
vocabulary development in, 446
Middle Eastern sexual attitudes, 529
Midwives, 142, 167
Mind, theory of (metacognition), 333–334, 417, 433, 472
Minimal parenting, 490
Minority groups. *See* Ethnicity and race; *specific entries, e.g.:* African Americans; Hispanics
Miscarriages, 102, 115–117, 122, 533
Mitosis, 53, 54
Modeling as educational technique, 450
Modeling theory, 20–21, 32, 368–369, 476
Modifier genes, 59
Monkeys, attachment in, 264
Monozygotic (identical) twins, 57, 58. *See also* Twin studies
Moral behavior, 600
Moral development
in adolescence, 591–600
and aggression, 371
in behaviorism and social learning theory, 366–370
in cognitive development, 366, 367, 370–371, 476, 592
in early childhood, 355, 366–375, 592
Kohlberg's theory of, 592–600
levels of, 593–596
in middle childhood, 476–479, 592
Piaget's theory of, 591–592, 594, 596
psychoanalytic perspective on, 366–368
Moral dilemmas, 592–596, 598, 599
Moral education, 598, 599
Moral reasoning. *See* Moral development
Moral rules versus social conventions 370–371, 478, 479
Morality
autonomous, 591–592
heteronomous, 591, 592
Moratorium as identity status, 587, 590
Moro reflex, 154, 155
Mortality. *See* Death
Mosaic pattern on chromosomes, 65
Mother–infant relationships. *See also* Parent–infant relationships
and attachment, 263–265, 270–272. *See also* Attachment(s); Attachment security
and drugs during childbirth, 143, 145
and personality development, 249–251
and postpartum depression, 164
and sibling attachment, 275
Mother–stepfather families, 493
Motherese, 241–242
Motherhood. *See* Parent *entries;* Surrogate mothers
Motion as depth cue, 200, 204
Motor development. *See also* Sensorimotor stage of cognitive development
in adolescence, 412, 541–542
in early childhood, 291, 302–307
fine, 184, 185, 188–189, 304–306
gross, 184, 185, 188, 302–304, 307
in infancy and toddlerhood, 155, 169–172, 183–190, 302, 303
maturation and experience in, 186, 187
in middle childhood, 409–417
of newborns, 155
promoting, 307
sequence of, 184, 185, 188–189
systems of action in, 184, 302
tests of, 228
voluntary reaching in, 188–189
Multiple attachments, 272, 274–275
Multiple births, 57–58. *See also* Twin *entries*
Multiple intelligences, Gardner's theory of, 441–442
Muscle–fat makeup, 172, 514–515
Muscular dystrophy, 63, 69
Musical intelligence, 441
Mutations, 61, 95
Mutual exclusivity principle, 345
Myelin, 175
Myelinization, 175, 176, 289, 291, 398
Myopia (nearsightedness), 400

Naming explosion, 224
Nation's Report Card, 568
Native Americans
alcohol abuse among, 115
childbirth practices of, 139
extended families of, 82
identity development among, 589
infant behavior among, 162
premarital childbirth among, 534
Native Hawaiian language styles, 443
Nativist perspective on language development (Chomsky), 235–236
Natural (prepared) childbirth, 138, 140–141, 167
Natural experiments, 41
Natural selection, 11
Naturalistic observation, 33–35
Nature–nurture controversy. *See also* Environment; Genetics
in child development theories, 7–8, 11, 32
in intelligence quotients, 442–443
in language development, 235–236
Navaho Indians
childbirth practices of, 139
language styles of, 443
NBAS (Neonatal Behavioral Assessment Scale), 162–163
Nearsightedness (myopia), 400
Neglected children, 385, 482, 483. *See also* Child maltreatment
Neighborhood impact
on child maltreatment, 387
on development, 78–79
Neonatal Behavioral Assessment Scale (NBAS), 162–163
Neonatal mortality, 150, 151
Nervous system development, 106, 107
Netherlands health care, 298
Neural tube, 106
Neurons (nerve cells), 106, 107, 174–175, 399
Neurotransmitters, 399, 400
Neutral stimulus, 19, 191
New York Longitudinal Study, 257–259, 262
Newborns. *See also* Infancy and toddlerhood; Infant *entries*
of adolescent mothers, 534
appearance of, 137
behavior of, assessing, 162–163
capacities of, 153–163
crying by, 160–162
emotions of, 252, 253
imitation by, 195–196, 219
operant conditioning of, 193
oxygen-deprived, 146–147
perceptual development of, 156–159, 198, 201–203
physical condition of, 137–138
reflexes of, 153–156, 188–191, 193, 213–214
sick, and attachment security, 271
states of arousal of, 159–162
Ngoni (Malawi), industry stage of development in, 466
Niche-picking, 91–92
Nicotine, 114. *See also* Smoking
Noble savage view, 11
Nocturnal enuresis (bedwetting), 404–405
Non-rapid-eye-movement (NREM) sleep, 159–160
Nonfunctionality of death, 323
Nonorganic failure to thrive, 181
Nonsocial activity, 362–364
Normal (bell-shaped) curves, 228
Normative approach to child study, 12–13
Norms in intelligence testing, 228
Norway, health care in, 298
NREM (non-rapid-eye-movement) sleep, 159–160
Nurse-midwives, 142, 167
Nutrition. *See also* Malnutrition
in adolescence, 526–529, 534
and attention-deficit hyperactivity disorder, 430
in early childhood, 293–296
and fraternal twinning, 58
in infancy and toddlerhood, 178–180
in menarche timing, 517
in middle childhood, 400
and physical development, 178–180, 293–296
and poverty, 120, 121, 178–181
during pregnancy, 118, 120–122, 534
Nyansongo (Kenya) gender typing, 485–486

Obesity, 179–180, 401–403, 527
Object-hiding tasks, 215
Object permanence, 215–219, 229, 266
Objects
attachment to, 264, 265
sorting (hierarchical classification), 317, 321, 324, 422–424

Observation, types of, 33–35, 37
Observational learning. *See* Modeling *entries*
Oedipus conflict, 16, 354–355, 367, 375
One-child families, 98, 99, 101
Open classrooms, 450
Operant conditioning, 19–20, 192–193, 235, 368
Operations (logical), 316–325, 422
Oral contraceptives, 115
Oral stage of development, 16–18, 248–249, 265
Organismic theories, 6, 11, 32
Organization
  in cognitive development, 211–212
  of information, 222, 331, 429, 431, 432. *See also* Memory strategies
Ova, 53–58, 70, 71
Ovaries, 55, 56, 513
Overextension vocabulary error, 238–239
Overregularization, 346
Overweight, 179–180, 401–403. *See also* Obesity
Oxygen deprivation (anoxia), 146–147, 150
Oxytocin, 144

Pacific Island sexual attitudes, 529
Pain, newborn sensitivity to, 156, 157
Painkillers during childbirth, 143
Palmar grasp reflex, 154, 155
Parallel play, 362–364
Parasitic diseases during pregnancy, 117, 118
Parent–child communication, 487
Parent–child relationships. *See also* Child-rearing practices
  and achievement-related attributions, 471, 472
  in adolescence, 522, 602–603
  of adolescent parents and their children, 534–535
  and aggression, 372–373
  and automobile injuries, 540
  after divorce, 489–492
  and eating disorders, 528
  and empathy development, 361–362
  and failure to thrive, 181
  and gender typing, 486
  and giftedness, 456
  and homosexuality, 532, 533
  and identity development, 590
  and maternal employment, 494
  and menarche reactions, 519
  and mental development, 338–339
  in middle childhood, 486–488
  and punishment, 370
  and school phobias, 497
  and self-esteem, 469, 471, 472
  and social class, 76–77
Parent–infant relationships, 76
  and attachment, 263–267, 272. *See also* Attachment(s); Attachment security
  development of, 163–164
  and emotional self-regulation, 255–256
  immediately after birth, 152–153
  in language development, 237, 241–242
  and make-believe play, 226
  and malnutrition, 121
  and Neonatal Behavioral Assessment Scale, 162–163
  operant conditioning in, 193
  and prematurity, 148–150
  and sleeping arrangements, 183
  and social referencing, 254
Parent–school involvement in academic achievement, 566
Parent–teacher communication, 459
Parental consent for research, 45, 46
Parenthood
  in adolescence, 83, 533–535
  advantages and disadvantages of, 98–99
  initial adjustment to, 163–164
  motivations for, 98–102
  preparing for, 126–128
  single, 83, 489, 505. *See also* Divorce
Parenting, minimal, 490
Parenting styles. *See* Child rearing; Child-rearing practices; Families; Family systems
Parents
  education involvement of, 38, 459, 460
  and infants, bonding of, 153. *See also* Mother–infant relationships; Parent–infant relationships
  in intervention programs, 342
  step-, 492–494, 505
  in temperament measures, 257–258
Parents Anonymous, 388, 391
Participant observation in ethnography, 37
Passive genetic–environmental correlation, 91
Pattern perception, 201–204
Pavlov's theory (classical conditioning), 19, 190–193
PCBs (polychlorinated biphenyls) during pregnancy, 116
Peddling and motor development, 303
Pedigrees in genetic counseling, 67
Peer culture, 480
Peer groups
  acceptance and rejection by, 482–484
  and cliques and crowds, 606–607
  and dating, 608
  in middle childhood, 480–484
Peer pressure in adolescence, 608–609
Peer relations
  and academic achievement, 566, 567
  in adolescence, 524–525, 561, 566, 567, 604–610
  and aggression, 372–373
  and attachment, 275
  and attention-deficit hyperactivity disorder, 430
  and delinquency, 616
  and distributive justice, 478
  in early childhood, 275, 362–365, 372–373, 378
  and gender-role identity, 485
  and gender typing, 378
  and mainstreaming of pupils with learning difficulties, 455
  in middle childhood, 478, 480–485
  and moral development, 597
  and self-esteem, 469, 471, 472
Peer sociability, 362–365, 480
Pendulum problem, 549, 551–552
Penis, 516
Perception
  depth, 198–201, 204
  face, 202–204
  intermodal, 203–204
  pattern, 201–204
  versus sensation, 197
Perception-bound thought, 317, 319
Perceptual development
  differentiation theory of, 204–205, 308, 309
  in early childhood, 305, 306, 308–309
  of infants, 195, 197–205, 308
  of newborns, 156–159, 198, 201–203
Permanence of death, 323
Permissive child rearing, 383, 565
Persian Gulf War, 496
Personal fable, 557, 613
Personal responsibility, 473
Personality
  and genetics, 88
  and identity status, 588–589
  in language development, 240
  Type A, 403–404
Personality development
  in adolescence, 584–585, 622–623
  in early childhood, 354–355
  in infancy and toddlerhood, 248–251
  in middle childhood, 466–467
  theories of, 15–19, 32, 248–251, 263–265, 466
Personality styles, 41–42
Perspective taking
  in adolescence, 475, 531, 557, 591–596, 599–600
  in early childhood, 475
  empathic, 599–600
  in middle childhood, 468, 474–475
Phallic stage of development, 16, 18, 354–355, 367, 511
Phenotypes, 52
Phenylketonuria (PKU), 59, 62, 95
Phobias, 360, 496–497
Phonics, 435
Physical abuse, 385. *See also* Child maltreatment
Physical activity. *See* Exercise
Physical attractiveness, 524–525. *See also* Body image
Physical development. *See also* Body growth; Psychosexual theory of development *entries;* Pubertal maturation
  in adolescence, 289, 509–542
  asynchronies in, 288–289
  in early childhood, 285–309, 392–393
  factors affecting, 177–181, 292–301
  failure of, 181
  in infancy and toddlerhood, 169–205, 282–283, 289
  and infectious diseases, 296–298
  information about, sources of, 207
  in middle childhood, 395–417, 506–507
  rate of, 173
  secular trends in, 396–398
Physical education, 416–417
Physical fitness, 416–417
Physical neglect, 385. *See also* Child maltreatment
Physical self-esteem, 469, 470
Piaget's theories
  cognitive-developmental. *See* Cognitive-developmental theory (Piaget)
  of moral development, 591–592, 594, 596
Pictorial depth cues, 199, 200
Pincer grasp, 188, 189
Pituitary gland, 291–293, 512, 513
PKU (phenylketonuria), 59, 62, 95
Placenta, 104–106, 109
  delivery of, 135, 136
  drugs crossing, 143, 145
Placenta previa, 146
Planfulness in attention, 428
Planning in adolescence, 558–559
Plastic sealants for teeth, 398
Play
  associative, 362–364
  in cognitive-developmental stages, 315–316, 324, 422
  constructive, 365
  cooperative, 363, 364
  in early childhood, 354, 363–365
  functional, 216, 365
  in infancy and toddlerhood, 217, 226
  make-believe. *See* Make-believe play
  and memory flexibility, 333
  in middle childhood, 413–417
  parallel, 362–364
  rough-and-tumble, 414, 416
  sociodramatic, 316, 364
  solitary, 362–364
Pollution
  lead, 116, 294, 430
  and pregnancy, 116
Polychlorinated biphenyls (PCBs), 116
Polygenic inheritance, 64
Popular children, 482, 483
Population growth and poverty, 100
Postconventional (principled) level of moral development, 594, 595
Postpartum depression versus postpartum blues, 164
Postponing Sexual Involvement program, 536
Postterm infants, 150
Poverty
  and academic achievement, 567, 568
  and adolescent depression, 611
  and adolescent pregnancy, 123, 533
  in African-American extended families, 83
  and AIDS during pregnancy, 119
  and alcohol abuse, 114–115
  and asthma, 405
  and attachment security, 271
  and body size, 397, 398
  and child development, 82–84
  and child-rearing practices, 77–78, 82, 83
  and day care quality, 231–232
  and delinquency, 616, 617
  after divorce, 492
  and dropping out of school, 569–570
  and drug abuse, 112–113
  and education, 78
  and educational television, 343
  and gun injuries and deaths, 541
  and health care, 124, 298
  and health problems, 399–400, 405
  and infant birth weight, 147–148
  and infant mortality, 151
  and infant nutrition, 178–181
  and infant/toddler intervention programs, 232, 233
  and infectious diseases, 296
  and injuries, 299–301, 541
  and intelligence quotients, 436–437, 442–444
  and intelligence testing, 337–339
  and KEEP schools, 451
  and lead poisoning, 294
  and learned helplessness, 471
  and malnutrition, 295, 400–401
  in menarche timing, 517
  and mental development, 339
  and nutrition, 120, 121. *See also* and malnutrition, *above*
  and population growth, 100

and preschools, 340–342. *See also* Project Head Start
and school problems, 487
and school transitions, 564
and sexual abuse, 498
and sexual activity, 531, 534
and tooth decay, 288
Praeder-Willi syndrome, 63
Pragmatics, 347, 447, 561
Preconventional level of moral development, 593–596
Preformationism, 9
Pregnancy. *See also* Conception; Prenatal development
in adolescence, 123, 124, 340, 532–536, 545
alcohol during, 114–115, 124
drugs during, 111–113, 534
emotional stress during, 122
exercise during, 118, 120
health care after, 151
health care during, 124–125, 131, 151, 534
high blood pressure during, 124
hormones during, 115, 122
information about, seeking, 126
marital relationship during, 128
maternal diseases during, 117–119, 124
and menarche, 516
nutrition during, 118, 120–122, 534
and pollution, 116
radiation during, 116
smoking during, 113–114, 194
weight during, 120, 122
Pregnancy rates by country, teenage, 533
Prelabor, 134
Premarital sex, 530, 531
Premature (preterm) infants, 147–150. *See also* Low birth weight
abuse of, 148, 161–162
attachment security of, 271
breast-feeding of, 179
caring for, 57–58, 148–150
causes of, 113, 115–117
and emotional stress, 122
habituation–dishabituation response in, 222–223
operant conditioning of, 193
stimulation of, 149
Prenatal development. *See also* Pregnancy
environmental influences on, 110–125, 430, 534
and malnutrition, 120, 121
periods of, 103–111
trimesters of, 104, 107–108
Prenatal diagnostic methods, 68–69
Prenatal health care, 124–125, 131, 151, 534
Preoperational stage of cognitive development, 22, 23, 314–327
evaluation of, 325
limitations in, 316–321
make-believe play in, 315–316, 324
mental representation in, 314, 316
and moral development, 594
recent research on, 321–322, 324–325
Prepared (natural) childbirth, 138, 140–141, 167
Prereaching, 188
Preschool intervention programs, 340–342, 351
Preschoolers. *See* Early childhood
Preschools, 339–342, 360
Preterm infants. *See* Low birth weight; Premature (preterm) infants
Preverbal gestures, 237, 238
Primary circular reactions, 214
Primary drives, 19, 263–264
Primary sexual characteristics, 515, 516
Principle of mutual exclusivity, 345
Principled (postconventional) level of moral development, 594, 595
Privacy as research right, 45
Private speech, 327–329
Privileges, withdrawal of, 369–370
Problem solving. *See* Social problem-solving *entries*
Production in language development, 240
Programming of computers, 452–453
Project Head Start, 340–342, 351
Propositional thought, 549–552
Proprioception, 188–189
Prosocial (altruistic) behavior, 367–369, 404, 476, 480
Prostate gland, 516
Proximodistal trend, 171, 172, 184
Psychoanalytic perspective
on gender typing, 375
on moral development, 366–368
on personality development, 15–19, 32, 248–249, 263–265
Psychological abuse, 385. *See also* Child maltreatment
Psychological distancing in adolescence, 522
Psychological impact of pubertal events, 518–525
Psychosexual theory of development (Freud), 16–17, 32, 248
in adolescence, 511
in early childhood, 354–355, 367, 368
Erikson's expansion of, 17–18, 32, 248–249, 251, 354–355
gender in, 354–355. *See also* Electra conflict; Oedipus conflict
and moral development, 367, 368
Psychosocial theory of development (Erikson), 17–18, 32
in adolescence, 584–585
in early childhood, 354–355
in infancy and toddlerhood, 248–249, 251
in middle childhood, 466–467
Pubertal timing, 522, 524–525
Puberty, 510, 512–525. *See also* Sex hormones; Sexual maturation
emotional and social behavior during, 520, 522–524
and gender typing, 601
Pubic hair development, 515, 516
Public health programs, 298
Public policy. *See also* Social issues
on academic achievement, 568
and child development, 82–86
on child maltreatment, 388
and childhood injuries, 301
and Children's Defense Fund, 85
on day care, 231, 341
on contraceptives, 545
on divorce, 492
on equal opportunities in education, 542
on health care during and after pregnancy, 151
information about, sources of, 95
about lead poisoning, 294
maternal employment, 495
and nutrition during pregnancy, 121
on preschool intervention, 342. *See also* Project Head Start
and reproductive choice, 72
and reproductive technologies, 71
on television advertising, 374
Pukapukan childbirth practices, 139
Punishment
and aggression, 369, 372
alternatives to, 369–370
corporal, 387, 478
in moral development, 367–370, 593–596
in operant conditioning, 20, 193
Punjabi childbirth practices, 139
Puritan doctrine, 10

Quantitative reasoning, 437, 438
Questionnaires, 34, 36

Race. *See* Ethnicity and race
Racial stereotypes on television, 373, 375
Radiation
and genetic damage, 61
during pregnancy, 116
Random assignment in experimental designs, 40
Range of reaction, 89–91
Rapid-eye-movement (REM) sleep, 159–160
Reaction range, 89–91
Reaction time in motor development, 410
Readiness to learn, 326
Reading
by adults, in language development, 242
in early childhood, 309, 335, 336
learning disabilities involving, 454
in middle childhood, 434–435
teaching, 434–435
Reading achievement, 451, 460, 559, 568
Realistic period of vocational development, 573
Reasoning
abstract, 548–552
hypothetico-deductive, 548–551
mathematical, 335–336
moral. *See* Moral development
quantitative, 437, 438
scientific, 568
spatial, 423–425, 437, 438
transductive, 317, 319, 322, 324
verbal, 437, 438
Recall in memory, 223, 330–331
Recasts in grammar development, 348
Recessive inheritance, 58–64
Reciprocity as fairness standard, 592–596
Recognition in memory, 223, 330–331
Reconstituted (blended) families, 492–494
Red–green color blindness, 61
Referential style of language learning, 240
Reflexes of newborns, 153–156, 188–191, 193, 213–214
Reflexive (unconditioned) response, 19, 190–192
Reflexive schemes in cognitive development, 213–214
Reformation, the, 10
Rehearsal of information, 331, 429, 431, 432. *See also* Memory strategies
Reinforcement
in language development, 235
in moral development, 368, 476
positive, 368
Reinforcers in operant conditioning, 19–20, 193
Rejected-aggressive children, 483
Rejected children, 482–484
Rejected-withdrawn children, 483
Relationships. *See specific entries, e.g.:* Bidirectional relationships; Family systems; Parent–child relationships; Parent–infant relationships
Relaxation techniques in childbirth, 140
Religious initiation ceremonies, 520
Religious practices and moral rules, 479
REM (rapid-eye-movement) sleep, 159–160
Remarriage, 492–494, 505
Reproductive choices, 67–73, 98–99
Reproductive organs
female, 55–56
male, 56, 57
Reproductive technologies, 70–71
Research. *See also specific entries, e.g.:* Information processing, research about, evaluation of; Twin studies
consent in, 45, 46
cross-cultural, and sociocultural theory, 29–31
ethics in, 44–46
Research designs, 37, 39–44
Research methods, 33–38
Research rights of children, 44–46
Resilient children, 502
Resistant attachment, 268–270
Resource rooms in schools, 455, 457
Respiratory distress syndrome, 147
Response
in classical conditioning, 19, 190–192
conditioned, 191, 192
habituation–dishabituation. *See* Habituation–dishabituation response
in operant conditioning, 193
unconditioned (reflexive), 19, 190–192
Reticular formation, 291
Retina, 158, 176n
Retrieval of information, 222, 431. *See also* Memory *entries*
Reversibility in cognitive-developmental stages, 317, 319, 322, 422, 423
Rh factor, 122–123
RhoGam vaccine, 122
Rites of passage in adolescence, 520, 521
Rooming in, 153
Rooting reflex, 154
Rough-and-tumble play, 414, 416
Rousseau's philosophy, 11
Rubella (three-day or German measles), 117
Rule-assessment approach to cognitive development (Siegler), 553–555
Rule-oriented games, 413–414
Running and motor development, 302, 303, 307, 409, 410
Russia, peer relations in, 604

Safety education, 406
Samoa, adolescence in, 511, 512
SAT (Scholastic Aptitude Test), 559–560, 568
Scaffolding, 328
Schemes in cognitive development, 210–214, 316, 426–427
Schizophrenia, 72, 88
Scholastic Aptitude Test (SAT), 559–560, 568
School(s). *See also* Academic achievement; Academic training; Day care; Education; Educational *entries;* Preschool intervention programs; Preschools
  ability grouping, 452, 459
  and attention-deficit hyperactivity disorder, 430
  attitudes toward, 606
  cluster groups in, 457
  computers in, 452–453, 463
  corporal punishment in, 387
  and delinquency, 616
  developmental impact of, 79–80
  dropping out of, 569–572
  educational philosophies in, 448, 450–451
  environments of, and academic achievement, 567–569
  in gender typing, 378
  governor's, 457
  in identity development, 590
  learning in, 434–436, 448, 450–457, 563–572
  in moral development, 598, 599
  problems at, dealing with, 487
  pubertal timing effects of, 525
  resource rooms in, 455, 457
  in suicide prevention, 613
  teacher–pupil interaction in, 451–452
  tracking, 569
  vocational, in Germany, 577, 578
School phobia, 496–497
School transitions, 563–565, 576–578
School year, length of, 459
Schooling. *See* Education
Science achievement, 460, 560, 568
Scientific reasoning, 568
Scripts in memory, 332
Scrotum, 56, 57
Sebaceous glands, 514–515
Second-language learning, 562. *See also* Bilingualism
Secondary circular reactions, 214
Secondary (learned) drives, 19, 263, 264
Secondary sexual characteristics, 515, 516
Secular trend
  in menarche timing, 517, 518
  in physical growth, 396–398
Secure attachment, 268–271. *See also* Attachment security
Secure base in attachment, 266–268, 590
Self, sense of, 250–251, 255
Self-awareness, 250, 276–279. *See also* Separation–individuation theory of development (Mahler)
Self-care children, 495
Self-categorization, 278
Self-concept
  in adolescence, 585–586
  in early childhood, 355–356, 359, 387
  in middle childhood, 467–468
Self-conscious emotions
  in early childhood, 357, 359, 361
  in infancy and toddlerhood, 254–255
  in middle childhood, 473, 474
Self-consciousness in adolescence, 556–557
Self-control, 279, 529
Self-development
  in adolescence, 585–590
  in early childhood, 355–357
  in infancy and toddlerhood, 276–279
  in middle childhood, 467–472
Self-efficacy, 20–21
Self-esteem
  and ability grouping in schools, 452
  in adolescence, 586–589
  in early childhood, 357
  and gender, 379, 564
  in middle childhood, 413, 468–472
  and motor development, 413
  and obesity, 403
Self-focusing in adolescence, 556–557
Self-fulfilling prophecies, 452
Self-help skills, 304–305
Self-recognition, 277–278
Self-reflective perspective taking, 475, 557
Self-regulation
  in adolescence, 434, 558–559, 561
  emotional. *See* Emotional self-regulation
  in middle childhood, 434, 452, 471–474, 496
Self-reports, 34–36
Selman's perspective-taking stages, 594
Semen, 56, 57, 516
Semilingualism, 449
Seminal vesicles, 516
Sensation versus perception, 197
Sensitive periods of development, 27
  for attachment, 270
  in brain stimulation, 174–175
  for language, 562
  prenatal, 110–111, 120
Sensorimotor activity and language, 314
Sensorimotor stage of cognitive development, 22, 23, 210, 211, 213–220
  circular reactions in, 213–216
  evaluation of, 219–220
  and language development, 238
  research on, 217–219
Sensory perception. *See* Perception *entries;* Perceptual development; *specific entries, e.g.:* Hearing; Touch
Sensory register, 221–222
Separation anxiety, 266–268, 490
Separation–individuation theory of development (Mahler), 249–251
Sequential processing in intelligence tests, 439
Seriation in cognitive development, 423, 424, 426
"Sesame Street," 343–344
Sex. *See* Gender *entries;* Premarital sex
Sex cells (gametes), 53–57. *See also* Ova; Sperm
Sex chromosomes, 56–57, 63–66
Sex differences
  in academic achievement, 559–560
  in aggression, 371
  in asthma, 405
  in attention-deficit hyperactivity disorder, 430
  in body growth, 514–516
  in body size, 170, 171, 286, 287, 396, 397
  in brain development, 399
  in cognitive development, 560
  in delinquency, 616, 617
  in depression, 611
  in divorce response, 489, 491
  in eating disorders, 527–529
  in emotional self-regulation, 256
  in friendship, 482, 606
  in homosexuality, 532
  in identity development, 588
  in initiation rites, 521
  in injuries, 299, 405–406, 540
  in language development, 240
  in learned helplessness, 471, 472
  in maternal employment benefits and problems, 494
  in mental development, 559–560
  in moral development, 599–600
  in motor development, 307, 413, 541–542
  in muscle–fat makeup, 172
  in psychosexual development, 354–355. *See also* Electra conflict; Oedipus conflict
  in pubertal timing, 512
  in remarriage adjustment, 493, 494
  in rough-and-tumble play, 414
  in school transitions, 563, 564
  in self-categorization, 278
  in self-esteem, 379, 470, 564, 586
  in sexual abuse, 497, 500
  in sexual attitudes, 530, 531
  in sexual maturation, 513, 515–516, 519–520, 522, 524–525
  in skeletal age, 173
  in skeletal growth, 288
  in suicide, 612
  in temperament, 260–261
  in vocational development, 575–576
  in weight, 170, 171
Sex drive, 529
Sex education
  in adolescence, 529, 532, 533, 535, 536, 538
  in middle childhood, 501
Sex hormones
  in adolescence, 513–515, 520, 611
  female (estrogens), 513
  male (androgens), 371, 399, 513
Sexual abuse, 385, 497–498, 500–501, 505
Sexual activity in adolescence, 529–536, 545
Sexual attitudes, 529–531
Sexual characteristics, primary and secondary, 515, 516
Sexual maturation, 513, 515–518. *See also* Pubertal timing, Puberty
  early versus late, 522, 524–525
  psychological impact of, 518–525
Sexual orientation, 532–533, 538
Sexually transmitted diseases (STDs), 537–538, 545
Short-term (working) memory, 222, 426–427, 429, 437, 438
Shoshone Indian child-rearing practices, 186
Shyness, 41, 42, 259, 260
Sibling caregiving, 81
Sibling relationships
  in adolescence, 603–604
  cross-sectional study of, 43
  in middle childhood, 488
  quality of, 274–275
Sickle cell anemia, 60, 62, 95
Sickle cell trait, 60
SIDS (sudden infant death syndrome), 193–195, 207
Sign language, 236
Simultaneous processing in intelligence tests, 439
Single parenthood, 83, 489, 505. *See also* Divorce
Siriono childbirth practices, 139
Skeletal age, 173
Skeletal growth
  in adolescence, 514
  in early childhood, 287–288
  in infancy and toddlerhood, 173–174
  in middle childhood, 398
Skinner's theory (operant conditioning), 19–20, 192–193, 235, 368
Skipping and motor development, 410
Skull growth, 173–175
Slang, 561
Sleep
  in early childhood, 182, 183
  in infants, 182, 183
  in newborns, 159–160
  non-rapid-eye-movement, 159–160
  rapid-eye-movement, 159–160
  and wakefulness (states of arousal), 159–162, 181, 183
Slow-to-warm-up children, 258, 259
Small-for-date infants, 148
Smell, newborn responsiveness to, 156, 157
Smile, social, 252
Smiling in infants, 252–253
Smoking
  in adolescence, 538–540
  and asthma, 405
  during pregnancy, 113–114, 194
  and sudden infant death syndrome, 194
Sociability
  peer, 362–365, 480
  stability of, 259
Social class
  and academic achievement, 566, 569
  and motor development, 413
  and child-rearing practices, 76–78
  and delinquency, 615
  and intelligence quotients, 442
  in menarche timing, 517
  and obesity, 401, 402
  and self-esteem, 586
Social-cognitive theory, 20–21
Social comparisons in self-concept, 467
Social contract orientation in moral development, 594, 595
Social conventions versus moral rules, 370–371, 478–480
Social development. *See also* Emotional development; Personality development
  in adolescence, 583–618, 622–623
  and attachment, 275–276
  and child-rearing practices, 382–388
  in early childhood, 353–357, 362–388, 392–393
  family influences on, 486–495
  in infancy and toddlerhood, 248–251, 276–279, 282–283
  in middle childhood, 465–502, 506–507
  and sports, 542
Social environment
  in adolescence, 511, 532, 601
  and gender typing, 378–379, 601

and motor development, 307
Social experiences
and cognition, 328–329
and memory skills, 332
and moral rules, 371
Social-informational perspective taking, 475
Social interaction
categories of, 362–364
in sociocultural theory, 30
Social issues. *See also* Public policy
academic achievement, 568
adult-organized sports, 414, 415, 419
bilingual education, 448, 449
child health care, 298
child-rearing practices, 14
children's causes, 84, 85
children's television regulation, 374
family planning, 100, 101
food programs, 400
infant mortality and health care, 151
intervention programs for at-risk infants and toddlers, 232, 233, 245
lead poisoning, 294
malnutrition, 180–181
and moral development, 597
prenatal AIDS transmission, 119
preschool intervention, 342. *See also* Project Head Start
reproductive technology, 70–71
war, 497, 499
youth gangs, 616, 617
Social learning theory, 20–21, 32
and gender-role identity, 379, 380
gender typing in, 375–376
moral development in, 366–370
Social networks in ecological systems theory, 29
Social-order-maintaining orientation in moral development, 594–595
Social problem solving, 476, 478
Social problem-solving training, 373
Social referencing, 254
Social relationships and newborn reflexes, 155
Social self-esteem, 469, 470
Social skills
and child maltreatment, 387
and peer acceptance, 483–484
and perspective taking, 475–476
Social smile, 252
Social systems
families as. *See* Family systems
schools as, 80
Social use of language (conversational skills), 346–348, 447. *See also* Pragmatics
Socially mediated process of cognitive development, 30
Societal perspective taking, 475
Sociocultural theory of cognitive development (Vygotsky), 29–32
in early childhood, 326–329
and elementary education experiments, 450
in infancy and toddlerhood, 225–227
in middle childhood, 426
Sociodramatic play, 316, 364
Socioeconomic status. *See* Social class
Sociometric techniques, 482
Soft spots (fontanels) of skull, 173, 174
Solitary play, 362–364
Sounds
infant responsiveness to, 156–158, 197–198
by infants, 236–237
and letters, 335, 435
newborn responsiveness to, 156–158
speech, 197–198, 236–237
Spatial intelligence, 66, 441, 442
Spatial reasoning, 423–425, 437, 438
Spatial skill development, 289, 560
Special learning needs, 453–457, 463
Specialized talents and giftedness, 456
Speech
egocentric, 327, 347
private, 327–329
telegraphic (two-word), 239
Speech sounds, 197–198, 236–237
Spelling in early childhood, 335
Sperm, 53–57, 70, 71
Spermarche, 516, 519
Spinal cord development, 106, 107
Sports
in adolescence, 541–542
adult-organized, 414, 415, 419
injuries related to, 541
Stage concept, 7, 11, 325
Stage theories of development. *See* Cognitive-developmental theory (Piaget); Psychosexual theory of development (Freud); Psychosocial theory of development (Erikson)
Stanford-Binet Intelligence Scale, 14–15, 437, 438
States
of arousal, 159–162, 181, 183
versus transformations, 317, 319, 320, 322
STDs (sexually transmitted diseases), 537–538, 545
Steering and motor development, 303
Stepparents, 492–494, 505
Stepping reflex, 154–156
Stereotypes. *See* Cultural stereotypes and vocational development; Gender stereotypes; Gender typing; Racial stereotypes on television
Sternberg's triarchic theory of intelligence, 440–441
Steroids and sports, 542
Stimulant drugs, 430
Stimulation
of brain, 174–175
infant tolerance for, 255–256
and physical growth, 181
Stimuli
conditioned, 191, 192
and habituation, 193, 195. *See also* Habituation–dishabituation response
neutral, 19, 191
in operant conditioning, 192–193
relations between, representing, 332–333
unconditioned, 190–192
visual, 189, 229, 454
Stimulus–response in classical conditioning, 19, 190–192
Strange Situation, 267–268, 273
Stranger anxiety, 253
Stress
and adolescent suicide, 613
and attachment security, 271
and child maltreatment, 386–388
and depression, 611
and emotional well-being, 293
in families, 271, 293, 386–388, 613
in middle childhood, coping with, 502
during pregnancy, 122
Stress hormones, 122, 137, 145
Stress-resistant children, 502
Structured interviews, 34–36
Structured observation, 34
Subcategories in cognitive development, 324
Subcultures, 81–82
Substance use and abuse, 112–113, 538–540, 545, 578. *See also* Alcohol *entries;* Drugs
Sucking reflex, 154, 155, 190–191, 193
Sudden infant death syndrome (SIDS), 193–195, 207
Suicide in adolescence, 612–614, 621
Suicide rates, 613
Superego, 16–17, 32, 355, 367, 511
Supplemental Food Program for Women, Infants, and Children, 121
Surrogate mothers, 70–71
in monkey studies, 264
Survival of the fittest, 11
Sutures of skull, 173, 174
Sweden
day care in, 231
divorce rate in, 489
food programs in, 295
pubertal timing effects in, 525
Swimming pools, fear of, 360
Swimming reflex, 154
Symbiosis in personality development, 250
Synapses between neurons, 174, 399
Syphilis, 537
Systematic observation, 33–35
Systems of action in motor development, 184, 302

Tabula rasa view, 10
Taiwan
academic achievement in, 459, 460, 471
education in, gender stereotypes in, 484
Taste preferences of newborns, 156, 157
Tay-Sachs disease, 62
Teacher–parent communication, 459
Teacher–pupil interaction, 451–452, 459, 567
and career choices, 574–575
and dropout prevention, 571–572
and moral development, 598, 599
Teachers. *See* School *entries*
Teeth. *See* Dental development; Dental health
Teething of infants, 174
Telegraphic (two-word) speech, 239
Television
advertising on, 373, 374
children's, 374, 391
educational, 343–344
and obesity, 401, 402
violence on, 373–375, 387
Temper tantrums of infants, 250
Temperament. *See also* Type A personality
assessing, 257–259
and attachment security, 271
and child-rearing practices, 257, 260–263, 271
and childhood injuries, 299
defined, 257
development of, 257–263, 271
and divorce, 489, 491
and environment, 260–263
and genetics, 259–260
in sibling relationships, 275
stability of, 259
Temperature, newborn responsiveness to, 156, 157
Tentative period of vocational development, 573
Teratogens, 110–119, 146, 430
Tertiary circular reactions, 215–216
Testes, 56, 57, 513, 516
Testosterone, 513
Tests as research method, 34, 36. *See also* Intelligence quotients; Intelligence tests; Mental testing; Scholastic Aptitude Test
Thalidomide, 112
Theory(ies)
child development, 6–32. *See also specific entries, e.g.:* Ecological systems theory of development; Psychosocial theory of development (Erikson)
defined, 5
general, in hypothetico-deductive reasoning, 548
of mind (metacognition), 333–334, 433, 471, 472
Thinking. *See* Cognition; Cognitive *entries;* Mental development
Third parties
in child development, 75
in microsystems, 28–29
Third-party perspective taking, 475, 557
Three-day or German measles (rubella), 117
Three-mountains problem, 318, 322, 325
Throwing and motor development, 303, 304, 409, 410
Thyroid gland, 293, 512, 513
Thyroid-stimulating hormone (TSH), 293
Thyroxine, 293, 512, 513
Tikopian (Melanesia) initiation ceremony, 521
Time out, 369
Toddlers. *See* Infancy and toddlerhood
Toilet training, 189–190, 249
Tonic neck reflex, 154, 155
Tooth decay, 288, 398
Touch
newborn responsiveness to, 156–157
in preterm infant stimulation, 149
Town, impact on development, 80–81
Toxemia (eclampsia), 124
Toxoplasmosis, 117, 118
Tracking in schools, 452, 569
Traditional classrooms, 450
Transductive reasoning, 317, 319, 322, 324
Transition in childbirth, 135, 136
Transitive inferences, 423–426
Traumatic events and obesity, 401, 402
Triarchic theory of intelligence (Sternberg), 440–441
Trimesters of prenatal development, 104, 107–108
Triple X syndrome, 66
Trisomy 21 (Down syndrome), 65, 95
Trobriand Islander (Melanesia) sexual attitudes, 529
Trust
in adolescence, 584
in friendships, 482
versus mistrust, as stage, 18, 248–251
TSH (thyroid-stimulating hormone), 293
Tubatulabel childbirth practices, 139
Turner syndrome, 66
Twin studies
of attention-deficit hyperactivity disorder, 430
concordance rates in, 87–89
of giftedness, 456
heritability estimates in, 88–89
of homosexuality, 532
of intelligence quotients, 442
of menarche timing, 517
of myopia, 400
and niche-picking, 92
of obesity, 402
of physical growth, 178

Twin studies *(continued)*
and psychological characteristics, 86
of temperament, 259–260
Twins
fraternal (dizygotic), 57, 58
handedness of, 290
identical (monozygotic), 57, 58
language development of, 242
premature birth of, 148
Two-word (telegraphic) speech, 239
Type A personality, 403–404

UCR (unconditioned or reflexive response), 19, 190–192
UCS (unconditioned stimulus), 190–192
Ulnar grasp, 188, 189
Ultrasound in prenatal diagnosis, 68, 69
Umbilical cord, 104–106, 109, 136, 146
Unconditioned (reflexive) response (UCR), 19, 190–192
Unconditioned stimulus (UCS), 190–192
Underextension vocabulary error, 238
Undifferentiated perspective taking, 475
Uninvolved child-rearing style, 383–385
Universal ethical principle orientation in moral development, 594, 595
Universality of death, 323
Unwanted children, 72
Urine alarms, 404–405
Uterine contractions in childbirth, 134–136, 144
Uterus, 55–56, 106
Utku Indian (Hudson Bay) moral development, 366

Vacuum extractors, 143–144
Values. *See also* Culture; Moral development; Moral education
in African-American extended families, 83
and child-rearing practices, 81
and conservation, 425
and educational philosophies, 448–449
and educational quality, 458, 459
in gender typing, 375, 377, 485–486
in infant sleeping arrangements, 183
and intelligence test performance, 441, 443, 444
and learned helplessness, 471–472
and moral development, 479
of peer groups,480,
in perspective taking, 475
and puberty, acceptance of, 521
and public policies, 82
and contraceptive use, 536
and social class, 76
in theories, 5
in vocational development, 573
Variables
dependent and independent, 39
in metacognition, 433
Vas deferens, 56, 57
Verbal ability tests, 559
Verbal communication, 328–329
Verbal intelligence, 66
Verbal reasoning, 437, 438
Vernix, 107, 109
Villi, 103–104. *See also* Chorionic villus sampling
Violence
and aggression, 373–375. *See also* Aggression; Wartime effects on children
and child maltreatment, 387
in gangs, 617
on television, 373–375, 387
Viral diseases during pregnancy, 117–119
Vision
and brain lateralization, 176n
problems with, 400
Visual acuity of newborns, 156, 158–159, 198
Visual cliff, 198, 199, 253
Visual development, 198–203, 308–309
Visual stimuli, 189, 229, 454
Vocabulary development
in adolescence, 561
in early childhood, 344–346, 357–358
in infancy and toddlerhood, 238–239
in middle childhood, 446
Vocational (career) development, 572–578
Vocational schools in Germany, 577, 578
Vocational training, 571, 590
Voice changes, pubertal, 516
Voluntary reaching, 188–189
Vygotsky's sociocultural theory. *See* Sociocultural theory of cognitive development (Vygotsky)
Walkers and perceptual development, 200–201
Walking
in individuation, 250
and motor development, 302, 303
Wartime effects on children, 497, 499
Watson's theory. *See* Behaviorism
Wechsler Intelligence Scale for Children–III (WISC–III), 439
Wechsler Preschool and Primary Scale of Intelligence–Revised (WPPSI–R), 439
Weight. *See also* Body growth; Body size
at birth, 112–117, 122, 147–151, 405
and environment, 178
and genetics, 178
over-, 179–180, 401–403. *See also* Obesity
during pregnancy, 120, 122
sex differences in, 170, 171
Weight loss and eating disorders, 527–529
West Indian (Jamaica) infant motor skills, 186, 187
Whole-language approach to reading instruction, 435
WISC–III (Wechsler Intelligence Scale for Children–III), 439
Withdrawal of privileges, 369–370
Word processing by computer, 452
Work–study apprenticeships, 577, 578
Working (short-term) memory, 222, 426–427, 429, 437, 438
WPPSI–R (Wechsler Preschool and Primary Scale of Intelligence–Revised), 439
Writing
development of, 334–336
learning disabilities involving, 454
and motor development, 305, 306, 308–309, 411–412
Writing achievement, 460, 568

X chromosomes, 56–57, 63–64
X-linked inheritance, 61, 63, 64, 532
X-rays during pregnancy, 116. *See also* Radiation
XYY syndrome, 66

Y chromosomes, 56–57
Yolk sacs, 103, 106, 109
Young adulthood, 431, 573
Youth (late adolescence), 512, 623
Youth gangs, 616, 617
Yurok Indian infant feeding, 17–18

Zambian infant behavior, 162
Zinacanteco Indians, 30, 186
Zone of proximal development, 225, 242, 328, 450
Zuni Indian self-conscious emotions, 255
Zygote, 55–58
period of the, 103–106, 108, 110, 111